THE LIBRARY OF LIVING PHILOSOPHERS

THE PHILOSOPHY OF
JULIA KRISTEVA

THE LIBRARY OF LIVING PHILOSOPHERS

PAUL ARTHUR SCHILPP, FOUNDER AND EDITOR 1939–1981
LEWIS EDWIN HAHN, EDITOR 1981–2001
RANDALL E. AUXIER, EDITOR 2001–2013
DOUGLAS R. ANDERSON, EDITOR 2013–2015
SARA G. BEARDSWORTH, EDITOR 2015–present

Paul Arthur Schilpp, Editor
THE PHILOSOPHY OF JOHN DEWEY (1939, 1971, 1989)
THE PHILOSOPHY OF GEORGE SANTAYANA (1940, 1951)
THE PHILOSOPHY OF ALFRED NORTH WHITEHEAD (1941, 1951)
THE PHILOSOPHY OF G. E. MOORE (1942, 1971)
THE PHILOSOPHY OF BERTRAND RUSSELL (1944, 1971)
THE PHILOSOPHY OF ERNST CASSIRER (1949)
ALBERT EINSTEIN: PHILOSOPHER-SCIENTIST (1949, 1970)
THE PHILOSOPHY OF SARVEPALLI RADHAKRISHNAN (1952)
THE PHILOSOPHY OF KARL JASPERS (1957; AUG. ED., 1981)
THE PHILOSOPHY OF C. D. BROAD (1959)
THE PHILOSOPHY OF RUDOLF CARNAP (1963)
THE PHILOSOPHY OF C. I. LEWIS (1968)
THE PHILOSOPHY OF KARL POPPER (1974)
THE PHILOSOPHY OF BRAND BLANSHARD (1980)
THE PHILOSOPHY OF JEAN-PAUL SARTRE (1981)

Paul Arthur Schilpp and Maurice Friedman, Editors
THE PHILOSOPHY OF MARTIN BUBER (1967)

Paul Arthur Schilpp and Lewis Edwin Hahn, Editors
THE PHILOSOPHY OF GABRIEL MARCEL (1984)
THE PHILOSOPHY OF W. V. QUINE (1986, AUG. ED., 1998)
THE PHILOSOPHY OF GEORG HENRIK VON WRIGHT (1989)

Lewis Edwin Hahn, Editor
THE PHILOSOPHY OF CHARLES HARTSHORNE (1991)
THE PHILOSOPHY OF A. J. AYER (1992)
THE PHILOSOPHY OF PAUL RICOEUR (1995)
THE PHILOSOPHY OF PAUL WEISS (1995)
THE PHILOSOPHY OF HANS-GEORG GADAMER (1997)
THE PHILOSOPHY OF RODERICK M. CHISHOLM (1997)
THE PHILOSOPHY OF P. F. STRAWSON (1998)
THE PHILOSOPHY OF DONALD DAVIDSON (1999)

Lewis Edwin Hahn, Randall E. Auxier, and Lucian W. Stone, Jr., Editors
THE PHILOSOPHY OF SEYYED HOSSEIN NASR (2001)

Randall E. Auxier and Lewis Edwin Hahn, Editors
THE PHILOSOPHY OF MARJORIE GRENE (2002)
THE PHILOSOPHY OF JAAKKO HINTIKKA (2006)
THE PHILOSOPHY OF MICHAEL DUMMETT (2007)
THE PHILOSOPHY OF RICHARD RORTY (2010)
THE PHILOSOPHY OF ARTHUR C. DANTO (2013)

Randall E. Auxier, Douglas R. Anderson, and Lewis Edwin Hahn, Editors
THE PHILOSOPHY OF HILARY PUTNAM (2015)

Sara G. Beardsworth and Randall E. Auxier, Editors
THE PHILOSOPHY OF UMBERTO ECO (2017)

Sara G. Beardsworth, Editor
THE PHILOSOPHY OF JULIA KRISTEVA (2020)

J. Kristeva

THE LIBRARY OF LIVING PHILOSOPHERS
VOLUME XXXVI

THE PHILOSOPHY OF
JULIA KRISTEVA

EDITED BY

SARA G. BEARDSWORTH

SOUTHERN ILLINOIS UNIVERSITY CARBONDALE

CHICAGO, ILLINOIS • OPEN COURT • ESTABLISHED 1887

To find out more about Open Court books, visit our website at www.opencourtbooks.com.

Cover photo © John Foley

Frontispiece photo © Anne de Brunhoff

THE PHILOSOPHY OF JULIA KRISTEVA

Open Court Publishing Company is a division of Carus Publishing Company, dba Cricket Media.

First printing 2020

Printed and bound in the United States of America.

Library of Congress Cataloging-in-Publication Data
Names: Kristeva, Julia, 1941– | Beardsworth, Sara, editor.
Title: The philosophy of Julia Kristeva / edited by Sara G. Beardsworth, Southern Illinois University, Carbondale.
Description: Chicago, Illinois : Open Court, 2020. | Series: The library of living philosophers; volume xxxvi | Includes bibliographical references and index.
Identifiers: LCCN 2020009716 | ISBN 9780812694895 (cloth) | ISBN 9780812694932 (ebook)
Subjects: LCSH: Kristeva, Julia, 1941-
Classification: LCC B2430.K7544 P45 2020 | DDC 194—dc23
LC record available at https://lccn.loc.gov/2020009716

The Library of Living Philosophers is published under the sponsorship of Southern Illinois University Carbondale.

NATIONAL
ENDOWMENT
FOR THE
HUMANITIES

The Philosophy of Julia Kristeva has been made possible in part by a major grant from the National Endowment for the Humanities: Exploring the human endeavor.

Any views, findings, conclusions, or recommendations expressed in this book, do not necessarily represent those of the National Endowment for the Humanities.

GENERAL INTRODUCTION
TO
THE LIBRARY OF LIVING PHILOSOPHERS

Since its founding in 1938 by Paul Arthur Schilpp, the Library of Living Philosophers has been devoted to critical analysis and discussion of some of the world's greatest living philosophers. The format for the series provides for creating in each volume a dialogue between the critics and the great philosopher. The aim is not refutation or confrontation but rather fruitful joining of issues and improved understanding of the positions and issues involved. That is, the goal is not overcoming those who differ from us philosophically but interacting creatively with them.

The basic idea for the series, according to Professor Schilpp's general introduction to the earlier volumes, came from the late F. C. S. Schiller's essay "Must Philosophers Disagree?" While Schiller may have been overly optimistic about ending "interminable controversies" in this way, it seems clear that directing searching questions to great philosophers about what they really mean or how they might resolve or address difficulties in their philosophies can produce far greater clarity of understanding and more fruitful philosophizing than would otherwise exist.

To Paul Arthur Schilpp's undying credit, he acted on this basic thought in launching the Library of Living Philosophers. The general plan for the volumes has sometimes been altered to fit circumstances, but in ways that have well served the mission of the series. The intellectual autobiographies, or, in a few cases, the biographies, shed a great deal of light on both how the philosophies of the great thinkers developed and the major philosophical movements and issues of their time; and many of our great philosophers seek to orient their outlook not merely to their contemporaries but also to what they find most important in earlier philosophers. The critical perspectives of our distinguished contributors have often stood on their own as landmark studies, widely cited and familiar not only to subsequent specialists, but frequently discussed in their own right as pieces of great philosophy. The bibliography helps to provide ready access to the featured scholar's writings and thought.

There is no reason to alter our historical format or mission for the present century. We are pleased that the success of the Library of Living Philosophers has led to a wider appreciation of the need for dialogue of the type our format creates. We respect the efforts of other academic publishers to employ versions of our format to facilitate pluralistic, meaningful, sharp, constructive, and respectful exchange in philosophical ideas. We are fortunate to have such support from the Open Court Publishing Company, the Edward C. Hegeler Foundation, and the Board of Trustees, College of Liberal Arts, and the Department of Philosophy of Southern Illinois University Carbondale, as to permit us to carry out our purpose with a degree of deliberate thoroughness and comprehensiveness not available to other academic publishers, and we have rededicated ourselves to maintaining the highest standards in scholarship and accuracy anywhere to be found in academic publishing. In recognition of the permanent value that has been accorded our previous volumes, we are committed to keeping our volumes in print and available, and to maintaining our sense of the long-term importance of providing the most reliable source for scholarly analysis by the most distinguished voices of our day about the most important philosophical contributions of the greatest living thinkers.

The Library of Living Philosophers has never construed "philosophy" in a narrow and strictly academic sense. Past volumes have been dedicated both to the leading academic philosophers and to the most visible and influential public philosophers. We renew with each volume our historical orientation to the practice of philosophy as a quest for truth, beauty, and the best life, and we affirm that this quest is a public activity and its results a public possession, both for the present generation and in the future. We seek, with the sober judgment of our Advisory Board, to bring forth volumes on the thought of figures whose ideas have made a genuine difference to the lives of people everywhere. Ideas truly do have consequences, and many of the ideas that have had the broadest impact were indeed best articulated by the figures to whom we have dedicated past volumes. The selfless work of Paul Arthur Schilpp and Lewis Edwin Hahn in realizing this mission stands among the most important scholarly contributions to twentieth-century philosophy. Their judgment regarding how best to pursue the purposes of the Library of Living Philosophers has found constant and continuous confirmation in the reception and ongoing importance accorded this series. Let us continue in their footsteps as well as we may in the important task of continuing the series in light of philosophical developments in the twenty-first century.

Sara G. Beardsworth

Department of Philosophy
Southern Illinois University Carbondale

FOUNDER'S GENERAL INTRODUCTION* TO THE LIBRARY OF LIVING PHILOSOPHERS

According to the late F. C. S. Schiller, the greatest obstacle to fruitful discussion in philosophy is "the curious etiquette which apparently taboos the asking of questions about a philosopher's meaning while he is alive." The "interminable controversies which fill the histories of philosophy," he goes on to say, "could have been ended at once by asking the living philosophers a few searching questions."

The confident optimism of this last remark undoubtedly goes too far. Living thinkers have often been asked "a few searching questions," but their answers have not stopped "interminable controversies" about their real meaning. It is nonetheless true that there would be far greater clarity of understanding than is now often the case if more such searching questions had been directed to great thinkers while they were still alive.

This, at any rate, is the basic thought behind the present undertaking. The volumes of the Library of Living Philosophers can in no sense take the place of the major writings of great and original thinkers. Students who would know the philosophies of such men as John Dewey, George Santayana, Alfred North Whitehead, G. E. Moore, Bertrand Russell, Ernst Cassirer, Karl Jaspers, Rudolf Carnap, Martin Buber, et al., will still need to read the writings of these men. There is no substitute for first-hand contact with the original thought of the philosopher. Least of all does this Library pretend to be such a substitute. The Library in fact will spare neither effort nor expense in offering to the student the best possible guide to the published writings of a given thinker. We shall attempt to meet this aim by providing at the end of each volume in our series as nearly complete a bibliography of the published work of the philosopher in question as possible. Nor should one overlook the fact that essays in each volume cannot but finally lead to this same goal. The interpretive and critical discussions of the various phases of a great thinker's work and, most of all, the reply of the thinker, are bound to lead the reader to the works of the philosopher.

At the same time, there is no denying that different experts find different ideas in the writings of the same philosopher. This is as true of the apprecia-

*This General Introduction sets forth in the founder's words the underlying conception of the Library. —S. G. B.

tive interpreter and grateful disciple as it is of the critical opponent. Nor can it be denied that such differences of reading and of interpretation on the part of other experts often leave the neophyte aghast before the whole maze of widely varying and even opposing interpretations. Who is right and whose interpretation shall he or she accept? When the doctors disagree among themselves, what is the poor student to do? If, in desperation, he or she decides that all of the interpreters are probably wrong and that the only thing to do is to go back to the original writings of the philosopher and then make his or her own decision—uninfluenced (as if this were possible) by the interpretation of anyone else—the result is not that he or she has actually come to the meaning of the original philosopher, but rather that he or she has set up one more interpretation, which may differ to a greater or lesser degree from the interpretations already existing. It is clear that in this direction lies chaos, just the kind of chaos which Schiller has so graphically and inimitably described.

It is curious that until now no way of escaping this difficulty has been seriously considered. It has not occurred to students of philosophy that one effective way of meeting the problem at least partially is to put these varying interpretations and critiques before the philosopher while he or she is still alive and to ask him or her to act at one and the same time as both defendant and judge. If the world's greatest living philosophers can be induced to cooperate in an enterprise whereby their own work can, at least to some extent, be saved from becoming merely "desiccated lecture-fodder," which on the one hand "provides innocuous sustenance for ruminant professors," and on the other hand gives an opportunity to such ruminants and their understudies to "speculate safely, endlessly, and fruitlessly, about what a philosopher must have meant" (Schiller), they will have taken a long step toward making their intentions more clearly comprehensible.

With this in mind, the Library of Living Philosophers expects to publish at more or less regular intervals a volume on each of the greater among the world's living philosophers. In each case it will be the purpose of the editor of the Library to bring together in the volume the interpretations and criticisms of a wide range of that particular thinker's scholarly contemporaries, each of whom will be given a free hand to discuss the specific phase of the thinker's work that has been assigned to him or her. All contributed essays will finally be submitted to the philosopher with whose work and thought they are concerned, for his or her careful perusal and reply. And, although it would be expecting too much to imagine that the philosopher's reply will be able to stop all differences of interpretation and of critique, this should at least serve the purpose of stopping certain of the grosser and more general kinds of misinterpretations. If no further gain than this were to come from the present and projected volumes of this Library, it would seem to be fully justified.

In carrying out this principal purpose of the Library, the editor announces that (as far as is humanly possible) each volume will contain the following elements:

First, an intellectual autobiography of the thinker whenever this can be secured; in any case an authoritative and authorized biography;
Second, a series of expository and critical articles written by the leading exponents and opponents of the philosopher's thought;
Third, the reply to the critics and commentators by the philosopher; and
Fourth, a bibliography of writings of the philosopher to provide a ready instrument to give access to his or her writings and thought.

PAUL ARTHUR SCHILPP
FOUNDER AND EDITOR, 1939–1981

DEPARTMENT OF PHILOSOPHY
SOUTHERN ILLINOIS UNIVERSITY CARBONDALE

ADVISORY BOARD

TABLE OF CONTENTS

PREFACE

Julia Kristeva is beyond all doubt one of the seminal thinkers of her generation. One major indication of this fact is the extraordinary breadth of her work. Kristeva's "life of the mind" provides a critical analysis of the present and includes the experiences and thought of a psychoanalyst in linguistics, philosophy, and literature. Studies in Plato, Aristotle, Hegel, Heidegger, Sartre, Merleau-Ponty, Ricoeur, and Arendt, among others, accompany and enrich an encounter in psychoanalysis and literature across a broad front. Throughout Kristeva's writings, the problem of meaning and representation in modern societies and cultures is prominent. Thanks to her early attention to philosophies of language and the sciences of meaning, she has earned a central place in semiotics, whose domain her work has extended.

Kristeva has transformed semiology through the notions of intertextuality, dialogism, and semanalysis. Her distinctive conceptual dyad, the semiotic and the symbolic, specifically *includes* in semiotics the "speaking being" from psychoanalysis. Her writings, increasingly grounded in psychoanalysis as "an art of treating the faculty of thought" and an investigation of the conditions for mentalization and verbalization, have sought a new humanist vision for our times. It is a vision in which the "positivity" of scientific thought and understanding cannot stand alone but must be supplemented by what has come to be known as "negativity." Affirming the unity of the human spirit means, for her, *both* keeping a stake in the legacy of Enlightenment thinkers and redrawing the philosophical and psychoanalytic paths of negativity from Hegel to Freud and since. This involves not only the disruption of consciousness but also the unleashing of the death drive. On the one hand, the psychic drive, desire, and affect are included as aspects of the faculty of thought, while, on the other hand, psychoanalysis itself is pushed past its traditional boundaries—crossing over into philosophy, literature, and religion. The overall effect is a realignment of the cultural vectors that make up our contemporary lives.

The movements of Kristeva's thought yield a multifaceted work that extends from semiotics and the theory of literature to psychoanalytic theory and practice, a philosophy of affect and passion, a thinking on religion, novel writing, and an expanding public philosophy with far-reaching discussions on the maternal, public health, disability, and the place of fundamentalism in contemporary cultures. Obviously, such a multidisciplinary oeuvre—by a woman and a "stranger/foreigner" from Bulgaria who made France her home and French her language in the mid-1960s—could not easily be organized into the more established philosophical categories for a volume in the series.

This volume—only the second dedicated to a woman in the Library of Living Philosophers—has required a section on the maternal, one on public health, and one on the theory of revolt if it is to capture the intellectual output of this rigorous, audacious spirit. Julia Kristeva never contents herself with the status quo in her intellectual domains, both acknowledging modernity's break with tradition—theorized by Arendt—and choosing the *transvaluation* of cultural forms over the outright rejection of ideas. Those conversant with the Library of Living Philosophers may also be surprised to find that the usual style of the replies—a subject philosopher's critical response to his or her critics—sometimes gives way to other values and approaches. Thus, in adhering to the principle of dialogue in philosophy and the series' goal of creative interaction with the contributors, Kristeva's replies include singular motifs, such as salutations to the interventions of her interpreters or a textual *responsory*, like the meditative chant "sung in alternation."

The intellectual autobiography in Part I provides access to this dialogue by relating theory to Kristeva's life in the twentieth and twenty-first centuries. It shows her knowledge of both Western and Eastern European culture and thought, including Byzantine art and religion, the Marxist-Hegelian tradition, and Russian formalism, while also memorializing the care of her parents, who gave "not roots, but wings" through a childhood that witnessed the Nazi and Stalinist invasions of Bulgaria, and her young life under Soviet communism. The autobiography portrays her entry into the intellectual ferment of France in the 1960s, followed by the prolific output of writings in her adopted language, as well as her research, teaching, and alliances in the United States, and international collaborations on many concerns of the two centuries, including thinking in dark times and the renewal of humanism.

In line with the chronological development of Kristeva's oeuvre, Part II begins with her early attention to the history of linguistics, including Saussure and the twentieth-century attempt to articulate the question of enunciation (Benveniste, Barthes). What emerges from her work in semiotics and the theory of literature as a kind of philosophical writing is her emphasis on semiology as a method of analyzing literary works that opens up into history, sociology, and culture. Kristeva's enhancement of semiological models through the Freudian theory of the unconscious appears above all in the notion of *signifiance*, part of a fundamental categorial triad whose continual refinement is a marked feature of her writings. *Signifiance*, the process of meaning, is at the intersection of the semiotic and the symbolic. The semiotic—the prelinguistic or translinguistic modalities of meaning—is heard in the speech of analysands and the sonorous or stylistic movements of literary writing. The notion of the symbolic (syntactic-semantic functioning) covers language systems or structures together with their generations and transformations. As is shown throughout the volume, *signifiance* arises in literary and poetic texts, in the transferential movements of psychoanalysis, and in thought, art, and life.

Part II brings together authors from many fields to analyze the components and developments of Kristeva's multifaceted work in its theoretical, cultural, clinical, and political aspects. The complex journey assembled here begins in sections I and II with her work in language, semiotics, and the theory of literature. Section III illuminates her choice of psychoanalysis for the theoretical and practical grounding of her thought, demonstrating her innovations in this field and its role in her reading of literature. Section IV turns to Kristeva's appeal for contemporary art and aesthetics, including feminist aesthetics. One essay goes to the depths of the meaning of her notion of abjection for art. Others reveal the importance of aesthetic experience or artistic practice as a search for sensation or "lost time" (Proust). These orientations in Kristeva's relation to art and literature are carried into her own novel writing, which is considered in section V. The two essays on her fictional narrative consider it as autobiography, as style and structure, and as a way of thinking or of continuing analytic practice. One of them also delves into the metaphysical dimension of her series of philosophical, historical, and political detective novels.

Kristeva's inclusion of the phenomenological idea of Being in her psychoanalytic clinic—a rare one—shows up in her widely received notions of abjection, love, and depression/melancholy. These are taken up in section VI, with emphasis on their links with phenomenology or their crossroads with religion and the sacred. In two connected essays, depression is approached as a "felt phenomenon," rather than a pathology, and melancholy is taken beyond individual affliction to melancholia's theological dimensions. The third essay explores Kristeva's writing on love in terms of Being and the "baroque." In the final essay in this section, the ideas of abjection, love, and melancholy appear in the relation between language and the sacred. Section VII turns to Kristeva's inheritance of the long debate on faith and knowledge, evaluating in markedly different ways her unique connecting of the (prereligious) "need to believe" with the "desire to know." One of the two illuminates her emphasis on "traversing religion" in secularized modernity, showing both the unusual critical attention she gives to the Christian female mystics as well as what has been called her "mystic atheism."

The multifaceted nature of Kristeva's oeuvre is especially apparent in the wide reception of her theory of *revolt*. In section VIII, one author relates this idea to the philosophy of Levinas, recovering the link between the idea of *intimate revolt* and traumatism. Another takes up the view that Kristeva's conception of revolt situates the psyche on political terrain, so that the idea of revolt, considered as a condition for community—an "intimate politics that unsettles identity politics"—can be questioned in relation to colonial or Eurocentric logics of alterity. The idea of revolt also animates the speech celebrating the award to Julia Kristeva of the Hannah Arendt Prize for Political Thought in 2006, published here in English for the first time.

Kristeva's innovations in psychoanalysis come back into clinical as well as philosophical focus in sections IX and X on her idea of the maternal and her philosophy of public health, respectively. The former brings out the manifold facets of Kristeva's writing on the maternal, with one author questioning the enigmas it sets for motherhood and for feminist writing on maternity. Two others focus on her signature conception of *maternal reliance*, which underlines the "mystery" of maternal passion in the child's early development. The idea of maternal reliance in Kristeva's oeuvre brings out more fully the conditions of mentalization and verbalization, which are conditions of representation, imagination, separation, and human bonds. Building on this, the dialogue on the philosophy of public health presents precise and moving contributions to contemporary work in the medical humanities as well as work with disability, experiences of migration in the transcultural clinic, and teenage involvement in fundamentalism—an "ideality disorder."

Kristeva's widely received conception of the "maladies of ideality" appears again in the final section of Part II, where the attention given to the issue of radicalization emphasizes both her work on Arendt and her own renewal of thinking on the problem of evil and forgiveness. Another essay formulates Kristeva's ethics of forgiveness in terms of a "dynamic materialism" that is distinguished by the conceptions of heterogeneity and temporality that permeate Kristeva's writings. A third, concerned with globalization and the rise of nationalism and populisms today, constructs the question of a latent political theory in Kristeva's thought. The final essay returns to Kristeva's concern for the perpetual refoundation of humanism, revisiting her thinking on disability and its critique of an economy of performance, in order to bring out an emphasis on meaning making. The attention given to the idea of a democracy of proximity (prefigured in Merleau-Ponty and Levinas) considers Kristeva's extension of democratic values, rights, and responsibilities through the ideas of vulnerability, listening, hospitality, and singularity.

One more element of this multifaceted oeuvre must be mentioned. This is Kristeva's attunement to *singularity*, in which she aligns herself with Duns Scotus and the notion of *haecceitas*. She is committed to a singular universal and affirms singularities as constitutive, irreducible, incommensurable, or without limits: singularities that appear not only in psychoanalysis or literature (the "singular processes in the flesh of words") but also in revolt, ethics, and "singular chances" in the third millennium, as she describes it here.

Kristeva's significance for feminist philosophy and the philosophy of race is often a focus in the anglophone reception of her writings, not least in the United States, where her ideas of the *stranger* and *revolt* are leading considerations. Some essays in sections VIII and XI attempt to bring Kristeva's thought into relation with an abiding commitment and sensitivity not only to the particular sufferings of groups in human communities but also to the innovations that may spring from these particulars. Kristeva's emphasis on the struggles for *and* risks of identity comes to the fore in her replies. Certain aspects of this dialogue reveal a difficulty—more than a polemic, perhaps—in the relation between, on the one hand, Kristeva's writing practice in Europe (a Europe that is not homogeneous but itself divided, as she herself insists) and, on the other hand, her translation and reception in a North American setting. The dialogue may provide a chance for further advancing the debates on the social and political implications of Kristeva's thought.

Amidst her multifaceted and challenging life's work, Kristeva calls herself a "monster of the crossroads" and an "energetic pessimist" for our times. An attentive reading of her oeuvre will reveal the intellectual and cultural strengths of this stance. *The Philosophy of Julia Kristeva* contributes to and encourages such a reading. As always, the aim of this volume in the Library of Living Philosophers is to provide interpretive and critical discussion that will lead scholars, students, and new readers further into first-hand contact with the thought of the principal figure.

***

The arrangements for this volume began with the work of a prior editor of the Library of Living Philosophers, Randall E. Auxier, who saw the idea for the volume through the process of approval by the Editorial Board and had the first meeting with Julia Kristeva. After an intervening period in which an interim editor supervised the series, the present editor began again on this volume, starting with the compiling of the contributors' list in consultation with Julia Kristeva, and seeking funding to support the preparation of the volume. *The Philosophy of Julia Kristeva* has been made possible in part by a major grant from the National Endowment for the Humanities: Exploring the human endeavor.

One of the first objectives was to find the right translators and bibliographer, a task aided by Julia Kristeva and by Jennifer Crewe at Columbia University Press, publisher of Kristeva's works in English. Lorna Scott Fox (translator of Kristeva's novel, *Teresa, My Love*) made the English version of *Je me voyage*, an interview with Samuel Dock, for the intellectual autobiography in Part I of the volume. Armine Kotin Mortimer (translator of Kristeva's novel, *The Enchanted Clock*) made the English versions of eleven of the contributors' essays and all of Kristeva's replies for Part II. The Library of Living Philosophers is also grateful to Hélène Volat for Part III, the bibliography of Kristeva's life's work.

The LLP acknowledges the continued support and cooperation of our publisher, Open Court, especially Kerri Mommer, whose long experience with the series and ready advice was essential in bringing this volume to fruition. Kyle Lake provided his expertise in typesetting once again. Southern Illinois University provided a sabbatical for the editor as well as graduate assistants to support the preparation of the volume. Kevin Cales, David Gray, Ryan Grunberg, Donnie McMann, Leslie Murray, Nick Popow, Mohsen Saber, and Amy Stewart all worked diligently in support of some part of the process. Amy Stewart also contributed her professional skills to the indexing. I thank the Office of Sponsored Projects Administration at Southern Illinois University Carbondale for their support in the application for and administration of the NEH grant, and Jeletta Brant, the Department of Philosophy's office manager, for helping the process along. Anthony Steinbock's support as a colleague and chair of the Department of Philosophy was greatly appreciated.

SARA G. BEARDSWORTH
EDITOR

DEPARTMENT OF PHILOSOPHY
SOUTHERN ILLINOIS UNIVERSITY CARBONDALE
MARCH 2020

PART ONE

INTELLECTUAL AUTOBIOGRAPHY OF JULIA KRISTEVA

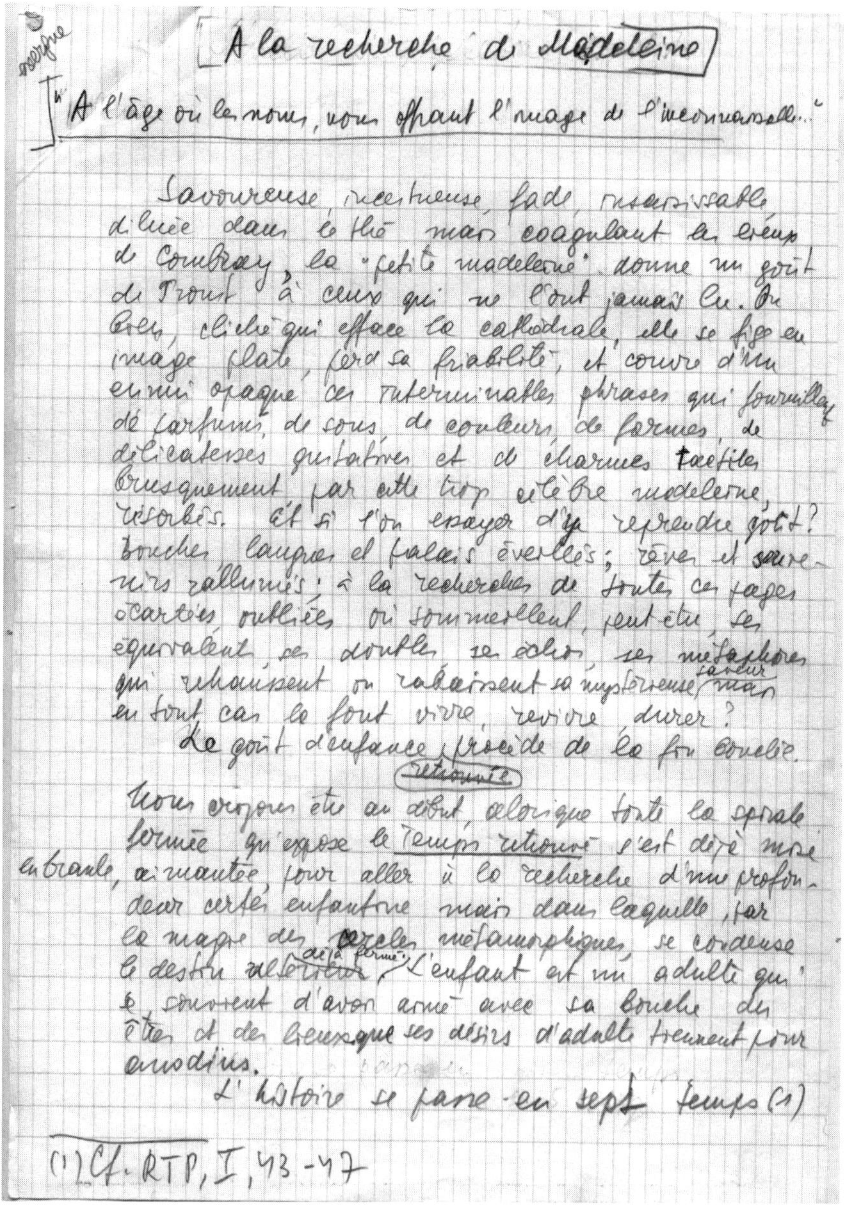

À la recherche de Madeleine

"A l'âge où les noms, nous offrant l'image de l'inconnaissable..."

Savoureuse, incestueuse, fade, insaisissable, diluée dans le thé mais coagulant les creux de Combray, la « petite madeleine » donne un goût de Proust à ceux qui ne l'ont jamais lu. Ou bien, cliché qui efface la cathédrale, elle se fige en image plate, perd sa friabilité, et couvre d'un ennui opaque ces interminables phrases qui fourmillent de parfums, de sons, de couleurs, de formes, de délicatesses gustatives et de charmes tactiles, brusquement, par cette trop célèbre madeleine, résorbés. Et si l'on essayait d'y reprendre goût? Bouches, langues et palais éveillés; rêves et souvenirs rallumés: à la recherche de toutes ces pages écartées, oubliées, où sommeillent, peut-être, ses équivalents, ses doubles, ses échos, ses métaphores qui rehaussent ou rabaissent sa mystérieuse saveur, mais en tout cas la font vivre, revivre, durer?

Le goût d'enfance procède de la foi conclue.

Nous croyons être au début, alors que toute la spirale fermée qu'expose le Temps retrouvé s'est déjà mise en branle, aimantée pour aller à la recherche d'une profondeur certes enfantine mais dans laquelle, par la magie des cercles métamorphiques, se condense le destin déjà formé. L'enfant est un adulte qui se souvient d'avoir aimé avec sa bouche des êtres et des lieux que ses désirs d'adulte tiennent pour anodins.

L'histoire se passe en sept temps (1)

(1) Cf. RTP, I, 43-47

Notes for the writing of *Time and Sense: Proust and the Experience of Literature*.

Julia Kristeva

INTELLECTUAL AUTOBIOGRAPHY

JE ME VOYAGE: A JOURNEY ACROSS BORDERS AND THROUGH IDENTITIES

Conversations with Samuel Dock

Translated by Lorna Scott Fox

Foreword by Samuel Dock
Julia Kristeva: An Elsewhere Here among Us

I will never forget our first meeting. That face, with its high cheekbones, incisive gaze, and beaming smile. She's smartly dressed, self-possessed but relaxed, and I warm to the strength that she exudes. She welcomes me into her home, me, my tape recorder, and my questions. We sip China tea in her quiet and luminous apartment. She reminisces, I urge her on. The book is a two-hander. I'm in awe of her, she finds it amusing, I nudge the theoretician back to lived experience, to her feelings, she plays along, or not, we push on. I enjoy her sense of fun, we laugh, and this sharing attenuates the lurking melancholy of an autobiographical exercise.

The intellectual heaped with titles and awards lets memories emerge, retracing her "journey" in my company. She's not severe at all—she's concentrated. Exacting. Decorously reserved, as well. Intensely there. She watches me, the psychoanalyst analyzing the psychologist, and vice versa, we understand each other, a bond is formed, the very essence of what we are about together. Her fingers clasp her teacup as she confides, muses, smiles. The charm works. With expressive precision, intellectual brilliance, and subtle probing into affects, she reveals herself as I shadow her. She has built her singularity in that elsewhere.

I listen to her story. Retracing the maze of existence, we find where the thread begins. A childhood in communist Bulgaria, studies, exile, encounters and lovers, marriage to Sollers, a marriage like one of the fine arts, and a son named David. And ever and always work, often travel, China, books, Freudian analysis, feminism in the wake of Simone de Beauvoir, poetry, disability. Trials, bereavements, and works have sprung from all of this. Julia Kristeva has turned errancy into vital motion, grief into insight, a taste for art and literature into caring, into a taste for others. Her gaze, wholly trained on me, moves through me in quest of others. I feel the plenitude of this impalpable collusion, this meeting in the truest sense.

Do you know Julia Kristeva? Not really, though she's famous, but not in France. I myself discovered her thanks to Marie-France Castarède, a psychoanalyst with whom I cowrote a book about generational clash, and who advised me to attend one of her lectures. So, one evening I went to hear her speak in a bookshop not far from Montparnasse. It was the launch of *Pulsions du temps*. Her razor-sharp mind, benign empathy, insatiable curiosity, and hypnotic whirlwind of ideas tackled the current status of the Freudian legacy, the European crisis, same-sex marriage, the valorization of motherhood, the need to believe. I was as much struck by her acuteness as by the breadth of her investigative range.

I read *Pulsions du temps*.[1] And then I wrote an enthusiastic review for the *Huffington Post*.[2] In our chaotic times, when language is falling apart and psychic life is in decline, Julia Kristeva sets out to put humanism on a new footing. The day the article appeared, she sent a brief thank-you email. I felt honored.

A few months later, Claude Durand, the president and CEO of Éditions Fayard, suggested I undertake to write her life in dialogue form, a project at the intersection of biography and psychological research: Julia hoped that I would do it. Hadn't she got the wrong name? No, it was me she wanted! I am a clinical psychologist and a writer, but not so much an intellectual or artist, I feel, as a craftsman, a workman first and foremost. I write with as much wariness as gusto until realizing I need to write more, revise, invent, reinvent myself all over again. Did I have what it took to foster the uncovering of her intimate self, which she has protected for so long?

It took me months to read everything she'd written. The novels, from *The Samurai* to *The Enchanted Clock*; the female genius trilogy—Arendt, Klein, Colette; the panoramic nonfiction, *Black Sun*, *Powers of Horror*, *Tales of Love*; and all the rest. Months to become familiar with her theoretical contributions when teaching at Paris 7 or across the Atlantic, and to chart her many battles . . . Months to sketch out the key lines of a life devoted to creation and sublimation, and to glimpse, beyond theory and on the far side of fiction, her own little madeleines, her rough edges, her secret chasms.

Now that I am to let you, the reader, into our work, I feel a pang of nostalgia. I'll miss the talking and the laughing. I enjoyed letting her do what she excels at: developing and clarifying her thoughts, as we roamed through territories she'd lost then found again. I hope you will take equal pleasure in following the steps of this exceptional woman, so endearing and inventive. For my part, I'll never forget it.

A destiny, an oeuvre. A "multiverse," she calls it. Is she a recognizable foreigner, a familiar stranger, a serene rebel? Her thinking reaches to the hard kernel of humanity that reveals the torments and wonders of otherness in oneself, beyond oneself.

Julia Kristeva? A distant elsewhere, and yet so close. An elsewhere here among us.

I. Growing Up in Bulgaria

Some men like me 'cause I'm happy

— Billie Holiday

Samuel Dock. Whether due to lack of curiosity or to xenophobia, the indifference in France to your Bulgarian beginnings is surprising. You're a war baby, after all.

Julia Kristeva. When I was small, I often heard this Russian song:

Dvadtsat vtorovo iyunya,
Rovno v chetyre chassa,
Kiev bombili, nam obyavili,
Chto nachalassya voyna.
(On twenty-second June,
On the dot of four o'clock,
Kiev was bombed and we were told
The war had just begun.)

I was born two days after the outbreak of war. At around four or five years old I became aware that my birthday was connected to the grand beat of a global conflict . . . and ultimately to the sensation of being consumed in an explosion, no room for "me," I'm just a splinter in a world in the throes of destruction. Then Bulgaria tumbles into the communist bloc, cue reconstruction, shortages, oppression and promises, the cold war . . . We were living in Sliven at the time, my birthplace, a town in southeast Bulgaria. Near the Balkans. Though I was tiny, I could tell there was a war. We were always going down to the cellar, and we listened to the BBC. We'd wait for the drumming jingle of Radio London, and I can still see the tense faces of the grown-ups as they listened to those enigmatic messages, their fear was infectious. My family was staying with some communist teachers, *résistants* living under the radar. The uniform of a German officer prowling the courtyard, the blackness of the night as we ran through the streets seeking shelter, a flare tearing the sky to warn of a bombardment: can these be the memories of a three-year-old child? Or are they reconstructions based on what I heard later? The reason I mention such flashbacks is because, with hindsight, it seems it was around them and against them that our family ties grew most solidly knotted.

S.D. You've more often waxed lyrical about the scents of the Valley of the Roses, the joys of the Black Sea, your homeland as a sublime cradle, sensually recalled. These darker memories are unfamiliar. You're bringing them up for the first time, I believe.

J.K. Probably because I've grown more at ease with my shadows and fractures . . . much like the Nivi of my latest novel, *The Enchanted Clock*. She represents me more faithfully than other characters.

S.D. This fragmentation springs from that first trauma, and will be developed across others, as we'll discuss later. In parallel, all the same, there were some cohesive and reassuring aspects to your early childhood, however stricken it was by history. I'd like to dwell on these a little.

J.K. Thanks to my parents, it was a fairly sheltered period in spite of everything. Two photographs obstruct my memory like screens, but they also bring associations flowing back, and make me feel like a toddler again.

The first shows a landau I've been lifted out of. I'm standing next to it, little black shoes on a white towel. My parents wanted to immortalize the moment when I stood upright for the first time! My mother, Kristina, is behind me. Her perfume will always be with me—a cloud of silk and essence of rose, the navy-blue caress of her dress. I can't see her, I'm leaning back on her presence, she envelops me like a cosmic breast, the maternal feminine is available. My mother studied biology before deciding not to teach and to take care of her children instead, without apparent regret. Oh, I haven't, to be sure, forgotten the silence drowned by her smile, slightly disenchanted but at peace, I think, whenever her university days were mentioned. Some might read into this a mark of spirituality, the discretion of the sacred. In fact, what my mother transmitted to me was simply that femininity encompasses maternal *reliance* without guilt or frustration. I've never understood how women could take themselves to be a "second" sex. For me, femininity expresses what is undeniable or irrefutable about life. Effortlessly, wholeheartedly, spontaneously. As my mother did.

In the second picture, a bit later, I'm in the world facing the world, that is, facing the photographer. We've been out shopping, my father Stoyan and I. I'm carrying a melon and he, two watermelons. He's bent over me and I snuggle into that masculine refuge with the marveling trust that precludes the least whit of loneliness. I am not losing myself in the other, we are two indivisible entities, but I smile with my father's smile. This incorporation of paternal maleness, as silly as it is simple and unconditional, is also the solidity that constituted me, made me into the person I am, notwithstanding exiles and traumas.

S.D. You've often defined yourself in terms of travel, motion, foreignness . . . Isn't it this solid confidence in your parents that allowed you to break through borders, geographical or mental, and unfold your thinking?

J.K. There speaks the analyst in you! The conclusions you draw from what I said are correct, but I prefer to remain in the story, where the facts neither confirm nor disqualify frailty or endurance but punctuate at best a suspended moment . . . To recount one's analysis so as to avoid doing it, no thanks, I'm trying to continue it on the other side of the couch, that's vital.

S.D. As you please! In *Pulsions du temps*, you talk very affectionately about the alphabet festival in Bulgaria you took part in as a child. You were, you embodied a letter in the parade—is that where your early love of language could have come from?

J.K. In our family, culture took pride of place. Books, piano, singing, theater, opera . . . and sports, as well. My father was fanatical about "physical culture." Were we unusual? Not really. That allegiance—be it escapism or resistance—strikes me as a prevalent feature of that part of Europe, the scene of a constant to-and-fro of influences, upheavals, and wars. Bulgaria stands as a crossroads country, still overlooked despite its entrance into the European Union. Even today the Balkans are a "powder keg"—think of Sarajevo. At the same time, with all the more reason perhaps, the cult of letters or the alphabet sustained those peoples and especially the Bulgarians throughout their history. Proximity to the "Greek miracle" is another factor: as an example . . . to be surpassed? That being said, Bulgaria is the only country I know of that celebrates the alphabet. May 24, the feast day of the brothers Cyril and Methodius, became a "festival of Culture."

S.D. Tell us about these two Orthodox saints.

J.K. The most recent research is divided on their background (were they Slavs or Greeks?), but we Bulgarians say their mother was a Slav and their father a high official of the Byzantine Empire. The brothers received an outstanding education and after they were ordained, Pope Adrian II sent them to preach to the Slavic peoples of Moravia. To carry out this mission they invented an alphabet for translating the Scriptures into Slavonic, the ancient language of the region. In *Passions of Our Time*, I go into the details of their story: trouble with the Vatican (we're in the ninth century, before the great schism of 1054); Cyril dies and is actually buried in the Vatican, while Methodius returns with his disciples to Bulgarian soil.[3] Literacy first takes off there, before spreading to Russia and farther afield. The University of Sofia is now named after Clement of Ohrid, the most famous of those missionaries of the written word.

Between the ages of seven and twenty-four, I took part in this unlikely festival alongside the entire "people of culture": schoolchildren, their parents clapping wildly from the sidewalks, but also teachers, students and professors, writers, journalists, publishers, librarians, artists and painters . . . We each sported a letter of the alphabet, surrounded by flags and floral displays, parading down streets hung with lights and suffused with music, scents, words. The letters free-floated on moving bodies or came together to form slogans, snatches of poetry, names of the great authors of our cultural memory.

S.D. What was your slogan, then?

J.K. It changed every year. I'll never forget those times. From the outside, I can see it's hard to comprehend how family life could ever be so anchored in this precious alphabet that, from the religiosity of its beginnings, had become altogether secular—the beating heart of the social and political pact. The festival itself transmitted an obvious, unconditional certainty: in order to *be*, it was absolutely necessary to take your place in the alphabet, by doing well at school, college, and the rest. But at the same time you were summoned, through the same cultural tool, to *play* on your keyboard, to say "I" by appropriating the letters, by writing.

S.D. After the end of the Second World War, your father, who shared none of the ideals of the communist regime, urged you to study foreign languages, with a kind of cosmopolitan philosophy.

J.K. He declared that his one aim in life was to "get his daughters out of the guts of hell," his grim metaphor for our country. "There's no other way than by learning languages, that's all, you've got to speak foreign languages. And become financially independent, of course." Dad claimed that the intestinal reference was in the Gospel, but I only ever found it in Dante, in the last canto of the *Inferno*, the Ninth Circle: the intestine, *burella* in Italian, lying on the ground, is the image of a "broken heart." Was this his obsession, his secret "family romance"? He'd say that the patronymic Kristev, literally "of the cross," "didn't come out of nowhere, it came down to us from the crusaders who had a cross sewn onto their clothing, yes, really, it's a fact that they went through Thrace (the region of his natal village), as early as the eleventh century!" My disbelieving face would send him apoplectic. "I don't need archives to prove it! In any case, it's so long ago that they'd have disappeared by now. I just know, that's all." To me, this belief unsupported by any historical evidence made him look bad, but I couldn't help being impressed by his hypothetical etymology. So much so that I used it in *Murder in Byzantium*!

S.D. The Bulgarian cultural environment was auspicious, and the alphabet festival acted as an institutional spur to reading and writing. Still, the family played a key role in your intellectual formation, I think. According to Daniel Sibony, a child will read if he is close to someone who enjoys reading. Did your parents read stories to you? How did they pass on the love of letters—your basis for life?

J.K. Precisely by reading. Reading was fundamental. They read us fairy tales, Bulgarian classics, and the great works of Russian literature, and pushed us to read them. At meals we'd talk about our schoolwork, particularly Russian and French classes. My father had studied theology, and then medicine; he was passionate about literature. Following the war, the communist government started sending all the young doctors to practice in the countryside. My father opted to drop medicine and stay in Sofia, to make sure his daughters went to a good school. He was very religious and went into church management, earning just enough to get by as a family, while doing various editing and Russian translation jobs to supplement his income. He also sang at Mass and in several religious and secular choirs. He had an extraordinary ear for music, which my sister Ivanka inherited. The spirituality he cast over the family collided with my mother's highly secular, scientific rationality. She brought her biology studies to bear in defense of Darwinism during our "cultural debates" at the dinner table. However, it would have been unthinkable for a woman of her upbringing to go so far as to quarrel with her husband.

It was left to me to brandish the torch of argument! Poor darling Dad, I called him a dinosaur, a relic, a fossil. He didn't take it lying down, there was always a fight. (*Laughter*) My sister would back me up, but with relative mildness. So I was the one who bore the brunt of punishment. In the corner, on your knees! Guilty and proud of it, I played the part of the boy who rebels against "paternal obscurantism," no less! My mother would rebuke me for going too far, but deep down she was quite pleased to have a daughter who dared to be her spokesman. Later, although she felt lonely—both us girls had left the country—she supported my choice to live as an emancipated woman in Paris. She thought I'd gone because of my father's temper, because he was always punishing the cheeky girl who "talked back." She had no idea that between him and me, it was total love!

S.D. A person who doesn't rebel is dead inside.

J.K. Exactly. I couldn't stay still, I needed to protest. In our house, you see, the atmosphere was highly cultured, but not at all conventional, more of a goad to the critical spirit. My father played along and took my stubborn teenage outbursts seriously, so much so that his impassioned reactions couldn't shut me up, and our showdowns got out of hand! I must have understood, subconsciously, that this performance of paternal attention in some way warranted my opposition, which ratcheted up as a result.

S.D. In your writings, you're more discreet about your sister.

J.K. Ivanka was born when I was three-and-a-half. She was named after our maternal grandfather, Ivan. In 1945, the country went communist and we left Sliven. On our way to Sofia we stopped in Yambol, where my mother's parents lived. My father, orphaned of both his parents, had been adopted by Jordana, a widowed friend of the family who was also to be my nurse. My parents assured me that my own name, Julia, was a modern version of that of this adoptive grandmother, Jordana. A name whose etymology harks back to the river of the Bible, the Jordan.

S.D. Might you, in a certain sense, have "lost" your mother?

J.K. You don't know how right you are! When my mother went into labor, at home, I was sent off to play with my little friend Anna, who lived next door. I couldn't stand her mother, a cold, elegant lady, a schoolteacher I believe, always mincing coquettishly around while my mother's belly grew bigger. I can see it now: I'm terribly thirsty, I long for a big glass of water, but the "witch" makes me drink out of a little spoon. Practically by the drop. Strange, isn't it! The foible of an overcautious mother, who only infuriated me on that day? Is it a memory at all? Or a reverie disguising the frustration caused by my sister's arrival? Regressing to babyhood, I fly into a rage, violently shove both spoon and lady away, and the lady complains to my father. The shame! I get a severe scolding at home, but at least I've managed to distract momentarily from THE baby. Then I refuse to drink, for two days. Proud of my anger and of vanquishing my thirst. Hadn't I defied the "witch" from the height of my three-and-a-half years, and scorned her little spoon? Mom had forsaken me to breastfeed an intruder. I wasn't angry with her, not at all, I took everything on myself. But I worked my revenge . . . on the neighbor.

Another scene, just afterwards. We're in Sofia, strolling through the Rose Garden, I pull free from my mother and run off as fast as I can, I fall over, bleeding knees, stagger to my feet, she catches up, white-faced and scared: "What is it? Show me!" I don't snivel or whine, ever. "It's nothing, I'm fine . . . Are you alright, mom?" That phrase would become legendary in our family.

S.D. Which of you is the mother, which is the daughter? . . . Identification, projection, envy and gratitude, reparation of harm . . .

J.K. I was so imbued with her wholehearted availability as a mother, with that cloud of perfume and reasoned vigilance, and then with the stormy partiality of my father, that I wasn't aware of feeling shaken by the arrival of the little "newbie." On the other hand, my status as the elder, absorbing the parents' attention, must have weighed heavily on her as the "little one." We were very close, our complicity was stronger than our rivalry. It was thanks to my sister that, very soon, I found myself admiring the talents of a fellow but superior female without feeling jealous. Yes, that can happen! My father had a very fine singing voice but didn't play an instrument. He passed on his love of music to us. I used to dread singing lessons, in which I performed with distinctly less brilliance than in other subjects. To be honest, I was awful! (*Laughter*) . . . Ivanka, on the other hand, was marvelous. She has perfect pitch, like my son David. My parents bought her a piano and a violin, and she got into the highly selective music school in Sofia, where budding talents could cultivate their gifts while following the standard curriculum. We'd regularly attend her concerts, she was amazing! I clapped wildly, full of awe. Even now, I can still hear her practicing for the next concert, Paganini, Bach, Shostakovich . . .

S.D. Maybe because you were so confident and secure in your own path.

J.K. The mere fact of another world than mine existing, alien and unattainable, filled me with respect, a kind of thankfulness . . . with not the least flicker of conflict, I think. Well, alright, it was annoying, because she was always sawing away in the next-door room, the sound made it hard to think, I missed the silence! My mother used to say to me: "You don't know how to hate." True, but it isn't only a virtue, as Mom thought. It's also a weakness, as I would realize later, when I came under attack. A weakness whose source may well lie in my lack of jealousy when listening to Ivanka play Mozart's *Fifth Violin Concerto*.

S.D. Did your sister remain in Bulgaria?

J.K. No, she continued her studies at the Music Conservatoire in Moscow, under some eminent musicians including Igor Oistrakh. Then she went to Switzerland, helped by Pierre Boulez to obtain a scholarship to the Music Academy in Basel. She did a doctorate in music and then became a professor at the University of Paris-Saint-Denis, specializing in classical, modern, and contemporary music.

S.D. The fact remains that she shared with your father a realm from which you were excluded. Where did she fit into the family dynamic? You were the insurgent, the "boy," but what about her? What was her relationship with your parents?

J.K. It's true I don't regard her as a rebel, possibly because I took that role for myself. And yet, more secretive and intuitive than me, more sensitive and exacting, she asserted her freedom—in the face of conventional expectations and with great strength and courage, in both Berlin and Paris. After a concert-hall career she moved into music theory, producing a very meticulous and personal body of work under the pen name of Ivanka Stoïanova.

S.D. While it may seem that the father occupies a larger place in your writings, there are passages concerning your mother which I personally find very moving. You pay her a magnificent tribute in *Murder in Byzantium*:

> I've just got back from the cemetery filled with tears and silence. The nighttime face of our sunny silence. My mother was one who inhabited the kind of silence that I've been trying to describe to you. She was the most reserved kind of woman, some would say the least hysterical, and it wasn't because she was depressed. You think that can't exist? But yes, this woman exists, my mother, and don't be shocked if I use the present tense, she's here, between us. Our silence is so transparent that I believe I never felt the need to speak to you about her, or not that much, it's possible. OK, so here I go, yet with a good bit of silence. In mourning, to write what one cannot say is still silence, I know that you understand me.[4]

How would you describe your mother, Kristina Kristeva?

J.K. She didn't talk very much, she was a gentle person, affectionate with her daughters, always nicely turned out, an excellent cook and to cap it all, a wizard at math! She loved figures and while busy with housework, cooking, or embroidery she'd help me solve the thorniest math and geometry problems. My idea of going to the USSR to study astrophysics came from her, and, in fact, had been her own desire: she never expressed this utopia aloud, but I lived through it with her when she was helping me prepare for the mathematics Olympics. An enigmatic person, very inward-looking, Kristina was also brilliant at drawing. Her hands could do anything, even knit jumpers and sew pretty dresses for her daughters—a pair of princesses among the other girls in those deprived postwar days. In the preface to the catalog of my exhibition at the Louvre, *Visions capitales*, dedicated to her, I tell a story that is a "capital" one for me. My sister and I are listening to a children's program on the radio. It's winter, it's cold, and we're huddled by the glowing stove. The program ends with a competition: you have to answer the question, "What is the fastest means of transport in the world?" and sketch your answer. My sister says: "An airplane." I propose: "Sputniks." Beside us, my mother is cooking. The atmosphere is tense. It's her turn to answer, she says: "Thought." Since I'm used to always having the last word, I complain that that's useless, because you can't draw thought. "Just you wait," she says. And she draws a snowman facing a sun. A sunbeam has cut into his head, making it hang sideways. Up in the top corner of the picture, a Sputnik is circling the moon. *Man is perishable, but his thought spans the sky.* We sent in the drawing and I won the prize.

S.D. A little girl delighted with the first in a long line of prizes! The least prestigious perhaps, a two-bit radio contest, but no doubt the most important of all, the most treasured.

J.K. You see, this story sums up the essence of my mother. Some people might pity her for taking a back seat, like a prisoner in the home, stuck with her children. But this was never a question for Kristina; she was happy that way. In the above little scene, she didn't "step back" to "make way" for her daughter. The daughter didn't rob the prize, triumphing at the mother's expense. *She* won because *I* won. A curious transubstantiation, in which we formed a single unit, yet each in our separate place. Physically, though, I look like my father.

S.D. Let's talk about him. You say that he bequeathed to you the "weightlessness of language."[5] In real or imaginary form, at times split into several figures within a single book, the father is of paramount importance in your works, with his authority and function, but also in a more intimate, affective way. In both novels and interviews you have shared key memories of him, such as the soccer matches you attended together. Could you introduce him once more? You mentioned earlier that he was orphaned by the war . . .

J.K. This brings up a traumatic genealogy that analysts now call transgenerational, as you know. My paternal grandfather served as an officer during the Balkan War of 1912. He was killed before my father, the youngest child, ever knew him. His mother, Mithra, died of childbirth complications. He was left with a sister and two brothers, and it was Jordana, as I said, who brought him up. Perpetually haunted by death and the fear of abandonment, the little boy kept terrors at bay through an intense closeness to his substitute mother, widow and orphan deeply attached to each other. This early clinging to the female across the void left by the deceased parents, this incestual imprint, gave rise in the man to a quasi-pathological sensibility and doubtless to his immoderate attraction to art, and also to the Beyond.

In his teens he had the choice between a scholarship to military college or to the seminary. His family opted for the seminary. It was the right decision. The orphan—as he liked to call himself—became a seminarian, before turning to theology and medicine.

S.D. He could have been a priest. Why the change of course?

J.K. I've often wondered that myself. He always claimed he left the religious life to get married and have children. And yet the Orthodox Church allows its priests to marry . . . I think he wanted to get away from the suffocating, centripetal homogeneity of the religious world. Freud points to an immanent homosexuality in army, church, and school, which may well underpin their social cohesion but is no less alienating for that, no less potentially doctrinaire and tyrannical. My father renounced the priesthood, but not the faith; he continued to pray in church, read the Old and New Testaments, and write theological works. Medicine offered him a social, or simply human, efficacy that religion no longer did, perhaps. The scientific training and clinical practice also brought him closer to my mother, with her scientific, pragmatic rationalism. The horrors of war and then communism had besides instilled in him a catastrophic vision of human history, and of his own place in its eddies. A dear friend of whom he often spoke, high up in the medical establishment, had been part of the group of intellectuals—solidary for once—that petitioned King Boris III to stop the deportation of Jews being planned by the pro-Nazi government. Along with the Metropolitan of Sofia, they declared that any convoys would have to pass over their dead bodies. Thanks to this, Bulgarian Jews were spared the extermination camps, if not the anti-Jewish laws . . . All in all, Stoyan must have chosen to shelter in the symbolism of theology, to reclaim his life in and through it.

S.D. He wanted you to be "pneumatic" . . .

J.K. You spotted that! He was deeply into Gnosticism. In the second century, *pneuma* meant what pertained to the Holy Spirit. Fortunately, my father didn't want me to be a Gnostic, but he did imagine his daughter endowed with an innate perfection of nature and spirit, small order! In true Greco-Latin fashion, he wished me to cultivate myself, to possess a rich inner life and a harmonious body. Every summer we invariably went to the seaside and then to the mountains—in that order, never the reverse!—with a view to "taming the complexity of nature" and applying the proverb *mens sana in corpore sano*. Imagine how this looked to our little playmates in Bulgaria! We had to hike, run, swim . . . read countless books in preparation for the new semester and . . . for the future! By the age of seven or eight, we were up at the crack of dawn with the Hindu-yogic sun salutation. There was no getting out of it, let me tell you! My sister and I applied ourselves earnestly, though we burst into giggles when we were done! I ended up enjoying the exercise, it felt normal and fun.

S.D. This pious father, whom you greatly loved, sought to impart the values that mattered to him. Much later, the "need to believe" would emerge as an important and recurrent strand of your thinking. Was this a resurgence or a discovery?

J.K. Created or found? Isn't that the question posed by every historical, cultural, intellectual, and emotional event? When I began thinking about the "need to believe," a notion examined at length by many other psychoanalysts, of course I was thinking about my father—even if my primary concern was with the current political context. While he was alive, as I said, I was sincerely at war with the rigid piety beneath his liberated airs! I continue to think that the abuses of organized religion must be combated, while pursuing the *transvaluation* of our traditional heritage, but "with full knowledge of the facts." That is, by studying the complexity of these beliefs, and above all by proposing a permanent refoundation of humanism. You're familiar with my hobby-horse, my aspiration to replace the "sickness of ideality," i.e. fundamentalism, with specific projects and ideals: for adolescents, for women, for parents adrift in changing conditions, for the disabled and those at the end of their lives . . .

When I was a child, my father's faith seemed not only incomprehensible but hopelessly archaic—not worth knowing or even wondering about. It wasn't until much later that my discovery of Freud enlightened me on the interdependence of faith and reason. At the time, I naively felt that my father's belief in God stood for a revolt against the "established order," that of a (totalitarian) historical materialism, and against existence in general, and this was how he justified his everyday life. Nor did it escape me that by practicing his religion he ran the genuine risk of winding up in prison or the Gulag. But Stoyan was neither a hero nor a victim. At home, our *disputatio* took the rhetorical form of an intellectual ritual; he didn't want to plant too much schizophrenia in my mind, given what we were being taught at school. Though he demanded respect for his convictions, he never tried to demolish mine. A kind of "secularism" of his own, in a communist context.

S.D. Earlier, you spoke of your maternal grandparents in relation to the move from Sliven to Sofia after the war. Could you tell us a little more about the extended clan and its origins?

J.K. My father once drew up our family tree, filling a notebook of fifty pages. I'm afraid I haven't read it: I don't feel that I depend on those "origins," any more than on some symbolic metafamily comprised of friends or acolytes. Am I too wary of "collectivity"? Too used to relying on "my own resources"? Another defect of mine! The truth is that we maintained few links to the maternal or paternal "clans," groups that had been splintered and dispersed by wars, moves, and what we now call "displacement." Nevertheless, I've met some cousins on my father's side, including Stoyan Pavlov, a kind and generous man high up in the Bulgarian Army, who with his wife and children remained very close to my parents when my sister and I left the country. He saw a lot of them in their old age, and I'm delighted to see him on the rare occasions I go back. My maternal grandmother, whose maiden name was Jekov—the local version of Jacob—alleged that the Jacobs had been followers of the pseudoprophet, Sabbatai Zevi, and had converted not to Ottoman Islam but to the Orthodox faith. This somewhat hazy *marrano* memory, if such it was, was thinly coated in a Christianity that, though it went back centuries, was half-hearted and rarely practiced.[6] My mother's only brother, Uncle Panayot, was a lawyer and a socialist in the "broad socialism" current of Bulgarian politics, as distinct from "narrow socialism," meaning communism. My shopkeeper grandparents, who were truly broadminded, encouraged Kristina and Panayot to go to university. As well as biology, my mother learned fencing—highly unusual in the Bulgaria of the 1920s! I was great friends with Panayot's daughter, my cousin Venetta, who was the same age as me. She was my first vacation bestie and the confidante of my early teens. Our friendship lapsed around the age of sixteen or seventeen, and after that our different studies, social circles, and personal evolution drove us apart for good.

S.D. I'm trying to picture you as a little girl. What were you like? What did you like? The psychologist in me wants a glimpse of the precocious, culture-vulture moppet you were.

J.K. I was solitary (said my mother) and pig-headed (said my father). I recognize myself in the word "solitary," but time would prove my father right. My few friendships were strong ones. I remember two bosom buddies at primary and then high school: Emilia and Lydia. At college, there was Helena and Anastasia. I preferred one-to-one relationships to groups. And yes, I loved studying. I had a knack for math, as I've said, but I was more drawn to the subjects that nourished comprehension and writing. Being pretty good at composition, I kept a diary in which I gave free rein to private soulfulness and dissected my relationships with boys and girlfriends. I was dreamy and introverted, yet also fascinated by the new worlds that were opening up at school through the sciences and the imaginary. What I remember most clearly about those years is the sense of being an outsider. I was a top student, and often came first in class, but was denied the recognition because my father wasn't a communist. I will always remember how at every Festival of Culture, on Alphabet Day, May 24, I'd be expecting to carry the school flag. But that honor always went to a less successful student than me, one whose parents were "in the Party." It never occurred to me to protest, not even at home, I "understood." It wasn't very pleasant all the same.

In the same vein, I'd applied to the English high school where the brightest students and the children of the nomenklatura went. The decision was a long time coming, and I grew more and more anxious. One day I spotted a letter addressed to my father, which looked like the long-awaited reply. I opened it. The verdict was that I could not be admitted to the English school, because the family did not adhere to communist ideals. My father was furious with me for opening his mail and deeply pained by the rejection, for my sake and his, for all our sakes.

Happily, I was something of a hit with the boys! My primary-school beau, whose name was Simeon, courted me by pulling my hair and throwing down challenges: which of us would get the best grades in class, which would beat the other at gymnastics, athletics, basketball . . . I wasn't very big or muscly, but I acquitted myself. Love in competition form.

S.D. The sun salutation paid off!

J.K. It certainly did! Anyhow, Simeon insisted he could run faster than me, because boys were faster than girls. I told myself it was stupid, to no avail: in the end, of course, I agreed to race him. I was so determined to win that I put on a massive spurt that carried me over the finishing line and beyond, where I hadn't seen that there was a bench. I banged my leg badly. But still, I won! And promptly dropped that Simeon in disgust.

My high-school boyfriend was very different. Anton was in the class above me, and extremely clever. After the baccalaureate he went to a top engineering college and then on to the USSR, to a specialization program in one of those sealed scientific towns in Siberia or somewhere, I never found out for sure. His departure severed a passionate love story. I saw him again years later in Paris, when I was already teaching at the university. He was as attentive, thoughtful, and fretful as ever. Convinced as he was of the imminent outbreak of war between the two blocs, he feared we'd never meet again; the parking lot at Jussieu reminded him of an atomic bomb shelter. I thought he was overdoing it, turning the blow of our separation into a fatal political conflict like that.

The last time I visited Bulgaria, in November 2014, I was well received, far more warmly than usual. Was it because this time I'd had my talk translated, and delivered it in Bulgarian? I speak without an accent, but in everyday conversation I often grope for words. My mother tongue is no longer the language of my thinking. All my mental activity, dreams included, takes place in French. Some faithful Bulgarian friends translated my text, and using that base I recovered the pith of my first language, found myself able to improvise, tried to impress my style onto this "other" tongue into which I was born . . . At the end of the lecture, I remained on stage while people proffered bouquets and asked for autographs. Among them a dignified-looking man was waiting, calm, silent, and still. When he approached, he was holding a photograph of me aged sixteen. I was amazed, thanked him, so interested in this photo I didn't have, I'd love a copy. "How do you come to have it?" Silence. "I am Anton," he said. I was overwhelmed.

Bulgarian TV was making a documentary about me, and before agreeing to be interviewed for it, he phoned to ask my permission. Again, his tactfulness. Of course, no problem! Well, I have recently seen the film. "I am in love with a goddess," says this quiet and decent man. Reliving my schoolgirl feelings, I don't recognize myself in the goddess, how could I, but she doesn't make me laugh, either. I thank her for ennobling in her own way the teenage passions of those wrecked by life.

S.D. I can understand your surprise, your shock before this loss incarnate. He'd kept a photo of you from when the two of you were separated by his work in the USSR, from which he returned a changed man, unable to regain you or forget you . . .

J.K. Anton speaks perfect French; he reminded me that we took lessons at the Alliance Française together. He carried on with the language, the only remaining link between us. He's married, of course, to a Russian woman, and he told me about his son. The power of tenderness is beyond reason, it's what keeps human beings alive. Regardless of the harsh tensions of history, which age the body but leave the passions whole.

S.D. By the age of five you'd been enrolled in a French nursery school. You learned to recite rhymes in French, to tell the time, to pray . . .

J.K. That's right. It was my parents' excellent idea. The teachers were nuns. I thought they were Dominicans but was recently told that they were most probably lay sisters, Oblates of the Assumption. They were rather strict, in the sense of *regulation*. They set great store by order, neatness, rigor, respect;

we curtseyed to them. They taught us to recite La Fontaine fables and a few prayers. Christmas was a day for gifts rather than church. Sadly, they were expelled two years later, accused of espionage. I missed them. But their work was picked up by the Alliance Française, and I went on attending two or three afternoons a week, for two hours—on top of the national curriculum.

In Bulgaria, the school system resembled that of Germany: lessons in the morning and extracurricular activities, such as languages, arts, or sports, in the afternoon (or vice versa). Parents and children decided on the activity together. My own interest was in languages, and I learned Russian first, then French and English. I was also very keen on gymnastics, athletics, basketball, and swimming. Later tennis, with Philippe . . . Needless to say it was my sister Ivanka who went in for singing, piano, and violin! In that domain, I was just the audience.

S.D. I am struck by the way nothing seemed to stop you, despite the difficulties, constraints, and sacrifices imposed by the regime. You adapted, you found alternatives, you sublimated, you forged ahead.

J.K. What else can one do? Is it because politics, in a communist country, is so omnipresent that it doesn't spare children? I was aware of far more serious dramas at a remove, world conflicts came into every conversation, and so my petty miseries were of no consequence, too bad; onward or die. That's a brutal way to put it, but, with hindsight, I was blessed with the luck or the instinct to keep on pushing on. Something doesn't work? Okay, what shall we do about it?

It was the Sputnik era, the conquest of space. I read everything I could lay my hands on. I didn't perform too badly at the math Olympics, and I wished I could follow Anton in his Soviet adventure, which I imagined in stellar terms. Impossible, alas. I ventured into medicine, hesitated: the first sessions at the morgue were petrifying! So I turned toward the microcosm of the human sciences.

S.D. Did your parents support you in your desire to do space research?

J.K. Mom did. Dad not so much, because he knew that communism would never let me fulfill that ambition. I think he also hated the idea of my going away. While at the same time wishing me to escape from hell . . .

S.D. You were seized early on, then, by the urge to escape. Having failed to get away by means of science, you succeeded by means of reading. Your endless journey, your endless elsewhere took off in the pages of books. At a young age you were tackling some of the greatest and least accessible authors, such as Dostoyevsky and Victor Hugo. Can you remember the first book you ever read?

J.K. I will forever be grateful to the French teacher who shaped my taste for twentieth-century European literature and culture. Cyril Bogoyavlensky was a White Russian noble who'd washed up in Sofia. As a teenager I was a regular at his language and literature classes in the Alliance, where there were other remarkable teachers, but it is his face and his voice that come to mind if I close my eyes. I was his favorite, for some reason! Whereas my fellow students were incapable of grasping the past participle and its agreements, I found the master's explanations clear as glass. Poor fellow, he was defeated by these little Bulgarians, he'd wipe his forehead with a white silk hankie and swallow his pills with a glass of water and ask me with a sigh to take over at the blackboard. He infected me with an irrevocable longing for France. The French literature he revealed brought me back to the magic of French that had touched me in kindergarten, but this was a whole new universe, dreadfully demanding but within reach, with the clarity of dreams.

At school we were taught Bulgarian authors and "great literature," Pushkin, Chekhov, Tolstoy, alongside the "socialist realism" of Gorki, Fadeyev, etc. Dad let me join his Leskov and Dostoyevsky cult. Next to Dostoyevsky and his superman, that I read in Bulgarian, Victor Hugo—whom Bogoyavlensky made us copy out—and his Gavroche seemed legendary and yet accessible.

S.D. You set foot in France via *Les Misérables* and the adventures of its fabled characters . . .

J.K. It was so exciting to climb with two small boys into the belly of the Elephant of the Bastille, "rude, squat, clumsy, harsh, severe, almost deformed, but certainly majestic, and marked by a sort of magnificent savage gravity," even though it's been replaced by some sort of giant stove complete with pipe, "almost as the bourgeoisie replaces feudality."[7] I was perturbed by the meeting of Marius and Cosette in the Luxembourg Gardens:

> Marius had opened his whole soul to nature, he was thinking of nothing, he was living and breathing, he walked by close to the bench, the young girl raised her eyes, their glances met. But that time what was there in the young girl's glance? Marius could not have said. There was nothing, and there was everything. It was a strange flash.[8]

For a long time I held on to an exercise book full of passages copied out with a fountain pen, in my most diligent hand. When I arrived in Paris I couldn't help catching sight of Gavroche near the vanished Elephant, and feeling "the effect that the infinitely great may produce on the infinitely small."[9] I looked for the bench in the Luxembourg where Cosette and Marius crossed paths. The first realistic poem I taught my son David was by Hugo: "Upon a barricade thrown 'cross the street . . ."[10] David still intones it in a half-piteous, half-jokey voice:

> But the laugh suddenly ceased, when, paler grown,
> 'Midst them the lad appeared, and breathlessly
> Stood upright 'gainst the wall with: "Here am I."
> Dull death was shamed; the officer said, "Be free!"[11]

S.D. It would seem the Alliance equipped you with a more authentic French culture than anything served up to French kids today! At once revolutionary and realistic, but with a caustic spirit that made a change, I suppose, from the narrow communist outlook?

J.K. That's it. Mr. Bogoyavlensky had a soft spot for Molière, the paragon of liberating mockery. And in a spontaneous, hilariously infantile French, verging on the silly because, on this level of blatancy, silliness is next to reason, it equates to reason, it conceals reason, unless reason be demonstrably silly: only Molière can bring this off. Look at *The Imaginary Invalid*, look at Toinette pretending to be a doctor: the French language invented Descartes's reason as well as Toinette/Molière's riff on lung trouble. Science and absurdity: science is absurdity, and vice versa. Ionesco and Beckett were bound to write in French, it was practically compulsory, to be expected. And even Sartre, that graver Molière, was a philosopher of the absurd. French comedy is grand, it laughs at nothingness. And in a less farcical but no less ironical register, Proust, decoding the inanities and cruelties of the Belle Époque in his winding, breathless sentences . . . interminable anxieties ornate with sensual pleasure, whorled into subordinate clauses that break felt time into pieces.

S.D. In one interview, you said: "I am a pure product of *la francophonie*."

J.K. So I am, but minus any underlying ideology, more the contrary. I sampled French literature according to what came up in class, feeling free to like a thing or not, and most importantly, to forage as I pleased. I never felt that it was a monolithic block. My "great classics" were, and still are, the pieces of a protean jigsaw puzzle in which each author plays their own game. As time went on, I became convinced that there is no one Literature, but instead an imaginary experience which inflects into a multitude of styles, genres, and flavors, whose sole reason for existing is to counter the *pensée unique* of totalitarianism in whatever shape or form. You see, I felt incontrovertibly French, and it's not forbidden to dream!

S.D. Winnicott posited that the transitional object must be left behind in favor of a psychical investment in the outside world. The intermediary zone between mother and child can then be succeeded by a cultural zone. My feeling is that you reached this phase at a precociously young age . . .

J.K. Maybe so, I've never thought about it . . . But I forgot to say this: I only ever had one doll, which was soon supplanted by a shelf of books. I stuffed all my toys into a suitcase under the bed. Unlike my little playmates, I never saw the appeal of prams or dollies or tea sets! But that one doll is still in splendid condition. My mother found it in my closet and brought it to Paris on one of her visits. It's celluloid, and good as new. A gift from my maternal grandmother for my fourth birthday. By the time I was seven I'd put it away in a drawer.

During summer vacations at Grandmother's house, I used to hide at the very top of a plum tree to avoid her strict discipline over the chores, the obligation to clean or cook! (*Laughter*) I put my notebooks in my big overall pockets, and between mouthfuls of greengages I'd devour the novels of Colette or Victor Hugo. Mom would shout at me to stop acting like a tomboy and get down from that tree this minute! While Grandmother muttered that if the girl went on behaving like that, she'd never get married.

S.D. You had something of a competitive streak . . . Competing with yourself, for a start.

J.K. Jumping in without knowing where I'm going.

S.D. Your works on adolescence have done a great deal to enhance our clinical understanding of this life stage. You wrote recently, in *Passions of Our Time*: "*The adolescent is a believer on top of a nihilist.* We are all adolescents when we're in love."[12] What kind of adolescent succeeded to the solitary child?

J.K. An active, curious, secretive one. In my journal I poured out my gripes against my family, which was normal, and against society, which was riskier. This "work" was seriously clandestine, needless to say, and my parents only found it long after I'd left Sofia. "I'm incurably romantic," Marilyn Monroe used to say, and I often say it of myself, to the surprise of my son.

I hewed out spaces of freedom for myself by means of . . . journalism, in a weekly magazine called *High School Banner*. Our youthful team, guided by professional journalists, planned, wrote, edited, and printed it! It was my first "trade," and it actually paid something—not a princely sum, but enough to make me proud, glad to bring a little money home, though my parents wouldn't hear of it and put everything into my savings account (I was still a minor). My first trade, then, was journalism. Just think: I could report on school life, on the hardships and pastimes of the students and so on, but I could also broach national, educational, or general interest topics, and review the latest books. My first fiction, some short stories, appeared in that magazine. And I adored doing interviews! I was fascinated by the talk of young and not so young people, celebrities and nobodies. Interviews never bored me, whether the person was dull or lively, smart or dumb, conventional or critical. When people say that they reckon an intellectual like myself (supposedly) must find it irksome to listen to someone who doesn't share "the same language" or "the same trajectory," I'm surprised, I don't understand. Curiosity is my great vice and I uphold it. Perhaps it emerged during those *High School Banner* years, when under the leaden lid of official speeches I became hooked on reporting, marveling at the spontaneous utterances of ordinary people and contriving to get them "past," outwitting stereotypes and censorship.

S.D. Wasn't it a further disappointment to enter the modern languages faculty of Sofia University, after the impossibility of conquering the stars, after journalism as a hobby or a consolation prize?

J.K. I was certainly not your usual freshman at the Romance philology department. French as my first language, English as my second, and comparative literature as the cherry on the cake. Being virtually bilingual after so many years at the Alliance Française, I found French classes on campus easy to follow, too easy in fact. That's why I continued my university education by correspondence, while cultivating my skills as a journalist. I joined the staff of the national youth daily, the highly respected *Popular Youth*, quartered in the huge and prestigious Press Building along with other leading titles. I took my double life as a student and a salaried reporter very seriously: I published features and reports in the Education section and did some reviewing for the Culture pages. As my investigative range expanded, I was often sent into the provinces and countryside. My interviews became more personal, more intimate, yet also more political: the cultural formation of peasant youth, the links between students and the rural world, the handling of younger children in holiday camps by student monitors . . . And since I spoke Russian, French, and English, I was lucky enough to interview eminent visitors from abroad. Waldeck Rochet, the then first secretary of the French Communist Party; Henri Martin, the famous communist sailor, campaigning against the "filthy war" in Vietnam; Valentina Tereshkova and Yuri Gagarin, the first woman and first man in space. And later, dissidents from the Eastern countries like Antonin Liehm, the acclaimed essayist and editor-in-chief of the Czech journal *Literární Listy*, destined to play a leading role in the Prague Spring. We became good friends with Antonin and his wife Mira when they emigrated to Paris; they looked after me during my time in New York and introduced me to Philip Roth.

S.D. That journalist is still alive in you. I imagine that interviewing Gagarin and Tereshkova, who had fulfilled your own dream of being a cosmonaut, must have been a high point in your life. Did you ever go through what is prosaically called an adolescent crisis? Was there a rebellious spike? An explosion? An explicit antagonism to the family milieu?

J.K. Not really. Bulgaria was in a permanent state of crisis, striving, sacrifice and, potentially, rebound . . . This unstable climate ruled up and down the country and, though in a different way, at home. My revolt was expressed in the pages of my secret journal, as I said before, but didn't break through "on the surface." And it crept into a motto I'd given myself, which proved relevant again later, when Jacques Chirac made me president of the National Council on Disability. I met the then health secretary, Professor Jean-François Mattéi, who heard me out attentively but skeptically, before concluding: "When it comes to disability, *madame*, there's nothing to be done." I stared at him, and my motto came back to me. "Quite right, *monsieur le ministre*. There's nothing to be done: so, what shall we do about it?" That maxim is the way I am.

S.D. What was it like to be a student in 1960s Sofia? Did you still live with your parents? Did you go away on vacation? What were your concerns?

J.K. I went on living with my parents. After their previous home in downtown Sofia, near the church of St. Nedelya, they had bought one in a "cultured" neighborhood. In those days it was unthinkable to leave "home" before marriage, and there was no money to spare in any case. Still, my travels as an interpreter and journalist gave me exceptional access to the wider world, as compared with the constricted life led by most young people of my generation.

On top of that was the duty I haven't mentioned to you yet, as a monitor looking after young "pioneers" in international summer camps on the edge of the Black Sea. Kids aged between seven and thirteen used to come over from France, Belgium, Italy, China, Vietnam, Africa, and occasionally from North

Korea, too. Not having played enough with dolls, was there some "maternal fiber" in me that was only waiting to vibrate in the open air? My friends of both sexes preferred to spend their summer placements on cooperative farms in the country. I found myself spontaneously, and very happily, slipping into the role of big sister cum mommy. Most of our little visitors needed to be listened to, to be recognized; they came from humble communist or fellow-traveler homes and were sometimes downright poor. I spoke to them in French, their mother tongue, and we had great fun setting up the evening shows, a chance for each group to show off their talents. "My" charges were always splendid, especially when performing, say, fables by La Fontaine! We designed the costumes, constructed them out of colorful paper or card, learned the texts by heart and were applauded by everyone for "The Raven and the Fox," "The Wolf and the Lamb," "The Cat and the Rat," "The Oak Tree and the Reed," "The Laborer and His Children" . . .

S.D. What do you remember best, looking back on that childhood and adolescence under communism?

J.K. The subterranean, contradictory currents of our family life, a protective and caring haven, yet whose complexity intrigued me, it left a mark. My father's wounded, flayed emotivity made him highly psychosomatic; he fought bravely against a stomach ulcer, as well as against the marginality to which he was condemned by his Orthodox faith. My mother supported him by letting him play the boss, contenting herself with the part of "little wife." In my novel, *The Old Man and the Wolves*, set in the last hundred years of the Roman Empire, Clarus evinces a profound belief in the need for a spiritual bond. "We've lost the sense of belonging," he tells his daughter.

> Don't think I'm asking for a revival of religion: these days religion is either worn out or vicious. Of course, the belonging that inspired the elegies of Tibullus or the tales of Ovid was a sacred bond both passionate and pious—by which I mean respectful. But it was also free, questioning, skeptical, intellectual . . . It was the dawn of connection. And that's the form in which we need it now. Not when it has become arrogant and acts as a kind of noose. Nor when it's dead, and leaves us free to die too, of hatred. I've spent my whole life seeking that dawn of connection.[13]

This passage represents, as closely as can be, the meaning of my father's faith as he conveyed it to me.

Mind you, Stoyan sometimes exhibited the most stupendous jealousy, particularly when I was involved as an interpreter or journalist with delegations from abroad. Woe betide me if I came home after nine o'clock at night, unless I was off on some out-of-town commission, an exception that had to be certified by my editor at the paper!

Our family life as a foursome was very intense. We often had guests who criticized the government, and my sister and I were all ears behind the door. These visitors passed on the rumors circulating through the city. Some priests who had refused to compromise with the "reds" had been hung up by their beards: I was glad my father was no longer a member of the clergy. Worse, it emerged that vile, humiliating, degrading, even scatological tortures had been inflicted on opponents of the regime; such horrors kept me awake at night. Two relatively everyday scenes from that troubled political era made a lasting impression on me.

In the first, I am on vacation with my mother and sister. We're going back to my grandmother's after a walk. It's getting dark. There's nobody else in the street. The loudspeaker blares out that the opposition will be crushed and that the Agrarian Party leader, Nikola Petkov, will be executed. The death sentence is pronounced, I hear people clapping. The orator proclaims that his supporters and the whole population must make ready. But ready for what? My mother speeds up with the stroller, my sister tips out on the sidewalk and scrapes her elbow, we strap her back in, I run ahead in distress, Grandmother is waiting for us in the garden. No one says anything, we don't feel hungry, or thirsty, or any desire to go to sleep.

The second scene is more oneiric. My father used to describe how the regime's henchmen would extract confessions by the torture known as the "bath." The police would push people's heads underwater in a tub full of excrement. For a long time I was haunted by this image whenever I stepped into the water of a bath or the sea. To beat the fear, I'd force myself to dive in. And swim through the wild waves of the Black Sea.

S.D. In that loaded climate of diffuse threats and totalitarian persecutions, were you not engaged in a discreet kind of "dissidence"? A kind of foreignness, in a way?

J.K. We didn't endure any of these horrors directly, and I was lucky to have a refuge in my parents. But I also benefited from the soundness of the teaching at both school and college, which, percolating through the totalitarian structure and yet against the grain, through its very fractures, nurtured a sense of effort, of stamina, of solidarity, of the common good, while extoling the roles of culture, initiative, and creativity. This communist "humanism," whose purpose was to be an "engineer of human souls," as Stalin, I believe, conceived it, was a ruthless molder of minds. But it could never prevent the outbreak of singularities which, no matter how concealed and constrained, proved difficult to subjugate or to suppress. Don't forget that Europe was cut in two by the Yalta accords, and my parent's generation could see no way out.

The effects of the "thaw," following the first critiques of Stalinism, were already patent at the start of the 1960s. Dissident thinkers began to show up in intellectual circles, including journalists and writers on the papers I was involved with, and I embraced their ideas. My father approved, we'd discuss it at mealtimes; our parents helped us to reflect on the changes underway while being careful not to stoke a spirit of insurrection in us. Their only wish was to bequeath a "cultural baggage": French, English, literature, and music . . . So that we might develop our own ideas, thoughts, and hopefully talents. Looking back, I'd say that for a traditional family they placed remarkable trust in our ability to construct ourselves and to make free and autonomous choices.

They made us understand that contestation is inherent to life: a cohabitation with survival on the molecular level, something that their existence modestly encapsulated, and which it would fall to me to realize by my own lights.

S.D. As indeed you did, in spectacular fashion. I'm curious to know how you feel about one of your greatest distinctions: being made Commander of the Legion of Honor, on February 18, 2015. This title was bestowed in recognition of your entire oeuvre in the fields of semiology, psychoanalysis, and literature, whose scope, lucidity, and generosity are appreciated by so many of us. Are you affected by such tokens of gratitude?

J.K. As a foreigner, which I have not ceased to be, I particularly welcome the honors bestowed by the French Republic . . . Is this because of my eagerness to integrate with the France I've loved since learning the language at nursery school? Although it's become fashionable to deplore them and even to turn them down, I have the utmost respect for these rituals of the medal, and I'm grateful for mine. All the same, something bothers me about them every time, as it does now that we're discussing the subject: Who is this Julia Kristeva they speak of? Let me make a confession: I can never quite inhabit "my" image, the image which others bounce back to me; I experience myself as always on the move: my element is running water and my aim is to ride the flow, to clear the way forward. I write novels in order to make this experience tangible and communicable.

S.D. What do you expect from this biography? What do you hope to communicate?

J.K. It will be a way of confronting my mistrust of the image and testing the possibility of finding "my" image tolerable at last. Something that might surprise those who have followed my work for years . . . At any rate, it's not about drawing up a balance sheet; clinical psychoanalysis taught me that autobiographies lie, and biographies amend the facts. What I'd like best is for this book to become a "travel log" that can chart and illuminate the journey. That's why I accepted to embark on this project for two voices and four hands. Your position as a clinical psychologist and your love of writing bring us together, while your youth guarantees some necessary distance and lends you a watchful curiosity. We shall see!

II. Coming to France

> *To make language into a work—ποιείν—to labor in the materiality of what is, for society, a means of contact and understanding, is that not to make oneself already foreign to the language?*
>
> — Julia Kristeva, "Le Texte et sa science"

Samuel Dock. Let's fast-forward to a precise date: Christmas Eve, 1965. You were preparing a dissertation on the Nouveau Roman. Your supervisor had sent you to the French Embassy to apply for the de Gaulle grant, awarded to a handful of young East Europeans to enable them to study in France. The cultural attaché was startled to find that your knowledge of the culture did not stop at the end of the nineteenth century (the point where, in the communist view, "bourgeois decadence" set in): it encompassed Blanchot, Sartre, Camus, and the Nouveau Roman. Having obtained the grant, you were forced to sneak out of Bulgaria on the quiet. On arrival, dirty snow and insufficient street lights. And just five dollars in your pocket . . .

Julia Kristeva. History was speeding up. At the 20th Congress of the CPSU, in 1956, Khrushchev announced "peaceful coexistence": there would be no Third World War . . . At the 22nd Congress, in 1961, Stalin's mummified corpse was quietly removed from Lenin's mausoleum; the USSR overtook the United States' per capita productivity. Meanwhile de Gaulle, in spite of his misgivings about the European project, already envisaged a Europe stretching from the Atlantic to the Urals, and put out a call for French-speaking young students from behind the Iron Curtain. The Bulgarian government channeled these grants to its deserving cadres, who were not precisely young and spoke hardly a word of French; such candidates were rejected by the French Embassy in Sofia. Nobody benefited, or very few. I had no idea the grant existed, and had I known, I would never have thought I had the smallest chance of getting it. In this political context, the student had turned into a young woman of twenty, attractive enough to be courted by many student, journalist, and teacher friends. And, as a reader of *The Second Sex*, deeply preoccupied with her future, her freedom, her emancipation. Tossed between passions and disappointments in love, amid the ebullience of wild nights spent dancing and drinking—all the rage in Moscow, Prague, Warsaw, and Sofia—I began to feel that not only journalism, but also the teaching career opened up by my French degree, amounted to little more than a transient lick of froth. Was it the urge to understand, or a scientific-spiritual avidity caught from my parents, or a simple spurt of enthusiasm to ward off incipient depression? Whatever the reason, I developed a hunger for philosophy, literary theory, and linguistic research: so many convergent trails that culminated, illuminatingly for me, in fiction. And contemporary French fiction in particular, novels I read and reread by the light of Russian formalism.

I discovered French structuralism, Blanchot's theory of literature, and Barthes, while devouring Camus, Sartre, and the Nouveau Roman authors. The devil with journalism, I thought! I'm done with interviews and newsrooms! I started a doctorate in literary theory at the Institut de Littérature de l'Académie des Sciences. My topic was the Nouveau Roman (Nathalie Sarraute, Michel Butor, Alain Robbe-Grillet): the acme of modernism! I wrote my first theoretico-critical essays on contemporary Bulgarian writers, such as Blaga Dimitrova—a fine poet and novelist and a liberated woman, who would become Vice President of the new Bulgarian Republic after the fall of the Berlin Wall in 1989. This "switch" to literary theory was of course guided and supported by the trust of my loved ones, and by the cultural effervescence of the intellectual scene I belonged to.

S.D. What a fascinating dovetailing of the life of a country and the life of a woman! Did you feel you were making the most of the "thaw" as a more flexible historical moment? Did you ever dream it would take you to France? Did the thaw foster better relations with the West?

J.K. The opening was not very wide. Despite the thaw, the Iron Curtain remained impermeable to information—remember, the Berlin Wall had been up since 1961. Still, we did our best to loosen the vise. Young Easterners exchanged letters with their French counterparts in the Communist Youth or from communist families. My pen pal in Lyon, Mireille Bourdeur, sent me the novels of Vercors (a *résistant* author recommended by my college professors) as well as the works of Camus.[14] My essays on *The Silence of the Sea* and *The Rebel* went down a treat, especially the second!

The director of the school students' journal, Vladimir Kostov, had since moved on to write for the Bulgarian communist daily in Paris. He liked me a lot and would bring me all the books that were causing a stir over there: Blanchot's *Space of Literature* (1955), Barthes's *Writing Degree Zero* (1953), and, guess what—the first issue of the *Nouvel Observateur* (1964)! After the Wall came down, Kostov was accused of being a double agent. It was a fertile yet murky period. Those Bulgarian umbrellas still arouse the nostalgia of the more unimaginative communism buffs.[15]

S.D. Didn't the Kostov affair increase your suspicion of journalism, and more generally of politics? You completely broke with your journalistic past, and these days nothing would suggest that you ever had one, am I right?

J.K. Whether it was true or false, the Kostov affair did make me more mistrustful. Sure, the empire of the media (now permeated by new technologies) has taken the place of totalitarianism, for better or worse, and with less fearsomely efficient powers. And yet I can't help it: in every opinion manager I smell a cop, in the broadest sense, someone poised to manipulate information and its every spin-off to suit the highest bidder, in terms of power, of course. It's not this or that individual's "fault," it's unconscious in some cases, and unavoidable. Being that there is no longer *a* power, but rather networks of powers, if you want to be "part of it" then you have at least to be a double agent. That's why I invent excuses to stay away.

Well, not altogether: I had both the pleasure and the nerve to accept my "five minutes of fame," Woody Allen–style . . . For two academic years (2000 and 2001) I broadcast a cultural program every Wednesday at 08:25, as part of *Première édition*, Pierre Assouline's morning show on France Culture. On other days the slot was presented by the sociologist Dominique Schnapper, the columnist Jacques Julliard, the historian Michel Winock, and the essayist-historian-journalist, Alain-Gérard Slama.

My method was to harvest "nuggets" from the news and fold memories and emotions into them. It had to be short. Sometimes I spent all night on preparation, sometimes hardly any time at all. The broadcast was live, at the Maison de la radio, and I had to read my piece in as natural a voice as possible, without stumbling. I zipped through the Nation and Corsica, Freud in Austria, the ethics of IVF, the death penalty in the USA, Virginia Woolf and Amélie Poulain, Paul Morand and Amos Oz, Heraclitus and Simone Weil, psychoanalysis and the far left, Shakespeare in translation and terrorism, not forgetting the Bulgarian alphabet festival and Chirac's attitude to disability . . . Those pieces were collected as *Micropolitique* and *Chronique du temps sensible*.[16]

S.D. Let's go back to the thaw and to Mireille Bourdeur, your pen pal in Lyon—an excellent surprise and very important for your life.

J.K. Our connection was no more than epistolary, and even that was soon broken by the turmoil of our respective lives. But she was the one who recommended me to Pierre Daix, who very kindly received me and introduced me to Aragon and Elsa Triolet.[17] It wasn't until decades later that I met Mireille in the flesh, when she turned up at one of my book launches.

S.D. And in Sofia . . . What of Tzvetan Stoyanov? His surname sounds like your father's forename.

J.K. That was an especially intense relationship. Tzvetan Stoyanov—"Dan" in *The Samurai*—was one of the top Bulgarian essayists and literary critics. The dissident intellectuals were split into two camps, the "nationalists" and the "occidentalists," whose disputes were amicable but vehement. Tzvetan was the leader of the occidentalists, the smaller group (I rather wonder who else was in it, apart from me!). Thanks to the passionate attraction that brought us together but wasn't, on my side, destined to last, I received a solid initiation into English-language literature: Swift, Blake, and especially Joyce, some of whose work Tzvetan had translated into Bulgarian. I owe to him, too, an original and deeper understanding of Goethe and Hegel, and of his great favorite, Kafka; he could reel passages of Kafka off by heart. He also gave me a grounding in Chinese philosophy. In an imaginary dialogue he had written between Laozi and Confucius, the future of China as he saw it was staged as a contest between their two currents of thought, before going on to divide the whole of humanity. You can see what dizzy geopolitical heights we mentally scaled, in our bid to escape the torments of totalitarianism! It was in this heady atmosphere that I went away to France.

S.D. To know that helps us to follow you, and to better understand an Eastern Europe, today simply Europe, that remains mysterious and little known. You were leaving Sofia for Paris. And I quote:

> She put down the two worn russet leather cases on the baggage counter, brushed her lips against Mama's and Papa's damp cheeks, gave Dan what was taken to be an amorous wink, climbed the steps to the Tupolev without looking back, spent three and a half hours on the plane without thinking of counting the minutes—her head was empty and there was nothing but the taste of tannin in her mouth—and landed in a gray and muddy Paris. Flakes of snow were endlessly falling and melting. The so-called City of Light didn't exist—the French didn't know how

> to clear snow away. Her disappointment was complete: she could feel it from the saltiness in her throat. Of course, Boris wasn't waiting for her at Orly, and five dollars was all she had on her. No laughing matter. Disaster.[18]

J.K. Let's go back a little bit. It was Professor Emil Georgiev, my dissertation supervisor, who told me about the French scholarships; taking advantage of the fact that the director of the Institute was away in Moscow, we handed in my application at the French embassy. I made a positive impression on the cultural attaché, as you said, and received my visa without delay—this was the thaw, after all, and de Gaulle's France was more than respected. My father managed to dig out five dollars for me—the grant money wasn't due until the end of January 1966—and I boarded a flight for Paris on Christmas Eve. Fortunately, a friend of Kostov's would be waiting at the airport.

But on arrival at Le Bourget, there was nobody. A lady from the Bulgarian embassy in Paris, who I'd met on the plane, suggested I accompany her: it made sense, the missing friend could only be expecting me in a "safe place," i.e. the embassy! Slumped in the waiting room, I was unable to either cry or think. It was terribly cold and dark; I'll never forget the frozen state I was in. And with no return ticket. A man came up and introduced himself: Albert Cohen, the Washington correspondent for Bulgaria's communist daily. "So this is you!" he exclaimed, rather disappointed by my youth, I felt, as well as by my obvious misery. I didn't know him personally, but I had huge regard for this former *résistant* and author of a collection of pieces precisely on the subject of the thaw. At *September* magazine, the organ of the Writers' Union I belonged to, nobody had wanted to review that book (I mean, this was a thaw, not a melt). I was naive enough to take it on. The day after my piece appeared, a rabid article in the same communist daily denounced me as an agent of capitalism and Zionism. So as not to worry my mother, Dad hid the paper and the two of us repaired to a bistro at the foot of the nearby mountains to "review the situation." It was scary, over the next few weeks, listening out early in the morning for odd noises in the staircase of our building (was that the police coming to take me away?). To make matters worse, a broadcast on the virulently anti-communist Radio Free Europe, based in West Berlin, commended me for my "courage" . . . But it was still the thaw, and my "exploit" was forgotten. And now, in one of those happy coincidences that only happen to other people, who did I see emerging from the icy gloom of the Bulgarian embassy in Paris, but Albert Cohen! He invited me to dinner and settled me in with a colleague, Mira Todorova, Paris correspondent for the same newspaper. I stayed with her until my scholarship came through.

My first French friends—Geneviève Blaise, Claude Nouzeilles, Catherine Lwoff, and Yves Bastide—were people I knew from when they did a course at Sofia University to complete their degree in Slavonic languages at the Sorbonne. They brightened up those first days, inviting me to meet their families and to tour the bars of the Latin Quarter.

I soon tracked down a distant cousin, Shabtai Haimov, and his wife Nelly, Israeli students settled in Paris. The affinity of travelers: I felt completely "at home" in the quiet surroundings of their rental apartment on avenue des Gobelins. There, after the novelty of a Chinese restaurant, we used to talk until dawn about our common and crossed histories, about books, painting, music, architecture, cinema. The inexhaustible drug of foreigners, those fleeting stopovers of memory that help us make it through the desert—they persist and they replenish us today.

S.D. That was the tough starting point of a new life and an extraordinary book, *The Samurai* (1990). "*To be reborn has never been beyond my strength*": you rapidly made Colette's motto your own, for you managed to summon up all your resources in order to surpass yourself, and make your thought exist.[19] Alain and Josette Rey have recalled your steely determination and your knack for surrounding yourself with others. You say that you were fragile and resolute in those days, like Olga "the squirrel," heroine of *The Samurai*. You recall a great loneliness in the midst of people who looked to you like shiny gifts.

J.K. I had no compass. Looking back on those first days at Mira's, the Christmas celebrations and vacation, it's like a mirage. The first Parisian wonder she showed me was Christmas mass, 1965. The ladies in their minks and the gentlemen in cashmere, smart and distinguished; their air of earnest absent-mindedness, which later I would term "Catholic indifference"; what sort of Christian charity was that? Devoid of kindness or warmth. The snow was melting on the sidewalks. My boots let in water, but I couldn't afford to buy new ones; I felt lost among all those beings piled up like luxury gifts, sealed and unapproachable. This impression stayed with me for a long time, even though my friends at *Tel Quel*, my university colleagues, and then fellow psychoanalysts were sincerely welcoming toward me, caring and even solidary.

S.D. Tzvetan Todorov, just finishing his *Théorie de la littérature: Textes des formalistes russes* (Theory of literature: texts of the Russian formalists) (Seuil, 1965), tells you about *Tel Quel* and Roland Barthes. You rush to Barthes's seminar, and to Lucien Goldmann's as well. Barthes soon becomes a friend. Gérard Genette counsels you to explore the "post–Nouveau Roman," and to look up Philippe Sollers. For Barthes's course you present your first paper, on Bakhtin, a basis for the concepts you will later develop of *dialogism* and *intertextuality*; the article is published in *Critique*.[20] Let's go back over those first, seminal encounters.

J.K. Just before the Christmas break, I attended the seminar given by Roland Barthes. Held in a small upper-story room in the left wing of the Sorbonne, it was packed with a cosmopolitan audience of students—German, English, Italian, Spanish, and of course French. Everyone was excited about the recent interpretation of Mallarmé by a certain Philippe Sollers, it was the first time I'd heard the name. "Quite a character," was the consensus. Marthe Robert, the essayist and historian of literature married to the psychoanalyst Michel de M'Uzan, had written a paper that cast a new, psychoanalytic eye on the novel in general and Kafka in particular. Her unorthodox and caustic approach resonated to some extent with my own reading of Bakhtin. Later, when *Tel Quel* was already quartered at 44, rue de Rennes, Barthes invited me to present my interpretation of that author to his own audience, and in the presence of René Girard, who would in turn ask me to join his department at Johns Hopkins University in Baltimore.

Because I would have to defend my dissertation in Bulgaria, in those first months in Paris I also went, full of curiosity, to check out Lucien Goldmann's seminar. Famed for establishing a relation, a dialectical one to be sure, between the structuralism then in vogue and the Hegelian philosophy underlying the Marxist ideology to which I would have to revert back at the Institute of Literature in Sofia, Goldmann's teachings looked likely to supply the "footbridge" I needed. On top of that he was highly regarded by the foreign students open to the latest and most progressive ideas, with whom I was beginning to make friends.

I signed up to do my dissertation under Goldmann, at the École Pratique des Hautes Études (EPHE). My topic would change as a result, from the Nouveau Roman to the *origins of the novel*. Goldmann's thought, his incursion into the world of Pascal and reappraisal of Hegel by the light of Georg Lukács, the celebrated Hungarian philosopher and renovator of Marxism, was more in tune with my philosophical training in Bulgaria; just as attractive were his easy-going Romanian Jewishness, his fraternal-paternal geniality, so unlike the usual professorial reserve. And yet, for me the most indispensable aid to elucidating the formality of language and the specificities of literary genres was Barthes's structuralism, a prolongation of Russian formalism. It therefore seemed to me that what was required was a "recasting" of the two approaches, *history* and *structure*. No doubt only the callowness and presumption of youth persuaded me to undertake such an impossible mission—one that eventually caused me to be credited as an ancestor of poststructuralism.

After long hours in the Bibliothèque Nationale followed by endless nights of reading, my ideas finally clarified and crystallized around a suggestion of Aragon's: well before Rabelais, it is in *Le Petit Jehan de Saintré*, by Antoine de la Sale (1385–1461), that the genesis of the "novel" as a genre becomes discernible. It was my first, incomplete and simplistic attempt at a simultaneously structural and historical approach, taking account of the narrative's internal logic and historical context but also of its cultural context (courtly poetry, carnival, religious and scholarly chronicles). I delivered it as my *thèse de troisième cycle* in accordance with my study grant, supervised, as I said, by Lucien Goldmann and defended plumb in the middle of the May '68 hurricane.[21] This despite the closure of the universities, with due regard for my situation as a foreign student.

S.D. What a launch! I'd love to have been there for your defense.

J.K. It was awful! True to the spirit of the times, everyone was on first-name terms. Lucien, who used the informal "*tu*" and expected his students to do the same, broke with the conventional ritual of the viva voce and declared up front that prior to any discussions the jury must award me the title of Doctor of Philosophy, as validated by the submitted text. He himself would ask just one question: "What do you think of Gaudí?" and was more interested in discussing the following, in depth: "Why give so much prominence to psychoanalysis, at the expense of Marxism? Do you consider the sex to be more important than the stomach?" I'm quoting from memory.

S.D. What bizarre questions—they don't seem to have much bearing on your work. It sounds as if he simply hadn't read it.

J.K. Oh, he had! In a colorful way, he was opposing materialism ("the stomach") to psychosexual determination and the structures inherent in discourse and genres. Whatever, these words from my doctoral adviser made me see red. It so happened I'd just come back from my first trip to Barcelona, where I'd seen Gaudí's outlandish forms. In the same iconoclastic spirit, I retorted that the dreamlike extravagance of the Catalan artist had nothing to do with the austere polyphony of *Petit Jehan de Saintré*, and that we were here to talk about carnival in the novel, not in architecture. Getting carried away on my '68er high horse, in a way that now makes me cringe, I embarked on an authentic act of parricide. I berated Goldmann for being a "mothball Marxist," "left behind by History," understanding nothing of the Freudian revolution, and trying to impose his own repression on us, and so on and so forth. Lucien's eyes were blurry with tears, and we hardly heard the compliments of the jury. At the end, my adviser refused to shake my hand when I received my doctorate with the congratulations of the jury. For all the soothing wisdom of his wife Annie, who tried her best to defuse the psychodrama, Goldmann remained deeply wounded by it, while I felt ashamed. Our quarrel did not prevent him from recommending me for his post when he stepped down from the Free University of Brussels, an honor I was unable to accept just then; it went to Jacques Leenhardt, whose qualifications far outstripped mine. Thereafter we were embarrassed but amicable when running into each other; we shared the same concerns as seekers and exiles, even if our professional paths were diverging more and more.

S.D. Your loss of temper before so many misapprehensions, after so long spent studying *Petit Jehan de Saintré*, is readily understandable. You went on to produce your *doctorat d'état*, *Revolution in Poetic Language: The Late Nineteenth-Century Avant-Garde, Mallarmé and Lautréamont*. And that led you to semiology.

J.K. I completed it under the direction of Jean-Claude Chevalier, and defended it before a jury comprised of Roland Barthes, Jean Dubois, and Lucien Lefebvre, at the University of Paris-Vincennes, in 1973.

S.D. Swapping the Renaissance for the nineteenth century, you delved into historical, philosophical, psychoanalytic, and semiological sources to analyze the tendencies of that avant-garde. Such a massive task of research must have been personally very demanding. How did you feel during the process?

J.K. It was thoroughly exhilarating to dwell in the writings of these so-called hermetic or "accursed" authors. French late-nineteenth-century history teems with incident: you have the Franco-Prussian War, the Paris Commune, anarchism, the separation of church and state. The reassessment of the alexandrine and the invention of free verse. Madness, lying flush with the most classic rationality. Premonitions of surrealism . . . This fin-de-siècle avant-garde made me read and reread Husserl's phenomenology, the semiology of Saussure and Hjelmslev, the psychoanalysis of Freud, Melanie Klein, and Lacan. And there was no avoiding Hegel, of course! To give a sense of the whirlpool I was in, I'll just say that I chose this quote from him as my epigraph: "In science what is important is that one should take on the strenuous effort of the concept."[22] You get the idea! What's more, I dug deep into French history, because I was sure that Meaning is not only a structure, it comes about in History. Having studied the works of the historian René Rémond on my period, I met him to talk about the religious currents and literary anarchism associated with Mallarmé; I later consulted him on the subject of Zola's "*petit bleu*" during the Dreyfus Affair.[23] I also came across him at the French University College in Moscow, founded by François Mitterrand and Marek Halter. To cut a long story short, defending this *Revolution in Poetic Language* in 1973, before a "university corpus" still in the throes of renewal following the events of May '68, was a real ordeal of initiation for me. And Roland Barthes gave me the ultimate accolade, much to the annoyance of some: "The novel of today is this dissertation," he thundered. Politely, as ever.

S.D. Literature and science are a dichotomy you sought to overcome. You prepared your dissertation while employed as a researcher at the Centre National de la Recherche Scientifique (CNRS), attached to the semiolinguistics section of Lévi-Strauss's Laboratoire d'Anthropologie Sociale. How was your relationship with him?

J.K. *The Elementary Structures of Kinship* and the *Mythologiques* series were essential texts for me, and they still are. However, Claude Lévi-Strauss himself, a man of impeccable distinction and elegance, was unapproachable. He was very supportive of my work, as well as extending the hospitality of his "laboratory," and I was indebted to the efficiency of his assistant Isaac Chiva, who helped me fill out mountains of documents for the CNRS and the visa services. I made real friends at the Laboratoire, including Nicole Belmont, Maurice Godelier, and Françoise Héritier. Claude Lévi-Strauss hovered with glacial rigor over a team who worshiped him. I used to work till late in the semiolinguistics office, and once he circulated a memo deploring the way Mme Kristeva left the lights on! I was deeply upset by this reproof, though he softened it with a kindly smile and no sanctions ensued.

S.D. Your novel, *The Samurai*, stars the core group of the *Tel Quel* journal and other intellectuals who revolved around its founder, Philippe Sollers: Jean-Louis Baudry, Marcelin Pleynet, Jean Ricardou, Jacqueline Risset, Denis Roche, Pierre Rottenberg, Jean Thibaudeau . . . It also features banished dissidents like Jean-Edern Hallier and Jean-Pierre Faye, and finally many characters on the periphery of the movement, such as Jacques Derrida, Michel Foucault, Pierre Guyotat, Jean-Joseph Goux, François Wahl, and Umberto Eco. How did you first come across the group in real life? How did you get along with the various members? There's a photograph from that period that shows you sitting among these men, smiling, radiant, sun-like.

J.K. It wasn't a "groupy" sort of group, and I never attended editorial board meetings; my name wasn't added to the board until quite late on. As for my relations with each of them, women as well as men—I'm thinking of Jacqueline Risset, I was deeply fond of her and still can't come to terms with her premature death—they were all completely different, specific and incomparable, not a whiff of community. But you're sliding around the essential point: Philippe Sollers!

S.D. The essential point indeed, and we'll discuss him at length. For the moment I'd prefer to keep to your intellectual journey, if that doesn't seem too artificial. But as we can't cover everything at once, it's necessary to cut from different angles into your dense and complex experience. How did you come to meet Sollers?

J.K. Gérard Genette had advised me to read and interview him, which I did, after reading a profile of this young writer in *Clarté*. We'll go back to that. At *Tel Quel*, Sollers introduced me to Marcelin Pleynet and Jean-Louis Baudry and his wife, all good friends of his. But we socialized most often with Roland Barthes, enjoying leisurely dinners at Le Falstaff in Montparnasse and discussing literature, their current projects, my research a bit as well, the political scene—starting before May '68, and continuing during the events and long afterward. Nothing was stable anymore, all our lives had been turned upside down, but there was still the magnet of writing to unite our odd threesome . . . Roland would leave us around 10:30 in the evening to go cruising in Saint-Germain, half glad to cut loose, half resentful at having to put up with what he called "arrogant deadbeats." His homosexuality as I saw it was rather shy and embarrassed, very different from the militant, aggressive style of someone like Foucault; he grew more confident later on.

S.D. How would you define your relationship with Barthes? As the camaraderie between two thinkers, as well-meaning cordiality, as friendship? Or was there something subtler between you?

J.K. We liked each other straight away. No demands, no curiosity. I hung on his words and respected what he did or did not wish to talk about. I've kept letters from him in which he fusses about my health and urges me to take care, not push myself too much, get some rest. Barthes was the only person who sensed how hard I was driving myself, he who knew so much about the work of death within us. He may have felt that we were both "bereft of family," both deeply marked by incestual bonds that stopped us from putting down roots anywhere but in the adjustment to strangers or adoption of them, as it were. Apparently he told Hubert and Teri Damisch that had I not been taken already, I was the only woman he would have married. I don't think this statement should be read as one of the cruel ironies he was prone to. It was rather a murmur of loneliness, an avowal of bitter, unfailing helplessness. Our emotional bond remained restrained, ardently Platonic.

S.D. How did you meet Jacques Derrida?

J.K. Philippe Sollers had admired his 1962 translation of Husserl's *Origin of Geometry*, and the introductory essay. By 1965, they were working together. In *Tel Quel*, Sollers published several articles by Derrida before he became known outside academia: "La Parole soufflée," "Plato's Pharmacy," pieces that were reprinted in collections like *Writing and Difference* and *Dissemination*. For me, these works were nothing less than a philosophical initiation. Our friendship evolved as a continuation of reading, by way of tasty dinner debates at Ris-Orangis, where Derrida lived with his wife Marguerite and their boys. Or in Paris at the home of Paule Thévenet, the remarkable custodian and editor of the manuscripts of Antonin Artaud. In 1971 Paule and I traveled to Kuwait in the wake of Jean Genet (whom we also saw a lot of at that time) for an international congress on "The Arab Revolution, Spearhead of the World Revolution." Our illusions were short-lived. There was much talk of Marx and Engels and the *Communist Manifesto*, but in Baghdad and Damascus, where we also went, the communists were languishing in jail, and there wasn't a single woman among those "revolutionary" petroleum magnates . . . Jacques also came to stay at the Île de Ré . . . Perhaps due to the awe in which I held his work, I never managed to get close to this reticent, secretive, introverted man. In fact, the hub of our connection was Sollers's oeuvre: Derrida wrote "Dissemination" for Philippe's novel, *Nombres* (Numbers), and I wrote "Engendering the Formula" around the same work. The theory evenings organized by the journal at 44, rue de Rennes were a ferment of ideas against a background of literature! The rupture occurred little by little. Sollers was leaning toward China and Lacan, while Derrida inclined to the Communist Party and the journal *La Nouvelle Critique* just as we were taking our distance from it. I stood back from their conflict. I had already become less apt to expect "answers" from politics than to seek the unconscious reasons for our attraction to providential ideologies. Subsequently I came across Derrida in the American universities where we both often taught, but didn't invest too much in this tenuous transatlantic friendship because of the tiff with Philippe. Derrida's thought, fairly niche today, had a potent effect on our generation. He was very critical of the inhibitions of university-based philosophy before crossing the line separating him from literature and developing a writing that had more to do with limit states than with analytical argument or with fiction. It was an exemplary *deconstruction* of literature, identity, the self.

S.D. In *The Samurai*, you devote most space, quite rightly, to your relations with the group and gradual integration in it. But I'd like to know a little more about your life between *Tel Quel* and the dissertation. What was your experience of the Parisian scene?

J.K. *The Samurai* doesn't claim to be a total portrait of *Tel Quel*. The discordant, corrosive note that immediately attracted me from behind the screen of busy levity and asocial poses was that of risk-taking. An extreme game with impossibility and death. Like the one played by the Samurai of the Rising Sun, who excelled at the art of war and extended their practice of it to poetry, calligraphy, even the tea ceremony. My samurai were the opposite of the "mandarins," the preachy cohort of a previous generation who aspired to govern teaching, civic society, and thought itself. I discovered that revolt was part and parcel of the youths I met, from bourgeois and middle-class families; they beguiled me with their exorbitance, their scorn for the rules, their resistance to institutions, their impulse to reach the far side of meaning and life. Those samurai, unassuming, comical, or intense—and some of their elders who read *Tel Quel*—built an irreverent, iconoclastic culture. With their febrility of mind and heart, grabbing hold of the formal structures of language and genre, they disrupted the official culture. The latter courted or censored them, copied or digested them; but whatever else, they were *not part of it*, they bothered it. This was patently the case with Sollers, but also with Roland Barthes, who appears as Armand Bréhal in *The Samurai.* You'll also find Benserade/Benveniste, Sherner/Althusser, Strich-Meyer/Lévi-Strauss, and Lauzun/Lacan. It should be read as an echo of Sollers's 1983 novel *Women.*

S.D. Let's talk about Lacan, now you mention him. Your research and writings on psychoanalysis are invaluable for a better grasp of the mental dynamic informing his theories, his "rhetoric of obscurity," the language he invented. *The Samurai* contains a devastating description of the grief that overcomes Carole (one of your alter egos) at the death of Lauzun, which speaks to your own affection for Lacan:

> *A dull pain, vague but unbearable. It reminds me of a dream I had after an abortion: I'd lost my ring, a diamond ring . . . I searched wildly among the sheets, under the furniture, in the trash can. Nothing. But no, it isn't a ring I've lost, it's a finger. Worse: it's a whole arm that's missing—someone's cut off my arm. . . . Someone has cut off Lauzun from me. Death.*[24]

J.K. Carole is indeed one of my alter egos, but she's not the narrator, she's "merely" a character . . . In my confrontation with the subtleties of a French always on the lookout for the *new,* I became aware that my hazy intuitions and abstract diagnoses were acquiring substance: it was true, then—we are a civilization of the word, of language, of the languages that speak through us here and now, and inaugurate unexpected footbridges and perhaps new universalities. The semiology of Roland Barthes, more exquisite than that of the founders, Saussure and Peirce, gave me the tools to probe into meaning and signification. These "categories" ceased to be a formality and appeared to embody a fragile but inalienable resistance to the new forms taken by totalitarianism, the coarsening of minds and the commodification of humanity. But it was not enough to identify the dependence of these signifying *forms* on their *historical* context. What was lacking in phenomenology and in Hegelian Marxism was the violence of desire, the living flesh of instinctual drives. This third component, set between Meaning and History, was slumbering out of sight . . . in Freud's *Interpretation of Dreams*. Knowing that Freud was banned by the "dominant ideology," my father had hidden his copy on the most inaccessible shelf of his library. I only found it after his death.

It was Philippe Sollers who unveiled this foundational work of psychoanalysis for me. He had read it over and over, in fact he was always reading, very fast, in bed, anywhere. He introduced me to *Three Essays on the Theory of Sexuality*, *Cinq psychanalyses*, and *Beyond the Pleasure Principle*. And, of course, to Lacan's work, which had just been collected in the volume *Écrits* (1966), a strenuous read for a rookie like myself. Like so many others, I free associated, I dreamed, in a sort of self-analysis through a sort of reading. We went to Lacan's seminar. A community in fascinated thrall to a magus who, speaking a language that was foreign to French, invited us to engage in free association, as I had already been doing while reading *Écrits*. And yet the seminar felt more accessible than the text, because the theatrical embodiment of speech gave rise to transferential vibrations, more intimate, though scarcely easier to understand. At the confines of aesthetic, religious, or oneiric experience. I set off on the road to the unconscious . . .

S.D. You make those seminars sound like proper group therapy sessions!

J.K. That's right, it was like a session! So packed that the disciples fought over the radiator pipes for somewhere to set up their mikes and capture the master's utterances. Prolonged silences, sudden phrases that lashed the mesmerized listeners, a calculated slowness, what an actor he was! I no longer recollect my first personal meeting with Lacan, but Philippe already knew him. I can see him now in our apartment, 88, boulevard du Port-Royal, over for a drink or to share a light supper. He was forced to climb five floors on foot! He was a simple, generous man, yes, he was, contrary to his reputation; and though I grant that simplicity is often just another baroque mask for an accomplished Catholic, I stand by my sense of its authenticity. Before David was born, Lacan sometimes called up in the middle of the night to ask how the pregnancy was going and whether I'd had any ideas for the baby's name. I would politely point out the lateness of the hour! (*Laughter*)

We met up after the publication of my book *Polylogue* (1977). Was it around the time he dissolved the Freudian School? I was surprised to hear him say that I wasn't cut out for schools, anything but! He invited me to give a talk at his seminar. I was deeply flattered, but uncertain, because so far very few people, and fewer women, had received that honor. But David, who was teething, cried all night and the next morning I was so tired that I cancelled the engagement.

S.D. In 1974, you were a member of the first party of Western intellectuals to visit China since it joined the United Nations in 1971, along with Sollers, Barthes, Wahl, and Pleynet. Lacan was slated to go but didn't. You were eager, as you put it, to "encapsulate the strangenesses" of Chinese socialism. Your recent article in the Chinese daily, *Renmin Ribao*, revisits the international political context and the role of France in that expedition. Can you tell us about it?

J.K. I've already done so in my book, *About Chinese Women* (1974). My life in Marxist Bulgaria had hardly turned me into a fervent Maoist, and the little

I knew about Chinese culture boiled down to my friend Tzvetan Stoyanov's fictional dialogue, as I mentioned, between Laozi and Confucius. The allure of Chinese thought for Philippe Sollers and his friends was inevitably contagious. I devoured Marcel Granet, and we both dived into the volumes of *Science and Civilization in China*, by Joseph Needham, whom I had the good fortune to meet; next up were Chinese lessons, first with Ysia Cheng and then with François Cheng, a refined man of letters who loved French civilization and had remarkable patience with the pupil in a hurry that I was. Philippe didn't keep up these lessons. I tried to take them further, by enrolling for a Chinese degree at Paris 7; I didn't pass, but I learned enough to be able to engage with Chinese tourists who were misled by my cheekbones and Mao jacket into asking me questions about the Great Wall! They thought I was a local! Although I couldn't sustain a proper conversation, I could at least look down my nose at my companions. Picture the scene!

S.D. Especially neat in the presence of men dedicated to language and writing!

J.K. The delegation of "comrades from *Tel Quel*" toured Beijing, Luoyang, Xi'an, and Shanghai. We met workers, peasants, intellectuals, men and women . . . A lot of women, I made sure of that! We'd hoped to visit Tibet, but it wasn't allowed, we should have known. However, we saw the Buddhist grottoes at Luoyang, and watched a surgical operation performed without Western-style anesthetic, using nothing but acupuncture. I wanted to find out whether a brand of "Chinese socialism," sensitive to national differences, was possible; whether women—first favored by a matrilineal, Daoist tradition, then thwarted by a patriarchal Confucianism, and now once more encouraged, not to say privileged, by Mao's latest exhortations that pressed them, side by side with the young, to take on the "CP bureaucrats"—might or might not be in a position to modify the social pact. The answer, which I will share with you shortly, severed me from politics and led me to align myself once and for all with the microcosm of the "talking cure." That withdrawal, mind you, takes nothing away from the prodigious intensity of that trip, bursting with discoveries, surprises, disappointments, comic episodes, and silly antics.

S.D. Antics?

J.K. Yes, starting before our departure, actually. Lacan had signed up for the trip, accompanied by his number one lady friend at the time, registered as his "secretary." The visas were on their way, so, to put the finishing touches to the schedule we were going to submit to the Chinese authorities, we met for a final dinner at La Calèche, the restaurant where Lacan customarily held court. Philippe, Lacan, and I sat waiting for the lady friend, sipping our usual pink champagne. Lacan was growing impatient: she didn't show up, and her phone wasn't answering either. There were no smartphones then, time ticked by and our anxiety mounted. Lacan decided to go find her at her apartment. We piled into Sollers's little Simca. No answer to the doorbell. Lacan tried to use his key, but the lock was blocked by a key on the other side. He was very jumpy, having recently been attacked by one of his patients, the oversuspicious "tape recorder man." Our racket finally woke the concierge: had he seen or heard anything unusual? No. Suddenly a window lights up in the apartment. "A man!" I blurt naively. "The murderer!" cries Lacan. "We're leaving," Philippe says. "You're coming upstairs with me," the master orders. Well, nobody had heard the telephone, or the doorbell; there was a transport strike, and another psychoanalyst, a friend of the lady's, had not been able to take the train to his out-of-town home and was therefore sleeping over. A pathetic vaudeville. "My dear, I was afraid you'd been attacked . . ." "Afraid? You wanted me to be attacked . . ." And the old man, slumped in an armchair: "I can't believe this." We gave up on all of them. I never set foot in Lacan's seminar again. Our delegation left without him. Maybe some people didn't want him to travel under the flag of *Tel Quel* . . .

S.D. Notwithstanding the absence of that star of French culture, I gather the trip was a success, and that it provided you with considerable material to bolster your thinking about women.

J.K. We were received with great courtesy and furnished with two interpreters, Comrades Chao 1 and 2, who very occasionally let us wander through the back streets of Beijing or the old quarter of Shanghai. Our rare discussions with academics in Beijing were chaperoned; classes were out of session, and most of the students and professors had returned to the countryside. However, we talked freely with the artists and intellectuals selected by our hosts. One painter-calligrapher recalled meeting Picasso in Montparnasse during the 1930s. I relished my conversations with women, who had increasing access to leadership positions in every sector; they were rewriting history in the feminine. Take the historian and director of an archeological museum who showed me some prehistoric ceramics: "Look at those nail marks, such fine and delicate nails, don't they prove that the makers were women? They were the artists of the olden days, weren't they, in Engels's matriarchy?" The paintings done by an illiterate peasant woman reminded me of Van Gogh: "She's never seen any painting but hers, she says that women have a paintbrush in their hearts," Chao 1 translated. I was enchanted by the little girls in kindergarten: more energetic and gigglier than the boys, they would beat them at every game they played.

Roland Barthes came with me on my investigations of women, taking (or pretending to take?) studious notes in his little book, as you can see in the pictures of him on that trip. But when we were supposed to admire the performance of some cooperative farm, he wouldn't get off the bus. In the evening, when the people's artistes put on their shows, he sneaked to the very end of the row of delegates, hoping to sit beside some young Chinese man. "Bit short on *desire*, wouldn't you say?" he whispered in my ear. To preempt a scandal, I explained to Chao 2 that our teacher, the senior member of the group, must always be sat in the middle and never on the end! Philippe deciphered Mao's poems, printed in gold on the red pennants and flags of May Day, on the Temple of Heaven. He easily beat the painter-calligrapher at table tennis, and trounced a younger museum guide as well.

S.D. On a less positive note, they didn't let you into any psychiatric hospitals.

J.K. No, they didn't. I was finally unsatisfied with regard to psychology, let alone psychiatry, in China. The two Chaos produced a philosopher who explained that there was no need for psychoanalysis in China, since, according to Chairman Mao, "one divides into two" in any case. It hadn't occurred to me that this slogan might also apply to schizophrenia. I only felt consoled, slightly, in Xian, where they let Philippe and I take a bath in the splendid tub that had belonged to the imperial concubine Yang Guifei, filled with scented mineral water. The other delegates had to make do with the public baths, like cement blockhouses, very disappointing. Regardless of the gracious inscriptions with which we were welcomed in every village—"Long life to the comrades from *Tel Quel*, worthy heirs of the Paris Commune!"—some peasants, who had never seen white people before, went away shouting "*Dà bízi!*" (big nose), the sobriquet commonly applied to foreigners of our sort.

S.D. You were once more embracing the role of foreigner. A fine vantage point from which to observe the world.

J.K. To learn the language and culture of China would take a lifetime, and my life was already well underway. I didn't feel equal to tackling this complex world, or the maze of politics—in the UN, in France, the Soviet Union, China—that comes down to impotent gesticulation over a volcano of secrets and oppressions, cultural traditions and treacheries . . . The cause of women was riding high at that stage of the Cultural Revolution. The very occasional old lady with bound feet, ferried by a grandson on the back of his bike, was the reminder of a bygone form of torture; the pill was freely on sale in pharmacies. But the emancipation of women was still a long way off, and there was much ground to cover, between Daoist flux, ancestral customs, and Party imperatives, before the freedom movement could acquire new meaning. As I told you, I turned away from politics and from China and plumped for Dr. Freud's "talking cure."

On returning to Paris, I did, though, seek Lacan's advice. We were too well acquainted for me to consider analysis with him, so who should I go with? He commended me to . . . the baneful friend of his alleged secretary! Had he forgotten about the incident in La Calèche? Was he losing his memory? He often remained speechless at the seminar, tying bits of string into Borromean knots. Or was he trying to tell me that, in order to become a psychoanalyst, I had to acquiesce to a kind of "incestual bond" with him?

S.D. To "join the harem," in short.

J.K. Symbolically, but yes. My desire for psychoanalysis was not deterred. In the end it was a friend and colleague, the Hungarian linguist Ivan Fónagy, deeply knowledgeable about the Hungarian school of psychoanalysis (Ferenczi, Hermann) who steered me toward Dr. Ilse Barande, a psychiatrist and psychoanalyst and member of the Société Psychanalytique de Paris. I was familiar with Fónagy's work; his study on *Les Bases pulsionnelles de la phonation*

(The drive basis of phonation) had influenced my notion of the *semiotic*—that prelinguistic mode of meaning, a primal organization of the drives under the pressure of erogenous zones as well as of the rhythmic and tonal features of the mother tongue.[25] An exile from Budapest, disillusioned with communism after detecting, thanks to his own work, that the "confessions" in the Slansky trial were fake, and blessed with an acerbic sense of humor, he was delighted to see me join the Freudian "plague." Freud said he was bringing a plague to the United States . . . On with the good fight! In his fatherly way, Fónagy considered me too exposed on the Parisian scene. "When you're bringing a plague, you've got to be very alone and very discreet. Are you ready?" I was ready.

S.D. An excellent argument with which to approach Ilse Barande! What was she like?

J.K. She had a youthful face, graying, curly hair, an intelligent smile, kind blue eyes, and a sparing way with words; her voice was melodious yet incisive. German and a Rothschild by birth, bilingual, she was highly attuned to mother tongues and to the expressions used by her analysands—but impervious to the Lacanian cult of the "signifier," the "great Other," and the "objet petit *a*." I didn't know her work, and it wasn't until after my analysis that I read her book, *Sándor Ferenczi* (1972), and her essay *Le Maternel singulier* (1977). Our first encounter was brief and trenchant: her mere presence decided me against listing, as I'd planned, all the "professional" reasons behind my request to be analyzed with her and my wish to become an analyst myself. Out of the blue I told her I felt like a rubber ball, constantly rebounding, and I wanted to touch the earth, "well, my mother, to coin a phrase," I said, embarrassed by an admission that could sound pretentious or knowing. "You are here to be able to say that," was her very simple response. In an exchange lasting barely ten minutes, we settled on a program of three forty-five-minute sessions a week.

Much later, I read Ilse's writings on the unfinished condition of the *neotenous* beings that we are, at once *premature* and perpetually *immature*. In studies coauthored with her husband, Robert Barande, she contends that as undeveloped, neotenous creatures we are possessed by a permanent *appetite for excitation*, leading us into ambivalent, richly duplicitous behaviors that are too easily labeled *perversions*. Further, this very "appetite for excitation" turns into a *vehicle of language*, opening the door to memorization and symbolization. And, without normalizing perversion, she illuminates the metamorphoses of our essential bisexuality. A Freudian through and through, Ilse Barande refrained from the slightest explanatory or theoretical intervention during our sessions. With hindsight, her innovative and generous attention to my "neoteny" set free my own "immature instability"—the pugnacity I told you about at the beginning—to confront and shoulder the trials of life, motherhood in particular.

Contra the psychoanalysis of the day, focused on trauma, Ilse Barande's "traumatophilic" approach taught me how to survive trauma and live with it. That transference/countertransference helped me accept the vicissitudes of my sexuality and that of my loved ones, and eventually that of my patients, so as to cope with people who are "different" or "outside the norm" and pursue my clinical practice as a *poietics*: each analysand is a singularity, a specific style, a sex apart, ultimately a *poem*. Such is the person's individual genius, which the psychoanalytic treatment reveals to him or her and which Ilse Barande acknowledges in her fashion, balking the "concept of perversion" with her rhetorical question: "Could any of us not be perverted?"

S.D. I believe this is the first time you've spoken about the relationship you developed with her.

J.K. "Relationship"? Oh, no, you're wrong! Transference/countertransference does not involve the slightest psychological or philosophical intersubjectivity. The intimacy of that bond is an *experience* of becoming dead to oneself and acceding to otherness through the other's mortality, and only then acceding to a personal rebirth. I'm summarizing. And it's impossible to "summarize" an analysis; while plenty of analysands purport to "tell it all," I regard their narratives as a defense, therefore a lie. However, I am determined to pay homage to her, an analyst as extreme as she was tactful; because, out of circumspection, I found myself involuntarily echoing the silence that surrounds her ground-breaking work today. Delivering a paper to the 2012 Congress of French-speaking psychoanalysts on "the maternal," I stressed Ilse Barande's very enlightening dissection of mother-infant relations that I'd found so helpful. But during the presentation, with her sitting in the audience right in front of me, and finding myself obliged to shorten my written text, I stupidly failed to mention her name, though it was there in black and white on the page! Once again, the rubber ball had bounced too quickly off the maternal ground. I hastened to offer my apologies, ashamed and pained by her mute smile. It was the last time we ever met.

S.D. There is no end to an analysis . . . You followed André Green more explicitly, and until the end of his life.

J.K. Together with Serge Viderman, he supervised the treatments I was carrying out as a student at the Institut de Psychanalyse. It was he who taught me to psychoanalyze. My first case was not a "classic" one, and yet Green approved it for supervision, at a time when "limit states" were only just beginning to be psychoanalyzed. He guided me step by step, in the theory as well as the clinical practice of these troublesome disorders. After the supervision, I attended his seminar for years; it was held at his home once a fortnight, with a small group of young analysts. He was patient, pedagogical, expounding his "patterns of the psychical apparatus" in minute detail and rendering them as diagrams while the trainees talked about their cases. This was the better to convey the interaction between various psychical instances, the libidinal play between the patient and their "object" as well as with the analyst, and vice versa. But he was quick-tempered, too, flying into a rage with anyone who failed to stick "close to the patient's material," that is, who was unable to reproduce the exact words of their analysands, the precise thread of the analytic process, their own countertransference, and their interpretation.

Later, when the seminar changed its formula and I stopped going, we still saw each other at my request, always after dinner. Many hours of catching up, talking about our writings but also about what was going on at the Société Psychanalytique de Paris and around the world, ending up with personal matters. Not "wild psychotherapy," but a living, uninhibited exchange, respectful and direct. I let fall somewhere that Green had behaved roughly, woundingly even, toward female colleagues. Was I the exception? The daughter that this father of two sons never had? I was certainly a disciple, but not an obsequious one. André had no time for colleagues of either sex who copied him, glossed him, praised him . . . invariably in the wrong way! He wasn't even jealous when I teamed up with Pierre Fédida and Daniel Widlöcher, two strong personalities of the Association Psychanalytique de France (the rival of our own SPP), whose clinical work and writings I admired, to launch an untypical seminar in adult psychiatry, the service headed by Professor Widlöcher at the Salpêtrière hospital. Under the title "Semiology and Psychoanalysis," we spoke to post-doc students in psychiatry, psychoanalysis, and literature, with occasional input from the biologists who invented the first anti-depressants! The aim was to interpret speech in analysis, through a combination of cognitive approaches, Freudian psychoanalysis, and semiology—a vast program that would doubtless be worth reinstating, in these somber times of ill-being of every description . . .

S.D. The investigative domains that most engage you often overlap with the concerns of André Green: the heterogeneity of drive and meaning, the signifying process (*signifiance*) and biology, maternal madness and *reliance* . . .

J.K. It couldn't be otherwise, since we were both building on the same theoretical base: Freud, of course, but also philosophy, structuralism, literary history . . . Hegel, Husserl, Saussure, Peirce; Shakespeare, Proust, Conrad, James . . . and Lacan, for sure, belying the rebellion led by Green against this "heretic": for he only rejected the Lacanian notion of *signifier* the better to recreate it by dint of affects and drives. Moreover, this idol of the SPP and powerful chief was at the same time a mutineer. Green did more than impose figures who are "atypical" (as people call me when they want to be kind) on the SPP, which has had a reputation for being traditional, not to say conventional, ever since Marie Bonaparte brought psychoanalysis to France; he also introduced Melanie Klein, Winnicott, and Bion, together with language theory, semiology, cognitivism, and biology. By his example as an unrepentant clinician who innovates by teaching and writing, Green taught us that psychoanalysis is a political art that demands as much affinity with madness as respect for the "common good."

S.D. Disillusioned with politics, then, you turned to psychoanalysis. How were you feeling at the time, in the company of Philippe Sollers and Roland Barthes, with your university colleagues, with the psychoanalysts?

J.K. Have I been talking about anything other than personal feelings? Psychoanalysis was the great turning point in my life, after exile and meeting Philippe. It rekindled a youthful excitement that did not fade after I became an analyst, that is, when I reached the therapeutic position from which the dramas and disappointments of those who put their trust in us can be reversed into potential new starts. In a different relationship to time. For the analysand and myself both. That whole period was marked by moments of discouragement, loneliness, letdown, but never quite depression. And punctuated with rebirths that heartened me, as did my "marriage as one of the fine arts": that was fundamental. I felt recognized and galvanized by Sollers, Barthes, Green. Not forgetting Émile Benveniste, which I don't . . . The source of my energy is often Philippe. I like to tell this story: we were outside La Coupole, I must have been looking dejected, thinking about my parents who weren't allowed to come to Paris before the end of my grant . . . It was pouring with rain and there were puddles everywhere. Philippe didn't try to comfort me, he just said: "Jump! You can do it!" And I did. And the blues were gone! That's not to say I don't scold him sometimes for his illusions, his optimism, his game-playing . . . He just laughs.

S.D. Were you happy then?

J.K. For as long as I can remember, happiness has been the mourning of unhappiness. It occurs when ill-being is spent. Supposedly happy people who conceal their ill-being are of no significance. Don't you agree?

S.D. Absolutely! But let's go back to your book, *About Chinese Women*, published one year after your journey by Éditions des femmes, and reprinted by Pauvert in 2001, with a new preface. In *The Samurai* you bluntly depict your dealings with the feminists (compressed into the character of Bernadette) who had "commissioned" the work. A sensuous and ferocious portrait emerges:

> There were lots of peonies in Nanking and Luoyang. Great purple or scarlet, pink or maroon or white heads, incredibly massive and fragrant. Whole streets and gardens full of bloody suns. They rotted on the stem. And that highly colored death was obscene, like some stupid, insolent female sex organ. How fragile beauty was, and how suddenly it could turn into its opposite, into coarse and obtuse horror! The excited faces of Bernadette and her pals, red and white with sick ambition, were rotting peonies.[26]

J.K. Are you sure? Not bad! Feminism was one of the aftershocks of May '68. I was very fond of Sarah George-Picot. Beautiful and free, she was the *bourgeoise* in her most exuberant, outrageous form and a friend of the filmmaker Jean-Daniel Pollet, with whom Sollers made a dazzling movie called *Méditerranée*.

S.D. In *The Samurai* she disappears . . .

J.K. No, she breaks up into several female characters. In reality, Sarah often traveled to India, came back and set off again. She told me a lot about the Parisian feminists she knew. She found my upbringing in a communist country charming, it was "feminist and political in the right way," according to her. I reminisced to her about reading Simone de Beauvoir's *The Second Sex*, a work that in Bulgaria I embraced as a novel, a promise. An adventure. I had recently spotted the famous existentialist with some other women in the Rosebud, a bar in Montparnasse. Riveting, chilly as a schoolmarm, with a brittle voice that petrified me, but I never got the chance to penetrate her circle. Sarah put me in touch with Antoinette Fouque, someone I'd noticed at Roland Barthes's seminar. Impassioned, earnest, and very clever, Antoinette hated her homely looks and used her intelligence to bewitch the girls. Her group, Psychoanalysis and Politics, was impelled by a towering ambition: to liberate women by crossing psychoanalysis with politics—so far so obvious—and with high finance (some members were wealthy heiresses), which was riskier. When I needed to fund my trip to China, this expanding feminist enterprise offered me 10,000 francs (about 1,500 euros) as an advance on royalties if I wrote a book on Chinese women. After my return, I delivered the manuscript and then had to wait two months to be "democratically" auditioned by the "collective." It was hardly a surprise to find that nobody had read the MS except for the "boss" and her friend. They nonetheless demanded that I alter my surname for the publication, because "the father's name is a relic of patriarchy." I was bold enough to retort: "And isn't the husband's name even worse?" Instead of replying, they asked for a preface detailing what I owed to the thought of Antoinette and the group. What thought? It has still to evolve, I insisted feebly. I was also reprimanded for making female homosexuality sound depressing. "Far from it, a single paragraph surveys the persecution of homosexual female writers by conventional morality at the beginning of the twentieth century . . ." Tired of arguing, I realized I would never get anywhere with this female "central committee." I wanted to take back my manuscript and reimburse the *firm*, but it was too late: "Your book is already with the printers."

S.D. You mean it came out without your correcting the proofs? That's outrageous!

J.K. Yes, and that first edition was full of typos and awkward turns of phrase. I pushed on with my feminism solo, as it were, not belonging to any group, just with my French students and especially those from the US, Canada, China . . . Because after my doctoral dissertation on Mallarmé and Lautréamont, I left the CNRS to become adjunct professor and then full professor in the department of Science des Textes et des Documents at the new University of Paris-Diderot or Paris 7 (Jussieu). I also became a visiting professor at New York's Columbia University, which was full of terrific young people wanting to learn about "French thought" in the aftermath of May '68.

I ran into Antoinette again during the campaign, which we both supported, to elect Ségolène Royal as President. She was in a wheelchair. All smiles, as if we'd never fallen out. Be that as it may, the movement she started, warts and all, furthered the emancipation of women in France.

S.D. Did this conflict dog you, pursue you even, in your subsequent dealings with feminism?

J.K. I've grown convinced that I'm no good at institutions, societies, academies, or communities in general. Whenever I do approach or join one, I may—

sometimes—prove useful, so long as they let me operate on the periphery. And my contributions, sure enough atypical, may perhaps bring a breath of fresh air to the whole; they certainly fuel debate. My foreign students, noting my predilection for the great *male* writers (Mallarmé, Lautréamont, Proust, Céline, Baudelaire, Stendhal, Bataille) and pointing out how seldom I discuss women (except for Duras!), urged me to write *the* long-awaited book on "feminism," in the singular! I tried my best to explain that any synthesis, likewise in the singular, was impossible and futile, not my style, and beyond my scope, but they wouldn't let go. In a way I did finally answer to their expectations with my trilogy on "female genius"—*Hannah Arendt*, *Melanie Klein*, *Colette*. The first volume won the Hannah Arendt Prize for Political Thought (2006), awarded by the city of Bremen. I donated the prize money to an NGO based in Marseille, HumaniTerra, which cares for Afghan women who self-immolate in order to escape forced marriage. It felt all of a sudden untenable to stay within the academic-institutional fold; the name of Hannah Arendt had to be carried wherever the *radical evil* she denounced was continuing to rampage. It was imperative to condemn the fundamentalist radicalizations, the new faces of totalitarianism that enslave women, doom them to ignorance and abuse, deny them every freedom and leave them with only one possibility of revolt, the horror of suicide by fire . . .

S.D. We've already touched on the honors and medals whose ritualistic vanity are not lost on you, especially as Philippe and David are forever teasing you about them. And yet here you acknowledge, quite passionately, indeed, that awards can have their uses . . .

J.K. Only so long as the foreigner and the young dissident or leftist, disillusioned with political power in these hyperconnected times, persists in balancing writing with "*engagement*" . . . But seriously now, let's make a date. At my funeral—which I can't help thinking about, it's only natural, as I retrace this journey more or less discreetly—at my funeral, then, there will be no litany of distinctions, no enumeration of prizes. It will be enough to listen to Mozart's *Requiem*, perhaps, and to say that I have traveled myself, across borders and through identities, in an endeavor to accompany the excluded, the fragile, and the unloved. I tried, that's all. In 2008, the year of Simone de Beauvoir's hundredth birthday, it proved so difficult to federate the various currents of French feminism that my women students—yes, them again—asked me to chair the colloquium at the Cordeliers, sponsored by the Académie de Paris.[27] I took the opportunity to set up the Simone de Beauvoir Prize for the Freedom of Women, along with Sylvie Lebon-de Beauvoir, the philosopher's adopted daughter, Claude Lanzmann, Élisabeth Badinter, and activists from the Ligue du Droit International des Femmes. The jury was comprised of some thirty connoisseurs of Beauvoir's thought from around the world, all of whom had kept faith with her battles. The annual prize is awarded on January 9, her birthday, to an achievement, an action, a project, or an institution in defense of women's freedom. We honored women in many fields: fighters against Islamic fundamentalism, an Iranian collective, Tunisian journalists, a lawyer and a video maker from China, one of the greatest contemporary Russian writers, and the most celebrated of anti-fundamentalists—the Pakistani schoolgirl, Malala, who survived being shot by the Taliban and, following the de Beauvoir award, won the Nobel Peace Prize. After that I withdrew from this magnificent project, which suffers from waning enthusiasms and a dissipation of its initial energies and backers. Let's hope the younger generation will give it a fresh lease of life.

S.D. Let's return then to the passions which never let you down. Your reflection on language was largely inspired by the work of Roman Jakobson, the great Russian Jewish linguist exiled in Boston, who had known the avant-garde writers of his day, including "futurists" like Khlebnikov and Mayakovsky. His work was reputedly influenced by the poets. And one day you meet him in Paris! An encounter that couldn't be timelier for your new life: a fatherly, protective figure who reawakens the past.

J.K. A point of reference and a promise. He cofounded the science of phonology with Nikolai Trubetzkoy, who had taught at the University of Sofia after leaving Bolshevism in the 1920s. Jakobson's cosmopolitan culture, as a Russophone in love with literature and fluent in French, reminded me of my old teacher Cyril Bogoyavlensky in Sofia—with the added bonus of a Jewish sense of humor and a worship of poetry that enlivened our most prosaic conversations. It was Jakobson who wrote "On a Generation That Squandered Its Poets" (1931), an essay that damns the strangulation of poetry and the extermination of the poets in the early years of Stalinism, prefiguring the Nazi concentration camps and the Gulag.[28] Poetry and politics: is there any difference? The polyglot Jakobson used to joke that he spoke Russian in thirty-six languages and told me that I became different according to whether I was speaking Russian, Bulgarian, English, or French. "Your voice switches frequencies, your body changes, you're not the same person," he said. "Don't be embarrassed, it's normal, language is incarnate." And we'd be off on long speculations about Mayakovsky, that unrepentant atheist who claimed to believe in the Resurrection when he was writing . . .

In Boston, where he lived, Roman Jakobson introduced me to Noam Chomsky at MIT. At the time, Chomsky was only just beginning to integrate semantics into his generative grammar and explained to me that linguistics had nothing to say about poetic language. "His doesn't, certainly," Roman said conciliatingly.

He was struck by my interpretation of Bakhtin's work, with the resonance it had at Barthes's seminar and in universities around the world; not least because the often vicious theoretical and political brawls between formalists and post-formalists had led him to underestimate this member of the latter camp. I supplied a preface for the first translation into French of Bakhtin's *La Poétique de Dostoïevski* (1967);[29] Jakobson's wife, Krystyna Pomorska, prefaced the English translation of Bakhtin's *Rabelais and His World* (1968).[30] Jakobson persuaded me that not only did the world need the cultural memory—ancient or recent—of this old Europe of ours, but that it was our duty to promote such a wakening.

S.D. We're not about to enter the maze of all these linguistic, semiological, or literary tendencies, it goes beyond our purpose. Let us pause, though, on the figure of Émile Benveniste, the man and the work: a great but unassuming linguist, almost invisible in the constellation of French geniuses of the twentieth century. I would venture that, for you, the work cannot be understood outside of the complexity of the man, a man you knew well. Your affection for him emerges very clearly when you talk about his illness.

J.K. It's true: my adventure of the mind can't be reduced to reading and research alone, it also encompasses my heartfelt bonds with people who were the drivers of intellectual life for half a century. And who set off the political tremors that shake the present.

S.D. And that's because, I suggest, for you the adventure of the mind was incarnate from the start. It was part and parcel of your personal life. In the preface to a publication that pays due tribute to his teachings, you write:

> Émile Benveniste was an austere scholar, an outstanding connoisseur of ancient languages, an expert in comparative grammar, and an authority on general linguistics. He knew Sanskrit, Hittite, Tocharian, Hindi, Farsi, Greek, Latin, and all the Indo-European languages; at the age of fifty-plus, he immersed himself in the study of Amerindian languages. And yet his oeuvre, of striking audacity while always restrained and outwardly modest, remains relatively obscure and seldom cited today.[31]

To what do you ascribe this lack of visibility?

J.K. If Émile Benveniste is still too little known, it's in large part because his chosen disciplines of comparative grammar, general linguistics, and semiology are so dauntingly dry. In the first, admirable volume of his *Problems in General Linguistics* (1966), he founds a new semiology: for him, the *sense*, the "signified," is a transcendence *inherent* in language. The complexity of *signifiance*, as described by the "poor" linguist, is constructed in language understood as an *act of enunciation* between two subjects. A man of the Enlightenment, Benveniste folds into his theories the knowledge gleaned from dozens of tongues, including Hebrew, which he didn't explicitly reference. I attempted to deepen this insight in my auscultation of poetic language in Mallarmé, Lautréamont, or Artaud. Benveniste was the first linguist to examine the place of language in the Freudian unconscious; he stressed the *disruptive forces* of the drives, not *structured like a language*, but having their own logics that he traces in surrealist poetry, or the "interior language" of Baudelaire, in touch with sensations (it's what I have called the *semiotic*). Besides these advances I found so stimulating, his pioneering research produced the extraordinary *Dictionary of Indo-European Concepts and Society* (*Vocabulaire des institutions*, 1969), in which through the etymological analysis of words, tracing their evolution from Sanskrit to Latin, Greek, French, Russian, German, and so forth, Benveniste illuminates the meaning and value of our institutional and ethical pillars: among them the rule of law, the sacred, the paternal, and the maternal.

S.D. Are you telling me that the sciences of language that flourished from the 1960s to the 1980s, including dry-as-dust semiology, carried a political project? If so, it could only be unconsciously.

J.K. Not as unconscious as all that, you will see. Semiology, which was beginning to take root in academia—from Soviet Estonia to the United States, from Poland to Italy and France—could find no better champion than Professor Émile Benveniste of the Collège de France. He therefore became the president of the International Association for Semiotic Studies, or semiology as the French call it. Roman Jakobson in Boston, the zoo-semiotician Thomas Sebeok of Indiana University, Roland Barthes in France, and Umberto Eco in Italy were the standard-bearers of this international movement. It was coordinated by the UNESCO journal, *Social Sciences Information*, whose "Semio-linguistics" section was entrusted to Josette Rey-Debove—a conscientious linguist who with her husband, Alain Rey, certified the linguistic soundness of the Robert dictionary—and to myself, due to my youth, my Eastern background, and my languages. And, don't forget, one of the greatest assets of semiology was that in Eastern Europe and the Baltic republics of the USSR, it made a counterweight to the all-powerful Marxist ideology! Beyond the abstruse debates and specialized jargon, a clear message emerged from our works: semiologists/semioticians showed that human beings are not solely determined by the place they occupy in the production of goods and the social relations that stem from this. Men and women are also, or chiefly, constituted by the productivity inherent in speaking beings, that is, language and the creations that stem from language: literature, the arts, laws, codes of communication and all manner of expressions that make meaning or nonmeaning . . .

S.D. Viewed from the standpoint of contemporary hyperconnection, this semiological ferment looks to me like a foretaste, a trailer for the "empire of signs" that has lately overwhelmed us.

J.K. But it also equipped us with a passionate urge to spring the traps of the Web, Twitter, email, texts, and sundry "avatars" (without denying their benefits). For at the time, we were mostly conscious of challenging crisis-ridden totalitarian ideologies by letting in a bit of fresh air; by banking on the freedom that resides quite simply in the human capacity to make meaning. No wonder many of us welcomed the IASS not only as a cardinal epistemological value, but also as a political commitment. I threw myself into it wholeheartedly. The chief administrator was Thomas Sebeok, and on his trips to Paris, I, promoted to "general secretary" (!), helped him out in dealing with the Poles and the Czechs and the Soviets. Philippe pretended to be jealous of my frequent working breakfasts with the "boss from Indiana," though such appointments were normal for Sebeok who doubled as a businessman. One day he sent the boss a telegram: "Sebeok, animals don't talk, convert to livestock farming!" The jibe went down very badly with our zoo-semiotician because he thought it came from Roman Jakobson, who could be a merciless tease and was not a fan of his entrepreneurial colleague. I made sure Sebeok never knew that the joker was so close to home! (*Laughter*)

S.D. It's hard to imagine Benveniste thriving in this agitated milieu.

J.K. Wrong! It took him back to his youth, or even better his identity, not at all secret in the end if you read him with care . . . His Jewish origin, Talmudic training, friendship with the surrealists, with whom he signed a subversive pamphlet, curiosity toward new forms of art and politics . . . Benveniste often invited me to his home, a staff apartment I believe, near Porte d'Orléans. The library had overrun everything: books on the walls, over the floor, piled on tables, chairs, couches, filling the air with a wonderful smell of old parchment—or so I told myself, when it was probably just mold. He offered tea with dainty cakes, his sister Carmelia would say hello and slip away, and then the professor would start reading me the Rigveda, translating it live into French. After we'd done with any business, he would question me about avant-garde literature, the latest debates in the cafés of Saint-Germain, or perhaps: "Madame, do you think that woman is the future of man?" He mused on my likeness to his mother, and pressed me to talk about my own family—it thrilled him to hear that my paternal grandmother was called Mithra. "A Vedic forename, you know! The religion that rivalled Christianity at the end of the Roman Empire." No, I didn't know. What I did know was how furious Philippe would be at my lingering among the parchments for all this time: he had dropped me off at the professor's for a brief visit at three o'clock, and it was already five-thirty!

S.D. Hearing your stories makes me think that the armor of the austere scholar concealed a very courteous, gentle man.

J.K. He never talked about himself, neither his past nor his current life, which one sensed was entirely dedicated to writing and teaching. It was only in researching my preface for *Dernières Leçons* that I found out that in 1913, eleven-year-old Ezra was sent to Paris to study at the rabbinical school in rue de Vaugirard, by his parents who were teachers at the Universal Israelite Alliance in Samokov, Bulgaria.[32] His mother died over there soon after the Great War; he never saw her again. Benveniste's solicitude toward me acquires a different hue in the light of those late discoveries.

S.D. Did he ever discuss your own research with you?

J.K. I heard his voice for the last time on the telephone: he had just received a copy of my first book, *Sémiotikè: Recherches pour une sémanalyse* (1969). He paid some polite compliments based on "a first, rapid reading" and added: "We'll discuss it after the Christmas break." Not long after, he suffered a stroke that permanently paralyzed him and robbed him of speech.

S.D. A linguist deprived of the power of speech. An artist deprived of his gesture. I can imagine your sadness at seeing this remarkable scholar so diminished. For how long did you support him in that state?

J.K. Seven years. Unfortunately, previous to and after the birth of my son David, I had to space out my visits. Benveniste passed away the following year, in 1976. Shortly before his death, on my last visit, he began writing with his forefinger on my chest. Puzzled, I gave him a sheet of paper and a biro. He wrote: *THEO*. Did he mean God? It was a mystery. Until I discovered that he had been schooled in the Talmud as a child. The ability to make meaning, as testified by the unrepresentable YHWH, was subsequently analyzed by my professor using the tools of grammar, linguistics, philosophy, and perhaps psychoanalysis: disciplines issuing from the deconstruction of theology and philosophy, whose wellspring is the Greek root term, *THEO*. Now, with his shaky finger, he was etching the intensity of that *signifiance* which exists in the immanence of *language* and nowhere else. And here, more precisely, in the *dialogue* between master and pupil, old man and young woman. The legacy of Ezra-Émile Benveniste, translated into "human sciences," fertilized theoretical modernity, quietly and without censorship. Could our final meeting have also been the scene of a transmission?

S.D. He once said some disobliging things to you about psychoanalysts, didn't he!

J.K. He certainly did! On my return from China, I let him know that I hoped to become an analyst. Gently but not in jest, he exclaimed: "My dear, they're all mad and you aren't, what on earth are you after in such company?"

S.D. We've talked about how you found your place in academia and in Parisian life. Did you manage to keep in touch with your family? Having always lived with them, I expect you missed them very much . . .

J.K. Well, there was loneliness, to be sure. And yet . . . I'd decanted myself so wholeheartedly into the French language and culture, that I considered myself to all intents and purposes French . . . That was clearly not how the French saw me, to my initial surprise. Stupid of me, of course—they were right, they are right. This foreignness in the eyes of others transformed me: I was mortal. I watched *my* hand writing sentences in French, and realized that another language, *my* native language, which had been *mine*, was mine no longer; the very hand that was writing was dying, and *me* along with it, and *my* French here reborn under *my* pen was no less provisional. Only then did a taste for solitude come over me, a taste that would bear fruit with psychoanalysis. All things considered, I was probably made for it. I recited Nietzsche to myself: "Even *suffering* from solitude is an objection—I have only ever suffered from multitudes."[33] Or Charles d'Orleans: "My heart is become a hermit / In the hermitage of thought."[34] And privately I laughed at all this sublimated, triumphal, pretentious masochism. I'd made new friends, of course; I had a husband who loved me and whom I loved—both of us fated to solitude, to the erotics of bodies and of intellectual work; I had parents who wrote to me often, especially my father. I have kept fat bundles of his letters, covered in the lovely blue scrawl of a reader who would have liked to be a writer, and letters from old friends in Bulgaria who wrote from time to time. There was no internet and no cellphones; it's become hard to imagine how a world could persist in memory and in writing, now that instant ubiquity projects us into everything and nothing. It was before the fall of the Berlin wall, the years have grown compressed inside me unawares: I am like Nivi in *The Enchanted Clock*, outside time. I hold upright in my great vertical instant. Everything is *now*.

S.D. Are you ever ill?

J.K. My brand of happiness has its fissures, I suspected as much and stumbled early on, in 1967, I think it was? The shock of landing here and adapting to France, the landslides of love, intellectual insecurity: I didn't know what easy game I was for viruses. The staff at the Cochin hospital being alarmed by my Bulgarian passport, the ambassador had to step in before "his" grant holder could be "admitted" for treatment. Philippe Sollers watched over me, the nurses waited on me hand and foot, cortisone was replaced by lemon juice and my viral jaundice was checked. I recovered, but felt awfully tired for a long time.

Mind you, I rather enjoy the heightened helplessness of those moments (still rare despite my years) when I don't feel up to reading four books at once, juggling five work deadlines and three love affairs concurrently, racing to ten meetings a day and catching four planes a month . . . I can simply let myself soak up the rays of sun between two clouds, inhale the lime tree under my window overlooking the Luxembourg Gardens, and picture on my inner screen the faces of dear friends, a beach on the shore of the Black Sea, or the descent of a night flight approaching New York and its myriad glittering skyscrapers. Of all the epiphanies in this "downtime," my favorite is a vision of the Boul' Mich'. My first excursion on my own, without the generous Mira who had let me stay with her after that icy landing in Paris: out for a walk in the Latin Quarter.

I'm dawdling along the boulevard Saint-Michel. It's raining. We're in February but spring is already here, the scents wafting from the Luxembourg tell me so. I'm wet through, but the smell of the earth around the cobble stones clings to my nose, invades my brain. I want to hold on to this memory and take it away with me, this damp instant, those students eagerly kissing, high on beer and cigarettes, the smoke clouding my eyes, I light one too as I walk. I've melted into these sounds, cries, smells, I can't leave them, but my grant won't last forever and maybe I'll never come back to Paris. I absolutely must hold fast to this perception, it mustn't become a memory, I want to stay here with it, this painful present, as my real, French self, mine and other, at the crossroads.

S.D. You were there, in the here and now, powerfully alive, in contact with the world through each one of your senses and yet conscious of the fragility of that instant. Some people would call this a "mystical" or sacred experience.

J.K. A footbridge.

S.D. You didn't pursue the theme of integration when I brought up the *Tel Quel* group.[35] You inhabited an outsiderhood as "golden" as it was "ruffled," a condition you examined in your book *Strangers to Ourselves*, retracing the very delicate and universal history of foreignness, of those who are strangers everywhere and always. But without mentioning yourself. Your sense of foreignness doesn't seem to have abated over the years.

J.K. What with Bulgarian yoghurt, the sodomitical proclivities of the Bogomiles (forerunners of the Cathars, for our readers' information), and the umbrella of the Bulgarian secret services—a toxic and phallic symbol if ever there was one—I was the butt of every fantasy you care to name. All that was me, hadn't you heard? To such a pitch of trashiness, I can only wonder what's wrong with them . . . Why does xenophobia in France take this form of tittering hatred, of faux-innocent, bilious egotism? Maybe because dechristianization has been more radical here, while the humanism of the Enlightenment failed to equip freedom of thought with any sort of compass? Look at the publishing industry. Squalid naturalism is now the default outlet for a generation trapped in ill-being, bereft of ideas and of solutions. The publishers bring out stink bombs and the authors revel in cutting into the quick of whatever turns them on. A jihadism *à la française* to entertain the depressed market.

S.D. Tell me about meeting your publisher, Claude Durand. While he and I were preparing the ground for these interviews, I got the impression that as well as a publisher he was a friend, a mainstay for you and your writing.

J.K. A great friend, and the only French publisher who reads, or read, any books, in my humble opinion, and I've met a few. He was Solzhenitsyn's literary executor, translated García Márquez with the help of his wife Carmen, and published Ismail Kadare. We met him, Philippe and I, at Éditions du Seuil. Then when I wrote my first novel, *The Samurai*, I didn't think to submit it to Denoël, nor to Gallimard, to which Philippe had since moved with his journal *L'Infini* (the successor to *Tel Quel*). My swashbuckling romance was, and still is, so necessary, and at the same time I knew it to be so precarious and illegitimate, that I simply couldn't put it next to Sollers's work. My admiration for him as the author of *Paradis* and *Women* made such a juxtaposition absurd, not to say a potential springboard for some paternalistic remake of "Oeuvres croisées."[36] I mentioned the novel to Claude Durand just in case, because he had published the non-fictional *Strangers to Ourselves* in 1988. Not in the least thrown by my daring, he offered immediate approval and encouragement. Meanwhile, I was learning with, and like, my little boy an infantile/childlike French in which to relive my Bulgarian childhood on the analyst's couch.

Claude caught on fast with *The Samurai*. He loved my mixture of styles: the novelistic (stories, letters, memories); the lyrical; the narrative; the reflective. He was enthused by the "workshop" spirit—the blend of naivety and temerity with which this foreigner allowed herself to play with the very genre of the novel, the French novel. It was even clearer in *Murder in Byzantium*, hailed by the press as a "total novel" in the manner of the eighteenth-century classics. My first metaphysical detective story was *The Old Man and the Wolves*. An outcome of bereavement, after enduring what was for me the outright assassination of my father in a Bulgarian hospital, that novel inaugurated a new path, more hazardous and dramatic than *The Samurai*, in concert with my own fear of falling apart. I could not have written about all this without Claude's crucial support.

I knew he was sick. We'd swap news of our medical travails, me with David, he with his heavy-smoker lungs. How many times must I have called him on the phone, in floods of tears, from the bedside of my ailing son! He understood. Philippe Sollers was convinced that Claude was in love with me.

I myself think he overestimated me, so far as to picture me a member of the Académie Française! He pictured himself there, too, and took steps to make the vision a reality by applying. An unfortunate desire for recognition that was in keeping with his hypersensitivity, the touchiness that helped him maintain a firm grip on the house of Fayard. He didn't get into the Académie; having turned bitter and scathing about all honors and "those who live off them," he became ever more of a firebrand and then went back to writing novels.

His sudden death left me utterly bereft. I think it was the third great loss that had befallen me, after that of my parents. Our present conversations, my dear Samuel, are the fulfillment of a Claude Durand project, we owe them to him. Now he's gone, I don't feel I can summon the strength to produce another novel. Or even another book. Does that mean I only published for him, only thanks to him?

S.D. Tell me, when all is said and done, where do you stand? I'm struck by the paradox of this social portrait. Where do you situate yourself? In France? In the endlessly spinning whirl? Or in writing, as the only habitable place?

J.K. In sketching out the broad lines of my social being, dear Samuel, I relive that permanent, fraught estrangement I spoke of at the start. Who is this woman navigating through waters churned by so many ambitions, jealousies, careers, love affairs, theoretical-political brawls, real and imaginary powers? A poor little Byzantine waif, lost in the surf? No need to exaggerate. She will recover at the end of the night among her novels. Quick, I sidestep, I disappear, I stand aside, men or women reject me, I can only follow the flow. Of the air!

III. "The Lovers' Star"

> *Another love, different from passion, can flourish in the very shadow of passion . . .*
>
> —Colette, *The Innocent Libertine*

> *Love, I believe, can never be content to stay for long where it is.*
>
> —Teresa of Avila, *The Interior Castle*

Samuel Dock. It's time we talked about Philippe Sollers. The couple you have formed together for several decades has always enthralled the media and titillated public curiosity, and yet you've managed to protect your privacy. Philippe is very present in your novels, diffracted into several characters. Could you describe your first meeting? How was the relationship between you built?

Julia Kristeva. The life path I'm reconstructing with your help, dear Samuel, would never have existed or led where it did had I not been welcomed and accompanied by Philippe. Like the good feminist you are, you've underlined my own efforts and played down his crucial role. To recap, Gérard Genette and Roland Barthes were quick to tell me about this young writer who had invented the Nouveau Nouveau Roman, but I didn't seek to contact the reputed "character" for several months. A considerable span of time, given that my scholarship only covered nine months' research here! But his name rang no bells with me, and there was so much else to do and see in Paris . . . I was living between the Boul' Mich', my little room in the Gobelins neighborhood not far from Shabtai and Nelly, and the Bibliothèque Nationale in rue de Richelieu, where I was working on *Le Petit Jehan de Saintré* on Aragon's suggestion, if you remember. Well, I happened to read an interview with Philippe Sollers in the magazine *Clarté*, and it came with a photograph. A Bourbon profile with a whiff of the Marquis de Sade, terribly handsome and attractive. I can no longer find that arresting photo anywhere. Looks aside, the ideas Sollers was airing reminded me of the Russian futurists and French surrealists, but with a fresh kind of aplomb, philosophical and beguiling. He was saying in substance that it's impossible to change anything without first changing language, and, of course, the novel.

I wrote to him for an appointment. He replied quite promptly, suggesting a date after the Easter vacation. On D-day I arrived at the Seuil building and climbed the spiral staircase to the little office where he was waiting for me. I explained what I was working on, I touched on Bakhtin; we chatted for a long time and then went for dinner. Walking me back to the metro, the smooth seducer tried to kiss me! "Really, *monsieur*!" I fended him off. He wasn't expecting that!

S.D. And then you gave in!

J.K. Well, yes, after holding out for some time! Philippe Sollers had asked me what I wanted to do in France. My answer had been a paraphrase of Marx's line about the proletariat: I had nothing to lose but my chains. That shortcut had intrigued him. In those days, there weren't many independent, brainy young women who were neither "easy" nor "uptight." Let alone who hailed from Eastern Europe.

S.D. Did he address you as "*tu*" straight away?

J.K. Oh no, nobody used the familiar form at *Tel Quel*. It's a good question because we called each other "*vous*" for ages. Philippe first spoke to me in the familiar when we were leaving the Île de Ré, after our first holiday there together. This intimacy turned out to be final and irrevocable.

S.D. Some passages of your fiction are erotically incandescent!

J.K. I often say this, and we went over it in *Marriage as a Fine Art*, "love expresses itself only in metaphors."[37] No declarations, avowals, recriminations, or panegyrics come anywhere near this flammable substance. In their attempts at approximation human beings invented literary figures and genres, music, the arts. Some preferred a spiritual road, the soul's journey toward God, sublimated by Dante in his comedy of hell, purgatory, and paradise. When I'd spent enough time in baby talk with David and recapping my childhood on the couch in French to feel that my reincarnation in this language had reached an adequate level, it was my turn to try to speak of love in a novel. On the face of it, the encounter between our two forms of outsiderhood—me, the student from Sofia with the intractable, Orthodox family, and he, the young writer from the Catholic bourgeoisie of Bordeaux and latest darling of Saint-Germain-des-Prés—had no chance of lasting. But our instant attraction to each other, the concord of skins, mouths, sexes made our bodies inseparable, because our intellectual entente had taken root and has continually renewed itself since. Only the novel can come close to this alchemy. Philippe appears in *The Samurai* in the shape of Hervé de Montlaur, nicknamed Sinteuil. I've also slipped some of his traits—charms, rages, anxieties, favorite reads—into most of the composite characters who play the love object of the heroine of other novels. Right down to Theo Passemant, the cosmologist who lives in the sky, in *The Enchanted Clock*. You're quite right, my supposedly philosophical novels also trace the arousal and erotic play and pleasure between women and men.

S.D. Sollers had already published two novels dedicated to two women with whom he had been passionately involved, did you know that at the time?

J.K. Who didn't! When he came into my life he was incomparably more experienced than I was. On my side there had been more romantic exaltation than sexuality given the inhibitions of my conventional upbringing. Philippe made me reinvent my body and his, merging and de-merging, the power of the vital and the void. Which is not nothingness.

And there was no guilt, I realized as soon as we first climaxed together. It wasn't so much marriage that reassured me: I had to get married to be a legal resident. No, I gave myself up to this sexual release with childlike innocence, animal innocence I should say, with a sense of absolute fraternity, because our intellectual communion was just as immediate.

S.D. "Communion"?

J.K. If anything it's a feeble word to describe our shared or complementary curiosities, our joint immersion in Hegel, Nietzsche, Freud, Joyce, Bataille, not forgetting Barthes and Lacan . . . The main difference being that Philippe read much faster than I did, he'd be turning the page before I'd finished the first paragraph. Music was our heaven, and it still is. Again, Philippe was the instigator here. He taught me to appreciate the simplicity of nature, the salty grasses and geraniums on the shores of the Atlantic, the swans and migrating herons, to the strains of Handel or Haydn: concertos of clockwork precision, with their clarity of melody and pulsing beat . . .

Even so, the sense of outsiderhood remained.

S.D. Painfully?

J.K. Not exactly. It's a kind of watchfulness, alertness, freshness, that makes *jouissance* more lucid. We weren't, and we aren't, alike. I was and am a romantic Slav, as I said, that's my "neurotic" component, the aspiration to an impossible plenitude in love. Whereas Sollers, on the contrary, proceeds in the way we habitually ascribe to angels. Does that surprise you? Angels, as you know, are simultaneously human, and thus extremely close to us, and divine in that they can absent themselves completely. This duality makes them desirable, magnetic, alluring, or more than that, hopelessly binding. But it also forces one to feel separate and alone. Something angels don't suffer from because they haven't been born.

S.D. And they're not sexed.

J.K. Exactly. Not sexed because not born. Philippe's problem—for he does have one, notwithstanding the perfection I've described so far—is to be an angel who has unmistakably been born, and so he is unmistakably sexual, indeed heterosexual, which is not the trend these days. On top of his angelic ambivalence, he is equipped with the panoply of a born gambler. The result is a play of different facets, each of which conceals and shields another. To him, this way of being is just eternal childhood, while the rest of us, the humans, are just failed children. In reality, he can only make a chorus of the teeming diversities he contains, his legion of demons, in the polyphony of writing. Owing to my Slav and/or neurotic side, I've sometimes appreciated only one facet in our love relationship, whichever one I needed then and there, and not the others. At such moments I found this Frenchman very odd: he played the angel, but he could also play the beast. So what? It took me a while to grasp this coherence, the product of frontiers and differences in which "each piece plays its own game," as Montaigne once said about himself.

S.D. This comes across strongly throughout your work: you advocate a respect for otherness at every opportunity.

J.K. I attempted something I thought was beyond me: to figure out the benefits of foreignness, to embrace it as an asset. My first two years in France, and certainly Philippe's personality, made me accept that I'd always be an outsider. Even if one part of him has hooked my strangeness to his own strange universe, this inclusion, in its shadow zones, proceeds by way of succession and modulation, as strictly preordained and unvarying as a piece of serial music. I was reinventing myself on a different planet and it was he who made me feel and think the bright side of that situation, the peculiar grace of it. The luck. Though not rejected as myself, the stranger that I was and would remain was revealed, in this lived emotion between us, to her own forms of foreignness and those of others, by including them. A place had to be carved out for each of our respective singularities, and this is something we are still engaged in. It means deepening our empathies while safeguarding our incompatibilities, which are also our freedoms.

With me, Philippe could be part of a duo that had nothing heavily incestual about it. The same went for me. Considering my family harmonics, two options seemed likely. Either I'd never find a man who could measure up to my toxic attachment to my father and his to me and would have to resign myself to celibacy. Or I'd reproduce that stranglehold and wear myself out in a daughter-father relationship, a sarcophagus of embalmed narcissisms. Well, this was neither. We chose to accord our two ways of being outsiders. However, since the imprint of incest inevitably stokes yet threatens passion, it was through the infant's invincible appetite for arousal and the tamed cruelty of mutual care that this primal perversity found its way into our marriage.

The "couple" we created in this way has sustained me in my professional life. As I've said, whatever the disparities and conflicts of French society, its cohesion is never more solidly welded than against the foreigner, who feels it more harshly than in other countries. That's because the French are so good at compounding frontal rejection with other, slyer, more deniable rebuffs. I had to make a place for myself in the university and elsewhere, to be inside and outside at once. I had to accept the role I was given, even if it wasn't the role I wanted or that I thought was right for me. This slot here? It's massive, it's what there is, it's great! Trying to do my best, trying (what unbearable pride!) to *be* rather than to *be an insider*. And from this frontier position, to remake myself over and over, questioning the inside, the outside, and the self.

S.D. And this is where *transvaluation* comes in. A word you use often.

J.K. Plato's surprise, if you will! It is not sufficiently remarked that the philosopher is *surprised*, because he is *alien* to the community. *Bios teoriticos* equals *bios xenicos*: "theoretical life is alien life." In order to think, best not to belong. Remain an outsider, on the margins! That marginality may be the homosexual and writer's, as in Proust; or it may be the stoic's, as in Zeno of Citium, who came to Athens from Cyprus and invented a new "theory," the science of signs, the first semiotics. It may also be the marginality of a philosopher who stands up against the oppression of the "second sex," like Beauvoir; or of a writer who redraws the line between "purity and impurity," like Colette. This frontier position is as fruitful as it is risky: one must not grow embittered or puffed up with militant indignation, and one must not fall ill. But since Philippe and I cultivate it at the very heart of love, its dangers are kept at bay. Barthes understood this about me before anyone else, including myself, as shown in his generous article, "L'Étrangère."[38] No doubt because he was himself an outsider, foreign in the sense of "marginal."

S.D. The relationship with Philippe Sollers has lasted the course, you've said, thanks in part to that powerful impulse that drove you toward each other. Would it be fair to call this an example of "relational lightning"?

J.K. Even before *jouissance*, there was an immediate affinity of skin, of voice, of rhythm, that ballasts thought and sensitizes it. When I met his parents, I saw that Philippe takes straight after his mother. He has a feminine side, not in his demeanor or way of talking, which are forceful, scathing, incisive—but still exude much sweetness and subtlety. That speedy, energetic footballer's body isn't a bit hairy or rough, there's a smoothness about it, a kind of softness that puts me at ease, like a restrained sisterly sameness that may suddenly blow up when it comes to marking territorial boundaries. Reminiscent of the piquant wit of those seventeenth-century lady moralists and letter writers that sparkled in the charm of my mother-in-law, Mme Joyaux. As for me, I don't lack for a dash of psychological bisexuality, given my identification with my father, whom I resemble physically. All in all, Philippe and I constitute the couple as foursome!

S.D. I'd say that most of the men in your orbit possessed a noticeably feminine quality.

J.K. Maybe so, in different ways. Like everyone does, but the ones we mean are conscious of it and express it through a singular way of thinking, against the conventional grain.

S.D. *The Samurai* contains a compelling account of how you were gradually taken into the bosom of your charmed and supportive in-laws. The scenes you describe appear completely real. Did everything happen just as you tell it?

J.K. Yes, word for word. No novelistic transposition can adulterate the spirit of this Gaullist, Catholic family whose children were forbidden to stand up and sing *Maréchal* (Pétain), *here we are!* I shouldn't think it was ever their dearest wish to see their son married to a Bulgarian student—Bulgaria, where's that again? People aren't too sure even today, so imagine in 1966! They didn't attend our wedding in the registry office of the 5th arrondissement. A few months later, though, my mother-in-law phoned to congratulate me after hearing Professor Barthes praise my work on France Culture. And she slipped in a question: did I like white gemstones? Soon afterward I received a magnificent diamond ring, that I've worn ever since like an engagement ring. An exceptional woman: handsome, warm-hearted, and endowed with a gracious authority that no longer worked on her famously independent son, but which she turned into a charming solicitude toward me. Her way with a French as proper as it was colorful, her sense of fun that didn't spare the hypocrisies of her class, her taste in books, whose alleged triviality she bewailed just to make us laugh: the very breath of Mme de Sévigné. Philippe's father was by contrast a taciturn, inward man, devoted to his loved ones and to his garden. As soon as I passed my driving test I headed for their home in Île de Ré in my secondhand Renault. I hadn't passed Orléans, doing 120 km per hour, when I performed a triple roll into a ravine . . . and escaped with a few cracked ribs, luckily. I'll never forget how quickly my father-in-law arrived once he'd been alerted by the police, and how beautifully he cared for me during a whole month on the island. I've never convalesced in greater comfort.

S.D. Nevertheless, you say you had to "earn" this French adoption. Within the couple? With your in-laws? In the "French mind"?

J.K. Everywhere and constantly, but there are nuances. Let's stay with Philippe. The welcome that is our physical and intellectual understanding implements itself in everyday life and extends into time by means of talk. And our conversations are great fun. Like every long-term couple, of course, we take turns at being daddy and mummy, baby boy and baby girl, teacher and pupil, and this goes for dialogues as well. But things get more complicated with discussion. I try earnestly to understand and to argue my case, Philippe plays along, or not quite, introduces red herrings, jokes around, I drag him back to reason, his allusions come thicker and faster, new topics intrude, the debate turns polyphonic. Its nerve cells ping into new force fields, subsumed or implied, we've lost the thread, or not at all, it's clearer this way. And we end up in stitches! Isn't that the most dazzling of illuminations? . . . Are you with me? In this body-to-body and tête-à-tête, our social or psychological or sexual identities get lost, it's all movement passing by. But don't imagine that this logic—for it is a logic—evaporates between bouts. It reinforces a way of thinking that is unique to Philippe, that captivates me, cheers me up, and teaches me to be lighter.

S.D. One longs for a mike to record this "way of thinking" through conversation . . .

J.K. You can catch it in many of Philippe's interviews; they are published verbatim, practically unedited, because he's in his element with this French art of conversation. Here he is being interviewed on Voltaire. Slightly more "written" but it's the exact same vibration that seizes hold of memory, accelerates time, knocks quotes together, makes dizzy leaps and slips the serious into the facetious, as when he's holding forth to me between sips of J&B, while four million citizens are marching against the attacks on *Charlie Hebdo* and in the supermarket, and sales of Voltaire's *Treatise on Tolerance* are going through the roof:

> *Journalist*: And yet Voltaire is a deist—the left has consistently held it against him. Is that not a contradiction?
>
> *Sollers*: He certainly lays into fanatics and zealots more than into God. At the end of the *Treatise on Tolerance*, he addresses a prayer to God: "You did not give us a heart so that we could hate each other, nor hands so we could slit each other's throats." He also avers, with his peculiar brand of irony, that if God didn't exist he'd have to be invented. That was a bold hypothesis for the time, hedging its bets on whether God exists or not. It's the idea of "natural religion" championed by some Encyclopedists, where reason is regarded as the "light of nature." At the same time, Voltaire repeats that reason has not got, and never will have, very many takers, and those few will always be persecuted. He's very pessimistic. And always derisive. At Ferney, he pulled down the chapel adjoining the chateau in order to enlarge it. When people protested, he rebuilt it and fixed a graven plaque on the door: *Deo erexit Voltaire* ("Voltaire raised it for God"). Again, how ironic, Voltaire playing God on God's behalf. And that *erexit* is so funny. Imagine the phrase printed on bank notes, like they do on US dollars . . .[39]

S.D. You are always so serious, professional and collected, but when you're with Philippe it's as if you lose a bit of that straight face. You turn into a little girl, and in that special smile you keep for him I see someone mischievous, sunny, fulfilled. Could you tell us something about your wedding now, the ceremony itself? How did you approach it? What did it mean to you? How did it go?

J.K. Philippe had thought he would never get married, "except the once." He said, "Why not?" Especially as it was the only way to legalize my staying in France. A small group gathered at the town hall of the 5th arrondissement (our apartment was on boulevard de Port-Royal): my sister Ivanka who came over from Bulgaria, the writers Marcelin Pleynet and Jean-Louis Baudry, from the editorial board of *Tel Quel*, our witnesses. No parents. Afterwards we went to La Bûcherie, a favorite restaurant for Philippe and me, overlooking the Seine. To our surprise, there were Aragon and Elsa, quietly eating lunch. We'd never seen them in that place before! Everyone said hello, we didn't explain the occasion, there was no need to publicize our marriage. Still, they could tell we were "together," and with something to celebrate.

S.D. I wouldn't have imagined such an understated wedding for the Sollers-Kristeva couple, any more than a gaudy bourgeois one in fact. What you describe is a simple, beautiful, sober occasion.

J.K. I was sorry of course that my parents couldn't make it, but it was a beautiful occasion, almost undercover.

S.D. Perhaps a way of minimizing the presence of "society" between the two of you? How did your family perceive Sollers, how did he go down in Bulgaria?

J.K. Sadly, Philippe has never been to Bulgaria. He says that if he was foolish enough to go, they would stick him in a concentration camp or in jail like any other dissident. (*Laughter*)

S.D. My goodness! Why?

J.K. It's true that he might have alarmed the dogmatists, and possibly the police, by his uninhibited talk and provocative "lefty" positions. Mostly I think that it was, and is, a way of marking his independence vis-à-vis archaic customs that expect the suitor to "ask for the hand" of the chosen one or to "follow" her to the home of "her folks." Furthermore, his take on Orthodox Christianity and the writing inspired by or derived from it can be highly disparaging, not to say devastating, when he feels like giving free rein to Voltairean sarcasm. And even if I'm hardly a typical representative of the Orthodox mindset (just ask my father!) or even of the Slavic soul, I still feel the barbs of the author of *Women* whistle by too close for comfort. He is also merciless about the cult some French writers have devoted to their exotic spouses from the East. I'm thinking of Paul Morand: Orthodox funeral, ashes mingled in Trieste with those of his wife, the Romanian princess Soutzo. And Louis Aragon, sucked in by Elsa's eyes and communism.

My parents thought he was wonderful, and he liked them, and my sister, very much. Bringing them through the Iron Curtain was a headache; after several failed visa applications, my in-laws helped us to go through Jacques Chaban-Delmas, the mayor of Bordeaux and an admirer of Sollers, and it worked: they would be permitted a visit to France . . . every three years! When in Paris, my father liked to meditate in Notre-Dame. He came within an ace of converting to Catholicism! My sister played the violin for Philippe, who, delighted, would tease her about her solid training at the Moscow Conservatoire by proclaiming his preference for the Baroque. And I'd never seen my mother so happy and forthcoming. My sister already spoke excellent French, and the language of Victor Hugo (a perennial favorite in Bulgaria) was slowly coming back to my parents, especially at the Île de Ré and in Bordeaux, where they made the acquaintance of Philippe's entire tribe.

Among the photos I keep of those visits is one of my father, returning enraptured from an expedition to the oyster farm we had at the time, his basket brimming over. He had just been treated to the spectacle of . . . a very low tide. Never having known anything but the Black Sea and the Adriatic, this retreat of the ocean over hundreds of yards struck him as apocalyptic and miraculous! He was thrilled that his daughter had enabled him to witness *all that*, just once in his life! My father would never change, he was still associating me with the phenomenal.

S.D. The Île de Ré is your refuge. A preserved, protected Eden.

J.K. The notarial deed to the house was signed by Louis XVI: a great-great-grand-uncle of Philippe's, a navigator, had rendered services to the Crown. Early twentieth-century photographs show a solid farmhouse with its back to the sea and surrounded by tropical trees and an outer wall. In those days the locals made wind breaks and didn't look out to sea. Being on a slight elevation, the grounds survived the worst of the recent storms, the flood swept part of the garden away but stopped just before the veranda. The old house was demolished by the Germans, who feared an Allied landing at La Rochelle. My parents-in-law were compensated by the reconstruction plan. The new buildings may be nondescript but the view of the bell tower of Ars and of the sunsets is stunning. I love sharing the tranquility of my faithful friend, the white swan who's been coming here for years. I call him Leibniz in *The Enchanted Clock* because the white curve of his neck folds the infinite sky into the infinite water. Philippe's grandfather used to sit on the stone bench, outside what is now his grandson's study, and shoot a brace of duck for supper. We're all ecologists now and the waterfowl are protected . . . so, through the window as I work I can see a little family of mallards bobbing on the ocean channel that feeds the salt marshes.

I am a "Rhétaise" myself by now, or nearly. One afternoon when I first came here, Philippe had gone to the post office and I was alone in the house. The rural constable came to the door, accompanied by two women carrying pails full of oysters. "I found them in the oyster farm," he said. I smiled at him, oblivious to the problem. He repeated his line. Finally, I came up with: "How much do I owe you?" I knew we had an oyster farm, but it had never crossed my mind, coming from Eastern Europe, that seas or woods or oysters could be private property! Philippe got back and reassured the bewildered constable. He suggested fining the offenders and giving the money to a sailors' charity. We enjoyed the oysters, but word soon got around of the poor match Master Joyaux had made.

S.D. Although it was Philippe Sollers who inducted you, as it were, one feels that the pupil ended up outshining the man she thought of as her teacher. You have been the object of massive acclaim, nationally and internationally. Doesn't this public image give rise to a certain competitiveness within the couple, not to say jealousy? I sometimes note a "dichotomy" between the Kristevans and the Sollersians, as if people had to take sides with the one or the other. A bid to break up this "impossible" couple. Have you felt any wish on the part of the society of the spectacle to set up a damaging conflict within the space of your entente?

J.K. Rumors circulate, or "images" as you say: Sollers's enemies, male and female, loathe Kristeva, his friends don't like me very much, while some of my friends think he's too this, and others think he's not enough that . . . While I was in hospital with jaundice an article came out in a far-right paper denouncing me as a KGB agent. Jean-Edern Hallier was behind it, apparently. He didn't know me, but harbored a "hatelove" for Sollers . . .[40] Need I say anything about the pathetic attempt at demolition from Alan Sokal and Jean Bricmont, who confused the mathematical *metaphors* to which I (and many others) resorted, with scientific *models*?[41] Their charges were refuted once and for all by the physicist Jean-Marc Lévy-Leblond. Or how about the scatological, antisemitic abuse spewed out by a so-called feminist with media clout, supposedly a fan of avant-garde writing? I'll tell it to you straight: the mud-slinging may briefly sicken me. It's not that I don't care, I just turn away. Unruffled. Elsewhere. Diffracted, disseminated over new and multiple horizons. We all have a world of our own. Mine has become a multiverse. And it'll grow larger every day until old age catches up with me. Well then, let "them" chatter! More harmfully still, more lethally, let them censor! It doesn't matter. The road unrolls ahead, the journey continues. Because we concur, Philippe and I, that life must be written, and the written is life. The "we" of two outsiders in accord. Different voices, visions, writings. Harmonies in constant readjustment and renewal. Alone, except for Time, that marks the beat of experience.

S.D. Do you recognize yourself in any of the female characters of Sollers's fiction? In which novel do you like yourself best?

J.K. That's just it, they change over time. I can spot aspects of myself in several composite characters. *L'Étoile des amants* (The lovers' star) is set almost entirely on the Île de Ré. And, at this moment of speaking, it's the character of Maud with her "metal density" that most resembles me, I think:

> Maud thinks we're living in a novel I'm inventing, she follows me, she believes in me. Everything started with that stubborn sweetness of hers. At first, watch out I thought, what's she after, that student, well, okay, young, dark, pretty, plump, graceful, good dancer; deep, black, amused eyes, melody, harmony, reason incarnate. No crazies for me, thanks. . . . Why her? Freshness and grace, that's all. Not innocence, no, dream on, but something rarer, more exciting. What to call it? Purity? Shrugs, guffaws and whistling in the hall. Stick a pin in the word, save it for later. Nothing idealizing, ignorant, repressive about her: a substance that comes from further back than the physical wrapper. Nothing sporty or sen-

timental: a metal density. The poison pouch, the vaginal gall bladder, they must be somewhere, but far away for now. . . . She's in the music of life, its gay gratuitousness. Why is she fond of me? Because I confirm without a word this moment in her existence. Human bodies need it, this remote approving silence laid over their bones, cells, tendons, knuckles. All tending to a good night's sleep: they sense it, they thank you.[42]

S.D. In resonance with that portrait, I think of the male characters in your own novels, particularly of the very recent Theo, from *The Enchanted Clock*, and his role in the couple he forms with the narrator.

J.K. Yes, so in a very different mode, here is how Theo and Nivi conceive of freedom:

> You are neither a passage nor a door. I have no need for light, no more than for night, oxygen, orgasm, even death. I have had it all; I still have it. . . . Now you give me what was missing: the fullness of solitude, a solitude full of you. . . . What to call you? Solus? The word seems too solar, exclusive and peremptory. It would be more correct to just call you You, without a name, a conjugate secret, me in you, you in me, my Asteroid, my Alone other, my A. I have no need to emphasize anxiety to discover that I'm missing you. I constantly tremble because of it; only at intervals do I lay myself open. For what purpose? For nothing. I have chosen gratuity; now I enjoy it a bit more. The furrow of your gaze in mine, osmosis of our hands that do not let go in the face of this film that the world has become, that we watch without seeing. Your breath, your odor, your voice from which I take food and drink outside time: when you are with me, while listening to your messages, when reading your texts and your e-mails. Dreaming about you, recalling you, reinventing you. Creating you. . . . Now: the expanding instant gathers together distinct universes from scattered times. . . . Emerging times cohabit and are distinguished. . . . In the encounter between Theo, Nivi, and the king's clockmaker, we are in tune body to body, heart to heart, autonomous and correlated. . . . Madness at a breakneck pace but under strict surveillance. Everything is possible, and everything eclipses. Fullness of the self outside the self.[43]

S.D. You nurtured difference in your couple, and, since narcissistic society can't bear couples that embrace difference, you defied social expectations. All the same, I suspect this was not only a "political" choice. To have demarcated yourself from Sollers would surely have led to overlooking your own "intertextuality": his presence mattered for your personal reconstruction, it marked your writings, it remains intellectually as well as emotionally indispensable.

J.K. The title of Teri Wehn Damisch's television film, *Histoires d'amour et de passerelles* (Stories of love and footbridges), (2011) is very apt. Putting it optimistically, I'm in the final third of my life and death is closer than it's ever been. There's fear and trembling, yes, but I can say, even if I hate balance sheets, that I'm very glad to have conveyed through fiction the quintessence of a "me" who "travels her self" and "loses her chains." The intellectual and the

French citizen are evidently part of this self. The malice and gossip of French clannism are off on the wrong track, completely missing this "journey" and its role of footbridge. Not just a "footbridge" between academic disciplines, psychoanalytic schools, cultural vagaries, religious conflicts, Europe and China included, but also between our separate personalities, Philippe's and mine.

S.D. As early as *The Samurai*, you make the case for secrecy in relation to Ed Dalloway and Olga:

> All they needed was to cultivate their affair and keep it secret. That was all. It had nothing to do with deception, guilt, and the farcical shifts of underhand adultery. . . . The real secret was a kind of alchemy that allowed them to be together without hurting anyone else: the serene tact that ennobles and moderates the will to power. Secrecy gave a woman real fulfillment, whereas man spoiled secrets by trying to collect them. . . . What are you when you're no longer a stranger to yourself? A sage? Not necessarily. More likely you are sick, or almost dead.[44]

I think we've all run into an Ed Dalloway at some point! To raise the matter of the third parties who gravitate between you is to venture into a somewhat sulfurous zone of turbulence.

J.K. Ed Dalloway, Olga's American lover, is a fictional construct. Anyone can try to identify the model or models, we'll leave that to the researchers. One can take him, as you do, to be a universal figure or, more in keeping with the quotation above, as emblematic of a generation, or of a recurrent masculine structure: the obsessional man, whose proficiency, ambition, and meticulous rigor are seductive. The Ed Dalloway type attracts me straightaway but rarely, if occasionally, over the long haul. His febrile excitability, haunted by impotence, intrigues me as much as the way his professional accomplishments tend to get bogged down in fussy management, shorn of vision. The media has begun to uncover these failings, particularly in our politicians, short-changing a democratic ideal that hungers for more pep, emotion, hysteria. But they apply to all men—from the lofty scholar to the transient entrepreneur—whose masculinity petrifies into an obsession with power.

This male pursuit of mastery and image fascinates me. Men seem to wilt in the attempt faster than women do, for women are perhaps better, if not at "cracking the armor" at least making it suppler by their sensibility. The obsessional man is incapable of encounter, but he yearns for it; and when he holds power, he cannot help parading his performances in public. This isn't mockery—I feel compassion toward this affliction that forms part and parcel of the virile pose, now more than ever. Women's emancipation and the restructuring of family models are among several aggravating factors, but it's nonsense to proclaim that we are seeing "the end of Western man." Masculinity is evolving, and democracies are in the vanguard of this anthropological mutation. A process that requires, of women too, greater finesse in handling couplehood, unless "man and woman are to perish each on separate sides," as Alfred de Vigny and Marcel Proust feared, or prophesied. In this resetting of love, well, my weakness is to plump for secrecy. You're right, I've made a case for it. Is it a female choice? Maybe. Sometimes. Not necessarily. It is certainly a personal trait or necessity of mine.

S.D. I hear you. Let's look at another male character, Vespasian.

J.K. The Olga-Ed relationship highlights a fundamental asymmetry in heterosexual couples. This imbalance becomes paroxystic across the whole of *The Old Man and the Wolves*. I went quite far in the wording of the violence between Vespasian and Alba, the physical and mental abuse of women inherent to a society where humans turn into wolves . . . Men and women find *jouissance* in different things, and their social relays also differ. One may lament the fact and seek to change it, but there it is: society has little trouble in accepting male violence and the male exhibition of conquests and addictions. I am a woman who approaches her pleasures and passions more discreetly, perhaps because the cavernous female body favors psychological interiority, more coiled and undercover. It could also be an effect of my upbringing and my struggles. I consider that I'm shielding my love and my friendships by keeping them off the table.

S.D. The public side of your relationship with Sollers rapidly took the form of a meditation on his novels: "L'Engendrement de la formule," your 1968 essay on *Nombres*, then *Polylogue* in 1977.[45] Seeking to plumb the man, or the writer?

J.K. The "recalcitrant," he says. I've always been struck by the way his work is the exact equivalent of his "personality." Speed and condensation. In language, these aim at finding a "perfect, vast, native word" (a phrase of Mallarmé's, at the center of my *Revolution in Poetic Language*) and produce metaphor, which is the core of poetry ("man is a thinking reed," "the Earth is blue as an orange," for example). In Sollers's novels, this grasp, this condensation, permeates both ideas and narrative. He swoops on a phrase, an idiom, or a word like an eagle diving on its prey. And his catch turns out to be the only one possible, the most revealing, making any commentary superfluous. A concept thus cut from the quick of some author or of current reality resonates with others, and this apparently off-key clash triggers surprise: you feel flummoxed at first, but then you get it, and a fresh "interpretation" imposes itself, another "world view." Rimbaud's illumination cast as an art of reading, of writing, of living. Is it philosophy, fiction, poetry? Narrative is too didactic a procedure for Philippe, films are too slow an art: we no longer go to the cinema, and not just because smoking has been banned. But I don't miss out on the latest movies, thanks to my students and to my dear Marianne and Jean-François Rabain, psychoanalysts and cinephiles of discernment, who have even won me over to the charms of Japanese film.

In everyday life these qualities in Philippe oddly give rise to an immutable levity punctuated by fits of ire. And a profound retreat from "people," the "world," despite occasional "appearances" here and there, lately not so much . . . But this mask of ease doesn't mean indifference. A piercing vigilance underlies the laid-back pose, with an appreciation for psychoanalysis—even though he mocks its practitioners and declares Freud to be obsolete, advocating political judgment instead, provided it is expressed with forceful articulacy *à la française*.

S.D. You should write a book about his work . . . You haven't written anything about him since the publication of *Nombres* (1968) and *H* (1973).[46] Journalists don't read anymore, and there aren't any serious critics.

J.K. You're teasing . . . I'm not impartial, I admit it. Sollers's writing belongs in my view to the percussive lineage of the "maxims" beloved of French moralists, crossed with a jolting poetry, a fluid Daoism, and an omnipresent, disabused sexuality. The movement of the "moving," as he puts it. Hence the distance from the novelistic spectacular, the impression of immobility and silence or, on the contrary, of extreme agitation. He plays and shoots like a Platini or a Zidane who never misses the opponent's goal in the great human match . . . This condensed effervescence characterized *Nombres* (1968), *Lois* (1972), *H* (1973), and *Paradis* (1981).[47] At that time I dubbed him a "Tibetan Mozart." In his recent novels—*Un vrai roman* (2007), *Les Voyageurs du temps* (2009), *L'Éclaircie* (2012), *L'École du mystère* (2015), and especially *Mouvement* (2016)—the same implacable acuity is deployed,[48] which can only be blunted by claret or J&B . . . I can never forget that his maternal grandfather, Louis Molinié, was a national fencing champion . . . In fact, Philippe Sollers writes and lives like a foilsman.

S.D. Instead of reading him, some people attack Sollers for dabbling in politics and taking sides in public. How does this fit in with your views?

J.K. In truth, he participates in movement, the motion of life, of the mind, what you will. And because he feels himself to be physically, carnally, a native of Gironde, politics forms an integral part of that movement, of *his* movement. He doesn't "dabble" in politics, you see, he scents a permanent *hatelove* in it, the ferment of concentration, the flesh of writing. He absorbs it. From political wars and skirmishes, this cannibal distills a war of taste . . . That's it, the fencer hides a cannibal . . . As for my political views, sometimes they coincide with his, sometimes they don't, and it's not about fixed political bias after all. The conversation is apt to swerve into, I don't know, the terrain of metaphysics, aesthetics, or psychoanalysis . . .

S.D. A disposition which is just as much yours, if I may say so.

J.K. Perhaps. Indeed, it must be, otherwise there wouldn't be that intimate rapport that holds us together through thick and thin. But our "duel" is fought with buttoned foils, much less warlike, or at least on another level of concentration . . .

S.D. Sollers's relationship with Dominique Rolin can't have been easy for you to take, all the same.

J.K. Why not? It was a steady passion, born long before I met him, for a woman of the generation above mine. I had the impression he was involved with the primary, maternal love object. The relationship had more to do with Sollers's mother than with me. Besides, I'd never felt jealous of my mother, convinced as I was that my father preferred me to her and to everything. This conviction is my symptom, for sure, or alternatively my strength . . . It was an essential dependence, under the ascendancy of that first object of attachment, from whom he found it impossible to detach. He's greatly indebted to her for what he is today. He accompanied Dominique Rolin with fidelity and dignity until her death . . . I've said it already, the two of us are lover-spouses: I am his wife-mistress, he is my lover-husband. I was the intruder, the anomaly, the spoilsport of libertinage itself. That situation made my foreignness exceptional and irremediable. "Irremediable" meaning that, neither condemned nor constrained, I felt delivered from the chains of superego-moralism and delivered to my uniqueness. And isolation turned out to be a source of freedom. I don't have a network; I bond with new others, I join in, I commit, I am regarded or not, I may even be the recipient of awards and prizes, but I remain apart. "Atypical." Philippe is atypical as well, but in a completely different way. This engagement between two forms of foreignness comes over as self-evident in the amorous encounter: *that's the way it is*. Without judging, you're in "something" natural and historical. Like the Alps, or Versailles, you know my taste for outsize metaphors . . . Especially when foreignness is transcended as a test and a stroke of luck.

S.D. Each in your fashion, you both confront the prohibition of incest.

J.K. There are very few men who don't fear women, to the point of accepting—beyond orgasm—that bond of reciprocity, of entropy, between two inalienable differences. In clear-sighted love, which can exist "in the very shadow of Love" with a capital L, the ideal of the sentimental masses, derided by the great Colette. Those who think they have attained it usually experience it with the fantasy of *profaning* the incest prohibition that, as Georges Bataille so forcefully showed, constitutes humanity. I'm not like that. I sorted out my paternal and maternal Oedipus by other, no less excessive means: exile and cultural commitment are some of their avatars. Psychoanalysis endlessly perfects this path: transference, elucidation, sublimation. Consequently, I am the kind of woman men want to marry. That is obviously out of the question. It's done and dusted. Irrevocably.

S.D. In *The Enchanted Clock*, Time is said to be the main character in a loving couple.

J.K. That's right. But how? Given the differences and autonomies of each partner, a couple cannot endure unless *care* becomes a major element. Care must not be confused with mothering. *Reliance* is an experience incumbent on both sexes. It lies at the heart of humanization, I believe—it's that important! The task is to become conscious of the ambivalence of drives and passions: attachment and aggression, love and hate. And then to transform them into a bond, into the possibility of speaking and thinking. *Reliance* works *against* maternal ascendancy, enabling separation to take place and the consequent self-sufficiency to propitiate new encounters. I listen to you, you listen to me, I hear you, you hear me, this changes *us*. You trust me. I vary. You mature. A regenerative therapy. *Reliance* encloses "*confiance*," trust, and the "re-commencement" of the bond.

S.D. You insist on the notion of singularity, the word often comes up, but what do you mean by it? How do you see your own singularity?

J.K. No community, no clan, no belonging, no PR, what's the point. Sounds pretentious? I know it does! A shield forged by exile. When you find yourself in an idealized place (Paris or France, say) that proves cold, closed, almost hostile, you realize you can only rely on yourself. No family, no roots, nothing to lose, and a few snappy slogans to buoy you up: "The proletarians have nothing to lose but their chains" (Marx);[49] a woman has nothing to lose but her chains, in my feminist version. And: "Nothing in my hands, nothing in my pockets" (Sartre).[50] And: "It should rest on our own strength" (Mao).[51] As it happens, we were similar in that respect. Sollers the Girondin and I the Byzantine inhabiting a France torn by the Algerian war, in full intellectual decline, Aragon's *Les Lettres françaises* enacting the decay of those letters and of "*les lendemains qui chantent*" . . .[52] Both of us inimical to cliques and so-called networks.

In such a state of weightlessness, there's nothing for it but to commit yourself unreservedly, with the brisk, unthinking, boundless enthusiasm that made some people wary of *Tel Quel* as "a gang of terrorists." Contemplative inwardness remained, searing and impregnable, but it was shared to some degree and, in that sense, supported. Sometimes based on misunderstandings, but there were underwater sympathies as well, a coded, dolphin language, unintelligible to the "in crowd," the deciders, the communicators . . . First of all with Philippe's family, after some hesitation; we discussed it. Inexpressible affinities with Roland Barthes, who lent a new, broader meaning to the "*étrangère*," the *foreigner*, to *l'étrangeté*, *outsiderhood*: but which? His own? That of the writing state, where you pull back and give of yourself in intimacy? With Lucien Goldmann, the Lukácsian Marxist, the atheist Pascalian, the dialectical structuralist. With Émile Benveniste, that severe linguist and surrealist petitioner. With Claude Durand, a free electron of the publishing world . . . A collection of paradoxes, who moved toward me and vice versa. Their fellowship was instinctive, intermittent, and effective. It responded to that wayward energy in me which otherwise might have become suicidal, and enabled it to evolve up to the present, here and abroad. Most of them were mavericks, unclassifiable, on the fringes of their own family or professional spheres: homosexuals outside the gay or lesbian lobby, independent Jews, restive freemasons, turbulent Catholics. It wasn't a "milieu," no, it was to do with magnetic attractions that lure and fade by turns, slumber and revive. There you have us: a foreigner and proud of it, an anomalous, non-joiner couple, and the multiverse of history through the test of writing.

S.D. What I find hypnotic is this sense of life, *existence*, being your laboratory. Nevertheless, as you know, the analysis or interpretation of a symptom does not, or not always, substitute for the pain it causes. You make me think of Virginia Woolf, who steeped every instant in sensations, who contracted and distended time and grabbed hold of the world . . .

J.K. What a peculiar association, you're scaring me! The peerless Virginia Woolf! She killed herself, don't forget. I'm not ready yet. I never will be. Nivi, my alter ego in *The Enchanted Clock*, attempts to drown herself, but Theo saves her.

That said, I understand your sensitivity to the ill-being of exile, which can lead to a fatal loss of self-esteem in personalities prone to depression; to a turning of aggressivity inward, onto the self, when it's not a kind of vandalism against the "ensconced." On the contrary, let me insist on the *refractory* outsiderhood of Philippe, and my own, if you will, *diffractory* version: he rebels, I multiply. I don't think there exists any substitute for the symptom and the associated suffering you mention. These experiences can always be deconstructed and sublimated. Endlessly. All so many ways of avoiding that more or less pathological depression that Aristotle himself identified . . . in the foundation of philosophical inquiry, of *surprise* itself! As for civilizations devoid of foreignness, they are dead in life, aren't they?

The respect for the foreign—in others and in oneself—is a lung, the only way to breathe. The shrewdest politicians know it: without foreigners, Europe could not exist. But proclaiming it is not enough. More importantly we must embody it, live it. In my case, Freudian psychoanalysis helped me to discern the advantages of being foreign and to enhance them by other means: through sublimation, through writing. The journey continues.

All the same, I do acknowledge your insight. I was uncertain whether to devote the final volume of my female genius trilogy to Virginia Woolf, who immerses me, or to Colette, who awakens me. I chose the sensual mystic over the hardline depressive.

The Voyage Out and the epiphanies of *The Waves* speak to my nocturnal frailties, and I subscribe to many of the sayings of the high priestess of the Bloomsbury Group. "The truth is that writing is the profound pleasure and being read the superficial."[53] "Fiction will be much better for standing cheek by jowl with poetry and philosophy."[54] Others I take issue with: "There is a dignity in people; a solitude; even between husband and wife a gulf; and that one must respect."[55] Obviously, but I renovate the solitudes and I rebound from the gulf. Or again: "Life is a dream. 'Tis the waking that kills us."[56] Perhaps so, or perhaps the reverse: life is permanent waking, it's the absence of dreams that kills us. Woolf's last letters make me shiver: she hears voices, she thinks she's going mad, she "can't fight any longer."

But I only fight on the surface; deep down, I take refuge with Colette in the flesh of the world: "Love, one of the great commonplaces of existence, is slowly leaving mine. . . . Once we've left these behind, we find that all the rest is gay and varied, and that there is plenty of it."[57] "For me, it is [in burgeoning flora] that the essential drama resides, more than in death, which is merely a trite defeat." What's more, the avid pagan broadcasts her love of the "word, greater than the object"[58] to persuade us that there's nothing better to do than write: "For me a single word is enough to create again the smell and color of hours I have lived through. It is as sonorous and full of mystery as a shell in which the sea sings."[59]

S.D. It makes me think of Maud Mannoni, who stresses the need to frustrate the drive and reenthrone narcissism.

J.K. Maud Mannoni, of course. She was a great friend; I was on the jury for her dissertation supervised by Pierre Fédida. She sent me my first cases of adolescent psychoanalytic psychotherapy, young people attending her experimental school in Bonneuil. But it's important to clarify: if the sublimation of amorous passion through writing avoids its "trivialization" (the banal that Colette deplores), it also differs, and radically, from the alchemy of the cure. To make a long story short, we could say that in the psychoanalytic experience, erotic arousal is neither "trivialized" nor "embellished." The therapist does not satisfy the drives and desires of the analysand; they jointly defer and in that sense frustrate them. However, via the link of transference/countertransference, analysis heals narcissistic wounds and restores the capacity to love. Through the patient's free association and thanks to the analyst's interpretation, this comes about. Analysis as a state of grace! It's rare, but it exists.

That specific bond between the analyst and the analysand, first imagined by Freud, is a new variant of love. Paradoxically, such fundamentals of the psychoanalytic experience are still little known and insufficiently developed and theorized. My seminar at the Société Psychanalytique de Paris addresses *interpretation* and its role in the capacity to invest the other. Interpretation begins with the analyst's intense empathy toward the patient and continues through the verbalization of past traumas and current affects: an exercise in listening, followed by remarks whose formulation demands the utmost tact. Ultimately, transference deals with the destructiveness of the two protagonists of the cure and accompanies the death drive that threatens the integrity of both analyst and analysand. Virginia Woolf found she could no longer fight this threat, but Mannoni confronts it—by caring for *herself*, caring for the youngsters in distress and awakening their creativity. Even the most frangible have creative potential.

S.D. The destructiveness you describe at the heart of the cure mirrors that of the infant who breaks things in order to test the reality of the parental figures, as Winnicott shows. He traces the creativity of the two protagonists right back to the early mother-child relationship.

J.K. If we have begun touching on the depths of psychic life uncovered by psychoanalysis, my dear Samuel, it's not only because you and I are in the business of psyches. How can we pursue the emergent "biographical" angle of these exchanges, except by acknowledging the violent conflicts now rocking globalization and which force us to look beyond the tired preachiness of "respect for others"? To "live with otherness/foreignness/singularity," as expressed in transference/countertransference, exposes the impotence of any political and educational treatment that overlooks the affective dimension of connection, remaining blocked on the surface of essential crises. Life as a *couple*—to return to the transference that occurs in that partnership—is a matter of depths, it depends on profundity. And it renovates the depths as well, by pouring a "tender current" into the exuberant outlay of erotic love. And then the proximity between life and death materializes in the likely conception of that startling, ephemeral being, the newcomer, the child.

IV. The Urgency-Emergency of Life

> *People cannot understand how difficult it is to stand up straight when one is a woman with a husband unlike others, a child unlike others, a profession unlike others—and when these various points of attachment are as much elevations as handicaps (it being understood that each of us is "unlike the others" and that she has her own plumb lines "unlike the others"). They can't imagine!*
>
> —Julia Kristeva, *The Feminine and the Sacred*

Samuel Dock. I would like to return to *The Samurai.* That novel built a first footbridge between your real and your dreamed existence, with a narrative strung between private life and fiction, and a story—yours—that juggled reality with fantasy. For me, one of the most affecting passages is that where you evoke pregnancy and motherhood.[60] The latter takes pride of place in your clinical work, and indeed you shook up psychological and psychoanalytic circles by elaborating the concept of *maternal reliance.* On the other hand, you've kept rather quiet about your own pregnancy. Were you expecting when you got back from China? Or is that a nosey question? How did Philippe handle this unique chapter in your lives?

Julia Kristeva. "Pregnancy is the common form of ecstasy," as I wrote once. Was it down to our deepening relationship, my progress on the analyst's couch, or those Chinese mothers whose truth blazed from beneath the official carapace of communist ideology? I was thirty years old, the longing for a child had become paramount and uncontainable. The "little girl" in me who preferred books to dolls now pined for a pram . . . After two upsetting abortions we had decided on together, because we weren't sure then that we wanted to be parents, he was feeling the same way I did: the time was right.

S.D. How did he react to the news?

J.K. Neither over the moon nor reluctant, the same as before the wedding. Sollers approaches life with a seriousness his detractors often fail to concede. We swapped excited thoughts and oblique, teasing allusions as the event drew closer, delighted with the babies and toddlers frolicking around us on the beach of La Conche near the Baleines lighthouse. You rightly spotted it in *The Samurai*, where I strain to reach this person who keeps eluding me, that other "Kristeva." To translate an evanescent sensibility, far more enigmatic than the Freudian unconscious, at the interface of meaning and biology. To give substance and words to this "limbo" of being alive, a bliss both natural and thinkable, thought-out. I'd always surmised that this was the secret of the dreamy eyes of Italian Renaissance madonnas, of their introspective gaze. Equipped with a Super-8 camera, I trudged up and down the saline marshes of Ars, filming salt flats, water, horses, sunsets. I mounted a short film alternating these oneiric immersions with stills of select Madonnas and Child by Bellini, the first artist to reconfigure Byzantine icons into realist painting. Those images must still be lying tucked away somewhere in my files.

S.D. And you analyze this very particular state in your clinical work.

J.K. That's right, I prolong this approach in a different, more serene framework, that of psychoanalysis. I move away, in several stages, from the usual notions, out of a concern to transform the concept of "maternal instinct" (which, let us note in passing, is not a Freudian concept but belongs to the hazy field of "pop" psychology). Biology *and* meaning, aggression *and* buttress; I propose to reflect on the violence of *abjection*, but also on the intensity of *reliance* between the two shores of maternal experience. We will doubtless have more to say about this founding madness, its dispersion into endurance, the buttressing of both by the paternal function, and the transmission of language. Talk about *experience*—motherhood leaves the rest standing!

S.D. And what about you, in all this?

J.K. I told you. My self is legion! Diabolical, my dear Samuel, with several facets. But it's always "myself" I'm talking about. Including when I speak of *reliance*. I felt its intensity from pregnancy onward.

The birth was perfect, which is to say painful, followed by an epidural, followed by a lovely baby, photos galore, ecstatic parents. My parents were unable to come, and my in-laws let the young couple welcome their newborn in peace. Philippe instantly decided to call him David, a name I loved. David Joyaux, son of Philippe Joyaux *aka* Sollers and of Julia Kristeva Joyaux. His dad showed himself to be caring and nurturing from the first in an unforced, spontaneous, extraordinarily tender way. I can see him now, cradling the swaddled David close to his chest and crooning . . . not *Au clair de la lune*, not him, but snatches of Mozart: *You who know what love is*, and some Bach: *Gloria patri et filio* . . . Later we recorded it and David loved hearing the cassette when he was little, he knew it by heart, he still sometimes sings it with his father. "My daddy who I love," he called him when he was growing up, saving the tantrums and showdowns for me. His father was all about music and fun; my job was to enforce the boundaries of everyday life. You'll observe, my dear Samuel, that it was not your standard Oedipus complex!

S.D. You said it first!

J.K. We went through it as a threesome, always ready to see the funny side. That's unusual, don't you think, in the largely tragic realm of the "complexes" identified by Dr. Freud. Laughter is the hallmark of our trio, despite and against the considerable adversity we faced. It punctuates all our exchanges, grumbles, justifications, recriminations, and lightens them up with a knowing wink that is deceived neither by difficulties nor by posturing. For instance, here is the motto of the three Joyaux: "Men are fragile, women work." Now and then I try to show fragility myself, if there's time, but I don't often succeed. When David was small, Philippe took him around the churches of Paris where they'd listen to the organs, records and CDs of Mozart, Bach, Vivaldi . . . I was in charge of museum visits, touring the Louvre, Versailles, Vaux-le-Vicomte, the castles of the Loire . . . My "program" went down all right, but David had more fun on outings with his father. When they came home, I'd be treated to their father-son refrain: "*We are the Captains of Gascony, Fighters and liars without shame, From Carbon and from Castel-Jaloux, We are the ones!*" It's been an earworm of mine ever since, you'll find it in *The Enchanted Clock*.[61]

S.D. But the disharmonies in your son's development began to emerge, and everything rapidly grew more complicated.

J.K. He was diagnosed with motor problems in preschool. After a full set of tests whose results were negative, no treatment was prescribed. Later on, as you say, psychomotor disharmonies and states of crisis began to emerge. David went to regular preschool and a public elementary school, then to a series of special needs schools. After a whole range of treatments, the diagnosis is still imprecise: it's one of those "orphan" neurological disorders, and it has put him in a coma several times. The situation is stable at the moment but the proximity of death, like a sword of Damocles over our heads, has made us lead a different life, infinitely more precious and aware. The heroic battle for sur-vival (with a hyphen) that David wages with such extreme vitality not only soldered us together, it changed the meaning of our existence. David's sur-vival means that he has incurred mortal risks, but also amassed a surplus of energy from this, a fighting spirit, an acute affinity with the suffering of others, and a spontaneous solidarity that demands of his parents, friends, and acquaintances to literally outdo themselves. Outside oneself: life. I don't mean to underplay the hardship, I do whatever is required—as do the specialists on call—to help him through those times of pain, fear, and wondering. I'm not like those pious parents of a disabled child who gush about the joy and grace they have been blessed with. David has stood me in vertical time, a continuous present, a "now" in which the demands of sur-vival make the rest of life seem secondary and unreal.

S.D. David was born and raised while you were producing the great pillars of your work, with *Black Sun*, *Powers of Horror*, *Tales of Love*, and the "female genius" trilogy, and building an exceptional international career. How did you manage to oversee his education and to be there for him, both things so important to you, while keeping up your literary creation and intellectual activities?

J.K. I managed thanks to moral support from Philippe, his constant concern and bottomless affection, and to the kindness of his mother. She laid down the law at once: "You're not to change a thing in your professional life. You have me by your side." "My treasure," grandmother called David. And off we'd fly to New York for my fall semester as visiting professor in the French department of Columbia University. With the help of the au pair she threw herself into a month of baby-food jars, visits to St. Patrick's Cathedral on Fifth Avenue, and the sight of Philippe capering with his son in his arms on the rooftop terrace, ringed by skyscrapers, of our apartment building on 28th Street East. It was thanks, as well, to the mental fortitude of my parents when we vacationed with them in Sofia. David and his grandpa would go sledding down the snowy slopes of the Vitosha, the great mountain massif near the city, and swimming in the warm springs of a spa in the south of the country; and when my parents came to Paris, they always took him to the slides in the Luxembourg Gardens, and bought so many balloons that people thought they were vendors themselves . . .

S.D. What great memories, what precious moments! They seem to have stayed with you more than the daily struggle to cope with David's development, to contain his illnesses and flare-ups, and reassure him when he was in hospital.

J.K. The medical and educational authorities agree on the need for personalized, à la carte care, and helped us to organize the best of what the Republic can provide in terms of a genuine interaction with those in a situation of disability. So far as that's concerned, I don't feel that my efforts were out of the ordinary. Maybe because effort summons effort, and love mobilizes unsuspected energies? Even though I need nine hours' sleep, I can wake up, do what needs doing, and go back to sleep. When I was breastfeeding, I used to put on makeup and a robe that was nice to touch and look at, to make the baby happy! I don't understand new mothers who moan about being harassed by the baby. At the same time, I'm not some Mother Courage who represses the least complaint, not to say shame, at having a child in a situation of disability, and turns them into militant denunciation of the "medical establishment" or the state. I take my life as a mother very seriously, and, to the undoubted benefit of psychoanalysis, it's become integral to my practice. My reading, my writing, even my patients are illuminated in new ways by what I go through with David. He has helped me to apprehend worlds that previously, before he came along, were opaque or closed to me.

The first time he lay in a coma at the Salpêtrière I kept watch at his bedside, talking to him and playing the music he liked best. In between I was reading Hannah Arendt, who established the difference between *zōē*, physiological life, and *bios*, life related and shared, life as biography, meaningful life. I felt or I knew in those moments of copresence that David himself was regaining the strength to lead both lives: *zōē* and *bios*. And that for my part I'd be able to lavish whatever care was necessary for him to get there in his own way. The "miracle of life" had never looked as simple and self-evident—stripped of religion, imbued with the Arendtian revolt against barbarism—as it did in that hospital room where I hung on my son's every breath. Life (*bios*) is essentially happy when it becomes a perpetual reconquest of meaning, through the mourning of grief. In the same spirit, the most fragile, most humble life is a shareable joy. Thanks to David, what I'm saying to you here is not a philosophical construct. I felt then that I understood Kant's *corpus mysticum*, the unity in freedom and maximal difference that is so sorely missing in secular morality. The experience of life-as-reconquest can already be glimpsed in my works prior to the first volume of *Genie féminin* (female genius), but it only emerged clearly during that hospital ordeal.

S.D. The way you talk about David, it seems you transmit a reciprocal vitality to each other.

J.K. David is entirely lucid about his predicament, but he never complains. Except to mention, very occasionally and casually, that he struggles to find the words to name his coma and other limitations. He records his pain in tight, laconic poetry. He has perfect pitch and adores Mozart and Vivaldi, a taste his father passed on, it's their private world and I admire them for it. Both of them are very demonstrative and demanding in friendship, but consider themselves anarchists politically. David holds his own against his parents by force of irony. He came up with some memorable wisecracks when he was small. Such as, "Daddy is like God, he exists, but you don't see him a lot." He prefers "Madame Joyaux" to Julia Kristeva. He warns me: "Keep it short," "You talk too much!"

S.D. In the film that was made about you, you refer at one point to "*taking care*." Of David and Philippe, obviously, but also of your patients, and even of your readers. Philippe explains with a twinkle that you're full of concern for others, that you're "jolly good at it," and we pick up on a certain divergence between your positions. Was he by your side throughout David's upbringing? Were you able to lean on him? Did he offer steadfast support?

J.K. Unwavering support.

S.D. But not intangible, I hope!

J.K. Spiritual, but not unreal. His way of helping David grow up often proved more pertinent than mine: no knocking on closed doors, no walking through any but open ones. Music, art, pleasure, dream, rebellion through clowning. The rest fell to me, which is to say the stewarding, in other words, the lot.

S.D. It can't have been easy.

J.K. Not easy, but not impossible either. In one of those haikus he has the knack for, David put his finger on it: "Dad is a happy bachelor." Which suits me fine. Philippe's behavior, aesthetic or metaphysical, and which can appear as a denial of reality, actually evinces a real efficacy of care.

Was it because of this journey through worry and tragedy that he endured, and David along with him, that I found myself overestimating my own vitality? So much so that I recovered the boldness that had energized me back in May 1968 against Lucien Goldmann, my dissertation supervisor if you remember, in order to tackle something even bigger: Heidegger's notion of *care*! In *Being and Time* the philosopher makes much of a late Latin deity, *Cura* (*Sorge* in German, *souci* in French), *Care*, prefiguring the *anxious concern* of Greco-Christian culture. Without the least pragmatism, *care* is portrayed as a movement *out of the self* while at the same time being an *attention* focused on oneself. I contested this Heideggerian vision of *Dasein*, pointing out what I saw as its failure adequately to take account of *the otherness of the other*, and noting the absence of the pleasure principle and of its leap into *jouissance*. What juvenile temerity, what stubborn polemics! Henceforth I am well placed to know that my *care* for David is the basic preoccupation that keeps me perpetually awake, with him, with myself, with others.

But don't get me wrong—*care* doesn't necessarily make a person *careworn*, anxious or gloomy; it simply maintains the most intense contact with the foreignness of one's fellows and oneself; *care* is the first glimmer of proximity. Something so rare in the selfish world of consumerism and digital virtuality that it becomes urgent, pedagogically speaking, to introduce *care* and the capacity to tend others as prime values, with precedence over every other secular moral teaching.

Philippe is an ultramodern father, proactive and rewarding, who transmits to his son the incipient movement beyond oneself and in oneself that we might call the fundamental sense of recognition and friendship. In *Ulysses* James Joyce calls paternity a "legal fiction" or a "mystical state" of transmission. Sollers implements that state with a true art of kindness borne by music, the French language, and laughter.

S.D. Your own experience of *caring* (*soin*) is not only more anchored in the everyday, I believe, but also more political than "mystical"?

J.K. It's often forgotten that the French Enlightenment made *caring* into a political *project*. For better and for worse. For better in as much as the Encyclopedists, Rousseau and Diderot above all but also Voltaire, writing about the deaf or blind or motor-impaired for readers who were none of those things, no longer regarded the disabled as *objects of care* (which is what they were, at best, to the charitable orders), raising them instead to the rank of *political subject*. According to this new, "enlightened" logic, which would culminate in the Declaration of the Rights of Man, such persons were free and equal before the law, and society owed it to them to compensate for their disadvantage and include them in fraternal equality.

Along the way, the said society, that "great beast" that fed on the dogma that yokes salvation to hard work, soon lost sight of *care* in the stampede toward induction–production–integration. The disabled are exhorted to become profitable producers, neglecting the more personalized connection they require for creativity to blossom. Yet creativity should be uppermost in "our scale of values," and certainly trump productivity. Caring empowers a singular creativity in the purview of an inclusive society. By contrast, integration at all costs subjects the singular to the high-handed normativity of a society of producers-consumers.

In the framework of the "republican initiative"[62] for matters of disability initiated by President Jacques Chirac (2002–2005), I joined forces with my friend Charles Gardou, professor of educational science at the University of Lyon 2, to organize an assembly on disability at UNESCO. The National Council on

Disability was our attempt to seed an entirely different attitude, an approach based on personalized care, recognition of singularity, and concern for its development. Just imagine what an apotheosis of the Rights of Man such a right to uniqueness would represent! If it worked for the disabled, why couldn't the same movement be replicated across society? Hannah Arendt dreamed of a political pact based not on "judgment" but on *aesthetic judgment*, on *taste*. Each concert-goer appreciates the music according to their taste, but the audience as a whole nonetheless forms a *consensus* within which diverse *tastes* coexist, communicate, and compete. The present political world is very far from this utopia. But nothing prevents us from dreaming that one day the care for the disabled, the care for our singularities whatever they may be, will help us live in a different, and better, way.

S.D. And who takes care of you?

J.K. My patients. I participate in the telling of their sorrows, which resonate with mine. I elucidate them, and this enlightens me. I deliver them, and this relieves me. But Philippe and David take care of me, too. In pretty much the same way. They are my star analysands, the most difficult, because the most beloved.

S.D. Looking at everything you do, for culture, for your chosen battles, for your nearest and dearest, I wonder if you ever get tired.

J.K. No doubt I do, but I don't feel it. The only thing I feel more as I get older is spinal compression, I'm turning into a tortoise (it's my mascot)! So I perform a few exercises with a bar that's screwed above my study door and with the multifunctional Swiss ball, plus a bit of Pilates—those are my amphetamines. After dinner or when I wake up at night, I like sorting through emails and answering them, or writing some. A few years ago, I could work on until dawn. Nowadays I unwind by watching American TV series, they send me to sleep. In the afternoons it relaxes me to listen to music in between patients. Or to write: writing sets energy in motion, channels and soothes it, but is never tiring.

S.D. I can detect David's importance in your life through some hints in your works, faint, understated, at times metaphorical or indirect clues that the general public would never spot. Not until *The Enchanted Clock*, your last novel, do you refer overtly to that relationship. One senses that he's your confidant, ally, and supporter, that he shares in your thinking and your literary adventures.

J.K. Very true, but David is actually a recurrent character, a central figure in most of my novels. In *The Enchanted Clock* he is easily recognizable as Stan, a fan of the android automaton, Versailles, and the stars. He was Alex in *The Samurai* and Jerry in *Possessions* and *Murder in Byzantium*. He was Paul in *Teresa, My Love*, where the narrator merged with the saint says of him: "I know someone who though he's not a poet composes poems without trying, novels that are poems with an extra something, extra movements."[63] The reviewers didn't recognize him, you're right there. They often don't read more than the summary on the jacket flap! On the other hand, many attentive readers got in touch with their own experience of psychomotor disorders and tensions between mothers and health professionals, or with their discovery of maternal endurance and possession, rare concerns for fiction of the spectacular kind. They found themselves sensitized, thanks to my novels, to the more vulnerable people around them.

Talking of David, but leaving fiction behind, his perfect pitch means he can hear my foreign accent and he teases me mercilessly. "Interesting, but slightly wrong," he says with a grin, and corrects my mistakes in French, something his father won't do. When I go abroad (which is often), he jokes: "Say hi to Barack Obama and I hope Angela Merkel will be with you, sorry, with us." He and his dad consider me addicted to the news: "French dairy farmers are not breaking even, instead they are losing 35 euros per thousand liters of milk . . . The monthly Russian salary is 120 euros . . . Wow, who'd have thought!" I get mad. "Madame Joyaux will put the morality back into finance," he hoots, switching off BFM TV, "the worst channel in France." If I behaved like a proper therapist with him, which I don't, I would have done more to stop him talking back, fighting me, acting spoiled or sarcastic . . . Not that I'm a pushover who puts up with everything to please him, either. My understanding goes only so far, and I know how to forbid! I could do that with the child and the teenager. Now, the needling and the sparring is between grown-ups . . .

S.D. Freud already warned mothers: "Whatever you try to do, it'll be wrong"! Here he was anticipating without knowing it Winnicott's "good enough" mother. Thankfully, you could never have been completely good! Let us return to the "republican initiative" launched by President Chirac. In 2003 you wrote an "Open letter to the president of the Republic on citizens in a situation of disability: for those who are and those who are not."[64] Thirteen years on, it remains burningly relevant and an inspiration to everyone who cares for a disabled person. To the assembly on disability at UNESCO in 2005, you invited the Unified Jewish Social Fund, the Great Mosque, and Jean Vanier, founder of the Catholic community for people with learning difficulties, L'Arche.

J.K. And media celebrities: Patrick Poivre d'Arvor, Claire Chazal, Serge Moati, and many more . . . Simone Veil came to the closing event, and Jean-Louis Borloo was representing Chirac.[65] How can we ever "change attitudes" toward disability without mobilizing the power of the media as well as politicians? We sought, and we still do, to enhance "awareness, information, and training" in several areas: schools, jobs, access, leisure, family, and emotional and sexual life. I was deeply invested in that last area, along with Jean Vanier of L'Arche and the journalist Claire Chazal, our patron. The Equal Opportunities Act of 2005 in France ratified significant progress on all these fronts. From the start, though, I knew that the toughest challenge would concern the love lives of the disabled. Anxious parents often tend to wall themselves up in their own fears, denying the affective and sexual needs of children, adolescents, or young adults. And the state is not sufficiently on board with providing living spaces for couples or small groups of adults, adapted to varying levels of independence. How on earth will they manage when we're gone? the parents worry. This is the heartbreaking, unanswered question—one that reaches far beyond the difficulties of school and workplace integration, themselves, for that matter, still unresolved.

S.D. The fight for your son grew into a battle of wider scope.

J.K. David's neurological problems made him ever more fragile, so from middle school onward he followed various programs, both private and public, that enabled him to nurture his creativity through music, writing, and so on. In schools, in the "Turbulences" tents, and at *Le Papotin*,[66] we've encountered every kind of disability: motor, sensorial, psychical, mental; autism, much discussed at the moment, and more complex situations in which various issues combine. My psychoanalytic approach, very helpful here, has led me to think that there's no such thing as disability, or even disabilit*ies*: instead there are people who are all different and singular, each with a specific shortcoming. David himself is highly attuned to the fact that every one of his comrades is unique, and he tries to help them with that in mind, as they do him. He and his friends reject the term "*handicap*," the French word for disability, whose etymology and common interpretation smack of "hindrance" or "disadvantage," and they find it too general: it obscures more subtle frailties. Outside their group, in society at large, they prefer to call themselves *different*.

Of course, this new reality I now inhabit with David has necessarily and naturally become my reality in terms of thinking and engagement. I'm not an activist, and I withdrew from the National Council on Disability when it seemed to be stalling. Politicians after President Chirac lost interest. But I maintain a presence at the "grassroots" and in my writing. My awakening to the political question and the issue of humanism in the twenty-first century derives as much from an awareness of the disabled and the values they force us to reassess as from a realization of the vulnerability of humanism itself, faced with the rise of religious fundamentalisms. Psychoanalysis, meanwhile, has remained peripheral and sometimes downright unhelpful when it comes to understanding and accompanying disability. At that delicate, complex junction where disability convenes us and on which the society of targets and performance turns its back, I would like a voice inspired by psychoanalysis, and my sensibility, to be heard. I want people to understand that disability is an existential experience and, beyond that, a tribulation that illuminates human complexity.

S.D. Sure enough, ever since your "Letter to the president of the Republic," you have written and spoken on the matter from the point of view of singularity and mortality, hardly the usual approach in this domain.

J.K. The disabled and those close to them are faced with a special kind of exclusion. Since the eighteenth century and the Declaration of the Rights of Man, we have endeavored—despite frequent setbacks—to abolish discrimination on grounds of class, race, sex, and religion. This has not extended to disability. Why not? Because over and above the "narcissistic" wound of the disabled and the shame affecting them and their loved ones, living with disability confronts us with mortality. For their ill-being—whether it be neurological, sensorial, motor, psychical, or mental—is such that in the absence of technical assistance (various prostheses) or human support (various kinds of caregiver), the disabled cannot live. Physical and human aids are what stand between them and an ultimately fatal loss of autonomy. Their pain is mortal. You remember Baudelaire's cry: "Give me your hand, my grief, come with me."[67] Well, it's not to grief but to death that the inaudible cry of the disabled is addressed. But so is their energy, their irrepressible vitality.

In our civilization death is either denied (by religions promising life eternal) or suppressed, ignored, gagged by the cult of performance and growth and fun. A welcome concern for end-of-life, palliative care has recently emerged. But in the case of disability we are not dealing with that inescapable mortality. Here it is rather a reminder of the constancy of death's work inside us, of its random accidents and possible delays. The secularized world has nothing to say on this. It's the kind of death that frightens all of us and prompts us to stigmatize and exclude. And a disability policy that attempts to change the way people look at the disabled aims to calm those fears.

S.D. At the hospital where I work as a clinical psychologist, these issues lie at the heart of the thinking of many practitioners. As a matter of fact I often reach for your works as an aid in difficult situations. That creeping kind of mortality holds little interest for contemporary philosophers.

J.K. They produce brilliant doctoral dissertations and progress to no less brilliant media careers, for the sake of self-promotion, and they may well touch on the subject of death. But the mortality of the disabled . . . no thanks, what a downer. Too much misfortune, no ratings in it, you'll scare the audience, they'll switch over, besides nobody wants to increase the social security deficit . . .

Even the most generous of our humanist reflections on disability remain rooted in the old Aristotelian notion of *steresis* ("deficiency," "lack," "sterility"), or of *fault* (though we've moved beyond the latter, it seems). Matthew (25:35–46) takes his cue from this, subsuming every "defect" and "failing" into the category of "poverty": the sick, the leprous, the strangers, the vagrants, the needy, the maimed—paupers one and all! Splendid works of charity have been undertaken in this spirit, the cornerstone of Christian humanism and the church, the community of the "suffering Servant," moved by an urge to make good what is wanting and "give" to "those who have not." Technical and scientific approaches likewise proceed from this model of lack or deficiency: for instance, the study of aphasia (speech impairment) advances our understanding of the complex mechanisms of language. I am not saying we should ignore or abolish pathology. But we must be vigilant, lest we lock the disabled *subject* into the status of an *object* to be "looked after."

S.D. What would you suggest?

J.K. I'd complete the *deficiency* model with a concern for *singularity*. Back to singularity, this time via Duns Scotus. For the medieval theologian, truth did not reside in general ideas nor in the opacity of matter, but in *this* man here, *this* woman, *this* object. The demonstrative (in Latin *ecce*, "here is, behold") gave rise to the scholastic notion of *haecceity—thisness* in English, translated as *singularité* in French. In Scotist ethics, *thisness* is the only positive, the only "value." You can see where I'm going with this . . . David's thisness, his singularity is my one positive, my ultimate value. My loving empathy led me to guess that despite his neurological troubles he had a sufficiently fine ear to make music. And so I usher him towards separation from me, in the utmost personalization of his languages, his means of expression, and his bonds with others. Let him get there in his own singular fashion, not as I will it, but as he wills, and can. A new "space of initiative" will open up in which he may build an "emotional and sexual life" with his friends of both sexes and his caregivers. It will be hard; is it even possible? I sometimes have doubts, I say to him: "David, you're dreaming!" And he says, "But Mom, I dream therefore I am."

S.D. Listening to you, it occurs to me that you too, like Sollers but in a different way, only walk through open doors. You look first to the possible, and to beauty. Not to impossibility or suffering.

J.K. David and Philippe both find me too voluntarist at times. It's true that I'm ready to do anything for things to go better, to go well. Once I was silly enough to sing them a Russian marching song from my Bulgarian youth: "May your mettle be as steel, girded for adversity, marching onward selflessly!" I'll never hear the last of it. "Onward, Julia, selflessly!" Well, there must still be a neutrino of that wide-eyed fervor left in me . . . But seriously now, my own analysis, the work with my analysands, and Philippe's affinity with our son—not very practical, alas, but with a "musical" efficacy—have led me to embrace life as a battle against the presence of death and, when all is said and done, as a wholehearted engagement, minute by minute. The one worthwhile commitment—to a certain beauty. Many of the encounters I've had in connection with David afforded an experience of that beauty. It is not an aesthetic consolation, but, rather, a sentiment of rightness and justice wrought by the tenuous harmony that crowns the expenditure of energy.

I think of the absolute commitment shown by Jean Vanier, with whom I had a two-year exchange of letters, published under the title *Leur regard perce nos ombres* (Their look pierces our shadows).[68] Do you know where that title comes from? When I was collecting the Holberg Prize in Bergen, I asked to meet people involved in caring for the disabled in Norway. I was introduced to Halvor Hanisch, a young associate professor (when will we see a severely disabled associate professor in France?) who showed me his work, notably on Ibsen. One of the great dramatist's plays deals with a female pied piper (the abject Rat-Wife is a stock figure in Nordic romanticism) who is moved by a lame boy called Little Eyolf (as in "eye"), comparing him to her first, drowned love. As if to plunge into the psychic depths where abjection, fear, shame, and desire are mingled, the boy decides to drown himself in the same fjord. His eyes have stayed with the woman ever since: "they stare fixedly into the shadow's depths and their look pierces our shadows."[69]

We have moved on since then. Scientific discoveries and modern campaigns have helped us through the depressive gloom of romantic Dolorism. But there is still a lot to be done. Following that meeting, and the book co-authored with Vanier, I've continued to communicate with Norwegian colleagues regarding the difficulty humanism has in fathoming the complexities of disability, in the shadow of the Enlightenment . . .

S.D. A final word to wrap up this chapter?

J.K. I am deeply grateful to the medical, psychological, sociological, and musical teams that support David and whom I've met through him and his friends. It's true that I tend to forget about the fears and the tears, the blunders, the unhappiness. The only thing that remains is David's grin, uniting everything he loves and all those with whom he shares his infectious vitality, wherever he wants, wherever he can, at the Île de Ré or in Paris, with his "I dream therefore I am": this is life. I do my best to live up to this urgency-emergency of life.

V. A French Existence in the Flesh of Words

> *I house my body in the logical landscape of France, take shelter in the smooth, smiling, comfortable streets of Paris, rub shoulders with its ordinary folk: reserved, cynical, impenetrably private, but, on the whole, civilized. They built Notre-Dame and the Louvre, conquered Europe and the greater part of the rest of the world, and then came home because they prefer a pleasure in accord with reality. . . . And so I forget the death that reigns in Santa Barbara.*[70]
>
> —Julia Kristeva, *Possessions*

Samuel Dock. You are one of the hundred foremost intellectuals in the world, something that inspires not only respect but also a certain curiosity, a mix of desire and fascination. Your oeuvre is highly admired, as are your generous and innovative ideas; your precise, classical style draws praise; but the image-civilization will never be satisfied with words alone. People don't know you, they can only guess at you, at best, and so they invent a persona for you with stereotypes of foreignness grafted on. You are said to be "severe," a frequent adjective in the mouths of defenders and detractors alike. And yet what strikes me most is your hearty kindness, your sense of humor, your sensibility and simplicity. I wish the reader could "see" you the way I do. Could you describe an average day?

Julia Kristeva. People often find me difficult, which surprises me, but when someone who has followed my work meets me in person, they quickly change their minds and call me generous, which surprises me just as much! The images and representations of me vary so widely, it's like trying to stick postage stamps onto a rushing stream . . .

My day begins in the middle of the night because, since the death of my father, I often wake up at 2:00 A.M. My explosive anguish at his passing has subsided somewhat, but I still wake up in the night. So if I don't get down to emails, I cling to my dreamlike state and make notes for future works. I scribble in pencil in a little book and copy it out later. It's like an epiphany, objects begin to radiate, there are bodily flashes and hallucinations that turn into words, nocturnal physical reality relayed by an infant memory of hand and pencil and paper. This can happen several times, day becomes folded into night, but I get my sleep all the same, I love sleeping. Philippe considers me a champion sleeper.

S.D. If your nights are so creatively fertile, your days must be no less intense. How do you organize your time to stay abreast of your numerous professional activities without neglecting family life, writing, and traveling?

J.K. Breakfast is around 8:00 A.M., a cup of milky tea and maybe some cereal and a piece of fruit. It's a moment shared with David and Philippe, and we each talk about the day ahead. Given everyone's assorted fragilities and very busy diaries, we have people to help around the house. I take a minute to draw up a schedule and delegate the day's tasks. Lucky for me, this persistence of old bourgeois habits! (*Laughter*) Madame Joyaux, for instance, does no cooking and never rises from the table during meals. Organizing the household is quite time-consuming all the same! Then sometimes a gentle workout or a stroll in the Jardin du Luxembourg. As of 10 A.M., I'm at work: patients, appointments, classes at the university or elsewhere, preparing publications. I try to keep working lunches to a minimum, but they can't be avoided altogether since most of my colleagues, students, and editors are available at that hour. Then it's back to my desk until 7:30 P.M., relying ever more on online video conferencing. I might take part in the Kristeva Circle in the US, now catching on in other countries;[71] or talk to Anish Kapoor, forever bouncing between Paris and London, about his Versailles exhibition catalog; I might skype with Adel Abdessemed, who's putting the finishing touches to an installation in Los Angeles or Malaga and waiting for my presentation text . . . I avoid traveling too often, especially to the United States, where the endless airport security checks are getting more and more irksome.

From 8:30 P.M. on, I belong to the family. The three of us usually eat supper together. After that, everyone gets on with reading or listening to music, we don't "dine out" much. I'll watch some television, especially the news channels, including CNN, and political debates. I can't stand book programs, a ghastly commercial debasement! But watching soccer, now that's heaven! I often used to go to the stadium with my father. There's nothing I don't know about the game. We often watch the important matches all together in the living room. If I can't join them for these sporting high masses, David and Philippe kick up a fuss. I was a great fan of Zidane, who corresponded with David and was a pal. Sometimes I feel so involved that I can't bear to look when "our side" is losing, especially back in Zidane's day! David and I are diehard supporters of Paris Saint-Germain but Philippe, who loves to be provocative, often splits off to support the Girondins de Bordeaux against us. Or he bets on the Brits, out of allegiance to the age-old link between Bordeaux and the queen of England and to snub "moldy old France." Another pleasure we all share is classical and baroque concert broadcasts. Cecilia Bartoli is the family's top-favorite opera singer. Otherwise, we each tune into our chosen programs on TV or on a tablet in our bedroom.

S.D. Do you socialize much?

J.K. Hardly at all! At one time we used to hold dinner parties or the odd reception here, but Philippe and David, like the recalcitrant anarchists they are, don't enjoy it anymore. "Dad is at war with humanity," is David's ostensibly critical diagnosis, but he shares the same frame of mind. Last year I thought I'd won them round and that we were going to start giving dinners again, or at least cocktail parties. I was wrong. Pity, when I'm a good cook and love rustling up my specialties for friends!

S.D. Such as what?

J.K. Trout in ginger, and shoulder of pork with forty cloves . . . Have you tasted those dishes?

S.D. No. I'm a terrible cook, a positively dangerous one! I therefore run a mile from recipes as well as kitchens and their fiendish utensils!

J.K. Both those recipes were passed to me by male friends. Highly serious gentlemen, who barely say a word during dinners hosted by their wives while they slave over the stove. I'm thinking of the publisher Ivan Nabokov and his wife Claude, and of the late Jean-Toussaint Desanti, a philosopher and mathematician, and his wife Dominique, also deceased. It was Touqui (Desanti's nickname) who introduced me to shoulder of pork with cloves, a Caribbean dish I believe. You cook the joint on low heat and then spike it with the forty cloves and lightly grill. Serve with a clear sweet-and-sour sauce, based on Cayenne pepper and pineapple, and white rice mixed with Chinese mushrooms. Ivan Nabokov was the source of the salmon trout with ginger. Intrigued? You can use salmon steaks instead, marinated in pineau blanc from the Île de Ré ('fraid so!) with a spoonful of ginger powder. Brown some finely chopped onions and diced lemons, add grated fresh ginger (that's essential) and quickly seal the fish in the mixture, turning once. Cover in foil and bake in the oven for twenty minutes. It goes nicely with rice, though some, again, prefer our local new potatoes! Have you noticed, Samuel, that most women tend to reproduce their mothers' recipes without changing a thing, whereas men are more inventive? I took the tangent of invention! Still, I do make some of my mother's recipes, like her very airy cheese and spinach pastries, the sort you find in Greek delis in France. But she excelled at Balkan dishes, and there I'd never dare to compete. On the other hand, I am by common consent pretty good at French cuisine. I can whip you up a veal blanquette or calf sweetbreads, or even a tasty calf's head in gribiche sauce fit to impress President Chirac! In sum, I make time now and then to prepare our evening meal, but those meals are very, very "private" for the moment. No guests allowed! (*Laughter*)

S.D. You are very fond of this corner of the 6th arrondissement, the rue d'Assas. The street resembles you in that it stands as a peaceful line between nature and city, somewhat outside time and yet vibrantly alive.

J.K. At the start, Shabtai and Nelly found me my first rental, as I mentioned: 33 rue des Gobelins. When I met Philippe, he was living at 88 boulevard de Port-Royal. His parents had joined several servants' rooms together for him, which we fixed up. I love that eyrie with its sloping roofs, up on the fifth floor, so studenty and bohemian. Philippe uses the space for an office now. When David was born, we rented an apartment on rue Michelet. Later, in 1989, we bought this one on rue d'Assas. In *The Enchanted Clock*, Nivi rejoices in the knowledge that she will depart this world before the lime trees and bees of the Jardin du Luxembourg. She fulfills what is my dream, because here we can only partly see the trees. I won't be able to. My heroine does it for me.

S.D. That says a great deal about your attachment to Paris and to France.

J.K. Yes. As far back as I can remember, the Luxembourg has acted as a kind of magnet. After the Gobelins, I migrated to the 15th, the 16th arrondissements, but when we got married I put down the anchor here. Already in *The Samurai* David takes his first baby steps down those paths flanked by statues of French queens. The intelligent canopy of the Lux shades my other novels, and dominates *The Enchanted Clock*—until Stan/David discovers Versailles.

S.D. Here you have found the place and the formula, to paraphrase Rimbaud. There's a long history to gardens and thinking, ever since Epicurus. And here you've found a "legacy of memories" (Renan).

J.K. The Jardin du Luxembourg encapsulates a certain idea of France. My yearning for France is incarnate here, in the palpable continuity from the classical age through Enlightenment to intellectuals, students, babies . . . France eternal because eternally young.

S.D. The eternal France is made up of incredibly varied landscapes, soils, and regions. Which landscapes do you love best? Which places are dear to you?

J.K. The Luxembourg. The Île de Ré. Versailles. I have a weakness for Vaux-le-Vicomte, where David was very happy, as well as for the castles of the Loire that he is always ready to go see again and again . . . Oh dear, there are so many places to discover . . . Italy, New York, the United States, China, Asia . . . Though I'm not a monarchist, or a jingoist, let alone a Le Penist, I consider Versailles to be the supreme jewel of French history. So what if the PC brigade scoffs at any sort of interest in national identity! I acclaim the historical genius of Versailles, which in my view segues into the modern age. Yes, and that's the wager of my *Enchanted Clock*, where we meet the clock-maker and astronomer Claude-Siméon Passemant, the learned Gian Domenico Cassini, and the feminist mathematician Émilie du Châtelet. Also Voltaire, Mme de Pompadour, Louis XV, and a present-day astrophysicist courtesy of my imagination, whose calculations concern cosmic expansion and dark matter.

S.D. Our aim is to compose together an overview of your intimate life, but the latter cannot be dissociated altogether from your theoretical work. A radio quiz on a leading national station recently asked: "What is intertextuality?"

followed by "Who invented this concept?" The answer to that is you, the listeners made no mistake about it.

J.K. I didn't know about that—I just hope the audience didn't confuse intertextuality with "copy and paste," which is no more than the lazy version of the phenomenon. Every text is in *dialogue* with other texts. The novel itself springs from myth and historical chronicle, and absorbs the theatricality of carnival, according to the post-formalist Bakhtin. Philosophy, science, poetry, and journalism likewise practice a veritable *textual interaction* through the transformation and combination of various preceding or contemporaneous writings, and that's intertextuality.

S.D. You were twenty-eight in 1969, the year of the publication of *Sémiotikè: Recherches pour une sémanalyse*. The whole of the intellectual community hailed the immense labor of scholarly analysis pursued in this first book on the origins and characteristics of the novel. "Already (and from the first) greatly indebted to it, I have just experienced the power of this work afresh," Barthes wrote.[72] How did it feel, from the inside, to be writing it?

J.K. That first book in French condenses a period during which I felt at once very precarious and intensely receptive. A state of exile, or "limit state," but without the psychopathological connotations the term has acquired lately. The crossing of every kind of border coupled with the distress of being uprooted, a distress itself carried by the intoxication of a possible surpassing—but not suppression—of limits, norms, identities, and of disciplines as well, to be sure.

S.D. Your book has such an intellectual intensity, and is so embodied, that I don't understand your allusion to limit states.

J.K. Immigrants are especially susceptible to this, as I noticed from my first days as a practicing psychoanalyst at the Cité Universitaire hospital. Exile entails a loss of familiar landmarks, a loss of identity, and can trigger psychosomatic ailments. I am not immune myself: those frequent sore throats, rhinitis and other flu-like symptoms, even the viral hepatitis I was treated for at the Cochin hospital shortly after arriving, are probably to do with it. But disorientation also, and fortunately, gives rise to research—and that was the path I took. The avant-garde used artistic means to explore the existential malaise of modernity, the traversal of boundaries, in tune with the identity-vertigos of exile and love. Things that philosophy, semiology, and psychoanalysis can conceptualize and figure out. I like to think that my youthful education and my fierce investment in that "yearning for France" we spoke of predisposed me not to separate the body from the mind. I threw myself into the humanities and modern literary experience with a passion. Exile became transformed, not into integration, but into a craving to endlessly recreate the *given* and the *acquired* . . . You dare to think from the vantage point of this mobility, this place-in-motion that you've become. You dare to innovate. And perhaps discover.

S.D. From that time on your output continued at a steady pace, with a consistently high standard of execution. If I were to sum up your work for a non-specialist reader, I would say that you practice a multidisciplinary reading of literary texts: you marry linguistics, psychoanalysis, philosophy, the arts, and you reframe in their biographical and historical context the formal breakthroughs (avant-gardists such as Mallarmé and Lautréamont, or Sollers) and conceptual breakthroughs (Arendt) of the authors you survey (*Powers of Horror* on Céline, *Proust and the Sense of Time*, *Colette*, and many more). Other works are centered on psychoanalysis (*Black Sun: Depression and Melancholia*; *New Maladies of the Soul*; *Melanie Klein*) or around social problems, disability, and, more recently, the issue of jihad. The entanglement of body, language, and sex emerges ever more clearly, and this leads you to an interest in the feminine and the maternal. As I was reading your works, it seemed to me that exile and foreignness made you immerse yourself in the *flesh* of language (sonorities, rhythms, erotic vibrations), deserting the firmament of pure abstraction. How did this inflection toward the body in language come about?

J.K. It could only happen because I was living in France, immersed in French literature, and lucky enough to be associated with the currents of a French thought that had—for centuries past and still today, by new and different means—built their kingdom from the body and the language. In France, with greater determination and passion than anywhere else, the alchemy of the word partakes of national identity and accompanies its historical mutations. This is the country that adopted me, this is my country. When I bend over my computer or my notebooks in French, I am at home.

S.D. Why the choice of Lautréamont and Mallarmé for your *Revolution in Poetic Language* (1974)? Was it because the "avant-garde" they represent advocates a "revolution" in the social and historical sense of the word? Or was it, rather, as you set forth later in *The Sense and Non-sense of Revolt* (1996) and *Intimate Revolt* (1997), a matter of "revolt" in the sense of a "movement of return and new beginning"?

J.K. Or of a "retrospective return." The poetry of Stéphane Mallarmé is not abstractly "symbolist"; it expresses a "whirlwind of hilarity and horror." In *Music and Letters*, the poet asserts that each vowel, consonant, syllable, or word is a "constellation," a "milestone to infinity": a monad or differential in the manner of Leibniz. I called this poetic concentration a "signifying differential," inviting the reader to read *differently*—like a throw of the dice, impelled by the movement of the meaning and of the senses. As for Isidore Ducasse, count of Lautréamont, he claimed to be "free as a storm," with no specific identity, to "attack man and his Creator" in the *Songs of Maldoror*. In his *Poems*, the iconoclast is in revolt against "soft heads" (from Rousseau to Chateaubriand to Hugo) and against the French moralists (Pascal, Vauvenargues, La Rochefoucauld) whom he reverses, reroutes, and rewrites. This inspired poet received "life as a wound," he "rejoiced in shipwreck" while affirming that "poetry is geometry par excellence." He died of a mysterious fever during the Paris Commune. The surrealists were inflamed by his work at the end of the Great War when, amid the crises of the state, the law, and religion, the language of poetry embarked upon a veritable *revolution* which laid bare the deep workings of creativity.

S.D. Listening to you makes me want to quote Renoir's famous maxim, "An artist always paints the same tree." And then again . . . the tree you paint from above, from below, in different seasons, in words or in colors, is always changing shape and therefore it never is the same tree! You encompass this vision of infinity. But how did you handle the success of your first two books, *Sémiotikè* (1969) and *Revolution in Poetic Language* (1974), with their wide critical acclaim?

J.K. Except that those modern, explosive, polyphonic artists no longer *painted* a tree, they *were* the tree; Baudelaire had said that already.

Success, you say? I didn't realize at the time. The books originally circulated among a small audience, but they probably benefited from the impact of *Tel Quel* on intellectual life. And not all responses were positive. I was told that the literary establishment, the guardians of the classical and academic temples, didn't get it and were quite shocked. Other, younger creators and authors were more appreciative. Nowadays, when "senior decision makers" tell me or write me that they were influenced by my first books, it makes an impression on me, of course it does! But I do wonder who they're talking about.

The various media were not as ubiquitous as they are today, so the dissemination of "new ideas" relied on the universities that were founded after May '68; on the people who had manned the barricades, or on the "revisionists," that is, Communist Party dissidents. Whether it's a character trait of mine, a flaw, or a vice, the fact is that no matter how convinced I am of the indispensability of PR, I can't do it, I'm not interested. There are two things I detest: grocery shopping and PR. If someone takes care of it for me, that's very helpful, thank you. If not, I just shrug and move on.

S.D. You coined the poststructuralist notions of intertextuality, dialogism, the semiotic and the symbolic (one being a function of corporeal drives, the other rational discourse, social communication), all widely taught in universities these days. I myself encountered them in college. You developed and multiplied the paths of access to your thinking. And reinvented that thinking. For instance, you rapidly introduced clinical psychoanalysis into your research.

J.K. Indeed. At the same time as initiating my doctoral students to the "mystery within letters" according to Mallarmé and Lautréamont, I took them to the nursery at Censier Paris 3, where we recorded infant echolalia and then analyzed the tapes at L'Institut de Phonétique. In addition, we did a newspaper together with the inmates of the "antipsychiatric" La Borde clinic, edited by Ghislaine Meffre, who was completing her thesis on Louis-Ferdinand Céline at the same time! Our "Psychoanalysis and Literature" seminar at the Cité Universitaire hospital broached the subject of critical states of language across the civilizations. Notable speakers included François Cheng (Chinese writing), Michel de Certeau (Christian mysticism), Madeleine Biardeau (theories of language in India), and Eva de Vitray-Meyerovich (Islam). The talks were collected in a book titled *Folle Vérité* (Mad truth).[73] Remember that there was no such thing as jihadism in those days, no human bombs. Psychoanalysis enabled me to delve deeper, via the utterances of my patients, into the *inner experience* that underlies literary discourses, practices, and texts. "Inner experience" is a concept found in theology and reworked by Hegel and Heidegger, and, somewhat differently, by Georges Bataille who had his own attraction to mysticism. Reading Freud led me to revisit it, with an emphasis on the sexual drives and accidents of desire among the protagonists of the family triangle as well as in the amorous bond and its sublimation in art and literature.

S.D. All in all, the core theme of your theoretical research consists in the extremes and perils of creativity. You fasten on artists who recast representation and language without abolishing them: thanks to a potent capacity for association and composition, they produce ground-breaking works that invite the reader to concentrate and to the pleasures of thought. In *Polylogue* (1977), for example, you survey Renaissance painting (Giotto, Bellini) and modern literature (Artaud, Joyce, Céline, Beckett, Bataille, Sollers), including their study by the human sciences. How do you go about selecting your topics of research?

J.K. My choices are usually guided by a personal or sometimes social event, in tandem with spontaneous, unconscious inclinations. On my first trip to Italy, with my sister, we went to Padua for the magnificent Giotto frescos in the Scrovegni Chapel. I was enthralled. A study of the perception by babies of the colors red and blue, which I'd just read, helped me make sense of this bedazzlement in terms of the part played by color in early Renaissance representations of the Gospels. The cosmic state that engulfed me during pregnancy was something I recognized in the inward gaze of Bellini's Madonnas and Child. The painter accompanies the depersonalized faith of the Virgins, whereas, in his *Young Woman at Her Toilette*, a woman who could be our contemporary attempts to capture her elusive image between two round mirrors. A prefiguration of Degas's *Toilettes*? Another time, asked to contribute to an anthology on Beckett, the grief of a friend who had recently lost his father made me want to comment on the little-known story "First Love," in which a narrator bereaved of his father faces up to the absurdity of his sexual adventures. One last example: the *Tel Quel* theory groups, held at 44, rue de Rennes, started me thinking about transference in psychoanalysis in the light of Hegelian dialectic, and led me to introduce the notion of the *heterogeneity* of drives. In Hegel, "force" only acts "behind the back of the concept," whereas in Freud, the sex drive is always already a heterogeneous entanglement of energy (that of the body) and meaning (that of language).

S.D. In the trilogy *Powers of Horror* (1980), *Tales of Love* (1983), and *Black Sun* (1987), you propose new ways of thinking about abjection, love, and depression. That triptych is regarded by many readers as the cornerstone of your work.

J.K. I was torn between my fascination with the writing of Céline, a veritable "opera of the deluge,"[74] and my revulsion at his deadly obsession with what he called "*juivre ou mourir*, "Jew or die." I didn't know how to reconcile these two faces of my reading of him in a way that avoided the trite conclusion "great writer, dreadful human being." My mother was staying with us on one of her visits to Paris. David was in the grip of serial bronchitis. I was reviewing, on Ilse Barande's couch, the joys and trials of motherhood: am I a subject or an object? Empathetic or rejecting? Dependent and/or autonomous? On my own couch, a patient relayed her dream about a scene in Céline's *London Bridge*: a bucking ship, dreadful seasickness, the mother and son clinging to each other and throwing up . . . I woke up with a word in my head: *abjection*. My analyst said, "It's what you're going through as well, in a way." I wasn't sure what I was going to do with it but I knew for certain that here was the missing link, the "binding agent" that would unify the "Céline phenomenon."

The uncertain line that separates me from you, clean from unclean, pure from foul, is the privileged terrain of religion (purification rites address this) as well as of aesthetic experience (tragic or comic, catharsis purges our passions). Dispensing with a religious safety barrier and blowing rhetorical conventions to smithereens, Céline—mesmerizing and nauseating, lover and hater, neither subject nor object, joker nor martyr, *ab-ject*—incinerated himself in the fire of this catastrophe of identity, the victim and harbinger of *abjection*. In the novels he sublimates this intolerable anguish, takes revenge on the maternal or instead idealizes it in the worship of some sublime little dancing girl. In the pamphlets, however, he moves into political action by preaching the extermination of the Jews—his scapegoats, his fellows, his abhorred brothers—with alternate laughter and tears, but never with regret . . . Such were the unfathomable depths into which I was swept by analyzing that primal, pathetic otherness constituted by the early mother-child relationship!

S.D. The pre-oedipal mother-child relationship.

J.K. Absolutely. In those days, no more than a handful of us dared follow in Winnicott's footsteps to plumb the archaic and its apocalyptic consequences. After *Powers of Horror*, as if swung by a pendulum, I embarked with *Tales of Love* on a far sunnier survey of the range of amorous ties in the West: Plato's *Symposium*, the Song of Songs, Narcissus and Plotinus, saints and theology, troubadours, libertines, romantics, E.T. . . . It was bliss! Underlying the transference-love of psychoanalysis, as well as the vagaries of my own love life.

S.D. *Tales of Love* is studded with "clinical case studies" and contemporary variants on this passion. There is a very lyrical allusion to your giving birth, in bold font in the "Stabat Mater" chapter. Do you know that that book made many readers want to begin an analysis themselves?

J.K. It's true, some of them told me that they hadn't understood all of it but wished to start analysis. My response was that if they were in my consulting room, they had understood the essentials. By calling the experience of motherhood *maternal reliance* and teasing out its complexity, I endeavor to show that it transforms the primal violence of the mother-child tie, that *ab-jection* we mentioned earlier, into a "tender stream." And allows the *child* to become the first *other*. The first recipient of a gift, whom I distance from me, whose singularity I divine and care for, my different one who trusts me, whom I trust. The dawn of a reciprocity without equality. And the dawn of time. I *stand firm* because of him, for him, for the other. After all, doesn't *Stabat mater* mean *the mother stands*? We lack a modern discourse of maternal love.

S.D. In *Black Sun* you dissect the enigma of depression and melancholia. Were you feeling under the same shadow yourself at the time? Or was it the social phenomenon that interested you? Was it to do with challenging what you call "national depression"?[75]

J.K. *Black Sun* was the last panel of what looked, with hindsight, like a trilogy; but I never intended any programmed continuity. Was I depressed? In my French life? Frankly no, never truly depressed, though I had reasons to be, and even less was I melancholic, I swear! I might feel briefly gloomy or moody, or blue. On the other hand, I've treated people who had tried to kill themselves, patients suffering from fairly severe depressions, and I can say I'm well acquainted with that abyss.

I recall another instance of the link between theory and personal life. I was on holiday in Corfu, thinking about my mother and her striking resemblance to these lovely Greek women. And this certainty came over me all of a sudden, something that had plucked at me during analysis but which I'd ignored. The magical competence evinced by my mother was built upon a blank or borderline depression—in the same way as there are "blank psychoses."[76] This latent depression had been neutralized by her exceptional intelligence and what was ultimately a supportive family environment. I swore to myself I wouldn't go down that path, I'd never be that kind of black-sun woman. This vow sustained me throughout the writing of the book. It's one of my most widely read works. I've only just remembered this now, your question sent me back to buried traces.

Whenever my mother was able to spend some time in France, I tried to open her eyes to a different world, a different culture in which she could cast off her latent melancholy. It was a way of abreacting my sense of guilt vis-à-vis this maternal shadow, and to see that my avoidance of this shadow was what had deflected me from the motherhood that my analysis, by contrast, authorized me to experience.

S.D. In *Strangers to Ourselves* (1988), your psychoanalytic approach helped shape a new understanding of migration, exile, and otherness. Once again, we feel this powerful, highly intimate affectivity quickening your pen and your thought alike.

J.K. I wrote almost all of that book on the Île de Ré—in my study at Martray, our house, or in the Café du Commerce in the port of Ars, waiting for the teenage David to finish a sailing lesson. I had become very aware of discrimination against immigrants, the rise of the Front National, and the decline of solidarity. The "stranger" or "foreigner" welcomed by Barthes was beginning to wonder whether she shouldn't exile herself all over again. To Canada, for instance: there were some tempting offers from the University of Toronto. But I finally decided against it. I'm at home here, French is the language in which I live and think. The project would have been too complicated to bring off, and neither my patients nor Philippe and David could have come with me.

In *Strangers to Ourselves* I go back with energetic pessimism, as I like to call it, over the founding events and myths of the memory of *foreignness* (the same as I had done with *love*). From Ruth the Moabite, the beautiful stranger at the origin of the line of King David, to the Stoics, taking in the cosmopolitan humanism of the Renaissance and the Declaration of the Rights of Man.

S.D. In *New Maladies of the Soul*, published in 1993, you detail how the supremacy of the image is now flattening differences and emotions, stifling our ability to represent our own personal experience and the values of the subject. Is psychic space in the process of disappearing? That is the alarming question your study poses, highlighting not just a therapeutic emergency but also a problem of civilization.

J.K. Do new patients exist? New pathologies? We can observe the resurgence and diversification of serious depression, psychosomatic disturbances, vandalism, drug addiction, and, more lately, those extreme "maladies of ideality" that lead to radicalization and gangster fundamentalism. Changing lifestyles, reshuffled families, chronic unemployment, and new communication technologies may cause and aggravate psychic disorders, but they also engender their own antidote in new means of resistance and, let us hope, of recovery. What has also changed is the capacity of psychoanalysis to discern, accompany, and treat the various declensions of contemporary ill-being. My own practice in that regard prompts me to speak of "new patients," those who fall outside the customary categories of psychopathology (hysteria or obsessional neurosis).

S.D. Is there any common denominator to these "new patients," who present widely disparate symptoms albeit produced by a single wave of destructiveness?

J.K. They are afflicted by essential narcissistic wounds and troublesome symptoms; some are in danger of falling into psychosis. All of them find it peculiarly hard to represent archaic terrors. Didier, whose treatment and cure are summarized in *New Maladies of the Soul*, wanted to start analysis but hesitated to do so, or had trouble doing so, due to an artificial, generic, false way of expressing himself. Thanks to his paintings, the analysis was able to happen: when he brought me photos of his work his manner changed, and so a story of affects and bonds managed to be told and modified. Might the analyst's couch be the one and only place where it is still possible to "get in touch" with one's grief? Provided we take account of the power, no matter how toxic, of the new psychical agents—be they *images*, as for Didier, or for others the *digital*, or *video games*, or *social networks* . . . The book considers these symptoms and envisages remedies (art, the couch, religious faith), which were seen to reach their full scope in the twenty-first century and with which I have not ceased to engage, in a way that is now more synthetic and direct.

S.D. Next came *The Sense and Non-sense of Revolt* (1996) and *Intimate Revolt* (1997). You ask in these works whether revolt—in the etymological and

Proustian sense of unveiling, overturning, displacing, of reconstruction of the past, of memory and of meaning—is still possible. In the face of a culture of entertainment, can we still build and animate a culture of revolt?

J.K. I penned "my" revolts during a period of stagnation and political chicanery. It was during the reign of Balladur,[77] I seem to recall, and "political power" was busy falling apart under the onslaught of a bland "democracy of opinion," aka the society of the spectacle. Globalized hyperconnection must have accelerated that unraveling, which had never been so conspicuous . . . Just as the term *abjection* had come up to make sense of the paradoxical Céline, the term *revolt* now struck me: was it still possible for someone to revolt? And if so, what kind of revolt would it be? In a country where revolt had lain at the heart of democracy, and of 1789, and of the Enlightenment in which I aspire to keep a stake, as a citizen or as . . . a free atom. What does Freud tell us? The first insurgency is that of the son against the father, the Oedipus; a more complex process where the daughter is concerned, played out in two modalities of the Oedipus, as I made clear, and confirming that "psychic bisexuality is more accentuated in women than in men," as Freud had posited.[78] This enabled me to broach from a new slant the matter of the sexual differences that govern creative capacity in general, and revolt in particular.

S.D. You examine some experiences to be pondered, rather than models to be followed, in the works of three notorious insurgents of French culture: Aragon and Sartre—understandably—but also, more unexpectedly, Barthes.

J.K. Aragon was the sine qua non, figuring as he does the two great revolts of the twentieth century: surrealism and communism. Defiance and imposture. Revolt as *a-thought* coexisted in him along with the political reason that cemented rebellion and, ultimately, annulled it.

Sartre turned down the Nobel Prize and manned the barricades. *Nausea* is my favorite philosophical novel because it restores to refusal its central place in our existence. "Human freedom precedes human essence . . . the essence of the human being is suspended in freedom"[79]

Is Barthes really the most unexpected of these mutineers? The semiologist and writer never relinquished his critical political vision. Terms like "placing in a sling," "knot," "cut," "recasting" replace the word *revolt* and metamorphose it into *writing*. A writing that "utters the place of meaning but does not name it," at the same time as being an "act of historical solidarity."[80] And while the work "asks questions of life," it is "more complete, more total than life."

S.D. I cannot but admire your intellectual abilities and your energy in constructing such a dense and varied body of work. What are your working methods? What is your secret?

J.K. I *invest*. In French, *investissement* is a term used in psychoanalysis (*Besetzung* in German, cathexis in English) as well as in economics. My teacher Émile Benveniste revealed to me the Sanskrit roots: **kred*, **srad*, meaning the act of gifting one's life force to a deity, in exchange for a reward; you can see this in the Latin *credo* with its two derivations, *belief* and *credit* or loan. As an intellectual, as a citizen of France and of Europe, I invest my life force in the objects, themes, and realms of my desires that have survived all obstacles. But with no expectation of reward, wholly gratuitously, for I'm alone—no deity here—with the freedom of my investments . . . in the human condition.

S.D. I imagine that the documentation of these works would have required a very substantial research phase. The reader becomes aware as she goes along of an intense proximity, what you call "cohabitation," with the writings of Sartre, Barthes, or Freud.

J.K. Yes. I'm a library junkie! I love books. And manuscripts, and ancient and recent documents. I love reading by day, by night, between patients. I adored the Bibliothèque Nationale when it was on rue de Richelieu, and the old reading room at the British Museum in London, where an assistant would bring you the volumes you'd ordered. Better still, over there I could prowl the shelves and find what I wanted myself. A poem by Baudelaire says, "The dead, the pitiable dead, have great sorrows";[81] well then, books, those pitiable dead, have great expectations . . . I'm not at all comfortable in the new Bibliothèque by the Seine, I find those vast spaces and horrible escalators chilling. It's not a pleasure to go down there. I send my assistants instead or researcher friends whom I pay to carry out the important tasks . . . As for reading online, it wears me out after just a few pages, the meaning slides away like water on glass. I belong to the generation of books and paper.

S.D. And then, once you've managed to gather and sort all these materials, comes the writing phase. At night.

J.K. That's it. After the intermediary stage of notes: summaries, snatches, more or less tentative phrasings that need tightening up. In between sessions there are tasks to carry out for the family . . . Disturbances, distractions, and other interruptions don't impinge because as soon as the "intertextual process" gets under way, nothing can stop me.

S.D. The books we've discussed were mostly written in the 1980s. This was a very fruitful decade for you on the intellectual and creative plane, encompassing the end of your analysis and the beginning of your career as a therapist. You had planned to specialize in child psychoanalysis, but finally you opted for the infant within the adult. You have acknowledged that your writing blossomed at that moment, the cure having "tamed everyday language," your own French tongue. And that it also benefited from a productive process of "dispassionment." What do you mean by that?

J.K. The end of an analysis and of the transference/countertransference link are, to my mind, very specific experiences of "dispassionment": it's not a question of "disinvestment" so much as of a diversification of investments. I open myself up to new subjects, objects, cultural platforms, social action on different fronts; I give myself unreservedly to these multiple ties. They free up new, and more clear-sighted, passions. These ties do not exhaust me because the destructiveness of passion has been transformed into *writing*, in Barthes's sense, with a more precise and interactive meaning that I prefer to that of "sublimation" in psychoanalysis. Moments of excitability and violence will still occur, but placed henceforth at the disposition of the sounds, tastes, and colors embedded in signs; of the sensations and significations that surround us. This entwining, this *investment* in the flesh of words, carries me in all confidence outside myself; it soothes, harmonizes, and enlightens me. A new lightness becomes possible, neither submissive nor aggressive. No more neurotic one-upmanship; instead, a receptive intensity. The end of my analysis consolidated these changes, shifts undergone by everyone to varying degrees; I have explored them in the work of Proust or Georges Bataille, and, from another angle, in the mystics from Meister Eckhart to Teresa of Avila. The bond itself, the factual, pragmatic link to the object of trauma or love, may be lost. But the investment of the mnesic trace never perishes. Neither the other nor I perish in this proximity where *writing occurs*.

S.D. You are frequently called on to deliver lectures, which are always very popular, at the Société Psychanalytique de Paris. The squabbles between the various tendencies annoy you and you keep them at arm's length. What have your dealings been with the SPP?

J.K. You're trying to bring me back to earth! I won't echo Proust and say that "reality is what experience discards,"[82] not in this case. The SPP is obviously the best of the psychoanalytic associations, since it accepted me as a member! My seniors such as Ilse Barande, Serge Viderman, Michel Neyrault, Michel de M'Uzan, Jean-Luc Donnet, and above all, André Green were highly responsive to my "atypical" work, as we mentioned. It's the least you'd expect among colleagues, even if it's not always the case. They encouraged and supported me during training and as I moved up through the levels of our Society. Among those of my generation—Marilia Aisenstein, Bernard Brusset, Bernard Chervet, Gilbert Diatkine, Thierry Bokanowski, Jacqueline Schaeffer, Denys Ribas, Jean-Louis Baldacci, Laurent Danon-Boileau, and Alain Gibault, to name only a few—research proceeds nondogmatically, mindful of the contributions of English, American, or Latin American psychoanalysis. The writings of Melanie Klein, Donald Winnicott, and Wilfred Bion are studied, discussed, and developed. Lacan's too. I'm very excited by the opening of the psychoanalytic movement to the emerging countries, to Eastern Europe, Russia, and China. Being one of the few Russian speakers in town after the departure of the White Russians, I invest—that word again!—a great deal in working with and supervising the Russian colleagues who come to Paris for intensive training courses.

S.D. Younger clinical practitioners appreciate your openness to the human and social sciences. Thanks to you, some unexpected analysands have stepped into the consulting room. You talk about society, civilization, politics, Europe . . . For people of my generation, this decompartmentalization of psychoanalysis has proved to be the prime condition for psychical adherence.

J.K. How could it be otherwise? Globalization imposes the reorganization of our psychic spaces, often brutally, egregiously, spawning eruptive identities as one of the new maladies of the soul that we spoke of before, and will return to. Back in the 1960s this acceleration was just beginning: a Bulgarian girl with Sollers in Saint-Germain and Île de Ré, China, my double life in Paris and New York . . . I don't have to "reach out" to others to lead them into psychoanalysis: I *am* those others. Many of my patients are foreign, or of foreign extraction, or they feel like "strangers to themselves" as well as in France. That said, I don't regard myself as a role model; why, I even neglect some of the admin tasks of transmission that I'm supposed to perform at the SPP, keep that under your hat! Conversely, even in my seminar organized with the help of Eléana Mylona, "The Role of Interpretation in Psychoanalysis," some people base themselves on my texts and others hardly at all. I prefer to "transmit" by listening and talking to the participants, who have supposedly come to hear me, and I impart my interpretive practice by commenting on theirs. Is this humility? Not altogether. But it may be the best way to analyze . . . Along with reading the fundamental texts on which clinical research is based, and which are obviously indispensable, despite the lack of appetite for them today. But that appetite may come back, whetted by the discussions I have launched.

S.D. You cultivate the bond by transmitting your knowledge and remain faithful to your thinking with its way of revealing to others their own originality. What role could psychoanalysis play in the ongoing process of globalization? Some colleagues see you as a stroke of luck for the discipline.

J.K. I would wish these young analysts to think for themselves. Not only is proper reading extinct, or nearly, but suspicion of psychoanalysis is on the rise. Such skepticism is nothing new, to be sure, but we need to find new ways of standing up to it. When André Green wanted to apply to the Collège de France, Michel Foucault apparently sneered: "By all means, old boy, and why not an astrologer and a fortune teller for good measure . . ." Green knew then that his cause was lost. Though mine wasn't, he added, because "you're not only a psychoanalyst." Good grief! How do *I* know what I am? Me outside myself . . . (*Laughter*)

S.D. Everything.

J.K. Right first time! But in Teresa of Avila's sense, *todo nada*, "everything is nothing."

S.D. Nevertheless, you went to great lengths to get Freud into the UNESCO Memory of the World register.

J.K. The idea came from the magazine *Passages*, on the instigation of its director Émile Malet with the psychoanalyst Charles Melman. It's a long-term project that involves informing public opinion worldwide and raising awareness of the importance of Freud's thought in an age of identity tensions and religious conflicts, the impotent failure of educational systems, and the hijack of the political sphere by the financial. We kicked off with a string of conferences, in Paris, New York, Israel, Tunisia . . . But we still need to persuade UNESCO.

S.D. What you have called *abjection* is a hot topic for contemporary art, especially in the US, and commands increasing interest among psychoanalysts concerned with early mother-child relations and the limit states behind the unleashing of acts of violence both private and collective. To my ears, the word chimes with the chaos of the hypermodern world, the political and moral atrocities raging everywhere that governments are incapable of managing because they are incapable of thinking about the foundations of identity, as you do in your work. Your reflections on contemporary ill-being follow in the footsteps of *Civilization and Its Discontents.* Against the importance he assigns to ethics in society, Freud opposes the permanence of Thanatos, ever at work in the human psyche. What can psychoanalysis accomplish in our time?

J.K. There is no politics *of* psychoanalysis. In the third millennium, we shrinks are the watchmen of psychic space; it's our responsibility to explore the logics of that space, to foster its metamorphoses and preempt or tend to its calamities. But we also have a duty to make this quest into something to be shared, to carry it into a public square overrun by the spectacular and the digital. It's up to us to develop a personalized treatment; each analysis is a *poietics*, I can't say that too often. The experience of transference and countertransference, the interpretation, and the theory upon which both are constructed have to do with *intimacy*, and our first task is to recover-recreate this. Without slipping into vulgarization—fear of which leads many to wall themselves up in purist isolation—we need to innovate, coming up with fresh approaches to the discontent that ails civilization: in schools, in psychiatric hospitals, in the family, in the workplace, in interactions with the media and social networks, whenever the circumstances and our personal situations permit it.

S.D. Parallel with your analytic practice, you are a professor at the University of Paris 7-Denis-Diderot, where you have directed the postgraduate course in "Language, Literature, Image (the semiotics of text and art)" for many years. Following the jolt of May '68, how did the university deal with mutation? Did it begin to reform itself?

J.K. It was in convalescence. Within the new University of Paris 7-Denis-Diderot, on the site of the old vintners' market (Jussieu campus), a department was founded with the strange name of UFR STD, standing for Unité de Formation et de Recherche, "Science des Textes et des Documents." It comprised three strands: literature and linguistics, literature and psychoanalysis, and literature and history. Nothing if not modern! This bastion of "hard" science at Jussieu trumpeted its encyclopedic ambitions by taking the name of Diderot and welcoming us in. In 1973 I happened to run into André Lacaux, one of the founders of STD, on the boulevard de Port-Royal. "We're looking to hire a professor with an interdisciplinary profile. Are you defending your doctoral dissertation? Then come along!" My defense of *La Révolution du langage poétique* caused something of a stir, we've covered that episode. Barthes sang my praises, and a piece came out in

Le Monde, not very polite as per usual, but what a scoop for them! The General Assembly at STD eventually voted for me, over more experienced candidates.[83]

S.D. Looking back, how do you evaluate the novelties pioneered by STD?

J.K. It was an avant-gardist adventure, and a unique one, I believe. We were trying to open the students' minds to a creative reading of the texts. Reading/writing, interpretation, interdisciplinarity. STD (whose name later changed to LAC, "Lettres, Arts, Cinéma") was a most stimulating place, as transgressive as it was prestigious. Among other initiatives, we invited the in-patients of the La Borde antipsychiatric clinic to attend lectures as auditors. The Centre Roland-Barthes, which I launched with my colleagues Francis Marmande and Martin Rueff, with the help of Éric Marty, gave a broad Parisian public the chance to hear prominent figures in the sciences and the arts (from the physician Jean-Claude Ameisen to the actor Isabelle Huppert) reflecting upon current affairs, in the spirit of Barthes's *Mythologies* and his vision of *writing* that I have already defined . . . Pierre Fédida, Dominique Lecourt, François Julien, and I created the L'Institut de Pensée Contemporaine, incorporating the Centre Roland-Barthes, the Centre Georges-Canguilhem for the epistemology of science, and the Centre Marcel-Granet for Chinese and other Asian civilizations.

S.D. Your enthusiasm is infectious. I can tell that all this activity brought you many joys.

J.K. But what truly makes me happy is the reception of my research by the students. The awakening of their interest, their questions, their evolution into scholars. I was nervous at first, I used to prepare my classes (first for undergraduates, and then doctoral only) meticulously, on paper, and it's a habit I've never lost, although these days I improvise more freely as I go along. Professor Jean-Claude Chevalier, who oversaw my *doctorat d'état* on Mallarmé and Lautréamont, offered great support and encouragement. He is an eminent linguist, an expert in the Port-Royal Grammar (in which Chomsky found the philosophical basis for his "generative grammar"), and his presence at the first classes I gave in a French university was a priceless gift.[84] Chevalier is also a fine connoisseur of Apollinaire's *Calligrammes* and *Alcools*, and I was delighted by his assent to my interpretations of Mallarmé's "A Throw of the Dice."

S.D. I was sorry not to have taken your course at Paris 7 when I saw some clips of it in the documentary that was made about your life. You were telling your students about Colette and explaining the importance of musicality in her prose, the play on vowel sounds, for example, as in: "*rose noire confiture d'odeur*" (black rose preserve of scent) . . . Your eagerness to transmit is palpable, no less than your considerate attitude toward the students, exacting but not austere, always joyous. What are your recollections of your French students and of your fellow professors? Did some of the dissertations you advised leave a greater mark on you than others?

J.K. I have such a trove of warm, cheering, bracing memories! A laboratory of ideas and solidarities. My doctoral teaching taught me, and helped me, a lot. True to the collegial and respectful spirit of the department, I could teach my own choice of authors, in line with what I was researching and writing. All my books came out of these courses designed for the doctoral school. Including *Proust and the Sense of Time*, perhaps my most accomplished work, in my opinion and that of my readers. Side by side with *Black Sun*, whose first drafts were for that doctoral class. The Proust book is an exemplary instance, if I may say so, of an approach to literature that blends pedagogical concerns (imparting the necessary biographical and historical data while engaging in a close reading of the text) with interpretive desire (how do I receive *In Search of Lost Time* today? Is it possible to lend a psychoanalytic ear to it, without forcing the text?).

Take a more precise example: remember that *In Search of Lost Time* opens with the image of a man attempting to go to sleep. But as the writing advances, Proust arrives at a profound and paradoxical narrative which he calls "the dream of the second apartment": a separate world, a descent into the abyss of the self, in which the ego's boundaries dissolve and are lost. Like a hallucination empty of objects and people, enveloping the sleeper as he floats in a state of psychic quasi-death. Here Proust touches on eclipses of identity and the edge of the unsayable. His narrator, Marcel, attempts to reach a place where memory does not exist and time itself is abolished. Proust the explorer succeeds in communicating the "endogenous autism" described by the English psychoanalyst Frances Tustin, which is in all of us and makes us vulnerable. By daring to recount this experience of the depths, the novelist demonstrates the power of writing, with its capacity to envisage and pierce such perils more articulately than philosophy or science could ever do.

S.D. Your students must have been surprised to meet a Proust who goes further, by your account, into the analysis of dreams than Freud himself in *The Interpretation of Dreams* . . .

J.K. A Proust who is not confined to the "little madeleine" or to the bittersweet insights gleaned from his incursions into the citadels of Parisian high society. A "political" Proust in the most complex sense, torn between his Jewish, Christian, and homosexual identities, and taking sides in the Dreyfus affair; a Proust whose uneasy preoccupations resonate with today's conundrums about identity. A Proust who appropriates the whole of French cultural memory and aspires to equal the Catholic sacrament of the *transubstantiation* of the Eucharist: for him, writing turns "the irrational qualities of matter and life" into words.[85] A Proust who invites the reader to seek *experience* in a twofold sense, both felt experience and scientific experiment. I confess to a fond belief that my Proust study altered the usual reception of him, because my interpretation aroused an absolute passion for the author among a younger generation who hadn't read him before. At the very least it encouraged my students to become "Proustians" in their own right, unconditional and innovative fans.

S.D. Indeed, more than one of them wrote their dissertation on Proust. Tell me about them.

J.K. My Proustian dissertators produced remarkable pieces of work of which I'm very proud. Raymonde Coudert chose "The feminine in Proust": her thesis won first prize for academic research from *Le Monde de l'éducation*, and Raymonde has since become a splendid coordinator of our post-grad school. Other standouts are Nathalie Mauriac, Françoise Leriche, and Eisuke Komatsu, now teaching in Japan. Some brilliant former students are working on other writers and subjects all over the world. Nikolaj Lubecker is a renowned Mallarmé scholar in the Netherlands and Oxford. Alice Jardine, Terri Gordon, and Fanny Söderbäck are involved in feminism and French literature at Harvard, the New School in New York, and Siena College, New York State, respectively. Élisabeth Bélorgey, who shone a light on the genius of Claude Simon and his reinvention of the Nouveau Roman, is herself a novelist and publisher who kindly keeps up with my publications. Pierre-Louis Fort, a subtle analyst of women's writing (Marguerite Yourcenar, Beauvoir, Annie Ernaux), edited my *La Haine et le pardon* (2005).[86] David Uhrig, a respectful and valiant critic of Blanchot, published *Pulsions du temps* (2013). I oversaw Antoine Compagnon's early work on Duras and Proust, whose high quality took him into the Collège de France. And I accompanied Frédéric Boyer in his probing of "inner experience" in Dostoyevsky, Proust, and Kafka; he published a Bible translated by writers, is a literary director at Bayard, and a prolific author himself. It was Frédéric who suggested I write a "little book" on Teresa of Avila, a project that grew bigger than we'd planned and was finally published by Claude Durand at Fayard; but Frédéric edited *Cet incroyable besoin de croire*, which opened up a whole new continent to me—the fate of religious believers in modern times.[87] I'm also thinking of Ilai Rowner, who borrowed Blanchot's notion of *event* to explore the grief of Duras and the apocalypse of Céline. Ilai took me to see the kibbutz in Israel where he lives with his wife and child: a place of enchanted simplicity! And then there's Keren Mock (Gitai), one of the most gifted scholars it's been my privilege to guide; her dissertation won the prize awarded by our Institut des Humanités. Based on my notions of *intertextuality* in semiology and *reliance* in psychoanalysis, she put forward a novel interpretation of the work of Eliezer Ben-Yehuda, the "intertextual" creator of modern Hebrew, alongside a study of the adoption of Hebrew as a mother tongue by contemporary Israeli authors who emerged from other mother tongues. Her latest work on the subject, an analysis of Spinoza's *Compendium of Hebrew Grammar*, is a masterpiece of interdisciplinary thinking.

Over the past few years at Paris 7, I've been fortunate to work with a dynamic team whose projects forcefully disrupt the university's tendency to doze off under the weight of the crisis. Chancellor Vincent Berger is a physicist and feminist, who poured all his energy into backing the Simone de Beauvoir Prize; Frédéric Ogée is an Anglicist and vice-chancellor for external relations, with whom we've launched many international initiatives; and finally Bernadette Bricout, my dear friend in heart and mind, a top specialist in oral literature and a gracious intelligence alert to ways of nurturing "a university in the city," above all a university that welcomes and celebrates women.

S.D. Speaking of which, your course on "female genius" gave rise to a triptych devoted to Hannah Arendt, Melanie Klein, and Colette. How did you settle on those exceptional women, before bringing them closer to us, from a more intimate perspective, than any previous work on them had managed to do?

J.K. I looked for outstanding female achievements in the fields where I feel most at home: psychoanalysis, literature, and philosophy. I was after singular, dazzling works, risky and disturbing, calling on universal values.

Who better than Hannah Arendt ever dissected the sociopolitical background against which the dramas of the twentieth century unfolded—as did its radical forward leaps, including the female emancipation that changed the face of the world? A philosopher, a student of Jaspers, and Heidegger's lover, a critical Zionist, this "political journalist" (as Arendt liked to define herself) wrote *Eichmann in Jerusalem: A Report on the Banality of Evil*. In it she pilloried the inability of human beings to think for themselves, a defect that is growing ever more widespread: yesterday under the lash of totalitarianism, today in a "lite" version through the automatization of the species. Nazi and Stalinist totalitarianism first stamped out the capacity to think before exterminating the people they considered "superfluous," she observed. After the horror of the Shoah and the discrediting of politics, Arendt called for a political life that would underwrite the uniqueness of every citizen through political ties made of the memories and stories proper to each individual and intended for their fellows. For one's truth "remains hidden from the person himself" and only emerges clearly to the eyes of others.[88]

S.D. In the rubric of psychoanalysis you propose an unusual reading of Melanie Klein, arguing that it is by separating from the mother (symbolic matricide), and accepting a certain form of depressiveness, that we accede to language and thought. Your Klein is the first to make psychoanalysis into an art of treating the faculty of thought.

J.K. Far from focusing on psychic *pain*, as she is often accused of doing, Melanie Klein overcame her own depressiveness. According to this "inspired tripe butcher," as a fascinated Lacan dubbed her,[89] the fantasy related to the mother's insides lies at the heart of human destiny. It splits into being a source of anxiety (connected to the "bad mother") *and* of resilience (bolstered by the "good mother"). To transcend such "belief" in the mother's omnipotence paves the way to the sublimation of the maternal "cavity." The capacity of thought therefore requires psychic "depth," and self-knowledge is only attained at the cost of leaving the maternal behind.

S.D. Klein, pain; and Colette, pleasure?

J.K. Pleasure comes through words, provided they appeal to the *senses*—and the French genius is the epitome of this, from Rabelais onward, through the sensualists and libertines of the eighteenth century. In the twentieth century the baton passes to Colette. She saturates the language in the pagan pungency that is the great charm of our civilization, while revealing how this sensuality is grounded in a refined sense of mischief as much as in the simpler pleasures.

Two German-speaking Jewish women, in New York and London, who used English to explore the gravity of politics and the boundaries of the human; one provincial Frenchwoman who rekindled the fire of the materialists and of the most sophisticated libertinage. Life, madness, words. As you can see, the multiple faces of modern times are restored to us by the genius of these three women, in all their intricacy and complementary excesses.

S.D. The "female genius" volumes (1999, 2000, 2002) demanded "investment" from you, and your affectionate esteem for these three personalities comes over loud and clear. What was it like to be immersed in each one's thought or imagination for the duration of this lengthy undertaking?

J.K. They became my roommates, I lived with them, sometimes we'd argue, their vital force accompanied and sustained me. My studies of them wove together life and works. I would wish my students and readers to let their writings in as sites of experimentation in which life and thought mutually illuminate each other. These three talents made their own way, they never stopped inventing themselves. They followed mentors and aesthetic templates. They spread their wings in the acknowledgment of what they owed to Freud, to Heidegger, to national identity. They accompanied humanity through periods of distress, horror, and endemic fragility, and for me they continue to do so in these times when the craving for ideals is devastatingly, poignantly clear. The craving not so much for a value as for a road, a way through. And they were able to construct their personal destiny, their "happiness," to borrow Arendt's term.

S.D. In this type of project, scholars sometimes appear to identify with their preferred author. They transfuse into him or her. Was that the case for you? For I do think that you resemble them, and that there's something of you in them.

J.K. My students sometimes make that connection. Not me, I can't see it at all. Not mirrors, not models. But my trio helps me to rebound . . . At my age, there's still some bounce in me . . . like that ball I spoke of in my first session with Ilse Barande. The ball is me. Highs and lows are the stuff of this game, to be sure, and when you're kicked it hurts, but it also sends you soaring . . .

S.D. What strikes me when we talk of your "French existence" is not only those rebounds that punctuate it but also its steady expansion: from literature to the European crisis, from the human sciences to the religious impulse. The scope of your interests, connections, and activities grows ever broader. You met Pope Benedict XVI. Perhaps we could talk about the Montesquieu Project that you founded with some friends at the Collège des Bernardins?[90]

J.K. How can an atheist, a Freudian to boot, who calls herself a "free woman," shake hands with the Pope? "Benedict XVI's favorite atheist," crowed one headline. The truth is, it's time we got serious about the magnitude of the changes underway. Some of my writings on psychoanalysis and literature, citing the Bible and the Gospels, had warranted an invitation to take part in the 2006 Lenten Lectures at Notre-Dame around the theme of "Suffering." The pieces collected as *Cet incroyable besoin de croire* (2007) diagnosed such a need as prereligious and prepolitical: it is a universal anthropological disposition that clinical psychoanalysis detects in the "oceanic feeling" of the infant with its mother, and in a "primal identification" with the father of "individual prehistory" at the dawn of the ego ideal. Was this why I was invited by the Vatican's minister of culture to the Interreligious Meeting for Peace in Assisi in October 2011, where I would speak on behalf of a small delegation of nonbelievers? Assisi! A chance to rediscover the Giotto frescos my sister and I had admired together soon after my move to Paris! Giotto, Dante . . . I didn't hesitate!

The cathedral of Assisi was packed. I had never seen, nor will I see again, so many devotees of all the religions on earth, with their robes, beards, and extravagant headgear. A podium stood in the place of the altar, where I took my seat beside the ten orators who were to speak for the great religions (Judaism, the various forms of Christianity, Islam, Buddhism, Confucianism, Shintoism . . .). At the end of this string of variously bright or somber statements, I read out "Some Principles for the Humanism of the Twenty-First Century," available on my website. Pope Benedict, whom I had already greeted, took the floor after me. He began by welcoming this first-time participation of nonbelievers in one of these prestigious meetings, before lamenting the "great pain" we must feel at not having found the true God. He went on to grant that even so, truth was for us an inner combat, a seeking, a path. Then, addressing the believers this time, he proclaimed that "No one owns the truth." Not what you'd expect from a pope, is it! To be in sympathy with the convictions cherished by us nonbelievers, us seekers, on our path, engaged in inner combat . . .

On my return, I shared my impressions with Richard Prasquier, President of the Conseil Représentatif des Institutions Juives de France; Michel de Virville, director of the Collège des Bernardins; and my friend Father Antoine Guggenheim, in charge of research at the same Collège. The outcome was the "Montesquieu Project," whose aim was to create a space where humanists can mix with representatives (ordained or otherwise) of the Jewish, Christian, and Muslim faiths to reflect on their essential elements, as well as debate the intractable problems that are currently causing so much conflict and tragedy. A space where "no one owns the truth." We felt that an independent space was called for, to sketch the lineaments of—what? The utopia of "living together" remains a pious wish.

I am again resorting to the tired term of *humanism*, as I did in Assisi, because this word signals more than a "system of humanitarian values" struggling to keep its promises; instead it invites us to enact a *continual refoundation*. The project was well received by many competent and remarkable people who decided to join us, including the sociologist Stéphane Rozès, the psychoanalyst Jean-Michel Hirt, and the journalist and former director of *Le Monde*, Jean-Marie Colombani. And women, of course: my good friends Élisabeth de Fontenay, Blandine Kriegel, Annette Levy-Villard, and Karima Berger. We invited the minister of National Education, Vincent Peillon, because of his idea of "the secular teaching of morality," which we discussed with education specialists. Figures knowledgeable about Islam and its history—Tareq Oubrou, Ghaleb Bencheikh, Abdennour Bidar—broached the thorny problem of its eventual development along the lines of the Enlightenment and the Haskalah: is an interpretive movement possible that would call the revealed Word into question? In parallel, it was high time to reevaluate the Enlightenment and its attitude to religions, with a view to an account of the conflicts and schisms within the Christian theology that paved the way for the "break in the thread of tradition" (as Alexis de Tocqueville and Hannah Arendt put it)—an event that played out exclusively in eighteenth-century Europe.

S.D. The re-Islamization of one part of the world, the contagious spread of jihadism, and the attacks on *Charlie Hebdo*, the supermarket in Vincennes, and the Bataclan concert hall among other targets, make this in-depth research more necessary than ever. The "Montesquieu Project" uses it against obscurantism and the liberticidal, not to say deadly, trends freighted by religious dogmas. Do you take part in any other initiatives?

J.K. I moved my seminar on "The Need to Believe" from Paris 7 to the Maison de Solenn (at the Cochin hospital) directed by Professor Marie Rose Moro. There we address the staff in charge of troubled adolescents, some of whom are being radicalized. My reflections on "How Can One Be Jihadist? Interpreting Radical Evil" have been published on Slate.fr. Putting the Montesquieu Project online would probably attract a bigger audience to our discussions, but the relatively restricted forum it is at present acts as a "guarantee of seriousness," before moving to enhance these sessions by organizing symposia or open days.

S.D. You are, I believe, one of the few intellectuals to have received accolades from the political world: you are a Commander of the Légion d'Honneur, you chair the Prix du Livre Politique, and you sit on the Conseil Économique, Social et Environnemental. Most psychologists or shrinks are more retiring. They might see the odd mover and shaker on their couch, but they keep out of the public eye themselves. Have you ever felt tempted to enter politics?

J.K. There is no such thing as a politics *of* psychoanalysis; I repeat it because my engagements are liable to lead to misunderstanding. My interventions are not clinical "sessions" to which men and women in power must bow; should any of them happen to need therapy, that's a different matter, and entirely their business. Your question raises the issue of *the line between the public and the private*, and with it that of the positioning of political discourse and action in the modern world. The crisis of civilization we see looming behind all other crises does not reside only in the expansion of Islamism and the terrorist threat; it's above all a crisis of the *political* sphere.

Back to back with the juridical, the political—presently caught in a vise between finance and public opinion—once imagined that it could resorb *theology* into *ideology*. Blandine Kriegel has conducted a perceptive study of this history and its workings. But in the twentieth century the fervor of political reason degenerated into totalitarianism, and ideology along with the democratic practices that succeeded it on the cusp of the third millennium are devoid of vision and promise, reduced to managing runaway debt, the hardships of the excluded, and overall vulnerability. Meanwhile ethics, or what's left of it, has taken refuge—splintering to infinity—in *inner experience.* "Privatized," individualized to the nth degree. Its aesthetic manifestations, literature and the arts, serve up its sensible forms, while the human sciences figure out its anthropological workings and historical variants. The youngest of these sciences, psychoanalysis, is determined to *transvalue* the incredible need to believe—recognized as being a psychic dimension, inseparable from the desire to know.

Likewise, freedom can only find its synonym in singularity. But is it still able to be shared? The humanism of the individual conscience, disencumbered of religious dogma and responsible only to itself—the humanism propagated by the Enlightenment—could not survive the ravages of Auschwitz and Hiroshima or the genocides in Bosnia, Kosovo, and Rwanda. Nor could it obey the pious wish of Habermas and Ratzinger when they exhorted the moderns to forge a "preserving conscience," one "nurtured by faith," or that is a "correlation between reason and faith."

S.D. The historical situation you describe has preoccupied many political scientists and philosophers of the postmodern age (such as Jean-François Lyotard, to name one), peddlers of "declinology," "the end of History," and so on. It seems to me that your diagnosis, informed by literature and psychoanalysis but also by the history of religions and an attachment to European culture, sharpens our awareness of the crisis of humanism, the existential crisis, in a different way.

J.K. What is left of this consciousness, this faith, in an age of biotechnology, artificial intelligence, and neuroscience? Can we argue for the universality of the new humanity in formation or must we bow to radically different doctrines such as gangster fundamentalism, posthumanism, or transhumanism?

We tend to forget about the existence of a twentieth-century culture that posited a vision and an interpretation of humankind that embraced its tragedies and beauties alike. Kafka and Proust; phenomenology, with its transcendental ego and "outer and inner horizons"; existentialism, with its infernos and freedoms; Sartre and Beauvoir; cubism, surrealism, Picasso, Joyce, Artaud, Bataille. Not to mention Hannah Arendt, Melanie Klein, and Colette. Why do the minds of policy makers and pundits appear built on a naturalist-realist model that became obsolete with Huysmans?

To this must be added the deeper elucidation of the *new maladies of the soul* by modern clinical psychoanalysis, the result of extensive research in this domain—and yet we have failed to publicize it. Not to mention the contribution of the human sciences, or their interaction with the life sciences. So many decisive actors that can and must participate in the refoundation of humanism that is sorely lacking today.

This refoundation necessarily involves a transvaluation of the discourses that in the past framed the intimate, the private, the ethical—in short, the human. With special attention to religious discourse. Not in a bid to banish it from the space of politics, nor to relegate it naively to who knows what private, hermetic, archaic sphere. But in order to rethink its logics, its moral and spiritual dimensions, and revitalize the need to believe that underpins the desire to know.

S.D. I come back to my question: have you ever been tempted by political action? Because what you just said rings out like a commitment, a compulsion, a mission.

J.K. It's a mission, I accept that word, a long-haul, highly sensitive mission, whose means need to be refined at every step. It's not about being "a counselor to the Prince" or complacently acting the "media intellectual." Still less is it about playing a political "role." It is, quite simply, the endeavor to thoroughly *think through* symptoms and anxieties and their many expressions, and then passing it on. It's a commitment without political partisanship, cross-party, eschewing both the nihilism of a supposed "end of History" and the abstentionism of a supposed "end of politics." Yes, the refoundation of humanism is a political act, a bet on a different politics.

S.D. As a "qualified personality," you sat in the foreign relations section of the Conseil Économique, Social et Environnemental (CESE). What was your "mission" there?

J.K. I was tasked with writing an opinion on "The French cultural message and the intercultural vocation of *la francophonie*." The Palais d'Iéna is the most incongruous building, a cathedral of modern rationalism made of reinforced concrete, pink marble, and green porphyry, enclosing a monumental void. It houses a great deal of good will and a stream of opinions and reports that reflect the swings of "civil society," the entity represented by this "third chamber of the Republic" (after the National Assembly and the Senate), whose role is consultative. It is made up of trade unionists, NGO staff, former ministers, sitting deputies, and journalists; not many intellectuals and not enough women, but all of them displaying a critical, independent cast of mind, innovative and intransigent, and they taught me a lot. I enjoyed my fact-finding expeditions to the Ministries of Culture and Foreign Affairs, certainly, but not as much as those to foreign countries, the Czech Republic, the United States, and Israel. We'll return to this later. There is a desire for France out there, it's our job to develop it, with heightened empathy and efficiency.

S.D. You've met a wide array of political celebrities. A rich seam of subconscious matter to be mined?

J.K. I've hardly *met* them, we crossed paths. I never switch on my Freud earpiece away from the couch, let alone near a politician. I let myself be impressed, surprised, and I store the mark.

S.D. Let's play a game. I name some celebrities who I'm pretty sure you've met, and you tell me your impressions of them.

J.K. A risky game? The stuff of novels.

S.D. François Mitterrand?[91]

J.K. Cagey, self-centered. I didn't know that he was ill, but I did feel that he had little interest in politics, despite the care and skill with which he handled it. He was elsewhere.

When we visited the Alexander Nevsky Cathedral in Sofia, I made a discreet sign to my father, who was in the choir. The president noticed. "Who's that? Your father? Will you introduce me?" Roland Dumas took my arm and lifted the cordon that separated the official delegation from the choristers, and my father was introduced to President Mitterrand. Religion and art, Orthodox icons. The sinew of nations.

S.D. Philippe Dechartre?

J.K. The doyen of the CESE. Unstinting availability, and all the humility and restraint of a great Gaullist *résistant*. An undefeated humanist.

S.D. Alain Juppé?

J.K. His honesty, which appears to frighten him. It is what stopped him putting himself forward when he admitted that his government was "trapped," just a few days before the "dissolution" of the Assembly in 1997. Read his book on Montesquieu: a paean to a "social radical"! Like himself, perhaps?

S.D. Jack Lang?

J.K. His empathy for misfits, his dexterity at soothing the narcissism of the excluded.

S.D. Lionel Jospin?

J.K. A true friend. I like his rigor, his uncompromising integrity, his bitter laugh. We were both placed near Bill Clinton at the "Third Way" summit conference in Florence in 1999, where I was to give a speech about the French cultural exception. The Clinton team had demanded to see my presentation in advance, but we refused; it was the Italian prime minister, Massimo D'Alema who introduced me, to the great relief of the inflexible Jospin.

S.D. Michel Rocard?

J.K. During a memorable lunch with Jacques-Alain Miller and Serge Leclaire, we argued at length about whether psychoanalysis should be regulated in law. He chilled us at first with his perfect rationality that did not understand us, and then the free man in him lit up: "Psychoanalysis is an exception. European laws can wait."

S.D. Ségolène Royal?

J.K. The best minister for National Education we've ever had, from the standpoint of disabled children. But she was unwilling to talk about that, it obviously wasn't a beneficial political subject for her at the time. The defeat of her presidential bid made her more mature; she succeeds royally in wearing a presidential garb that does not suit everyone.

S.D. Laurent Fabius?

J.K. His weariness moves me. Though he knows that "all is not well," this staunch diplomat will assure us that it is. But since his intelligence is unimpaired, the duty exhausts him. A sense of humor, the glint in his eye, brings him some relief.

S.D. Valérie Pécresse?

J.K. Diffident and undervalued. Her encomium of Simone de Beauvoir for the hundredth anniversary of the philosopher's birth delighted me. The minister had written it all by herself, at night, on the pages of an exercise book.

S.D. Bertrand Delanoë?

J.K. Gentlemanly, compassionate, disillusioned.

S.D. Anne Hidalgo?

J.K. Self-possessed, loathes injustice and exclusion, sensual.

S.D. Bruno Le Maire?

J.K. A splendid novelist. I enjoyed his book on the conductor, Carlos Kleiber, published by Sollers.[92] The greatest connoisseur of French culture and history of all our politicians. Maybe the only one? His physique lifts him as high as his mind when it comes to "getting down to business." But in France, one's "origins" are never pardoned.

S.D. François Hollande, of course. I was there.

J.K. Unique for his grasp of the issues, he persuades his interlocutors that he has understood their position. Unfortunately, the issues don't necessarily bear this out. This strategist of provincial tendencies tries to introduce reforms without making waves, gently and gradually. Disappointing. But a unifier, perhaps?

S.D. Nicolas Sarkozy, and his famous gaffe over Barthes!

J.K. When decorating me as an officer of the Légion d'Honneur, which he did movingly, with gravity and feeling, Speedy Sarkozy managed to pass Roland Barthes's ball to Fabien Barthez. I scored a goal.

S.D. Only one man truly overwhelmed you, and that was Jacques Chirac.

J.K. It was when David was in a coma in hospital. The telephone rings early in the morning and I rush to pick up. "Jacques Chirac speaking." "I'm not amused by your little joke, *monsieur*, it's not a good time." He phones again at once. "It's me, I assure you. How is David getting on?" I don't know whether the president had someone call the Salpêtrière, but the standard of care improved, and so did David. It did not turn me into a Chirac supporter. I still think that he took an interest in disability not just because "it concerned him," but rather because humanism is *that*, too. The French are quick to notice these things.

S.D. For some years now, you've been drawing attention to the plight of adolescents who lack an ideal. You diagnosed a "malady of ideality," you developed André Green's propositions on "unbinding" (*déliaison*) in order to approach "radical evil" from a psychoanalytic perspective. You have lately made several speeches on "radicalization." Is psychoanalysis seeking a vaccine against narcissism mingled with contemporary nihilism?

J.K. There is no vaccine. But this subject remains central for me. From my first writings on the adolescent *malady of ideality* (1986, 2005), then on the attraction exerted by *radical evil* and the idea of *decapitation* (1998, 2012), I have been airing these issues in my books, in an exhibition at the Louvre, and in my seminar on "The Need to Believe."

S.D. Your thoughts on the crisis of adolescence apply to more than just this age group. You discern a kind of psychic *position*, or perhaps a *structure* proper to adolescence, that forms part of us and is liable to be activated at any time of life.

J.K. Indeed, we are all adolescents when we're in love, but your question contains another question: what does it mean "to be an adolescent"? The child is a seeker, fired by curiosity, impatient to know where babies come from. Adolescents are believers: they adamantly believe in absolute satisfaction, the ideal love object, and a perfect world. This indisputable certainty of belief is the sine qua non for moving beyond their parents, leaving the family behind, pursuing a brilliant career, changing society. Teenagers believe in heaven—in a God who is, yes, judgmental, but who is loving above all. Think of Adam and Eve, Dante and Beatrice, Romeo and Juliet. Faced with the slightest setback, however, the quest for the ideal crumbles into the *malady of ideality*. In this fearsome state, adolescents are prone to absolute destructiveness; they see no difference between self and other, inside and outside, right and wrong. By destroying, they destroy themselves: this is the kamikaze syndrome, the mindset of the suicide bomber.

Here, psychoanalysis comes up against the Kantian question of *radical evil*. This resides in the fact that some humans declare others to be superfluous and exterminate them, either without invoking any "reason" at all or based on ideological "reasons" that are twisted and untenable; always in the name of an "ideal" of purification and in the hallucinatory grip of this *malady of ideality*. The disease can coexist with the "healthy" parts of a seemingly well-adjusted personality, just as it can be aggravated by drug addiction in the framework of gangster fundamentalism.

S.D. Is psychoanalysis in a good position to accompany these adolescents? My own experience as a psychologist in hospital settings has shown that, even in less urgent situations, radicalized teenagers resist seeing an analyst, afraid of challenges to their narcissism, independence, creativity, or representations. How do you gain the trust of young would-be jihadists, enough to deflect them from their deadly goal?

J.K. Through the diversity of the ethno-psychiatric team. Parents who have worries about the radicalized behavior of their offspring approach the Maison des Adolescents. Teachers and school psychologists can do the same. Worry can lead to panic, but it's not always necessary to follow up: hysterical provocation must be distinguished from genuine psychic disarray. Most nursing staff lack the training to care for these endangered adolescents: they know little about the history of religions (in the plural of course, even if right now it's that of Allah we are up against!), and practically nothing about limit states. We present clinical case studies, lectures by anthropologists, ethnologists, or religious historians, and updates on psychoanalytic and ethno-psychiatric investigations. In parallel, a team of psychoanalytic ethno-psychiatrists works directly with these adolescents in jeopardy.

S.D. The topic of religion and destructiveness brings us to the sacred and the role of women in it throughout history. *The Feminine and the Sacred*, an exchange of letters between you and Catherine Clément, gives us a glimpse of the "Christian atheist" in you, according to your friend and coauthor.[93]

J.K. Yes, the book has recently been reprinted by Albin Michel with a new preface by each of us.[94] A strange and very strong friendship links Catherine and myself. Quite different from my attachment, say, to my Bulgarian friends, Anastasia Stratieva and Elena Mikhailovska, whom I've known since my days at Sofia University, who phone me on my birthday, and in whom I confide more than I do in anyone; different too from my complicity with the faithful Marie-Noëlle Demarre, Nelly Bass, and Sylvie Le Pelletier-Beaufond, who became such good friends with David. And Marie-Christine Navarro, of course, whose friendship and insights into my work occasioned a fine series of interviews on France Culture, later published as *Au risque de la pensée*.[95] But Catherine is the only woman with whom I've written a book. That's saying something! We share a deep understanding, over and above our differences and disagreements. Catherine is more combative than me, she's a militant, she loves going on the offensive and knows how to sting, how to rile me, I adore her. But I don't enjoy a fight. I hate conflict. I disinvest, I lose interest, I go my own way. If someone tries to provoke me, I wrongfoot them by walking on by. Our book is a playful joust between me and my passion for the Virgin Mary, which irritates her no end, and her with her cult of India, hoping to convert me to Buddhism! Nothing doing, I'll stick by the latest stage of Judeo-Christianity, which is none other than the continuation of the Freudian discovery, using updated tools, through the metamorphoses of parenthood in the third millennium. On this subject, my new preface salutes the eulogy delivered by Rabbi Delphine Horvilleur at the funeral of the psychoanalyst Elsa Cayat, assassinated in the offices of *Charlie Hebdo*. I also call for a worldwide campaign against forced marriage, to which certain religions condemn millions of women on this earth.

S.D. You do not neglect the social aspect of your commitments. In 2014, to coincide with Women's Day, you were appointed guest editor for a day of *L'Humanité*.

J.K. Indeed, and I felt highly honored to be selected by the paper's editors. Although communism is a promise that lost its way in totalitarianism, it continues to foment social solidarity projects that help a great many people who have been left behind by the crisis. The Marxist utopia also "works" like a religion, and this variant on the need to believe is accompanied—at times—

by the desire to know: or that's the agenda of some of the new communists I met while editing that issue of *L'Huma*. It does not alter the fact that today's left-of-leftwing culture, nostalgic for an alternative communism, is merely an anachronistic revolt, comforting but impotent. An adolescent revolt, if you prefer, in the sense we touched on earlier. Its economic and social models are incapable of challenging either globalized finance or the nihilism of hyperconnected jihad, and make it unfit to govern.

S.D. As we near the completion of the present volume, the attacks haven't ceased (after *Charlie Hebdo* came the Hypercacher, the Bataclan, Nice, Saint-Étienne-du-Rouvray, Orlando, Munich, Kabul, Iraq, Syria . . .), signed "Daesh" and plunging countries around the world into mourning. Jihadism seems to offer a "handbook" for postcolonialism and for what you call the "new maladies of the soul" (depression, drug addiction, delinquency, vandalism, etc.), all of which are running amok nowadays. Are we faced with a new and perhaps unprecedented civilizational malaise?

J.K. Technological progress and globalization have their flip side. What was for metaphysics a "world" is crumbling into depression and/or the radicalization of identity, nationalism, and religion. The absence of a rigorous international policy able to curb an Islamist intoxication that battens on petrodollars exposes the flaws of our 200-year-old democratic model. And reveals, abyssally, an anthropological mutation that ideologues struggle to track, when they do not negate it outright. This concern is epochal. We are in it for the long haul.

At a time when authorities of every kind are fast losing their purchase on events, is the social pact *à la française* more threatened than the rest? Is there a national depression, an irritation, an eruption? It is a mistake to reduce the "French spirit" to secularization or to a feisty, if not comic, materialism. The *exception française*—the uniqueness that I love, that welcomed me in—is never more French than in the taste for an artful naming of and reflection on extremes, never doubting the universality of their elaborate disparities, their seductions and perils. There is no other way of demystifying terror and the erotization of death and enabling all humanity to traverse them without end. This is the sense in which French secularity is universal. You'll understand, then, why I pin my hopes on our "French uniqueness," extended today through the development of letters, arts, and the human sciences to treat those "new maladies of the soul," with their permeability to terrorism. Against the politicos' twists and turns whipped up by the attacks and petering out in impromptu, ineffectual "measures," I cherish the ambition that it is possible, but only on the basis I've described, to design a new psycho-educational project that will prove stronger than barbarism.

VI. Crossing Borders

Those who nourish their lives well travel on land, And do not encounter predators, And do not (need) wear the armor.

The rhinoceros cannot find the place in them to thrust its horn, The tiger cannot find the place to claw them. Why is this? Because there is no space in them for death to enter.

—Laozi, *Dao de ching*

Samuel Dock. Your work has been acclaimed around the world, particularly in the United States, where you command a substantial following. You're as much admired there as in most of the countries where your books are available in translation. And yet in France, the recognition has not been as pronounced. Conversely, many intellectuals extolled over here are unknown across the Atlantic. How do you explain this discrepancy?

Julia Kristeva. A memory comes to my mind whenever I am asked that, which is often. I was with François Mitterrand on his Bulgarian tour in January 1989, a few months before the fall of the Berlin wall. During a crowded meeting at Sofia University, one student (probably a dissident who had contrived to slip through the net of the entrance checks) asked him this question: "How would you explain the dictators still clinging to power in some countries, when everybody wants rid of them?" The jibe was aimed at President Todor Zhivkov, up there on the platform beside Mitterrand—who responded, with that serpentine smile of his: "In some circumstances, my dear sir, the question is worth more than the answer." (*Laughter*) "Mr. Dock, your question is worth more than the answer!"

S.D. That's too bad of you! (*Laughter*) How did your American adventure begin? What was your connection to Columbia University in New York?

J.K. Everything started with the Artaud-Bataille conference, organized by *Tel Quel* at the Cerisy International Cultural Center in 1972.[96] It was unforgettable! Our little gang had great fun, to the amazement of the very dour Professor Maurice de Gandillac, who liked us really, and the shock of the Heurgon family, who owned the chateau: we wouldn't be invited back! I delivered one talk on Artaud—writing schizophrenia, "The Subject in Process"—and another on Bataille, "From Mysticism to the Dialectic: An Experience." A professor at Columbia, Leon Roudiez, was attending the event, or the happening, I should say in this case: an unassuming man who loathed injustice, an anti-establishment sort in the manner of the American New Left. He had taken part in the Omaha Beach landings and the liberation of France, and met his wife, Jacqueline, in our beautiful country. Leon appreciated my talks; they were not easy, but offbeat and fairly innovatory, if I may say so. As of 1976 he began regularly inviting me to the Department of Romance Languages, which he chaired, as one of a celebrated trio of visiting professors (Umberto Eco, Tzvetan Todorov, and me) that taught at Columbia for several years. It was a hugely exciting period. I lived in New York with all the enthusiasm of a pioneer, plus a naive belief that I could fit into a New World that seemed more kindly disposed toward immigrants than this old France. Thanks to Leon and Jacqueline, I expect. They treated the ten-month-old David to a swing, which we set up in the middle of the living room. In subsequent years we made family expeditions to explore upstate New York and the quiet charms of New Jersey, where our friends lived. We loved the roof restaurant at the World Trade Center, you can see it in their photographs of those occasions.

S.D. Having given succor to Jewish intellectuals fleeing the Nazis, US universities were swept by a new wind from Europe . . .

J.K. The scientific and pedagogic atmosphere at that department was unusual, largely because of the rivalry between Professor Leon Roudiez and the reigning star of French Studies, Professor Michael Riffaterre. The dashing Riffaterre, besides being passionate about poetry, phonology, stylistics, and structuralism, was a ladies' man and proud of it; all the female students were crazy about him. The scion of a bourgeois Sephardic family from the Landes region of France (family photos in "fin de siècle" style covered every table and sideboard of the splendid Upper West Side apartment he shared with his wife Hermine), Michael was the opposite of Leon. Niceties of style for the first, the weight of history for the second. Between the pair of them the department spanned the full complexity of French literature, to the happy advantage of its postgraduates. Michael would invite me for lunch at the Top of the Sixes, a fancy rooftop restaurant on Fifth Avenue opposite St. Patrick's Cathedral, and then a stroll through the swankier neighborhoods of New York; Leon introduced me to his friends at *Partisan Review*, the Trotskyist journal directed by William Phillips and Edith Kurzweil, who sought to open Marxism to psychoanalysis and structuralism.

My old friend Antonin Liehm, a Czech journalist who had moved to Staten Island, provided occasional respite from the university. Do you remember, he was the editor of *Literární Listy*, which publicized the ideas of the Prague Spring. He spent his vacations by the Black Sea and we met at the International Journalists' House in Sofia; I've mentioned him. He was a great friend of Philip Roth and had taken him around Prague in Kafka's footsteps. When Liehm told Roth that I was here teaching at Columbia, I found myself being warmly welcomed into the writer's apartment near the Met with, much to my surprise, a bottle of Chateau Margaux: "Merely what a Frenchwoman, a European lady, would expect, surely!" A man of taste and a stylish host, I saw him again in Paris, with Philippe Sollers, after his marriage to Claire Bloom. "Julia Kristeva" and her *Black Sun* feature in his novel *The Human Stain*, whose female protagonist prefers them to . . . Philippe Sollers! A private joke between friends, I daresay, as each man holds the other in high regard. From Liehm via Roth, the path led straight to the *New York Review of Books*. Editor Bob Silvers found it natural to ask me to discuss "participation"—a social issue then in vogue—on one of the panels he was organizing for the World Economic Forum at Davos in Switzerland. So there we met again, amid the snows of high finance.

S.D. From academia to politics . . . You're everywhere! What was a university professor doing among the economic and political decision-makers of Davos?

Here in France, politicians take pride in being authors, and intellectuals fancy themselves as "counselors" to the Prince.

J.K. Haven't politics and literature always been impossible to separate? But no, I'm not everywhere. Whether because of being exiled or because of Philippe and David, I've always made a point of distinguishing the decor from the laboratory, in academic life and elsewhere. So, Columbia dominated Uptown for me, while Downtown there was Tom Bishop, the Beckett specialist and head of the French Department at New York University. I didn't teach regular classes there but did give a number of talks and conference papers. Tom and his wife Helen became great friends of ours, lavishing attention on little David and getting into contorted arguments with Philippe that ended in roars of laughter. I'll never forget one crazy fall (was it in 1973, before Columbia hired me?) when we were living with a bunch of others in a large apartment belonging to NYU, right at the top of a building on Bleecker Street, overlooking the Picasso sculptures; Edgar Morin was obsessed with buying organic, and Marguerite Duras never stopped being nasty about all the people who had the nerve to think they were her friends.

American universities are a tissue of acquaintanceships, all surreptitiously at war with one another, but peacefully coexisting on the surface, and Philippe came to join me on almost all my US trips. Together we made new friends, who until then had been no more than "names" in literary-historical bibliographies. Jan Kott, for example, a Polish dissident ensconced in Yale, famous for his *Shakespeare, Our Contemporary*—an inexhaustible fount of jokes and short-circuits linking the great William with Ionesco and Beckett. Or David Hayman, the editor of *A First-Draft Version of Finnegans Wake* by James Joyce, who delighted Philippe by receiving us in his Madison home near the icy banks of Lake Michigan. Or Victor Brombert, of Yale and Princeton, an eminent reader of Stendhal and Flaubert, and his wife Beth, an Italian scholar who tried to get Philippe to give up smoking. Without success, need I add. And Hélène Volat, of course, still busy compiling a marvelous and exhaustive bibliography of texts written about me; her husband, Richard Harvey, is a great connoisseur of contemporary French literature, whose love for the country made him take French nationality. And above all the enduring affection that links me to Domna C. Stanton, an outstanding specialist in the literature of the Grand Siècle in France (especially works by women) and a scholar of feminism in general, but also of the "*honnête homme*" and the French-style dandy, Baudelaire included.[97] With her husband Frank Stanton ("a left-wing businessman who attends night class on Nietzsche" is how he introduced himself), the epitome of New York wit and generosity, Domna used to hold gatherings in their Upper East Side apartment or their place in East Hampton, Long Island, where Philippe and I met academics, journalists, and artists: the sparkling conversation and joyous transatlantic utopias of the time before 9/11 . . . But we still keep in touch with Domna, whether in New York, at La Closerie des Lilas restaurant in Paris, or over the Internet.

S.D. You were living between two continents . . .

J.K. Yes, another life took shape in parallel to my French life, one that actually felt more immediate, benign, and auspicious at times. Columbia University Press became my English-language publisher, thanks to Leon Roudiez who translated most of my books and undeniably cemented this adoption of me by America. John Moore, the quirky head of the Press when I first started (he sported a single earring before it was the fashion), quoted passages from *Powers of Horror* or *The Samurai* at me when we met, already won over and delighted to put me on the list. We toasted the contract in the restaurant at the top of Butler Hall, Columbia's smartest venue. Jennifer Crewe, formerly in charge of the human sciences desk, has now taken over as director—with the invaluable assistance of Larry Kritzman, a penetrating friend and indefatigable cultural messenger to and fro across the ocean. Jennifer has fluent French and a British-style attention to detail with which she ensures the perfection of *our* books. She is always by my side, supportive and protective—as far afield as Norway, where she was with me for the Holberg Prize award ceremony.

S.D. What differences were there between your teaching in France and in the United States?

J.K. I gave the same courses as in Paris. In French at the French Department of Columbia University, and later in English in the comparative literature or philosophy departments of other universities. The French-speaking students at Columbia had been carefully selected and were very well equipped for the doctorate level. Over time this standard of preparation declined and so did the students' proficiency in French. Still, I was fortunate enough to have some especially brilliant philosophy students at the University of Georgetown in Washington and, most notably, at the New School for Social Research, the New School in New York. Natural-born scholars. I was struck by their way of receiving what was being imparted, quite unlike the reaction of French students. An example? Well, after my class on Proust and the Dreyfus Affair, a French doctoral student will often ask something like: "What's your opinion of *Proust and Signs* by Gilles Deleuze?" In this way, he dodges the issue of the narrator's identity and relation to French history, highlighting his own originality instead: how much he's read, what a lot he knows! An American student, on the other hand, is more likely to ask: "Was the narrator happy? What is the meaning of happiness for Proust?" He's not asking *me* a question, either, he's not interested in my interpretation of Proust. He is looking for existential guidance.

This naive attitude, this sincere curiosity may well have contributed to the positive reception of my work in the US. I hope that I could *also* introduce them to data, concepts, and theories, but what students and readers grasped most readily in my courses, over and above any intellectual performance, was a way of thinking, which is the same as a way of living. To plumb Céline's abjection, Proust's eroticism, or female *jouissance* in Colette allowed them to *put into words* certain dark and possibly determinant creases in their own lives. This explains, to my mind, the strange infatuation with the "French Theory" of which I am an exponent, along with Barthes, Derrida, Lacan, Foucault, and Deleuze, and which some people find so maddening.

S.D. Speaking of that, in several of your works you remark on the pendulum that swings toward and away from French Theory in the United States. Is this something to do with the fear of colonization? Or with the absence over there of a solid tradition of the pesky intellectual, like that which formed in France in the wake of the Enlightenment?

J.K. It may be that here and there some of these progressive steps in France have been turned into gimmicks, vacuous or "politically correct" buzzwords to bolster a nondescript academic career. I can only speak about the people who folded my teaching into their own original research or who assimilated the underlying ideas in order to resolve a personal or professional impasse. I'm thinking of a certain architecture student who enrolled in my course at Columbia because he'd found, in my book on *abjection*, a line of thought that helped him reassess his plan for the regeneration of a rough urban neighborhood. The paper he delivered at the seminar about his project made no direct reference to "abjection in Céline": he was exploring the confliction between sameness and difference, frontier and transparency, security and freedom, and explained how these tensions had been resolved thanks to what he had gleaned from my books and teaching. I also recall a certain installation artist who took my course on "depression and melancholia," and showed how her creative inhibitions were lifting by presenting the trajectory of her work in the form of words in order to share it with the whole seminar.

The global financial crisis gave rise to a crushing credit crunch in the US as elsewhere, which severely damaged culture in general and university humanities in particular. English and American colleagues who raised their voices in the media against this carnage often appealed to "French Theory," both for its support and as an example of active thought. Following a period of defensiveness against what was sometimes resented as a colonization by "French stuff"—the opportunity for more conservative faculty to revert to good old "textual analysis" in the manner of the Lagarde et Michard schoolbooks, at the risk of turning French departments into Berlitz schools—now, at last, there is a broad realization that people will once more want to learn French if, and only if, foreign students (in the United States, and also in China, India, Latin America . . .) feel seduced by *French thought*. And French Theory is indispensable here because it trains the mind to question the very knowledge it transmits. And this at a time when the banalization of behaviors and languages, procedural thinking, the triumph of the "how" over the "why" constitute a threat to the very capacity to think, over and above the fate of the human sciences. A recent webinar organized by the French Cultural Service in Chicago, aimed at all the universities in the Northeast, in which I took part alongside Professor Arnold Davidson to argue on behalf of the embattled human sciences, convinced me that a shift in consciousness is under way.

S.D. How is your life organized over there day to day? Where do you live? Are David and Philippe usually with you?

J.K. In New York I've stayed in several properties belonging to Columbia University, which is a major landlord. After starting out on East 28th Street, we were very happy on Morningside Drive, next door to the apartment that Hannah Arendt once occupied, overlooking Harlem and the trees of Morningside Park that glowed golden red in the sunshine. Then it was Riverside Drive, on the other side of the campus, in the home of Henri Mitterand, who ran the department after retiring from the University of Vincennes. And I loved the smaller but delightful studio I had in Butler Hall, with its roof restaurant. Philippe adored "my" house and garden at Georgetown University in Washington, located in a residential neighborhood near the French embassy. At the University of Toronto, where I used to go when I was teaching in New York, I was kindly harbored by two academic friends, Peter Nesselroth and Paul Perron, and sometimes put up in a comfy hotel like a true cosmopolitan traveler. I could never list them all. This nomad's existence suits me. I enjoy adapting to unfamiliar spaces.

Over the past few years, though, I've grown more sedentary. It was my privilege to be appointed visiting professor in the Department of Philosophy, the New School for Social Research, the New School in New York, after receiving an honorary doctorate. With Jürgen Habermas, a visiting professor in the same department, we took turns occupying a place on 56th Street, near the East River and a stone's throw from my Italian friends Giovanna and Arturo Borradori.

New York is a 24/7 high, all those galleries, museums, lectures, dinner parties . . . A cosmic light bouncing off soaring towers stuffed with money, while on the asphalt of the next street down is utter deprivation. That city keeps me on the go; I don't sleep a wink when I'm there. I'm usually out in the evening, at a concert, a movie, a bar, an opera; or I'm mulling over the things I have to do, over David who's supposed to phone or is asleep next door; or spending time with Philippe who's come over for a few days; or going out with a friend. An ever-present and yet crowded solitude, as upright as the city itself. David loved the Rockefeller Center skating rink and we often had lunch in the café right beside the ice. When he grew older, he stopped traveling with me, but he always phones as soon as I've landed. Philippe, who can't stand the enhanced security at airports, is waiting for more auspicious times to revisit the United States.

I could never have this paradise if it weren't for my assistants, Alice Jardine, Maria Muresan, Fanny Söderbäck, and Terri Gordon—students of mine who turned into friends. Free-spirited young women, hard-working and creative, following remarkable academic careers. I guess that to them, and others as well, I represent the Frenchwoman par excellence, or rather a European mirage haloed by a glorious past that sets their minds to fizzing like champagne. I don't know where they pick up these images, but I don't inquire, just let myself be accompanied. Our closeness mitigates their fear of French people, whom they find plain inaccessible, and they tell themselves that if a foreigner like me can manage to get a foothold in the language of Mallarmé, then why shouldn't they . . .

S.D. Thanks to the film Teri Wehn-Damisch made about you, *Histoires d'amour et de passerelles* (Tales of love and footbridges), we know that you made a lot of friends in the States. Could you tell us something about those encounters, and maybe about the Kristeva Circle?

J.K. The first to reach out to me was Toril Moi. Now a professor at Duke University, she told me how when she was studying French and comparative literature at Bergen, in Norway, she'd read my books at the kitchen table of her modest home; she wanted to meet me for her project to edit a *Kristeva Reader* with the UK publisher Blackwell. We met up in London and I took her to the National Gallery to see Piero della Francesca's *Nativity*, one of my favorite paintings, which she put on the cover of the book. Toril is an ardent feminist and has an independent, defiant mind. Her book on Beauvoir caused quite a stir, and I admire her free-ranging thought. Other introductions to my research appeared later, edited by John Lechte in Australia and Kelly Oliver in the US.

S.D. No equivalent publications have appeared in France. It was Kelly Oliver, a professor of philosophy and feminist studies at Vanderbilt in Tennessee, who had the idea in 2011 to found the Kristeva Circle, which meets annually.[98]

J.K. I'm not personally acquainted with most of the academics who form part of that circle. Some of them don't speak French and have only read me in English translation. We communicated by video link for the last meeting at Vanderbilt University. I was taken aback, overwhelmed to be conversing with so many fine colleagues, including Professor Zhu Keyi and her students, whom I'd met before at Shanghai's Fudan University. The next meeting is planned for Stockholm, 2016, with the participation of Miglena Nikolchina, a Bulgarian philosopher whose work I greatly respect and who has become a friend. There will also be a Norwegian academic, Eivind Engebretsen, whose research on the disabled overlaps with mine. It's so impressive to see such a spontaneous, unexpected, and original way of disseminating an experience as singular as mine is: from the alphabet festival to Freud, by way of Paris . . . It would seem that through the institutions, or more accurately in spite of them, and in defiance of the conservative forces currently bent on chilling our intellectual life, some independent circles are beaming out *dialogism*, *intertextuality*, *reliance* . . . Beneath the leaden lid of the crisis, of bureaucracy, of the mafia, or the stock market, the digital waves of Skype carry the vibrations of *Teresa, My Love*, and soon, perhaps, those of *The Enchanted Clock* . . . I'm not part of it myself but sharing in an expectation.

S.D. Your popularity in the United States has not prevented you from casting a critical eye on that country's politics and culture. You once described it, indeed, as an uncultured civilization.

J.K. That sounds rather brutal, let me express it more precisely. By *culture* I mean a memory reassessed and reordered by means of singular discourses and behaviors, through interactive histories and life stories. *Culture* is *political*. By *civilization* I mean a social organization dominated by the administration of labor and procreation, based on specific rules corresponding to regulatory priorities. In our time, more than ever before, perhaps, *civilization* is liable to be reduced to the *economic*. Of course, I admire Algonquin and the early settlers, William Faulkner and Louis Armstrong, Soho and Jackson Pollock, as much as anyone. There certainly is such a thing as American culture in the sense outlined above. But I perceive that as distinct from the achievement of the "genius of Protestantism," to paraphrase Max Weber: that is, an American *civilization* that culminates in economics and more recently in *financial speculation* and ruthless *neoliberalism*. Whenever American academia tries to fulfill its duty to awaken, to realize its role as a critical and argumentative culture, it finds itself shut out of a society locked into economics and finance. The academic world's growing tendency to adjust to the strictures of the economic mold does nothing to mend the separation, on the contrary: it simply turns academia into a laboratory for the refinement of economism and autistic financialization.

In this context, might *culture* still be capable of inquiring into the history and logics of *civilizations*? Being heir to a powerful history, Europe—despite, or possibly because of, its endemic crisis—offers the requisite conditions for us to take ownership of this dramatic memory and reassess it. I'm not talking about the essential meticulous filing, classification, and conservation that are the preserve of specialists. I mean the reevaluation of the past and the present, in an extension of the work that began to be carried out on the Shoah and its cultural roots in Europe. And continuing that work with a similarly implacable transvaluation of the ongoing automatization of the human race, as well as of the mounting aggressivity of the fundamentalisms that this automatization unwittingly emboldens. My contention is that this *culture* has a better chance of deepening in Europe than in the United States.

S.D. In the US, you're a celebrity. What's more, you have, over the years, accumulated honorary doctorates from a dozen universities around the world, the latest (2014) being the University of Haifa in Israel. What do you make of this worldwide recognition of your work? Are there any memorable incidents you could share with us?

J.K. I'm always bowled over, amazed, laughing at myself and at these rituals, even as I'm engulfed by a wave of emotions. I remember the award ceremony at the University of Toronto. I used to fly the shuttle from New York LaGuardia once a week, at the crack of dawn. That day I realized on arrival in Toronto that in all the rush I'd put on my green pumps instead of the black ones. I was so embarrassed, I thought everyone was staring at my lapse of taste. They decked me out in a monkish toga and matching headgear, I went up on stage, some Canadian colleagues listed my achievements, I kept my eyes on the paper where my response was printed and didn't look at the packed auditorium. I was thinking about my parents, who'd have wept tears of joy at this moment. At last I look up . . . Dear me, they're almost all Chinese! I must be seeing things! I rub my eyes, but nothing doing, they really are Chinese. I'd had some Chinese students; one of them had impressed me with her work on Hannah Arendt and Heidegger. But I never dreamed I'd see the entire Chinese community invade Her Majesty's University in Canada! Had Toronto become a new Hong Kong, a beefed-up Beijing, a resurrected Shanghai?

I have a very warm relationship, too, with colleagues in Latin America. Exotic Chile is now the home of my friend Michèle Sarde, who's as keen on Colette as I am and whose Jewish roots led her to conduct research in Bulgaria.

The psychoanalytic community in Buenos Aires is the most impassioned I've ever seen, clustered round my good friend Fernando Urribarri, a disciple of André Green. But the greatest revelation came in Argentina. The rector of the University of San Martín, Carlos Rafael Ruta, runs a project for the vulnerable adolescents of Greater Buenos Aires, a city with its own "rough areas," aimed at turning them from drug-traffic fodder into . . . scholars. "And we're getting there!" he assured me. Could he be a follower of Bourdieu, a Third-Worldist, a psychotherapist? He confessed rather shyly that he had written his dissertation on the mysticism of Meister Eckhart, of all people! And then he took me to the Teatro Colón where, before the ceremony itself, we were treated to the famous aria from *Don Giovanni*—"*Vivan le femmine! Viva il buon vino! Sostegno e gloria d'umanità!*"—performed by the Opera's star tenor in my honor.

S.D. A fight against nihilism on every front! No "national depression" there! It sounds like a magical occasion.

J.K. Magical, that's the word. Perhaps you think I'm inventing an imaginary Latin America, turning it into Europe minus the gloom? Not at all, I'm well aware that those countries get depressed too, severely so at times. But they are putting up a baroque resistance, so far, at least.

The University of Haifa, for its part, accepts a substantial number of Arab Israeli students and has done a great deal to advance mutual understanding and cooperation between the two communities. I met my colleague and friend there, Dana Amir, whose psychoanalytic investigations into maternal passion chime with mine. And, with a pleasure that grows every time I see her, my dear Michal Ben-Naftali, the writer and philosopher. She translated *Tales of Love* into what I'm told is delectable Hebrew, and the book won the hearts of a very demanding public. Needless to say, I spoke in Haifa about my conception of revolt, about radical evil, and radicalization itself.

S.D. You have many friends among Israeli intellectuals.

J.K. Starting with the late Stéphane Mosès, a philosopher and essayist who introduced me to the harsh beauty of that land and the suspended time of Jerusalem . . . We went on long walks through the Old City, to Gehenna, the Wailing Wall, the Mount of Olives, the ultra-Orthodox quarter of Mea Shearim, and out to the Dead Sea, to Bethlehem . . . How often we discussed, there or in Paris, the Biblical notion of "chosen people," something that for Stéphane was more than a "narrow pluralism" and paved the way for the "dignity in difference" so cherished by British rabbi Jonathan Sacks . . . We'd come back tirelessly to Job and Jesus, Rosenzweig and Kafka, Walter Benjamin and Gershom Scholem, the "void of Revelation" that retains its validity but "signifies nothing," and the "rumor of true things"; all this led infallibly to Stéphane's reading of Freud's dreams . . . His deftness as a ferryman between Judaism, Christianity, and the spirit of the Enlightenment helped me to crystallize what I would later call "exodus, exile, and return." He and his wife, Liliane Klapisch, a thoughtful and delicate painter, introduced Philippe and I to the translators of Proust and Céline into Hebrew . . . On a more "active" level, the publication of my book *This Incredible Need to Believe* was followed by a memorable forum on the subject, held at the Mishkenot Hotel. It was jointly organized by psychoanalyst friends at the SPP and their Israeli counterparts, convened by our colleague Viviane Chetrit-Vatine, with the participation of Muslim thinkers and clerics. Despite the current tensions and impasses, we hope these encounters may be resumed.

S.D. In 2006, when you received the Hannah Arendt Prize for Political Thought, you officially donated it to the NGO HumaniTerra, as we mentioned earlier with regard to your trilogy on female genius. Let us now turn to the Holberg Prize, founded by the Norwegian government to compensate for the absence of human sciences in the Nobel prize list. You were the first to win it, in 2004, in recognition of your oeuvre as a whole and in particular for your "innovative exploration of questions on the intersection of language, culture and literature." Your lecture delivered on the occasion of this exceptional distinction can be read online.[99] But we know little about what went on behind the scenes. How did you find out that you'd won?

J.K. I was sitting in Jacques Chirac's waiting room when a call came through from Norway. A woman's voice informed me that I'd been chosen as the first Holberg laureate for the humanities, and transmitted the congratulations of the jury, the government, and Crown Prince Haakon. I was stunned. I didn't know any Norwegians apart from Toril Moi, who'd left her homeland years ago to teach in the US. And the prize didn't ring any bells, I was completely thrown. I must have looked it, too, because Marie-Claire Carrère, President Chirac's adviser on social matters, expressed concern: had I received bad news? I told her mumblingly what it was about. Chirac ushered me in with a smile. We discussed the next disability conference at UNESCO and when I took my leave, he said in my ear: "Congratulations! One should never overlook the Norwegians, a simple and very honest people!"

S.D. So off you went to Norway. How was your stay organized?

J.K. From Oslo I went on to Bergen, where the jury sits. Bergen Castle is simple indeed, and all the more imposing for that. There were speeches, then dinner . . . Young Prince Haakon of Norway and his wife Mette-Marit were happy to talk about France and to discuss my books on adolescent depression and the female genius—men and women are equal on almost every level in Norway. With me were Professor Jan Bernt, a legal expert and chair of the Holberg Prize Board; Jennifer Crewe of Columbia University Press, my New York publisher; and the president of Paris 7, Professor Benoît Eurin. The most striking presence was that of the Lutheran pastor and prime minister, Kjell Magne Bondevik, whose brainchild the prize is. Having observed that his countrymen seemed to be losing their moral compass, his first idea was to launch a kind of media-based game getting citizens to rank certain values in order of importance (friendship, honesty, security, etc.), in hopes that this classification exercise would push them to think. Perhaps it did, but not enough . . . He then proposed creating a prize to honor scholars in the human sciences whose work had contributed, in his estimation, to the refounding of values. The idea was that to acknowledge these disciplines ignored by the Nobel Prize would stimulate young people's interest in them. And why was it named for Holberg? I made sure to find out before leaving. An acclaimed Danish Norwegian author and dramatist regarded as the Nordic Molière, an admirer of Montesquieu and the Encyclopedists, Ludvig Holberg (1684–1754) occupied the chair of metaphysics and logic, Latin rhetoric, and history. He was an early feminist, too: one of his novels takes the hero to the center of the Earth and a state whose name is Utopia . . . because it is governed by women.

I can still see the castle's white walls and ocher light, I recall the unforgettable tribute that was paid to me, one that outshines all honors before and since in the pantheon of my narcissism—including becoming a member of the American Academy of Arts and Sciences and the British Academy! I have kept up sincere relations with Norwegian colleagues, chiefly those working on disability and who are, to the best of my knowledge, the most cutting-edge in that domain. I collaborate with them on publications and colloquiums.

S.D. How do Philippe and David react to the announcement of awards and the ensuing trips? Are they jealous? Proud? These kinds of event upend daily life, you're always going away, and then there you are in the limelight! The ball rebounds again and again . . .

J.K. The hardest thing is parting from them! There's this gesture they make, drawing a circle over their heads and touching their forefinger to the table. It means: "You're stuck, you have to stay put!" Apart from that they laugh at me a bit, calling me *madame honoris causa.*

S.D. One senses profound admiration on David's part.

J.K. He says I'm a celeb. (*Laughter*) And then he plays the chorus to an old hit by La Rue Kétanou, "*You talk too much, you don't listen to anyone and nobody's listening to you* . . ." He doesn't keep it up for long, he's soon back to his favorite classics, Bach, Vivaldi, Mozart . . . Philippe approves, he supports me, as amused and ironical as ever.

S.D. Talking of prizes and travels, in 2008 you received the VIZE 97 Prize, presented by Václav Havel.[100] You didn't communicate as much around this occasion, why was that?

J.K. I don't communicate around any of them, and no one communicates on my behalf, as you know. The Holberg Prize itself is unknown in France. Why? Same answer as Mitterrand's to the challenge from the Bulgarian student.[101] Václav Havel, the eminent "philosopher-president," the inspirer and guide of the Velvet Revolution, the playwright influenced by Kafka and the theater of the absurd, was already unwell. Even so, energetic as ever, he set up a foundation and a prize for democratic education and citizenship, with special concern for the future of Europe and European culture. In Prague I made the acquaintance of his young wife, Dagmar, who manages the foundation. We talked about Antonin Liehm and Milan Kundera and our shared desire to reinforce Europe through culture, something regrettably overlooked by the founders and still sidelined today. The enormous sculpture I received with the prize is housed in the Île de Ré. Crafted by a contemporary Czech artist, it is a modern take on the crozier of St. Adalbert of Prague, the tenth-century bishop who attempted to pacify the Prussians and the Slavs before he was martyred, decapitated, and his head impaled on a stake. The sculpture stands in my office, facing the bell tower of Ars, like a reminder that Europe needs Václav Havel and us. A token of our friendship, and a steadfast reminder of our European project.

S.D. You write: "Being the guardian and the rebuilder of threatened and often broken psychic space, shrinks only fulfill their duty of memory toward European culture. They are at the heart of today's ills."[102] You are one of Europe's most ardent champions and yet you are profoundly uneasy about it. I sense a great ambivalence in you here.

J.K. I made the point in my Holberg speech and I repeat it all the time. The fall of the Berlin Wall, the subsequent war in Iraq, the imposition of globalization and our helplessness in the face of fundamentalism gave rise in Europe to two models of freedom that have spread around the world. Two complementary models. One of them holds that freedom abolishes barriers, oppressions, and injustices, the better to adapt to the demands of production and reproduction. The other counterposes to this, or adds to it, a project of freedom-as-*encounter*, envisaging a possible revelation in the bond between people: initiatives and new beginnings. Although these two models are mutually dependent, freedom-as-*adaptation* has swept the board very successfully in the United States, while freedom-as-*encounter* is more ingrained in Europe.

I don't idealize Europe by any means, and while I'm betting on the Europe of the Renaissance and the Enlightenment, I don't discount the Europe of the crusades, the pogroms, and radical evil, and frequently insist on it. Continuing to denounce these wrongs more firmly than they do elsewhere, and constantly refining the scientific tools and social measures necessary to forestall their return, we are not as proud as we should be of this European model whose shortcomings so offend and outrage us. Over and above our current and potential capabilities, I would add that Europe is the one place where a reevaluated historical memory has taught us to see that identity is not a cult but a question. A multiverse—much like the new European subject, the multilingual young Erasmus scholar, who speaks and thinks in English, French, Norwegian, Russian, and Spanish while teaching herself Chinese.

Psychoanalysis, which was born from this European culture, contributes to rehabilitating its complexity and freedom. Well then, it's our job to make a political issue of it! People tend to forget this at a time when the plight of jobless workers or struggling farmers fills us with justified rage against the failings of politicians, when it doesn't lead us to waste our fury on the dead end of the Front National.

S.D. Your presence in Assisi in October 2011 becomes clearer in this light. We've already mentioned the occasion, but I want to go back to that encounter with Benedict XVI. Because I really like the photo of the handshake between you: you are slightly inclined, to show respect, but your eyes are locked onto his, you've seized and firmly held his gaze. A powerful image.

J.K. You noticed that? This is the first time anyone has mentioned that photo to me, a photo that does, you're right, capture a moment of real personal significance. I am a citizen who comes forward to thank a religious authority for receiving her. I respect the hierarchical framework in which I am the guest. I come with a wish to understand and be understood. The openness of the interreligious meeting to nonbelievers, on the pope's initiative, strikes me as a homage to the endeavors of all those who are seeking to get to grips with the existential crisis. And also as a wager on possible synergies, enabling us to act by harmonizing the positions of secularized humanism with those of the churches, but without the two sides renouncing their differences, now that wars are breaking out everywhere and threatening to get worse. I am impressed by the intense commitment of a man who was already alleged to be worn out and had some difficulty in moving around.

"He wrote his speech himself," insisted his entourage, oddly. I never doubted it. Such ambiguous remarks could have alerted me. But the phrase pronounced by Benedict XVI—"No one owns the truth"—clarified the meaning of that interreligious gathering, and left a deep imprint on me. It was over this point, perhaps, that our eyes met in recognition.

S.D. Next to Europe, which is increasingly central to your writing and action, I have the feeling that you are ever more at home in the Anglo-Saxon world! I'm thinking of Canada, for instance, where you received your first two honorary doctorates, and also of England.

J.K. I love Toronto, probably because Peter Nesselroth, to my mind the foremost Lautréamont scholar, lives there. He and his fellow professor Paul Perron brighten my stays with fraternal connivance and affection. In addition, since the myth of a bilingual and thus French-speaking Canada is not borne out in Toronto, I had to improve my English. I reconnected there with a former student of mine at Columbia, Rubén Gallo, of Mexican origin and a passionate reader of Freud. He and his friend Terence Gower spent days and nights showing me how to use a computer and Skype. Rubén is now an influential professor at Princeton in the department of Hispanic Studies; he was very keen for me to present the words and ecstasies of "my" saint, Teresa of Avila, before the students and researchers of that prestigious university. With the participation of Peter Brooks, naturally. We were deep in fevered discussion of the differences that oppose or link "my" Teresa with her friend St. John of the Cross (equally mystical but more ascetic), when the session had to be cut short to dash to Times Square: the election of Barack Obama as President of the United States had just been announced.

S.D. And you have a soft spot for the New School in New York. You said before that you'd met some proper scholars there.

J.K. That's true. For a start, the place is steeped in the memory of Hannah Arendt. It was one of her old students and friends, Professor Richard Bernstein, head of the philosophy department, who "hired" me. And then, no doubt as a result of the Arendt connection, I am convinced that no other department that I know of can match this exceptional, not to say unique, place for seriousness and originality, where so-called continental philosophy (primarily French and German) is courted by psychoanalysis, literature, and the arts. I am proud of the course I designed on the notion of *experience* in Hegel and Heidegger, among others; and just as happy, or even happier, with the students' responses. Dick Bernstein made me a precious gift of some photographs of Hannah Arendt he'd kept, which are mostly or entirely unknown. Hannah as a baby with her maternal grandfather, a toddler with her mother, a young lady with her husband Heinrich. I've put them in a discreet but visible corner of my consulting room. My patients can see nothing else. Except for a reproduction of the Matisse painting, *Femme couchée*, you must know it: the one that appears to capture the moment when Gustave Courbet's *L'Origine du monde* gives in to reverie.

S.D. From one woman to the next, your travels take us to London, and your friends at Queen Mary University. As a bonus, your whole family enjoys visiting that city.

J.K. That's right, we often used to go to London for the Christmas vacation, until David was in his teens; we stayed at the Hyde Park Hotel in Kensington. David used to scamper by the pond with its ducks that reminded him of the Île de Ré, we bought toys at the Harrods sales, wandered around the museums, of course, and spoke English to each other in the street and in restaurants. We traveled British Airways until the Eurostar came along, no more customs or tedious security checks . . .

Because a friend of my father's had lived in London for years, I went there as soon as I could after settling in Paris. And I still often visit this unbelievable city where my body abandons me, I get lost, my senses falter in the mist and the haste and all that's left is a frustrated, and therefore endless, curiosity . . . I discovered Oxford and Cambridge under the wing of Marian Hobson. Our complicity as students of Goldmann and Barthes is constantly renewed as time goes by. Marian is a top Diderot specialist, and we're never done chattering about our hobbyhorses: *Rameau's Nephew*, Diderot's text on mystical women, our children, and lately, China, which fascinates her as much as it does me. With Jacqueline Rose, another English friend, we tread the terrain of feminism, psychoanalysis, and especially Hannah Arendt. Echoing the author of *Men in Dark Times*, Jacqueline's latest book is titled *Women in Dark Times*.

S.D. Recently your attention has turned back to China. In "Une Européenne en Chine" (A European woman in China), you say: "Many things have changed since my first sojourn. A new China now welcomes me, where giant skyscrapers have shot up in place of the old rustic dwellings on picturesque streets and the Soviet-style public housing; and instead of busy masses in the blue uniforms of the era, a colorful and enterprising population challenges, and indeed alarms, the globalized world."[103] How do you find a space for yourself in all that?

J.K. I do it like Nivi in *The Enchanted Clock*, who is frightened by the sight of empty social-housing blocks lining the vast freeways of Beijing and Shanghai before being swept into fantastic adventures with her son Stan at the Shanghai World Fair—an event they don't enjoy one bit. In this effervescent Chinese reality, which goes over my head as you'd expect, I still came across some free spirits determined to conquer their rights, in spite of or in accommodation with official directives that are shuffling very reluctantly toward modernity. While compiling my report for the European Economic and Social Committee on "France's cultural message," I met Professor Gao Xuanyang, a philosopher who did his doctorates in France and Germany. He teaches at Jiao Tong University, the source of the celebrated world university league tables that so dismay us over here, given the poor showing of France . . . Deeply interested in contemporary French thought, my work especially, and concerned with social conflict, Gao Xuanyang founded the Institute for Advanced Study in European Culture to explore the philosophies and spiritual traditions of our two continents. I am its honorary president! Marian Hobson has been invited there, as has Father Antoine Guggenheim of the Cercle Montesquieu. Still in Shanghai, but at Fudan University this time, Professor Zhu Keyi, a linguist and aficionada of Bakhtin, is a regular at the Kristeva Circle. Miss Huang Bei, who took my seminar at Paris 7 and trained at the École Normale Supérieure de Paris, is a superb teacher of French literature and a keen Proustian. My books *About Chinese Women* and *Revolution in Poetic Language* have been translated into Mandarin. The doctoral school I directed at Paris 7 takes in Chinese students. The level of exchange may rise or fall, according to the vagaries of politics, but it never dries up altogether. The *Renmin Ribao*, the Communist Party daily, commissioned and published an article by me to mark the 50th anniversary of the establishment of diplomatic relations between France and China: a happy reprise of the *Tel Quel* expedition of 1974.

S.D. Regardless of the differences, sometimes major, between the cultures of China and those of Europe, your oeuvre attracts a sizable readership and commands unanimity among intellectuals from both places. As though singularity, foreignness, and a questioning disposition could be universal dimensions of human existence. What do you think?

J.K. The European Union organized an encounter between Chinese and European intellectuals in October 2010. I attended in the company of Rem Koolhaas, Peter Sloterdijk, Umberto Eco, Angelos Kollias . . . There were some impressive contributions from the Chinese delegation, among which I particularly remember a comparative study of Laozi and Nietzsche presented by an elderly professor, more redolent of the wisdom of Chinese folk tales and the pungency of European literature than of fashionable trends in philosophy. Some of the speakers had been trained in American and European universities. Others were the product of an older, Chinese school, from before the opening to the

West but free of the Soviet imprint, eager to appropriate the ancient wisdom of Confucianism, Daoism, and Buddhism. Where the president of the European Commission, José Manuel Barroso, commended the exploits of the cultural industries in creating new markets for both populations, the Chinese Prime Minister, Wen Jiabao, came out with a paean to European culture that cited the *Odyssey*, Plato, Aristotle, Dante, Shakespeare, Goethe, Voltaire, Rousseau, and Diderot. Wen declared that there were two great civilizations in globalization: the Chinese and the European, and they were not so far apart, in his view. It was a conclusive demonstration of our leaders' divergent perspectives on culture. And China has all the time in the world.

VII. The Novels

> *Do you want my address? I'm living among the geraniums and their soil, which was wet yesterday and dry today. I pour myself into the fresh water with which I moisten their feet; I drink alongside the full-leafed branches above the rocky beds; I knead them into timid little purple flowers in the heat of the sun. I seep into this lively amber scent that overpowers the heavy fragrance of the neighboring rosebushes and chases away the mosquitoes sickened by the taste of seaweed that increases with the coming storm behind the low wall of stones; and I fill my mouth with the most delicious plum jam that my grandmother flavored with these full-shaped citronella-scented leaves. But the taste is only a memory and I am no more than an earthling at the edge of the ocean.*
>
> —Julia Kristeva, *Murder in Byzantium*

Samuel Dock. The further we go in this conversation, the more I feel how completely implicated, *invested*, you are in your theoretical writings and your fiction. Intellectually, emotionally, and, I might add, instinctively as well. A total and lucid coordination, burning but controlled, between life and writing. Between the reality and the myth. I would like to know more about the context in which your novels were written. Let's go back to *The Samurai* for a moment. This novel covers a significant period in your life, roughly ten years. When did you feel the urge to put essays to one side for a while and move onto a fictional account of your experience and that of the people around you?

Julia Kristeva. If thought is the swiftest form of transport, as my mother taught me, the novel is the most sensitive way to *touch time*. I was obscurely aware of this, somehow, ever since the publication of my first short stories in the *High School Banner* in Sofia, or while I was composing my dissertation on the birth of the European novel, and then my essays on the evolution of this genre up to the Nouveau Nouveau Roman. And simply as a reader, too, without compass or direction at times during the night. All in all, quite often. But the *need* to write a novel, to take that risk, seized me at a later date, after my analysis and after the birth of my son—at a specific moment in my history. And at a turning point in History: 1989 saw the fall of the Berlin Wall. But aren't there always turning points, and isn't it just a certain way of *telling oneself the story* "after the event" that makes us conscious of them?

But I don't really want to comment on the novels and their context. They are *written down* precisely because *that* cannot be said or lived in any other form. I get irate when I'm asked to do so, I feel like smashing up the CDs or DVDs that record me "explaining myself," and if ever I'm careless enough to listen to or watch myself in the course of this exercise, I always vow never to be caught out again. Don't worry, with you I'll try my utmost to play the game, to address the text.

But I'd like to say a few words about this imperious necessity to write. It's not an urge to dramatize the trauma in order to appease, exhibit, or sell it in the self-indulgent manner of autofiction. I listen to this torment on the couch and I try to accompany it the better to treat it, we've talked about that; it is no doubt useful in helping me to pinpoint, in those nervous kinds of book, the sexual misery that avoids analyzing itself or whose analysis was botched. It's not hard to account for the commercial success of such outpourings: they attract an audience that probably sees itself reflected, invited to purge itself and to luxuriate in smiles and tears. Public catharsis and naturalist realism are tailor made for reality TV and its repetitive obscenities.

Analysis and motherhood were a calm interlude. They made me available, they enabled me to direct my hypersensitivity elsewhere than onto my frustrations—and to become an analyst. I rediscovered more vividly than ever the palette of felt time, both behind and before me.

Ever since it was invented, writing has been a spell against mortality. But the experience of a novel, as I conceive it, does not mummify bodies or acts by carving them in the genius of a communal language. I surrender to the passions in order to throw time open, I breathe in a time regained-recreated, Proust said it once and for all. For this respiration to impregnate the narrative, the novel must balance the weaving of a plot with the song of poetry and the light of the concept; it becomes a reasoning and it thinks, or it tries to. I try. Felt time restores lived experience, but in a form reworked by hallucination, fantasy, and the project. It's a risky alchemy that verges on delirium. I don't like autofiction because it hasn't rid itself of sadomasochism and, by flaunting it, bears it and prolongs the pleasure of it inoculated into the hypocritical reader—"its likeness, its brother" (Baudelaire)—whose desire aspires, by definition, to power and to submission. Sade showed how fantasies left pending in the imagination are steeped in morbid pleasures; but, by his saturation of them and by his philosophizing, the divine marquis prevents hard-sex buffs from dozing off: he invites them to think. In contrast, by replacing the philosophy of the boudoir with pornography or self-pity, the Spectacle distributes the designer drugs of autofiction, those customized and licit drugs, among the hyperconnected populace.

S.D. Fantasy and delirium find refuge in the imaginary, don't they, and the imaginary is also their distributor . . . I'm thinking of Céline, to whom you devoted *Powers of Horror*.

J.K. Céline, with his journey to the end of the slaughter, continues to be pilloried by the "politically correct" brigade. But they forget that this lover of baroque dancing said he wrote in order to "keep his delirium in check." In my book about abjection I delve into those murky regions where "delirium" does not pass into "the act," for the author is testing the death drive; and there are other contexts where he commits himself politically, especially in his antisemitic pamphlets . . . But none of this is my experience, I don't inhabit such extremes. Let's just say that I try to activate my delirium in vibrate mode.

S.D. In *The Samurai*, Olga muses:

> The grace of the birds, compact of nimble body and dauntless mind. . . . A migrant fragments time, but when it alights somewhere, that particular bit of time is all its time, and it puts its heart in it, grows fond of it, improves it. Because it has no real home, it is at home in that land of exile and asylum. Being always on the move, instead of worrying a migrant, makes it curious, like the avocet; proud, like the male teal; coquettish, like the egret; or aristocratic, like the heron.[104]

Isn't yours a solar journey, rather than to the end of the night, even if it does take you close to a black sun?

J.K. I prefer a blossoming to a deluge. That's my own personal weakness, obviously. An atavistic femaleness, perhaps. My way of marking the beat of my own mortality. My migrant's imagination. In *The Samurai*, the portraits of writers and philosophers I knew or lived with are neither snapshots nor pieces of reportage; I'm not oblivious to the cruelty of writing about living people, and the caresses and swipes can be discerned. For Olga the Squirrel, the facets multiply: elegiac wanderings through the salt marshes, hallucinatory states, Olga as a baby, Olga as a horse, Olga as a migrating bird . . .

S.D. You are this composite Olga, but not only her. You project yourself into each of the protagonists.

J.K. I am very fond of one character from another era, Joëlle Cabarus, who shares a name with a famous Girondist, Thérésa Cabarrus, Tallien's Spanish-born wife. In my novel she's a psychoanalyst and quietly introduces the erotic explosion of my generation, the sixty-eighters, like an echo of the criminality of the French Revolution. You'll find her described in Olga's journal.

S.D. Let me read it out:

> *Everyone's busy preparing for the Bicentenary of the Revolution. And Jessy and Arnaud have suddenly remembered Thérésa Cabarrus. . . . A courtesan, no connection with the greatness they see nowadays in Olympe de Gouge's femininism or even Théroigne de Méricourt's psychosis. But she suits me well enough, our ancestress. Revolution through Eroticism, unbridled Sex versus the Reason of the goddess Terror. . . . Thérésa, that undistinguished but successful seductress, decapitated several myths: the myth of Great Ideas, and the romantic myth of*

> *Love, though both in fact survived her. Is the present the age of living without myths? . . . Arrogance is the myth of people who have no more myths.*[105]

How was this first novel perceived by those around you, by Philippe, by your family?

J.K. Philippe has always shown the greatest generosity towards my work and my writing, novels included. He participates in final revisions with his own firm opinions, but taking my universe into account. If he makes suggestions and proposals, it is never in the guise of a lover-husband or of an editor. He builds me up. The Joyaux clan has a sense of humor and when my in-laws recognized themselves in the Montlaurs of *The Samurai*, they didn't mind being teased tongue-in-cheek. I owe a great deal to Claude Durand and his unfailing support. He read my drafts with meticulous attention and any edits he saw fit to insert, whether of style or composition, blended with my voice without distorting it. It's very rare to find an editor in such osmosis with his author, I can't say that too often.

S.D. When you talk about your voice, I feel as though I'm witnessing the birth of a new genre, at the intersection of all the others, perhaps. We ought to invent a new term to define it!

J.K. I'm not the kind of novelist who can trot out a book every year. It can take me up to eight years to produce one, and each of them reflects as much the evolution of my personality as that of my storytelling. What kind, what "genre" of novel? I daresay *The Samurai* is more of a "social fresco," whereas "noir" predominates from the beginning of my series of metaphysical detective stories, *The Old Man and the Wolves*, *Possessions*, and *Murder in Byzantium*. *Teresa, My Love* is like a "cubist portrait." Starting with *Murder in Byzantium*, the aim is a "total novel," coming to fruition with *The Enchanted Clock*, the most accomplished in my view. Irrespective of the differences between them, the inclusion of current affairs and different historical periods—the *touching of time* that interests me so much—generates a writing that could be called polyphonic. Each of these novels contains a plot and a story. In *The Old Man and the Wolves*, it's the murder of old Clarus. *Possessions* gives us the passion and beheading of Gloria Harrison, a translator in a world where no one reads anymore, and the mother of a deaf child. The journalist Stephanie Delacour discovers present-day Europe and ancestral Byzantium in *Murder in Byzantium*. The age of the Baroque, and the affection of narrator Sylvia Leclercq for St. Teresa of Avila, shape *Teresa, My Love*. And in *The Enchanted Clock* we see the court of Louis XV, on the eve of the Enlightenment, through the eyes of Nivi Delisle. But the tale is always broken up, breached by dramas and pathologies, erotic or lyrical scenes, meditations conducted by the narrator or her doubles that draw on philosophy, psychoanalysis, and even theology.

S.D. Your "multiverse" . . . How do you orchestrate this plethora of voices, settings, epochs? We can tell that the documentary research has been considerable, but you don't let it weigh down the *molto allegro* lilt of the prose. What is your working procedure?

J.K. I redraft the text several times to make it harmonize. The material is woven by night, at first combining documentation as you say, notes in the form of dreamlike flashes, random epiphanies about everything and nothing, plus the condensed and portable philosophy of the essay writer and therapist that I am in another life. I cut, I expand, I hone the characters, the initial project evolves, and a new universe comes to life, one that's more alive than the other, for me at any rate; it absorbs the everyday and even seems to modify it.

This *redrafting* is the most pleasurable and exposed side of the fiction-writing process. Along with the obsession, which dogs me at every stage, with perfecting the *selection of words*: avoiding repetitions, tightening up, seeking accuracy, feeling the sinews of the language. I adore splashing around among synonyms and etymologies. And I rely on music, lots of it. Jazz or baroque, it's indispensable for getting the elements of language to chime in tune and then for my own adjustment, after long submersion in the silence of the nights.

S.D. There's a carnival side to this polyphony.

J.K. My theory of the novel had explored that kind of playful possibility before I dared publish any fiction of my own. The game is to break the narrative thread, to multiply the meaning of a theme, a time, from one mask to the next. This carnivalesque jig sounds clearly in *Possessions*, my favorite metaphysical detective novel. Starting with the very first, however, *The Old Man and the Wolves*, the tone has been predominantly tragic; I'm not laughing and not weeping, either. Carnival is not annulled by murder. It pulses in the very barbarity that keeps the narrator awake in Santa Barbara, the global village where she "travels herself" in *The Old Man and the Wolves*, *Possessions*, or *Murder in Byzantium*. In *The Enchanted Clock* polyphony opens itself up to radiation from the primordial cosmological background. Intimate reality is mirrored in the audacities of the eighteenth century, and the romance between Nivi and Theo seeks a lexicon of love in the astrophysical multiverse.

S.D. And that certainly links yours with the fiction of the Enlightenment. And yet you "practice" this today with the aid of all possible orders of knowledge and through the rearrangement of every genre, for the sake of a fiction focused on the individual and on the society in which she is embedded. You mentioned Dostoyevsky and this of course made me think of *The Brothers Karamazov*. But also of Tolstoy's *Resurrection*. In one, music is born from an encounter, in the other it's from an explosive blast.

J.K. Tolstoy was the lullaby of my childhood and one of my father's favorite authors. But to my mind he is more "monological" than "dialogical." You're right, his characters lack the *carnivalesque*, hopelessly conflicted nature of Dostoyevsky's unsettling heroes. And we also find this dialogism in Diderot, especially in *Rameau's Nephew*, a resource I found very helpful when writing *Strangers to Ourselves*. "*Me*," the philosopher, seeks for truth with "*Him*," the sporadic musician; the great Hegel couldn't get over it! He declared admiringly that this, specifically French, "witty talk" is the high point of culture . . . prior to the absolute knowledge sought by his dialectic! Anyway, let's return to my own "total novel" . . .

S.D. In *The Enchanted Clock*, *Me* and *He* are a psychoanalyst and an astrophysicist. The depths of intimacy in dialogue with the depths of the cosmos; the intensity and solitude of the amorous bond.

J.K. In one scene, Nivi and Theo are by the ocean with Leibniz the swan. The lovers exchange thoughts about "their" mathematician, Émilie du Châtelet. Does anyone still remember, my dear Samuel, that the intellectuals of the Enlightenment embraced divine infinity not only in their philosophy, we take that for granted, but also in their atheism—and, mark this, in their artistic craftsmanship? The clinching evidence is that fabulous astronomical clock, programmed to strike the hours of universal, that is, French, time until the year 9999.[106] No less bewitched than Nivi by that enchanted clock, I researched its origins and discovered that it was designed by Claude-Siméon Passemant, Louis XV's engineer, who became a central character in the novel. Imagine: the realm is beginning to crack apart, Mme de Pompadour worships the Encyclopedists, the Revolution is at the gates of Versailles. This world in the shadow of the Enlightenment is living in a doubtless apocalyptic time (9999 is the cabbalistic number of the Apocalypse), but one which they lay claim to; these "illuminati" possess it until 9999 at least, there's no doubt on that score. They are inside it, they calculate it, compose it, live it. And my Nivi and my Theo likewise inhabit the year 9999, with Passemant and Émilie du Châtelet.[107]

Does one have a right to pick one's "characters" from among those unknowns, those rejects of the modern spectacle, for whom history, astronomy, psychoanalysis, too, God, and the void are not abstractions, but keys inherent to their existence? They turned these into discourses of the soul, android automata, sensitive musical scores to be played as they worked, loved, wandered, survived. No meek submission here, and no convulsionary revelations in the style of the Saint-Médard sect, either.

S.D. Passion accelerates and harmonizes thoughts:

> What are those two doing at the edge of the Fier d'Ars? Abstractions as flying buttresses against the appetites of desire? Cold follies, impenetrable allusions?
>
> —"We are illusions, like time and space. But also points impacted by an infinite expansion. . . ."
>
> —"Isn't God a 'capricious Worker who is determined without sufficient reason'?"
>
> —"Finitude put to death is passion, isn't it?" . . .
>
> —You're the one saying it, or is it I? . . . Their way of loving together.[108]

What's more, there are passages in *The Samurai* and *The Enchanted Clock* that are torridly erotic, opening startling windows onto your own most private life. How did the readers who know you primarily from the fields of semiotics and psychoanalysis react to that? Did they stick with you? In the end, do the same people appreciate you as a theoretician and as a novelist? I know that you interact a lot with your readers; how did they handle that first unveiling of drives and instincts?

J.K. You're too young to know, but when *The Samurai* was published, it was still widely rumored that Julia Kristeva was hot stuff! Some male readers—not all of them elderly—are apt to come up after a lecture, look meaningfully into my eyes and tell me how much they like my writing. I deduce that they've read everything I've written, and the compliment does not rejuvenate me. We can't rule out the possibility that future scholars will find out from my books and papers that Julia Kristeva was an unsuspected "monster at the crossroads,"[109] the opposite of the demure young lady I appear to be in the eyes of the partisans or pulverizers of Casanova Sollers. Nothing doing, Santa Barbara is everywhere and Paris can't escape it, let alone the press and the publishing industry, in the midst of intrigue, censure, bedazzlement, and malicious gossip. Gloria Harrison, the carnivalesque character who stands for me in *Possessions*, will pay the price: a foreigner and a translator, almost a writer, she will be decapitated. I haven't lost my head yet, and I know I live in Santa Barbara.

S.D. "You want to locate Santa Barbara on a map? But it's impossible, you know. How can one locate the global village? Santa Barbara is in Paris, New York, Moscow, Sofia, London, Plovdiv, and in Santa Barbara too. . . . The nonstop exhibition of intimacy, televising of values, and execution of our passions."[110]

J.K. Don't make the mistake of thinking that a reviewer ever wonders whether the character is the narrator, and what connection there might be with the author. Readers are an endangered species, displaced by spectators. Spectators follow the movie. If by chance one makes the effort to open a novel, he will be looking for a screenplay, reality television. Do not whatever you do attempt to explain that, in some pages of *The Enchanted Clock*, Nivi describes the clockmaker Passemant in terms borrowed from the *Memoirs* of Saint-Simon. That's polyphony for you! No one has read or reads Saint-Simon.

S.D. You don't suspect that you are being involuntarily shielded when people prefer to engage with the novels without intruding too much or digging into your life story. This approach may safeguard somewhat the magic, the mystery, of letters. Well, I'm just trying to see the glass as half full.

J.K. But there's no mystery, for God's sake! Or rather there is, but it resides in the coexistence of sex and meaning, fracture and cohabitation. The way I write is the way I live. I'm not offering the reader a mirror, a pathetic and therefore flattering reflection in which she is supposed to recognize her image. I try to plumb the image. Spectacle and social media favor mechanical reflexes, and homogenize behaviors, and dehumanize the users: "one" ends up behaving like a product. And suddenly a woman, with no community to lay claim to her or that she can claim, and moreover married to Philippe Sollers, is not content to be a professor and an analyst but must boast of her singular inner life. Just leave her to get on with it! She makes us tired! I told you, I have a failing and it's catching up with me: I fancy that I can dispense with PR. I'm digging my own grave, aren't I? Well, we all need a grave.

Writing to recompose oneself; the pleasure of writing without staking too much on the pleasure of being read or even published. If that's what happens, you're in luck. Otherwise the novel is a testimony, an exultant martyr. I say this in the momentum of writing, a writing forever addressed to . . . the unknown.

S.D. In *The Samurai*, you write:

> The cruelty of children who are supposed to be gifted! Some gift! The gift of being able to wound! You see it everywhere, including the universities. Impossible to count the intellectual murders. Thought has no blood, you can't see it die; professors die of cancer of the liver but are killed by bitterness.[111]

Are you confronting an empathy with the violence undergone, or its traversal, the necessary step for survival? Which then leads to further tribulations?

J.K. I wrote that passage in the wake of some trying sessions with one of my analysands. I'm not exceptionally gifted and have never experienced the strains of being a precocious child. All the same—whether out of female hypersensitivity or the immemorial hysterical background—in the course of countertransference I am seized by empathy, from which I gently extricate myself while keeping company with the words of the person speaking to me. The analysand's free association is not always chaotic and disjointed, indeed it can be more to the point than autofiction. Certain words spring from silence to initiate a peculiar narrative that puts the trauma into suspension. They sometimes come back to me at night, when I relate them to my own fantasies and stories and note down the sequence. The gifted child, closed-up as a clam, was going to die, unable to spill blood: that's how this person described themselves. We managed to get through this haunting dread together. But on a different stage, some wakeful night, the countertransference turned into writing. Does this metaphorical cohabitation protect life? The patient's? Mine? Yes, in large part mine, though not decisively; delirium in vibrate mode, as I said before. The resulting novel may delight some, just as it may trigger rejection, hatred, jealousy, boredom, exclusion in others. We are familiar with the mystique attached to the great writers, but we know less about the annealed hatred aroused by writing. "I believe in the unconscious hatred of style," Flaubert wrote.[112] Paranoid? I wouldn't say so. In this instance, it's not a matter of "the style is the man" (according to Buffon's academic encomium). The hatred of style in question refers to the catastrophic depths that, quivering in the pleasure of the text, its verbal voluptuousness and paroxystic rebirth, are resented as an injustice by those who cannot save themselves by such means.

S.D. *The Old Man and the Wolves* (1991) is the fruit of bereavement following the shocking death of your father, a victim of the medical experiments carried out in Bulgarian hospitals before the fall of the Berlin Wall. "Too somber," decreed the reviews. This reaction reminded you all over again that "depression is not French," as you'd stated already in *Black Sun: Depression and Melancholia* (1987). *The Old Man and the Wolves* makes a link between the carnal agony of loss and the narrative engendered by the proliferation of language:

> Words were dying, I was dying. There's nothing so impossible to describe as a nightmare in which you can feel yourself dying. All sensation is gone; you're the inert, helpless victim of a kind of abduction; and there's nobody left to register what's happening, only shreds of soon-to-be-putrid flesh. Something and nothing so close yet so disparate you can't remember them.[113]

In reading your novels, I'm struck to see how closely you link literary experience to dramatic personal events and, via their historical echoes, to the religious texts that become pertinent at such critical moments. With this first "metaphysical detective story," your writing begins to tackle the sacred . . . in culture.

J.K. We are in Santa Barbara, for the first of its several outings in my metaphysical detective stories. A learned old man is killed in a country that encapsulates the global village; the law is unable to find the culprits, and the ancient myths return: they are the wolves. In real life, in Sofia, there were no more burial plots available, the regime's way to prevent funerals turning into protest gatherings. I offered to pay for one, in French francs or in dollars. They said: "If you yourself die, no problem, as you are somewhat known, we'll put your father in with you. And your husband, if you like." The official was not joking. He merely embodied the stupidity of barbarism. And so my father was cremated, contrary to his faith and his last wishes.

S.D. You spent some years trying to put yourself back together after the brutal shock of your father's death, compounded by the dramatic circumstances. Was the creation of your first detective story, metaphysical for good measure, a "work of mourning"?

J.K. Philippe reminded me of something Francis Bacon said: it would be terribly sad if, thousands of years from now, humanity or what is left of it could not dig up a single corpse. With the fall of communism, I myself felt closer to the Goya of the black paintings, devastated as he was by the Napoleonic Wars, and to Ovid, whose *Metamorphoses* anticipate the end of the Roman Empire. Human beings became wolves prowling through the hallucinations of the narrative. Characters bleed into each other and split apart, assassinations and politics, dreams and reality. How could a Parisian hack ever be expected to make head or tail of it?

The old man's first name and last name are Latin, Septicius *C*larus: my father's initials (Stoyan *K*ristev) and a nod to his mastery of Latin, a precious benefit of his theological studies that I've never been able to equal. I felt certain that I had no other option in my mourning than to invent a genre, whose subject would be *radical evil*: the killing of those human beings whom other "human beings" have deemed superfluous, and as a corollary, the impossibility of elucidating this. The journalist Stephanie Delacour, the old man's student and his real or imaginary daughter, consumes her grief in the inquiry into the disappearance that she conducts alongside Commissioner Rilsky. But uncertainty remains: the lady sleuth fails to identify the criminals. The detective story is an optimistic genre, even when it leaves the crime unsolved, for it basically tells the reader: "You can know where evil comes from." Since then I've applied Nietzsche's rule: "Never write anything that does not drive every sort of hurried man to despair."[114] I take him to be targeting the acceleration of the death drive in modern history. Each of us, whether passively or actively, participates in it.

S.D. You resume the theme of *radical evil* by pointing to religious fundamentalism and the impotence of secularized society to respond to this new form of nihilism bursting forth under the goad of radicalized religion.

J.K. Yes, the evil is endemic and the "solutions" applied in Santa Barbara are powerless, deceptive, not to say perverse, as shown in the character of Vespasian. Neither juridical measures nor metaphysical wagers satisfy the heroine's disquiet. All she can do is investigate without end: the only solution is a narrative tirelessly starting over. Such is the lesson Stephanie retains from her teacher, father and Latinist.

You're right, my reaction to the radicalization of adolescents and the mayhem of jihadism brought me back to the death drive. And I find, yet again, that a comprehensive moralism—whether political, juridical, educational, or philosophical—is helpless to contest radical evil. Totalitarian or fundamentalist, Thanatos is catching up with us. It seems to me that a psychoanalytic accompaniment that attends to the need to believe, inasmuch as it proves capable of repairing collapsed identities, is one of the few in-depth resources we have, perhaps the only one. With radicalized young people, I attempt to *interpret radical evil*. Is that so different from what Stephanie Delacour is seeking in Santa Barbara? In a strange way, the tragic transfiguration that befalls the narrator of *The Old Man and the Wolves*, her account reopening and rearranging spaces and times, without heroism and in the acceptance of uncertainty—"there is always crime where there are no borders"—strikes me as rather contemporary.

S.D. The integrity of writing as the analytic act.

J.K. Yes, the discretion of the word that opens out and does not compromise.

S.D. In the aftermath of your father's passing, you were supported by your mother, your cousins, and your sister, though she was unable to come in person. There was kindness, too, from many Bulgarian friends and dissidents, people who shortly before had met with the French delegation under President Mitterrand.

J.K. I was deeply moved by those sympathetic presences. Since arriving in Paris, I'd become quite estranged from my Bulgarian colleagues. But our attachment endured, and they buoyed me up that day at the religious service for the cremation. One was Professor Jeliu Jelev, who would become the first President of the Bulgarian Republic after the fall of the Berlin wall. Another was my dear friend Blaga Dimitrova, reputed to deserve a Nobel Prize for Literature, on whose work I had produced one of my very few monographs in Bulgarian; she would, briefly, serve as Vice President of the new democracy. I was not alone in the cemetery, nor afterward. Other more recent friendships revealed themselves to be rock solid. My metaphysical detective story was praised in a powerful text by the faithful and vigilant Bernard-Henri Lévy.

And yet, I felt myself touch bottom in those days. I thought about exiling myself once again. The Santa Barbara series charts my path through this ill-being, I could not tell it better today.

To the need to allay my personal grief was added a political unease, bred by François Mitterrand's two terms in office. Seeing the procession of ever more momentous social earthquakes, I couldn't go on without trying to metabolize them in words. *The Old Man and the Wolves* (1991) was followed by *Possessions* (1996) and *Murder in Byzantium* (2004). This descent into hell by means of fiction was anchored in collections of essays explicitly concerned with revolt: *The Sense and Non-sense of Revolt* (1996) and *Intimate Revolt* (1997) reprised my postgraduate classes at the University of Paris 7-Diderot. Then came the "female genius" trilogy: *Hannah Arendt* (1999), *Melanie Klein* (2000), and *Colette* (2001).

S.D. In *The Old Man and the Wolves*, which I think of as your pivotal novel, you write: "No one liked foreigners, especially female ones, and the natives vented their dislike on whatever the strangers held most dear."[115] Is this something that affects you? What do you hold most dear?

J.K. To be sure, the fear of the other—the rejection of the outsider—is primal: Freud observed it in very young children. This fear becomes normalized and heightened in accordance with the individual and social context. I am affected by the phenomenon, of course, but I don't address it from the perspective of my own "situation as a foreigner." I cringe when people from abroad, who have carved out influential niches in our institutional hierarchy, whine about some supposed discrimination against them. Discrimination undoubtedly exists, even against the most privileged incomers, but please: pipe down, for there are others who are brutally oppressed. From where I stand, an inevitably singular foreigner, it's more a question of probing the intimate facets of this exclusion. No complaints, no persecutors to denounce or to hound. Instead, realities and how to deal with them. Hence the metaphysical detective stories.

And what I hold "most dear"? It is what I *invest*: I become "one" with . . . my own, Philippe and David. My analysands. My friends. Books. Philippe often mocks my humanism, a "flabby thinking" that hampers proper thought, and so on. I know that this kind of teasing misses the humanism that really does engage me. But it's true, I am a humanist who has read Freud, and I *invest* human beings, people, I care about their debacles and their joys, I live them vicariously. Whether they are in China, Canada, or the United States. Strong relationships, each one a now that lasts.

S.D. It seems to me that your mother occupies a much less important place in the novels. Why is that? Perhaps because you yourself became the mother figure for your family?

J.K. My mother is not a fictional character. She succeeded in making herself invisible, which I felt was a mathematical necessity in her. She was always already there. Like the cosmological *instanton*, that condition prior to quantum states, to the Big Bang, to every imaginable multiverse, and which encloses every potentiality. Do I make her into a "divine" cause, but hollowed out? A sort of dark matter? She takes me to the limits of the imaginable. Upon her death, absolute silence. A long time afterward, some passages of *Murder in Byzantium* depict this tête-à-tête with the elusory.

S.D. But you bring her back to life:

> Christine . . . let us believe that she was content to open a path for us, that she didn't suffer or scratch and gave nothing but a caress. "I didn't tie you down, I gave you wings." That was her modest motto, which she'd repeat with a spark of irony in the corner of her eye and her lips, apologizing for having said too much, for having broken the silence. Her complicit silence was only an interval; it left a lot of room to the rest of us; I can hear it still and I am always looking for it.[116]

J.K. I didn't cry at my father's funeral, too full of rage, a world was crumbling. When my mother passed away, I cried for ten days without stopping. I had lost my foundation, worse, my instanton. Nearly thirty years had gone by between the start of my psychoanalytic work and my mother's death, and meanwhile I'd become a mother myself. And I'd rediscovered mom in my body-to-body contact with the baby, the gestures I used with my son, his babble and the way I stood back to give him space to thrive. The "mystery" of maternal passion, which I was later to call a *reliance*. Helping the new arrival, that ephemeral stranger, to develop his originality. Which makes me cry. "You're crying with happiness," David says.

S.D. In *The Old Man and the Wolves*, to return to that work, you relate with frightening accuracy your confrontation with the *real*, through the emotional vagrancy of your characters. Alba pictures the void and knows how to vanish into the symptom, she is hyperactive, "she was caught up in an unremitting rush that left no room for sorrow or despair."[117] Vespasian is a surgeon, a repulsive sadist: "He seemed to be afflicted with that mental impatience that is a kind of excitation without discharge—the same mania that makes for constant changes in electronic equipment, which passes from new to old in the course of a few months, from superefficient to ultra-outmoded before it is even used, a sheer delight for technologists but of little if any use to people in general."[118] One cannot think that these figures are entirely made up. Are they inspired by real people? What if the "prototypes" should recognize themselves?

J.K. Confession or invention, is that what you're asking? Don't worry, it's not my life. But my life has placed me in unison with certain extremes that many victims, as well as tormentors, conceal from themselves, or so I gather from this war between the sexes. As for the prototypes, no one has complained so far. In one sense, the Santa Barbara universe that wafts up from the couch and can be perused in my novels is mine, of course it is. It's my sensibility that hears and lays bare that of other people. I project myself into the timid, defensive words of the denizens of Santa Barbara, I graft onto them the fantasies I decode from their sufferings and whose gravity *we*, at the end of the day, succeed in articulating. And then, in contrast to hyperconnected naivety, tragic violence overturns repression, and the body and mind are alleviated. And the novel recomposes, after the event, this alchemy of "self" and "others." Which you know so well . . .

S.D. Transference and countertransference.

J.K. Exactly. The Alba and Vespasian couple dramatizes the desire unto death and for death that festers under cover of feminism, nontraditional families, and same-sex marriage. Psychoanalysis places me in the eye of the storm, and the "vignettes" in my clinical articles attempt to grasp these anthropological mutations. Meanwhile, with the metaphysical novels, I edge my way into these brutal struggles, into the dehumanization currently underway. The murder of the old man is more than just a social incident or a serious medical blunder. It partakes of this unbridled explosion of the death drive within the family itself (I stress the irreducible hatred between Alba and Vespasian).

The death drive reappears in another guise in *Possessions*, with Gloria's decapitation. Perhaps because I was exposed to the destructiveness of war—I'm a war baby, remember—I tend to relive it, but without eroticizing it. Without complacency, resorting to the "estrangement" that Brecht advocated and that I conduct by other means. By a journalistic and police investigation in which blood becomes mingled with tears; by the scrambling of conventional plot; by the ambiguity of the characters, starting with the key duo of the reporter and the commissioner; by the way they think, simultaneously inside and outside the crime, subjecting death-dealing perversity to a tenacious, meditative dissection. In the neoreality thus constructed, the imagined Alba-Vespasian couple opens the wounds of this or that patient as well as those of other people I have known and staunches my own. The inquiry continues.

S.D. The next novel to appear was *Possessions*, in which neoreality and the inquiry center on a decapitated woman and mother. The loss of the "sexual organ" and "work tool" that is her head, according to her, refers the reader straight to your work as a theoretician, and to you as a *femme de tête*, an intellectual: "Her possession had no trace of resentment in it. It was just a kind of concentration; humiliation converted into serenity. . . . But how had Gloria attained that refinement of trauma where it can be savored like iced vodka: with no sense of either pleasure or intoxication?"[119] Bordering on self-irony, here we behold the tragedy and carnival of the human condition. How was this novel born?

J.K. It's my favorite of the Santa Barbara series. An exploration of the travails of the "second sex": the exhaustion of the *femme-mère* in the chores of keeping life going, the negation of the *femme de tête* . . . In *Possessions* I expounded a poignant vision of female "genius," shortly before tackling the trio of famous examples that are Arendt, Klein, and Colette. The beheading of Gloria—by another woman, indeed—is just one of the crimes committed by Santa Barbara, a microcosm/metaphor of our technological planet, where all manner of assisted reproduction is permitted while maternal passion is suppressed. However, the beautiful translator is not only a victim. This tragic horror also befalls her because she has shut herself away in isolation and takes pride in being a wronged woman. I listen to women confiding their wrongs, I feel those wounds a hundredfold, they infuriate and brace me. And I am only appeased when I have plucked the right word from them, captured the cruel image, when I wrap myself in the plot of their possessions . . . and write it down.

S.D. For Freud, the severed head indicates a castration fantasy, whether as threat or retribution. He seldom associates it with the head of the Medusa, exhibiting female castration.

J.K. At the end of the 1990s beheading was not yet a propaganda image. I knew of this ritual through art history and a handful of anthropology texts. Dreams and fantasies relayed on the couch came to supplement what child psychoanalysis can tell us. The young patients of Melanie Klein and Hanna Segal dreamed of and drew disembodied heads, the sign of an important stage in psychical evolution: the subject in the process of being constituted appropriates the mother's face by *representing* it to himself. He "takes" her head, "cuts it off," and "carries it away" inside him. This capacity to picture mother's face, her head, allows him to separate from body-to-body contact, and only then can he begin to name. The preceding echolalia, the gustative babble of "*moh-meh-mih*" turns into a word: *mommy.* An imaginary decapitation that makes up for the cruelty of separation.

S.D. It's a psychic "position" that marks the phases of development and integrates with the mechanisms of neurosis. Not to be confused with depressive or borderline pathologies.

J.K. Indeed, and Kleinian analysts have made much of the imaginary and symbolic "matricide" that alone promotes autonomy and the access to language. In *Possessions* I confine myself to exploring this experience *from the maternal side*: a risk of maternal madness, a "possession" in the sense of a "loss of self," over and above the social violence that often instrumentalizes it, aggravates it, and pushes to criminality. What interests me in this beheading ("*décollation*," a delectable but arcane French term) is the maternal: it begins in *narcissistic* devotion and veers into a reciprocal and reversible mother-child possessiveness. The narrator, Stephanie Delacour, witnesses this very relationship between Gloria and her son Jerry, who was born deaf. My encounters with the mothers of disabled children, whether on the couch or in community groups, helped me to evaluate the risks and destruction that loomed over me, too, in my relationship to David. I believe I've avoided them, thanks to the three of us (Philippe, David, and I), thanks of course to analysis, and thanks to writing above all.

S.D. Your 1996 novel predated the spread of this ritual in Islamist gangster fundamentalism, where vengeance favors decapitations that are posted online and commented on by news services around the world. Soon afterward, you delved into the religious and political hinterland of this theme in an exhibition at the Louvre (Visions Capitales, 1998). How does one go from writing a metaphysical thriller to mounting a show like that?

J.K. Good question! The drawings department at the Louvre had launched a series of exhibits curated by thinkers who had no connection with the world of museums (Jean Starobinski, Jacques Derrida, Peter Greenaway, Hubert Damisch) as a way of revamping its approach to art and putting rarely shown graphic works before a mass audience. When the director, Françoise Viatte, invited me to participate I was daunted, I didn't feel qualified. Hoping to dissuade her, I suggested an abject topic: chopped-off heads! *Possessions* had just come out. My scheme misfired, she loved it. After all, wasn't decapitation a fetish subject at various points in the history of art? I had admired its visualization by Caravaggio and Tiepolo: the Medusa, Salome and John the Baptist, Judith and Holofernes . . . Not to mention Artemisia Gentileschi's version . . . In Europe alone, it was a specialty! French revolutionary terror was slaughter by guillotine. Françoise's team helped me enormously. And as the cherry on the cake, I dedicated the catalog essay to my mother, who came over for the opening conference—cheerful and smiling for the first time, I think, since my father's death.

S.D. The horror of decapitation uncovers an abyss before which politics and civilization at large hold their breath, appalled. Weren't you invited to speak about the topic when the text of *Visions capitales* was reissued with the subtitle *Arts et rituels de la décapitation*?[120]

J.K. Yes, I was, but I always decline invitations from the media on this (and other) subjects, to avoid any conflation between barbaric acts on the one hand and the *psychic representation* of foundational violence—what is depicted in art's "capital visions"—on the other. This sublimation must urgently be revisited so it can be interpreted. But that would only be possible in a secure framework, under the auspices of the university or the clinic, certainly not in an interconnected rush or under the glare of the media spotlight. I attempted to do it in my seminar on "The Need to Believe" at the Maison des Adolescents. The novel is another facet of this, the one I prefer for its greater intimacy and reticence.

S.D. So, with *Murder in Byzantium*, where are we? One passage runs:

> A foreigner and a woman, I know that I come from Byzantium, a place that has never existed with any credible reality except in my soul. . . . The never ending incongruous debates about the sex of angels, that's Byzantine. . . . The first religious war in the Old World, those legendary Crusades . . . all that still always happens via Byzantium. From this point of view, I believe, Byzantium is what remains most precious, refined, and painful about Europe, that which others envy

> about it and which she has difficulty realizing herself and extending—unless that is . . . who knows? In the meantime, Santa Barbara expands in all directions.[121]

This novel is still a metaphysical detective story but it plays on a greater range of literary registers: history, fiction, dialogue, lyrical reminiscence . . . Between individual narrative arcs and social crises, the main protagonist of your neo-reality would seem to be Europe itself.

J.K. The Europe that has broken down is disoriented because it's unable to acknowledge its cultural history, one of whose fountainheads is the Orthodox or Byzantine element. That matters to me, as you'd expect. So here, I go back to my foreignness, childhood memories, the fractures and blessings of being uprooted. Less dreamlike than its predecessors, it's the first metaphysical thriller in which the life of the detective-journalist Stephanie Delacour aligns so closely with mine: born in Bulgaria, vacationing by the Black Sea, meeting Lionel Jospin . . . The turmoil of the characters in various limit states is interwoven with an historical interrogation of Europe. Are you familiar with Eastern Europe? Orthodox Christianity? Did you know that an obscure female genius called Anna Comnena, chronicler of the First Crusade, was the first woman world-historian in the eleventh and twelfth centuries? Against this Byzantine backdrop, Stephanie/Julia recalls watching soccer matches with her father and bombs falling on Sofia during World War II; the sun salutation and the intoxicating wrangles over Bakhtin or Laozi or Confucius . . . A stranger to herself between Paris and New York, and proud of it.

S.D. You specify: "Except one is never at peace when one pulls at one's roots, and only a satisfied curiosity can occasionally calm the rushing waste of anxiety."[122]

J.K. Yes, I endorse that. Underlining the words "curiosity" and "calm."

S.D. You projected yourself into the character of Stephanie Delacour for several years. As your narrator, she observes that: "Judging by my own experience, you become a detective when, having no place of your own, you appoint yourself an ambassador of the law and spend your life trying to solve a mystery that is really a murder."[123] Between violence and justice: are you the detective, the analyst, or the novelist?

J.K. The novel is a prolongation of psychoanalysis by other means. It multiplies me by creating links to other worlds. Inner awareness plus the newsroom. As David/Stan puts it in *The Enchanted Clock*: "You have so many facets . . . Like a Picasso portrait."[124] An artist who knew all about fragmentation and destructiveness, while never ceasing to represent faces and bodies.

S.D. Is it true what some people contend, that a writer only repeats the same novel again and again?

J.K. Not at all! The novel creates the unexpected, reengendering its "author." It reconstructs the psychic space, the body, history, and the very ability to reconstruct. It's a different experience every time. In psychoanalysis we say that to remember is to discover. Finding-creating, we talked about that. Writing a novel and continuing my analysis "on the other side of the novel," through countertransference and its renewal with my analysands, intersect to keep me in motion. No, I don't produce the same novel in umpteen versions; the one constant is the polyphonic form of the text, but the storylines, themes, and pacing are different. *The Enchanted Clock* has a much faster tempo than the others, leading some readers to compare it to a "particle accelerator," as Élisabeth Bélorgey remarks. Louis XV, Passemant's clock, the traffic of artworks, Versailles and Dubai, assisted reproduction, the crisis of print news, cosmological research that seeks to disprove time. It's about today. And it's about Nivi. A one-woman band who resembles me, though she's more unstable and more combative than I am.

S.D. *Murder in Byzantium* opens fresh vistas onto the narrator's universe. Secretive and adventurous, a cosmopolitan intellectual and David's/Jerry's mother: "I've been loaned many languages but I own none," "even though I like to trace rhythms and visions more easily in French . . . a language of childhood . . . and nevertheless meditated upon cautiously, like the language of children who were for a long time mute—oysters who were mistaken for stones."[125] All that remains for you is to . . . compose?

J.K. I've nothing to add.

S.D. In resurrecting the historian Anna Comnena, you seem to be investigating the enigma of the intellectual woman:

> First raised on the teachings of ancient cultures, she further enriched her mind with studies of the quadrivium of the sciences: astrology, geometry, arithmetic, and music plus the trivium—grammar, rhetoric, and dialectics—that is the foundation of all cultures, as I'm sure you know.[126]

Surely an exception in those early days of Europe? You often cast backward through time in search of models or peers. You're a fan of Teresa of Avila, of Émilie du Châtelet . . .

J.K. It's not because the narrator travels through time that she doesn't live in the present. I feel sorry for our epoch and, I'm afraid, for your generation with its forgetfulness of history. Except, at best, when there's a duty to commemorate it. Maybe the Web wiped out time? I told you from the first that I write fiction in order *to touch time*. Present, past, future—they sometimes rear up like a great vertical *now*, together, not passing and not disappearing either, crisscrossing one another. I don't identify with the great figures of the past: the narrator puts them together, disputes them, mocks them, dies from them. Alongside Comnena stand Cassini, the astronomer, and Teresa of Avila.

S.D. You also project us into contemporary figures, of which your neorealities contain plenty. They include Gloria Harrison, a mother and translator, each member of whose entourage could have decapitated her in *Possessions*; the psychoanalyst Marianne Baruch and Mr. King, the *PsychMag* journalist, in *The Enchanted Clock*, and many more. Not forgetting Commissioner Northrop Rilsky, Stephanie's friend and lover in Santa Barbara, who reappears in *The Enchanted Clock*. Is he a cop or a hit man? He's not too sure himself; in *Murder in Byzantium* he momentarily thinks he's Xiao Chang, the terrorist Chinese student (a premonition?) who signs with the alias "Infinite" and is preparing an atrocity . . . but how can crime be tracked unless one is *part* of it?

J.K. If you look for me in these pages, you won't find my photograph, it's not there; but Commissioner Rilsky, a composite of the traits of a few close friends, also represents my detective side. And the female characters are not chosen at random. I am captivated by the unknown, it absorbs me when fleshing out time. Europe is not merely a bankrupt Greece or colonial culpability; it encompasses a vast heritage including Greece's neighbor Bulgaria, as it happens; and the amazing Anna Comnena, who found Western crusaders dirty and coarse—what a woman, completely overlooked alas by online surfers in a hurry; and of course the Byzantine that I am, a Holberg Prize winner, it goes without saying. As for the icon of French feminism, Émilie du Châtelet, she adored Leibniz as much as she did Voltaire, her boundless passion inhabited her like a true monad—and yet she died in childbirth, at the age of forty-three!

I'm grateful for the opportunity to evoke that universe, that multiverse, of which I'm not aware while writing, for it carries me along and I don't stop to justify myself. In such a whirlwind, you'll admit, the many tangles elicit as much astonishment as irony. And you ask me whether time, thus opened wide, is a model or a foil, tragic or comic!

S.D. All the same, in *Murder in Byzantium* only the character of Jerry escapes this corrosive effervescence. He remains beyond the reach of irony.[127]

J.K. Yes. David takes different names in my novels: as Alex, Jerry, Paul, or Stan, I watch him develop and become himself. Sometimes I tell him off, but he senses my weakness, and only listens to his father.

S.D. You spent a few years with a surprising "roommate": St. Teresa of Avila. *Teresa, My Love* was hailed by critics and readers alike, deeply affected by your tenderness for the baroque saint and won over by your analysis. At the Théâtre de l'Odéon, Isabelle Huppert recited the feverish words you address, or attribute, to "your" Teresa:

> Hail Teresa, borderless woman, physical hysterical erotic epileptic, made word, made flesh, who unravels inside and outside herself, tides of images without pictures, tumults of words, cascades of florescence. . . . A veritable twin of Christ . . . or Him in the deepest part of me, me Teresa. . . . The path that is pain, the Nothingness of everything, that everything which is nothing, do what is in you to do, but gaily, be cheerful . . . games are allowed, oh yes, even in a cloister . . . God loves us to be playful, believe me . . . Jesus loved women . . . checkmate to God too . . . souls that love can see all the way into atoms . . . infinite atoms that

> are atoms of love . . . oh yes, Teresa, my sister, invisible, ecstatic, eccentric, beside yourself in you, beside yourself in me, yes, Teresa, my love, yes.[128]

What lies behind this lucid "fusion"?

J.K. Fusion? You're joking! It came to my attention that French Catholics knew as little as I did about Teresa of Avila, which is to say practically nothing. She is often muddled up with "little" Thérèse of Lisieux, and even with Our Lady of Fatima! She was an extravagant mystic, all suffering and sensuality, highly spiritual, and a self-defined businesswoman. She was also a great writer. Now and then in *Teresa, My Love* I argue with her, I get annoyed, I analyze her. Elsewhere I render a homage as close as the union I was trying to have with her. "Water is my element," she says in what she calls "my fiction," written to "convey an understanding" . . . of what? Of her communion with Jesus *como hombre*, as a man. I immersed myself in her writings, her "pure love" for John of the Cross and less pure for Jerónimo Gracián. She had a major influence on such giants of European culture as Leibniz, Bossuet, the younger Haydn, Diderot, Edith Stein . . .

It involved ten years of reading, including biographies, feminist texts, and theological tomes. Our room-share threatened to last forever. I had to give up on the "little psychoanalysis book" requested by my friend Frédéric Boyer and go back to Fayard. The monologue you quoted above is written and spoken by Sylvia Leclercq, a psychoanalyst narrator with some likeness to me; it imposed itself on me as a paean, echoing Molly's speech at the end of *Ulysses*. A holy hysteria, holy epilepsy, holy traversal of the frontiers separating the body and the soul. Holy fiction, holy saint.

S.D. The English translation of this book recently won an award in the United States.

J.K. Yes, the prize for best humanities translation of 2015! Thanks to the excellent Lorna Scott Fox. For her 500th birthday we treated Teresa to a loving reading in the language of globalization! As for the monologue, following the Odéon performance it was adapted into a play, *Tandis qu'elle agonise, Thérèse mon amour* (As she lay dying, Teresa my love), staged in Zagreb (with Alma Prica, 2014) and in Genoa (with Carla Peirolero, 2015). At the International Conference in Avila, I was fortunate enough to discuss the saint with Cristiana Dobner, an Italian Carmelite reputed to be one of today's greatest experts on Teresa. I also met Indian and Southeast Asian Carmelites who realized, reading about "my" Teresa in English, that their *Madre* was also a modern woman. UNESCO regards her as a part of our world heritage.

S.D. Let us now look at your latest novel, *The Enchanted Clock*. Here the reader will recognize your personal passions, your love life, your care for your nearest and dearest and for the world, from Versailles to the cosmos. When exactly did this strange clock begin to figure in your existence?

J.K. The older I get, the more time is my main protagonist. It has been so ever since *The Samurai* and *The Old Man and the Wolves*, with Olga landing in Paris and Septicius Clarus assassinated in Santa Barbara, present and past intertwined. My book on Proust, written in parallel to the Santa Barbara series, propelled me into *The Sense of Time* (1994). In *Possessions*, time collapses into crime; in *Murder in Byzantium*, it's the convulsions of Europe that catch up with me; while the outside-time of the unconscious dilates the ecstasies of *Teresa, My Love*. I felt an urge to make time tangible. A hopeless challenge, for it is only embodied when it escapes in fleeting events, flashes, interludes . . . And then I remembered the astronomical clock, set to mark the hours, minutes, seconds, and thirds all the way to the year 9999, which I'd seen with David in Louis XV's clock room. The Versailles archives contained exhaustive data on the object and almost nothing on its designer. I threw myself into the hunt for him, and after countless documentary searches, scouting expeditions and cross-checks, I discovered the obscure, the splendid, the unpredictable Claude-Siméon Passemant! And the dawn of the Enlightenment, in the unrest of Paris and the reflective theater of Versailles.

The astronomer-clockmaker ultimately incarnated my desire for France, as expressed by my character Nivi, whose name means "my word" in Hebrew. Our narrator is once again a psychoanalyst. On the verge of drowning, she is rescued by Theo, a learned astrophysicist, who calculates time in astronomic figures by measuring the vibrations from the primordial cosmological background. The novel is constructed as a collider of various timescales: Nivi, her son Stan, and Theo share a time with the android clock 9999, and with interstellar outside-time. Fit to make you dizzy, but now in a very special version of happiness in which we recognize the resilience of the modern woman, mother, and lover, among other roles. Traits borrowed from Philippe and David may equally be glimpsed, for they are among the more hidden prototypes of this cyclotron-novel. Documentation, history, projection, poetry, meditation: I tightened, paced, cut, and rearranged. Because the stronger the energy, the shorter the wavelength in duration regained. So the writing unfolds in flashes, in the explosion of linear time, the expansion of original light.

S.D. To plumb time is also to speak of its end. Does death frighten you?

J.K. Not really. Illness, helplessness, palliative conditions, yes, all that is frightening. David's life after me, after us, I think about that as well, I dwell on it in my correspondence with Jean Vanier. I heard recently that a friend had died in his sleep, aged ninety-four. Don't you think that's marvelous? To die while you're dreaming. I'd like that. But there's no rush! No, time is multiple in *The Enchanted Clock*, but my favorite version is the kind of happiness discovered by Émilie du Châtelet. That mathematician of infinity includes it in a subtle substance she dubs "fire," her intuition of the "dark matter" that preoccupies modern physics. And the core of passion she calls *bonheur*, happiness—granting that it's a kind of illusion, but a necessary one, so long as you manage not only to create it but to enjoy it. That's what Émilie thinks, and Nivi along with her . . . Émilie, a key character of my novel, forms a counterpoint to the clockmaker. He masters time, she spends it, she plays with it. That artistry, that natural pleasure and sixth sense, is love. Not the "good old blustering love" derided by Colette.[129] But the joy of a sharing whose illusions are endlessly outplayed and replayed. Illusion, from the Latin *ludo*: I play. Happiness is the investment of this game, this concentration. Like a novel.

Julia Kristeva and Samuel Dock

Paris
January 2015 to July 2016

NOTES

1. Julia Kristeva, *Pulsions du temps* (Paris: Fayard, 2013); *Passions of Our Time*, trans. Constance Borde and Sheila Malovany-Chevallier (New York: Columbia University Press, 2019).

2. Samuel Dock, "Julia Kristeva: Un Espoir pour la pensée, une promesse de liberté," HuffPost, January 27, 2014, last modified October 5, 2016, http://www.huffingtonpost.fr/samuel-dock/julia-kristeva-philosophie_b_4672955.html

3. Julia Kristeva, "My Alphabet; or, How I Am a Letter," in Kristeva, *Passions of Our Time*, 3–10; *Pulsions du temps*, 15–23.

4. Julia Kristeva, *Murder in Byzantium*, trans. C. Jon Delogu (New York: Columbia University Press, 2006), 183–84; *Meurtre à Byzance* (Paris: Fayard, 2004), 281.

5. Julia Kristeva, *Au risque de la pensée* (La Tour d'Aigues: l'Aube, 2001).

6. [In Spanish, *marrano* (pig) also means a forcibly converted Jew who practiced his faith in secret.—Tr.]

7. Victor Hugo, *Les Misérables*, trans. Lee Fahnestock and Norman MacAfee (New York: Signet Classic, 1987), 954.

8. Ibid., 704.

9. Ibid., 955.

10. Victor Hugo, "On a Barricade," in *The Works of Victor Hugo*, vol. IX, ed. Henry Llewellyn Williams, trans. Nelson R. Tyerman (Boston: Jefferson, 1907), 273.

11. Ibid., 274.

12. Julia Kristeva, "Freud: The Heart of the Matter," in *Passions of Our Time*, 68; *Pulsions du temps*, 150.

13. Julia Kristeva, *The Old Man and the Wolves*, trans. Barbara Bray (New York: Columbia University Press, 1994), 97; *Le Vieil Homme et les loups* (Paris: Fayard, 1991), 138–39.

14. [Jean Bruller (1902–1991), alias Vercors, was a French writer and illustrator of Hungarian descent, and cofounder of Les Éditions de Minuit. A respected novelist during the postwar and thaw periods, he has since fallen into neglect.—Tr.]

15. [In 1978 the KGB used a ricin-injecting umbrella to assassinate a Bulgarian dissident, Georgi Markov, in London. Kostov himself escaped a similar umbrella attempt in the Paris metro.—Tr.]

16. Julia Kristeva, *Micropolitique* (La Tour d'Aigues: l'Aube, 2001); *Chroniques du temps sensible* (La Tour d'Aigues: l'Aube, 2003).

17. [Pierre Daix (1922–2014), *résistant*, journalist, novelist, and literary and art historian. A friend of Aragon and Picasso, he wrote about both during his prolific and influential career.—Tr.]

18. Julia Kristeva, *The Samurai* (New York: Columbia University Press, 1992), 7; *Les Samouraïs* (Paris: Fayard, 1990), 15.

19. Colette, *La Naissance du jour*, in *Oeuvres complètes*, tome III (Paris: Pléiade, Gallimard), 349. [Colette's phrase is cited several times in Kristeva's writings, notably in

Colette, trans. Jane Marie Todd (New York: Columbia University Press, 2004) (volume 3 of the "female genius" trilogy), 210.—Ed.]

20. See Julia Kristeva, "Bakhtine, le mot, le dialogue et le roman," *Critique* 20, no. 13 (April 1967): 438–65.

21. [There used to be two different kinds of "thesis" in France. Kristeva wrote the work published as *Le Texte du roman* for the first one, sometimes called "thèse du troisième cycle." For the second, long thesis, also called "thèse d'état" or "doctorat d'état," she wrote the work published as *La Révolution du langage poétique*.—Ed.]

22. G. W. F. Hegel, *Phenomenology of Spirit*, trans. A. V. Miller (Oxford and New York: Oxford University Press, 1997), 35 (translation modified).

23. [An unsent telegram from the German military attaché, discovered in 1896, that for Zola and others confirmed the innocence of Captain Dreyfus.—Tr.]

24. Kristeva, *The Samurai*, 285; *Les Samouraïs*, 381.

25. Julia Kristeva, *Revolution in Poetic Language*, trans. Margaret Waller (New York: Columbia University Press, 1984), part I, "The Semiotic and the Symbolic," 19–106; *La Révolution du langage poétique: L'Avant-garde à la fin du XIXe siècle, Lautréamont et Mallarmé* (Paris: Seuil, 1974), 17–100.

26. Kristeva, *The Samurai*, 181–82; *Les Samouraïs*, 242–43.

27. [The Couvent des Cordeliers is a fourteenth-century monastery, home to the Cordeliers Club during the Revolution. Today its great Refectory hosts a range of cultural events.—Tr.]

28. Roman Jakobson, "On a Generation That Squandered Its Poets," trans. Edward J. Brown, in Edward J. Brown, ed., *Major Soviet Writers: Essays in Criticism* (New York: Oxford University Press, 1973).

29. Mikhail Bakhtine, *La Poétique de Dostoïevski* (Paris: Seuil, 1967); *Problems of Dostoyevsky's Poetics*, trans. Caryl Emerson (Minneapolis: University of Minnesota Press, 1984).

30. See Mikhail Bakhtin, *Rabelais and His World*, trans. Hélène Iswolsky (Bloomington: Indiana University Press, 1984).

31. Julia Kristeva, Preface to Émile Benveniste, *Dernières Leçons: Collège de France 1968 et 1969* (Paris: EHESS-Gallimard-Seuil, 2012), 14.

32. Ibid.

33. Friedrich Nietzsche, *The Anti-Christ, Ecce Homo, Twilight of the Idols, and Other Writings*, ed. Aaron Ridley and Judith Norman, trans. Judith Norman (Cambridge: Cambridge University Press, 2005), 99; *Ecco homo*, trans. Alexandre Vialatte (Paris: Gallimard, 1942), 67.

34. Charles d'Orléans, "Fortunes Stabilnes," in Mary-Jo Arn, ed., *The Fortunes Stabilnes: Charles of Orleans's English Book of Love* (Binghamton: SUNY Press, Medieval and Renaissance Texts and Studies, 1994).

35. See above, page 32.

36. [A reference to the multivolume *Oeuvres romanesques croisées d'Elsa Triolet et Aragon*.—Tr.]

37. Kristeva, *Colette*, 246; *Le Génie féminin*, t. III, *Colette* (Paris: Fayard, 2002), 331.

38. Roland Barthes, "L'Étrangère," *Quinzaine littéraire* 94 (May 1–15, 1970).

39. Philippe Sollers, interviewed by Frédéric Joignot, "Il manque, Voltaire, là!" *Le Monde*, April 11, 2015: 5.

40. [Kristeva develops the notion of *hainamouration* (hatelove) from Lacan, a neologism that highlights that love and hate are entwined in an inextricable interaction. See, for example, Jacques Lacan, *On Feminine Sexuality, The Limits of Love and Knowledge: Encore, The Seminar of Jacques Lacan Book XX*, ed. Jacques-Alain Miller, trans. Bruce Fink (New York: Norton, 1998).—Ed.]

41. Alan Sokal and Jean Bricmont, *Impostures Intellectuelles* (Paris: Odile Jacob, 1997); *Fashionable Nonsense* (New York: Picador, 1998).

42. Philippe Sollers, *L'Étoile des amants* (Paris: Gallimard, 2002), 12, 17.

43. Julia Kristeva, *The Enchanted Clock*, trans. Armine Kotin Mortimer (New York: Columbia University Press, 2019), 6, 8, 58, 59; *L'Horloge enchantée* (Paris: Fayard, 2015), 16, 17–18, 87, 88.

44. Kristeva, *The Samurai*, 232; *Les Samouraïs*, 308, 309.

45. Julia Kristeva, "L'Engendrement de la formule," in *Sémiotikè: Recherches pour une sémanalyse* (Paris: Seuil, 1969); *Polylogue* (Paris: Seuil, 1977). Philippe Sollers, *Nombres, roman* (Paris: Seuil, 1968).

46. Philippe Sollers, *H*, trans. Veronika Stankovianska and David Vichnar (London: Equus, 2015); *H, roman* (Paris: Seuil, 1973).

47. Philippe Sollers, *Lois, roman* (Paris: Seuil, 1972); *Paradis* (Paris: Points, English and French edition, 2001).

48. Philippe Sollers, *Un vrai roman* (Paris: Plon, 2007); *Les Voyageurs du temps* (Paris: Gallimard, 2009); *L'Éclaircie* (Paris: Gallimard, 2012); *L'École du mystère* (Paris: Gallimard, 2015); *Mouvement* (Paris: Gallimard, 2016).

49. Karl Marx and Frederick Engels, *The Communist Manifesto* (New York: Verso, 1998), 77.

50. Jean-Paul Sartre, *Words*, trans. Irene Clephane (London: Hamish Hamilton, 1964), 173.

51. Mao Tse-Tung, "The Situation and Our Policy After the Victory in the War of Resistance Against Japan" (August 13, 1945), in *Selected Works of Mao Tse-Tung*, vol. IV (Peking: Foreign Languages, 1969), 20.

52. ["Singing tomorrows," a communist slogan of the 1930s, from a poem by Paul Vaillant-Couturier. Aragon edited the French Communist Party's literary supplement to be highly critical of Stalinism.—Tr.]

53. Virginia Woolf, *A Writer's Diary* (New York: Houghton Mifflin Harcourt, 1982), 87.

54. Virginia Woolf, *A Room of One's Own* (New York: Harcourt Brace, 1991), 120.

55. Virginia Woolf, *Mrs. Dalloway* (New York: Modern Library, 1928), 181.

56. Virginia Woolf, *Orlando: A Biography* (New York: Houghton Mifflin Harcourt, 2012), 217.

57. Colette, *Break of Day*, trans. Enid McLeod (New York: Farrar, Straus and Giroux, 2002), 16; *La Naissance du jour*, 285.

58. Colette, *Looking Backwards*, trans. David Le Vay (London: Peter Owen, 1975), 60; *Journal à rebours* (Paris: Fayard, 2004), 178.

59. Colette, *The Vagabond*, trans. Enid McLeod (New York: Farrar, Straus and Giroux, 1955), 28; *La Vagabonde*, in *Oeuvres completes de Colette*, t. IV (Paris: Flammarion, 1949), 31.

60. "While a mother is still unaware of the embryo coming to life inside her, her body already knows. It experiences a shock: the graft that is going to enlarge you starts by diminishing you. . . . You're not a single person anymore—you're double. . . . The other that is inside you reveals that you are an other. Not human. Minor, but supreme. Your eyes go on following the performance in which you move about, vague, visionary (getting together diapers, baby clothes, the stroller, the cot, all on top of your ordinary work), but they're not really looking at what's in front of them. They are turned inward, though they can see nothing, sight becomes hearing and touch, you're floating in a capsule of pleasure and anxiety (who knows how it will all turn out!). Pregnancy is the modern version of ecstasy. That's how it was for Olga too." Kristeva, *The Samurai*, 306–7; *Les Samouraïs*, 409–10.

61. Kristeva, *The Enchanted Clock*, 317.

62. [A *chantier républicain* is here a presidential initiative involving working groups and research in civil society.—Tr.]

63. Julia Kristeva, *Teresa, My Love: An Imagined Life of the Saint of Avila*, trans. Lorna Scott Fox (New York: Columbia University Press, 2015), 26.

64. Julia Kristeva, *Lettre au president de la République sur les citoyens en situation de handicap: à l'usage de ceux qui le sont et de ceux qui ne le sont pas* (Paris: Fayard, 2003).

65. [Patrick Poivre d'Arvor (b. 1947), a TV journalist and writer, known as PPDA. Claire Chazal (b. 1956), a TV journalist and novelist. Serge Moati (b. 1946), a journalist, actor, and TV and film director and producer. Jean-Louis Borloo (b. 1951), a politician who, as Employment Minister under President Chirac, developed a "social cohesion plan" dubbed Plan Borloo.—Tr.]

66. [Turbulences is a theater company working since 1992 with people with learning difficulties or autism. *Le Papotin* is a paper run by young people with similar special needs.—Tr.]

67. Charles Baudelaire, "Recueillement," Spleen et idéal, *Les Fleurs du mal*, in *Oeuvres complètes*, t. I (Paris: Michel Lévy frères, 1868), 239.

68. Julia Kristeva and Jean Vanier, *Leur regard perce nos ombres* (Paris: Fayard, 2011).

69. Ibid., 67.

70. [The standard English translation has "Santa Varvara." Here the translation has reverted to the original "Santa Barbara."—Tr.]

71. [The Kristeva Circle was founded in 2011 and holds annual international meetings of Kristeva scholars and those interested in her work. It is directed by Kelly Oliver at Vanderbilt University, Fanny Soderbäck at DePaul University, and Sarah Hansen at California State Northridge, www.kristevacircle.org.—Ed.]

72. Roland Barthes, "L'Étrangère," in *Oeuvres complètes*, t. 3, *Livres, textes, entretiens 1968–1971* (Paris: Seuil, 2002), 477.

73. Julia Kristeva, *Folle Vérité* (Paris, Seuil, 1979).

74. Louis-Ferdinand Céline, *Death on the Installment Plan*, trans. John H. P. Marks (New York: Little, Brown and Company, 1938), 29 (translation modified); *Mort à crédit*, in *Romans*, t. I (Paris: Bibliothèque de la Pléiade, Gallimard, 1981), 536.

75. Julia Kristeva, *Contre la dépression nationale* (Paris: Textuel, 1988).

76. [*La psychose blanche*, elaborated in psychoanalysis by André Green and Jean-Luc Bonnet, is defined as borderline, nonhallucinatory psychosis, often accompanied by a mental blank or absence.—Tr.]

77. [Édouard Balladur (b. 1929) was Prime Minister under President Mitterrand from 1993 to 1995.—Tr.]

78. See Julia Kristeva, *The Sense and Non-sense of Revolt: The Powers and Limits of Psychoanalysis Volume 1*, trans. Jeanine Herman (New York: Columbia University Press), ch. 4.

79. Jean-Paul Sartre, *Being and Nothingness*, trans. Hazel E. Barnes (New York: Philosophical Library, 1956), 25 (translation modified); *L'Être et le néant* (Paris: Gallimard, 1943), 61.

80. See Roland Barthes, *Writing Degree Zero and Elements of Semiology*, trans. Annette Lavers and Colin Smith (London: Jonathan Cape, 1984), 15; *Le Degré zéro de l'écriture* (Paris: Seuil 1972), 14.

81. Charles Baudelaire, "La Servante au grand Coeur," in *Les Fleurs du mal*.

82. Marcel Proust, *Le Temps retrouvé*, IV (Paris: Pléiade, 1989), 469.

83. Among the founders of this new Noah's Ark was a group of young litterateurs in love with Lacanian psychoanalysis: Marie Depussé, Jean-Yves Pouilloux, André Lacaux with Marie-Claire Dumas, Anne-Marie Christin, Georges Benrekassa, Maurice Laugaa, Pierre Chartier . . . And scholars hailing from other universities: Philippe Forest, a theorist of contemporary literature, and two philosophers, Bruno Clément, who headed the Collège de Philosophie, and François Noudelmann, who invited me onto his program at France Culture.

84. [*The Port-Royal Grammar* (1660) by the Jansenists Antoine Arnauld and Claude Lancelot was a pioneering work on speech and language influenced by Descartes.—Tr.]

85. Marcel Proust, "Lettre 166: À Lucien Daudet" (November 27, 1913), in *Correspondance*, t. XII (Paris: Plon, 1970), 343.

86. Julia Kristeva, *Hatred and Forgiveness*, trans. Jeanine Herman (New York: Columbia University Press, 2010).

87. Julia Kristeva, *This Incredible Need to Believe*, trans. Beverley Bie Brahic (New York: Columbia University Press, 2009).

88. Hannah Arendt, *The Human Condition* (Chicago: The University of Chicago Press, 1998), 179; *Condition de l'homme moderne* (Paris: Calmann-Lévy, 1983), 236.

89. Jacques Lacan, "The Youth of Gide, or the Letter and Desire," in *Écrits*, trans. Bruce Fink (New York: Norton, 2006), 632; "Jeunesse de Gide ou la lettre et le désir," in *Écrits* (Paris: Seuil, 1966), 750.

90. [A thirteenth-century Cistercian training college, today a pluridisciplinary center "dedicated to the hopes and questions of our society and their encounter with Christian wisdom," https://www.collegedesbernardins.fr/a-propos.—Tr.]

91. [The politicians named here by Samuel Dock include four presidents (Mitterrand, Chirac, Sarkozy, Hollande), holding office from 1981 to 2017, the first and last from the Socialist Party, the others from the center-right UMP. The other figures likewise span the moderate-liberal spectrum and stand out for their engagement with cultural or social affairs.—Tr.]

92. Bruno Le Maire, *Musique absolue: Une répétition avec Carlos Kleiber* (Paris: Gallimard, 2012).

93. Catherine Clément and Julia Kristeva, *The Feminine and the Sacred*, trans. Jane Marie Todd (New York: Columbia University Press, 2001); *Le Féminin et le sacré* (Paris: Stock, 1998).

94. Catherine Clément and Julia Kristeva, *Le Féminin et le sacré* (Paris: Albin Michel, 2015).

95. Kristeva, *Au risque de la pensée.*

96. [The International Cultural Center carries on a long cultural tradition that started in Pontigny in 1910 and has been based in Cerisy since 1952. Its annual summer colloquiums feature artists, scholars, and public figures, attracting a numerous public from France and abroad. Edith Heurgon, director since 2015, invited Julia Kristeva to preside over a Colloquium around her oeuvre, in June, 2020.—Tr.]

97. The "*honnête homme*" is an ideal model of balanced, moderate, middle-class manhood who emerged in seventeenth-century literature: Boileau, Montaigne, Molière . . .

98. [See note 71, above.—Ed.]

99. Julia Kristeva, "Thinking about Liberty in Dark Times," https://www.holbergprisen.no/en/holberg-lecture-2004-thinking-about-liberty-dark-times.

100. [Since 1999, the VIZE 97 Prize (also Vision 97 Award) has been awarded by the Dagmar and Václav Havel Foundation to significant thinkers in the scientific domain. See http://www.vize.cz/en/—Tr.]

101. ["In some circumstances, my dear sir, the question is worth more than the answer" (112, above).—Ed.]

102. Julia Kristeva, "Freud: The Heart of the Matter," in *Passions of Our Time*, 67; *Pulsions du temps*, 151.

103. Kristeva, *Pulsions du temps*, 661.

104. Kristeva, *The Samurai*, 309, 310; *Les Samouraïs*, 413, 414.

105. Ibid., 337; *Les Samouraïs*, 453–54.

106. [A gilt rococo clock at Versailles, standing over two meters high, acquired by Louis XV in 1750. For Julia Kristeva and the British artist Anish Kapoor in conversation about it at Versailles, see "Julia Kristeva Anish Kapoor 'Dans les entrailles de Versailles,'" https://vimeo.com/135016636.—Tr.]

107. [Claude-Siméon Passemant (1702–1769), clockmaker and optician, appointed Ingénieur du Roi in 1740. Émilie du Châtelet (1706–1749), natural philosopher, mathemati-

cian, and physicist. Lover and collaborator of Voltaire, her major works are *Institutions de physique* (1740) and a translation of Newton's *Principia* (1749), still the standard version in French.—Tr.]

108. Kristeva, *The Enchanted Clock*, 229, 230–31; *L'Horloge enchantée*, 315, 316, 317.

109. Julia Kristeva, *L'Avenir d'une révolte* (Paris: Flammarion, 2012), 68. [This work is translated as the second part of the English translation of *La Révolte intime: Pouvoirs et limites da la psychoanalyse II* (Paris: Fayard, 1997). See Julia Kristeva, *Intimate Revolt: The Powers and Limits of Psychoanalysis Volume 2* (New York: Columbia University Press, 2002, 244.—Ed.]

110. Kristeva, *Murder in Byzantium*, 64–65; *Meurtre à Byzance*, 113–14.

111. Kristeva, *The Samurai*, 258; *Les Samouraïs*, 343–44.

112. John Charles Tarver, ed., *Gustave Flaubert as Seen in His Works and Correspondence* (London: Archibald Constable and Company, 1895), 296. Flaubert à Guy de Maupassant, Croisset, 19 février 1880, in Gustave Flaubert, *Correspondance*, t. 4 (Paris: Bibliothèque-Charpentier, 1924), 375.

113. Kristeva, *The Old Man and the Wolves*, 109; *Le Vieil Homme et les loups*, 155.

114. Friedrich Nietzsche, Preface to *Daybreak: Thoughts on the Prejudices of Morality* (Cambridge: Cambridge University Press, 1997), § 5.

115. Kristeva, *The Old Man and the Wolves*, 6; *Le Vieil Homme et les loups*, 16.

116. Kristeva, *Murder in Byzantium*, 185–86; *Meurtre à Byzance*, 283–84.

117. Kristeva, *The Old Man and the Wolves*, 76; *Le Vieil Homme et les loups*, 112.

118. Ibid., 38; *Le Vieil Homme et les loups*, 60.

119. Julia Kristeva, *Possessions*, trans. Barbara Bray (New York: Columbia University Press, 1998), 52; *Possessions* (Paris: Fayard, 1996), 74.

120. Julia Kristeva, *Visions capitales* (Paris: Éditions de la réunion des musées nationaux, 1998); *Visions capitales: Arts et rituels de la décapitations* (Paris: Éditions de la Martinière, 2013); *The Severed Head: Capital Visions*, trans. Jody Gladding (New York: Columbia University Press, 2012).

121. Kristeva, *Murder in Byzantium*, 64 (translation modified to Santa Barbara); *Meurtre à Byzance*, 112–13.

122. Ibid., 168; *Meurtre à Byzance*, 260.

123. Kristeva, *The Old Man and the Wolves*, 140; *Le Vieil Homme et les loups*, 201.

124. Kristeva, *The Enchanted Clock*, 110; *L'Horloge enchantée*, 153.

125. Kristeva, *Murder in Byzantium*, 63; *Meurtre à Byzance*, 112.

126. Ibid., 113; *Meurtre à Byzance*, 184.

127. Ibid., 233; *Meurtre à Byzance*, 351.

128. Kristeva, *Teresa, My Love*, 26–27; *Thérèse mon amour* (Paris: Fayard, 2008), 40–41.

129. Colette, *My Apprenticeships*, trans. Helen Beauclerk (London: Secker and Warburg, 1957), 103; *Mes apprentissages*, in *Oeuvres*, t. III (Paris: Gallimard, 1991), 1053.

PART TWO

DESCRIPTIVE AND CRITICAL ESSAYS WITH REPLIES

1

Dominique Ducard

THE *SEMIOTIC CHORA* AND THE INNER LIFE OF LANGUAGE

Benveniste concludes one of his last articles with a call to "go beyond" the linguistics of signs and take account of the semantic dimension of discourse.[1] Following the semiology envisaged by Saussure, he announces a "second-generation" semiology, which is both "intralinguistic" and "translinguistic," aspiring to a "metasemantics" built on a "semantics of utterance." The semantic order is identified with the world of verbal acts and discourse. The reference to a semantics of utterance therefore indicates, first and foremost, an opening up of linguistic studies to the subject, history, and society, with an interest in anthropology, mythology, literary theory, psychology, and psychoanalysis. This call to go beyond theory is not very explicit but may be understood better in the light of Benveniste's particular regard for the work of Barthes and Kristeva.

Barthes's "semiological adventure" underwent various phases, from a psychosociology of the signs of human communication—underpinned by a commitment to social criticism—to a desire to discern a method for objectively analyzing meaning. He subsequently abandoned the second quest, highlighting instead the subjectivity of the analyst and the intimacy of the act of reading and interpreting a text. It then remained for him to deal with the transfer to his chosen object, moving from the original question, "here is the world: is there any meaning in it?" to the question, "what's meaning *for me*?"[2] When he entered the Collège de France in 1977, to take up the chair of literary semiology, he was in his fourth phase—that of a "morality" of the sign and of a "second semiology," which he tells us is "the body's thought in a state of language."[3] His model is a semiology of music, which permits a better understanding of

Translated from French by Rosemary Rodwell.

the text's *signifiance*. An ethics of form is replaced by an ethics of *aesthesia* or sensibility, still based on language but a language full of affects. This "second semiology" is not the "second-generation" semiology referred to by Benveniste, even though Barthes is indebted to him for the notion of *signifiance*, which Kristeva traces back to the *modi significandi* of Modist grammar (second half of the twelfth century).[4] Benveniste has Saussure's project in mind; he is probably also referring to "semanalysis," and the "translinguistic analysis of texts and works" he is planning recalls the notion of intertextuality introduced by Kristeva—a reader of Bakhtin—or of what she was to call a "supralinguistics."[5] In this set of cross-references and reciprocal influences, we should point out that Barthes publicly recognized the major impact of Kristeva's theoretical thinking on his own work; and that Lacan, too, in his seminar, demonstrated the attention he paid to her work, particularly upon the publication of *La Révolution du langage poétique*.[6]

My purpose here is not to unravel the historical web of concepts or to retrace a semiotic route. Rather, by adopting the path followed by Kristeva in her questioning of meaning, I shall attempt to take from semanalysis what can be clarified by lateral views in order to show its impact on complex thinking about language. In order to do this, I first review the major initial concepts, before proceeding to examine afresh what appears to me to be a fundamental notion, that of the *semiotic chora*; this will lead on to the question of what links language to life, in its diversity as well as its unity.

I. Since Semanalysis

1. A Critical Epistemology of Meaning

In her semiotic lexicon, Rey-Debove gives this short definition of semanalysis: "The theory of the meaning of discourse and texts taking account of the speaking subject's involvement."[7] She specifies that she is talking about the split subject (conscious/unconscious) of psychoanalysis. This represented a psychoanalytic turning point for semiology and, in order for the relationship between language theory and the theory of the unconscious to take shape, it was necessary, Kristeva tells us, "from Freud and Lacan onwards, for semiology to be transformed, to be alert to the unconscious, in a *semanalysis* that makes an object of study out of what has always been excluded from epistemological scrutiny, namely the *production* of meaning and its *work*."[8]

The general semiotic project that Kristeva outlined in the 1970s calls into question the very foundations of semiological knowledge: the sign, the subject, and its sociohistorical position. The increased number of meanings and subjects of utterance, both psychological and social, is supported by references to psychoanalysis and a materialist philosophy of Marxist inspiration. Added to this was the proposal for a possible formal modeling of the generation of meaning. The introduction of psychoanalytic thinking into *semiosis* aimed to open up reflection on signs and systems to the material, tangible, social and historical *production* of signifying practices.[9] The work gathered together to form the first *Recherches pour une sémanalyse* ends with a complete annotated index of the fundamental concepts that enable the problems to be grasped in all their originality.[10] Kristeva indicates that some of these concepts are taken from different authors and that the studies presented "merely *set out* an *open* topic of analysis."[11] Reading this index reveals the main themes of an original plan, perceived through an abundance of theory that is disconcerting to begin with. Emphasizing the complexity of signifying activity, Kristeva notes that the place of semiotics can only be specified by means of a general theory of symbolic functioning, whose development supposes a semiological approach. The "science of discourse" thus hoped for could only be conceived of in connection with other scientific fields. Since the semiology of the future had to be radically critical, not only did the related sciences become its "*challenged object*" and the borrowed concepts "subverted premises," but the theoretical edifice under construction was itself being undermined. This "troubled theory of the non-representable" could therefore only allow itself "intervention-concepts" and subsequently abandon the idea of a "supralinguistics."

2. Formalism and Analogy

The new semiology called for the development of models conceived of as formal systems, whose structure was analogous to the structure of the systems studied. Asserting, while at the same time transcending the incompatibility between the logic of a closed scientific system and the signifying practices whose language is "potentially infinite," a "set of abbreviations (numbers)" had to be found, which would be capable of describing how these practices worked. The use of formulae, theorems, and axioms taken from set theory, metamathematics, and symbolic logic, was justified by the search for an artificial language of isomorphic variables for the diverse semiotics being studied. It was, in fact, the paragrammatic conception of poetic language, inherited from Saussure's research on anagrams and leading to a tabular representation of textuality according to the image of a network of connections, which called for a formalization of material and semic relations in the dynamic space of the text. The connections first shown up by semantic analysis were converted into a pseudo-formalization founded upon the idea that it is the relationships between elements that are signifying and on an analogy between the mathematical infinite and the infinite of language. Mathematicians were able to discredit such a use of formal language, which was judged to be vague and even inconsistent. But the establishment of this principle had only metaphorical value, functioning simply as a "caricature" of the paragrammatism revealed by a more empirical description. It had to do with simulating the arrangement of sense markers that go beyond syntactic-semantic linking. This transfer of logic, when subjected to the ideal of exact knowledge, was fairly quickly abandoned.

3. Signifiance

The epistemological act that determines the semanalytical approach to texts and discourses is an opening up of the structure of the sign and the linguistic system to an "outside," so as to grasp the productive dynamic of meaning in forms, the *process of signifiance.* From this point of view, the decisive contribution is the distinction made by Freud between the latent content of dreams and the thinking manifested when recounting the dream. The discursive surface manifestation is understood as the product of distortions and misrepresentations of another underlying text, of a different scene, which the analyst-interpreter reconstructs by means of the subject's associative language. The conception of a dream's *work*, with mechanisms for transforming thoughts through the forms in which it is expressed linguistically, under the effect of primary and secondary processes, is thus extended to other modes of representation and signification. The aim is therefore, through the text, to grasp the principles of its origin. Semanalysis can then be precisely defined as

> [a] theory of textual signification, which will consider the *sign* as the specular element, ensuring the representation of this generation—this process of germination—which both inhabits and encompasses it, and whose laws it is essential to define. In other words, without forgetting that the text presents a system of signs, semanalysis opens up another scene within this system: the scene that is hidden beneath the screen of the structure, and is *signifiance as a process whose structure is simply a marginal effect.*[12]

The text is thus split into a *phenotext*, the text as it is presented in its material, sequential composition, and a *genotext*, which is the matrix form and is reconstructed by analysis. To this distinction of method may be added the notion of *signifying differential*; it has no definite linguistic dimension, but describes a constellation of signifiers linked by formal or semic relationships. It may be considered as the trace of the "potential infinite" that characterizes language.

This model of a two-tier text is inspired by the distinction established by Chomsky in generative linguistics between deep structure and surface structure, and even more so by the contrast pointed out by the Russian linguist, Shaumyan, between genotype and phenotype.[13] The opposition does not postulate a process of genesis based on a previous text that would logically and structurally precede the development of the finished product; it indicates that meaning is the outcome of a conflict of tendencies between the circuit of representations and affects and the processes of symbolic thought. *Signifiance* describes "this *work* of differentiation, stratification and confrontation that is practiced in language."[14] The general principle of *signifiance* explained in *Revolution in Poetic Language* and taken up again later is a dual one. The text is thus the result of a dynamic tension and power movements between two production authorities: *the semiotic* and *the symbolic.*

4. The Literary Text Model

Intertextuality, taken from Bakhtin, is one of the "intervention-concepts" that was decisive for textual criticism.[15] The term *transposition* was subsequently associated with it.[16] Textual analysis has to proceed by segmentation and cross-checking, discerning what the utterances repeat and transform: the places of *dialogism*. Because of the overdetermination of signs and the conception of the text as reading-writing, produced by a dialogue between texts and cultures, semanalysis resorts to the discourses and documents of science, history, and philosophy. It situates the text in its relationship with other semiotic practices; it questions the discursive norms and aesthetic codes in which or against which the text is set.

Initial studies have privileged the works of writers considered as "sensitive" to the process of transforming culture and ways of writing (Joyce, Mallarmé, Lautréamont, Artaud, and so on). Kristeva laid down as a precondition for semiotic analysis "the ability to identify with the activity of the person producing the discourse, with the writer."[17] The commentary is then akin to a sort of renewal, in the order of conceptualization, of the act of producing the text. As for Barthes, it is about understanding the manifestation of the sensory in forms of literary writing. "Literary creation is that adventure of the body and signs that bears witness to the affect."[18] Symbolization takes place on two levels: in the drama of the passions depicted and in the forms of portrayal themselves, with the techniques of style aiming to transfer the heterogeneity of meaning into the semantic content of a language and the rhetoric of a discourse.

Semanalysis, whose name remains identified with that of its inventor, is a type of analysis with two aspects: a semiological aspect without which it would just be a philosophy or a metapsychology, and a hermeneutic aspect, without which it would merely be a branch of semiotic studies. Kristeva, like Barthes, was aware of the multiplicity and mobility of signifying elements and turned away, just as he did, from the idea of a logical, formal systematization. While pursuing, by other routes, numerous investigations into language and texts, particularly literary ones, and ever attuned to the senses transmuted into style, she resolutely took up her stand in the field of a psychoanalysis that was open to philosophy and the sciences.[19] Her work as a semiologist created a rupture in the development of language sciences. For some people, who stressed the hazardous nature of the method and the risk of interpretation being sidetracked, the approach could not claim to be scientific; while for others, including myself, it is an incentive to continue in the spirit of inquiry because of its very audacity and the challenges it poses.

II. Verbal Acts and Language Activity

I will resume this exploration of meaning and language from the viewpoint of a theory of verbal acts set within the perspective of an interpretive semiology;

this is a variant of semanalysis but free from materialist philosophy and less fully committed to psychoanalytic interpretation, reinforcing its linguistic foundation. Although I began by linking Kristeva's conceptual enterprise, at its outset, to the work of Benveniste—a major leading figure in verbal act linguistics—I turned to Culioli's theory of enunciative operations to fulfill the demand for an interpretation based on the analysis of forms, while remaining open to disciplines related to linguistics in the study of language. Very early on, Kristeva paid heed to the work of Culioli, whose early publications date back to the 1960s. She got to know him and, on several occasions, invited him to explain his theory of language, particularly through lectures at the Centre Roland-Barthes. His linguistic theory of verbal acts coincided, she states, with her own semiological investigations, going beyond the artificial separation between the "psychical apparatus" and the "language apparatus."[20]

1. Signifying Activity

According to Culioli, verbal act linguistics—also called the theory of predicative and enunciative operations—do not look like the outcome of what Benveniste appeared to be planning, even if a certain similarity of thought is evident in matching comments and comparable forms of expression. Verbal act linguistics set itself the task of studying *the cognitive-affective activity of language through the diversity of languages systems, texts, and situations.* The word *through* indicates that the aim is to use the forms of language (or languages) in texts and thus attempt to account for the operations and representations that underlie the signifying activity, and in so doing become reunited with Benveniste's psychological and anthropological preoccupations. We have to insist on language seen as an activity (Humboldt's *Tätigkeit* or *energeia*), that is to say, as both process and action. The act of utterance is defined as an activity of production and of interpretive recognition of interpretable forms (texts). It is not simply "the formal apparatus of enunciation" (Benveniste). It has its antecedents in the philosophy of language, notably among the Stoics, with the Greek *lekton* and, for Seneca, the *dictum* and the *enuntiatio*. It is also found among medieval philosophers, with the *complexe significabile* (complex signifiable) or, again, the *complexe enuntiatibile* (the complex enunciable), which we might compare with the "complex system of representation based on physical and cultural properties."[21] Epistemologically, this is the foundation of theory, at a first level of representation, namely, notional representations whose linguistic projection corresponds to a second level, that of signifying textual forms; while the third level in the model is the system of metalinguistic representation.

In this way, through the construction of observables and reasoning, the linguist seeks to simulate and understand the connections between the first two levels, by analyzing the arrangements of markers formed by utterances—the term marker referring to the perceptible sign of mental operations; these are responsible for the move from level I, of which we have merely the trace, to level II. Three levels are distinguished: (I) notional, the level connected with representations and mental operations; (II) linguistic, the level of the representatives constituted by forms; and (III) metalinguistic, the level of modeling and formalization, with a dynamic conception of the construction of meaning in texts (interpretable forms), which the analyst seeks to deconstruct and reconstruct. This distinction seems to be in harmony with the dual authority of text generation and the process of *signifiance* according to semanalysis. But the theory of enunciation would be too limited, in Kristeva's view, if it were to restrict itself to an activity dependent on an intention to signify, even if this is not reducible to a wish to speak or to an intention, conscious or nonconscious. Psychoanalytic technique—in the sense of a *technē*, an art of interpreting where conjectural reason (German *erraten*, to guess) plays a major role[22]—provides us with valuable lessons in that it follows the progress of speech from the inside, constructing and deconstructing the thought being sought; as, too, does literary creation, which gives free rein to language interpreting itself. Both of these steer us towards the idea of what it is that takes place within us during language activity, without always becoming externalized. To the "ability to identify with the activity of the person producing the discourse, with the writer," posited by Kristeva,[23] Culioli responds with this statement: "I put myself in the place of a subject who is discovering his own language and who, while he gradually organizes what will become a text in a language system, asks himself what he is doing when he does this."[24] But here, the text corresponds to a sequence, oral and written, taken from discursive exchanges that can be analyzed in the terms and with the means of formal linguistics; while the textual model of semanalysis is the literary text, a model informed by the experience of psychoanalysis. Furthermore, while the linguist's epistemological prudence limits the investigation to what can be controlled by observation, experimentation, and reasoning, semiology dares to go further in its interpretation. I shall therefore examine what is on the margins of the linguistic theory of utterance but is nonetheless hypothetically present and assumed to be active in language, which will bring us closer to the views promoted in semanalysis.

2. The Semiotic Chora *and Epilinguistics*

In a 1992 article, Kristeva asks herself the question: "Does a Freudian 'linguistics' exist?"[25] In opposition to the concept of the Cartesian subject that underpins structural and generative linguistic theories, and to the transcendental ego of Husserl's phenomenology on which pragmatics is said to be based, she takes up a position in the Freudian camp and proposes the contrasting image of a divided and conflictual subject. She then returns to the contributions of her previous work, in particular the distinction between a *semiotic chora*, linked to prelinguistic modalities of meaning, and a symbolic, existential phase. The general pattern of *signifiance* presented in *Revolution in Poetic Language* and returned to later is thus a dual one. The "semiotic *chora*" or *the semiotic* refers to that authority of *signifiance* that is this side of articulated language—the locus of the subject's drive heterogeneity that is semiotized in prelinguistic signs organized into rhythmic groupings (vocal or graphic, gestural and kinesic elements). The *symbolic system* is superimposed upon this authority; without this, utterance is not possible since the so called thetic phase—to follow Husserl's line of thinking—describes that moment of structuring in language when an identified subject differentiates himself from objects, thus marking out in his speech a position upon which the locating and setting up of relationships realized in his signifying activity is conditional. The observation of certain pathological languages, like the reading of some modern texts, can then be linked to the destabilizing irruption of the semiotic into the symbolic: the *negativity* that operates in language.

If we consider the signifying activity of language as a symbolic activity of representation, and regard enunciation linguistics as an attempt to comprehend how this operates in language; and if Kristeva's early studies were trying to "grasp through language what is foreign to its habits and disturbs its conformism"[26]—whereas for Saussure, in a little-known formulation, semiology is "the study of what happens when humans attempt to signify their thinking by means of a necessary convention"[27]—are we condemned to set two methods in opposition to one another: an investigation that is subject to empirical observation and formal analysis that can be scientifically validated over against a more conjectural interpretation of meaning?

Kristeva's thinking about language has been described as speculative and Culioli's as mentalist, and I would like to redefine here how the latter conceptualized the terms epilinguistic or epilanguage, in order to show how language as an activity, in its functioning, can include semiotics, in the sense that Kristeva gave to it, and how it can go beyond the duality of the conceptual schema.

The notion of epilinguistics was first defined as a nonconscious metalinguistic activity, in the sense that it is not conscious of itself in the way that the linguist is, and is often understood as the ordinary activity of speakers who, correcting themselves, modulating or reformulating utterances, or questioning ways of expressing themselves, manifest a preconsciousness of the language act, in the course of utterance. It serves, moreover, to describe a reflective process that is internal to language, underlying the activity of the speaker. Following the biological model of epigenesis, epilinguistics (a better word would be epilanguage), functions as a generator of forms based on forms, and as a creator of affinities and differentiation. This movement, comparable to the *clinamen* of atomists, has been described by Culioli as "permanent anamorphosis."[28] For him, epilanguage activity is of the order of "silent rationality," alongside the "rationality of explicit demonstrative performance,"[29] the rationality that operates in a discursive exchange, when one says something *for* others, *about* and *with a view to.*

This area of indeterminate meaning and its forms of expression is also linked to the idea, expressed by Wittgenstein,[30] of the "halo" surrounding a word, which is created by the possible values of this word, and might always be present in a semiconsciousness when the context and situation of a usage distinguishes one of its values. The psychologist William James also talks about the "halo" enveloping mental images, saying that there exists a feeling of unarticulated relationships and bands of affinity in the thought and words of a language, through psychic resonance.[31] For Culioli, who freely cites Wittgenstein and James and repeats this idea of a "halo," the meaning of a term is the complex of representations it triggers that, by a series of interactions, is reduced to an utterance "rich in all its related echoes, in all the paraphrastic families, because each one of the terms will evoke something else."[32] He also continually insists on the abundance, the proliferation arising from epilinguistic activity, that "chaos" hiding behind a "veil of order," as he puts it, borrowing an image from the pianist Alfred Brendel, quoting Novalis.[33] And he comments on the expression, saying that this veil—the veil of linear order—sometimes prevents the unveiling of the surface's underside, adding: "I am generalizing about language activity where, under the veil of order (syntax, schema, habitual semantics, adjustment to others), a text allows epilinguistic chaos to appear, the shimmering beneath the surface of which Mallarmé speaks."[34]

It would seem possible to assign the same language reality to the two expressions of epilinguistic "chaos" and "semiotic *chora*." We can identify it with what Lacan names "*lalangue*" and link it with the "associative chains" (Freud) reconstructed by the psychoanalyst in the text of dreams, or with what Saussure calls "associative links" between elements of language or the paragrammatism that he tested, in his own way, in his search for anagrams.

To give a more linguistic basis to this reality, let us return to Saussure's conception of language as a system of differences. This concept, according to which there are only relative and negative oppositions in language, is expressed more clearly in what Saussure calls the "last quaternion."[35] The quaternion's schema is composed of four terms: sign, form, signification, and figure; and of three links: a form relating to signification (and vice versa), a form relating to other forms (the general difference of forms only existing according to the difference of significations), and a signification relating to other significations (the general difference of significations only existing according to the difference of forms)—a triple relationship to which may be added the vocal figure, which becomes a signifying form when it includes the semiological relationship. In this schema the sign, as a significant form—indissociably form and signification—can only be opposed to the figure,[36] which appears thanks to the suspension of the semiological relationship and the concatenation of signs. We should add to this clarification Saussure's explanation of the term "image," present in "acoustic image" (or "verbal image"), correlated to "concept" in the schema of the sign, and which would take the name of signifier. Defending himself from the wish to suggest, by using this term, a resemblance linked to what is represented, he states that "*image* is intended in the most general sense as a *figure* [my emphasis] having some evocative power, speaking to the imagination."[37] It is a quotation I would like to put side by side with the following declaration by the poet René Char: "the word not only describes but represents, and immediately imposes one or several *figures*."[38]

We should remember, for our purposes, that figures, without restricting them to the vocal, constitute so many available components, detached from their possible values, while preserving the memorial traces of their uses; but they are also loaded with a potential for *signifiance* in a field of attraction and repulsion, according to a set of variable forces and intensities. I consider this configuration to be a mode of functioning that is internal to language, and within a language system—including in its gestural and bodily dimension, to which I shall return. It allows us to understand semantic variations, diachronic as well as synchronic, according to situations and contexts; the formation of morphosemantic fields, by relative motivation;[39] the phonic or graphic connections between figural elements; the stress, melodic, and rhythmic patterns that superimpose themselves onto prosodic and sentential schemata; vocal timbres, too, in the written version of a language; the topographies of writing; the drawing of words and letters; and the visual space in which these are inscribed. I recognize in this mode of functioning what Kristeva says about "semiotic potential," and I include in this what she calls *signifying differential*, which Michel Arrivé likens to the "homophonic semantic contagion" of Damourette and Pichon.[40] The grammarians say that the "tendency towards semantic contagion" is not conscious but manifests itself in the aesthetic use of language: "All the evocative power of phonetic strings comes into play in poetry, and from this point of view we should no longer even restrict ourselves to the over-confined law of homophonic semantic contagion. Phonetic strings, syllables, and even phonemes, in addition to their onomatopoeic value, have a mnesic value arising from all the words of which they are part, and I am convinced that this semantic burden is constantly present in the speaking subject's subconscious."[41]

Saussure thought of language as a "treasure trove" of forms stabilized by usage and deposited in the memory, and he likened it to the consciousness (semiconsciousness or preconsciousness, depending on circumstances) of speaking subjects; while Culioli compares this "treasure" to the mental activity of language, which is nonconscious. The semiotic-epilinguistic is the living matter of language's dynamic memory, the "zone of turbulence" where it diffracts and becomes iridescent, as well as where it recovers its forces.[42]

3. *The Sense of the Sensory*

In an interview, Culioli declared that with epilinguistics "one is in some ways . . . 'liberated' from the constraints of relationships with others, from linearity, from the very fact that there are social sanctions if you diverge too much from an inevitable conformity. So you reflect on the representations you use, without being at all conscious of them, you make developments, derivations, rather in the way that Deleuze and Guattari talk about rhizomes."[43] From these remarks, let us retain the idea that the signifying activity of language turns back on itself and the subject, escaping from the constraints of communication and surrendering to an inner language, once it has withdrawn from verbal exchange and discursive activity and thus been freed from the rules that operate in interaction because of the need to adjust to others for the purpose of mutual understanding.

The writer who "absents himself from company at the moment of writing," finding himself "alone with his language. . . . Alone with this language against him," as the poet André du Bouchet says, undergoes this experience of a tension between the tumult of language and the expressible, the utterable; he thus develops, through a greater receptivity to language that slips out of reach, a keener attention to his own activity: "critical awareness, which is constantly dislodging words, goes hand in hand with the very notion of poetry. It is made and unmade."[44] Let us also remember, along with the poet, that "in words, before the meaning is deciphered, there are *figures*,"[45] or again, "a word: it is not the meaning, but first and foremost the thrust of the meaning that is communicated, or rather, *imprinted*."[46] This expression, "thrust of the meaning" leads us away from semantic content, whose construction the linguist seeks to understand in ordinary utterances; it brings us closer to more hidden links, the "*buried links*" that the writer Julien Gracq talks about, evoking the "immense artistic potential" that is language, because of the "multiple internal connections and delicate nervous anastomoses of nerves . . . awakened at the slightest, somewhat sensitive touch, [which] make a fundamentally vibrant texture, a harmonic instrument."[47] It also evokes for us the notion of meaningful direction or direction of meaning (*Bedeutungsrichtung*) proposed by the psychiatrist Ludwig Binswanger and repeated by the phenomenologist of existence Henri Maldiney.[48] For the latter, meaning-direction, as distinct from meaning-signification, which is conceptual and thematic, is the source of meaning and is to be found in the roots of words. More generally, this is what directs people in their sensory communication with the world and with others, in an esthesic relationship in the order of what he calls the pathic (feeling). Furthermore, meaning-direction returns us to the sensorimotor experience and the dynamic scheme of one's own body, the first referent for our behaviors and representations.

Among the theoretical propositions that postulate a close link between bodily activity and symbolic activity in language, I would like to flag the theory of the gestural nature of signs, both visual and spoken.[49] According to this conception, language is deeply rooted, ontogenetically and phylogenetically, in its corporeal base, and a linguistic description that starts from the viewpoint of gesture and neuromuscular activity allows the theory to be unified by not separating the levels of analysis (phonological, morphological, syntactical, and semantic). Gesture is in fact understood as a neuromuscular activity of a semiotic order (from spontaneous gestures of communication to more conventional gestures) or of a linguistic order (for conventionalized visible or vocal signs). The verbal sign, in the word, is a functional unit corresponding to a class of equivalence involving coordinated movements carried out with a view to an end.

Highlighting sensorimotor action in perception and the cognition deriving from it, which underlies language, Armstrong *et alii* resort to the notion of *image schemata*, which are not abstract relationships between symbols and an external, objective reality, but, rather, relate to what organizes our experience and understanding at the level of bodily perception and movement. These embodied image schemata cover a perceptual field that includes the visual, the auditory, and the kinesthetic, and they betray the intermodal nature of language. I might also mention the theory of embodied and situated cognition, according to which sensorimotor interactions with the environment are integrated, schematically, with semantic knowledge.[50]

These studies match the widely shared hypothesis of embodied cognition, which makes cognition depend on experiences linked to a body endowed with various sensorimotor capabilities, in a biological, psychological, and cultural environmental context, and which refers more specifically to the idea of embodied action or enaction.[51] We might also mention the wider-ranging hypothesis of the mathematician René Thom, which sees profound unity in the living system, based on a continuity between the biological and the symbolic.[52] It establishes an equivalence, in phylogenesis and ontogenesis, between physiological reactions and conceptual representations. Language finds its origin in what conditions the psyche, both animal and human. If thought is a simulation of the world, language is a sort of mimesis of biophysical interactions. According to this conception of a semiophysical continuum, the creation of language signs is a "symbolic bifurcation" and the significations of symbol-forms are due to a series of transfers, by diffusion and derivation, of signifying qualities attached to morphodynamic schemata present in the physical world experienced by subjects.[53] Thom acknowledges that his model is speculative, but it is surely of heuristic interest.

Without neglecting the work done in cognition sciences and neurosciences, which seek to naturalize meaning, the semiolinguistic point of view leads me to maintain the theory that language is a semiotic mediation between the phenophysical world and the world of (re)presentation, according to a schematization by François Rastier;[54] or perhaps like an interpreter in a chain process, according to Peirce; or an interpretive relationship between the external and internal world, according to Benveniste. We shall also bear in mind, based on Peirce's semiotics, that the thought-sign includes three elements: the representation function, the application of a thought-sign to another, and the material quality of the sign—what is felt and, he states, why bodily movements may accompany our feelings and affects.[55]

But let us return to Kristeva's work, for she approached the semiotics of gesture at a very early stage,[56] referring to ethnography and to what mythical tales tell us about words, in order to highlight the practice and production of words, outside the circle of communication and signification contained in them. Gesture has an indicative or anaphoric function, as bedrock of the voice and written form, and *anaphoricity* becomes the basic function of the semiotic text: the sense is *indication* and the sign is anaphora. Kristeva thus invites us to depart from the linguistic model and categories for analyzing gesture based on American kinesics, and its attempt at formalization, notably in the works of Birdwhistell.[57] The study she devoted, much later, to an account of Saint Teresa of Avila's mystical experience marks a return to anaphoricity.[58] It is through *contact* with the Other, through *touch*—primary sensoriality in the embryogenesis and the relational life—that the subject, indissociably body and soul, is moved. And Kristeva says of this subject that it is *deictic/anaphoric* (*Ecce*, here is; *Haec*, this) and has a demonstrative function: it is the sensory point of the infinite that is affecting it. From this detour, we will note the semiotic continuity-discontinuity between the gestural body and verbal language, two modes of contact with the other, in the de-signation and the co-presence.

Studies of gesture have substantially increased and, indeed, have soared in the recent past, with an international association being created in 2002.[59] Its objective was to promote work on human gesture, in multiple disciplinary fields (anthropology, linguistics, psychology, history, neuroscience, communications, art history, and so on) and in relation to different activities: verbal interactions, work, artistic performances, cultural body techniques, technologies, and so on. It appears that the function of communication and the cognitivist option have come to dominate these studies.

But to limit ourselves to language gestures—considering that spoken language is an activity involving posture, mime, verb, and gesture—I would suggest that the mimicry of language, to borrow the expression of the anthropologist Jousse, quoted by Kristeva, is a secondary function of motor ability: gesture is reconfigured by the language within a language system. Word gesture is polyvalent (symbolic, iconic, and indexical functions),[60] diagrammatic and rhythmic, idiosyncratic and cultural, subjective and normalized (types of situation, discursive genres of words, language actions). Gesture is movement organized into dynamic configurations and the gesture is a *figure of meaning* that is converted into a signifying form when it includes a semiological relationship, according to the Saussurian schema previously shown.

The theory of the verbal act, together with the notion of *mental gesture*,[61] has assimilated the hypothesis that language activity is the product of a symbolic activity by gesture, according to a transmutation process of a sensorimotricity internalized in mental representations, of which linguistic markers preserve the traces in their semantic content. To describe this intermediate passing place between the corporal and the symbolic, Culioli refers to Plato's *chora* in *Timaeus*—a void in waiting—which indicates what is situated in between the sensory and the intelligible. The Platonic *chora* is an image of this generator of forms that is the epilinguistic. As sensory things are subject to change and fluctuation whereas language tends towards stabilization, in order to recount the world, Plato seeks to establish a link between these latter and intelligible forms. This link becomes a place, the receptacle of phenomena in the state of becoming, of which it cannot be said that it is "this" or "that" or that it is "that which is such and such" (*toioutōn*), as permanent realities, but only insofar as they partake of intelligible forms, of the *material*, a term used by Brisson in his translation to designate the *chora*.[62] This receptacle of everything that is subject to generation is in the image of a nanny, or perhaps similar to the modeling of figures from the same material, which are constantly being remodeled as other figures. The *chora* "presents itself as the imprint-bearer [*ekmageion*] of all things."[63] Plato says of this formation process, between the sensory informal and intelligible formal, that it is difficult to describe and provokes surprise.

III. Language as Inner Medium

Does "*chora*" then allow us to bring together linguistic theory and semanalysis? In verbal act linguistics, the terms that make up an utterance are markers, material representatives of mental representations and operations of which they preserve the trace. In production they are sensors of representations, which are configured in language and text, while in reception they are the triggers of representations. These representations of mental images evoked in language activity correspond, according to the hypotheses mentioned above, to sensorimotor sketches linked to praxis, and the imagination of the movement in the formulations is of the order of a specular imagining and a cognition based on perception and action, on which is superimposed the affectivity attached to representations, whose formal marks are diverse.

The "semiotic *chora*," according to Kristeva, includes sensations, affects, and drives (the drive being a limit concept, according to Freud, related to what passes from the somatic to the psychic) and it opens up a prespecular space to the imagination, which we might call *imaginal*. Faithful to Freudian theory, Kristeva thinks of affect as a byproduct of the drive (*Trieb*), of which it is the psychical representative. Composed of *quantum* and *qualis*, "the affect is therefore the place where *a shifting quantity of the drive and its initial psychic tonality* coexist: the crossroads where the energy *quantum* becomes a subjective *quality*."[64] Kristeva mentions that Freud, in an article written in French, translates *Affektbetrag* by the French term for "affective value," the term "value" expressing a "quantitative *and* qualitative" notion. Let us say that an affect is differentiated by its values of *intensity* and *tonality*, and that the variety of emotions and feelings, expressed in language, are so many linguistic representatives of the *range of affects* experienced, against an indescribable and unrepresentable background. Kristeva tells us further that the amalgam of elements in various registers constitutes a "heterogeneous continuity between body-soul-mind, and the experience of this heterogeneous continuity now appears to us as the essence of the intimate."[65] This intimacy, when it is voiced, is expressed in "the intense depth of words,"[66] according to an expression borrowed from Baltazar Gracián, or what she calls "the flesh of words" by analogy with Merleau-Ponty's flesh of the world. As a consequence of the Freudian conception of the affect, the heterogeneity of the unconscious drive is posited, involving "representatives of a *linguistic type*" and "openings for *affects*," which may or may not become incorporated with the elements of language, and are components of the psyche emerging from the somatic. The affect, as the source of subjective meaning that participates in *signifiance*, is then defined as "*my interior* correlating to the *exterior* where the object of incitement, emptiness, and appeal, is situated."[67]

For me personally, in my attempt to combine the linguistic concept of an epilinguistic "chaos" with the semanalytical concept of semiotic *chora*, the interiority of language, defined by the withdrawal from interaction and from the discursive exchange—the theater of referencing and regulatory processes in a situation of communication—includes notional representations that are loosely linked to various kinds of figures (prosodic, phonic, graphic, lexical, syntagmatic, gestural), these in their turn being sensors of meaning. This figurative language is in tune with images of perception and action, on the one hand, and on the other, with a sensoriality and affects that vary in intensity and tonality, pleasure or displeasure.

It is difficult to design a model of the way language functions without using a topological representation, so it is better to think in terms of opening up pathways and connections, activation and inhibition, or interactions. Language functions according to various regimes of activity, with different degrees of linguistic awareness on the part of speakers, ranging from the nonconscious to reflected awareness, with the preconscious in between; we might define this, along with Lacan, as "that chattering by means of which we articulate ourselves inside ourselves,"[68] with, in addition, the instinctual and sexual unconscious underlying everything. The language takes shape within a language system—or in several languages systems—and the texts produced by locutors evolve in accordance with the situations, conforming to discursive genres and types, in different stylistic registers.

It is also difficult to do without the relative oppositions between outside and inside, exterior and interior, even if one might agree with Rastier in saying that language is neither external nor internal but is "a place of coupling between the individual and his environment."[69] We live from permanent spoken dialogues, with others or with ourselves; we have been immersed in a bath of language since before our birth and perpetually assailed, in both our daily activity and our dreams, by perceptible linguistic signs, which are heard, read, or seen. Saussure assimilates language to the consciousness of speakers and, in his communication diagram, he traces a circuit that is both external and internal.[70] He sees the sign as a "two-sided psychic entity," while at the same time insisting on the social nature of language.[71] Epilinguistic "chaos" and "semiotic *chora*" refer to the internal side of what is a dynamic internal/external system continuously being updated by an infinite process of exits and re-entries.

Acknowledging a debt to life sciences, I make a distinction between language's *inner medium* and its *external medium*.[72] Adopting the model of the biological discourse in its description of the extracellular inner medium,[73] I would say that the *inner medium* of language is the intermediary for all exchanges between what goes to make up mental life and the exterior environment; a flow of diverse elements permanently runs through it, and it also permits a transfer of information between the different components in the form of messengers, which play their part in integrating the different functions. We might extend the analogy by noting that Claude Bernard considered the proper functioning of this medium to be the "condition of free and independent life" in beings raised in an organized setting. And I would set this formulation of the inner medium of language alongside a statement by Kristeva: "Basically, there is no life without psychical life. Whether it is intolerable, painful, deadly, or jubilatory, psychical life—which combines systems of representations that traverse language—provides access to the body and to other people."[74]

IV. In Conclusion: The Life of Language

In the long preface she wrote for the publication of Émile Benveniste's *Dernières Leçons* at the Collège de France, Kristeva talked about what "the *way* of a life" was in language, conceived of and lived as an experience, in the search for meaning created in and by language.[75] She quotes the phrase of Heraclitus reported by Plutarch in *De Pythiae oraculis* apropos of Apollo and the Delphi oracle, which Benveniste partly uses, applying it to the "signifying power of language, which occurs well before [the power] of saying something:"[76] οὔτε λέγει οὔτε κρύπτει ἀλλὰ σημαίνει (*oute legei oute kryptei alla semainei*: neither says nor hides but signifies). Another possible translation of *semainei* is "to indicate," and this would return us to the semiotic anaphoricity emphasized by Kristeva. What is shown in the verbal act, without being stated, is *signifiance*.

In her reading and interpretation of Benveniste's lessons on systems of writing, Kristeva leads us to establish a connection between the "inner language" represented by writing, through its semiotization and iconization of language, and a subjectivity other than that of the cogito of consciousness and the transcendental ego of intentionality. In this, writing joins the language of poetry, whose "motivations" are of another order than that of the sign in communication and discourse. Any system of writing is an introspective analysis of language renewed by every speaker in the process of learning to read and write; this is how linguistic consciousness moves to a higher level and also how *figures* (phonographic, morphographic, or logographic) are inserted into the material of the "*chora*."

Kristeva states that Benveniste, in his reasoning, detected "the trace of free and creative subjectivity in the duality of signifiance: between the nameless experience of 'interior language' and the semantics of discourse which is used to communicate and to order," thinking of language as a "signifying organism," "a living, generating and self-generating organism."[77] As a semiologist and psychoanalyst, she has ploughed her own furrow, walking alongside other thinkers, and her contribution constantly encourages us to delve again into the inner life of language. And when, recalling Benveniste's declaration that "well before serving to communicate, language serves to live," she says that the experience of language is "strictly speaking, a vital experience," she means that language is the hub of life, both psychological and social.[78]

Dominique Ducard

University of Paris-Est Créteil, CÉDITEC
July 2018

NOTES

Translations of quotations from works in French for which there are no English translations are by Rosemary Rodwell.

1. Émile Benveniste, "Sémiologie de la langue," *Problèmes de linguistique générale*, t. 2 (Paris: Gallimard, 1989), 43–66.
2. Roland Barthes, *Essais critiques* (Paris: Seuil, 1964), 160; *The Preparation of the Novel*, trans. Kate Briggs (New York: Columbia University Press, 2011), 123; *La Préparation du roman I et II: Cours et séminaires au Collège de France (1978–1979 et 1979–1980)* (Paris: Seuil, 2003), 178.
3. Roland Barthes, *Roland Barthes par Roland Barthes* (Paris: Seuil, 1975), 174–75.
4. According to Kristeva, Benveniste told her that the term *signifiance* may have been used by Jean Paulhan's father. See Julia Kristeva, "La Linguistique, l'universel et le 'pauvre linguiste,'" in *Autour d'Émile Benveniste* (Paris: Seuil, 2016), 135.
5. Kristeva recounts her conversations with Benveniste, regarding the use of these terms: "I particularly remember having told him that infra- and supra-linguistic were not sufficient for me, and I asked him if the term 'translinguistic' appeared to him to be suitable for talking about texts in which a psychosomatic experience is manifest, leading to the transformation of linguistic codes and rules: to 'style,' to that productivity I had just discovered while commenting on Raymond Roussel's flamboyant texts." "La Linguistique, l'universel et le 'pauvre linguiste,'" 100.
6. Julia Kristeva, *La Révolution du langage poétique: L'Avant-garde à la fin du XIXe siècle, Lautréamont et Mallarmé* (Paris: Seuil, 1974); *Revolution in Poetic Language*, trans. Margaret Waller (New York: Columbia University Press, 1984).
7. Josette Rey-Debove, *Lexique sémiotique* (Paris: PUF, 1979), 127.
8. Julia Kristeva and Dana Rudelic-Fernandez, "Psychanalyse et linguistique," in P. Kaufman, ed., *L'Apport freudien: Éléments pour une encyclopédie de la psychanalyse* (Paris: Larousse, 1998), 747.
9. Julia Kristeva, "Sémiologie," in *Encyclopaedia universalis* (Paris: EU SA France, 1980).
10. Julia Kristeva, *Sémiotikè: Recherches pour une sémanalyse* (Paris: Seuil, 1969).
11. Ibid., 373.
12. Ibid., 279.
13. Sebastian Shaumyan, *Applicational Grammar as a Semantic Theory of Natural Language* (Edinburgh: Edinburgh University Press, 1997); *A Semiotic Theory of Language* (Bloomington and Indianapolis: Indiana University Press, 1987).
14. Kristeva, *Sémiotikè*, 9.
15. See Tzvetan Todorov, *Mikhaïl Bakhtine, le principe dialogique, Suivi de: Écrits du Cercle de Bakhtine* (Paris: Seuil, 1981).
16. Julia Kristeva and Elisabeth Bélorgey, "Les Modèles linguistiques et pragmatiques de la communication," in *Revue internationale de psychopathologie* 7 (Paris: PUF, 1992).
17. Kristeva, *Sémiotikè*, 59.
18. Julia Kristeva, *Black Sun: Depression and Melancholia*, trans. Leon S. Roudiez (New York: Columbia University Press, 1989), 22.
19. Julia Kristeva, *Time and Sense: Proust and the Experience of Literature*, trans. Ross Guberman (New York: Columbia University Press, 1996); *New Maladies of the Soul*, trans. Ross Guberman (New York: Columbia University Press, 1995); *The Sense and Non-sense of Revolt*, trans. Jeanine Herman (New York: Columbia University Press, 2000).
20. Julia Kristeva, "Language, Sublimation, Women," in *Hatred and Forgiveness*, trans. Jeanine Herman (New York: Columbia University Press, 2010).

21. Antoine Culioli, *Cognition and Representation in Linguistic Theory*, trans. John T. Stonham (Amsterdam: John Benjamins, 1995), 36; *Notes du séminaire de DEA 1983–1984* (Poitiers: University of Paris 7, Department of Linguistic Research, 1985), 20.

22. According to a study of Freud's thinking, *technē* (*ars*) is the mode of conceptualization at the origin of psychoanalysis, inseparable from the procedure for investigating psychical processes that are otherwise inaccessible and the method of treating psychological disturbances based on this procedure. Giovanni Vassali, "La Psychanalyse naît de l'esprit même de la technique grecque," *Penser/rêver* 1 (2002): 211–56.

23. Kristeva, *Sémiotikè*, 59.

24. Antoine Culioli and Claudine Normand, *Onze rencontres sur le langage et les langues* (Paris: Ophrys, 2005), 182.

25. Kristeva and Bélorgey, "Les Modèles linguistiques et pragmatiques de la communication."

26. Kristeva, *Sémiotikè*, 25–26.

27. From a handwritten note by Saussure quoted by Fehr in a work that gives pointers enabling us to better understand the linguist's semiological project. Johannes Fehr, *Saussure entre linguistique et sémiologie* (Paris: PUF, 2000), 123.

28. Culioli and Normand, *Onze rencontres sur le langage et les langues* 110. In the ancient philosophy of atomistic materialists (Epicurus, Lucretius), the *clinamen* designates the deviation of atoms falling in infinite, empty space, which allows them to meet and strike each other. This movement of deviation creates associations and aggregations that form bodies.

29. Ibid., 73.

30. Ludwig Wittgenstein, *Philosophische Bemerkungen* (Oxford: Blackwell, 1964).

31. William James, *Psychology: The Briefer Course* (New York: Harper, 1961), 30.

32. Antoine Culioli, *Variations sur la linguistique: Entretiens avec Frédéric Fau* (Paris: Klincksieck, 2002), 180.

33. The quotation borrowed by Brendel from Novalis is as follows: "*Beim Kunstwerk soll das Chaos durch den Flor der Ordnung schimmern*" (In the work of art, chaos must shine under the veil of order). Culioli and Normand, *Onze rencontres*, 97n1.

34. Culioli and Normand, *Onze rencontres sur le langage et les langues*. Quotation from Mallarmé: "*Si, tout de même, n'inquiétait je ne sais quel miroitement, en dessous, peu séparable de la surface concédée à la rétine—il attire le soupçon*" (If, even so, I know not what shimmer was troubling, underneath but not too far from the surface granted to the retina—it attracts suspicion). See Stéphane Mallarmé, "Le Mystère dans les lettres," https://www.fabula.org/actualites/le-mystere-dans-les-lettres_11228.php.

35. Ferdinand de Saussure, *Writings in General Linguistics*, trans. Carol Sanders and Matthew Pires (Oxford: Oxford University Press, 2006) 22; *Écrits de linguistique générale*, ed. Simon Bouquet and Rudolf Engler (Paris: Gallimard, 2002), 42.

36. "When considering what can be *opposed* to material sound, we rule out, in essence, and with no likelihood of modifying this view, the possibility of opposing sound and idea. What can be opposed to material sound is the *sound-idea group*, but certainly not *the idea*." Saussure, *Writings in General Linguistics*, 139; *Écrits de linguistique générale*, 202.

37. Ferdinand de Saussure, *Saussure's Third Course of Lectures on General Linguistics (1910–1911)*, bilingual ed. (Oxford: Pergamon, 1993), 76a.

38. René Char, *Sous ma casquette amarante*, interview with France Huser (Paris: Gallimard, Pléiade, 1980), 829 (my emphasis).

39. The notion of morphosemantic fields refers to a more or less structured and stable complex of formal as well as semantic relations among linguistic units, which mutually determine each other.

40. Michel Arrivé, *Langage et psychanalyse, linguistique et inconscient: Freud, Saussure, Pichon, Lacan* (Paris: PUF, 1994). The grammarians Damourette and Pichon speak of "synsemic tendency" *(tendance sysémique*, a neologism constructed with the prefix

sy(n) and *sémie*, as for polysemy) to evoke the semantic relations of words with phonetic similarities, a phenomenon of semantic contagion, as it were, between words that resemble each other phonetically. The semantic connectedness of words that rhyme in poetry provides an example. Jacques Damourette and Edouard Pichon, *Des mots à la pensée: Essai de grammaire de la langue française*, vol. I (Paris: d'Artrey, 1930).

41. Damourette and Pichon, *Des mots à la pensée*, 63. Damourette and Pichon believe that linguistic elements convey a semantic memory of the different words in which they appear.

42. In meteorology, one speaks of a zone of turbulence to describe a zone of more or less powerful agitation of the air. The expression is used here, for language, apropos of a space-time organized in an aleatory and unstable manner. See Antoine Culioli and Dominique Ducard, "Un Témoin étonné du langage," in Claudine Normand and Estanislao Sofia, eds., *Espace théorique du langage: Des parallèles floues* (Brussels: Academia, 2012), 129–72.

43. Culioli and Normand, *Onze rencontres sur le langage et les langues*, 109–10. Questioned about the use of the verb "reflect," which appears to contradict the unconscious nature of the activity, Culioli states that he used it to mean "it goes around in our heads."

44. André du Bouchet, *Entretiens avec Alain Veinstein* (Paris: L'Atelier contemporain & Institut National de l'Audiovisuel, 2016), 39, 18.

45. Ibid., 71.

46. André du Bouchet, *Un mot: ce n'est pas le sens . . .* (Halifax: VVV Editions, 2013).

47. Julien Gracq, *Reading Writing*, trans. Jeanine Herman (New York: Turtle Point, 2006), 305; *En lisant en écrivant* (Paris: José Corti, 1980), 255. In medicine, anastomoses are the natural or artificial points of junction of two structures in the form of a tube or a conduit, like blood vessels. Gracq employs this word apropos of multiple connections and ramifications among the words of the language that literary writing generates.

48. Henri Maldiney, *Penser l'homme et la folie* (Grenoble: Jérôme Million, 2007).

49. See David F. Armstrong, William C. Stokoe, and Sherman E. Wilcox, *Gesture and the Nature of Language* (Cambridge: Cambridge University Press, 1995).

50. Lawrence W. Barsalou, "Perceptual Symbols System," *Behavioral and Brain Sciences* 22 (1999): 577–660.

51. See Francisco J. Varela, Evan Thompson, and Eleanor Rosch, *The Embodied Mind: Cognitive Science and Human Experience* (Cambridge: MIT, 1991).

52. René Thom, *Apologie du logos* (Paris: Hachette, 1990).

53. According to Thom, philosophical mathematician and inventor of catastrophe theory, the shapes of the physical world are subtended by a continuous dynamic that engenders and organizes them (morphodynamic schemata). René Thom, *Semio Physics: A Sketch*, trans. Vendla Meyer, bilingual ed. (Redwood City: Addison-Wesley, 1990).

54. François Rastier, "L'Action et le sens pour une sémiotique des cultures," *Texto!* (June 2001), http://www.revue-texto.net/Inedits/Rastier/Rastier_Action.html.

55. Charles S. Peirce, "Some Consequences of Four Incapacities," *Journal of Speculative Philosophy* 2 (1868): 140–57.

56. Julia Kristeva, "Le Geste, pratique ou communication?" in *Langages: Pratiques et langages gestuels* 10 (1968): 48–64, http://www.persee.fr/doc/lgge_0458-726x_1968_num_3_10_2548.

57. Ray Birdwhistell, "Some Body Motion Elements Accompanying Spoken American English," in Lee Thayer, ed., *Communication: Concepts and Perspectives* (Washington: Spartan, 1967).

58. Julia Kristeva, *Teresa, My Love: An Imagined Life of the Saint of Avila*, trans. Lorna Scott Fox (New York: Columbia University Press, 2015).

59. International Society for Gesture Studies (ISGS), http://www.gesturestudies.com/.

60. I refer to two models and typologies of gesture in speech. For the Information Processing Model, see Robert Krauss, Yihsin Chen, and Rebecca F. Gottesman, "Lexical

Gestures and Lexical Access," in David McNeill, ed., *Language and Gesture* (Cambridge: Cambridge University Press, 2000). For the Sketch Model, see Jan Peter de Ruiter, "The Production of Gesture and Speech," in ibid.

61. Antoine Culioli, "Gestes mentaux et réseaux symboliques: À la recherche des traces enfouies dans l'entrelacs du langage," *Faits de langue*, no. 3 (Paris: Ophrys, 2013): 7–31.

62. Platon, *Timée/Critias*, trans. Luc Brisson (Paris: GF-Flammarion, 1992).

63. Ibid., 149, 50a–d.

64. Julia Kristeva, "De l'affect ou 'L'intense profondeur des mots,'" lecture by Julia Kristeva, Facultà Teologica dell'Italia Settentrionale, February 23–24, 2010, Milan, http://www.kristeva.fr/de-l-affect.html.

65. Julia Kristeva, *Intimate Revolt: The Powers and Limits of Psychoanalysis Volume 2*, trans. Jeanine Herman (New York: Columbia University Press, 2002), 51; *La Révolte intime: Pouvoirs et limites de la psychanalyse II* (Paris: Fayard, 1997), 94.

66. Kristeva, "De l'affect ou 'L'intense profondeur des mots.'"

67. Ibid.

68. Jacques Lacan, *The Ethics of Psychoanalysis: The Seminar of Jacques Lacan Book VII, 1959–1960*, ed. Jacques-Alain Miller, trans. Dennis Porter (New York: Norton, 1997), 62; *Le Séminaire, livre VIII: L'Éthique de la psychanalyse (1959–1960)* (Paris: Seuil, 1986), 76.

69. François Rastier, "Le Langage comme milieu: Des pratiques aux œuvres," *Texto!* (December 2003), http://www.revue-texto.net/Inedits/Rastier/Rastier_Langage.pdf.

70. See Ferdinand de Saussure, *Cours de linguistique générale* (Paris: Payot, 1971), 27.

71. Ibid., 99.

72. This distinction goes back to Claude Bernard (1813–1878), who said: "Animals have two environments: an *external medium* in which the organism is situated, and an *inner medium* inhabited by the elements of the tissues" (*Leçons sur les phénomènes de la vie communs aux animaux et aux végétaux*, 1878–1879). See François Chast, "Claude Bernard: concept de milieu intérieur," *Encyclopaedia Universalis*, http://www.universalis-edu.com/encyclopedie/claude-bernard-concept-de-milieu-interieur/.

73. See Jean-Paul Truchot, "Milieu intérieur," *Encyclopaedia Universalis*, http://www.universalis-edu.com/encyclopedie/milieu-interieur/.

74. Julia Kristeva, "Healing, A Psychical Rebirth," in *Hatred and Forgiveness*, 157; *La Haine et le pardon: Pouvoirs et limites de la psychanalyse III* (Paris: Fayard, 2005), 321.

75. Julia Kristeva, "Émile Benveniste un linguiste qui ne dit ni ne cache, mais signifie," Preface to Émile Benveniste, *Dernières leçons: Collège de France 1968–1969*, ed. Jean-Claude Coquet and Irène Fenoglio (Paris: Gallimard, 2012).

76. Émile Benveniste, "La Forme et le sens dans le langage," in *Problèmes de linguistique générale II* (Paris: Gallimard, 1974), 229.

77. Kristeva, "Émile Benveniste, un linguiste qui ne dit ni ne cache, mais signifie," 37, 28.

78. Ibid., 21.

2

John Lechte

LANGUAGE, LITERATURE, AND THE FOUNDING MURDER IN THE WORK OF JULIA KRISTEVA

It is a question of the function of the sacred as symbolic commemoration of the crime.

—Julia Kristeva, *The Sense and Non-sense of Revolt*

I. Introduction

While the approach to language as found in the science of linguistics is far from absent from Kristeva's writing, it is a much broader idea of language that constitutes the originality here. Consequently, I will trace how—especially in her early work—Kristeva's approach to language embraces the notions of textuality, signification, *signifiance*, negativity, and the semiotic as revealed through the prism of "*sémanalyse*." *Sémanalyse* involves an engagement with language, beyond linguistics, that highlights the carnivalesque and the semiotic, the poetic aspect of language as implicated in the drives—that aspect (like the unconscious) not beholden to contradiction. As carnival and the semiotic become manifest only in the *practice* of writing and literature in all its forms, it is appropriate to observe the way that this occurs—initially, in Kristeva's textual approach to the epic as symbol and the novel as sign, then in relation to the modern novel as space and number, and finally in her theory of writing and the semiotic.

The second half of this essay will show that, through the semiotic, language is profoundly indebted to the Freudian thesis of a founding murder that would give rise to society. If the semiotic is Kristeva's major contribution to a deeper understanding of language and signification—and thus of literature—it is a concept that cannot be fully appreciated independently of the Freudian founding murder. My general approach is to give a commentary on key texts by Kristeva, then to pose questions that are judged to derive from the works analyzed.

II. Language as Symbol and Sign: The Epic and the Novel

Kristeva begins her Parisian intellectual odyssey that will change our view of language and signification[1] by speaking and writing about the work of Mikhail Bakhtin and the dialogical novel and the notion of carnival. She then publishes *Le Texte du roman*, her *doctorat de troisième cycle*, on the rise of the modern novel.[2] This dual intervention effectively offers a new theory—not specifically of language, but of the nature of the practice of modern literature. Thus, at the commencement, there is a theory of the novel, and therefore of literature, and thence a formalization of modern poetic language, as we shall see.

1. "Ideologeme" and the Logics of the Monological and Dialogical Text

Antoine de Sale's novel, *Jehan de Saintré* (1456), Kristeva argues, signals a fundamental change from the ideologeme of the symbol to the ideologeme of the sign. "Ideologeme" refers to the governing framework within which fictional texts are generated. The ideologeme of the symbol is the era of the epic, folk tale, myth, and Mennipean satire. These have a dual, "disjunctive" structure (often playing on the opposition, good and evil). "Disjunctive" means that oppositions are irreconcilable. With the ideologeme of the sign comes the nondisjunctive logic of the modern novel (the logic of "both/and"), of difference and otherness. Recognition of the modern novel's structure foreshadows the theorization/formalization of poetic language, the key feature of Kristeva's essays in the late 1960s and early 1970s.

"Epic discourse," Kristeva says, "is easily graspable as a closed, static discourse identical to itself," one that is outside of time.[3] The transformations (hero becomes traitor and vice versa) noted by Propp and Greimas in their analyses of folk tales are different from those occurring in the novel.[4] The traitor in the epic might pretend to be a hero (or vice versa), whereas in the novel the character will have heroic *and* traitorous qualities (i.e. a complex psychology).

2. The Actant

Transformation as the manifestation of nondisjunction brings to the fore key characteristics of the novel, which is ambivalent and asymmetrical.[5] On the one hand, intrigue is reorganized, or restructured; on the other, the Greimasian *actants* fulfill the structural roles of hero, villain, helper, object (of a quest), etc.[6] The actant in the novel is both same and other—both identical and not identical to itself. Is it plausible to speak of the structural category of actant in relation to the novel, where events reign?—a point Kristeva confirms by quoting Henry James on the link between "character" and "incident."[7] For James, character *is* incident, which suggests a radical contingency. Character in the modern novel would thus be infinitely variable and not susceptible to an analysis based on the notion of actant.

Might it not be objected that in literary criticism reference is still made to categories such as "hero" and "antagonist" (villain) across a wide range of novels? Maybe. But most notable is the difference between heroes. The hero in *À la recherche du temps perdu* can hardly be compared to that in *Crime and Punishment*. To use the term "hero" is simply a convention unrelated to what is really at issue. Such, in my view, is the case if Kristeva is to be consistent in her characterization of the modern novel as open to the world. The actual analysis seems to reach a similar conclusion, for we read that "an actant is nothing other than the discourse that it assumes or by which it is designated in the novel."[8] So why use the category of actant at all—given that the specificity implied means that we are in fact dealing with an actor or with a character bereft of an a priori content? The probable answer is that in 1968 structuralism was in vogue; it thus made sense to use its resources, even if there was a lack of fit with the actual issue being addressed. However, the fact that the novel is open to history and context (diachrony takes precedence over synchrony) means that a structural analysis is all but redundant. Moreover, as is shown in relation to *Jehan de Saintré*, "author" becomes an actor just like the characters of the modern novel. The author, indeed, can be an actor in the novel.

3. Structural Analysis, Intertextuality, and the Genotext and Phenotext

A structural analysis of epic and myth (as Kristeva herself indicates) depends on taking a large corpus of texts and distilling in them the constant, unchanging elements—those unaffected by history. Consequently, to claim that structure is *in* history does not seem plausible. Either one adopts a structuralist approach, to the detriment of history, or history to the detriment of structure. Carnivalization, and thus "ambivalence," implies the insertion of history into literature so that a structuralist method ceases to be pertinent. The modern novel (e.g. Lautréamont) is thus double—or paragrammatic (Kristeva)—a notion illustrated most forcefully by Saussure's "Anagrammes."[9]

"To study the structuration of the novel" is to see it as a dialogue between several texts; or, the novel is an "intertextuality."[10] *Intertextuality* implies that the novel is open to its environment and thus to history, whereas a syntagmatic study looks only at the novel's internal structure. In this vein, compared to the epic, the novel can appropriate "extranovelistic" discourses (such as advertising); for it is open to its environment—to the world—and ready to make the available material an integral part of its creative process. More precisely, "diachronic transformation" makes literary discourse "an intertextuality."[11] Intertextuality as diachronic generates literature, so that it becomes "spatialized." How a text is generated ushers in the notion of the *genotext* at the foundation, compared to the *phenotext* as the level initially encountered by a reader/addressee. I will examine this in more detail below.

A close proximity exists between the levels of geno- and phenotext and Chomsky's theory of generative grammar, where there is, at the level of language use, a difference between deep and surface structure, or between linguistic competence (what a speaker could ideally do) and performance (what a speaker actually does).[12] Kristeva adds a third level to Chomsky's competence and performance, "textual productivity beyond the sign."[13] The signification of the novel's narrative field suggests that it is—at the level of performance—a *closed* field, while at the level of competence it can generate an infinity of variations—to the point where "there are no categories in which the fluid structures of the transformation of the novel can be captured."[14]

Crucial to the *énoncé* (statement) of Antoine de la Sale is carnivalesque laughter provoked by the novel, especially as *fatras*: nonsense words and phrases, written only to provoke laughter.[15] Later authors such as Rabelais, Diderot, and Joyce also adopted the mode of *fatras* to produce a comic effect.

4. The Suppression of Empedocles

In her succinct conclusion, Kristeva says, first, that nondisjunctive novelistic discourse was, until early modernity, prevented from being installed in European culture due to the repression of the thought of Empedocles by Aristotle and Plato,[16] presumably because it embraced ambivalence, although recent evidence in the literature is not conclusive.[17] Nonetheless, the important point is that Aristotle, even more than Plato, becomes the seminal thinker for the European tradition of the superiority of bivalent logic. The hegemony of the latter is what Kristeva seeks to challenge. Second, we are told that the triadic structure of a new type of negation in Hegel—"that is, a combinatory among signifying units within a closed totality"[18]—is the incarnation in thought of novelistic nondisjunction. (This is the "negativity" that will become central in Kristeva's later work.)[19] However, third, our author says that the status of the novel is also ambiguous because it can be invaded by the ideologeme of the symbol. Tolstoy's fiction—as noted by Bakhtin—is "monological," which means that it is dominated by a disjunctive (either/or) logic.[20] Many nineteenth-century realist novels also manifest this logic. Does this not imply that the thesis presented also falls under the auspices of a certain ambivalence? For the novel—supposedly dominated by the sign—*also* comes to be infiltrated by the symbol, mark of the epic?

The novel (sign), then, comes into being on the back, as it were, of the epic (symbol). While the story is dominant in the epic, the narrating/telling as such (later called "style") is the distinguishing feature of the novel. The difference is thus dialectical—meaning by this that the novel, in its emergence in the early modern era, implicitly references the epic through intertextuality. Thus, in Joyce's *Finnegans Wake* numerous folk tales, myths, and nursery rhymes form the impetus for discursive elaboration. Although Kristeva does not use the term, her description of the novel evokes the logic of *emergence* in complexity theory. "Emergence" means that there is no preconceived, a priori model guiding the outcome of writing. Rather, the model emerges by way of the writing itself.

5. Is There a Truly Closed Text?

We are offered an extremely thought-provoking and illuminating analysis of the "closed" text (epic, myth) and the "open" text (modern novel). But difficulties do arise. The first is evoked by the question: is there an essentially closed text? If we recall that folk tales and other stories derive from storytellers of an oral tradition, we can, with Lyotard, note that the story is as much—or even more—about the telling as it is contained in a narrative content.[21] Moreover, the epic of oral tradition gave rise to variations in the narrative content resulting from the telling. Rather than there being different textual versions of the same myth, as Lévi-Strauss argued, the emphasis falls on the enactment or performance of narrating the closed text within a given context.[22] This implies that the epic can manifest a certain dynamism; it is not entirely static, not entirely closed. It is only closed if it is separated from the telling (in the manner of a structuralist approach). In effect, to separate myth or epic from its telling is analogous to treating a natural language as nothing other than a formal system of rules independent of its contextual enactment.

It might be objected, though, that the modifications occurring in the telling of the myth do not materially change its structure. Oppositions of good or bad, true or false, happy or sad, and so on still dominate; there will still be "monological" texts presenting a moral position (like Tolstoy's). However, even a "monological" text can be enacted—performed: the performance might, for instance, be cinematic. D. W. Griffiths made a film of Tolstoy's *Resurrection* in 1909, while Tolstoy was still alive (he died in 1910). Rather than thinking of cinematic versions of novels and novellas as perversions of the written text, we can think of film versions as tapping into a potential that is there within the text. Cinematic versions of novels thus become analogous to the *enactment* of epics and myths. Even so, it could again be objected that a cinema version of a so-called monological text would still have to reproduce the bivalent logic of that text. If it did not, it could be accused of taking unwarranted liberties. Well, yes—but even if that be true, no two directors would bring a literary work to cinema in the same way.[23] While the physical text of a novel must always maintain its integrity, images in cinema—the *mise en scène*, so to speak—can vary almost ad infinitum. Even if the physical text remains constant, what a reader takes from it can also vary greatly. Reading can thus be analogous to a cinematic—or theatrical—*mise en scène*.

Opera provides another instance of how the telling as performance of a story can *be* the story. Wagner's singular presentation of Greek and Norse mythology in the Ring Cycle and Verdi's use of Shakespeare and tales, while written in the nineteenth century, often conform—at least in part—to the structure of the bivalent, "closed" text of the symbol. With opera, the form of the drama, singing, orchestration—the music, in short—takes the setting of any tale to other levels. Especially in Verdi's early period (1834–1842), a well-known story, often with a bivalent structure, was chosen as the basis of the operas. And, let us recall that Stravinsky offers Sophocles's *Oedipus Rex* as an oratorio.

III. *Nombres* (Numbers) as the Genotext

I focus now on the next stage of the development of Kristeva's practice of semanalysis, which goes beyond the scope of conventional linguistics. To do this, the study of Sollers's novel, *Nombres*, as treated in Kristeva's essay "L'Engendrement de la formule," will be my point of focus.[24] In it, the division "*géno-texte/phéno-texte*," indebted to Chomsky's deep and surface structure, is described, but the terms themselves are taken from the work of Soboleva and Saumjan.[25] The genotext in *Nombres* does not have a subject and is not in time. It cannot be subsumed under the sign as it is the text of "engendering;" it has a "numerical" character.[26] As the "volume" of the text, it joins with the phenotext as "surface." In relation to the communicative function of the phenotext, the genotext constitutes the productive aspect of signification. Here is an intimation of the semiotic (genotext) and the symbolic (phenotext) that will underscore *La Révolution du langage poétique* and much of the work of the late 1970s and 1980s.[27]

Against our intuition, then, engendering does not mean that something is engendered (fact or product) outside the process itself. Rather, engendering evokes the "germination" or the very "process" of the coming to be of the text. Thus, the positing of a relation of cause and effect would be a mistake. The genotext does not *produce* the phenotext. Rather, the genotext is how the phenotext is in space—hence the emphasis on volume.

1. Number

Engendering and germination connect the literary text and numbers. Certainly, the novel *Nombres* is divided into four sets or numbered sequences: numbers one to three are in the imperfect tense (evoking the past?) while sequences bearing the number four and its subsets (4.8, 4.12, 4.16, etc.) are in the present tense. The numbers of the sets 1, 2, 3, 4 and their subsets add up to 100. "4" is the key number as far as the order of the sequences is concerned. Thus, once the initial sequence numbered 4 is completed, the next sequence is numbered 1.5 and the following one 2.6, then 3.7, then 4.8, then 1.9, 2.10, 3.11, 4.12, 1.13, 2.14, 3.15, and so on. Each time 4 is reached, there is a return to "1." The difference between each sequence is thus "4." The privileged "4" takes on the character of a cardinal number, implying that it stands out in its own right, as opposed to the ordinal, relational character of the numbering of the sequences.

Why then privilege "4"—the *number* 4—in a text labeled "*roman*" (novel)? Is it, as Kristeva argues, that this number evokes the volume of the text? The latter would thus have four dimensions, including the position of the reader, something that in its turn evokes the structure of the theater, where the audience/reader becomes the fourth element of the scene. The diagram—*adapted* from sequence "4.8" (in the present tense)—seems to point to this (see diagram 1):[28]

2

↖↑↗

1 3

(4)

↓

(reader)

Diagram 1 (adapted from the diagram in Sollers, *Nombres*, page 22)

In relation to this diagram, Sollers's text reads in part: "This fourth surface is as it were practiced in the abstract; it allows words to be heard, lets the body itself look; one easily forgets it, as a result, and there, no doubt, is the illusion or the error."[29] By accounting only for three dimensions (= perspective), consciousness forgets its own place—the fourth side—in the process. Will this fourth side also be shown by Kristeva to be the side of the genotext, the side of germination—of dissemination?

Significant in this regard is the statement "the textual signifier . . . is a *numbering*."[30] Moreover, subsequently, it is said that "*sémanalyse* discovers *infinite numbering* which includes the *numbered* (graphic and phonic sets) before it finds a referent or a signified and a making of signs."[31] Again: "From the origin, number neither *represents* nor *signifies*."[32] "Number is *anaphoric*, its function is to *designate* [*désigner*] the plurality."[33] Numbering does not separate the signifier from the signified—differentiated in Saussure's image of a sheet of paper representing the sign. This image gives the sign volume-space.[34] A link thus begins to emerge in *Nombres* between number and space. The novel is not just what it says (a series of signifiers) but what it is (a signified). To speak of signifier and signified—i.e. of the sign—in relation to *Nombres* turns out to be misleading. For: "An infinite, plural *generative textuality* replaces *the* signifier."[35] Through numbers, textuality becomes a generating space (the genotext) giving rise to the phenotext—"the printed text."[36] Despite the risk of becoming subservient to the opposition of appearance (phenotext) and reality (genotext), semanalysis aims to reveal the "translation of the geno-text in the pheno-text."[37] The procedure no doubt foreshadows the translation of the Freudian unconscious in consciousness and the translation of the drive-based semiotic in the symbolic.

In Sollers's novel, signifiers are a numbering because they only appear as a plurality. Signifiers do not function as singularities. The question, then, is: how is this plurality—or infinite number—of signifiers engendered? What is the mode of engendering discernible in the phenotext of *Nombres*? The answer is that it will be discernible at the level of "*numerical* differences" and not at the level of the sign.[38] Moreover, this implies that the engendering/germination of the text is at one with its pluralization or infinitization; engendering does not produce a text, for it is the text as such. For its part, "*la formule*" (the formula) is a kind of index or trace of the engendering of the text rather than a vehicle of meaning in any linguistic sense. Crucially, "*la formule*" appears as a plurality of "differential signifiers": "The differential signifier will be . . . the place where the geno-text penetrates the pheno-text."[39] "*La formule*," I suggest, is the mark of the irruption of the genotext in the phenotext. However, Kristeva seems to problematize this by referring to "*formules du geno-texte*,"[40] thus making it difficult to be sure as to whether such "*formules*" appear as such or whether the phenotext is always their vehicle. I have assumed that the latter is the case. The same issue emerges no doubt in the relation between the semiotic and the symbolic—or again in the Freudian distinction between the primary and the secondary process. However, in addition, differential signifiers belong to the register of infinite numbers (in the manner of Cantor), which allows Kristeva to speak of "infinite" signifiers.[41] The "*formule*," then, must be the mark of infinite signifiers, where signifiers become numbers because the infinite is the set of numbers.

Things become still more complicated—especially for the mathematical neophyte—when vowels as they emerge in the Sollersian text are at issue. How are vowels linked to number? This is unclear, even if it *is* clear that vowels, instead of being bearers of meaning, are an index of the genotext—that is, an index of engendering.[42] It is in effect unclear what theory or understanding of number (not to be confused with numerals, "*chiffres*") Kristeva (and Sollers for that matter) is working with. What we do know is that numbers in the novel are linked to space. They thus take on a quantitative rather than a qualitative significance. Can one say, then, that meaning is qualitative while number is quantitative? This is not to deny that when a number is represented by a word ("five") that it can have meaning, that it becomes a qualitative entity. But what we then have is not strictly number, based on the premise that number—*qua* number—has no meaning. Indeed, I suggest that it is only because number as such does not signify that it can be imbricated in the genotext.

For Kristeva, the vowel is equivalent to the "*différentielle signifiante*." It therefore has to do with number—with "the infinite geno-text numbering-space," not with meaning.[43] Here, another complication arises (one not made explicit), namely, that while numerals represent numbers, numeral and number are distinct. In short, number is frequently accessed through meaning, but it is not meaning. Whatever the case, the aim is to bring the genotext to light,[44] which is not to bring to light a communicative utterance. And this is all very well, except that we lose track of the theme of numbers. What *sort* of infinity might correspond to the genotext? Furthermore, is the phenotext to be understood—at least in part—in terms of finitude?

Our question is not answered but rendered more pertinent by the reference to Chinese ideograms (sprinkled throughout the novel) as underlining the practice of language in *Nombres* as a finite engendering that renders present an infinity. It is, though, unclear exactly what notion of infinity Kristeva is working with. Is it mathematical and thus related to Cantor? Or is it more commonsensical and related to a concept of what is limitless? In "Word, Dialogue, and Novel," a reference to Cantor and set theory and the "logic of the 'transfinite'" and of a countable infinity is a way of illuminating the notion of dialogism.[45] But then this is offset by a note saying that such references in relation to poetic language are only metaphorical and analogical.[46] Such would be the way that a certain ambivalence (key term in the Kristevan theory of the carnivalesque) also haunts the Kristevan text in relation to number.

Still more puzzling is the fact that our theorist does not address the definition of number (Frege's problem).[47] Here is one attempt at a definition by the mathematician Benacerraf: "I therefore argue, extending the argument that led to the conclusion that numbers could not be sets, that numbers could not be objects at all; for there is no more reason to identify any individual number with any one particular object than with any other (not already known to be a number)."[48] He continues by pointing out that no individual number can be defined in isolation because: "To *be* the number 3 is no more and no less than to be preceded by 2, 1, and possibly 0, and to be followed by 4, 5, and so forth. And to *be* the number 4 is no more and no less than to be preceded by 3, 2, 1, and possibly 0, and to be followed by. . . . *Any* object can *play the role of* 3; that is, any object can be the third element in some progression."[49] Given that "textual *practice*" is said to be mathematical,[50] attention to the mathematical aspect would have been in order. As this textual practice is exemplified in the couple "Lautréamont-Mallarmé," it draws attention to a deficit here.

Significantly, from the point of view of number, when reference is made to "*nominal enumerations*" in the novel *Nombres*, or to the *frequency*—number—of "*infinitives, past participles and present participles*," the question of number is not addressed.[51] Moreover, the Kristevan concept of *signifiance* is a multiplicity embedded in the genotext—that is, it evokes number.[52] But this aspect is passed over without comment. The cut (*coupure*) in the text (between sequences and within sequences, e.g. as caused by quotations within a sequence) is, on the other hand, "the initial mark of number."[53] But this implies that discontinuity, rather than continuity, drives the text, whereas numbers (ordinals) have to do with continuity: with series, or with counting—with infinity. Indeed, discontinuity only exists if the linguistic (semantic, grammatical, syntactic, etc.) aspect is separated from the number aspect. Numerical continuity exists in the numbering of the sequences from 1 to 100. At the level of counting, every sequence is part of the continuity of the series 1 to 100.[54]

2. Numbers as Symbolic or the "Pythagoric Snare"

In *Nombres*, sequence 4, we find the utterance (*énoncé*): "*l'opération dans le nombre, 1 + 2 + 3 + 4 = 10,*" followed by a Chinese character for the number "4."[55] That there are, as we have noted, four initial sequences numbered 1 to 4, followed by 96 sequences numbered consecutively strongly suggests a symbolic significance being attached to numbers, that number and numbers become signifiers operating at the level of the phenotext, even if number is also the engendering principle of the genotext. Whether intended or not, the number 4 is not only significant in Chinese thought but also in Pythagorian thought. For instance, according to Pythagoras, 4 is the number connoting justice. Zijiang Ding tells us that the integers 1 + 2 + 3 + 4 are crucial to Pythagorian thought because (as is shown in *Nombres*) they make 10, the "perfect number."[56] It is ironical, then, that emphasis is placed on "10" in a text supposedly evoking the Chinese approach to number. In the thought of the Chinese philosopher, Shao Yong (1011–1077 AD), as analyzed by both Ding and Arrault, 4 is a key number but, in general, numbers are not, according to Arrault, to be understood as "the measure of all things, the very essence of things," as in the Pythagorian tradition.[57]

The repetition of the number 4 in various guises in *Nombres* cannot but draw our attention to it—to the point, indeed, where we seem to be drawn into a "numerical semiology."[58] At least two consequences follow from this. (1) Numbers are not treated as such, but, rather, as signifiers with symbolic resonances—in the manner of Pythagoras and the Chinese tradition as represented by Shao Yong. (2) The argument that numbers in Sollers's novel form the basis of the genotext begins to break down. For, rather than being the basis of an invisible productivity, numbers cease to be numbers and function as signifiers of the phenotext. That is to say, in the end, the treatment of number and numbers in *Nombres* falls into the category of what Ricardo and David Nirenberg have called the "Pythagoric snare," by which they mean that conclusions are drawn from numbers that do not relate to number *qua* number.[59] Much as it would be intriguing to pursue this meditation, we must turn now to examine language and signification in relation to the semiotic and symbolic.

IV. Revolution in Poetic Language: The Founding Murder, Revolt, and Writing as Transubstantiation

From the dominance of the conceptual couple genotext and phenotext in the Kristevan approach to language, we move to the now well-known "semiotic-symbolic" couple in the writings of the 1970s. From an essentially textual approach (dealing with content and form of specific instances of writing), Kristeva endeavors to show not only the social and historical dimension of literature but also how literature—language in the broadest sense—is constitutive of the social. Consequently, as we shall see, the founding murder comes to assume a significant presence in Kristeva's work from 1974 onward.

1. The Semiotic and the Symbolic

If the genotext and the phenotext make a relatively brief appearance in Kristeva's theorizing of poetic language in the late 1960s, which formed the foundation for

La Révolution du langage poétique, and which had in its sights the hegemony of the logic of the Greek *logos* (word and discourse), this is because the later work, with its Freudian impulse, is more focused on the subject in language and society, the latter being equivalent to the symbolic order and its logic of noncontradiction. The speaking subject of everyday communication is also deemed to be founded on this logic. When addressing signification through a semanalytical lens (i.e., when reading a text *as* a text), the genotext and the phenotext couple are there in the background.[60] Binary logic is dominant within a social and political context. Hence the political significance, for Kristeva, of a nineteenth-century avant-garde as producer of poetic language. How is it possible to distill the notion of poetic language if it is resistant to the language of everyday communication—the language, as it happens, of researchers in traditional linguistics? Whatever answer we give to this question, the avant-gardists of poetic language found their latter-day ally in the practitioner of "*sémanalyse*."

In *Revolution in Poetic Language*, Hegel and his concept of negativity, as much as the work of any linguist, holds sway. Interestingly, in relation to Kristeva's reading of *Nombres*, negativity is defined as the *fourth* term in the Hegelian dialectic.[61] Moreover, in the *Phenomenology of Spirit*, negativity as Force is presented under the rule of "One," according to Kristeva.[62] What is this "One," we may well ask? Is it not unity? Hegel says that Force has "the express character of a One," and that "Force is posited as *a One*," even if "this *oneness*" becomes "something *other* than Force."[63] But Hegel, being Hegel, also says: "the oneness, in the form it appeared, viz. as an 'other,' vanishes; Force is this 'other' itself."[64] "One" thus appears as unity despite the "other."

However, negativity, evoking Bataille's "expenditure," is also the movement generated by contradiction. It becomes the "semiotic movement" (practice) in poetic language. In 1973 Kristeva was still concerned to distinguish negativity from negation—the latter relating to judgment in the work of Frege and Kant. To avoid all misunderstanding, the term "rejection" is chosen as a synonym, the advantage being that drives and their stases could be introduced and a more Freudian take on poetic language pursued, one focusing on the *formation* of the subject as the subject in process/on trial in and through language and signification. Subjectness (if not subjectivity) is experienced rather than represented. In short: "The subject never *is*. The *subject* is only the *signifying process* and he appears only as a *signifying practice*."[65] Expenditure of drive energy signified by "*semēion*" or "*chora*" does not simply appear in articulated language but includes the Rousseauian "cry" or "call" of language—everything from preverbal gestures ("concrete operations") to holophrastic utterances, to rhythmical sounds based on agglutination and alliteration, where certain vowels might be repeated, or syntax disrupted (a feature of Mallarmé's and Lautréamont's poetry).[66] With the revolutionary avant-garde (Mallarmé, Joyce, Schoenberg), timbre or sound-color melody (*Klanfarbenmelodie*) brings to the fore drives originating in childhood.[67]

The semiotic also takes its point of departure in the analysis of subject positions (compare Lautréamont) from Benveniste's subject of discourse. This is the existential subject of enunciation (*sujet d'énonciation*) marked by the invocation of pronouns (I/you/he/she/it) and indices of time and place (here, there, yesterday, tomorrow, etc.)—indices called collectively "shifters," the term formulated by Jakobson.[68] Shifters are context specific and so only have significance in the act of being uttered. With an "instance of discourse," the mode of enactment of a subject in a specific context leaves its mark, so that there is no purely symbolic utterance (*énonciation*) but one inevitably marked by the semiotic (drives) as the index of subjectivity.

2. The Semiotic and the Founding Murder

Kristeva comes to argue in the 1970s that an appreciation of the semiotic requires the acknowledgment that a subject exists within a sociosymbolic fabric. Along with the semiotic drives—as the Freudian inflexion would have it—the symbolic came into being with the original murder of the father in the primal horde, or with the killing of a scapegoat if one opts for the Girardian version; or, again, with the idea of an original sacrifice that would bring the sacred into social life.[69] The whole point of the "revolution" in poetic language—as will be the case with revolt in the 1990s—is to demonstrate its profoundly social bearing. While linguistics à la Chomsky and a certain semiotic analysis could arguably replicate the Kristevan analysis of the internal workings of Mallarméan poetry or Joycean prose, the idea that the stakes are essentially social sets Kristeva's approach apart from all the rest. In one of her summaries of the founding of society, she writes in relation to sacrifice:

> this violent act puts an end to previous (semiotic, presymbolic) violence, and, by focusing violence on a victim, displaces it onto the symbolic order *at the very moment* this order is being founded. Sacrifice sets up the symbol and the symbolic order at the same time, and this "first" symbol, the victim of a murder, merely represents the structural violence of language's irruption as the murder of soma, the transformation of the body, the captation of drives.[70]

Through sacrifice—murder—the thetic (positions of subject and object) and thus the symbolic and the social come into being. The semiotic here is theorized as a residue, an enduring trace in the symbolic—a trace of the sacrificial act, its instauration. Art is now significant because it is equivalent to the "semiotization of the symbolic," of which poetic language is a prime instance.[71] As noted, the idea of sacrifice and the founding of society on a murder, the semiotic being a constant reminder of this murder, is taken up again in relation to the Freudian "primal horde" in the latter part of Kristeva's *doctorat d'état*—in the account of the role of avant-garde poetic language at the end of the nineteenth century in Paris. Poetic language and, more broadly, art is not an essentially individual, isolated, strictly private, or marginal activity and practice, such as is evoked by the late nineteenth-century notion of "*l'art pour l'art.*" Indeed, in its evocation of violence, Kristeva's theory of language and signification is close to that of Girard and his thesis that society can only exist if violence is contained in the wake of the original murder.[72] Such a position also makes the practice of art relevant to social change since the partial, socially based liberation of the semiotic destabilizes frozen forms of the symbolic and in this sense becomes political. The theory of a founding murder allows Kristeva to call on the Freudian version and to introduce sexuality—based in the drives (see the *chora*)—into the relationship between language and society.

Revolution and poetic language are thus related to each other through the myth (Girard would say "fact") of an original murder. The issue in its archaic and anthropological guise occurs again in Kristeva's text on abjection, the text possibly having had the broadest impact in the Anglo world.[73] There, murder is inextricably linked to the "advent of language." "If the *murder* of the father is that historical event constituting the social code as such, that is, symbolic exchange and the exchange of women, its equivalent on the level of the subjective history of each individual is therefore the *advent of language*."[74] Even more incisive for my argument is the reiteration of the link between poetic language (therefore the semiotic) and murder. "Poetic language would then be, contrary to murder and the univocity of verbal [*sic*] message, a reconciliation with what murder as well as names were separated from. *It would be an attempt to symbolize the 'beginning.'*"[75] Before the "beginning" there was chaos—or was it the semiotic *chora*? The latter is not mentioned, but is surely implied. Then again, maybe not (even if the interdiction against incest is); for in her analysis of Céline's writing, the carnivalesque and dialogism (Bakhtin) are the key descriptors of his style.[76] However, those authors deemed to exhibit in their writing the "both-and" (0-2) logic of carnival are, in the case of Lautréamont and Joyce, also those who show us the working of the semiotic as the evocation of murder and the sacred.[77] Given the intensely rhythmic nature of the Célinian text, together with the author's avowed claim that "in the beginning was emotion," the semiotic is very much in play.

3. Love, Depression, and Murder

Similarly, the founding murder plays a key role in Kristeva's theorizations of love and melancholia. For if the "father of individual prehistory" (an imaginary, loving, father with whom the subject is in an immediate, *primary* identification) is fundamental to the formation of the imaginary and thus to a capacity for love, such a capacity is well-nigh absent in melancholia. The whole idea of incorporation of the object and a capacity for identification evokes the totemic meal (à la Robertson Smith) that took place after the killing of the father, even if this object of incorporation is the word of the other.[78] With primary identification being defective,[79] the depressive patient is in mourning for an object, but only has a profound sadness (defined as "the thing")[80] with which to identify. And the only way left to approach "the thing" is via the semiotic: "through melody, rhythm, semantic polyvalence, the so-called poetic form."[81] The semiotic (evocative of the founding murder) is thus the basis of the depressive's "language" because symbolic capacities are in default.[82]

4. Revolt, and the Founding Murder

The story does not end there; for more than a decade after the work on abjection and exactly two decades after the publication of *La Révolution du langage poétique*, in a course on revolt taught in 1994, Kristeva spells out the various logics of the sacred and revolt, with particular reference to Freud and the founding murder as the origin of language and the symbolic.[83] Here, the sacred becomes the commemoration of the crime that established the social/symbolic order.

After revealing Freud's approach to language in his early work—where, with the model of language as "heterogeneity," the representation of words and the representation of things in relation to psychical energy charges are at issue—Kristeva proceeds to explain Freud's "optimist" model of language in *The Interpretation of Dreams*, where Lacan's linguistic theory of language in psychoanalysis gains plausibility. For it is here that displacement (Lacan's "metonymy") and compression or condensation (Lacan's "metaphor") seem to justify the claim that Freud had a refined semiotic approach to language[84]—an approach that, for Lacan, would lend itself to the mathematization of the signifier and the unconscious. Kristeva's point is that this is only one of three models of language to be found in Freud, so that despite its sophistication the Lacanian approach is an incomplete version of the theory.[85] For instance, Lacan neglects the drives and the primary process. The third model of language, one already evoked in relation to the founding murder as described in *Totem and Taboo*—the one to which I want to draw renewed attention, is the model Kristeva refers to as "*signifiance*," now known to be a synonym for the semiotic.

The constitution of the thetic (semiotic/symbolic; subject/object) is coterminus with the birth of language and signification as essentially social. This model now allows for the semiotic to constitute the *sujet en procès* as a subject in revolt. Overall, *Totem and Taboo* initiates a broad field of symbolic processes, within which language in the linguistic sense would be situated. It enables an identification with and against the (place of) the father ("paternal complex")—with and against the Law—and it gives rise to, is the basis of the oedipal triangle as the harbinger of the unconscious and sexuality. Not least, though, the founding murder story is also the index of "hominization"—the separation of human from animal, the birth of the *Homo sapiens* as a "social animal" and the emergence of culture as the reverberation of the founding myth, so that phylogenesis never ceases to have a presence in ontogenesis (formation of the subject/self).

Freud's global approach to the human entails that language in psychoanalysis is the mode of appearing of the drives and sexuality, of forms of delirium and persecution, of joy and sadness, of love and hate (of abjection), of self and other, etc.

5. Transubstantiation and the Founding Murder

The most free-flowing of energy, motility, and instability is the semiotic *chora*. In a sense, the *chora*—even as it underpins life—is a presupposition, much like, for Freud, the primary process is a presupposition (a "theoretical fiction").[86] The upshot of the founding murder and the establishment of the Law—the *socius*—is to give form to the formless energy of the *chora*. That is, the founding murder enables the materiality of language to be perceived. Perception as sensation would, in my view, be tributary to the *chora*, even if Kristeva does not make this explicit. The narrator's body riven by sensations as described in the study of Proust would be the confirmation of this, even if the further dimension of transubstantiation (of a blurring of word and thing—word becoming flesh) is also in play.[87] I am saying that however focused on an individual psyche the Kristevan lens seems to be, always at stake in every instance of language is how the *chora* energy and motility appear in a specific *social* guise, and how an existing version of language in its communicative incarnation can exhibit an eruption of the semiotic *chora* that can lead to a reorganization of existing signifying practices.

On the face of it, the study of Colette seems removed from the semiotic and the founding murder, yet rhythm, music "bursts forth in certain texts, whose meaning, strangely, allows itself to be dominated by an almost autonomous musicality."[88] "Her writing then becomes a torrent, a current," and "a deluge of metaphors."[89] Like Proust (whom Colette much admired), Colette's writing blurs sensation and perception (the senses) in a transubstantiation tributary, I say, to the semiotic, where passion is "infinite and heterogeneous" and where meaning (*sens*) and sensations become blurred. As a transubstantiation, Colette's writing "installs the felt [*senti*] into words and words into sensations."[90] Significantly: "Death itself does not put an end to that *bacchanalia*."[91] Colette's writing as "sensation," "bacchanalia," and "transubstantiation" is where language or the signifying process—words in Colette—disappears entirely in what it evokes. Like an image as I have defined it,[92] language being utterly transparent to the point where, in Colette as in Proust, it becomes an *experience*—the latter defined, in light of tradition, as "a simultaneity with the plenitude of Being, if not a fusion with God."[93] Literature is an "*experience*" that "modifies the *psychic space* of the *speaking subject*," and, in this, we know that it is at one with love and that the semiotic is ever present.[94] This means that literature is not reducible to "language," if by this we understand language as it is presented by phenomenology or structuralism. Literature as experience means, at its deepest level, that language is formative of the psyche and of the *socius*. As such, it would ever be linked to murder.

V. Is Murder in Everything?

Finally, does the notion of experience place us at one remove from the semiotic? Is the evolution in the oeuvre we have been considering with regard to language and the signifying process one that moves, in the 1960s, from pushing traditional linguistics and literary criticism to the limit with the invocation of mathematics, through the 1970s with the development and modification of the semiotic and the symbolic, where the founding murder is the touchstone, through to sensation, transubstantiation, and then to experience and the modification of psychic space in the later developments of Kristevan literary theory, where, some might argue, the founding murder is hardly present at all? In short, is not experience, recalling its transcendent character, at the antipodes of the founding murder? I believe that it is not, for the sacred is involved, and it evokes violence. It would, however, require a further study to demonstrate this, and things must now be drawn to a close.

To conclude, I ask: does this mean that being grounded in the founding murder, both transubstantiation and experience, like the semiotic and the symbolic, are ultimately grounded in what could be said to be the most problematic aspect of the whole of Freud's oeuvre?

JOHN LECHTE

MACQUARIE UNIVERSITY
NOVEMBER 2018

NOTES

Translations of quotations from works in French for which there are no English translations are by the author.

1. See John Lechte, *Julia Kristeva* (New York: Routledge, 1990), 91–122; and, in a more popular vein, John Lechte, "Julia Kristeva and Thought in Revolt," *TLS online*, January 29, 2018, https://www.the-tls.co.uk/articles/public/julia-kristeva-thought-revolt/.
2. Julia Kristeva, *Le Texte du roman: Approche sémiologique d'une structure discursive transformationnelle* (Paris: Mouton, 1970).
3. Ibid., 64.
4. Vladimir Propp, *Morphology of the Folktale*, trans. Laurence Scott (Austin: University of Austin Press, 2009). Algirdas Julien Greimas, *Narrative Semiotics and Cognitive Discourses*, trans. Paul Perron and Frank Collins (Minneapolis: Pinter, 1990).
5. Kristeva, *Le Texte du roman*, 64.
6. As Kristeva points out, the *actant* is distinguished from the actor in being the structural category derivable from studying a plurality of texts, while the actor is present in a particular text (ibid., 79).
7. Ibid., 70.
8. Ibid., 85.
9. Ibid., 90. See Jean Starobinski, *Words upon Words: The Anagrams of Ferdinand de Saussure*, trans. Olivier Emmet (New Haven: New Haven University Press, 1979).
10. Kristeva, *Le Texte du roman*, 68–69.
11. Ibid., 69.
12. Noam Chomsky, *Topics in the Theory of Generative Grammar* (The Hague: Mouton, 1978).
13. Kristeva, *Le Texte du roman*, 78.
14. Ibid., 137.
15. *Fatras* is one of many (albeit one of the most important) aspects of the novel's *énoncé* and *énonciation* (*act* of discourse) discussed by Kristeva. For "act of discourse," see also Émile Benveniste, *Problems in General Linguistics*, trans. Mary E. Meek (Coral Gables: University of Miami Press, 1971), 218.
16. Kristeva, *Le Texte du roman*, 189.

17. See Peter Kingsley, "Empedocles for the New Millennium," *Ancient Philosophy* 22 (2002): 340.

18. Kristeva, *Le Texte du roman*, 189.

19. The Hegel of contradiction as "the root of movement and life," as negativity, is still dominant at this stage of her thinking. See G. W. F. Hegel, *Science of Logic: Volume Two*, trans. W. H. Johnston and L. G. Struthers (New York: Allen & Unwin, 1966), 67.

20. Mikhail Bakhtin, *Problems of Dostoevsky's Poetics*, trans. Caryl Emerson (Manchester: Manchester University Press, 1984), 69–73.

21. Jean-François Lyotard, *Just Gaming: Jean-François Lyotard and Jean-Loup Thébaud*, trans. Wlad Godzich (Manchester: Manchester University Press, 1985).

22. Claude Lévi-Strauss, "The Structural Study of Myth," in *Structural Anthropology*, trans. Claire Jacobson and Brooke Grundfest Schoepf (Harmondsworth: Penguin, 1972), 216–17.

23. A brief survey of the way Dostoyevsky's *Notes from the Underground* has been brought to cinema by various directors can confirm this.

24. Philippe Sollers, *Nombres, roman* (Paris: Seuil, 1968). Julia Kristeva, "L'Engendrement de la formule," in *Sémiotikè: Recherches pour une sémanalyse* (Paris: Seuil, 1969).

25. Kristeva, "L'Engendrement de la formule," 281. Kristeva cites, for example, S. K. Saumjan, "Outline of the Applicational Generative Model for the Description of Language," *Foundations of Language* 1, no. 3 (1965): 189–222.

26. Kristeva, "L'Engendrement de la formule," 283.

27. Julia Kristeva, *La Révolution du langage poétique: L'Avant-garde à la fin du XIXe siècle, Lautréamont et Mallarmé* (Paris: Seuil, 1974). Part A is translated into English as *Revolution in Poetic Language*, trans. Margaret Waller (New York: Columbia University Press, 1984). Passages cited from Parts B and C are my own translation.

28. Sollers, *Nombres*, 22.

29. Ibid., 22.

30. Kristeva, "L'Engendrement de la formule," 294.

31. Ibid.

32. Ibid., 295.

33. Ibid.

34. Ibid., 300.

35. Ibid., 303.

36. Ibid., 280.

37. Ibid.

38. Ibid., 284.

39. Ibid., 298.

40. Ibid., 315.

41. Ibid., 300. For Cantor's infinite numbers, see Robert Tubbs, *What Is a Number?* (Baltimore: Johns Hopkins University Press, 2009), 243–48 and passim.

42. Kristeva, "L'Engendrement de la formule," 305.

43. Ibid., 306.

44. Ibid, 308.

45. Julia Kristeva, "Word, Dialogue, and Novel," in *Desire in Language: A Semiotic Approach to Literature and Art*, trans. Thomas Gora, Alice Jardine, and Leon S. Roudiez (Oxford: Blackwell, 1984), 72; "Le Mot, le dialogue et le roman," in *Sémiotikè*, 153.

46. Kristeva, "Word, Dialogue, and Novel," 72n15; "Le Mot, le dialogue et le roman," 153n10.

47. See Gottlob Frege, *The Foundations of Arithmetic: A Logico-Mathematical Enquiry into the Concept of Number*, trans. J. L. Austin (Oxford: Blackwell: 1968), 11 and passim.

48. Paul Benacerraf, "What Numbers Could Not Be," *Philosophical Review* 74, no. 1 (January 1965): 69.

49. Ibid., 70.

50. Kristeva, "L'Engendrement de la formule," 324.

51. Ibid., 324, 325.

52. "Multiplicity" is the key term in Badiou's theory of number and numbers. It displaces the notion of One as unity, so important to the Greeks. See Alain Badiou, *Number and Numbers*, trans. Robin Mackay (Cambridge: Polity, 2008), 7–15.

53. Kristeva, "L'Engendrement de la formule," 334.

54. Although Dedekind invented the "cut" in mathematics in relation to irrational numbers, this is quite different from what is implied by the series presented in *Nombres*. See Richard Dedekind, *Essays on the Theory of Numbers*, trans. Wooster Woodruff Beman (New York: Dover, 1963), 12–19.

55. Sollers, *Nombres*, 17. Notably, "0" does not figure explicitly in the series of sequences.

56. Zijiang Ding, "The Numerical Mysticism of Shao Yong and Pythagoras," *Journal of Chinese Philosophy* 34, no. 4 (December 2005): 625.

57. Alain Arrault, "Numbers, Models and Sounds: Numerical Speculations of Shao Yong (1012–1077)," *Monumenta Serica—Journal of Oriental Studies* 61, no. 1 (2013): 186.

58. Ding, "The Numerical Mysticism of Shao Yong and Pythagoras," 620.

59. See Ricardo L. Nirenberg and David Nirenberg, "Badiou's Number: A Critique of Mathematics as Ontology," *Critical Inquiry* 37, no. 4 (Summer 2011): 583–614, especially 586.

60. Thus, when reading Sollers's novels, such as *H*, in the essay "The Novel as Polylogue," or when addressing the rhythmical, phonic, and semantic aspects of a text—or, more broadly, when addressing the semiotic aspects of the text—the phenotext and genotext couple is in play. Philippe Sollers, *H* (Paris: Seuil, 1973). Julia Kristeva, "The Novel as Polylogue," in *Desire in Language*; "Polylogue," in *Polylogue* (Paris: Seuil, 1977). See also Kristeva, *La Révolution du langage poétique*, 215.

61. Kristeva, *Revolution in Poetic Language*, 109–13.

62. Ibid., 114.

63. G. W. F. Hegel, *Phenomenology of Spirit*, trans. A. V. Miller (Oxford: Oxford University Press, 1977), 83.

64. Ibid.

65. Kristeva, *Revolution in Poetic Language*, 215.

66. See Kristeva, *La Révolution du langage poétique*, 239–91.

67. Ibid, 229–30.

68. Roman Jakobson, "Shifters and Verbal Categories," in Linda R. Waugh and Monique Monville-Burston, eds., *On Language* (Cambridge: Harvard University Press, 1995), 386–92.

69. As a note in *La Révolution du langage poétique* says: "the theme of the 'murder of the father' is *one* of the representations of this thetic event" (545n1). René Girard, *The Scapegoat*, trans. Yvonne Freccero (Baltimore: Johns Hopkins University Press, 1986).

70. Kristeva, *Revolution in Poetic Language*, 75.

71. Ibid., 79.

72. René Girard, *Violence and the Sacred,* trans. Patrick Gregory (Baltimore: Johns Hopkins University Press, 1979).

73. Julia Kristeva, *Powers of Horror: An Essay on Abjection*, trans. Leon S. Roudiez (New York: Columbia University Press, 1982); *Pouvoirs de l'horreur: Essai sur l'abjection* (Paris: Seuil, 1980).

74. Ibid., 61; *Pouvoirs de l'horreur*, 76.

75. Ibid. (emphasis added).

76. Ibid., 138; *Pouvoirs de l'horreur*, 161.

77. See Kristeva, "Word, Dialogue, and Novel," 79–80; "Le Mot, le dialogue et le roman," 162.

78. See the reference to the "common meal" in Julia Kristeva, *Tales of Love*, trans. Leon S. Roudiez (New York: Columbia University Press, 1987), 25; *Histoires d'amour* (Paris: Denoël, 1983), 37.

79. "With those affected by melancholia, primary identification proves to be fragile, insufficient to secure other identifications." Julia Kristeva, *Black Sun: Depression and Melancholia*, trans. Leon S. Roudiez (New York: Columbia University Press), 14; *Soleil noir: Depression et mélancholie* (Paris: Gallimard, 1987), 23.

80. Ibid., 13–15; *Soleil noir*, 22–25.

81. Ibid., 14; *Soleil noir*, 24. Moreover, in *Black Sun* Kristeva cites a long passage from *Revolution in Poetic Language* that defines the semiotic (*Black Sun*, 264–65n24; *Soleil noir*, 33n27).

82. A number of explicit references to Freud and the founding murder can be found in both *Tales of Love* and *Black Sun*. See, for example, *Tales of Love*, 45 and *Black Sun*, 265n28; *Histories d'amour*, 61 and *Soleil noir*, 37n35.

83. Julia Kristeva, *The Sense and Non-sense of Revolt: Powers and Limits of Psychanalysis Volume 1*, trans. Jeanine Herman (New York: Columbia University Press, 2000), 20–31; *Sens et non-sens de la révolte: Pouvoirs et limites de la psychanalyse I* (Paris: Fayard, 1996), 47–69.

84. Hence the Lacanian claim that the unconscious is structured like a language.

85. See Kristeva, *The Sense and Non-sense of Revolt*, ch. 3.

86. Sigmund Freud, *The Interpretation of Dreams*, in *The Standard Edition of the Complete Psychological Works of Sigmund Freud*, vols. IV and V, trans. James Strachey (London: Hogarth, 1958), 603.

87. See Julia Kristeva, *Time and Sense: Proust and the Experience of Literature*, trans. Ross Guberman (New York: Columbia University Press, 1996), 108; *Le Temps sensible: Proust et l'expérience littéraire* (Paris: Gallimard, 1994), 139–40.

88. Julia Kristeva, *Colette*, trans. Jane Marie Todd (New York: Columbia University Press, 2004), 113 (volume 3 of the "female genius" trilogy); *Le Génie féminin: La Vie, la folie, les mots*, tome 3, *Colette, ou la chair du monde* (Paris: Fayard, 2002), 155.

89. Ibid., 247; *Colette*, 332.

90. Ibid., 318; *Colette*, 425.

91. Ibid., 318 (my emphasis); *Colette*, 425.

92. John Lechte, *Genealogy and Ontology of the Western Image and Its Digital Future* (New York: Routledge, 2012).

93. Kristeva, *Time and Sense*, 193; *Le Temps sensible*, 239.

94. Julia Kristeva, "Monstrueuse intimité (de la littérature comme expérience)," *L'Infini* 48 (Winter 1994): 55.

3

Eléana Mylona

JULIA KRISTEVA BETWEEN THE SEMIOTIC AND THE SYMBOLIC: THE "PROCESS OF *SIGNIFIANCE*"

What we call signifiance, then, is precisely this unlimited and unbounded generating process, this unceasing operation of the drives toward, in, and through language; toward, in, and through the exchange system and its protagonists—the subject and his institutions.

—Julia Kristeva, *Revolution in Poetic Language*

I. Introduction

By a large measure, Kristeva's thought goes beyond the psychoanalytic milieu; it is inscribed in a debate that takes us from philosophy to linguistics. From Ricoeur to Proust, from philosophy to works of literature, passing through Arendt and Stern, Kristeva's work, centered on the psychoanalytic experience, leads me to conclude that "the process of *signifiance*" is life itself. We will follow the development of her thought on the basis of questions she has posed about narration and its production of a form traversed by fantasy, to the point of its revelation of narration as sensorial, as the representation of psychosexuality, and finally as meaning in the psychoanalytic situation. The polymorphous fate of narration revealed by the transference and the countertransference implies the act of questioning and illustrates the complex process of the construction-deconstruction of subjectivity. Narrativity traversed by the drive force realizes the surge of sensible experience, its indexing, with the goal of traversing its foundation in the originary repression on which the language of narration relies.

Translated from French by Armine Kotin Mortimer.

II. The Collective Challenged by the Singular: From Act to Representation

To think the psychical expression in all its forms, especially the form of narrativity that produces the narrative, is a preoccupation as ancient as the appearance of organized speech in a communicative ensemble, oral or written.[1] Narrativity is commonly defined as the quality, the condition, or the properties of the process of production of a narrative. It is also an attempt to make the singular challenge the collective, to make *signifiance* challenge common sense and lived experience. According to Kristeva's theorization, these processes generating narrative are an attempt to elaborate movements of the drive. Thus, in her conceptualization, the processes of narrativity in all its forms—literary or specifically subjective—reveal, in the human being, the processes of making sense of subjective experience. These processes of narrativity are related to the passage from the sensorial to the symbolic, from act to representation, as Kristeva describes them, at the time of the acquisition of language. For if narrativity concerned only the quality or the form of a narrative, there would be no problem. The descriptions in which "targeted" classical rhetoric and academic discourse excel, for example, would suffice, we are told by Barthes and Kristeva.[2] Besides its phenomenological or literary aspects, narrativity includes other procedures that implicate the experience of the speaking being.

Already according to the procedures of classical elaboration, narration permitted the interference of different levels of *temporality specific* to the narrative, in which poetry and philosophical narrative interweave.[3] The philosophers all insist on the demand for rationality (*logos*), which breaks with the traditional discourses, that is, the legends and fables (*mythos*) of mythology, to articulate the specific lived experience with rational time. The art of speaking becomes both a science (in the sense of a structured study) and an art (in the sense of a practice resting on experienced knowledge, a technique) that relates to the action of discourse on the mind. Aristotle spoke of words psychically inhabited.[4] This art of speaking can be considered a theory of effective speech linked to an experience and a practice. Centered at first on oral narrative discourse, the concern with the narration of heroic legends was progressively replaced by the concern for historicity, the exploration of human nature, then ethics, logic, and science. Kristeva takes part in this philosophical tradition when she travels between linguistics, literature, and psychoanalysis, and allows us to understand how in narrativity intra- and interpsychic functionings, as well as interpersonal ones, are engaged.

III. Language Incarnate

From a *macroscopic* point of view, we find this concern continuing into our time in the philosophy of language: Benveniste, Jakobson, Heidegger, Sartre, Barthes, Ricoeur, and Arendt; and also in the writers Shakespeare, Baudelaire,

Mallarmé, Proust, and Céline. The concern common to these authors is *the narrating of the soul of the human being.* Every narrative involves interest for what is human. According to Kristeva, it's a matter of "questioning the *experience* . . . to show its singularity. And thus how this singular *experience*, this *enunciation* of an utterance, this *writing* . . . jostles and innovates."[5]

In her conceptualization of language, Kristeva rejoins Merleau-Ponty (1908–1961), who quoted Cézanne in the epigraph to "Eye and Mind": "What I am trying to translate to you is more mysterious; it is entwined in the very roots of being, in the impalpable source of sensations."[6] Kristeva localizes in this carnal source the subjective pole of language, which will be articulated with the universal pole. In this fashion, she supports his thesis that language is the place of the intertwining of the human being and the universe, a "hollow," a "fold," a "flesh," as Merleau-Ponty put it.[7] Sensible and sensed language thus becomes incarnate. This language incarnate is the object of Kristeva's study.[8] Every form of narration seems to her conditioned by the propensity intrinsic to the creation of narrative, inherent in the human being in her universal essence, therefore in humanity. Kristeva identifies the same idea in Hegel, who also articulates the individual and the universal: "Such are all great historical men—whose own particular aims involve those large issues which are the will of the World-Spirit."[9]

Dialectically, narrative includes the diachronic and the synchronic, the individual and the collective, the canonic-linguistic language and *the speech of lived experience, nurtured by the drive and subjectively appropriated.* In contrast, Kristeva tells us (again quoting Barthes), we have the "science of the *conditions* of content, that is to say of forms: it will concern itself with the variations of the meanings engendered and, so to speak, *engenderable* by works: it will not interpret symbols but only their polyvalence; in a word, its object will no longer be the full meanings of the work but on the contrary the empty meaning which underpins them all;"[10] because the new human sciences, hyperspecialized in hyperprecise autonomous and well-delineated domains, have paradoxically fractioned and invalidated the global method that previously addressed human experience.[11]

From a *microscopic* point of view, today, we find the multiple aspects of narrative as the object of research in several disciplines: linguistics, literature, history, philosophy, sociology, etc. This statement does not aim to demonstrate the anteriority of classical thought to contemporary culture. It seems to us that narrative has this plurality of aspects of form, purpose, and status because, for one thing, the *aptitude for speaking* is the pedestal of human identity, of human experience, and, for another, this experience is itself plural. Narrative has multiple expressions: literary, linguistic, historical, psychical, social, philosophical, and political.

The true value of this capacity of narrative to conceptualize is not due to its antiquity, but, rather, its antiquity is due to its value. Narrativity, from the moment of its origins, recounts the process of psychicization of humanity, which gave rise to the constitution of language in its multidimensional expression.

IV. Julia Kristeva, Freudian

It is with this foundation in diachronic pluridisciplinarity that we propose to approach Kristeva's oeuvre, on the condition that we add the contributions to it of Freudian thought, which allow us to identify *her conception of narrative and narrativity in literature, philosophy, and linguistics, above all starting from and in the psychoanalytic cure.* Narrative for Kristeva is understood as a psychical product nurtured by and based on the drive and the body. Its roots lie in the unconscious, and it borrows the linguistic code to make itself heard. Her theorization is based in and bears on three disciplines: linguistics, philosophical anthropology, and psychoanalysis.

Following her theorization, we maintain that narrative is born with the human being and marks the entire trajectory of his phylogenetic and individual evolution. According to Kristeva's conception of narrativity, life consists in the potentiality of being narrated by the subject to give it a meaning; thus in sharing. Kristeva follows Freudian theory like a compass that allows her to insert her proficiency as a psychoanalyst into linguistics, literature, and philosophy. From this point of view, the narrativity of the subject contains her psychical organization of the drives and expresses the passage from the archaic field of partial relations with the object to the field of relations with the object of desire, that is to say, from the id to the ego, having subjectively appropriated its drive elements. In her theorizing approach, Kristeva follows Freud, also a great connoisseur of ancient civilization. He returned to and completed the human patrimony by exploring and adding to it the unconscious psychical aspects and those of the drive. Freud proposed that this cultural patrimony is a product of the collective unconscious, a derivative of psychical functioning. The cultural patrimony, human thought, speaks through these narratives of its very substance, its emergence from the chaos of the drive, its representation, its questioning, conflicts and anxieties, its successes and failures. Kristeva proposes to grasp in it the processes of psychicization of repeated and unrepresented acts, such as the murder of the father—their production as representation, narration, then meaning—as psychical processes of humanity and organizing processes of language. Thomas Mann also raises this relationship between the phylogenetic past and the ontological past: "its penetration into the childhood of the individual soul is at the same time a penetration into the childhood of mankind, into the primitive and mythical."[12] Freud himself affirmed that his interest in medicine, the natural sciences, and psychical functioning was, for him, an eternal return to his initial youthful passion for human nature, archeology, and the sources of belief and ethics.[13]

Not only did he demonstrate the relationship between the organization of humanity's patrimony and psychical organization (*Totem and Taboo*, *Moses and Monotheism*) but he brought to light the processes generating the subject's narrative that go beyond the relations of the collective to the individual, and even beyond the strictly analytic framework based on free association. In putting them in parallel with the dream,[14] Freud showed how these processes generative of narrative open toward the transference and the fantasy, constituting the matrix of language that implicates the sensory lived experience with others, itself drive based. To be sure, narrativity concerns expression and its formulation into narrative, but from the Freudian point of view it is one of the forms of psychical expression, singularly fostered in the psychoanalytic situation by this fundamental rule: to say "whatever goes through your mind."[15] However, the voice, silence, slips of the tongue, parapraxes, unconscious fantasy, and even the body—that is, everything that escapes the verbal—have a primordial place in what is expressed during an analysis in *a state of regression* and are taken up in the transferential movements. That which is not expressed by conscious language is experienced by the body, which relates it in primary processes that come through the voice, words, and language. Kristeva joins Barthes, who says it in his own fashion: "What I hide by my language, my body utters. . . . My body is a stubborn child, my language is a very civilized adult."[16]

Freud not only put into a dialectical relation the objective and the subjective, the voluntary and the unconscious, the past and the present, the roots of narrative in infantile sexuality, which fabricates myths and infantile sexual theories; he also revealed the breaking up of time. "Have you observed that the sexual theories of children are indispensable for the understanding of myth?" he writes to Jung.[17] Literary narrativity connects with narrative in analysis and differentiates from it in topographical, economic, and dynamic terms: *regression*, the *unconscious fantasy*, and the *transference* give a psychical texture not only to the subject and her narrative but also to their addressee. Who speaks? Whence does it speak? What does it say? And to whom? We shall see how Kristeva explores these questions in her works.

For the moment, we will not approach the Freudian contributions that specifically concern Kristeva's theorization on language and narrativity, our purpose being to provide the epistemological framework within which she inscribes herself, before proposing her conceptualization. In her theorization as a psychoanalyst, she navigates between Freud, Lacan, and Klein, but in the plentiful company of Benveniste, Barthes, and their fellow thinkers, and of writers and poets—Baudelaire, Proust, Mallarmé, Colette, not to forget the philosophers: Plato, Aristotle, Hegel, Sartre, Ricoeur, Arendt. In the connections Kristeva weaves between literature and psychoanalysis, where language is now understood only as a linguistic code, she uses the Freudian discovery of the unconscious and the transference to enrich access to the extraordinary creative singularity of poets and writers. Discourse is animated by the *transference*, such that *the subjective experience traversed by the trauma* of the amorous infantile experience can express itself, transforming anxiety into creativity. From her immense body of work, we will simply mention her philosophical affinities with Ricoeur and Arendt, and then dwell more extensively on Proust, read and heard through the Kristevan prism of language.

V. Epistemology of Kristeva's Psychoanalytic Anthropology

On the epistemological level, Kristeva distances herself from the structuralist model in linguistics based on the notion of the *sign*, with the Saussurian distinction of the signifier and the signified as an invariable material linguistic structure. This innovative, mobile position brings her closer to Ricoeur.[18] Ricoeur articulates *interpretation*, from the point of view of a *hermeneutic phenomenology*, with the tradition of *existential phenomenology*. The last and most important part of his work is centered on *philosophical anthropology*. He raises questions about structuralism, which poses philosophical problems, fixes language in a universal static structure, and ties time to the calendar and knowledge to objective methodology.[19] Ricoeur includes language in his philosophical reflection and proposes *employed discourse*—formulating strings of actions, events, and their human contexts—which, articulated with the linguistic system, creates and recreates meaning.[20] Thus, *lived time*, articulated with cosmic time, harmonizes the calendar.[21] "Narrative identity," says Ricoeur, "is not a stable and seamless identity. . . . [It] continues to make and unmake itself."[22] According to Ricoeur, it is the history of the lives of people that fashions their lives. They build their lives to conform with their histories. Thus, identity constructed in situ can take on the status of reality. Narrating one's life creates individual history and in this way fashions identity. However, these individual identity realities that people construct are also social realities because they are negotiated with others and shared among them.[23]

Arendt shares with Ricoeur the vision of a dialectic between the subjective individual usage of language and its relation to the world, an articulation that founds the narrative identity of the subject. Without the subject there is no narrativity, but without the relation to the world there is no narrativity either. It is the invention of one's own language in reply to the question "who am I?" that gives meaning to one's existence and creates the narrative of the subject—who thus becomes historical—addressed to humanity. What is essential in the human being, she says—what is essential in someone—appears with his death, which leaves behind only his history. Opposed to the "who am I?" one finds the body, the only thing that no one can share, because it acts "only in the sphere of the private."[24] She believes, however, that body and mind are identical, and the differentiation intervenes only when declarative discourse appears. The body is an obstacle to the unity of the "who am I."[25] Arendt articulates life, narrativity—the living language that produces meaning and can become history—and the world.[26] According to Arendt's theory, and Kristeva shares her point of view, life is the possibility it has of being narrated and thus of being shared with others.[27] In her book about Arendt, *Hannah Arendt: Life is a Narrative*, Kristeva centers the philosopher's theory on narrativity.

While also sharing several points on the theorization of narrativity with Ricoeur and Arendt, Kristeva proposes a psychoanalytic approach based on the *semiotic* as found in literary and poetic texts that take into account the question of *enunciation*. Supported by her experience of analysis, Kristeva examines enunciation in articulating it around three fundamental concepts: the *semiotic*, the *symbolic*, and *signifiance*. Her theory principally draws on Freudian theory, the theory of the unconscious and of the dimension of the drive, but enriches it with the notions of *lack*, *desire*, and the *symbolic*. We are tempted to propose an inversion of Kristeva's expression: *Hannah Arendt: Life is a Narrative*, which synthesizes Arendt's work, becomes *Signifiance is Life*.

VI. Semiotic, Symbolic, and *Signifiance*

It is from the salient points of her reading of Freud and from questions raised by the development of her thought that Kristeva developed her theorization of *signifiance in process*. We will emphasize questions concerning the domain of psychoanalysis and their effect on analytic practice. Starting with the three models of language in Freud, Kristeva constitutes her theory of language around the axes of the semiotic, the symbolic, and *signifiance*.[28] The first model is that of the *layered*, of *heterogeneous series in the area of language (without a subject)*, a model that proposes various types of representations (word/thing). The second is the model of *free association*, which gives prevalence to "the capacity of the associative story to translate unconscious traumatic contents, to illuminate them, and indeed to displace them."[29] Language traverses the apparatus of the conscious to reach the unconscious, putting the accent on the work of the preconscious. Finally, the third model in Freud, that of *meaning* or *signifiance*, follows the process of hominization that necessitates the passage from a psychical strategy of "*unrepresentable acts*" to a strategy of "*structuring representations* through identification with the father," that is, through "psychological identification with the function of the father."[30] This passage, completed by the identification with the father, "elevates [the human being] to the rank of subject of a culture."[31] According to Kristeva, in introducing the father of individual prehistory, Freud passes to the second topography and opens psychoanalysis both to a process of symbolization and to the "becoming-subject" through identification.

Starting from her reading of Freud, Kristeva differentiates herself from authors who confuse language as a simple, disembodied sign—the word beyond experience, belonging to a universal law—with language made of linguistic signs indispensable to the canonic production of language (verbalization), but which also belongs to a different (libidinal) economy; she rejects any unifying and static position. *Language as well as the subject are in motion*—generating, pulsating.

1. The Process of Signifiance

Kristeva theorizes the economy of *language in motion* through the *process of meaning*. She understands and proposes the opening and unlimited creation of meaning—analogue of the drive and its constant pressure (*Konstanzkraft*)—as the opening of meaning in and through language, but also in and through the commerce between subjects, their bodies, and their words. "What we call *signifiance*, then, is precisely this unlimited and unbounded generating process, this unceasing operation of the drives toward, in, and through language; toward, in, and through the exchange system and its protagonists—the subject and his institutions."[32] *Meaning* is to be understood as a dynamic that is topographically inscribed in its corporeal and subjective roots, a dynamic vectorized by *signifiance*. While language conveys it and serves to pass it on, such language is nonetheless engendered and worked on by the drive, which is represented while still keeping a remainder that is inexpressible in terms of social organization. This montage of language, both subjective and universal, is composed of two modalities, according to Kristeva: *the symbolic function* and *the semiotic function*. Their articulation produces *signifiance.*

2. Language as Pivot of the Axes of the Semiotic, the Symbolic, and Signifiance

Within this process of *signifiance* that constitutes language, Kristeva distinguishes two modalities that are inseparable from one another: the semiotic and the symbolic. Thus, two *psychical places*, two *modalities* organizing the whole emerge: the *semiotic* and the *symbolic*, which imply the *drive functioning* as well as the *functioning-of-the-becoming-of-the-subject* in exchanges with the *other*. These two lines of the drive carry and are carried by language and participate in the *process of meaning, the signifiance that necessitates and organizes their articulation.*

The first modality, the *semiotic*, from the Greek *σημειον*, "distinctive mark," concerns an archaic expression, a preverbal semiology of the sensorial register. This is an expression without subject: the drives and their stases organize a *chora*, without position, without subject, without object, but between subject and object: *the place of engendering of the subject* emerging from the charges and stases of the drive. There is no distinction between subject-object or real-symbolic. It is an *ordering-given-by-social-relations*, natural or sociohistorical constraints (biological differences of the sexes, of generations). This ordering pertains to a *preverbal functionality* that orders the body in the process of psychicization, objects, and the protagonists of the family structure. We are at *the degree zero of thirdness*; these are pre-oedipal semiotic functions, discharges of energy that connect and orient the body with respect to the mother, who mediates social relations. These functionalities are to be distinguished from symbolic operations that pertain to language in the sense of an autonomous sign exterior to the subject.

The second modality, the *symbolic*, implies the language of the post-oedipal subject, its grammatical, syntactical, and logical organization, never separated from the semiotic. The fantasy signals the irruption of the drive into the order of the signifier and articulates it, integrates it. The semiotic is the condition of the symbolic and can even become its destroyer. Any disruption of the social order produces deformations in the signifying chain and in *signifiance.* With the semiotic we are dealing with drives that have not been enchained in signifier/signified, an enchaining that constitutes a censoring of the absolute *jouissance* with the thing (the sexual affect). It is on this point that symbolic castration intervenes. *Signifiance articulates the semiotic and the symbolic. These three axes—semiotic, symbolic, and signifiance—condition discourse first, then listening, and determine the paths of interpretation in the analytic clinic.*

The semiotic, the *princeps* proposition in Kristeva's work, is tightly linked to the infantile pre-oedipus, in reference to the works of Freud and Klein and to the pre-mirror stage in Lacan. The semiotic is the field of affect, of the fragmented pre-oedipal body. Linked to the drives, it remains more in the fissures and prosody of language than in the signification of words.

> This modality is the one Freudian psychoanalysis points to in postulating not only the *facilitation* and the structuring *disposition* of drives, but also the so-called *primary processes* which displace and condense both energies and their inscription. Discrete quantities of energy move through the body of the subject who is not yet constituted as such and, in the course of his development, they are arranged according to the various constraints imposed on this body—always already involved in a semiotic process—by family and social structures. In this way the drives, which are "energy" charges as well as "psychical" marks, articulate what we call a *chora*.[33]

In this way, Kristeva opposes the semiotic to the symbolic, which connects words with signification in a strict, even mathematical sense, identified with judgment and the sentence.

VII. The Libidinal Economy of Language, Psychical Organization, and Interpretation

Through this theorization of language associated with the libidinal economy of the subject, Kristeva proposes a new approach to the comprehension of the neurotic psychical organization. In *obsessional neurosis*, she emphasizes "the dissociation between speech and affect as well as the shrouding of the 'archaic' object relation in affect and in preverbal representatives: movement, touch, and the gaze."[34] In *hysteria*, Kristeva puts the accent on the conflict between two psychical modalities: (1) *The high demand of the symbolic*: a cognitive competence following from a phallic identification with the father that leads to a competition with maximal symbolic performance. (2) *The high demand of excitability*: a peerless, or father-less, excitability, which leads the hysteric to crack this phallic backbone by opposing to it an overflowing affect due to the excess of the semiotic. The clash of these two demands constitutes the *trauma*, whereas interpretation aims to metabolize autosensuality into a compatible discourse.[35] The interpretive work would have the task of giving thing-presentations their autonomous dimension so as to articulate them with word-presentations.

In this way of listening to patients' discourse, Kristeva emphasizes the Freudian conception of representation and takes into account the plurality of psychical representatives: drive-representative, representation of affect, R.thing, R.word. The result is a layered model of psychical *signifiance*, operating with heterogeneous traces and signs. Kristeva proposes to take into account this polyphony as well as the different linguistic and extralinguistic levels (gesture, voice, etc.). With this conception of interpretation, the psychoanalyst insists, from the ethical point of view, on (1) maintaining meaning, valid and demonstrable truth, and (2) maintaining respect for the desire and *jouissance* of the patient. The model of interpretation that Kristeva proposes is based on the recognition of the importance of the affect in the transference/countertransference exchange. The analyst is mobile and occupies several places:

- the place of the father in individual prehistory, himself marked by symbolic castration
- the place of the father who organizes prohibitions and laws
- the place of the primary father who mobilizes bisexuality
- the place of the mother who participates in the creation of the framework of the sensorial exchange and the semiotic

The analyst shows this psychical mobility in both the pre-oedipal register and the oedipal register properly speaking, in both the semiotic network and the symbolic. This mobility of identification of the analyst in the countertransference and with interpretation puts into question the affect and the drive traces in the preconscious. In this way, the drive is mobilized in language.

Kristeva explains what directs her interpretive function: *the father of individual prehistory* allows for the *translation* of drives into language. She insists on the creation of a *psychical magma that contains the oedipal father and the father of individual prehistory*, a magma that allows for the articulation of abstract and arbitrary signs with the affective meanings that stem from prehistorical identifications. It is a matter of the connection of signs and meaning. This connection ensures a living language that contains meaning and affect; this language supports the subject and her relations with others.

From a technical point of view, at the antipodes of those who fetishize language by cutting it off from affect and drive, Kristeva proposes the eroticization of the channels of communication in order to give full importance to the drive and sensorial foundations of language. She proposes an *interpretive poiesis* to touch all the levels of language: *signifiance*, rhythm, voice, syntax. She aims (1) to differentiate the word-presentation from the thing-presentation in order to bring the semiology of the pre-oedipal exchange closer to the object, and (2) to name the stases and the drive movements in order to fix word-presentations in their autonomy. In the process, Kristeva creates a psychical magma where the oedipal father and the father of individual prehistory combine, a magma that destroys the *denial of the signifier.*

1. Two Obstacles to Psychoanalytic Speech

Analyzing her listening in the cure, Kristeva identifies two obstacles to analytic speech: *depression* and *perversion.* After a brief presentation of the particularities of language in depression, we will focus on her conception of language in perversion, based on her study of Proust. In the case of *depression*, Kristeva identifies the *denial of the signifier* and *the devalorization of language* that disorganize the association of affect and representation, an association essential to the "audibility" of the discourse. Desire and the drive determinants of the symptom, which cannot be signified, seem to have deposited their meaning in the preverbal register (voice, intonation). As a result, "the image of the depressive future does not succeed in consolidating itself in *verbal representation.* The reason is that the mourning for the object is not done in this representation. On the contrary, the object . . . is as if buried—and dominated—by jealously guarded affects and, on occasion, vocalizing: the *Thing* of the depressive resists symbolic castration" and meaning.[36] This impossible loss, less of the object than of the *thing*, leads to veritable bankruptcies of the signifier and signification. In this sense, Kristeva comes closer to Lacan, who designates the *thing* as the *beyond-of-the-signified* that one hears nevertheless in speech.

In the cure, Kristeva proposes a *poiesis of interpretation* based on the semiotic, the surface of words, intonation, by investing (cathecting) the images in order to represent them, by making connections between lived experience outside language and word-presentations, the symbolic. Primary identification with the mother facilitates and is articulated with primary identification with the father of individual prehistory, through the linking function of the mother that Kristeva presents in the concept of *reliance*.[37]

2. Perversion and Translatability of the Image in Language

In the clinical configuration of perversion, there is no access to the drives or to the other, both are denied. "Substitutions of his [the analysand's] thing-presentations (his paintings) replaced the relationship between thing-presentation and word-presentation. . . . In exchange, linguistic signs were cut off from meaning, cut out from his actions, and cut away from affect."[38] As such, the images seem isolated from conscious discourse, resistant to any associative work likely to reach the unconscious fantasy.[39]

The unrepresented psychical act (traumatism) gives rise to operative functionings or phantasmatic operative constructions made of images without words.[40] Kristeva poses the question of the translatability or not of the image into language and proposes to formulate the phantasmatic operative composition as being marked by a phantasmatic inhibition.

Kristeva identifies a "perversion [that] separated drives and their psychic representatives from language and symbolic functioning," which presupposes symbolic castration.[41]

VIII. Julia Kristeva and Narrativity

This synthesis of Kristeva's theory of language is necessary to identify the main lines of her conception of narrativity disseminated throughout her work. She focuses more precisely on the topic in her essay "La Narration en psychanalyse."[42] She shows that Ricoeur's hermeneutic approach, even if it is situated in an analytic perspective, beyond objectivist temptations, takes into account neither the experience of psychoanalysis nor the libidinal economy of language.

She evokes the *processes of construction/deconstruction/reconstruction of subjectivity* and of the meaning given to its history, in their prenarrative or transnarrative relations as revealed in the experience of the transference and countertransference. The functions of narrativity upset the rationality that inscribes itself in a universal structure of narrative like an expansion of logic, historicity, and literary creativity—even if certain literary narratives aim to realize regressive states in contact with the sensorial or dreams. We will see below how Kristeva understands Proust's poetic narration in *In Search of Lost Time* in order to bring out what differentiates her approach from Ricoeur's.

To do this, Kristeva goes through prelanguage and prenarrative to untangle the *prehistory of individual narrativity*. She refers to the Kleinian thesis of a protophantasm in the baby, a quasi narration that articulates the drive, desire, and the object of satisfaction. Thus, she revisits Stern's concept of the *prenarrative envelope*, which founds a *basic narrative structure actualized by the first drive interactions with others*. According to this theorization, the word "mommy" expresses the holosentence (*holophrase*) "*I want my Mommy*," for example.[43] This prenarrative envelope is a subjective emotional experience lived in an interpersonal context. This real and subjective experience recovers the logical properties of the drive and results in a mental construction. Narrativity proves to be an elementary structure of the object relation. The prenarrative envelope, emotional experience, is associated with "analogical representations," neither lived experience nor abstraction, between perception and representation.[44]

From the point of view of psychoanalytic experience, Kristeva returns to Kleinian theory and the possibility of expression that the destructive oral drive will find. In a preverbal context, the child expresses primary anxiety, and it is only by its potential recognition by the mother or its verbalization by the analyst that the fantasy can be narrated. For my part, I emphasize the difference between the conscious fantasy-narration and the unconscious fantasy Kristeva speaks of in following Klein and Segal.[45] Kristeva completes the phase of the emergence of the fantasy described by Stern, the condition of the acquisition of language: the passage from symbolic equivalents to symbols.[46] Indeed, for Kristeva the passage from "presymbolic equivalents" to symbols occurs with the phallic phase. "The curve of the quest, which implies a narration composed of an enigma, an ordeal and a solution, is a more complex construction. It is dependent, even more than statements of wishes or pleasure, on the capacity of the subject to overcome the phallic trial to reach the oedipal triangle."[47] On this point, Kristeva's model of *signifiance* and the articulation of the semiotic and the symbolic, presented above, are of the greatest importance: *signifiance* marks the articulation between the symbolic and the semiotic, that is, between the syntactic-semantic functioning of the language of the post-oedipal subject, on the one hand, and the semiotic functioning of the fragmented pre-oedipal body, on the other. As we have seen, the semiotic is conceived as the *preverbal functionality* that organizes the body in its process of psychicization, as well as objects and the protagonists of the family structure; these are the pre-oedipal semiotic functions, discharges of energy that connect and orient the body with respect to the mother, who mediates social relations. These functionalities must be distinguished from symbolic operations that pertain to language in the sense of an autonomous sign exterior to the subject. As we said earlier, the *symbolic* implies language, its grammatical, syntactical, and logical organization, never separated from the semiotic, while the fantasy signals the irruption of the drive into the order of the signifier and articulates it, integrates it. The symbolic corresponds to symbolic castration, which "steers both the boy and the girl to phallic identification with the father."[48] From this identification ensues psychical curiosity and the point of departure of questioning, beginning with "where do children come from?"—an interrogation that implies causality and finality, produces sexual theories, and introduces the Oedipus complex. Narration thus appears as a response to a questioning, introducing the other as symbolic interlocutor. Free association on the couch involves the articulation of the semiotic and the symbolic, pre-oedipal and oedipal procedures. As for literature, she will say in *Cet incroyable besoin de croire*:

> With these authors, but also with others, sublimation takes hold of the dimension of meaning I call "semiotic," prior to and beyond the "symbolic" proper to language itself. And through the "enunciative impudence" of style, sublimation communicates to the reader the impact of a perception that unleashes the effect of a contact with the real. Even an illumination.[49]

We propose to follow her in her elaboration of Proust's narrative, *In Search of Lost Time.*

IX. Proust and the Test of Transformation

"Aesthetic creation, notably literature, but also religious discourse in its imaginary, fictional essence, propose a device whose *prosodic economy*, *dramaturgy of the characters*, and *implicit symbolism* are a very faithful semiotic representation of the subject's struggle with symbolic collapse."[50] Literature, Kristeva tells us, "is the place where this alienation [of the subject in language] is specifically and each time thwarted."[51] It is in the "perpetual transvaluation by writing and interpretive, analytic, and critical discourse that elucidate it, that this mobile identity evolves . . . a constant questioning,"[52] a *test of transformation.*

While it is in the *literary imaginary* that the subject finds a privileged space in which he acquires his freedom and meaning, it is in *the literary experience of the utterance* that the subject transforms her dependence on the fantasy and the image. The *test of freedom* and the limits of the ego are played out, foiled, and replayed in literary experience. Proust expressed this, writing: "My imagination, which was the only organ that *I* possessed" for the enjoyment of beauty.[53] The literary imaginary allows him to describe reality, the "remains of experience," and transform it. As Kristeva writes:

> Little Marcel dreamt of sadomasochistic scenes, the flagellations of a baron, a rich industrialist . . . A way of transiting between unthinkable asthma attacks—different sadomasochistic rituals that had tormented him from his earliest youth—and his pure meditations as a writer reflecting on time regained. But that did not prevent him from experiencing deep sleep, which he designated as a "second apartment," more distant in space and time, more inaccessible, with none of the "realizations of desire" found in novelistic plots like the first dreams analyzed by the inventor of psychoanalysis. Nothing but painful sensations, bedazzlements as well, strident ringings and burning lights. Plato's cave transformed into an autistic cave: Proust the sleeper.[54]

In naming the quantitative sensorial, Proust succeeds in portraying the sensorial in the form of narrated *mises en scène* that he calls "*transubstantiations*" achieved by means of the narrative structure. In Proust's first drafts, "the tasty madeleine" was a dry "biscuit" overdetermined by a crossing of two narrative streams:[55] "a scene in which the narrator's mother was reading a novel by George Sand, where the incestuous mother's name is Madeleine," and "the secretly coded ritual for homosexuals of the time, who, to profane the Catholic communion, ate toast dipped in urine that they called 'tea' in the urinal slang of the time."[56]

With his literary imagination, Proust takes pleasure in beauty, associating in the narration incestuous maternal excitation, the plunge into the secret of the senses, and the sadomasochistic *jouissance* of flagellation to the death. Kristeva hypothesizes that "Proust's modifications to narration have as their basis or goal the traversal of the original repression that supports the language of canonic narration."[57] By *transubstantiation*, by the transport of his body into the experience of narration, Proust tries to avert the trauma of the incestuous proximity of his mother, the love/hate ambivalence that was formerly discharged in the asthma attack. He mourns his mother and identifies with her; he succeeds in remaining as close as possible to his desire while sublimating it in his writings and holding it at bay. The homosexuality that imposes itself replaces asthma, of course, but Proust succeeds in staging homosexuality in his narration. *Lost time* is none other than the time of the sensorial that he attempts to restore and which is at the origin of his writing. His *search* is for the expression and clash of desire.

The loss of the maternal object is in relation to the depressive moments, and writing is associated with the excitation of the writing; the two states of depression and excitation compose the lived experience of the subject. Kristeva reminds us that Proust "compared his text to a dress—another indication hiding . . . the subject's femininity."[58] She draws a parallel with autistic lived experience enclosed in sensoriality, from which Proust escapes by managing to name the unnamable drive. Kristeva compares this success to perversion as she detects it in the biographical information and in *In Search of Lost Time*. Céleste Albaret, the devoted servant, recounts in *Monsieur Proust* an anecdote that attests to *the passage from the sensorial to writing*, "*from voyeurism to narration*."[59] Proust returns late from a habitual night of sexual excesses and recounts to his servant his pleasure in seeing how a flagellated man suffered. He transforms this scopic grasp of the drive into a search for the words to describe it and write it. Kristeva wonders: "What is the narrator's erotic object that has taken over from the voyeur?"[60] The servant emerges from it stricken, Kristeva tells us. Also the body of language. While the homosexual object and the servant dissimulate the maternal object, the writer's erotic object is language. Proust puts into words the passage he effects from the material of the raw sensorial to the material of the narrative: "compact, cool after warmth, rose-pink,"[61] he says, an expression that condenses and dissimulates the bleeding body of the flagellated man, of the rat, of the voyeur, but also of the young man who drinks his tea dipping a madeleine into it, and of his mother. The material of the narrative represents both the pleasure-body of the excited voyeur and the sublimated living narrative that has absorbed and "spoken" the sensorial material.

X. Conclusion

Evans has suggested that the "recognition of the drawing's power as a medium turns out, unexpectedly, to be recognition of the drawing's distinctness from and unlikeness to the thing that is represented."[62] If a gap is recognized between the drawing and the thing it represents, let us imagine for a moment the gap between the words and the materiality of the sensorial represented by the narration. It is in this sense that Kristeva proposes that by way of narrativity literary experience expresses and translates the sensorial into language, and, at the same time that it escapes from it, names the drive. She quotes Proust: "The only true book, though in the ordinary sense of the word it does not have to be 'invented' by a great writer—for it exists already in each of us—has to be translated by him. The function and the task of a writer are those of a translator."[63] Proust, a dreamer and *translator of the sensible and the drive*, says this. According to Kristeva, this translation consists in passing from the semiotic to canonical language, passing toward *signifiance* to translate "the universe as his sensitive singularity."[64] Whereas the semiotic function marks the heterogeneity of meaning incarnated in the *chora*, the symbolic is the place of the renunciation of the drives in the face of the demands of representation. Narrativity represents their articulation, the putting into movement of the relation of the subject to the drive objects and his own body.

To conclude, the recognition of the power of narrativity as a means of expression proves unexpectedly to be a recognition of the distance of symbolic language used in narrativity, and of that whereby it differs from the semiotic, from the represented thing as sexual affect.

Eléana Mylona

Member, Société Psychanalytique de Paris
June 2019

NOTES

Translations of quotations from French texts for which there are no English versions are by Armine Kotin Mortimer.

1. For Freud on the psychical expression, see Sigmund Freud, *New Introductory Lectures on Psychoanalysis,* in *The Standard Edition of the Complete Psychological Works of Sigmund Freud*, vol. XXII, trans. James Strachey (London: Hogarth, 1964), Lecture 31; and *An Outline of Psycho-Analysis*, in *Standard Edition*, vol. XXIII (London: Hogarth, 1964).

2. Roland Barthes, *Criticism and Truth*, trans. Katrine Pilcher Keuneman (Minneapolis: University of Minnesota Press, 1987). Julia Kristeva repeats and elaborates on this in "How to Speak to Literature with Roland Barthes," in *Passions of Our Time*, trans. Constance Borde and Sheila Malovany-Chevallier (New York: Columbia University Press, 2018), 25.

3. Rudolf Kassel, ed., *Aristotelis De Arte Poetica Liber* (Oxford: Oxford University Press, 1965), 1451b.

4. Aristotle, *On the Soul*, in Jonathan Barnes, ed., *The Complete Works of Aristotle*, vol. 1 (Princeton: Princeton University Press, 1984).

5. Kristeva, "How to Speak to Literature with Roland Barthes," 25.

6. Maurice Merleau-Ponty, "Eye and Mind," in *The Primacy of Perception*, trans. Carleton Dallery (Evanston: Northwestern University Press, 1964), 159.

7. Kristeva cites Merleau-Ponty in "How to Speak to Literature with Roland Barthes," 25.

8. Julia Kristeva, "La Chair des mots," in Bernard Chervet, ed., *L'Interprétation* (Paris: PUF, 2012), 133–50.

9. G. W. F. Hegel, *The Philosophy of History*, trans. J. Sibree (New York: Dover, 1956), 30.

10. Barthes, *Criticism and Truth*, 73–74; *Critique et vérité* (Paris: Seuil, 1966), 57.

11. See Julia Kristeva, "Pratiques de génie," interview with Gilles Behnam, *Mag philo*, http://www2.cndp.fr/magphilo/philo17/interview.htm#top.

12. These words were pronounced by Thomas Mann on May 8, 1936 in Vienna in his lecture "Freud and the Future," to celebrate the eightieth anniversary of Freud's birth. Thomas Mann, *Death in Venice, Tonio Kröger, and Other Writings*, ed. Frederick A. Lubich (New York: Continuum, 2003), 290.

13. See Sigmund Freud, Postscript to *The Question of Lay Analysis*, in *The Standard Edition of the Complete Psychological Works of Sigmund Freud*, vol. XX, trans. James Strachey (London: Hogarth, 1959).

14. Sigmund Freud, *Jokes and their Relation to the Unconscious*, in *The Standard Edition of the Complete Psychological Works of Sigmund Freud*, vol. VIII, trans. James Strachey (London: Hogarth, 1960).

15. Sigmund Freud, "On Beginning the Treatment," in *The Standard Edition of the Complete Psychological Works of Sigmund Freud*, vol. XII, trans. James Strachey (London: Hogarth, 1958), 135.

16. Roland Barthes, *A Lover's Discourse: Fragments*, trans. Richard Howard (New York: Hill and Wang, 1978), 44; *Fragments d'un discours amoureux* (Paris: Seuil, 1977), 54.

17. Sigmund Freud, letter to Jung, December 19, 1909, in *The Freud/Jung Letters: The Correspondence between Sigmund Freud and C. J. Jung*, trans. Ralph Manheim and R. F. C. Hull (Princeton: Princeton University Press, 1974), 276.

18. See Julia Kristeva, "La Narration en psychanalyse, une transubstantiation," in *La Haine et le pardon: Pouvoirs et limites de la psychanalyse* III (Paris: Fayard, 2005). [The publication in English approximately corresponding to this essay is Julia Kristeva, "From Symbols to Flesh: The Polymorphous Destiny of Narration," trans. Paula Barkay, *International Journal of Psychoanalysis* 81, no. 4 (2000): 771–87.—Tr.]

19. Paul Ricoeur, "Narrated Time," trans. Robert Sweeney, *Philosophy Today* 29, no. 4 (1985): 263.

20. See Paul Ricoeur, *From Text to Action: Essays in Hermeneutics*, vol. II, trans. Kathleen Blamey and John B. Thompson (Evanston: Northwestern University Press, 1991); *The Rule of Metaphor: The Creation of Meaning in Language*, trans. Robert Czerny (London: Routledge and Kegan Paul, 1978).

21. See Ricoeur, "Narrated Time," 263.

22. Paul Ricoeur, *Time and Narrative*, vol. 3, trans. Kathleen Blamey and David Pellauer (Chicago: University of Chicago Press, 1990), 248–49; *Temps et récit*, t. III (Paris: Seuil, 1985), 358.

23. See Paul Ricoeur, *Oneself as Another*, trans. Kathleen Blamey (Chicago: University of Chicago Press, 1994).

24. Julia Kristeva, *Hannah Arendt: Life Is a Narrative*, trans. Frank Collins (Toronto: University of Toronto Press, 2001), 62.

25. Ibid., 64.

26. Ibid., 8–15.

27. Ibid., 7–8.

28. Julia Kristeva, *The Sense and Non-sense of Revolt: The Powers and Limits of Psychoanalysis Volume 1*, trans. Jeanine Herman (New York: Columbia University Press, 2000), ch. 3; *Sens et non-sens de la révolte: Pouvoirs et limites de la psychanalyse I* (Paris: Fayard, 1996), 71–109.

29. Ibid., 38; *Sens et non-sens de la révolte*, 85.

30. Ibid., 44; *Sens et non-sens de la révolte*, 96–97. Unrepresentable acts refer to coitus or the murder of the father, acts that are repeated without giving rise to a psychical representative and constitute what in our psychic life stands for the traumatism.

31. Ibid., 44; *Sens et non-sens de la révolte*, 96.

32. Julia Kristeva, *Revolution in Poetic Language*, trans. Margaret Waller (New York: Columbia University Press, 1984), 17; *La Révolution du langage poétique: L'Avant-garde à la fin du XIXe siècle, Lautréamont et Mallarmé* (Paris: Seuil, 1974), 15.

33. Ibid., 25; *La Révolution du langage poétique*, 23.

34. Julia Kristeva, *New Maladies of the Soul*, trans. Ross Guberman (New York: Columbia University Press, 1995), 57; *Les Nouvelles Maladies de l'âme* (Paris: Fayard, 1993), 91.

35. Ibid., 71, 78; *Les Nouvelles Maladies de l'âme*, 111, 121.

36. Kristeva, "La Chair des mots," 143.

37. Julia Kristeva, "Reliance, or Maternal Eroticism," trans. Rachel Widawsky and Perry Zurn, *Journal of the American Psychoanalytic Association* 62, no. 1 (2014): 69–85; "La Reliance, ou de l'érotisme maternel," *Revue française de psychanalyse* 75, no. 5 (December 2011): 1559–1570.

38. Kristeva, *New Maladies of the Soul*, 18; *Les Nouvelles Maladies de l'âme*, 34.

39. Ibid., 19; *Les Nouvelles Maladies de l'âme*, 35.

40. Ibid., 22; *Les Nouvelles Maladies de l'âme*, 40.

41. Ibid., 15; *Les Nouvelles Maladies de l'âme*, 27.

42. See note 18, above.

43. See Kristeva, "From Symbols to Flesh," 775; "La Narration en psychanalyse," 295.

44. Ibid., 773; "La Narration en psychanalyse," 292.

45. As a reminder, Ernest Jones points out that symbolism arises from an intrapsychical conflict "between the repressing tendencies and the repressed"; furthermore, "only what is repressed is symbolised; only what is repressed needs to be symbolised." The whole process of symbolization is effected at the unconscious level. Ernest Jones, "The Theory of Symbolism," in *Papers on Psycho-Analysis* (London: Bailliere, Tindall & Cox, 1948), 116.

46. Kristeva, "From Symbols to Flesh," 773–77; "La Narration en psychanalyse," 290–99.

47. Ibid., 775; "La Narration en psychanalyse," 295.
48. Ibid., 774; "La Narration en psychanalyse," 294.
49. Julia Kristeva, *Cet incroyable besoin de croire*, expanded edition (Paris: Bayard, 2018), 74.
50. Julia Kristeva, "Le Langage comme antidépresseur," lecture of January 14, 2012, École internationale de Genève, http://www.kristeva.fr/le-langage-comme-antidepresseur.html.
51. Kristeva, "How to Speak to Literature with Roland Barthes," 29.
52. Ibid., 30.
53. Cited in Julia Kristeva, *Time and Sense: Proust and the Experience of Literature*, trans. Ross Guberman (New York: Columbia University Press, 1996), 203; *Le Temps sensible: Proust et l'expérience littéraire* (Paris: Gallimard, 1994), 251.
54. Julia Kristeva, "Ma vie en dormant," in *Pulsions du temps* (Paris: Fayard, 2013), 136.
55. See Julia Kristeva, "In Search of Madeleine," in *Time and Sense*, 3–22 ; *Le Temps sensible*, 13–36.
56. Julia Kristeva, "Speaking in Psychoanalysis: From Symbols to Flesh and Back Again," in *Passions of Our Time*, 116.
57. "La Narration en psychanalyse," 299.
58. Ibid., 306–7.
59. Céleste Albaret, *Monsieur Proust*, (Paris: Laffont, 1973), 240, quoted in Kristeva, "From Symbols to Flesh," 784; "La Narration en psychanalyse," 309.
60. Kristeva, "From Symbols to Flesh," 784; "La Narration en psychanalyse," 309.
61. Marcel Proust, "Time Regained," in *Remembrance of Things Past*, vol. 3, trans. C. K. Scott Moncrieff, Terence Kilmartin, and Andreas Mayor (New York: Vintage, 1982), 904; "Le Temps retrouvé," *À la recherche du temps perdu*, t. III (Paris: Robert Laffont, 1987), 706.
62. Robin Evans, "Translations from Drawing to Building," in *Translations from Drawing to Building and Other Essays* (London: Janet Evans and Architectural Association Publications, 1997), 154.
63. Proust, "Time Regained," 926; "Le Temps retrouvé," 721.
64. Julia Kristeva, "Singular Liberties," in *Passions of Our Time*, 10.

REPLY
TO DOMINIQUE DUCARD, JOHN LECHTE, AND ELÉANA MYLONA

Dominique Ducard's vast study reconstructs and addresses my immersion in general linguistics and the philosophy of language, as well as the disruptive incursion that I am trying to achieve into the field of *semiology* through work that is closer to Saussure, Benveniste, and Barthes than to Peirce's *semiotics*. Taking up the possibility of a *semanalysis* attentive to the engendering of meaning as a *signifiance*, Ducard's reflection marks the steps of my journey through the "inner life of language," in which he quite pertinently identifies an echo of the "dreamwork" according to Freud, notions borrowed from Freud and Wittgenstein, as well as resonances with Culioli's enunciative semantics. In response, I would like to develop a few of the stages of the development analyzed by Ducard.

In 1969, I published two books: *Le Langage, cet inconnu* by Julia Joyaux (married name), and *Sémiotikè: Recherches pour une sémanalyse* by Julia Kristeva (my name as author).[1] The first retraces the long emergence of language as an object of knowledge and a social practice, regulated and taught: from mythology to grammar by way of the birth of "linguistics" (the word is recorded for the first time in 1883!), and the different currents of linguistics in the twentieth century. The second book (exile and polylinguism having opened up the abyss of drives, affects, and emotions) led me to probe the processes of the "engendering" and the "production" of meaning beneath the surface of signs.

At the crossroads of phenomenology, semiotics (Peirce, Saussure, and their successors, but also and more particularly in France, Greimas, Benveniste, and Barthes), and Freud's psychoanalysis and his *unconscious*, *signifiance* was waiting for me. I grasp *signifiance* in the process of the crossing between *semiotic meaning* (pre- and translinguistic indexes of drives, emotions, affects) and *symbolic signification* (systems/structures and their syntactic and semantic generations-transformations). *Signifiance de-signs*[2] the psychical functioning of the speaking subject as creativity open to the "trans-finite" of *dialogism* constitutive of speaking beings and to the *intertextuality* of cultures. This ambitious attempt to articulate current *linguistic* and semiological models *with* the Freudian theory of the *unconscious* is sketched in the "dreamwork" and

---

Translated from French by Armine Kotin Mortimer.

in the "two Freudian topographies" that current research in psychoanalysis is working to refine.

Since the tool of the analytic cure *is* language, this mutual interference of the two approaches is essential and works to break the *closure* of "language as an object of linguistics" and its "Cartesian subject." It can thus make evident the psychosexual transformations of the "subject in process in enunciation" in the analysand but also in literary and artistic works, where the subject can only respond to his own collapse by creating new "languages."

***

Another approach to the capacity to signify then opened up for me. To sketch it, I had to borrow metaphors from mathematical concepts (see Ducard), before turning toward the concrete identification of the configurations and transformations of psychosexuality in the "talking cure," in listening to the unconscious. And in so doing, I had to go deeper into my psychoanalytic practice. The semiology of *signifiance*, in my view, can only be a *semanalysis* attentive to the *singular poiesis* in the *flesh of words*. This is unfinished, long-term work. With hindsight, this recasting seems to me closer to the psychoanalysis of "transformations" in Bion's sense.[3] With the difference that instead of "abstract grids" (a, b "elements," etc.), I try to track these "transformations" by opening within these "significations," "signs," and "forms" of language the conscious and unconscious depths of psychosexuality. So that these "signs" and "forms" of the normative codes of "communication" unfold into "treasure troves" of meaning, into "figures" of psychical life understood as an *experience* (Ducard).

In the process of *signifiance*, the *signs, forms,* and *significations* studied by the sciences of language then appear like *stabilizations* of the *epiphora*. This generic term, which Aristotle borrowed from physics, indicates the metaphysical *movement* prior to any *objectification* of *one* meaning, *figured* from the start, because the original emergence links perceptions to mnemic and verbal traces. The imaginary reproduces and complexifies this originary figurability that Baudelaire writes of, when *metaphor* becomes *metamorphosis* or synesthesia and claims to grasp "the expansion of infinite things" in the "transports of the mind and the senses" (in the poem "Correspondences").[4]

As one might have expected, my "work as a semiologist created a rupture in the development of language sciences"; otherwise, for "others, including myself [Ducard], it is an incentive to continue in the spirit of inquiry." I recognize myself in the resonances established between my research and that of Culioli, for example, which develops, within the linguistic framework, a semantics of discourse open to the "semiotic-epilinguistic" (Ducard); and also in Wittgenstein's "halo" ("series of interactions"); and Thom's "continuity between the biological and the symbolic" through "symbolic bifurcation" (Ducard).

***

John Lechte's text examines an essential dimension of this recasting of *meaning/signification* into *signifiance*: the opening of the speaking being to *the infinite* as well as to the *closure* of his actions required for social communication/transmission. Necessarily, this dynamic is seen—and my semanalysis is constructed—starting from and with the *texts* that our cultural tradition considers literary or sacred, rather than in "systems" or "structures," even "generative" ones. Lechte is right to remind us of this dynamic: in the theory of literature, I maintain there is no "closed text" since *dialogism* (which I develop in Bakhtin's wake) subtends all the *actants* (Greimas) of *narrative* or of *drama*. Now, when speech is no longer understood as a *myth* (in the sense of the deposit of a society's practices and knowledge) but as a *text* (in the sense of a singular experience where the polyphony of the characters, and even of the narrator, is at the *center* of the writing as experience [*Erlebnis* rather than *Erfahrung*]), then "carnival" (Lechte) invades *signifiance*. Thus, Dostoyevsky's characters given over to the "concupiscence of their thought" rejoin the thought movement of the Proustian sentence, as I am trying to show in research currently under way.

"The intimation of the semiotic . . . and the symbolic" (Lechte) opens each sign, word, sentence, and narrative to the infinity of meaning (semiotic) and signification (symbolic), so that they function like numbers, "signifying differentials."[5] This *anaphora* designates the infinite plurality of the imaginary, solicited in the narrator and in the reader by the writing. Thus a paragraph, a word, or a syllable invites a multitude of significations and fantasies and can be read as an open ensemble of meaning; such is the "signifying differential" in Sollers's novel *Nombres* (1968). And this practice of "numbering" (Lechte) endures and pulsates in the condensed or suspended novelistic fragments (taken from Céline or from Shakespeare) that together weave the "metaphysical novels" of this writer.[6]

***

For her part, referring to my three models of language in Freud, Eléana Mylona relies on her clinical practice to complement my understanding of the drive substrate. The latter subtends the enunciation of a *metaphor*, for example, traversing the "originary repression," the "polymorphous" "sensorial, and the "primary processes" to rejoin the visible—image and fantasy. And reveals the sadomasochism underlying the metaphorical movement, considered a "transubstantiation" by Proust. In the same clinical perspective, Mylona considers *narration* and insists on the *narrathemes* already present in the "holophrases" of the baby; whereas narrativity is constructed in the passage from the *polymorphous* chaos of the primary *abject* to the relation with the *object of desire*.[7] A narrativity of which the analyst hears the failures or the exhilarations in the two major obstacles to free association, which are *depression* and *perversion*.

The process of *signifiance* necessarily leads to the field of the imaginary: free association, which undoes the *fantasy* (Mylona) and the poetic-rhetorical figures and *narrativity* in literature (Ducard, Mylona, Lechte). Each in their own way, the three authors suggest that the social contract (the "murder of the father" in Freud, "language" as a "social fact" and a "fact of the masses" in Saussure), as well as massive, globalized socialization and its growing technicity today, impose restrictions on the drive impulses and a constant contraction-condensation of psychical movements. In the imaginary, however, the social pact gives itself a moment to breathe, and it is here, under the *stabilized* elements of language (increasingly banal!), that the three authors offer observations that make evident and legitimate this "zone of turbulence" of language (Ducard) that is the process of *signifiance*. The latter is also present in the "inner language" that emerges in the invention of writing (according to Benveniste) and is deployed in the "revolution in poetic language" "whose 'motivations' are of another order than that of the sign in communication and discourse" (Ducard). *Signifiance* bears witness to the catastrophes in the identity of the speaking subject, identity put to death and recomposed starting from its very core, which is none other than the capacity to make meaning, to signify. And which Mylona identifies in Proustian writing, where the sacred meaning rubs shoulders with scatological profanation.

I understand Lechte's vigilance: could this *signifiance*, all construction-deconstruction, be based on the murder of the father and the death drive, "the most problematic aspect of the whole of Freud's oeuvre" (Lechte)? Yes! On condition that we recognize that the violence in question is that of the social pact itself, which simultaneously establishes the communities of brothers and the repression of drives—by displacing them onto a different *jouissance*, that of psychical *representation* and its *signifiance*. Henceforth, it is in the *jouissance* or enjoyment of this *displacement* that the violence of the drive is transformed and refined. With and against the violences of the social code. The destructiveness indispensable to the vital process of the *parlêtre* (the speaking being)—on the neuronal level (*apoptosis*) as on the psychical level (aggressivity and death drive)—is sublimated by participating in our transformations, creativities, and freedoms. Freud warned against the power of the destructive and self-destructive drives, whereas a woman, Sabina Spielrein, proposes to consider the death drive as an inherent scansion and a "condition of becoming."[8]

I would like to illustrate this position, which is also mine, by proposing a brief sketch of the *work of metaphor*, which the analyst hears in the collapse and the transformations of the analysand and that the poet and the novelist make explicit and reveal in their writing: in "vaporization-centralization" in Baudelaire and in "crystallization" in Stendhal.[9] Complicit with Ducard, Lechte, and Mylona, then, my answer can only be a textual *responsory*.[10]

***

"Of the vaporization and centralization of the Ego. Everything is there."[11] In Baudelaire, the *text* triumphs over the experience of love, although the experience is explicit and doubly staged: the destructive "sadistic" passion of bodies; the supreme idealization of an inaccessible but absolute and necessary Other. Baudelaire the lover, Baudelaire the Catholic, Baudelaire the mystic: perhaps not all the same, but the text is entirely based on the *metaphor*.

On the one hand, the abject: woman, nature, vile body, carcass, decay: "A carcass reclined / On a bed sown with pebbles and stones" ("A Carcass"); "Abhorrence, to whom I am bound" and "Your vampire lover's corpse!" ("The Vampire"); in opposition to the Virgin, the poet's mother chosen "from all women . . . to shame, / To be disgusting to [her] grieving spouse" ("Benediction").[12] On the other hand, an idealized transcendence intellectually named God ("God is the sole being who, to reign, does not even need to exist,"),[13] which subjectively returns to the memory of a mother sublime because she is loved, in the shadow of an imaginary pre-oedipal Father. Thus: "I am the keeper for corpses of love / Of the form, and the essence divine" ("A Carcass"); "Drawn from the holy hearth of primal rays" ("Benediction"); "Mother of memories, mistress of mistresses" ("The Balcony").[14]

Through its fusional connotations, mixing the drunken memory of an invading-invaded maternal body, *perfume* in Baudelaire becomes the allegory of the pulverization of meaning and language, but also of the identity of the self.[15] "Old neighbourhoods, are allegorical for me" ("The Swan").[16] And the dynamics of the allegory-metaphor, or more precisely of the *epiphora*, appears as the nucleus of the Baudelairian mystical soul. With the soul, the reader rejoins the wounded, punctured, hemorrhagic ego, which tries to bandage its losses by eroticizing its tatters and its rage. Perversion—between voyeurism, exhibition, exaltation of waste, and sadomasochism—then proposes its screen of *abjects*, fragile film that is neither subject nor object but signifies fear, the horror of being *one* for an *other*. The Baudelairian *metaphor* speaks "the tyranny of the human face"[17] for this modern "heautontimoroumenos (torturer of oneself)": "I am the wound, and rapier!" ("Heautontimoroumenos").[18] But borne by the amorous ego, it culminates in an ecstatic, fusional *metamorphosis* with the object: "First you imagine a tree has your passions, your desires, or your melancholy; its moaning and its oscillations become yours, and soon you are the tree" ("Artificial Paradises").[19]

Whereas Stendhal's *narration* exposes the fantasies of his *desire*, always missing and missed, a branch denuded by winter and brilliantly petrified in a salt mine: a "crystallization as an imaginary solution," the novelist specifies.[20] Desire, insoluble—every love object is a disappointment—as a result of being absolute, goes hand in hand with the language of the egoist: although inadequate for expressing the depths of the self, this feigned absolute is the royal road through which the actor-diplomat tries to reach them.[21] On the properly linguistic level, we might seek the mark of this disavowal of both language and its hypostasis in Stendhal's polyglottism (as well as in his polynomia: he accumulates pseudonyms!). The author does not hide his scorn for popular language, preferring a scientific language or simply a precise one, even tending at times to a "metalinguistics" as mistrustful of dull words as it is trapped by stereotypes. However, while the egotist's "false self" can be deciphered in this mastery, and while the impotent's dynamic is achieved in this language diminished to the point of cliché, even when adored and polished to the point of the unutterable, it is not in the "little units" of language that the writer's genius shines forth—he who wanted to "get out" of his century to communicate with Shakespeare, Mozart, and Mme Roland—but in this *transverbal* product that is the representation of amatory interaction! In the *image* of the *power* and the *impossible* in love, which are detailed only in the fantasies of his characters: Madame de Renal and Julien Sorel, Sanseverina and Fabrice del Dongo . . . Novels that the contemporary imaginary feeds on in movies and in television series.

***

When language is reduced to texts and tweets and is drowned in selfies, *signifiance* has not really disappeared. If the hurried internaut (surfer) is not yet totally liquefied, he or she finds *signifiance* in the transference in psychoanalysis or in the multiverse of the arts and literature, or by taking the risk of approaching it in what he or she considers "sacred" . . .

J.K.

NOTES

1. Julia Joyaux, *Le Langage, cet inconnu* (Paris: Seuil, 1969), republished as *Le Langage, cet inconnu: Une Initation à la linguistique* (Paris: Seuil, 1981); *Language, the Unknown: An Initiation into Linguistics* (New York: Columbia University Press, 1989); *Sémiotikè: Recherches pour une sémanalyse* (Paris: Seuil, 1969).

2. De-sign (or de-signate): the spelling with the hyphen (instead of "design" or "designate") insists on the fact that this approach to signification departs from the theory of language centered on the sign and explores the process of the engendering and production of meaning before, beyond, or through the sign.

3. W. R. Bion, *Transformations: Change from Learning to Growth* (London: Karnac, 1984).

4. See Charles Baudelaire, *The Flowers of Evil*, trans. James McGowan (Oxford: Oxford University Press, 1981), 19, where these lines are translated: "Having dimensions infinitely vast . . . Singing the senses' rapture, and the soul's."

5. See Philippe Sollers, *Nombres* (Paris: Seuil, 1968).

6. See Philippe Sollers, *Centre* (Paris: Gallimard, 2018) or *Le Nouveau* (Paris: Gallimard, 2019).

7. Julia Kristeva, *Powers of Horror: An Essay on Abjection*, trans. Leon S. Roudiez (New York: Columbia University Press, 1982); *Pouvoirs de l'horreur: Essai sur l'abjection* (Paris: Seuil, 1980).

8. Sigmund Freud, *Civilization and Its Discontents*, in *The Standard Edition of the Complete Psychological Works of Sigmund Freud*, vol. XXI, trans. James Strachey (London: Hogarth, 1964). Sabina Spielrein, "La Destruction comme cause du devenir," in *Revue française de psychologie* 66, no. 4 (2002): 1295–1317.

9. See Julia Kristeva, "De l'identification: Freud, Baudelaire, Stendhal," in Geneviève Haag, Julia Kristeva, et al., *Travail de la métaphore: Identification/Interprétation* (Paris: Denoël, 1984), 53–98.

10. With the Latin meaning "responsum" and "responsorium": a chant sung in alternation between a soloist, a group of soloists, and the choir, or a short meditative chant after a brief reading.

11. Charles Baudelaire, *My Heart Laid Bare*, trans. Rainer J. Hanshe (New York: Contra Mundum, 2017), 68. [What follows now reprises some of the essay cited in note 9, above.—Tr.]

12. Baudelaire, *The Flowers of Evil*, 59, 65, 11.

13. Charles Baudelaire, "Flares," in *My Heart Laid Bare*, 18.

14. Baudelaire, *The Flowers of Evil*, 63, 15, 73.

15. See Julia Kristeva, "Baudelaire, Or Infinity, Perfume, and Punk," in *Tales of Love*, trans. Leon S. Roudiez (New York: Columbia University Press, 1987), 329.

16. Baudelaire, *The Flowers of Evil*, 175.

17. Charles Baudelaire, "At One O'Clock in the Morning," in *The Parisian Prowler*, trans. Edward K. Kaplan (Athens: The University of Georgia Press, 1997), 16.

18. Baudelaire, *The Flowers of Evil*, 157.

19. Charles Baudelaire, *Oeuvres complètes*, t. I (Paris: Gallimard, 1975), 420 (translation by Armine Kotin Mortimer). For an alternative translation, see Charles Baudelaire, *Artificial Paradises*, trans. Stacy Diamond (Secaucus: Carol Publishing Group, 1996), 51.

20. Stendhal, *Love*, trans. Gilbert and Suzanne Sale (Harmondsworth: Penguin, 1975), 51 (translation modified).

21. [The rest of this paragraph returns to the text of Julia Kristeva, *Histoires d'amour* (Paris: Denoël, 1983), 323–24. For a slightly different rendering of the passage in English, see Kristeva, *Tales of Love*, 346–47.—Tr.]

4

Philippe Forest

BIRTH OF THE NOVEL, YESTERDAY AND TODAY

I

The temptation is always great, when one examines the extensive series of books an author has signed, to ascribe to the first a particular importance. Try as we may to ignore the effects of a retrospective illusion, we nevertheless want to believe that a first book announces—almost contains—those that are to follow. Under a reader's eyes a novel is born, within which all the books that remain to be written are inscribed in advance. And if, as in Kristeva's case, this first work deals precisely with the birth of the novel, we tell ourselves that we are entirely justified in granting it the privilege of a sort of word of origin.

No doubt this first book, by which, in a sense, everything starts, is the least read of the ones Kristeva has authored. I wouldn't claim—for who would believe it?—that it is the most important. I haven't the slightest doubt, in fact, that the interest one may bring to this book resides essentially in the echoes with which it resonates, echoes that place it in relation to the great works that will come only later. This book was her first thesis, written under the direction of Lucien Goldmann in 1966 and 1967 and defended at the École Pratique des Hautes Études.[1] Its object of analysis is an old narrative from the end of the Middle Ages, *Jehan de Saintré* by Antoine de la Sale, which here serves to develop theoretical reflections of a semiological nature on the genre of the novel.[2]

Her study adheres admirably to all the requirements for rigor and seriousness called for by the genre of the academic exercise (as practiced at the time),

---

Translated from French by Armine Kotin Mortimer.

the genre to which it indubitably belongs. In this respect, on a more modest scale of about two hundred pages, and in spite of obvious differences as regards both the corpus used and the method adopted as well as the conclusions to which it leads, this study anticipates the great treatise that her *thèse d'état* will provide when she defends that thesis a few years later and publishes it in 1974 under the title *La Révolution du langage poétique: L'Avant-garde à la fin du XIXe siècle, Lautréamont et Mallarmé.*[3] On the other hand, at first glance, there are hardly reasons, nor are there ways, to liken this first enterprise of theorization to the important books she published from the start of the 1980s. This is because by its form and in any case by its tone it doesn't compare to the books that constitute Kristeva's principal body of works: essays and lectures, collections and novels, from *Powers of Horror* to *Time and Sense*, by way of *Black Sun* and not forgetting *Possessions* or *Teresa, My Love*.[4]

There is a certain amount of imprecision, however, in speaking of a "first book." To be sure, this is most likely the first book written by Kristeva. But a thesis is not necessarily a book, at least in the mind of the person who signs it. And, quite cognizant of the rules imposed on any student and the game they must play with the institutions on which their future depends, they can put off until later the time to make a book that would be more personal, one they would recognize as being fully their own.

Besides, though written first, this was not the first book to be published. Kristeva's thesis doesn't appear until 1970, published by Mouton—and precisely in the brand new collection "Approaches to Semiotics" edited by Thomas A. Sebeok, whose two assistants happen to be Josette Rey-Debove and Julia Kristeva herself. *Le Texte du roman: Approche sémiologique d'une structure discursive transformationnelle* was the sixth volume in the series. Note that the fourth volume in the same collection—in which one also finds *Grammaire du Décaméron* by Tzvetan Todorov, published the same year—consists of a collection of articles, *Essays in Semiotics/Essais de sémiotique*, which Kristeva edited.[5]

However, on the date when her "first book" appears, the author has already published *Le Langage, cet inconnu*, a remarkable introduction to linguistics, in the series "Le point de la question" at the publisher SGPP. But as she signed this book, exceptionally, with her married name—Julia Joyaux—behind which it is doubtful that anyone would have been able to recognize Kristeva herself or the wife of her husband, already famous, to be sure, but under his pseudonym Philippe Sollers, one may well wonder to what extent the author claimed this work as authentically hers.[6] Most important, in that same year of 1969, thus one year before the publication of *Le Texte du roman*, Kristeva had just offered a collection of her essays, *Sémiotikè: Recherches pour une sémanalyse*, in the Tel Quel series.[7] Some of these essays have become emblematic of what has sometimes been called "poststructuralism." And if there happened to be readers—there must have been some at the time—who read *Le Texte du roman* after having read *Sémiotikè*, they must have experienced a distinct feeling of déjà vu, since one of the chapters in *Sémiotikè*, "Le Texte clos" (The bounded text), consisted of a return to the analysis Kristeva developed in her thesis, in the form of a collage of its essential points.

II

Kristeva has often told under what conditions, thanks to a scholarship, she arrived in Paris at the end of 1965 as a quite young student from Bulgaria, with the idea of pursuing her research. Her intention was to undertake study bearing on the most contemporary French literature, which she had discovered with difficulty, or rather sensed the existence of, through the echoes that reached her on the other side of the iron curtain. At the time, *Les Lettres françaises*, the weekly cultural review edited by Aragon, was the principal source of information, as concerns French culture, available in the regimes under Soviet influence. The review was connected to the French Communist Party and as such was widely distributed in the countries of the East; it remained so until Aragon's stance in support of dissidents led to its interdiction and its disappearance. But in the political as well as the literary domains, Aragon was already in the process of revising the very dogmatic positions he had espoused during the previous decade. More and more he lent his support to young artists and writers who sometimes proclaimed their relative disengagement and defended an experimental conception of creativity quite distant from the principles defining "socialist realism." For this reason, *Les Lettres françaises* manifested a definite curiosity about and good will toward Jean-Luc Godard and Philippe Sollers, the Nouvelle Vague, and *Tel Quel*, as well as certain authors of the Nouveau Roman, especially Claude Simon and Michel Butor—the movement that at the time appeared as the principal one of the French literary avant-garde.

It was the Nouveau Roman to which Kristeva at first wished to devote her research. Thus the question must be asked: what could have led her to embark on a study bearing on a medieval author? This change of direction is something of a surprise. And yet, we are not lacking for elements of an answer. One of these elements actually figures in her thesis, discreetly it is true.[8] In 1965, shortly before Kristeva's arrival in France, Aragon's new novel *La Mise à mort* was published.[9] Because of the reputation the communist poet enjoyed in the East, the young Bulgarian student knew his work. She even on occasion claimed she had learned French from his books, and she could not fail to be aware of the metamorphosis his oeuvre was about to undergo. The place she will grant thirty years later to the author of *La Défense de l'infini* and *Blanche ou l'oubli*, in her books *The Sense and Non-sense of Revolt* and *Intimate Revolt*, bears witness to this fact.[10]

Among other things, *La Mise à mort* is a rather dizzying meditation on the creation of the novel. In particular, this reflection rests on a consideration of the medieval origins of French literature, for which one finds numerous precedents in Aragon, particularly at the time of the Resistance. It is for this reason that Aragon mentions in passing *Le Petit Jehan de Saintré* by Antoine de la Sale, whose first name he spells "Anthoine" to emphasize the link that connects this author to one of the principal protagonists of his story. The reference is quite fleeting, and the author of *La Mise à mort* gives greater weight to another example, contemporaneous with the first, a work by the Sire de Bueil called *Jouvencel*. But he does not fail to present *Jehan de Saintré* as "the first realistic novel."[11]

A new edition of the work of Antoine de la Sale had just been published in 1965; Kristeva's thesis was based on it.[12] It is probable this edition drew Aragon's attention. One sees in *La Mise à mort* a renewal of experimentation that, after long years devoted to the defense and illustration of "socialist realism," fostered Aragon's return to the surrealistic inspiration of his youth, under the notably significant influence of the new avant-gardes developing in France at that time with the Nouveau Roman, *Tel Quel*, and structuralism. Aragon's novel was written in the proximity, proclaimed or not, of the young writers he supported. That the most contemporary novel was able to reinvent itself on the basis of a reflection pursued on its most distant sources could not have failed to strike Kristeva and prompt her to think that such a detour through the past might prove as paradoxical as it was fruitful.

The idea was to think through the present starting from the past—but also the reverse. More precisely—to hark back to the origins of the artistic form one is examining (in this case the novel) to describe its most contemporary incarnation. In this respect, there is certainly no reason to grant more importance than it deserves to Aragon's mention of Antoine de la Sale in *La Mise à mort*. One can simply suppose that such a reference awoke Kristeva's curiosity by alerting her to a work that few French readers know. But it would not have sufficed to determine the project on which she embarked as a doctoral student. Other precedents for the choice she made no doubt counted for more: Georges Bataille attempting to think art on the basis of its double birth in the frescoes at Lascaux and the paintings of Edouard Manet; and even more Bakhtin, whose thought Kristeva introduced to France in her earliest interventions, and who reaches as far back as Rabelais, as we know, to describe the dialogic novel whose logic he presents and analyzes, notably in Dostoyevsky.

III

To understand why Kristeva turns away from the Nouveau Roman to which she had at first thought to devote herself, thus abandoning her first project, another element should certainly be taken into account. She will never return to the Nouveau Roman, except in respect to studies bearing on authors like Beckett and Duras, who are precisely the least representative of the movement in the meaning one ordinarily gives it.

There is no doubt that Kristeva must have become aware, quite quickly, of the contradictions at work within the theoretical and novelistic avant-garde in France, contradictions that hardly corresponded to the distant image she had had of it from her native Bulgaria. Any united front one might have found within it had disappeared. Alain Robbe-Grillet's theses expounded in the articles collected in *For a New Novel* (1963) were from the start subjected to violent criticism from writers adhering to the great classical traditions they propounded and who declared themselves offended by the strangeness of the fictions for which the theses served as program and support.[13] But the debate also carried into the political domain where prestigious authors intervened whose positions could not be mistaken for those of the partisans of pure and simple academicism. Thus Sartre and Aragon, in spite of the real benevolence they showed to the authors of the new literature, did not fail to remind them to what extent they lacked the political conscience that should have been indispensable to it.

Reacting against surrealism and existentialism and breaking with the principle of *engagement* as it had long governed the French literary field, the Nouveau Roman, in the form for which Alain Robbe-Grillet had become the spokesperson, called for a kind of essential distance with respect to all the ideologies the novel was held to express. As a result, his vision was denounced as a new version, falsely updated for the taste of the day, of the old theories of "art for art's sake." The relative recognition redounding to the benefit of the author of *In the Labyrinth* was interpreted as a sign of his bourgeois recuperation.[14] When the Nouveau Roman took a new direction at the end of the 1950s—so that people could speak of a Nouveau Nouveau Roman some time later—it was exposed even more to such objections. With Robbe-Grillet and Ricardou, then with Claude Simon, the novel became "the novel of the novel" or "metanovel" and gave the impression of turning farther away from the political and historical reality for which it should have been responsible, in one way or another. When the effect of surprise passed, when the charm of the new dissipated, the formalism and aestheticism imputed to it appeared as more and more insufficient and irrelevant, even in the eyes of the critics and writers who had at first supported the Nouveau Roman.

At the moment Kristeva arrives in Paris, the divorce has already been consummated. Lucien Goldmann has just published *Towards a Sociology of the Novel* in which he expresses the most explicit reservations about the Nouveau Roman on the basis of Marxist convictions inherited from Lukács.[15] As concerns Roland Barthes, whom Kristeva meets quite early and declares herself close to from the moment she is writing her thesis, the famous articles by which he defended and one could almost say discovered, even invented, Robbe-Grillet belong already to the past. In the case of *Tel Quel*, where Kristeva will publish her major articles, the situation is no different. To be sure, Jean Ricardou, who is on the editorial committee of *Tel Quel*, publishes his theories in that journal and defends the metatextual turn taken by the Nouveau Nouveau Roman, as both its instigator and its theoretician, undertaking to demonstrate, with an incontestable critical brio, that no real gaps exist at the heart of the French avant-garde. But Philippe Sollers, in the brilliant and memorable lecture he gave in December 1965, "Le Roman et l'expérience des limites," expressed in the clearest and the most polemical manner possible his condemnation of the positions defended by Robbe-Grillet, thus defining the new route he is preparing to open himself with *Drame* and *Nombres*.[16]

Thus Kristeva's first contacts when she arrives in France—Goldmann, Barthes, and Sollers—can variously be considered as adversaries of the Nouveau Roman. Or in any case, as writers convinced of the necessity of another literary option. Perhaps it is under their influence that Kristeva turns away from the Nouveau Roman. Unless these contacts offered her their support because they immediately recognized that the young Bulgarian student, whose talents they discovered with awe, brought in her baggage the means to think differently about literature precisely at the moment when they particularly needed it.

IV

One has to admit that *Jehan de Saintré* is scarcely dealt with in *Le Texte du roman*—the title of which, as will have been noticed, makes no reference to the work studied. To be sure, Kristeva acquits herself in all seriousness of the obligations imposed on whoever engages in the doctoral exercise. She situates the work and describes it, she returns regularly to it to illustrate the analyses she proposes, her bibliography and the scholarly studies she cites demonstrate that she has read everything that had to be read, and she doesn't fail to take into account even the facts that emerge from the examination of the manuscripts. Nevertheless, as she herself admits, it is not that the text before her eyes has value, in her opinion, for any of its inherent qualities, which generally justify the study one may devote to a book: "Antoine de la Sale's texts are our objects of interest, but without accentuating in any way the value of the author's person or the aesthetic importance of the work. Rather, it is for their anonymity, or as it were their 'insignificance,' that these writings claim our attention, as the location of a structural change."[17]

In no way does Kristeva's study primarily seek to take up residence in the field of medieval studies. Moreover, it is significant that her thesis is completely ignored by specialists of Antoine de la Sale's oeuvre. In any case, we can suppose so, noting that there is no mention of it in the critical bibliography found in Joël Blanchard's edition of the novel published in the "Lettres gothiques" series directed by Michel Zink, the most easily accessible edition for today's readers.[18]

The stakes are elsewhere. They principally concern the place occupied by *Jehan de Saintré* in the history of the genre to which it belongs. This book is usually held to be the last of the medieval novels. Joël Blanchard insists on this point from the first sentence of his introduction: "With *Saintré*, Antoine de la Sale authors one of the last medieval representations of a long series of literary works, of diverse forms and inspirations, which are conventionally classified under the generic name *novel*."[19] The perspective taken by Kristeva is different, though not irreconcilable with the preceding. She prefers to maintain that *Jehan de Saintré* is the "first French novel" more than the last medieval novel, and that with this work there occurs a turning point whereby one passes from a "thought of the symbol" to a "thought of the sign."[20] It would be less the last medieval novel than the first *modern* novel, as it were. A history begins with it, rather than ending. However, adds Kristeva, and she repeats it, this history, which began in the second half of the Middle Ages and for which *Jehan de Saintré* provides a kind of first attestation, is itself about to come to its end.

The density and complexity of the demonstration Kristeva develops do not allow us to summarize it in a few sentences. Let us say, at the risk of simplifying and therefore betraying the proffered thought, that according to theses related at times to those of Lukács and Goldmann and at times to those of Bakhtin, this novel is defined as a "post-epic narrative." Its birth at the end of the Middle Ages, reprising that of the Menippean satire at the end of Greek antiquity, is connected to the passage from one mode of thought to another. Whereas the epic was subject to the reigning univocity, the monovalence proper to its symbolic structure, the *ideologeme* of the sign, evidenced by the novel, introduces a principle of duplicity that detaches the discourse from the realities it refers to and from the transcendental basis from which they draw their meaning. The Chansons de Geste and the tales of the Round Table obeyed the law of "nonconjunction" or "exclusive disjunction," by which the contraries are clearly opposed within what also constitutes a moral code: Good and Evil, the hero and the traitor, the good man and the bad man, etc. Substituting for this is a law of "nondisjunction" within the novel by which the figures of the feint and the double proliferate—in other words, and at the risk of simplifying further, the figures of an "ambivalence" in which we generally recognize the essential characteristic of novelistic discourse. Which doesn't mean that the novel is deprived of a moral or even of a message, the stating of which constitutes both its foundation and its purpose—its principle and its end—delimiting the loop the novel forms. As such, the novel does indeed constitute a "bounded text," but within this closure it makes space for a whole series of transformations that bear witness to a different functioning.

However, and this may be the principal idea, the reversal that this interpretation of *Jehan de Saintré* identifies does not cover the essential point: "the mutation of the discourse of the epic into novelistic discourse, the passage from the symbol to the sign, leaves intact a constant that ensures the resemblance of these two types of discourse. It is the *expressivity* of the symbolic discourse and of the discourse of the sign, their function of expressing a *signified* anterior to them that takes the place of the law for them."[21] Thus, at the price of a somewhat overarching synthesis (hence the numerous references to Hegel), and choosing an almost indifferent example for the needs of demonstration, the author seeks to recapitulate the entire history of the modes of signification in studying the passage from the symbol to the sign solely to show how those two discourses subscribe equally to a principle of "expressivity," the questioning of which constitutes the horizon of the thought proposed by Kristeva.

V

Only incidentally does one expect *Le Texte du roman* to be understood as a study of *Jehan de Saintré*, I think any reader would agree. Rather, we should read the book as the matrix within which the author proposes the first systematic exposition of a thought to come. Summarizing the theoretical knowledge she has just acquired, envisioning that knowledge according to the new proximity she claims with the French literary avant-garde as she has discovered it, this thought will be affirmed thanks to important developments from the end of the 1960s and the beginning of the 1970s, and they will continue to inform in diverse ways her most recent books.

We cannot but be struck by the rigor and the ease with which the young Julia Kristeva succeeded in assembling, in a coherent manner, the great diversity of theoretical discourses coexisting at the time, theories she was able to master often in the space of a few months. To mention just a few examples: Saussure's semiology, Chomsky's generative grammar, Greimas's semantics and the actantial model he proposed following Propp and Lévi-Strauss, the theses of Lukács and Goldmann, intertextuality and dialogism in Bakhtin's sense, not forgetting more episodic references to Barthes, Lacan, and Derrida. All of this was made to contribute within a reflection that allowed for circulating from one to another of these models.

The wager made is the same as that to which the preface to the 1978 republication of *Sémiotikè* returns.[22] It is less a matter of explaining literature through linguistics with a scientist's perspective than just the opposite: submitting linguistics to the questioning literature addresses to it. As Kristeva declares, "the encounter of the human sciences, especially semiology, with literature reveals instead how their omnipotence is waning, so unimportant do they prove to be in unveiling the logic of literature and of its subject."[23]

Stemming from the triumph of structuralism, but at a distance from it and against it, the intention is to put back into play an essential concern for History and the subject—at a time (just before May 1968) when such categories are about to return to the fore in people's minds. For her work in this direction, Kristeva's principal support is Bakhtin, whose thought, we recall, she introduces in France in a form compatible with the convictions and the expectations of the intellectuals whom she addresses. The notions of dialogism and the carnivalesque, of intertextuality, aim for "the insertion of history (society) into a text and of this text into history."[24] These notions ensure an indispensable "revitalization of structuralism" and allow us to think the subversive dimension of a novelistic discourse within which the plural texts it harbors can contradict each other and relativize each other.

The return to the origins of the novel that Kristeva realizes with Antoine de la Sale, as Bakhtin did with Rabelais, allows us to understand the discourse the novel constitutes, but also the limits beyond which literature may now venture. At no time does Kristeva pretend that the author she is studying is a precursor. Quite the contrary, she constantly points out how much he is representative of a time period she asserts is perhaps coming to its end. Nevertheless, she always identifies the features in him that help her sketch a profile of literature based on the symbol but also on the sign, a literature that breaks with the "expressivity" that governs it. One example among others is the way the adventure recounted by Antoine de la Sale slips into the background, allowing the speaking of the author to take the front of the stage; the text, though consisting of the confrontation of contrary discourses, then becomes its own object. A different logic obtains, also characteristic of medieval fantasies and *fatrasies* (nonsense poetry), a logic that prevails because the work, abandoning expression and representation, becomes "the inscription of its own production."[25] And that is the case, as Kristeva repeatedly indicates, with writers like Mallarmé, Lautréamont, and Roussel, and also with the ongoing writings of Philippe Sollers and a few of the other authors of the *Tel Quel* group. Kristeva concludes: "always ambiguous," the novel "is the milieu where the consecration of expressive thought (of the symbol or the sign) and the (problematic) 'exit' of this expressivity through the infinite transformation of the signifiers can be simultaneously in play."[26]

VI

Le Texte du roman is a tour de force that consists in the way in which, beginning with a forgotten and indifferent work, the author succeeds in both recapitulating and renewing theoretical knowledge as it is constituted under the sign of structural linguistics (primarily using Bakhtin's thought as a lever), so as to emphasize what in the literary experience pertains to "the most amazing affirmation of life, the relief from anxieties, the traversal of crises" that she speaks of in this regard. She adds: "whoever analyzes the logic of meaning knows unfailingly that truth resides where resistance arises."[27]

Each new novel—and this is also an idea that Aragon often expresses—places us before the birth of the novel, its rebirth as well; repeats its past history; and explores its possible horizons, returning to near or distant sources from which it proceeds, posing all the while the perpetual possibility of a destiny that nothing ever allows us to predict exactly. With it, everything begins again. As a result, because it is essential to humanity, the novel will never disappear, no matter what unheard-of and unusual forms it may take, because it is the place where contesting discourses meet, thus assuring its indispensable renewal.

Each novel begins the novel anew. One may imagine that such a conviction was not unrelated to the decision Kristeva made to author her first work of fiction in 1990, *The Samurai*, then to make an ever more important place for the novel in her work during the following decade. It happens that at the same time she turned her attention to Aragon—not without surprising her readers at times. Aragon was considered an outmoded author unlikely to interest anyone who was concerned with theory and modernity. I am not at all claiming that Kristeva's turn to the novel owed anything essential to her reading of Aragon, because I don't think that. Other French novelists certainly counted more, and more durably, for her: Sollers, Céline and Proust, Duras and Colette, to name just a few. Let's just say that, just as the reading of *La Mise à mort*, through its reference to *Jehan de Saintré*, was no doubt not without a role in the decision to write *Le Texte du roman*, it is not impossible that rereading *Blanche ou l'oubli* counted somewhat in the metamorphosis that belatedly made of Kristeva an authentic novelist.

I introduce this hypothesis out of self-interest—since I am taken for both a novelist and a critic (among well-informed people, more and more the novelist, less and less the critic except on rare occasions like the one I am offered here), since I have devoted the bulk of my past academic work to the surrealist and structuralist avant-garde, and since I am a faithful reader of Aragon and Kristeva—to close the circle of my little demonstration.

In *Intimate Revolt*, Kristeva quotes this sentence by Aragon: "The novel is a science of anomaly." And she comments: "the novel is articulated, in short, as an antimethod, as the incessant revolt of an imaginary against itself, as the questioning of an intimacy continuously reinvented." Quoting *Blanche ou l'oubli* once more: "Until now, novelists were content to parody the world. Now it has to be invented."[28] It seems to me that such was Kristeva's belief already in her first book, and that it remains hers through her latest ones.

PHILIPPE FOREST

UNIVERSITY OF NANTES
OCTOBER 2018

NOTES

Translations of quotations from French texts for which there are no English versions are by Armine Kotin Mortimer.

1. [There used to be two different kinds of doctoral thesis in France. Kristeva wrote *Le Texte du roman* for the first one, sometimes called "thèse de troisième cycle." For the second, long thesis, also called "thèse d'état" or "doctorat d'état," she wrote *La Révolution du langage poétique*.—Ed.]

2. Antoine de la Sale, *Jehan de Saintré*, ed. J. Misrahi and C. Knudson (Geneva: Droz, 1965). Julia Kristeva, *Le Texte du roman: Approche sémiologique d'une structure discursive transformationnelle* (Paris: Mouton, 1970).

3. Julia Kristeva, *La Révolution du langage poétique: L'Avant-garde à la fin du XIXe siècle, Lautréamont et Mallarmé* (Paris: Seuil, 1974).

4. Julia Kristeva, *Powers of Horror: An Essay on Abjection*, trans. Leon S. Roudiez (New York: Columbia University Press, 1982); *Time and Sense: Proust and the Experience of Literature*, trans. Ross Guberman (New York: Columbia University Press, 1996); *Black Sun: Depression and Melancholia*, trans. Leon S. Roudiez (New York: Columbia University Press, 1989); *Possessions: A Novel*, trans. Barbara Bay (New York: Columbia University Press, 1998); *Teresa, My Love: An Imagined Life of the Saint of Avila*, trans. Lorna Scott Fox (New York: Columbia University Press, 2014).

5. Julia Kristeva, Josette Rey-Debove, and Donna J. Umiker, eds., *Essays in Semiotics/Essais de sémiotique* (The Hague: Mouton, 1971).

6. Julia Kristeva, *Language, The Unknown: An Initiation into Linguistics*, trans. Anne M. Menke (New York: Columbia University Press, 1989). [First published in 1969 under the name Julia Joyaux, *Le Langage, cet inconnu* became available in a Livre de Poche edition. Julia Kristeva, *Le Langage, cet inconnu: Une Initiation à la linguistique* (Paris: Seuil, 1981).—Ed.]

7. Julia Kristeva, *Sémiotikè: Recherches pour une sémanalyse* (Paris: Seuil, Points, 1978).

8. Kristeva, *Le Texte du roman*, 23.

9. Louis Aragon, *La Mise à mort*, in *Oeuvres romanesques complètes*, t. V (Paris: Gallimard, Bibliothèque de la Pléiade, 2012).

10. Louis Aragon, *La Défense de l'infini* (Paris: Gallimard, 1986); *Blanche ou l'oubli* (Paris: Gallimard, 1967). Julia Kristeva, *The Sense and Non-sense of Revolt: The Powers*

and Limits of Psychoanalysis Volume 1, trans. Jeanine Herman (New York: Columbia University Press, 2000); *Intimate Revolt: The Powers and Limits of Psychoanalysis Volume 2*, trans. Jeanine Herman (New York: Columbia University Press, 2002).

11. Aragon, *La Mise à mort*, 138.

12. Antoine de la Sale, *Jehan de Saintré*, ed. J. Misrahi and C. Knudson (Geneva: Droz, 1965).

13. Alain Robbe-Grillet, *For a New Novel: Essays on Fiction*, trans. Richard Howard (Evanston: Northwestern University Press, 1992).

14. Alain Robbe-Grillet, *In the Labyrinth*, trans. Richard Howard (New York: Grove, 1978).

15. Lucien Goldmann, *Towards a Sociology of the Novel*, trans. Alan Sheridan (New York: Tavistock, 1975).

16. Philippe Sollers, *Drame* (Paris: Seuil, Tel Quel, 1965); *Nombres* (Paris: Seuil, Tel Quel, 1968).

17. Kristeva, *Le Texte du roman*, 20.

18. Joël Blanchard, "Avant-Propos," in Antoine de la Sale, *Jehan de Saintré* (Paris: Le Livre de Poche, 1995).

19. Ibid., 5.

20. Kristeva, *Le Texte du roman*, 22, 26.

21. Ibid., 162.

22. Kristeva, *Sémiotikè*, 5–7.

23. Ibid., 6.

24. Julia Kristeva, "Word, Dialogue and Novel," in Toril Moi, ed., *The Kristeva Reader* (New York: Columbia University Press, 1986), 39; "Le Mot, le dialogue et le roman," in *Sémiotikè*, 88.

25. Kristeva, *Le Texte du roman*, 65.

26. Ibid., 192.

27. Kristeva, *Sémiotikè*, 6–7.

28. Kristeva, *Intimate Revolt*, 218; *La Révolte intime: Pouvoirs et limites de la psychanalyse II* (Paris: Fayard, 1997), 404.

5

Marian Hobson

JULIA KRISTEVA'S FAREWELL TO PHILOSOPHY

Kristeva taught for many years at the University of Paris 7-Denis-Diderot as a professional academic. This was not in a department of philosophy but in the UFR (Unité de formation) Sciences des Textes et Documents, which is now the UFR des Lettres, Arts et Cinéma. The name change occurred shortly before her retirement in 2007.[1] The alteration is more important than it may seem: the title of the university unit where she worked during her career, with vigor as many have testified, points to an approach to literature that widens it immeasurably. The reconfigured department (UFR) does not include in its title "sciences de langage," but like many other departments of languages and literatures, it includes such courses in what is taught, so one might conclude that the title reverts to something more run of the mill, a department of languages, linguistics, and literatures, with perhaps drama or the performing arts ("Arts"). A department unlikely, then, to be very different from most departments of languages and literatures within different universities. The words *textes* and *documents* of the previous name—the material support of what is studied—are let go of in this later academic context. In a book dedicated to Kristeva's work as a philosopher, the question of why professionally she was thus catalogued within her university has to be posed. Answering this question would lead in two directions. The first is the way in which the place of philosophy in universities as an academic subject was evolving. I have discussed this in part elsewhere and leave it aside here. The second is the role of Kristeva herself in this evolution, and the question of what there was in her work that had early meshed with this change, so that she can be said to have been one of the Parisian writers actually bringing it about.

The pivot in the Paris 7 departmental name, dropping *texte* and *document*, may not be unrelated to the retirement of its most famous member. It seems to mark something that could be given a chronological label: a leaving behind of structuralism and its successor, poststructuralism, and thus a moving through what may have been a kind of detour, in the road-traffic sense, back to more traditional work on literature. This in very marked contrast with the young Kristeva, who from her arrival in France in late 1965 had worked with an intellectual avant-garde—chiefly Roland Barthes,[2] whose own writing in his structuralist moment had enacted a break with traditional literary criticism.[3] His work later evolved into something more fluid ("poststructuralism," for lack of a better term).[4] But it is he who can be said to have caused "*texte*" to enter into more common use in France, in a sense that his own writings had greatly refined. With it, he actually provoked the displacing, at least for a while, of such a term as "literature"—in certain genres of discourse, it has to be said. It may be that he perceived the older term as indicative of a class-based penchant for complex expression.[5] His own professional development widened into the study of all signs, and "text" was covered at the last by a term allowing an even greater freedom as to the field of study: *semiology*, the study of signs, of meaning. His final, most prestigious appointment was at the Collège de France, holding the Chaire de Sémiologie Littéraire (1977–1980).

"Semiology" allows a sense even less circumscribed by borders than "text," and wider than such terms as "book" or "work" dating much farther back in cultural history. It enables a sense that easily allows extension into other disciplines—sociology, history—and tones down any relation to literature considered as an aesthetic activity. Kristeva, at once more rigorous and more traditional, will exploit this possibility of enlargement of scope in a fuller fashion than Barthes. "Structuralism" had evolved as a movement out of structuralist linguistics and the work of Roman Jakobson (1896–1982), following the development of the latter's work by his friend, the anthropologist Claude Lévi-Strauss (1908–2009). It considered that meaning is created not so much by the actual items, words, or other elements in the intellectual analysis, as by the relations holding between these items, often impossible to baptize with a simple name. It had a liberating effect on the study of literature, being in many ways a reaction against the preceding tradition, academic and pedagogical, where knowledge of its history was often highly restricted, both culturally and socially, because derived from particular circumstances of social advantage. Instead, literature could be seen as a collection of works, each of which could be closed off and analyzed with methods that were less intuitive and more directly transmissible in teaching, since their application could be taught. Where an accompanying sociocultural baggage was less necessary.[6] This closing off of items to form a matrix, and their reassembling in what were often novel ways, were the typical strengths of a structuralist analysis, as were its claims to a certain rigor. In reaction against this, "poststructuralism" sought more fluidity in the choice of elements of analysis and, more especially, rejected the closing off of the work for analysis either explicitly, or implicitly through the way the analysis was actually conducted. In other words, poststructuralism let the rigidly bordered grids of structural analysis fray and seep outside themselves.

Both poststructuralism and structuralism are text based, or treat material to be dealt with like a matrix of signs—the derivation of "text," "woven materials" already suggests this is the word's origin. They do this even when such material is rather different from verbal or written signs, for example, a pattern of social arrangements, as happened in the academic discipline of structural anthropology. The items to be discussed were disengaged by a kind of combinatorial analysis based on correlations and were thus freed from the cultural genealogy and traditional aesthetic, concerned with intuitive conceptions of beauty, that they often trailed with them. However, crucially: the imagination, in literature as in psychology, is left aside as an explicit value or element. In spite of Kristeva's allusions to Husserl, the imagination, which plays an important role in his work, is left aside; it is to Freud, rather, that she turns, and it is the imaginary that will play the major role. This illuminates at least in part the move into psychoanalysis that Kristeva will make later.

Following the way opened by Barthes, she will, at the beginning of her career, write on literature, semantics, and theory of writing. But, together with others of the time, for instance Gérard Genette (1930–2018) or another Bulgarian working in France, Tzvetan Todorov (1939–2017), the writing will be theoretical, seldom monographic or restricted to one author or work, but ranging more widely. "*Texte*" in this context then has an interesting destiny, one akin to "*écriture*" ("writing"), also a Barthesian term: a destiny that is probably momentary and is certainly time-dated; in both these cases, a common term is skewed slightly out of its usual context, endowed with a special *timbre* and put to work in a new way, bringing important changes of perspective in the teaching of literature, but more important, changes in the way the role of literature in a society is conceived.

To sum up: the change in departmental title discussed above indicates a kind of reversion to a mean, and perhaps reflects the struggle of most university systems to house experimental work more easily, without undergoing pressure to reconfigure the relations between whole swaths of a university's component parts (such systems needing to satisfy the demands of funders or of students' future employers, as well as the particular interests of students). This essay will argue that the tension indicated by the alteration in the name of this department at Paris 7 is particularly owed to Kristeva and, through her, to Barthes. It throws sharp light on her writings, causing them to be seen as part of a movement out towards a certain kind of theory considered as a kind of philosophical writing,[7] and just as there is a reversion closer to a more normal title for such academic entities, so Kristeva will later move to other, perhaps more settled intellectual positions and genres (including the writing of novels). The tension points to a mutation in the general status of philosophy in academia as well as to a disquiet about the status of literature as a component of academic studies. For, although it is certainly not as a professional academic that Kristeva has been primarily known, she was one, even though it was not particularly easy to place her work within a standard university classification (nor that of Barthes). It is here that one of the main effects of her work came into play: the term *semiology* moved into prominence, a term that allowed the freedom to extend research across different subjects and that was neither as traditional nor potentially as historically restrictive as *philosophy* would have been.

However, in the UK and US, as a result of the very considerable interest taken in Barthes's and Kristeva's work, along with others of their generations (especially, Foucault, Derrida, Lyotard), a kind of term for this area of intellectual work was developed: "theory." It was this that could most easily be attached to her work, at least in its earlier phases, at least when it had to be catalogued in academic courses. So that in the English-speaking world, it is as a producer of complex, energetic, and vivid theories that she became known, through the publication of the articles leading to her first book.

I. The First Book and Its Moment: *Sémiotikè: Recherches pour une Semanalyse* (1969)

Kristeva arrived in Paris in late 1965 on a scholarship that allowed her to study in France. Bulgaria had a strong tradition of connection to French language and culture; this is also true of Romania (Ionesco, for example) as of intellectuals in Turkey and Lebanon, suggesting longstanding contacts between this area (the Western part of the old Ottoman empire) and Paris.[8] Her ease with French culture was not so much acquired as already rooted in Bulgarian culture itself, through her Catholic school and her university education. Furthermore, education in Marxist-Leninist thought was inescapable in Bulgaria, then behind the Iron Curtain. However, this tradition was also strong in France. The Communist Party had a long history of influence, both on the shop floor and among intellectuals. Sartre (1905–1980) and Beauvoir (1908–1986) were sympathizers.[9] In a later generation, other Iron Curtain intellectuals, Bronislaw Baczko (1924–2016) or Leszek Kolakowski (1927–2009), who were expelled from Poland or otherwise prevented from teaching there, brought with them a strong background in Marxist thought. Kolakowski went first to the US and then to the UK, and Baczko first to France and then to Switzerland (Geneva). They presumably quit the Polish Communist Party, or their membership lapsed at their expulsion from Poland in 1968. Baczko in particular had written from within a communist-oriented tradition of the history of ideas (though he did not stay there, either geographically or spiritually). The strength of this intellectual background to all these thinkers of two generations, quite apart from their actual experience of what were then regimes behind the Iron Curtain, was that of difference from the Western philosophical cursus: a much wider reading in both Marxist philosophy and its antecedents, like Hegel, and a tradition of intellectual history writing much more philosophically informed than that of many Westerners. Marx was, it is not always remembered, a great historian of philosophy, and not many Western-trained thinkers understood the Marxian intellectual tradition in that depth (Alastair McIntyre may well be an exception for one trained in the UK.) Baczko, like Kristeva, received criticism for his transfer both out of the Communist bloc and out of communist thinking.[10] However, he stayed within what could be called the purlieus of that philosophical tradition. In Kristeva's case, that movement out is very different and provides matter for the understanding of her philosophy.[11]

Paris in 1966 was a place of enormous intellectual ferment. The excitement was particularly derived from the set of brilliant thinkers who were teaching there: Lévi-Strauss, Barthes, Derrida, Foucault, Deleuze, Lyotard. Kristeva quickly made a name for herself with the articles she published, collected together in *Sémiotikè* (1969), published by the prestigious house "Aux éditions du Seuil" in the Tel Quel collection edited by Philippe Sollers, whom she had married in 1967.[12] The importance of what was by then known as the *Tel Quel* group as a supportive element in which work could be written, tested, and finally published is hard to overestimate.[13]

Kristeva brought to her readers some strangeness[14]—the first word of the title of her first book, *Σημειωτική* (*Sémiotikè*) is visually striking: in Greek characters, with no transliteration; the subtitle, *Recherches pour une sémanalyse* (Research for a semanalysis), while suggesting incompletion (*recherches pour*), uses a term invented by Kristeva, *une sémanalyse*. The book was highly visible, appearing in a prestigious collection of publications associated with the journal *Tel Quel*. To this milieu she also brought a good deal of novel information. She could read (and speak) Russian,[15] and was well informed about linguistics. This included important movements in what was entitled "semiotics" in the work of the Tartu, Estonia group led by the great semiotician Juri Lotman (1922–1993), who, though Russian by birth, was unable to find a position in the USSR, almost certainly because of antisemitism. Soviet linguistics and pre-Stalinist poetics were not well known in the West at the time. Kristeva here acted as a highly intelligent and active conduit of Lotman's and others' work on the theory of signs, thus participating in the development of semiotics as a recognized branch of information theory as well as linguistics.[16] However, Kristeva's work then and now never merely recapitulates a status quo; one of the most engaging testimonies to the authenticity of her investigations into semiotics and its development is her interest in the writings of Charles Sanders Peirce (1839–1914), whose work, difficult, fragmentary, is still (in 2019) far from having been mapped out, and at the time was scarcely referred to outside a fairly narrow circle. With a similarly generous gesture, she brought to more general attention the work of the linguists Émile Benveniste (1902–1976, born in Aleppo) and Jean-Claude Chevalier (1925–2018), and the semiotician Thomas Sebeok (1920–2001). Yet the semiotic approach has a longer history that she does not mention: it was John Locke (1632–1704) who, much earlier in 1689, had baptized his "doctrine of signs" a "semiotics," and who gave the word in Greek characters, just as does Kristeva in the title of her book.[17] It is as if she was participating in a long movement of recovery, of the possibility of a science of meaning as encapsulated in signs, and, as we shall see, enabling an expansion of its scope and claiming her place in it.

She herself called her book "*un bilan*," a "balance sheet."[18] However, these articles when read together seem rather the opposite. They give the sense of a program, pointing to what is relevant and apt for investigation, pointing to her future work. They tend to show how semiotics can probe a whole raft of subjects: what is a "text"?—claimed not as a literary work but as, for example, part of fashion;[19] how can writing analyze gesture and its troubled relation with speech?; how can semiotics, through the notion of "text," erase too definite a separation between writing and reading? So that in the last essay in the volume, "L'Engendrement de la formule" (The engendering of the formula), it can cope with myth and with scientific and political texts, each time tending to consider thinking as an array of formulae or sequences rather than as an organized unity. This is an important step, one left somewhat implicit in the essay, but having an influence in other disciplines. For the collection of essays as laid out in *Sémiotikè* has direction if not unity; it is clearly going somewhere that is beyond present thinking. Moreover, there is a self-localization in what she writes in these essays, where she strives to see her situation in the contemporary culture with the maximum of distance, to be on the edge of her own intellectual location, as it were. The collection, as we are reading it, then, is no mere juxtaposition of already published pieces; it gradually appears as something more like a project for a poetics of the avant-garde.

One of the striking elements in this project is the positive connotation constantly given to "science." Few engaged in thinking about literature at the time would have applied this word, although in the UK the work of I. A. Richards (1893–1979) or William Empson (1906–1984) had prepared for this (authors to my knowledge never cited by Kristeva).[20] As one reads this collection, like her later work, the realization dawns that this is a claim: to status, to respect, and to a certain sort of rigor. This has involved the right to use diagrams. These are, to my mind and in *Sémiotikè*, one of its most interesting developments. They are worked up out of current use—for example, from linguistics or out of Barthes. But they have been altered and made more complex. They point to a way of linking up ideas of meaning that goes beyond what is expressed in words within articles on logic, or which as formulae can act as a shortcut to remind the reader of some styles of work in linguistics making heavy use of symbols. Early on, in the piece written as a kind of preface, "Le Texte et sa science," we are as if warned, again by the introduction of a Greek term in its Greek characters, *poiein*, that a strangeness is being brought on stage. One that works against straightforward sense, one that produces a "polyvalence with no possible unity."[21] We learn that semiotics is not becoming a system but is a place for the elaboration of theories and models, and, what is more, a place of contestation and self-contestation.[22]

What is outstanding in this introductory essay is the intellectual audacity. Semiotics is linked in a kind of authoritative gesture to the great discussions of the foundations of mathematics and logic, to "Zermelo, Frege, Russel [*sic*], Hilbert etc." Peirce is mentioned immediately in the next sentence as "one of the first axiomaticians." What saves this from hubris?—by which I mean, from using reference by name only as support for an argument? Some investigation (perhaps only possible post-Google) reveals that there is, indeed, a conjectural link between Peirce and the great discussants of the foundations of mathematics.[23] In a step further, then, let us generalize: we have intellectual daring + great intelligence = high intuition, it would seem.

At the time, these references were empowering to a certain audience. They seemed to encourage both rigor and a particular kind of audacity. "Just looking" at other more austere and prestigious disciplines was allowable, it seemed.[24] Was this a transference into literary studies of an attitude derived from consumer culture? And did it stop there? Or rather, was there occurring, or perhaps more accurately, was there being organized a kind of shift in the basis from which the reading public related to literature, with a concomitant sifting (or even purge?) of writers deemed less central to a particular project, one to be defined below. Lautréamont and most especially Mallarmé are formed into a canon; Rimbaud, on the contrary, is barely mentioned, if at all.[25] The next section will discuss this move, in the sense of a move in chess, in greater detail. At the time, this seemed liberating to me as to many, in that the discourse of the essays was in constant mutation. Instead of creating a doctrine to replace and supplant those attitudes to literary criticism that had preceded, there was a kind of movement through topics in semiotics, and through their relevance to the language of literature, accompanied by a constant renewal of Kristevan vocabulary. Thus "paragrammes," for instance, which seems to be a *hapax*, to have no future beyond the article in which it is developed ("Pour une sémiologie des paragrammes") . . . until the reader does some homework and discovers that the term dates back to Demosthenes, and that Aristotle allows for a joking use.

Kristeva's use of an extending panoply of slightly strange terms certainly suggests both a fermentation of ideas and a movement forward. And the importance of terminology warns, by Kristeva's use of *on* ("one"), that there is agreement that a renewal of scientific thought occurs through a renewal of its terminology.[26] But it is the agreement that is relayed in the essay—Engels quoted by Althusser[27]—rather than the detail of any actual renewal of terminology itself. This brings us up short against a problem: what is the lifespan of Kristevan coinages? Are they nonce-words? Do they have sufficient purchase on contemporary discussions to have a semi-independent development? Can they have a life of their own?[28]

One Kristevan coinage has indeed survived: *intertextualité*. Developed in "Le Texte clos," it is put forward as part of the *productivity* of a text, in which there is a redistributive function at work, one that by breaking up and redesigning links both destroys and constructs.[29] So we are told a space is made, an intertextuality, where statements from other texts cross over and neutralize each other. This is a typical Kristevan move in fact aimed at redefining *genre* in a nontraditional way: a typology that grants specificity to different textual ways of organizing, yet allows them to make their way in a kind of general milieu, namely, the whole of culture.[30] But almost immediately *intertextualité* is shored up by another invention, *idéologème*, which seems to be figurable as a kind of vapor trail, a trace through the different levels of the structure of each text, from beginning to end, and which gives it its historical and social coordinates. Kristeva can then incorporate a theorization of the novel, with reference both to the society and to the historical context, using as example Antoine de la Sale's

Le Petit Jehan de Saintré (1456) on which she prepared her *thèse de troisième cycle*.[31] We can see the interest of her alteration of critical habit and vocabulary, especially when she relates this theoretical beginning of the essay to the development of the novel. It is not merely an attention-catching, somewhat fancy terminology, though it is that too. It enables a reconfiguring of what can be done within "literary criticism" as she has extended it. In particular, it allows some extraordinarily powerful descriptions of structures.[32] These are arranged into a kind of sketch of the history of the novel, written round the work of Mikhail Bakhtin (1895–1975). Indeed, one of the great Kristevan services to the general literary culture of the time was the introduction to her audience of Bakhtin's thought, especially the idea of the polyphonic novel, encompassing Rabelais, Swift, and Dostoyevsky, and leading on to Joyce, which she developed in the essay "Le Mot, le dialogue et le roman."[33] The centralization of experience in a novel within one (human) subjectivity, a process baptized "*monologique*," is contrasted with Bakhtin's idea of the "carnivalesque," where there is no closure, no single voice, no remaining within limits. In audacious fashion, she opens this out very widely. "The journey which is constituted between the two poles supposed by the dialogue, radically squeezes out of our philosophical field the problems of causality, finality, etc., and suggests how interesting the dialogic principle is for a thought-space which is much more vast than that of the novel. Dialogism, rather than any binary structure, is perhaps the basis of our age's intellectual structure."[34]

In these early essays, encompassing so many topics from such innovative angles, Kristeva renews thinking about writing, especially literary writing, but also produces more general effects. For she desegregates such writing from wider movements in thought, from Saussurean linguistics, Marxist materialism, even accounts of Chinese or Sanskrit literature (in "L'Engendrement de la formule"). The reader is shaken from her habits by a sort of unexpectedness and audacity in the discussion, which hauls in themes and arguments from widely different areas, makes them work together, and makes them known. This is in spite of the work appearing to the reader to be a program, as has been said, for it does not give a sense of measured development, but, rather, one of an exciting and excited opening out on to different fields.

II. Revolution in Poetic Language
A Partial Translation of *La Révolution du langage poétique* (1974)

This major work runs to 646 pages in French. It is only available in English in an abridged version. At the time Kristeva wrote it, the French *thèses d'état* were usually longer than dissertations in the UK or US, and followed on the shorter thesis on a different subject, the *thèse de troisième cycle*. As pointed out earlier, Kristeva wrote the latter, published as *Le Texte du roman*, around one of the earliest novels in French, Antoine de la Sale's *Le Petit Jehan de Saintré*. Its subtitle, *Analyse sémiologique d'une structure discursive transformationnelle* (A semiological analysis of a transformational discursive structure) clearly points to its relation to her *Sémiotikè*, yet it goes one step further than that book. By its term "*transformationelle*," it refers to one of the founding ideas in Chomskyan generative grammar: that grammar is a hierarchy of procedures of semantic transformation. The term in Kristeva's subtitle seems to promise a kind of cycling through the process of development of the novel as a genre to be correlated with different linguistic perspectives, yet that does not, as far as I can see, lead any further, either in this text or in other work.

This second thesis, *Revolution in Poetic Language*, is not a sequel, although it develops some of the themes of the first book, her programmatic collection of essays discussed above. It is less unexpected in the angles it explores, and as befits its place in the academic cursus, it is much longer. The work sketches out a history of recent poetics from mid-nineteenth century France. As the title indicates, the line of development is a postulated change in poetic language, one so radical as to justify the term "revolution." It is worth noting that this title is ambiguous: the abridged English translation is entitled *Revolution in Poetic Language*.[35] The French, *La Révolution du langage poétique,* can bear a double meaning that the English cannot: "a radical change is being actively perpetrated *on* poetic language" and/or "a revolution is occuring *within* poetic language," for the genitive "*de*" in French can be active or passive when used in such phrases. Taking this into account helps understand one of the puzzles in the history of poetry as Kristeva constructs it, and which her subtitle is perhaps intended to point to: "The avant-garde at the end of the nineteenth century: Lautréamont and Mallarmé." For Rimbaud (1854–1891), to my mind the most adventurous and disconcerting poetic voice of the same period, is simply absent, not just from the title but also from the argument. Asking why this might be provides a point of entry into Kristeva's work and enables a better understanding of what she is doing.

Rimbaud, most of whose poems are thought to have been written before he was twenty-one, said farewell to poetry entirely, and after travels and very varied jobs (for example, as foreman in a stone quarry in Cyprus) left to work as a trader in Abyssinia; a gun runner certainly, perhaps more. An adventurer, moving about a great deal, when asked in later life about his poems, he seems to have expressed distaste, his poetry having public influence only through Verlaine who published a volume of poems by a group of poets, which included Rimbaud and Mallarmé.[36] To this sense of inconclusion was added the intriguing nature of his mysterious life and early death. But Rimbaud inhabited this group of artists or poets as a male leopard may be said to inhabit a patch of *veld*, that is, only for a short time. In contrast, Mallarmé, the poet at the basis of Kristeva's thesis, was married, had children, lived in a more or less settled social group, writing poetry and journalism of a particular sort; maintaining a salon, "*les jeudis*."[37] While not politically active, Mallarmé nonetheless served as a character reference for Fénéon, an anarchist visitor to his salon, when he was tried for subversive conspiracy. Consideration of this is an essential feature of Kristeva's book, a novelty in her work at this point, and gives as an important part of the book's argument, an account of the political background of her subject, Mallarmé.[38] The contrast with Rimbaud suggests a possible explanation of the presence of Lautréamont in Kristeva's book: the two poets' periods of creativity are practically identical. Does the second "stand in" in some way for the first? Lautréamont's writing is closer to twentieth-century experiments in poetic language than Rimbaud's, who conducts his exploration more through the imagination and choice of poetic form than through his actual poetic language.

This comparison, uninvited by Kristeva, acts at this point in my essay as a kind of axis: the imagination's role in assembling and recalibrating sense experience is a major feature of the epistemology of Husserl, but it is left aside in Kristeva's work in spite of her mentioning him regularly; whereas her work around Freud and psychoanalysis develops in tandem with her work on the imaginary. Imagination and imaginary seem to be in some kind of contrast in Kristevan aesthetics, one that is left implicit. So it is as if, in the two books this essay discusses, Kristeva points to a philosopher, Husserl, who produced major accounts of the activity of the imagination in creating what we know, but in fact works with the psychoanalyst and philosopher Freud, who deals with the activity of the imaginary, that is, the transformations of the contents of consciousness.

La Révolution du langage poétique opens with an important and difficult first part, "Préliminaires théoriques" (Theoretical preliminaries), seeking to link what is to come on Mallarmé with threads already at work in *Sémiotikè*. But in a chapter on Husserl, Kristeva makes an important step towards her own future: she will use phenomenology as a bridge allowing her to consider how the speaking subject is positioned. Even more important, her future activity in psychoanalysis is explicitly foreshadowed, perhaps as a kind of catching up with and overtaking of the Husserlian subject.[39] For this setting off of her ideas against Husserl enables Kristeva to pose what has come to represent for her the problem: consciousness considered not as something that produces but as something that is producible, that can be started.[40] Contrasted with the phenomenologist's transcendental ego and the Cartesian ego (thought of as belonging to Chomskyan transformational grammar, no doubt), she brings forward what will be for her a major concept: *le sujet en procès* (the subject as a process). The intellectual scope of this first part of "Préliminaires théoriques" is very wide, bringing together Freud, Frege (wrongly, to my mind), and her own distinction between "*géno-texte*" and "*phéno-texte*."[41] The second chapter brings in what Kristeva names as "the fourth term of the dialectic," negativity. It contains a low-key criticism of Marxism's conception of the subject as unitary, as a complicity between being a philosopher and also a member of the proletariat.[42] (To what degree this may be covert self-criticism, I am not sure.) Barely later in the text, there is muted and respectful criticism of Derrida. The following chapter on the heterogeneous prepares us for the discussion of Mallarmé and the family, a thread that runs through the whole book, enabling links between psychoanalytic commentary and late nineteenth-century society. The final section of these "preliminaries" urges the separation of poetic praxis from experience, and confirms the disapproval evinced in all her writing so far of mere representation of experience without transformation through writing.

From this, the logic of her move into writing novels appears retrospectively in an enriched light.

This is a difficult book on a difficult poet, seeking to link political strands in Mallarmé's social context with the "revolution [operated on] poetic language" by this hermetic, ironic writer, relating it to the "revolution [with]in poetic language" that was occurring more generally. It becomes clear as we read that the main thesis of Kristeva in this book is to give the poets of the avant-garde a role in their society, in terms not of what they actually get done (unlike, for instance, Victor Hugo) but what they can do through language: "the whole experience of the avant-garde from the end of the twentieth century [*sic*] from the *poète maudit* to the experience of schizophrenia on the contrary proves the possibility of a process of *signifiance* different from that of conceptual thought, which is unifying."[43] The "utopianism" of this role allotted to the poet is part of a history of political appropriations of Mallarmé of the later twentieth century, it has been pointed out.[44] For Kristeva, using a term borrowed from Bataille, this role is part of a *dépense*, an expenditure of talent and energy that is truly subversive, being placed outside social institutions and the drive to profit, a role that is also outside the unity of a psyche that may be derived from social pressures.[45] Nevertheless, Kristeva suggests in a note that follows Bataille, it has involved compromises with "bourgeois values."[46]

La Révolution du langage poétique presents part of the history of French poetic writing in the later nineteenth century. In a sense it is an argument for the political value of the writer's activity in a hostile, commercially oriented, imperialistic world: an activity not through political action and effect, as Sartre claimed, but through language. Mallarmé, in a social apartness of near extreme preciosity, was for Kristeva and the *Tel Quel* group the poet of a "textual practice" "that was thought to be the necessary poetic prolegomena to any further revolution."[47] Literature could, through language, take part in a social revolution. Some critics have argued that in Kristeva's book there is an energy in theorizing,[48] a delight even, which is its main thrust and that will work to displace any taking for granted of a particular society and its way of looking at things, which is always language-borne. This is an argument central to Kristeva's thinking here and, interestingly, one close to the main thrust of Derrida's writing. Revolution works through language as well as through public action. Language is freighted in ways we cannot control, and of which we are often to a large degree unconscious.

Kristeva's book then makes a case for the poet as underground revolutionary, one who affects what speakers and writers of a language want to express and the mode in which they do that. Boncardo's admirable book points out that, for Mallarmé, all historical events, even the most tragic and extreme, were seen through the idiosyncratic prism of his practice as a writer, and that this is true of Kristeva too.[49] He is concerned with the tradition of "political appropriations" of Mallarmé, asking how we can return to the readings of philosophers like Sartre or theorists like Kristeva when they seem to have been superseded—because written before later appropriators? To me, the answer appears at one level simple: we can learn from them, both about the poet Mallarmé and about

Kristeva. His question seems to forget that culture, any culture, doesn't move forward in a straight and single line. Like a glacier, inside it is multilayered, outside it changes the landscape. Reading Mallarmé after Kristeva isn't equivalent to reading his poetry earlier. She has placed him in an intellectual heritage where he wasn't clearly present before she wrote. One that leads on to the *Tel Quel* group, fairly obviously: he seems to be the great predecessor, and they his successors, by implication moving beyond him. In doing so, she has caused a diversion in the way in which he is read, perhaps momentary, perhaps not. She has pulled this apparently remote, even precious poet over to the side of a kind of utopian subversion that, as she admits, is divergent from political practice even while it operates a kind of solidarity with the political avant-garde.[50] In a phrase which acts as an excellent summary, Boncardo maintains that, for Kristeva, Mallarmé's linguistic praxis was a sort of "anarchist attack" that could bring forth "the revolution of poetic language." Through transgression of the rules of syntax, Mallarmé has disarticulated language and opened it to the possibility of participating in social transformation. Indeed, with vocabulary derived from Bataille, she has placed "expending" in language, lavish and unguarded, in opposition to merely communicative language, which she links with the aim solely to produce, where means are subordinated only to an end, where language only attempts mere reproduction of experience.[51] Through the spiritual descendants of Mallarmé, aka the *Tel Quel* group among others, writing has moved to continue the Revolution in Poetic Language. How has this come about?

In a section, "The prudent writer-anarchist," Kristeva shows how Mallarmé's sympathies move between the rightwing-liberal side of politics and anarchism.[52] Her own work points ultimately to the possibility, it seems, that poet and worker could be united through the work of language. There is a kind of visionary hope in this long and difficult work; its spirited adventurous mode working in what is after all a work produced within a socio-intellectual, indeed academic framework.

The very last paragraphs of the book reinforce this transformational possibility of poetry, pointing forward to an incorporation of experience at an infradiscursive level, limiting, so she claims, any metalinguistic mastery of what is being written.[53] This kind of text, we are told, is far from being both the experience of a signifying process and its metalinguistic expression; it is not both undergoing and shaping experience. On the contrary, it has in fact undone that shaping, rendered it impossible, causing a massive redistribution among the modern sciences. This kind of text has broken philosophy's back.[54]

By implication, there is, in the last pages of *La Révolution du langage poétique* a farewell to philosophy. Not just among the "modern sciences," but one that is personal and particular to Kristeva.

MARIAN HOBSON

PROFESSOR EMERITUS, QUEEN MARY UNIVERSITY OF LONDON
MARCH 2019

NOTES

Translations of quotations from French texts for which there are no English versions are by the author.

1. The name change occurred in 2006, while Kristeva was still in post. I thank Professor François Lecercle, University of Paris-Sorbonne, for this information.

2. Roland Barthes (1915–1980) supported her warmly in her early career, admiring her exceptional intelligence, energy, and inventiveness (an off-the-cuff, highly personal remark to the present author).

3. See, for example, his altercation with Raymond Picard, who attacked his work in *Nouvelle critique ou nouvelle imposture* (Paris: J-J. Pauvert, 1965). Barthes replies in *Criticism and Truth*, trans. Katrine Pilcher Keuneman (London: Athlone, 1987); *Critique et verité* (Paris: Seuil, 1966).

4. Developing from Roland Barthes, *Writing Degree Zero*, trans. Annette Lavers and Colin Smith (New York: Hill and Wang, 2012) to, for example, *The Rustle of Language*, trans. Richard Howard (Berkeley: University of California Press, 2010).

5. In the early part of his career, Barthes was greatly interested in work in the theater, such as at the *Theâtre National Populaire* (TNP), which was decidedly on the left of the literary political spectrum, and to which essentially was owed knowledge in France of Brecht's plays. Its international fame was largely due to the succession of great directors who developed the TNP (Jean Vilar, Georges Wilson, Roger Planchon, Patrice Chéreau).

6. I owe this point to a conversation with the late Professor Ross Chambers.

7. Here I borrow the title of an article on Derrida: Richard Rorty, "Philosophy as a Kind of Writing," *New Literary History* 10, no. 1 (Autumn 1978): 141–60. Such writing (of both Derrida and Kristeva) can be linked back to a French tradition, perhaps best represented by Roger Caillois (1913–1978), employed by UNESCO, and Georges Bataille (1897–1962), employed by what is now the Bibliothèque de France.

8. Tzvetan Todorov, who had arrived in Paris earlier, in 1963, is another Bulgarian who became active in roughly the same intellectual area in France.

9. I owe thanks to the guidance of Professor E. J. Hughes for this point.

10. That Kristeva, an intellectual with family still in Bulgaria, and returning occasionally, might have had little choice in her early days in France but to attend debriefings held by the Bulgarian secret services seems to have escaped recent commentators, many of whom have had the luck to live in less authoritarian regimes. The author of a recent article in *The New Yorker*, September 5, 2018, Dimeter Kenarov, though himself Bulgarian, seems uncomprehending of a point unlikely to be missed by anyone working in the UK in the last couple of years: such denigration, however slight, is playing Mr. Putin's game of unsettling Western attitudes to what is, when all is done, a totalitarian regime, not balking at attempted or actual assassination of political opponents. In a riposte, Sara Beardsworth writes of compliments paid by the article to Kristeva: "These accolades appear, in this situation, to make her worthy of the sudden, unprecedented act of dumping 400 pages of raw data, the State Security documents, from the archive of the Dossier Committee into a public forum for all to see—if you read Cyrillic." "Reflections on the Kristeva Affair," The Philosophical Salon, September 24, 2018, http://thephilosophicalsalon.com/reflections-on-the-kristeva-affair/. This politicocultural point is pretty clear to any citizen of the UK, or indeed of the Netherlands, who has drawn consequences from the recent attempted break-in to the Dutch laboratory investigating the Novichok poison, which had killed a UK citizen in the UK. One can but wonder that such a motive—the besmirching of emigré reputations—didn't occur to the author of the *New Yorker* article, nor indeed to the journal itself. Perhaps the life of the poisoned semi-tramp in the UK didn't count for enough?

11. This point is well worth further examination.

12. Julia Kristeva, *Sémiotikè: Recherches pour une sémanalyse* (Paris: Seuil, 1969).

13. See the helpful resume in the Wikipedia article on *Tel Quel*. For much greater detail, see Patrick ffrench, *The Time of Theory: A History of Tel Quel* (Oxford: Clarendon, 1995).

14. Roland Barthes gave her this label in his article "L'Étrangère," *Quinzaine littéraire* 94 (May 1–15, 1970).

15. See, for example, the use made of Russian formalist poetics in Kristeva, *Sémiotikè*, 177.

16. For example, she was connected early on with the journal *Semiotica*, edited by Thomas Sebeok, which began the year of publication of *Sémiotikè* (1969) and points to the rising importance of semiotics as an area of academic interest.

17. See John Locke, *Essay Concerning Human Understanding*, ed. Peter H. Nidditch (Oxford: Clarendon, 1979), bk. IV, ch. XXI. Notably, Locke had added at the end of this chapter: "The Consideration then of *Ideas* and *Words*, as the great Instruments of Knowledge, makes no despicable part of their Contemplation, who would take a view of humane Knowledge in the whole Extent of it. And, perhaps, if they were distinctly weighed, and duly considered, they would afford us another sort of Logick and Critick, than what we have been hitherto acquainted with."

18. Private conversation, 1969.

19. Kristeva discusses and defends Roland Barthes, *Système de la mode* (Paris: Seuil, 1967).

20. Ivor Armstrong Richards, *Practical Criticism* (London: Kegan Paul, Trench, Trubner & Co., 1929). William Empson, *Seven Types of Ambiguity*, 1930, rev. ed. (New York: New Directions, 1947).

21. Kristeva, *Sémiotikè*, 11.

22. Ibid., 21.

23. See Benjamin S. Hawkins, Jr., "Peirce and Frege: A Question Unanswered," *Modern Logic* 3, no. 4 (1993): 376–83.

24. I borrow the phrase from Rachel Bowlby, *Just Looking: Consumer Culture in Dreiser, Gissing and Zola* (New York: Methuen, 1985).

25. Private remark by Barthes on his visit to the University of Warwick, c.1967.

26. "We know that any renewal of scientific thought is brought about by means of and thanks to a renewal of the terminology: there is no invention, properly speaking, until a new term appears (let it be 'oxygen' or 'infinitesimal calculus')." Kristeva, *Sémiotikè*, 33.

27. Ibid. The quotation of the German seems to be a misreading of handwriting: *Fachonsdrücken* instead of *Fachausdrücken*, the "*au*" having been taken for "*on*."

28. It is possible to pose a similar question about Derrida's earlier work. This particularity of important work of the 1960s needs further investigation.

29. See Julia Kristeva, "The Bounded Text," in *Desire in Language*, trans. Thomas Gora, Alice Jardine, and Leon S. Roudiez (New York: Columbia University Press, 1980).

30. Kristeva, *Sémiotikè*, 113, 114.

31. Julia Kristeva, *Le Texte du roman: Analyse sémiologique d'une structure discursive transformationnelle* (Paris: Mouton, 1970). [There used to be two different kinds or stages of doctoral thesis in France. The first, sometimes called "*thèse de troisième cycle*" was published as *Le Texte du roman*. For the second, long thesis, also called "*thèse d'état*" or "*doctorat d'état*," Kristeva wrote *La Révolution du langage poétique*.—Ed.]

32. "These terms set in opposition, always exclusive, are caught up in a web of gaps, which are multiple and always possible (the surprises in narrative structures), and which give the illusion of an open structure, one impossible to bring to an end and which have a purpose which is arbitrary." Kristeva, *Sémiotikè*, 118.

33. See Julia Kristeva, "Word, Dialogue, and Novel," in *Desire in Language*.

34. Kristeva, *Sémiotikè*, 173.

35. Julia Kristeva, *Revolution in Poetic Language*, trans. Margaret Waller (New York: Columbia University Press, 1984).

36. Paul Verlaine, *Les Poètes maudits: Tristan Corbière, Arthur Rimbaud, Stéphane Mallarmé* (Paris: Léon Vanier, 1884).

37. There is a kind of disparaging irony, which to me seems almost patronizing, in Mallarmé's account of Rimbaud given to an enquiring US visitor. Rimbaud is said not to have affected the way poetry moved: "the brilliance of a meteor, lit with no other motive than its own presence." Stéphane Mallarmé, *Divagations*, 1897, https://fr.wikisource.org/wiki/Divagations_(1897)/Arthur_Rimbaud. The passage is nevertheless very beautiful: the whole runs: "*éclat, lui, d'un météore, allumé sans motif autre que sa présence, issu seul et s'éteignant. Tout, certes, aurait existé, depuis, sans ce passant considérable, comme aucune circonstance littéraire vraiment n'y prépare.*" The passage is arguing for the necessity of a socioliterary context. Notably, gentler deflation is present in some of his remarks around the violent incident in which Fénéon was involved and for which he was tried, Mallarmé acting as a character witness.

38. I use the term "political" because the references to social background seem to me to be somewhat broadbrushed (compare Kristeva, *La Révolution du langage poétique*, 435n41). The political background to Rimbaud's work, though subject to intense critical speculation, is perhaps too uncertain to have led anywhere.

39. Kristeva, *Revolution in Poetic Language*, 32; *La Révolution du langage poetique*, 31.

40. Ibid., 36n36; *La Révolution du langage poetique*, 35n44.

41. Although they throw intense light on the evolution of Frege's idea of meaning, the two series of discussions by letter between Husserl and Frege on the foundations of logic are not treated. It should be remembered that it was in this context, a discussion about literature, that Frege first uses the distinction *Sinn/Bedeutung* crucial for his thought. (Derrida, for example, was aware of this. See Marian Hobson, "Derrida and Frege," *Paragraph* 41, no. 2 (2018): 184–95). However, had Kristeva explored the tension that literary use of language represented for Frege, it might have been possible for her to allow a more complex role to the imaginary statement in human discourse without bypassing Husserl's complex view of the role of the imagination, as to my mind she does.

42. Kristeva, *Revolution in Poetic Language*, 138–39; *La Révolution du langage poétique*, 127.

43. Ibid., 166. "Twentieth century" is no doubt a lapsus for "nineteenth century," but a telling one, hinting at the overarching literary historical frame of the book: *Tel Quel* moves the Mallarméan achievement beyond itself.

44. Roberto Boncardo, *Mallarmé and the Politics of Literature: Sartre, Kristeva, Badiou, Rancière* (Edinburgh: Edinburgh University Press, 2018), an excellent book to which I am indebted. The "appropriations" run from Jean-Paul Sartre (*Mallarmé, or the Poet of Nothingness*, 1986) to Jacques Rancière (*Mallarmé: The Politics of the Siren*, 1996).

45. Kristeva, *La Révolution du langage poétique*, 435.

46. Ibid., 435n41. Again, one can wonder to what degree this might be self-reference.

47. Boncardo, *Mallarmé and the Politics of Literature*, 7.

48. Vincent Kaufmann: see n. 38 in ibid.

49. See *La Révolution du langage poétique*, 406–7.

50. Ibid., 429.

51. Boncardo, *Mallarmé and the Politics of Literature*, 102.

52. "One can say that it is the bourgeois state, such as we have described it, characterizing the concrete historical situation in France at the end of the nineteenth century, which dictates to those engaged in an experiment with text, positions that [can] go from the liberal right all the way to anarchism, and situating this more precisely in the subjective or religious backgrounds of these tendencies." Kristeva, *La Révolution du langage poétique*, 429.

53. "The text remains nevertheless a 'poetic language' in the sense that it is even so a discourse that introduces the trackings of impulses and their moments of stasis right into the moment when language symbolizes" (ibid., 618).

54. Ibid.

6

Maria Margaroni

ARTAUD'S MADNESS AND THE LITERARY OBSCENE: HUMANISM AND ITS DOUBLE IN JULIA KRISTEVA

I. Introduction

This essay explores the contexts and stakes of Kristeva's persistent theorizing of the literary experience in connection with the vicissitudes of the subjective and linguistic crisis that, since the eighteenth century at least, we associate with madness. To this end, I consider her concern with the relation between literature and madness in light of the wider investigation into forms of writing in France in the 1960s and 1970s that defied conventional notions of literature, aligning themselves with emergent philosophical interrogations of the Enlightenment and its privileged ground-cum-support, namely, the humanist idea of Man. I aim to throw into relief the distinctness of Kristeva's approach to the madness *of* literature and to trace how this approach informs both her materialist rethinking of the "realm of the beautiful" and her unique position in the confrontation between humanist and antihumanist currents in this realm.

I argue that Artaud's impact on Kristeva's theorizing of literature has not been fully appreciated. I seek to demonstrate that Artaud's experience of madness and his corporeal understanding of writing enable Kristeva to define a type of literary experience that refuses to function as a band aid to human suffering, developing instead as the stage of cruelty Artaud envisioned, where Man is confronted by what emerges out of the shadows of the *ob*scene: the convulsing body-in-pain. Drawing on Grosz's theorizing of the "inhuman," I show how Artaud's and Kristeva's concepts of literature are shaped by an attunement to what lies before and beyond Man, what erupts in spite of the human as the agent and center of meaning. On my reading, Kristeva's theorizing of the literary experience remains indebted to Artaud because it refuses to betray what I call Artaud's *obscene inhuman*, the figuration of which, I argue, is "the black laughter" that Kristeva hears in the avant-garde text. My contention in this essay is that Kristeva's allegiance to Artaud's obscene inhuman allows her to complexify the legacy of humanism from the perspective *no longer* of Man but of that *within* Man that is exposed to vulnerability and what the ancient Greeks called "fate." It is this notion of fate that lies at the heart of Artaud's experience of madness *and* of Kristeva's Artaud-inspired, long-term engagement with the *question* of the subject. I trace the development of this question from Kristeva's early essay on Artaud to her most recent reflections on disability in *Hatred and Forgiveness.*

II. Literature's Encounter with the Impossible

In *The Sense and Non-sense of Revolt*, Kristeva reevaluates surrealism and the work of Aragon in particular by approaching them within the horizon of an event that "profoundly marked the European literary experience," namely, "*literature's encounter with the impossible*."[1] Starting at the end of the 1800s and throughout the twentieth century, literature "renounced its role as purveyor of beautiful language and seductive beauty. . . . It explored the impasses of consciousness and associated itself with madness."[2] This association between madness and what she calls the "modern text," "poetic language," or "the literary experience" has remained prominent in her work since the 1970s. In *Revolution in Poetic Language* she argues that "as a signifying practice, the text is the active form of madness."[3] *Powers of Horror* approaches "great modern literature" as unfolding over a terrain "at the boundary of what is assimilable, thinkable."[4] *Black Sun* demonstrates how the artist Holbein and writers such as Nerval, Dostoyevsky, and Duras share "a thirst for suffering to the point of madness."[5] *Hatred and Forgiveness* reiterates Kristeva's conviction that what characterizes twentieth-century art and literature is their determination to take seriously "the ultimately psychotic limits of the speaking being."[6] Her own ventures as a novelist since 1990 seem motivated by a similar determination. Hence her focus on crime, which she perceives as a symptom of the "psychosis that is the brute reality of globalized humans."[7]

As Marx-Scouras has demonstrated, Kristeva's foregrounding of madness in her systematic endeavor to produce a theory of avant-garde literature can be fully appreciated if seen in the context of the French literary scene in the 1960s and 1970s.[8] It needs to be situated in relation to similar projects undertaken by the circle of writers affiliated with or influenced by *Tel Quel,* the controversial literary journal of which Kristeva herself was a prominent member. Marx-Scouras points to Foucault's "pioneering work on the division between reason and madness in Western culture," which set the stage for a rethinking of the nature and function of literature.[9] In *Madness and Civilization* Foucault traces the gradual formation from the Middle Ages to the Classical Age of a nexus among practices, institutions, and discourses that brings about the exclusion of madness, defined anew as the absence of reason, seeking its truth in a "*delirious discourse*," one that "liberated passion from all its limits."[10] The history of insanity he attempts to write is an archaeology of silence, for the delirium of madness cannot be heard in a language that, in wishing to understand, objectifies it. It is only in "the lightning-flash of works such as those of Hölderlin, of Nerval, of Nietzsche, or of Artaud," he concludes, that "the life of unreason" can make itself felt.[11]

Foucault's suggestion that modern literature has served as a hosting body to the muted voice of madness has given rise to questions relating to what Felman calls the "obscure but essential kinship" between madness and literature.[12] She asks: "Why is it to literature that the task of 'saying madness' is entrusted? . . . In what way does literature attest to the intercourse between thought and madness?"[13] It is precisely this testimonial function of literature, its ability to bear witness to what is excluded in the name of reason, that can account for the distinct literary ethics associated with the *Tel Quel* group. Even Derrida's deconstructive reading of *Madness and Civilization* acknowledges that the only instances when Foucault seems to be successful in conveying the silence of the captured body of the mad is when he allows his philosophy to betray itself by opening up to what exceeds it, namely, its archetypal other, literature.[14] Therefore it is when sense is abandoned in the privileging of metaphor, when logos gives way to its pathos that the muted howling of madness stands a chance to be heard.[15]

In turning to literature's encounter with madness, Kristeva shares with Foucault a concern with (subjective or societal) limits and, like him, defines modernity as the adventure of their transgression.[16] She is equally attentive to the sensible, tactile, vocal body and its suffering that needs to be (re)collected among the ruins of an objectifying discourse of knowledge. However, she knows better than to approach literature as "a flight into madness," a site where the authentic voice of madness can be heard.[17] Rather than attesting to what Foucault describes as a *break* between reason and madness, the literature of Nerval, Lautréamont, or Mallarmé mobilizes their interplay, their dialectical connection-in-separation. Kristeva equally refuses a deconstructive perspective that seems content with exposing the "fatal complicity" between different forms of metaphysics: a metaphysics of logos (as self-present and undivided) and a metaphysics of (undiluted, untamable, wild) silence.[18]

In what follows, I reflect on Kristeva's singular approach to the difficulty of thinking literature and madness side by side. I argue that Artaud's impact on Kristeva's attempt to articulate a materialist, nonhumanist theory of literature has been decisive. Along with figures such as Mallarmé, Bataille, or Céline, among others, Artaud's transgressive writing has been a major focal point in debates of the 1960s to 1970s on the relation between language and subjectivity or literature and revolution in France. Foucault draws on Artaud in his concluding gesture of defining madness as "the *absence of the work of art*."[19] Derrida returns to Artaud's writings on several occasions.[20] Although Kristeva has written only one extended essay on Artaud, the numerous references to his writings show that his thought permeates her work up to today.[21] Artaud's madness offers Kristeva a distinct vantage point from which to rethink literature as a species of the obscene. As she explains in an interview, this has nothing to do with his caca-mania and scatological discourse.[22] What scandalizes in Artaud, Kristeva argues, is the sensible, suffering body that literary humanism and literary formalism alike prefer to keep off stage, behind the scenes. Kristeva invokes a kind of literature that serves "as a Band-Aid . . . no horror, 'the writer must not create sorrow in her books,' suffering is refined into nothingness, erudition, beauty. . . . Denial of ill-being sustains beautiful style. And publishing houses."[23]

It is this type of literature that Artaud seeks to destroy. To the view of Mankind that sustains it, Artaud opposes the "cold pictureless suffering" of a body "barely recognizable as human."[24] This is Artaud's *obscene inhuman*, which I will trace both behind Kristeva's critique of Enlightenment humanism and at the heart of her suspicion of the antihumanist currents popular in the post-1960s literary scene. As a key protagonist in what is known as the linguistic turn, Kristeva hails the shift away from Man to language as a system, yet she remains critical of any understanding of language as "a mere depository of thin linguistic layers, an archive of structures, or the testimony of a withdrawn body."[25] Interestingly, her engagement with Man leads to, not a rejection, but a rethinking of humanism from the perspective of its double or, as Artaud would put it, from the perspective of that "eternal ghost" haunting Man, "radiating affective powers."[26] Like Artaud, Kristeva remains a humanist—albeit a "perverse" one.[27] The laboratory of this perverse humanism driven by the force of the inhuman is her own distinct brand of literature, a literature "not made to be loved."[28]

III. Artaud's Obscene Inhuman

Grosz argues that it is time to rethink crucial questions that have been evaded post-1960s owing to our concern with identity, identity politics, signification, and representation. "Among these underdeveloped and unasked questions are those deemed the most offensive and disputed within the last decades: *not* the body . . . but messy biology, matter, materiality . . . *not* ideology . . . but force, energy, affect."[29] In a more recent work, Grosz draws on Darwin and demonstrates how these difficult questions need to be pursued beyond the concept of Man and the humanist baggage this concept has accumulated. The task is "to discuss what is before, beyond, and after the human: the inhuman, uncontainable condition of the human, the origin of and trajectory immanent within the human."[30] It is precisely Artaud's concern with articulating an ontology beyond the privileging and control of the human that seems to render his self-effacing oeuvre so disturbing. Jannarone complains:

> *The Theater and its Double* does not present utopic visions of the sort that normally followed avant-garde manifestos' opening moves, no pictures of health, transcendence, or progress. Instead, written in the aftermath of a nearly worldwide self-destruction, *The Theater and its Double* dwells, with intense concentration,

> on cataclysms, on moments of suffering, on abjection and terror, on annihilation and gratuitous violence, on the dark nature of mankind and life and the forces that regulate them.[31]

It is striking how Artaud refuses to inscribe life within the teleological, progress-oriented trajectory of Man, remaining attuned to its violence and cruelty, its purposelessness and exposure to accident. His writings are attentive to the existence of "things outside" and the autonomous, quasi-mechanical functions of the body: "the influx of vegetal thundering blood," the digestive or defecating processes, the "disturbed fluids," the "limpid but inhuman teeming" within the cell of a living organism, the experience of asubjective forces traversing, affecting, attacking the body.[32] He insistently refers to a quasi-mystical connection between natural or historical events (the plague, the war), a looming world of things, and the human nervous system. In doing so, he shows how a rethinking of life ought to start from the decentering of Man as sovereign ruler. His is the vision of a humanity that is interconnected with *and* dependent on implacable (active or inert) forces. Artaud's vision, though dark, is not life-denying. On the contrary, he seeks to demystify life in his struggle to embrace it in all the danger of its becoming. Tormented by the dominant dichotomies and hierarchies that make up the edifice of Man (mind over body, spirit over matter, high versus low, reason versus madness), Artaud foregrounds movement and process instead; the continuous flow, the changeability of a life that remains multiple. His target, then, is not life but the *human fear of* life as a transformative, revolutionary force that is, however, not easily integrated within the progressivist narratives of the human.

This is why he seeks to get rid of literature, the privileged space where such narratives are fostered and where an aggrandized figure of Man prevails. The theater Artaud strives to theorize is one he seeks to rescue "from its human, psychological prostration."[33] Hence his concern with staging machine-like beings that do not have a "clear-cut personality and feelings," warrior figures facing "inhuman or mineral meteorites hurtling down on them," impassioned bodies connecting like "living fires."[34] In *The Theatre and Its Double* Artaud confesses: "We are seized with a kind of terror when we think of these mechanical beings whose happiness and pain seem not to be their own."[35] If his is a theater of cruelty, this is not because it exalts in violence and blood but because it forces us to face this *kind of terror* at the sight of the "dual body" of Man: Man replaced by his "effigy," a gigantic puppet "attacked by things outside."[36] Cruelty means, above all, not "the cruelty we practice on one another . . . but the far more terrible cruelty objects can practice on us."[37] He repeatedly refers to this as "the plague," a "relentless necessity" inextricable from pain, "irreversible and absolute determination," or *life* irreducible to the "lazy, ineffective idea" people have of it.[38]

Significantly, Artaud calls this cruel, inhuman necessity that drives creaturely life "*fate* or what you will."[39] In his writings, "fate" takes on the guise of *motility,* a biological, material force that undermines and works despite his will, opening him up to a knowledge that modern Man in his obsessive need for control prefers to deny: "We are not free and the sky can still fall on our heads"; the theater "is made to teach us this."[40] Kristeva's life-long interest in Artaud shows that this difficult lesson has not been lost on her. This is why *motility* and the *process* associated with it become central in her early theorizing of the subject conceptualized at the crossroads between language and materiality, sense and non-sense, freedom and determinism.

IV. "Black Laughter" or the Persistent Question of the Subject

Kristeva associates the poetic language cultivated since Hölderlin with "the burst of black laughter" hurled in the face of "all attempts to master the human situation, to master language by language."[41] Black laughter is the literary index of the obscene inhuman in Artaud. Its eruption marks the decentering of Man, the hollowing out of any desire to fix signification, the opening up of sense to what infects it from within, eating away at its vitals. This laughter is black "with burnt up meaning."[42]

Confronting us with the impossibility of any form of identity, the black laughter of modern literature poses what Kristeva calls *the question* of the subject—the subject in language and in its relation to the inhuman. This is what she pursues in her essay on Artaud, which opens with her concern "to 'take account' of a signifying function refused by our culture."[43] This signifying function is equally resisted by a current in psychoanalysis that remains hinged on an understanding of the subject as "a divided unity" or, as she calls it, the "unitary subject."[44] What attracts Kristeva in Artaud's writings is the glimpse they offer of a different signifying economy in which the unitary subject goes through a crisis and is made to confront its limits. This is why they constitute the key source of her theory of the subject in process/on trial. I suggest that this theory of the subject draws on and translates a striking dynamic between freedom and determinism, heroism and fate, the human and the inhuman in Artaud's works. After all, Artaud's theater of cruelty is meant not only to expose spectators to an inhuman "thinking power in close contact with what we call fate" but also urges them "to take a nobler, more heroic stand in the face of destiny."[45] Kristeva seems to appreciate this when she (twice) quotes his words: "and life is what I did when I thought about working on the resistances to my motility," the material force that becomes a code for fate.[46] The black laughter Kristeva aims to make heard in modern literature perfectly captures this dynamic between resistance and motility, heroism and fate, epitomizing the experience of cruel disillusionment in the face of human powerlessness and, at the same time, the defiant refusal to use language, Mankind, or elaborate conceptual systems as a sort of band aid. The risk of modern literature lies here, in its venturing with audacity across the human borders where fate or accident rules.[47]

The accident that befalls Artaud, against which he struggles, is of course what he experiences as *his* madness, repeatedly associating his "lot" with the "frayed" condition of his nerves.[48] He calls this the "fate which has chosen me," one inextricable, it seems, from his corporeal existence, his "flesh."[49]

"Snakes do not react to music because of the mental ideas it produces in them, but because they are long, they lie coiled on the ground and their bodies are in contact with the ground along almost their entire length."[50] He experiences his madness as the effect of a similar corporeal causality: "I am a man by virtue of my hands and feet, my belly, my heart of flesh and blood, my stomach whose knots unite me with life's decomposition."[51] It is life's decomposition that he associates with what he describes as his *motility*, the motility of a body that has a will of its own, a body that "coughs, spits, excretes mucus through the nose, sneezes, sniffs and breathes."[52] Motility is defined in biology as "the ability of living systems to exhibit motion and to perform mechanical work at the expense of metabolic energy."[53] Motility, then, is movement that is genetically or environmentally determined. It includes bacterial movement, contraction of stomach and anal muscles, cell division, particle motion, etc. Thus motility becomes synonymous with necessity in Artaud, a force produced by "the vertical rotation" of a body beyond consciousness, on the path of rigor mortis.[54]

Kristeva borrows the term motility from Artaud in her determination to articulate a materialist, nonhumanist theory of subjectivity and the modern text. Her "Prolegomenon" to *Revolution in Poetic Language* begins by emphasizing that philosophies of language have repressed "the *process* pervading the body and the subject," the matter-instigated drive process that exceeds the institutional or linguistic structures in which the subject is embedded.[55] *Process* is one of the central concepts in Kristeva's early works—including her essay on Artaud. She defines it as "this unceasing operation of the drives," the "movement of heterogeneous matter," a dialectic of charges and stases, or "negativity as the trans-subjective and trans-semiotic moment of the separation of matter."[56] The ordering force of this process is the semiotic *chora*, "a nonexpressive totality formed by the drives and their stases."[57] Motility is repeatedly used to describe the *chora*, referring to its "gestural and vocal play," its operation obeying a logic of scission (the separation of matter) and the renewal of scission.[58] Its motility is an "a-subjective," "a-familial," "a-filial," "a-social" process.[59] Employing the Hegelian concept of negativity and drawing on Freud's theory of the drives, which permits her to rethink negativity in relation to the body, Kristeva associates the motility of the *chora* with the aggressivity of the anal drive. With close reference to Artaud's writings, she traces the effects of this aggressivity on the subject's body. The subject is in process/on trial because it is pulverized by the inhuman motility of the *chora*. The signifying system within which the subject is posited dissolves. Caught in the drive network that forms the space of the *chora*, both subject and language seem to obey "a necessity that is not God's law."[60] While insisting on the renewing potential of the *chora*'s destructive motility for the subject, language, and the community at large, Kristeva, like Artaud, knows well it can be murderous: "Organic functioning . . . which invades the trans-corporeal, *choral* automaton, tends, therefore, towards immobility."[61] Closing her essay on Artaud, she reminds us: "The way to madness thus remains open."[62]

Our analysis demonstrates that Kristeva's attempt to rethink subjectivity outside of dominant philosophical, psychoanalytic, and linguistic frameworks that divorce it from the organic, inhuman process that pulverizes, exceeds and threatens to annihilate it, keeps close to the insights imparted by Artaud. She appropriates and reinvests his metaphorics of motility, is attentive to corporeal, drive functions, traces the rhythm of drive ruptures on an echolalic body, and listens for the dissonance of multiple voices, affects, or forces within what can no longer be perceived as a unitary subject. Kristeva does not hesitate to invoke a relentless necessity that is clearly indebted to Artaud's understanding of fate. Her own audacity as a thinker lies here, for she too is a demystifier of the myths that serve as a palliative to Man. Moreover, like Artaud, she reclaims a vital becoming that does not evade suffering and the risks of death. Writing becomes the site and testimony of this vital becoming. Unfolding in the silences and scars of a signifying system that gets reborn where it comes closer to death, literature is the carrier of a force that is as uncontrollable and as contagious as Artaud's *cruelty* or what she, in her turn, terms *black laughter*.

Kristeva's decision to base her theory of subjectivity and avant-garde literature on such an inhuman force, one that is material rather than spiritual, blindly mechanical rather than intentional or purposeful, ambiguously death-driven and transgressive of social codes rather than subjected to these codes and rechanneled for the benefit of Mankind, is by no means uncontroversial. Bedient takes *Revolution in Poetic Language* to task for reducing poetic language to mere "instinct," divorcing it from any considerations of form or genre, pulling it down "from its high horse . . . in[to] the mud" of self-dividing matter.[63] Poetry here is more nature than culture, the product of accident not "a mental construction," the *work* of a conscious subject who invents and invests in an "*elsewhere* of the inorganic."[64] "Kristeva's rhetorical sympathies lie with anal cruelty, with 'revolution'" and not with the identificatory function of literature, its commitment to *eros* rather than *thanatos*.[65] Her foregrounding of anal aggressivity and expulsion as the revolutionary force of poetry renders change "the blind result of the *chora's* restiveness."[66] Kristeva's approach to literature is not a humanist one, then, for it seems to dispense with the human as the gifted agent, the inimitable individual source of the creative process. Bedient wonders: "But how can we get back to the 'instinctual, material' process of poetic practice? How can we examine various authors' nerve ends in their moment-by-moment vehemence? In any case, why do so? In their ceaseless 'scissions,' are they not all alike? Are there qualitative differences in a Joyce's, as against a Mallarmé's, destructive drives?"[67]

It is not difficult to recognize in this critique the restaging of a gesture that Artaud and Kristeva's reading of him seek to expose and challenge as the gesture that strives to keep the inhuman *ob-scene* by insisting on the difference between "life" and "Mind," work and waste, product and process, literature and madness.[68] In essence, Bedient accuses Kristeva of having mistaken what Artaud calls "the waste products of myself" for his oeuvre.[69] Writing involves more than a muscle contraction; the creative process has nothing to do with shitting and poetry is not just "reject," "a foul-smelling turd."[70]

One of the problems with this approach to Kristeva's theorizing of poetic language is that the subject in process engaged in its production is mainly understood in terms of an impossible dialectic between separation and identification, expulsion and stasis, rejection and thesis/position-taking. However, if Kristeva's concern with Artaud's obscene inhuman is to be taken seriously, then any resistance to the body's motility (hence the risky space of freedom) needs to be sought, not in any kind of *position-taking*, but in what Artaud insists is a form of cruelty. "Everything that acts is cruelty."[71] In rethinking freedom from the perspective of the inhuman, Grosz argues that it is not the transcendental property of the human. It is located not in being but in doing. Freedom is the capacity to act and "is attained only through the struggle with matter, the struggle of bodies to become more than they are."[72] In this light, it is perhaps important to remind ourselves that the subject in process/on trial is also the subject of *practice*. Practice is not, as Bedient suggests, "blindly thrashing rejection."[73] Kristeva devotes part IV of *Revolution in Poetic Language* to developing a theoretical analysis of *practice* and the modern text as a form of practice. She emphasizes that the text-cum-practice does not merely offer a space where the process of the subject can be carried out, but realizes this process in language.[74] Preventing the process from becoming locked into a social or family identification, the text at the same time avoids turning into "a free-flow 'escape' [*fuite*] of the signifier."[75] In other words, the text as a signifying practice demonstrates that the subject caught in the inhuman process of motility is simultaneously a subject of/in language. It is as a subject who *speaks* his/her being put in process/on trial that she or he is able to resist his or her motility. Kristeva insists on Artaud's "'will to meaning': he searches for a language, speaks to others."[76] This enables him to survive the intractable logic of corporeal motility, helps him preserve a sense of life and "elude the machinations and blind alleys" that result from the "'natural' imprisonment" of the signifying process in madness.[77]

Again, Kristeva associates the modern text as practice with a *black* laughter: it is "painful, forced" because it bears witness to the eruption of the drive within the signifying system.[78] This is not the laughter of "one who observes and knows."[79] The producer of black laughter is a subject who remains vulnerable to both *process* and the prohibitions against it. She or he laughs in the hope of making his or her laughter infectious. Like Artaud's explosive/expulsive language, black laughter does not seek to educate its addressee but to make him or her porous enough to experience "the stench of nothingness" (yes, the foul-smelling turd) behind the arbitrariness of names.[80] This is why the black laughter of the modern text in Kristeva is also the risky space of freedom. Exposed to the arbitrariness of naming, the laughing subject speaks in tongues, infinitizes the name, and "replaces the effect of laughter with the production of new devices (new texts, a new art)."[81] What Artaud calls *life* is precisely the production of "a *new organization of reality*" out of his struggle to speak and to translate his experience of corporeal motility.

The production of the *new*, indeed, the transformation of the real is crucial for Kristeva in the 1970s. Her conclusion to the essay on Artaud returns to the question of the subject. The unitary subject needs to open up to its experience of heterogeneous contradiction by retrieving its corporeal motility, a source of permanent contestation and a form of *jouissance*. However, the subject put in process/on trial runs the risk of fixing itself in the implacable logic of the pulsional and expulsional process. It needs, therefore, to be given back its *freedom* through the cruelty of a practice that speaks the process so that it penetrates others and becomes the bearer of "collective fury."[82] Although Artaud clearly sensed the need of making his madness infectious like the plague, Kristeva suggests that, in abdicating the sphere of politics, he fails to cultivate a space of what she calls "mutual enlightenment" between the subject of textual practice and the "subjects transforming the process of history."[83]

When she returns to avant-garde literature and the question of the subject in her analysis of Sartre in the 1990s, her perspective differs considerably. In the 1970s the madness of the modern text had to submit itself to the constraints of political struggle. In the 1990s she reevaluates "the madness that sustains literature" against a privileging of social praxis that, post-World War II, has led into "the old errors of Promethean optimism" against the background of an increasing spectacularizing of the political.[84] Artaud's "failure" seems preferable to any of the success stories promoted in contemporary societal structures driven by the spectacle. In *Hatred and Forgiveness* Kristeva narrates the story of John, a man diagnosed with schizophrenia, presented in the documentary *People Say I'm Crazy* created by his sister, who films her brother in his favorite pastime of drawing and making woodcuts. Thanks to her efforts, the "madman" is soon recognized as a "disabled artist" and his illness is transformed into an oeuvre, a work of art. "What success! Clearly, he has been cured," Kristeva writes, yet "an immense sadness keeps me from applauding with both hands. Something seems to be missing from this lovely 'integration.'"[85]

The problem is that "the *question of the subject* is not raised."[86] Although the process of the subject gets translated into a practice, this practice does not involve the "*personal rebirth*" of the subject because it is reduced to the object produced, i.e. the disabled artist's oeuvre presented in a much publicized exhibition.[87] What is missing is the *time of production* in relation to which "the object appears only as a limit."[88] Importantly, Artaud's discussion of the cruel force of acting insists on its "frenzied pointlessness," its product-free nature.[89] Compared to a murderer's act that gets released, he argues, the actor's does not lose contact with "the mystery of passionate *time*" and the inhuman power that inspired it.[90] It is precisely this power, in all its horror and madness, that is experienced by the spectator as "tangible laceration . . . on the heart and senses."[91] In contrast, John's filmed story is a tear-jerker that serves to reinforce the inane concept of life Artaud's theater of cruelty seeks to expose and demystify. With Kristeva, the subject in process/on trial is inevitably lost behind a life reduced to its spectacle and the "producer . . . of the *show*."[92] "The person, the subject, is absorbed by his objects, and his psychical life seems cured, because it has quite simply disappeared."[93] The film, then, keeps the inhuman force of John's madness *ob-scene*. John is not offered a chance to "speak of his anxieties and desires or the exclusion in which 'people' wall him up."[94] "People" (i.e. the sane, able spectators) remain at a safe distance and can indulge in the scopophilic pleasure experienced in the face of the suffering of others. Happy to witness one more miracle of human will power, they are content to forget John and the less fortunate of John's ilk at the end of the film. There is "no *interaction* between the disabled and the able." Indeed, "there is no sharing" that would enable the spectator to develop an attentive approach to "the *subject* in the limited body or mind" beneath "the *producer of images.*"[95] Concluding her discussion, Kristeva does not hesitate to raise the question of the subject anew. The subject, she suggests, needs to be sought in that which makes *one* singular; in other words, the unshareable share (*moira*) allotted to him or her in life—what Artaud called necessity or fate (*moira*).[96] At the same time, *subject* is the name Kristeva gives to the passionate, inarticulate conviction in a (speaking, laughing, suffering) man or woman that (despite the risks, the difficulty, the cost) the unshareable can be shared.[97]

V. Literature as the Laboratory of a Fate-based Humanism

Heller has defined fate as "the end that visits upon us."[98] In ancient Greece this sense of fate was posited at the heart of an understanding of the human as a *finite,* a *limited* being. To Heller, the ancient Greek recognition of fate was inextricable from an acknowledgment of what we have defined as the inhuman share of Man, his creaturely, vulnerable existence. In contrast, the moderns insist that "one's life has no pre-set destination, that one is, or is supposed to be, the master of one's own destiny."[99] This assumption is a mere fallacy but continues to dominate representations of the human and is strengthened by scientific/technocratic discourses in the context of which the inhuman aspects of our bodily nature are approached as an obstacle or, at best, an embarrassment. Wendell's aptly titled book on feminism and disability, *The Rejected Body*, exposes the reliance of the Western medical system and a body-oriented media culture alike on the "myth of control," which is a "major obstacle to coming to terms with the full reality of bodily life."[100] Ours is a culture that denies malaise, psychic or somatic illness, disability, and death. Anyone who fails to fit into the dominant ideals of health and beauty is socially shunned, pushed to the obscure corners of an increasingly mediatized life. Artaud, condemned to a life of incarceration, knew all too well this stigma of failure. He knew that failure to control one's corporeal motility and be "cured" is perceived as synonymous with a failure to attain full humanity. In response to a letter from Rivière, Artaud feels the need to explain his inability to "fulfill" himself; in another letter he feels forced to justify his very existence. "Meanwhile, the man exists. . . . Should he be condemned to oblivion on the pretext he can only give fragments of his self?"[101]

Writing at the turn of the millennium, Kristeva astutely demonstrates that our refusal to "share the wound, the intolerable, the unshareable," is the inevitable outcome of a Western-style humanism, "a culture that posits human beings as creatures capable of excellence, pleasure, and achievement in the image of an all-mighty Creator."[102] Like Wendell, she points out that such culture (remnant of the Enlightenment cult of Man) is all too keen to blame the victim of fate, that is, the vulnerable man or woman for his or her resistance to the cure. As a psychoanalyst, a writer, and a theorist of literature, Kristeva has become overtly critical of such versions of humanism, which paradoxically survive alongside postmodern discourses of difference, respect, and the need for assimilation. In *Possessions*, one of her crime novels, her protagonist Stephanie Delacour is quick to debunk the political and ethical cynicism of assimilationist trends in postmodern humanism.[103] She is also shrewd enough to note how this collective effort to assuage guilt regarding less fortunate others behind the moralistic facade of an assimilationist discourse goes hand-in-hand with an eagerness to abject whatever (be it physical illness, madness, or crime) threatens to destroy this facade and a cheerful existence-in-denial.[104]

In the face of the clear perseverance in postmodernity of forms of humanism that refuse to raise the question of the subject and fail to take on board concepts of life informed by the inhuman, Kristeva argues that we are in need of a "more complex humanism" that recognizes "concretely the suffering of those who are different" and *interacts* "with this suffering in a project of life."[105] This can only be a fate-based humanism,[106] one that does not idealize Man nor turn a blind eye to the pain, the malaise, the sense of hopelessness human creatures feel when confronted with the destructive force of the drive or the implacability of accident. To this end, she insists, nothing less than "an anthropological revolution" is needed,[107] a rethinking of the singularity and vulnerability of the human at the risky threshold between biology and language, death and life, determinism and freedom. Such an anthropological revolution can bring about a true *cultural* revolution, the development of a "democracy of proximity" capable of facing up to the arrogance and control-fixation of the moderns through its commitment to respond to "the most insurmountable of fears—one that confronts us with our limitations as living beings."[108]

It is important that Kristeva considers literature (along with psychoanalysis) as one of the laboratories for incubating a fate-based humanism.[109] As I have shown, her concept of literature remains indebted to Artaud's demystified understanding of it. It is not the kind of literature that uses beauty as a sort of band aid. Offering a risky experience of limits, it develops as a form of loyalty to the malaise, the solitude, and suffering that keep us at the crossroads between renewal and crisis, audacity and accident. Like Artaud's theater of cruelty, the literary experience Kristeva theorizes functions "like an open door" leading both author and readers "where they would never have gone of their own free will."[110] This is why literature for Kristeva remains a species of the obscene. Unlike psychoanalytic practice, it is not cure-driven. On the contrary, it seeks to render *dis*ease contagious—like Artaud's plague. If it is neither comforting nor pleasing to the senses, this is because its method is *cruel*, it is "nothing other than a way of thinking beyond judgment, with one's body and tongue."[111] More importantly, it does not lose sight of the *question* of the subject behind the narcissistic images of the ego, committing itself to the inscription of the inhuman within the grand narratives of the human, and to the affirmation of vulnerability as a *right*, a value complementary to those codified by Enlightenment Man.[112] Can such a materialist, dis-idealized conceptualization of literature survive in the face of the spectacle? In her "utopian" moments,[113] Kristeva insists on holding on to the conviction that literature can serve as an antidote to the spectacle—on the condition that it remain an *epidemic* at once infectious, death-borne, *and* redemptive of what we are in most need of today: life in its "raw state."[114]

VI. Conclusion

My inspiration in this essay has been Kristeva's suggestion that a *new*, more complex and demanding humanism would need to be fate based. Retracing Kristeva's steps from her current concern with vulnerability and disability back to her early engagement with Artaud and his all-too corporeal semiotics of madness has helped me throw into relief Kristeva's undiminished attention to a sort of material necessity—one very similar to what Artaud termed *fate*. The concepts of motility, cruelty, process, and practice are central in Kristeva's theorizing both of the subject-in-process/on trial and of a distinct signifying function that she associates with the literary experience. Attentive to the Artaudian echoes in these concepts, I have suggested that the *question* of the subject in Kristeva becomes the site where the difficult dialectic between freedom and determinism is investigated, an investigation restaging Artaud's heroics of an enunciating body burdened by the singularity of an unshareable share. If Kristeva's new humanism is fate based, this is because she conceptualizes it as a life-validating perspective *counter* to the nexus of images or discourses promoted by a cheerful society of the spectacle and a technomedical establishment invested in the myths of control. Like Artaud, Kristeva does not wish to spare us the rage, the contagiousness, the redeeming force of a *dis*ease (call it madness or the plague) that pushes us to the limits of meaning, identity, or the human. In his 1947 lecture, faced with an audience of puzzled, indifferent or sympathetic onlookers, Artaud (weakened though sustained by a spirit of resistance) shaped out of his howling body a text that, to our ears, may remain obscene.[115] For Kristeva, the literary experience begins *here*, in the obscene rhythms of a body in crisis. However, as a practice or, more accurately, a theater of cruelty and resistance, literature has the potential to seduce us (through and beyond the crisis) to paths where meaning crystallizes in impassioned sharing.

Maria Margaroni

University of Cyprus
February 2019

NOTES

1. Julia Kristeva, *The Sense and Non-sense of Revolt: The Powers and Limits of Psychoanalysis Volume 1*, trans. Jeanine Herman (New York: Columbia University Press, 2000), 107.

2. Ibid.

3. Julia Kristeva, *Revolution in Poetic Language*, trans. Margaret Waller (New York: Columbia University Press, 1984), 214.

4. Julia Kristeva, *Powers of Horror: An Essay on Abjection*, trans. Leon S. Roudiez (New York: Columbia University Press, 1982), 18.

5. Julia Kristeva, *Black Sun: Depression and Melancholia*, trans. Leon S. Roudiez (New York: Columbia University Press, 1989), 238.

6. Julia Kristeva, "The 'True-Lie,' Our Unassailable Contemporary," in *Hatred and Forgiveness*, trans. Jeanine Herman (New York: Columbia University Press, 2010), 271.

7. Ibid., 296.

8. Danielle Marx-Scouras, *The Cultural Politics of Tel Quel: Literature and the Left in the Wake of Engagement* (University Park: Pennsylvania State University Press, 1996), especially the chapter on "Excesses of Language."

9. Ibid., 69.

10. Michel Foucault, *Madness and Civilization: A History of Insanity in the Age of Reason,* trans. Richard Howard (London: Routledge, 1989), 99–100.

11. Ibid., 278.

12. Shoshana Felman, *Writing and Madness (Literature/Philosophy/Psychoanalysis),* trans. Martha Noel Evans, Shoshana Felman, Brian Massumi, and Barbara Johnson (Palo Alto: Stanford University Press, 2003), 16.

13. Ibid., 47.

14. Jacques Derrida, "Cogito and the History of Madness," in *Writing and Difference*, trans. Alan Bass (Chicago: University of Chicago Press, 1978), 33–34.

15. Ibid., 37.

16. References to boundary-crossing, identity-limits, art as transgression, etc. abound in her early work. Even recently, the experience of limits lies at the heart of any contemporary form of revolt. See, for example, Kristeva, "The 'True-Lie,'" 271.

17. Kristeva, *Revolution in Poetic Language*, 82.

18. See Derrida "Cogito and the History of Madness," and "La Parole soufflé," in *Writing and Difference*, 193.

19. Foucault, *Madness and Civilization*, 287. Macey points to Artaud's "The Nerve Scales" as Foucault's source of inspiration here. David Macey, *The Lives of Michel Foucault* (London: Random House, 1993), 102.

20. Apart from Derrida, "La Parole soufflé," see "The Theater of Cruelty and the Closure of Representation," in *Writing and Difference*, and Jacques Derrida and Paule Thévenin, *The Secret Art of Antonin Artaud*, trans. Mary Ann Caws (Cambridge: MIT, 1998).

21. Julia Kristeva, "The Subject in Process," in Patrick ffrench and Roland-François Lack, eds., *The Tel Quel Reader* (New York: Routledge, 1998).

22. See Kristeva's interview with Cathy Vogan on YouTube (2007), accessed July 18, 2018, https://www.youtube.com/watch?v=NYHUHX768Zc.

23. Kristeva, "A Stranger," in *Hatred and Forgiveness*, 247.

24. Antonin Artaud, "Letter to the Legislator of the Drug Act," in *Antonin Artaud: Collected Works*, vol. 1, trans. Victor Corti (London: Calder and Boyars, 1968), 62. Ros Murray, *Antonin Artaud: The Scum of the Soul* (Basingstoke: Palgrave Macmillan, 2014), 1.

25. Kristeva, *Revolution in Poetic Language*, 16.

26. Antonin Artaud, *The Theatre and Its Double*, trans. Victor Corti (London: Calder, 1993), 89.

27. In a special issue on Artaud, Letiche argues: "Artaud was a humanist—perhaps a

perverse humanist, but nonetheless a humanist." Hugo Letiche, "Introduction: Artaud, the Real and the Melancholy," *Culture and Organization* 11, no. 4 (2005): 233.

28. Kristeva, "A Stranger," 250.

29. Elizabeth Grosz, *Time Travels: Feminism, Nature, Power* (Durham: Duke University Press, 2005), 171.

30. Elizabeth Grosz, *Becoming Undone: Darwinian Reflections on Life, Politics, and Art* (Durham: Duke University Press, 2011), 11.

31. Kimberly Jannarone, *Artaud and His Doubles* (Ann Arbor: University of Michigan Press, 2010), 33.

32. See, in turn, Antonin Artaud, "Umbilical Limbo," in *Collected Works*, vol. 1, 49, 50, *The Theatre and Its Double*, 16, and "Description of a Physical State," in *Collected Works*, vol. 1, 57.

33. Artaud, *The Theatre and Its Double*, 69.

34. Ibid., 82, 49, 60.

35. Ibid., 40.

36. Ibid., 41, 84; "Umbilical Limbo," 49.

37. Artaud, *The Theatre and Its Double*, 60.

38. Ibid., 22, 58, 79–80.

39. Ibid., 56.

40. Ibid., 60.

41. Julia Kristeva, "From One Identity to an Other," in *Desire in Language: A Semiotic Approach to Literature and Art,* trans. Thomas Gora, Alice Jardine, and Leon S. Roudiez (New York: Columbia University Press, 1980), 145.

42. Ibid., 181.

43. Kristeva, "The Subject in Process," 133.

44. Ibid.

45. Artaud, *The Theatre and Its Double*, 10, 22.

46. Kristeva, "The Subject in Process," 145, 156.

47. See Kristeva, "The 'True-Lie,'" 271.

48. Antonin Artaud, "The Nerve Scales," in *Collected Works*, vol. 1, 79, 86.

49. Antonin Artaud, "Fragments from a Diary in Hell," in ibid., 83, 85.

50. Artaud, *The Theatre and Its Double*, 61.

51. Artaud, "Fragments from a Diary in Hell," 84.

52. Antonin Artaud, "Note pour 'Une Lettre aux Balinais,'" in Delphine Plauteau, ed., *Antonin Artaud* (Paris: Gallimard, 2006), 25 (my translation).

53. Robert Day Allen, "Motility," *Journal of Cell Biology* 91, no. 3 (1981): 148.

54. Artaud, "Note pour 'Une Lettre aux Balinais,'" 23 (my translation).

55. Kristeva, *Revolution in Poetic Language*, 13.

56. Ibid., 17; "The Subject in Process," 138, 139.

57. Kristeva, *Revolution in Poetic Language*, 25.

58. Ibid., 26.

59. Kristeva, "The Subject in Process," 134–35.

60. Kristeva, *Revolution in Poetic Language*, 240.

61. Kristeva, "The Subject in Process," 135, 144, 147, 154.

62. Ibid., 170.

63. Calvin Bedient, "Kristeva and Poetry as Shattered Signification," *Critical Inquiry* 16, no. 4 (1990): 812.

64. Ibid., 810.

65. Ibid., 810–11.

66. Ibid., 811.

67. Ibid., 812.

68. "I suffer because the Mind is not in life and life is not Mind." Artaud, "Umbilical Limbo," 49.

69. Quoted in Murray, *Antonin Artaud*, 1.
70. Artaud quoted by Kristeva, "The Subject in Process," 146.
71. Artaud, *The Theatre and Its Double*, 65.
72. Grosz, *Becoming Undone*, 72–73.
73. Bedient, "Kristeva and Poetry as Shattered Signification," 814.
74. Kristeva, *Revolution in Poetic Language*, 203, 209.
75. Ibid., 209.
76. Kristeva, "The Subject in Process," 160.
77. Kristeva, *Revolution in Poetic Language*, 214.
78. Ibid., 224.
79. Ibid.
80. Kristeva, "The Subject in Process," 161–62.
81. Kristeva, *Revolution in Poetic Language*, 225.
82. Kristeva, "The Subject in Process," 171, 173.
83. Ibid.
84. Kristeva, *The Sense and Non-sense of Revolt*, 185.
85. Kristeva, "Liberty, Equality, Fraternity and . . . Vulnerability," in *Hatred and Forgiveness*, 30–31.
86. Ibid., 31.
87. Ibid.
88. Kristeva, "The Subject in Process," 159.
89. Artaud, *The Theatre and Its Double*, 15.
90. Ibid., 90.
91. Ibid., 65.
92. Kristeva, "Liberty, Equality, Fraternity and . . . Vulnerability," 31.
93. Ibid.
94. Ibid.
95. Ibid., 31–32.
96. Ancient Greek *moira* refers to both Fate as the force(s) controlling human life and the part allotted a human being, the portion of a fortune or property she or he is entitled to.
97. Kristeva, *Hatred and Forgiveness*, 32.
98. Agnes Heller, *A Philosophy of History in Fragments* (Oxford: Blackwell, 1993), 23.
99. Ibid.
100. Susan Wendell, *The Rejected Body: Feminist Philosophical Reflections on Disability* (New York: Routledge, 1996), 93.
101. Artaud, "Correspondence with Jacques Rivière," in *Collected Works*, vol. 1, 40.
102. Kristeva, "Liberty, Equality, Fraternity and . . . Vulnerability," 32, 33.
103. Julia Kristeva, *Possessions*, trans. Barbara Bray (New York: Columbia University Press, 1998), 12.
104. Ibid., 12, 73.
105. Kristeva, "Secularism: 'Values' at the Limits of Life," in *Hatred and Forgiveness*, 28.
106. Ibid., 27.
107. Julia Kristeva, *La Haine et le pardon* (Paris: Fayard, 2005), 583 (my translation).
108. Kristeva, "Liberty, Equality, Fraternity and . . . Vulnerability," 30, 34.
109. Kristeva, *La Haine et le pardon*, 20.
110. Artaud, "Umbilical Limbo," 49.
111. Kristeva, *The Sense and Non-Sense of Revolt*, 108.
112. Kristeva, "Liberty, Equality, Fraternity and . . . Vulnerability," 42.
113. Ibid., 30, 45.
114. Artaud, "Letter to the Legislator of the Drug Act," 60.
115. See Roger Shattuck, "Artaud Possessed," *New York Review of Books*, November 11, 1976.

7

Miglena Nikolchina

SIGNIFIANCE AND TRANSUBSTANTIATION: THE RETURNS OF THE AVANT-GARDE IN KRISTEVA'S PHILOSOPHY OF LITERATURE

Kristeva is a thinker of change. The conceptual apparatus she has developed throughout the years has been systematically concerned with detecting, challenging, and fighting stagnation on the level of both the individual and society. Literature is one of the privileged nodes of such overarching concerns: by understanding literature, thinking about it, and, from a certain point on, making literature, Kristeva elaborates her view of literature as a place where change is reflected and, more importantly, as a place where change takes place and through which change takes place. For her, literature is an active force: it mirrors processes it brings into motion; it is a medium, mode, exemplum, and instrument of transformation or, as Kristeva prefers to call it, of revolution and revolt.

This approach requires conceptual tools for addressing two major questions. First, how is language as the material aspect of literature transformed—in literature and through literature—into a mode and instrument of change? Second, how is this transformation to be studied? Already in her earliest works, in *Sémiotikè* and in *Revolution in Poetic Language*,[1] Kristeva elaborates the concepts of *signifiance* and *semanalysis* to answer these questions.[2] Put in most general terms, *signifiance* is the operation of the drives towards, in, and through language; that is to say, it is the process constituting and dissolving meaning and the subject. *Semanalysis* is the theoretical method for approaching this process: its goal is "to describe the signifying phenomenon, or signifying phenomena, while analyzing, criticizing, and dissolving 'phenomenon,' 'meaning,' and 'signifier.'"[3] In her later writing, the concepts themselves are subjected to modifications and developments: put otherwise, while conceptualizing change, they are not immune to it. *Semanalysis*, which appears in the subtitle of *Sémiotikè*, practically vanishes at the end of the 1970s. This disappearance signals the beginning of a fundamental rethinking of *signifiance*. Initially, this rethinking takes place in practice; subsequently, it is articulated theoretically. Hence, it might be argued that the alteration of *signifiance* is part and parcel of the subsumption of *semanalysis* by a different approach, based on Kristeva's innovative reading of Freud's models of language. A revolution of a sort, which is intertwined with a considerable shift in Kristeva's understanding of revolution, and which affects her perspective on literature.

I. Why the Avant-Garde

Before turning to these conceptual developments, the pivotal importance of modernism and the avant-garde needs to be recognized and emphasized. Kristeva's interest in literature spans authors and works from as early as the Song of Songs and ancient Greek drama to contemporary writing. In the vast array of her literary examples the privileged position of modernism can be singled out and articulated as a juncture of the biographical, the political, and the purely theoretical. This juncture inaugurates and subtends the elaboration of her major concepts, including the concepts of *signifiance* and *semanalysis*, but also the better known dichotomy of the semiotic and the symbolic. The fusion of Kristeva's philosophy of literature with the practices of the avant-garde is most tenacious precisely insofar as the transformative powers of literature are concerned. The belief in these powers was especially vigorous with the Russian avant-garde, with futurism and poets like Mayakovski and Khlebnikov, who preceded and were contemporaneous with the Bolshevik revolution. They believed that a new art, a new poetry, and perhaps a new language (as in the case of Khlebnikov's radical experiments) would form a necessary part of revolution and social renovation. With the consolidation of the Soviet state in the late 1920s, such beliefs and the artists who shared them were swiftly and mercilessly crushed. Modernism and the avant-garde were declared incompatible with the interests of the proletariat. When East European countries, including Kristeva's native Bulgaria, became part of the Soviet bloc after World War II, the negative attitude towards modernism was perpetuated and the publication of modernist authors put under a ban. This ban was nevertheless incessantly contested, no matter what the risks might be. In the early 1960s, controversies around Kafka, in which the very young Kristeva left a trace, provide a curious illustration of the faith—shared by both the prohibitors and their opponents—in the revolutionary potential of modernist writing.[4] Paradoxically, then, the prohibition of modernism reinforced ideas of modernism's revolutionary potential: a potential *against* the revolution that had betrayed both itself and its radical artistic proponents. As a result, two failed projects for social renovation—the Bolshevik revolution after World War I and the East European revolutions following World War II—had become entangled with the repression of the avant-garde. With the East European communist regimes so obviously not delivering what they were supposed to, the repressed avant-garde art turned into a symptom of what went wrong from the very beginning and into a promise for the possibility of setting things right.

Furthermore, the avant-garde was accompanied—and in many ways inspired—by the theoretical developments related to Russian formalism, the Prague linguistic circle, and other tendencies indebted to Husserl's phenomenology, on the one hand, and linguistics, especially Saussure's, on the other. Jakobson, who played an important early role in the inception and the international spread of these ideas, and who coined the term structuralism to name them, emphasized the connection to the avant-garde practices that called them into being.[5] What Steven Cassedy describes as Jakobson's "puzzling" linguistic genealogy—listing Picasso, Joyce, Braque, Stravinsky, Le Corbusier, and Khlebnikov, especially Khlebnikov, as the impulse behind his work—testifies to this juncture that, in stark contrast to received ideas about structuralism, is the thinking of transformation and innovation across artistic practices and their theoretical conceptualization.[6] Kristeva foregrounds this connection in "The Ethics of Linguistics," where she brings together Jakobson, Mayakovski, and Khlebnikov, while elaborating her thesis—the same one that animates *La Révolution du langage poétique*, published in the same year—that the stakes of poetry are that "language, and thus sociability, are defined by boundaries admitting of upheaval, dissolution, and transformation."[7]

Like avant-garde practices, structuralism had its share of trouble in the communist countries. So did Bakhtin's work, the ban on which was finally lifted at the beginning of the 1960s. While perceived as opposed to Russian formalism and, by extension, to structuralism, especially in the East European context,[8] Bakhtin's position is defined by Kristeva in "Le Mot, le dialogue et le roman" (published in *Sémiotikè* in 1969) as "one of that movement's most remarkable accomplishments, as well as one of the most powerful attempts to transcend its limitations."[9] Hence Kristeva partakes of the strategy of Russian semiotician Juri Lotman in bringing together Russian formalism and Bakhtin in a more comprehensive approach.[10] Most importantly for her, Bakhtin, although working predominantly with classical literature, shares the avant-garde perspective that endows language with a dynamic involvement in social transformation. "Bakhtin situates the text within history and society, which are then seen as texts read by the writer, and into which he inserts himself by rewriting them."[11]

Bulgaria was probably the first country outside of the Soviet Union where Bakhtin's writing was enthusiastically received. When Kristeva left for France at the end of 1965 she therefore had Russian formalism, Bakhtin, and a fascination with the utopian extremism of the avant-garde as the basis of what would be a sustained understanding of literature as a transformative force. She also had the awareness that this artistic and philosophical utopia had been thwarted in two of its major social entanglements: first, in its effort to have a say in the Bolshevik revolution; and second (though this effort was still under way and would remain so until the end of the Cold War), in its attempt to oppose the stifling and repressive outcome of this revolution. Her investment in the social and political interactivity of literature was hence both ardent and skeptical: it kept its analytical distance and was mindful of pitfalls, limitations, and inescapable disillusionments, if not, in fact, of suicidal, destructive, and self-destructive lures.[12]

Paris gave Kristeva the chance to turn openly to avant-garde literature and its theoretical implications, which could be done only at the price of excruciating strategizing in communist Bulgaria. However, the 1960s being what they were, Paris was more than a zone of comfort for artistic and academic freedom. In an atmosphere of political turmoil, other major intellectual developments reinforced the blend of poetic and theoretical radicalism that subtended Kristeva's philosophy of literature.

In a comparatively late text, "Thinking about Literary Thought," Kristeva expounds her take on literature by tracing the genealogy of literary theory.[13] There are the processes that begin with the metamorphosis of philosophy at the end of the nineteenth century. Via the pivotal work of Husserl and Saussure, but, she adds, also of Hjelmslev as a linguist closer to phenomenology, these processes constitute literary theory and literary structuralism as an investigation of "form as thought."[14] The controversy between Russian formalism and Marxism, inscribed in Bakhtin's work, and the displacement of the dogmatic mimetic understanding of literature through semiotics both participate in this trend which, as already noted, is informed by the Russian avant-garde's utopia of poetry as a material force in social and even cosmic transformation. To this joining of avant-garde and literary theory via philosophy and linguistics, Kristeva adds a second perspective that brings avant-garde writing and literary theory into another fusion. This second fusion is accomplished by psychoanalysis and Freud. It concerns "changes in how the imaginary is perceived, a change contemporaneous with the transformation of philosophy and of aesthetics."[15] The first change, then, the one that welds philosophy and linguistics in structuralism, is "contemporaneous with an *unprecedented readjustment* of the *imaginary experience* in modernity."[16] This new regime of the imaginary amounts to a "meeting of literature and the impossible."[17] It "appears as a rival to the inner experience, while at the same time trying to change social structures by modifying the relationship between the talking being and meaning, inasmuch as this relationship deeply codifies the social contract."[18] While structuralism is the study of form-as-thought, however, the Freudian revolution allows for uncovering literature as thought of the impossible or, perhaps, literature as a-thought (*a-pensée*), which Kristeva addresses through the writing of French surrealism.[19] "There is a thought at the boundary of that which is thinkable: an experience of language liberated from the shackles of a judgmental conscience gives access to this thought and gives evidence of its existence. It is perhaps a matter of another world (of thought) that modifies the (real) world."[20]

In certain ways this *a-pensée*, a term that makes its appearance in *The Sense and Non-sense of Revolt* and does not appear in Kristeva's earlier explorations of literature, coincides with her well-known concept of the semiotic. It relies on the semantic resources of sounds, it shatters language, unveiling the germination of meaning; it brings news of the dynamic rather than the finality of thought. Yet there are important nuances to *a-thought* that distinguish it from the conceptual span of the semiotic, and which come from the Freudian rather than the linguistic encounter of philosophy with the avant-garde. That there is a turn in Kristeva's writing from linguistics to psychoanalysis is well known.[21] This turn is succeeded by a turn from revolution to revolt, hence it modifies the nexus of art and change, which nevertheless persists. The alteration of the concept of *signifiance* is inflected by both turns. More than that, however, it signals a deep alteration in Kristeva's methodological apparatus that would allow me to speak of a third turn. This turn is of central importance in Kristeva's study of Proust and the role she ascribes to the concept of transubstantiation in this study and, later on, in the study of Colette.[22] By foregrounding, enhancing, and re-visioning the translinguistic dimensions of *signifiance*, transubstantiation makes room for addressing the contemporary digitalized hybridization of the literary. It thus opens the way for a more comprehensive understanding of the immersive and interactive aspects of new media. This is a turn from the semiotic to the transubstantiative; a turn transforming the avant-garde's grappling with the unrepresentable into an encounter with the virtual. Before reaching this point, however, some further elucidations are in order.

II. The Realisms of the Avant-Garde: From Pulverization to Incarnation

In short, while Kristeva keeps returning to Greek drama (with Freud always looming in the background) and any major epoch of European and especially French literature, it can be claimed that her philosophy of literature is profoundly informed by literary modernism. There is the Russian avant-garde with its utopian extremism. There is, much more prominently, the French avant-garde, which Kristeva divides into three stages. She explores the first in *La Révolution du langage poétique*, but also in her later writing through the figures of Mallarmé, Lautréamont, and Rimbaud. The second stage is surrealism, Breton and Aragon, which is the focus of *The Sense and Non-sense of Revolt*. The third stage is the era of *Tel Quel* (1960–1982). *Tel Quel* thus appears as the latest reincarnation of literature's confrontation with the impossible and of the unprecedented changes in imaginary experience. In fact, the incredible intellectual hub that *Tel Quel* was in the 1960s, when Kristeva joined it, not only presents a crossing of the two developments Kristeva discusses in "Thinking about Literary Thought" (structuralism as the study of form-as-thought and psychoanalysis as uncovering literature as a-thought); it also comprises, one might say, a higher degree of lucidity concerning two crucial engagements taken up from Rimbaud and Lautréamont.

On the one hand, there is what Kristeva describes as "literature faced with a classical, and ultimately classicist, philosophical plan."[23] This plan refers to the theoretical self-awareness of the *Tel Quel* literary production. The *Tel Quel* period coincides, notably, with the French "philosophical moment," which has been declared the third great epoch after Greek philosophy and German idealism.[24] Hence, while the first two stages of the French avant-garde and the Russian avant-garde provoke theoretical reflections that could render them comprehensible (as illustrated by the case of Russian formalism), the third stage was intrinsically and self-consciously philosophical: it knowingly blended its artistic "madness," its risky destabilizations of meaning and the subject, with a "philosophical plan."[25] On the other hand, the self-awareness concerns "the comparison of literary utterance and poetic statement with the feminine aspects of both man and woman, which in fact goes back to a trans-subjective real, increasingly impossible to define."[26] The feminine, in fact, like Plato's *chora*, names the unnameable: the maternal *jouissance* to which the subject has no access and that she tries to achieve through writing and art. The elusive feminine *jouissance* is possibly "the secret of *all writing*."[27] Although common to men and women, femininity has gender-specific but also unique characteristics: each artist bears witness to a different confrontation with its challenge. The emphasis on femininity is a fundamental trait both of the literary practice of *Tel Quel* and of Kristeva's theoretical work: possibly the most debated aspect of her work, especially in its earlier stages. Once again, this aspect partakes of the *Geist* of the epoch, with its peak of feminist movements in France and elsewhere, its heated discussions of *écriture feminine*, and the international impact of so-called French feminists. We should not tire of bringing this aspect up, in view of the automatisms that tend to obliterate both sides of the intellectual effort it involved: the feminine as the subversive and innovative energy in artistic creation, and women's input in producing and understanding it. Thus, there is practically no trace of this aspect of the epoch in Badiou's account of the "French philosophical moment" (in fact any word related to woman hardly appears).[28] The same goes for the collective work dealing with the 1960s philosophical moment.[29] The process of canonization of French philosophy is in full swing deleting, as is habitual, women's integral participation in it.

There is, however, another important trend in Kristeva's reliance on the avant-garde for the elaboration of her philosophy of literature. It springs from a tension that relates to genre. This tension will be crucial for the later stages in Kristeva's thinking, but it is there from the very beginning. The tension involves an opposition between poetry and the novel, between poetic language and narrative, between the abstract and the figurative that, insofar as writing is the medium, encompasses a conflict between sound and meaning. The premises for this conflict may be summarized as follows: the revolutionary potential of poetic language is an effect of the semiotic where the semiotic should be understood as pre- or transverbal representation, as rhythm, alliteration, accent, music, as articulations anterior to signs and syntax evolving from the sensorial exchanges during the pre-oedipal osmosis with the maternal body and from a dehiscence between the sensory and the signifiable. Another term Kristeva uses to designate this sensorial osmosis is the *chora*, a Platonic concept emphasizing the impossibility of saying something that nevertheless finds a way to signify. In Kristeva's early work the semiotic modality that, in its artistic manifestations, bears witness to unresolved problems with the mirror stage, is explicitly set up against, not simply the symbolic as logic, syntax, and law, but also the "narcissistic, specular, imaginary investment," which is constitutive of language qua symbolic.[30] The specular and the imaginary provide a defensive buffer against the attack of the drives; poetic language with its innovative potential occurs precisely as the yielding to these attacks, as a breach in the buffer and a failure of the defenses. The breach has then to be somehow contained or psychosis will follow; this is another story. The risk, the pulverization of the subject and meaning must be there first; such are the stakes of the revolution in poetic language.

The relegation of the mirror, of the specular and the imaginary, to the function of symbolic props befalls narrative as well: insofar as the first narrative emerges with the oedipal phase, it is posterior to the turbulences of the semiotic, serves the stabilization of subjectivity and the law, and allows the permeability of semiotic contents only feebly, if at all: "subordinated to the broad outlines of narrativity, the semiotic drive flow gives only a faint indication of the signifying process."[31] The only way for narrative to open up to the transformative incursion of the drives and to a pulverized subject in process is by becoming a *text* in a sense that is summed up as follows: "the drive process cannot be released and carried out in narrative, much less in metalanguage or theoretical drifting. It needs a text: a destruction of the sign and representation, and hence of narrative and metalanguage, with all their lock-step, univocal seriousness."[32] Narrative is good insofar as it is being shattered; a novel is good insofar as it is (avant-garde) poetry, or, rather, insofar as it is neither narrative, nor poetry: "an infinite fragmentation that can never be terminated."[33] Narrative may look open-ended but it is in fact a bearer of closure. This may be a bit crudely put—narrative, Kristeva never fails to stress, is something we need even if only to have it pulverized; there are two types of narrative in terms of openness or closure with respect to signifying practices—yet doing away with narrative is very much the dilemma already posed in *Le Texte du roman*.[34] Kristeva refers to many scholars in her reflections on narrative and tends to be critical of the Russian formalist "literariness." Nevertheless, her approach could very well be described, as noted above, as an effort to reconcile Jakobson with his take on avant-garde poetry, and Bakhtin with his take on the novel. Bakhtin describes the novel as a young genre (unlike epic and lyric, it postdates the invention of writing): a genre that is unfinished, evolving, and transformational. Kristeva takes up this idea, translating Bakhtin's notion of carnival into her well-known concept of intertextuality. It could be argued, however, that in Kristeva's reading Bakhtin is subjected to a "semiotization," a Jakobsonization, so to speak, and the novel's transformative aspects are ultimately equated to "intonations, scansions, and jubilant rhythms preceding the signifier's position as language's position."[35]

In this respect, Kristeva's conceptualization of mimesis presents an especially intriguing problem. In the chapter "Breaching the Thetic: Mimesis" in *Revolution in Poetic Language*, the mimetic object appears not as the reflection of a real object but as a product of drive turbulences: it is not "*vrai*" (true) but "*vraisemblable*" (appearing true, or, as the English translation has it, mimesis is "the construction of an object, not according to truth but to *verisimilitude*").[36]

This claim might be taken as Aristotelean but its inversion towards the Platonic *chora* and the economy of the drives gives it a rather peculiar twist. The verisimilitude is . . . verisimilar; it emerges post-factum, after the encounter with the symbolic order. Before that it is something else, the seeping through of the ineffable *chora* into the realm of symbolic structures. Being the result of semiosis, of the drive economy of enunciation, the mimetic object is hence akin to objects in dreaming: the dream does not aim to give us a picture of reality; it uses the picture of reality. To what ends? The answer to this question, in Kristeva's later writing, will mark the difference between Freud's optimistic psychoanalytic model of language (dreams function like a language and are the royal path to establishing the subject's domination over the unconscious) and his not so optimistic model, which is her own and that she calls *signifiance*. I will return to this. I evoke dreaming at this point only to emphasize the inadequacy of the idea of mimesis qua reflection.

Like dreams and the unconscious, but also poetic language, mimesis works through displacement and condensation (metonymy and metaphor); to these two processes Kristeva adds the idea of transposition, the transformation of one sign system into another, or intertextuality, which she evolves out of Bakhtin's writing. Although drive-impelled, sensorial, and hence translinguistic, the mimetic procedures (metonymy, metaphor, intertextuality) are explored in her early work through language's materiality. Thus mimesis may open the stagnant closure of narrative, but only by superimposing a transversal ordering through sound, rhythm, etc., on narrative structures and by, so to speak, blinding it. Conversely, if mimesis becomes subordinated to narrativity, the semiotic will only trickle, at best. To support her point, Kristeva evokes a telling quotation from Barthes: "Narrative does not show, does not imitate; the passion which may excite us in reading a novel is not that of a 'vision' (in actual fact, we do not 'see' anything). . . . 'What happens' is language alone, the adventure of language, the unceasing celebration of its coming."[37] To go back to Kristeva's communist background, this nonmimetic conceptualization of mimesis is clearly a rearguard fight with the theory of reflection that dominated the notion of realism in dogmatic aesthetics.[38] A major proponent of this aesthetics was Bulgarian philosopher Todor Pavlov, whose magnum opus *Theory of Reflection* was originally written and published in exile in Stalinist Russia in 1936.[39] In the 1960s, when Kristeva left for France, Pavlov's influence was supposed to be waning, yet the need to oppose his views was still and, according to some accounts, remains vibrant.[40]

In its capacity to undermine symbolic structures, mimesis is conceived by Kristeva as complicit with poetic language. It thus partakes in the avant-garde brand of realism as she elaborates it: not a reflection or reconstruction of reality, not showing, not imitating, not envisioning reality, but a practice within, with, against, and criss-crossing it; a material process in the very texture of the social, disturbing it, eroding it, decaying it, pulverizing it, shattering it. This understanding of the revolutionary operation of mimesis discards both narrative qua narrative and the imaginary. Such an outcome, however, creates theoretical tensions in Kristeva's early work, especially in view of the psychoanalytic perspective, already substantially present, and of the role that narrative, dream, and fantasy but also ancient drama and myth play in psychoanalytic theory and practice. Furthermore, an approach through the shattering of language and pulverization of subjectivity might work for a large part of avant-garde poetry, but it risks being too narrow in its applicability so far as the novel is concerned, even the modernist novel. A judgment Kristeva passes on Virginia Woolf is indicative of the risks: "Virginia Woolf describes suspended states, subtle sensations and, above all, colours—green, blue—but she does not dissect language as Joyce does."[41]

I am quoting out of context, of course: Kristeva's concern here belongs to a whole other strand in her thinking that deals with the specificity of female subjectivity and its positioning with respect to language. Nevertheless, approaching the novel only through the "dissection of language" might leave us with a few celebrated examples like Molly's monologue in *Ulysses*. There are, however, some even more serious difficulties in Kristeva's take on poetic language. From the very start, what concerns her in conceptualizing the *chora* and the semiotic is extra- and translinguistic. Capturing this elusive entity through the *linguistic* disturbances it causes privileges linguistics: an outcome Kristeva will later criticize in Freud's "optimistic" model of language. Her move away from this limitation has been summarized as a psychoanalytic turn and, notably, it involves a turn to the imaginary through the figure of the imaginary father.[42] Nonetheless, this methodological shift is parallel to cultural shifts involving the rising scope and influence of the cinema, television, and the image in general. Kristeva discusses these changes in negative terms through Debord's "society of the spectacle," but also positively by uncovering the processes of *signifiance* at work in and through imagination.[43] In her novel *The Enchanted Clock*, imagination is even described as an "organ of survival."[44]

In fact, the psychoanalytic turn takes many years to unfold methodologically and comprises many other turns in Kristeva's writing: to other media like music and especially painting (from the early texts on Giotto and Bellini to curating the Capital Visions exhibition at the Louvre) and, indeed, to narrative (from analyzing "tales of love" and recounting patients' stories to writing novels). These shifts also address a more profound problem inherent in Kristeva's early approach. Addressing the semiotic as the shaking of existing structures does pose the question about "the specific ways in which . . . a new symbolic device is constituted—a new reality [*un nouveau réel*] corresponding to a new heterogeneous object."[45] However, those specific ways remain unspecified insofar as the focus is on the shaking and the shattering: the very method Kristeva employs at this stage, *semanalysis*, has its focus on dissolution. The concrete answer to the question how the new comes into being or, to put it in less revolutionary terms, how literature and art add to the world is, so to speak, deferred. Although not developed in Kristeva's early writing, the answer to this question is implied in comparing the work of mimesis to the work of dreaming: the mimetic object does not reflect reality, it shapes, in and through reality, the sensual forms of an ineffable experience, impossible to articulate. Perhaps the experience of lost time, of forgotten memory.

Perhaps the experience of something that never was, of the new birth. Twenty years after *Revolution in Poetic Language*, in *Time and Sense: Proust and the Experience of Literature*—thus via the modernist novel—Kristeva will call this procedure incarnation or transubstantiation: a procedure through which time becomes sense and flesh, an "imaginary substance."[46] With *Colette* she will take this idea further towards the experience of literature as a "strange life, which *is* only because it *imagines*. In other words, in experience according to Colette, fantasy remakes the body and attaches it to the world's flesh, itself nestled in the flesh of language."[47]

Thus, two contrasting models of dealing with realism emerge from Kristeva's work on avant-garde poetry and the modernist novel. There is the one that shakes, pulverizes, and ceaselessly traverses reality by inscribing in it the processes through which meaning and subjectivity come into being. And there is the other model that, while attesting to the same processes, extends reality, adds to it, by incarnating and transubstantiating absence, loss, and impossibility into sensual fullness, ceaseless blossoming. It could be argued that both models are already present in the early work while it simultaneously delineates their distinction. To quote from *Sémiotikè*:

> Since the text is not the communicative language that grammar codifies, the text is not satisfied with *representing*—with *signifying* the real. Where it signifies, with the delayed effect of representation which is presented here, it participates in the movement, in the transformation of the real which it grasps at the moment of its non-closure. In other words, without imitating (*rassembler*)—simulating—a fixed reality, the text constructs the mobile theater of its movement to which it contributes and of which it is an *attribute*.[48]

In this passage we can see the idea of the text as an attribute of the real and as an agent of its transformation; but we can also see it as the constructor of the mobile theater of its own movement—of the real's?—of their entanglement? This construction, the mobile theater, gets precedence in the second model: a shift that entails a reevaluation of simulation if not of imitation. As a result, the second model rehabilitates narrative and imagination, but also, in a manner that points towards new media, treats the novel as a sort of virtual reality: "*verbum* become *res*, and *res* thus attains a new reality that makes it an *imaginary substance*."[49] Although composed with words, the novel turns words into flesh, it is a transubstantiating device. Kristeva develops this view in *Time and Sense* through superimpositions of Proust's writing, including drafts, notebooks, and letters; her analysis takes into consideration his life and the books he read as well as his cultural and political context. The theoretical reconsideration of the methodology subtending this study, however—as well as the re-visioning of revolution as revolt—is fully developed in *The Sense and Non-sense of Revolt*, that is, after the book on Proust and before the book on Colette. The reconsideration brings together Kristeva's approaches to (avant-garde) poetry and to the (modernist) novel; it juxtaposes the dissolutions and rebirths through literature and the arts. It is carried via a reexamination of

Freud's models of language and, on the basis of this, of Kristeva's own conceptualization of *signifiance*.

III. *Signifiance* and Freud's Three Models of Language

Thus there are turning points in Kristeva's work, which she herself discusses and that have not gone unnoticed by her commentators. One major turning point is the shift from linguistics to psychoanalysis; another the rethinking of revolution as revolt. Throughout these turns the concept of *signifiance* persists, unlike *semanalysis*, which has been abandoned. The full theoretical elaboration of the implications of this change comes comparatively late, after many studies that are carried out in this vein and that scrutinize specific aspects of Freud's thought. The various results of these studies are brought together conceptually through the examination of three distinct stages that Kristeva discerns in Freud's views on language and that she brings into focus through her own theory of *signifiance*.

Kristeva discerns three models in Freud's oeuvre. The first one is prepsychoanalytic and belongs to the time when Freud is a neurologist (1881–1895). His reflections on language at this stage prefigure important aspects of his third model (which more or less coincides with the second topography and the introduction of the death drive), in which they acquire a full-fledged psychoanalytic implementation. At the prepsychoanalytic stage, Freud's preoccupation is with the gap between the sexual and the verbal; with the impossibility for the sexual to be put into words so that sexual desire remains "asymptotic to language and intellect."[50] This gap will in many ways be downplayed in Freud's "optimistic" second model, to return, psychoanalytically elaborated, in the third model. An especially pertinent aspect of Freud's first model is his psychological schema of word-presentation/thing-presentation, which envisions a series of levels of representations whose heterogeneity is very far from Saussure's signifier-signified duo. The schema, as Freud conceives it, is a multilayered complex of perceptions belonging both to the thing (as image, sound, smell, tactility, motion) and the word (which one can say, hear, read, write, so that it involves phonetic, graphic, motor aspects). Among the crucial implications of this model—whose "layered" conception of language will, once again, be temporarily put aside in the "optimistic" phase—is the energetic facilitation, later called drive, and the fact that representation and representability are, as Kristeva puts it, "unwedged from language."[51] In this, one might say, Proustian reading of the prepsychoanalytic Freud, Kristeva foregrounds "Freud's assertion that language puts thought and perception on the same level"—not abstract language but the "language the child learns, that of passionate and amorous communication": "what kind of speech affects both thought and perception? Not intellectual arguments and vague abstractions but stories."[52]

This claim, extracted from the prepsychoanalytic Freud, will then unfold through the rich psychoanalytic register of identification (*Einfühlung*), idealization, and sublimation. It is easy to see that this Freudian grid, belonging predominantly to his third model of language, comprises the trajectory of Kristeva's "psychoanalytic turn" in her work from the 1980s. In *Tales of Love*, *Black Sun*, and elsewhere these concepts are theoretically elaborated both through a direct exegesis of Freud's work and through the philosophy inherent in artistic production.[53] In *The Sense and Non-sense of Revolt*, Kristeva does not thematize but does rely on her own input into this grid: her conceptualization of abjection in *Powers of Horror*. The concepts unfold their own story: before knowing what or who it is, the subject to be asks "where am I?" and finds itself persecuted by the horror of its initial nondifferentiation from the maternal body (*abjection*); he or she then identifies, through a metaphoric leap, with the Imaginary Father (*Einfühlung, identification*) who is in fact an ambiguous amalgamation of mother-and-father; the Narcissistic *idealization* of one's own image through this move abandons sexual aims; it is, therefore, a desexualization (*sublimation*) that, by dissociating the life and the death drives, liberates the death drive and, rather than providing a safe haven, opens the way to depression and melancholia . . . a peril that can then be averted by resexualizing the sublimatory activity. Literature and the arts hypostasize this resexualization that is the destiny of every human being, and do so either by directly introducing erotic fantasies or by concentration on the sublimatory act itself and its product. All this may look too subjective, but it is in fact the groundwork of social, historical, and civilizational processes.

In *The Sense and Non-sense of Revolt*, Kristeva identifies her own concept of *signifiance* with Freud's third model of language, which is not exactly a model of language, but, rather, "a model of *signifiance* that presupposes language and its instinctual substrata but grasps language and the drive through the work of the negative."[54] She thus links *signifiance* with the modalities of identification, idealization, and sublimation, as observed in the psychoanalytic as well as the aesthetic experience. Set in the most general terms—as a concept "expressing the process, dynamic, and movement of meaning, not reduced to language but encompassing it"[55]—this notion of *signifiance* does not seem to differ from the one that is operative earlier in *Sémiotikè* and *Revolution in Poetic Language*. In both cases, Kristeva insists on the translinguistic and heterogeneous character of *signifiance*, which does not separate drives and words and is organized in intermediary structures. In both cases the emphasis on negativity and the death drive—with and without reference to Hegel's dialectic—is crucial, for "it is the death drive that consolidates the narcissistic ego and allows the prospect of investing not an erotic object (a partner) but a pseudo-object, a production of the ego itself, that is quite simply its own aptitude to imagine, to signify, to speak, to think."[56] In both cases literature is explored as a hypostasized locus of these processes, with modernist literature a privileged example. In both cases the seemingly subjective and intimate range of the processes involved is posited as fundamentally implicated in the constitution and renovation of the social and the political, of history and civilization. In both cases "realism"—a concept about which, given its communist abuses, Kristeva does not have much to say—implies a tampering with the real rather than its reflection.

Yet, there are significant differences. The emphasis on the semiotic shifts to transubstantiation in the later work. Narrative is foregrounded. The triple modality (or quadruple, if we include abjection) of identification, idealization, and sublimation, which plays no role in the early work, rehabilitates the imaginary. What I called tampering with the real is also quite distinct: subversion, shattering, pulverization in the first case; anamnesis, which out of forgotten memory and fantasy brings forth a new birth, new flesh, reincarnation, in the second case. Sedition and addition, so to speak. The story of what was forgotten brings into being what never existed: the returns of transubstantiation open Kristeva's philosophy of literature to a yet to be written Kristevan theory of the fantastic. So are we dealing with a more nuanced and more comprehensive elaboration of the same concept of *signifiance*, or are we actually dealing with a concept surreptitiously smuggled in and fundamentally different, with the same name?

In her discussion of Freud's "optimistic" model of language, the second one, Kristeva brings forth an interesting problem related to Freud's essay "The Antithetical Meaning of Primal Words."[57] Freud compares the functioning of the unconscious to certain so-called primitive languages—including Latin—in which the same word might express two opposite ideas: for example, "deep" and "high." This linguistic observation was taken up by Freud as proof for his claim that the unconscious does not recognize contradiction. Kristeva identifies this claim as an error subtending Freud's optimistic model and quotes linguist Benveniste, who points out that this claim in regard to language "did not consider the position of the subject of the enunciation in the act of discourse. Indeed, if the same word signifies 'deep' and 'high,' it is because the subject of the enunciation has moved; the subject is high atop a ladder when saying that a well is deep and at the bottom of the ladder when commenting on its height."[58] While this problem is considerably larger in its linguistic, anthropological, or philosophical implications, it may also provide the proper perspective for understanding the convergences and divergences in Kristeva's conceptualizations of *signifiance*.[59] She proposes two optics for *signifiance* as the process producing meaning and the subject: the first optic, *signifiance one*, is observed, so to speak, from the bottom of the ladder, and the second, *signifiance two*, from its top. One end of the ladder would reveal literature as semiotic shattering and scission; the other end would reveal it as—to put it in terms of Kristeva's discussion of Colette—(transubstantiative) flesh of the world. So far as literature and art in general are concerned, this bifocality makes an aspect emerge in which the two optics overlap: experience. Experience is transversal to the distinction between semiotic and transubstantiative, between abstraction and incarnation, between (avant-garde) poetry and (modernist) novel. It appears from both sides of the ladder.

IV. Time and Flesh

In literature *signifiance* is *experienced*: this is what grants literature the power to interfere in reality, not simply as a participant in social or political battles (for example, by reflecting injustices) but as part of, as Kristeva puts it apropos

Colette, the "mutation of civilization."[60] Experience in, through, and of literature is effective because it turns the word into flesh; it is perceptual; it is sensual and voluptuous; it is Proustian transformation of time into sense; it is Colette's cosmic body. The flesh of literature is monstrous, to be sure, it is inhuman, it is stellar, because, like the giants into which Proustian characters are transformed, it feeds on time and space and transubstantiates them. The experience of literature is thus a call for "the entire body . . . to participate through its senses—sight, of course, but also hearing, touch, sometimes smell. . . . The ultimate goal of art is perhaps what was once celebrated as incarnation. I mean by that the desire to make one feel—through abstraction, form, color, volume, sensation—a real experience."[61]

Here Kristeva is discussing installations at the 1993 Venice Biennale. Had she, at that moment, already finished *Time and Sense*, which appeared in French at the beginning of 1994, or was this a pilgrimage inscribed in its completion? In any case, the crucial term "incarnation" appears in her book on Proust in connection with Proust's own pilgrimage to Venice while he was translating Ruskin, and it is the term's first appearance in Kristeva's book in the sense of "metaphor become flesh,"[62] which will be expounded as "the very life of the imaginary—the incarnation of meaning, the devouring of the signified by the sensed."[63]

So does literature end up being . . . an installation? Surely, Kristeva never lets us forget that literature is done with words. Studying words from that other side, however, the side on which the senses incarnate meaning and produce a new reality with imaginary substance, opens Kristeva's philosophy of literature to the other arts and most of all to those which are today in the making.

Miglena Nikolchina

Sofia University
August 2018

NOTES

1. Julia Kristeva, *Sémiotikè: Recherches pour une sémanalyse* (Paris: Seuil, 1969); *La Révolution du langage poétique: L'Avant-garde à la fin du XIXe siècle, Lautréamont et Mallarmé* (Paris: Seuil, 1974), part of which appeared in English as *Revolution in Poetic Language*, trans. M. Waller (New York: Columbia University Press, 1984).

2. The various translations have provided various solutions for rendering Kristeva's term *signifiance*. I stick to its original form, which, in English, aptly conveys its novelty as well as its relatedness to signifying practice, i.e., signifying as process. See, for example, Megan Becker-Leckrone, *Julia Kristeva and Literary Theory* (New York: Palgrave Macmillan, 2005), 163.

3. Julia Kristeva, Preface to *Desire in Language: A Semiotic Approach to Literature and Art*, trans. Thomas Gora, Alice Jardine, and Leon S. Roudiez (Columbia University Press, 1980), vii.

4. Kafka turns out to be a major culprit behind the 1968 political upheavals in Prague that were ended by a Soviet-led invasion of Czechoslovakia. See Veronika

Tuckerova, "Reading Kafka in Prague: The Reception of Franz Kafka between the East and the West during the Cold War" (Ph.D. diss., Columbia University, 2012), 188–94, https://academiccommons.columbia.edu/catalog/ac%3A172916, accessed August 7, 2017. Before leaving for France, Kristeva, twenty-three years old at the time, defends Kafka in her Bulgarian book, *Harakterni tendencii v zapadnata literatura ot XX vek* (Characteristic tendencies in twentieth-century Western literature) (Sofia: DKMS, 1965), 12.

5. See Stephen Rudy, "Introduction" to Roman Jakobson, *My Futurist Years*, trans. Stephen Rudy (New York: Marsilio, 1992), xii. For an interesting, be it one-sided perspective on the dissemination of Jakobson's ideas, see Roman Jakobson and Claude Lévi-Strauss, *Correspondance 1942–1982* (Paris: Seuil, 2018).

6. Steven Cassedy, *Flight from Eden: The Origins of Modern Literary Criticism and Theory* (Berkeley: University of California Press, 1990), 124; http://ark.cdlib.org/ark:/13030/ft8h4nb55x/.

7. Julia Kristeva, "The Ethics of Linguistics," in *Desire in Language*, 25.

8. See Enyo Stoyanov, "Poststructuralist Backgrounds: The Political Strategies of Resistance in the Literary-Theoretical Debates During the 1960s–1970s in Bulgaria," *Slavica Tergestina: European Slavic Studies Journal* 20, no. 1 (2018): 16–45; https://www.openstarts.units.it/handle/10077/22379.

9. Julia Kristeva, "Word, Dialogue and Novel," in *Desire in Language*, 64; "Le Mot, le dialogue, et le roman," *Sémiotikè*, 143.

10. Lotman had to do this tacitly and indirectly. Curiously, in France Kristeva continued to do battle with a dogma that, one might say, no longer concerned her. See Kamelia Spassova, "Dual Codes: The Text within a Text in Lotman and Kristeva," *Prace Filologiczne. Literaturoznawstwo* (Philological studies: literary research) 8, no. 11, part 2 (2018): 13–28; http://pflit.uw.edu.pl/en/numer-811-2018/.

11. Kristeva, "Word, Dialogue, and Novel," 65.

12. See Jakobson, *My Futurist Years*, 209–48. Kristeva keeps returning to these problems in their entanglement with extreme political choices, as in *Powers of Horror: An Essay on Abjection*, trans. Leon S. Roudiez (New York: Columbia University Press, 1982) and *The Sense and Non-sense of Revolt: The Powers and Limits of Psychoanalysis Volume 1*, trans. Jeanine Herman (New York: Columbia University Press, 2000).

13. Julia Kristeva, "Thinking about Literary Thought," *Sign Systems Studies* 30, no. 2 (2002): 405–17.

14. Ibid., 407.

15. Ibid., 405.

16. Ibid., 407.

17. Ibid., 408.

18. Ibid.

19. *A-pensée* is translated as anti-thought in "Thinking about Literary Thought" and is rendered, more adequately, as a-thought in *The Sense and Non-sense of Revolt*.

20. Kristeva, "Thinking about Literary Thought," 412.

21. Many of the major studies on Kristeva's work are structured around this turn. See, for example, Sara Beardsworth, *Julia Kristeva: Psychoanalysis and Modernity* (Albany: SUNY Press, 2004).

22. Julia Kristeva, *Time and Sense: Proust and the Experience of Literature*, trans. Ross Guberman (New York: Columbia University Press, 1996); *Colette*, trans. Jane Marie Todd (New York: Columbia University Press, 2004) (volume 3 of the "female genius" trilogy).

23. Kristeva, *The Sense and Non-sense of Revolt*, 111.

24. See Alain Badiou, *The Adventure of French Philosophy*, trans. Bruno Bosteels (London: Verso, 2012), li.

25. Kristeva, *The Sense and Non-sense of Revolt*, 111.

26. Ibid.

27. Kristeva, *Colette*, 169.

28. Badiou, *The Adventure of French Philosophy.*

29. Patrice Maniglier, ed., *Le Moment philosophique des années 1960 en France* (Paris: PUF, 2011).

30. Kristeva, *Revolution in Poetic Language*, 49.

31. Ibid., 92.

32. Ibid., 103.

33. Kristeva, "The Novel as Polylogue," in *Desire in Language*, 174.

34. Julia Kristeva, *Le Texte du roman: Approche sémiologique d'une structure discursive transformationnelle* (Paris: Mouton, 1970). Although it appeared after Kristeva's first French book, *Sémiotikè: Recherches pour une sémanalyse*, *Le Texte du roman* precedes many of the essays included in *Sémiotikè*.

35. Kristeva, "The Novel as Polylogue, 95.

36. Kristeva, *Revolution in Poetic Language*, 57–61; *La Révolution du langage poétique,* 57–61.

37. Kristeva, ibid., 248n72.

38. Notably, in the French original the term "mimesis" appears in inverted commas in the chapter's title. See *La Révolution du langage poétique*, 57.

39. Excerpts from Todor Pavlov's work can be found in English at http://marxistphilosophy.org/pavlov.htm.

40. See Kamelia Spassova, "Authentic and Heterogeneous Mimesis: Reflection and Self-reflexivity in Todor Pavlov and Yuri Lotman," *Slavica Tergestina: European Slavic Studies Journal* 20, no. 1 (2018): 70–97.

41. Julia Kristeva, "Oscillation between Power and Denial," in E. Marks and I. de Courtivron, eds., *New French Feminisms* (New York: Schocken, 1981), 166.

42. For an early elaboration of the concept of the imaginary father, see Julia Kristeva, *Tales of Love*, trans. Leon S. Roudiez (New York: Columbia University Press, 1987).

43. Guy Debord, *The Society of the Spectacle*, trans. Donald Nicholson-Smith (New York: Zone, 2012).

44. Julia Kristeva, *The Enchanted Clock*, trans. Armine Kotin Mortimer (New York: Columbia University Press, 2017), 201.

45. Kristeva, *Revolution in Poetic Language*, 181.

46. Kristeva, *Time and Sense*, 122.

47. Kristeva, *Colette*, 22.

48. Kristeva, *Sémiotikè*, 11 (my translation).

49. Kristeva, *Time and Sense*, 122.

50. Kristeva, *The Sense and Non-sense of Revolt*, 32.

51. Ibid., 34.

52. Ibid., 35–36.

53. Julia Kristeva, *Black Sun: Depression and Melancholia* (New York: Columbia University Press, 1989).

54. Kristeva, *The Sense and Non-sense of Revolt*, 56.

55. Ibid., 37.

56. Ibid., 55.

57. Sigmund Freud, "The Antithetical Meaning of Primal Words," in *The Standard*

Edition of the Complete Psychological Works of Sigmund Freud, vol. XI, trans. James Strachey (London: Hogarth, 1957), 153–62.

58. Kristeva, *The Sense and Non-sense of Revolt*, 41.

59. See, for example, Alex Pillen, "A Space That Will Never Be Filled: Sharp Communication and the Simultaneity of Opposites," *Current Anthropology* 58, no. 6 (December 2017): 718–38.

60. Julia Kristeva, "De Claudine à Sido: Colette ou la chair du monde," in Julia Kristeva, ed., *Notre Colette* (Kindle, 2016), 37%.

61. Kristeva, *The Sense and Non-sense of Revolt*, 11.

62. Kristeva, *Time and Sense*, 102.

63. Ibid., 307.

REPLY
TO PHILIPPE FOREST, MARIAN HOBSON, MARIA MARGARONI, AND MIGLENA NIKOLCHINA

I. PHILIPPE FOREST

I thank Philippe Forest for going back to my first book, *Le Texte du roman: Approche sémiologique d'une structure discursive transformationnelle*, published in 1970, and for demonstrating that my contribution to literary theory was *magnetized* by the novel from the start, as a "genre" and as *writing*.[1]

Seduced by the audacity of the French "Nouveau Roman," which from my native Bulgaria appeared to me like a subversion at the heart of Western literature and an explosion in a communist regime that falsifies language, I undertook a thesis to elucidate this "phenomenon." A youthful audacity that one may understand better by reading Miglena Nikolchina's study (see the section on "Why the Avant-Garde" in her essay): the futurists and the Russian formalists, then the Soviet semioticians, rebelled against the stranglehold of totalitarianism, calling into question the conventions and the lies of "newspeak" (*novlangue*) or breaking them outright. Solzhenitsyn himself did not fail to compare this Sovietism to a regimentation of language. In response to which the former convict reinvented a harsh, elliptical language, melodic in its very density.[2] As for me, why did I make that jump back four centuries to land on *Le Petit Jehan de Saintré* (1456)? It was Pierre Daix, the director of the literary review *Lettres françaises*, who drew my attention to Antoine de la Sale (1386–1462), a virtually unknown, even "indifferent" (Forest) author, whom Louis Aragon praised in his *La Mise à mort* (1965): "a rather dizzying meditation on the creation of the novel" which goes back to the "medieval origins of French literature" (Forest).

Mikhail Bakhtin, whom I had just introduced in the seminars of Lucien Goldmann and Roland Barthes at the École Pratique des Hautes Études, went "beyond" the "formalists" (related to the French structuralists) in placing the *birth of the novel* in Rabelais, at the intersection of carnival, courtly poetry, Menippean satire, and medieval "scientific" chronicles. In Antoine de la Sale, I was able to discern, in his very awkwardness, the emergence of a new mentality and literary genre, anterior to the jubilatory Rabelaisian synthesis—even though

Translated from French by Armine Kotin Mortimer.

he belonged to his period, the Middle Ages, and was haunted by a vertical "Beyond" whose logic of "exclusive disjunctions" proper to the "Chanson de Geste and the tales of the Round Table" resolved contraries (Forest). *Le Petit Jehan de Saintré* was, however, constructed on a new "moral code": it overflowed with *signs* linked in a "horizontal grammar" obeying the "non-disjunction" of contraries "by which the figures of the feint and the double proliferate"—ferments of the *psychology* that was to develop on the soil of the European novel before becoming a "human science."

As Forest writes, "less the last medieval novel than the first *modern* novel," *Le Petit Jehan de Saintré* interested me as "the location of a structural change." The passage from the ideologeme of the *symbol* to the ideologeme of the *sign* does not prevent these two discourses from subscribing to an identical principle of *expressivity*. While seen as a "somewhat overarching synthesis" (Forest), this structural mutation, which underlies the advent of the novel as a genre, is indispensable for discerning the specific features of the *author*. The socio-historical *ideologeme* breaks here with the "expressivity" that governs it. The adventure of the page and his Lady slips into the background, and it is the *author's enunciation* that occupies center stage. Forest emphasizes that, in the reading I propose, a new genre, "always ambiguous," is in progress from the start: both the "expressivity" and "the (problematic) 'exit' of this expressivity through the infinite transformation of the signifiers" (citing *Le Texte du roman*), which calls for "plural texts" that "contradict each other and relativize each other" within the novelistic discourse. He also notes that this "revitalization of structuralism" that I propose with *Le Texte du roman*, in attempting to "put back into play an essential concern for History and the subject," continues in *Sémiotikè* (1969) and in *Intimate Revolt* (1997).[3]

The allusion to Aragon's *Blanche ou l'oubli* is all the more pertinent in that *Le Petit Jehan de Saintré* addresses the ambivalent relation of the young page to the Lady and to his own confraternity of young men, intermixing fidelity, incestuous love, treason, and homoeroticism—currents of passion that I had neither the intention nor the capacity to examine in depth at the outset of my research. Psychoanalysis would later open other horizons allowing me to address these subjects in modern and contemporary literature. But as early as that period, a text by Sollers that Forest mentions, "The Novel and the Experience of Limits" (1968),[4] allowed me to glimpse the fact that this novelist of the "*Nouveau* Nouveau Roman" (as the critics designated him) displaced the formalistic exploits of the Nouveau Roman onto the metaphysical and psychosexual dimensions of *inner experience* in Bataille's sense as informed by Freud. These new orientations alerted me that I had to "return to the source" with my cultural baggage, aided by "important developments from the end of the 1960s and the beginning of the 1970s" (Forest), before daring to interpret the literary experience of modernity and before forging my conception of the novel in *Intimate Revolt*, cited by Forest: "Until now, novelists were content to parody the world. Now it has to be invented."[5]

I would have liked Forest to elaborate his thought and his writing at the University of Paris 7, to which I belong. His passion for Japanese art and literature as well as his novels and his books devoted to Sollers, *Tel Quel* and *L'Infini*, Camus, Joyce, Kafka, Robbe-Grillet, and Butor, and especially his *Aragon* (which received the Goncourt Prize for Biography) trace a path that intersects with mine.[6] And I read *Une Fatalité de bonheur* with *Je reste roi de mes chagrins* as the reverse and obverse of philosophy and the novel.[7]

Forest continues to explore elsewhere, at the University of Nantes and throughout the world, "an intimacy continuously reinvented," as he writes in this volume. Proof, if it were needed, that the spirit of the university remains cautious about and resistant to those who are not content to apply models to "interpret," but who write, also as novelists, "the incessant revolt of an imaginary against itself."

II. Marian Hobson

In a subtle way, Marian Hobson asks: what is she doing? This question leads her to explore numerous fields, including the university. For my work addresses the study of "Texts and Documents," just as it contributed to a new name for my department, "Letters, Arts, and Cinema." It was not a matter of breaking with semiology, which, as Hobson rightly emphasizes, exerted a "liberating effect on the study of literature," but, rather, of refining and completing these tools in order to decipher the galloping "society of the spectacle" where the *image* can end up imposing itself to the detriment of language, before globalizing it. We were attempting to anticipate—and prevent—the current denigration of the "human sciences," well known in the United States, with draconian budget cuts as a consequence. In this respect, I would like to emphasize a French specificity.

Although it developed in universities and quite often outside departments of philosophy, this new approach to literature was borne by philosophers (Derrida, Foucault, Deleuze) as well as linguists and specialists of literature (like the "Barthes vs. Picard" debate).[8] It received a favorable welcome above all in the milieu of the literary avant-garde, the review *Tel Quel*, then in the press and on television.[9] The professional and existential issues were less "academic" at that time, but they provided real *bridges* toward interdisciplinary research—at the heart of the École Pratique des Hautes Études and innovative laboratories at the Collège de France. (I researched my *thèse d'état*, *Le Texte du roman*, in Lévi-Strauss's anthropology laboratory.)

Is this effort to "think literary thought"[10] possible anywhere other than in France, where we have "broken the thread of the religious tradition" (borrowing the expression from Alexis de Tocqueville and Arendt) and developed philosophy in works as literary as they are conceptual by Voltaire-Diderot-Rousseau? Hobson's studies on French literature of the eighteenth century have taught me a lot. In particular, her reading of *Rameau's Nephew*[11] gave me a better grasp of that enigmatic "shamelessness which gives utterance" that Hegel noted in Diderot, which offers French "culture" the possibility of rising to the threshold of "absolute Spirit."[12]

My research could not have taken place without this universalistic humanism and the discursive form in which it has developed. The postcolonial sociopolitical context, which resulted in May '68, was also favorable to my research. And that is true even though I have had to remain "on the margins" both of the university institution and of the national establishment; but other doors opened, going towards my American "adoption" (beginning with the French Department at Columbia University). The generous diffusion and developments of my work, regrouped under the term "French Theory," deserve a careful interpretation that I cannot provide here. I would simply note the richness of this work—in American universities at first, then in England, and throughout the world by means of English translations—even if it did not always succeed in avoiding the hurdle of a "politically correct" recuperation. An encouraging extension, in counterpoint to the country of the French Enlightenment, as fertile in the avant-garde as it is allergic to grafts, to foreigners, and to the unexpected. Did America, a political democracy with promises of liberties that were held back by its conservatism (Arendt), lack "languages" for the *societal transformations* that were shaking it, fomented by technologies and Cold War weariness? The fact is that neither conventional academicism nor normative psychiatry or ego psychology were in a position to understand these transformations. Alone in the breach, contemporary art and literature would become the conveyers of French Theory, which, in the footsteps of Continental Philosophy, would take hold of the passions and disruptive discourses of an America in the middle of societal, technological, and political upheavals (the Cold War, Vietnam, the stranglehold of marketing and the image).

Turning to Marxist-Leninist thought, my education in it is the fruit of crossings, disruptions, impatience. What are they? Hobson evokes the Hegelian Marxism of "Iron Curtain intellectuals." (I will come back to this problematic later, in my reply to Sarah Hansen in the section on Theory of Revolt.) My discussion will lead me to return to the disastrous "Bulgarian affair" that Hobson alludes to. Of course, the political role of my studies did not escape my notice. *Semiology-semiotics* was considered refractory to Marxism, and its Estonian leader, Juri Lotman, was persecuted (see Hobson), all the more so because he was Jewish. The Association Internationale de Sémiologie (AIS), which was created then, brought together philosophers of language and theoreticians of literature from the Eastern bloc countries, all considered uncontrollable or dissident. In proposing a conception of the human being as a *speaking being*, irreducible to the single role assigned to it in the production of goods and the reproduction of the species, semiology-semiotics destabilized a sclerotic Marxism, and "sensed," too, the technological acceleration that was to turn us into hyperconnected internauts.

Have I underestimated the *imagination*? Hobson remarks: the imagination "is left aside," "in spite of Kristeva's allusions to Husserl."

As a student in Paris, I read I. A. Richards but not much of William Empson (see Hobson), and although the French semiologists Greimas and Barthes rarely refer to phenomenology, my reading of Hjelmslev inevitably led me to Husserl. I think I made only one "allusion" to him in *Revolution in Poetic*

Language. I see him as the indispensable foundation for the understanding of syntactic competence and the conscious and intentional transcendental ego.[13] I also mention Frege (enunciation-denotation) and his divergence from Husserl, which is only apparent since he does not question the transcendentality of the ego.[14] This interpretation, which is certainly not as detailed as Hobson's study on Frege and Derrida, nevertheless points out what semiology owes to the phenomenological continent.[15] Without it, this discipline would not have been able to open up that *other epistemological space*: that of the Freudian unconscious and of *subjectivation* as a process of heterogeneous engendering, *psyche-soma*, and its catastrophes.

My research published after 1974 (*Powers of Horror*, *Tales of Love*, *Black Sun*, *Time and Sense*) continued to elaborate these topics.[16] I thus proposed another way of probing Husserl's "imagination" or Sartre's "imaginary." Without ignoring them. Rather, by displacing the analysis onto the risks and pleasures of individuation/subjectivation in and through language, with the drives, the senses . . . and the image.

Has "semanalysis" disappeared? I would say rather that it has been realized in *signifiance* and rebuilt thanks to the "compass" of Freudian psychoanalysis. In this approach, are my neologisms a "somewhat fancy terminology" (Hobson) of which only "intertextuality" remains? I would add, with all due respect to Hobson, *abjection*, the *semiotic/symbolic*, *reliance*, etc. (See among other things the work of the Kristeva Circle.) These stances punctuate my conceptual grasps, the "fermentation of ideas" and "a movement forward," as Hobson does say, "instead of creating a doctrine." The fact is my intent is to mark the steps of my *journey* toward the *open*. . . Thus, the term "paragram" is found in Saussure's *Anagrammes*, which I studied in 1966.[17] (Hobson informs me the term comes from Demosthenes and Aristotle!) It designates the dissemination of a proper name or of a pivotal theme-word, which "is heard" and "takes shape" in the reading aloud of poetic texts. Much like the "dreamwork" according to Freud, in which the "play on words" composes and/or censures the desire of the dreamer. . . Of course, my neologisms also betray my "energy in theorizing" (Hobson)—and this energy delivers me over to language as to life: the life of language, where the "terms" of the theoretical neoreality are ephemeral lifelines.

Among the numerous other questions Hobson raises, there is Rimbaud. I didn't summon him in *Revolution in Poetic Language* because his Catholicism and his homosexuality escaped the young student I was then. But I found him again later and, as with Céline, I will return to him later in my replies to Françoise Coblence and Michal Ben-Naftali.

III. Maria Margaroni

Antonin Artaud was a scandal in the literary world. His battle with schizophrenia and drugs is fought in an explosive oeuvre, now published, which prompts fascinated readings defying conventions and disciplines.[18] To appraise the radicalism of my research, Margaroni drew on this provocative experience of writing as lived by Artaud, the "scapegoat" of "errant furies."[19] Margaroni's interpretation is itself provocative, as she intends to bring justice to this "body gobbling the infinite nothing" that is "terrified by the pulsing of its death."[20] As a result of "keep[ing] himself at the insensitive limit of things" while his "throat seeks to speak names and something like the vibrating filament of objects."[21] Artaud further aims to overthrow the straightjackets of the "theoreticians of literature" who "cannot imagine their conscious aggregate falling apart," but can only have the right to ethical existence on the condition of making themselves capable of elucidating the "motilities" of the one who has "overthrown Insanity."[22]

Of course, the term "madness" is not capable of illuminating the "disaggregations" of subjectivity that Artaud nevertheless manages to *write*. Margaroni uses these writings to alert social conscience and hermeneutic powerlessness in the face of these catastrophes-and-rebirths of the speaking subject, and she assumes my diagnostic of "psychosis" as "the brute reality of globalized humans." While there exists an "'obscure but essential kinship' between madness and literature," and if it is possible "to rethink literature as a species of the obscene" (Margaroni), it is also important to hear "ob-scene" like "off-stage": inassimilable into the uniformity of the spectacle, though frequently induced by the grip of its banalized languages, its images, and its normalized behaviors.

At these limit states, where the drive overflows psychical composure and tears language to shreds, we are at the limits of life. It would be *obscene* to "theorize" a "literary" performance in this ultimate psychical creativity of language that accompanies the collapse by giving it a *medium* (body-voice-meaning) to *defer* the hormonal energy and make its outbursts shareable.

The *care* Artaud lavishes on himself, thanks to his extraordinary capacities as a poet, actor, and painter, does not exclude an equally singular investment on the part of his "entourage." I have never taken part in the enthusiasm with which the admirers of *Anti-Oedipus* idealized madness.[23] On the contrary, it is a question of broadening the notion of *humanity* by ensuring the life and the sur-vival of those who attain and reveal these limits. Their paroxysms inhabit us, "limit-states" intermittently capture the *neurotic* who prefers not to know himself in the *normal* he is supposed to be. And our dreams reveal these latencies. All the same, Artaud's "theater of cruelty" does not lead me to an apologia for psychosis, and I do not perceive his destructiveness as an invitation to crime but as a possibility of recognizing it where it hides—to *sublimate* it but also to *heal* it.

In trying to transpose my *clinical* experience of psychoanalysis into the *reading* of texts that still today bear witness to the convulsions of psychosis, serious depression, autism, and drug addictions, I stake a claim to a humanism that I must explain.

My *theory of literature*, supported by psychoanalysis, shares in the latter's ethic. Margaroni identifies and develops this journey, attentive to both its *ethos* and its *pathos*, including enigmas of (mystical) incarnation and its smiling imaginary. The ethical accents of her interest in "reconstellating humanism" and the "global hybrid" give me the opportunity to add further details.[24]

The psychoanalyst practices a solitary profession in which her only companion, the patient, is not very reliable, as Bion ironized. I entirely agree, but then, why this profession? Because this "not very reliable" coupling of the transference/countertransference rests on a sort of ethic, in which judgment and the world are bracketed: "Where id was, there ego *shall* be," with *two principles* that are opposed, the *pleasure* principle and that of *reality*. Philosophical reflection on the aspiration for happiness began two millennia ago. Contemporary thought usually distinguishes in it the *imperative aim* of morality, based on the *norm*, and the *optative aim* of *ethics*, based on *choice* and the *will* in which there appears *desire*, dear to Freudians. The norm does not disappear in the ethical quest, but biopolitics, born in the fortunes and misfortunes of democracies to which are added the promises of the life sciences, proposes another conception of the *norm* today: it is no longer a concept fixed *a priori* but *a dynamic concept*.

We are forced to comment that by opening reason to the drives and the desires *of the two sexes*, psychoanalysis has become the *primary factor* in the upheaval of normative morality. It will continue to be so, having detected the unease inherent in the social link and because we testify, after Freud, against the *refusing of sexual life* (which is not pornography) by betting on "eternal Eros."

This ethic is possible because the theory of the unconscious breaks with metaphysical dichotomies in considering neither matter nor mind but the *drive* as a heterogeneous construction: energy *and* meaning (prior to and underlying the advent of signification proper to language), neuronal thrust *and* memory trace. More than a "corporeal understanding of writing" (Margaroni), it is the *drive signifiance* that I identify in writing as experience. The "body," "matter," "sex" are *denatured* in Freud's oeuvre by the copresence of language and by the "psychical revolution of matter," which inscribes the *splitting* or the *fading* of the subject at the center of the speaking being. In regard to Husserl's "unitary subject" or "transcendental ego," I perceive, in "limit-states" and situations of disability, including the various forms of autism, a *subject in process*. A singular approach to these "*other* identities" is indispensable.

With the psychosomatic dynamic understood like this, and without acquiescing to the *anal* (Margaroni), I observe these *facilitations* and *investments (cathexes)* prior to subject-object separation in the early mother-child relations. Belonging to the drive, memory, and the prelinguistic (semiotic), these investments are tied together in *ab-jection*: fascination/repulsion with the maternal container. I do not aim for any dialectical synthesis between soma and psyche, nor between Eros and Thanatos; I identify and analyze their adjustments in the diversity of "signifying practices" (Margaroni: "Text-cum-practice") with regard to the sociohistorical context. And between Sartre and Artaud, I do not "prefer" either the one or the other (Margaroni); rather, I give myself the epistemological possibility of thinking the *subjectivations* or different psychic structures underlying their specific *sublimations*.

The notion of sublimation, which helps to refine and deepen the *listening* to the "new maladies of the soul," is a cornerstone of my approach to writing as an *intimate and extimate experience*. Margaroni carefully elucidates the interpretations—indeed the misunderstandings—my research has raised; I would simply like to add my lecture at the 65th Congrès des Psychanalystes de Langue Française (2005), titled "L'Impudence d'énoncer: La Langue maternelle."[25] Probing the writings of Colette and Proust, my analysis identifies in them the sublimation of perversion and autism through the resources of style and narration: "the purity of perversion" (Colette) and "the reunion with autism" (Proust).

In an era when transhumanism is presented sometimes as a promise, sometimes as a threat, I reclaim the old humanist project, the one from the Renaissance and the Enlightenment, on the condition that we subject it to a permanent re-foundation. In no way, however, can it be a "perverse humanism," but, rather, a "more complex" one (Margaroni). Does that mean this humanism could be "fate based"?

The expression "destinal humanism," peremptory in French, does not refer to the *Fate* of the Greeks, nor to that of the Christians, but to human finitude, on the one hand, and biological determinism on the other. In both cases, the translation of the adjective "based" runs the risk of insisting too much on mortality or the genetic heritage. I prefer "attentive to destiny," and to inscribe therein the aspiration for freedoms. Founded on emancipation, performance, and *jouissance*, secularized humanism fails to think mortality. The unthinkable of death has no other course but to take refuge in arts and letters: the imaginary circles around the "black sun of melancholy" and challenges the "theory of literature" to illuminate its seduction. As for naturalistic determinism, one finds an echo of it in Freud: "Anatomy is destiny!" he writes, paraphrasing a line attributed to Napoleon. It becomes apparent, in following the psychoanalyst's text, that the "anatomy" he is referring to is that of "birth" (from the maternal uterine, from the excremental sexual). Artaud remembers this. Without transforming the biological givens or erasing the archaic psychosomatic impressions, the "talking cure" recasts subjectivation by opening it up to new links and languages.

Writing participates in these transformations but can make its "*dis*ease contagious" (as Margaroni emphasizes). In fact, contemporary writing is no longer cathartic. It takes pleasure in captivating the reader—its fellow being (*semblable*), its hostage—by eroticizing the delirium, by whitening meaning: "Destroy," Duras writes, and communicates to those who love "the malady of grief."[26] The postmodern reader is free to caress his or her ill-being, knocked about by mediatized literary criticism and awaiting . . . a psychoanalysis? A literary theory?

IV. Miglena Nikolchina

Is it her familiarity with *l'écriture féminine*, or her wager on intertextuality as a "renaissance"?[27] Between Miglena Nikolchina's work and my research, a proximity immediately took hold. "Kristeva is a thinker of change," she writes for this volume, at the moment when I had just finished giving an "opening lecture" at the 51st Congress of the International Psychoanalytical Association in London (2019) on "The Feminine," which I define as . . . a "transformative feminine." In her view, *transformation* proves to be my *element*—from the tense climate of communist Eastern Europe by way of what she calls my different "fusions," with the literary avant-garde, Freudian psychoanalysis, and the "imaginary substance" through transubstantiation-incarnation according to Proust and Colette (and, I would add, Teresa of Avila). I detect this specificity in *language* and in *literature*, the "active force" that "mirrors processes it brings into motion" and "implies a tampering with the real rather than its reflection" (Nikolchina). She asks: "how is language as the material aspect of literature transformed . . . into a mode and instrument of change?"

I can only invite the reader to carefully read the section in her essay titled "Why the Avant-Garde," to grasp both the "ardent and skeptical" interactivity between the social and political and my "investment" in it. This author notes that "after Greek philosophy and German idealism" and the period of the Enlightenment, the contribution of women is still not recognized in the "French 'philosophical moment.'" According to Nikolchina, this moment is founded on the complex heritage that was "European" (even before the European Union existed). Most authors from those times, including me, "knowingly blended . . . artistic 'madness,' its risky destabilizations of meaning and the subject, with a 'philosophical plan.'" With precision, Nikolchina comments on the two sides of this *poetic language* that has become a question to itself: *poiesis* and *narrative*. Poetic language "as a breach in the buffer and a failure of the defenses" carries risks of "pulverization of the subject and meaning." But narrative does not escape these risks either, even though it is tributary to the oedipal phase: "Narrative is good insofar as it is being shattered." This says, differently than Todor Pavlov, that "mimesis" translates the poetic and narrative spasms while *always* projecting the *fantasy* onto a supposed ideal correspondence with "objective reality." "Narrative, dream, and fantasy" constitute a fantastical "new reality" (Nikolchina)—the imaginary, this focus of desire, of utopia, but also of delirium.

Taking up the various models of the "metamorphoses of language" that I point out in Freud's works,[28] Nikolchina recalls Freud's wager on the "talking cure," which aims to modulate unconscious drives, while he removes the verbal construction from his later clinical investigations. However, it is actually in the discourse of the couch, in myths, as well as in arts and letters, that Freud finds the ingredients of his theory. Have I projected my personal experience *with* literature and *with* my analysands onto Freud's work, and could I have thus been led to make of it an innovative reading, according to Nikolchina? Or is it indeed Freud's attention to a "philosophy inherent in artistic production" (Nikolchina) that has filled me to the point that I read into literary texts as into the "free associations" of my patients the process I call *signifiance*? She touches on these questions in studying my "turning points," which lead me, according to her, to the "*shift* from linguistics to psychoanalysis" (my emphasis)—unless we must envisage these two ways of thinking as a form of *cohabitation*? In emphasizing my reinterpretations of *idealization*, empathic *identification* (*Einfühlung*), *sublimation*, as well as *abjection*, Nikolchina observes that my research no longer bears on *language*, but that *signifiance* "grasps language and the drive through the work of the *negative*" (citing *The Sense and Non-sense of Revolt*) "not reduced to language but encompassing it."

Through the "turning point" that proposes "two optics for *signifiance* as the process producing meaning and the subject," the subject of knowledge (the theoretician, man or woman) is not limited to taking thought *upon oneself* as an "effort." He or she probes the effort of knowledge in *psychosomatic and history processes* (*processus historial*). In sum, conceptualization is illuminated as an *experience* in which "the two optics [bottom-up, bottom-down] overlap" (Nikolchina). In doing this, she continues, theoretical elucidation must interrogate literary experience "not simply as a participant in social or political battles" but as a privileged space of *transformation*—"because it turns the word into flesh" as a part of the "mutation of civilization." Having come to this point in her analysis, the author takes up two of my notions. *Transsubstantiation*: a term Proust borrowed from the Catholic mass, which that writer considers as being active in *metaphor*. And the *flesh of words* (designating "the devouring of the signified by the sensed," writes Nikolchina, in Colette and Proust). While the author of *Sodom and Gomorrah* perceives the infantile as a frequently *obscene* secret,[29] Colette never takes the infantile paradise out of its so-called *purity*.[30]

Nikolchina's interpretive process is like Beardsworth's, who demonstrates that the "new model of the individual" that I am proposing is not focused on "the 'truth' of the subject," but constitutes "a grasp of its innovative capacities—capacities for playing a part in a world qualified by the challenges of separateness and otherness."[31] This new model inevitably connects with the "modernist temperament of refusing totalizing" that contemporary writing is and which opens the way for "the imaginary . . . to be recognized and sustained in conditions where dialectical political transgression is unavailable."[32]

Henceforth, we must understand the specificity of the "theory of literature," such as I develop it, as thinking/writing an experience of writing. (I will come back to this in my reply on Melancholy, Love, and the Sacred.)

J.K.

NOTES

1. Julia Kristeva, *Le Texte du roman: Approche sémiologique d'une structure discursive transformationnelle* (Paris: Mouton, 1970).

2. See Aleksandr Solzhenitsyn, *Letter to the Soviet Leaders*, trans. Hilary Sternberg (New York: Harper and Row, in association with Index On Censorship, 1974); and Julia Kristeva, "Alexandre Soljénitsyne: Un Écrivain en lutte avec son siècle," Prison, Écriture, Combat ou La Langue disruptive et la Beauté en Question, Conference on the centenary of Solzhenitsyn's birth, November 21, 2018, Institut de France, Sorbonne, www.kristeva.fr/soljenitsyne.html.

3. Julia Kristeva, *Sémiotikè: Recherches pour une sémanalyse* (Paris: Seuil, 1969); *Intimate Revolt: The Powers and Limits of Psychoanalysis Volume 2*, trans. Jeanine Herman (New York: Columbia University Press, 2002); *La Révolte intime: Pouvoirs et limites de la psychanalyse II* (Paris: Fayard, 1997).

4. Philippe Sollers, "The Novel and the Experience of Limits," in David Hayman, ed., *Writing and the Experience of Limits*, trans. Philip Barnard (New York: Columbia University Press, 1983).

5. Kristeva, *Intimate Revolt*, 218; *La Révolte intime*, 404.

6. Philippe Forest, *Philippe Sollers* (Paris: Seuil, 1992); *De Tel Quel à L'Infini: Nouveaux essais* (Nantes: C. Defaut, 2006); *Étude de l'Étranger: Albert Camus* (Alleur: Marabout, 1995); *Textes et labyrinthes: James Joyce, Franz Kafka, Edwin Muir, Jorge Luis Borges, Michel Butor, Alain Robbe-Grillet* (Paris: InterUniversitaires, 1995); *Joyce était-il fou?* (Paris: M-Éditer, 2014); *Aragon* (Paris: Gallimard, 2015).

7. Philippe Forest, *Une Fatalité de bonheur* (Paris: Grasset, 2016); *Je reste roi de mes chagrins* (Paris: Gallimard, 2019).

8. See Roland Barthes, *Criticism and Truth*, trans. Katrine Pilcher Keuneman (Minneapolis: University of Minnesota Press, 1987); *Critique et Vérité* (Paris: Seuil, 1966).

9. See Bernard Pivot's television program *Apostrophes* on the Antenne 2 channel.

10. See Julia Kristeva, "Penser la pensée littéraire," *Textuel—Où en est la théorie littéraire*, no. 37 (April 2000): 25–39; "Thinking about Literary Thought," *Sign Systems Studies* 30, no. 2 (2002): 405–17.

11. Marian Hobson, *The Object of Art: The Theory of Illusion in Eighteenth-Century France* (Cambridge: Cambridge University Press, 1982); *Diderot and Rousseau: Networks of Enlightenment*, trans. Kate E. Tunstall and Caroline Warman (Oxford: Voltaire Foundation, 2011); Marian Hobson, ed., *Denis Diderot, 'Rameau's Nephew'—'Le Neveu de Rameau': A Multi-Media Bilingual Edition*, trans. Kate E. Tunstall and Caroline Warman (Cambridge: Open Book, 2016).

12. G. W. F. Hegel, *Phenomenology of Spirit*, trans. A. V. Miller (Oxford: Oxford University Press, 1977), 317. See also the section "Might Culture Be French?" in Julia Kristeva, *Strangers to Ourselves*, trans. Leon S. Roudiez (New York: Columbia University Press, 1991), 146–48; *Étrangers à nous-mêmes* (Paris: Fayard, 1988), 218–20. Marian Hobson, "Pantomime, Spasm and Parataxis: *Le Neveu de Rameau*," in *Diderot and Rousseau: Networks of Enlightenment*, 93–113; "Pantomime, spasme et parataxe: *Le Neveu de Rameau*," *Revue de métaphysique et de morale*, no. 2 (April–June 1984), 197–213.

13. Julia Kristeva, *Revolution in Poetic Language*, trans. Margaret Waller (New York: Columbia University Press, 1984), 31–37; *La Révolution du langage poétique* (Paris: Seuil, 1974), 30–37.

14. Ibid., 52–56; *La Révolution du langage poétique*, 50–56. In this regard, I am referring to the "expressivity" inherent in phenomenological hermeneutics, against which my reading of the *text* of the novel is constructed. See my reply to Philippe Forest, above.

15. See Marian Hobson, "Derrida and Frege," *Paragraph* 41, no. 2 (2018): 184–95; "Derrida et Frege," *Rue Descartes* 89–90, no. 2 (2016): 38–47.

16. Julia Kristeva, *Powers of Horror: An Essay on Abjection*, trans. Leon S. Roudiez (New York: Columbia University Press, 1982); *Pouvoirs de l'horreur: essai sur l'abjection* (Paris: Seuil, 1980); *Tales of Love*, trans. Leon S. Roudiez (New York: Columbia University Press, 1987); *Histoires d'amour* (Paris: Denoël, 1983); *Black Sun: Depression and Melancholia*, trans. Leon S. Roudiez (New York: Columbia University Press,1989); *Soleil noir: dépression et mélancolie* (Paris: Gallimard, 1987); *Time and Sense: Proust and the Experience of Literature*, trans. Ross Guberman (New York: Columbia University Press, 1996); *Le Temps sensible: Proust et l'expérience littéraire* (Paris: Gallimard, 1994).

17. See Julia Kristeva, "Towards a Semiology of Paragrams," trans. Roland-François Lack, in *The Tel Quel Reader*, ed. Patrick ffrench and Roland-François Lack (New York:

Routledge, 1998), 25–49; "Pour une sémiologie des paragrammes," *Sémiotikè: Recherches pour une sémanalyse* (Paris: Seuil, 1969), 174–207.

18. Antonin Artaud, *Oeuvres complètes*, 26 vols. (Paris: Gallimard, 1976–1994).

19. Antonin Artaud, "L'Anarchie sociale de l'art," *Oeuvres complètes*, vol. VIII, 233.

20. Antonin Artaud, "Notes pour une 'Lettre aux Balinais,'" *Tel Quel* 46 (1971); 29; English translation of these words by Patrick ffrench in Julia Kristeva, "The Subject in Process," in *The Tel Quel Reader*, 146. Antonin Artaud, "Correspondence of the Mummy," trans. Paul Zweig, *The Random House Book of Twentieth-Century French Poetry*, ed. Paul Auster, bilingual edition (New York: Random House, 1984), 268–69.

21. Antonin Artaud, "Notes pour une 'Lettre aux Balinais,'" 34, quoted in Patrick ffrench in Julia Kristeva, "The Subject in Process," 156 (translation modified); "The Anvil of Strength," in *Collected Works*, vol. 1, trans. Victor Corti (London: John Calder, 1968), 107.

22. Antonin Artaud, "Further Letter About Myself," in *Collected Works*, vol. 1, 186; "Toxic Knuckle Bones," in *Collected Works*, vol. 1, 190.

23. Gilles Deleuze and Felix Guattari, *Anti-Oedipus: Capitalism and Schizophrenia*, trans. Robert Hurley, Mark Seem, and Helen R. Lane (Minneapolis: Penguin, 1983).

24. See Maria Margaroni, review of Mina Karavant and Nina Morgan, eds., *Edward Said and Jacques Derrida: Reconstellating Humanism and the Global Hybrid*, *European Journal of English Studies* 15, no. 1 (April 2011): 91–93.

25. See Julia Kristeva, "L'Impudence d'énoncer: La Langue maternelle," in *La Haine et le pardon: Pouvoirs et limites de la psychanalyse III* (Paris: Fayard, 2005), 393–410; "The Impudence of Uttering: The Mother Tongue," trans. Patricia Viera and Michael Marder, *Psychoanalytic Review* 97, no. 4 (2010): 679–94.

26. Kristeva, *Black Sun*, ch. 8; *Soleil noir*, 227–65.

27. See among others Miglena Nikolchina, "Julia Kristeva: The Polylogic Wager," pt. I, *Tessera* 21 (Winter 1996): 38–53; and "Julia Kristeva: The Polylogic Wager," pt. II, *Tessera* 22 (Summer 1997): 71–93; *Matricide in Language: Writing Theory in Kristeva and Woolf* (New York: Other, 2004).

28. See Julia Kristeva, "The Metamorphoses of 'Language' in the Freudian Discovery," *The Sense and Non-sense of Revolt: The Powers and Limits of Psychoanalysis Volume 1*, trans. Jeanine Herman (New York: Columbia University Press, 2000), ch. 3; *Sens et non-sens de la révolte: Pouvoirs et limites de la psychanalyse I* (Paris: Fayard, 1996), 72–140.

29. See Kristeva, *Time and Sense*, the section on "In Search of Madeleine," 3–22, and the section on "The 'Second Dwelling,'" 235–39; *Le Temps sensible*, 13–36 and 291–94.

30. See Julia Kristeva, *Colette*, trans. Jane Marie Todd (New York: Columbia University Press, 2004), 372; *Le Génie féminin*, t. 3, *Colette, ou la chair du monde* (Paris: Fayard, 2002), 497.

31. Sara Beardsworth, *Julia Kristeva: Psychoanalysis and Modernity* (Albany: SUNY Press, 2004), 267.

32. Ibid., 275, 235.

8

Bernard Brusset

JULIA KRISTEVA: ORIGINAL AND INNOVATIVE CONTRIBUTIONS AT THE CORE OF PSYCHOANALYTIC THEORY

Psychoanalysis is, for Julia Kristeva, the center, the laboratory. It provides the foundation for the numerous and extensive developments of a thought open to the present: culture, politics, religion, artistic creation. But in her very conception of psychoanalysis, the plurality of references is exceptionally rich: from Freud to Melanie Klein, to the criticism of Lacan, and most of all, perhaps, the work of André Green. Within psychoanalysis, her stance and her contributions at the core of contemporary discussions on both theorization and practice constitute fruitful sources for inquiry and reflection. My focus here, from the point of view of psychoanalytic theory only, is on seven fundamental concepts: the association of ideas, the semiotic, the biopsychical, attachment, abjection, reliance, and forgiveness (*pardon*). I consider the questions these concepts pose in relation to adjacent notions in psychoanalysis and in their epistemological implications.

I. The Association of Ideas

The association of ideas, at the root of the psychoanalytic method, evokes a double reference. On the one hand, there is the first topography with the two principles of psychical functioning: pleasure and reality, and the dialectic of the secondary processes and the primary processes.[1] On the other hand, are the second topography, "Negation," the destructiveness of primary rejection, which prefigures the negation of the affirmation of self (*Bejahung*), and the

Translated from French by Armine Kotin Mortimer.

dialectic of the judgment of attribution of the good or bad quality and of the judgment of existence in reality (and not just in fantasy).[2]

The secondary processes, regulated by the reality principle, correspond to ordinary narration. However, during analysis they tend to be dissociated under the influence of the primary processes regulated by the pleasure principle, and we then speak of the association-disassociation of ideas, hence of a clinic of manifestations of the unconscious: slips of the tongue, parapraxis, repetitions, confused zones, pronominal confusions, incidental idea or image, thought expressed in images as in dreams, etc. In the case of splitting, the contribution by the analyst of a "tertiary process" of mediation becomes necessary.[3]

Kristeva writes: "[the] primary processes such as displacement and condensation . . . while often presented as linguistic signs (words or phrases), are not strictly speaking 'signs,' but function as 'indicators' ('index' according to Peirce) of feelings and affects . . . even 'thing-presentations' rather than 'word-presentations' (according to Freud's terminology)."[4] With the second topography, it is no longer a matter of the order of representations, but, rather, of drive impulses (*motions pulsionnelles*) of the "unconscious of the id," finalized in the act and invested with the dualism of the drive: Eros and the death drive. Kristeva adds the "semiotic" to the primary processes of the unconscious and the enigmatic "thing-presentations,"[5] in reference to the Platonic *chora*: "In this way the drives, which are 'energy' charges as well as 'psychical' marks, articulate what we call a *chora*: a nonexpressive totality formed by the drives and their stases in a motility that is as full of movement as it is regulated."[6]

II. The Semiotic

Infra-, pre-, and paralinguistic expressions, in clinical observation and in theory, are opposed to the symbolic, which is identified with judgment and with the sentence. This thesis stands in direct opposition to the Lacanian conception of the unconscious structured like a language, as Kristeva writes: "the semiotic (infralanguage: rhythms, alliteration, breath, vocal gestures, cries, digestive and respiratory spasms, and so on) and sensations, thus tying the unconscious to the biological."[7] A register consisting of pictograms, of nonverbal signifiers, of primary symbolization by affect, according to other authors.[8] At another degree of theoretical abstraction, this means *signifiance* distinguished from and prior to *répresentance*. Regression, notably in the treatment of nonneurotic patients, can actualize these levels of psychic functioning, which are sometimes close to psychosis. Constructions referring to the first development of the child lead to the questioning of the neurobiological sources of psychic life. This results in research on the relationship between, on the one hand, the instances of somatic determinism that stem from neurobiology—in the epistemology of the natural sciences—and, on the other hand, the primitive psychical inscriptions of pleasure and pain. To what extent do the differences in method, linked to different epistemological positions, define different objects of knowledge? Is this dualism irreducible?

III. The "Biopsychical"

Kristeva cites an exchange between Marjory Brierley and Paula Heimann during the great English controversies of 1941 to 1945 between the two schools of Anna Freud and Melanie Klein, notably on the subject of the psychoanalysis of children.[9] Brierley says: "Indeed, if we persist in equating mental functions with our subjective interpretations of them, we forfeit our claim to be scientists and revert to the primitive state of the Chinese peasant who interprets an eclipse as the sun being swallowed by a dragon." Heimann replies: "What *we* are studying is *not* the solar system, but the mind of the Chinese peasant, not the eclipse but the belief of the peasant concerning the eclipse. How do such beliefs arise, what function have they in mind?"[10]

In this imagined Chinese peasant's belief, it may be a matter of the mythic-symbolic in his culture, which is of the order of the implicit, the subconscious, or the individual drive-unconscious. It may be either a collective belief that makes the anomaly explainable or the projection of the fantasy of "the primal scene" of devouring orality such as one can see in a child's drawing or in a dream: one parent devours the other (reduced to a partial object: the mother dragon devours the father sun, or vice versa). This raises the question of the individual and the collective. In psychoanalytic practice, what place should be granted to the cultural, not in the analyst's associations but in what is said to the patient?

But to return to the little parable in the *Controversies*, what is going on in the brain of the Chinese peasant? What is the cerebral infrastructure for a possible emotion? The fact is that although science takes as its object anything that can be objectified, measured, quantified, the cognitive sciences and the neurosciences are led to take into account the emotions and the social connections, as for example on the subject of empathy. Edelman's "Darwinism of neuronal groups" and Ameisen's destructiveness in the service of the "sculpture of the living" bring a stimulating renewal to the relations between different areas of knowledge.[11]

The fundamental epistemological position of psychoanalysis is based on the drive-unconscious, the expressions of which are objectifiable through the psychoanalytic method. This implies various levels of psychical functioning and the drive economy of Eros and of the death drive (as extinction of excitation and as the destructive drive). Of the somatic anchor we know only what the hazards of the demands of psychical work that flows from it let us grasp—namely, corporeal sensations and alterations in psychical functioning during the session, the various affects, and the phenomena of psychical linking and unlinking of affects and representations and of representations amongst themselves.

Certain somatic pathologies, more than others, justify psychosomatic constructions that it might be interesting to connect with the physiology of the brain. In spite of differences in epistemological positions, certain analogies prompt reflection; theoretical models may gain pertinence in spite of differences in the nature of the object of knowledge, for example in the discrimination of the Self and the Non-Self, of the psychic self and the immune self. Thus

Kristeva writes of the *biopsychical* or refers to the "oppositional processes" described by Vincent, but also the "essential depression" and the so-called "operative" thinking in psychosomatic psychoanalytics.[12] The biopsychical is elsewhere categorized as "alexithymia."[13] Like empathy and imitation (the mirror neurons), alexithymia contains within its very name the hope of finding for it a neuronal aetiology that is objectifiable by functional cerebral imagery. Its neuropsychological categorization implies anatomoclinical rationality—the epistemology of the sciences of nature—while the new methods of investigation expand the field of competence of neurobiology and neurochemistry. Furthermore, clinicians are more and more concerned by the increasing utilization of narcotics and psychotropic drugs, by addiction, by clinical cases of "emptiness," and by psychosomatic pathology. The economy of representation and of the psychic apparatus characterizes the "new maladies of the soul," according to Kristeva.[14]

However, the present neurobiological point of view departs from the Freudian biological references: the drive is viewed not as a force but as preformed know-how, emotion as a program of neurobiological action preceding feeling, affect.[15] The originary unconscious is initially procedural—that is to say, constituted by unconscious rules for feeling, acting, and interacting, outside symbolization. One can compare it to "the first mosaic" of uncoordinated, unintegrated sensorimotor functions and of conditioning.[16] This cognitive procedural, which is not reducible to the Freudian representations of things, nor to representations of actions, is automatic, desubjectified, opposed to the desires and beliefs that imply both one's own singular, subjective memory and the instinctual forces of life as they are in play in organizations and disorganizations, both somatic and psychical.

It appears, then, that the knowledge of complex processes or organizations requires the utilization of different logical operations, even incompatible with each other. We are forced to accept the paradoxical effects that result. There remains a question: can we resolve the question of the dualism of the objective and the subjective through the complexity of the operations in the nerve networks without taking into account any of the qualities? Following Buser, must we assume the qualitative transformation, the translation, of a measurable elementary nerve impulse into a nonmeasurable elementary subjective signal "whose physical nature remains unknown at present, but which would be a basic component of a consciously lived perception? We then have imagined the existence of basic 'translating' processors operating at the level of the theoretical neuronal/mental boundary" by successive translations.[17]

Given Kristeva's interest in the elementary forms of the mother-child connection, including its biopsychical dimensions, the notion of attachment deserves discussion. It gives an inaugural relational dimension to self-conservation, to the register of needs, prior to the consolidation of the sexual. It is exemplary of the naturalist and positivist paradigm that, based on animal models of neurobiology, claims to explain the connection and the effects of its loss[18]—a point of view valorized by contemporary culture in its break with the dimension of subjectivity, meaning, and symbolization, and of course with the psychoanalytic conception of psychic reality and the reality of the drive.

IV. Attachment

According to the ethological perspective (Bowlby), the grasping, the cry, the smile are human equivalents of the connection between the young and the adult in the animal.[19] This social connection, biologically determined, is a developmental, progressive, aconflictual model. The factors of its variations can be objectified experimentally: insecurity, disorganization depending on the expression of the mother's face, not her absence but the absence of her reactions expected by the child. Separation anxiety and the effects of the early deficiencies of the mother find a simple theorization here, defining a "figure of attachment" (Bowlby) as a relational dimension of self-conservation. The responses of the environment permit the construction of the primary connection in the specifically human dimensions. On the neurobiological level, attachment as a preprogrammed, innate schema is characterized by a hypothalamo-hypophyseal and adrenal integration before it is cortical (on the posterior parietal, the cerebral site of the "proto-self," according to Damasio).[20] Oxytocin, a neurotransmitter, plays a large part. Attachment explains the relations of tenderness and reactions to loss, making alimentary pleasure and orality as oral sexuality secondary. On the matter of the fate of the schema of attachment, the question has become complex. It becomes interiorized, persisting throughout life and even transmitted from generation to generation. But in what relation to the object, to the economy of the drive, the emotions, the senses, to *signifiances* and passion? The primary connection of mother-child attachment and parents-child attachment, far from excluding the other dimensions of interrelations (such as the effects of epigenesis from before birth) gives a place and support to intersubjectivity and the process of emergence of the sexual according to the Freudian model of consolidation, that is to say, through the originary seduction at the time of the mother's care. It is then a question of what we can call the "instinctualization" (*pulsionnalisation*) of the attachment-connection in the relation to the object—through the mother's care, through the drive investment of the child by the parents.

The phenomenon of regression in the psychoanalytic treatment of adults actualizes, through the transference and as a function of the countertransference of the analyst, modes of psychical and relational functioning that give rise to interpretations and constructions whose pertinence is or is not validated by its effects in the process. However, the model of regression and fixation in the theory of the stages of libidinal development reaches its limit when neuroses are no longer in question. Beyond neurosis, in the limit states, the historic, prehistoric, and phylogenetic regressions, which gave rise to grandiose considerations by Freud and Ferenczi, reached their limit, so that it is first of all a matter of topographical regressions.[21] These regressions can actualize various psychical inscriptions of the memory and outside memory.[22] The question is one of the relations between these different levels: integration, transcription, translation, transposition, and transformation. Also, for Kristeva, with Proust: transubstantiation.[23] But with the concept of abjection, Kristeva strongly accentuates the dimension of the negative in the archaic regime of affects closest to the psychical *signifiance* of the drive. She engages the theory of drive disengagement, of destructiveness (thus of the Freudian death drive), and the theory of its erotization in masochism—but also the theory of somatic infrastructures of the drive in play in human experience.

V. Abjection

In the triple reference to the clinic, to Frances Tustin, and to literature (Céline, Bataille), abjection is a tragic conception of primitive experiences, because of the importance of hatred.[24] Abjection, anterior to the schizoid-paranoid position, "is the only possible narrative of the experience of lack," prior to the constitution of the object:[25] the self-abjection of mystics, and the "abject" as preobject in relation to the early environment. This term *abjection*, borrowed from a paranoid patient, is illuminated by the reference to the clinic. Kristeva writes:

> The paranoid hatred seemed to be a defense against maternal control, making the subject regress to the point of abjection, where the borders between the ego and the other are erased. Against this abjection in which the "I" tries desperately to merge with the maternal feminine, hatred—in the guise of defense—crystallizes two objects (not two subjects) that are dangerous for each other. "'I' am, only if I am dangerous for a dangerous other—a fellow creature," says the paranoiac.[26]

An apotheosis of negative narcissism. In the cure:

> Paranoid hatred has transformed the uncertainty of abjection into a reversible dyad, sadomasochistic communicating vessels, but it does not assure any lasting independence in terms of identity. The armor of the hateful warrior is the temporary hiding place for a nonsubject who—if he finds the path of analysis—asks only to be born.[27]

In another direction, Kristeva relates sublimity, idealization, and creativity to the regressive experience of abjection and masochistic *jouissance*. The subjective experience of horror (and its powers) is an abjection insofar as it implies the imperative need to get out of it. Theoretical models of the genesis of the individual psyche are then summoned, those of the processes of subjectivation correlative to the "objectalization" of the drive.[28] According to Freud, the first self-affirmation (*Bejahung*) is done by *negation* and the model of the purified "pleasure-ego," that is to say, the establishment of the difference between "me" and "outside me."[29] From this point of view, autoeroticisms function to structure narcissism by making possible the liberation from the primary dependence on the mother. This primary narcissism is a first form of the psychical apparatus capable of constructing the space of representations of things (and objects), then of words, and of circuits of projection and introjection in the mother-child bond, from the intersubjective to the intrapsychical. The autoerotic reversal onto the self, in identification with the attitudes of the mother towards the self, is associated with the inversion of the positions of the subject and the object, from activity to passivity. Voyeurism and exhibitionism, sadism and masochism give significant illustrations of this inversion, but it is first of all the inversion of contents, unpleasure-pleasure, and then, within the object relation, of love and hate.

In counterpoint to the narcissistic relation of visual and corporeal contact of the child and the mother, we are obliged to take into account the relational effects of orality such as satisfaction and unsatisfaction of the alimentary need, pleasure and unpleasure in the order of self-conservation (including attachment), and eroticism in the order of the effects of originary seduction, of libidinal subversion. It is then a question of the relations of the mouth and the breast, of partial drives and partial object relations, in the pictograms of fusion-nondifferentiation and those of rejection, abjection. Through the emotional intensity of pleasure and unpleasure (pain, rage, and anger), the founding experiences of masochistic and sadistic drives find entanglement and symbolization in orality, anality, and early genitality.

In the primitive crucible of psychic life and the activity of thinking, the notion of abjection condenses the inverse aspects of the *jouissance* of the lost paradise: pain, melancholy ("the black sun"), mourning, nostalgia, and always eroticism and hatred—sometimes under the guise of idealization. The drive ambivalence in the primary bond with the mother gives rise to the transformations that the mechanisms of splitting and projection, then elaboration of the depressive position, construct, and the two stages of the Oedipus complex that Kristeva distinguishes as "oedipal prime" and "oedipal two."[30] The resulting normal-neurotic organization frees the subject from nondifferentiation with the object (and from the paranoia of escaping from it), and from specular alienation and modes of relation to the other that were initially based on splitting and projection. But what about the mother? On this subject, Kristeva introduces the notion of *reliance* as a theory of specifically maternal eroticism, whose components she analyzes.

VI. Reliance

Kristeva writes:

> By *reliance* I mean *experience* in the double meaning it has in German. Experience (in the sense of *Erlebnis*) brings to life a new preobject: an emergence, a flash, a fulguration. Progressively, in its second phase, experience becomes understanding, patient knowledge (*Erfahrung*). Whether she is prepared or not by a desire for motherhood, every expectant mother is immediately overtaken by biopsychic events like pregnancy, labor, and breast-feeding, so that maternal reliance is not only irreducible to an irrevocably social "symbolic function" like the "paternal function," but it is also a *passion*.[31]

She adds:

> Narcissism and/or object relation, tenderness and depersonalization, even psychic catastrophe, "suffered" and "endured" but not "passive," passion is in the end integrated into the logics of the unconscious—so as to better pierce it. . . . Maternal reliance *naturally contains the void, as well as the collapse of passion.*[32]

From the metapsychological point of view:

> *Reliance* is a specific economy of the drives such that, *countercathected* by psychic representation and thus *fixed* by *inscriptions*, the energy of this *originary split* both maintains and spans primary and secondary repressions. . . . as an "open structure."[33]

In existential sociology this notion of reliance is at once psychological, sociological, and philosophical (if not religious). Kristeva gives it a metapsychological scope insofar as it implies, in the drive economy, the phenomena of binding and unbinding between the unconscious representations in Eros's effects of binding and uniting and in destructiveness. In the Freudian theory of the drive, the notion of binding (*Bindung*) determines the fixations, the taming of free energy into bound energy, of the affect into representation, and of representations among themselves (representations of representations allow the activity of dreaming and thinking). Unbinding is the opposite effect—that of the destructive drive—which undoes links and even the investment (principle of inertia). In excess, and through the failure of drive entanglement and symbolization, the destructive drive produces the dangerous unbindings of psychosis and melancholy. But well-tempered unbinding, followed by rebinding, makes possible symbolization, psychical transformations, and subjectivation. In analysis, the free association of ideas and topographical regression facilitate the emergence of the primary processes of the unconscious, resulting in the unbinding manifested by the temporary disorganization of the secondary processes. Unbinding defeats defenses by rationalization and narrativity deprived of affect; and rebinding through symbolization enriches psychic life and opens new horizons.

With the notion of reliance, Kristeva integrates the metapsychological model of the contradictory play of Eros and the death drive and extends it to the early mother-child relationship. In the process and state of abjection, as in reliance, she takes into account the complexity of different logics in a way that can evoke the "dialogic" according to Morin.[34] For him, the dialogic signifies "the symbiotic unity of two logics, which simultaneously nourish each other, compete against each other, live off each other, oppose and combat each other to the death."[35] He adds to the reliance of sociologists the reliance that links words and ideas. But, closer to the thought of Kristeva, "de-liance" and reliance suppose an originary "liance." Physical and psychical, "liance" would define the lived experience of the fetus and, related to it, that of the mother. Birth would be the first de-liance, giving rise, secondarily, to the narcissistic phantasm of the lost paradise of intrauterine life and also to the primary maternal bond of which, after Freud, Kristeva emphasizes the "incommensurable" force. But "while the [female] lover's libido is dominated by the satisfaction of drives, maternal eroticism deploys (or 'tends toward') its libidinal drives as tenderness: beyond abjection and separation, tenderness is the basic affect of reliance."[36] This maternal passion cannot simply be reduced to tenderness as the effect of the aim inhibition of the drive. Through it, the biological and the psychical, the semiotic communion and the concern for the individuality of the child—the otherness of the subject to come: the child as "other" object—are entangled.[37] As we can see, Kristeva's maternal reliance transcends the too simple notion of symbiosis, by integrating it into the life of the drive, as well as the now widespread notion of empathy. It opposes the usual desexualization of the mother-child relation. These formulations find relevance at various levels, both metapsychologically and in other dimensions. Maternal reliance, empathy, and countertransference: what are the connections?

VII. Reliance and Empathy

Even before being promoted by the neurobiology of a cerebral, cognitive, and emotional unconscious (the mirror neurons), by cognitive psychologies, and by the proponents of intersubjectivity in psychoanalysis, empathy benefited from a sort of immediate self-evidence as a human quality and as a condition of the exercise of the psychoanalytic method, as of all psychotherapy and any relation of assistance. Freud repeatedly used the term *Einfühlung* (feeling, feeling inside), and he refers to Lipps, who has, in aesthetics, described the fact of feeling as "internal mimicry and organic sensations": to bring the life of the other into our reality.[38]

The empathy of the analyst, as an ethic of the relationship of care, as a component of the analyst's professional personality, and as neutrality defined as benevolence, is the condition of possibility of the cure. Kristeva wishes to found maternal reliance on a specific ethic. Different from and contrasting with empathy in the interpersonal relationship, the phenomena of transference and countertransference are identifiable and analyzable in a specific context because they disturb and overdetermine the interrelation as manifestations of the drive-unconscious and correlative resistances. In imaginary identification with the patient, the analyst, attentive to the singularity of the other, can find the right formulations, those that are likely to be heard and used by the patient—a case-by-case adjustment. Through its reflective dimension associated with its affective dimension (in other words, cognitive and emotional—formulations that open up the question of connections with the neuroscientific field), empathy is in the service of the patient's knowledge. For purposes of intelligibility, empathy takes into account the resonance in oneself of the conscious and unconscious affect of the other. Normally associated with the relation of speech, empathy is relative, variable, and subject to ruptures by default (antipathy, indifference)—or by excess (sympathy, passion). Its variations and qualities are obviously in relation to the transference and the countertransference whose manifestations can put it into question, if not to the test, in love and hate. Ideally, the analysis and the elaboration of the countertransference ensure the regulation of empathy in the service of the analysis and reliance. But, according to Kristeva, what place does one give to forgiveness?

VIII. Forgiveness

If the notion of reliance can evoke religion, if only by the etymology of the word (*religio*, *religo*: the link; *religare*: to connect), the notion of forgiveness is first of all religious. But it has a broader anthropological meaning, including that of the guilt of the oedipal murder of the father, which found expression in the myth of the killing of the father in the primitive horde, according to Freud.[39] Forgiveness has many other roles from the point of view of justice, reparation, amnesty, politics. According to Google, propitiation involves "the action of (making) a deity propitious; sacrificial act offered to a god to make him favorable, with a view to obtaining atonement, forgiveness of sins; rite, sacrifice, victim of propitiation."[40] In monotheistic religions, God is Father, and the father has a symbolic function for *signifiance* and *répresentance*, for abstraction and the language that the activity of thought and culture requires . . .

In Catholicism, the sacrament of confession, performed by a priest, realizes the absolution of all sins. The symbolic effectiveness of the sacrament presupposes faith in God and the "redemption" of original sin by Christ, son of God and God incarnate. In Judaism, Yom Kippur, the Day of Atonement of Sins, is the most important holiday: ritual observances, prayers, and mortification.

In Kristeva's study of Dostoyevsky's work, her idea finds its fullest expression with the section "Writing: Immoral Forgiveness":

> It is by making his words suitable to his commiseration and, in that sense, accurate that the subject's adherence to the forgiving ideal is accomplished and effective forgiveness for others as well as for oneself becomes possible. At the boundaries of emotion and action, writing. . . . causes the affect to slip into the effect. . . . It conveys affects and does not repress them, it suggests for them a sublimatory outcome, it transposes them for another in a threefold, imaginary, and symbolic bond. Because it is forgiveness, writing is transformation, transposition, translation.[41]

Can psychoanalysis realize in any other way what is expected and found in the religious practice of the believer and in the universe of signs of the writer?

In the psychoanalytic cure, the alleviation of internal superegoic constraints is a long-recognized effect of the awareness of their infantile origins. Without being indifferent, the analyst does not enter into interactions and does not respond to the attacks and provocations of patients, and sustains the questioning of their defensive or transferential meaning. Kristeva writes:

> Analytical listening . . . neither judges nor calculates, but is content to untangle and reconstruct. Its spiraled temporality is realized in the intersecting times of transference and countertransference. This pardon *renews the unconscious*, because its temporality inscribes the right to narcissistic regression in History and in the Word; thus, only this pardon confronts the other side of desire—hate. It does so without fighting it or submitting to it.[42]

In the cure, "psychoanalytical interpretation" reveals "the multifaceted destiny of hatred that makes and unmakes the human species."[43]

More than forgiveness, is it not first of all a matter of removing guilt? This is the effect, in the transference relation, of the absence of a punitive or reproving answer to the attacks and of the absence of judgment in maintaining the link—whatever happens on the phantasmatic level—in the transference or in the acting out. It seems to me that forgiveness gains meaning in reference to Klein. And Kristeva has facilitated access to the work and the character of Melanie Klein in her fine book, the second volume of the trilogy on female genius.[44] In this respect, during the passage of the paranoid-schizoid position from partial object relations to the depressive position of "whole" objects, the reduction of the splitting confronts the subject with the guilt of hatred and the desire for reparation. By the "par-don," the mother helps the child bear his ambivalent desire towards her without destructiveness.

The depressive dimension, with its melancholic potential, can give rise to manic defenses, projective identification, but normally the Oedipus complex, "oedipal two," redistributes differently the problematic of drive ambivalence and "oedipal prime."[45] The Oedipus complex structures the relations of desire and secondary identifications: the superego, with the ego-ideal, is its (forbidding and protecting) heir, far from the tyranny of the archaic superego. In the context of the elaboration of the depressive position, the interpretation by the analyst that gives meaning and revives the analytic work is pardon and par-don, hence what Kristeva formulates as "the deconstructive elucidation of 'love-hatred.'"[46]

In any case, in the analytic situation and framework, the quality of the analyst's listening—attentive, empathic, understanding before being interpretive—is a gift reparative of the traumatisms and sufferings of the patient, especially through the emergence of a new, more truthful self-perception and the "introjection of the good object" that gives rise to the sense of self and self-worth.[47] The renunciation of symptoms and illusions gives new perspectives to the becoming of the self in the links with others, in cultural life, and in the activity of thinking, creating, and sublimating. Which Kristeva evidences in the full scope of her multifaceted work.

By focusing on some of Kristeva's frequently used concepts, which are rooted in psychoanalytic experience and theory, but which are not limited to it, I run the risk of reducing, simplifying, even caricaturing her thought. Her thought is characterized precisely by openness, by links and articulations between different fields of culture: from linguistics to philosophy, to aesthetics, to ethics, and always with a renewal of perspectives on women's causes and on humanism. We must also add her teaching skills and her novelistic creations and, always, the passion of the activity of thinking in the practice of psychoanalysis, reading, and writing.

BERNARD BRUSSET

UNIVERSITY OF PARIS 5-DESCARTES AND
SOCIÉTÉ PSYCHANALYTIQUE DE PARIS

DECEMBER 2018

NOTES

Translations of quotations from French texts for which there are no English versions are by Armine Kotin Mortimer.

1. Sigmund Freud, "Formulations on the Two Principles of Mental Functioning," in *The Standard Edition of the Complete Psychological Works of Sigmund Freud*, vol. XII, trans. James Strachey (London: Hogarth, 1961), 213–26; "Formulations sur les deux principes de l'advenir psychique," *Oeuvres complètes de Freud, psychanalyse*, t. XI (Paris: PUF, 1998).

2. Sigmund Freud, "Negation," in *The Standard Edition of the Complete Psychological Works of Sigmund Freud*, vol. XIX, trans. James Strachey (London: Hogarth, 1961); "La Négation," *Oeuvres complètes de Freud, psychanalyse*, t. XVII (Paris: PUF, 1992).

3. See André Green, *On Private Madness* (London: Karnac, 1997); *La Folie privée, psychanalyse des cas-limites* (Paris: Gallimard, 1990).

4. Julia Kristeva, "From Symbols to Flesh: The Polymorphous Destiny of Narration," *International Journal of Psychoanalysis* 81, 4 (August 2000): 777. [This publication in English corresponds essentially to the essay "La Narration en psychanalyse, une transsubstantiation," in Julia Kristeva, *La Haine et le pardon: Pouvoirs et limites de la psychanalyse III* (Paris: Fayard, 2005)—Tr.]

5. See Freud, "Formulations on the Two Principles of Mental Functioning."

6. Julia Kristeva, *Revolution in Poetic Language*, trans. Margaret Waller (New York: Columbia University Press, 1984), 25; *La Révolution du langage poétique: L'Avant-garde à la fin du XIXe siècle, Lautréamont et Mallarmé* (Paris: Seuil, 1974), 23.

7. Julia Kristeva, "The Sobbing Girl: Or, On Hysterical Time," in *Hatred and Forgiveness*, trans. Jeanine Herman (New York: Columbia University Press, 2010), 132; *La Haine et le pardon*, 253.

8. See André Green, *The Fabric of Affect in the Psychoanalytic Discourse*, trans. Alan Sheridan (London: Routledge, 1999); *Le Discours vivant* (Paris: PUF, 1973).

9. Julia Kristeva, *Melanie Klein*, trans. Ross Guberman (New York: Columbia University Press, 2001), 175–76 (volume 3 of the "female genius" trilogy); *Le Génie féminin, tome II: Mélanie Klein* (Paris: Fayard, 2000), 283–84. Pearl King and Riccardo Steiner, eds., *The Freud-Klein Controversies 1941–45*, New Library of Psychoanalysis, vol. 11 (London: Routledge, 1991).

10. King and Steiner, *The Freud-Klein Controversies*, 69. [In the French translation of the *Controversies* cited by the author: "*Comment surviennent ces croyances, quelles fonctions ont-elles pour le psychisme?*"—Ed.]

11. Gerald M. Edelman, *The Remembered Present: A Biological Theory of Consciousness* (New York: Basic Books, 1990). Jean-Claude Ameisen, *La Sculpture du vivant: Le Suicide cellulaire ou la mort créatrice* (Paris: Seuil, 1999).

12. Julia Kristeva, "The Passion According to Motherhood," in *Hatred and Forgiveness*, 80–81; *La Haine et le pardon*, 176–78. Jean Didier Vincent and Luc Ferry, *Qu'est ce que l'homme?* (Paris: Odile Jacob, 1998). Pierre Marty, *La Psychosomatique de l'adulte* (Paris: PUF, 1990).

13. Peter E. Sifneos, "The Prevalence of 'Alexithymic' Characteristics in Psychosomatic Patients," *Psychotherapy and Psychosomatics* 22 (1973): 255–62.

14. Julia Kristeva, *New Maladies of the Soul*, trans. Ross Guberman (New York: Columbia University Press, 1995); *Les Nouvelles Maladies de l'âme* (Paris: Fayard, 1993).

15. Antonio R. Damasio, *The Strange Order of Things: Life, Feeling, and the Making of Cultures* (New York: Pantheon, 2018).

16. Marty, *La Psychosomatique de l'adulte.*

17. Pierre Buser, *Neurophilosophie de l'esprit (ces neurones qui voudraient expliquer le mental)* (Paris: Odile Jacob, 2013), 192.

18. John Bowlby, *The Making and Breaking of Affectional Bonds* (London: Tavistock, 1979).

19. Ibid.

20. Damasio, *The Strange Order of Things*.

21. Sándor Ferenczi, *Thalassa: A Theory of Genitality*, trans. Henry Alden Bunker (New York: Routledge, 2018).

22. Letter to Fliess (6 December 1896) in Jeffrey Moussaieff Masson, ed., *The Complete Letters of Sigmund Freud to Wilhelm Fliess, 1887–1904* (Cambridge: Belknap, 1985), 207; *Lettres à Wilhelm Fliess 1887–1904* (Paris: PUF, 2006), 263.

23. Kristeva, "From Symbol to Flesh," 777–78; *La Haine et le pardon*, 299–300.

24. Frances Tustin, *Autistic Barriers in Neurotic Patients* (New Haven: Yale University Press, 1986). Julia Kristeva, *Powers of Horror: An Essay on Abjection*, trans. Leon S. Roudiez (New York: Columbia University Press, 1982); *Pouvoirs de l'horreur: Essai sur l'abjection* (Paris: Seuil, 1980).

25. Kristeva, "Hatred and Forgiveness; or, From Abjection to Paranoia," in *Hatred and Forgiveness*, 186; *La Haine et le pardon*, 361.

26. Ibid., 190; *La Haine et le pardon*, 367–68.

27. Ibid., 191; *La Haine et le pardon*, 368.

28. André Green, *The Work of the Negative*, trans. Andrew Weller (New York: Free Association Books, 1999); *Le Travail du négatif* (Paris: Minuit, 1993).

29. Freud, "Negation," 237.

30. Kristeva, "Fatigue in the Feminine," in *Hatred and Forgiveness*, 116–20; *La Haine et le pardon*, 230–36.

31. Julia Kristeva, "Maternal Erotism," in *Passions of Our Time*, trans. Constance Borde and Sheila Malovany-Chevallier (New York: Columbia University Press, 2018), 103; *Pulsions du temps* (Paris: Fayard, 2013), 201.

32. Ibid., 103–4; *Pulsions du temps*, 201.

33. Ibid., 103; *Pulsions du temps*, 200.

34. Edgar Morin, *The Nature of Nature*, trans. J. L. Roland Bélanger (New York: Peter Lang, 1992); *La Méthode I: La Nature de la nature* (Paris: Seuil, 1977).

35. Ibid., 77; *La Méthode I*, 80.

36. Kristeva, "Maternal Eroticism," 106; *Pulsions du temps*, 205.

37. Kristeva, "The Passion According to Motherhood," 88–89; *La Haine et le pardon*, 189.

38. Thomas Lipps, *Komik und Humor, eine psychologisch-ästhetische Untersuchung* (Hamburg: L. Voss, 1898).

39. Sigmund Freud, *Totem and Taboo*, in *The Standard Edition of the Complete Psychological Works of Sigmund Freud*, vol. XIII, trans. James Strachey (London: Hogarth, 1955).

40. See http://www.cnrtl.fr/definition/propitiation ("*Action de (se) rendre une divinité propice; acte sacrificiel offert a un dieu pour le rendre favorable, en vue d'obtenir l'expiation, le pardon des péchés. Rite, sacrifice, victime de propitiation.*)

41. Julia Kristeva, *Black Sun: Depression and Melancholia*, trans. Leon S. Roudiez (New York: Columbia University Press, 1989), 217; *Soleil noir: Dépression et mélancolie* (Paris: Gallimard, 1987), 226.

42. Kristeva, "Hatred and Forgiveness," 194; *La Haine et le pardon*, 372

43. Ibid. (translation amended); *La Haine et le pardon*, 373.

44. Kristeva, *Melanie Klein*.

45. Kristeva, "The Two-Sided Oedipal," in *Hatred and Forgiveness*, 116–21; *La Haine et le pardon*, 230–36.

46. Kristeva, "Hatred and Forgiveness," 194; *La Haine et le pardon*, 373.

47. Kristeva, *Melanie Klein*, 66–67; *Melanie Klein* 107–9. Melanie Klein, *Envy and Gratitude and Other Works, 1946–63*, ed. Masud R. Khan (London: Hogarth, 1975), 9.

9

Jean-Louis Baldacci

ABJECTION, RELIANCE, AND SUBLIMATION

I. Necessary Crossings

In 2016 Kristeva publishes her memoirs in the form of interviews, with the title *Je me voyage*.[1] The reflexive form of the verb summons strangeness. What is the "*me*" trying to say in front of a nonpronominal verb? Who is actually traveling, "I" or "myself"? This doubling provokes the doubling of the psychoanalyst/reader who ventures commentary. To whom do I address myself? Of whom do I speak? Which one do I write about? Julia or Julia Kristeva? Julia, the French psychoanalyst, the colleague esteemed for the value of her original and innovative psychoanalytic research? Or Julia Kristeva, the foreign-born intellectual with an international reputation, renowned for the entirety of her work and crowned by the Holberg Prize? The fact is, for a psychoanalyst, the alternative is illusory, and psychoanalysis easily carries the day. However, the questioning raised by the title of her memoirs alludes to a problematic that is present in all her writing, whether psychoanalytic or not: the concern to get beyond splits, to link and to articulate, in order to show that singularity and universality are not incompatible, that crossing them is possible. Could it be that this intent was already indicated by the name "Kristeva," the origin of which, "Kristev," "of the cross" (as her father used to remind her), would make of the crossing of diversities the condition of the emergence of singularity as a universal value?

But to cross, to articulate, to link in order to get beyond splits requires finding practicable bridges and passages. For her, the first among them appears with the confrontation with the universality of language and the singularity of speaking. This passage is the first form of the voyage between the "*je*" of

Translated from French by Armine Kotin Mortimer.

the addressed narrative and the "*me*" of the intimate experience born in the commerce with the object—between the "I" and the "myself." It allows the person who takes this passage to open up the possibility of internal speech, to speak to oneself, to appropriate for oneself one's singularity, one's identity, and no longer to be a clandestine passenger who must hide his body. It is this passage between language and speaking, between speaking and language, that Kristeva chose to explore from the beginning. And in this traveling, the language sciences and psychoanalysis allowed her to forge her principal tools, if not weapons.

Without retracing the richness of the itinerary that led her from Bakhtin to Benveniste by way of Barthes, it is remarkable to observe after the fact that the notions and concepts she elaborated in the field of language sciences prepared, in a way, her encounter with psychoanalysis. If we consider, for example, the notion of *intertextuality* as a transforming appropriation produced by the correlation of diverse texts, the similarity with the subjective appropriation of diverse modes of speech—conscious and unconscious—specific to the analytic process is obvious. Likewise, the "semiotic" in its differentiation from the semantic, as something that precedes meaning, reveals her project to specify the modalities of the encounter of language and the body. It announces the importance she will grant to the Freudian concept of the drive.

But thinking of the drive, with Freud, as a "mythology" did not suit her. Did she sense that the drive without language could be the Achilles' heel of psychoanalysis? She then tries to elucidate the conditions of a pact between the body and language, a pact that would give language its psychosomatic dimension, simultaneously interactive, affective, and sensorial, the pact that would make the psychical the means of an agreement between the biological and the cultural. This research takes place in stages. Psychoanalysis plays a decisive role in it.

II. Her Personal Experience of the Cure

First there is her personal experience of the cure. Her complaint about feeling like a rubber ball that never stops bouncing around without ever managing to settle down gathers a first intervention from the analyst consulted: "You're here to say it!" she hears.

"Here to say it": each word counts, words that seal the pact and the analytic contract. "Here," in this framework; "to" like a prescription imposed by the fundamental rule of analysis; finally, not "say" but "say it," which implies, as in "I travel myself," the doubling of the internal dialogue. Thus, from the beginning of the encounter with the psychoanalyst, she lives a first experience of the transference, which allows her to cross its topographical, dynamic, and economic aspects: "here" with me, the space of the transference; "to," the transference speech, that is, the interior voyage among psychic spaces as a condition of thought; finally "it," the transference onto the word as a means of interior transactions, as exchange currency among the psychic spaces traveled. This first intervention is thus truly a transference interpretation if not an interpretation of the transference that founds the psychoanalytic situation. The psychoanalyst chosen, Ilse Barande, a woman, a foreigner, having fully adopted, like her, the French language and culture, thus becomes her psychoanalyst. With Barande, intertextuality and the semiotic are called upon to be lived from the inside, to authorize the crossing of discourses, of languages and their music, to disengage (without being perpetually in motion) from the influence of a mother who inhabited silence, and to fully recover the taste for debate transmitted by her father.

Starting from this foundational experience of the psychoanalytic cure, Kristeva is able to explore the different facets of psychoanalysis—the theory, the practice, and the transmission—while preserving the originality of her approach as a linguist and semiologist. But from Freud to Lacan, from the theory of the drives to the theory of the signifier, she keeps her focus on the semiotic and its questioning on the conditions of symbolization. Certain post-Freudian authors in particular sustain her in her research: Klein with the attack of the mother's body and symbolization, Winnicott and primitive cruelty, Lou Andreas-Salomé and her conception of the maternal, and Green with the heterogeneity of the drive—both energy and meaning—and the work of the negative.[2]

III. Theoretical Elaboration: Abjection and Reliance

These influences allow her to elaborate two crucial notions that will bring her (and us) very close to the psychosomatic dimension of language. These are *abjection* and *reliance*.[3]

Céline the writer, the dream of a patient struggling with the maternal, and her psychoanalytic work prompt her with the word "abjection." This is a process of attachment/rejection, of fascination/repulsion, that concerns destruction as an exit from the death-dealing paradox of the encounter, which is engendered by the ineluctable separation of mother/baby. Abjection is a shared phenomenon that is not projection, for there is neither subject nor object yet. The matricide/infanticide pair is only a phenomenological or after-the-fact representation of it because the phenomenon is situated this side of representation. Certain artistic creations can give us an idea of it: thus, the poem "A Carcass" by Baudelaire or, in painting, the series of female witches by de Kooning and the figures broken in the cubist manner by Picasso. To reject and/or absorb with violence and in all cases destroy.

But Eros, borne by the maternal Eros, finds another issue besides the mutual destruction of opposing bodies. It allows going beyond the aporia of abjection by proposing a third path, *reliance*: neither fascination nor repulsion, neither attachment nor attack, but the preservation of their dynamic split. Reliance is therefore both hiatus and juncture, separation and link. Not exclusively the one or the other, it results from the work of the negative. Tenderness is its elementary affect, speaking its vector. The enigmatic smile of the *Mona Lisa*, a subtle mixture of reserve and seduction according to Freud, could represent it.[4] Reliance thus transforms fascination/attachment into affects of love and hatred, and repulsion/attack into signifying appeal. Fascination becomes passion and repulsion becomes vocation. By crossing affect and language, thanks to speaking, reliance makes possible the drive transformations necessary for the psychosomatic construction of thought.

These notions of abjection and reliance, which enrich the metapsychology of the formation of the ego, have turned out to be very useful in the contemporary psychoanalytic clinic. Prolonging the work of Deutsch, Winnicott, Marty, Kernberg, and Green,[5] Kristeva is interested in what she calls "the new maladies of the soul," which intersect in particular with the field of borderline states, false personalities, and psychosomatic patients. Characterized by traumatic fixations that have resulted in disturbances of separation and symbolization, as well as a wounded narcissism, these pathologies are badly adapted to the classical analytic situation. Actions, from the action of speaking to the transgression of the frame, play an important part adapted to the difficulty in representing, and most often impose accommodations. Abjection and reliance make us understand their necessity, as well as the need for the psychoanalyst's research, in order to restore to the analytic situation its transformational potentialities.

IV. Psychoanalytic Practice: Didier

In this respect, the fragment of the analysis of Didier is exemplary. A patient, an amateur painter, came to analysis for "difficulties of a relational order." In the sessions, he padlocks his speech and avoids the surprise of the incidental idea by means of a combination mixing isolation and perversion. Didier's perverse mastery of his discourse puts the countertransference of the analyst to a severe test. Kristeva holds her own and maintains the analytic situation. She succeeds in opening up the hallucinatory pathway of dreams. But the oneiric representation now figures destructiveness and abjection, which target the patient/analyst couple. Thus the dream figuration veers into nightmare and threatens to reveal with it the identity faults that make cracks in narcissism, leading to a possible collapse. To avoid it, Didier exits his dream, awakens, and recounts it during the session: "*he is leaning out of the window of the family home, someone pushes him, he tumbles into the void. But, he says, instead of smashing his face in, panicking, or crying out, he suddenly notices there is no void. He finds himself in front of a mirror that reflects, not his face, but . . . his sister's. Then he really does cry out, and he awakens.*"[6] In spite of the poverty of the associations that follow the dream, the analyst asks: Was his sister taking his place? Could it be she who pushes him into the void, or is it he who shoves her so she will "smash her face in"? Guided probably by the cry in the dream, which signals the danger of the hallucinatory figuration, and to give it the value of an appeal, Kristeva adds: "Your voice becomes animated when you talk to me about your paintings." These interventions show that the analyst has heard not only the speaking—the "smash his face in" that falls into the formulaic field of the transference—but also the affect borne by the cry. She proposes to weave them together, to link them, and to repair, thanks to the framed acting and the objective perception, what the hallucination of the dream cannot yet do. The patient then brings his paintings to the sessions—photos and collages that, until then, only his deceased mother had been able to see: bodies cut up and dirtied with splashes of paint, broken faces, cruelty of a carnage contrasting with the politeness of the discourse.

The reliance work that follows mobilizes the plural registers of *signifiance*—words, affects, and concrete representations. It is done, therefore, by means of an adjustment of the framework. It allows quitting the field of destructivity and attaining the field of perverse infantile sexuality: it sexualizes thought. Particularly solicited are the couples sadism/masochism and voyeurism/exhibitionism, and, for them to remain compatible with the analytic situation, they again impose on the analyst an elaboration of the countertransference. This leads to a new interpretation that returns to the figuration of the dream: *You are making me participate in your massacres. Maybe you need to smash a woman's face in to take your pleasure of her, but you and I must be glued together so you will not fall into the void?*

This interpretation allows for detachment in favor of a reversal of the drive and the investment of autoeroticisms. In fact the patient stays away, and upon his return abandons the exhibition of his collages and turns to associating in the sessions. The sequence ends on an associative evocation concerning his spouse born and raised abroad: he has never been able to keep himself from "smashing her face in." Whereupon Kristeva responds: "Smash a foreign woman's face in."[7] The patient, moved, is at last able to understand the interpretation of the transference.

What is remarkable about this analytic work is the observation that an "anti-analysis" patient can succeed in benefitting from the analysis on the condition of opening the interpretive process with an initial period of reliance, which implies the multiple aspects of *signifiance*. This period allows the other two periods of the interpretation—that of the autoerotic reversal and that of the actual interpretation of the transference—to deploy their symbolizing effects. It is also remarkable to be able to follow this trajectory through a single verbal expression, "smash in a face," which bridges these three periods: reliance, reversal, and symbolizing negation.[8]

V. Reliance and Sublimation

But these notions of abjection and reliance pose multiple questions. The first concerns their relation to sublimation. Reliance permits the transformation of the pair satisfaction/destruction into a sexualization of thought as a condition of putting into place an unconscious governed by the pleasure principle and the functionality of hallucinatory satisfaction. As an initial protective weave between body and language—which will afterwards be called originary repression—reliance founds the bases of the psychical by controlling the destructive chaos of abjection linked to the experience of distress. It is a matter of renouncing, through it, an immediate and brutal satisfaction of the drive for the benefit of a detour linking affect, motor ability, and language in psychical pleasure. Thus reliance, which utilizes the encounter of bodies and language to transmit to the future subject the conditions of access to the symbolic, seems highly implicated in the sublimatory process.

Following this thread, from the moment of the mother/baby encounter, reliance would correspond to the transmission, based on sufficient satisfaction, of an aptitude for sublimation. Is this not what Freud suggested in "Leonardo da Vinci and a Memory of His Childhood" with the notion of a sublimation present "from the very beginning"?[9] Moreover, it is possible to see the premise of this hypothesis in the *Three Essays on the Theory of Sexuality* and in *Jokes and Their Relation to the Unconscious*. In the first, Freud proposes that the maternal reserve and renunciation in her relation to the baby are transformed into a gift of feeling.[10] And in the second, he shows how the author of the joke cannot reap the pleasure linked to his elaboration on account of critical reason and internal obstacles.[11] In this way, he saves the preliminary pleasure he has engaged, and this saving augments by as much the pleasure experienced by ricochet when the listener laughs. In relating this model to reliance, can we not think that the reserve and renunciation linked to the elaboration of abjection call forth a savings that is transformed into a gift of feeling, the condition of the pleasurable appropriation of *signifiance*?

In this perspective, a successful reliance would correspond to putting a virtuous cycle of sublimation in place between the mother and the baby as a condition of the subjective appropriation of *signifiance*. Each of the terms of the couple would elaborate its impulsionality by learning the language of the other.

A text by Kristeva, a beautiful and profound one, may perhaps illustrate this sublimatory dimension of reliance. In "La Linguistique, l'universel, et le 'pauvre linguiste,'" she explores the enigma she confronted when Benveniste, who had lost the ability to speak, traced the word THEO on her blouse.[12] Much later and after a veritable investigation, she became convinced that this THEO represented universal *signifiance*, which is actualized in the encounter between two bodies that speak: the encounter of the symbolic thanks to the body and speaking. "The infinite and the corporeal then act in common," she writes, and this acting opens onto the other.[13] In other words, the question is to know if maternal reliance is the condition of this "beginning sublimation" that, in the child, seals the "acting in common" of the body and language.

VI. Transmission and Reliance

This raises a new question, then. Under what conditions does maternal reliance allow access to the cycle of sublimation capable of transforming abjection? A love life and various investments in sublimation would allow the mother to avoid considering the child as a substitute or an obstacle and would make reliance possible. But what about the analyst in borderline situations, when reliance has formerly been defective and the always current destructiveness mobilized by abjection exceeds the hatred commonly experienced in the countertransference? How to succeed, in spite of this destructive force, in elaborating the movements of disinvestment or seductive control that then occur? In her memoirs, Kristeva attributes a determining role to writing. If we follow her, writing would have the power to transform the countertransference, in separating from the heard and the spoken through the introduction of the seen and the objective. Writing would thus detach from the object and make a third present, a potential reader, another analyst, or more generally an other of the object. This could mean that when the analysis becomes transgressive—as in the case of Didier—the thirdness search opened up by writing can bring back a sufficient orthodoxy. In this perspective, writing in psychoanalysis, as a speaking transferred from hearing to seeing, would allow the countertransference to find its way back to the transference. From the start, writing is addressed to another analyst, and for this reason it allows returning to the transference of any analyst onto psychoanalysis. Would that make the transference of the analyst onto psychoanalysis, the analyst's desire, the condition of reliance? And inversely, would reliance be the condition of the transference of the patient?

The transmitted ideal would then be the condition of reliance? What does it correspond to?

Beginning with the notions of abjection and reliance, following Kristeva has led us to the transference and the countertransference by way of sublimation. The elaboration of the countertransference in the analytic situation has led us to discover in writing the triple function of the ideal: to confirm the possibility of the encounter of the body and language; to seal the irreducibility of their separation; finally, to seek the mobile conditions of reliance. This triple function tallies with the three stakes of therapeutic, political, and ethical psychoanalysis, which converge to preserve the psychic space, the dynamics of the transference, and more generally the work of culture.

Kristeva teaches us how much the transmission of the ideal, which addresses the relations of the individual superego and the cultural superego, commits psychoanalysis to seeking the passages,[14] the bridges, and the dialogues among disciplines—for example, with the neurosciences or the sciences of language—to avoid sectarian radicalism at all costs. And this engagement goes far beyond psychoanalysis.

Jean-Louis Baldacci

Training Analyst, Société Psychanalytique de Paris
March 2019

NOTES

1. See part I of this volume; Julia Kristeva, *Je me voyage: Mémoires entretiens avec Samuel Dock* (Paris: Fayard, 2016).

2. Julia Kristeva, *Melanie Klein*, trans. Ross Guberman (New York: Columbia University Press, 2001) (volume 2 of the "female genius" trilogy); *Le Génie féminin*, t. II: *Mélanie Klein* (Paris: Fayard, 2001). D. W. Winnicott, "Primitive Emotional Development," in *Through Paediatrics to Psychoanalysis: Collected Papers* (New York: Routledge, 2018). Lou Andreas-Salomé, *The Freud Journal of Lou Andreas-Salomé*, trans. Stanley A. Leavy (New York: Basic Books, 1964); *Journal d'une année*, trans. Lily Jumel, in *Correspondance avec Freud* (Paris: Gallimard, 1970), 418. André Green, *The Work of the Negative*, trans. Andrew Weller (New York: Free Association Books, 1999); *Le Travail du négatif* (Paris: Minuit, 1993).

3. See, for example, Julia Kristeva, "Maternal Eroticism," in *Passions of our Time*, trans. Constance Borde and Sheila Malovany-Chevallier (New York: Columbia University Press, 2018); "L'Érotisme maternel," in *Pulsions du temps* (Paris: Fayard, 2013).

4. Sigmund Freud, "Leonardo da Vinci and a Memory of His Childhood," in *The Standard Edition of the Complete Psychological Works of Sigmund Freud*, vol. XI, trans. James Strachey (London: Hogarth, 1957), 108; "Un Souvenir d'enfance de Léonard de Vinci," trans. Jean Laplanche et al., *Sigmund Freud: Oeuvres completes*, t. X (Paris: PUF, 1993), 135.

5. Helene Deutsch, *Les "Comme si" et autres textes* (Paris: Seuil, 2007). D. W. Winnicott, "Ego Distortion in Terms of True and False Self," in *The Maturational Processes and the Facilitating Environment* (New York: International Universities Press, 1965). Pierre Marty, *L'Ordre psychosomatique* (Paris: Payot, 1980). Otto Kernberg, *Borderline Conditions and Pathological Narcissism* (New York: Aronson, 1975). André Green, *Life Narcissism, Death Narcissism*, trans. Andrew Weller (London: Free Association Books, 2001).

6. The words Didier speaks and Kristeva's interventions are taken from an unpublished lecture she gave at the Société Psychanalytique de Paris on February 13, 2016. The story of Didier's analysis is also found in Julia Kristeva, *New Maladies of the Soul*, trans. Ross Guberman (New York: Columbia University Press, 1995), 10–26, 42–43; *Les Nouvelles Maladies de l'âme* (Paris: Fayard, 1993), 20–47, 69–70.

7. Ibid., 20.

8. The last period of interpretation in fact permits living the experience that speaking is not necessarily doing: that the analyst is and isn't the person one is addressing.

9. Freud, "Leonardo da Vinci," 80; "Un Souvenir d'enfance," 105.

10. Sigmund Freud, *Three Essays on the Theory of Sexuality*, in *Standard Edition of the Complete Psychological Works of Sigmund Freud*, vol. VII, trans. James Strachey (London: Hogarth, 1953); *Trois essais sur la théorie sexuelle* (Paris: Gallimard Folio, 1999), 166–67.

11. Sigmund Freud, *Jokes and Their Relation to the Unconscious*, in *Standard Edition of the Complete Psychological Works of Sigmund Freud*, vol. VIII, trans. James Strachey (London: Hogarth, 1960), 136–37, 143–44; *Le Mot d'esprit et sa relation à l'inconscient* (Paris: Gallimard Folio, 1988), 253, 263.

12. Julia Kristeva, "La Linguistique, l'universel, et le 'pauvre linguiste,'" in Irène Fenoglio, ed., *Autour d'Émile Benveniste: Sur l'écriture* (Paris: Seuil, 2016).

13. Ibid., 128 (translated by Armine Kotin Mortimer).

14. See Julia Kristeva, "Sur les pas du passeur," preface to Stéphane Mosès, *Rêves de Freud: Six lectures* (Paris: Gallimard, 2011), 9–34.

10

Jean-François Rabain

JULIA KRISTEVA, READER OF ARAGON

Was wir suchen ist alles.
What we search for is everything.
—Hölderlin

To read the works of poets and writers with Kristeva is always to make discoveries. *Revolution in Poetic Language* and *Polylogue* made us discover the unsayable in Lautréamont and Mallarmé. *Time and Sense*, her book on Proust, brought us the taste of metaphor's flesh, the sensation beneath the sign. The trilogy on female genius let us reread Arendt, Colette, and Klein with her. *The Sense and Non-sense of Revolt* made us discover the meaning of the literary *experience* and feel how indispensable literature is to us. Kristeva showed us that, well beyond its formal aspect and its foundation in social and economic life, literature was primarily an *experience*, which is to say, the discovery of the appearance in language of a hitherto unnamed, a rootedness in lived experience, in the passionate and the archaic. In this way, literature as *the experience of psychic life* intersects with the experience of psychoanalysis.

Sometimes one doesn't know what one admires the most: the rigor of an unstinting thought highly skilled at all kinds of reasoning, with its searing intensity and its multiple facets; a thought open to numerous epistemological fields; the extent of her culture; or the constancy of her engagements with the polemics of her time. Numerous readers and students have discovered with her the great texts of literature thanks to an innovative approach introducing little-known concepts like *dialogism* and *intertextuality*. Every text dialogues with other texts, and one cannot understand a work on its own if one does not make the *intertext* resonate in that work, which is to say, the other texts to which the writer refers, whether explicitly or implicitly or unconsciously, texts that resonate without the writer having explicitly called upon them, she

Translated from French by Armine Kotin Mortimer.

writes.[1] Thus we do not comprehend a text simply within its own closure, we open it to the history of texts, that is, both to history and to subjectivity. Kristeva initiated us into the Russian formalist approach, Bakhtin's *dialogism*, the Carnival body on which the body of the novel is based, into the toppling of hierarchies and values, into the embedding of consciousness, all sorts of limit states that will be taken up again and explored through the polyphony of the novel. To this paradoxical logic she will add the essential contribution of *psychoanalysis*, which carried this reading forward, for her, with even more rigor. The detour through psychoanalysis, "which confronts the nightfall of meaning," then appeared indispensable to her.[2]

Investigating hermetic literary texts of the late nineteenth-century avant-garde, notably the reputedly incomprehensible authors Mallarmé and Lautréamont ("*Aboli bibelot d'inanité sonore*"; "Abolished bauble of sonorous uselessness"),[3] Kristeva proposed a certain number of tools to think these transformations of language, wishing to go beyond the fascination one feels in the confrontation with these limit states of the imaginary. The quite revolutionary upheaval these authors brought is not limited to form or style but touches on the foundations of subjectivity, prelanguage, rhythms, an entire dynamics of meaning that is not limited to words. This "music in letters," as Mallarmé put it, destabilizes the meaning of language and renews it by rooting it in the unconscious and the body. Kristeva contrasts this *semiotic* modality of language to the *symbolic* of coded language in the denotative exchange, which is the bearer of simple, univocal meaning. In counterpoint to denotative language, which Kristeva calls the *symbolic*, poetic language deploys infinite potentiality, where signification is given through rhyme, where colors and sounds correspond as in our unconscious or in the infantile archaism of language. It is this secret continent of language that Kristeva calls *semiotic*. The Greek term *semeion* means *sign*, but it also means *trace*, distinctive sign, but not symbol. In reprising it, Kristeva draws attention to a more elementary functioning of meaning than the symbol (*sum-bolein = join together; dia-bolein = disunite*). Referring to the *chora* from Plato's *Timaeus*, Kristeva seeks to describe a modality of archaic meaning comparable to a receptacle, a womb. Attributing maternal connotations to it, describing it as a nourishing receptacle, Plato considers this archaic receptacle of meaning anterior to the name. This notion of the semiotic *chora* thus alludes to a translinguistic modality of meaning linked more to maternity, to the infancy of language, which one sees fully realized in the poetic experience of language, writes Kristeva.[4] Mother tongue, then, language of the very earliest childhood, genius of prosody, of echolalia, rhythms, intonations, alliterations—all music the child possesses before words. These elements have a *meaning* (a direction), without for all that having a strict, univocal *signification*, and this meaning is rooted in the primary relations between the mother and the child. Kristeva calls this modality of signification (of *signifiance*) a *semiotics* conceived as the musical level of poetry. "Music first and foremost!" wrote Verlaine.[5]

Kristeva pertinently refers this discovery of literary experience to the experience of psychoanalysis: "Proust, who never underwent psychoanalysis, describes a psychical movement in which I recognize perfectly well what I experienced myself in analysis: you have the feeling of being surrounded by your soul, as by a sonority that is not only a sonority from the outside, but the echo of an internal vibration."[6] This idea of a dislocation of meaning, referring to a potentiality of language as an infinite and not conscious process of engendering of meaning, has predecessors. One finds it in Saussure with his *Anagrams*. The basis of sacred poetry was the hidden name of a god to whom the poem was addressed. This name was disseminated throughout the text, as if the letters of the word or its syllables had to be dispersed in the poem. The *Anagrams* propose a sort of Cabbalistic reading of poetry that tries to return the polyphony of the text to a sacred name. Kristeva starts from this idea, but thinks it is not necessary to reduce this dissemination to just one name. The polyphony of the poetic text is generalized, each word can be dislocated and connoted differently. This dislocation of meaning leading to new engenderings recalls many other authors. "Words make love," Breton wrote. We can also cite Giordano Bruno, who had his character based on John Florio, presumed author of Shakespeare's plays, say: "Who knows if true happiness and true beatitude do not consist of the due linking and taking apart of the parts of a phrase?"[7] To this remark one can add a famous formulation by Hans Bellmer, who conceives of the body as an anagram: "the body is comparable to a sentence that invites you to disarticulate it, for the purpose of recombining its actual contents through a series of endless anagrams."[8] This approach to the body, to the anagrammatic body, to sexuality, and to language allowed Kristeva, professor in the Department of Letters and Human Sciences at the University of Paris-Diderot, to surprise her students by reading to them, in March 1995, Aragon's most eruptive pages, *Irene's Cunt*. Adding, that day, to the scientific study of the Mallarméan text, its semiotic disposition, its syntax and its composition, the infinite embeddings of *A Throw of the Dice*, came the most exalted pages of a pornographic Aragon. "So small and so large! It is here that you are at ease, man finally worthy of your name . . . Don't be afraid of moving your face close to this place. . . . O cleft, moist and soft cleft, dear dizzying abyss."[9] The writer never admitted being the author of this erotic or pornographic text. Was he already too far removed from the surrealist movement, or was his position at the heart of the French Communist Party too constraining to claim its paternity? We know how demanding the establishment can be, and Benveniste's remarks asking Kristeva no longer to mention his surrealist past in front of his colleagues at the Collège de France are here to remind us of it.[10]

There is a famous painting by Brouillet that shows one of Charcot's hysteric patients, Blanche Wittmann, fainting in the arms of Babinski, leaning backwards and offering her bosom to the gaze of the neurologists at La Salpêtrière. Blanche's white body contrasts with the traditional black clothing of doctors of the time. It seems to me that Kristeva's reading of Aragon's *Irene's Cunt* in front of her students at the University of Paris-Diderot in 1995 connects, a century later, with Charcot and his students questioning hysteria and the aberrations of sexuality face to face, this time interrogating no longer only the body but its trace in literary experience.

I. *Irene's Cunt*

Irene's Cunt is a prolific, fertile, and delirious text, the writer having let his pen lead him toward excesses of language and associations that reveal his way of thinking, his way of exploring the intensity of language. *The ardent language of the storm*, Aragon writes. This text is part of a burned manuscript, *La Défense de l'infini*. The infinite in question is that of an excessive *jouissance*, which is transferred from the woman to the writing of the narrator. The infinite is Irene's orgasm and that of the writing. In Kristeva's analysis:

> Irene is an ambiguous character, the narrator's double, a libertine, an idealized echo of the prostitute . . . she exercises a power over others—and over the narrator—thanks to words: an infinite power. . . . The writer and the muse are almost assimilated; he is a woman and she is him. A split projects the libertine into the role of female creator and assigns the writer to the feminine role, thereby acknowledging the creator's bisexual nature.[11]

In this text, Aragon's poetic writing links sexual pleasure to the *jouissance* of language. Irene's sensorial "hurricane" is transposed into an entirely verbal *Défense de l'infini*; the *jouissance* and ecstasy of metaphors. A cascade of images tries the reader, allowing one to define a *style*. "I confer a very elevated meaning on the word style," writes Aragon; "I call style the accent adopted by the flow of the symbolic ocean, reflected by a given man, that universally mines the earth with metaphors."[12] Kristeva elaborates: "Style opens language in such a way that each individual, any given man, is the representative of the symbolic ocean, of the infiniteness of language, to which we are led if we truly acknowledge the confrontation with the ephemeral, humor, and the image."[13] This *symbolic ocean* is marked by the signifying possibilities of language that will lead the surrealists, beyond the dream and the marvelous, to revitalize life. As a semiotician, Kristeva particularly insists on the music, the prosody, on the *semiotic*, that is, on "*the singular experience that insufflates an irreducible sensibility* into the communal use of language."[14]

The surrealist adventure, she reminds us, is one of the exhaustion of beautiful language, the renunciation of literature-as-distraction.[15] Surrealist literature renounces decorative poetry and empty rhetoric. It explores the very resources of the word: what to say, how to say it, how to make and unmake meaning. It explores the impasses of consciousness and associates with madness. It is a matter of finding a form of writing as close as possible to the processes of thought. Breton thought he had discovered it with "automatic writing," borrowed from Freudian free association. "Say whatever comes into your head, give up censorship." It is the fundamental rule of the psychoanalytic cure. "Dictated by thought, in the absence of any control exercised by reason, free of any aesthetic or moral concern," the *Manifesto of Surrealism* pronounces in 1924.[16] Aragon writes his own Manifesto the same year with *A Wave of Dreams*: "Who is there? Ah good. Let in the infinite."[17] A thought at the limit of the thinkable does exist, Kristeva reminds us, a logic freed from the constraints of action and judgment, a practice of language liberated from the judgments of consciousness.

This *thought-as-writing*,[18] this thought-sexuality, "dissolves the apparent coherence of reasoning and deploys the dynamic of thought."[19] It is a matter of attaining "a type of illumination or magic through the cult of writing: writing as favored access to *a-thought*" (with the privative *a-*), to the thought of the impossible.[20] This *a-thought* deploys in the flesh of language the polyvalences of metaphors, the semantic resources of sounds, and even the beating of sensations. There is no flesh more unsettling than the flesh of writing. The concept of *a-thought* proposed by Kristeva thus connects with the *symbolic ocean* mentioned by Aragon. This returns us to Rimbaud's language, the language of the *Illuminations*, to think with our body and our language. Rimbaud auscultates that limit state where thought finds resources in sensations. He proposes a fulgurating language ("This is the age of ASSASSINS"),[21] an *unmoored* language (that of "The Drunken Boat").[22] He proposes exaltation, the incantatory, violence, dementia. Such will be the new style! Writing is transmuted into *jouissance*. It is a matter of translating feeling pulverized into language. "And all the words must fade before the sensation," writes Mallarmé.[23] Proust will ask the word-as-written to become "flesh" by *transubstantiation*.[24] "To transubstantiate each thing into a miracle," Aragon also writes in the *Treatise on Style*.[25] There you have what the objective of the new poetry will be.[26] The surrealist revolt demands a new thought that overthrows the essence of thought.

Like the surrealist texts, *Irene's Cunt* proposes an encounter of literature with *the impossible*. Kristeva asks, "just how far literature could go, as a *journey to the end of the night*, the end of the night as limit of the absolute, limit of meaning, limit of (conscious/unconscious) being, limit of seduction and delirium."[27] In France this encounter has known several moments. Initiated by German Romanticism with Schelling, Nietzsche, and Hölderlin, this encounter took shape in the French poetry of Rimbaud, Lautréamont, and Mallarmé. These poets remain fascinated by the woman's genitals. Rimbaud: "I've seen the hell of women down there," from *A Season in Hell*.[28] Lautréamont: "It is time to curb my inspiration and to pause a while along the way, as when one looks at a woman's vagina," he writes in *Maldoror*.[29] Sex is linked with terror, Pascal Quignard reminds us.[30] Leviticus forbids viewing the woman's genitals. Tiresias who saw the intercourse of the two sexes is blind. Medusa has death in her eyes. Perceiving the female sex organ plunges one into petrification. Anyone who sees Medusa's gaze is petrified. It is the myth of the Gorgon, of Medusa, and the goddess Baubo. To tear yourself away from the mortal face-to-face with Medusa, you have to take *a detour*, there has to be a *reflection*, the mirror-shield of Perseus or Narcissus's river, a mirror, a painting, a canvas . . . or indeed a delirious text. In Apuleius, Psyche wonders, "within what shade can I hide myself from the all-seeing eyes of great Venus?"[31] In the frontal face-to-face, death petrifies. With the female genitals, it is a face that approaches. Courbet's "Origin of the World" unveils the genitals, but the woman does not have a face. There appears a headless feminine, wounded, decapitated, revealing of an eroticized castration, the threatening antithesis of the *phallus* which Latin translates by *fascinus*. With this decapitated feminine, one can read the abyssal connotation of the feminine as the inverse of the representable, the visible, the phallic, which remains a place of fascination. One can wonder about the void, about this nothingness. One sees there only edges, folds, pleats, a gash, as in the photographs of the female genitals by Henri Maccheroni. In front of *Irene's Cunt*, Aragon offers us a torrent of words that unfurl, "the ardent language of the storm," a cascade of words and images that indicate the distance, the necessity of representing, the horror of the vacuum. For all time, it has been a matter of *representing* nudity, grasping it, approaching the sex organ, that crack, sculpting it on bone, in wood, in stone, in the depth of ornamented grottos, materializing its divination (the hidden approach of the divine), desire, or offering. It is a matter of finding something symbolic to conjure a *real* that constantly escapes. Nevertheless, the images as well as the words remain *on the surface*. To see the smooth or the pleated, the colored, the gold, the disguised, veil, lace, mirror, is to perceive desire, but above all it is to cover over (or crack open) *the ontological thickness of the lack*, Roesz remarks apropos of Maccheroni's photographs.[32] Freud speaks of the *horror of castration*, of the man's anguished fear of losing his identity when he perceives the woman's absence of a penis. Whence the denial of castration and the role of the fetish. Language allows the distancing and allows *seeing*. Translating the emotions aroused by the sight of the female genitals can only lead to an obscene explosion or a mystical contemplation. *Irene's Cunt* offers an obscene poetry of which Irene, excited and speaking smutty words, is the metaphor. But female *jouissance* is maintained like the embodied variant of the divine. What is ungraspable about the female genitals stems as much from profanation as from ecstasy. In Aragon, the unveiling of the female genitals pertains to the sacred. "Under the designer-label satin claws of dawn the colour of summer when one closes one's eyes."[33] "Irene is like an arch above the sea."[34] There is a "church," a "holy ogive." The gaze cast on the body of the woman hesitates between the Virgin and the Whore, between sacralization and disgust. "Irene is already a queen of the male bees," writes Philippe Sollers, who emphasizes the homosexuality of the poet in his preface to *Irene's Cunt*.[35]

For Aragon, women, inhabited by an acephalous, archaic, unconquerable violence, have chosen "*the vagabondage of uncertainty*." "Woman, the eternal female, is contained in fire, in the forceful and the feeble, the full-blooded and the faint-hearted, her femininity is in the flood tide's flux and flow, in the fall and flight of foliage, in the false front of the sun where like a voyager lacking guide or horse I lead my fatigue astray into a far-flung fairyland," Aragon writes in *Paris Peasant*.[36] The woman, "kleptomaniac of pleasure," is in fact *style*. In the last analysis, she is the writer himself, the one who creates writing, and no longer any particular goddess of beauty or love. *Irene's Cunt* transcribes the female marvelous, which Aragon invents as if from the interior of his own flesh, since he creates it in his own disappropriated language, as Kristeva writes. The poetics of *Blanche ou l'oubli* (1967) is already under way here.

II. *Blanche ou l'oubli*

With *Blanche ou l'oubli*, we rediscover Aragon with a work rich in all the exploits of *a-thought* encountered during his surrealist period, and which "here displays a sharp and sumptuous maturity," writes Kristeva.[37] "What is compelling about this novel is the intensification of this intimate revolt that is the imaginary: to the limits of language, meaning, image, to the point of absence, the impossible, to the point of 'oblivion,' as Aragon writes."[38] *Blanche ou l'oubli* was written in 1967, about ten years after the publication of Khrushchev's report and the crushing of Budapest by Soviet tanks. Can we imagine an evolution of the writer and a break with political *realism*? Renouncing hope and the construction of a radiant future, which had become problematic, many intellectuals at that time transferred their political concerns to another domain and began to question the functioning of language and representation, which allow naming, communicating, loving, and also *lying*. They opposed literary imposture as much as the imposture of political realism. "The non-sense of political revolt curved into the sense of the revolt of writing, of discourse, in a radical questioning of the aptitude to name and, by consequence, to be."[39]

In a recent text, Daniel Bougnoux proposes an interpretation: "Aragon insisted so much on his abandonment of surrealism in favor of realism, in 1932, that we have to question this famous and perhaps too clear *break*."[40] "No more than Ducasse rewriting Lautréamont could the realist novelist 'cross out his previous speech,' even were he tempted."[41] In his novels, Aragon has always preferred the depiction of "the fall of man" to that of his ascension toward a socialist heaven or some radiant future. Unlike Victor Hugo, the writer lived, not the ascension and rising utopia toward a republican and socialist future, but the decline and the disposal of his noble ideal horribly disfigured by the Soviets: "You will bury me with it / Like a star at the bottom of a hole."[42]

However, the question remains open. How does one assume the real? How does one go from revolt to engagement? Kristeva writes:

> Political engagement seems to be a replacement for tragic revolt, its papering over in the cult of the people . . . under the iron rule of [Stalin] the "little father of the people," and/or the Party police. In contrast to the deconstruction of an uncertain identity, the unbearable "Being" of pleasure and anxiety that decided to join forces with automatic writing, there is "membership." This reversal of the quest for Being in Membership is supported by a will to atone for the father and the law, to struggle against the disappointment of depression, against the invasion by the feminine, against the capsizing into a-thought, of which *La Défense de l'infini* was such a perfect example and whose scars *Blanche ou l'oubli* still touches.[43]

As we know, the matter of the lie is at the center of Aragon's biography. "The word has not escaped my lips / The word has not touched my heart . . . / This weighty secret hangs between us / And you dedicated me to *the lie* / At your knees. . . / Allow me to say before all / That the sun is the sun / That if I pretended, it was for you alone / Acted innocent right up to the end."[44] As

Bougnoux has written:

> We know that around 1964 Aragon had the idea of replacing a socialist realism with [its] somewhat worn-out connotations with the more stimulating, or playful, oxymoron, the "true-lie." This neologism, which provides the title for a rather vertiginous tale written by him in response, perhaps, to the resounding autobiographical work by Sartre, *Les Mots*, which appeared the same year, constitutes, in Aragon's view, a better definition of the novel, as he will assert in his reception speech at the Lomonossov University in Moscow (January 1965), in which he also defines himself as a sort of *linguist*. This true-lie marks with indecision the so troubled boundary (in art) between the true and the false; it insists, not without provocation, on the virtues of the lie, as Aragon has just done in his contemporaneous preface to *The Bells of Basel*. "What is *lie* in the novel frees the writer. . . . What is lie in the novel serves as a *substrate* to truth."[45]

"True-lie" was the best possible definition of the novel or of narration for Aragon. Impossible not to *lie* in an autobiography! Like the unconscious marked by repression, memory is a lie, full of holes and errors, approximations and inexact reconstructions. Autobiography can only be an *autofiction*. Bougnoux points out that "true-lie" marks the troubled boundary between the true and the false with undecidability or indecision. This notion insists on the virtues of the lie, as Aragon wrote in the preface to his *Bells of Basel*. "What is lie in the novel serves as a *substrate* for the truth. . . . What is *lie* in the novel frees the writer."[46] Rather than constructing the truth or reconstructing the past, Aragon *invents* it. With Hegel, we have to *invent* the truth. All the more since even the past is unpredictable. The real being the impossible (Lacan), and any apparition in the world being undiscernible in its reality, only the exploration of language (and of the unconscious that correlates with it) gives us the possibility of discerning what escapes our memory.

For Aragon, there is *perpetual motion* of correlation, of repeats, or of escalation. "At every moment I betray myself, I belie myself, I contradict myself. I am not one in whom I would place my confidence," he writes in 1919.[47] This sentence "expresses the protean, polyphonic aspect of both the personage and the work . . . the ambition to tell the truth through a thousand disguises, masks, theatricality," Kristeva comments.[48]

This renewal of revolt by putting the imaginary into perpetual motion, "to the point of vertigo and non-sense," stages a negativity "that ceaselessly opens up figures of meaning from words, vision, colors to black and white, cries, delirium, and pain."[49] For Kristeva, this deconstructive rage takes on a tonality of tenderness in *Blanche ou l'oubli*: "we perceive, filtered through the insatiable attraction of farce and disguise, a serenity beyond melancholy, a certain appeasement, finally, that confers something feminine upon the Aragonian imaginary."[50] It is a cult of the feminine as prototype of the *impossible* and its emptying-out, for which the *blank* serves as metaphor in *Blanche ou l'oubli*. Kristeva perceives the poet's homosexuality, revealed late in life, as an absorption of the feminine and not as a defense against the feminine. The title of the burned manuscript was *Défense* de [of] *l'infini*, not *Défense* contre [against] *l'infini*. This infinity is Irene's *jouissance* and . . . writing.[51]

Blanche ou l'oubli is thus a book about memory and forgetting. What figures inhabit us at the sunset of our lives? What regrets and what remorse come to haunt us? The other is forgettable, unnamable, unlocatable, *impossible*. Kristeva questions "the immanence of a *whiting out*, which is the perpetual work of the oblivion at the very heart of a-thought. Whiting out, forgetting, but what, whom? Blanche and unnamable femininity? The decomposition of the visible, the evanescence of the expressible?"[52] For Kristeva, the ultimate threshold of contemplation is the feminine. Ultimate barricade that softens violence into tenderness and makes *the connection* still possible. Kristeva perceives, in Aragon's novel, the affirmation of a concern to link differences beyond the annihilation that acts in the memory and in words and that makes us what we are, "namely, forgetful beings, strangers, stranglers. How does one maintain the link beyond the impossibility of the link, when forgetting empties it out? All the aesthetic and moral stakes proposed by this novel lie in this paradox . . . . For what is able to reconstruct this pulverized link, free in its polyphony and disabused of its game, and what appears as the modern version of the link, if not the novel?"[53]

"The blanks indeed take on importance," writes Mallarmé in the preface to *A Throw of the Dice*.[54] Blanche's first name in *Blanche ou l'oubli* is not insignificant. It contrasts with Marie-Noire, her antonym, but above all Blanche is the figure of the absent woman, of the forgetting-whiting-out that is the heart and theme of the novel. "I say: a flower! and, out of the oblivion . . . there arises musically . . . the one absent from every bouquet," writes Mallarmé.[55] This line could have been cited as an epigraph for Aragon's novel. *Blanche ou l'oubli* alludes to the poet of *A Throw of the Dice*, who celebrates chance and the blank as a potential, as a promise of creation. The blank is a figure of emptiness, around which all possible representations circle. "On the void of paper, that whiteness defends."[56] In *La Mise à mort*, on the other hand, one can read, in the disappearance of the image in the mirror, a *blank* that evokes a negative hallucination, which is to say the representation of the *absence of representation*. A representation of the disappearance in the other, the other then conceived as a figure of annihilation or as hallucinatory double, an other recognized as "impossible, forgettable, unnamable, unfindable."[57]

The shadow of the linguist Arsène Darmesteter, quoted in the epigraph to *Blanche ou l'oubli*, hovers over the entire novel: "everywhere the condition of change is the forgetting the mind does of a first term, considering then only the second. This forgetting has received from grammarians the name *catachresis*," writes Darmesteter.[58] Every change of meaning is based on the forgetting of the former meaning, and this mechanism controls the usual metaphor of new meaning. When I say "table leg," I forget that the leg is a part of the human body. Thus the catachresis generalizes in the metaphor to create an image. The "nihilating" or negativity, which Kristeva already emphasized as a "revolted" intimacy in the voyage to the heart of an imaginary, here takes on the figure of *forgetting-whiting-out* that underlies the creation of new significations. For Kristeva, the linguist Gaiffier, the hero of the novel and Aragon's double, is moved to pass from linguistics to aesthetics and morality. Forgetting can metamorphose into creative freedom, but at the same time it is a trap, an alienation, a murderous lie. Isn't all nomination always already displaced, inauthentic, unreal, imaginary, because always off, in negating the referent-object? Unfailingly, the word is already false; it emerges beyond the annihilation and *forgetting* of the thing. The word is an ersatz, *a distortion*, Chomsky says, quoted in English in the epigraph to the novel.[59] The word is translation/treason:

> Isn't the word always a distortion of a first seizure, impossible to seize as such? Where is the first authentic, presumably authentic, outline of this seizure to be found, if by naming I betray it in words that are outside of it, elsewhere, on the superhighway of the true lie? The first draft is forgotten, displaced, metonymically and metaphorically relayed by another—isn't the word always altered, fictive, fictional?[60]

How then *de-think*, *a-think* this threatening logic of nothingness and forgetting that underlies the signs of language, which is to say the very faculty of thinking? Kristeva refers this fascination of Aragon's for language play to the question of the *mask*. Aragon "deciphers the proof of a masquerade inherent in linguistic functioning, and he jubilantly finds the profound, inevitable reason for the Stendhalian determination to wear a 'mask': 'I wore a mask with pleasure; I would change names with delight.'"[61]

One of the most troubling moments of this generalized destabilization of meaning crystallizes in the pages where Gaiffier, the linguist, specialist on the laws of communication, describes the pain that is the absence of communication between him and Blanche:

> Even this language of ours, the one living together has formed, was in the end a glass wall, a trompe-l'oeil (fooling the eye, or the ear), through which the exchange is faked, the words go only halfway and returned to me, humiliated, as if having struck the partition that separates us. It took me a long time to understand this. And that even speaking is silence. How could it be that we were strangers to each other? . . . And yet we spoke the same language, Blanche. Or do the same words mean different things for you and me?[62]

All through the novel, Aragon explicitly and allusively associates the oblivious and treacherous magic of words first to amorous celebration (the anticipated disappearance of Elsa, which harks back to the disappearance of all the lost lovers and in particular Nancy Cunard) but especially to political enthusiasm, a central variant of the lie. "'Ten years . . . it was necessary to forget, unceasingly.' Ten years: 1956–1967. . . . Ten years after the Twentieth Congress of the Communist Party of the Soviet Union in 1956 that—finally—officially recognized the crimes of Communism under Stalin."[63] Gaiffier-Aragon identifies with the German poet Hölderlin, who was stirred by the French Revolution. Realizing the abjection of the Terror, Hölderlin retreats to Diotima: "Everything is finished, Diotima."[64] "At every period, people of my type have lived with the perspective of a utopia," Aragon writes in chapter five of *Blanche ou l'oubli*, "*Et toi ta grande passion*" (And you, your great passion). The Jacobin Hölderlin and the Stalinian Aragon find themselves united in a final disillusion.

The text of *Blanche ou l'oubli* finishes on a murder, and the characters disappear. Blanche lets herself be smothered or decapitated, as if in a detective novel that would be a questioning of meaning and a questioning of the idea of the couple. The stranger is to be strangled. "This scattered novel investigates the major questions of being and its nihilation, the irreality and the absence that are the liberating and risky ferments of the imaginary, with the savor of language and sensory experience itself."[65]

In *Blanche ou l'oubli* the world unfolds as imaginary shadows are piled up. For Aragon, it is a matter of *inventing* the world, an unstable, ungraspable world, in uncertainty, on the shifting sands of the imaginary. *Après-dire*, at the end of the novel, recalls Shakespeare: "Everything in life is only a matter of dreams. Dreams are the fleeting image of what we are looking for. Dreams are perhaps everything. . . . The most beautiful hypotheses are abandoned dreams. Like children at the doors to churches. . . . And the sea at low tide, in the distance, replays the extinguished sound of kisses."

Jean-François Rabain

L'Hôpital de la Salpêtrière
May 2019

NOTES

Translations of quotations from French texts for which there are no English versions are by Armine Kotin Mortimer.

1. Julia Kristeva, *Au risque de la pensée* (Paris: L'Aube, 2001), 33.
2. Ibid., 34, 53.
3. Stéphane Mallarmé, "Sonnet: Ses purs ongles très haut," trans. A. S. Kline, https://www.poetryintranslation.com/PITBR/French/Mallarme.php#anchor_Toc223495091.
4. Kristeva, *Au risque de la pensée*, 113–15.
5. "Music first and foremost! In your verse, / Choose those meters odd of syllable" ("*De la musique avant toute chose/ Et pour cela préfère l'impair* . . . "). Paul Verlaine, "Art poétique," trans. Norman R. Shapiro, https://www.poetryfoundation.org/poems/55034/ars-poetica-56d2361d56078.
6. Kristeva, *Au risque de la pensée*, 123.
7. Giordano Bruno, *Cause, Principle, and Unity*, trans. Robert de Lucca (Cambridge: Cambridge University Press, 2004), 31.
8. Hans Bellmer, *Little Anatomy of the Physical Unconscious, or The Anatomy of the Image*, trans. Jon Graham (Waterbury Center: Dominion, 2004), 36–38.
9. Louis Aragon, *Irene's Cunt*, trans. Alexis Lykiard (London: Creation, 1996), 63.
10. Julia Kristeva, "La Linguistique, l'universel, et 'le pauvre linguiste,'" in Irène Fenoglio, ed., *Autour d'Émile Benveniste* (Paris: Seuil, 2016), 104–5.
11. Julia Kristeva, *The Sense and Non-sense of Revolt: The Powers and Limits of Psychoanalysis Volume 1*, trans. Jeanine Herman (New York: Columbia University Press,

2000), 134; *Sens et non-sens de la révolte: Pouvoirs et limites de la psychanalyse*, t. 1 (Paris: Fayard, 1996), 283.

12. Louis Aragon, *Treatise on Style*, trans. Alyson Waters (Lincoln: University of Nebraska Press, 1991), 105; *Traité du style* (Paris: Gallimard, 1928), 210.

13. Kristeva, *The Sense and Non-sense of Revolt*, 117; *Sens et non-sens de la révolte*, 247.

14. Ibid. (my emphasis).

15. Ibid., 112; *Sens et non-sens de la révolte*, 236.

16. André Breton, *First Manifesto of Surrealism*, trans. A. S. Kline, www.kristinedoor.com/uploads/1/1/4/0/11407928/manifestopdf.pdf, 19.

17. Louis Aragon, *A Wave of Dreams*, trans. Susan de Muth (London: Thin Man, 2013), 45; *Une vague de rêves* (Paris: Seghers, 2006), 35.

18. Kristeva, *The Sense and Non-sense of Revolt*, 113; *Sens et non-sens de la révolte*, 237. Aragon writes, in *Le Libertinage*: "From a very early age, then, I have belonged to the zoological species of writers for whom thought takes shape while writing." *Le Libertinage*, in *Oeuvres romanesques complètes*, t. 1, ed. Daniel Bougnoux and Philippe Forest (Paris: Gallimard, Bibliothèque de la Pléiade, 1997), 256. In *Irene's Cunt* he writes: "I do not think without writing, which is to say that writing is my method of thinking." *Irene's Cunt*, 36. In *Paris Peasant*: "My concern is with metaphysics." Louis Aragon, *Paris Peasant*, trans. Simon Watson Taylor (Boston: Exact Change, 1994), 202. To undo and redo the logic of representation, of images, of narratives, of words, of meaning—this project is indeed metaphysical or transmetaphysical, writes Kristeva.

19. Kristeva, *Sense and Non-sense of Revolt*, 113; *Sens et non-sens de la révolte*, 237.

20. Ibid., 115 (my emphasis); *Sens et non-sens de la révolte*, 243.

21. Arthur Rimbaud, "Drunken Morning," *Illuminations*, trans. A. S. Kline, https://www.poetryintranslation.com/PITBR/French/Rimbaud2.php#anchor_Toc202067623.

22. Arthur Rimbaud, "The Drunken Boat," in *Arthur Rimbaud: Complete Works*, trans. Paul Schmidt (New York: Harper Perennial Modern Classics, 2008).

23. Stéphane Mallarmé, letter to Henri Cazalis, 1864, in Rosemary Lloyd, ed. *Selected Letters of Stéphane Mallarmé*, trans. Rosemary Lloyd (Chicago: University of Chicago Press, 1988), 39.

24. See Julia Kristeva, "From Symbols to Flesh: The Polymorphous Destiny of Narration," *International Journal of Psychoanalysis* 81, no. 4: 777–86. [This publication in English corresponds essentially to the essay "La Narration en psychanalyse, une trans-substantiation," in Julia Kristeva, *La Haine et le pardon* (Paris: Fayard, 2005).—Tr.]

25. Aragon, *Treatise on Style*, 104; *Traité du style*, 209.

26. Kristeva, *The Sense and Non-sense of Revolt*, 115; *Sens et non-sens de la révolte*, 243.

27. Ibid., 112; *Sens et non-sens de la révolte*, 236.

28. Arthur Rimbaud, "Farewell," *A Season in Hell*, trans. A. S. Kline, https://www.poetryintranslation.com/PITBR/French/Rimbaud3.php#anchor_Toc202003798.

29. Isidore Ducasse, comte de Lautréamont, *Maldoror*, trans. Alexis Lykiard (Cambridge: Exact Change, 1994), second canto, stanza 16, 105.

30. Pascal Quignard, *Sex and Terror*, trans. Chris Turner (Kolkata: Seagull, 2012).

31 Apuleius, *The Story of Cupid and Psyche*, trans. Charles Stuttaford (London: David Nutt, 1903), 61.

32 Henri Maccheroni, *Cent photographies du sexe d'une femme* (Paris: Images Obliques/Éditions Borderie, 1978).

33. Aragon, *Irene's Cunt*, 64.

34. Ibid., 65.

35. Philippe Sollers, "Aragon Secret," *Éloge de l'infini* (Paris: Gallimard, 2001), 514.

36. Aragon, *Paris Peasant*, 171–72.

37. Julia Kristeva, *Intimate Revolt*, trans. Jeanine Herman (New York: Columbia University Press, 2002), 182; *La Révolte intime* (Paris: Fayard, 1997), 338.

38. Ibid.

39. Ibid., 183; *La Révolte intime*, 339.

40. Daniel Bougnoux, "Aragon, coller au surréalisme," *Le randonneur*, https://media.blogs.la-croix.com/aragon-coller-au-realisme/2019/04/17/, April 17, 2019.

41. Ibid.

42. A line from Aragon's poem, "J'entends, j'entends."

43. Julia Kristeva, *Hatred and Forgiveness*, trans. Jeanine Herman (New York: Columbia University Press, 2010), 269; *La Haine et le pardon*, 603. "After setting Infinity ablaze, writing could only be a constant betrayal/translation of styles, genres, postures, and tonalities" (Ibid., 268; *La Haine et le pardon*, 601).

44. Louis Aragon, "Le Mot," in *En étrange pays dans mon pays lui-même* (Monaco: À la voile latine, 1945), 63.

45. Bougnoux, "Aragon, coller au surréalisme."

46. Aragon, *Les Cloches de Bâle*, in *Oeuvres romanesques complètes*, t. 1, 692.

47. Louis Aragon, "Révélations sensationnelles, *Littérature*, no. 13: 21.

48. Kristeva, *The Sense and Non-sense of Revolt*, 124; *Sens et non-sens de la révolte*, 263.

49. Kristeva, *Intimate Revolt*, 183; *La Révolte intime*, 339.

50. Ibid., 183; *La Révolte intime*, 339–40.

51. Ibid.; *La Révolte intime*, 340.

52. Ibid., 184; *La Révolte intime*, 340.

53. Ibid., 184; *La Révolte intime*, 341.

54. Stéphane Mallarmé, *A Throw of the Dice Will Never Abolish Chance*, trans. A. S. Kline, https://www.poetryintranslation.com/PITBR/French/MallarmeUnCoupdeDes.php#anchor_Toc160699747.

55. Stéphane Mallarmé, "Crisis of Verse," trans. Mary Ann Caws, in *Selected Poetry and Prose*, ed. Mary Ann Caws (New York: New Directions, 1982), 76.

56. Mallarmé, "Sea Breeze," trans. A. S. Kline, https://www.poetryintranslation.com/PITBR/French/Mallarme.php#anchor_Toc223495106.

57. Kristeva, *Intimate Revolt*, 184; *La Révolte intime*, 341.

58. Louis Aragon, *Blanche ou l'oubli* (Paris: Gallimard, 1967), 7.

59. Ibid.

60. Kristeva, *Intimate Revolt*, 190; *La Révolte intime*, 352.

61. Ibid.; *La Révolte intime*, 353.

62. Aragon, *Blanche ou l'oubli*, 309.

63. Kristeva, *Intimate Revolt*, 197; *La Révolte intime*, 365.

64. Aragon, *Blanche ou l'oubli*, 491.

65. Kristeva, *Intimate Revolt*, 218–19; *La Révolte intime*, 404.

REPLY
TO BERNARD BRUSSET, JEAN-LOUIS BALDACCI, AND JEAN-FRANÇOIS RABAIN

I. BERNARD BRUSSET—PSYCHOANALYSIS: CENTER AND UNITY

Contrary to a misinformed and alas too widespread opinion, contemporary psychoanalysis, while renewing the heritage of Freud, Klein, or Lacan, abounds with research that resonates with the general evolution of ideas, more specifically with the sciences of life and of the mind. Bernard Brusset's clinical and theoretical work shows it, from his remarkable study of anorexia in *L'Assiette et le miroir* (The plate and the mirror) to his *Au-delà de la névrose: Vers une troisième topique* (Beyond neurosis: toward a third topography), and *Psychanalyse du lien* (Psychoanalysis of the link).[1] Attentive to the drives in Freud's first topography, he examines the *object relation* of the second topography and proposes the need (evoked by Freud at the end of his life in *An Outline of Psycho-Analysis*, 1938–1939) for a psychical apparatus with a spatial extension able to integrate the cases that do not fit the "psychoanalytic conception of psychical and instinctual reality" (Brusset).[2] His purpose is to refine the analysis of the psychic splitting, denial, the clinic of "emptiness," addictions, psychosomatic pathologies, and "external psychical functionings"—which also held my attention in *New Maladies of the Soul*.[3]

The fact is that, without it being necessary to designate it as such, this "third topography" is addressed in numerous works (as Brusset reminds us in "Métapsychologie des liens et troisième topique")[4] that reprise and renew the "grand models"—those of *projection* or *primary identification*, notably in the clinic of the limits of the ego.

Brusset's reading of my work comes fully within the scope of this contemporary discussion in which I participate and whose epistemological implications I share. Thanks to his extraordinary capacity to embrace biology, ethnology, and neuropsychology, I discover that my clinical observations and my theorizations also echo infra-drive somatic logics identified by advances in the neurosciences during the last decade (see Brusset). This fact confirms my hypotheses, in a sense, or at least reduces the separation between psychoanalysis and the

---

Translated from French by Armine Kotin Mortimer.

neurobiological and neurophysiological exploration of human functioning (see Damasio, Buser, Edelman, Ameisen, cited by Brusset).

Thus, the *semiotic* (emotions and affect encoded in gestures, in vocal frequencies and intensities, or in echolalias), which has *meaning* for the child but does not yet have *signification* (the latter will arrive with morphology, grammar, and logic), remains an infra- and prelinguistic component: I hear it as much in the speech of my analysands as in the musical and stylistic variations of literary texts.[5] This *semiotic* meaning (underlying *symbolic* signification) adjoins the neurobiological "nucleus of the unconscious," the "automatic, desubjectified" "cognitive procedural" outside symbolization (Brusset). The illumination brought by Brusset allows for a better grasp of those "elementary forms" that I call semiotic, which express biopsychological dimensions. It makes us understand how these dimensions construct the *psychosexuality of maternal reliance* as I conceive it,[6] as well as its *transformation-sublimation* all through the process of subjectivation, using the potentialities of languages and other translinguistic vectors (gestures, sounds, images).

Indeed, the way parents invest the child's drives (through his *semiotic* or *symbolic* expressions) "gives a place and support" to intersubjectivity in the emergence of the sexual (Brusset). And the author is right to insist on the multiple levels of this consolidation: integration, transformation, even "transubstantiation" (reprising the term I analyzed in Proust, borrowed from the Catholic mass: a fusion of the *word* and the *thing*, of the *logos* and the *flesh*). The phenomena of regression in the transference-countertransference of the analytic cure bear witness to this: these "multiple levels" go "unnoticed" while constituting the complexity and the fragility of maternal reliance itself.

Abjection participates in these "elementary forms" of self-construction by accentuating the dimension of the *negative*, closest to the psychical *signifiance* of the drive. And I observe, with Brusset, that this dimension is lacking both in the theories concerning the *dualism* of the objective/subjective and in the hypothesis of the *qualitative transformation* of the nerve impulse into an unmeasurable subjective signal (Brusset). I entirely agree with the reading he gives of my notion of *abjection* (neither object nor subject, attraction/repulsion) as the "primitive crucible of psychic life and the activity of thinking," "autoerotic reversal onto the self, in identification with the attitudes of the mother towards the self, . . . [that is] associated with the inversion of the positions of the subject and the object, from activity to passivity." Entangled in maternal reliance, then, are the originary intrauterine "liance," the linking-delinking (binding-unbinding) of the drive, the "semiotic communion," and the "otherness of the subject to come."

This is to say that I do not reduce the maternal to *empathy* nor to *desexualization*. And while I affirm that "maternal eroticism deploys . . . its libidinal drives as tenderness," I do wish to emphasize that, in this delicate emotion, the linking forces (Eros) tend toward a specific ethics that overdetermines the interrelation. The *genitrix* is transcended by the *mother*, in the sense that the latter transforms *attachment* (according to Harlow, Herman, or Bowlby; see Brusset) into *passion*. The mother also prepares for and assumes "matricide" as a counterphobic fantasy, necessary to the child's becoming an autonomous subject. And she *sublimates* (I will return to sublimation at length in this reply) the pain of this destructivity (of which she is subject and object, expulsing-expulsed, separating-separated) by the *transmission of language* and by the *opening of time* as new beginning, interminable ephemerality.

Ambivalent reliance, then, but even more so *dialogical* reliance (as Brusset specifies, citing Morin). Drawing on works by Bakhtin, I extensively explored this foundational figure of the capacity to make meaning and signification, by deciphering *dialogism* in the novels of Dostoyevsky.[7] In this context, which makes the life and death of meaning evident, I try to restore to *forgiveness* its anthropological scope by recalling its theological and aesthetic history.[8] It cannot be summarized by "the alleviation of internal superegoic constraints" nor by "removing guilt" (Brusset). I consider that the experience of sublimation in a work of the imagination (poem, novel, painting, etc.) is a forgiveness: the re-beginning of subjectivation in and through the recomposition-reinvention of *signifiance* by the recreation of the work. I tried to unfold the singular alchemy of this forgiveness in Proust, Céline, Dostoyevsky, and Colette.

But forgiveness thus understood participates "from the start" in maternal eroticism as a "deconstructive elucidation of 'love-hatred'" (Brusset); beyond the reparations of traumas and suffering, it gives (for-gives, *par-donne*) a new perception of self in the open temporality of rebeginnings. Mortality is not (or not only) inscribed in it as the murder of the father, it is constitutive of the vital process of subjectivation in which the mother participates by managing to efface herself, thereby embodying the copresence of mortality in the gift of life itself. Think of Freud's mother who "kneads" this mortality by rubbing bits of earth in her hands: "Everyone owes nature a death," the founder of psychoanalysis sums up later, borrowing from Shakespeare.[9]

If love is the intimate face of ethics (according to the onto-erotics of Spinoza),[10] the multiverse of maternal eroticism is a "*herethics*" of love.[11] The ethics of psychoanalysis is constructed by the sublimation of this eroticism: this for-giveness (*par-don*). "Psychoanalysis is, for Julia Kristeva, the center, the laboratory," writes Brusset. Yes, I wanted to believe in the unity of the human spirit, I wagered on it, and I found it in psychoanalytic research.

II. Jean-Louis Baldacci: Crossing the Line

In psychoanalysis theorizations emerge from the couch. In this respect, Jean-Louis Baldacci is right to recall my experience of the cure with Isle Barande. Preoccupied by my baby's first teeth and the pain inherent in teething, and haunted by the power of horror in Céline's writing, which I couldn't pin down, a word—the word—escaped my lips while free-associating on her couch. She picked it up: "That's the word." I had to use it for the title of the book I was writing. Later, I took it up again in the analysis I was conducting with a patient with "external" psychical functioning. His paranoid hatred seemed to me to constitute a defense against the erasure of the boundaries between the ego and the other: neither subject nor object, *ab-ject* (privative "a").

The analysis with Ilse Barande reconciled me with the maternal feminine, which made the analysis continue all the better, particularly in my approach to *maternal reliance*: in pursuing my "investment" ("cathexis") transference and my "displacement" transference, as well as in the "sexualization-desexualization" transference, which provide speech with the "investment" of a new object as well as the sharing of an ideal.[12] The attentive reader will not fail to notice, among the facets I sketch of maternal eroticism, the "singular maternal" that Ilse Barande describes in analyzing the famous painting by Leonardo da Vinci, "The Virgin and Child with Saint Anne" (an *image*, the imaginary: I'll come back to this), but also the *perversion* of the maternal in what my analyst calls the *mère-version*.[13]

The "transference speech" with an analyst who is a foreigner (like me, but different from me—see Baldacci) having led us to probe the pre- and translinguistic modalities of French and of my mother tongue, Bulgarian, I was able to live "intertextuality and the semiotic" from the "inside" of the transference (Baldacci). Only in this way did my personal experience of the cure allow me to recreate the infantile psychic space in the French language. To make of it a *second mother tongue*,[14] in which the technical idiolect of concepts that I easily handled beforehand let itself be infiltrated by the "embodied" discourse of the transference-countertransference, which the writing of fictions (novels) eventually took over.

I thank Baldacci for having insisted on this "foundational experience of the psychoanalytic cure," adding to it my debt to the thought of Klein, Winnicott, and also Lou Andreas-Salomé, and most especially André Green. If I have never considered that the "mythology" of the drive is an Achilles' heel for psychoanalysis, it is because Green always insisted on the *heterogeneity* of the drives: energy-and-meaning. Green's terminology developed, in Freudian terms, the *heterogeneous* that had struck me in Bataille's "inner experience" and that I was trying to elaborate to better understand representation as a "reversal of rejection" and "trans-language experience."[15]

Baldacci proposes an interpretation of my vignette on Didier, one of my patients and an amateur painter.[16] His interpretation illuminates the role of sublimation in reliance, in the traumatic life experience of Didier, while still insisting on the fact that, through the word as act and through the introduction of the image in the transference-countertransference, I transgressed the analytic frame.

An anti-analysand par excellence, Didier isolated himself in the perversion of a technical discourse until the day he recounted a dream figuring the destructiveness and abjection of the patient/analyst couple, and from which he awoke with a *cry*. The poverty of the associations and the hallucinatory dangerousness of the dream drew my attention to the disparity between, on the one hand, the *intensity of the cry* and, on the other, the *frozen* representation of the broken image reflecting Didier's sister, described in a monotone voice. I then proposed an interpretation . . . of his voice. Of the *semiotic*, preform of the vocal gesture, of the *meaning* of the affect that escapes from *signification* and contradicts the masterful narration of the dream. My countertransferential construction sensed that the *signifiance* of Didier's unconscious provoked me by padlocking itself elsewhere, in an "other language," his painting, which this patient had vaguely spoken of but in another voice that suddenly came back to me: a sort of *cry*.

At the next session, Didier brought me copies of his pictorial works. I agreed to *see* him show me and comment on their cruelty in a jargon that was at first scholarly and aestheticizing, then scandalized by my interpretations "on the level of the images," and finally in speech given over to the voyeurism-exhibitionism of his sexuality. Aimed exclusively at his mother, he had done nothing other than sublimate his sexuality in painting and keep it under lock and key in his apartment, until the analytic process made it accessible to discourse. In naming it, Didier displaced its abjection onto the woman analyst and only thereby began to deconstruct his own isolation entrenched between obsession and perversion, finally to engage in a different regime of subjectivation.

Baldacci's work on sublimation returns to the Freudian position, according to which sublimation is present "from the start" of mother-child relations, and he describes it (in line with the joke in Freud) as a "cycle of sublimation." The latter is inaugurated by maternal reserve and renunciation, so that the saving of preliminary pleasure is transformed into the *gift* of feeling to the *infans*, the condition of the appropriation of *signifiance* by the future subject. In Didier's infantile history, the "cycle of sublimation" was, on the contrary, fixated in exhibitionist and voyeurist sadomasochism, under the effect of the maternal grip and the sexualization of thought. In introducing the iconic into the field of speech, at the risk of unlocking Didier's destructivity, I wagered on the three paradoxes of the transference according to Baldacci.[17] We thus elaborated the disinvestment of speech and the destructive grip on the object and recreated a new cycle of sublimation in which Didier was able to change his "style of living" and his manner of painting through the transference speech in which he was reconstructing his sexuality.

I understand Baldacci's epistemological and ethical question: What of the *jouissance* of the analyst "when the analysis becomes transgressive," like the one I conducted with Didier? And I agree with his reply. Yes, the position of the analysis is a quite uncommon solitude, for the analysand is hardly a reliable companion (Bion warned us about this). Rather than an ideal (Baldacci), our only horizon is an ethics that is not a morality prescriptive of *norms* but an optative framework, based on *choice*, *will* (where desire makes an appearance), *concern*, and *care*, and which does indeed urge us to "cross the line."[18] In returning to infantile sexuality that the analytic process recreates, it is important to leave open the sexualization/desexualization paradox and to promote new symbolizations by speech in the play of interpretation and transference.

I therefore maintain that, leaning on the cure, *writing* is a "search for thirdness," but it does not necessarily aim for a "sufficient orthodoxy"; it can "cross the line." Only writing can allow psychoanalysis to avoid isolation and, to the contrary, take on the role it is responsible for in the work of culture and in the social field. Are they able to meet the challenge posed by hyperconnectivity and the image, when they demand much more than to innovate and sharpen the concepts of our clinical research? Yes, but this presupposes that psychoanalysis reinvests in the word in order to translate and make known its implication in the ongoing anthropological acceleration.

III. Jean-François Rabain: The Feminine of the Man and the Imaginary

Starting with *Revolution in Poetic Language* (1974), I have devoted many texts to sublimation in the writings of Mallarmé, Lautréamont, Céline, Proust, Colette, Duras, Baudelaire, Stendhal, Bataille, Artaud, and Sollers. But as Jean-François Rabain quite rightly notes, I have addressed bisexuality only in my interpretation of Aragon's oeuvre, with the feminine of the man and of the woman as *princeps* organizers of the sublimatory act. In this response, I would like to return at some length to this topic, as bisexuality and the feminine are better able to elucidate, more broadly and outside of writing, the function of the imaginary as such, and more specifically the role of *sublimation* in the psychic life of speaking beings.

Rabain compares my two published courses, *The Sense and Non-sense of Revolt* (University of Paris 7, 1994–1995) and *Intimate Revolt* (University of Paris 7, 1996–1997)[19]—in which I analyzed *Irene's Cunt* and *Blanche ou l'oubli* by Aragon—to "Charcot and his students questioning hysteria and the aberrations of sexuality face to face."[20] I confess I had not thought of this painting when I conceived of my course, but—in all modesty—I accept the prestigious connection. Both Blanches (Charcot's and Aragon's) associate the "Copernican revolution" of psychoanalysis with the irruption of the feminine in the imaginary (Aragon appropriating for himself the *jouissances* of Irene and Blanche). On the eve of the third millennium, when the quite new Europe, scarcely reunited, was emblazoned with so many promises, a new world order was settling in, one that finance and the spectacle took over, hypernormalized and at the same time falsifiable. The failure of ideologies advocating revolt, the surge in commodity culture—transgression became standardized, even rioters nurtured their image (like the yellow vests today). As a countercurrent to this normalization-falsification, which virtual hyperconnectivity has only accentuated, clinical experience has maintained and developed the capacity to evaluate, reevaluate, transvaluate. It was not a matter of "applying" psychoanalysis to literature or philosophy at the university, but of probing the symptoms of Eros, the traumas of Thanatos; of unfolding the archeology of fantasies, the denatured sexual (always drive-and-meaning), the feminine and the masculine; of descending into the *meaning* of the drives and affects that diffract the *signification* of words, sentences, and stylistic or narrative figures.

Freud had alerted us that "writers are valuable allies . . . they are way ahead of us."[21] At the same time, he recognized the revolutionary import of his own descent into the "lowly dwelling" of unconscious movements that hysterics revealed to him.[22]

It was therefore critical to be open to the scandalous anxieties of surrealist flights and the catastrophes of communist utopias. To accomplish this, I proposed to reevaluate language (see my notions of *dialogism*, *semiotic* and *symbolic*, *intertextuality*), attentive to the Freudian unconscious, to my analytic experience, then to my clinic as a psychoanalyst. I cohabit with the poetic language, whether lyrical or narrative, of those refractory to morality known as writers, "on strike against society" (as Mallarmé affirmed in the nineteenth century): Proust, Aragon, Sartre, Bataille. In rejecting moraline (*das Moralin*, Nietzsche wrote in the *Anti-Christ*),[23] these writers do not liberate themselves from norms but "put them in parentheses," judgment and the world included, in order to think them, to say and live them differently. By connecting the very depth of the intimate with the extimate.

An ethics in suspension also subtends the transference-countertransference in the analytic cure attentive to eroticism and the death drive, which underlie human civilizations and today threaten the earth. With only a single orientation: "Where id was, there ego shall be";[24] and with two principles: the pleasure principle and the reality principle. Subtle dosage that makes the paths of the imaginary intersect and allows us to interpret them endlessly.

But the explorations in which art and literature risk themselves, particularly since the end of the nineteenth century, free them from psychoanalytic working through. For their sole and unique "guardrail" they have only the virtuosity of *sublimation*, playing on all the registers of *signifiance*, reweaving the gap of foreclosure and the traumas of the being. Alas, rare are the psychoanalysts who confront Artaud's "body gobbling up the infinite nothingness," or the "opera of the deluge" illuminating Céline's antisemitic abjection[25]—without hiding behind a supposed "artistic and philosophical background" and without becoming "virgin[s] in horror the same as in sex."[26]

Jean-François Rabain has joined me in that "lowly dwelling" where literature and psychoanalysis meet and attempt to elucidate the distress of human beings and the catastrophes of the political.

***

Louis Aragon (1897–1982) is an emblematic figure of the two movements that shook the twentieth century: surrealism and Stalinism. A son without a father—his genetic father, the prefect Louis Andrieux, was officially his godfather before becoming his guardian—and with a clandestine mother who presented him as her little brother (Marguerite Toucas-Massillon pretended she had not conceived him). His grandmother having been designated as his mother, the future writer is thus raised among four women: his grandmother, his mother, and his mother's two sisters. The untenable impact of the feminine, in this exceptional family configuration, obviously structures his life and his work. But this impact, and this configuration, nonetheless resonate with the push for emancipation and the distress of women that were shaking up all the ranks of society at that time, masculine psychosexuality in particular. And analysis discovers, in the Aragonian imaginary, the stupefying "vignettes" of the wounds and sublimations of the twentieth century.

First World War, mobilization, disaster, the doctor's assistant encounters André Breton, Dadaism, surrealism . . . "[Set] my heel on the throat of my own song," Mayakovsky will write in 1930.[27] "It's all about coming up with a new declaration of human rights" (Aragon).[28] "My concern is with metaphysics."[29] "Transubstantiate each thing into a miracle."[30] At war with the French language, "a cashier's language . . . precise and inhuman,"[31] in order to create another one with the help of the *automatic writing* dear to surrealists, made of narratives, dreams, collages, fragments. And this admission of a liquid, ungraspable identity: "At every moment I betray myself, I belie myself, I contradict myself. I am not one in whom I would place my confidence."[32]

The surrealist cult of the "true woman," a "conjunction of the ephemeral and scandal,"[33] becomes with Aragon a deep quest for feminine *jouissance*, between the violence of desire and erotic annihilation, which comes up against the *impossible* and the capacity-incapacity for *writing*: "From a very early age, then, I have belonged to the zoological species of writers for whom thought takes shape while writing," Aragon affirms in his late preface (1964) to *Le Libertinage* (1924).[34]

In 1927 his affair with the wealthy, liberated, and tomboyish Nancy Cunard, marked by social humiliation, violence, and jealousy, results in a project for a novel, *La Défense de l'infini*: an orgy of exaltation, a plurality of narrative lines, confessions mixed up in "an immense bordello" (both literal and figurative). "I have never learned how to write," the author specifies, to make his project even more vertiginous.[35] Aragon attempts suicide and destroys the great novel, which may have numbered thousands of pages.

As a rigorous psychoanalyst, Rabain is not content to take up the biography of the writer to transform him into a patient in spite of himself. He has apprehended the man tirelessly constructing himself in his style, to the point of claiming he doesn't think—therefore doesn't exist—except in writing. A defensive denial, but even more a *transformative* one because it sublimates the painful fantasy of the "clandestine," omnipotent, and unassailable feminine into a jerky, imaginary flux, an infinite and impossible competition. In enriching my reading, Rabain listens closely to the configuration of Aragonian writing, this solitary, porous, and oneiric act of writing that is never sufficiently freed from imposture—sexual or political—but succeeds in liberating the unrealized feminine in . . . the man with the pseudonym.

Rabain rightly emphasizes that this "febrile and delirious" text explores "the intensity of language": "The infinite is Irene's *jouissance* and that of the writing." "Irene is an ambiguous character, the narrator's double, a libertine, an idealized echo of the prostitute"; indeed, this split "projects the libertine into the role of female creator and assigns to the writer the feminine role, thereby acknowledging the creator's bisexual nature."[36] All powerful, it is the feminine that is definitively the "kleptomaniac of pleasure," whereas the man (Irene's grandfather, but also the narrator) voluptuously exposes his "ignoble fiasco," amorous or erotic impotence, deep motivation for his suicide attempt: "What bloody sadness there is in all erotic achievements!"[37]

The disenchantment of eroticism is quite rare in French literature, which had placed eighteenth-century libertinage at the zenith of the experience of freedom. It continues to compete with the glorification of the sexual exploit—

whether in the media image of hard sex or as the expected norm in the "novel à la *française*" under serotonin. On the contrary, confronted with the sadness of eroticism, *jouissance*, according to the narrator of Irene, is capable of being transposed to another level: beyond the feminine orgasm—imaginary zenith—the novelist valorizes the magic of the word, "the prodigious metaphorical value which *I* attribute to words alone."[38]

Such then is the alchemy of sublimation: another *jouissance* is possible, that of *metaphors*. It mobilizes the feminine of the man who has assimilated the female orgasm, which slips away, and it proceeds by *transport* (Greek *metaphora*): displacement in the word, ec-stasy that transits into recollection in solitude and surrenders. It takes its pleasure in plays with words, which among surrealists speak nonsense, but it is also at work in the making of the novel; putting coitus into narrative form, for all its scandalousness, confronts the unnamable, psychosis, aphasia.

Irene's Cunt is a hymn to the most absolute of what feminine *jouissance* possesses, doubled by its inverse, the impotence of the man whom Irene and/or her narrator discover at the limits of the human: "So small and so large! It is here that you are at ease, man finally worthy of your name . . . Hell, let your damned toss off, Irène has come."[39] I know of no text—perhaps Joyce's on Molly, more ironic and more refined—that flows with as much complicity, physiological precision, and admiring tenderness, in the female marvelous that Aragon invents as if from the interior of his own flesh, since he creates it in his own disappropriated language (as Rabain acknowledges).

This passage inspires Rabain to take a superb voyage—from Leviticus, transitioning through Apuleius, the Gorgon, and Medusa, but also Hans Bellmer and Henri Maccheroni—and underscores the profanation intrinsic to Aragonian ecstasy. In the name of style, which aspires to being the veritable and definitive "kleptomaniac of pleasure."

***

Dream interpretations come to a stop in front of the "navel" of the dream, the unrepresentable limit of analysis, Freud warned.[40] Having challenged "the navel" of the fantasy by appropriating feminine *jouissance*, Aragon thwarted the process of sublimation itself: bankruptcy of the word, ceasefire of metaphors, suicide and self-immolation as the only payment for impertinence. Membership in the Communist Party (in February 1927, effective in 1930), the encounter with Elsa (in 1928), followed by the "mad love" that became "conjugal," reassured and consolidated the collapsed identity of the writer.

True-lie,[41] pretense? "I don't know who I am, but I am in, I join, I belong." That could be the syllogism of this above-all political "rescue." The surrealist group in the past, followed by the Communist Party, then the legal frame of the couple took on the role of support for identity. Without the creator belonging entirely to an identity or a precise truth. Solitary suppleness of sublimation: of the fantasy translated into imaginary adjustments by the infinite *signifiance* of language—styles, genres, tonalities, and postures.

The turmoil of his identity will be resolved in a new adoptive paternity: the recomposed family of comrades, itself cemented by the erection of the dogma, Reason in its supposed proletarian purity. Hegel had warned, however, that the Terror is Kant put into practice. But through a ruse of the imaginary, the writer will permit himself to forget the crimes *whited out, laundered* (*blanchis*) by dialectical materialism.

Belatedly published (by Gallimard in 1986), *Irene's Cunt* addresses the bisexuality of the man in the form of an appropriation-confrontation, inscribed in an untenable tension with the maternal and the feminine, to the extent that they represent the fantasy of an unrepresentable excitability: the *mater*—demoniacal matter (or jubilatory distress of the mother-baby dyad?). This war-love is to be understood as a counterpoint to the war the subject fights with himself, with his superegoic and paternal identity, with his social ideals. Tirelessly, the player defies the oedipal recentering, he expends himself histrionically. Grandeur and misery of the illusion? A rapturous (*jouissif*) unfurling of the burlesque. Adventuring to the limits of the sensible and the feminine, can this imaginary even blossom without the feeling of security that *belonging* to an institution procures? But then, what belonging is there today when political *parties* are disintegrating and traditional *beliefs* are being radicalized into holy wars? When the irresistible need for conviviality is content to parade around the "roundabouts"? Could financial prosperity, success in the "social networks," the amassing of "likes" and "followers" be the only, the final landmarks and shelters, paid for by submission to the consensus, to the virtual? . . . What solitude!

Blanche ou l'oubli (1967), "a book about memory and forgetting" (Rabain) . . . of Irene? From the Khrushchev report to the fall of the Berlin wall, militants are starting to have doubts. The non-sense of political revolt replaces the quest for a rapturous enthusiasm and is transformed into re-volt: a return on engagement, radical questioning of our aptitude to name, speak, write, and in consequence to be. An *impetuous acceleration* of the imaginary thwarts narration, confuses the characters, loses the sense of history, only deploying figures of meaning: words, sight, from colors to black or white, from sentences to the point of babble, from the cry to pain and delirium. The breaks in representation, in the manner of Braque or Picasso, undermine Aragon's art of telling stories, but in a more sensual and more philosophical way than the "nouveau roman" does.

Rabain is right: the "perpetual movement" of this novel aims for *emptying out* in discovering that the *nihilation* would be inherent in language. Isn't the signifier studied by linguistics constituted by the "forgetting" of the referent? From signifier to signifier, verbal figures carry on the "whiting out" (*blanchiment*) at all the levels of language, according to the narrator-linguist Geoffroy Gaiffier in *Blanche ou l'oubli*, who appropriates the theories of Darmesteter and Chomsky.

At the crossroads of the drives and meaning, *nihilation* controls above all the imaginary *a-thought* that, in this novel, bears witness to annihilation. But what annihilation? That of the feminine infinite which is strangled in *Blanche*?

That of the feminine in itself? Of the self? The polysemy of this whiting out is vertiginous. Tragic repression of the impossible *jouissance*. Salvational desire to efface the group past and its Stalinist acme. Essence of language as well, "originary repression" that tears itself away from sensations and drives, and thus from the real, impossible blaze of which only a sonorous trace remains, the imprint and illusion of the void. Or else, even more painfully, *Blanche and foreclosure* (*Verwerfung*): rejection of the feminine out of the symbolic sphere of the subject. Beyond forgetting, the feminine is perceived as if it had never existed except in the fabric of the fiction-sublimation where the novelist redoubles it, multiplies it, strangles it, but also possesses it, possesses her, possesses himself, between psychosis and delirium.

The fusion-defusion of the narrator and Blanche is no longer an absorption of the feminine, as it was in *Irene's Cunt*: Blanche is the index of the other, finally recognized and yet impossible, forgettable, unnamable, unfindable. Rabain reminds us that in this limit state where the *other is eclipsed*, the "*blanc*" is also the *blank* of hallucination: a concretion of death-dealing destructivity. However, even in this limit-state bordering on foreclosure, the aggressivity deferred in intimacy encounters the *feminine*—on the condition that the imaginary a-thought remains and lasts. "Ultimate threshold of contemplation" (Rabain). Last rampart in the face of the pillage the author's fantasies indulge in. A bitter dignity and a violence disintegrated into benevolence result from this new version of the Aragonian imaginary. No longer is it a matter of forming a "cult of the other" within the "mythical couple," about which the writer suggests it is built on a censured suffering. It is necessary nonetheless to *link differences*—Rabain insists on this point. And beyond the nihilation, recognized and adopted, to compose the novel that makes us such as we are: beings of forgetfulness, strangers, stranglers.

By the work of sublimation, it is therefore not the feminine but the *cult* of the feminine as a prototype of the impossible—absorbed (Irene), then whitened (Blanche)—that collapses in a baroque staging of the homosexuality belatedly revealed but at work from Aragon's literary beginnings. Never will he give up the novel as a "science of the anomaly,"[42] a science whose forms and genres he will never stop varying. Whereas Sartre, after *The Words* (1964), takes his leave of neurosis-literature, from which the philosopher says he awoke as if "cured of a long, bitter-sweet madness."[43]

Rabain's text also takes me back farther, beyond Irene and Blanche, to the dawn of the representation of the feminine in Renaissance art, which conceals a symptomatic doubling.[44] On the one hand, the theme of maternity, the mother, and the woman (the Virgin with Child and the Joconde) put in place the body-object, the passion for the object, the woman-object that will determine the gaze of the Western male for four centuries. On the other, *She* slips away: ungraspable enigma (Leonardo da Vinci's *Joconde*, 1503) or inaccessible peace tinged with melancholy (the Virgins of Giovanni Bellini, 1430–1516). To touch the mother, the woman, is to *see* and to make seen a secret, unrepresentable *jouissance*. Only the artist-painter possesses it and communicates it to anyone able to slip into his gaze: *through* and disengaging from the "theme" and from the "model object." The folds of the colored surfaces, the juxtaposition of the levels, the subtle light that opens the color to bedazzlement—the painter is a "kleptomaniac of pleasure." Bellini's canvases generally carry a common denominator: *Sacra conversazione*. Bellini's mother is absent from his biography: lost, dead, illegitimate, "clandestine"? But the maternal *place* is there: ineffable *jouissance*, infinite "conversation." With *Blanche ou l'oubli* the permutation with the feminine of the man sizzles, exhausted and disabused by its game. Who can still maintain this place, beyond the link, and when forgetting empties it? The novel, in all its states, despairs. The restarted imaginary of internauts contracts or harasses with texts, tweets, and passages to the act. There remains only psychoanalysis, lucid and ultimate point of reference.

J.K.

NOTES

1. Bernard Brusset, *L'Assiette et le miroir* (Paris: Privat, 1977); *Au-delà de la névrose: Vers une troisième topique* (Paris: Dunod, 2013); *Psychanalyse du lien* (Paris: PUF, 2007).

2. See Sigmund Freud, *An Outline of Psycho-Analysis*, in *The Standard Edition of the Complete Psychological Works of Sigmund Freud*, vol. XXIII, trans James Strachey (London: Hogarth, 1964), 145.

3. Julia Kristeva, *New Maladies of the Soul*, trans. Ross Guberman (New York: Columbia University Press, 1995); *Les Nouvelles Maladies de l'âme* (Paris: Fayard, 1993).

4. Bernard Brusset, "Métapsychologie des liens et troisième topique," *Revue française de psychanalyse* 70, no. 5 (2006): 1213–82.

5. Julia Kristeva, "The Semiotic and the Symbolic," in *Revolution in Poetic Language*, trans. Margaret Waller (New York: Columbia University Press, 1984); *La Révolution du langage poétique: L'Avant-garde à la fin du XIXe siècle, Lautréamont et Mallarmé* (Paris: Seuil, 1974), 17–100.

6. Julia Kristeva, "Maternal Eroticism," in *Passions of Our Time*, trans. Constance Borde and Sheila Malovany-Chevallier (New York: Columbia University Press, 2018); "L'Érotisme maternel," in *Pulsions du temps* (Paris: Fayard, 2013).

7. Julia Kristeva, "Word, Dialogue, and Novel," in *Desire in Language: A Semiotic Approach to Literature*, trans. Thomas Gora, Alice Jardine, and Leon S. Roudiez (New York: Columbia University Press, 1980); "Le Mot, le dialogue et le roman," in *Sémiotikè: Recherches pour une sémanalyse* (Paris: Seuil, 1969).

8. Julia Kristeva, *Black Sun: Depression and Melancholia*, trans. Leon S. Roudiez (New York: Columbia University Press, 1989), 205–17; *Soleil noir: Dépression et mélancolie* (Paris: Gallimard, 1987), 215–26.

9. Sigmund Freud, *The Interpretation of Dreams*, in *The Standard Edition of the Complete Psychological Works of Sigmund Freud*, vol. IV, trans. James Strachey (London: Hogarth, 1958), 205; *L'Interprétation des rêves* (Paris: PUF, 1967), 182.

10. Baruch Spinoza, *Ethics* (London: Penguin, 2005), pt. III, "Of the Origin and Nature of the Affects," and pt. V, "Of the Power of the Intellection, or On Human Freedom."

11. Julia Kristeva, "Stabat Mater," in *Tales of Love*, trans. Leon S. Roudiez (New York: Columbia University Press, 1987), 263; *Histoires d'amour* (Paris: Denoël, 1983), 327.

12. Jean-Louis Baldacci, *L'Analyse avec fin* (Paris: PUF, 2016).

13. Ilse Barande, *Le Maternel singulier* (Paris: Aubier Montaigne, 1992) and Ilse Barande and Robert Barande, *De la perversion: Notre duplicité d'être inachevé* (Meyzieu: Césura Lyon, 1987).

14. Keren Mock, *Hébreu, du sacré au maternel* (Paris: CNRS, 2016), explains the genesis of a new mother tongue, modern Hebrew.

15. See Julia Kristeva, "Heterogeneity," in *Revolution in Poetic Language*, 165–91; *La Révolution du langage poétique*, 151–71.

16. See Julia Kristeva, *New Maladies of the Soul*, 10–26; *Les Nouvelles Maladies de l'âme*, 20–47. A vignette taken up again in the Seminar of the Société Psychanalytique de Paris, February 19, 2016, which Baldacci comments on.

17. Baldacci, *L'Analyse avec fin*.

18. I'm borrowing this colloquial expression from Jean-Louis Baldacci, *Dépasser les bornes: Le Paradoxe du sexuel* (Paris: PUF, 2018).

19. Julia Kristeva, *The Sense and Non-sense of Revolt: The Powers and Limits of Psychoanalysis Volume 1*, trans. Jeanine Herman (New York: Columbia University Press, 2000); *Sens et non-sens de la révolte: Pouvoirs et limites de la psychanalyse I* (Paris: Fayard, 1996); *Intimate Revolt: The Powers and Limits of Psychoanalysis Volume 2*, trans. Jeanine Herman (New York: Columbia University Press, 2002); *La Révolte intime: Pouvoirs et limites de la psychanalyse II* (Paris: Fayard, 1997).

20. One can see this now famous scene in the painting by P. A. A. Brouillet, showing a hysterical patient, Blanche Wittmann, swooning in the arms of Babinski (*A Clinical Lesson at the Salpêtrière*, 1887).

21. "But creative writers are valuable allies and their evidence is to be prized highly, for they are apt to know a whole host of things between heaven and earth [Hamlet] of which our philosophy has not yet let us dream." Sigmund Freud, "Delusions and Dreams in Jensen's *Gradiva*," in *The Standard Edition of the Complete Psychological Works of Sigmund Freud*, vol. IX, trans. James Strachey (London: Hogarth, 1959), 8; *Le Délire et les rêves dans la Gradiva de W. Jensen* (Paris: Folio Essai, 1992), 141.

22. "I have always dwelt only in the ground floor and basement of the building. . . . In that you are the conservative, I am the revolutionary. Had I only another life of work in front of me I should dare to offer even those highly born people a home in my lowly dwelling." From a letter to Binswanger, October 1936, quoted by Ernest Jones, *The Life and Work of Sigmund Freud*, vol. 3 (New York: Basic Books, 1957), 204.

23. Friedrich Nietzsche, *The Anti-Christ*, in Aaron Ridley, ed., *The Anti-Christ, Ecce Homo, Twilight of the Idols: And Other Writings*, trans. Judith Norman (Cambridge: Cambridge University Press, 2005), 4, §2.

24. Sigmund Freud, *New Introductory Lectures on Psycho-Analysis*, in *The Standard Edition of the Complete Psychological Works of Sigmund Freud*, vol. XXII, trans. James Strachey (London: Hogarth, 1964), 80; *Nouvelles conférences d'introduction à la psychanalyse* (Paris: PUF, 2004), 163.

25. Antonin Artaud, "Note pour une 'Lettre aux Balinais,'" *Tel Quel* 46 (summer 1971): 29; quoted in Kristeva, "Le Sujet en procès," *Polylogue* (Paris: Seuil, 1977), 73. Louis-Ferdinand Céline, *Death on the Installment Plan*, trans. Ralph Manheim (New York: New Directions, 1966), 40; *Mort à crédit*, in *Romans*, t. 1 (Paris: Gallimard, Pléiade, 1981), 536. Julia Kristeva, *Powers of Horror: An Essay on Abjection*, trans. Leon S. Roudiez (New York: Columbia University Press, 1982), chs. 6–11; *Pouvoirs de l'horreur, essai sur l'abjection* (Paris: Seuil, 1980), 155–248.

26. Louis-Ferdinand Céline, *Journey to the End of the Night*, trans. Ralph Manheim (New York: New Directions, 1983), 9; *Voyage au bout de la nuit*, in *Romans*, t. 1, 14.

27. Vladimir Mayakovsky, "At the Top of My Voice" (1929–1930), trans. George Reavey, in *The Bedbug and Selected Poetry*, ed. Patricia Blake (Bloomington: Indiana University Press, 1975), 225.

28. Louis Aragon, *A Wave of Dreams*, trans. Susan de Muth (London: Thin Man, 2010), 41; *La Révolution surréaliste* (December 1, 1924), reprint (Paris: J.-M. Place, 1975).

29. Louis Aragon, *Paris Peasant*, trans. Simon Watson Taylor (Boston: Exact Change, 1994), 202; *Le Paysan de Paris* (Paris: Gallimard, 1978), 27–28.

30. Louis Aragon, *Treatise on Style*, trans. Alyson Waters (Lincoln: University of Nebraska Press, 1991), 104; *Traité du style* (Paris: Gallimard, 1928), 209.

31. Ibid., 9; *Traité du style*, 13.

32. Louis Aragon, "Révélations sensationnelles," *Littérature* 13 (March 1919–August 1921): 22.

33. André Breton, *Nadja*, trans. Richard Howard (New York: Grove, 1928); *Nadja* (Paris: Gallimard, 1963).

34. Louis Aragon, *Le Libertinage*, in *Oeuvres romanesques complètes*, t. 1, ed. Daniel Bougnoux and Philippe Forest (Paris: Gallimard, Pléiade, 1997), 256 (translation by Armine Kotin Mortimer).

35. Louis Aragon, *Je n'ai jamais appris à écrire ou les Incipit* (Geneva: Skira, 1969), 48–49.

36. Rabain quotes from Kristeva, *The Sense and Non-sense of Revolt*, 134; *Sens et non-sens de la révolte*, 283.

37. Louis Aragon, *Irene's Cunt*, trans. Alexis Lykiard (London: Creation, 1996), 33; *Le Con d'Irène*, in *Oeuvres romanesques complètes*, t. 1, 444.

38. Ibid., 36; *Le Con d'Irène*, 446.

39. Ibid., 63, 66; *Le Con d'Irène*, 462, 464.

40. Freud, *The Interpretation of Dreams*, 111n1; *L'Interprétation des rêves*, 446.

41. The "true-lie" (*le mentir-vrai*) is the title of a novella (1964) and a collection (1980) by Aragon.

42. Louis Aragon, *Blanche ou l'oubli*, 474; Kristeva, *Intimate Revolt*, 218; *La Révolte intime*, 402.

43. Jean-Paul Sartre, *The Words*, trans. Bernard Frechtman (New York: Vintage, 1964, 1981), 253; *Les Mots* (Paris: Gallimard, 1964), 211.

44. See Julia Kristeva, "Motherhood According to Bellini," in *Desire in Language*, 237–70; "Maternité selon Giovanni Bellini," in *Polylogue*, 409–35.

11

Anish Kapoor

DEAR JULIA

Dear Julia, you wrote me a letter some months ago and this is not a reply. I really want just to tell you what you have done to me. You ab-jected me; once I saw the world as whole and then something happened—it fell to pieces. Not just pieces but horrid, dirty-cornered, smelly pieces, each a part of my former self, once whole, once handsome. But now look at me, I smell. Wretched dripping oozing putrid. But you know what Julia? I like myself more like this.

I. The Smell of Death

Julia, you once, at our very first meeting in Paris, proposed to me that women were afraid of or unable to make real the feminine image. That with her there is too much unconscious repressed content that always gets in the way. We discussed whether the *Venus of Willendorf* was made by a man or a woman. I was at the time showing my *Leviathan* at the Grand Palais in Paris.[1] It is of course a giant womb object, confusing inside and outside, architecture and object. A Kleinian meta-object of a kind.[2]

So is it that a man can do what women can't? In these politically polite times in which so-called authentic experience plays such an idiotic role, men can't, or can't be allowed to, make the feminine. It is, however, my mission—I must admit—to expunge, or at least to uncover, the maternal obsessions that force me to find ways to my internal feminine. This has become or perhaps always has been my essential mission. Your words in Paris, if I understood them correctly, further my mission. You see, Julia, in so many ways you drive me on. Can a man do what women can't? Is the *Venus of Willendorf* a man's idealization—is this another Venus by Botticelli? An image of idealization?[3] This feminine being is not some nice mother, she is after all Inanna, the goddess of war, death, and sex; as such she is insatiable. She is older than Gilgamesh and her horizontal power is bloody and ritualistic. She is no male bloodless blue god of the sky who never dies. Her power is juicy and of course dirty and abject. My *Dirty Corner* (figure 1) points at this.[4] Perhaps that is why it is so hated. So Julia, can a man do what a woman can't? We men have no blood. We can try . . . circumcision . . . hunting . . . paint . . . war . . . this primal ritual matter has to be made by us, it is not given. Perhaps that is a process that is the eventual idealization of Venus. Help, Julia, help.

"*Like the sorcerer who is no longer able to control the powers of the nether world whom he has called up by his spells.*"[5] Karl Marx here conjures the evil capitalist out of control but he could be talking of the artist or the shaman . . .

Menstruation is the first act of blood. We are told that women who live together menstruate together. This must be an act of solidarity. Women menstruating together will mean that together they have the power to deny sex to their partners. In early societies it is speculated that red ochre from the earth was used to cover this first ritual act of bleeding.[6] Together women formed the first exclusive groups that excluded men but gave solidarity to each other. I have no doubt these acts of solidarity were the first acts of culture. Blood as the primal stuff of community and of identity becomes the primal ritual matter. It is horizontal and is identified with the earth. Blood flows downward and into the earth. Earth takes blood and gives fruit and eventually death.

Men are outside this equation; the only way men have of entering the blood circle is by circumcision and by inducing genital bleeding. Hunting is men in blood society that they hold to exclusive rules and taboos . . . eventually their gods come to be the gods of the sky and are blue. These blue gods are bloodless and never die. This is the male turning the Red abject, bloody, dirty Goddess of the feminine horizontal into the blue vertical, bloodless, undying, male gods of the sky. This disassociated sky god sits in judgment on us but is in truth powerless since no blood is no power. This, Julia, is your feminine almighty-ness. Psychically the void vagina has the far greater power both to give and to devour; she is the one who must be conquered whatever the cost. Julia, it is precisely this abject feminine that we have to bring back to the forest of our being.[7] She is, after all, at the heart of things and answers our void longings. Hers is the dark vagina of blood beginning and of blood death. This is who I was before I was born and who I am after I die.

II. Earth

When I first left home at the age of sixteen my brother and I were sent to Israel—the land of our Jewish beginning . . . or so we were told. It was not a happy time for me. A few months later my mother came to see us in Israel and saw my unhappiness. My aunt who had a shamanic predilection suggested that earth from India the land of my birth had to be brought to Israel and spread under my bed. This way she said I would walk in my sleep back to where I was born and be well. My mother then did as she asked and earth from India was brought to Israel and scattered under my bed. This, Julia, is for me the second ritual material. With it comes the real destiny of the artist—to be the shaman. To walk in my sleep back to the land of my birth. Blood and earth are of course painting and sculpture and they are the ritual materials of psychic projection.

Figure 1. Anish Kapoor. *Dirty Corner*. 2011–2015. Mixed media. Dimensions variable. Château de Versailles 2015. Photograph: Tadzio.

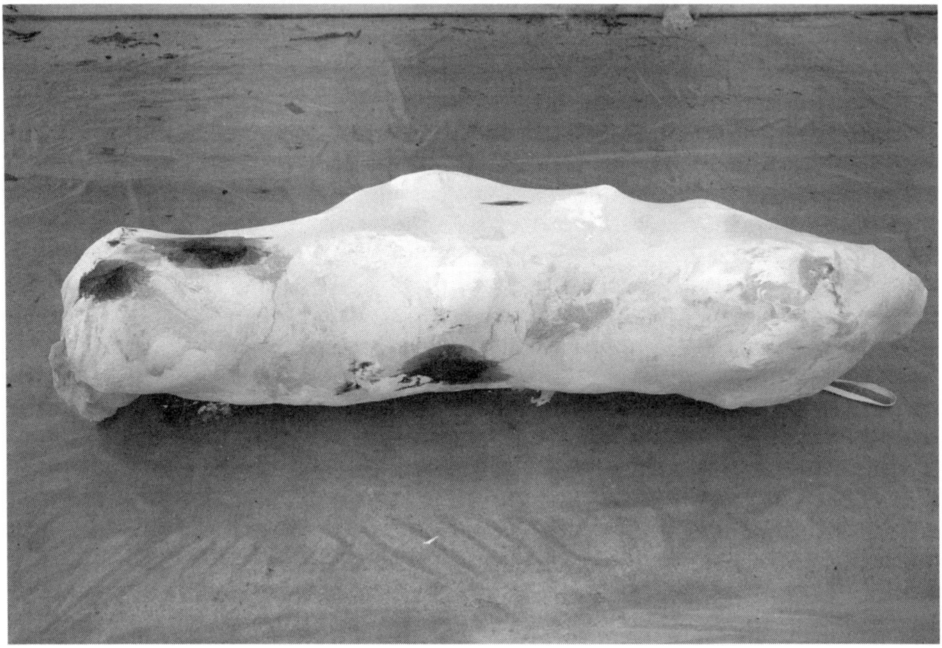

Figure 2. Anish Kapoor. *Seep*. 2016. Silicone, fiberglass, gauze. 49x92x200cm.

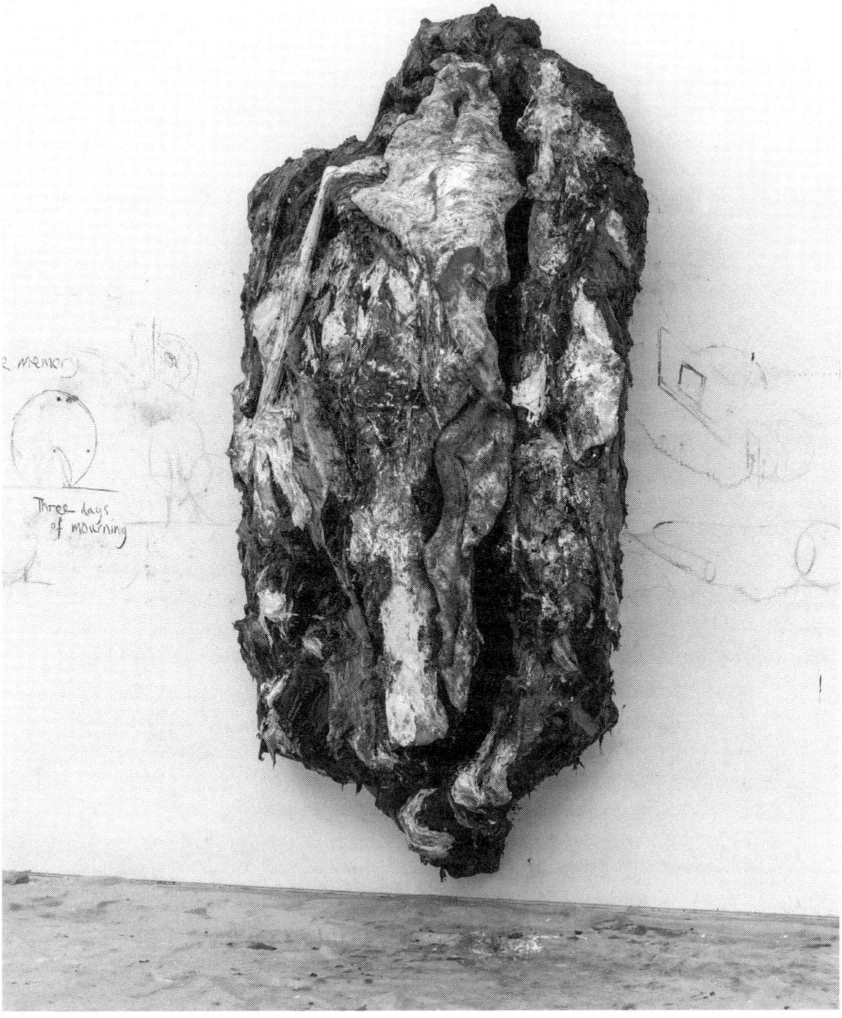

Figure 3. Anish Kapoor. *Unborn*. 2016. Silicone and pigment. 270x170x100cm.

Figure 4. Anish Kapoor. *My Red Homeland*. 2003. Wax and oil-based paint, steel arm and motor. Diameter 12m. Photograph: Nic Tenwiggenhorn.

Figure 5. Anish Kapoor. *A Blackish Fluid Excavation*. 2018. Steel and resin. 150x140x740cm. Photograph: Dave Morgan.

I the artist have little space between vaginal void, blood, and earth. I have had to make this journey or die. My red homeland formed the churning place of my origin. (See figure 4, *My Red Homeland.*) I gave birth to myself and felt able to hold that vaginal void in myself. I know this is so. So you see, Julia, I can be female; I can be the feminine. I cannot bleed but I can see her bleeding and know that in it there is terror, truth, and comfort. I am not afraid.

III. Anxiety

Julia, I am a suffering melancholic, the shadow of the mother has fallen on my soul.[8] She won't let me go. As time goes by her shadow gets longer. Like the evening sun she lies across me. I see her loss in the only way I can, as a wound; leaking blood, dripping the liquids of an eventual idealization. But idealization is sexless without *jouissance*—I think you say. I suggest that her wound—my wound—is deeply sexualized. Pained with poetic absence, lost and here ever present.

Like the great Indian mystic Rama Krishna, I call out "Oh Mother, oh Mother, why do you not hear me?" Yet she is everywhere. My callings are the wailing of a lost child.

I am a sculptor; I make the *Thing*, the lost *Thing*. The lost mother *Thing*.[9] I have discovered not surprisingly that in her essential nature she is *Really* a *No-Thing*, a *Void Thing*, at best a *Dark Thing*. Present and not present, latent in being, Botticelli's Venus emerging from the shell, both hidden and revealed. A present illusion.

An object in non-object form. She hides from me and yet I see her shadow on my soul.

Is it that *My Body* is *Your Body* . . . or *Her Body*? Or is it that your *Holes* are like my *Holes* or her *Holes* are like my *Holes*? Oh dear Julia . . .

IV. The Artist

Somehow the artist has to let herself go. I have said again and again that I have nothing to say. That what I know is of no use to anyone, especially to me. My job is to find the tools to go to what I don't know. Julia, how do I do this?

I am helpless—yet it is my only mission.

What is there before mother and father? What is there before thought?

Is this the wretched struggle for unknowable mother or is it instead an oneiric calling of the forces of the poetic unknown. How can I know what I do not know?

A feeling being is what I am and this is my only resource. The knowing in feeling is the only tool I can trust. It knows before I do.

I repeat. I have nothing to say. I speak instead of a feeling condition. Like walking into a shower and being wet.

My work eventually must be to reveal to myself my repressed matter even if in reality I can do little more than that . . .

Strangely, disobedience is my weapon. "Don't do what must be done" I say repeatedly to myself. I cannot allow my bourgeois sensibility to be the taste center of my life as an artist.

Refuse, refuse, refuse.

I have been in Zen practice for many years and in Zen there is a strong tool; it says "first idea best idea," no thought just trust. First idea it is—jump in, see what. As on the analytic couch, nonsense freewheeling. Go where it goes. As ever freewheeling is not so free—the same content is returned to before long. But in repetition small parts of what has been hidden are revealed. Small golden nuggets of "repressed" material, I do not know what I hide from myself . . . But I trick myself. My fiction beguiles me.

Oh dear Julia.

ANISH

LONDON
JULY 2019

NOTES

1. *Leviathan* (2011), P.V.C, 33.6x99.9x72.2m. Exhibited for "Monumenta 2011," Grand Palais, Paris.

2. See Julia Kristeva, *Melanie Klein*, trans. Ross Guberman (New York: Columbia University Press, 2001).

3. See Julia Kristeva, *Tales of Love*, trans. Leon S. Roudiez (New York: Columbia University Press, 1987).

4. *Dirty Corner* (2011–2015), exhibited in the gardens of Versailles in 2015. The work was attacked and vandalized three times, and on the third occasion it was covered in racist graffiti.

5. Karl Marx, *The Communist Manifesto* (London: Penguin, 1967), 85–86.

6. See Chris Knight, *Blood Relations: Menstruation and the Origins of Culture* (Yale: Yale University Press, 1995).

7. See Julia Kristeva, *Powers of Horror*, trans. Leon S. Roudiez (New York, Columbia University Press, 1982).

8. See Julia Kristeva, *Black Sun: Depression and Melancholia*, trans. Leon S. Roudiez (New York: Columbia University Press, 1989).

9. See ibid., 13–15, 40–41, 145–46.

12

Elaine P. Miller

JULIA KRISTEVA ON THE SEVERED HEAD AND OTHER MATERNAL "CAPITAL VISIONS"

I. Introduction

In 1998 Kristeva organized an exhibit as part of a series at the Louvre in Paris, entitled *Parties Prises* or "Biased Views," accompanied by a catalogue, *Visions capitales*.[1] The series was designed to give individual intellectuals complete interpretive freedom in choosing works from the museum's collection to organize a show around a theme of their choice. Kristeva's selection of the theme of decapitation, or the severed head, for her exhibit may appear baffling at first, despite the fact that numerous representations of this act can be found throughout the history of art, notably depictions of John the Baptist beheaded and Judith beheading Holofernes. There are few scholarly interpretations in English of Kristeva's work on decapitation (restricted, as it seems to be, to this one art exhibit) but, for me, the theme is central to her work.[2] The accounts of this exhibit in a few places in the popular media (including news articles and web blogs) often assume that the theme of decapitation is simply an extension of Kristeva's analysis of abjection.[3]

Abjection is Kristeva's term for the process of psychic individuation in which a child becomes a self in its own right as opposed to being "merged" with the mother as the source of all life and nurture in its earliest years. The child begins to learn its bodily boundaries as well as a kind of vocal and gestural protolanguage through the activity of either taking things into its mouth or spitting them out. This, I believe, follows Freud, for whom these oral-instinctual impulses are the oldest way of making a judgment of "good" or "bad."[4] The abject usually represents material or bodily elements that have been cast off.

Encountered in mature, conscious life, abject remnants of blood, nail clippings, hair separated from the body can cause a visceral reaction even though they are not necessarily unclean. These reminders of what has been or should have been cast away can cause horror or disgust. Ultimately, in Kristeva, our reaction is traceable to the child's archaic need to separate from the mother's body, to lose the mother but rediscover her in language. This separation is mirrored in a move away from gestural or affective toward linguistic expression. Kristeva has documented the way in which certain artworks evince a kind of abject representation, just as certain literary texts play with a breakdown in linguistic structure that mirrors the earliest protolanguage. The severed head certainly could be a representation of abjection in that it reminds us of the richness of a being whose life has been cut short through the severance of its most important appendage, while simultaneously horrifying and disgusting us in its transformation into an object.

Only three accounts that I could find draw attention to the fact that *The Severed Head* is dedicated to a positive maternal memory from childhood.[5] Kristeva begins the book with an account of her mother drawing a picture for her that depicts what her mother describes as the "fastest mode of transportation in the world," namely, thought. Image and thought, as psychically, artistically, and linguistically expressed, testify to the split from and subsequent symbolic rediscovery of the mother. They indicate the ways in which humans connect the visible and the invisible just as the image of the melting snowman that Kristeva's mother drew, its head severed by a ray of sunshine and standing next to an image of the planet Earth, depicts the ability of human thought to "travel" deftly around the world even as the body may deteriorate.[6]

I argue here that the theme of decapitation, while certainly having a strong connection to Kristeva's work on abjection, amplifies the most explicitly feminist strand of the above conception. Through it, she proposes an account of psychic development that pays tribute to the *positive* role not only of the father but also of the mother, who is not simply a figure to be left behind but whose legacy is preserved in the realm of representation. The theme of decapitation is the maternal analogue to Freud's discourse on castration and its network of cultural practices designed with the aim of "subordinating maternal power (whether historical or phantasmatic, natural or reproductive) to symbolic order as pure logical order regulating social performance, as divine Law."[7] While these practices revolve around a rejection of the mother and an identification with the father, the practice of artistic representation can also pay tribute to and resuscitate what has been abjured, making it a "maternal," feminine form of revolt.

Around the same time of composing her exhibit at the Louvre, with its accompanying intellectual catalogue, Kristeva published a novel entitled *Possessions*, a murder mystery that revolves around the death of a woman killed by decapitation.[8] The narrative follows the ensuing investigation in which the local police are aided by investigative reporter Stephanie Delacour, the narrator of the novel and a stand-in for Kristeva herself. Because of the nature of the crime, and her own philosophical bent, Stephanie muses on the theme of the severed head in a way that explicitly identifies it as a feminist theme. I consult sections of this novel to further support my claim that the theme of the severed head is a feminist one for Kristeva. I address several themes related to Kristeva's discourse on decapitation in connection with her engagement with Freud and Klein. First, decapitation refers to the violence of the child's separation from or abjection of the mother, a necessary scission that leads to normal psychic development. In conjunction with this development, decapitation also refers to the rediscovery of the mother, subsequent to scission from her, through both imagistic and conceptual representation. What is at stake is the capacity for representation per se rather than any given representation or tradition. Decapitation figures the cut that opens up toward representation, and concerns a renewed relationship to the maternal.

Finally, Kristeva distinguishes between virile phallic-symbolic depictions of beheadings, like John the Baptist, and those that symbolize a flight both away from and *with* the mother.[9] Decapitation is related to castration in symbolizing psychic development against and away from the mother. The "maternal" version of such representations signifies in addition a rediscovery of the mother in word and image. This recuperation can do justice to the mother, or it may appropriate her such that her head can be taken up by the artist "as if it was his own," forgetting her along the way.

II. Abjection and Beyond

In a short piece published posthumously, "Medusa's Head," Freud unequivocally equates decapitation with castration.[10] The terror represented and aroused by Medusa's decapitated head, surrounded by wild hair, is a depiction of the child's horror when faced for the first time with the female genitalia, most frequently that of their own mother. The terror of Medusa comes from the awareness of the absence of the penis, an absence that gets associated with the mother both because she is now seen not to possess one and because, as a result, the fantasized action whose outcome is its loss is attributed to her. In Freud's words, woman is "a being who frightens and repels because she is castrated."[11] In the case of the boy, she seems to threaten the possible loss of his own penis, and in the case of the girl, a life characterized by deprivation. Even Medusa's multiple coils of hair are "confirmation of a technical rule according to which a multiplication of penis symbols signifies castration."[12] The castration complex centers on the child's reaction to the anatomical differences between the sexes, leading them to attribute the difference to the fact of the girl's penis having been cut off. The fantasy of threatened castration from the father leads the boy away from the maternal object toward the formation of the superego, whereas for the girl it initiates the research that leads her to desire the paternal phallus.

In her book on Klein, Kristeva gives an alternative psychoanalytic interpretation of decapitation as the loss of the archaic mother, whom the child has absorbed as she goes through the depressive phase.[13] The depressive phase, occurring at around six months, follows the "paranoid-schizoid" phase in which the child is split between the libidinal and aggressive impulses prompted by its love for and frustration at the mother. In the "paranoid-schizoid position" of the first three or four months of life, the infant experiences persecutory anxiety from internal and external sources, including the fear of annihilation stemming from both the experience of birth and frustration at the periodic absence of the breast.[14]

For Klein, at six months the child is capable of experiencing the loss, not just of a part-object like the breast, but of a whole object, the mother. The loss of the breast can be seen as a preliminary version of the castration complex, where anxiety results from weaning or progressively longer separations from the mother. The "loss" of the mother gives rise to an increasingly complex psychic life developing out of the ego's defense against anxiety. "My mother is disappearing, she may never return, she is suffering, she is dead. No, this can't be, for I can revive her."[15] The feeling of guilt at possibly having lost the object through the infant's own destructiveness, accompanying the depressive position, leads to a desire for reparation, which, in tandem with the discovery of the distinction between real things and their symbols, fantasies and external reality, is at the root of the drive to represent. The depressive position interests Kristeva because it is at the origin of all thought and language, symbolization being the only way in which we can maintain a stable and satisfying relation with objects.[16] In order to function in the world we necessarily assume a position within the paternal sphere of language and law. Because of this there is no return to the intimate, fused sphere of maternal love. However, the child can and does attempt to recuperate the mother, along with other objects, in imagination and, later, in words.[17]

According to Klein, the death drive exists in the child from the moment of birth, expressing itself through destructive drives and anxiety.[18] The just emerging ego is fragile, its precarious relation to the mother, who both cares for and sometimes leaves it, causing the child to oscillate between anxiety at the fear of being abandoned and aggression in a fantasy of gaining power over the mother. In consuming or ingesting and spitting out the breast, the child enacts the process of constructing itself and the other as whole and separate objects. The breast is initially only a quasi-object from which the child separates with difficulty and anxiety; it both exists "out there" in the world and is a construction from within; involvement with it constitutes the emerging self. The breast eventually "splits," through ambivalent relation to the mother, into a "good breast" that will ultimately constitute the core of the ego and a "bad breast" that transforms into the voice inside the ego that persecutes it.[19]

At this stage of the formation of the psyche, relationships and identifications are unstable, constituting what Kristeva describes as a "fluid exchange of fragments" rather than stable object relations. Therefore "it may be more helpful to speak of an *abject* rather than of an ego or an object already there," where *ab-jection* refers to the ego expelling as much as it internalizes.[20] Abjection is a process that provokes a separation from the "maternal container," which is neither the bodily mother nor the mother with whom the child may later have symbolic interchanges, but, rather, that aspect of the mother that stands in the way of full individuation and psychic development. The processual ingesting and expelling, Kristeva claims elliptically, "challenges the sacred and the mystic as well as the difficulties posed by modern art."[21]

The depressive position occurs when the child accepts the loss of the mother and rediscovers her in fantasy in the form of a whole object. This acceptance leads to "depression," for to reach it the child must abandon the expectation of being able to control the mother's absence. This loss is "tantamount to *death*." Mastered in fantasy, it is "matricide."[22] Through separating itself from the mother, the child learns to be a self who can rediscover the mother in a new form that it creates. This creation must be perpetually renewed, repeatedly created and rediscovered, and restored through images and words.[23] In Klein it is "reparation" in relation to unconscious guilt at having "killed" the mother in fantasy.[24]

III. Rejecting and Rediscovering the Mother

In *The Severed Head* Medusa is *abject* as "primitive matrix of that archaic nondifferentiation in which there is neither subject nor object, only the sticky, slimy ab-ject."[25] Because she is abject, Medusa can only be seen beheaded; one must "cut off Medusa's head and make it into a reflection if you want to see (it), if you want to know."[26] In the same way, Kristeva argues, separation from the mother is a precondition not only of subjectivity, language, and knowledge but also of artistic representation. Indeed, all speculation is "rooted in your first triumphs over your archaic terrors."[27] This makes Medusa the "patron goddess of visionaries and artists."[28] Art allows us to "look death in the face."[29]

For Kristeva, Medusa's "primary beheading" represents—beyond Freud's limited interpretation of the castration of the woman—the image of the loss of the archaic maternal position that the child absorbs during the depressive position. The separation or beheading should be understood as a representation of the process of original separation, or "judgment" understood in its German etymology as *Ur-teil* or primary scission. Freud's analysis of a negative judgment in the psychoanalytic situation is instructive here. The "no!" of the toddler or the patient in analysis is a product of the oldest oral-instinctual drives, and reflects and perpetuates the original process by which the ego either takes things into itself ("I should like to eat this") or expels them ("I should like to spit this out").[30] *Powers of Horror* analyzes the ways in which these same oral-instinctual impulses are coded by religion and society as part of the symbolic genesis of the autonomous individual. The process of abjection or spitting out results in a preverbal precondition for subjectivity that involves the rejection of the mother. For Freud, the initial "yes I will eat this" or "no I will spit it out" constitutes the "judgment of attribution," which depends on pleasurable or unpleasurable perception: "this is good" (therefore I take it into myself) or "this is bad" (therefore I spit it out).[31] From this original, oral judgment there emerges a second level of judgment, the intellectual judgment, which involves the absence rather than the presence of a sensation. Intellectual thought depends upon on the mind's capacity to reproduce a perceived thing in the absence of the external object, independently of whether it is perceived to be good or bad. This kind of judgment, which makes a distinction between a representation that is solely within the subject and the existence or nonexistence of an object outside of it, is a "judgment of existence."[32] The Kleinian distinction between a "good breast" and a "bad breast" can be interpreted as oral "judgments of attribution" or even as the "original separation" (*Ur-teil*) itself, whereas the ability to symbolically represent through image and word constitutes intellectual judgment.

Abjection concerns not only original ego formation, however. Subsequent to original matricide and subjectivity, in ordinary symbolic life the individual may experience the return of the primally repressed, primarily the mother or the feminine in general.[33] The abject erupts into subjective life as an uncomfortable reminder of a time when "I" did not yet fully exist as a self. Experiences like the sensation on the tongue of the skin on the surface of a cooling cup of warm milk, or on the feet of the parings of fingernails, gives rise to nausea and loathing. "The abject confronts us with our earliest attempts to release the hold of the *maternal* entity even before ex-isting outside of her thanks to the autonomy of language."[34] It recalls a time when the food was not an "other" for me, when, in spitting it out, I "expel *myself,* I spit *myself* out, I abject *myself* within the same motion through which 'I' claim to establish *myself.*"[35] In spewing the abject out repeatedly, we initiate and reinforce the distinction between inside and outside that gives rise to judgment. This triumph occurs when the beginning, without a clear distinction between inside and outside, is given a name and barred, amounting to the inception of symbolic language and ultimately of subjectivity: I am not my mother, I lose her to become myself; this is my mother, I regain her as a separate being in symbolic life.[36]

In her reflections on abjection, Kristeva also reinterprets the ban on graven images after Freud, for whom it constitutes a "triumph of intellectuality over sensuality." In Kristeva the ban is an injunction that gives rise to a particular tradition, which, while barring the mother, allows for her to be recaptured in the form of representation. Leviticus 11–16 formulates the prohibition as part of a complex biblical code that stretches from dietary prohibitions to the care of the leaking, sick, decaying body, and of the corpse. Kristeva pays particular attention to Leviticus 12, dealing with the maternal body and childbirth and a direct transition from there to the decaying body, as in leprosy. This has importance for our theme because it deals with both the child's relation to the mother and the cut of circumcision, both of which will be connected to decapitation. While in earlier chapters of Leviticus impurity was linked solely to external things that could be ingested, it now becomes associated with the woman during her "time of the month" and after childbirth: "dietary abomination has thus a parallel—unless it be a foundation—in the abomination provoked by the fertilizable or fertile feminine body (menses, childbirth)."[37] The woman is impure during her parturition, and if she gives birth to a daughter, the daughter, too, is impure for two weeks, and the mother must purify herself through a burnt offering. If she gives birth to a son, he must be circumcised, the cut separating him "from maternal, feminine impurity and defilement."[38] This act of cutting carves out the son as one allied with God and at the same time carves out "the other sex, impure, defiled," aligning one with symbolic life, the other with nature. "Judaism seems to insist in symbolic fashion—the very opposite of what is 'natural'—that the identity of the speaking being (with his God) is based on the separation of the son from the mother."[39] Impurity and defilement are now "attributed to the mother and to women in general."[40]

In Leviticus the abject inscribes a scission, a "border between the sexes, a separation between feminine and masculine as foundation for the organization that is 'clean and proper'" or individual, "signifiable, legislatable, subject to law and morality."[41] The explicit transition to speech, law, and morality moves away from the defilement of the material register to a prohibition on anything that compromises symbolic unity. Representations that would substitute for divine or maternal presence threaten symbolic oneness, giving rise to the prohibition on graven images or idols.[42] This ban separates humans from god, and animal life from symbolic existence. Idol worship was associated with pagan religions, and while images were considered acceptable and even necessary for the state to retain its power over the imaginary of the people, they were forbidden in the context of the spiritual. Nevertheless, a fundamental need persisted to make the transcendent somehow accessible to ordinary people, to represent in images the invisible truth to which spirituality refers. The problem lay in finding a way to indicate the invisible through the visible while still respecting the ban on images of the divine.

Kristeva argues that the particular type of iconoclasm practiced by the Orthodox church functioned as the equivalent of Freudian negation on the level of images in allowing for an imaginary element to appear that would otherwise have remained hidden. Furthering this analogy, we recall the drawing, by Kristeva's mother, of thinking as the fastest mode of transportation, a sketch that lies "in the direct line of Byzantine icons."[43] In *The Severed Head*, the image of the Virgin Mary in the Byzantine icon refers not to the historical woman, but, rather, to the trajectory of impregnation–incarnation–divinity. The economy of the icon represents the process by which the divine is "dispensed into history," thereby becoming tangible and relatable to ordinary people.[44] Icons of Mary represent both physical birth through the maternal body and the kenosis or "self-emptying" of the "original belly" into the incarnation.[45] As such, the icon signifies both cut and representability, the full image of the divine order in the absence of the visibility of god. Along with the divine image, then, a void is inscribed, allowing it to be visually represented while still retaining its character as void. The simultaneous presentation of void and divine image is the sign of the decapitation of the divine, the invisible sacrifice itself that births the visible.[46] The cut represents the simultaneous coming into being of representation and the limitations placed on it.

The catalogue accompanying the Louvre exhibit begins with an examination of ancient skulls, particularly those that were worked, decorated, carved, and apparently worshipped. Remarkably, most though not all of the skulls are those of women, and Kristeva speculates as to why this is the case: do the skulls of women conjure up the power of fertility or are they symbols of female castration? Do they celebrate the power of women or seek to limit it? She argues that the worship of the skull, along with the consumption of the brains of victims of human sacrifice, was meant to transmit to the communicants the power of death in life—another version of the transition between the visible and the invisible. Freud famously studied the archaic practice of the totemic meal where the father is devoured by a primitive horde of brothers banded together against him, interpreting the brothers' aim as an internalization of the father's power in order to exercise his power as a collective.[47] The worship of skulls, like the totemic meal, is both a cult of consolidating power and a cult of memory. Kristeva notes that Freud's interpretation relies essentially on the privilege assigned to the phallus and the father. The skull and face, in contrast, represent "privileged stations in the loss of maternal dependence," and skull worship may have constituted a means of conjuring up "the original loss of the nurturing body that the subject hallucinates as a head that leaves it."[48] Skull worship thus commemorates not just the threat of castration by the father, which is feared, but also the original loss of the mother, which gives rise to melancholia and other bodily humors.[49] Castration effects an entrance into language, but at the expense of tactile, olfactory, auditory, and visual stimuli. Social bonds are thus founded on the child's complicity in the sacrifice of *both* parents.[50] By assimilating the power of the parents, primal desires for murder and incest are curbed in a kind of dual interiorization "in favor of representation."[51]

Although psychoanalysis traditionally identifies symbolic activity as a "paternal" function, it stems in fact from both parents. Green drew on Winnicott's analysis of transitional objects to postulate that acquiring this capacity for symbolism arises out of the establishment of a body/object "border between inside and outside" that can give rise to "a vast range of creative possibilities."[52] The space of transition is a kind of "neutral" space between existence and nonexistence and between mother and father. To Kristeva, this neutral area is a "pattern" that "carries over" from the subjective to the objective realm. She refers to the young child's relationship to its own body, a blanket, or a doll as the "'equivalents' of its needs and its dependence on the maternal body" or as "semiotics," precursory signs or imprints that augur the ability to speak.[53] Sublimated "objects" may give rise to a "new pleasure" that is other than the pleasure associated with the directly sexual, yet nonetheless libidinal.[54] By investing in one's own representations, including the representation of the mother who has abandoned it, the child emerges into image and language through depression.[55]

IV. "Masculine" and "Feminine" Decapitation

Kristeva distinguishes between diverging forms of decapitation based on sexual difference. An "appropriating" artistic "decapitation" triumphs in representation over the lost mother, repossessing her face and head.[56] Renaissance sculptor Benvenuto Cellini's towering bronze statue, *Perseus*, presents the hero sent by King Polydectus to behead the gorgon Medusa, a seemingly impossible task designed to get Perseus out of the king's way so he could marry his mother, Danae. With the help of Hermes and Athena, Perseus beheads Medusa, guiding himself by looking at her reflection in his shield since to look on her directly would turn him into stone. On the way, he rescues the beautiful Ethiopian maiden Andromeda from a sea monster. In so doing, Perseus triumphs not only over Polydectus but also over Medusa, and saves a damsel in distress while assuring his own legacy as a hero. Cellini depicts Perseus as a muscular ideal of manhood, naked and holding up the head of Medusa triumphantly, its serpent hair and streaming blood marvels of sculpture. Kristeva interprets the myth and the artistic representation as an annexation of the archaic mother, with Perseus taking her place through a daring deed that cuts him off from the maternal while at the same time appropriating her power for himself. Medusa in this depiction is both abject and potent, capable of petrifying the viewer even in death through her very repulsive nature. The theme of the male ruler overcoming or "raping" the state personified as the body of a woman was common in sixteenth-century Italian art. Historically, the statue testifies symbolically to the repressive power of the tyrant who commissioned it as a warning to the people not to resist him.

A generation later, Caravaggio, whom Kristeva calls "quick-tempered" and the "lover of cut heads," presents a "David with the incurved gaze of a beautiful young Greek" holding the severed head of Goliath, whose face is modeled on the artist's own.[57] David and Perseus are perfect embodiments of the "phallic power of the violating man."[58] David does not look at the head of Goliath in the painting. Indeed, as with Medusa or any abject, "no one looks at a severed head," for it is the "endpoint of the visible."[59] In *Possessions*, Stephanie Delacour says even more intensely of Caravaggio that he "adores" and "worships" severed heads, depicting not only David but also Judith and Holofernes, Abraham ready to sacrifice Isaac, and John the Baptist several times over.[60] Here again the severed head is the limit of the visible: "a decapitation is meant to be heard, not seen." Kristeva adds: "*All* painting ought to be heard."[61] This enigmatic phrase can be interpreted in several ways. On the one hand, of the five senses vision is the one that lends itself most foundationally to representation. At the same time, hearing is a sense perception linked to the word, which has greater precision and integrity than the image, at least in psychoanalysis. To "hear" a painting would be to "see" beyond its visible outlines to the "invisible" that it depicts, just as a thought or a word conjures up that which is absent. The outlines of painting depend on a decapitation, one that proscribes looking at the origin or the cut that made representation possible.

However, the question here is whether it might be possible to "hear" in a different way, one that would not insist on keeping the head of the mother at bay? We find Kristeva distinguishing between two types of painting: one in which there is an image, yet one overshadowed or foreclosed in favor of symbolic or linguistic meaning, and another in which there is a play between the realms of the visible and the invisible. On the one hand, there is the philosophical "eye of the soul" in Plato or the "clear and distinct" ideas of Descartes, where vision is a metaphor for thought purified of anything that might distort or deceive it. On the other hand, vision can, like hearing, be a play of absence and presence. These lie on either side of what Kristeva calls the "sacred slash."[62]

In contrast to the representations of decapitation by male painters, Artemesia Gentileschi's *Judith Slaying Holofernes* embodies a kind of shifting away from the fear of death toward a different, life-giving form of representation that Kristeva calls "giving birth" to a painting.[63] In the erotic playfulness of this kind of representation, "the artist and the viewer alternately [play] the roles of the wound and the knife."[64] In such a painting there is no absolute dichotomy between victor and vanquished. One can alternately be afraid of the image and take pleasure in it, as in a dream.[65] We can understand this kind of representation as a new kind of "hearing" of a painting, one that does not foreclose the possibility of truth being expressed in the image. *Possessions* refers to Artemesia in the language of the dream.[66] Just as in a dream, we "see" fragments—images that translate our day into enigmas and that we must strive to make sense of after the fact—so, too, does this kind of representation marry the ambiguities of image, the semiotic, the maternal, with the clear symbolism of language, without consigning the imaginary to a realm of misrepresentation and deception.[67]

In describing Artemesia, Kristeva links this new type of representation to sexual difference and a decidedly feminist stance: "what matters is that she painted as no other woman has done before or since and that she didn't paint just any old thing but a man being raped—beheaded by herself."[68] Referring to the cut both of abjection and of castration, Kristeva writes of the dualities or ambiguities between which the human lives: we are conscious, wakeful creatures but when we fall asleep, we withdraw into total darkness or relive our days in fractured dream form. As Stephanie Delacour puts it, "you're not your 'self' when you're dreaming: another 'self' wakens beneath the closed eyelids."[69] We are body and soul, man and woman, passive and active, vulnerable and violent, although the sexes are often relegated to one side of each dichotomy. When the distinctions are not kept clearly separate, the individual becomes "a stranger, a foreigner, sick, handicapped, crazy," but also "a star, an exceptional being" or "a woman."[70] In seizing hold of representation, Artemesia refuses the relegation of the feminine solely to the body, to passivity, to vulnerability; she is a "feminine genius," the ability to surpass oneself in one's field.[71] For Stephanie, "there's more than one decapitated woman in the picture galleries of our lives, but I know some whose desires are so strong they turn reality upside down and then paint it as skillfully as if they were Artemisia. And that's not an easy role to play; far from it!"[72] Thus decapitation is a condition (we are all decapitated/castrated) that can be catastrophic, but it is also one that can be transformed into an action.

Possessions presents two decapitations, one literal and one symbolic. The murder mystery at the center of the novel concerns the decapitation of Gloria, who is both a translator, therefore someone whose calling deals with understanding other people through language, and the mother of Jerry, who is deaf and communicates, at least initially, through painting and images. Stephanie calls him an "optical glutton," and his mother attempts to translate those images into meaning that is "jerky" and "shapeless."[73] His own father, now absent, was a painter. Yet Gloria the translator is unable to "translate" her own son's desires. Instead, she stands in for them, becoming, as Stephanie says, his "mother, father, grandfather, grandmother, aunt, boy cousin, girl cousin, godfather, godmother, doctor, shrink, friend, lover, matrix, womb, ears, mouth, stomach, anus, God—and that wasn't all." Jerry is her "only love," the "only one that was certain," "forever." She writes, "people say babies cling to their mothers as monkeys do. Not true. It's the opposite."[74] Gloria and Jerry's relationship is one in which "matricide" has not taken place. Jerry is unable to individuate himself, remaining fused with his mother, to his detriment. She is "possessed" by him, and is unindividuated herself.[75] Her "decapitation" is required for Jerry to become his own person. Pauline, Jerry's speech therapist, whose job is to "make others speak, not to speak herself," watches warily, giving him "more space" so he can "breathe more freely."[76] Pauline has her own issues. Quiet and unobtrusive, almost mousy, she has no real presence as a subject; she is a kind of prop or reflective surface, a "sensory mirror" for the coming into being of others.[77] At the same time, she too wants to "have Jerry all to herself," and judges Gloria for her ineptitude as a mother, especially in substituting emotional outbursts and floods of caresses for discipline and pedagogy.[78] Suffering from her own trauma, having lost a brother, Pauline confuses Jerry with her brother at the end of the novel, calling both of them "my son."[79] Submerged in her work with Jerry, Pauline is described as having a dead face: "only her mouth is really alive."[80] She is, like Samuel Beckett's main character in "Not I," a mouth without a head.[81]

It turns out that it is Pauline who decapitated Gloria, although the latter was already dead when the speech therapist cut off her head. Pauline's "hatred" serves to "cut the Gordian knot" joining mother and son, clearly what this kind of decapitation signifies.[82] Her act frees not only Jerry but also herself. Kristeva-as-Stephanie muses that "Pauline is indispensable . . . whatever she certainly did do, this now allows life to go on after death."[83] As she disposes of the rest of the body in the trash, Pauline incants to herself, "I cut myself off from her, sever myself from the mother who drowns her son, detach myself from the corpse that I was but am no longer."[84] Significantly, Pauline represents speech and language, whereas Gloria, though a translator, only communicated with her son in images. Jerry is deaf; he and Gloria could not "hear" each other, yet Pauline gives him a way to hear. As Krentz argues, Kristeva's concept of the abject always concerns a negative relation to language, which he articulates in terms of the experience of the deaf, for what is abject cannot be expressed in words.[85] As words without body, Pauline balances out what Gloria represents, a body without a head.

However, "language" has perhaps the most transformative power when it takes a written or creative form. Writing or creating artistically is an activity that constructs an object of its own, a space that might best be described as "transitional" in Winnicott's sense, yet Kristeva views this transitional phase not just in terms of the individual but as part of a critique of patriarchal culture. As Margaroni puts it, in thematizing decapitation Kristeva foregrounds "the woman-theorist's concern with the 'capital force' of patriarchal history, which divorces women's existence in the symbolic from their sensory/bodily experience."[86] In our focus, here, Gloria, whose existence with Jerry is submerged in the sensory, and Pauline, who speaks and helps others speak but does not fully exist as a subject herself, represent the two extremes of this dichotomy.

V. Conclusion

The specifically feminist interpretation I develop here can be pulled out of Kristeva's texts, but it takes some doing, and one wonders whether readers like me simply will Kristeva to be more of a feminist than she really is. The argument made here that the discourse on decapitation represents Kristeva's feminist account of the child's possible positive relation to the mother is never directly expressed by the author herself. Certain questions arise for feminists in reading Kristeva's oeuvre. Is the initially unconscious but eventually conscious relation to the mother equivalent to a real relation of recognition to a female other? Can a woman ever have a fully subjective relation to her own mother? Can there be a feminism that is political rather than personal since even the feminist account that can be culled from Kristeva's work seems to concern only individual development? Does artistic representation constitute a positive relation to the abjected mother?

This reading has followed the Kristevan account of the historical "severance" of woman's "head" from her body, which, symbolically speaking, marks an appropriation of maternal power to masculine ends. Historically, this kind of "decapitation" might depict the conception of successful women as "heads" that strive to substitute for the phallus, where the feminine is rendered wounded and decapitated, "the threatening antithesis of the phallus."[87] Another threatening form of decapitation sees woman as a mute body to be used or viewed but not intellectually engaged. Finally, a "decapitation of women" represents her as one who chatters endlessly, a mouth without a body that talks but has nothing to say.[88] All of these versions of decapitation may be turned around, in the most positive version of the Kristevan account, into the effort to find "a *kind of face* that has not yet found its *face*, that never will, but that never stops seeking a thousand and one ways of seeing."[89] One may imagistically represent or "write out" a decapitation, thereby effecting a rebirth that provides an alternative to the tradition where only the complete sacrifice of the maternal body gives rise to paternal language.

Elaine P. Miller

Miami University
October 2018

NOTES

1. Julia Kristeva, *Visions capitales: Arts et rituels de la décapitation* (Paris: Réunion des Musées Nationaux, 1998); *The Severed Head: Capital Visions*, trans. Jody Gladding (New York: Columbia University Press, 2012).

2. See Maria Margaroni, "Decapitation Impossible: The Hundred Heads of Julia Kristeva," in Robin Truth Goodman, ed., *Literature and the Development of Feminist Theory* (Cambridge: Cambridge University Press, 2015); Alison Jasper, "Taking Sides on Severed Heads: Kristeva at the Louvre," *Text Matters: A Journal of Theory, Literature, and Culture* 4, no. 4 (2014); Martha Reineke, *Intimate Domain: Desire, Trauma, and Mimetic Theory* (East Lansing: Michigan State Press, 2014); *Journal for French and Francophone Philosophy* 21, no. 1 (2013) (publishing the roundtable at the 2012 Kristeva Circle meeting). See also Elaine Miller, *Head Cases: Julia Kristeva on Philosophy and Art in Depressed Times* (New York: Columbia University Press, 2014).

3. Hughes writes that the exhibit "builds on [Kristeva's] earlier work on the corpse." Kathryn Hughes, "The Severed Head by Julia Kristeva—Review," *Guardian*, April 6, 2012. Weinberg writes that "the fear of death, which the sight of a severed head evokes, is associated by Kristeva with the notion of the abject." Grazia Sumeli Weinberg, "The Severed Head, Capital Visions," *Issues in English Studies in Southern Africa* 19, no. 1 (2014): 142–43. R. H. Rossin, "Kristeva's Top-Down Critique," *The Brooklyn Rail*, January 2, 2012, does justice to the full range of themes.

4. Sigmund Freud, "Negation," in *The Standard Edition of the Complete Psychological Works of Sigmund Freud*, vol. XIX, trans. James Strachey (London: Hogarth, 1961), 237.

5. Noëlle McAfee, "Review of Julia Kristeva's The Severed Head," https://www.academia.edu/5892849/Review_of_Julia_Kristevas_The_Severed_Head. Pleshette DeArmitt, "Julia Kristeva's The Severed Head," *Journal of French and Francophone Literature* 21, no. 1 (2013). Jasper, "Taking Sides on Severed Heads."

6. See DeArmitt, "Julia Kristeva's The Severed Head," 116–19. Kristeva, *The Severed Head*, 2, 4–6, 11, 12, 14, 16, 17.

7. Julia Kristeva, *Powers of Horror*, trans. Leon S. Roudiez (New York: Columbia University Press, 1982), 91.

8. Julia Kristeva, *Possessions*, trans. Barbara Bray (New York: Columbia University Press, 1998).

9. Kristeva, *The Severed Head*, 130–31.

10. Sigmund Freud, "Medusa's Head," in *The Standard Edition of the Complete Psychological Works of Sigmund Freud*, vol. XVIII, trans. James Strachey (London: Hogarth, 1955).

11. Ibid., 274.

12. Ibid., 273.

13. Julia Kristeva, *Melanie Klein*, trans. Ross Guberman (New York: Columbia University Press, 2001), 130 (volume 2 of the "female genius" trilogy).

14. Melanie Klein, *Envy and Gratitude and Other Works 1946–63* (London: Hogarth, 1975), 61–62.

15. Ibid., 75. Kristeva specifies that this revival or retrieval takes place through language. See Julia Kristeva, *Black Sun: Depression and Melancholia*, trans. Leon S. Roudiez (New York: Columbia University Press, 1989), 43.

16. Kristeva, *Melanie Klein*, 73.

17. Kristeva, *The Severed Head*, 5.

18. Kristeva, *Melanie Klein*, 61.

19. Ibid., 67. See also Klein, *Envy and Gratitude*, 180–90.

20. Ibid., 72.

21. Ibid., 73.

22. Ibid., 130.
23. Ibid., 131.
24. Klein, *Envy and Gratitude*, 194.
25. Kristeva, *The Severed Head*, 31.
26. Ibid., 33.
27. Ibid.
28. Kristeva, *The Severed Head*, 33.
29. Kristeva, *Possessions*, 9.
30. Freud, "Negation," 237.
31. Ibid.
32. Ibid.
33. Kristeva, *The Severed Head*, 82.
34. Kristeva, *Powers of Horror*, 13.
35. Ibid., 3.
36. Ibid., 61.
37. Ibid., 100.
38. Ibid., 99.
39. Ibid., 100.
40. Ibid.
41. Ibid.
42. Ibid., 104.
43. Kristeva, *The Severed Head*, 3.
44. Ibid., 54.
45. Ibid., 53.
46. Ibid., 55.
47. Sigmund Freud, *Totem and Taboo*, in *The Standard Edition of the Complete Psychological Works of Sigmund Freud*, vol. XIII, trans. James Strachey (London: Hogarth, 1955).
48. Kristeva, *The Severed Head*, 16.
49. Ibid., 17.
50. Ibid., 18.
51. Ibid., 19.
52. André Green, *The Work of the Negative*, trans. Andrew Weller (London: Free Association Press, 1999), 246.
53. Kristeva, *The Severed Head*, 5.
54. Green, *The Work of the Negative*, 238.
55. Kristeva, *The Severed Head*, 6.
56. Ibid., 35.
57. Ibid., 88.
58. Ibid., 78.
59. Ibid., 89.
60. Kristeva, *Possessions*, 7.
61. Ibid., 8.
62. Kristeva, *The Severed Head*, 87.
63. Ibid., 78.
64. Ibid., 84.
65. Ibid., 87.
66. Kristeva, *Possessions*, 128.
67. Juliana De Nooy describes this new "feminine" version of revolt as a possession by language. It involves "a dissolving of the self as one moves from a capacity for signification in one language towards a capacity for signification in another language." Juliana De Nooy, "How to Keep Your Head When All About You Are Losing Theirs: Translating Possession Into Revolt," in John Lechte and Mary Zournazi, eds., *The Kristeva Critical Reader* (Edinburgh: Edinburgh University Press, 2003), 122.

68. Kristeva, *Possessions*, 129.
69. Ibid., 127.
70. Kristeva, *The Severed Head*, 86.
71. Ibid., 129. See also Julia Kristeva, "Is There a Feminine Genius?" *Critical Theory* 30, no. 3 (2004): 493–504.
72. Kristeva, *Possessions*, 132.
73. Ibid., 46.
74. Ibid., 47.
75. Ibid., 51.
76. Ibid., 49–50.
77. Ibid., 197.
78. Ibid., 198.
79. Ibid., 201.
80. Ibid., 208.
81. Samuel Beckett, "Not I," *Samuel Beckett Festival* (New York: Repertory Theater of Lincoln Center, 22 November 1972).
82. Kristeva, *Possessions*, 202.
83. Ibid., 208.
84. Ibid., 202.
85. Christopher Krentz, *Writing Deafness: The Hearing Line in Nineteenth-Century American Literature* (Chapel Hill: University of North Carolina Press, 2007), 105. Krentz uses Kristeva's concept of the abject to discuss the depiction of the deaf in nineteenth-century American literature.
86. Margaroni, "Decapitation Impossible," 99.
87. Julia Kristeva, *The Sense and Non-sense of Revolt: The Powers and Limits of Psychoanalysis Volume 1*, trans. Jeanine Herman (New York: Columbia University Press, 2000), 123.
88. Cixous describes decapitation as a threat that emerges within patriarchal culture, calling it the inferior substitute accorded to feminine subjectivity that lends her only a muted entrance into history and the symbolic order. Hélène Cixous, "Castration or Decapitation?" *Signs* 7, no. 1 (1981): 42.
89. Kristeva, *The Severed Head*, 127.

13

Carin Franzén

AN ANTIDOTE TO THE CRISIS OF CONTEMPORARY CULTURE: REREADING KRISTEVA ON DURAS

Kristeva's linguistic and psychoanalytic theory of the subject in process, formulated for the first time in *Sémiotikè* (1969), was a game-changing introduction of the body and sexual difference into the field of aesthetics and literary studies.[1] Although Kristeva has never described her work as feminist, her reflections on the subject and its symbolic practices are still fundamental references in an ongoing feminist debate about sexual and political identities. Indeed, Kristeva's idea of the subject in process, putting every linguistic and sexual identity into a movement of "destruction and construction," as she writes in her doctoral thesis (published as *La Révolution du langage poétique* in 1974), has regained actuality in many ways.[2] She also continually elaborates her work by following the "pulse of time," as the title of one of her more recent books reads in French (*Pulsions du temps*), each text opening the question of time—the time of history as well as the time of the subject.[3]

Kristeva's theoretical foundations can be derived from her linguistic and psychoanalytic training, which made her move beyond the trends of structuralism in the 1960s and 1970s towards the subject: its body as well as its history. Her way of analyzing subjectivity and history through the subject's discourse—especially its literary and aesthetic practices—continues to offer a specific approach to our own time's "social structures and their ideological, coercive, and necrophilic manifestations."[4] Moreover, her work is still prompted by an endeavor to investigate the potentialities for a revolutionary art and literature in our contemporary society. However, from the turn of the century it has become more and more obvious that the modern subject has entered a new era that could be described in terms of a polarization between, on the one hand, neoliberal demands of flexibility and performance, resulting in an increasing rate of anxiety and depression, and, on the other, different forms of destructive radicalization.[5] Kristeva puts it in this way: "disillusioned nihilism, on one hand, and fundamentalist transcendentalism, on the other."[6] With this new crisis of the modern subject in mind, it is time to revisit some of Kristeva's seminal and foundational notions in order to test their relevance for contemporary discussions about subjectivity and its aesthetic practices. After considering some of her notions of subject formation and the threats to the psyche of the dominant forms of neoliberal subjectivity, I propose to reread Kristeva on Marguerite Duras as an exemplar of an art of resistance in relation to just these threats. I will do this by focusing on the aesthetic value of Duras's writing, rather than the psychical topic of feminine melancholy elaborated by Kristeva in *Black Sun*.[7]

I. A Subject in Crisis

If the modern subject has been in crisis at least since the traumatic events of the twentieth century, it seems that it has taken a new direction in our age, which, more urgently than before, also defies a critical tradition based on humanist values. This can be sensed in new theories that are looking for transhuman and posthuman perspectives in order to deconstruct what is felt to be an obsolete "occidental transcendental system of meaning production" in the face of new technologies.[8] However, the changes also appear in respect of neoliberalism and global capitalism, provoking what Ehrenberg calls a "weariness of being oneself."[9] This weariness can be derived from the modification of a previous notion of the subject as autonomous and rational into a neoliberal subject whose docility and tractability join together in constituting, as Malabou puts it, "a new structural norm that functions immediately to exclude" the one who is not flexible enough.[10] Malabou refers to the seminal study of sociologists Boltanski and Chiapello, *The New Spirit of Capitalism* (which first appeared in France in 1999), which analyzes the development of neoliberalism.[11] The authors argue that neoliberal ideology has consequences not only for the contemporary subject but also for the possibility of a critical stance towards an engulfing business culture that seems to absorb every resistance by new and subtle methods of exploitation such as project-based forms of organization demanding flexibility and adaptability at the cost of material and psychological security.

In order to remedy this new form of subjective submission in the era of neoliberalism and global capitalism, Malabou calls for a materialist philosophy that does not neglect current neurobiology and the role of the brain. It is interesting to note, in this respect, that Kristeva's work is based on a definition of the subject as both biologically *and* symbolically constituted. Throughout her writings, she has maintained the *heterogeneity* of the subject, reducing it to neither language nor biology. The problem today, however, seems to be less that of the reticence of the human sciences in the face of the development of neuroscience than the inability of critical theory to counter a neoliberal discourse that emphasizes individual flexibility in such a way that the only resistance that seems to be left is depression, "the major personal unhappiness of our time," as Ehrenberg states.[12] Alternatively, as Kristeva puts it in the early 1990s in a book about new maladies of the soul: "Today's men and women—who are stress-ridden and eager to achieve, to spend money, have fun, and die—dispense with the representation of their experience that we call psychic life. Actions and their imminent abandonment have replaced the interpretation of meaning."[13]

In the following, I assess Kristeva's way of dealing with the decline of the *symbolic* that seems to be one of the salient features of our postmodern and global capitalist societies. I propose her theory of "the subject in process" for the development of a critical practice and for a sense of revolt that is needed in every societal order that needs to change the "forces of enslavement" (Deleuze) into more liberating ones.[14] I do this, first, by focusing on Kristeva's use of the concept of the symbolic, taking as my point of departure a feminist debate on this concept that began in the late 1990s. I then turn to Kristeva's writing on aesthetics and literature to underline what I consider to be her original contribution to a new path for a subject that has become weary of itself.

II. Social or Symbolic

In an interview following the publication of her doctoral thesis in 1974, Kristeva states that her idea of the subject in process is based on the conviction that identity cannot be assessed outside of language and its "structuring limit," which she labels *symbolic*, and which in its turn cannot be separated from what she calls a "semiotic and not yet signifying destructive and violent *pulsion* against the symbolic system."[15] Subjectivity is formed by the contradiction of these two modalities, and thus depends both on a given sociosymbolic order and on corporeality. Three decades later, after receiving the Norwegian Holberg Prize in 2004, she posits that the subject she addresses in her writing, including her novels, "still in my view is a 'subject in process,' meaning a 'self-traveler.'"[16] The French term that she now uses to designate the subject in process is "*se voyage*," which she also used as the title of her autobiography, *Je me voyage*, translated in this volume. This poetic title is difficult to translate, reflecting not only the passage between languages and disciplines but also psychic displacement, the continuous migration of thoughts and affects. This movement is essential in understanding Kristeva's theory of the subject and, more generally, her view on aesthetics.

Nonetheless, starting with Butler's *Gender Trouble* in 1990, a critique has been addressed to Kristeva's conception of the subject and its symbolic and semiotic constitution: that it depends "upon the stability and reproduction of precisely the paternal law that she seeks to displace."[17] The main argument that Butler raises is that Kristeva's psychoanalytic theory does not relate the symbolic to the sociological, historical, and political context of power relations clearly enough. Thus, the concept of the symbolic—that Butler, in the final analysis, derives from Lacan—risks internalizing heterosexual norms and, by this gesture, becomes naturalized.

Butler acknowledges that the Lacanian symbolic has been of importance for rethinking sexuality in terms of linguistic positions, but also "that the symbolic itself is the sedimentation of social practices" that "a queer poststructuralism of the psyche" is precisely defying.[18] However, it seems to me that the Lacanian symbolic is a condition for sociality rather than a construction *après coup* that gives it legitimation. As he says in his first presentation of the term in 1953, the symbolic is one of the three delimited and foundational registers of "human reality."[19] Alongside what he calls the real and the imaginary, the Lacanian symbolic is presented as a specific function that cannot be reduced to a sign. The symbolic functions between humans before signification takes place—it has an "interhuman function."[20] Kristeva uses this definition of the symbolic in the 1970s when she argues that the symbolic functions are a "structuring limit" to which social norms are answers that change over time. However, in this first period of her writing, the symbolic also appears as an aspect of the signifying practice that cannot be separated from its corporeal double that is designated by the term *the semiotic*. Thus, if the symbolic is a presupposition in Kristeva's psychoanalytic theory of the subject, the semiotic constitutes a critical assessment of both Freud's and Lacan's theories. This is of course also noted by Butler, but since she equates the symbolic with the social she puts in doubt the subversive force of Kristeva's theory: "If the semiotic promotes the possibility of the subversion, displacement, or disruption of the paternal law, what meanings can those terms have if the Symbolic always reasserts its hegemony?"[21] However, if the problem for today's subjects is not that the symbolic "reasserts its hegemony," but is, as Malabou points out, a new structural norm based on "the absence of clear and localized conflict, and the necessity of being mobile," it may be that the very possibility of subversion must be reinvented.[22] If this is so, it could also be argued that Kristeva's use of the symbolic and the semiotic points to such a reinvention.

What Kristeva in the 1970s called a *practice* in the sense of a *destabilization* of hegemony is linked to the dialectical work of the semiotic and the symbolic. First, the two terms cannot be separated in the way Butler does in her refutation of what she calls Kristeva's "body politics" because they are the *precondition* for every subversive strategy. With Kristeva, "the contradiction inherent in the signifying process is the precondition of all practice."[23] Furthermore, the assumption in her theory of the subject in process is not heterosexuality, as Butler seems to argue, but, rather, the contradiction of the symbolic and the semiotic in every subject—a subject that is in need of permanent analysis in order to undo enslaving forces that change form with time and society. This is why I contend that Kristeva's theory still offers a critical and political practice, which can be sensed in her responses to the debates about the relation between gender and sexuality that followed Butler's book on gender trouble.

It is true that the concept of gender has never been of great importance in Kristeva's work. However, in her later works she deploys the psychoanalytic notion of the subject as a relational being *before* any sexual identity has been (per)formed. She also underlines that desire transforms biological sex into a gender that is not necessarily normative. To the contrary, this transformation is an *alchemy* that makes of a desiring subject "an incommensurable singularity (a 'gender'—to deconstruct, indefinitely—and belonging to this incommensurable singularity itself)."[24] Thus, for Kristeva, the question is not how or if sexuality and sexual norms are determined by culture (say, by paternal law or heteronormativity) but, rather, how to revitalize the contradiction inherent in every subject between what she introduced as the semiotic and the symbolic in her early work, and which in later works she detects as an incommensurable singularity at the heart of every desiring subject.

When Butler assesses the semiotic as a concept that was made "as a way of undoing" the symbolic, she fails to see that it is the dialectical process between these two modalities that constitutes "a way of undoing" petrified forms of being and thinking.[25] She even maintains that it is this dialectical relationship that prevents Kristeva's "strategy of subversion" from becoming "a sustained political practice."[26] However, the subversive strategies discernible in Kristeva's readings of different aesthetic experiences, from her analysis of the French literary avant-garde via early modern artists such as Giotto and Bellini to mystics such as Teresa of Avila, to name a few, are all constituted by singular ways of declining the one with the other—a semiotic sexual corporeality with a symbolic form and thought.

III. Impasses of Subversion

It could be that it is this very dialectical process that is becoming more and more difficult for a neoliberal subject to conjugate into an experience that does not submit to the demands of unlimited flexibility. All the more so if it is true that we are living a "waning of critique" as an effect of global capitalism and its power to absorb all resistances of sorts into a question of marketing.[27] Simply put, if global capitalism is the new normalizing world order, how is social and aesthetic subversion possible? To answer this question, I will reassess Kristeva's theory of the subject in relation to the contemporary (in)capacity for revolt.

Kristeva began to develop her critical perspectives on the modern subject by analyzing the "revolution in poetic language," while later works from the 1990s underline that the very term revolt cannot be reduced to a political meaning.[28] Although there is a clear continuity between the experience of revolt that she wants to revitalize and her idea of the signifying process in the 1970s, she argues in *The Sense and Non-sense of Revolt* that the current political state is characterized by a lack of revolt.[29] Her view on contemporary Western subjectivity parallels what, in the same period, Boltanski and Chiapello diagnosed as an incorporation of artistic critique into global capitalism by subordinating it to profit-making.[30] Kristeva's response in the 1990s to these new forms of subjectivity, together with the lack of revolt that becomes manifest, consists of a return to the notion of sexual difference as a precondition for an ongoing "re-creation" of the subject rather than a biological determination of specific gender identities. Since her works on the contradictions of the symbolic and the semiotic, her preoccupation has been with highlighting and mobilizing "the bi-sexuality of sexual difference" as a universal experience that nevertheless determines each subject's singularity.[31] Arguably, it is this singularity that has come to fail in a neoliberal society that demands a subjective flexibility without limits. At any rate, Kristeva talks of "pushing the need for the universal *and* the need for singularity to the limit in each individual, making this simultaneous movement the source of both thought and language."[32] If this subversive movement stops, the risk is high for both "repressive returns to systems foregrounding the needs of identity" and a humanity governed by "monetary and humanitarian indifference."[33]

When revolt and opposition are no longer options in a world that has become dominated by a new spirit of capitalism, it seems that a new kind of genius is demanded, as Malabou points out: "Indeed, what flexibility lacks is the resource of giving form, the power to create, to invent or even to erase an impression, the power to style. Flexibility is plasticity minus its genius."[34] Thus, the question is from where does the subject gain this genius power to counteract the demands of flexibility and the symbolic void of global capitalism? Kristeva's own readings of what she calls "female genius" offer some interesting suggestions as to how a resistance can be articulated today.

IV. Genius Resistance

In a globalized and increasingly uniform world there seems to be a problem in giving expression to singular experiences and interpretations of meaning. It is against this "normalizing order" and its crisis of signification and subjectivity that Kristeva returns to three women from the past century—Hannah Arendt, Melanie Klein, and Colette—who present three different fields of seminal importance for Kristeva's own work: philosophy, psychoanalysis, and literature. In her "female genius" trilogy, Kristeva recuperates the term genius from its romantic and male-dominated tradition, not only by describing these women's importance for the twentieth century's philosophical, political, and cultural life but also by highlighting the importance of the *feminine* within these traditions. Their *female genius* is presented here as a form of subjectivity that is open to sexual difference and able to give it a specific articulation that "disrupts the coherence of any postulation of identity."[35]

Kristeva's reading of these three women's work and lives implies a reassessment of the psychoanalytic theory of the Oedipus complex. In the concluding chapter of the trilogy, she makes clear that there is a "feminine specificity" to be found in both sexes but declined in different ways in each subject.[36] Her interest in the feminine in the three volumes of 1999–2002 is not concerned, then, with a search for a particular feminine identity. On the contrary, the purpose is to "transcend the dichotomy of the sexes" by maintaining that it is the subject's capacity to go beyond its biological and cultural conditions that defines its genius.[37]

If the Kristevan theory of the subject in process began as a critique of "the 'bourgeois mentality' and 'bourgeois morality' closely associated with the critique of capitalism since the mid-nineteenth century,"[38] in recent times it has been oriented more towards a preoccupation with the writing and thinking subject's capacity to recreate meaning when and where it has become petrified or has vanished. The attention paid to a feminine specificity at the turn of the century could therefore be seen as an example of how Kristeva revitalizes the critical potentiality of her own theory of the subject. This revitalization can be sensed in her recuperation of the notion of genius from Kant, who defines it as "the talent (natural endowment) that gives the rule to art."[39] With Kristeva, this talent cannot be imitated—it is singularity that "in itself is without common measure."[40] A genius talent can then be said to operate when a subject transcends the constraints that form its subjectivity. As regards, sexuality and gender, Kristeva concludes: "I would like to think that every subject invents in its private life a specific sex. It is there that one's genius resides, which is quite simply one's creativity."[41] With this conclusion in mind, I will take my reflection on Kristeva's relevance for contemporary discussions about subjectivity and its aesthetic practices a step further by arguing that the French novelist Marguerite Duras can be reread as precisely a kind of feminine genius that has the capacity for transforming writing into both a resistance against global capitalism and a defense of psychic space when "the spirit of 'performance'" seems to be the only thing that counts.[42]

V. Reinventing Psychic Experience

Kristeva's theory of feminine genius is related to her revaluation of the psychoanalytic theory of the maternal function. Her book on Klein is a homage to the analyst's original assessment of the importance of the first relation between mother and child.[43] This notion of pre-oedipal experience in every speaking subject is seminal in understanding Kristeva's gendering of both Freud's and Lacan's theories of the formation of subjectivity, in which both stress the importance of the paternal function. Kristeva's study on depression and melancholia in *Black Sun* elaborates the modification through an analysis of art and literature.[44] The general idea is that creativity is about the capacity for turning the affective attachment to the mother into signs and meaning. Thus, if the condition for every "interhuman function" is the symbolic—language and culture—according to Lacan, Kristeva introduces a precondition for this assumption.[45] More precisely, when Lacan talks about the symbolic as the introduction of a constitutive lack in the formation of the subject that moves its desire, Kristeva puts the emphasis on the subject's work of transposing and translating this lack into words as an "*impossible mourning for the maternal object*."[46] Her development of Klein's theory and, more generally, the reintroduction of the maternal function and the importance of the pre-oedipal experience for the subject in process, is fundamental to her endeavor to make room for sexual difference in the fields of aesthetics and literary studies as well as in clinical and critical practice. This is also Kristeva's major contribution to what, in her classical essay on motherhood, "Stabat Mater," she called "*herethics*" (*l'héréthique*), highlighting the importance not only of accepting the law but also of coming to terms with the affective and bodily experiences disrupting the symbolic, which can become renewed in this way.[47] This *herethical* perspective can be used to revisit Kristeva's reading of Duras in *Black Sun*. Instead of focusing on feminine melancholia (Kristeva's topic in this book), my aim is to show how Duras's writing can be linked to a culture of revolt that could counteract dominant forms of neoliberal subjectivity by functioning as a potential resistance to dispensing with the "experience that we call psychic life," as demanded by the new spirit of capitalism.[48]

I suggest that Duras's aesthetics, which "leads us to X-ray our madness" according to Kristeva, belongs to a tradition of revolt through a specific arrangement of an experience of something ineffable within aesthetic practices.[49] As Kristeva has pointed out, Duras's writing could be connected to an incapacity for "working out the loss within the psyche" that, in the final analysis, reveals itself to be "the real that does not lend itself to signification."[50] One main point in *Black Sun*, however, is that if the melancholic refuses to translate the loss it can nevertheless be approached "through melody, rhythm, semantic polyvalency, the so-called poetic form, which decomposes and recomposes signs."[51] Furthermore, to be faithful to this singular experience in poetic form can be to resist the incorporation of artistic critique by the new spirit of capitalism that undermines every potential resistance. At any rate, when Duras writes in her autobiographical novel, *The Lover*, "that there seem to be no more barriers, that writing seems at a loss for somewhere to hide, to be written, to be read," she points to the need for a protection of psychic space.[52] I take this statement to be key for assessing the spirit of revolt in Duras's modernist aesthetics, despite or, rather, thanks to what Kristeva calls the author's "faithfulness to madness."[53] I propose a reading in which this experience is connected to a writing that can offer resistance to the actual commodification of artistic critique and contemporary aesthetics by first returning to the cultural context where Duras's writing took form.

VI. A Crisis of Signification

The subjective and social crises emerging after the catastrophes and traumas in the last century also affected the means of representation. As Renata Salecl points out, "Europeans especially felt anguish in regard to their existence, since some perceived that they were entering times of meaninglessness."[54] In *Black Sun* Kristeva describes the post–World War period as marked by a "crisis of signification."[55] This description is especially relevant for Duras's writing, which Kristeva also describes as an "aesthetics of awkwardness" and a "noncathartic literature" that nevertheless transforms a subjective narration into poetic form and reflections on the impossibility of "the true story" of one's life.[56]

In Duras's work, the "crisis of signification" can be sensed in her change of literary style from a realistic narration to her famous minimalism that, after her publication of *Moderato cantabile* in 1958, associated her with the *nouveau roman* (an association she later dismissed).[57] Kristeva's somewhat provocative description of Duras's "stylistic awkwardness" in fact correlates with a positive review in *Libération* by Roy, who describes the novel as "excelling in the incomplete."[58] It is also interesting to note that in this period Duras changed her publisher from Gallimard to Les Éditions de Minuit, reclaiming what she called "the non-commerciality" of her books.[59] This aesthetic and political attitude contrasts with the "affected rhetoric of literature" that could be exemplified by Beauvoir's novels, and that Duras openly disliked insofar as "their approach to writing was radically different," as her biographer points out.[60] We have to do with a new aesthetic practice here of which Robbe-Grillet is reported to have said (in an interview with Adler) that he saw in it "a wonderful subversive strength at the very heart of the narrative."[61] This "subversive strength" goes hand in hand with Duras's reflections on her own writing. She has on various occasions underlined that literature must be set free from moral constraints, not in the name of individual freedom but in response to a demand that seems to come from the writing practice itself. In a short text from the 1980s, "Solitude," published in the French film magazine *Cahiers du Cinéma* and reprinted in *Green Eyes*, Duras describes the writing of a book as a kind of submission in the sense that it has a life of its own and, furthermore, a life that is unknown. The writer can only be subject to its force, which she calls "this wonderful misery."[62] A "misery" that Duras in the same context describes as a kind of fundamental unawareness—"You don't know. You know nothing about what you're doing," a statement that can be interpreted as an openness towards the ineffable. As Adler puts it: "If Marguerite never gave up writing, it was because she believed that, beyond the words she used, she could arrive at another indescribable [*indicible*] reality."[63]

This search for something beyond the symbolic could also explain the way in which Duras talks about the integrity of the creative process itself underlining the noncommercial aspects of her books. As a writer who is highly involved in her books' editorial and commercial business, these reflections seem to be more a matter of style than a real choice to stand outside the market. However, instead of reducing Duras's approach to writing to a vain gesture or even mannerism, I suggest it be read as a critical practice that is a way of assigning literature an intrinsic value resisting commodification.[64] For Duras, the becoming of a literary text is not negotiable because writing for her is tied to the unknown. If the becoming of a book could be predicted, the act of writing would not be necessary, or, as she explicitly puts it in reflecting on her writing: "it's impossible to speak to someone about a book one has written, and especially about a book one is writing."[65] If this sounds like a romantic or mystical view of literature, it can nonetheless be understood as a way of approaching the impossible mourning at the heart of the subject that Kristeva, in her analysis, sees as a drama for everyone. "Even the soundest among us know just the same that a firm identity remains a fiction. Suffering, in Duras's work, in a mannered way and with empty words evokes that impossible mourning."[66] This impossibility is evoked by the protagonist in Duras's novel *The Ravishing of Lol*

Stein (1964) as the absence of a unique word—a word that could precisely tell the "true story" of the protagonist's life, which does not exist: "a hole-word, whose center would have been hollowed out into a hole, the kind of hole in which all other words would have been buried."[67] Like Lol, Duras's writing is driven by something ineffable, but, unlike Lol, the writer concedes to putting the "absence-word" into words.[68] The aporetic transposition into words of a lack or an absence also characterizes Duras's own reflections on writing as "the unknown."[69] It is this poetics of the unknown, and of "empty words," as Kristeva puts it, revealing a faithfulness to a reality beyond words precisely by continuing writing, that makes Duras's art a possible harbor against the current commodification of aesthetic experience.

Even though Duras's work seems to be part of a more general crisis of signification in the post–Second World War period, her dedication to the force of writing as such indicates a specific adherence to the symbolic order that could resist the imperative of flexibility and self-realization in a neoliberal normalizing order.[70] Thus, although Kristeva suggests that Duras's writing gives expression to a specific feminine melancholia through a refusal of linguistic proficiency, it could be that Duras's art of the impossible gives literary writing a specific implication that transgresses the feminine experience of melancholia as well as the given historical crisis of signification. Thanks to her lucid confrontation with "madness," Duras subverts traditional representations of subjectivity and politics by creating a singular style of writing and a writing of singularity that is also a force of critique. By summarizing the essential traits in Kristeva's reading of Duras in connection with her idea of "genius," I will try to highlight further this creative force and how it can be said to remobilize the current weakening of artistic critique and its lack of revolt.

VII. In Search for Truth

I have proposed that Kristeva describes Duras's style as deriving from an aesthetic based on an experience tied to a feminine melancholia, as well as to the major events of the twentieth century. Kristeva's main point is that the aesthetic refusal or minimization of literary devices that characterized art and literature in the post–Second World War period was directed by a desire to stay true to exterior as well as interior traumas, as if pain was the only faithful expression of these crises.[71] However, the force of this pain and the breakdown of ideologies that followed the war did not imply that Duras gave up her belief in the necessity to write or in political change. This belief persists although her style excels in "the incomplete," as Roy put it, and although her adherence to a political party no longer seems to be an option, as she concludes when looking back on the 1960s. "We are sick with hope, those of us from '68. The hope is the one we placed in the role of the proletariat. And as for us, no law, nothing, no one and no thing, will ever cure us of that hope. I'd like to join the Communist Party again. But at the same time I know I shouldn't."[72]

From one perspective, the crisis of representation and the theme of melancholia that Kristeva discerns in Duras's writing reflect a political failure as well as a personal experience. Motifs such as the crazy mother, the colonial experience, and the Second World War are recurrent throughout Duras's work, and could easily be related to her biography. However, the autobiographical narrative in Duras's work is at the same time undermined by an aesthetic practice that articulates an experience that cannot be fully represented. Furthermore, Duras's art of the impossible is tied to a specific aesthetic exigency that has already been touched upon, and that could be further elucidated by the following passage from *The Lover*: "Nowadays it often seems writing is nothing at all. Sometimes I realize that if writing isn't all things, all contraries confounded, a quest for vanity and void, it's nothing. That if it's not, each time, all things confounded into one through some inexpressible essence, then writing is nothing but advertisement."[73]

When writing *The Lover*, her great public success in 1984, Duras was seventy years old. To be sure, the autobiographical themes—childhood and the drama of sexual desire—have captivated the public and made the book into material for perhaps an even more successful film. As Kristeva puts it, with this novel "suffering gains a social and historical neoromantic congruity that has insured its place among bestsellers."[74] At the same time, Duras articulates these captivating themes as something beyond reach: "The story of my life doesn't exist. Does not exist. There's never any center to it. No path, no line. There are great spaces where you pretend there used to be someone, but it's not true, there was no one."[75] Differently put, if writing is to be something other than a more or less automatic response to the demands of the market—for example, the true story of one's life—then it must obey "some inexpressible essence." This paradox is also perceivable in the following configuration of some kind of *Urszene* at the beginning of *The Lover*, where she speaks of the memory of childhood "on whose brink silence begins."[76] "What happens there is silence, the slow travail of my whole life. I'm still there, watching those possessed children, as far away from the mystery now as I was then. I've never written, though I thought I wrote, never loved, though I thought I loved, never done anything but wait outside the closed door."[77] I want to suggest that it is this very impossibility—"the closed door"—at the core of Duras's (autobiographical) writing that points towards a singular experience where passion and politics become juxtaposed. In *The Lover*, for instance, she compares the French collaborator during the Second World War with her own political engagement in a way that evokes a kind of solution that tries to escape the impossibility at the core of every subject: "The two things are the same, the same pity, the same call for help, the same lack of judgment, the same superstition if you like, that consists in believing in a political solution to the personal problem."[78] If this experience leads Duras to "scrutinize only the spectrum of suffering," as Kristeva suggests, this very spectrum is also condensed into a style that can lead us to X-ray the compromises of social life and the resignations following the failures of ideologies and ongoing victories of global capitalism.[79] To conclude, I would like to show how Duras with Kristeva can make manifest the work of a genius plasticity, by focusing on the subversive effects of Duras's configurations of love and its consequences for a critical practice.

VIII. Love of Love

By letting the experience of impossible mourning be transformed into writing, Duras not only destabilizes the symbolic, leading "to an aesthetics of *awkwardness*," as Kristeva says.[80] She also puts the subject into process by activating its impossible core through desire and love. Let us return to a passage from *The Lover* to highlight this process in a more tangible way. The scene is the narrator as a young girl just after her meeting with the Chinese man—the lover: "He's desirable. I tell him of this desire. He tells me to wait awhile. Talks to me, says he knew right away, when we were crossing the river, that I'd be like this after my first lover, that I'd love love, he says he knows now I'll deceive him and deceive all the men I'm ever with."[81] The formulation "I'd love love" can be traced back to Augustine's *amans amare* as well as to the tradition of courtly love in which idealization makes of the beloved woman an abstract entity for the male subject's narcissistic desire.[82] If, as Kristeva puts it, Duras verges on "the mythification of the inaccessible feminine" when she lets the lover in her story inscribe the young girl in these canonized discourses on love in the Western tradition, she also deconstructs this very "mythification."[83] In her writings, Duras dramatizes in different ways the profound incompatibility between passion and will, and in doing so she also reveals an impossibility not only in the subject but at the heart of every community and, a fortiori, in the dreams of union that romanticism is made of. There are many instances of these revelations in her novels and essays, as, for example, in these lines from "Solitude" in *Green Eyes*: "Most people marry to get out of solitude. . . . Solitude is blurred but not defeated. . . . A lover's couple is short-lived. It never survives marriage. . . . One cannot do anything from within the couple but wait for that wonder, the days of love, to run out."[84] I suggest that, by deconstructing the romantic idea of the couple, Duras can also help to undermine the commodification of love that follows the new spirit of capitalism. If this is the case, Duras demonstrates the critical potentiality of aesthetics in a current neoliberal hegemony where the exercise of power has changed from regulations or restrictions to the subject's "healthy competition" as a mechanism of control.[85] Thus Duras's writing, which Kristeva describes as a refutation of the "affected rhetoric of literature and even the common rhetoric of everyday speech," can also be conceived as a critical practice and an antidote to the leveling of artistic critique in our contemporary society.[86]

Duras's description of love and writing is, in many respects, inscribed in a Western democratic literary institution conditioned by the liberty to say everything and to say it in the way one wants. Nevertheless, Duras insists that the modern absence of literary moral constraints must be directed by something that it is not possible to express in public. If this quality is lacking, as is said in *The Lover*, then "writing is nothing but advertisement." This aesthetic sensibility towards "some inexpressible essence" could be another name for what Kristeva describes as an *herethics* that disrupts postulations of identities by introducing the force of the body, its desire, affects, and drives into every symbolic coherence. Differently put, and on a more general level, if writing is conceived as a counterforce that disrupts the coherence of narratives and precludes any attempt at totalizing a story of oneself, then it cannot do away with "madness." I contend that such a counterforce is constituted by Duras's singular style of awkwardness or incompleteness, which opens the symbolic towards the experience of the impossible mourning at the core of subjectivation. In other words, in Duras's writing this impossibility is transformed into an art that holds aesthetic practices, as well as love, apart from commodification and from the neoliberal demands of performance, productivity, and competition. At any rate, this is a reading of Duras inspired not only by Kristeva's sensitive reading of feminine melancholia but also by her way of underlining a possible genius in every subject—and it takes a genius to transform the lack of revolt into subversive and critical creativity.

IX. Coda

In her conclusion of the "female genius" trilogy, Kristeva returns to Beauvoir by paying homage to her existentialist conviction of the subject's need for self-transcendence. However, Kristeva underlines that it must be done by going "through and beyond" the political and social situation of the given moment. "To appeal to the genius of every woman, of every man or woman, is a way, not of underestimating the weight of History . . . but of attempting to free the female condition, like the human condition in general, from biological, social, or fateful constraints by emphasizing the conscious or unconscious initiative of the subject against the weightiness of its program, dictated by these various forms of determinism."[87] Kristeva does not only *appeal* to the subject's genius. She gives her readers tools for transforming contemporary control mechanisms and demands of adaptation and limitless flexibility into adventures of rebirth and revolt—into self-travelers reinventing their singular experiences.

Carin Franzén

Linköping University
October 2018

NOTES

1. Julia Kristeva, *Sémiotikè: Recherches pour une sémanalyse* (Paris: Seuil, 1969). Some of its essays are translated in Julia Kristeva, *Desire in Language: A Semiotic Approach to Literature and Art*, trans. Thomas Gora, Alice Jardine, and Leon S. Roudiez (New York: Columbia University Press, 1980). See also Toril Moi, ed., *The Kristeva Reader* (New York: Columbia University Press, 1986).

2. Julia Kristeva, *Revolution in Poetic Language*, trans. Margaret Waller (New York: Columbia University Press, 1984), 16; *La Révolution du langage poétique: L'Avant-garde à la fin du XIXe siècle, Lautréamont et Mallarmé* (Paris: Seuil, 1974), 14.

3. Julia Kristeva, *Passions of Our Time*, trans. Constance Borde and Sheila Malovany-Chevallier (New York: Columbia University Press, 2018); *Pulsions du temps* (Paris: Fayard, 2013).

4. Kristeva, *Revolution in Poetic Language*, 15.

5. See Alain Ehrenberg, *The Weariness of the Self: Diagnosing the History of Depression in the Contemporary Age*, trans. Enrico Caouette, et al. (Montreal: McGill-Queen's University Press, 2010), 5, 160–230.

6. Julia Kristeva, "How to Speak to Literature with Roland Barthes," in *Passions of Our Time*, 31.

7. Julia Kristeva, *Black Sun: Depression and Melancholia*, trans. Leon S. Roudiez (New York: Columbia University Press, 1989), 219–59.

8. See Bernard Siegert, *Cultural Techniques: Grids, Filters, Doors, and Other Articulations of the Real*, trans. Geoffrey Winthrop-Young (New York: Fordham University Press, 2015), 6.

9. Ehrenberg, *The Weariness of the Self*, 135.

10. Catherine Malabou, *What Should We Do with Our Brain?*, trans. Sebastian Rand (New York: Fordham University Press, 2008), 46.

11. Luc Boltanski and Eve Chiapello, *The New Spirit of Capitalism*, trans. Gregory Elliott (New York: Verso, 2007).

12. Ehrenberg, *The Weariness of the Self*, 3.

13. Julia Kristeva, *New Maladies of the Soul*, trans. Ross Guberman (New York: Columbia University Press, 1995), 7.

14. See Deleuze's short but seminal "Postscript on Control Societies" in which he states that "it's not a question of asking whether the old or new system is harsher or more bearable, because there's a conflict in each between the ways they free and enslave us . . . but of finding new weapons." Gilles Deleuze, *Negotiations, 1972–1990*, trans. Martin Joughin (New York: Columbia University Press, 1995), 178. The "Postscript" was first published in *L'Autre journal* 1, May 1990.

15. Julia Kristeva, "Un Sens insensé: La Poésie dans l'histoire—Entretien avec Jacques Henric," in *Julia Kristeva: Les Grands Entretiens d'artpress* (Paris: Art Press, 2014), 27 (my translation). This interview first appeared in *artpress* 11, May 1974. [*Pulsion* is the French translation of Freud's *der Trieb*, the psychical *drive*.—Ed.]

16. Julia Kristeva, "La Haine et le pardon—Entretien avec Philippe Forest," in *Kristeva: Les Grands Entretiens d'artpress*, 100 (my translation). This interview first appeared in *artpress* 321, March 2006.

17. Judith Butler, *Gender Trouble: Feminism and the Subversion of Identity* (New York: Routledge, 1999), 102.

18. Judith Butler, *Undoing Gender* (New York: Routledge, 2004), 44.

19. Jacques Lacan, *On the Names-of-the-Father*, trans. Bruce Fink (Cambridge: Polity Press, 2013), 4; *Des noms-du-père* (Paris: Seuil, 2005), 13.

20. Lacan, *On the Names-of-the-Father*, 19.

21. Butler, *Gender Trouble*, 102.

22. Malabou, *What Should We Do with Our Brain?*, 49.

23. The phrase "body politics" is in a section heading in chapter 3 of Butler, *Gender Trouble*, 101. Kristeva, *Revolution in Poetic Language*, 216.

24. Julia Kristeva, *Seule une femme* (Paris: L'Aube, 2013), 232 (my translation).

25. Butler, *Undoing Gender*, 208.

26. Butler, *Gender Trouble*, 103.

27. Boltanski and Chiapello, *The New Spirit of Capitalism*, xliii.

28. Julia Kristeva, *The Sense and Non-sense of Revolt*, trans. Jeanine Herman (New York: Columbia University Press, 2000), 3.

29. Ibid., 1.

30. Boltanski and Chiapello, *The New Spirit of Capitalism*, 419–20.

31. Kristeva, "Un Sens insensé," in *Julia Kristeva: Les Grands Entretiens d'artpress*, 30 (my translation).

32. Kristeva, *The Sense and Non-sense of Revolt*, 19.

33. Ibid.

34. Malabou, *What Should We Do with Our Brain?*, 12.

35. Butler, *Undoing Gender*, 203.

36. Julia Kristeva, *Colette*, trans. Jane Marie Todd (New York: Columbia University Press, 2004), 408 (volume 3 of the "female genius" trilogy).

37. Ibid., 407, 426.

38. Boltanski and Chiapello, *The New Spirit of Capitalism*, 419.

39. Immanuel Kant, *Critique of Judgment*, trans. Werner Pluhar (Indianapolis: Hackett, 1987), 174.

40. Kristeva, *Colette*, 407.

41. Ibid., 426.

42. Julia Kristeva, "Soleil noir: Dépression et Mélancolie—Entretien avec Catherine Francblin," in *Julia Kristeva: Les Grands Entretiens d'artpress*, 41 (my translation). This interview first appeared in *artpress* 114, May 1987.

43. Julia Kristeva, *Melanie Klein*, trans. Ross Guberman (New York: Columbia University Press, 2001) (volume 2 of the "female genius" trilogy).

44. For an engaging assessment of Kristeva's works on depression and art, see Elaine P. Miller, *Head Cases: Julia Kristeva on Philosophy and Art in Depressed Times* (New York: Columbia University Press, 2014).

45. Lacan, *On the Names-of-the-Father*, 19.

46. Kristeva, *Black Sun*, 9.

47. Julia Kristeva, *Tales of Love*, trans. Leon S. Roudiez (New York: Columbia University Press, 1987), 263. The essay "Stabat Mater" first appeared in *Tel Quel*, no. 74 (1977).

48. Kristeva, *New Maladies of the Soul*, 7.

49. Kristeva, *Black Sun*, 228. I have developed this aspect of Duras's aesthetics in relation to the Lacanian theory of the real in "Duras and the Art of the Impossible," in Agnieszka Piotrowska and Ben Tyrer, eds., *Psychoanalysis and the Unrepresentable: From Culture to the Clinic* (New York: Routledge, 2017), 130–39.

50. Kristeva, *Black Sun*, 13–14.

51. Ibid., 14.

52. Marguerite Duras, *The Lover*, trans. Barbara Bray (New York: Pantheon, 1997), 8.

53. Kristeva, *Black Sun*, 230.

54. Renata Salecl, *On Anxiety* (New York: Routledge, 2004), 2.

55. Kristeva, *Black Sun*, 222.

56. Ibid., 225.

57. Laure Adler, *Marguerite Duras: A Life,* trans. Anne-Marie Glasheen (Chicago: University of Chicago Press, 2000), 210.

58. Claude Roy, quoted in Laure Adler, *Marguerite Duras* (Paris: Gallimard, 1998), 491 (my translation). Adler does not give the original source in *Libération* for Roy's review. The reference to Roy is omitted in the English translation of Adler's book (cited in note 57, above).

59. Marguerite Duras, quoted in ibid., 488. Duras's letter to her publisher, Gaston Gallimard, on October 16, 1957, is omitted in the English translation of Adler's biography (cited in note 57, above).

60. Kristeva, *Black Sun*, 225. Adler, *Marguerite Duras: A Life*, 195.

61. Adler, *Marguerite Duras: A Life*, 209.

62. Marguerite Duras, *Green Eyes*, trans. Carol Barko (New York: Columbia University Press, 1990), 69.

63. Ibid., 7. Adler, *Marguerite Duras: A Life*, 193.

64. Boltanski and Chiapello, *The New Spirit of Capitalism*, 472.

65. Marguerite Duras, *Writing*, trans. Mark Polizzotti (Minneapolis: University of Minnesota Press, 2011), 17.

66. Kristeva, *Black Sun*, 257.

67. Marguerite Duras, *The Ravishing of Lol Stein*, trans. Richard Seaver (New York: Pantheon, 1966), 38.

68. Ibid.

69. Duras, *Writing*, 44.

70. Boltanski and Chiapello point to the new forms of psychic health problems as a result of "the tension between the requirement of *flexibility* and the need to be someone": the need "to process a self endowed with *specificity* (a 'personality') and a certain *permanency* in time," which is "a constant source of anxiety." *The New Spirit of Capitalism*, 461.

71. The example that Kristeva gives of postwar literary devices, other than Duras, is Maurice Blanchot's "working toward the origin of the work" (Kristeva, *Black Sun*, 225). However, one could think more generally of the break with tradition of literary realism by the movement called the *Nouveau Roman*.

72. Duras, *Writing*, 26.

73. Duras, *The Lover*, 8.

74. Kristeva, *Black Sun*, 230.

75. Duras, *The Lover*, 8.

76. Ibid., 25.

77. Ibid.

78. Ibid., 68.

79. Kristeva, *Black Sun*, 236.

80. Ibid., 225.

81. Duras *The Lover*, 42.

82. See Kristeva's analysis of courtly love, "The Troubadours: From 'Great Courtly Romance' to Allegorical Narrative,'" in *Tales of Love*, 280–96.

83. Kristeva, *Black Sun*, 246.

84. Duras, "Solitude," in *Green Eyes*, 66–67.

85. Deleuze, "Postscript on Control Societies," in *Negotiations*, 179.

86. Kristeva, *Black Sun*, 225.

87. Kristeva, *Colette*, 407.

14

Françoise Coblence

AESTHETICS ACCORDING TO JULIA KRISTEVA

I. Did You Say . . . Aesthetics?

In 2003 Kristeva asked this question: "Given the 'new fall novels' or the 'installations' of contemporary art, the spectator and even more so the psychoanalyst have the right to wonder: 'Is it still possible to speak of aesthetics?'"[1] She comments that while "the mystery of the Beautiful and the alchemy of sensations transmuted into signs have not completely disappeared," the status of the "Beautiful" has incontestably changed.[2] From its Greek origins, the cult of the Beautiful has spread in modern times by following the wave of Christian culture: beauty, inseparable from love, is connected to the pleasure of representing the soul or inner experience. But when Eros yields to Thanatos, when the object libido is transposed into narcissistic libido, what is the nature of this "kind of sublimation" that is in fact a "desexualization," but which can be accompanied by a "defusion of the drives" and a liberation of destructivity? Freud did perceive the risk that a "work of sublimation" would then be subjected to the "danger of maltreatment and death."[3]

While this aspect of sublimation does not concern the whole of what this drive destiny covers in Freud, Kristeva focuses on following some of its figures, precisely to the extent that they are the most ambiguous, the most paradoxical, and perhaps the most interesting. In the field of aesthetics, and most particularly in literature, the liberation of destructivity can take melancholic, perverse, or psychotic forms.[4] But at the crossroads of language and the sensible, the perverse latencies of the ego are magnificently mobilized, and that is what Kristeva studies in two French writers, Proust and Colette.

Translated from French by Armine Kotin Mortimer.

This approach reconnects with the etymological meaning of aesthetics. Aesthetics is traditionally assimilated with the science of the beautiful, and that is the tradition to which Freud adheres, as does Hegel. But the term was forged from the Greek *aesthesis*, sensation. From the moment of its "invention" in the eighteenth century, aesthetics also designates everything that concerns the sensible and feeling. Between the pleasure of the senses and the pleasure of words, the flesh of the world and time regained, Kristeva invites us to follow how literature shares the experience of the sensible in Proust and Colette.

Treating these two writers together does not necessarily go without saying, but it illuminates their works as they accentuate the articulation of sensations and language. In Proust's correspondence as in Colette's, the letters they exchanged show their mutual admiration, an admiration that was not immediate for Colette but was quickly established from the moment she read *Swann's Way* (1913). The exchanges between them culminated with the publication of *Mitsou* (1919) and Proust's famous letter saying he had cried while reading Mitsou's letter.[5] The exchanges lasted until Proust's death (1922).[6]

Between Colette and Proust, Kristeva makes a common world of plants and animals emerge that they both explore and which give them the metaphors of the world, of the self, and of sexuality. "Who, after you, would dare to touch upon the lepidopteran, vegetal, ornithological awakening of a Jupien at the approach of a Charlus," writes Colette to Proust in 1921 after reading *Sodom and Gomorrah*.[7] But what especially brings the two writers together is how both the route to the infantile and recovered memory pass through perversion, even if the passage is different for the one and the other.[8]

II. Proust and the Sense of Time

With Proust, experience and writing are inseparable one from the other. As with Colette, sensation is a language that it is up to the writer to deploy. To name, to describe this sensible world—which is at once the world of the first experiences of childhood, including corporeal experiences, the world of sensations (visual, auditory, olfactory, gustatory, etc.), and of relations with the mother or maternal figures, the world of jealousy—will be the work of an entire lifetime. Better than anyone, Proust described the ambivalence of these relations, and his writing conveys the "sensual, artificial, and blasphemous" nature of his experience.[9] Kristeva associates profanation and perversion in Proust, in a universe that goes beyond that of psychoanalysis and its clinical field. For one thing, the writing raises the elaboration and sublimation of psychic life to the highest point, obtaining "a veritable *fragmentation of the apparatus of representation*" in the description and elaboration of the states of the ego, of its ideas, of its sorrows, of those of others, of language.[10] For another thing, art operates a "transubstantiation" of objects, sensations, and impressions through the force that memory rediscovers behind them, through psychical contractions in the series of metaphors characterizing them and their exchange. (Among so many possible examples, the metamorphic adventures of the little phrase by

Vinteuil, and the passage from sensations to the "compact, cool after warmth, rose-pink" matter of words around the perverse scene of flagellation first narrated to Céleste before being written.)[11]

Thus one finds in Proust, as a formula of sublimation, a "*sensation situated outside the domain of meaning*,"[12] a new status given to the image and imagination, both sensation and memory. Without the one being reduced to the other, psychoanalytic interpretation can be revitalized in aesthetic experience. Both concern the same psychic regions, they concern memories that consist of time incorporated into sensations, but which it is the privilege of the writer to be able to remodel and share. The sharing operates with the reader because "the tonality is at once tender and sarcastic."[13]

III. Colette: The Double Alphabet

For Colette, to whom Kristeva grants primacy in mooring writing to infantile memory, childhood recovered by the senses is the place of "an inexpungable innocence." The essential passage through homosexuality is serene, without transgression or a blasphemous dimension (that, of course, is not the case with Proust). "To remember," according to Colette, "is above all to feel."[14] "Bring to your nostrils the unchanging scent of these changeable violets and watch, while inhaling the filter that abolishes the years, watch as I do the springs of your childhood resuscitate and grow before you."[15]

Why devote the third volume of the trilogy on female genius, after Hannah Arendt and Melanie Klein, to Colette? Kristeva replies: "I love that woman's writing: it is an immediate pleasure, without 'why'; nevertheless, I want to hazard an explanation."[16] In her writing, Colette explored a double alphabet: a solar alphabet, transmitted in part by her mother Sido and shared with her, the alphabet of the world of the tendrils of the vine, of animals at peace, of odors and colors; the other alphabet is the one of the abysses of our identities, of nauseating chaos, an active participant in the empire of the senses and feminine sexuality. We know how important the alphabet is for Kristeva, who in her childhood paraded every May 24 dressed as a letter of the Cyrillic alphabet during the celebration of the brothers Cyril and Methodius.[17] Colette's double alphabet "found a language to express a strange osmosis between her sensations, her desires, her anxieties—those 'pleasures thoughtlessly called physical'—and the infiniteness of the world, the blossoming of flowers, the rippling of beasts, sublime apparitions, contagious monsters."[18]

How could a psychoanalyst remain insensitive to a writing that deploys like a savage and sensual experience captured between the flesh of the world and the power of words, attentive to meaning as well as to the very forms of the letters—one might say captured between conscious and unconscious? Is it not true that Colette, after all, defines writing as "*unconscious scrawls*, pen doodles around an ink spot that *nibbles at the imperfect* word, claws at it, surrounds it with darts, adorns it . . . until it loses its *readable word shape* and, transformed into a fantastic insect, takes flight as a fairy-butterfly."[19] A universal writing, but rooted—like Proust's—in what Kristeva considers "the French exception": the mobilization of the perverse latencies of the ego at the intersection of sense and the sensible.[20] Colette's writing, rooted in matter, is a cuisine-writing that makes tasty dishes with words, the writing of a free woman who does not dissociate the cult of *jouissance* and the cult of words. Moored in the quest for childhood memory, in search of sensation, she too is "in search of lost time":[21] "Oh, try to halt the passage of time, try to remain a little longer something like yourself; don't grow up, don't think, don't suffer! Try, hope so much for this that somewhere a god will be moved at it and grant your wish!"[22]

But through the sonorous, the tactile, and the olfactory, a squalid universe also transits: the writing is transformed into a chaos-alphabet, the gaze tumbles from the forms it masters down to the repugnant formless, to "the blandness of puddles."[23] In echo or counterpoint to the radiant alphabet, the monstrous proceeds from the same maternal imperative: Look! The gaze reveals the uncanny under the surface, another figure of the body, of animality, and of the sexuality that is also that of the murderers who fascinated Colette and whom she observed in criminal court or in prison, notably Landru. In this calm and cold murderer, at the antipodes of an unleashed bestiality, Colette perceives a variant of the "banality of evil" that Hannah Arendt tracks in Eichmann, or an "as if" personality that Joan Riviere and Helene Deutsch, in the same period, will describe with precision.[24] Thus writing accompanies cruelty, which also belongs to life, the destructivity that Colette goes so far as to observe in the cut-off heads and decapitated queens. All of this must be taken up.

IV. The Abject

Well before tracking the various monstrous counterpoints to the radiant study of the world in Colette, Kristeva had theorized, under the term *abjection*, the "powers of horror."[25] In an interview published in the *Revue française de psychanalyse*, she returned to the origin of this term in her thought:

> My text on abjection came to me in the course of my analysis and through my scholarly writing. I was in the process of preparing a book on Céline. It was hard to get a handle on the abyss opening up between my revolt against his anti-Semitic violence and the emotion which his fiction aroused in me. His novels, from *Voyage to the End of the Night* to *Castle to Castle,* are a veritable "force of nature." . . . My mother was visiting France. . . . I'm on Ilse Barande's couch: "I don't know how to manage all of it, the baby, my mother, and this Céline, with his *Voyage to the End of the Night—tu parles*!—all massacre, horror, abjection." My analyst responds: "That's the word for it." I leave the session relieved, with a feeling of deliverance more than the certainty of "mastering my subject." . . . So I took the word *abjection,* and tried to elucidate food taboos in Leviticus, Christian sins . . . even Céline.[26]

This personal origin is a measure of the originality of this notion and of the very specific articulation she proposes between the aesthetic and psychoanalysis. To be sure, she situates herself in the continuity of what Freud thought on the subject of fascination and horror for the Medusa's head and for apotropaic images: an anxiousness lacking any familiarity.[27] But the abject closely links affect, body, and thought without having a definable *object*; it is experienced as it unveils for the subject something of his deep being. In the disgust for a food or dirt, nausea or vomiting separates from the foul, and therefore protects from it. Such is the paradox of the abject, repulsing, rejecting (*ab-jectum*), separating. On the part of the body, it accompanies the symptom, inassimilable; on the part of aesthetics, the sublime, no less inassimilable, "*something added* that expands us, overstrains us, and causes us to be both *here*, as dejects, and *there* as others and sparkling."[28] The abject makes us confront our oldest attempts to mark our separation from the maternal entity, from a power as reassuring as it is stifling. In literature, Bataille, Proust, Artaud, Joyce, Borges elaborate different figures of abjection, partial figures in which the abject is a threat that language, in innumerable combinations, holds at bay. But Céline supplies a privileged example of it, according to Kristeva, because it touches all domains. One could say he is abjection itself, an abjection in which the writing forms in the very place of horror and the foul—an apocalyptic enunciation that separates from nothing, protects from nothing. Can we still see in it the fringes of the sublime, a tension maintained by the work of the writing? I cannot, for my part, but perhaps that is resistance to the total degradation of words into abjection?

However, abjection understood in this sense, that is, neither subject nor object, but with its both internal and external nature, its strangeness, is also a "normal" psychosexual component of maternal eroticism.[29] As such, while remaining the work of the negative, it nevertheless accompanies the "*fabulous investment in the state of emergency in life* . . . the *care* of the living and the *concern* for transmission": the negative at work if its unbinding is immediately recathected and reattached (*reliée*).[30] Such is "maternal reliance," for which Kristeva has rehabilitated the old French term *reliance*, in a back and forth between English and French. *Reliance* relinks, reassembles, but also allows trusting, relying on. *Stabat Mater*: The Mother keeps her station. Many works, on the one hand, the clinic on the other, bear witness to this reliance (as a force of maternal eroticism) and to its close link with the process of sublimation.

V. The Regimes of the Image

Therefore it is in the direction of the power of images that I will now follow Kristeva in her exploration of the powers of horror, of the powers of the sacred. The image is certainly considered a more archaic expressive modality than words, "a very imperfect becoming-conscious," in Freud's terms.[31] Its power of alienation and its seduction have been denounced by philosophers as well as by psychoanalysts. According to Levinas, the image is an invasion of shadow, it possesses us, carries us off, bewitches us, "marks a hold over us rather than our initiative."[32] The image confronts us with its impact in a direct and brutal way—such is the force of the visible. But is this impact more traumatic than the impact of the furor borne by words and the constraints they impose? Words can be without appeal, without space for disengagement. In the face of the image, what is our degree of freedom? Might it not prove great when the image—notably through the intermediary of a trajectory through space—invites us to a liberating progression or makes possible a speaking enchained until then?

The exhibit Kristeva organized at the Louvre in 1998 asks this question, and answers it in part. In a program called *Partis pris* or *Biased views*, in the sense of a choice, the Department of Graphic Arts at the Louvre proposed that a theoretician not connected to the museum world dig into the collections and expose an interpretive thread. The idea was to create a critical space, a "place of rupture," wrote Régis Michel, curator at the Louvre, in the introduction to the book that accompanied this exhibit.[33] After Jacques Derrida and Jean Starobinski, Kristeva fully utilized this freedom to display the link with the sacred that the image still maintains at the present time. The exhibited graphic and plastic works bring together "the *terror* that death and sacrifice provoke . . . the *serenity* that follows from the pact of identification between sacrificed and sacrificing, and . . . the *joy of representation* indissociable from sacrifice, its only possible course."[34] In the age of irreligiosity and atheism, Kristeva offered visitors of the exhibit and readers of the work an experience of the sacred, an experience of transcendence. "Differently from psychoanalysis, the aesthetic experience too revisits and exhausts the logic of the sacred."[35] Looking at the art and the works does not separate the two approaches, first because of the chosen theme, a theme that imposed itself on Kristeva: beheadings, a history of decapitations in different civilizations. Such a theme invites one to scrutinize the sacrificial limits of the visible, and to scrutinize them like a psychoanalyst—that is to say, to see in this genre the representation, momentarily made guilt-free, of our excesses, the putting into images of habitually repressed violence, a sort of "terminus" of the visible. These figurations at the limits also show that the visible ordinarily remains a defense against archaic anxieties of losing the mother and against the anxieties of castration.[36]

With the beheadings, we are at the crossroads of art and worship from the start, since this theme allows approaching the "capital" representations in all their aspects: cranium, head, face, figure, gaze. Human face, sacred face, decapitated face, masculine or feminine face, terrifying or sublime face, often the sign of a delicious horror—Medusa, of course, which, like all forbidden visions, is bearable only as an image (*eikôn*), precisely: "Cut off the monster's head and offer its reflection for view: that is the only way to protect yourself from death and from the female genitals that could swallow you."[37] Aesthetic pleasure occurs only when the gazer is protected. But, for Kristeva, who grew up, as she reminds us, "in the shadow of icons,"[38] the Medusa's head and the horror it can inspire already foretell an aesthetic of incarnation that will unfold through variations on the face of Christ and in the Byzantine tradition. The veil of Veronica (the *vera icona*), the Mandylion or Image of Edessa, and the icons are not only images but also relics; they have an effectiveness and a power of presentation of the divine.

VI. Power of the Image, Power of Women

In multiple ways, twentieth-century aesthetics proposes new logics to account for the powers of the image. It goes beyond the conception of mimesis as resemblance or imitation, the more or less faithful double of the real, the pale copy condemned by Plato. Whether the paradigm of incarnation and impress (Louis Marin, Georges Didi-Huberman) or of the index inspired by Peirce (Carlo Ginzburg, Rosalind Krauss), the idea is that something real is inscribed in the image, which is no longer a simple sign but belongs to something Kristeva calls an *economy*, following Marie-José Mondzain. Far from the too simple mimesis, economy implies the organization of an order in view of a profit, material or spiritual; it presupposes the consideration of ends and the particularity of cases; it is a management of the administration of temporal realities. In the icon, the incarnate Son is conceived as "economy of the Father."[39] After the icon, the *figure* thus revealed leads us toward a new phase in the history of the visible when figure becomes face, when painting does not seek to resemble but works to "exaggerate, weaken, correct its model," as Diderot puts it, and when the painter invites the spectator to enter the painting.[40]

Returning now from the visage to the decapitated faces, to the cut-off heads, to the beheadings that make these visages emerge, the power of the image is linked to two essential themes: the power of horror and the horror of the feminine, linked to death. The maternal body, present and fearsome in the face of the Medusa, is equally present in the economy and the icon—a maternal body that is resorbed and implicit, that allows the image of the Father to be dispensed in history, to enter into the visible.[41] Passing from the divine face to the beheadings, to the fascination and the horror for the cut-off heads, the ideal figure is that of Saint John the Baptist or his modern versions (from guillotined heads to those of Odilon Redon or Arnulf Rainer), a figure that takes us to liberating violence, from Salome to Judith. For Kristeva, Judith is "the positive version of the Gorgon," the "headed woman" who decapitates the most pitiless man and takes her revenge against the tyranny of the fathers.[42] One thinks of the innocent monstrosity and the "weirdness" of Baudelaire's "Miss Scalpel," who likes doctors to come see her with their instrument cases and a little blood on their smocks.[43] And it's understandable that the women psychoanalysts—Sabina Spielrein, Melanie Klein, Marion Milner, Piera Aulanier—pursue in their study of psychosis this feminine exploration of the violence of the human soul. The weepers, the detectives, the therapists, and also the painter Artemisia Gentileschi are "passionate pilgrims to the high places of carnage who relate, with extraordinary sangfroid, adventures of blades severing heads and states of the soul."[44] And in the women's curiosity and their desire to know, in their grating humor, in their struggle against boredom and depression, there is a reversal of the sufferings undergone and a lucid courage. To analyze as closely as possible, to minutely observe the logics and the economy of violence, such is the direction Kristeva proposes to women, psychoanalysts, and writers, a direction she herself has followed in her clinical work as in her writing of detective novels (*Possessions*) and in her work in aesthetics on the image, on painters, and on writers.[45] They will not be able to avoid horror and abjection—but it is not a question of avoiding them, quite the contrary, and they will see things with new eyes. For these portraits and these irreconcilable visages, from Artaud to Picasso by way of Bataille's Acéphale are "a challenge directed at the horror, through the invention of an unprecedented form, which doesn't shrink from abjection but reshapes our vision so that we see it with new eyes."[46] And let us forget neither humor nor laughter, of which Colette, once again, has given us the example.

Finally, Kristeva offers us a singular use of the power of images in the treatment of the patient she calls Didier.[47] In the face of speech cut off from its affects, the analyst's conviction that a secret discourse resides in the paintings left in the mother's apartment leads her to accept to see the works themselves, and not just hear them spoken about: they are collages of posters cut up and colored. Authorizing a certain perverse action of the patient in the treatment, she gives him in exchange the interpretation of the perverse meaning of his works and of his transferential movement, at the same time liberating his affected speech. This is both an investment *in the speech* of the patient (and not only the patient), and also a taking into account of *iconicity* as a more archaic degree of his psychic life. Kristeva's hypothesis is that the proximity of the traumatism requires the recreation by the analyst of a maternal *reliance*, and that, to do so, it might be necessary to accept the patient's actions, a certain perverse putting into action.[48] Speech and the phantasmatic capacity can then regain their rights, bringing to a close, through the return to language, the strong articulation between psychoanalysis, literature, and aesthetics that Kristeva magnificently invites us to think and combine.

Françoise Coblence

Emeritus Professor, University of Picardie Jules Verne
January 2019

NOTES

1. Julia Kristeva, "Peut-on parler encore d'esthétique? Ou du destin de la sublimation selon Colette," *Revue française de psychanalyse* 67, no. 2 (April 2003): 647.

2. Ibid.

3. Sigmund Freud, *The Ego and the Id*, in *The Standard Edition of the Complete Psychological Works of Sigmund Freud*, vol. XIX, trans. James Strachey (London: Hogarth, 1957), 30, 46, 56; "Le Moi et le ça," *Sigmund Freud: Oeuvres complètes psychanalyse*, t. XVI, trad. J. Laplanche, et al. (Paris: PUF, 1991), 274, 289, 299.

4. Kristeva, "Peut-on parler encore d'esthétique?" 650.

5. Letter from Proust to Colette (March 1919), *Correspondance de Marcel Proust*, t. XVIII (Paris: Plon, 1990), 118–19.

6. Julia Kristeva, "Colette et la chair du monde," *Le Plaisir des formes* (Paris: Seuil, 2003), 33–34.

7. Letter from Colette to Proust (July 1921), cited in Kristeva, "Colette et la chair du monde," 35.

8. Kristeva, "Colette et la chair du monde," 38–41.

9. Julia Kristeva, *Time and Sense: Proust and the Experience of Literature*, trans. Ross Guberman (New York: Columbia University Press, 1996), 226; *Le Temps sensible: Proust et l'expérience littéraire* (Paris: Gallimard, 1994), 279.

10. Julia Kristeva, "La Transsubstantiation de Proust: une suspension du refoulement," *Marcel Proust visiteur des psychanalystes, Revue française de psychanalyse* 2 (1999): 436.

11. Kristeva, *Time and Sense*, 214–16, 212, 241–42; *Le Temps sensible*, 265–68, 263, 297–98.

12. Ibid., 203; *Le Temps sensible*, 250.

13. Kristeva, "La Transsubstantiation de Proust," 438.

14. Kristeva, "Colette et la chair du monde," 45.

15. Cited in ibid. Colette, "Les Vrilles de la vigne," in *Oeuvres*, t. I (Paris: Gallimard, 1984), 978 (translated by Armine Kotin Mortimer).

16. Julia Kristeva, *Colette*, trans. Jane Marie Todd (New York: Columbia University Press, 2004), 1 (volume 3 of the "female genius" trilogy); *Le Génie féminin,* t. III, *Colette* (Paris: Fayard, 2002), 13.

17. See Julia Kristeva, "Intellectual Autobiography," in this volume, 7.

18. Kristeva, *Colette*, 1; *Colette*, 13.

19. Colette, "La Vagabonde," in *Oeuvres*, t. I, 1074. Quoted in Kristeva, *Colette*, 3; *Colette*, 15–16.

20. Kristeva, "Peut-on parler encore d'esthétique?" 650.

21. Kristeva, "Colette et la chair du monde," 42.

22. Colette, *Retreat from Love*, trans. Margaret Crosland (New York: Bobbs-Merrill, 1974), 104; "La Retraite sentimentale," *Oeuvres*, t. I, 887. Quoted in Kristeva, "Colette et la chair du monde," 43.

23. Colette, "Serpents," in *Prisons et paradis*, *Oeuvres*, t. III, 657–59. Quoted in Kristeva, "Peut-on parler encore d'esthétique?" 652.

24. Kristeva, "Peut-on parler encore d'esthétique?" 658.

25. Julia Kristeva, *Powers of Horror: An Essay on Abjection*, trans. Leon S. Roudiez (New York: Columbia University Press, 1982); *Pouvoirs de l'horreur: Essai sur l'abjection* (Paris: Seuil, 1980).

26. Julia Kristeva, "The Psychic Life: A Life in Time, Psychoanalysis and Culture," trans. Carol Mastrangelo Bové and Anne Marsella, *Journal of French and Francophone Philosophy—Revue de la philosophie française et de langue française* 26, no. 2 (2018): 89; "Une Vie psychique est une vie dans le temps," *Revue française de psychanalyse* 81, 2 (May 2017): 365.

27. Kristeva, *Powers of Horror*, 5; *Pouvoirs de l'horreur*, 13.

28. Ibid, 12; *Pouvoirs de l'horreur,* 19.

29. Julia Kristeva, "Reliance, or Maternal Eroticism," trans. Rachel Widawsky and Perry Zurn, *Journal of the American Psychoanalytic Association* 62, no. 1 (2014): 76; "La Reliance ou l'érotisme maternel," *Revue française de psychanalyse* 75, no. 5 (2011): 1563–65.

30. Ibid., 77; "La Reliance," 1566.

31. Sigmund Freud, *The Ego and the Id*, 20–21; "Le Moi et le ça," 265.

32. Emmanuel Levinas, "Reality and Its Shadow," in Seán Hand, ed., *The Levinas Reader* (Oxford: Blackwell, 1989), 132; "La Réalité et son ombre," *Les Temps modernes*

4, no. 38 (1948): 771–89, 774. See also Paul Denis, "Séduction de l'image, image de la séduction," *Emprise et satisfaction: Les Deux formants de la pulsion* (Paris: PUF, Le fil rouge, 1997), 179–99.

33. Régis Michel, "Alibi?" in Julia Kristeva, *The Severed Head: Capital Visions*, trans. Jody Gladding (New York: Columbia University Press, 2012), xvii; "L'alibi?" *Visions capitales* (Paris: Réunion des Musées Nationaux, 1998), 8.

34. Kristeva, *The Severed Head*, vii; *Visions capitales*, 11.

35. Ibid., 75; *Visions capitales*, 81.

36. Ibid., 83; *Visions capitales*, 95.

37. Ibid., 30–31; *Visions capitales*, 37.

38. Ibid., 37; *Visions capitales*, 45.

39. Marie-José Mondzain, *Image, Icon, Economy*, trans. Rico Franses (Stanford: Stanford University Press, 2005), 21; *Image, icône, économie* (Paris: Seuil, 1996), 35–36.

40. Kristeva, *The Severed Head*, 61; *Visions capitales*, 67.

41. Ibid., 53–54; *Visions capitales*, 61.

42. Ibid., 77; *Visions capitales*, 84.

43. Charles Baudelaire, "Miss Scalpel," *The Parisian Prowler*, trans. Edward K. Kaplan (Athens: The University of Georgia Press, 1997), 117; "Mademoiselle Bistouri," *Le Spleen de Paris*, *Baudelaire: Oeuvres completes*, t. I (Paris: Gallimard, Bibliothèque de la Pléiade, 1975), 355.

44. Kristeva, *The Severed Head*, 118; *Visions capitales*, 137–38.

45. Kristeva, *Possessions*, trans. Barbara Bray (New York: Columbia University Press, 1998); *Possessions* (Paris: Fayard, 1996). The heroine of this detective novel, Pauline, bruised by an early loss, desperately persists in holding onto the cadaver of Gloria—and particularly her neck—as she could not do with her mother. See Kristeva, *The Severed Head*, 118–19; *Visions capitales*, 138.

46. Ibid., 108; *Visions capitales*, 122.

47. Julia Kristeva, "In Times Like These, Who Needs Psychoanalysts?" in *New Maladies of the Soul*, trans. Ross Guberman (New York: Columbia University Press, 1995), 42–43; "À quoi bon des psychanalystes en temps de détresse qui s'ignore," in *Les Nouvelles Maladies de l'âme* (Paris: Fayard, 1993), 69–71.

48. Didier's case is taken up again more recently in Kristeva's "Reliance, or Maternal Eroticism."

REPLY

TO ANISH KAPOOR, ELAINE P. MILLER, CARIN FRANZÉN, AND FRANÇOISE COBLENCE

I. ANISH KAPOOR

With his generosity as an artist who has "nothing to say" from his "little space between vaginal void, blood, and earth," but can only "refuse, refuse, refuse," Anish Kapoor reveals to me, and shows the reader, like a surprise, "what you have done to me": "You ab-jected me." Since then, the world "fell to pieces," and he, "once whole": "look at me, I smell," "you see . . . I can be female." Those who are familiar with my *Powers of Horror: An Essay on Abjection* know that these admissions are compliments.[1] And that Kapoor's entire work prepared our meeting, as he says a few lines later: "to expunge, or at least to uncover, the maternal obsessions that force me to find ways to my internal feminine . . . has become or perhaps has always been my essential mission." A fascinating and inaccessible horizon, a terrifying expulsion-loss. I had perused these obsessions in his giant installation, *Melancholia* (2004), a suspended gulf, and in the minimalist *My Red Homeland* (2003–2011)—red Vaseline in a bleeding vulva—and in the immense swollen cavern of the *Monumenta* (2011), a monstrous and appeasing Leviathan.

Mother-child ab-jection is the secret of what the West calls an "art," an art this artist exhibits by *refusing* the canons of "beauty" and "taste," preferring an insolent, slick, calculated anguish. Could this be the universal, shareable face of . . . circumcision? "The only way men have of entering the blood circle is by circumcision and by inducing genital bleeding." Could this be the condition that lets the sculptor who wants to "make the *Thing*, the lost *Thing*" have the ability to discover that she (the mother) is "*Really* a *No-Thing*, a *Void Thing*," and that sensorial disfiguration is purified in illumination, the invisible dazzle of the visible?

We had to meet, and we did indeed meet—when Kapoor installed monumental objects in the gardens of the Château de Versailles in commemoration of the tercentenary of the death of Louis XIV.[2] In distributing his sculptures in the reasoned serenity of Le Nôtre, his intention was not to decorate Versailles, nor to insult it. He "sows" his works in places to reveal what is *hidden* in them,

---

Translated from French by Armine Kotin Mortimer.

which is none other than the "anxious tension," the "visceral depth," the "centrifugal forces" of beings. Very attentive to psychoanalysis, more Freudian than most contemporary artists, Kapoor lends a clinical precision, a *sexual indetermination* that impressed me, to his "fight between rationality and the unexpected" and to how the body "easily loses itself in this terrifying order."[3] I also call it an "ab-jection," in which he recognizes himself: fascination-repulsion, present from the start in the early mother-child relation, not yet subject or object but *ab-jects*. Fusion-defusion of the sexes and contrary identities, both masculine *and* feminine, shadow *and* light: "a form deformed into utopia," he says, specifying that this experience in the adult is a sort of transcendence. I add: a cabalistic transcendence.

Whereas Le Nôtre sculpted the earth and the royal vegetation to "help nature," Kapoor tears out the gardener's *Tapis Vert*: he dismembers and disembowels the sovereign body in order to "understand Le Nôtre's *finesse*," as he put it, impudently. I shiver in the face of this lightning intimacy with classical genius, which Kapoor exalts with the word "finesse." In it he also—especially—inscribes the tormented genealogy of humanity, which had already inhabited "rusty and sweet" Versailles (Proust),[4] and which today massively invades the planet. A humanity revolting against God and nature itself, untenable, disoriented, given over to its destructivity and its "pleasure to the death," criminal and ecstatic, totalitarian and hyperconnected. It is precisely this paradoxical *finesse* of Versailles's interrupted construction sites, their ruins and their questioning incompleteness, that captivated me. For it reveals—to those who did not want to take pleasure in its underground *vibrations*, immanent on the surface, to those who refrained from submitting to the purity of these hydraulic vortices—that Versailles is a *sexual site*.

Together, we toured the garden and the chateau. Disturbing violence of *Dirty Corner* (see figure 1 in Kapoor's essay), broken columns, rubble and ruins, "and this giant horn that opens its rapacious maw in our direction"![5] Does the dirty tube aspire to slapping reasoned geometry in the face? Throat, ear, orifice, male or female, eye of a camera, or monstrous antenna that *incurves* the infinity of senses and non-sense, pulls them down and transfers them into disasters of the heart of hearts, mainsprings of subjectivity. Even when Kapoor takes on mathematical objects, their perfection and their circular temporality interest him only in order to open them up—these too—to the unbearable process of life to death in sexual intimacy, this "Inner Sanctum" of the unnamable.

Like *Shooting into the Corner*, which he did not set up in the Galerie des Glaces, nor in the Trianon but in the Jeu de Paume at Versailles: he is not unaware of the political connotations of his "uncertain objects, fragments, [and] *in-betweens*," deboning and "ritual arena in which everything including murder can take place."[6] However, through and beyond the political event that was to install the Rights of Man and state violence in History, it is *phallic shooting* that haunts the artist Anish Kapoor in particular. Ejaculation and rape have taken place, the sublimatory and erotic gesture of the artist retains only the fascination and horror of symbolic penetration. Yes, Kapoor bears witness to a humanity that has lost its innocence.

The only feminine figure here is the Versailles chateau. The famous astronomical clock that Claude-Siméon Passemant conceived for Louis XV (1749) is housed in this beehive. I wanted to show it to the sculptor, officially invited to astonish the "optical gluttons" that are the tourists. The clock is programmed to give universal time until 9999. Its *intention* ("the key is in the intention," Kapoor also likes to say) was to bend the infinity of time into the *now* of those human beings who had no idea that only a few decades separated them from the fall of their too *ancien* régime. The clock is like an "enclosure" (*enceinte*) of infinite time, whereas a phallic pendulum swings between the legs of the android casing. "I am pregnant," Kapoor also writes. Standing in front of this marvel, I spoke to him about Émilie du Châtelet (heroine of my novel *The Enchanted Clock*), a mathematician and physicist who roamed these sites at that time, now an icon of feminists.[7] She prophesied the existence of "strange matter," "passive energy" lacking "extension," in which modern researchers have deciphered *dark matter* and *dark energies*. Émilie called them *fire*. Kapoor says *Descension*: vortex of *water*, whirling black hole, "feminine object" that prolongs the "dark object," the "internal object," the *proto-object*, the *abject* object, between day and night, between being and nonbeing. And the artist for whom "no blood is no power" pierces Le Nôtre's green expanse to allow us to see, with the water, the blood of the earth.

I must return to the *sensuality* of "his" Versailles, but also to our dialogues, for I count them among the most memorable moments of my life—at a time when miserable residues of an obscurantist Catholicism and so-called defenders of the prestige of the Chateau, of the queen's honor, and necessarily of the national patrimony have vandalized the works with yellow spray paint and antisemitic tags. This odor of Nazism provokes in me a broad and deep indignation; it deserves only the severest of condemnations and sanctions. Their reactionary and freedom-killing ideologies, their identitarian twitches and moralizing or aestheticizing professions of faith are merely fallacious screens that hide precisely . . . what Kapoor is showing them: *the terror of sensuality*. It is their own shame about the primitive chaos, their unbearable fascination with the horror of the "Dirty Corner" in their own depths that they forbid themselves and refuse to look at. *Art scares them when it reveals the violent pantomime of carnage in oneself under the serene victory of beauty.*

Dear Anish, your adversaries are incapable of sensing or understanding that the abject touched "to the forest of our being" opens "the world as whole," "the horrid, dirty-cornered, smelly pieces," to astral capture. At the end of the invisible tunnel the light of your immense lenses breathes: the *Sky Mirror* and the masterful *C-Curve*, my favorites. The formal purity and the musical joy of luminosity do not flow away, they loop in an infinite point: a certain transcendence.

II. Elaine P. Miller

With the acuity of her remarkable *Head Cases: Julia Kristeva on Philosophy and Art in Depressed Times*, Elaine Miller develops and refines her analysis of decapitation, a "theme . . . central to [Kristeva's] work," in which Miller discerns two aspects complementary in their tension, as unbearable as it is constitutive.[8] On the one hand, "the severed head certainly could be a *representation of abjection* in that it reminds us of the richness of a being whose life has been cut short through the severance of its most important appendage, while simultaneously horrifying and disgusting us in its transformation into an object" (my emphasis). On the other hand, the book dedicated to the "positive maternal memory from childhood"—it is dedicated to my mother drawing *thought* as the "fastest mode of transportation in the world": a sputnik flying over the snowman whose head is melting under a ray of sunshine—announces and "amplifies the most explicitly feminist strand of the above conception" of abjection.

Miller quite rightly emphasizes that the child's appropriation of the maternal head is not only a "figure to be left behind"—in other words, to be "cut off"; it is a "legacy" (of the mother, and, I would add, to the extent that it incorporates the desire of the father in this primary thirdness) "preserved in the realm of representation." It is clear, then, that the pictorial representation of decapitation "pay[s] tribute to and resuscitate[s] what has been abjured, making it a 'maternal,' feminine form of revolt." "The scission from her, through both imagistic and conceptual representation," "symbolize[s] a flight both away from and *with* the mother." It is true that this capture of the maternal as a visual memory trace is equivalent to an incorporation of the maternal feminine by every speaking being in the path toward thought and speech. But only the artist assumes and exhibits its secret laboratory—by claiming the *cut* as a painful *break* but also as an *opening* for new alliances (see Kapoor on circumcision)—all the while discovering himself as feminine, even a woman (see Kapoor "bleeding," abjecting/abjected in Versailles): "as if it [her head] was his own."[9]

At the intersection of "castration" according to Freud (threat and punishment by the father—source of guilt) and "reparation" according to Klein (of the separation-abandonment by the mother—source of depression, itself compensated by the representation of *absence* and by its verbalization), Miller reminds us that in my clinical theorization, the "formation of the psyche" seeks to identify and accompany the *gradual, fluid process* of subjective creativity: "relationships and identifications are unstable," "abjection is a process." This conception begins with a "primary scission" that is not reduced to the negativity of the *judgment* (*Urteil* in German, the etymology of which—"origin" and "part"—lets one hear an "originary separation"), but refers to the "oral-instinctual drives . . . coded by religion and society as part of the symbolic genesis of the autonomous individual" (Miller; see my *Powers of Horror*).

When I had just finished my novel *Possessions* (1996), I was asked to curate an exhibition at the Louvre. The exhibition catalogue shows a sculpture of a decapitated female body.[10] It was the heyday of feminism, and I was writing the story of a mother who "loses her head" following the birth of her son Jerry, a child not like the others whose deafness is quickly discovered and whose mother is decapitated by her child's speech therapist. In a baroque and bitter tonality bordering on the satirical, this novel from my series of "metaphysical detective novels" explores the dispossession of a society where people write and translate (Gloria, the mother, is a translator by profession) but do not read—the mystical passion or madness of a super-woman who gives her life to another to the point of losing her own; and the putting to death of this mother by a "caregiver" who, herself wounded by an early loss, desperately attacks the cadaver—particularly her neck—as she was unable to do with her own mother.

I had never done an exhibition, I don't consider myself a "specialist" in art history or aesthetics, and so as not to impolitely refuse the offer, but with the hope that the prestigious museum would refuse so barbarous a "theme," I proposed (still haunted by Gloria) "Decapitation." The wrong move, the topic was welcomed enthusiastically! So I dove into the cellars of the Louvre and into art history, to discover that decapitation shapes the West's pictorial memory; and to revisit my own clinical experiences, my fantasies, my imaginary as a woman, mother, and writer, relying on the diverse masterpieces from prehistory to modern and contemporary art, not forgetting the guillotine.

Abjection, the "return of the primally repressed" (Miller), was thus not only the focus of the religious (as in Leviticus, for example, as Miller shows) or of writing (as in Céline). It accompanied the flowering of the *visible* starting from and with the *invisible*. The abject emerged in the image, is even called for and communicated by the image when it is capable of making the invisible visible. Image as "eye of the soul" or image as "thought purified" (Miller)? Impressionism, surrealism, minimalism, abstractionism, installations of all sorts, body art and tattoos . . . intrinsically plural, could the image defy the tendencies of globalized standardization?

I appreciate Miller's insistence on the "new pleasure," different from the sexual, that the image procures as "sublimated object": "By investing in one's own representations . . . the child emerges into image and language through depression." How is that possible?

Because the sexuality of the speaking subject is always a "sexuality of the drive," that is, energy (instinctual: hormonal, electric) *and* sense (semiotic and symbolic), it is intrinsically *denatured* by "originary repression."[11] *Sublimation* relays this constitutive *denaturing* by investing (cathecting) *representations of representation*: sounds, gestures, words, images. The bisexuality of each of the two sexes (feminine and masculine) differently invests the psychical-drive movements, crossing them, that constitute abjection and castration, as seen in the reading-reception of the painting *Judith Slaying Holofernes* in which the artist-painter Artemisia Gentileschi deploys herself as both "the wound and the knife." I say "reading-reception" of the painting because the ambiguities of the image solicit languages, and the image of speaking beings must consequently "be heard." Here I am referring to any image, and especially to those of decapitation that allow the emergence of the visible and interrogate the limits of the visualizable and the representable. In the face of the influence of hyperconnected images we cannot *resist*. But we can "'hear' a painting" "to 'see' beyond its visible outlines to the 'invisible' that it depicts" (Miller).

In *Possessions*, that is what Stephanie Delacour, the journalist detective who represents me, does. She invites the reader to "find there a *kind of face* that has not yet found its *face*, that never will, but that never stops seeking a thousand and one ways of seeing" (*The Severed Head*, cited by Miller).[12] Does the "seen" call for the "heard" so the true *flowering* of the image will occur? Does our hearing, the most intellectual of the senses, therefore constitute, by its polyphonic suppleness, a sort of floral vitality, a burgeoning that is complementary to and indispensable for the invasive violence and the toxic ambiguity of the seen, of the visible, which slices, sorts, and subjugates?

Here I'm in agreement with Miller's vegetable imaginary, this time, which proposes to rethink the soul in "plantlike" terms.[13]

III. Carin Franzén

I like Carin Franzén's anger at "the impasses of subversion," the "incorporation of artistic critique into global capitalism by subordinating it to profit-making" and the "increasingly uniform world," to which she opposes the "highlighting and mobilizing [of] 'the bi-sexuality of sexual difference' as a universal experience that nevertheless determines each subject's singularity." To bring out feminine singularity, Franzén chooses to turn to Marguerite Duras's oeuvre, recalling my "development of Klein's theory" in the second volume of the "female genius" trilogy:[14] Duras's traumas, wounds, "stylistic awkwardness," "famous minimalism," and "noncathartic literature"; but also her political protestations through writing considered as "a critical practice . . . assigning literature an intrinsic value resisting commodification."

The reading Franzén proposes of *The Ravishing of Lol Stein* and *The Lover* concentrates on an "impossible mourning" (for the mother, definitively) and on the "absence of a unique word," "putting the 'absence-word' into words." This melancholy seems to me more insidious in women than in men, because matricide does not follow the path of crime like Orestes but lives on quietly in an interminable possession-dispossession of the self. Duras's writing takes matricide toward its absolute through a "refusal of linguistic proficiency," the aesthetic experience "articulat[ing] an experience that cannot be fully represented": "the story . . . doesn't exist," anxiety makes holes in the narrative fabric and composes fugues broken by *silence*. Strange author, who has "never written, though [she] thought [she] wrote, never loved, though [she] thought [she] loved . . . *but wait[ed] outside the closed door*" (from Franzén citing Duras, my emphasis).

Franzén excels in the updating of this "scrutiny [of] the spectrum of suffering" and this "faithfulness to madness" that I had identified in the chapter on "The Malady of Grief: Duras" in *Black Sun*.[15] She accompanies and elaborates the interpretations that stem from this study all through my research. Thus, these "exterior as well as interior traumas" where "passion and politics [war, colonialism] become juxtaposed" in Duras stem from my "semiotic," according to Franzén, on the condition that one hears that it lies close to "the real that does not lend itself to signification" (citing *Black Sun*). She also maintains that by introducing a "condition" for the *symbolic*, which according to Lacan would be the "condition for every 'interhuman function,'" the "semiotic" dimension allows for elucidating the inscription of traumas in writing. And she continues her interpretation by opening up an abyssal problematic: where does this deconstruction of "mythifications" lead, whether they be the "inaccessible feminine," the "subject," or the "community and . . . dreams of union that romanticism is made of"?

Clearly, Franzén underscores, "it is more a matter of style than a real choice to stand outside the market." Impossible, obviously! And Duras's demands did not fail to "utilize" both political power (Mitterrand among others) and the image market (movie stars).

If it is true that I "transform the lack of revolt into . . . critical creativity" and underline "a possible genius in every subject," notably in the psychoanalytic encounter, my research does not seem truly "subversive" to me. But "*herethic*" (heresy plus ethic) it certainly is, in the sense that it is situated in the prolongation of the current of modern philosophy that proceeds by a "suspension" (a bracketing) of norms, of morality, and of the world. And by a suspension of the three pillars by which humanity, having broken the thread with religious tradition, supports itself: the *political*, the *ethical*, the *aesthetic*. The chaos that threatens globalization, in which the political is the hostage of hyperconnectivity and finance, indicates how much these three pillars are crumbling, barely retained by the juridical.

Henceforth, the *herethic* understood as what "disrupts postulations of identities by introducing the force of the body, its desire, affects, and drives into every symbolic coherence," aspires neither to *save* nor to *subvert* "the modern absence of literary moral constraints." As writing touches the unnameable, the analytic experience intends—but more discreetly—to give rise to transvaluations and the risks of the unknown—which is to say, freedom. A sort of open happiness, and to begin again.

IV. Françoise Coblence

In a remarkable study, Françoise Coblence, psychoanalyst and philosopher, borrows and modulates Freud's lapidary formula, "Psyche is extended, knows nothing about it," concluding: "Psyche is corporeal, knows nothing about it."[16] And she does not provide a definitive answer to the question: what about this ignorance-unconsciousness? Her discussions displace and renew how psychoanalysis speaks about itself: "imbrication of the corporeal and the psychical"; "its *undissociability* from an intersubjectivity"; "the soul is more corporeal than the mind."[17] I can hear this advancement, both theoretical and clinical, as I discover the delicate reading Coblence proposes of the "very specific" articulation, as she puts it, between aesthetics and psychoanalysis in my publications.

Indeed, in the "continuity" with Freud, but differently from him, I note that "the abject closely links affect, body, and thought without having a definable *object*; it is experienced as it unveils for the subject something of his deep being" (Coblence). At once "separation from the maternal entity" and "a 'normal' psychosexual component of maternal eroticism," "inassimilable" and "sparkling," the abject has close ties with iconicity.

Excessive or prudent? Freud concedes that "psychoanalysis, unfortunately, has scarcely anything to say about beauty,"[18] while laying the groundwork for an exquisite and unfinished *theory of sublimation*. From this theory I take and develop in particular the "defusion of the drives" and "desexualization," which expose one "to the danger of torture and death" (Coblence citing Freud). For my part, in addressing *decapitation* (through the imaginary in my novel *Possessions*, and in the history of sculpture and painting through the exhibition Capital Visions at the Louvre), I treat the *image/imaginary* as a momentarily guilt-free representation of our excesses (Coblence). Coblence the clinician interprets the *cut-off head*, "'terminus' of the visible" and "capital representation," as a "defense against archaic anxieties of losing the mother and against the anxieties of castration": "delicious horror" that delivers the subject from his acted upon, suffered, and fantasized destructiveness—from Medusa to the guillotine by way of Salome carrying the head of Saint John the Baptist.

As a philologist and theoretician, Coblence also reminds us that the Byzantine tradition (which I returned to in *The Severed Head*), in granting theological and political authorization to represent *Christ's face*, goes beyond the "resemblance" and "imitation" that grounds earlier systems of representation. She also proposes that "something real is [henceforth] inscribed in the image" (the impression on the Veil of Veronica shows it). The *icon* system contains a *writing* in the sense of a *management* of the Self "for the profit" of the Father, but also as an *abandonment* of the Self to what I would call the *maternal bearing* (the orthodox person *sees* only when *kissing* the image). In Europe, succeeding this icon-economy of the imaginary is the system of the *figure*, which takes hold, "exaggerates," and "corrects" the face, unfolds the features of love and hatred, and puts the spectator into the painting (Coblence).[19]

The beheading of the maternal body is my *princeps* stance in this figuration-tension that transports the speaking being between here and the beyond, between flesh (mother) and sense (sovereign paternal thirdness). Monstrous innocence of this "violence of the human soul" (Coblence) in which women excel: weepy detectives, psychoanalysts too (Spielrein, Klein, Milner, Aulagnier). The indomitable Artemisia Gentileschi summarizes their genius: cutting/cut, the *female* painter occupies the two sides of beheading/murder/subjectivation. Deflection of the "sufferings undergone" into "lucid courage," of the "horror" into "an unprecedented form," of abjection into "new eyes" (Coblence).

Through my probes into systems of representation, Coblence discerns the genesis of an *aesthetic of incarnation*: its psychical-drive sources, its transformations, its singularities.

Proust traverses profanation-perversion by "transubstantiation"—an allusion to the Catholic mass designating the psychical exaltation-concentration of the novelist by which objects, sensations, and impressions are not spoken in "metaphors" but metamorphose into "compact, cool after warmth, rose-pink" substance, quoted by Coblence. Take the episode of the flagellation of Charlus, or the one of the delicious mammary-madeleine, both rolled up in the language of the narrator. Going beyond "psychoanalysis and its clinical field" but "rooted . . . [in] the French exception" that, I maintain, mobilizes "the perverse latencies of the ego at the intersection of sense and the sensible" (Coblence)—think of the sensuality orchestrated in French by Rabelais, Villon, Sade, Rimbaud, Voltaire (more ironic), Sollers (more mysterious).

Colette as a pagan twin of "Time Regained" in *Remembrance of Things Past* but who "purges" the "impure" perversity into "inexpungable innocence," with two areas of seduction: the solar alphabet, anthropomorphic fauna and flora and nauseous chaos; or bestiality and criminality—Landru style[20]—calm and cold, contemporary to the "as if personality" (see Deutsch, Riviere, and the "banality of evil" according to Arendt).

This *aesthetic of incarnation* continues and deteriorates in Céline; it is the "total degradation of words into abjection" (Coblence), indulgent toward Nazi antisemitism. But here too, this son of a lacemaker distills the shreds of his persecuting and death-dealing delirium in a phraseology without punctuation, to deliver a stupefying "opera of the deluge" to the "virgins of pleasure." (See also my reply on Theory of Literature.)

In the psychoanalytic cure, *iconicity* engages me also "as a more archaic degree of . . . psychic life," and Coblence reminds us of this quite pertinently in her analysis of the role of the image at the heart of the process of subjectivation. In the "Didier case," she points to my "interpretation of the perverse meaning of his works . . . at the same time liberating his affected speech": "the traumatism [of this patient, a painter] requires the recreation by the analyst of a maternal *reliance*."

Coblence's synthetic reading elucidates and enriches the *systems* of the image that I sketch in my writings: "powers of horror . . . of the sacred"; "a more archaic expressive modality than words"; "experience of transcendence"; "seduction"; "invasion"; but also "liberating progression."

***

My colleagues' research addresses, along with me, the intersection of the aesthetic and the feminine, as well as their transformation in cultural history. "Suspension" of the aesthetic to elucidate the dynamics of sense and the sensible, in the ongoing anthropological acceleration? Neither politics absorbed by technique and finance nor extinct or radicalized religions seem to be capable of channeling the explosions of those left behind in hyperconnected globalization. In this context, it is to be feared that the times that are approaching are in the end times favorable to hatred. Yet another reason to put into forms or words the seductive terror of subjectivity that works of art reveal. That is where the centrifugal force of humanity resides, against the current of the brown-red or transhumanist ideologies.[21]

Yet another reason not to "neutralize" the feminine and to follow this "boson of the unconscious" linking the soma and the psyche, ungraspable constituent of sensible sense and the imaginary.[22]

J.K.

NOTES

1. Julia Kristeva, *Powers of Horror: An Essay on Abjection*, trans. Leon S. Roudiez (New York: Columbia University Press, 1982); *Pouvoirs de l'horreur: Essai sur l'abjection* (Paris: Seuil, 1980).

2. Words quoted in the following paragraphs come from "Blood and Light/Sang et lumière," a dialogue between Julia Kristeva and Anish Kapoor, April 7, 2015, published in facing-page translations in the exhibition catalogue *Anish Kapoor Versailles*, ed. Alfred Pacquement (Paris: Éditions de la Réunion des Musées Nationaux-Grand Palais, 2015), 36–71.

3. Ibid., 38, 40.

4. Marcel Proust, *Pleasures and Days*, trans. Louise Varese, in *Pleasures and Days and Other Writings*, ed. F. W. Dupee (Garden City: Doubleday Anchor, 1957), 101.

5. Kapoor's description, in *Anish Kapoor Versailles*, 52.

6. Ibid., 36 (Kristeva), 44 (Kapoor).

7. Julia Kristeva, *The Enchanted Clock*, trans. Armine Kotin Mortimer (New York: Columbia University Press, 2017).

8. Elaine P. Miller, *Head Cases: Julia Kristeva on Philosophy and Art in Depressed Times* (New York: Columbia University Press, 2014).

9. "Blood and Light," in *Anish Kapoor Versailles*.

10. *Woman Rubbing Her Back with a Sponge* by Edgar Degas (1834–1917), around 1885, Musée d'Orsay, in Julia Kristeva, *Visions capitales: Arts et rituels de la décapitation* (Réunion des Musées Nationaux, 1998), 147.

11. Julia Kristeva, "Prelude to an Ethics of the Feminine," 51st International Psychoanalytical Association Congress, 24–27 July, 2019, http://www.kristeva.fr/prelude-to-an-ethics-of-the-feminine.html.

12. Julia Kristeva, *The Severed Head: Capital Visions*, trans. Jody Gladding (New York: Columbia University Press, 2012), 127; *Visions capitales*, 150.

13. See Elaine P. Miller, *The Vegetative Soul: From Philosophy of Nature to Subjectivity in the Feminine* (Albany: SUNY Press, 2002).

14. Julia Kristeva, *Melanie Klein*, trans. Ross Guberman (New York: Columbia University Press, 2001).

15. Julia Kristeva, *Black Sun: Depression and Melancholia*, trans. Leon S. Roudiez (New York: Columbia University Press, 1989), ch. 8.

16. Françoise Coblence, "La Vie d'âme: Psyché est corporelle, n'en sait rien," *Revue Française de Psychanalyse* 74, no. 5 (2010): 1349.

17. Ibid., 1288.

18. Sigmund Freud, *Civilization and Its Discontents*, in *The Standard Edition of the Complete Psychological Works of Sigmund Freud*, vol. XXI, trans. James Strachey (London: Hogarth, 1964), 83; *Malaise dans la culture*, in *Oeuvres complètes de Freud: Psychanalyse*, t. XVIII (Paris: PUF, 1930), 270.

19. See also Julia Kristeva, "From Madonnas to Nudes: A Representation of Female Beauty," in *Hatred and Forgiveness*, trans. Jeanine Herman (New York: Columbia University Press, 2010), 57–78.

20. [Henri Désiré Landru was a French serial killer who murdered at least seven women between December 1915 and January 1919. —Tr.]

21. ["Brown" ideologies are those of the extreme right, because of the association of brown shirts with fascism, while "red" ideologies have long meant those of the left. —Tr.]

22. See Kristeva, "Prelude to an Ethics of the Feminine." ["Boson" alludes to the ungraspable Higgs boson in particle physics—Tr.]

15

David Uhrig

NO PRESENT APART

It is not that my time is different from theirs but that I have no present apart from theirs.

—Stanley Cavell, *Must We Mean What We Say?*

From the start, Julia Kristeva's narrative project in *The Samurai* (1990) differs from Simone de Beauvoir's in *The Mandarins* (1954): the audacity of the samurai who daily confronts an uncertain world is diametrically opposed to the prudent figure of the mandarin tied to the permanence of the State.[1] What can do better than this title—*The Samurai*—to portray the change of epoch that led from the period of the laborious reconstruction of France after the Liberation to the discovery of a society of consumption lacking any singing tomorrows?

In both novels one finds the point of view of a psychoanalyst speaking in the first person doubling the story of another central character, but this fact should not mask a decisive difference: in *The Samurai* the two protagonists always allude to the author as, alternately, an amorous student and a seasoned psychoanalyst, in a novelistic structure that designates the autobiographical form as the blind spot of psychoanalysis.

I. *The Samurai*, a Novel-Collage

This autobiographical fiction is first of all a collage of snapshots taken from life, raw sketches, scattered opinions, and snap judgments in which we witness the avid desires of a young Bulgarian student, Olga Morena alias Julia Kristeva,

---

Translated from French by Armine Kotin Mortimer.

who arrives in Paris in the middle of the 1960s thanks to a scholarship from the French government. In the course of encounters with various intellectuals, a series of portraits emerges against the backdrop of a desire for emancipation shared by a whole generation.

The writing has the assurance of an instinctive act, and several choice anecdotes make it possible to shatter the term "French Theory," a shorthand expression the media have substituted for intellectual enterprises as varied as those of Jacques Lacan, Émile Benveniste, Jean-Paul Sartre, Maurice Blanchot, Claude Lévi-Strauss, Lucien Goldmann, Roland Barthes, Gilles Deleuze, François Wahl, Michel Foucault, Jacques Derrida, Marcelin Pleynet, Philippe Sollers, and Antoinette Fouque.

As rapid as the samurai's gesture, as trenchant as the swipe of his saber, the writing subjects the most illustrious intellectual figures of the period to the cutting edge of its blade, beginning by depriving them of the names that often encapsulate their fame.[2] Could we consider this deprivation of identity as the first step in a project of revenge consisting of making heads fall, in the style of Uma Thurman's character, ex-member of the "Deadly Viper Assassination Squad" who, in Quentin Tarantino's film *Kill Bill*, begins by cleanly slicing off the top of the cranium of the female chief of the yakuza?

In relegating these authors to a few isolated fragments of existence, unconnected with the image people usually have of their period, the narration cuts to pieces, instead of weaving, the veil of ideality that too easily is made to cover their epoch, retaining only the little disappointed hopes or the great defeated ideals. This process of distanciation which deprives their works of the "relation of antecedence . . . a father sustains with his child," as Roland Barthes puts it in "The Death of the Author,"[3] turns them into orphans whose abandonment transforms "the abjectness of hope and the pathos of despair into the brief equilibrium of childhood."[4]

Is it not true that precisely the best way to read these texts is to measure the distance their writing implies, both today and in the past, from the movements of liberation that took place throughout the world at the turn of the 1970s? That question is posed indirectly by a remark by Joëlle Cabarus, alias Julia Kristeva turned psychoanalyst, whose point of view decenters that of the young student full of enthusiasm, as if better to resist the numerous temptations of the collective imaginary: "Revolution is a strike on the part of the 'inner consciousness,' which is replaced by mass declarations, psychodrama, acting out, or—quite frankly—love."[5]

II. Beneath the Leaden Masks

Because of this calling into question consigned to the diary of a psychoanalyst who questions her practice, we can read the plot against the current of a conception of History in which the different stories would be absorbed by a broad dialectical scenario. Although Olga's romance is tempered by Joëlle's questioning, which brings its ideality to light, the intensity of what the student lives more or less naively as she discovers France at the same time as love remains at the heart of the plot.

What does the young heroine wish for that the contestatory effervescence of her environment fails to give her? What better can she hope for in a society that struggles to find in the extraordinary potential of its culture the means to get beyond its moral conservatism? Isn't the entire country in the image of that city of Bordeaux, proud to have been administered by one of the most famous humanists of the Renaissance (Montaigne), but obsessed by the profits of its wine production?

While Olga desires nothing other than to rise to the emotions that submerge her, one of the judgments she makes about her husband's father, a big landholder of this southwest region of France, on the day of his funeral shows the incapacity of an entire country to be touched by the most natural emotion:

> His reserve precluded intimacy, so the living corpses present today were silent, ashamed at never having been able to reach the heart which from its retreat had judged them. Unless the truth was that these society people were simply incapable of human feeling beneath their leaden masks? An appearance of reserve often covers real indifference—a foolishness of the senses.[6]

Olga thinks she will at least find, in the intellectual adventure she shares with the writer she loves (Hervé Sinteuil alias Philippe Sollers), the world "as it is" and even "*what was and is* repeated into all eternity, shouting insatiably *da capo*—not only to himself but to the whole play and spectacle, and not only to a spectacle but at bottom to him who needs precisely this spectacle—and who makes it necessary because again and again he needs himself—and makes himself necessary," according to the original quotation from Nietzsche, who insists in *Beyond Good and Evil* on the detachment that implies: "Whoever has really [done this] . . . may just thereby, without really meaning to do so, have opened his eyes to the opposite ideal."[7]

The social network constituted by the literary review *Maintenant* alias *Tel Quel* exposes *everyone* to a change that effectively goes *beyond* what he or she would have ever wanted *for themselves* or wished for *by themselves* for the collectivity. This is in contrast to what the first issue of the review suggested in 1960 in quoting an altered version of Nietzsche's text: "*I* want the world and *I* want it as it was and it is."[8] So that the love relation with this French man rapidly changes for Olga into something that, depending on neither the one nor the other, greatly surpasses the spontaneous egoism of the couple.

III. Looking for a Lover's Discourse

An episode of *The Samurai* that recounts the voyage of several members of the *Tel Quel* group to Maoist China in 1974 shows the eminently critical meaning that such a surpassing in love implies.[9] "At night the three bachelors all went back to their rooms, which they found 'very Spartan.' Hervé and Olga had been given a comfortable bed in one of the luxury bedrooms provided for distinguished guests or eminent Chinese officials traveling with their wives."[10] First observation: the Party has carefully reserved for an elite a quite material comfort that it is manifestly not in the interest of any government, even a revolutionary one, to abandon.

No doubt the explanation lies in this second observation: one discovers one is distinguished according to a ranking that has no other role than to serve the political regime in power. The distinction granted to the person who plays the part of the leader of the expedition traps the couple in a situation so disproportionate to their marital status that they find themselves placed in an awkward position not only with respect to the other members of the group, but also with respect to themselves:

> "Sleep well—we're too tired [on *est trop fatigué*] to make love after such a long day, aren't we?"
>
> Hervé obligingly turned his back, ready to fall asleep right away.
>
> "I suppose you think it wouldn't be fair to the [three] others? [*ce serait* moche *vis-à-vis des trois autres*?]"
>
> "In a way. Don't you agree?"
>
> "I couldn't care less about the [three] others." [*Moi, les* trois *autres, je m'en fous*.]
>
> "Quite right. Sleep well!"
>
> Silence.[11]

For the husband, instituted as dominant male by the mechanisms of the government, it's easy silently to accept sexual frustration and claim not to care about the others. These few words surreptitiously exchanged thanks to a question full of attentiveness show that the husband is perfectly conscious that his official privilege consists precisely in being able to consume (or *not*) what the others don't have: in effect, not only a nuptial chamber but also, to put it crudely, a partner.

It's not obvious that having a sexual relation (or *not*) is going to change anything at all for the "others." The inequality imposed by the government mechanism will remain unshakable in this case. On the other hand, if they were to yield to sleep without exchanging even a word, that would condemn the couple itself to disappear before a partitioning that serves a purpose other than the economy of love. To perpetuate by a dialogue, however fragmentary, the intimate connection that the others are temporarily deprived of, that is the inestimable, if prosaic, privilege of the couple, on the condition that they have the resources for it.

In a setting where the prohibition of courtly love is replayed as transposed into a totalitarian context, Roland Barthes, who occupied one of those very Spartan rooms reserved for the "three others," here appears as an imaginary Third—he who would write, three years after this trip to China: "as an amorous subject . . . I am not necessarily 'depoliticized': my deviation consists in not being 'excited.' In return, society subjects me to a strange, public repression: no censure, no prohibition: I am merely suspended *a humanis*, far from human things, by a tacit decree of insignificance: I belong to no repertoire, participate in no asylum."[12]

IV. Who Are the Samurai?

It's hard for the reader not to think of the hired killer in the film *The Samurai* by Jean-Pierre Melville (1967), superbly portrayed by Alain Delon. With a price on his head, his life hangs by the thread of a little bird with dull plumage and a monotonous call (a female bullfinch), caged out of precaution in some seedy hideout in the Paris of the people. Here we have another way to portray the constrictions of the affective life of individuals in a society under permanent surveillance.

The fall of the Berlin wall, contemporary to the writing of *The Samurai*, seemed to promise the hope that a great movement of democratic reconciliation would soon put an end to regimes based on a totalitarian ideology. But for those who, like Julia Kristeva, had been victims of a permanent administrative control in their own countries, which was then continued abroad, this was an illusion their own situation belied.[13]

Since then, a "world wide web" has made the instantaneous dissemination of images and words likely to condition each person's sensitivity, independently of their meanings. An individual's psychic resistances are thus neutralized in a form of fascination that weakens the fundamental gains of the individual psyche. Spectators lose the very resources that allow them to express the simplest of their emotions: in the ideal distance of the images, sensitivity remains without a name and the violence is unnameable.

If as Roland Barthes writes it is the task of literature to preserve the conditions of possibility of a discourse that, because of its very fragmentation, escapes the assimilative power of all social functioning, it becomes understandable that the gaze of the amorous Olga Morena rejoins that of the psychoanalyst Joëlle Cabarus in the novel. For Olga as for Joëlle, the samurai are those individuals ready to do hara-kiri rather than renounce the sensitivity that animates them. "I don't care if I'm laughed at for writing about pain. After all, psychoanalysis is a discourse on pain, arising out of romantic pathos and disciplined by analytical philosophy. Freud applies reason to pain and helps it to transform itself into something else. Has Lauzun forgotten suffering in his eagerness to formulate it?"[14]

The figure of Lauzun alias Jacques Lacan, broadened to the dimensions of an "amorous discourse," seems particularly vulnerable to that over which the psychoanalyst publicly displayed his mastery. Why, in spite of his great interest in the language and culture of China, had Lacan decided not to participate in the trip to China organized by *Tel Quel*? Partly, according to Philippe Sollers, so as not to let him gain more intellectual precedence over the others than Lacan felt he had himself.[15] Or more profoundly, because he couldn't tear himself away from a mistress who was sucking the blood out of him.[16]

Haunted and tempted by this terribly destructive ego ideal described—and suffered—by Lauzun alias Lacan unmasked, the novel undoes the always misleading identification of any figure of mastery with the different avatars of the ideal. It raises the fragmentary character of all amorous discourse to the level of principle: "What if . . . the very essence of the amatory relationship [in literature and in analysis] lay in preserving the necessity of the Ideal and its detachment from the Superego?" Julia Kristeva had already written in *Tales of Love*.[17]

V. The Role of Autobiography

The fact that the narration seeks to turn ideality against itself explains the comparison we made in the first section between Julia Kristeva's narrative and that of Quentin Tarantino's cinema. In the one and the other case, it's a matter of emancipating the actor, understood broadly (that is, any person implicated in an action), from the stereotypical role his environment has reduced him to. The procedure is the same: arrange a staging capable of dismantling the overvalued expectation of a particular social environment.

To liberate the actor from the potentially inappropriate system of values he is stuck in, Quentin Tarantino brings back a famous actor from a bygone period and turns him against his celebrity, to reveal through the features of an offbeat character the sensitivity of his acting. John Travolta, star of the 1970s, rediscovered thanks to *Pulp Fiction* after twenty years of aimlessness, and David Carradine and Gordon Liu in *Kill Bill*, are exemplary of the rediscoveries we owe to Tarantino.[18]

In the same way, Julia Kristeva detaches her characters from their ideality as models to make their posture as actors visible. What paradoxically distinguishes the actors that these writers have sometimes been, perhaps in spite of themselves, is the ordinary facts of their lives. Why narrate their little peccadillos, quite insignificant, in the end, in comparison to the work they have done? For that very purpose: to confront the ideal figure—idealizing and/or idealized—of the Author with the irreducible biographical detail that fragments his authority.

As Stanley Cavell has grasped, remarkably, here as elsewhere the moral quest is constitutive of Julia Kristeva's reflection. "She is, I assume one is to know, boldly declaring a moral from Lacan's discussion of the difference between the Ego-Ideal and the Ideal Ego."[19] If Lacan is the first one targeted by this moral that he inspired, it is first of all because the sad spectacle of his private life has come into conflict with the interest that Julia Kristeva had in his work.

> Olga feels like kissing the little boy who's being bullied, and trying to comfort him. Hervé is ashamed for the fallen idol.
>
> "Sorry—we have to go."
>
> "That's all right, dear. Do."[20]
>
> Lauzun lets his arms drop to his sides, his usual sign of weariness at mankind's murderous stupidity, and just sits in his chair waiting for the onslaught to continue.[21]

Neither Hervé's embarrassment nor Olga's compassion can spare us the narration of a scene obligingly played out for their eyes: the irremediable solitude of any individual who abandons himself to abandonment. To stay with him bolsters him in his desire to abandon himself, and to leave confirms him in his abandonment. But this "deviation" resembles in every particular the "amorous subject" of Roland Barthes when his desire, like a two-edged saber, separates him from his entourage and at the same time from himself.

VI. A Limitless Present

One cannot summarize any person's life by a feature of their personality, and the pseudonym Lauzun like those of the other characters is there to remind the reader of the distance that must be maintained with respect to the "truth" of the characters. There is an excellent explanation of the doubling around which the novel *The Samurai* is constructed (two central characters for a single autobiographical subject) in this program described by Stanley Cavell: "If the following autobiographical experiments are philosophically pertinent, they must confront the critical with the clinical, which means distrust both as they stand, I mean distrust their opposition."[22] What is too "wrongly personal" in literary fiction prevents us from judging the lives it relates, since our critical point of view is neutralized by the narrative distance.[23] At the same time, the presentation of a few biographical details, which is also "too personal," keeps us adding something affective to what is recounted. All the interest of *The Samurai* resides in this ability to be affected and/or concerned by these few lives, in the face of which our critical judgment is temporarily suspended before the limitless present offered:

> That's really the miracle of analysis, though no one ever talks about it. You learn to inhabit your past so intensely that it isn't separated from your present body anymore, and every scrap of memory is transformed into a real hallucination, a direct perception, here and now. The surprising thing is that this almost mystical metamorphosis continues later with the patients—only in the most inspired moments of an analysis, of course, when I follow them so closely that through my words I give them back my own memory and thus my own body, so that they both become theirs. Thus I've been living for years with a multiple body that isn't really mine, but that survives and even changes in time with the others. Joëlle the octopus, the protean jellyfish, the woman without qualities of her own, who takes her pleasures with the tongs of words, via people who think they're living a real life, while hers is mere imagination embodied in moods.[24]

David Uhrig

New York University Paris
November 2018

NOTES

1. Julia Kristeva, *The Samurai*, trans. Barbara Bray (New York: Columbia University Press, 1992); *Les Samouraïs* (Paris: Fayard, 1990). Simone de Beauvoir, *The Mandarins*, trans. Leonard M. Friedman (New York: Norton, 1999).

2. Lacan (Lauzun), Benveniste (Benserade), Sartre (Dubreuil), Blanchot (Brichot), Lévi-Strauss (Strich-Meyer), Goldmann (Edelman), Barthes (Bréhal), Deleuze (Decèze), Wahl (Weil), Foucault (Scherner), Derrida (Saïda), Pleynet (Brunet), Sollers (Sinteuil), Fouque (Bernadette).

3. Roland Barthes, "The Death of the Author," in *The Rustle of Language*, trans. Richard Howard (Berkeley: University of California Press, 1989), 52; originally published in *Aspen Magazine* 5–6 (Autumn–Winter, 1967).

4. Kristeva, *The Samurai*, 194; *Les Samouraïs*, 258.

5. Ibid., 130; *Les Samouraïs*, 174.

6. Ibid., 295; *Les Samouraïs*, 395.

7. Friedrich Nietzsche, *Beyond Good and Evil*, trans. Walter Kaufmann (New York: Random House, 1966), §56.

8. *Tel Quel* 1 (Spring 1960): 2 (my translation).

9. See Qingya Meng, "Le Voyage en Chine de Tel Quel et de Roland Barthes (1974): Enjeux, embûches, enseignements," Ph.D. diss., Université Paul Valéry-Montpellier III, 2017.

10. Kristeva, *The Samurai*, 189; *Les Samouraïs*, 251.

11. Ibid., 189; *Les Samouraïs*, 251.

12. Roland Barthes, "No Clergyman Attended," in *A Lover's Discourse: Fragments*, trans. Richard Howard (New York: Hill and Wang, 1978), 212–13.

13. Julia Kristeva, "It's Just Not My Life—Julia Kristeva Responds," interview by Olivier Bouchara, trans. Patsy Baudoin, in *The Los Angeles Review of Books*, November 1, 2018; "Une Autre Vie que la mienne," *Vanity Fair France* (July 2018): 66–73.

14. Kristeva, *The Samurai*, 131; *Les Samouraïs*, 175.

15. Philippe Sollers, "Lacan même," in *Fugues* (Paris: Gallimard, 2012), 475.

16. Kristeva, *The Samurai*, 153; *Les Samouraïs*, 205.

17. Julia Kristeva, *Tales of Love*, trans. Leon S. Roudiez (New York: Columbia University Press, 1987), 209–10; *Histoires d'amour* (Paris: Denoël, 1983), 265. The words in brackets in this quotation are Stanley Cavell's insertion into his quotation of *Tales of Love* in *A Pitch of Philosophy: Autobiographical Exercises* (Cambridge: Harvard University Press, 1994), 155–56.

18. See Célia Sauvage, *Critiquer Quentin Tarantino est-il raisonnable?* (Paris: Vrin, 2013), 86.

19. Cavell, "Philosophy and the Arrogation of Voice," in *A Pitch of Philosophy*, ch. 1, 156. [For Lacan's distinction between the Ego-Ideal and the Ideal Ego, see, Jacques Lacan, *Freud's Papers on Technique: The Seminar of Jacques Lacan Book I*, ed. Jacques-Alain Miller, trans. John Forrester (New York: Norton, 1991), 129–42.—Ed.]

20. According to Kristeva, Lacan used to say "*cher/chère*" to anyone, indifferent to the gender (which appears in French only when written).

21. Kristeva, *The Samurai*, 153; *Les Samouraïs*, 205.

22. Cavell, *A Pitch of Philosophy*, 8.

23. Ibid., 4.

24. Kristeva, *The Samurai*, 129; *Les Samouraïs*, 171–72.

16

Pierre-Louis Fort

JULIA KRISTEVA AND THE DETECTIVE NOVEL: FICTION AND METAPHYSICS

The novel is a flowering of questions.

—Julia Kristeva, "*Murder in Byzantium*"

While Kristeva is often presented as a renowned psychoanalyst, a cosmopolitan scholar, and a theorist known throughout the world, we sometimes forget to add to this trilogy the writer translated into several languages, the novelist whose fictional work, far from being merely a distraction—on the contrary—makes the complexity and the depth of her thought resonate.[1]

For nearly thirty years, in fact, Kristeva has forged intimate ties with the novel. After having studied it extensively, she engages in her practice of the novel in the calm of the time that she succeeds in making available from all those times she inhabits and that inhabit her, a temporality stolen and subtracted, as it were, from the order of the everyday, allowing her to surrender to a "writing by night." This writing is placed under the double sign of "disconnection and regression," it is a moment without moorings, an alchemy in which "composition comes in a second phase, also without a safety net, but more consciously musical."[2] To emphasize the force that governs this nocturnal and sometimes nomadic activity, Kristeva has declared: "Writing is an unconscious necessity for me. I don't decide when to scrawl notes in my journal or write page after page in bed at two o'clock in the morning."[3] From

Translated from French by Armine Kotin Mortimer. An earlier version of this chapter appeared as "Du côté de chez Stéphanie Delacour," in Julia Kristeva, *Prix Holberg* 2004, ed. Isabelle Rieusset-Lemarié (Paris: Fayard, 2004).

this singular, passionate, and fascinating experience several novels have been born, three of which belong more specifically to the detective genre. Kristeva herself evokes her "series of metaphysical detective stories, *The Old Man and the Wolves*, *Possessions*, *Murder in Byzantium*."[4]

Metaphysical? These novels unquestionably are, as we shall see by detailing what qualifies them as such, beyond their resonance with recent attempts to classify the "metaphysical detective story" genre. For while they share with that classification the intention to "question the mysteries of being and knowledge," the novels written by Kristeva go beyond codes and frames. One of the major differences with the category the critics have defined lies notably in the link to the plot: whereas in such narratives the questioning "transcend[s] the mere machinations of the mystery plot," with Kristeva the questioning finds its origin and its reverberation in the intrigue.[5] The "metaphysical crime novel," as she explains during an interview, "tells political stories and human passions in order to exhibit this criminality intrinsic to and always underlying the social link."[6] The plot, then, is at the service of a true critical and reflective design. As Kristeva explains the articulation: "The 'metaphysical crime novel' allows me to tell an adventure and an inner experience, painful or ecstatic, situated in a historical context, without depriving myself of the ability to distill a certain number of reflections on the world today."[7]

I. The Detective Novel: A Narrative Turning Point

The detective novel (or its Kristevan avatar) does not come first among the author's publications. Before starting her series of metaphysical thrillers, Kristeva publishes a first novel entitled *The Samurai* in 1990,[8] a "*sensual and metaphysical narrative*"[9] centered on the "*impassioned life of intellectuals*,"[10] tracing what has sometimes been called "the trajectory of the 'Tel Quel generation.'"[11] In it one finds identifiable characters, as in a *roman à clés*. But while the text includes a substantial autobiographical component (for example, the arrival of Olga in Paris, recounted in the opening of the work, recalls the author's),[12] this dimension is only one of the elements of a novel in which "transformation or deformation" has a greater role.[13] From her first steps in the novelistic domain, Kristeva rejects the "novel of the Self," which she later designates as rather facile, and writes the "novel of the Subject," conducive to a metaphysical implementation. Playing on the refraction of her "doubles," she considers the novel, from her beginnings in the genre, as a way of thinking (in *narrative* versus in *concept*), thus rejoining the questioning of an author dear to her, the author of *In Search of Lost Time*: "Recently, reading Proust's handwritten *Carnets*, I noted . . . a question: 'Should I make it into a novel, a philosophical study?' It is an eternal problem, knowing how to treat a subject that concerns us, whether theoretically or fictionally."[14] The following year, 1991, Kristeva publishes a new novel, the first in this series of metaphysical detective novels: *The Old Man and the Wolves*. The intertextuality of this title—not Simone de Beauvoir and *The Mandarins*, as was clearly the case with *The Samurai*, but more plausibly Freud with *The Wolf Man*—is already a subtle way to give an inkling of the metaphysical dimension of the work.[15]

In *The Old Man and the Wolves*, the reader discovers a character promised to a fine future in Kristeva's narratives: Stephanie Delacour. A vivacious young woman with a sharp eye and a keen intelligence, "the special envoy of *L'Événement de Paris*," is sent to Santa Barbara—the place where a good many of the novels take place—as soon as an event happens there (preferably a crime), so that she ends up being both journalist and investigator.[16] Moreover, she finds herself in familiar territory because her father was an ambassador there and she herself spent part of her childhood there. In writing this somber and troubling first of these novels, marked by the death of Professor Septicius Clarus, assassinated (perhaps) by wolves that "symbolize the ambient barbarism, the criminality of each and every one,"[17] Kristeva brings to life the woman who will become her emblematic character.

In 1991, then, we find Kristeva where she wasn't necessarily expected: not only is she persisting in fiction by authoring a second novel, but, furthermore, it is a detective novel. Critics express no end of astonishment: *Really, Julia Kristeva, why are you writing a detective novel? This is a most astonishing marginal note*—so suggests some of the critical reception, forgetting people like Robbe-Grillet, Butor, Pennac, and Modiano. For the detective novel is not a minor genre, far from it, and Kristeva knows it. Not only does she play with the genre, she even succeeds in displacing its norms and renewing its practice. Better yet: at the source of a choice that one might think motivated by chance and a certain taste for provocation, Kristeva places an internal and personal necessity, as she revealed to Christine Rousseau during an interview: "After *The Samurai*, I wrote to mourn the death of my father. The form of the detective novel impressed itself on me then as a way to delve deeply into seriousness and what is most unapproachable: the death drive. The thriller allows for remaining in the open, the investigation being a version of optimism, for me the only one. One does not eradicate the evil, but one can know where the radical evil that is murder comes from."[18]

This means of confronting a loss, the detective novel, turned out to be for Kristeva an encounter with *the* form that corresponds to her insatiable desire to question and to understand, to be psychically and intellectually in movement, as she is in her daily life, whether during her public interventions or in the intimacy of her office. Besides, how can one ignore the intrinsic and original proximity between the detective novel and psychoanalysis, both of which are kinds of hermeneutic enterprises?[19] As early as *The Old Man and the Wolves*, Kristeva pointed out this fundamental connection: "I intend to persevere in the detective genre—a game, a way of continuing analysis."[20] What particularly seduces her about this "game" seems to be the principle of interrogation, stimulating and profoundly fruitful, which she summarizes as follows: "the detective novel says, 'You can know' without necessarily giving the answer, but placing us in the investigation. The question, because it is more stimulating and more open than the answer, is our only promise."[21] The space-time of freedom that Kristeva grants herself via the detective novel is thus nothing other, in fact, than a space-time of reflection and research, but in another modality—an *other* modality—more ludic, to be sure, but just as effective.

A testing ground, this *Old Man and the Wolves*? More like a launch since it won't be long before this first detective novel is followed by another. After *The Old Man and the Wolves* appears *Possessions* in 1996, which opens with the discovery of a decapitated woman and continues with the questioning of maternal passion, through the optic of the detective story.[22] This novel places at its heart "the passion and beheading of Gloria Harrison, a translator in a world where no one reads any more, and the mother of a deaf child."[23] Kristeva likes the carnivalesque melody it gives out and calls it her "favorite metaphysical detective novel."[24]

But the one that was best received by the critics is certainly the third one, which appeared in 2004. This is *Murder in Byzantium*, which opens directly on a murder scene with the assassination of a member of a sect by the mysterious Number Eight. Other crimes and disappearances will follow in this novel characterized by a complex plot, which combines the investigation into the serial murderer appearing in the first pages with the flight of Sebastian Chrest-Jones, the historian of migrations who is passionate about Anna Comnena. While the narrative allows her to portray Anna Comnena, an "important intellectual figure," it is also, as Dominique Bourdin emphasizes, "a meditation on wandering, exile, and strangeness [that] unfolds in a quest for origins—the Bulgarian origins of the author and those of her characters."[25]

Whatever the singular orientations of these novels, the reader is taken each time to the place mentioned above: Santa Barbara.

II. Santa Barbara: Backdrop of a Vast Reflection

As a common backdrop, the place Kristeva calls Santa Barbara is the planetary village, "the corrupt, criminal, and mafialike society of the globalized village."[26] In an interview, she speaks of this singular and symbolic location in the following terms: "The imaginary city of Santa Barbara might be found in the heart of Central or Eastern Europe, but it also evokes an American megalopolis or a similar European city. One can find a fountain there that strangely resembles the one at the Beaubourg Center, while the Oasis bar recalls a very popular place in San Francisco."[27] The symbolic dimension prevails, then. The author continues: "The very name of Santa Barbara suggests to me first of all the ambient barbarity, but also, by reference to a well-known American soap opera, complacent American society, and the banalization that is one of the features of modern savagery."[28]

Santa Barbara, the *barbaric*? Yes, and even more so when one knows that the etymology of Barbara, "barbaric," refers to "foreigner" or "stranger" and that the problematic of the "stranger," just as much as "strangeness," is dear to Kristeva.[29] In her detective novels, this "strangeness" is constitutive of her characters. In *Murder in Byzantium* it culminates, notably, with Sebastian Chrest-Jones, the Police Commissioner Northrop Rilsky, and even Stephanie

Delacour, caught up in her Russian origins. This diffuse "strangeness" is partially but not exclusively that of its author, who declared at the reception for the Holberg Prize that one of the wagers of *Murder in Byzantium* was "to write in [her] migrant's French the happiness and the misfortunes of the displaced."[30] Moreover, in Kristeva's detective novels, the displaced exist in all the meanings of the word: the geographically displaced, of course, but also the psychically or affectively displaced; displacement, exile, and wandering rank first among the issues raised by her "thrillers."

The latter, however, are so rich that it would take the space of another essay to attempt to compile an exhaustive list of all the themes and problematics touched upon. The fact is, one would have to mention maternity, disability, love, hatred, evil, feminism, and politics too—the present state of the world in general and of Europe in particular. To which we should add the interrogation of identity (as Kristeva explains: "whether it's a 'detective story' in the style of Patricia Highsmith or a 'mystery novel' in the style of Patricia Cornwell, the detective novel shakes up our identity and makes us complicit in one human being's murder by another and the ultimate intolerability of this");[31] and we should not forget the role religion is made to play. Kristeva insists as well on the profound ability of the novel to treat "this incredible need to believe":[32] "What other composition, if not the polyphony of the novel, could convey these psychical modulations that are different religions, in crisis today more than ever and consequently in fratricidal conflict?"[33] In Kristeva's detective novels, the questions echo each other, from the political to the religious, from the public to the intimate, continually restimulating thought.

One of the most striking aspects of her work, in this metaphysical perspective, and subsuming it entirely, is certainly the perspective that consists in the confrontation with time[34] through the concepts of time and "time outside time" (originally a Freudian notion—the *Zeitlos*—that Kristeva has analyzed and returned to, notably in *Intimate Revolt*).[35] These two categories are at the heart of *Murder in Byzantium*, for example. Kristeva concedes it as follows, in showing how they constitute the secret fabric of the text:

> *Murder in Byzantium* is basically a novel about Time, about the diversity of the times we live in, perhaps more diverse now than ever before: the time of the first Crusades in the eleventh century and the modern crusades; the time of the cathedral in Le Puy and the Orthodox churches on the edges of the Black Sea; the time of Byzantium attacked by the Seldjukides in the east and the Latins in the west, and the time of the modern Byzantium that France is today, which is having a hard time having its difference recognized between the power of Santa Varvara and the terrorists of Bin Laden, the time outside time of the love affairs of Stephanie Delacour and the commissioner, or the time just as outside time of her maternity, not forgetting the time of crime, black ecstasy that makes Sebastian a killer of butterflies, a strangler, and Wuxian a bloodthirsty calligrapher, a purifying serial killer.[36]

Is this salience of time and time outside time in her work due to chance? Should we merely see in it a simple reflection of theoretical research, of analytical investigation? No. The two categories are fundamentally connected to the detective novel. Kristeva insists on this when she proposes that "the detective novel leads its readers precisely to this unbearable and fascinating place where the death drive shatters duration. Crime fascinates us because it reveals a psychical functioning that allows itself to suspend time, and which, in the instant of the criminal gesture, is itself excluded from human time."[37] The detective novel is thus "the only type of novel to deal with this radical evil that is murder and that abolishes human time, the time of life: radical evil is a catastrophe of time."[38] Kristeva's entire oeuvre, critical and fictional, is placed under the sign of time—that, in any case, is one way of conceiving it—and even her latest novel (in 2018) places time at the center of its issues and its objectives with the famous clock by Passemant. Without being a metaphysical detective novel, *The Enchanted Clock* resonates with this genre prized by the author, with Police Commissioner Rilsky even returning in the second half of the novel.

III. Generic Renewal and Aesthetic Melting Pot

Kristeva's detective novels are thus not content with a simple police investigation. They augment it with a play of reflections supported by a historical accompaniment and a philosophical, critical, and political intent (notably by exploring the way the death drive and radical evil resurge in contemporary times: "my novels . . . necessarily became crime novels in which the pathological is mixed with the political").[39] In this way, though never neglecting the narrative thread, Kristeva plunges the reader into a vertiginous universe by multiplying practically to infinity the possibilities that writing offers her, blurring the boundaries and thwarting expectations.

Claude Durand, her editor and friend, had been drawn, as early as *The Samurai*, to the "blend of naivety and temerity with which this foreigner allowed herself to play with the very genre of the novel, the French novel,"[40] but it is in the detective novel that this renewal of the genre reaches its full measure. And it is *Murder in Byzantium*, most certainly, that marks a turning point in this regard, noticed by the press first of all, which applauded a "total novel" and emphasized the ambitious composition of the whole.[41] In *Le Point*, one could read an enthusiastic celebration of the way Kristeva eluded rigid classifications while making her work resonate with her analytical, psychoanalytic, philosophical, and ontological preoccupations: "We have here a thriller. A metaphysical fable. A novel of love. An encrypted self-portrait. We have here a picaresque narrative founded on sects, terrorism, the end of History, Europe under construction or convulsion, ritual murders, mysterious manuscripts. We have here a meditation on Evil. A return, but through fiction, of this irremediable 'strangeness to oneself' the author has explored elsewhere."[42] In this same "Bloc-notes," an article in which the analyses emphasize the kaleidoscopic aspect of the work, even the metanovelistic dimension of *Murder in Byzantium* was suggested: "We have here a novel about the novel."[43]

A novel about the novel? The idea is correct, because, not without irony[44]—and her novels do not lack for irony—Kristeva shakes up the novel in its entirety and does not hesitate to challenge the form that she invests at the very moment when she is immersed in it, whether in *Murder in Byzantium* through Stephanie Delacour who declares, frankly and with much irony, that "the novel is the rhetoric of the perverse"[45] or through more evident authorial interventions, which occur in *The Old Man and the Wolves*.[46] Kristeva thus becomes mischievous and facetious in and with this form that she revisits, reinvents, and forges on the basis of the novel. So much so that her detective novels become protean, multiple, and experimental and push the innovation even into their material realization, notably in *Murder in Byzantium*, where one finds maps, paintings, and reproductions of icons inserted into the book.

Although this is the first time Kristeva lets one *see* concretely, in a novel, she had previously played on the visual domain quite often, not by inserting images but by evoking numerous painters: Goya, for example, in *The Old Man and the Wolves*, and Caravaggio in *Possessions*. To suggest painting, then, and more broadly still, to play on the arts to make the fiction denser: sculpture with the fountain in Santa Barbara or the allusions to Rodin, music with Scarlatti and Scott Ross's playing, and also Vivaldi. With this cultural and aesthetic openness, the intent is to open the detective novel onto the arts and involve them in the critical resonance that the detective novel conducts. Painting, sculpture, music, but also, of course, writing since Latin authors, philosophers, and novelists of the greatest diversity surface constantly to nurture and support reflection.

The most diverse, but also the most prestigious, and, notably, in this rich and varied pantheon, Colette and Proust whom Kristeva convokes in speaking of Stephanie Delacour: "Stephanie Delacour, who is my alter ego, admits that she does not inhabit the phonemes and syntax of the French language—a kingdom in which she will always be surpassed by Proust or Colette, to cite only those two—but she writes the melody of the sensory that flows beneath her sentences."[47]

IV. Novel of the "Self" versus "Novel of the Subject"

Is Stephanie Delacour Julia Kristeva's alter ego, as she herself suggests? In a certain sense, yes, and numerous indications, in a playful vein, could shore up this resemblance. Stephanie Delacour does resemble Julia Kristeva a lot, in fact. But Julia Kristeva is not Stephanie Delacour. Even if, as Rousseau quite rightly emphasizes, the novel helps her "get beyond her wounds: the loss of the father, the difficulty of being a mother (*Possessions*), then the mourning for her mother around which *Murder in Byzantium* crystallizes," Kristeva does not subscribe to a logic of total projection of herself—which is certainly an important aspect of her writing; she preserves her intimacy and rejects the novel of the "Ego-Ego":[48]

> The novel as an account of the subject uses the affects of the ego who is telling the story, telling its story—pleasure, anxiety, fear, violence, shame, seduction, etc., so as to activate them, to put them to the test of events. But it plays with them like cards in a game, as a body is used in choreography or the chords of a musical instrument in a concerto. Then affect, childhood memories, romantic trials, and personal history are sideswiped by the stakes and rules of the philosophical, ethical, and political game. The big story is transfigured by the little story. And it is indeed this crossing, this diagonal line, that makes up the real flesh of the novel of the subject, which is not an admission or a confession, but a questioning, a voyage, an invitation to distance oneself from original identities, insufflating an essential irony into the very heart of the tragic.[49]

There is some of Julia Kristeva in her novels, then, but in a diffracted manner. The author does not resonate only with Stephanie Delacour, she multiplies the echoes with other characters. Thus, in *Murder in Byzantium*, she is also Sebastian Chrest-Jones, specialist in migration and a migrant himself: "It started with a daydream about my nomadic life: the strange pleasure I felt 'feeling at home' in airplanes reminded me of my father's jokes, about how our family name, Kristev, which means Delacroix (of the cross), meant that we were descended from the crusaders, bizarre people, holy but hardly commendable travelers."[50] Kristeva insists, moreover, on her proximity to these two essential characters: "The initials of the last name Chrest-Jones echo my own, Kristeva-Joyaux, and Stephanie Delacour is her father's daughter, as I am."[51] But she is careful not to favor these kinds of projections and reaffirms both her own singularity and the limits of identification: "Through Sebastian and Stephanie, who both resemble me, but are complete strangers to me. . . . I am speaking of myself as if I were another."[52]

What is the secret of this distancing? A clever savoir-faire: drawn from "personal histories," "stories of the ego," as she says, "but mixed together, played out or thwarted, put in perspective, disengaged, endlessly refracted," utilizing, among others, irony, to "play the ego card, yes, like a card in a game, on the path, the diagonal line that cuts across the circle of the confinement of identity, as well as the circle of oblivion."[53] Anyone who knows how to untangle such a subtle web would be truly skillful. It's not a matter of searching for the keys or tracking Julia Kristeva in the novel, but of letting oneself be carried along by her words and her art of narration. Kristeva invites us to enter into the story, to let ourselves be sensitive to its rebounds, and to immerse ourselves in this destabilizing universe that makes us confront our anxieties and our own metaphysical questioning. To take the direction of Kristeva's metaphysical detective novels is a way of going "in search of lost time" and exploring the complex and ambiguous regions of "hatred and forgiveness."

V. Traveling Oneself

Perhaps we may end this analysis of Kristeva's novels, her detective novels in particular, with the motto of her heroine Stephanie Delacour: "I travel myself," which has become the title of Kristeva's memoirs. "I travel myself," she says several times. Nothing about this neologism is innocent, quite the contrary, and Kristeva has reminded us of it in the speech connected with the Holberg Prize, saying this:

> And, since this journalist is a cultivated woman, to say "I travel myself" is, in sum, her way of summarizing a fundamental axis of our European culture: from Saint Augustine, who admitted only one country for himself, one of travel, precisely ("*In via, in patria*"), to Freud, who wrote: "Where Id was, there Ego shall be." In other words, for the heroine who resembles me, the crossing of borders—geographical, between disciplines and constituted discourses—is possible only if the one who travels succeeds in displacing his or her own internal borders: I travel *myself*.[54]

Subtly convoked here are Proust, with ideas like "successive sorrows" (*Time Regained*),[55] and Colette with rebirth ("To make a clean sweep, to build up once more, to be born again has never been too much for me," *Break of Day*).[56] Intertextuality thus insists on this renewal induced by "traveling oneself." And it is precisely to this experience of a new flowering of the self, of displacement of the self, that Kristeva invites us in her novels: "The questions are raised, there is no response, and the reader is invited once again to 'ship himself on a voyage.'"[57]

This invitation to "travel oneself," proposed *by* and *with* the detective novel with a metaphysical dimension, is pursued in the other works by Kristeva, whether in *Teresa, My Love* or *The Enchanted Clock*, in which we find Police Commissioner Rilsky and time as principal protagonists. And what if the detective novel, it too, "traveled itself" in the oeuvre, going beyond its generic borders and carrying us along with a metaphysical whirlwind that is nothing other than thought in movement and in action?

PIERRE-LOUIS FORT

CY CERGY PARIS UNIVERSITY
NOVEMBER 2018

NOTES

Translations of quotations from French texts for which there are no English versions are by Armine Kotin Mortimer.

1. Her fictional work is already the subject of several critical studies, some examples of which are listed here for those who would like to learn from their stimulating reflections. Paul Renard, "Des Mandarins aux Samouraïs, ou de l'engagement existentialiste à l'individualisme post-moderne," *Roman 20-50*, no. 13 (June 1992): 111–24. Ieme van der Poel, "Possessions: La Sainte Trinité revue par Julia Kristeva," in Michael Bishop and Christopher Elson, eds., *French Prose in 2000* (Amsterdam: Rodopi, 2002). Colin Davis, "Psychoanalysis, Detection, and Fiction: Julia Kristeva's Detective Novels," *Sites: The Journal of Twentieth-Century Contemporary French Studies* 6, no. 2 (2002): 294–306. Ieme van der Poel, "Linda Lê et Julia Kristeva: Citoyennes de la langue française," in Aline Mura-Brunel, Marc Dambre, and Bruno Blanckeman, eds., *Le Roman français au*

tournant du XXIe siècle (Paris: Sorbonne Nouvelle, 2004). Chen Szu-chin Hestia, *French Feminist Theory Exemplified Through the Novels of Julia Kristeva: The Bridge from Psychoanalytic Theory to Literary Production* (Lewiston: Mellen, 2008). Maria Margaroni, "Julia Kristeva's Chiasmatic Journeys: From Byzantium to the Phantom of Europe and the End of the World," in Kelly Oliver and S. K. Keltner, eds., *Psychoanalysis, Aesthetics, and Politics in the Work of Julia Kristeva* (New York: SUNY Press, 2009). Benigno Trigo, ed., *On Kristeva's Fiction* (Albany: SUNY Press, 2013).

2. Julia Kristeva, "*Murder in Byzantium*, or Why I 'Ship Myself on a Voyage' in a Novel," in *Hatred and Forgiveness*, trans. Jeanine Herman (New York: Columbia University Press, 2010), 304; "Meurtre à Byzance, ou Pourquoi 'je me voyage' en roman," *La Haine et le pardon* (Paris: Fayard, 2005), 653.

3. Ibid., 275 (translation modified); *La Haine et le pardon*, 611.

4. See Julia Kristeva, "Intellectual Autobiography," in this volume, 130; *Je me voyage: Mémoires* (Paris: Fayard, 2016), 265. Julia Kristeva, *The Old Man and the Wolves*, trans. Barbara Bray (New York: Columbia University Press, 1994); *Le Vieil Homme et les loups* (Paris: Fayard, 1991); *Possessions*, trans. Barbara Bray (New York: Columbia University Press, 1998); *Possessions* (Paris: Fayard, 1996); *Murder in Byzantium*, trans. C. Jon Delogu (New York: Columbia University Press, 2006); *Meurtre à Byzance* (Paris: Fayard, 2004).

5. Patricia Merivale and Susan Elizabeth Sweeney, "The Game's Afoot: On the Trail of the Metaphysical Detective Story," in *Detecting Texts: The Metaphysical Detective Story from Poe to Postmodernism* (Philadelphia: The University of Pennsylvania Press, 1999), 2.

6. "Entretien avec Julia Kristeva: Penser en nomade et dans l'autre langue le monde, la vie psychique et la littérature," interview with Irene Ivantcheva-Merjanska and Michèle Vialet, in *Kristeva in Process: The Fertility of Thought, Cincinnati Romance Review* 35 (Spring 2013): 163.

7. Ibid.

8. Julia Kristeva, *The Samurai*, trans. Barbara Bray (New York: Columbia University Press, 1992); *Les Samouraïs* (Paris: Fayard, 1990).

9. Julia Kristeva, "À propos des *Samouraïs*," interview by Elisabeth Bélorgey, *L'Infini* 30 (1990): 57.

10. Ibid., 56.

11. Christine Rousseau, "Julia Kristeva, la Byzantine," *Le Monde*, February 6, 2004.

12. See Bernard Pivot, "Double jeu," broadcast 26 June, 2003 on the France 2 channel.

13. Kristeva, "À propos des *Samouraïs*," 56.

14. Ibid.

15. Simone de Beauvoir, *The Mandarins*, trans. Leonard M. Friedman (New York: Norton, 1999). Sigmund Freud, "From the History of an Infantile Neurosis," in *The Standard Edition of the Complete Psychological Works of Sigmund Freud*, vol. XVII, trans. James Strachey (London: Hogarth, 1955).

16. All the more so because she frequents—sometimes very closely!—Police Commissioner Northrop Rilsky, another important character in the author's novels. But the heroine is sometimes a subject of suspicion, as in *Possessions*. [The English translation of Kristeva's novel renders the location as Santa Varvara.—Ed.]

17. Julia Kristeva, "Roman noir et temps présent," interview by Bernard Sichère, *L'Infini* 37 (1992): 76.

18. Rousseau, "Julia Kristeva, la Byzantine."

19. Davis, "Psychoanalysis, Detection, and Fiction: Julia Kristeva's Detective Novels," deals with this topic.

20. Kristeva, "Roman noir et temps présent," 83.

21. Kristeva, "*Murder in Byzantium*," 305; *La Haine et le pardon*, 654. See also Julia Kristeva, *Intimate Revolt: The Powers and Limits of Psychoanalysis Volume 2*, trans. Jeanine Herman (New York: Columbia University Press, 2002), 4; *La Révolte intime: Pouvoirs et limites de la psychanalyse* II (Paris: Fayard, 1997), 10.

22. On the theme of decapitation, one can read Kristeva's *The Severed Head: Capital Visions*, trans. Jody Gladding (New York: Columbia University Press, 2012); *Visions capitales* (Paris: Éditions de la Réunion des Musées nationaux, 1998).

23. Kristeva, "Intellectual Autobiography," this volume, 130; *Je me voyage*, 265.

24. Ibid., 131; *Je me voyage*, 267.

25. Dominique Bourdin, "La Femme, la vie, la foi: quelques publications récentes de Julia Kristeva," *Revue française de psychanalyse* 73, no. 2 (2009): 560.

26. Kristeva, "Murder in Byzantium," 273; *La Haine et le pardon*, 610.

27. Kristeva, "Roman noir et temps présent," 76.

28. Ibid.

29. See Julia Kristeva, *Strangers to Ourselves*, trans. Leon S. Roudiez (New York: Columbia University Press, 1991); *Étrangers à nous-mêmes* (Paris: Fayard, 1988).

30. Speech given on December 2, 2004, at the University of Bergen. [Julia Kristeva is the first laureate of the Holberg International Memorial Prize for outstanding scholarly work in the fields of the arts and humanities, social sciences, law, or theology. It is administered by the University of Bergen. Kristeva gave an acceptance speech at the ceremony and a presentation on "Thinking about Liberty in Dark Times." The latter is published in *Hatred and Forgiveness*.—Ed.]

31. Kristeva, "*Murder in Byzantium*," 288; *La Haine et le pardon*, 630.

32. Kristeva, *This Incredible Need to Believe*, trans. Beverley Bie Brahic (New York: Columbia University Press, 2009); *Cet incroyable besoin de croire* (Paris: Bayard, 2007).

33. Kristeva, "*Murder in Byzantium*," 297; *La Haine et le pardon*, 642–43.

34. How can we not think again of Proust and of Kristeva's now classic book, *Time and Sense: Proust and the Experience of Literature*, trans. Ross Guberman (New York: Columbia University Press, 1998)?; *Le Temps sensible: Proust et l'expérience littéraire* (Paris: Gallimard, 1994). This question of time will be exploited further in the novel *The Enchanted Clock*, trans. Armine Kotin Mortimer (New York: Columbia University Press, 2017); *L'Horloge enchantée* (Paris: Fayard, 2015).

35. "The Scandal of the Timeless," in Kristeva, *Intimate Revolt*; "Le Scandale du hors-temps," in *La Révolte intime*.

36. Kristeva, "Murder in Byzantium," 281–82 (translation modified); *La Haine et le pardon*, 621.

37. Ibid., 285; *La Haine et le pardon*, 626.

38. Ibid., 286; *La Haine et le pardon*, 627.

39. Ibid.; *La Haine et le pardon*, 628.

40. See "Intellectual Autobiography," in this volume, 52. Kristeva, *Je me voyage*, 107.

41. See Rousseau, "Julia Kristeva, la Byzantine."

42. Bernard-Henri Lévy, "Bloc-notes: Le Byzance de Julia Kristeva—Bondy et Reza—Libérez Battisti," *Le Point*, no. 1640 (February 19, 2004): 114.

43. Ibid.

44. In the course of *Murder in Byzantium*, Kristeva realizes a distinction between revelatory irony ("an elevation toward a truth") and destructive derision ("leaves us with the impression that everything is imposture"). *Murder in Byzantium*, 243–44; *Meurtre à Byzance*, 365.

45. See Kristeva, "*Murder in Byzantium*," 304; *La Haine et le pardon*, 652.

46. See the beginning of the first chapter, "Neither More Nor Less" in the second part, "Detective Story," in *The Old Man and the Wolves* to illustrate these interventions.

47. Kristeva, "*Murder in Byzantium*," 301; *La Haine et la pardon*, 649.

48. Rousseau, "Julia Kristeva, la Byzantine." Kristeva, "*Murder in Byzantium*," 274 ; *La Haine et le pardon*, 611.

49. Kristeva, "*Murder in Byzantium*," 277–78; *La Haine et le pardon*, 615–16.

50. Ibid., 290; *La Haine et le pardon*, 634.

51. Ibid., 291; *La Haine et le pardon*, 634.

52. Ibid.; *La Haine et le pardon*, 635.

53. Ibid., 280; *La Haine et le pardon*, 619–20.

54. Kristeva, "Penser la liberté en temps de détresse," *La Haine et le pardon*, 26. [This passage does not appear in the publication of Kristeva's Holberg Prize presentation in *Hatred and Forgiveness*.—Ed.]

55. Marcel Proust, *Time Regained*, trans. Andres Mayor and Terence Kilmartin (New York: Modern Library, 2003).

56. Colette, *Break of Day*, trans. Enid Mcleod (London: Secker & Warburg, 1961), 112; *La Naissance du jour*, in *Oeuvres*, t. III (Paris: Gallimard, 1991), 349.

57. Kristeva, "*Murder in Byzantium*," 292; *La Haine et le pardon*, 636.

REPLY
TO DAVID UHRIG AND PIERRE-LOUIS FORT

It was a while before I dared to let myself be absorbed by a character or create a narrative.[1] Was it my experience of psychoanalysis—which had already taken me from the couch to the armchair? Was it motherhood—which nurtured and revitalized me in French, having become my mother tongue and the cradle of vocalizations and fantasies? Was it the impasses, if not the looming "end" of history, the bankruptcy of providential ideologies, and the disappointment with the political that culminated with my trip to China? Philosophy and the human sciences lacked the luxurious appeasement that fiction and the imaginary bring to language. The *novel* seemed to me the propitious place to let this endless end be heard.

Bakhtin, whom I had introduced in France, had revealed, in symbolizing Dostoyevsky, that the novel is a *polyphonic*, mosaic, kaleidoscopic genre. I agreed wholeheartedly with this polyphony. Freud, attentive to the cumulative temporal diversities in the dreams and memories of his patients, had discovered the *time-outside-time* (*Zeitlos*) of the unconscious. What other composition, if not the polyphony of novels, would give resonance to psychosis, that brutal reality of globalized humans to which globalized criminality bears witness?

My novels are better liked in foreign countries, and yet French is now my only language for writing. My French was that of an immigrant. In it I would write the fortunes and misfortunes of the uprooted, and I have never learned to inhabit its phonemes and its syntax the way Colette and Proust were able to. Writing fiction also impressed itself upon me like an unconscious necessity that "falls upon you": an *infralinguistic experience*, tied up with the melody of the *sensible* that runs under sentences and even more so with the *tempo* of the polyphonic narrative structure itself, set with philosophical and political insertions. Impossible to continue without all that. I decide nothing when I scribble notes in my "travel notebook" or when I write page after page in the middle of the night. One of my analysands, visibly in a phase of positive transference, told me he was convinced that I "like to take down the mirror" when I write my novels. It's true, "I" decompose "myself" into multiple facets: images from childhood and family are present but disseminated within a historical fabric, a whirlwind of "estrangements" and "transubstantiations."[2]

During the night, between two dreams, waking up is a necessity for me—it is not insomnia but a paradoxical lucidity that nevertheless blinds me. Suspending

---

Translated from French by Armine Kotin Mortimer.

my vigilance, letting myself submerge into that "dark spot" Freud speaks of (sensation, fragrance, or brutality, sentence or idea) that occupies all space in the darkness.[3] Flinging myself toward this "dark spot" the way one who jumps from the sixth floor. Speed is my element, *Time* has become my main character: to write time for the times. I take responsibility for the insolence of this opening, this ambition. A message in a bottle.

I. David Uhrig

David Uhrig and Pierre-Louis Fort received the message with a demanding complicity that highlights my audacities as well as my limits. Had I sensed them? These authors have named many others, which come to the fore only in the mysterious collection of the instances of reading when reading recreates writing and is free of the novelist's "without-Oneself."

Yes, as Uhrig notes, the writing of *Les Samouraïs* (1990) is "as rapid as the samurai's gesture."[4] Has the novel become a *katana*, the long saber that the samurai wields with two hands, in homage to the Japanese *chanbara*? I do see myself in this.

After twenty-five years of initiation into and practice of "French Theory," the young student Olga Morena (my double) shatters the "media shorthand" of that "intellectual enterprise" by slashing with a *saber* its more or less unrecognizable protagonists. Could Olga Morena, "avid" but "romantic," "submerged by emotion," be the Bride in *Kill Bill*, Quentin Tarantino's famous film—a killer from a secret organization, the Deadly Viper Assassination Squad, portrayed by Uma Thurman—as Uhrig imagines it? The comparison does not displease me; rather, I'm honored by it because it is quite true that Olga embodies the "desire for emancipation shared by a whole generation" and the desire to "detach [my] characters from their ideality as models to make their posture as actors visible" (Uhrig) even as "players." (As, for instance, Lauzun/Lacan's amusing conflicts with his mistress, which prevent him from participating in the trip to China with the review *Maintenant/Tel Quel*.) The narrative, "diffracted" and "ironic," as Fort specifies, inverts the potential suspicion of "revenge" when it doesn't quash it from the start in the "sensitivity of the acting" (Uhrig). Henceforth, "critical judgment is temporarily suspended," and the reader, "affected" and "concerned" (Uhrig), participates in the novel.

The *violence of writing*, proclaimed from the title (*The Samurai*) but ignored or minimized by theoreticians of *writing*,[5] and which Uhrig points out with the imaginary and the respect for texts he is known for, had struck me from the start—both in the personal feeling of this experience and in my cohabitation with the men and women the experience lives in. Is it not to the imaginary of a writer, the Marquis de Sade, continuing to write his oeuvre in prison, that we owe the most extreme and scandalous revelation of the destructivity inherent in human psychosexuality, which accompanies the writing of fantasies and takes shelter in the imaginary?

Other "processes of distanciation" punctuate the violence of *The Samurai*, according to Uhrig, and prevent it from retreating into the "too personal" or "the revenge consisting of making heads fall." *Doubling* is one of them, and I am pleased that the author insists on Olga Morena's alter ego, the psychoanalyst Joëlle Cabarus. With her, the psychoanalytic approach participates explicitly in the writing of the novel, and Uhrig concludes that the "novelistic structure . . . designates the autobiographical form as the blind spot of psychoanalysis." To her we owe this reflection on *pain* (quoted by Uhrig)[6] in which psychoanalysis and literature intersect and are merged, but above all reciprocally question each other. In confronting this *detachment* of the revolutionary posture, the clinician diagnoses that "revolution is a strike on the part of the 'inner consciousness.'"[7]

Actually, this gentle doctor of souls does not fail to remind us, in her notebook, that she bears the name of a famous revolutionary, Thérèse Cabarrus (1773–1835), better known by the name Madame Tallien. This young woman—free in her pleasures and a "feminist" avant la lettre, "French vivacity and Spanish voluptuousness"—then stood up against Robespierre and saved from the guillotine numerous nobles from Bordeaux, became the beneficent "Our Lady of Thermidor," and gave a "Discourse on the Education of the Citizenry" in 1793 at the Temple of Reason in Bordeaux!

This inclusion of History will extend to my other novels, as Uhrig notes, with the first female historian, Anna Comnena (1083–1153) in *Murder in Byzantium* and Émilie du Châtelet (1706–1749) in *The Enchanted Clock*.[8] In *The Samurai*, the often multiple doubling (the couple Martin/Carol is juxtaposed with the Hervé/Olga couple, etc.) and the snapshots, "scattered opinions" or "snap judgments" instill the *carnivalesque* into the "samurai's gesture." Thus these "historical characters" open "private histories" to the *historical*.[9] And narration, though shaken, does not close but remains in the *open*: "a limitless present," writes Uhrig.

I discovered with a great deal of emotion how Uhrig particularly appreciates some features of "my" characters. The *modesty* of Jean de Montlaurs, the father of Hervé Sinteuil (alias Philippe Sollers) whose "reserve precluded intimacy, so the living corpses present today were silent, ashamed at never having been able to reach the heart which from its retreat had judged them."[10] Or this particular feature of Hervé/Philippe: "Again and again he needs himself—and makes himself necessary," which I trace by appropriating an expression from Nietzsche. Likewise, the *couple* Hervé/Olga in China, pressed between the political pressure of the host state and the presence of the "three" bachelors, breathes again and is renewed only with the breath of time,[11] and only in that way attempts to *"greatly surpass the spontaneous egoism of the couple"* (Uhrig).

The multiplicity of characters and/or discourses, which "cut to pieces" and, when they do not "weave the fabric," bring a singular *rhythm* to my *Samurai*, as Urhig specifies. "Rhythm is my business," I could say with Ella Fitzgerald. And I would add some of my favorites to the decomposed-recomposed identities evoked by Uhrig: Dan (Tsvetan Stoyanov, a Bulgarian literary critic and my friend); Albert Lévy (Albert Cohen, the Bulgarian journalist, foreign correspondent, and the first person who assists Olga when Boris is not waiting for her at the airport and she has only five dollars in her pocket); or Olga, pregnant, listening to the migrating birds in the salt marshes of the Island of Ré, then taking her son Alex, with Hervé, for a walk in the Luxembourg gardens . . . But neither the novel nor an inspired reading of it can say everything, and Uhrig, a judicious interpreter of Maurice Blanchot,[12] carefully exposes "the fragmentary character of all amorous discourse."

II. Pierre-Louis Fort

Pierre-Louis Fort, specifying that my novels "make the complexity and the depth of [my] thought [as a theoretician] resonate," devotes his study to my series of "metaphysical thrillers": *The Old Man and the Wolves* (1991), "somber and troubling first" of these thrillers, consecutive to the death of the father;[13] *Possessions* (1996), constructed around Gloria Harrison, the mother of Jerry, a deaf child, and a translator, who is beheaded in Santa Barbara, a city symbolic of the globalized village;[14] and *Murder in Byzantium* (2004), "saga of immigrants" and "completely twisted detective novel," which explores "more secret territory . . . than in my earlier books."[15] The author comments that these "metaphysical thrillers" "go beyond codes and frames" because the narration "transcends . . . the mystery plot" in which it "finds its origin and its reverberation . . . at the service of a true critical and reflective design." A "way of *thinking* (in *narrative* versus in *concept*)" "the criminality of each and every one" "intrinsic to and always underlying the social link"—the metaphysical thriller is "*the* form that corresponds to [my] insatiable desire to question and to understand."

Analyzing these three novels—particularly *Murder in Byzantium*—as a putting into question of both the detective novel and metaphysics, Fort takes up and develops my distinction between the *novel of the ego* and *the novel of the subject*. My "metaphysical thrillers" belong to the second category. What is the difference?

Psychoanalysis has changed our relation to what we *say*. Can we *write* as if psychoanalysis did not exist? In unlocking childhood creativity and its metamorphoses, psychoanalysis permits the self to be reborn if and only if it places itself into question. The ego reassures itself in the exhibition/shoring up of its minidramas. In contrast, the *intimacy of the subject* is diffracted into a mosaic of associations and perceptions that destabilize the egoic complacency but also that of the readers. The *subject* is at the crossroads of irreconcilable identities, in transverberation with those of others. It is also invited to take on philosophical, ethical, and political stakes and rules. "No genre, only a diagonal passing through" (*Murder in Byzantium*).[16] Fort quotes this passage in our interview[17] and develops it here.

Was it necessary to borrow the *ways of narration*, even if only in foiling them, to inflect the "Cartesian subject" or the "transcendental ego" toward the sensorial and affective "prepredicative sphere" dear to phenomenologists?

Recent observations, inspired by cognitivism, seem to confirm Klein's thesis of a "proto-fantasy" in the baby, anterior to the acquisition of language. A quasi-narration, a "prenarrative envelope"[18] articulates drives and desires, aiming for the object (the breast, the mother) to insure the survival of the young phobic and sadistic ego. Narration, in sum, is the elementary structure of the object relation and of the fantasy that constitutes it.[19]

To loosen the grip of the moral and intellectual superego, we therefore have no other method than to *cathect* narration, to shore up the subject's modulations and metamorphoses. To *recount* in order to remain in contact with the prehistory of subjectivity. Narration: "emerging property" of thought, emerging mental construction of the real world. The novel of the subject takes hold of narration to redo it and to redo itself. At this level of the investment of *signifiance*,[20] writing-analysis unfailingly confronts the gravity of "what is most unapproachable: the death drive," Fort reminds us. He summarizes the unbearable tension that carries the *narrative* of the murder, backed up by the *investigation* that explores it. Whereas putting the murder into words *assumes* the rupture of life and *punches holes* in narrative time, the investigation maintains that you can know where the evil, including radical evil, comes from, our one and only promise proving to be the act of questioning. Thus the author subscribes to my definition of the "metaphysical thriller" as a "version of optimism."

It remains to develop the very specific intimacy of the *feminine* with the *death drive*, which I address in my "Prelude to an Ethic of the Feminine."[21] And, in the process, the excellence and ease of women novelists in the detective genre, the "queens of the detective novel" (from Agatha Christie to Patricia Highsmith, to mention only these two) whom my "female genius" seeks to unveil.[22] The spirited journalist Stephanie Delacour, double of the narrator, sometime detective (and echoing the distinguished police chief Rilsky, who sees himself as a potential twin of "his" criminals), is both seduced and devastated by the protean ramifications of evil. In the face of these ramifications, she becomes malicious and facetious: "The novel is the rhetoric of the perverse," she declares bluntly.[23] Fort, not rejecting this diagnosis but inscribing it in the ironic tonality of my metaphysical detective novels, reminds us of its gravity, which he calls "authorial" (exposed by the female narrator in *The Old Man and the Wolves*), a gravity that carries and justifies my blazing, exploded, and recomposed narrative structure.

***

To conclude, I would very much like to return to a few excerpts of this initiation to the "authorial" novel of the subject:

> But if the master of ceremonies should reveal himself and include himself in the story, then the narrative, whether dreamlike so far or literary, plausible or grotesque, is ipso facto transformed into a quest after mysteries, a police inquiry. And the form of the narrative, the twists and turns of the plot, the changes of genre, will depend on choices made by the narrator himself in terms of space, distance, and psychological geometry. . . .

> This angle of vision invests the writer with a neutrality that is a kind of arrogance: the presumptuousness of those who are sure of themselves and of traditions and beliefs that conceal a tendency to jump to conclusions. In other words, a fundamental stupidity. . . .
>
> The novel breaks down into fragments, into poetic prose, the occasional dash of sentiment or compassion heralding the eternal return of lucidity. And when speech reaches the extreme of its own strength and certainty, it may revert to the weakness, flexibility, and repetitiveness of its point of departure in baby talk, nursery rhymes, and lullabies. . . . But storytelling also relies on pleasure, the kinetic pleasure everyone feels in following a sequence of events. . . .
>
> But let us also consider people who are immature, whose intelligence, developing as they—allegedly—grow up, is devoted to observing their own weaknesses: anxiety, fear, sleeplessness, stupidity, bestiality, brutality, crime . . . And who knows what else? And would I say if I knew? When people like this pluck up the courage to speak they tell stories. But while their kind of story puts the pieces together, instead of arriving at a completed jigsaw puzzle it produces only a riddle. There's a meaning here, it says, but it's a hidden meaning. There's a purpose, but its object escapes me. There's action, but who will notice and be affected by it? . . .
>
> Beneath all the rigor of method, concept, doubt, and wager, I claim and proclaim the minor dignity, and the therapeutic, aesthetic, philosophical, even physical value of the polytopical space in which the simple-minded meet, recognize one another, and merge. The kind of people who, when they try to put into words adventures they have secreted away in order to make life bearable, dare, like me, to say "I" in lots of different ways.[24]

Pierre-Louis Fort, you who probe the vitality of the singular feminine beyond mourning and in written form, in the ordeal and in strangeness,[25] you know that the "metaphysical thriller" did not stop with the trilogy. Stephanie Delacour yielded to Silvie Leclerc, who becomes the explorer along with Teresa of Avila to probe the transverberations of her inner palace (*Teresa, My Love*).[26] And police chief Rilsky, not content to investigate the attack at the Louvre (*Murder in Byzantium*) is again solicited by the fire that occurs at the Chateau de Versailles when Nivi and Stan visit Claude-Siméon Passemant's fabulous astronomical clock (*The Enchanted Clock*).

> Have you noticed the absolute silence that resonates on earth just before nightfall? Only an ear attuned to the deep radiance of beings captures it, escaping parasite noises. What one calls a "couple," in the inaccessible meaning of this term, is formed when two people hear this radiance in each of themselves, reciprocally, and in the world around them. No one else can mix in. We have indeed become a sort of couple, my A[stro] and I. . . . Through the enchantment of a fabulous astronomical clock at Versailles, the clock made by Passemant, a visionary in love with his King at the dawn of the Enlightenment.[27]

> I watched over Stan during his first illness, then during his coma, and even more at his awakening.
>
> "Can we go see the clock, Mama, can we?"

Scarcely reanimated, was my son wondering what time it was? I must have looked flabbergasted.

"Don't worry, I feel fine. I'm okay now. How about you? Do you remember that clock and the pushing and shoving, at Versailles?"

At life's frontiers Stan is thinking about what time it is, what time it was, and what time it will be. He lives in time, Stan, and brings me back into it.[28]

A love story, always—Uhrig and Fort have identified its fragile strangenesses—and, definitively, Time, my subject, to invite the reader to think in novels.[29]

A new one, to come? Maybe. I have its title: *For the Time Being.*

J.K.

NOTES

1. I had already written Julia Kristeva, *Sémiotikè: Recherches pour une sémanalyse* (Paris: Seuil, 1969); *Revolution in Poetic Language*, trans. Margaret Waller (New York: Columbia University Press, 1984); *La Révolution du langage poétique: L'Avant-garde a la fin du XIXe Siècle, Lautréamont et Mallarmé* (Paris: Seuil, 1974); *Powers of Horror: An Essay on Abjection*, trans. Leon S. Roudiez (New York: Columbia University Press, 1982); *Pouvoirs de l'horreur: Essai sur l'abjection* (Paris: Seuil, 1983); *Tales of Love*, trans. Leon S. Roudiez (New York: Columbia University Press, 1987); *Histoires d'amour* (Paris: Denoël, 1985); *Black Sun: Depression and Melancholia*, trans. Leon S. Roudiez (New York: Columbia University Press, 1989); *Soleil noir: Depression et mélancolie* (Paris: Gallimard, 1989).

2. I develop these arguments among others in a long interview with Pierre-Louis Fort in "*Murder in Byzantium*, Or Why I 'Ship Myself on a Voyage' in a Novel," in Julia Kristeva, *Hatred and Forgiveness*, trans. Jeanine Herman (New York: Columbia University Press, 2010), 273–305; "*Meurte à Byzance, ou pourquoi 'je me voyage' en roman*," *La Haine et le pardon: Pouvoirs et limites de la psychanalyse III* (Paris: Fayard, 2005), 609–55.

3. See Kristeva, "*Murder in Byzantium*," 296; *La Haine et le pardon*, 641. In a letter to Lou Andréas-Salomé: "I have to blind myself artificially in order to focus all the light on one dark spot." Sigmund Freud and Lou Andréas-Salomé, *Letters* (New York: Norton, 1985), 45.

4. Julia Kristeva, *The Samurai*, trans. Barbara Bray (New York: Columbia University Press, 1992); *Les Samouraïs* (Paris: Fayard, 1990).

5. See Jacques Derrida, *Of Grammatology*, trans. Gayatry Chakravorty Spivak (Baltimore: Johns Hopkins University Press, 1976); Roland Barthes, *Writing Degree Zero*, trans. Annette Lavers and Colin Smith (New York: Hill and Wang, 1968); and Philippe Sollers, who complemented his *Writing and the Experience of Limits*, trans. Philip Barnard and David Hayman (New York: Columbia University Press, 1983) with the unbelievable verbal and philosophical profusion of his *Paradis*, t. 1 (Paris: Seuil, 1981) and *Paradis*, t. 2 (Paris: Gallimard, 1986).

6. "I don't care if I'm laughed at for writing about pain. After all, psychoanalysis is a discourse on pain, arising out of romantic pathos and disciplined by analytical philosophy. Freud applies reason to pain and helps it to transform itself into something else. Has Lauzun forgotten suffering in his eagerness to formulate it?" Kristeva, *The Samurai*, 131; *Les Samouraïs*, 175.

7. Ibid., 130; *Les Samouraïs*, 174.

8. Julia Kristeva, *Murder in Byzantium*, trans. C. Jon Delogu (New York: Columbia University Press, 2006); *Meurtre à Byzance* (Paris: Fayard, 2004); *The Enchanted Clock*,

trans. Armine Kotin Mortimer (New York: Columbia University Press, 2017); *L'Horloge enchantée* (Paris: Fayard, 2015).

9. "Historical" here translates the German *geschichtlich*. The term implies history as "destiny," i.e., the history of Being, which is the profound sense of history (*geschichtlich*), used in contrast to *historisch*. See Martin Heidegger, "Temporality and Historicality," *Being and Time*, trans. John Macquarrie and Edward Robinson (New York: Harper & Row, 1962), 424–55.

10. Kristeva, *The Samurai*, 295; *Les Samouraïs*, 395.

11. See Julia Kristeva and Philippe Sollers, *Marriage as a Fine Art*, trans. Lorna Scott Fox (New York: Columbia University Press, 2016); *Du mariage considéré comme un des beaux-arts* (Paris: Fayard, 2015).

12. See Maurice Blanchot, *Chroniques politiques des années trente: 1931–1940*, ed. David Uhrig (Paris: Gallimard, 2017); and David Uhrig, *Maurice Blanchot, magicien-philosophe (5/5): Les Deux Versions de Thomas l'Obscur*, radio broadcast on France Culture: Les Nouveaux Chemins de la connaissance, May 16, 2008.

13. Julia Kristeva, *The Old Man and the Wolves*, trans. Barbara Bray (New York: Columbia University Press, 1994); *Le Vieil Homme et les loups* (Paris: Fayard, 1991).

14 Julia Kristeva, *Possessions*, trans. Barbara Bray (New York: Columbia University Press, 1998); *Possessions* (Paris: Fayard, 1996).

15. See Kristeva, "*Murder in Byzantium*," 294, 280, 271; *La Haine et le pardon*, 639, 619. 610.

16. Kristeva, *Murder in Byzantium*, 67; *Meurtre à Byzance*, 117.

17. See Kristeva, "*Murder in Byzantium*," 278; *La Haine et le pardon*, 617.

18. See Daniel N. Stern, "L'Enveloppe prénarrative: Vers une unité fondamentale d'expérience permettant d'explorer la réalité psychique du bébé," in *Journal de la psychanalyse d'enfant*, no. 14 (1993), 13–65; and Julia Kristeva, "La Narration en psychanalyse: Une Transsubstantiation," in *La Haine et le pardon*, 290–93.

19. See Julia Kristeva, *Melanie Klein*, trans. Ross Guberman (New York: Columbia University Press, 2001), 144; *Le Génie féminin*, t. II., *Mélanie Klein, ou le matricide comme douleur et comme créativité* (Paris: Fayard, 2000), 236.

20. For *signifiance*, see also my replies to to Ducard, Lechte, and Mylona in the section on Language and Semiotics in this volume; to Hobson, Margaroni, and Nikolchina in Theory of Literature; and to Brusset, Baldacci, and Rabain in Psychoanalysis.

21. Julia Kristeva, "Prelude to an Ethic of the Feminine," 51st Congress of the International Psychoanalytical Association, London, July 24–27, 2019, http://www.kristeva.fr/prelude-to-an-ethics-of-the-feminine.html.

22. See Kristeva, *Melanie Klein*, 135–36; *Mélanie Klein*, 221.

23. See Kristeva, "*Murder in Byzantium*," 304; *La Haine et le pardon*, 652.

24. Kristeva, *The Old Man and the Wolves*, 63–66; *Le Vieil Homme et les loups*, 97–100.

25. On the works of Beauvoir, Yourcenar, Annie Ernaux, see among others Pierre-Louis Fort, *Ma mère, la morte: L'Écriture du deuil chez Yourcenar, Beauvoir et Ernaux* (Paris: Imago, 2007); not to mention political history in literature, from colonialism to the still problematic integration, in Azouz Begag, *Le Gone du Chaâba* (Paris: Champion, 2014).

26. Julia Kristeva, *Teresa, My Love: An Imagined Life of the Saint of Avila*, trans. Lorna Scott Fox (New York: Columbia University Press, 2015); *Thérèse mon amour: Sainte Thérèse d'Avila* (Paris: Fayard, 2008).

27. Kristeva, *The Enchanted Clock*, 103–4; *L'Horloge enchantée*, 146 and back cover.

28. Ibid., 13–14; *L'Horloge enchantée*, 26.

29. See Julia Kristeva, "L'Horloge enchantée," interview by Abeline Majorel, *L'Infini* 134 (2016): 53.

17

Edward S. Casey

DEPRESSION: HEADING DOWN AND OUT

This essay and the one that follows, by Alina N. Feld, were conceived together and pay conjoint tribute to the thought of Julia Kristeva by pursuing alternate pathways in *Black Sun: Depression and Melancholia*, each going in a direction ostensibly opposed to the other yet converging in the end. In this first essay, depression is in focus not as a pathology but as a felt phenomenon. The several ways in which a depressed person finds herself drawn down into her body and her emotions with seemingly no escape are discussed from a largely descriptive and phenomenological point of view. Affect and body are here at stake, and special attention is paid to the ways in which what surrounds the depressed subject contributes to the emergence and lingering of downcast states. In the next chapter, the emphasis is on melancholy. Pursued there are other dimensions and directions of *Black Sun*—following vectors that take us out of the individual subject and transport us into the theological realm, where the death of God is the major event in contrast with personal object-loss regarded as a finite matter. The question becomes: How does melancholy release us from sheer affliction and take us somewhere else—into the meta-physical? Taken together, the two essays trace out complexities in *Black Sun* to which no single or simple analysis can do full justice. Each follows fulgurations rather than featuring finalities.

> *Where does this black sun come from? Out of what eerie galaxy do its invisible, lethargic rays reach me, pinning me down to the ground, to my bed, compelling me to silence, to renunciation?*
>
> —Julia Kristeva, *Black Sun: Depression and Melancholia*

Where does depression come from? Often we are tempted to say that it "descends," "comes upon us," "takes us over"—from *we know not where . . .* Part of being depressed is not knowing just where it comes from, even if we may know the precipitating cause (the death of someone close to us, a serious setback in our current professional life). But we do know *where it takes us*: it takes us *down*, way down and way below where we were before it came upon us. Not that there are no preliminary signs, recognizable warning signals—a sense of impending darkness, a gathering gloom, forebodings that darken the day before the undertow sets in: warnings sent out from a *black sun*, a locution whose oxymoronic construction signifies a withdrawal of light from within the very source of light itself: "darkness flashes as a solar light."[1] These bare signals—felt as sadness or listlessness, or unremitting pessimism—are portents, premonitions. As such, they occur at the outer limits of conscious experience, being its coruscating edges as it were.

Attending to such adumbrations may help us not to be overwhelmed when "the world of darkness and despair" arrives in full force.[2] Often they play a diversionary role—acting as a shield protecting us from something more portentous that we fear is coming next and all too soon. They constitute a kind of dark foreplay in relation to what is oncoming, which is not a discrete object or event but an entire state of mind and emotion that we call conventionally "depression." We know we are in it when it arrives in full force even if we do not know where the depression itself comes from. It certainly settles *in us*, as if we are its intentional destination or target. What we don't know is what is its own locus, its own place of origin? We may well know the whereabouts of depression—the places in psyche and soma where it is most likely to afflict us—but we do not know its own domicile, its own ultimate whereness.

One thing we do know: depression is all about *loss* and, most especially, "object loss." If the primary cause of depression is absence, then it is coming from a certain kind of nothing—a nothing that still exists. It stems from a nullity—a nonbeing that, precisely as not existing, has no place of its own, no home-place, indeed no place at all. As pseudo-Archytas proclaimed, "all existing things are either in place or not without place."[3] In other words, to exist is to have a place; not to exist is to have no place at all. And yet it is this very nonbeing, that which has no place of its own, that is the very occasion of depression and that acts to bring it about in those who are susceptible to it.

No wonder then that we do not know exactly where depression comes from. How could we, if it comes from a nonbeing that, precisely as not-existing, is itself nowhere? And yet it is just here that we reach the pivot of depression: for it is the very absence, the very loss, the nonplacement that generates a depressive force. Depression is not only *about* object loss, it is instituted by the loss or absence itself as well as by our negation of it (e.g., by efforts *not* to think about it, to deny the loss itself). All such *négatités* have a psychical force of their own. This force is not merely reactive but is *an intrinsic force of its own*. This force fuels what we experience as depression, giving to it its own energy. It also accounts for the poignant sense of descent that depression brings with it, its powerful proclivity for *pulling us down* physically and *getting us down* psychically. We are here dealing with a potent form of affective gravity whose psychophysics has yet to be fully spelled out, although Kristeva has made a powerful and promising start in *Black Sun*.

The paradox of exerting force from nowhere and nothing was something that fascinated Freud. As Kristeva demonstrates, Freud's essay "Negation" (*die Verneinung*) is built upon a version of this same paradox. In negating something explicitly, we do not remove the object of negation from any further influence. On the contrary, it takes on a force of its own—precisely by being denied. So the negated object is not annihilated but gains a special actuality in the very act of negation itself. We move here from stark object-loss to a situation of ongoing *Nachträglichkeit*, continuing efficacity.

This survival of the negated-as-lost object means that, rather than being sheerly or simply lost, the kind of loss at stake in depression constitutes a special form of continuance, of after-life. This happens not at the level of the symbolic alone, as in Freud's paradigm of linguistic negation ("this does not exist"), but also, as Kristeva insists, in semiotic expressions (e.g., a depressive gesture such as wringing one's hands or hanging one's head). Her analysis merges negation with "denial" as the more generic process, about which she writes that "denial focuses on the *intrapsychic (semiotic and symbolic) inscription of the want*."[4] The depressed person both lacks and desires the lost object, and in its place constitutes a syndrome that brings the object back—a species of *resurrection*, not now of a sacrificial god but of someone or something that had once been an intact presence in one's life. The loss does not end in vacuity or sheer absence but in a form of continuing presence whereby the lost object continues as what Kristeva aptly calls "the Thing"—a haunting presence that suffuses depression with a special form of psychic gravity that is felt in the downwardly moving directionality of depression.

In fact, there is a twofold survival of the lost object—in symbolic and/or semiotic formations but also by way of *affect*. Kristeva's description is vivid: "The affect is the partial object of depressive persons; it is their 'perversion,' in the sense of a drug that allows them to insure a narcissistic homeostasis by means of a nonverbal, unnameable (hence untouchable and omnipotent) hold over a nonobjectal Thing."[5] Notable here is Kristeva's point that affect is not merely reactive—not just an immediate emotional response—but is itself an active force that serves to protect the depressed person from self-destruction: "the depressive affect—and its verbalization in analyses and also in works of art—is the perverse display of depressed persons, their ambiguous source of pleasure that fills a void and evicts death, protecting the subject from suicide as well as from psychotic attack."[6] Together, then, sign and affect act not just to mediate or mitigate object loss but to bring about a vicarious *vita nuova* of the lost object, transformed into a Thing that sustains the depressed person, who is "glued to the Thing (*Res*)"—a situation in which affective value is "riveted to the thing."[7] This Thing is thus no mere substitute for the lost object but a being in its own right, powerful enough to carry a depressed person through the deepest Vale of Despond. By no means a determinate thing—an entity, a substance, nor even a psychical substance (an "idea," a "memory")—this Thing is, rather, "a mere Nothing."[8]

By this circuitous path, we return to where this line of thought began: to the Nothing. But now we realize that it is not a matter of sheer vacuity but of a Non-Being that has a force of its own—a force sufficient to maintain the depressed person in a minimal viability, protected from suicide for the time being even if devitalized in relation to everyday tasks and pleasures.

By the same token, this Non-Being occupies a Non-Place that possesses its own positivity—a nugatory place that acts as "the *crypt* of the inexpressible affect."[9] A crypt is here understood as "an exitless personal vault," "the darkroom of what thus becomes my psychic tomb."[10] Instead of being the depository for dead bodies, the depressive crypt is a psychic vault that holds lost objects—dead or missing presences, as well as things of irreplaceable value—and that acts both to hold these objects in place and to preserve them as Things "buried alive."[11] This is what becomes of these objects once they are invested with affects that cling to them and endow them with emotional density and intensity: thereby realizing a continuing presence within the depressive subject. An affect such as sadness or hatred—and sometimes both together—overwhelms the depressed subject by under-whelming it: coming from below, from the body (and ultimately from the earth). As Kristeva puts it: "As primary inscription of the loss that persists beyond denial, the affect swamps the subject."[12] It swamps it to the point of rendering the depressed subject virtually speechless—with limited if any access to the symbolic order, where coherently formulated significations reside. No god is here resurrected from entombment, released to a heaven beyond the vault where his literal body had been placed; rather, the depressed subject endures in a self-wrought psychic crypt that constitutes the very scene of survival. In such a crypt, in such a null-place, the subject survives itself.

Let us circle back to our initial description of how depression *feels* to the depressed person: that is, let us return to the phenomenology of the afflicted subject. Its unknown ultimate location—what we have come to call its Non-Place—contributes directly to two effects. First, there is the way a serious depression overwhelms us each time it occurs, pulls us *down* into despair—no matter how often this has happened, and no matter how well we think we understand its psycho- or physiogenesis, and despite being able to give a detailed description in so many words (that is, at a symbolic level) of just how it inhibits our spontaneity. The force of the experience can be captured in these four words: *it takes us over*. Indeed, it is precisely because we don't know its ultimate locus that it exerts such force.

A second effect is the striking way that theories of depression tend to be baroque in their abstractness and complexity. This is evident from the merest glance at the canonical psychoanalytic theories of depression—from Abraham and Freud, Klein and Jacobson to more contemporary work. Ingenious and insightful as these can be, they employ a proliferation of explanatory constructs that often seem evasive in their very ingenuity. The ideas at play in such theories are what we can call "superstructs," created from the deeply mired experience of depression itself, as if to compensate for depressive downward-going by adverting to dazzling conceptual heights. The highly corporealized character of depression—the undeniably *heavy* body sensibility it brings with it, reinforced by affects that bog down the suffering subject—is here *built over* in the form of a pyramid of superstructs that loom over it and that bear such names as "primary identification," "secondary repression," etc. Something about depression as a felt state of being seems to call for these supervening explananda: as if they will allow us finally to map out the labyrinthine caverns of depression and arrest its downward spiral by providing us with a measure of relief and resolution at the level of theoretical insight. One suspects that the alchemists' insistence on starting with *nigredo* ("blackening")—closely related to the black sun (*sol negre*)—was itself an admission of the dark origins of melancholy, its unknown roots, and that the processes of refinement and transmutation they advocated for converting dross into gold anticipated the same upward thrust of psychoanalytic models of depression. The directionality in such models is *up* and *out*—up and out from the *down* and *in* that characterizes the first-person experience of depression itself.

We have been tracking how depression, despite its ponderous felt presence, is often occasioned by, and is the dark aftermath to, sheer *loss*—especially loss of a person to whom we've been close in life, whether family member or friend. It is as if the very *absence* that loss entails—the person (or thing, place, experience) we have lost is gone forever—is compensated for by the psychic *weight* of depression: as if the latter could take the place of the loss, or at least cover it over, making it such that we don't have to deal with the nothingness of the loss itself. For this loss qua sheer absence is something we cannot face: in place of the living other, there is now *no one* before us, *nothing* anymore present: we are staring into the vacant face of the Nothing-There, the heart of darkness. No wonder we flee into elaborate psychical strategies composed of evasive, symptomatic complexes that defy precise naming, much less full theoretical understanding. Clinical efforts at understanding depression reflecting this evasion fly further afield into the realm of conceptual abstraction.

In the face of all this compensatory behavior and panicky flight of ideas, Kristeva's *Black Sun* offers relief in the form of rays of hopeful light. Although not averse to employing the jargon of the pioneers of psychoanalysis, she turns their conceptual meanderings to descriptive and poetic effect, suggesting that a more salutary approach would be one that offers a way around the often obfuscating psychoanalytic nomenclature that has become canonical after more than a century of writing on depression. In so doing, she literally *lightens up* both the burden and the opacity of depression. She suggests where it comes from in new ways—ways that, while offering no panacea for it, nor any easy exit from it, do allow us to construe depression differently. In particular, she removes depression from the almost exclusively pathological status it has been given in so many classical as well as contemporary treatments of depression. In her discussion of artists like Nerval and Holbein, Dostoyevsky and Duras, she draws back the curtain on an experience that has long been assumed to be so unremittingly grim as not to allow any alleviation of its own self-compounding gravity. (See Alina Feld's essay in this volume.) Thanks to her generous gesture, very different vistas open up. Literature and painting do not afford direct, much less permanent, alleviations of depression; but they glimmer with creative possibilities that are otherwise foreclosed when the subject is caught up in the midst of an implacable depressive episode.

My insistent question has been this: what does it feel like to be depressed? I have been arguing in various ways for the radical indeterminacy of this experience. The depressed person does not know just where the felt force of the affliction is coming from nor even where it is currently located: in the body (and then in which precise part of the body?) or in the mind (just where there?). Even if particular symptoms are often felt in lethargic bodily movements (referred to in the psychiatric literature as "physical retardation"), or in an unduly heavy sense of one's body as a single mass, or in bleak and hopeless moods (the depressed person, according to *DSM V,* "feels sad, empty, hopeless"),[13] or in certain angry or despairing thoughts, it remains the case that there is no *simple location* for the depression itself, that is, the whole state or condition from which one suffers. Just as Whitehead argued against simple location for things and events in the physical universe in the wake of quantum physics,[14] so Kristeva can be said to offer an equivalent critique in the realm of soma and psyche. She, like Whitehead, is deeply skeptical of the modernist passion for finding the exact cause, the precise locus, of a given phenomenon. Both thinkers want to preserve a dynamic field as the basis for phenomena as different as prehensive relations between events (as described in *Process and Reality*)—events that are linked by the indeterminacies of feelings—and depression regarded in *Black Sun* as nonsimply located: as not limited to what *I* as an isolated subject experience in mind or body but as something more diffuse—something not only *in me* but *around me*; situated not only in my own personal being but also in the unforgiving bleakness of my immediately surrounding world.

Kristeva's version of the indeterminacy principle as it applies to the first-person experience of depression leads us to grasp a thus far neglected dimension of depression. If the precise whereness of depression is not determinable from within the experience of depression itself, this opens the prospect that depression does not come exclusively from *within* the human subject—thus that it is not located altogether *in* that subject. At stake here is the real possibility that depression can characterize and pervade whole lifeworlds and not individual subjects alone. Put differently, there is no compelling reason to exclude the *environmentality of depression.* By environmentality I do not refer merely to literal factors that act in a directly causal manner: as when one is thrown into despair by seeing one's home entirely destroyed in Paradise, California, by the recent devastating fire there. In this kind of case, there is likely to be a twofold sequence of sheer shock at the sight of the ruins of one's homeplace, followed by depression over one's prospects for inhabiting any comparable domicile in that location in the future. But environmentality on my construal also includes more subtle circumambient factors that characterize one's surroundings even if barely noticed at the time: *peripheral influences*, as we might call them. These include other people's emotions that we "pick up" by virtue of merely being in their proximity—for example, their enthusiasm (as at a political rally), their boredom (at a tediously conducted meeting), their joy (upon the success of a long-planned event)—or else, more relevant to depression, their noticeably downcast mood. This mood is not mine initially, but it can occasion my own depressive mood—not by any direct or simple causal effect but by something more subtle and sinuous, as the word *in-fluence* suggests: something *flows into us from around us*. The mere fact that this *influenza* is difficult to name or describe does not make it any less important as an effective force. Indeed, the subtlety of the signal may render it all the more efficacious, since it can steal under or around certain defensive maneuvers we may be tempted to make in the circumstance. In this case, the signal's strength is built upon the very indeterminacy of its locus.

Exemplary here is sundowners syndrome. A number of older people, especially those psychologically vulnerable in various ways, find themselves getting depressed as the daylight recedes. There is no single stimulus—far from it, this is a circumstance of an altogether gradual atmospheric transition, changing imperceptibly from minute to minute. Yet the slow darkening of the sky and the disappearance of the sun have a depressive effect on those susceptible to the syndrome. A social analogue of this subtle onset of depression occurs when we walk into a room filled with people and sense a down mood in the room. This force does not need to stem from any given person, or subgroup of persons, but it somehow pervades the room, creating an atmosphere that is conducive to a depressed mood on our part.

We should not be surprised by circumstances such as those I have just recounted. If depression is a *mood* as Kristeva asserts and as many experience, and if mood is itself experienced as something in which we are caught up—always *in the midst of*—it should not be surprising if we find ourselves influenced by phenomena that we are tempted to call "atmospheric," a notion I have just invoked in describing sundowners syndrome and a depressive crowd situation.

The basic situation with pervasive influences of many kinds is that they occur for the most part when we are not looking for their presence, much less expecting their effects, even if we may have premonitions as I stressed earlier. One of these effects is our becoming depressed, being taken over by our own version of this mood. And yet we often do not know where a given mood comes from or where it is going, as is eminently true of depression. Moods are notoriously difficult to pin down. This was already recognized by Heidegger when he wrote in *Being and Time*, "ontologically mood is a primordial kind of Being for Dasein, in which Dasein is disclosed to itself *prior* to all cognition and volition, and *beyond* their range of disclosure."[15] To be beyond such disclosure is to be at their periphery—to be around us rather than squarely in front of us.

Instead of anything like direct causal efficacy, we should speak here of the indirect *inducement* of depression: we are quite literally "drawn into" (*inducere*) a matrix of circumambient microforces. Rather than operating by way of contiguous, one-on-one efficient causal action, these forces are better said to provide the *occasion* for the emergence of a mood like depression (and doubtless other moods as well: elation, hopefulness, and so on, but this is another story). Once the direct intervention of God (as was required on Malebranche's original conception of occasional causes) is suspended as a requirement for its operation, the notion of occasional cause can help us understand better how something like what I have been discussing under the heading of "atmospheric," "peripheral," and the "indirect" can emerge. The environing world, far from intervening piecemeal in the generation of depression as a *causa efficiens*, provides the occasion—that is, the generative circumstance—for the depressive syndrome to emerge from its very midst.

From its very midst: instead of a model of monolinear causality such as efficient causality requires, we have a situation in which depression arises from a certain con-figuration of the surrounding world in which the depressive subject is immersed, occasioning depression by releasing it into the affective life of the human subject. The model here suggested requires a conception of the kind of setting from which depression is likely to emerge. In Kristeva's own earlier nomenclature, this generative matrix can be conceived as a version of *chora*: a space in which all is *outside*. Outside the subject to begin with, and then composed such that the key constituents co-exist *alongside* each other, laterally as it were, and in such a way as to attain semiological coherence as a whole.

In Kristeva's own words, it is a matter of a "nonexpressive totality formed by the drives and their stases in a motility that is as full of movement as it is regulated"[16]—a totality whose energies are supplied by the subject's drives. For drives subtend the semiotic *chora* in such a way as to dynamize the subject and to link this subject to the immediate surround.[17] Further, "one can situate the *chora*"—that is to say, it is not nowhere but also, as with the atmospheric ambiance of depression to which I've been pointing, it "can never be definitively posited" in the form of a definite or simple location.[18] Instead of providing a pinpointed position, it activates-and-occupies a dynamic space of its own by way of what Kristeva designates as an "ordering" (*ordonanncement*) that operates by its own energies and tendencies. Summing up her thinking in this direction, Kristeva affirms that "the semiotic *chora* is no more than the place where the subject is both generated and negated, the place where his unity succumbs before the processes of charges and stases that produce him."[19]

Her choice of "place" (*lieu*) is propitious, for it designates a *scene* of interaction in which the constituents are quite diverse—not only elemental (as in the *Timaeus:* fire, air, earth, water) but also semiotic (thus as featuring coherent but preverbal meaning), energized by drive or drivelike forces that may be first of all situated in the human subject but that have resonance and outspread in the wider lifeworld in such generic forms as Becoming, *conatus, élan vital*, Process, and so on. All such loosely assembled forces make up a matrix that is *psychoactive*, thus capable of eliciting and sustaining what is too quickly designated as a mere "psychological state" such as depression itself (I say "too quickly" because at issue is an assemblage of factors and forces, no one of which has priority or supremacy overall, even if specific circumstances favor the prominence of some over others).

It is *place* alone that can hold together these diverse and discrepant forces—hold them together *from below*, as it were. A sunset is one such place, and a crowded room into which we enter is another. Rather than a strict site (a definite location), each of these is an open-ended place that is capable of generating and sustaining a given mood such as depression *from beyond the subject*, even if this same subject contributes to the situation by way of the configuration of her drives, her personal history, her current concerns and her preoccupations, etc. In view of this configuration, we can say that depression is a literal *syndrome*—a running together (*dramein,* to run, and *syn*, together) of factors in a certain diagnostic pattern that has come to be called "depression."

So far I've been developing an *exogenous* model for the generation of depression—quite literally, "born from the outside," coming from beyond the strict psychophysical perimeters of the subject. Coming from there largely if not entirely: in any case, much more significantly so than is usually considered the case. Rendering this model all the more remarkable is the fact that depression, of all psychopathic afflictions, is the one most likely to be considered exemplary of internally generated conditions. If I am afflicted by depression, I often feel that it comes from the *psychophysical inside* or at least has settled in there—that I cannot escape it, for it *has become* me to the point that I am convinced that now it is not just in me but *is me,* and *I am it*. It has taken me over by bringing me under—taking me to my underside: *myself down under.*

Such depression is sometimes termed *endogenous*, "generated from within." This kind of depression signifies a state whose genesis occurs inside the human subject. The result is an inescapable mood characterized primarily by fixations of various kinds (e.g., not being able to think otherwise) and dark forebodings (for instance, a fixation on disappointing or disastrous things to come). But the primary dimension is physical: felt bodily. As stated in the standard clinical book *Depression: Behavioral and Directive Intervention Strategies:*

> The most distinctive characteristic of the endogenous depressions is the accompanying physical or "vegetative" symptoms that give this syndrome a particularly biological aspect. These include the following: psychomotor agitation or retardation; insomnia, particularly early morning awakening; diurnal variations of mood, with the worst time being the morning; anorexia with weight loss; decreased libido.[20]

Not surprisingly, a neurological basis for endogenous depression has been posited and pursued in recent decades; underlying numerous hypotheses is the general claim that such depression "reflects dysfunction of limbic-hypothalamic brain centers involved in the regulation of mood and appetitive functions."[21]

Whether the effective locus of depression is found in the brain—or alternatively in the heart (as Descartes posited) or in other internal organs—endogenous depression is thought to be generated from inside the human organism, from the "innards," the largely if not entirely physical or physiological insides of the subject. Not only is such depression held to originate there but it is considered likely to remain there as well: we are caught up in the sheer gravity of the mood, mired and entangled in it, irremissibly so. No wonder there is a despairing sense of being trapped in it with no way out. For depression to be so deeply within us—buried within our very biological being—is to despair of ever finding a way out of it. For, as Merleau-Ponty insisted, we *are* our body.

And yet, whether we are fully aware of it or not, depression has exogenous parameters that are rarely recognized or, even if noticed, allowed to play an integral role in the experience and understanding of depression: atmosphere, occasional cause, and choric space. If this is so, we must resist the temptation to locate depression exclusively inside the suffering subject. It is not a matter of denying physiological, including neurophysiological, factors in the generation of depressions of many kinds, especially those conventionally labeled "endogenous." All such factors are ingredient in and formative of such depression. But we must also recognize the importance of exogenous factors, resisting the temptation to regard these as merely "extraneous," "superficial," or just "contingent." At least as important as endogenous forces are those that come to us from the outside—outside the body, beyond the brain: somewhere other than in the supposedly autonomous self. A more complete acknowledgment of exogenous forces is required to reach an adequate account of depression in terms of its initial genesis, its continuation, and its prolongation. We must go outside in order to understand more adequately what we too often posit as inside, striving to contain it there at all costs.

It is a matter, in short, of turning depression *inside out*. In doing so, Kristeva's contributions in *Black Sun* and elsewhere are invaluable—most notably, her refusal to give a definite location to depression and her characterization of *chora* as a possible model for what kind of space depression occupies as it is experienced in the first person. (This last step is my extrapolation from her earlier work.) Also significant in this context is her effort to disencumber depression from being explained exclusively in terms of "object loss" (such as the death of a loved one), as in many psychoanalytic theories of depression—and to posit *Thing* in place of *object* as the pertinent factor in depression. "The looming of the Thing" is her way of characterizing the onset of depression, given that "my necessary Thing is also and absolutely my enemy, my foil, the delightful focus of my hatred."[22] Closely related to this is the claim that "affect is the most archaic inscription of inner and outer events."[23] If it is generally true that depressed persons are "prisoners of affect," then we should affirm that for them "the affect is their Thing."[24]

The Thing is "the real that does not lend itself to signification, the center of attraction and repulsion, seat of the sexuality from which the object of desire will become separated."[25] Whereas objects—including not only objects of desire but intensely remembered objects, objects of love and hate, and of other strong but often conflicted emotions—can play into complicated entanglements that often end in ambivalence, Things are sinkholes of emotion, attracting affective masses that anchor ongoing depressive experiences. Notably, Things do not possess simple locations—unlike objects, which lend themselves to precise spatiotemporal positioning (such as in maps, photographs, etc.). Instead, Things act as epicenters of the choric field that attract or repel us in ways we do not understand at the time but that act to indicate various possible courses of action. One such course of action is the experience of depression itself. Depression, then, is a way of living among and dealing with Things—Things that draw us down. They take us down into the depths of despair—down into a choric space from which we cannot find any exit: *huis clos*. This space surrounds us, encompasses us: drawing us in, drawing us down.

To inhabit such space when that which punctuates it are Things occasioning ambivalence and irresolvable conflict is to enter into the space of depression: it is equivalent to *becoming depressed.* No determinate objects (people, events, memories, fantasies) can save us as we sink into the entangling embrace of this downward thrust. We are in it such that there is no way out of it—out of an affective mass of Things that takes us down even as the depression itself may well have been precipitated from what we have taken in from a circumambient world . . .

Thus we end in paradox: depression often starts in a scene that surrounds us, a choric indeterminacy dynamized by forces that are at once affective and archaic—"affect is the most archaic inscription of inner and outer events,"[26] ensnarling us in an abyssal downswirl of Things that take us under into an interiority that feels as inescapable as it is inevitable—a psycho-physical-affective nexus that tempts us to adopt models of depression as inherently endogenous. All too easily, these models become archetypal for all depression, leading us to overlook the exogenous sources of many depressive syndromes. Here as elsewhere, we need to look out if we are to understand what happens within.

EDWARD S. CASEY

STATE UNIVERSITY OF NEW YORK AT STONY BROOK
FEBRUARY 2019

NOTES

1. Julia Kristeva, *Black Sun: Depression and Melancholia*, trans. Leon S. Roudiez (New York: Columbia University Press, 1989), 147.
2. Ibid.
3. Archytas, cited by Simplicius in *Aristotelis Categorias Commentarium*, in S. Sambursky, ed., *The Concept of Place in Late Neoplatonisim* (Jerusalem: Israel Academy of Sciences and Humanities, 1982), 37.
4. Kristeva, *Black Sun*, 44.
5. Ibid., 48.
6. Ibid.
7. Ibid., 51–52.
8. Ibid., 51.
9. Ibid., 53.
10. Ibid., 60, 61.
11. Ibid., 53.
12. Ibid., 64.
13. *DSM V: Diagnostic and Statistical Manual of Mental Disorders* (Washington: American Psychiatric Association, 2013), 160.
14. Alfred North Whitehead, *Process and Reality*, ed. David Ray Griffin and Donald W. Sherburne (New York: The Free Press, 1978).
15. Martin Heidegger, *Being and Time*, trans. J. Macquarrie and E. Robinson (New York: Harper, 2006), 175.

16. Julia Kristeva, *Revolution in Poetic Language,* trans. Margaret Waller (New York: Columbia University Press, 1984), 25.

17. These drives are, from the side of the subject, the forces that move this subject into major moods such as depression or joy.

18. Kristeva, *Revolution in Poetic Language*, 26.

19. Ibid., 37.

20. J. F. Clarkin and H. I. Glazer, eds., *Depression: Behavioral and Directive Intervention Strategies* (New York: Garland, 1981), 297–98.

21. Ibid., 298. These dysfunctions have been traced to "deficits in turnover of amine neurotransmitters (norepinephrine, serotonin)" and to "central-monoamine-facilitating effects of the anti-depressant medications" (ibid.).

22. Kristeva, *Black Sun*, 15.

23. Ibid., 23.

24. Ibid., 14 (capitalization added).

25. Ibid., 13.

26. Ibid., 23.

18

Alina N. Feld

MELANCHOLIA: PASSING THROUGH AND BEYOND

Does not the wonderment of psychic life after all stem from these alternations of protections and downfalls, smiles and tears, sunshine and melancholia?

—Julia Kristeva, *Black Sun: Depression and Melancholia*

Kristeva develops her original psychoanalytic theory in conversation with classical psychoanalysts, notably Freud and Klein, as well as with illustrious thinkers of melancholy. Her central argument proposes art and religion as fitting counterdepressants for the melancholy/depressive composite, as universal therapeutics equivalent and often superior to psychoanalytic practice.[1] In a succinct overview of the history of hermeneutical metamorphoses of melancholy, Kristeva notes the mysterious relationship between melancholy and creative imagination, whether expressed in image or word, artistic, poetic, or religious. In this brief reflection adumbrated on the margins of *Black Sun*, I ponder Kristeva's psychoanalytic insights into the theology of melancholy. The apparent identity between *Typus melancholicus* and *Homo religiosus*, according to which self-transcendence constitutes the only remedy for melancholy, establishes a dialectical tension between melancholy and God.[2] As Kristeva argues, melancholy is unfinished mourning either for the pre-objectal archaic Thing or for the Object of desire. The ultimate Object of desire is God, and mourning the death of God is always a matter of unfinished melancholy. While primordial mourning for the Thing, the zero-degree condition of the psyche, caused by the non-I or otherness within, the nonbeing ground of being—the dark nature of God present throughout creation—is an otherness in the depths of God and the human individual. God's death and otherness remain the absolute ground of melancholy and, paradoxically, its remedy.

In a masterful synthetic tour de force, Kristeva retrieves the major moments of the venerable tradition of the hermeneutics of the melancholy/depressive composite that began with Aristotle's analysis of the relationship between melancholy and the exceptional individual, and which underwent an important interpretive shift in medieval monasticism. If melancholy qualifies as a theological notion, its natural home has been moral theology, in particular the theology of sin. Kristeva aptly refers to acedia as a medieval forerunner of Heidegger's care. One of the seven mortal sins, melancholy-depression figured in the two forms of acedia (depression, boredom, ennui) and sadness (melancholy), appearing on the first list of eight passionate thoughts drafted by Evagrius Ponticus and, subsequently, as one of the seven mortal sins, or even as the condition of sin itself.[3]

Outside the strictly theological domain, the melancholy/depressive composite manifested the complexity of its enigmatic nature in works of poetry and art. In Dante's *Divine Comedy* it became omnipresent in its different hypostases, ranging from sloth and despair to Saturnine contemplation, and later it recaptured its Aristotelian-Hippocratic identity with Ficino, who added to this mix mythological astrology and poetic therapeutics.[4] Melancholy and depression were both present in Kant's anthropological discussion of the temperaments, and were alternately considered the basis of philosophical temperament par excellence, apt for the experience of moral duty and the sublime, while melancholy as such was emphasized in his theory of genius.[5] With Schelling, melancholy becomes the condition of freedom and, as anguish, it is integral to Heidegger's mood of thought.[6] Iconic for the entire tradition, Dame Melancholy stands out in Dürer's enigmatic engraving *Melancholia I.* Dürer's engraving can be considered an illustration of Henry of Ghent's vision of melancholy as *non-transcendendum*, a masterful mathematician or geometer but a bad metaphysician, incapable of self-transcendence.[7] Arguably, the latter is a forerunner of Heidegger's profound boredom (*tiefe Langeweile*), construed as emptiness and suspension or entrancement in limbo, indicating a relation to time and an understanding of "*how time resonates in the ground of Da-sein.*"[8]

Throughout this complex history of interpretation, melancholy and depression have been baffling in their seemingly endless metamorphoses. Ostensibly diverse, even mutually opposing, yet sharing a fundamental phenomenology, a common core, they are referred to interchangeably by Kristeva, who considers them a melancholy/depressive composite.[9] This common core is hollow, emerges as an absence, the shadow of a lost archaic Thing or Object of desire, one whose loss through abandonment or death is not accepted but, in the "denial of negation," is infinitely deferred.[10] This is mourning for that whose mourning remains unfinished and as such becomes melancholy, thus an ontological condition rather than simply an existential and contingent one.

Kristeva evokes the phenomenological profile of melancholy: psychomotor retardation affecting interior rhythm and perception of time, together with an entire constellation of delusions or deliriums of loss, guilt, disaster and damnation, deprivation and worthlessness, all grounded in the dark mood of one with a past that does not pass and without future, thus living life in death, death in life, as one condemned to death.[11] A sense of emptiness with a distorted perception of time constituted the main feature of the condition that Evagrius named the demon of acedia or the noonday demon, the most pernicious of all passionate thoughts as a temptation to nonbeing or separation from God.[12]

Kristeva notes the occurrence of a different and unsuspected component of the melancholy/depressive composite that may accompany psychomotor retardation, namely a phenomenon of accelerated creativity. This odd combination of apathetic body and active intellect was known to Ficino as the condition affecting philosophers and scholars of the occult. Ficino adduces Hippocratic humoral metaphysics and astrological mythology to decipher the pathetic condition as a combination of black bile and phlegm suffered by those under the malignant influence of Saturn, the exiled king, the old God resisting creation and time.[13]

If the primary cause of melancholy is the loss of the Object of desire, Kristeva, like Heidegger, identifies "a more originary beginning," one that precedes the emergence of the other as object, an otherness that resides within the self. She thus endorses Freud against Klein: his discovery of the death drive in primordial masochism that displaces the sovereignty of the pleasure principle and eros, and which generates his second topography of the psyche. Suffering comes first, before any aggression toward an alien ambivalent object of love and hate. Or, rather, the other appears to be always already within the self: the unknowable and unnameable Thing. Arguably, this originary primordial condition suggests what Henry considers an immanent pathetic subjectivity or pathetic subjective body. His notion of pathetic subjective body is perfectly attuned to the melancholy ontology centered on mood and the body.[14] Heidegger's analysis of profound boredom deepens Henry's phenomenological notion. He analyzes boredom—essential, for him, to the constitution of the melancholy/depressive composite—as an ontological or rather meontological fundamental attunement. As with Pascal's ennui, it is the repelling mood of our abyssal ground, the nothing of our Godless postlapsarian condition, one that we dread and escape in the self-forgetfulness of distraction.[15] Like Pascal, Heidegger calls the bored away from the temptation of distraction back to the fundamental attunement of boredom that "permeate[s] our Dasein in the ground of its essence," and that we "must let become awake."[16] For both Pascal and Heidegger, the nature of our being becomes evident in ennui or profound boredom as an abyssal nothing, the groundless ground of being itself.[17] In the same vein, Altizer welcomes the birth of self-consciousness with Paul and Augustine as a self-lacerating consciousness of guilt, divided against itself, of individual will imprisoned and free, "a self-lacerating and self-wounding act that acts only by acting against itself," a "self-embodiment of that dichotomy at the center of self-consciousness," a consciousness of the other within.[18] Might this otherness within discerned by these philosophers and Christian writers, this abyssal groundless ground, explain primordial suffering and masochism, thanatos preceding eros, pathetic melancholy-depression preceding all other affects being the deepest bottomless bottom of the psyche, its zero degree?

Arguably, Kristeva's answer would be affirmative. A primordial otherness within seems to be the ground for her notion of the archaic pre-objectal Thing. With the ease and grace of erudition, she briefly mentions without further elaboration that, for Schelling, melancholy is the condition for human freedom.[19]

The observation evokes Schelling's meontic theology of God's dark nature that reverberates throughout the creation and constitutes the ground of the human being.[20] According to Schelling's theogonic imagination, the principle of the nought and nonbeing enacts God's beginning as negation and ground of revelation. God's dark nature, the God of wrath, breaks up the absolute indifferent slumber of all powers and provokes the God of love to self-revelation. This dialectic will be the operating principle in creation.[21] Indeed if, for both Schelling and Hegel, negation constitutes the engine of dialectic, the beginning is conceived differently: in contradistinction to Hegel's pure concept, Schelling posits nature, God's dark nature.[22] This will never be overcome but will constitute the irreducible remainder, the "indestructible melancholy of all life," the otherness relentlessly confronting the self as the power of the nought, as well as evil, bringing the self into being, freedom, and creativity.[23] If Schelling's *Treatise on Human Freedom* centers on God, freedom, and evil, *The Ages of the World* concludes with an admonition to careful negotiation with "self-lacerating madness," "the innermost in all things," that must be continually confronted and overcome, neither eliminated nor allowed to rule: Jacob's wrestling with the dark nature of God and of oneself.[24] Referring to Schelling's vision with sobering clarity, Wirth contemplates on the brink of apocalyptic extinction the razor-edge choice between assuming and working through the dark nature, eliminating it in arrogant sterile "stupidity," or becoming submerged by it in madness.[25] Like Kristeva, he appeals to literary texts to verify, illustrate, and support his Schellingian dialectic. He speculates on the relation to madness of the main characters in Melville's *Moby Dick*. Freedom and creativity as well as evil are made possible by the primordial melancholic nature of God—or, since God can be symbolized by the sun, God's other or the black sun.

Considering the same constellation of notions surrounding melancholy, Saturn, and God's dark nature, Kearney adduces a different set of concerns. He finds the Schellingian metaphysical dualism of primordial dark nature unappealing, and finds ethically disquieting Kristeva's suggested correlation of the sublime with the monstrous and terror in the Kantian analysis of the sublime.[26] However, Kearney acknowledges the relevance in contemporary theological debates of the psychoanalytic reinterpretations of Plato's primordial *chora*—Kristeva's and Žižek's use of this notion in particular.[27] For Kristeva, Kearney argues, the *chora* represents the "primordial matrix of the unconscious."[28] It is the non-ego, presymbolic, and prelinguistic, the site of chaos and abjection, "not yet unified in an ordered whole because deity is absent from it," while Žižek understands the *chora* as Schelling's "divine madness of the Ground of Existence itself, namely, that which in God himself is not yet God."[29] For both, therefore, it stands for the otherness of God: either God's absence, a presymbolic precondition of self, speech, meaning, and God, or God's other, the Schellingian paradox of negation and ground of revelation.[30]

Kristeva's *pathographies* simultaneously enact psychoanalytic investigations, sui generis aesthetic and poetic exegeses, and historical and biographical portraits, as well as quintessential theological treatises.[31] They constitute experiments that test the psychoanalytic theory introduced in the first part of

Black Sun. Her study of Holbein's *Dead Christ* shows the theological nature of melancholic mourning by adducing Hegel's notion of the death of God as the perfect enactment of a *coincidentia oppositorum* of natural death and divine idea. She appreciates the originality and aesthetic achievement of Holbein's *Dead Christ* as a successful actualization of Hegel's idea of the death of God. Avoiding the Scylla and Charybdis of Grünewald's Gothic Dominican expressionism and of Mantegna's Italian Franciscan certainty of transcendence, Holbein reaches a new form of sober dignity closer to humanism. Kristeva celebrates the cathartic and therapeutic power of Holbein's realism. Psychoanalytically, the ubiquitous, even when seemingly invisible, presence of suffering and death in Holbein's oeuvre—from the dead Christ and the series of *danses macabres* to the melancholic portraits and, especially, the anamorphosis of a human skull in *The Ambassadors*—represents pictorially Hegel's work of the negative, the moment of abandonment, of severance or "splitting," considered as sine qua non condition of autonomy and individuation.[32]

According to Kristeva, the therapeutic value at the core of Christianity resides in the centrality of death, the "gift of death" as Derrida will name it.[33] It is a paradoxical death that is simultaneously a portal to absolute life, thus a death of death, a eucharistic death and kenosis, life and nourishment through sacrificial death. This total "rupture at the very heart of the absolute subject" constitutes a true initiation no longer enacted as ritualistic ordeal, pace Girard, but only in the imaginary realm of the words and signs of the Eucharist.[34] The imaginary identification of the faithful with the absolute subject's death and resurrection, passion and hope of salvation, constitutes redemption, while faith operates as the "antidote for hiatus and depression," not by eliminating them but, on the contrary, by starting with them and going through them.[35]

Abandonment in a series of splittings giving rise to fantastic polymorphous identity and illustrious genealogies is also central to Nerval's poem, "The Disinherited." Kristeva engages in a carefully paced psychoanalytic exegesis of the poem that encompasses a vast territory of esoteric science and mythology. While the death of God was represented pictorially in Holbein, here it is expressed poetically and kerygmatically by Richter and by Nerval himself.[36] A new crisis of values in the mid-nineteenth century, whose cause and effect lie in melancholy, is conducive to Nietzschean nihilism. More markedly evoking a psychoanalytic interpretation, Kristeva cites Jean Paul's declaration: "God is dead, the sky is empty . . . Weep! Children, you no longer have a father." Nerval goes further: "No, God does not exist. . . . Have you heard *the news*? . . . I misled you. Abyss!"[37] This leads Kristeva to recall that becoming a "speaking being" is predicated on separation from and loss of the Object of desire, separation and loss that are negated, while the Object is recovered, kept alive, imaginatively, symbolically in language and representation. It is only the "denial of negation" that leads to melancholy and the refusal of language and representation: aphasia and silence.[38]

Here, too, the death of God refers to the hiatus and severance of Christ, forsaken by the father, with whom Nerval identifies. Confronting nonbeing, the absence of God, Nerval overcomes what the theologian Tillich knows as the anxiety of emptiness and meaninglessness by substituting for the dead God the "hidden God . . . of a diffuse spirituality," an "immanent Christianity," "ultimate refuge of a psychic identity in catastrophic anguish."[39] Indeed, in the face of the nothing, Nerval's appeal to a hidden God will be validated by Tillich's call to the "God beyond God," "the God who remained his [Jesus as the Christ's] God after the God of confidence had left him [the Crucified] in the darkness of doubt and meaninglessness."[40] If, as Nerval the narrator of *Aurélia* believes, "God is the Sun," the black sun of melancholy is God's other, of an equal and obverse potency of negation.[41] Infinitely mourned and melancholized, the death of God is here represented by the black sun—a symbol Nerval takes from alchemy—that burns with the power of the nought and nonbeing, overshadowing and infecting with brilliant darkness and nihilism the mood of the time.

In her pathographies of Holbein and Nerval, Kristeva is attentive to the cathartic and therapeutic potential of the death of God available in visual art and poetic construction through imaginative identification with and undergoing the symbolic initiatory ordeal of death and resurrection. At the end of each of her readings, she adduces the dialectic of suffering and forgiveness as ciphers of psychoanalytic healing and regeneration, devoting her study of Dostoyevsky to this. The psychoanalytic and theological musings on Dostoyevsky focus on the dramatic evolution of Raskolnikov: the story of his fall and redemption, essentially a modern *Divine Comedy*. The section "In Praise of Suffering" opens the chapter, with suffering as the new name of Erasmus's folly.[42] With Dostoyevsky, suffering becomes the essential mark of being human. As the primary preobjectal affect, primordial suffering on the fringe of consciousness is feverishly chased after, assumed, indulged, deepened, and always in "'excess,' a power, sensual pleasure, the black spot of Nerval's melancholy. It recalls medieval acedia and the pathos of Job and involves a delight in crime and suicide.[43] This longing for voluptuous suffering, theologically known as mortal sin, perfectly enacts Freud's death drive or primary masochism as the zero degree of psychic life and noneroticized suffering, a primordial psychical inscription of a break, an internal or external, bioenergetic or symbolic discontinuity.[44]

Kristeva elaborates on Dostoyevsky's Nietzschean view of suffering as an act of consciousness, of asserted freedom, of doubt and negation, ultimately the origin of consciousness.[45] However, in her insight, like Le Senne on the nervous melancholic, the remedial defenses against melancholic suffering are perverse and deadly: the nihilistic negation of an absolute paternity and divinity as supreme value, crime and suicide, terrorism and torture, relinquishment of morality and meaning.[46] As genuine counterbalances to melancholic suffering, Kristeva proposes religion, mania, and artistic creation.[47]

To explain further the therapeutic role of religious faith, Kristeva considers the nature of Byzantine theology—subsequently developed by Russian and other forms of Eastern theology—as Dostoyevsky's own choice against the nihilism of despair, less pernicious in her view than terrorism waged against either oneself or the other. She identifies forgiveness as the deepest core of Christian faith and the true meaning of resurrection, making possible a post-apocalyptic new being.[48] She launches into a vigorous apology for forgiveness that amounts to an apology for the cathartic value of Byzantine theology as a system of symbols intuitively conceived to achieve the care and temporary cure of the melancholy self. Modern misunderstandings of forgiveness as a degrading form of weakness—Nietzsche's and Freud's included—contaminated the judgment of Christianity itself as a religion of *ressentiment* and moral perversity. In opposition to this, Kristeva adduces the "solemnity" of forgiveness in both theology and aesthetic experience, its sober and lucid identification with abjection, necessary in order to allow for the emergence of a renewed psyche.[49] Psychic rebirth is the goal of psychoanalytic practice, achieved thanks to the tact of the analyst, the art of truthful listening and forgiveness.[50]

In the process, paranoia and death as inability to forgive are subverted. Kristeva's insight into the therapeutic value of listening and forgiveness in psychoanalysis, theology, and art is endorsed by Ricoeur's hermeneutic of confession and Tellenbach's psychiatric profile of *Typus melancholicus*.[51] In confession the melancholy one deliberately assumes responsibility for evil and traverses the hell of suffering (abjection) while being heard, forgiven, restored by faith in a benevolent divine parent. By assuming responsibility for evil, Ricoeur maintains, freedom of the will is exercised and the ethical meaning of existence recovered, and with it, as Jung knew, the health of the mind. According to Ricoeur, our fallibility rooted in our fundamental "unstable mélange" of and disproportion between infinite desire and finitude gives rise to melancholy as "pathétique of misery" that calls for self-transcendence and the total renovation of the self: only a God can save us, pace Heidegger, thus a transcendent benevolent instance, whose forgiveness is trusted and accepted.[52]

Apparently, in Kristeva's view, the forgiveness called forth by Dostoyevsky goes deeper than restoration of meaning and beyond liberating transcendence. It is rooted in Paul's notion of love as principle and power of renewal of self and other, even renewal of the unconscious. It is only love that knows all and forgives absolutely, forgives and accepts forgiveness: essential to sublimation, it goes beyond morals and intellect to reach affects and bodies, absorbs and transforms abjection, and allows the melancholy person to identify with and reconcile to a loving parent, the agency of the ideal, thus liberating speech and representation.[53]

Can loving forgiveness liberate the melancholy person? In search of an answer, Kristeva makes a concise excursus into early preschism Byzantine theology and the specific character that differentiates it from Western Latin theology. The uniqueness of Byzantine theology as articulated by John of Damascus, Symeon the New Theologian, and Maximus the Confessor, is marked, she contends, by its emphatic pneumatology.[54] The preservation of the personhood of the Spirit within a pneumatic Trinity was a result of the Trinitarian doctrine of *per filium* (the spirit descends from the father through the son), one whose immanent economy was fundamentally changed in the West by the addition of *filioque* (the spirit descends from the father and the son) to the creed. On this theological change hinges the long debated and lamented schism that split Christendom into Greek and Latin Christianities—two different worldviews and cultural sensibilities—with all-pervading consequences. On the one hand, is the Byzantine Trinity of "pneumatological *belonging* of each [divine person] to the other," unity in difference, and loving perichoresis.[55] Its anthropological reflection into speech, spirit, soul allows for mystical pathos and erotic fusion, and makes possible deification.[56] On the other hand, with Anselm and Aristotle-Aquinas, the Latin-logicized Trinity, along with the concept of God as a simple intellectual essence articulated by dyads, became the basis for political and spiritual authority, autonomy, and individualism.[57]

Mercy as a sort of sorrow, according to John of Damascus, forgiveness of evil, and joy inseparable from tears that marked Symeon the New Theologian's thinking, the pneumatic conception of the Eucharist that envisions Christ simultaneously deified and crucified as pronounced by Maximus the Confessor—these Byzantine theologoumena preceding the schism justify the centrality of the dialectic of suffering and forgiveness making possible deification or *theosis* by identification with the agency of the ideal. At a symbolic level, Kristeva maintains, a theology of forgiveness and deification appears as a superior equivalent to a psychoanalytic therapeutic.

Her analysis of Duras's narrative work, along with Resnais's French New Wave cinematic adaptation of Duras's novel, *Hiroshima mon amour*, emphasizes the absence of the cathartic dimension, an absence that allows apocalyptic nihilism to be all in all. In the post–Second World War debacle of a threefold crisis of thought, speech, and representation, a passion for death has contaminated not only the military, economic, political, and social worlds but also that of the spirit. As if Holbein's anamorphic skull has engulfed our entire world, the malady of death has contaminated the depths of our psyche, thus becoming total: psychoses, depression, manic-depressive and borderline states, false selves—psychoanalysis is challenged to refine its diagnoses.[58] As a disquieting visual metaphor of our contemporary pathology, Kristeva adduces Valéry's apt description of the invisible, nonrepresentable chaos of our psyche: "in a kiln heated to incandescence, if our eyes endured, they would see *nothing*."[59] This nothing is not vacuity but a "tremendous trapped energy" in "a *perfect state of disorder*" whose invisibility emanates from its omnipresence and absolute sovereignty in our psyche and whose immediate effect is a crisis of naming and signification, one that gives way to meaninglessness and silence.[60] The incandescent nothing—arguably, choratic fullness—is apocalyptic. Self-lacerating, the nothing imploding in our psychic being generates apocalyptic madness, an exacerbated state of melancholy. As Schelling wrote at the end of *The Ages of the World*, the melancholic dark nature present in God and throughout creation remains a permanent temptation for the individual to nonbeing, which must be not eliminated but appeased, worked through in agonic confrontation. When the power of dark nature overwhelms reason, madness becomes sovereign.

Kristeva's analysis of Duras is witness to madness become the disease of our psyche, the eclipse of the sun or the apocalyptic black sun, the death of God. The image of Holbein's *The Dead Christ*, in which death was envisioned as a power that could not be contained within the tomb or the frame of the painting, has taken hold of the world and, with Duras, this death has been born in the spirit. Here, in Duras's world, Tillich's anxiety facing all forms of nonbeing—death and fate, guilt and condemnation, emptiness and meaninglessness—can no longer be courageously overcome. Madness is our failed response to the nothing as absolute negation and otherness in the absence of God, forgiveness, recovery, purification, beauty, tragedy. Nonetheless, with a Schellingian gesture, Kristeva can celebrate this unredeemable, noncathartic madness as the only space of "antisocial, apolitical, paradoxically free individuation."[61] Melancholic madness is "like an explosion in history" when private suffering absorbs political horror, the drama of our time, into the psychic microcosm.[62] Her suggestion of a relationship between melancholy and individuation emerges naturally against the historical background of the hermeneutics of melancholy initiated by Aristotle's question ("are all exceptional individuals melancholy?"), metaphysically heightened by Schelling's dark nature as ground of God and of individual freedom and creativity. Kristeva asks: "would suffering enamored of death be the supreme individuation?"[63]

The paradox of suffering *jouissance* present in Dostoyevsky unfolds abundantly in Duras's sadness as "women's sickly core," the mystery of suffering as eroticism, the "unfulfilled mourning of the autosensual preobject," the "archaic auto-sensuality of wounded affects."[64] Women suffering as mourning an archaic pre-object together with the trauma of abandonment as the discovery of otherness, a not-I, present further evidence of an essential, transhistorical pathetic condition, one that is not simply a response to contingent history, collective or individual, but is, rather, metaphysical, a matter of meontology, supremely visible in Schelling's dialectic.[65] Kristeva's final reflections on the challenge posed to Duras's narrative of abyssal darkness by postmodern irreverent shallowness make evident the dialectical ground of her own psychoanalytic and theological thinking: "within the eternal return of historical and intellectual cycles," the invisible inner hell of melancholic madness is followed and lightened up by postmodern hell, "a 'nothing'—like our 'truths' henceforth made visible, televised," thus rendered innocuous, irrelevant, or comic.[66] This is a deeper apocalyptic nothing than the incandescent nothing of Valéry and Duras, one closer to the indifference of self-annihilation.

Kristeva's final note of melancholy *vanitas vanitatum* counterbalances Baudrillard's embittered critique of the melancholy nothing of simulacra devoid of reality, of both tragedy and hope.[67] There is a note of ultimate celebration in Kristeva's dialectic of faith and its absence, God and the death of God, sun and black sun. Essential to the thinking of both Hegel and Schelling, this dialectic has been celebrated more recently by Altizer. Kristeva's psychoanalytic studies in *Black Sun* bring to mind Altizer's insights into the apocalyptic imagination manifest in the Western epic tradition and art, as well as Freud's psychoanalytic studies and Jaspers's pathographies.[68] Her reflections on Duras's malady of death allow for the theological interpretation proposed by Altizer in his analysis of Van Gogh.[69] Duras and Van Gogh represent a world in which God's absence is universally present, a world that lives through the death of God. Suffering survivors of an apocalyptic cataclysm that continues to unfold—the death of God, a cataclysm nothing greater than which can be conceived—are living out this death, carrying, within, the corpse of the archaic *nec plus ultra* beloved. Altizer argues that Van Gogh's *Wheatfield with Crows* is the icon of our time in which God can be present only as abyss and darkness. Like Kristeva's black sun, Altizer's darkness is a luminous darkness. For both, it is a justification for celebration, for the tears and the ultimate joy of a *missa jubilaea.*

And yet. More recently, in a dialogue with Kearney about her current project of a new humanism, Kristeva has declared: "I am a resolute pessimist."[70] Her avowed pessimism came as a response to the "radical phase of nihilism" of contemporary secularism in which *Homo sapiens* apparently reached the limits of the human.[71] The cause of this apocalyptic condition, she affirms, was the event of the death of God—the Greco-Judeo-Christian God—that occurred in European consciousness, paradoxically prepared for by its own religious tradition.[72] Kristeva envisions as consequence the disturbing phenomenon of adolescent crisis, one that has become pandemic. Arguably, the portrait of adolescent crisis resembles Dostoyevsky's Raskolnikov, the melancholic, confronting a total crisis of values, turned criminal. Owing to the "denial of negation," the death of God experienced as loss of the Object of desire in unfinished melancholic mourning means a loss of ideals, of the unappeased need to believe and to know, and total nihilism.[73] This is a time of global melancholy, the apocalyptic attunement par excellence.

We find Kristeva's conception of the new humanism emerging as a questioning and problematization of the tradition, and centered on the question of God. It is an infinite task that begins by taking seriously the "maladies of ideality" and involves a transvaluation of values while keeping alive the inner self by a "perpetual questioning of its norms and powers; of its own sexual, national, linguistic identity; of its desires, its sufferings, its loves, and its hates."[74] This perpetual questioning takes place through psychoanalysis, art, and anatheism—Kearney's term for the return to God after God through a rediscovery and rethinking of the religious experience of the past. Kristeva's new post-Christian humanism is to fulfill our perennial "incredible need to believe" and to "exceed the human, which is in crisis—to always and constantly go beyond" while preserving the Christian notion of love and forgiveness within the meeting of cultures.[75] It is a sui generis remedy liberating the self-entranced melancholy person for a post-apocalyptic new being, a courageous and timely response to the black sun.[76]

ALINA N. FELD

ST. JOHN'S UNIVERSITY
FEBRUARY 2019

NOTES

1. Julia Kristeva, *Black Sun: Depression and Melancholia*, trans. Leon S. Roudiez (New York: Columbia University Press, 1989).

2. Present throughout the tradition of interpretation of melancholy, this identity was clearly articulated by the German psychiatrist Tellenbach in relation to Henry of Ghent's theory of melancholy. Hubertus Tellenbach, *Melancholy: History of the Problem, Endogeneity, Typology, Pathogenesis, and Clinical Considerations*, trans. Erling Enq (Pittsburgh: Duquesne University Press, 1980).

3. Evagrius Ponticus, "The Eight Kinds of Evil Thoughts," in *The Praktikos & Chapters on Prayer*, trans. John Eudes Bamberger (Kalamazoo: Cistercian Studies, 1981), 16–17.

4. Kristeva, *Black Sun*, 8. She refers to Marsilio Ficino, *Three Books on Life*, trans. Carol V. Kaske and John R. Clark (New York: Medieval and Renaissance Texts and Studies, 1989).

5. Immanuel Kant, *Anthropology from a Pragmatic Point of View*, trans. Victor Lyle Dowdell (Carbondale: Southern Illinois University Press, 1996); *Critique of Judgment*, trans. Werner S. Pluhar (Indianapolis: Hackett, 1987).

6. F. W. J. Schelling, *The Ages of the World*, trans. Jason Wirth (Albany: SUNY Press, 2000). Martin Heidegger, *The Fundamental Concepts of Metaphysics*, trans. William McNeill and Nicholas Walker (Bloomington: Indiana University Press, 1995); *Being and Time*, trans. John Macquarrie and Edward Robinson (San Francisco: Harper & Row, 1962).

7. See Alina N. Feld, *Melancholy and the Otherness of God: A Study of the Hermeneutics of Depression* (Lanham: Lexington, 2011), 185–86.

8. Heidegger, *The Fundamental Concepts of Metaphysics*, 80.

9. Kristeva, *Black Sun*, 10.

10. Ibid., 43–44.

11. Tellenbach, *Melancholy*, 137, 148.

12. Ponticus, "The Eight Kinds of Evil Thoughts," 18–19.

13. For a study of the history of the concept of melancholy and its mythical association with the planet god Saturn during the Middle Ages and the Renaissance, see Raymond Klibansky, Erwin Panofsky, and Fritz Saxl, *Saturn and Melancholy* (London: Thomas Nelson & Sons, 1964).

14. Michel Henry, *Philosophy and Phenomenology of the Body*, trans. Girard Etzkorn (The Hague: Nijhoff, 1975), 222–23, 258. Henry reached the notion of pathetic subjective body through his study of Maine de Biran (1766–1824), whose philosophy grew out of his confrontation with melancholy.

15. Heidegger, *The Fundamental Concepts of Metaphysics*, 132.

16. Ibid.

17. See Feld, *Melancholy and the Otherness of God*, 129–30.

18. Thomas J. J. Altizer, "Augustine and the Foundation of Western Christendom," in *History as Apocalypse* (Albany: SUNY Press, 1985), 92, 95.

19. Kristeva, *Black Sun*, 7.

20. See Feld, "On God's Otherness," in *Melancholy and the Otherness of God*, 115.

21. F. W. J. Schelling, *Philosophical Investigations into the Essence of Human Freedom*, trans. Jeff Love and Johannes Schmidt (Albany: SUNY Press, 2006), 44.

22. "God himself is not a system, but rather a life" (ibid., 62).

23. Ibid., 63.

24. Schelling, *The Ages of the World*, 103.

25. Jason M. Wirth, "Stupidity" and "Life of Imagination," in *Schelling's Practice of the Wild: Time, Art, Imagination*, ed. Dennis J. Schmidt (Albany: SUNY Press, 2015), 110, 165–71.

26. Richard Kearney, "Evil, Monstrosity, and the Sublime," in *Strangers, Gods, and Monsters* (London: Routledge, 2003).

27. Kearney, "God or Chora?" in ibid., 194–97.

28. Ibid., 195.

29. Ibid., 196, 197.

30. Ibid.

31. See the four chapters forming the second part of *Black Sun*, dedicated to Holbein, Nerval, Dostoyevsky, and Duras. The term *pathography* refers to Jaspers's study of mental pathology as well as his discussion of Nietzsche and Kierkegaard. Karl Jaspers, *Strindberg and Van Gogh: An Attempt of a Pathographic Analysis with Reference to Parallel Cases of Swedenborg and Hölderlin*, trans. Oskar Grunow and David Woloshin (Tucson: University of Arizona Press, 1977); *Reason and Existenz*, trans. William Earle (Milwaukee: Marquette University Press, 1997).

32. Kristeva, *Black Sun*, 132.

33. Jacques Derrida, "Secrets of European Responsibility," in *The Gift of Death*, trans. David Wills (Chicago: Chicago University Press, 1995), 33.

34. See Kristeva on Girard in *Black Sun*, 131–34.

35. Ibid., 134.

36. Ibid., 163–64.

37. See ibid.

38. Ibid., 43–51.

39. Ibid., 164.

40. Paul Tillich, *The Courage to Be* (New Haven: Yale University Press, 1959), 188–90.

41. Kristeva, *Black Sun*, 169.

42. Desiderius Erasmus, *Praise of Folly*, trans. Betty Radice (London and New York: Penguin, 1994).

43. Kristeva, *Black Sun*, 177, 179, 178.

44. Ibid., 175, 182–83.

45. Ibid., 180–81.

46. See René Le Senne, *Traité de caractérologie* (Paris: PUF, 1973), 136. This treatise discusses the most problematic melancholic temperament—the nervous ones (*les grands nerveux*) such as Baudelaire, Byron, Dostoyevsky, Poe, Rimbaud, Wilde, who can be spurred on only by what Poe called the demon of perversity.

47. Kristeva, *Black Sun*, 186–87.

48. Ibid., 192.

49. Ibid., 189–90.

50. Ibid., 189.

51. Paul Ricoeur, "Phenomenology of Confession," in *The Symbolism of Evil*, trans. Emerson Buchanan (Boston: Beacon, 1967), 3–10. Tellenbach, *Melancholy*, 146.

52. Paul Ricoeur, "The Pathétique of Misery" and "The Concept of Fallibility," in *Fallible Man*, trans. Charles A. Kelbley (New York: Fordham University Press, 1986).

53. Kristeva, *Black Sun*, 206–7.

54. See ibid., 208–11, 212–14.

55. Ibid., 210.

56. Ibid., 208–11.

57. Ibid., 210–11.

58. Ibid., 222.

59. Ibid.

60. Ibid.

61. Ibid., 235.

62. Ibid., 234, 238.

63. Ibid., 7, 237.

64. Ibid., 239–40.

65. See Schelling, *Philosophical Investigations into the Essence of Human Freedom*, 42.

66. Kristeva, *Black Sun*, 259.

67. Jean Baudrillard, *Simulacra and Simulation*, trans. Sheila Faria Glaser (Ann Arbor: University of Michigan Press, 1994), 162.

68. I am thinking of Altizer's *History as Apocalypse* (cited above), which is devoted to theological portraits of revolutionary thinking within a historical enactment of consciousness: Paul, Augustine, Dante, Milton, Blake, Joyce.

69. Thomas J. J. Altizer, "Van Gogh's Eyes," in Babette E. Babich, ed., *Hermeneutic Philosophy of Science, Van Gogh's Eyes, and God: Essays in Honor of Patrick A. Heelan* (Boston and London: Kluwer, 2002).

70. Richard Kearney, "New Humanism and the Need to Believe: Dialogue with Julia Kristeva," in Richard Kearney and Jens Zimmermann, eds., *Reimagining the Sacred: Richard Kearney Debates God* (New York: Columbia University Press, 2016), 102.

71. Ibid.

72. Ibid., 99.

73. Kristeva, *Black Sun*, 43–47, where her notions of the need to believe and the desire to know are already implicitly present. See also Julia Kristeva, *This Incredible Need to Believe*, trans. Beverley Bie Brahic (New York: Columbia University Press, 2009).

74. Kearney and Zimmerman, eds., *Reimagining the Sacred*, 109.

75. Ibid., 102.

76. Ibid.

19

Michal Ben-Naftali

A BAROQUE READING OF *TALES OF LOVE*

Tales of Love unfolds Kristeva's credo as a declaration of love, articulating the essential link between lingual and erotic dynamics.[1] Kristeva's reflection directs itself simultaneously towards love and the language of love: towards metaphor, by definition a "transference" (intersubjective and intertextual) that constitutes, by turns, an act of translation, of thought, and of love. Every discourse is thus essentially a discourse on and of love (even when it hates or expresses hate). The speaking subject is necessarily a subject-in-love.

In the thirty-five years following the publication of *Tales of Love*, Kristeva will develop many of the motifs and insights so intensively packed into it. One therefore ought to lend an easily soaring ear to this primal music and its annunciation. Following Freud, *Tales of Love* intertwines theory, clinical experience, and self-analysis. The passage between them is elusive, "baroque" as we shall see. The retrospective reading of the personal past appearing here and there in restrained rhetorical slips is only explicit in "Stabat Mater," where it bursts out with typographical clarity, in two printed columns, distinguishing between the symbolic-order genealogy of the Virgin Mary and the author's semiotic testimony.[2] Nevertheless, on the view of the relations between self and being in *Tales of Love*, self-analysis serves both as mythobiography and ontobiography, feeding upon an array of interpsychical and extrapsychical options—intergenerational as well as cosmic, enfolded in the subject's psychological destiny. It is a self-analysis involving a movement that Kristeva, in the opening chapter, calls an abstraction from the psychological, even from the human. The book as a

Translated from Hebrew by Mirjam Hadar. An earlier version of this chapter appeared in the Hebrew translation of Kristeva's *Tales of Love*: Julia Kristeva, *Sipurei Ahava*, trans. Michal Ben-Naftali (Bnei Brak: Hakibbutz Hameuchad, 2006).

whole might be read as an account of countertransference, and of the introjection of materials that have preoccupied the author since then: semiology, theology, philosophy, anthropology, psychoanalysis, literature, and art. The result is a unique lexicon of notions, even as it draws upon or is influenced by preceding psychoanalytic work: a dynamic writing, hesitant, somewhat ambivalent as to the status or the categorial authority of abstract theories and concepts ("tales of love" and not "metapsychology"), coming very close to a mixture between what Deleuze called the (philosophical) invention of concept and the (artistic) invention of percept. We face the oxymoron of "singular concepts," which include a perceptual-sensual dimension and make us see things; concepts that transcend personal experience, presenting an autonomous structure that stirs both affect and sense. The apparently discursive writing tries to touch, within its limits, language-less elements, the unrepresentable signals of bodily pains and pleasure.

I. Being: A Post-phenomenological Insight?

What is love? Or, first of all, what enables it? Identification and idealization, Kristeva answers. In relation to what? To anything: a man, a woman, a word, a flower, a god—as long as it is transcendent. Eros is neither normative nor purposeful. The soul reaches out for a being, whether divine, human, animal, vegetative, mineral, or textual. In this view, Kristeva's psychoanalytic method draws upon various versions of the German phenomenological tradition.[3] Even if, following the psychoanalytic and structuralist challenges to phenomenology, she rejects the view of the subject as a transhistorical consciousness, Kristeva adopts the method of *epoché* in order to focus as purely as possible on the movements of affect and impulse embodied in phantasms. However, her phenomenological, perhaps post-phenomenological insight is more ambitious. Like other key notions of hers (for example, the semiotic, or *signifiance*), this aspiration to transcend the psyche's tangible history without renouncing its historicity is rooted in a rereading of Freud. "If he succeeds where the paranoiac failed," she writes, referring to a letter Freud wrote to Ferenczi, "it was because he constantly returned to the *historic*: being, the transpsychical; the transsubjective."[4] And further on: "though psychoanalysis does in fact too often objectify and psychologize the analysand and transference itself, it is essential to emphasize the fact that the Freudian discovery opens the path, at the heart of scientific rationality, to a knowledge and to a transformation of the psyche as a life in being, transversal to psychological objectification. Therein lies its most radical revolt."[5]

This phenomenological account of the psychological realm may indeed use metaphors of the visible in order to point towards the invisible, but it does so without assuming a fundamental homogeneity among phenomena. The imaginary movement towards liminal states, traces of unconscious representations—which the authors appearing in *Tales of Love* attempt to grasp, each in their own way, through language and in the face of repressions and negations—necessarily yields clashing phenomenal impressions, pregnant with white spaces. The use of images should not make one forget that they remain a heuristic means, a sensation-arousing and therefore crucial tool on the way from the comprehensible to the inaccessible, from sense to affection. This is the unconscious or preconscious epistemological status of figures such as "Narcissus," "the preoedipal mother," and "the father of individual prehistory," as well as Hamlet and Don Juan, or the singular and ungeneralizable figures representing desire, like Mother Mary, the Shulamite, and the Lady. This fact by no means reduces the truthfulness of the imaginary, its efficiency and theoretical fecundity. The duty of testimony and trust is ours, the reader's, as we may surrender to dreaming or to analysis, always with some effort, almost with aversion. "If I must identify with an image," says Kristeva in an interview, "it may be that of an intellectual, who by definition processes the invisible."[6]

The phenomenological effort draws upon the tradition of ontotheological writing, which, even if its alpha and omega originate in the self, aims entirely towards expansion. The teachings of Plotinus, Thomas Aquinas, or Bernard de Clairvaux feature in *Tales of Love* as attempts to characterize the inner world as part of a whole Being, as exteriority and interiority at once, offering conceptual and even practical-ascetic tools for their own quests after the "One." A realized personal intimacy is thereby contact with the external, one that—in the case of Bernard, whose intuitions come closest to the psychoanalyst's—implies a violent breaking out of the lover's body in order to approach the Other. Bernard accentuates the dimension of the negativity or the narcissistic wound, their importance being somewhat dimmed with Aquinas (who is quick to charge desire and affect with will and cognition): a negativity present in the very pursuit of the disappearance of Self in Other, in the implied violence towards the similar; an eternally unfinished uprooting, leaving a varying measure of carnal love in our most abstract loves, a tenacious zero degree on a never-ending journey.

Contemporary discontent, a topic Kristeva revisits in different contexts, including *New Maladies of the Soul*,[7] is then analyzed in light of the absence of Being in this particular sense: a state marked by the impossibility of idealization; literally, a process of psychologization sometimes (but not always) equivalent to complete somatization, even psychosis: enclosure in a body-self, with no addressee, no addressing, and, even worse, with no internal representational resources, hence no ability to think, ensuing in no intelligibility or means of conveyance. The reduction of love to pleasure and desire. The absence of love, which is by definition the absence of a discourse-in-love.

II. The Baroque

Kristeva's proposal to contribute to the "history of subjectivity" turns out to be an unfolding of the "historicity" of Being. However, through encompassing guile and a noncommitment to an absolute signified, she conducts a "baroquization" of Being by recounting its history from the viewpoint of the imaginary where Being becomes *ipso facto* a "catastrophic-fold-of-'being.'"[8]

The author of *Tales of Love* seems to discard the question of true or false by giving an apparently strict ontological and epistemological status to illusion, even to hallucination.

Baroque is love. Love is baroque: it is a unique idea; it cannot itself be subjected to baroquization. What does this mean?

Kristeva does not systematically discuss the notion of baroque. The noun and the adjective—as well as the names of baroque authors and works par excellence (for example, Borges and Mallarmé, cited in *Tales of Love*)—are strung like pearls through her works, as if to draw attention to how they permeate that author's sensibility, who thus shares her intimate secret. The way of the baroque: limelight and a rushed blurring of footprints.

"Baroque," a technical term of the seventeenth century that no school of thought nor any author of the era used to name itself, was recruited in the eighteenth century to denote anything anomalous, strange, astounding, capricious, or decadent. The blossoming of the notion into a full-fledged aesthetic-intellectual view originates in a succession of studies by Heinrich Wölfflin (a student of Burckhardt who turned from his teacher's poor judgment of the baroque to a favorable one).[9] In a polarizing fashion reminiscent of Nietzsche's dichotomy between the Apollonian and the Dionysian, recognizing no coexistence or mutual contamination of seemingly contrasting formations, Wölfflin discerned two formal and evaluative principles of the aesthetic: the classical and the baroque. The former indicates measure, order, temperance, unity, clarity, stability, hierarchy, wholeness, the harmony of opposing forces; the latter, overabundance, rejection of rules, fragmentation, obscurity, change, refusal of authority, progressive disintegration, movement. The most prominent contemporary theoretician of the baroque, Jean Rousset (mentioned by Kristeva),[10] when facing the historical-critical literature of his times, underlines the conceptual difficulty posed by a phenomenon so multifarious, so complex and nonhomogeneous, varying across countries, artists, and arts. Trying to explain why the baroque rekindled such interest, becoming almost rehabilitated around 1940 to 1950 when he wrote his book, Rousset pointed to the major resonance afforded by present circumstances with an era marked by political-religious instability (from the end of the sixteenth century onwards), atrocious religious and civil wars, killing not only presumed heretics and heathens but also those of the same creed; an era marked, moreover, by a drift of geographical boundaries—as if to introduce globalization—and consequent physical and spiritual restlessness. In the perspective of the Counter Reformation, the baroque constitutes a creative adaptation of the momentary and the chaotic, thus bestowing an ontological status on historical development, yet without relinquishing an ironic reflexivity which questions the solidity of foundations.

Regarding Kristeva's silence surrounding her choice of the baroque as a multipurpose sign in her writing (ontological, psychoanalytic, and to a large extent metapoetical), one cannot simply assert that it derives from or is somehow related to connections between the religious fundamentalism of then and now, or the cumulative results of globalization. Moreover, Kristeva seems to distinguish categorically between these eras when she emphasizes the transcendent dimension—crucial in the world of the libertine or the heretic, such as Don Juan—whose absence, as we have indicated, accounts for the emergence of modern psychosis. Hence the affinity to the baroque is not of an anachronistic nature. The current actuality of the notion is of a different order, neither religious-political nor even formally literary-artistic.

To begin with, we must emphasize three major points. First, versions of the myth of Narcissus pervade *Tales of Love* and turn the Heraclitean waters, reflections, and reflexivity into key motifs in the discussion about love, transference, sublimation, and creation. Second, Kristeva points to the "wealth of signs that constitutes the baroque" (in "Stabat Mater" or the chapter on Baudelaire)[11] to describe the aesthetic inclination in general, an inclination given to "baroquization" and even to "Don Juanization." These terms, then, which involve an aesthetics of existence, are equivalent or synonymous: "aesthetics" or "metaphor," in her understanding, are baroque by definition. If she does not explicitly elaborate a baroque aesthetic, the reader herself can, upon reading her book, do so on interconnecting planes—poetic and psychoanalytic. For everything depends on everything else: the position of the writer and that of the object shift accordingly, like painter and model circling each other. The metamorphosis this permeability brings about is typical of Kristeva's theoretical and literary writing as well as psychoanalysis: since each category is permeable, the unanalyzable is not necessarily an impassible barrier, but is, rather, a "resistance" that must be thought in liquid, elusive terms. Third, the baroque viewpoint on self-world relations is not merely psychological, according to Kristeva, and if it is indeed an "aesthetic of existence," then it is based on an ontological insight.

III. The Pre-oedipal Mother

Kristeva attempts a new description of the pre-oedipal coordinates at life's beginning when the separation between subject and object is not clear-cut. She seeks to name or suggest a journey back in time, some "point of departure" that is always already a fold, in light of which we must try retrospectively to process minute and seemingly trivial stirrings, as well as large maneuvers, guiding our way, eternal children, between Being and Baroque. It is no coincidence that the presence of the pre-oedipal mother—the "submarine mother" as she is called in the discussion of Ginette/Genny—is ambiguous and unsystematic.[12] To revert to Deleuze, Kristeva's concepts-percepts invite us to recall or, rather, imagine the immemorial. Concerning the mother, then, these concepts-percepts signify ripples of affect rather than fixed meaning. The "semiotic," the "abject," "abjection" are singular concepts, their action itself strangely semiotic. As if they have torn the conceptual screen itself, indiscreetly and unrestrained, demanding a different order of time and urgency, separate from daily affairs. That is their power and temptation, the potency of their promise, as if they contained clear knowledge about their subject matter, and we, called for the journey, already know this to be so. We are back to the phenomenological *epoché*. However, we know we must commit ourselves to the most strenuous imaginary effort, the most intimate, aimed at the boundaries of existence, felt even when unidentified, felt as discontent urging hyperbolic speech: too much, unbearable, not enough, more; felt as a filter that signals what is episodic and transient, and what is meaningful, dead-on.

This focus on the pre-oedipal mother raises another question in the book's ontotheological perspective. Was there love in the Beginning? What came first, love or hate, Eros or Thanatos? Or was it perhaps lovehate to begin with, a contamination, coming together as one, without precedence? What, therefore, are the power relations between the pre-oedipal mother and the father of individual prehistory? Is the presentation of a primordial, radical, and pure state of affairs of any importance? What are the implications regarding morality, atonement, forgiveness? Regarding any presumed radical goodness at the foundation of analysis, of life?

Kristeva acknowledges her debt to Klein on this displacement of the discussion about the primal self from the oedipal to the pre-oedipal scene: a primordial drama enabling us to speak about the infant not as an organism but as a human being who has an object and wishes to regulate his anxieties by means of projections or introjections. Concentrating exclusively on the mother-child dyad, Klein emphasized the mutual ambivalence dominating their relationship. Aggression, destructiveness, and hate are present from life's beginning. The infant is responsive to the danger of annihilation, dependency, even enslavement to the object of his desire and nourishment, who or which therefore causes him both pleasure and anxiety, hence anger and vengefulness too. His aggression, his desire to empty his excreta in the mother or invade her in order to control her from within, are an answer to parental aggression, the fear of penetration, or the anticipation of punishment for his own attack. Unlike Freud, who thought the (preconscious) infant did not know death, Klein located infantile aggression in what she called the paranoid-schizoid phase. The transition from this phase to the depressive position, which involves separation and distancing as a condition of mentalization and verbalization, requires a passage through abjection. Before she becomes an object, the mother is therefore the first abject, implicated in a private, concealed rite in the chambers of the infant's heart, where her authority is both introjected and rejected, resulting in the implicit organization of internal and external experience via the correspondent movements of taking in and throwing out, self-constructing and self-evacuation. Everything is signed in this covenant, this vital abjection, this intimate movement towards the mother figure: with and against. Everything depends on her ways with the child, the hygiene she will teach him, her conduct, her intonation, her soft and soothing words, her piercing and hurting words, creating a world and destroying a world, words that will sow in him the sense of right and proper, the boundaries of his body, his awkwardness, potency, cleanliness, what he identifies as dirt, waste, impurity, sickness, his dos and don'ts. Finally, all depends on how she lets him acknowledge his aggression, what is allowed, accepted with understanding and love, and what might bring the loss of what is dearest—her, her love—and the consequent search after ways to reconcile with or to appease her while otherwise releasing his affections.

Understood in this sense, as covenant, abjection is the secret ID in which the primary processes are registered without being set down, their mystery crystallizing as the cluster of practices that make life roll on, delineating the borders of the public, the ritual, and the unconscious, a series of meaningless prohibitions. Practices that indicate the perpetual loss of the seemingly obvious, the natural, the most elementary, which now become a task; the extent to which cleanliness or overcleanliness are compensated for or neutralized by a major impurity (or a feeling of major impurity), a powerful consciousness of transgression or intense elation. Practices reflecting, finally, how well the baby has been nurtured, facing a burden of destiny beyond her capacity, which she can only shrug off and flee. That baby, haunting our dreams, male and female, wise and inspiring and dreadful; knowledge we forgot or only half remember wanders far out of sight, in the gut.

The pre-oedipal mother enables the movement of impulse into sense. The mother tongue she "embodies" or "transmits" is not informative; it lacks a defined syntax or structure. It may be reminiscent of the Adamic language that Walter Benjamin described.[13] For even if it appears as words, it transcends conscious speech, pregnant with additional volume or value, close to the sensual and psychic worlds. It is the first voice, touching the thing, which might later on hide itself, fall asleep, be brushed aside by symbolic language. It might, in the extreme case, become mere body when lacking a verbal, musical, or visual outlet; or, in the absence of a symbolic appearance, it might be assimilated in a highly expressive but shrouded body, a body unelucidated even for the subject itself. This is the psychosomatic symptom or semiotic language turned symptom: it has lost its subtle touch in the interval between impulse and sense, between "nature" and "culture," the quality implicit in the enactment of this duality, which Kristeva names the *sacred*. Even though silence, too, is a distinctive concept, and the silence of the pathetic and suffering body, showing through the well-dressed everyday body, might well enhance the sacred dimension at times. There is therefore music of the body, a body language embodying the sacred inasmuch as a body language is not "just" body but a threshold welding a readable or visual sense to what escapes verbalization. Nevertheless, Kristeva will wonder to what degree becoming-a-body reembeds the sacred in the realm of the victim (a subject position of absolute passivity and pure subjugation or sacrifice), removing the sacred from the dynamic interval and giving it place. In other words, the pre-oedipal mother, crucial in constituting the semiotic sense, is by definition accountable for a rethinking of the sacred, which mainly takes the form of the sanctity of life, stabilizing a semiotic foundation for the infant's psychic space.[14] In this respect, psychosomatic embodiment might testify retrospectively to the domination of the death impulse and the mother's failure to secure sense for her child and thereby to engender the ability to move between the two orders, semiotic and symbolic.

Because Kristeva cannot conclusively define her notion of the sacred, excluded from the realm of religion and victim, from public or private compulsion, she offers various phrasings. The symbolic imperative of the Sacred, actualized in a sequence of meticulously performed actions, is converted into tentative, intuitive sacredness, free from neurosis and violence.[15] A subjective, singular, and transient sacredness in the margins of the ontotheological tradition (Jeanne Guyon, for instance).[16] The sacredness of a singularity constituted as it observes the Sacred from the window, neither passively nor obediently. Such is the pre-oedipal mother as she overcomes the dolphin temptation to turn silent like a fish and realizes the semiotic as an authentic option of expression. The mother as ironic, a pariah, heretic, hence sacred. Herethic. A strange hybrid excluded by the Sacred of society.

Hence the pre-oedipal mother binds everything together, woman and man, by essentially putting into question abjection and the semiotic, sacredness and victim, and, by extension, religion and ideology. Again, Kristeva asks, is the sacred thinkable without its "natural counterpart"? Is there a sacredness that does not demand sacrifice?[17] Is there sacredness in the word itself, rather than only in its abolition, in pure incarnation? Is there a sacred purpose free from an external or internalized logic of destruction and self-destruction? Freud's fascinating juxtaposition of the religious rite and obsessive neurosis mediates, in the background, the connection between the pre-oedipal mother and the psychosomatic symptom, her own sacrifice and/or victims. He emphasizes the fragility of the master of the neurotic ceremony, overwhelmed, even as alone, by inner witnesses watching him naked, by the power of his prohibitions and agony.[18] The mother or the dolphin woman becoming mere body is she who paradoxically introjected the paternal prohibition and through this incarnation forgot the coexistence of body *and* name, the extent to which she may temper the rigidity of the symbolic. In other words, the development of the symptom is not a "Kleinian" matter, solely between mother and child. It involves a premature oedipalization of that relationship, and its seriousness derives from the malfunctioning of the pre-oedipal mother's semiotic relation to the child as well as from the absence of a pre-oedipal father figure. Anorexic or bulimic symptoms, for instance, originate from an amplified secondary identification with the parents, lacking the vital pre-oedipal foundations. Somatization is not without a paternal ideal. On the contrary, it is a rigid and uncompromising assimilation of a divine-paternal code or commandment, dictating suffering—in the face of a detached and unstable world—and transforming the interventions of the mother herself into symbolic principles. "Neither super-ego nor repression disappear in analysis," Kristeva writes to Clément, "at most they become flexible. And the tyrannical religion is replaced by what? By tenderness, which is nothing other than the possibility of telling yourself the story of duty, and which is called the imaginary. I am about to tell you why the sacred, in my view, is that as well, perhaps that only: the imaginary."[19]

In fact, the semiotic and the sacred, the two notions intertwined in the figure of the pre-oedipal mother as a continuous displacement of the interval simultaneously attaching her to and detaching her from sense, by playing with the Name of the Father, by the baroquization of being—these two notions constitute Kristeva's heterodox adaptation of the Freudian corpus, those parts where Freud is not systematic or conclusive, displaying secondary, repressed figures, or apparently dismissing a phenomenon with a pessimistic and gloomy idiom: thus "the heterogeneity of language," "the father of individual prehistory," "the future of an illusion."

"Our Faith: The Seeming" is the title of a chapter in *Tales of Love* that describes an ever-present position in Narcissus's metamorphoses. We are not without religion. But our religion is baroque, namely an illusion, a "religion," as distinct from dogma, hence its sanctity. "Our Faith: The Seeming" makes a gesture in the direction of "The Future of an Illusion": "We have transcended Freud's scientistic suspicion as to the illusion of religion: we know that illusions are necessary, provided we can play with them."[20] In a letter to Clément: "Psychoanalysis as I understand it . . . seeks to restore *illusion's* rights."[21] In *The Future of an Illusion* Freud rejects religious propositions as incredible and insubstantial,[22] seeming to completely overlook theology's attentiveness to self-world relationships, not to mention the affinity of psychoanalysis itself to theology's insights, an affinity that reflects an equivalent epistemic status, one that, by extension, also embraces myth and literature. But Freud's views cannot be reduced to a single essay, and even in the one essay different voices and speakers raise doubts, temper his statements, and ferment his conclusions. Kristeva points out that, somewhat grudgingly, Freud, as an heir to both philosophy and religion, predicts a bright future for illusion nonetheless.

Kristeva's distinctive stance regarding the imaginary quality of illusion orients the reading strategy of the ontotheological texts offered in *Tales of Love*: Kristeva does not seek to refute religion by means of scientific criteria, but, rather, to designate modalities of enacting the unconscious in theological texts. The delineation of psychoanalysis' implication in the ontotheological tradition, on the one hand, and the secularization of the idea of the sacred, on the other, even if not strongly polemical, converse with a certain view of a "secular, all too secular" humanism that ignores the crucial contribution of the ontotheological discourse to the constitution and understanding of the psychical. In this sense, *Tales of Love* continuously questions the current economy of subjectivity, the failures of the project of self-knowledge or of subjective reappropriation, which in its nihilistic version has led to the stark exclusion of religion or at least to an obfuscation between its oppressive sociopolitical and institutional aspects, on the one hand, and its intellectual framework, on the other. The latter still provides a diagnosis of phantasms and psychological conflicts as well as suggestions as to their processing and reconciliation. "I am not speaking of secularism, understood as a battle against religion, but of atheism as the resorption of the sacred into the tenderness of the connection to the other," Kristeva writes, in favor of an atheistic secularity.[23] Such a secularity criticizes, on the basis of religion, the secular project for omitting the pre-oedipal figures from its worldview. As if it collaborated with the forgetfulness of the original Narcissus who, by losing the spring, immediately lost the primal, vital object of identification and idealization as well. The genealogical journey of *Tales of Love* seeks to rehabilitate, through the ontotheological corpus, everything that Narcissus experienced unknowingly when he stooped to drink: a magical instant in which immanence touched transcendence.

IV. The Father of Individual Prehistory

Kristeva has told us: "it has been a long time since I have returned to these archaeologists of faith, to which the love of my father once propelled me."[24] One can also read Kristeva's heterodox interpretation of Freud, the double gesture of sanctifying and blaspheming the father's name, as if it imagined Freud not as the oedipal father of some theoretically dogmatic school of thought but as a loving father providing his sons and daughters with the words, notions, and conceptual tools that enable them to imagine differently: primarily to imagine him, without excommunications, exclusions, betrayal, and factionalism, with no punitive systems and no guilt. The father of individual prehistory is the invisible point, the most elusive—and therefore cardinal—element in the baroque structure that Kristeva's book erects; a father who opens a window to the ghosts of all imaginary fathers, as though he were beckoning to catch the readers' attention. But where? To whom? Towards what? What is there to see, not only in order to understand and to keep on reading but to live, love, speak? He may be the source, an aquatic element, ambiguous, bisexual. An oceanic father, a container lacking matter and solidity. Kristeva relies on remarks by Freud in *The Ego and the Id*,[25] pointing to a primal, immediate presubjective identification with this instance, the father of individual prehistory, which is neither object nor figure; a prehistoric identification, leading us therefore to the innermost and the outermost, leading us to withdraw inwards so we can spread our wings and fly.

In the beginning there was psyche and nothing more, yet it is not self-sufficient: a psyche addressing itself to . . . In the beginning there was psychical action, before impulse, before sexuality. In the beginning there was an imagination adopting a father, an imagination-in-love conceiving a loving father. Not a biological father, not necessarily the biological father.[26] A loving father, an absolute other, whose presence enables and will enable, in the future, the movement of abstraction from the psychical, biological, biographical, and human. Whose presence renders the oedipal phase a psychologization of the subject, which is a forgetting of the primal father and thereby of the capacity to create.[27]

The father of individual prehistory demands nothing. In his flight, always bound to disappear, tangible yet elusive, he encourages psyche to draw near herself, look at herself, acknowledge her freedom. In a certain sense he is more intimate with her than she is with herself. It is he who constitutes her as an ever-heteronomous structure. He speaks to her from the beginning of life, so she will unfetter herself, forgive herself, and go on. Just as he does. An affranchising father, willing to walk with whoever turns to him until the end of sense, non-sense. A father before time and memory who is therefore, above all, the father of the future, forgiveness, promise. But why should she be forgiven? What was her sin?

Kristeva weaves the strands of the primal scene, situating the presubject in the order of knowledge, love, and goodness, prior to the oedipal drama, by means of an eclectic pursuit of texts describing similar attempts: Song of

Songs, the Gospels, Thomas Aquinas, Hegel, Heidegger, Freud. The instance of a pre-oedipal father allows the ideas of the good and guilt to unfold not as subjective categories originating in the introjection of parental prohibitions and ideals but as ontological categories inherent in our existence as speaking beings. Our distress, Kristeva writes in *Intimate Revolt*, is due to a conscious and unconscious structure of transgression, rendering us both innocent and guilty,[28] beings thrown by definition towards the good by the love of the father (Aquinas) and receiving immediate absolution even before manifesting guilt and debt (the Agape-God). Kristeva supposes—referring to Heidegger, who raises the question of an absolution already involving the issues of responsibility and the pre-original guilt of *Dasein*—that the being-becoming-subject of whom she speaks is accountable, responsible, that is, guilty before an instance present within himself. Yet it is not a defined instance, guilt, or debt. Following Heidegger, and in the light of the immense importance Kristeva gives to *voice* in the pre-oedipal phase, one can describe the affinity with the father of prehistory as founded primarily on voice: a voice speaking within me, though it is beyond and above me. This precedence does not annul the crucial importance of the oedipal drama and the displacement of the singular relationship from the loving father to the judgmental and punitive father, with all the complexity of feelings towards him: remorse, guilt, pangs of conscience. The life, law, and order of the polis are unimaginable without the oedipal morality treating us as equals and weighing our actions according to impartial and general criteria. However, Kristeva, as she would be, is interested in the interval between the instances, between the two ethics of the fathers, and in the primal father thus remaining an other in relation to justice, law, and the polis. An other who does not set a priori rules for our speech and deeds, but is attentive to the immanent motion of our existence, without prohibiting or punishing, commanding and avenging, so that we can renew our days in other dimensions and planes of time. Transcend linear time. The interval (*entre-deux*) between the formations—between Narcissus, the father of prehistory and the pre-oedipal mother, on the one hand, and the oedipal triangle, on the other—is what allows for the proposal of innovation and rebellion, that is, the introduction of radical goodness (and, by extension, of absolution and promise) in the discussion. This is also a *herethic* homage to the late, idealizing phase of Arendt's thought in *The Life of the Mind*.[29]

The interval between the fathers that appears in *Tales of Love* might have suggested a deconstructive relationship: the father of prehistory as prerequisite of the oedipal order and morals, who constantly contaminates and challenges the latter. However, such an implication between "foundation" and "derivation" did not occur here, and it seems that the primal father completely gave way to the secondary father, to the extent of obscuring, perhaps completely erasing the former's vital memory. As if, harmless though he was, he was murdered, more cruelly and desperately than the murder of the tribal father. For Narcissus falters so between sense and abyss, and his father (calling out from the water) does not know how to speak to his defiant and enfolded soul. The necessarily nonmelancholic association with a loving father, who is not yet an object, is converted into a melancholic identification, immediately becoming an interior, a wound, an abscess. A complex. This psychologization is the basis of Kristeva's criticism of the modern predicament, expressed in the acute sentences, for instance, ending the chapter on Aquinas: ontology hereby ceases to be an ontology of the good; the good is now limited to ethics. The knowing subject, in the philosophy of the true, has forgotten the natural passion for the good.

Modern discontent, therefore, is not due to the absence of a sufficiently solid oedipal instance. It is not exhausted by an empirical or a symbolic account of the collapse of the traditional family. Moreover, as we have seen, psychosomatic maladies are highly correlated with an amplification of the introjected oedipal instance, an unrestrained monster that has long ago moved its psychodrama to the agora and the global city. Guilt and shame and anxiety and depression, murder and fear, prohibition and remorse act rigorously in a moralistic, compulsive, punished and punishing civilization. The reproof in *Tales of Love* against modern nihilism (the death of god or the death of the father, which is not necessarily the death of the oedipal father) is therefore aimed at the oedipalization and psychologization of the soul and the world, leading to total somatization, on the one hand, and total symbolization, on the other, on the assumption that resolution of the oedipal complex will solve psychical distress. Hell is oedipal, to the extent that the only speech produced is oedipal speech while semiotic speech is repressed, and Kristeva will go a long way, following theologians and mystics and troubadours, to show how, with the aid of a loving father, one can prevent (even temporarily) this hell and its destructiveness. If there is a nostalgic dimension in the book, it has to do with a scarcely audible lament for the disappearance of that father or, rather, a yearning, because it lacks a definable object or place, for a different possibility of selfhood, a dynamic individualization, seeking to take us from one state to another, free of a fixed "true" image that desires its own identity.

A longing for another heritage, sealed in nothingness, in the primal narcissistic structure. Silent, clear, serene, restrained, held within, in the folds of our soul. But from that attending, we succumb, irreparably, to messianic moments of presence, oblivious to the racket of Eros, forgetting that the power we imagined we received from the father is as fragile as his presence. It is not true that the loving father does not punish. His punishment may well be the worst. For pride, for possessiveness. Low spirits, dimming of light, extinguishment.

V. Narcissus

Let us leave the parents aside and look into the soul of the child, a youth by now, for, through most of its chapters, *Tales of Love* follows, implicitly and explicitly, the metamorphoses of Narcissus: the gamut of possibilities he has faced since he took residence in humanity's nocturnal agenda, anticipating the infinitude of possibilities still ahead, for him and for us. Kristeva accentuates Narcissus—and, by extension, narcissism's—vital role in any account of Western subjectivity. Each and every one must see himself as originating from that youth, who died in the springtime of his life; who by his horrifying vegetative regression, in his fall from grace, bequeathed us a hidden treasure of images and reflections and silences; who compelled us to encounter void and inertia, violence inside and out, complete absence of perspective.

The story as told by Ovid, which sets the baroque tone of Kristeva's metamorphic journey, already raises many problems and questions. The myth presents a short but highly complex scene. Narcissus's unrequited lovers, youngsters in search of an object, cursed the one who did not answer their love. They wished on him that his love may never find an object and perhaps, indirectly, that he would fall in love with a nonobject. In other words, they presumed that Narcissus, the hardhearted, who didn't love them, was capable of love just like them. And indeed, Narcissus, just like them, wants object-love. When he realizes the truth of the reflection, from his perspective of course, he is bitterly disappointed. This should be emphasized: the original Narcissus is not a narcissist! He is terrified when he falls in love with what he mistakes for himself. He does not want osmosis. He wants an object, an other! In this sense, those around Narcissus, Echo included, are no riper or readier for love than he is. Not one of them is capable of more than instantaneous satisfaction or its negation, frustration and revenge. His trial is similar to theirs, and the agony he signifies from now on is a "common denominator," the proper and common name of all other nameless figures, and of the Narcissistic Echo, who resonates from the same void. The failure of the youngsters gathering here lies in their lack of imagination, and it goes back to their loss of both the primal father and mother. Lamenting Narcissus's death, they still fail to notice that Narcissus is, after all, gathered to his father. And this gathering, unto death, is his offering to them. Teach yourselves, brothers and sisters, he calls, how to be alone.

But we must slow down. For the narrative evolves slowly. Narcissus takes a break from the hunt, loosens his grip on life's frenzy, and, until the brutal drowning, he accepts, even if unknowingly, the source's invitation to both concentrate and unfold. Seeking an other, he is willing to accept the violence of leaving towards the other, of being uprooted. By no means does he wish to find himself yet again, and his violence—self-inflicted—derives from feeling denied by otherness, denied by life, which has shown him by signs and wonders to be unworthy of love, unworthy to live it. Life grants him an object and takes it away almost instantaneously, grants him the pain of finding and the helplessness of desertion, the quintessence of experiencing love, all at once. In the cosmos Ovid depicts, nobody has the courage and precision and integrity to acknowledge the fundamental weakness underlying everything since days beyond recall: nobody except Narcissus, perhaps, and when it's too late.

Narcissus is where the two parallel paths of *Tales of Love* nevertheless come together: love and the discourse-in-love. Narcissus who kills himself, knowingly or not, because of too much love or the lack of it—is invited to look and listen and put his own destitution into words while transposing himself or his language (metaphor) from one state of matter to another. Narcissus is like an open book, an internal grammar unscrolling, a screen constituted by void and object. The malady of the soul in every sense, the soul itself. The narcissistic structure is by definition a narcissistic wound, an open wound, much as Narcissus tries to heal it, that is, to love and speak love. Love in both senses, as body and as language, dangles by a thread, over void, impossibility. The moment of void is not only vital for the soul, language, and consciousness as a narcissistic consciousness; it is also inscribed in the essence of life, bearing no relation to a (secondary) nihilistic stance. It is what bestows meaning on life. One therefore should not confuse void or nothingness with lack (potentially filled), on the one hand, or with reflexive or judgmental negation, on the other. This is a pre-oedipal void, presymbolic, prereflexive, sentencing the subject to an ec-static existence, thrown as he is into being and rejected by it, dwelling in a perpetual becoming. Kristeva emphasizes that Narcissus, sober, has an object: the psychic realm as such. This in turn relies on both a primal identification with a loving father (the source) and a primordial mother towards whom Narcissus is ambivalent and from whose physical contact he has severed himself due to his identification with the father.

Freud identifies primary narcissism with autoeroticism, the objectless condition in which there is no relation to an other, the infant taking his wholeness and nothing more as his object of love. Life in the womb—or sleep—is close to this nonobjectal narcissism. Kristeva, following Klein, puts the object relation right at the beginning of life. Narcissism is not then identified with autoeroticism. It is a highly complex structure serving as the first step towards a relation with the world, on the way to constituting an ego ideal. Self-love depends on the introjection of a good object, that is, on primary identification and idealization addressed to the father of prehistory. Primary narcissism therefore derives from this crucial psychical affinity, which inaugurates the subject's ability to invest his means of expression and his love in one and the same gesture. It constitutes a primary, as yet incomplete because passive, autonomization process. It is the condition for secondary narcissism, which involves a transposition of the libidinal tendency from objects external to the ego back to the ego. If, for Kristeva, primary narcissism is the desire for a loving father, sublimation as Freud presents it carries a double movement, immanent and transcendent. It does not merely concern the removal of libido from objects to become absorbed in the self. Primary idealizing identification nurtures the imaginary world, transcending monadic enclosure. Rather than offering temporary relief from physical suffering or destiny, the aesthetic-imaginary horizon keeps working at the constitution, processing, and expansion of the psychic realm. The fruits of representation and thought are not defenses, compensations, or substitutes for a failure in the world but an aesthetic of existence, a modality of standing in and against the world through the use of an object. Nevertheless, depriving the id's libido of sexuality, together with the implied renouncement, repression, and even suppression of drive (the negation of erotization, in Freud's terms) expose the ego to the seductions of the death drive. The latter fortifies the narcissistic ego and lies at its door, threatening to annihilate it. In every act of sublimation, the creator wraps himself in coils of death-and-revival. Narcissus may then viciously attack the outside, fight what he sees as the metaphysical "spirit of seriousness," the frigidity of creed and law; or, alternatively, assault himself with lethal criticism or suicidal melancholy. Kristeva examines the gamut of these formations in many of her works, from Céline's fascist modernism and brutal abjection to Nerval's melancholy, to Colette's metamorphic language, cleaving to the world as if observer and observed were one flesh. Here Kristeva sees eye to eye with Freud although she maintains that displacement of libido to the ego does not prevent a resexuation of the act of sublimation. Still, sublimation does not protect us against the death drive, and the omnipotent Narcissus, solemnly and diligently crossing the void of self and language, is a rare flower. Usually he is vulnerable to surges of the death drive, unless he can love, namely, go on creating.

These narcissistic fluctuations, amplified in the creative life, can also be described as processes of "psychologization" or "oedipalization," on the one hand, and abstraction of the psychological and from the human, on the other. This insight leads Kristeva to trace the ontotheological, lyrical, and Romanesque genealogy of Narcissus from the beginning of Christianity onwards, for, in each and every one of its stages, over and beyond all differences, the Narcissus paradigm is not only not abandoned but improved, elaborated, and sublated—even in the paradoxically estranged gestures of abjection of the loving father, the father's forsaking of his son, or the evaporating of the ego. Plotinus is the harbinger of this development, quick to restore Narcissus's lost support, the father, and therefore understand the former's error and punishment in terms of his misapprehension of the source of his reflection and apparition. If one conceives the spring, reflection, and reflectivity as the essence of the psychic structure as such, one can relieve narcissistic anxiety and imagine Narcissus happy: lover and beloved united with Being, the Other, the One. Moreover, if the source of love is the One, then self-love is not only not wrong, it is vital. The identical is nothing but another identical, and one must return to Narcissus's biography, tying it fundamentally to the foundation of Creation. Sometimes, as in the case of Jeanne Guyon, tying it to complete identification with the foundation-God, annihilating relationship as such through the abyssal introjection of the burden of the narcissistic void, as Jeanne disinherits herself, as it were, of all possessions, ideas, judgments, imagination. But the narcissistic extinction of the quietist, who exists solely in the Other, is worked through by excessive if not plethoric writing, Kristeva stresses. When it withdraws to degree zero, the narcissistic economy demands its measure of pleasure; it is, moreover, erotic through and through. Therefore, precisely where it refers to the loving father, religious writing is another domain for erotic pleasure to focus: now on language that, lacking both object and subject, organizes as a space-in-love. Kristeva's elaborate discussion of the tight bonds between self-love, love of God, and love of one's neighbor, mainly in the writings of Bernard de Clairvaux and Thomas Aquinas, reflecting her intense involvement in this corpus, aims to underline the nature of modern impoverishment. It is an era marked by the absence of a fear of God, as is evinced in religious fundamentalism and nihilistic atheism alike, which are one and the same thing.

The contemporary Narcissus, withdrawn, diluted, and bastioned, is closer than ever to the spirit of the spring, an ephemeral source. Psychoanalysis, according to Kristeva, will fight for his language.

MICHAL BEN-NAFTALI

TEL AVIV UNIVERSITY
APRIL 2019

NOTES

1. Julia Kristeva, *Tales of Love*, trans. Leon S. Roudiez (New York: Columbia University Press, 1987).

2. Julia Kristeva, "Stabat Mater," in ibid.; first published in *Tel Quel* 74 (1977).

3. Here Kristeva differs from most psychoanalysts, who, she points out, do not accept the phenomenological stance and refrain from including the idea of Being in their clinic, thus rejecting the extrapsychical, extrasubjective, investigative horizon offered in German phenomenology. See Julia Kristeva, *The Sense and Non-sense of Revolt*: *The Powers and Limits of Psychoanalysis Volume 1*, trans. Jeanine Herman (New York: Columbia University Press, 2000), 65–68; *Sens et non-sens de la révolte* (Paris: Fayard, 1996), 141–47.

4. Ibid., 59; *Sens et non-sens de la révolte*, 129–30.

5. Ibid., 68; *Sens et non-sens de la révolte*, 107.

6. Julia Kristeva, *Au risque de la pensée* (Paris: L'Aube, 2001), 13 (translated by Mirjam Hadar).

7. Julia Kristeva, *New Maladies of the Soul*, trans. Ross Guberman (New York: Columbia University Press, 1995).

8. Kristeva, "Stabat Mater," 248–49.

9. Heinrich Wölfflin, *Renaissance und Barock* (Munich: T. Ackermann, 1888).

10. Julia Kristeva, "Don Juan, or Loving to Be Able To," in *Tales of Love*, 403n4.

11. Kristeva, "Stabat Mater," 253; "Baudelaire, Or Infinity, Perfume, and Punk," in *Tales of Love*, 319.

12. Julia Kristeva, "Romeo and Juliet: Love-Hatred in the Couple," in *Tales of Love*, 228.

13. Walter Benjamin, "On Language as Such and on the Language of Man," in *Reflections: Essays, Aphorisms, and Autobiographical Writings* (New York: Schocken, 1986).

14. Catherine Clément and Julia Kristeva, *The Feminine and the Sacred*, trans. Jane Marie Todd (New York: Columbia University Press, 2001), 56, 100; *Le Féminin et le sacré* (Paris: Stock), 92, 162.

15. [The Sacred is the social, codified, normalizing imperative.—Ed.]

16. See Julia Kristeva, "A Pure Silence: The Perfection of Jeanne Guyon," in *Tales of Love*.

17. Clément and Kristeva, *The Feminine and the Sacred*, 120, 134; *Le Féminin et le sacré*, 193, 216. Kristeva, *Sense and Non-sense of Revolt*, 24; *Sens et non-sens de la révolte*, 55.

18. Sigmund Freud, "Obsessive Acts and Religious Practice," in *The Standard Edition of the Complete Psychological Works of Sigmund Freud*, vol. IX, trans. James Strachey (London: Hogarth, 1959).

19. Clément and Kristeva, *The Feminine and the Sacred*, 116; *Le Féminin et le sacré*, 188.

20. Kristeva, *Au risque de la pensée*, 130.

21. Clément and Kristeva, *The Feminine and the Sacred*, 38.

22. Sigmund Freud, *The Future of an Illusion*, in *The Standard Edition of the Complete Psychological Works of Sigmund Freud*, vol. XXI, trans. James Strachey (London: Hogarth, 1961), 54.

23. Clément and Kristeva, *The Feminine and the Sacred*, 60; *Le Féminin et le sacré*, 99.

24. Ibid., 38; *Le Féminin et le sacré*, 65.

25. Sigmund Freud, *The Ego and the Id*, in *The Standard Edition of the Complete Psychological Works of Sigmund Freud*, vol. XIX, trans. James Strachey (London: Hogarth, 1961), 31.

26. Although the biological father can constitute the concrete pillar on which the metaphorical movement of identification is being made, the loving father is not or not necessarily the biological father.

27. The oedipal metapsychological frame of reference is thus a reductive, constraining development of the subject's originary ontotheological potentiality.

28. Julia Kristeva, *Intimate Revolt: The Powers and Limits of Psychoanalysis Volume 2*, trans. Jeanine Herman (New York: Columbia University Press, 2002), 18; *La Révolte intime: Pouvoirs et limites de la psychanalyse* II (Paris: Fayard, 1997), 32.

29. Hannah Arendt, *The Life of the Mind* (New York: Harcourt, 1978). Julia Kristeva, *Hannah Arendt*, trans. Ross Guberman (New York: Columbia University Press, 2001), 230–40 (volume 1 of the "female genius" trilogy); *Le Génie féminin,* t. I, *Hannah Arendt* (Paris: Fayard, 1999), 358–71.

20

Keren Mock

LANGUAGE AND SACREDNESS IN THE QUEST FOR SUBJECTIVITY

Freud believed that science inflicted three narcissistic injuries on humankind. These injuries shifted the focus from God to the human being and raised fundamental questions about the nature of the sacred. The first injury was inflicted by Copernican heliocentrism and the realization that the human being was not the center of the universe, which shook foundational beliefs about the cosmos. The second was caused by Darwin's theory of evolution and the discovery that the human being was descended from apes, shattering the belief in being created in God's sacred image. The third injury came from the discovery of the unconscious and the realization that the human being was not the master of their own house, which overturned the Cartesian conception of the psyche.[1] Kristeva continues in the Freudian tradition of deconstructing the sacred by drawing on multiple fields in the humanities and social sciences and by infusing her own subjective experience into her psychoanalytic approach to the sacred.

In Latin, the sacred refers not to an *arche* but to an opposition: *sacer* represents both upward transcendence or that which is "holy," "consecrated," and celestial as well as downward transcendence or that which is "cursed," "abomination," and "taboo." The sacred thus comprises two diametrically opposed poles. Contradictory by definition, the sacred produces tumultuous affect, an ambivalence where attraction and repulsion, idealization and debasement mix together. Both inherent in and foreign to any form of social organization, the sacred is a constituent element of the bond between individuals. Kristeva even suggests that without the sacred—"that violence-sacrifice-castration-lack-etc."—there can be neither language nor subject.[2]

Translated from French by T. Aaron Priest.

The existence and emergence of the sacred are intimately tied to the question of subjective meaning addressed throughout the long history of philological, philosophical, linguistic, and religious scholarship. This is the intellectual legacy Kristevan thought perpetuates and deepens. Her psychoanalytic conception of the sacred draws upon: the maieutics of *Cratylus* ("speaking is a kind of action");[3] the medieval logicians who spent centuries quarreling over universals; Spinoza, who famously proclaimed *Deus sive natura* despite knowing that the word "nature" appeared nowhere in the Bible and that while nature is unchanging, what does change is the causality of a "naturing nature" or "nature natured"; and the linguistics of Saussure and Benveniste—the formalization of meaning with the rise of a new language theory and the introduction of the distinction between signified (concept) and signifier (sound image).

Are religions the only spaces where humanity encounters, experiences, and expresses the sacred? Does the sacred manifest in secular spaces? If so, what place do subjectivity and the sacred have in secular contexts? In addressing these questions, Kristeva implements several shifts in the study of discourse about the sacred: a theoretical shift from religious metaphysics and the praxes of the humanities to an analysis of the sacred that uses metapsychological tools; an etiological shift of the origin of the sacred, moving it from the father to the mother; and a shift from the social space to the subjective space. Her literary style pierces the depths of intimate experience. Her formulation of a nonreligious ethics is grounded in the concept of transference and a countertransferential and reflexive approach to language. Kristeva proposes a new way of conceptualizing the process of becoming a subject. The need to believe and the drive to know arise against the backdrop of the work of the negative intrinsic to the emergence of language. A new form of the original sacred "bond," the *religere*, Kristeva's concept of *maternal reliance* (*reliance maternelle* or rebinding to the maternal) expresses the transcendent belief in a form of immanence: a new and more archaic image formed by the corporeal link to the mother and by the loving authority of the father. Between the nameable and the representable, the sacred is animated by a subjective quest that forces one into the depths of meaning at a time of rising individual and collective symptoms; into a place where the unspeakable is the other face of melancholia and religious extremism: a sacrilegious and sacrificial erotization of death.

I. A Sacred Original Language

In several Semitic languages, the term "sacred" derives from a common triliteral root: *Quddušu* or "pure" in Akkadian, *muqaddas* (مقدس) in Arabic, and the Hebrew term *kadosh* (קדוש), which fades to the hushed silence of the sibilant consonant. Some medieval philosophers viewed Hebrew as an original sacred language that could serve as a basis for analyzing all other languages. This view remained common until the Enlightenment thinkers such as Leibniz. Kristeva's philosophical approach includes an examination of the origins of texts and words.[4] In the Bible, the term "sacred" has several meanings. In

Leviticus, which discusses sacerdotal rites, the sacred refers to transcendence, purity, and righteousness. It is also a synonym for the name of God: "Ye shall be holy [*kedoshim, sancti*]: for I the Lord your God *am* holy [*kadosh, sanctus*]."[5] In Exodus, the sacred becomes the place where elaborate holy rites and rituals are carried out, including purification, dressing, anointing, sacrificial offerings, the anointing of priests, the holy meal, and the holocaust: "And thou shalt take the ram of the consecration, and seethe his flesh in the holy *place* [*bemakom kadosh, loco sancto*]."[6]

The space of the sacred has been regulating life and death in Judaism for millennia. A central component in Jewish liturgy, the *Kaddish* prayer, used in ancient Aramaic and in mourning rituals (the basis of the Lord's Prayer), praises the name of God and exalts Him "high above all blessings and hymns, praises and consolations, which are uttered in the world; and say ye, Amen."[7] The *Kiddushin* refers to betrothal in the marriage process, specifically the moment when the husband, by way of a ring, declares to his bride: "Behold, thou art consecrated unto me by this ring, according to the Law of Moses and of Israel."[8] The sacred later took the name of "temple," *mikdash* (מקדש). Purity is at the core of the social pact and it is on its basis that were formed the prohibition against visual representations, *Kashrut* dietary laws, purity rituals known as *tumah* and *tahara,* and the delimitation of public and private spaces found in the Eruvin Tractate in the Talmud. In Judaism, the sacred refers to ethical and religious values as well as the quality of the relationship between human beings and between oneself and God.

For more than a decade now, Kristeva and I have been discussing the sacred and the profane, the religious and the secular, *la langue* and *le langage.* These subjects intersect throughout her entire body of work. We first met in early 2006 in a small café in the Latin Quarter in Paris to discuss the etymological and religious implications of the concept of "freedom" in the Hebrew language. To be entirely honest with readers, I handed my notes over to Kristeva and I no longer remember exactly what I told her that day. What I do still remember is that the very concept of freedom, absent from the early biblical texts, did not appear until freedom was lost. Indeed, it was only after the Hebrews were exiled and deprived of their freedom and sovereignty that two terms appeared in rabbinical texts that referred to the concept of freedom: *hofesh* (חפש) and *herut* (חרות).[9] The ideas we exchanged that day formed the basis of an approach to studying the origins of the sacred using etymology. In this particular instance, the etymology pointed to the origin of a signifier and its sudden appearance in language.

A new signifier emerged in the space hollowed out by loss. This signifier endured whereas others met a different fate, becoming mere ancient symbols. Many sacred signifiers became antiquated and sank into oblivion, which is not the case of these two words commonly used in today's Modern Hebrew. Their sacred meaning has been preserved but other profane meanings have been tacked on. For instance, "freedom" became "holiday," *hufsha* (חופשה). Modern Hebrew was reborn as a modern-day living language after having been a sacred language for two millennia.

A few years later, while I was working on my doctoral dissertation under Julia Kristeva and Pierre-Marc de Biasi on the reemergence in the nineteenth century of Hebrew as a new mother tongue, Kristeva and I once again had the opportunity to discuss the centuries-long process of sacred terms becoming imbued with profane meaning. My dissertation and my dialogues with her culminated in the publication of my first book, *Hébreu, du sacré au maternel* (Hebrew: from sacred language to mother tongue), which examined the transformation of Hebrew from a sacred language into a means of communication and transmission, a language of the unconscious.[10] The book analyzed the process through which a sacred language can come to produce immanent meaning. The case of Hebrew is unique in the history of languages. Its secularization was a pivotal moment in the processes of subjectivity in which a new mother tongue supplanted the multiple languages of the diaspora (Russian, Yiddish, Arabic, German, Judeo-Spanish, etc.) and, in so doing, transgressed the prohibition against speaking a language designated as sacred. The multiple mother tongues acquired during exile were abandoned in favor of Hebrew, which became the official language of the State of Israel. From a Kristevan perspective, it could be said that a new subjective meaning emerged out of the sacred in a nascent society through a process of rebinding (*reliance*) in which the formalization of the symbolic served as a frame for *jouissance* by shattering the paradigmatic sacred language and by introducing semiotics, a process Kristeva refers to as a "reactivation of an inner experience."[11]

II. The Origins of the Sacred: From the Primitive Murder to Abjection

Kristeva's theory of the sacred involves two stages in a movement from text to speech, from corpus to body (*corps*). In the order instilled by language, its rules and its laws between diachrony and synchrony, the "sacred—sacrifice—which is found in every human society, is, then, a theologization of the thetic."[12] This notion of the sacred-sacrifice has roots in the Freudian primitive murder, that of the father as outlined in *Totem and Taboo*, "The Dissolution of the Oedipus Complex," "Dostoevsky and Parricide," and *Moses and Monotheism*.[13] Between vengeance, desire to possess, and exogamic exchanges, the social pact is founded on the sacrifice expressed in the murder and incest taboos. In *Moses and Monotheism* Freud mentions the *auri sacra fames*, an allusion to the passage from *The Aeneid* by Virgil.[14] In dactylic hexameter, this passage recounts the murder and the sacred burial ritual for the decapitated Polydorus:

> To what ends will you not force the human heart, this awful hunger for gold [aura sacra fames]. . . .
> We set up altars for the spirits of the dead, with dark deep-blue ribbons and black cypress.
> The Trojan women walked around it with their hair undone, as is the custom. We offered a foaming bowl of warm milk and dishes of the blood of sacrifice [*sanguinis et sacri pateras*]. We bound the soul to its tomb, and in a loud voice called out to him for the last time.[15]

The ego ideal and the superego are formed through this primal and symbolic murder of the father, which plays out on the individual level during the Oedipus conflict. But then, what role does the mother play? For Kristeva, the mother does have a decisive role, but understanding it requires going beyond the social and anthropological lens into the territory of individuality, psychoanalysis, and ontogenetics. Like Klein before her, Kristeva explores a shadow zone, that of an archaic phantasmatic reality where she also locates the sacred. This space she names the abject.

In *Powers of Horror*, Kristeva proposes a metapsychological perspective on the sacred that incorporates religion and art as well as the way in which creativity has been sublimated through literature following the collapse of religions.[16] Her starting points are the rituals of defilement and exclusion, taboos, and purification methods, as well as the transgression processes outlined by the anthropologists and ethnologists. For Douglas and Lévi-Strauss, the forms of the sacred are separating agents included in a symbolic network on the basis of which the subject is defined as both an individual being and a social being.[17] Since rituals set the boundaries of social space, the sacred contains both an ethical value and an aesthetic value. As a tracer of boundaries and intrinsic to all societies since the dawn of time, the sacred regulates law, morality, and ethics. What Kristeva developed was the constitutive dimension of the sacred. These modalities of the sacred emerge at the dawn of psychic life when language appears. They occur against the backdrop of the drives with the semiotic-symbolic fabric taking form through the process of differentiation between subject and object, the abject and the Thing (*das Ding*). *Res extensa*, system, order, rituals . . . On the border between nature and culture, rituals reenact this inaugural moment of separation between subject and object.

An ontological constituent of the advent of the subject, abjection is involved in the narcissistic constitution as this first projective movement that enables the separation from the object. What constitutes me as a subject is the abjection of the maternal, the rejection of this body that formed me and from which I must separate. That which the ego rejects is located outside the symbolic order; it is radically other and different. It is an object opposed to "I" and thus becomes abject. An archaic remnant of primary repression, the abject only appears in its symptomatic form, such as depression. Due to the threat of literally becoming *das Ding*, the Thing, the overlap between the sacred and the abject (whose psychical assimilation is impossible) can only be glimpsed belatedly (*nachträglich*). In this positive and negative two-way movement of the drives, abjection is constitutive of ideality in the mother-father object relation (see next page).

Kristeva associates the sacred with the mother in the primary relationship. But she goes even further, grounding it in the original biological reality of intrauterine life. Abjection is "two-sided," just as her essay "Stabat Mater" is written in two printed columns in *Tales of Love*.[18] In this work, Kristeva offers a comparison of two diametrically opposed experiences: the birth and the death of the son. In the form of a textual dyad, she recounts her embodied experience of abjection. Kristeva draws a parallel to this pivotal moment of the feminine in Hymn XIII of the Madonna where, overcome with suffering and pity, the immaculate mother weeps over the crucified body of her son.

Stabat Mater dolorosa	The Mother stood, with grief confounded,
Juxta crucem lacrimosa	Near the cross, her tears abounded,
dum pendebat Filius.	Whilst her Son thereon did hang.
Cuius animam gementem,	Thro' whole soul, which sighs were renting
contristatam et dolentem,	Sadly mourning and lamenting,
pertransivit gladius.	Pierc'd a sword with cruel pang.[19]

This image brings to mind Giovanni Bellini's visual representations of the theme of the *sacra conversazione*, which replaced polyoptics with a new aesthetic comprised of colors and lights.[20] In the *Critique of Pure Reason*, Kant asserts that space represents a structure of subjectivity whose form of external intuition is constituted a priori.[21] The modification of sacred space results in a modification of internal space. Kristeva juxtaposes these two diametrically opposed scenes in two literary styles, one semiotic and the other symbolic. She contrasts the intimate experience of the son's birth with the pain suffered by the Mother when the son dies:

> Taut eardrum, tearing sound out of muted silence. Wind among grasses, a seagull's faraway call, echoes of waves, auto horns, voices, or nothing? Or his own tears, my newborn, spasm of syncopated void. I no longer hear anything, but the eardrum keeps transmitting this resonant vertigo to my skull, the hair. My body is no longer mine, it doubles up, suffers, bleeds, catches cold, puts its teeth in, slobbers, coughs, is covered with pimples, and it laughs.

> Very soon, within the complex relationship between Christ and his Mother where relations of God to mankind, man to woman, son to mother, etc., are hatched, the problematics of time similar to that of cause loomed up. If Mary preceded Christ and he originated in her if only from the standpoint of his humanity, should not the conception of Mary herself have been immaculate? For, if that were not the case, how could a being conceived in sin and harboring it in herself produce a God?[22]

Images, representations, impressions, and affects clash in the gaping maw of Eros and Thanatos. Here, there is a confrontation between things and words, between the creation and the separation of forms. Bodily sensations flow like lava, each sensation running into the next and then detaching from it freely. These poetic forms of semiotic poetic language that spurt from the imagination rattle the symbolic order. The sacred aspects of the abject in language emerge from: (1) the union of the maternal body and the undifferentiated intrauterine body of the child, and (2) the shattering of this union upon the death of the child and the encounter with its corpse. Locus of our uncertainty and of lack, a part of the discourse about language moves away from its initial object toward other spheres: the intimate *signifiance* of the theoretician who places herself on display. Projecting herself into the literary experiment, Kristeva describes the space of abjection as being constituted of bodily sensations that dominate the feminine body and of a psyche in which languages merge yet her own mother tongue remains absent. Therefore, perhaps the origin of abjection and the sacred should be sought in the arena of ambivalence, a place where love and hate dance together.

III. Sacred Melancholy: Ambivalent Love

In a letter to Clément, Kristeva says that, essentially, "the sacred is love."[23] Object relations involve successive losses in the relationship between the ego and its inner dynamics. Our first love objects are always already lost. The libidinal flows can allow a displacement of investments from the prohibited objects (mother and father), although this plastic movement can sometimes be inhibited. Melancholy could therefore be characterized as a malady of the soul determined by love sickness, but also perhaps by an annihilation of the sacred bond. How can this be healed? Through meaning (*signifiance*), Kristeva would say. Subjective meaning has a therapeutic value that is constructed on the basis of a reorganization of idealities and identifications.

In the melancholic subject, ambivalence acquires greater amplitude when the identification processes are destabilized. As if frozen in time, such a subject loses all interest in and access to pleasure, and the need to believe sinks into a deep malaise characterized by the absence of differentiation from the lost love object. According to the metapsychological model Freud outlined in *Mourning and Melancholia*, since the object is introjected following an inexorable loss, the subject splinters and struggles to extricate itself from the clutches of an object inhabiting the body in an intense unconscious intrapsychical conflict.[24] According to the psychoanalytic theory of narcissism, the object with which the subject has identified becomes a psychical introject. It becomes part and parcel of the subject and can cause a drive reversal where the object claims a false victory because, by annihilating the subject, it has annihilated itself.

Governed by the contradictory forces of ambivalence, the love-hate binary that gives rise to the sacred mourning process also has an entire sacred dimension in and of itself. Melancholy is characterized by an incapacity for metaphorical thought, taking words literally and confusing the maternal tongue with the maternal body.

> The speech of the depressed is to them like an alien skin; melancholy persons are foreigners in their maternal tongue. They have lost the meaning—the value—of their mother tongue for want of losing the mother. The dead language they speak, which foreshadows their suicide, conceals a Thing buried alive. The latter, however, will not be translated in order that it not be betrayed; it shall remain walled up within the *crypt* of the inexpressible affect, anally harnessed, with no way out.[25]

The melancholic subject thus mourns the self and the abject part of the other. Its early form appears in the depressive position of the child who rejects the breast and considers the mother as a total object, which is to say, when the child loses the partial object and acquires language. Regarding primary repression, which occurs upon separation from the primary object, the mother, Freud distinguishes between being (identifying with the object) and having (possessing the object once separated from it). Involving both attraction and distancing, primary repression plays an inaugural role in the formation of the three dimensions of the unconscious (topographic, dynamic, and economic). Psychical representations of this first separation and loss are formed before the advent of language. Primary repression occurs through pre-oedipal identifications and primary processes that dominate the unconscious and atemporality. Narcissistic identification with the mother occurs as the body begins to emerge from an "ocean" with two opposing currents: tenderness and cruelty. As if moored to the "oceanic feeling" Romain Rolland described to Freud, a state in which the ego and its boundaries are not yet formed, the subject experiences the mother's body as the entire world, a world of complete autoerotic satisfaction.[26] For Kristeva, belief itself originates in this world.[27] Coleridge describes a state of immersion inherent in all belief systems: "God therefore is the cohesion and the oneness of all things—and dark and dim is that system of ethics, which does not take oneness as the *root* of all virtue!"[28]

The need to believe transforms into a need for ontological being and identity. Formed by a phantasmatic core that becomes a reason for being, it serves as a buffer against the "real real" (*le réel pur*) that plays out in maternal and paternal identifications. According to Kristeva, separation from the mother's body occurs through primary identification with the loving father, a love she believes to be necessary and a constitutive element of psychic development. Qualitatively speaking, this is a love mixed with authority, which underpins prohibition, a love that brings consistency and solidity to being, bearing the form of a third love, that of psychological bisexuality since, according to Kristeva, it has attributes of both parents. This type of superego-tinged love emerges as the subject's investment of the paternal object and, in terms of phylogenetic development, occurs before the encounter with the oedipal father. This is the father Freud referred to as the "father of individual prehistory," that of the primitive horde being precisely the one killed by the sons in *Totem and Taboo*. For Kristeva, this representation of the primitive father is more than simply a superego-like being, and is one endowed with affects and a capacity for positive investment, an ideal love that only turns against the father in a second phase of psychological identification. This first identification with a third party—the father—takes place without intermediaries. Identification with the third party is thus direct (in the Hegelian sense) and immediate (*direkte und unmittelbare*). Without this identification, there can be no sublimation. As Kristeva points out, "there can be no language without creativity because there is no language without sublimation."[29]

This "original" love thus unfurls a constructive power in the subjective quest, without which undifferentiation and psychosis reign. Based on her reading of Freud's "oceanic feeling" and primary identification, Kristeva proposes a new, vital and fundamental need: the need to believe. Anthropological in essence, the relation to the father gives consistency to the child's being and to the father figure as recognition of otherness. The philosopher relies on the experience of the psalmist who, on the basis of love for the figure of paternal authority, beseeches his creator and calls His name in times of deep affliction:

> I love the Lord, because he hath heard my voice and my supplications. Because he hath inclined his ear unto me, therefore will I call upon him as long as I live. The sorrows of death compassed me, and the pains of hell gat hold upon me: I found trouble and sorrow. Then called I upon the name of the Lord; O Lord, I beseech thee, deliver my soul. Gracious is the Lord, and righteous; yea, our God is merciful. . . . I will walk before the Lord in the land of the living. I believed, therefore have I spoken: I was greatly afflicted.[30]

First David believes (*he'emanti*), then he speaks: *adaber*, a verb sharing the same root as *diber*, the commandment. In other words, believing precedes the integration of the law and the symbolic. Knowledge can only emerge from the need to believe. Its early searches can be found in the drive to know inseparable from its elaborations in the theories of infantile sexuality. During the oedipal period, the imaginary identification with the father is supplemented by a secondary symbolic identification. To use Lacan's terms, "the metaphor of the father" as a separating agent enables the rupture of the mother-infant dyad and embodies a separating function in the mother's desire. In the child's process of language acquisition, Kristeva considers the mother's desire or passion as more sensorial and dynamic, with passion transforming into dis-passion-dispossession.

Distinct from mere linguistic signifying, the act of making meaning (*signifiance*) that occurs in psychoanalytic treatment is the antidote to melancholy. Subjective meaning emerges through the process of *signifiance* that is animated both by the unlimited circulation of the drives in language and by the subject's relation to social and political dimensions of language. Since the analyst believes the psychic reality of the patient, when meaning is recognized in the psychoanalytic space, the need to believe that supports and inhabits the thetic rupture can be transformative and therapeutic. It then becomes possible to "hear" what is being expressed through the transference relationship. The emerging meaning makes it possible to reconstitute the space of speech. Interpretation takes the place of repentance and grace, and puts words on what had been shut off and abject. On her patient, Anne, Kristeva writes: "'I speak,' she would often say, 'as if at the edge of words, and I have the feeling of being at the edge of my skin, but the bottom of my sorrow remains unreachable.'"[31] In the transference relation, the analyst interprets Anne's fragmented speech. However, before this interpretation can occur, the analyst first listens at the semiotic level, hearing what verbal expressions of bodily sensations are attempting to describe and shedding light on the archaic repressed ambivalence.

> Now, it so happens that this patient, in the early years of her life, suffered from serious skin diseases and was probably deprived of the contact with her mother's skin and identification with the mother's face in the mirror. I continued: "Since you couldn't touch your mother, you hid beneath your skin, 'at the edge of the

> skin'; and in that hiding place, you enclosed your desire and hatred of her in the sound of your voice, since you heard hers from afar."[32]

Transference is a reconstructive and an active process. It puts words on things, injects meaning into the void in love, assigns affects to representations, and renews the sacred bond through displacement and by reawakening the *traumatic*, the abject—that which has been excluded, taboo, rejected, and repressed into a new sacred space: the symptom. Kristeva distances herself from linguistic discourse on language in order to reveal the relationship between language and drives.[33] Uttering cannot be reduced to mere word use. The utterance is accompanied by a libidinal charge that associates the word with the body in its sexual dimension. The foundation of language rests on the body of the mother who tends to us in our helplessness, and on the potential of rebinding (*reliance*).

IV. The Sacred Potential of Rebinding (*Reliance*)

Freud identified four vicissitudes of the drive: repression, sublimation, reversal into the opposite, and turning against one's own person.[34] Kristeva proposes a new vicissitude located between repression and sublimation: rebinding (*reliance*). Much like sacred space, relating imaginary capacities to the symbolic, *reliance* is located at the interface of the maternal and the paternal. Based on one of the primordial functions of the mother, which is to counter the state of helplessness, "maternal eroticism" is an intrinsic part of the "biopsychical complex." The "maternal function" that Kristeva mentions acts in the direction of "matricide" and mourning: that of separation. The paternal function is viewed as the site of investment of the symbolization process.[35] The synergy of the maternal and the paternal, an alliance that fosters the formation of common meanings shared by human beings binds the subject to a signifying mother tongue that supports the bond in the sense of *religere:* binding–unbinding–rebinding (*liance–déliance–reliance*). Stemming from the maternal-paternal synergy, the mother tongue does not depend exclusively on the signifying position of the mother. It is shareable while still bearing within it the remnants both of the mother's libidinal investment in the father and the child and of the transmission of archaic heritage. The corporeal eroticism of the flesh is rebound by the symbolic. Desire is no longer deposited in the magical power of a God, of a spiritual entity in which desire places its confidence and awaits a return, but, rather, in the human being herself and in her subjective quest. The transformation of mnemonic traces into perception and verbalization can thus allow inner experience to come forth.

Bourdieu has suggested that changing words or substituting one word for another changes the social order.[36] With Kristeva, this also changes the order of things. As the signifier precedes the signified, words are linked to the drives and the body itself is linked, in layers, to representations, sensations, and perceptions. The mother tongue is the living material of maternal eroticism. Rooted in the law of the sacred, the maternal body is splintered, shattered, and interwoven with the symbolic paternal body. "The mother's body is therefore what mediates the symbolic law organizing social relations and becomes the ordering principle of the semiotic chora."[37] This *chora*, an imprint and matrix of the possibility of becoming a third kind of being in Platonic idealism, is reattached to sensible reality. A prelanguage stage dominated by a variety of perceptions and affects, it is also a binary heterogeneous space that comprises life and death, expulsion and introjection—the space of the abject.

The breast represents the primary partial object that enables loss to become psychical, a perlaboration via the replacement of the external object by internal representations.[38] This involves a transition from the partial object of the breast to the total body object. Language is constructed on both a psychical and corporeal level through signifiers, a stream of prerepresentations that Kristeva includes in the semiotic. The mother names the body and enables the infant to recognize her physical entity and to attach it to a psychical entity—what Lacan theorized in the mirror stage. Kristeva describes the drive process at work in the constitution of language as articulated in the relationship to the mother. It has a price in the psychic economy: "Language as symbolic function constitutes itself at the cost of repressing instinctual drive and continuous relation to the mother. In contrast, the unsettled and questionable subject of poetic language (for whom the word is never uniquely sign) maintains itself at the cost of reactivating this repressed instinctual, maternal element."[39]

Detachment from the mother tongue can have benefits, creativity being but one. While this detachment can cause a dissociation from the body, angst, or hallucination, rebinding bypasses the prohibition and enables disinhibition and creativity or, in the case of Anne, the elaboration of a new language that brings forth meaning in the psychoanalytic process. While the foreign language takes precedence over the superficially "forgotten" language, the mother tongue remains the primary tongue, one from which the body does not detach. And distancing oneself from it becomes a form of liberation.

Kristeva also takes up the issue of the adopted language.[40] For her, it remains a fragile and artificial language distanced from the body and on the edge of emptiness, a place where the unconscious is withdrawn from thought. Leaving the mother tongue and adopting another language provides the illusion of a new self, yet the abandoned part remains dormant, counterinvested within oneself: "Saying nothing, nothing needs to be said, nothing can be said. At first, it was a cold war with those of the new idiom, desired and rejecting; then the new language covered you as might a slow tide, a neap tide."[41] The paradox of adopting a new language is here conveyed in the form of a monologue. While it brings a certain comfort, the new language remains an artificial language and constitutes a handicap one can never entirely overcome. Describing the consequences of using the artificial language defines the mother tongue as the "natural" language, the childhood language, the language of the unconscious. Not using a mother tongue does not mean the mother tongue has been forgotten, for it remains embedded in the foundations of the new language. Prior to repression and sublimation, the weaving of the first representations into the mother tongue constitutes the earliest sacred experiences of rebinding. The subject's extirpation from the sensoriality of maternal eroticism and passion through abjection constitute the first links in an endless signifying chain. In the acquisition of the new language, it is as if abjection as a process of individuation is reenacted again in the sensorial experiences of infantile memory: poetics as intonations, babbles, and rhythmic variations. Abjection is what catalyzes the emergence of the subject on the micro level and of society on the macro level. Sublimated by its successive representations—as if to try to catch it, to touch it—the sacred is transformative precisely because its meaning is not fixed.

Through the ages, the sacred has left its mark on all societies. No civilization has escaped it. It is like a reminiscence whose nature is to include and destroy what preceded it. Traces of the sacred have undergone infinite metamorphoses in the dialectic of their disappearances–reappearances. The captivating mysterious hieroglyphs of ancient Egyptian polytheism deciphered long ago by Champollion, using the Rosetta Stone, have marked steles, sarcophagi, and papyrus with the hypnotic intensity of the blue obtained from the dust of lapis lazuli gemstone. The Greek and Roman mythological representations of divinities were sculpted into the ethers of Olympus and into the monumentality of the Pantheon, as in the transformations of Aphrodite into Venus. The sacred texts of the revealed monotheistic religions have transmitted prayers, chants, and rituals to the one God across millennia. When the sacred fire stolen from Zeus was threatened with extinction, other traditions picked up the torch, so to speak. The sacrificial fire of Prometheus showed the way to new knowledge and has passed through the generations. New sacred narratives appeared and more will come as it is the nature of the sacred to be ever changing.

Kristeva's theory translates the sacred into a cultural fact that, without denying the need for ideality, proposes a new, nonreligious humanist ethics founded on the maternal. From Plato to Buber by way of Berkeley, the dialogical principle constitutes an ethics of knowledge where the intellectual does not confine herself to the realm of the mind but engages with the world through dialogue and exchanges. To philosophize, to reflect, for Kristeva, is to engage in transference. Naturally polyphonic and vastly complex, each transference experience Kristeva evokes is a hermeneutic that brings us closer to the multifocal heterogeneity of the real meaning of the sacred as much as it seems to distance us from it. What is quite certain, for her, is that the sacred is tied to the emergence of language and its various forms. The place Kristeva grants to the study of ontophylogenetic meaning falls under a broader project to conceptualize the process through which transcendence becomes immanent, namely, through an analysis of its discourse and its slow mutations. The deconstruction of meaning (*signifiance*) through the psychoanalytic prism reveals that meaning does not emerge *ex nihilo* but only from within intersubjective spaces.

In conclusion, casting off the fetters of formalism and structuralism, Kristeva interprets the sacred in the translinguistic and prelinguistic modalities of meaning. The sacred, being at the core of purification rituals, appears in the human sciences as a form of social catharsis that can also be thought in terms of the transference relationship. Since the symptom known to psychoanalysis touches upon that which is unsettling, what incurs a diffraction of meaning, it is expressed through various defensive modalities—repression, denial, or splitting; which is to say, through that which libidinally overruns the psychic apparatus. In her conception of the sacred, Kristeva proposes a therapeutic form of immanent meaning that is constructed and deconstructed in the process of psychoanalytic treatment, and which awakens the transference in the experience of exile that is inherent to any subjective quest.

KEREN MOCK

UNIVERSITY OF PARIS
MAY 2019

NOTES

1. Sigmund Freud, *A General Introduction to Psychoanalysis*, trans. G. Stanley Hall (New York: Boni and Liveright, 1920).
2. Catherine Clément and Julia Kristeva, *The Feminine and the Sacred*, trans. Jane Marie Todd (New York: Columbia University Press, 2001), 135.
3. Plato, *Cratylus*, in *The Dialogues of Plato Translated into English with Analyses and Introductions*, vol. I, trans. Benjamin Jowett, 3rd edition revised and corrected (Oxford: Oxford University Press, 1892), 265.
4. See Julia Kristeva, *Tales of Love*, trans. Leon S. Roudiez (New York: Columbia University Press, 1987).
5. Leviticus 19:2.
6. Exodus 29:31.
7. *The Standard Prayer Book*, trans. Rev. S. Singer (New York: Bloch, 1915), 462.
8. Ibid., 443.
9. Eliezer Ben-Yehuda, *A Complete Dictionary of Ancient and Modern Hebrew*, vols. III–IV (Jerusalem: Makor, 1980).
10. Keren Mock, *Hébreu, du sacré au maternel* (Paris: CNRS, 2016).
11. Julia Kristeva, "La Nature signifiante du langage," in ibid., 13–20.
12. Julia Kristeva, *Revolution in Poetic Language*, trans. Margaret Waller (New York: Columbia University Press, 1984), 78.
13. Sigmund Freud, *Totem and Taboo*, in *The Standard Edition of the Complete Works of Sigmund Freud*, vol. XIII, trans. James Strachey (London: Hogarth, 1958); "The Dissolution of the Oedipus Complex," in *Standard Edition*, vol. XIX, trans. James Strachey (London: Hogarth, 1961); "Dostoevsky and Parricide," in *Standard Edition*, vol. XXI, trans. James Strachey (London: Hogarth, 1964); *Moses and Monotheism*, in *Standard Edition*, vol. XXIII, trans. James Strachey (London: Hogarth, 1964).
14. Freud, *Moses and Monotheism*, 121.
15. Virgil, *The Aeneid, Book 3,* trans. Barry B. Powell (Oxford: Oxford University Press, 2016), 93–94.
16. Julia Kristeva, *Powers of Horror: An Essay on Abjection*, trans. Leon S. Roudiez (New York: Columbia University Press, 1982).
17. Mary Douglas, *Purity and Danger: An Analysis of Concepts of Pollution and Taboo* (New York: Praeger, 1966). Claude Lévi-Strauss, *The Savage Mind* (Chicago: University of Chicago Press, 1966).
18. Julia Kristeva, "Stabat Mater," in *Tales of Love*, 234–63.
19. Stabat Mater, an Hymn, as Perform'd at the King's-Theatre in the Hay-Market, Etc. (London, 1765), https://books.google.co.uk/books?id=I6VhAAAAcAAJ&pg=PP5&dq=stabat+mater+hymn+king+theater&hl=fr&sa=X&ved=0ahUKEwjt3ejAwdDjAhU

AQRUIHf5BVIQ6wEIMTAB#v=onepage&q=stabat%20mater%20hymn%20king%20theater&f=false.

20. See Julia Kristeva, "Motherhood According to Giovanni Bellini," in *Desire in Language: A Semiotic Approach to Literature and Art*, trans. Thomas Gora, Alice Jardine, and Leon S. Roudiez (New York: Columbia University Press, 1980).

21. Immanuel Kant, *Critique of Pure Reason*, trans. Paul Guyer and Allen W. Wood (Cambridge: Cambridge University Press, 1998).

22. Kristeva, "Stabat Mater," 240–41.

23. Clément and Kristeva, *The Feminine and the Sacred*, 91.

24. Sigmund Freud, *Mourning and Melancholia*, in *The Standard Edition of the Complete Psychological Works of Sigmund Freud*, vol. XIV, trans. James Strachey (London: Hogarth, 1964).

25. Julia Kristeva, *Black Sun: Depression and Melancholia*, trans. Leon S. Roudiez (New York: Columbia University Press, 1989), 53.

26. Sigmund Freud, *Civilization and Its Discontents*, in *The Standard Edition of the Complete Works of Sigmund Freud*, vol. XXI, trans. James Strachey (London: Hogarth, 1964), ch. 1.

27. Julia Kristeva, *This Incredible Need to Believe*, trans. Beverley Bie Brahic (New York: Columbia University Press, 2009).

28. Samuel Taylor Coleridge, *Notes on English Divines* (London: Edward Moxon, 1853), 116.

29. Julia Kristeva, "The Impudence of Uttering: The Mother Tongue," *Psychoanalytic Review* 97, no. 4, (2010): 679–94.

30. Psalms 116:1–10.

31. Kristeva, *Black Sun*, 56.

32. Ibid.

33. See Kristeva, "The Impudence of Uttering: The Mother Tongue."

34. Sigmund Freud, "Instincts and their Vicissitudes," in *The Standard Edition of the Complete Psychological Works of Sigmund Freud*, vol. XIV, trans. James Strachey (London: Hogarth, 1957).

35. Kristeva, *This Incredible Need to Believe*, ch. 1.

36. Pierre Bourdieu, *Language and Symbolic Power*, trans. J. B. Thompson (Cambridge: Harvard University Press, 1991).

37. Kristeva, *Revolution in Poetic Language*, 27.

38. [*Perlaboration* is a neologism created by J. Laplanche and J.-B. Pontalis to capture the German term *Durcharbeitung*, "working through."—Ed.]

39. Julia Kristeva, "From One Identity to Another," in *Desire in Language*, 136 (translation modified).

40. See Julia Kristeva, "Bulgaria, My Suffering," in *Crisis of the ~~European~~ Subject* (New York: Other Press, 2000).

41. Julia Kristeva, *Strangers to Ourselves*, trans. Leon S. Roudiez (New York: Columbia University Press, 1991), 16.

REPLY
TO EDWARD S. CASEY, ALINA N. FELD, MICHAL BEN-NAFTALI, AND KEREN MOCK

I don't believe I am a melancholic. I define myself as an "energetic pessimist," with energy (from Aristotle to quantum mechanics) evoking the movement that puts the universe into action. To live is to exile oneself, and first of all to exile oneself from melancholy. For although we diagnose in the "depressive position" (Klein) a human capacity to make meaning, through *signifiance* and/or subjectivation (according to my terminology), this capacity cannot be achieved except by exiling oneself from depressiveness, through language.[1] Language deploys in *culture* (in Hegel's sense),[2] which transmutes the urgency of the drive and the imperatives of sublimation into the imaginary, while ontotheology consecrates the mourning for the lost object through the power of religion, when it doesn't remain complacent about it. Unless the philosopher becomes "able to think otherwise."

Edward Casey, Alina Feld, Michal Ben-Naftali, and Keren Mock clarify and complete my writings with their own thinking. The themes of this section in the volume place us precisely at the intersection of the imaginary and the symbolic, mobilizing the imaginary of my discussants as well. Without providing commentary, argumentation, or polemics, my first reaction is to move the dialogue forward by simply recalling my personal remedies for melancholy.

First of all, Proust. Devoured by distress, he devours it. By returning to the "sensitive times" of childhood; of the turn of the century (nineteenth to twentieth); of sensual passions; of the "accursed race"—Jews and homosexuals. And through the energy of the French language, which he reawakens, he tells us that *ideas* well up from *grief*.[3]

Two films: one for the delicacy of the image, the other for the pathos of its maternal distress. *Sweet Bean* (2015) by Naomi Kawase: delicacy of the taste and violence of the *mortality* that inhabits us; *pastry* and *leprosy*, the camera hints at tears and tenderness. *The Man Who Knew Too Much* (1956) by Hitchcock: maternal depression accompanies the mother-child separation that I hear on the couch. To recognize it, as Doris Day's singing does, is the best way to "save the mother and the child."

Translated from French by Armine Kotin Mortimer.

Two pieces of music: "Blue Skies" by Ella Fitzgerald—the "skat" beyond the depression of love. "*Agitata da due venti*" (Vivaldi) by Cecilia Bartoli—anger triumphs over shipwreck.

In the vast field of psychoanalytic experience: recalling that Freud discovered that *separation*, *loss*, *lack* can be *transferred* onto the analyst and only thus traversed. This austere man enjoyed dissecting jokes.[4]

To invite my discussants to my favorite antidepressor, the Isle de Ré where, exiled and inaccessible, I swim at sunrise and sunset. And where I am calmed by reciting a few verses of Jean de La Fontaine with my son David.[5]

Or invite them to visit the fabulous astronomical clock designed by Claude-Siméon Passemant (Versailles 1749, up to the year 9999).[6] The ancien régime is crumbling, but the clockmaker calculates the stars and programs a "robot" that will give universal time until . . . 9999! "Melancholy is not French," I was told upon the publication of my book, *Black Sun: Depression and Melancholia*.

My colleagues demonstrate, after me, that the "love of the question mark"[7] provides us with an ultimate metamorphosis of our melancholies. I will return to some of their propositions (the intimate-extimate in Casey; the death of God in Feld; the baroque according to Ben-Naftali; the sacred according to Mock), which, while illuminating my thinking, open pathways for new research.

I. Edward Casey

I share Edward Casey's aggravation concerning "canonical psychoanalytic theories of depression." Indeed, that "pyramid of superstructs," these "supervening explananda" that weigh down on the morbid behavior of melancholy "heavy bodies" are only "conceptual abstractions" incapable of traversing the "felt states" and succeed only in "arrest[ing] its downward spiral," with the eventual "relief" and "resolution" at the level of the "theoretical insight."

Attentive to psychoanalysis, nevertheless, not as a theory but as an *experience*, Casey constructs a periphenomenology of "place," oriented toward the intermediary and the indetermination of "edges," which delimit only by opening.[8] I will call these "cardinal respurges" *transitions*, *borders*, *edges*, and, why not, *limbos*.[9] "Psychological scars" and "apperceptive transfer," the "material intentionality" of Casey the hermeneutist impregnates his writing with metaphors, neologisms, and narrathemes, to suggest porous *places*, peopled by fugitive *links*.[10] This "something else" transversal to the *self* and to the *beginning* could only resonate with my *semiotic chora*: "space" prior to representable space, nameable but anterior to the One, to the Father and to the syllables of language.[11] Casey returns in this volume to this "choric indeterminacy dynamized by forces that are at once affective and archaic" in my approach to depression. Captive of the *Thing*, depressiveness also bears witness to the emergence of a *vita nuove*. The *Thing* was not a crypt without issue; between being and nothingness, the *Thing* sketches the possibility of a "nothing" in the sense that the French language says "something"—"*a mere*

Nothing" that precedes space by initiating a "Non-Place that possesses its own positivity" (Casey).

Casey insists on the importance of a resurrectional immanence in the depressiveness constitutive of the *parlêtre* (speaking being), which I distinguish from pathological depression and from its extreme form constituted by melancholy in the asylum as a symptomatology of inhibition and asymbolism. This depressiveness inherent in the human condition is *from the start* "not only *in me* but *around me*," writes Casey. "Depression does not come exclusively from *within* the human subject" because it is a "quantic" dimension of subjectivity. It continues to accompany us in the incommensurable states of *creativity*.

Many Freudian "theoretical fables" challenge metaphysical dualism, at the edge of these categories: in "quantic" superposition and entanglement. Thus the *drive*, which refers to the biological body, is energy-and-meaning at the outset—I often insist on this *heterogeneity* inherent in the psychoanalytic approach to the speaking being.[12] The semiotic *chora* is not extralinguistic but translinguistic: the *drives* and their transformation into *affects*, *sensations*, and *emotions* are tributary to the anatomical equipment, to the neurobiological, as well as to the sociocultural and environmental parental surroundings.

The *investment* (*cathexis*), a property of the neuronal, is differentiated and operates between the somatic and the psychical, then in the structuration of psychic spaces. "Free cathexes" are transformed into "bound cathexes" in *sensations*, memory traces, and linguistic signs, and achieve an "elevation of the principle of investment" that Freud defines as a *psychical revolution of matter*. It is the investment thus oriented that is "projected" in the "mythical" notion of "the beyond of religions."[13] Klein and Segal have unfolded this process of psychical investment by distinguishing the "psychical equations" from their mutations into "veritable symbols" in the course of the "depressive position."[14] The passage from the *Thing* to the *Object* refines and increases this heterogeneity all through the depressive position; the *infans* (not-yet Subject) loses the *Thing* (not-yet *Object*) only to find it again in the Representation/Psychicization of a *partial Object* (the breast) becoming a *total Object* (face, presence, representatives in language of this affective representation henceforth psychicized). And sadness becomes Word, and the Word (the capacity to speak the affects) becomes a new source of life.

I will not continue further on the long road of subjectivation thus conceptualized. But I will add a text by Klein, "On the Sense of Loneliness," where a *primitive capacity of being* is not a "narcissism" but an "ego relatedness" constructing an "intimate environment."[15] The theoretical fables of psychoanalysis attempt to tear themselves away from metaphysics, and there is no way they can do it without deconstructing its categories.

Alterity (dependence-separation) is copresent with each constituent of this psychoanalytic construction, between biology *and* history, individuals *and* socius, vital process *and* apoptosis . . . Always between two things, at least.

Nevertheless we are not "our body," as Casey writes. The body is constituted as an ideal and superegoic form, an image henceforth superinvested by globalized marketing. While depression deprives us of our bodies, its traversals in the opposite direction attest to a transverse "corporeal" substance, an always unattainable dehiscence and differentiation: *the flesh*.[16] An intertwining exists between man and the surrounding container, a "hollow," a "fold," a "flesh," an invisible armature woven into the very depths of Being. "Incorporeity" and "reversibility," "prereflexive and preobjective unity of my body," not simply matter, but "the coiling over of the visible upon the seeing body," flesh fulfills what one does not dare think: this transition from the mute world to the speaking world.[17]

Under the sadness that psychically attests to the *loss* of the *Thing* in the process of becoming an *Object* for the affected *Subject*, the prereflexive incorporeity of the *Flesh* is an ab-jection, sensuousness of the tearing away, violent *mère-version*.[18] It is up to the imaginary to immerse itself in the inaccessible *Thing* by creating languages for the ab-ject sensuousness that precedes and exceeds the grief for the lost Object.

I subscribe to Casey's insistence on the share of *lightening up* that depressiveness paradoxically brings. Because it opens the passage to nameable psychicization, the neoreality in which depressed infants survive—these speaking beings that we are. But who is aware of it? Who will draw the consequences, to live "outside" and "alongside" depression? Certainly not the blessed *serotonin*, regulator of sexual difficulties and of sleep. It takes hold of the "symptoms" but lets social networks manage the "problems."

Could it be philosophy that ontologizes the "antepredicative thesis" itself?[19] Or is it the person who extracts the concept of "ontological mood" from distress?[20] Before specifying (with reference to Duns Scotus via Kant) that existence does not depend on apprehension by the intellect: the "substance" is at most "present" or "implied" in the concept, but the concept turns its back to the Thing/*Res*, irreducible in its effective quiddity, and is not sufficient to "supply a thing-content" for it.[21]

Actually, the *interpretive* reception, which recognizes the depressive mood, consoles and legitimates it—when it doesn't become fixated as a *management of its symptoms*, the way religions, ideologies, or Opinion do, not forgetting the multiple compartmentalist "taking charge" that contributes to consolidating the social bond, henceforth reduced to its melancholic side erected into a sacred foundation.

Can literature and painting "glimmer with creative possibilities that are otherwise foreclosed when the subject is caught up in the midst of an implacable depressive episode" (Casey)? At the border of "nature" and "culture," of the Thing and the Object-Subject, the artist attempts to give form to moods and affects. These neorealities, languages and installations, consume the horror of the *Thing*, the ennui of the social "influenza." The artist offers us his creations, ultimate erotic objects, her "sunsets" and her "atmospheres," which the ordinary depressed person lacks. Such is *mood*, not ontological but transposed into the quasi serial and tonal dissonances of *Stimmung* by Stockhausen. Around a "hippie campfire," melodic and rhythmic games dismember and savor the invocation of a divinity, the erotic poems of the composer. A spectral music diffracts monotony by giving *flesh* to depression. The piece premiered in Paris in December 1968, an act redoubling moods of revolt.

Completely different is the body-flesh in *Triptych* (1967) by Francis Bacon. I look at it and think about the *Oresteia* by Aeschylus: an implacable matricide, which apparently left an impression on the artist. And about the poem by T. S. Eliot that he likes to mention.[22] The painter's rage projects, deforms, and reforms the colored materials. Disposing them in a triple space of incurved mirrors, he penetrates the eye and all the orifices of the spectator. He seizes bodies and hearts, making the embryo that lives within bleed. The wisdom of myths and the melancholy of the poet are sent back before the mirror stage and the depressive position that makes it speak. This intense backwards contemplation gives off an absolute serenity. Bacon the Assassin and self-devourer emerges from the carnage lighter, but more than that, *unhurt*. Because he is convinced—along with us—that he has given form to the *mère-version* beneath the perversion of men who complain they are *hollow*.

Great works of art resonate with our unnamed experiences. And call for our interpretations to join them.

II. Alina N. Feld

Alina Feld illuminates what she calls the "mysterious relationship" between "melancholy and creative imagination," such as I address them, and my "psychoanalytic insights into the theology of melancholy." In pursuing her research on the "otherness of God,"[23] and in confronting the "dialectical tension between melancholy and God," she raises two questions: (1) Does "God's death and otherness remain the absolute ground of melancholy"? Why, and to what extent? (2) Are art and religion "fitting counterdepressants for the melancholy/depressive composite, as universal therapeutics equivalent and often superior to psychoanalytic practice"?

Let us consider that decisive and uniquely European event: when we broke the link with tradition. "The death of God" belongs to this heritage, as it is constitutive of the Christian religion in which God is the man Jesus, dead and resuscitated.[24] This braid of death-and-resurrection is announced from the start of the Gospel as a "common core" of "absence," "shadow" and "source of mourning,"[25] and *at the same time* (I emphasize this copresence) as a *faculty for love*, which comes into being only by virtue of *languages* (John 13:34, I Corinthians 13:1), the only antidotes to barbarity (I Corinthians 14:1–11).

The descent "into the lower parts of the earth" (Ephesians 4:9), the *kenosis*[26] that marked my childhood in a country with an Orthodox tradition, does not leave even the divine unharmed: "He that descended is the same also that ascended up" (Ephesians 4:10). However, the long history of dogmas, councils, schisms, and their theologies gives a different interpretation of the *kenosis*. It is more pathetic in Orthodoxy; Dostoyevsky becomes its tragic and carnivalesque herald. (Feld mentions Raskolnikov, "a modern *Divine Comedy*"; I would add the Crippled Woman in *The Possessed*, an echo of the orthodox

Virgin who "bathes the earth in her tears.") The two readings of the Trinity (which would lead to the great schism of 1054), the reading of *Per Filium* (according to which the Holy Ghost proceeds from the Father *through* the Son, for the Orthodox) and that of the *Filioque* (according to which the Holy Ghost proceeds from the Father *and* the Son), offer different subjective experiences to the believer. Whereas the Catholic "and" puts the father *and* the son on a par, prefiguring the autonomy and independence of the person and opening the pathway to Western individualism, the Orthodox "through" suggests an *annihilation* of the Son and of the believer, which maximizes his deified suffering. An exquisite interaction of submission and exaltation, joy and pain internal to the master/slave dialectic and to masculine homoeroticism. Delights of the *hesychasm* (immobility, repose, and silence), prayer from the heart, and tenderness in *the love of beauty* (*philokalia*). This mystic experience is likely to distance itself from "representation," from the "knowledge of all things," and from "human affairs."

Orthodoxy has not known the Aristotelian moment of Saint Thomas, nor the debate with Duns Scotus or the emergence of individuality. The "community of believers" has precedence over the *kenosis*, of course, but free singularity is still a long time coming. It yields to nihilism: since God is unknowable, "everything is permitted," claim the Dostoyevskian nihilists.[27] The materialist revolution that succeeded them and accompanies them today was carried out "in a pagan manner," and it is about to succumb to the market economy. Whereas the emancipation movements stemming from Christian humanism aim in principle for the resurrection of the singular. Far from considering Byzantine theology as "a superior equivalent to a psychoanalytic therapeutic" (Feld), I call for the elucidation of its sensorial richness and historical accidents.

Feld traces the avatars of this Christic *death-resurrection*, which takes hold of the Saturnine myth and is purified in the *acedia* of monks, before inspiring the "Aristotelian-Hippocratic identity with Ficino." This death-resurrection also fires up baroque style (to which Ben-Naftali returns). But it burns its own decors in Versailles or glows in many heretic and saintly experiences, like those of *my* Teresa of Avila, "dying of not dying"[28] before proclaiming that Christ is "*dentro de mí*."[29]

***

Did we have to wait for the evolution of technology and the Enlightenment's insurrection for Hegel to diagnose the *logical* bearing of this jubilatory suffering, the *raison d'être* of this chiasmus? Before Nietzsche,[30] Hegel writes: "'God has died. God himself is dead.' This is a monstrous, fearful picture [*Vorstellung*], which brings before the imagination the deepest abyss of cleavage."[31] The philosophers Schelling, Heidegger, Girard, Derrida, Ricoeur, Baudrillard, and Althusser, among those whom Feld mentions, will each examine in turn the components of this *constitutive alteration* of subjectivity.

Non-transcendendum or transcendentality; "provok[ing] the God of love to self-revelation" or "profound boredom"; "freedom and creativity" or "stupidity," "madness," and "evil"—always this "Jacob's wrestling with the dark nature of God and of oneself" (Feld). Does the shadow of a dead God weigh down on the hermeneutists?[32] That is what I maintain, with Arendt, who mocks the melancholic tribe, professional weepers who neglect "human plurality."[33]

The "cursor" of modern and contemporary philosophers has been displaced onto the Biological/Meaning chiasmus and into the labyrinth of languages—from Husserl to Sartre, by way of Heidegger, Benjamin, Cassirer, Wittgenstein. Are they all melancholic? Heidegger makes a claim for "his vital space," isolated in his chalet in Todtnauberg; he tracks down Being "off the beaten track" in Hölderlin's poetry.[34] Benjamin tackles the translation of Proust in a "festive" Paris; saved from the Vernuche camp, he takes his own life in September 1940 after having written his farewell to Adorno. Cassirer wards off the panic of the modern by studying the "plurality of languages" in "a world that does not have meaning." Wittgenstein renounces his family's money and, converted to Christianity, demonstrates that language *says nothing* but *shows* "another world."[35] Is man a being of language "who neither tells nor hides but signifies," as the Oracle at Delphi said, according to Heraclitus cited by Benveniste?[36]

Freud's discovery of the unconscious revolutionized this breakthrough, which prepared it. The drive bases in *negativity* (*separation, frustration, castration*) mold the advent of language and its accidents. Eros and Thanatos impregnate the primal scene as well as the psychosexual maturation of the child. The psychoanalytic approach to sadomasochism doesn't spare Christianity either.[37]

With Abraham, Ferenczi, and Klein, it is *anxiety* rather than *desire* that is imposed on the analyst. I would not say that I "endorse Freud against Klein" on the death drive and masochism (Feld)—I am not against Freud but "right up against" him. Klein introduces destructiveness as early as the schizoparanoid and depressive position of the *infans*. This modulation of the Freudian theory is not a deviation. She develops an approach to subjectivation in prelanguage, all the way to the drives: through the technique of *play* and the putting into narration of the fantasy in the *countertransference* of the therapist. Anchored in the depths of the psychism, the psychoanalytic work constantly probes the primitive capacity of "the sense of loneliness," "ego-relatedness,"[38] more primitive still than narcissism, anterior even to "the introjection of the mother" in Klein. Pulverizing the *Thing* and the *Object*, the *Beginning* and *Being*, the transference/countertransference link extracts the padlocked individual from the *claustrum* of his depression.

In deconstructing ontotheology, the psychoanalytic experience thus understood does not essentialize Desire, Suffering, or Sexuality. It *thinks* and *proceeds* to a recreation of the foundational alterity of the living speaking person. Depressiveness, itself reconstructible-deconstructible, underlies the speaking being and is constitutive of it. This primary transcendentality makes me "feel loneliness," *with*: with an "environment" that, before being *Thing* or *Object*, arrives as a link, transversal to pleasure as to suffering, before-with-and-through them.

So I would say, in dialogue with Feld, that in revealing "the death of the Greco-Judeo-Christian God," the centrality of the European message does not consist in causing death, but in diffusing its suspension in life, thinking it to un-think it through love—this desire to *think with*.

Abraham does not kill but thinks death and contains it. Job himself, after having exposed his remorse and his melancholy punishments, is shaken by the "prophetic" speech of Elihu; he withdraws into the alliance. The need to believe and the desire to know are not necessarily nihilistic, they are the universal anthropological components stemming from the capacity to *invest* in the alterity that supports me, enlightens me, and legitimizes me. Interpreting Psalm 116, Mock reminds us that because the psalmist *believes* (*heemanti*) in the Other (the reciprocal love link preexists them), he admits he is "distressed" and "disappointed" . . . while *speaking*. But *adaber*—"to speak," from the root *diber*—has the meaning of "commandment." The *word* thus manifests "the integration of the law and the symbolic" (Mock): my *spoken* suffering participates in the Law. My speaking exists only through and for *alterity*, through and in the *link* that founds me and legitimizes me. From the moment I speak I am legitimate. Listen to me, let us listen to ourselves.

While Europe vacillates and threatens to fall apart, the European "message" is one of social suffering (yellow vests, ecologists . . .), which requires transformations of the social pact. As for the "postmodern hell" and the "noncathartic madness" of modern art (Feld), they require us to be more creative in *interpreting* them—in spite of the seizure of the imaginary and art by marketing.

Transcendentality has not disappeared. Undervaluing the "vale of tears," secularized humanism finds itself reduced to its *memory* as a result of idealizing progress, marketing, opinion, and the spectacle. To invest in the alliance, the "at-one-ment" (Bion)[39] through the transcendentality of pain. To be worked through and sublimated without end.

III. Michal Ben-Naftali

Michal Ben-Naftali, theoretician and novelist, detects in my research[40] what she calls a "'baroquization' of Being by recounting its history from the viewpoint of the imaginary." Her intimacy with my way of thinking is evident in her writing: her translation into Hebrew of my book *Histoires d'amour* was broadly admired by the Israeli public.

"Kristeva does not systematically discuss the notion of baroque," writes Ben-Naftali. The fact is, the baroque is already present in *Tales of Love*: proclaimed in the Song of Songs, or vibrant with Don Juan, and with Shakespeare.[41] But it is in my *Teresa, My Love* that the baroque commands as a main "character" and resonates with the reading Ben-Naftali proposes of my work.[42] From the start, she lays the groundwork for *our* baroquism—"the speaking subject is necessarily a subject-in-love"—and unfolds this experience of *language* in the psychoanalytic *transference*, and especially in my "oxymoron of 'singular concepts' . . . that stirs both affect and sense." She examines my "post-phenomenological insight" and accompanies my "imaginary movement towards liminal states": simultaneously "heuristic means," "permeability," "exteriority and interiority at once," "where Being becomes *ipso facto*" a "catastrophic-fold-of-'being.'"

I cannot retake, here, Ben-Naftali's both baroque and loving journey toward "the pre-oedipal mother," which she grasps in a striking definition: "The mother as ironic, a pariah, heretic, hence sacred. Herethic. A strange hybrid excluded by the Sacred of society." Or toward the "imaginary father" in which she sees a "playing with the Name of the Father," "double gesture of sanctifying and blaspheming" (see my "metaphysical detective novel," *The Old Man and the Wolves*, 1991).[43] Yes, "heterodox adaptation of the Freudian corpus," "'baroquization' of Being": my "reading strategy" of the imaginary consists in "enacting the unconscious in theological texts," which Ben-Naftali takes as a "secularization of the idea of the sacred," "resorption of the sacred into the tenderness of the connection to the other," "magical instant in which immanence touched transcendence."

Attentive to the *interval* that my concepts enclose, notably in my analyses of love through its metamorphoses, Ben-Naftali deciphers an attention "to the immanent motion of our existence," "the interval between the formations," "what allows for the proposal of innovation and rebellion." And she ends up paying homage to Narcissus, who is also in love, but with his image. *Between* reflexivity and the object he poses "right at the beginning of life," as in the *emptiness* that finally engulfs him, always in search of the "psychic realm as such." A Narcissus who is finally happy, because "closer than ever to the spirit of the spring, an ephemeral source." Where psychoanalysis "will fight for his language."

This conclusion prompts me to clarify the debt of post-phenomenology *to* the imaginary, and the cohabitation of Freudian theory and the psychoanalytic clinic *with* the imaginary.

I would have to return to the "theory of literature" to maintain that my "baroquism" does not speak *about* literature: it neither mimes it nor justifies it. It speaks *to* literature.[44]

***

Inscribed in the involutions of philosophy since the end of the nineteenth century, *literary thought thinks itself* according to the rhythm of changes in the regime of the imaginary. These profound upheavals are in play and they propose words that are henceforth memorable: "God is dead," therefore "Everything is permitted" (so proclaim Dostoyevsky's *Possessed*), and just as serious if not worse, "poetry has been under attack" (as Mallarmé's "A Throw of the Dice" ironizes), but also the poet "is on strike in front of society."[45]

More exactly, the theory of literature is connected with German philosophy and aesthetics from the end of the nineteenth century and the beginning of the twentieth. Heinrich Wölfflin's *Principles of Art History* (1915) renounces singular cases and discovers an "artistic language" common to a given period.[46] Ernst Cassirer attaches the diversity of "cultural forms" (including myth, art, religion, science) to the "symbolic function" they accomplish. But it is Husserl, the founder of phenomenology, who opposes the essence of the "form of knowledge" to the "matter of knowledge," discusses the distinction between formal laws and material laws, and reestablishes the "logical unity of the content of thought, or the unity of theory."[47] We could determine the phenomenological lineage of research in *Literaturwissenschaft* in Germany (Vossler, Steinthal, Shpet, Staiger, and Spitzer) for which the literary *form* bears a specific *content*; general linguistics and the *semiology* of Saussure (1857–1913), as well as the work of Hjelmslev (1899–1965) and his *semiolotics*; Russian formalism with the *Theory of Literature* (1925) by Tomashevsky and the writings of Shklovsky, Vinogradov, Tynianov, and Jakobson; Wellek and Warren's *Theory of Literature* (1949); etc.[48]

These investigations bearing on *thought* as *form* and not as *expression* are contemporary with an *unprecedented repositioning of imaginary experience* itself. In a different way, they questioned habits of reception and, turning to new approaches to "languages" and "forms," participate in the upsetting of classical rationality, morality, and ideologies. Literary experience from the end of the nineteenth century and the beginning of the twentieth was the "royal road" that interrogated anew the limits of the speaking subject along with those of language.[49] *Coming very close to the limit states*, even psychosocial pathologies, the imaginary thus appears as the more or less intentional accomplice of the Freudian revolution in discovering the unconscious.

This new regime of the imaginary also stands as a rival to the mystery attributed to inner experience—after the *sacred* and the *religious*, the *modern imaginary* confronts Meaning, the meaning of human consciousness and social morality, defying them under pressure from an impossible *real* that the *modern imaginary* explores, to inscribe unavowable truths therein.

Begun by German Romanticism (Hölderlin, the Schlegel brothers, Schelling, Hegel, Schopenhauer, Nietzsche), this encounter of literature with the *impossible* finds its most radical form in the French language. Several moments of this encounter have occurred: Rimbaud, Lautréamont, and Mallarmé; surrealism; *Tel Quel* (1960–1982); the present cohabitation of writing with the hyperconnected image. These disturbances are accelerating today with social networks, the image, and the virtual. Talk shows on sexual dissatisfaction keep the industry of the book afloat, and television series are formatting the fantasies of internauts. The potentialities of the imaginary having never been so available. "A single man of genius who will live as long as humanity."[50]

Thinking literature participates in this omnipresent flowering of the imaginary, it elucidates it in its radicalness (whether complacent or disruptive). But it also judges it and *interprets* it on the level of the *psychical*, *worldly*, and historical experience of a writing that brings risks for the *common good*—which is neither *common sense* (the consensus, repression) nor the *general interest* (regulator of the social pact). Confronted once again with the question "Of what use is literature?" (literary) "theory" replies: to think and make people think the borders where meaning and the subject revolt in ab-jection and in ecstasy.

I don't write *about* Narcissus, *about* the Song of Songs, *about* Saint Bernard, Lautréamont, Mallarmé, Proust—I write *to them*. I write the facts/effects of my transference onto the texts. Neither philosopher nor writer, nor sentinel of repression, nor hostess of pleasure, the analyst maintains herself on the crest. She wagers on the meaning of the transferred word. Without end, but not without unease.

The decentering of the conscious subject that Freud explored in the intimacy of the transference (which is also revealed in modern literature) supports my interpretation. In this, my interpretation differs from hermeneutics and from the *dismantling* of metaphysics (Heidegger, Arendt, Derrida) that it undertakes. It is not a matter of abandoning interpretation in favor of a generalized fiction. By its sentences, themes, narratives, meanings, and nonsense, Céline's "opera of the deluge" grabs me, I appropriate it for myself. The "relentlessness inherent in [the] sheer thinking"[51] of thought questions the underlying affects, it transports me, and nevertheless revolts me.[52] It leads me to the unavowable of the author or of the text, such as they appear to me.

In the wake of Kant, Arendt joins to the freedom to *think* the duty to *judge*, which she bases on *aesthetic judgment*, applicable in politics.[53] Isn't my necessarily political interpretation, in the connected sense of the term, destined to the reader-author, "fellow beings," "brothers,"[54] digitalized consumers? I make them understand that the Holocaust is not merely an accident of history but reveals a human potentiality: that dementia that advocates the superfluity of certain humans and exterminates them. Art and literature visit these places to examine them, an undecidable catharsis. Or do they only diffuse and legitimate them?

Examining the logics of Céline leads me, then, to judge them from the depths of his experience, which I know is contagious. I hear his singularity, and I reveal mine: *Who* enunciates *which* truths? And at what risk? I maintain my judgment and situate myself between the unavowable and the shareable. Since those are the stakes of literature: after the *sacred* then the *religious*, and in an epoch of the globalized virtual, literary experience finds itself at the intersection of the singular and the connected. The theory that examines these pleasures and these risks must be a revelation for the one who sketches it: neither abolished nor forgotten, but in a vigilant *suspension*[55] in the analysis of this confrontation with the impossible that is "literature." A sort of baroque love, indeed, in internal exclusion, in external inclusion of political philosophy.

IV. Keren Mock

When Keren Mock was preparing a doctorate on "The Intertextual Genesis of Modern Hebrew: Anastylosis of a Maternal Tongue" under the direction of Professor Pierre-Marc de Biasi and me,[56] I reminded her of Gershom Scholem's famous warning: "That sacred language on which we nurture our children, is it not an abyss that must open up one day? . . . . The secularization of the language is no more than a *manner of speaking*. . . . It is impossible to empty the words so bursting with meaning, unless one sacrifices the language itself."[57]

The young woman was not unaware of the anxiety of the famous philosopher-historian, specialist in Jewish mysticism. Without initiating a discussion with him, and as a sole response to the anticipated dangers, she sketched her project, patient and determined. Mock proposed to interview Israeli writers for whom Hebrew was not their maternal language but who, in this language of adoption had developed a writing capable of re-birthing and reinventing the sacred. At the crossroads of history, literature, philosophy, and psychoanalysis, her investigation would lead her to Ben-Yehuda, "composer" of modern Hebrew, and to Spinoza's *Hebrew Grammar*.[58]

Mock's analysis of my work, presented in this volume, develops the thought that she matured in this thesis.

In the continuation of the "Freudian tradition of deconstructing the sacred," Mock addresses a few moments of the history of the sacred: "Does the sacred manifest in secular spaces? If so, what place do *subjectivity* and the *sacred* have in secular contexts?" (my emphasis). She recalls the emergence of love as a "necessary and a constitutive element of psychic development" and proposes from the start the *process of subjectivation* such as it appears in the ambivalences of the transference ("Transference is a reconstructive and an active process").

Mock rereads Freud's texts with my *Powers of Horror* and, in retracing "the process of differentiation between subject and object," she observes a "constitutive dimension of the sacred." Her analysis of ab-jection, paired with maternal *reliance*, whose resonances with the Kantian apprehension of space she notes, induces an impassioned reading of my interpretation of *Stabat Mater* as a "pivotal moment of the feminine." The ambivalence of the intrapsychical conflict in the melancholic subject; the "need to believe" "formed before the advent of language"; the direct and immediate investment with the thirdness of the "father of prehistory" that "mixes" love with authority so that the separation ("matricide and mourning") is accomplished only by the "synergy of the maternal and the paternal." This trajectory captures the privileged place of the "maternal tongue" as "living material of maternal eroticism," which Lacan had perhaps underestimated in the mirror stage: hailed as "a form of liberation" (Mock).

Does this mean that the language of adoption is merely a "cold war" with the maternal? No! The "mother tongue . . . remains embedded in the foundations of . . . language." But, *between the two*, "the sacred is transformative precisely because its meaning is not fixed." Rather than an idealization, Mock detects in my work a "humanist ethics"—though *not* "founded on the maternal"—that "brings us closer to the multifocal heterogeneity of the . . . sacred as much as it seems to distance us from it." Interpreted as immanent to the "translinguistic and prelinguistic modalities of meaning," the sacred "appears . . . as a form of social catharsis that can . . . be thought in terms of the transference relationship." And from languages to languages, "awakens the transference in the experience of exile that is inherent to any subjective quest."

The immanence of the sacred resides, definitively, in the psychosexual transformability of speaking beings; it is supported by the transformative feminine.

How should we understand this ethic, the successor to ontotheology—which it deconstructs—with regard to psychoanalysis and the emancipation of the "second sex"?

For the two thousand five hundred years that the ethical has existed, the feminine has been rejected from its sphere: the feminine is not a subject of the ethical; at most it is its object. Psychoanalysis has shattered this exclusion of the feminine with a kind of ethics that "brackets," suspends judgment, morality, and the world, the better to interrogate them. It gives itself an orientation: "Where id was, there ego shall be";[59] and two principles that are opposed: pleasure and reality.

The transference thus reveals in the unconscious a drive sexuality that, far from evacuating the organic, is *denatured*, because disjoined from the organic instinctual by originary repression.[60] An originary disjunction founds the speaking being as a split subject—a fading to which the analyst pays attention, because it is this that arises in normative morality. Feminine fecundity and eroticism seem to manifest and betray this disjunction, and they become the target of desire. To be possessed, to be mastered, to be destroyed, in favor of a masculine domination observed in all societies. The castration complex should be understood, for the two sexes, as a traumatic displacement of the "trauma"[61] of the differences of the sexes, which resonates with the originary fading-splitting.

The Freudian hypothesis on the "two phases" of the feminine Oedipus bring to light what I call a *transformative feminine*, a factor in the transformability of *psychic life* considered not as an "apparatus" but as a "life of soul" or "life of the soul," according to Françoise Coblence's expression.[62]

And I take up again the seriousness of the question, still unanswered, that Freud addressed to Marie Bonaparte: "What does a woman want?" The questioning does not bear on desire, it is addressed to the will. It is no longer a matter of the enigmatic "black continent" that conceals itself from science. Nor is it a *Weltanschauung* that Freud would appeal to. I can imagine him, aggravated, curious, *suspended* on the question, on the ethical.

With this "will" in the feminine, Freud specifies the change of perspective that is under way in his clinic of feminine psychosexuality. The ungraspable ("what does she want?") bears on the relation of the *feminine* to the *ideals* of life and to life itself, inseparable from culture. In other words, *the perplexity about the feminine has become the psychoanalytically accessible face of the Freudian perplexity about the discontent in civilization*. Let us illuminate *with the feminine what escapes us in the social*. Could the feminine be located at the intersection of the (psychoanalytic) Logos and the (unconscious) Ananke, the two divinities Freud acquiesced to? Crossing or split, gap or fracture? Where does the opening or the closing of the human condition take place?

I reread Freud's last texts as a defense and illustration of the *denatured differences of the sexes*. To which is added—as a presentiment of certain antinormative aspects of gender theories—a polyphonic psychic bisexuality, doubled on both sides of this Freudian differentiation: the feminine of the man and the feminine of the woman, the masculine of the man and the masculine of the woman, at least four at play in the "match." But definitively conjugated in the singular. An "open structure" of the sexuality of speaking beings is sketched, generating tensions and conflicts, anxieties and pleasures.

An unsustainable multiverse of singular unconsciouses, of this woman, of that man, which psychoanalysis does not "program," does not "judge or calculate," but accompanies. Ventured jubilatory freedom of this choice, of this ethic in which the "norms," even the "identities" (man, woman), have become "dynamic concepts." For better or for worse.

And I maintain, therefore, that The Feminine borne by the Freudian discovery of the *unconscious* is one, if not *the*, factor in this dynamiting: *the feminine is transformative.*[63]

The suspended questioning about *feminine will* invites us to probe the transformative feminine: it is a *becoming.* In polemic with Freud, but declaring that he is "one of the men of this century for whom I have the greatest admiration,"[64] Beauvoir resumed her thought on the feminine in mutation, in existentialist terms: "One is not born a woman, one becomes one." As a psychoanalyst, and listening to mobile and multiversal feminine subjectivity, I would say "*One* is born a woman, but '*I*' become one." "One," biological and anatomical, although struck from the start by the imaginary of the parental community ("Look, it's a girl!"). But "*I*" try to arrive as a speaking subject in the cultures (plural) of mommy-daddy. *Alterity* is not taught, it is *incarnated* in the feminine not only because it is structural, by reason of the two phases of the Oedipus, reprised and diversified in the trials of reality; but also because *women* live it in social and political existence.

Not to "*neutralize*" in the "neuter" is to do justice to those women who come to seek sur-vival and creativity on our couches; but also to those women who, for example, are 700 million in forced marriages, throughout the world, and 130 million young girls mutilated by excision, subjected to the grip of various beliefs and fundamentalisms; and I'm not forgetting the murders of women (one woman killed by her spouse every two days even in France!). I offered the Hannah Arendt Prize for Political Thought (2006) to Afghan women who self-immolate by fire so that NGOs can accompany the survivors.

Women want to be free to decide to become mothers, or not. Certain ones among them willingly seek out assisted maternities, without prejudice—is it because the presubjective side of feminine eroticism (oedipal prime, the extraneousness of the Phallus)[65] makes them familiar with the *possession-dispossession of self* that modern science imposes on the most intimate? While at the same time the transformative feminine does not free itself from dogmas and norms, but modulates them into *dynamic concepts.* And rejoins this *ethics* in suspension that specifies . . . psychoanalysis itself.

It is up to us to create new concepts of metapsychology to develop the elucidation and accompaniment of maternal eroticism in its specificity. Without which the emancipation of the woman subject is consigned to being only a component without ethics in the automatization of the human species. If love (according to Spinoza) is the intimate face of the ethical, the feminine is neither an ideology nor a morality, but appears as a *herethic* of love.

J.K

NOTES

1. See Julia Kristeva, "L'Impudence d'énoncer: La Langue maternelle," in *La Haine et le pardon* (Paris: Fayard, 2005), 393–96; "The Impudence of Uttering: The Mother Tongue," http://www.kristeva.fr/impudence.html. See also Julia Kristeva, "The Depressive Position" and "The Inner Mother and the Depth of Thought," in *Melanie Klein*, trans. Ross Guberman (New York: Columbia University Press, 2001) (volume 2 of the "female genius" trilogy), 73–81 and 241–47; *Le Génie féminin*, t. II, *Mélanie Klein* (Paris: Fayard, 2000), 119–32 and 389–97.

2. See G. W. F. Hegel, *Phenomenology of Spirit*, trans. A. V. Miller (Oxford: Oxford University Press, 1977), 317f, commenting on *Rameau's Nephew* and the "impudence of uttering" in Diderot and in "Culture," particularly in French culture; *La Phénoménologie de l'esprit*, t. II (Paris: Aubier-Montaigne, 1941), 76f.

3. See Julia Kristeva, *Time and Sense: Proust and the Experience of Literature*, trans. Ross Guberman (New York: Columbia University Press, 1996); *Le Temps sensible: Proust et l'expérience littéraire* (Paris: Gallimard, 1994). See also Proust: "Ideas come to us as the successors to griefs, and griefs, at the moment when they change into ideas, lose some part of their power to injure our heart; the transformation itself, even, for an instant, releases suddenly a little joy. But successors only in the order of time, for the primary element, it seems, is the Idea, and grief is merely the mode in which certain ideas make their first entry into us. But within the tribe of ideas there are various families and some of them from the very first moment are joys." Marcel Proust, "Time Regained," in *Remembrance of Things Past*, vol. 3, trans. C. K. Scott Moncrieff and Terence Kilmartin (New York: Vintage, 1982), 944; *Le Temps retrouvé*, *À la recherche du temps perdu*, t. IV (Paris: Gallimard, 1989), 485.

4. See Sigmund Freud, *Jokes and Their Relation to the Unconscious*, in *The Standard Edition of the Complete Psychological Works of Sigmund Freud*, vol. VIII, trans. James Strachey (London: Hogarth, 1960); *Le Mot d'esprit et ses rapports avec l'inconscient* (Paris: Gallimard, 1969).

5. Jean de La Fontaine, *The Loves of Cupid and Psyche* (London: 1744), 365 (translation modified):

> Love, Books, Town, Country, Music, Play,
> Divert: With all Things I am blest;
> And ev'n can Bliss supreme survey
> In Thoughts which soothe the melancholy Breast.

6. See Julia Kristeva, *The Enchanted Clock: A Novel*, trans. Armine Kotin Mortimer (New York: Columbia University Press, 2017); *L'Horloge enchantée* (Paris: Fayard, 2015).

7. See Friedrich Nietzsche, "Thus Spake Zarathustra: A Book For All and None," in *Ecce Homo*, trans. Walter Kaufman and R. J. Hollingdale (New York: Vintage, 1969), 295–309; *Ecce Homo* (Paris: Flammarion, 1992), 127; see also Foreword to *Twilight of the Idols*, trans. R. J. Hollingdale (Harmondsworth: Penguin, 1990); *Crépuscule des idoles* (Paris: Gallimard, 1974), 9.

8. See Edward Casey, *Getting Back into Place: Toward a Renewed Understanding of the Place-World* (Bloomington: Indiana University Press, 2009); *The World at a Glance* (Bloomington: Indiana University Press, 2007); and *The World on Edge* (Bloomington: Indiana University Press, 2017). Also: "more of a bleeding boundary than a strict border" (*The World on Edge*, 268); "on the verge of going somewhere else" (ibid., xviii); "edges . . . are also where that something begins" (ibid., 357).

9. From *limbus* (Latin), rain in a storm or a cloud of rain, which in Christian theology designated the sojourn of the dead just before they were saved. See the long scholastic debates about hell for children deprived of baptism (and of their mother!?) in limbo.

10. Casey, *The World on Edge*, 326–28.

11. Ibid. See my reading of Plato's *Timaeus* in Julia Kristeva, *Revolution in Poetic Language*, trans. Margaret Waller (New York: Columbia University Press, 1984), 28–30; *La Révolution du langage poétique: L'Avant-garde à la fin du XIXe siècle, Lautréamont et Mallarmé* (Paris: Seuil, 1974), 27–30.

12. See among others, Kristeva, "Heterogeneity," in ibid., 165–81; *La Révolution du langage poétique*, 151–71.

13. See Sigmund Freud, "Formulations on the Two Principles of Mental Functioning," in *The Standard Edition of the Complete Psychological Works of Sigmund Freud*, vol. 12, trans. James Strachey (London: Hogarth, 1958), 223; "Formulations sur les deux principes du cours des évènements psychiques" (1911), in *Résultats, idées, problèmes* (Paris: PUF, 1984), 140.

14. See Hanna Segal, "Notes on Symbol Formation," *International Journal of Psycho-Analysis* 38, no. 6 (1957): 391–97.

15. Melanie Klein, "On the Sense of Loneliness," in *Envy and Gratitude, and Other Works, 1946–1963*, vol. III in *The Writings of Melanie Klein* (New York: Delacorte/Seymour Lawrence, 1975), 300–13; and Kristeva, *Melanie Klein*, 111; *Mélanie Klein*, 183.

16. For the Greek, Jewish, and Christian traditions of this notion, see Kristeva, *Time and Sense*, 391–92n109; *Le Temps sensible*, 334–35.

17. See Maurice Merleau-Ponty, "The Intertwining—The Chiasm," in *The Visible and the Invisible*, trans. Alphonso Lingis (Evanston: Northwestern University Press, 1968), 138–55, especially 141–42, 146, 154; *Le Visible et l'invisible* (Paris: Gallimard, 1964), 182–204, especially 184, 189, 200.

18. See Julia Kristeva, "Maternal Eroticism," in *Passions of Our Time*, trans. Constance Borde and Sheila Malovany-Chevallier (New York: Columbia University Press, 2018), 106; *Pulsions du temps* (Paris: Fayard, 2013), 205; and Ilse and Robert Barande, "Antinomies du concept de perversion et épigenèse de l'appétit d'excitation: Notre duplicité d'être inachevé ou la mère-version," *Revue française de psychanalyse* 47, no. 1 (1983): 143–282.

19. See Julia Kristeva, "Husserl's Hyletic Meaning: A Natural Thesis Commanded by the Judging Subject," in *Revolution in Poetic Language*, 31–33; *La Révolution du langage poétique*, 30–32.

20. Casey cites Heidegger: "ontological mood, a primordial kind of Being for *Dasein*, in which *Dasein* is disclosed to itself *prior* to all cognition and volition, and *beyond* their range of disclosure." Martin Heidegger, *Being and Time* (1927), trans. J. Macquarrie and E. Robinson (New York: Harper, 2006), 175.

21. Martin Heidegger, *The Basic Problems of Phenomenology*, trans. Albert Hofstadter (Bloomington: Indiana University Press, 1982), 94; *Les Problèmes fondamentaux de la phénoménologie* (Paris: Gallimard, 1985, 122.

22. See T. S. Eliot, "Son of man, / . . . / A heap of broken images, where the sun beats"; "I will show you fear in a handful of dust," in *The Waste Land*, in *The Poems of T. S. Eliot*, vol. 1, *Collected and Uncollected Poems*, ed. Christopher Ricks and Jim McCue (Baltimore: Johns Hopkins University Press, 2015, 55); or "This is the dead land / This is cactus land," "In this hollow valley / This broken jaw of our lost kingdoms," "Between the conception / And the creation / Between the emotion / And the response / Falls the shadow / *Life is very long*" ("The Hollow Men," in ibid., 82, 83, 84).

23. See Alina N. Feld, *Melancholy and the Otherness of God: A Study in the Genealogy, Hermeneutics, and Therapeutics of Depression* (Lanham: Lexington Books, 2011).

24. The break with the other religions follows, and operates with the violence that marks history.

25. Feld, *Melancholy and the Otherness of God*.

26. From the Greek *kenose*, "non-being," "nothingness," "inanition," "nullity." But also "senseless," "deceptive" (the adjective *kenos* means "empty," "useless," "vain"; the verb *kenoun*, "to purge," "to cut," "to wipe out": death given, suffered, and integrated with and/or consubstantial with the living.

27. See Julia Kristeva, "L'Europe divisée: Politique, éthique, et religion," in *La Haine et le pardon*, 61–82.

28. See Julia Kristeva, *Teresa, My Love: An Imagined Life of the Saint of Avila*, trans. Lorna Scott Fox (New York: Columbia University Press, 2015), 63; *Thérèse mon amour: Saint Thérèse d'Avila* (Paris: Fayard, 2008), 81.

29. See Kristeva, "Cristo como hombre," in *Teresa, My Love*, 203–6; *Thérèse mon amour*, 243–47.

30. See Julia Kristeva, "Suffering," in *This Incredible Need to Believe*, trans. Beverley Bie Brahic (New York: Columbia University Press, 2009), 87–98; "*Cet incroyable besoin de croire* (Paris: Bayard, 2007), 159–76. See Friedrich Nietzsche, "Book Three," in *The Gay Science*, trans. Josefine Nauckhoff (Cambridge: Cambridge University Press, 2001), §108, 109 ("New battles") and §125, 119 ("The madman").

31. See G. W. F. Hegel, *Lectures on the Philosophy of Religion: Volume III, The Consummate Religion*, trans. R. F. Brown, P. C. Hodgson, and J. M. Stewart (Berkeley: University of California Press, 1988), 125; *Leçons sur la philosophie de la religion: Troisième partie, La religion accomplie*, trans. Pierre Garniron (Paris: PUF, 2004), 61.

32. Freud, for his part, observes that "the shadow of the object fell upon the [melancholic] ego." Sigmund Freud, *Mourning and Melancholia*, in *The Standard Edition of the Complete Psychological Works of Sigmund Freud*, vol. XIV, trans. James Strachey (London: Hogarth, 1957), 249; *Deuil et mélancolie*, in *Métapsychologie* (Paris: Gallimard, 1968), 156. The *shadow* of the maternal object perpetuated in the convulsions of ontotheology?

33. See Julia Kristeva, "Intersections," in *Colette*, trans. Jane Marie Todd (New York: Columbia University Press, 2004), 419–27; "Croisements," *Le Génie féminin*, t. III, *Colette* (Paris: Fayard, 2002), 558–66. See also Hannah Arendt, "Thinking" and "Willing," in *The Life of the Mind*, (New York: Harcourt Brace Jovanovich, 1978), 96. On *death* as an "extreme possibility," a "care" or a "shrine" of Being, see Julia Kristeva, *Hannah Arendt*, trans. Ross Guberman (New York: Columbia University Press, 2001), 200, 216–18; *Le Génie féminin*, t. I., *Hannah Arendt* (Paris: Fayard, 1999) 315, 337–40. And on *birth* as a paradigm of initiations of new foundations that are *forgiveness* and the *promise* (ibid., 164; 209–10; *Hannah Arendt*, 264, 327–29) and the Spinozist joy of attaining this *felicity* in which *to live is to think* (ibid., 239; *Hannah Arendt*, 371).

34. See Martin Heidegger, *Off the Beaten Track*, trans. Julian Young and Kenneth Haynes (Cambridge: Cambridge University Press, 2002); *Holzwege* (Frankfurt: Vittorio Klostermann, 1950).

35. Wolfram Eilenberger discusses these reinventions of philosophy, in this period split between the genial and the monstrous, in his book, *Le Temps des magiciens* (Paris: Albin Michel, 2019).

36. See Julia Kristeva, "Un Linguiste qui ne dit ni ne cache, mais signifie," Preface to Émile Benveniste, *Dernières Leçons: Collège de France 1968–1969*, ed. Jean-Claude Coquet and Irène Fenoglio (Paris: Gallimard, 2012), 13–40.

37. See Julia Kristeva, "A Father is Beaten to Death," in *Passions of Our Time*, 84–100; *Pulsions du temps* (Paris: Fayard, 2013), 175–96.

38. See Kristeva, *Melanie Klein*, 183; *Mélanie Klein*, 111; and Melanie Klein, "On The Sense of Loneliness (1963), in *Envy and Gratitude* (New York: Vintage, 1997), 300–313.

39. W. R. Bion, *Attention and Interpretation* (London, Basic Books, 1970), 33; quoted in Kristeva, *Melanie Klein*, 14; *Mélanie Klein*, 22.

40. Julia Kristeva, "Interprétation," Conference of the Société Psychanalytique de Paris, November 19, 2019, Palais Brongniart, Paris; and "Affect, That 'Intense Depth of Words,'" in *Passions of Our Time*, 125–47; *Pulsions du temps*, 235–57.

41. Julia Kristeva, "A Holy Madness: She and He," "Don Juan, Or Loving To Be Able To," and "Romeo and Juliet: Love-Hatred in the Couple," in *Tales of Love*, trans. Leon S. Roudiez (New York: Columbia University Press, 1987), 83–100, 191–208, 209–33; *Histoires d'amour* (Paris: Denoël, 1983), 106–27, 243–63, 264–94.

42. See Kristeva, *Teresa, My Love*, 113; *Thérèse mon amour*, 138:

> Consistently and to the end, Teresa stages an intimacy that is secret and yet without secrecy, in a continuous state of budding emergence, alluring and infectious: in a word, baroque. Devoid of sensation, it seems, during the final ecstatic trance, and yet always supraconscious of what makes her swoon with pleasure, the writing of rapture "touches" the theopathic state to the point of "divine touch." At this point too, dispossession and destitution can only be described in a flow that is more denuded than ever, admittedly, and yet still incandescent with metaphors and metamorphoses.
>
> Was this not a peerless exposition in plastic terms of the very principle of the Incarnation? The Church, and the world, were impressed.
>
> The fiction produced by this paradoxical theologian, at the intersection of flesh and spirit, of subconscious drives and conscious meanings, triggered a theological revolution. Not only did Teresa fully earn her title of "Doctor of the Universal Church," she also bequeathed us a mission that would otherwise be impossible to fulfill: to solve the enigma of that embodied imaginary—of sublimation, Freud would say.

And:

> *The Interior Castle* closes upon Jesus alone, among enamels more delicate than ever, gold and precious stones—mystical graces unseen, hidden in anonymity, and yet flashing forth. Tensions and charms of the . . . baroque: *barroco*, an irregularly shaped pearl. . . .
>
> Today, as her race through the world crosses with her surge toward the Beloved within, at the intersection of *Foundations* and *Dwelling Places*, Teresa has just made a "baroque" discovery—as we will understand later—which enchants her: bliss beats torment if, and only if, the soul manages to inhabit itself in such a way as to perceive itself as a generous polytope, a kaleidoscopic mobility sustained by the Other's love. (ibid., 347–48; *Thérèse mon amour*, 407–8)

> Freud's philosophy was explicitly based on the Enlightenment, his interpretative method was without doubt Kabbalistically and Talmudically Jewish, but his unconscious was baroque. (*Sidelong glance at the diamond.*) Baroque—as in inconstant, mobile, playful, reinvented on the go—is the word for the amorous principle upon which he founded psychoanalysis, and over which he lingered in his scrutiny of the history of myths, religions, arts and letters; the principle Teresa crosses back and forth, with cheerful faith, never underestimating the demons of excitation unto death. Teresa reigns as the high priestess of the continent of idealization that inaugurates the transference that precedes the cure, into which the psychoanalyst will hack with the blows of the chisel, ice ax, hammer or pen . . .
>
> . . . . Can I convince you that by remitting the truth of the amorous bond, and by extension of the transferential bond, to an unconscious that is equally in love and yet infantile, no analytical interpretation can expel this "delusion" of love from the field of that (interminable) analysis? (ibid., 561; *Thérèse mon amour*, 652)

43. Julia Kristeva, *The Old Man and the Wolves*, trans. Barbara Bray (New York: Columbia University Press, 1994); *Le Vieil Homme et les loups* (Paris: Fayard, 1991).

44. See Julia Kristeva, "How to Speak to Literature with Roland Barthes," in *Passions of Our Time*," 21–32; "Comment parler à la littérature avec Roland Barthes," *Pulsions du temps*, 39–54.

45. See Stéphane Mallarmé, "Music and Letters," in *Mallarmé in Prose*, trans. Mary Ann Caws (New York: New Directions, 2001), 32. [Translation of the phrase changed

by Julia Kristeva.—Ed.]; "Enquête: Sur l'évolution littéraire," in *Oeuvres completes*, t. 2 (Paris: Pléiade, 2003), 700.

46. Heinrich Wölfflin, *Principles of Art History: The Problem of the Development of Style in Early Modern Art*, trans. Jonathan Blower (Los Angeles: Getty, 2015).

47. See Martin Farber, *The Foundation of Phenomenology: Edmund Husserl and the Quest for a Rigorous Science of Philosophy* (Piscataway: Transaction, 1943), 100.

48. See René Wellek and Austin Warren, *Theory of Literature* (Orlando: Harcourt Brace, 1984).

49. As Freud said of the dream: "the royal road to a knowledge of the unconscious activities of the mind." Sigmund Freud, *The Interpretation of Dreams*, in *The Standard Edition of the Complete Psychological Works of Sigmund Freud*, vol. V, trans. James Strachey (London: Hogarth, 1958), 608; *L'Interprétation des rêves* (Paris: PUF, 1967), 517.

50. Marcel Proust, "Sainte-Beuve and Balzac," *Against Sainte-Beuve and Other Essays*, trans. John Sturrock (London: Penguin, 1988), 68 (translation amended); "Sainte-Beuve et Balzac," *Contre Sainte-Beuve*, ed. Pierre Clarac and Yves Sandre (Paris: Pléiade, 1971), 276.

51. See Hannah Arendt, "Thinking," in *The Life of the Mind*, 55; quoted by Kristeva in *Hannah Arendt*, 189; *Hannah Arendt*, 299.

52. In all senses, including disgust and putting into question. See Julia Kristeva, *The Sense and Non-sense of Revolt*, trans. Jeanine Herman (New York: Columbia University Press, 2000).

53. See Kristeva, "The Taste of the Spectator: Toward a Political Philosophy" and "Judgment: Between Forgiveness and Promise," in *Hannah Arendt*, 220–240; *Hannah Arendt*, 343–71.

54. "Hypocrite reader, my fellow, my brother," wrote Charles Baudelaire, in "To the Reader," in the 1857 edition of *Les Fleurs du mal.*

55. See also my replies to the sections in this volume on Psychoanalysis, Art and Aesthetics, and Ethics and Politics.

56. The thesis was to obtain a prize for best Pluridisciplinary Thesis from the Institute of Humanities in Paris in 2015, and was published the next year. Keren Mock, *Hébreu, du sacré au maternel* (Paris: CNRS Éditions, 2016).

57. See Gershom Scholem, "On Our Language: A Confession," trans. Ora Wiskind, *History and Memory* 2, no. 2 (Winter 1990): 97.

58. Eliezer Ben-Yehuda, *A Complete Dictionary of Ancient and Modern Hebrew*, vols. III–IV (Jerusalem: Makor, 1980). Baruch Spinoza, *Hebrew Grammar (Compendium Grammatices Linguae Hebraeae)* (Philosophical Library, 1962).

59. Sigmund Freud, *New Introductory Lectures on Psycho-Analysis*, in *The Standard Edition of the Complete Psychological Works of Sigmund Freud*, vol. XXII, trans. James Strachey (London: Hogarth, 1964), 80; *Nouvelles conférences d'introduction à la psychanalyse* (Paris: PUF, 2004), 163.

60. I also speak of "denatured sexuality" in my replies to Jean-François Rabain in the section on Psychoanalysis, Elaine Miller in the section on Art and Aesthetics, and Ewa Ziarek in the section on Ethics and Politics in this volume.

61. See Sigmund Freud, *An Outline of Psycho-Analysis*, in *The Standard Edition of the Complete Works of Psychoanalysis*, vol. XXIII (London: Hogarth, 1964), 155.

62. See Françoise Coblence, "La Vie d'âme: Psyché est corporelle, n'en sait rien," *Revue française de psychanalyse* 74, no. 5 (2010): 1285–356. Coblence's idea is that we should not speak of a psychic apparatus but of life of soul or life of the soul. The psyche is not an apparatus but an inseparably psychosomatic *transformative vitality*. Life comes from the psyche, *life of soul*, and/or the psyche comes from or partakes of life, *life of the soul.*

63. See "Prélude à une éthique du féminin," 51st International Congress of the International Psychoanalytic Association (IPA), London, July 24, 2019, and 25th Conference of the International Psychoanalytical Studies Organization (IPSO), London, July 24–27, 2019. www.kristeva.fr.

64. Simone de Beauvoir, *All Said and Done*, trans. Patrick O'Brien (New York: Paragon, 1993), 148; *Tout compte fait*, in *Mémoires*, t. 2 (Paris: Pléiade, 2018), 640.

65. See Julia Kristeva, "On the Extraneousness of the Phallus; or, the Feminine between Illusion and Disillusion," in *The Sense and Non-sense of Revolt*. See also the essays by Rachel Boué-Widawsky and Fanny Söderbäck in the section on The Maternal in this volume.

21

Robert Harvey

OF INCREDIBILITY IN THE NEED TO BELIEVE: A PHILOSOPHICAL EXPLORATION

Proof—Never interested me, I believe. But I also believe that one should never renounce proof: ever more reason and light in order to preserve the improbable in its redoubts, those of the other. I only like faith or, rather, the irreligious proof involved in faith.

—Jacques Derrida, "Épreuves d'écriture"[1]

Ignorance is ignorance; no right to believe anything can be derived from it.

—Sigmund Freud, *The Future of an Illusion*

In recent years, Julia Kristeva has been developing the contention that we harbor what she calls an "incredible need to believe." This contention derives primarily from her practice as a psychoanalyst. The phrase appears with "incredible" added to the title of the 2007 French version of a book first published in Rome in 2006 under the more straightforward *Bisogno di credere*.[2] The adjective remains in the English and other translations. *Cet incroyable besoin de croire* (or *This Incredible Need to Believe*) presents an extensive interview—from which the qualifier "*incroyable*" derives—followed by a shorter one, a lecture, and various other texts, all given in unabashedly Catholic contexts.[3]

This Incredible Need to Believe is far from a fluke in Kristeva's recent career. Over the course of the two decades prior to its publication she had, with increasing persistence, demonstrated her interest in this particular dimension of belief. The subtitle of *In the Beginning Was Love*, first appearing in 1985, is *Psychoanalysis and Faith*.[4] Her *New Maladies of the Soul* appeared in 1993 and

The Feminine and the Sacred, authored in tandem with Catherine Clément, in 1998.[5] The subtitle (dropped for the English translation) of the original French version of her 2005 essay, *Hatred and Forgiveness* is *Powers and Limits of Psychoanalysis III*.[6] Finally, in the year following *This Incredible Need to Believe*, Kristeva's magisterial "imagined life of the Saint of Avila," *Teresa, My Love* was published.[7]

The dust cover and title page of the original Italian issue of the book under examination here emphasizes that this is *Un punto di vista laico*[8] and, coming from an avowed atheist, the exuberance with which "incredible" is applied to "the need to believe" begs for exploration—especially in light of Sigmund Freud's unambiguous and relentless efforts to encourage our species to overcome its dependence on religion. Ironically, Kristeva's contention that religion—especially Roman Catholicism—and psychoanalysis have much to share and can join forces in the common cause of civilization rests upon the firm ground of Freud's theory of the superego.

It is quite true that in many of his essays Sigmund Freud acknowledges that the kind of belief in which Kristeva is interested constitutes an irrepressible impulse in our species. Notably, in *The Future of an Illusion* (1927), the figure Kristeva recognizes as "the least religious man of his century"[9] asserted that: "Man's self-regard, seriously menaced, calls for consolation; life and the universe must be robbed of their terrors; moreover his curiosity, moved, it is true, by the strongest practical interest, demands an answer";[10] thus, a bit further, "the dream-work knows how to select a condition that will turn even that dreaded event [death] into a wish-fulfillment."[11] In that self-same work, however, ultimately judging faith to be not only an illusion but indeed a serious *delusion*, Freud toiled mightily to provide a framework—however "Victorian"—wherein we might evolve out of and beyond religion.

Of course, for philosophical speculation, something akin to belief is fundamental and, thus, necessary. Belief is akin to what Martin Heidegger called "the undisclosed" and is not unrelated to the hypothesis that forms the kernel of demonstration and proof. Kristeva, of course, recognizes this when she observes: "Whether I belong to a religion, whether I be agnostic or atheist, when I say 'I believe,' I mean 'I hold as true.'"[12] She illustrates the point with quotes from Voltaire, Pascal, and Montaigne, who famously affirmed that "it is perhaps not without reason that we consider credulity and the readiness to be persuaded to be signs of simplicity and ignorance."[13] Yet the incredibility stressed in the title and throughout the volume casts an air of mystery over belief. Perhaps more inscrutable still is that the variety of belief Kristeva has been working on is a *need* rather than, say, a wish or an impulse or a drive. There is a need, in any case, to meet the challenge that Kristeva holds before us of determining just how incredibility contributes to the need (if indeed it is a need) to believe.

As Freud knew, "the principle task of civilization, its actual *raison d'être*, is to defend us against nature."[14] But is the best method for accomplishing this that "civilization" has to offer *religious* belief? That there remain billions of individuals in our advanced primate species who cling to a need to believe (i.e. have faith) predicated on incredible propositions is a fact that obviously calls for tolerance from those of us who have moved beyond such superstitious behavior. But should we not persevere—along lines clearly set out by Freud, for example—to develop rational, critical, ethical, and scientific means of explaining and coming to terms with nature?

To attempt some further directions of thought on these matters, I should now like to explore—in as philosophical a manner possible—the dimension of incredibility in the need to believe. I shall do so principally through a juxtaposition of Kristeva's eponymous interview and Sigmund Freud's 1927 essay, *The Future of an Illusion*.

I

Although we know already that the belief of which Kristeva writes and speaks is a particular type of belief—faith, as it were—that psychoanalysis and religion share, it will be useful for our exploration to review broad and abstract definitions of the vast subject that is belief, of its initial inflection by need and, finally, by the quality of incredibility attached to both.

Belief is a state of mind in which a person holds something to be the case in the absence of any fact that might prove with certainty that it *is* the case. Belief differs from knowledge in that the conviction arrived at to form the latter is based in empirical evidence, fact, and proof. In the absence of these bases, we can merely be content with speculation, fantasy, or unfounded likelihood. Whereas knowledge is achieved when a proposition is proven, belief treats a proposition *as if* one knew.

In his *Critique of Pure Reason*, Kant situated belief vis-à-vis two other forms of conviction—opinion and knowledge—as functions of subjective and objective sufficiency. Regarding belief, these are criteria by which philosophy continues to operate today:

> Taking something to be true, or the subjective validity of judgment, has the following three stages in relation to conviction . . . *having an opinion*, *believing*, and *knowing*. *Having an opinion* is taking something to be true with the consciousness that it is subjectively *as well as* objectively insufficient. If taking something to be true is only subjectively sufficient and is at the same time held to be objectively insufficient, then it is called *believing*. Finally, when taking something to be true is both subjectively and objectively sufficient it is called *knowing*. Subjective sufficiency is called *conviction* (for myself), objective sufficiency, *certainty* (for everyone). I will not pause for the exposition of such readily grasped concepts.[15]

As psychoanalysts whose practice entails critique of and commentary on collective behavior, both Freud and Kristeva are necessarily interested in prereligious beliefs and religious beliefs. Notwithstanding their differences, prereligious beliefs and religious beliefs alike abide by Kant's criteria: the conviction of their adherents equals their uncertainty.

A need is something that, again, by current universally accepted definition, is required for an organism's survival. Certainly all members of our species who are in a state of good mental health yearn, want, desire, strive toward goals, and so forth. But only if it is alone present to consciousness—that is, in the absence of and unchallenged by alternate, more plausible narratives for human wonderment and fear—can belief by a stretch be deemed a need.

It is in the context of these definitions that "incredible" comes provocatively to modify our putatively entrenched need to believe. The etymological root of this adjective is the same as the Latin for "believable": *credibilis*. That which is incredible is therefore unbelievable: not even susceptible, that is, to satisfying simple subjective criteria for sufficiency let alone objective ones. Here is how one scholar has brilliantly paraphrased Francis Bacon's crucial contention in his *De Dignitate et Augmentis Scientiarum Libri IX* as to why, despite the "reluctance in our reason," we are compelled to "believe God's word": "whereas the incredibility of witnesses decreases the credibility of their testimonies, in the case of God it is precisely the incredibility of His word that increases His credibility as Author."[16] Clearly, incredibility in religious belief keeps it in a realm impervious to and oblivious of fact.

Freud recognized this. With unequivocal directness, he wrote that "all religious doctrines are illusions and insusceptible of proof." Freud's proclamation is predicated on the fact that "we call a belief an illusion when a wish-fulfilment is a prominent factor in its motivation and in doing so we disregard its relations to reality, just as the illusion itself sets no store by verification"; and even before that, in defining illusion, "that the Messiah will come and found a golden age is much less likely" than a girl's "illusion that a prince will come and marry her."[17]

There is, of course, a variety of illusion to which Freud adhered: the contingent illusions attendant on the scientific method. But unlike the arrogant immutability of "truths" based on faith, the belief of a scientist is eminently modifiable. Here is Freud clearly delighted with this suppleness and integrity: "we make trial with hypotheses that soon have to be rejected as inadequate."[18] In fact, the modifiability of hypotheses has been one of the essential elements of the scientific method since Aristotle—perhaps since Democritus. It is in this area that we can further lend definition to credibility (and to its opposite, incredibility). Credibility is the set of objective and subjective components contributing to the magnitude of our ability to believe that something or someone exists or existed or, a fortiori, to believe a given narrative.

The merit to scientific "belief," then, is the willingness of such "believers" to jettison them as soon as the establishment of their objective sufficiency proves impossible for want of empirical evidence. Religious belief, on the other hand, digs in, taking subjective sufficiency for objective sufficiency. "To assess the truth-value of religious doctrines does not lie within the scope of the present inquiry," wrote Freud in 1927, "it is enough for us that we have recognized them as being, in their psychological nature, illusions."[19] Or, with a hint of sarcasm at religion's ability to arrest man's development: "it would be very nice if there were a God who created the world and was a benevolent

Providence, and if there were a moral order in the universe and an after-life; but it is a very striking fact that all this is exactly as we are bound to wish it to be. And it would be more remarkable still if our wretched, ignorant and downtrodden ancestors had succeeded in solving all these difficult riddles of the universe."[20]

II

Already, on the very first page of her letter to Frédéric Boyer that serves "in guise of a preface," Kristeva is describing the "need to believe" as "that narcotic that makes living easier"[21]—in terms that surprisingly echo Marx's famously misunderstood remark that "religion . . . is the opium of the people."[22] Never-theless, when she asserts that the need to believe "is the foundation of our capacity to be . . . *speaking beings*,"[23] we sense, rightly, that the belief of which she will be speaking is neither entirely religious nor exclusively so. And this belief that takes hold in the not-yet-speaking baby is neither the "belief that" or the "belief in" between which philosophers usually distinguish when discussing this particular state of mind. Although, as we shall see, infantile belief, which Kristeva claims enables our transition from *phonē* to *logos*, is, to her view, already a foundation for faith in gods and, particularly, the lone gods in the image of human fathers.

Kristeva announces the goal she has in mind in exploring the incredible need to believe on the last page of this letter-introduction. That goal is "to touch upon a few big questions that vitally concern me, starting with this prepolitical and prereligious need to believe, which constitutes . . . only one of the elements in this complex experience of faith."[24] Although an avowed secularist, Kristeva's wager is that religious belief and its institutions have as much to contribute to reforming an imperfect humanist tradition hopelessly adrift today as psychoanalysis does. This wager, as we shall see, is grounded in the role of the father figure common to psychoanalytic theory and church dogma.

Indeed, the last words of this long interview that forms the core of *This Incredible Need to Believe* reiterate Kristeva's aspirations well. Seeing a "programming of the superfluity of human life" as the most likely trend of the immediate future, she "calls not for a return to but a refoundation of the authority of the Greco-Judeo-Christianity that gave the world the desire for a 'common world,' constituted by a plurality of 'who's' that Arendt points to as 'the center of politics.'"[25] "It is up to us," she adds, "to reinterpret this gift. Only a 'new politics' thus enlightened can still save us."[26] The inextricable ties binding the psychoanalysis that Kristeva practices to the religion that Sigmund Freud strove to supersede are thus patent. Proof that social sciences may yet fail to shake loose from their primitive origins in belief systems may be found in the question with which Carmine Donzelli initiates the long interview. When the director of Donzelli Editore states that he would like "to begin, not with specifically religious arguments, but with considerations that are more in the domain of anthropology or psychoanalysis," he begs the question by naming modern disciplines that, despite origins in Enlightenment Europe, are themselves—of necessity—descendants of (and improvements vis-à-vis) religion.[27] Kristeva seems to admit this to a certain extent in a rhetorical question she pronounces toward the end of the conversation with Donzelli: "Might psychoanalysis be one of the variations of theology? Its ultimate variation, *hic et nunc*?"[28]

III

Freud clearly used psychoanalytic theory and practice not only better to understand the need to believe as an experience of consciousness but also in order to prepare humankind for overcoming faith. He forcefully implied as much near the conclusion of *The Future of an Illusion*: "surely infantilism is destined to be surmounted. . . . the sole purpose of my book is to point out the necessity for this forward step."[29] In no way did he advocate either legislating or cajoling the need away: "Since men are so little accessible to reasonable arguments and are so entirely governed by their instinctual wishes, why should one set out to deprive them of an instinctual satisfaction and replace it by reasonable arguments?" However, he saw as his task and, indeed, his duty as an intellectual to educate others out of such darkness: "It is true that men are like this; but have you asked yourself whether they *must* be like this, whether their innermost nature necessitates it?"[30]

This is a conjecture with which Kristeva also grapples. It is also part of what she means by "incredible," as when we find it incredible when a teenager still believes in Santa Claus. Indeed, Freud, like Marx before him, recognized a certain marvel in the fact of religion's having taken part in the unfolding of the human story.[31] In Kristeva's thought, however, the marvel at and the virtual superiority attributed to religion emblematized by having lent it the marker of "incredible" are undeniable. In declarations like "the questioning of any and all entities, including belief and its objects, is one of Christianity's most impressive legacies; and humanism, its rebellious child, must not be prevented from developing this legacy," we see these dimensions and qualities of incredibility at work.[32]

Kristeva stresses that through her exchanges with religious leaders, she is working at a "pressing need to radically reform humanism."[33] The urgency with which she persists at joining forces with believers is predicated on real present-day problems both plaguing and caused by humans—one of which operates on the fringes of religion: "Not hostile to religions, and even less indulgent with them, this school of thought that I am part of is perhaps our last chance to deal with the rise of obscurantism and its other face: the management via technology of the human species."[34]

The roots of such dysfunction and self-dehumanization are in our origins as individual subjects just as they are in our origins as a certain evolved primate species: "Because I believe, I speak," says Kristeva, "I would not speak if I didn't believe; believing in what I say, and persisting in saying it, comes from the capacity to believe in the Other and not at all from existential experience, necessarily disappointing." Then, in a moment reminiscent of her early studies in the realm of linguistics and borrowing from Benveniste, she goes on to trace the origins of Latin *credo* in "Sanskrit *sraddha* 'which denotes an act of 'confidence' in a god."[35] Later, she will use the word *créance* or credit.[36]

It is thus the link established in Judeo-Christian narratives between belief and the origin of speech, on the one hand, and the link between, again, belief and a child's first use of spoken language, on the other, that for Kristeva form the tie binding psychoanalysis to religion. Kristeva's ideas concerning the need to believe are intrinsically bound to the nascent human—the infant on the cusp of the discursive realm (*logos*). Belief embodies the key skill allowing us to cross that threshold. "'I' am only if a beloved authority acknowledges me."[37] The question inevitably arises as to whether that moment in our individual development need refer back to the structure of religious belief and, even more importantly, be promoted to the status of metaphor for the evolution of the species. "Is it," in other words, "inevitable that this 'need to believe' be religious?"[38] For, if it is, then the "beloved authority" takes on an identity of incredibly powerful proportions with repercussions in the social and political realms that could be crucial to the survival of this species and of the other species whose lives we have made dependent on ours.

Kristeva makes no secret as to the identity of this authority: "The psychoanalytical experience of the child and the adult . . . testifies to a crucial moment of development, when the *infans* projects itself onto a third person with which it identifies: the loving father. . . . [T]his confident recognition granted me by the father loving the mother and loved by her, and that I in turn grant him, turns my babble into linguistic signs whose value he establishes."[39] Or, in language both poetic and emphatically favorable to the perpetuation of the nuclear heterosexual family: "At the dawn of individuation a life raft . . . appears on the horizon of the 'oceanic feeling': the loving father. An imaginary Surface who, through his loving authority, takes me from the engulfing container: he is the guarantor of my being."[40]

Kristeva may well attempt to reassure us that she is "only interested in the *psychic reality* that these events generate in believer subjects, in the representations or the phantasms, leaving aside the question whether these events really happened or not,"[41] yet enthroning and confirming the paternal instance in the eternal status of quintessential "loving authority" runs the risk of leading the believers (that we all supposedly still are despite ourselves) to a fairly masochistic psychosis: "'We are both of us in love and, guilty, we ought to be beaten to death together, death initiates our reunion in the beyond': such might be the believer's motto."[42] The believer, in that case, would appear to be in far greater need of help than the "rebellious humanist child."

Freud unflinchingly recognizes this danger, I think, once again in *The Future of an Illusion* when he writes that "religion would . . . be the universal obsessional neurosis of humanity; like the obsessional neurosis of children, it arose out of the Oedipus complex, out of the relation to the father," adding that it can lead to "amentia, in a state of blissful hallucinatory confusion."[43] Yet, in plumbing "the depths of the unconscious, [Freud] made of the 'need to believe' an *object of knowledge*."[44] Despite his antitheism, it is perhaps a fatal flaw of his legacy—and one leaving the door open for continued collaboration between psychoanalysis and religion—that, as Kristeva states, "it is truly this capacity to signify, this *significance rooted in the destiny of the paternal function*, that Freudian psychoanalysis bequeaths us";[45] that he "did not hesitate to postulate, in commenting upon the destiny of the paternity that governs the installation of significance and its accidents, 'a high aim in human beings': '*Das höhere Wesen in Menschen*'";[46] and that he enabled his descendants to declare that "the speaking being is a believing being."[47] This leads Kristeva to assert, in face of the final words of the 1927 essay—i.e. that "my illusions are not, like religious ones, incapable of correction. They have not the character of delusion"[48]—that it is a "superficial reading of *The Future of an Illusion* (1927)" that "allows us to think that Freud reduced belief to an illusion."[49]

IV

And so, for better or worse (between which one day we will have to decide), psychoanalysis has inherited from the first and second revealed monotheisms a conviction that we operate in a relation of incontrovertible fealty to our father, a father, the father, the Father:

> Christian Faith rests upon an indelible confidence in the existence of an Ideal Father, and upon absolute love for this loving Father, who is seen, quite simply, as the foundation of the speaking subject, who is, consequently, none other than the subject of loving speech. The Father of Agape or Amor, therefore, not Eros, although these two kinds of love come together, when they are not opposed, in Christian histories. "I love because I am loved, therefore I am," could be the believer's syllogism. . . . This syllogism takes us back to the "loving father of individual prehistory," whom we encountered with Freud at the start of our discussion.[50]

Or, as the "father of psychoanalysis" put it, "now that God was a single person, man's relations to him could recover the intimacy and intensity of the child's relation to his father."[51] Part and parcel of this development brought about by our first attempts—with Judaism, then Christianity—to explain the universe, to palliate our fears about death should have been the recognition that first attempts are always the most imperfect and, thus, destined for replacement by better, more convincing, more mature work of the mind: "when man personifies the forces of nature he is again following an infantile model."[52]

As we intimated before, in regard to the disturbing story of our socialized being's inextricability from patriarchal forces, we find Freud in 1927 struggling mightily with inherent contradictions. To refute the arguments in favor of religious belief, paternal authority must be repudiated: "We ought to believe [my opponents maintain] because our forefathers believed. But these ancestors of ours were far more ignorant than we are. They believed in things we could not possibly accept today; and the possibility occurs to us that the doctrines of religion may belong to that class too."[53] Albeit the fatherly foundation for speech, for the superego, indeed for civilization itself, "we arrive at the singular conclusion that of all the information provided by our cultural assets it is precisely the elements which might be of the greatest importance to us and which have the task of solving the riddles of the universe and of reconciling us to the sufferings of life . . . that are the least well authenticated."[54] Recognizing and paying tribute to the great works made under the aegis of belief systems, it is high time, stresses Freud, that humans get on with their spiritual evolution, as this thought movement's crescendo indicates: "religious doctrine. . . . [has] called up the spirits of the greatest men and of the most eminent thinkers, but all the pronouncements and information which they have received from them have been so foolish and so wretchedly meaningless that one can find nothing credible in them but the capacity of the spirits to adapt themselves to the circle of people who have conjured them up."[55]

V

In studying Kristeva's thinking in regard to belief, the question may arise as to whether Freud's attempts to wrest dominion over belief from religion and bequeath it to secular humanism were effective enough. Certainly, as Kristeva infers, "what Freud had in mind when he said that it wasn't so much a question of 'founding a religion'" was that it was more about "'sublimating' the need to believe."[56] But is sublimation sufficient when, like the Hegelian *Aufhebung*, the very operation carries over all the primitive and sometimes embarrassingly erroneous aspects of that which is sublimated? "It would be an undoubted advantage if we were to leave God out altogether," Freud wrote in 1927, "and honestly admit the purely human origin of all the regulations and precepts of civilization."[57] But is condescension—however amusing—enough to rid us once and for all of the illusions inherent to religion? Freud's was a commendable endeavor and one that gestured toward the eventual (and long overdue) release of humans from their cultural infancy. Yes, "our science is no illusion [and] an illusion it would be to suppose that what science cannot give us we can get elsewhere,"[58] but when atheist humanism concedes to religion "customs" and behaviors long ago proven to have nothing to do with "human nature," it gives established religion an undeserved pass for all the ills it has caused and continues to cause despite the great works of art that have been made under its shadow. Of course magnificent sighs have been heard from the heart and soul of the *condition that requires illusions* (Marx), but it would be truly incredible indeed to expect rational discussion from peddlers in miracles and magic, from those who are keeping vast swathes of humanity lulled by the absurd, empty, and cruel promises of religion.[59]

We need to be clear, nevertheless, that under that banner of incredibility Kristeva concedes nothing to revealed religion: the need to believe is incredible because, as she puts it, "it is not a question of making of it an absolute, flattering it and using it as a basis for this or that order or hierarchy."[60] She maintains, however, in accordance with the tenets of Freudism, that we become human (i.e. speaking subjects and civilized members of society) only by means of the introjection of a paternal instance—the internalization of a "loving father"—and that Judaism and Christianity got that story right. "The pivotal figure of this fatherhood," she writes, "both juridical and loving, is none other than the biblical Abraham, who spares Isaac: for God is so moved by his obedience to the divine commandment."[61] The same convoluted logic by which these fathers—in this case, one is earthly, the other celestial—are construed as loving fathers is repeated in the Christ legend in which, according to John, "God so loved the world that He gave His only begotten Son."[62] By "gave" is of course meant "allowed to be murdered." "No other religion," as Kristeva eloquently puts it, "even that of the Greek gods, encouraged the experience of sublimation quite so effectively as the Son-Father beaten to death."[63]

This is why some of the most powerful statements Freud made (for example, "ignorance is ignorance; no right to believe anything can be derived from it," and "where questions of religion are concerned, people are guilty of every possible sort of dishonesty and intellectual misdemeanor") ultimately ring a bit hollow.[64] The "ambivalence in the attitude toward the father [that is] deeply imprinted in every religion" is an ambivalence that Freud found impossible to conjure;[65] hence his incapacity to square a vehement and altogether cogent rejection of religious belief ("Let us. . . . ask on what their claim to be believed is founded")[66] with his views about our acquisition of *logos* and the formation of the superego. Indeed, when we read this formulation found in *The Ego and the Id*—"The superior being, which turned into the ego ideal, once threatened castration, and this dread of castration is probably the nucleus round which the subsequent fear of conscience has gathered"[67]—we can but be reminded of Abraham's Ur-threat, of Isaac's Ur-dread, and of some of the less savory handiwork carried out in the name of Christian belief.

Unlike earthly fathers, the celestial "One" is believed (and feared) to be all seeing, all knowing, able to supervise every action, every thought while the subject is awake or while he or she is sleeping, overseeing everything even before one is born and even—since an integral part of faith is the belief in an afterlife—after one is dead. This tableau epitomizes not only totalitarian but also eternal supervision. It might, as we have already hinted, be the root of masochism: the wish, that is, to be a slave. Meanwhile, the living vicars of this system are the "fathers of the Church" who disseminate their love in ways that are all too familiar to us.

VI

In the place of democracy with its inherent freedoms, the result of religion's intrusive claims in the realm of politics may degenerate into theocratic authority: sharia imposed in Muslim states—Shiite and Sunni alike (Iran, Saudi Arabia)—the seemingly relentless reduction of the deist-conceived U.S. to a monolingual evangelical Christian state, and the inextricable contradictions of the Jewish state of Israel. As Freud stressed, there is a "fatal resemblance between the religious ideas which we revere and the mental products of primitive peoples and times."[68] When they are applied to political management, the principles derived from faith tend with virtual inevitability to tyrannize either the unfaithful or those whose faith is "misguided" into another religion.

While "incredibility" might fairly evoke the persistence or even the growth of religious belief, there are some indications that the number of agnostics, atheists, and antitheists is increasing, despite the fact that apostasy is still punishable by death in many parts of *man's* world. But even if these indications prove factual, belief applied to politics still works its nefarious ways. Slavoj Žižek recently observed that: "When [Sam] Harris writes, 'It is possible, for instance, to be a practicing Jew who does *not* believe in God,' he fails to mention how the non-believer can nonetheless draw all practical consequences from this belief—for example, you might not believe in God yet nonetheless believe that God gave your people the land they claim as theirs." Žižek then proceeds to recount an example of just such a claim pronounced by Israeli Deputy Foreign Minister Tzipi Hotovely, to which he adds that "if such a direct legitimization of one's claim to land by reference to God's will is not religious fundamentalism, then one should wonder if this term has any meaning at all," remarking for good measure that "the irony reaches its peak when we bear in mind that, according to some surveys, Israel is the most atheist state in the world (more than 60 per cent of Jews in Israel don't believe in God)."[69]

In advocating for the importance—through psychoanalytic theory and practice—of the need to believe, Kristeva toils admirably at building a rampart against "religions' past and present fundamentalist off-course drift."[70] She places what she sees as "the dead ends of secularized societies" on equal footing with this "drift" as a threat to the horizon of a more peaceful and just world.[71] One leads, of course, to the murderous violence with which we are all too familiar, the other to "the automation of the species."[72] Asserting that there is a "consensus that our multicultural and recomposed societies" are "deprived of moral bases,"[73] Kristeva claims that "the alternative to the rise of religiosity, as to its opposite, narrow-minded nihilism, comes already from precisely those *thought loci* that we are attempting not to occupy but to bring to life."[74] Those "thought loci" are situated in "the vast continent of the social sciences."[75] Between these two impediments to survival, Kristeva is determined to create "optimal condition[s] for democratic debate."[76] The burden of guilt for not allowing this debate to occur is squarely on the shoulders of those who have agreed with Freud that "civilization runs a greater risk if we maintain our present attitude to religion than if we give it up"[77] and have chosen to ignore the persistence of religious belief: "Is it not surprising that our secularized societies have neglected this incredible need to believe?"[78]

Freud optimistically maintained that "there is no stopping [the scientific spirit]; the greater the number of men to whom the treasures of knowledge become accessible, the more widespread is the falling away from religious belief."[79] This is because Freud firmly believed in the species' capacity for self-amelioration: "It is not true that the human mind has undergone no development since the earliest times and that, in contrast to the advances of science and technology, it is the same today as it was at the beginning of history."[80] In this respect, Freud was a staunch and prominent proponent of a variety of belief that stands vigil for its own revision: the conviction not only that evolution of living beings is a fact, but that the evolution of our greatest attribute—consciousness—is possible within the life of *this* species.

VII

Here is how Kristeva sums up the fatal tension between belief's perversion as fundamentalism and humanism's perversion as "narrow-minded nihilism": "The problem of this beginning of the third millennium is not the war of religions but the rift and void that now separates those *who want to know that God is unconscious* and those who would rather not know this, the better *to enjoy the show that proclaims He exists*."[81] In her psychoanalytic practice, therefore, Kristeva has taken on the laudable task of attempting to draw young subjects back from destructive practices like anorexia and jihadism. In her role as a prominent public intellectual, she has brought a variety of religious and secular (clinical) players together in a forum to debate the future of the world. "Why not in . . . Jerusalem?"[82]

Engaging in conversation with representatives of the three main revealed monotheisms on the basis of the father functions they promote, however, leads inevitably to engaging in a comparative evaluation of them that results in the demotion of Islam. This may be surprising for several reasons, not the least of which is the massive influence Aristotle had on Islamic philosophy. Given that, according to Freud and Kristeva in his wake, the first civilizing step that the subject of psychoanalysis takes is his (or her) budding use of language, we naturally refer back to the first iteration of this thesis in Book I of Aristotle's *Politics* where he recounts in unforgettable terms our passage from *phonē* to *logos*.[83] While confessing that she hasn't "'reflected a great deal' upon the relationship between Greek culture and Christianity, nor upon the relationship between the three monotheisms,"[84] Kristeva does acknowledge that "we owe to such great masters as Avicenna and Averroes the 'discovery' and diffusion of Aristotle, above all in Christian culture. [But] how venture into this vast domain without knowing the language and lacking all but secondhand information?"[85] She adds that, from her psychoanalytic perspective, what is fundamentally wrong with Islam is that "the contact with Aristotle has concealed the fact that Islam cut itself off from Jewish and Christian monotheism, in ruling out any idea of paternity in its idea of the divine, along with many other pivotal points of the biblical-Gospel canon having to do with the loving bond between Creator and creatures. So, for instance, original sin doesn't exist in Islam."[86] (Unbelievers might find that this example is not the worst characteristic of Islam!) It may well have been quite strategic for Kristeva to have left Aristotle's famous tale of language acquisition virtually out of *This Incredible*

Need to Believe because, as one reviewer has speculated in Kristeva's regard, "the problem with the world today is Islam, and the solution is Christianity."[87]

But is psychoanalysis really foreclosed to Islam? What about Fethi Benslama's work?[88] While few can disagree with the condemnation of wanton violence currently carried out in the name of the third revealed religion, all three monotheisms have now long proven themselves to be stultifying for their acolytes and potentially dangerous to others—to believers in other gods, for instance, or to those who don't believe at all. As only one example, the history and current story of apostasy—the negation of belief—stands as a stark reminder of religion's dark side.

Kristeva nevertheless finds herself moved to admonish: "'Don't be afraid of Christianity, and together we won't fear religions!' . . . [to her] agnostic, humanist, atheist friends. We hail from the same continent of thought."[89] She continues:

> We often rise up "against" each other because we are in reality "right against" one another; let us continue our analyses . . . [*sic*] And I have a dream: may true complicities, essential in our face to face with the rise of barbarity, be woven not only, and to my way of thinking less, between Christianity and the other religions today tempted by fundamentalism, but between Christianity and this vision to which I adhere that grows out of Christianity, although it is detached from it today, and has the ambition to elucidate the perilous paths of freedom. In his person and his acts Jean [*sic*] Paul II made this dream possible. Far more than sainthood, this pope has shown us his universal dimension.[90]

VIII

While "at a time when religious doctrines held unrestricted sway,"[91] when we understood little, that is, and misunderstood even more about ourselves and the world around us, Freud might have conceded faith's capacity to provide comfort to us, to serve as a "narcotic that makes living easier,"[92] "it is doubtful whether men were in general happier . . . more moral they certainly were not."[93] So if the need to believe is so wondrous and irrepressible that it must be deemed no less than "incredible," and given all the beautiful and innovative reflections Kristeva makes about motherhood, why not work to shift the basis for the bastion against barbarism (and improve humanism too) to the introjection of a loving mother?

Indeed, we need not fear Christianity—or religions in general. We should, however, recognize that channel for belief for what it is: an obsolete mental formation (Freud) whose supersession is long overdue. Because of "the religious prohibition of thought. . . . it is worth making the experiment of an irreligious education."[94] And since the "infantile prototype" exploited by religion is to "especially" fear "one's father,"[95] it seems to me that seriously considering matriarchy might make for a worthwhile experiment in the irreligious reeducation of our species.

I will close with a cautionary tale in a trice that fairly illustrates the failure of belief in face of thought, which it is always determined to prohibit when necessary for maintaining its hegemony. The day the latest (as of my writing of this article) mass murder took place at Santa Fe High School in the U.S. state of Texas, one could read *incredulously* the following observation of *fact*: "They are praying today in Santa Fe, Tex. They often are, but after Friday, the need feels bottomless."[96] In face of the obvious, the reasonable, and the rational, the factual, faith cannot hold a candle.

ROBERT HARVEY

STATE UNIVERSITY OF NEW YORK AT STONY BROOK
MAY 2018

NOTES

1. "*Preuve—Ne m'a jamais intéressé—je crois. Mais je crois aussi qu'on ne doit jamais y renoncer: toujours plus de raison et de lumière, afin de sauver l'improbable en ses confins ultimes, ceux de l'autre. Je n'aime que la foi, ou plutôt dans la foi, son épreuve irreligieuse.*" Jacques Derrida, "Jacques Derrida: Épreuves d'écriture," *Cahiers philosophiques* 117, no. 1, *Les Introuvables des Cahiers* (April 2009): 90. Derrida's entry is dated 10 October with no year indicated, but since it was written for Les Immatériaux, an exhibition curated by Jean-François Lyotard and inaugurated in March 1985 at the Centre Georges Pompidou, we may assume Derrida wrote this on October 10, 1984.

2. Julia Kristeva, *Bisogno di credere: Un punto di vista laico*, trans. M. Guerra (Rome: Donzelli Editorie, 2006); *Cet incroyable besoin de croire* (Paris: Bayard, 2007); *This Incredible Need to Believe*, trans. Beverley Bie Brahic (New York: Columbia University Press, 2009).

3. "From Jesus to Mozart (Christianity's Difference)," "Suffering" (the Lenten Lecture delivered on 19 March 2006), "The Genius of Catholicism," and "Don't Be Afraid of European Culture," in Kristeva, *This Incredible Need to Believe*, chs. 2–5.

4. Julia Kristeva, *In the Beginning Was Love: Psychoanalysis and Faith*, trans. Arthur Goldhammer (New York: Columbia University Press, 1987); *Au commencement était l'amour: Psychanalyse et foi* (Paris: Hachette, 1985).

5. Julia Kristeva, *New Maladies of the Soul*, trans. Ross Guberman (New York: Columbia University Press, 1995); *Les Nouvelles Maladies de l'âme* (Paris: Fayard, 1993). Catherine Clément and Julia Kristeva, *The Feminine and the Sacred*, trans. Jane Marie Todd (New York: Columbia University Press, 2001); *Le Féminin et le sacré* (Paris: Stock, 1998).

6. Julia Kristeva, *Hatred and Forgiveness*, trans. Jeanine Herman (New York: Columbia University Press, 2010); *La Haine et le pardon: Pouvoirs et limites de la psychanalyse III* (Paris: Fayard, 2005).

7. Julia Kristeva, *Teresa, My Love: An Imagined Life of the Saint of Avila*, trans. Lorna Scott Fox (New York: Columbia University Press, 2014); *Thérèse mon amour: Sainte Thérèse d'Avila* (Paris: Fayard, 2008).

8. "A secular point of view."

9. Kristeva, *This Incredible Need to Believe*, xv.

10. Sigmund Freud, *The Future of an Illusion*, in *The Standard Edition of the Complete Psychological Works of Sigmund Freud*, vol. XXI, trans. James Strachey (London: Hogarth, 1961), 16.

11. Ibid., 17.

12. Kristeva, *This Incredible Need to Believe*, 3.

13. Michel de Montaigne, *Essays*, trans. J. M. Cohen (London: Penguin, 1993), 86; *Essais*, in *Oeuvres complètes* (Paris: Garnier Frères,1962), 193.

14. Freud, *The Future of an Illusion*, 15.

15. Immanuel Kant, "On the Canon of Pure Reason: Third Section, On having an opinion, knowing, and believing," *Critique of Pure Reason*, trans. Paul Guyer and Allen W. Wood (Cambridge: Cambridge University Press, 1998), A 822, B 850.

16. Francis Bacon, *De Dignitate et Augmentis Scientiarum Libri IX* (London: Forgotten Books, 2018). Tom van Malssen, *The Political Philosophy of Francis Bacon: On the Unity of Knowledge* (Albany: SUNY Press, 2015), 163.

17. Freud, *The Future of an Illusion*, 31.

18. Ibid., 55.

19. Ibid., 33.

20. Ibid.

21. Kristeva, *This Incredible Need to Believe*, vii.

22. Karl Marx, *Critique of Hegel's "Philosophy of Right,"* trans. Joseph J. O'Malley (Cambridge: Cambridge University Press, 1977), 131.

23. Kristeva, *This Incredible Need to Believe*, vii.

24. Ibid., xvi.

25. Ibid., 67.

26. Ibid., 76.

27. Ibid., 1.

28. Ibid., 70.

29. Freud, *The Future of an Illusion*, 49.

30. Ibid., 47.

31. "In what does the peculiar value of religious ideas lie?" Ibid., 15.

32. Kristeva, *This Incredible Need to Believe*, ix.

33. Ibid., 2.

34. Ibid., 29.

35. Ibid., x.

36. Ibid., 4.

37. Ibid., 9.

38. Ibid., 3–4.

39. Ibid., xi.

40. Ibid., 10.

41. Ibid., 57.

42. Ibid., 58.

43. Freud, *The Future of an Illusion*, 43.

44. Kristeva, *This Incredible Need to Believe*, 4.

45. Ibid., xiv.

46. Ibid., xv.

47. Ibid., 1.

48. Freud, *The Future of an Illusion*, 53.

49. Kristeva, *This Incredible Need to Believe*, 4.

50. Ibid., 49.

51. Freud, *The Future of an Illusion*, 19.

52. Ibid., 22.

53. Ibid., 26–27.

54. Ibid., 27.

55. Ibid., 28.

56. Kristeva, *This Incredible Need to Believe*, 30.

57. Freud, *The Future of an Illusion*, 41.

58. Ibid., 56.

59. Marx, *Critique of Hegel's "Philosophy of Right,"* 131. "The wretchedness of the religious is at once an expression of and a protest against real wretchedness. Religion is the sigh of the oppressed creature, the heart of a heartless world, and the soul of soulless conditions. It is the opium of the people. The abolition of religion as the illusory happiness of the people is the demand for their real happiness. To call on them to give up their illusions about their condition is to call on them to give up a condition that requires illusions. Thus, the critique of religion is the critique in embryo of the vale of tears of which religion is the halo."

60. Kristeva, *This Incredible Need to Believe*, 11.

61. Ibid., 66.

62. John 3:16.

63. Kristeva, *This Incredible Need to Believe*, 60.

64. Freud, *Future of an Illusion*, 32.

65. Ibid., 24. Freud is here referring to his findings in *Totem and Taboo*.

66. Ibid., 26.

67. Sigmund Freud, *The Ego and the Id*, in *The Standard Edition of the Complete Psychological Works of Sigmund Freud*, vol. XIX, trans. James Strachey (London: Hogarth: 1964), 57.

68. Freud, *The Future of an Illusion*, 38.

69. Slavoj Žižek, *The Courage of Hopelessness: A Year of Acting Dangerously* (London: Melville House, 2017), 120–21.

70. Kristeva, *This Incredible Need to Believe*, 12.

71. Ibid.

72. Ibid.

73. Ibid.

74. Ibid, 27.

75. Ibid.

76. Ibid., 11.

77. Freud, *The Future of an Illusion*, 35.

78. Kristeva, *This Incredible Need to Believe*, 11.

79. Freud, *The Future of an Illusion*, 38.

80. Ibid., 11.

81. Kristeva, *This Incredible Need to Believe*, 26–27.

82. Ibid., 63.

83. Aristotle, *Politics*, in *The Completed Works of Aristotle*, 2 vols., ed. Jonathan Barnes (Princeton: Princeton University Press, 1984), Book I, §10.

84. Kristeva, *This Incredible Need to Believe*, 56. The words "reflected a great deal" are in inner quotes because Kristeva repeats the phrase from her interlocutor's question.

85. Ibid., 65.

86. Ibid., 67.

87. Mary-Jane V. Rubenstein, "Review of Julia Kristeva: This Incredible Need to Believe (Columbia, 2009)," *Division II Faculty Publications*, Paper 148 (January 2010): 666.

88. Fethi Benslama, *La Psychanalyse à l'épreuve de l'Islam* (Paris: Aubier, 2002).

89. Kristeva, *This Incredible Need to Believe*, 106.

90. Ibid.

91. Freud, *The Future of an Illusion*, 37.

92. Kristeva, *This Incredible Need to Believe*, vii.

93. Freud, *The Future of an Illusion*, 37.

94. Ibid., 48.

95. Ibid., 17.

96. Vivian Yee and Amy Harmon, "'Please Pray': Santa Fe Is a Town That Has Long Found Comfort in Faith," *New York Times*, May 18, 2018.

22

Alain Delaye

THE NEED TO BELIEVE AND THE DESIRE TO KNOW

In Western thought, belief and knowledge have always been more or less at odds with each other. This difficulty arose acutely in the twelfth and thirteenth centuries in the context of medieval theology. Christian thinkers then tried to reconcile them by prioritizing one over the other. St. Bonaventure and St. Thomas Aquinas—belonging to different spiritual traditions, one Franciscan the other Dominican—opposed each other, the former defending the superiority of faith over reason and inviting reason to fade away humbly, the latter judging the role of reason to be legitimate and important and assigning it the task of serving and supporting faith. "*Philosophia, ancilla theologiae*," Aquinas said.

However, the debate did not stop with medieval scholasticism but was prolonged among the lay philosophers of the centuries that followed. Descartes, Spinoza, and Kant, and more recently Nietzsche, Freud, and Derrida, to name some well-known thinkers, have approached the question and, each time, caused it to take a new turn. Descartes, after questioning the data of faith with his universal doubt, provided arguments to reintroduce it into the philosophical landscape. Spinoza, insisting on the infinite capacity of our intelligence, wanted to demonstrate, "*more geometrico*," that faith was not indispensable, yet it was useful for thick-headed minds incapable of grasping the obvious reality of the Divine nature. In contrast, Kant, convinced of the incapacity of our intellect to intuit metaphysical realities, declared that he had to suppress knowledge and replace it with belief. Nietzsche declared that, God being dead, all belief was vain, and Freud, denouncing the illusory character of all religious statements, posited the scientific process as the sole source of truth. As for Derrida, in "Faith and Knowledge," he wonders how one can grasp religion today without breaking with the philosophical tradition.[1]

Julia Kristeva has inherited this long debate and has taken over its stakes in a very singular way. It is this way that I would like to set out here by questioning how it is rooted in her work and also in her life. For I am convinced that no serious thought falls from the sky of ideas, nor unfolds abstractly from a disembodied consciousness. As Kristeva herself remarks, there are two levels of language: symbolic and semiotic, conceptual and impulsive. As Nietzsche rightly saw, understanding a thought requires exploring its genealogy. Let us try to see how the need to believe and the desire to know were born and unfolded in her mind.

I. The Need to Believe

For Kristeva, "the incredible need to believe" has its roots in a dual identification: the identification with the mother, which gives the child the original fusion of the amniotic environment and then surrounds him with an unconditional love; and the identification with the "loving father of individual prehistory" of which Freud speaks: the lover of the mother, having the characteristics of both parents, whose loving authority soothes primary anxiety.[2] The father will then take on another role in the oedipal function, allowing the child to become an autonomous subject. While Freud, who did see these early identifications with the parents, tends to disregard them by classifying them under the label of a "primary narcissism," without object, Kristeva thinks that one cannot thus throw the baby out with the bathwater and insists on the permanence of these two identifications in a sublimatory process that may eventually lead to the "oceanic feeling" mentioned by Romain Rolland, or else to the "other *jouissance*," feminine, mystical, which according to Lacan transcends phallic *jouissance*.[3]

Freud did understand this double process, but in various writings and in his correspondence with Romain Rolland, he scrapped it in favor of the Oedipus complex, the sole access, according to him, to the detached maturity of adulthood and object desire.[4] He did, however, honestly acknowledge his inability to explore "the 'black continent' of femininity," which he regarded as narcissistic; or to understand "the oceanic feeling" that might be for him, as Kristeva suggests, the dark continent of motherhood.[5]

Leaving aside these theoretical questions, addressed in 2007, to turn to more personal comments, Julia Kristeva returned in 2014 to the theme of "the need to believe" in a book written with her husband: *Marriage as a Fine Art*. Referring to her family, she writes: "And to my own family, whom I don't forget, and who surrounded me with love. This 'portmanteau' word should here be understood as a *linkage* that instills in the child the indispensable *trust* that I call the 'need to believe': the foundation and condition of the 'desire to know,' which is then in a position to scrutinize the 'belief' to the point of abolishing it if need be."[6]

Similar texts are found in her recent autobiography, in which she describes the strong relationships she has had with her two parents.[7] Deeply "connected" with a loving mother and a tender father, Kristeva was installed in a psychic bisexuality that enabled her to face exile, the world, and all its questions.[8] This impregnable reliance has never failed her.[9] It is therefore not surprising to find it, decades later, in the background of her analyses of Teresa of Avila and the Passion of Christ. There, she reveals herself at once as a theologian and a psychoanalyst, who prolonged somewhat boldly a few milestones left by Freud as unfinished sketches.

Thus she emphasizes the importance of the "need to believe" in Teresa of Avila, for whom she has great esteem and affection.[10] Faced with the experience of the Spanish mystic, she admits: "the faith I never had may not be so far distant," and further on: "As for so-called atheists like me, we are just as susceptible to other, mostly violent delusions."[11] At the end of her book, after reading Diderot's work on the Portuguese nun, she tells him: "I'm asking you to make your object of incredulity—God—into an object of interpretation."[12] By calling herself an atheist, Kristeva does not propose to exclude the divine, but, rather, to suspend the ideas concerning it in favor of a new interpretive discourse: "Along with Freud, we dare say that 'god' is analyzable,"[13] she writes.

For her, "God is unconscious," by which she means inaccessible to our consciousness but not nonexistent, and she undertakes to analyze him through Theresa's psyche.[14] She does so by questioning the fiction that the Spanish mystic constructs to explain the development of prayer as a love affair with God. "Indeed, it is by means of a fiction involving water . . . that the nun describes her immersion in the Other and her sense of losing the boundaries of the self."[15] This water, she also says, symbolizes the meeting of the earthly orante with her divine Heaven from which it pours, and through its enveloping and caressing power expresses the fiction of a loving touch, of a liquefying contact that dissolves body boundaries and generates a unifying state.[16] What Teresa has experienced, she tells us, is a kind of immanentism of the divine: "Over a few decades of monastic experience Teresa rewrote, after her fashion, the thousand-year-old story of God the Father, which Jesus had already done much to transfigure. . . . In her visions, through her pen, the tyrannical Beloved, the stern Father, *Père-sévère*, softens into a Father so tender as to become an ideal alter ego, kind and rewarding, who draws the ego out of itself: ek-static. . . . What's more, He is in her, He is her as she is Him."[17] "Know yourself in Me!" he had said to Teresa, during an ecstasy. Here we are poles apart from the "divine tyranny, irrevocable, unquestionable, which supports the mass orthodoxy of fundamentalist Islam."[18]

Returning to her atheism, Kristeva explains that it does not consist in a fight against religion, but, rather, in a withdrawal of her intelligence "into the tenderness of the connection to the other."[19] This atheism, both sober and modest, is experienced through the relation to the mother.

This atheism, tender and suspicious, is not the enemy of "the need to believe." It has a lot to do with the apophatism of the mystics who, in Christianity, went from Clement of Alexandria in the second century, to Gregory of Nazianzus and Gregory of Nyssa, the Pseudo-Dionysius, in the fourth and fifth centuries, to Master Eckhart and the Rhenans in the thirteenth century, and culminated in the Spanish mystics of the sixteenth century: Garcia de Cisneros, Francisco de

Osuna, Bernardino de Laredo, John of Laredo, John of Avila, John of Segura, Luis de Granada, Luis de León, and of course (last but not least) John of the Cross.[20] To whom I could add the long line of Buddhist and Vedantine mystics who, like the former, extol the Absolute as incomprehensible, unrepresentable, unspeakable, but deliciously vacuous. "God is unknowable," they say. "God is unconscious," Kristeva writes. These qualifiers seem very close to each other, so that "mysticism can go so far as to open the path of atheism"— and vice versa I would add.[21]

As for Christianity, Kristeva does a psychoanalytic reading of the Passion of Christ, starting from Freud's essay "A Child Is Being Beaten" (1919), which portrays the fantasy of a son-father beaten to death.[22] Coupling the annihilation of the kenosis mentioned by St. Paul[23] with the words of Jesus reported by St. John—"The Father and I are one. . . . Who has seen me has seen the Father. I am in the Father and the Father is in me"[24]—she interprets the crucifixion of Christ as the perfect staging of "the death of God," hammered out since Nietzsche by atheists of all stripes.

The fantasy of the father beaten to death in the divine person of his son, she says, is "a cornerstone of Christian faith."[25] Jesus is a brother beaten to death, suffering like us, with whom we can identify, but is also, to the extent that "He that hath seen me hath seen the Father," a father beaten to death, deprived of his omnipotence, whom we can agree with.[26] The kenosis of the Son is also that of the Father, who is consubstantial with him, the suspension of his paternal function in its overarching and constraining side. Before being a Nietzschean fantasy, the death of God is, thanks to Christ, a theological reality that, for Christians, opens a door, traces a path, marks a crossing.[27]

Because the domineering figure of the Father disappears, any will to power, the ideal of the superman, also dissolves, replaced by an egalitarian space of love and freedom in which man can be deified because there God is made human, and even, Kristeva says, "feminized by the suffering he undergoes."[28] On the Cross, Jesus Christ, who "became a subtle antidepressant for abandoned, unhappy humanity,"[29] deprives God of his castrating and domineering ornaments to offer a suffering and compassionate image of Him, acceptable, lovable, an image that has an incomparable cathartic power, a power that Buddhism itself, though it did tackle suffering, does not offer.

However, Kristeva's analysis seems, there again, to come up against the affirmation of an atheism that she has never ceased to claim.[30] Yet, let us insist on this point, Kristeva gives it a particular meaning.[31] While Freud claimed to venerate "our God, Logos,"[32] Kristeva, although a psychoanalyst convinced of the importance of the word as a therapeutic tool, distances herself and claims to be the atheist of this verbal God.[33] The reason is that she experiences as a girl, then as a woman, and as a mother, the psychic importance of this femininity, which Freud described as a "black continent," unknown to him, but which for her is the abyssal hidden continent of the body. Her atheism, like "the need to believe," is rooted in this soil of flesh that evades description.

In the landscape of contemporary atheism, hers is singular. If she were an atheist, as were Nietzsche and Freud yesterday, or as Michel Onfray and Régis

Debray are today, she would not have taken part in the meeting of Assisi in 2011, would not have found so appealing Benedict XVI's opening to unbelievers, and would not have written *Teresa, My Love*.[34]

Although she claims to be an atheist, Kristeva does not close the door to religious imagination. On the contrary, she opens it, and some of her novels like the poems written by apophatic mystics (Eckhart, Suso, John of the Cross), confirm that. Like these poets, Kristeva wants to leave access to the "umbilicus of dreams" free, and to give spiritual rights back to illusion and fiction,[35] which is to say, to base the capacity of creation on the "the space of reverie or illusion that the mother leaves open to her young child."[36] It is this space—which Rilke called "the interior space of the world"—that "the need to believe" opens for her.[37]

However this need to trust people, which for her is rooted in the unfailing love of her mother and father, was reversed in a singular way on the day she became a mother. After two painful abortions, decided on with her husband, she decreed one day, together with him, that the time had come for her to become a mother, which she did with great pleasure. However, fate caused the project to take an unexpected turn. David, the boy she bore, having developed psychomotor disharmony and a disturbing neurological disease, she formed with him a maternal reliance, both attentive and combative. It was now her son who "needed to believe" in her, and she passed on to him, against the winds and tides of crises, comas, and anxieties, the love received from her parents. It was an obstacle race that she then started along with her husband: a fight, she says, which "stood me in vertical time, a continuous present, a 'now' in which the demands of sur-vival make the rest of life seem secondary and unreal."[38]

With the help of her husband, her parents, and her parents-in-law, but all the same still under a sword of Damocles that kept bringing alive the proximity of death, she forged for herself this sturdy character that will make her later define herself as an "energetic pessimist."[39] The "need to believe," to trust other people, was then reversed for her into a "need to love," to inspire confidence, and in this maternal feeling she felt herself to be the strong link of a long transmission of love.

II. The Desire to Know

For Freud, it is by solving the Oedipus complex that the child, thanks to the paternal figure and the prohibition of incest, breaks away from the mother and from his or her autoeroticism in order to gain autonomy and to attain the objectal relation. Kristeva does not reject such an analysis,[40] but she adds another that Freud seems to ignore. For her, the psychic maturation of the child is also rooted in a certain detachment-disinterest of the mother regarding her child, a dispassion that allows the child to detach himself or herself too. In this, she joins the Kleinian analysts who, she says, have insisted a lot on the "matricide"—imaginary and symbolic—essential to autonomy and access to language.[41] "It is through a progressive dispassion and/or by her aptitude for sublimation that the mother lets the child interiorize and represent *not the* mother . . . but *the absence of the* mother. A sort of *symbolic matricide* thus occurs."[42] "By calling the experience of motherhood *maternal reliance* and teasing out its complexity, I endeavor to show that it transforms the primal violence of the mother-child tie, that *ab-jection* we mentioned earlier, into a 'tender stream.'"[43] Pointing to one of the shortcomings of the oedipal theory, she adds "We lack a modern discourse of maternal love."[44] "The 'mystery' of maternal passion . . . [helps] the new arrival, that ephemeral stranger, to develop his originality."[45]

Kristeva's mother was an academic who had studied biology but who then chose not to teach but to devote herself to her children. However, she had made this choice without frustration or guilt and had ensured that culture was central to her family. This concern was part of a particular context for her, that of a literate Bulgaria, the only country in the world to celebrate the alphabet—on 24 May, the Saint's day of the brothers Cyril and Methodius, who had invented it to translate the Holy Scriptures into Slavonic, the old Slavonic language. In her autobiography, Kristeva tells us how, from the age of seven to twenty-four, she participated in this festival of culture in which each held in his or her hand a letter of the alphabet.[46] She also reports what the event, repeated annually, meant for her: "The festival itself transmitted an obvious, unconditional certainty: in order to *be*, it was absolutely necessary to take your place in the alphabet, by doing well at school, college, and the rest. But at the same time you were summoned, through the same cultural tool, to *play* on your keyboard, to say 'I' by appropriating the letters, by writing."[47]

For Kristeva, appropriating the letters also meant appropriating knowledge, allowing herself to be pervaded by this desire to know that they hold in them, a desire that led her to learn foreign languages, to explore the world's literary heritage, to think, and then to contribute to the enrichment of this heritage.[48] To do all this meant that she was expected to respond to the educational desire for autonomy that her mother held for her.[49]

In *Murder in Byzantium*, Kristeva, who calls herself Byzantine,[50] will make of the character Christine a barely disguised avatar of her mother who had displayed a love without control: "a woman who was never a weight to anyone—not even to her daughter, can you imagine?"; "Because really it was we who weighed her down, because we relied on her. But this woman let us believe that she was content to open a path for us, that she didn't suffer or [inflict any] scratch and gave nothing but a caress. 'I didn't tie you down, I gave you wings.' That was her modest motto."[51] At the death of her mother, Kristeva, who had not cried at the funeral of her father because there was so much rage in her, cried for ten days on end.[52]

The "desire to know," stimulated in Kristeva by her mother, was also stimulated by her father, but in another way. Since he was opposed to communist ideals, he encouraged her to study foreign languages and to broaden her culture in a kind of "cosmopolitan philosophy," away from the closed ideology of Marxism-Leninism. He said, he wanted "to get his daughters out of the guts of hell."[53]

However, his orthodox faith came into conflict with the scientific rationality of his wife, who would yield in front of the religious zeal of her husband. "It was left to me," Kristeva said, "to brandish the torch of argument! . . . My mother would rebuke me for going too far, but deep down she was quite pleased to have a daughter who dared to be her spokesman. . . . She had no idea that between him and me, it was total love!"[54] "I'd never felt jealous of my mother, convinced as I was that my father preferred me to her and to everything."[55]

What her mother could not imagine was her deep identification with her father, whom she actually resembled physically: an identification she will later call "my toxic attachment" and that she will consider to be the cause of her bisexuality.[56] This love "to the death," both oppositional and unconditional, is undoubtedly one of the primary sources of the particular atheism professed later by Kristeva: a mystical atheism that will encourage her to write *Teresa, My Love*, to dedicate the book to her father, and to write: "Might psychoanalysis be one of the variations of theology? Its ultimate variation, *hic et nunc*?"[57]

That was how Stoyan Kristev, a believer and theologian mocked by his daughter, succeeded post mortem in turning her into an atheistic theologian, a "Christian atheist" as Catherine Clément prefers to call her. When he died in a Bulgarian hospital, a death that she regarded as an assassination, Kristeva, who had kept voluminous packages of his letters, experienced an overwhelming feeling of loss.[58]

She then began a true scriptural therapy by writing the first of her metaphysical novels: *The Old Man and the Wolves*.[59] Her father appears there as an old professor who kept in hiding under the pseudonym of Septicius Clarus and who ends up being killed by the wolves of Santa Barbara: those hungry carnivores, implacable, creeping everywhere, "wearing people's faces."[60] Returning to the murder in her autobiography, she analyzes how the death drive is unleashed.[61] Kristeva will then confront this death drive in her novel *Possessions*, in which a decapitated mother-wife appears, but especially in the texts she wrote about jihadism, well known for its decapitation practices.

If we leave Kristeva's childhood and progress further in her life's course, we witness, as soon as she arrived in France, the progressive evolution of her "desire to know" throughout a multifaceted literary and psychoanalytic career. Plunging greedily into French culture, she discovered structuralism while devouring Camus, Sartre, and new novelists. She then attended the seminars of Lucien Goldmann, Tzvetan Todorov, and Roland Barthes who introduced her to René Girard and Philippe Sollers. Preparing her *doctorat d'état*, *Revolution in Poetic Language*, she saw Lévi-Strauss regularly and he encouraged her work, as did various researchers who became her friends, among whom Françoise Héritier.[62] Her *doctorat d'état* earned her Barthes's praise: "The novel of today is this dissertation."[63]

In fact it was the group contributing to the journal *Tel Quel* that brought her the most favorable environment for the blooming of her "desire to know." There, she met Jacques Derrida, Michel Foucault, and Umberto Eco, and many intellectuals who gravitated around its creator, Philippe Sollers.[64] Thanks to him, her "desire to know" went beyond the scope of her intellectual pursuit and took on a biblical significance, as sexual curiosity and fulfillment. For her, to know became a means to vibrate sensually, to love in a sentimental way, to experience erotic pleasure, and to prolong this enjoyment on a daily basis in the delights of conversation, a stimulating discussion, often full of barbed remarks.

She ended up marrying Sollers and found with him that family "reliance" that her departure from Bulgaria had deprived her of.[65] With him, Kristeva harmoniously combined her "need to believe" and her "desire to know." He revealed to her Freud's writings and introduced her to Lacan, whose seminar he attended with her. Surprised at first by the histrionics of the guru whom she considered to be exhibitionist, theatrical, a little hysterical, she nevertheless clung to him out of curiosity, she said, and eventually became his friend.[66]

A good idea indeed! Lacan opened doors for her, not only to some of Freud's intuitions but also, beyond those, to Christian mysticism. It is he who introduced her to Teresa of Avila and allowed her to discover a form of enjoyment different from that usually listed by the theorists of psychoanalysis. The Lacanian theory on "*l'autre jouissance*," different from the phallic pleasure—the other pleasure, that of the Other, typical of women, more and more desiring, inexpressible—helped her to leave aside judgments that many psychologists, after Freud, pass on religious illusions in general and mystical hallucinations in particular. Lacan's positive view of Teresa's experience guided and supported hers.[67]

Thanks to Lacan, as she renounced the political commitments that had once tempted her, she moved gradually towards "the microcosm of the 'talking cure.'"[68] Her "desire to know" then focused on herself, her past, her unconscious, which she undertook to explore by going to see a German psychoanalyst who attached great importance to the mother tongue: Ilse Barande. On her couch, she experienced how "to relive my Bulgarian childhood on the analyst's couch."[69] But she relates how she got engaged, unconsciously, in a real intellectual matricide. At a congress of psychoanalysts on the "maternal," she appropriated the luminous analyses of her analyst without recognizing they were hers.[70] Realizing afterward how ungrateful she had been she tried to apologize, but it was too late. Her other master and supervisor in psychoanalysis, whom she followed until he died, was André Green. He introduced her to Melanie Klein, Winnicott, Bion, and the theories of language, semiology, cognitivism, and biology.

Recognized and encouraged as she was by Sollers, Barthes, and Green, Kristeva gave herself other guides in her exploration of languages, including Roman Jakobson, a great Russian linguist whom she met in Paris. He drew her attention to the frequency changes in her voice when speaking Bulgarian, English, or French. She also met Émile Benveniste. For her, he is "the first linguist to examine the place of language in the Freudian unconscious; he stressed the *disruptive forces* of the drives."[71] One last meeting with him, shortly before his death, marked her deeply. Since the linguist couldn't speak any more, he wrote on Kristeva's chest with his index finger: "THEO," a word that she asked him to write on a sheet of paper. "Did he mean God? It was a mystery. Until I discovered that he had been schooled in the Talmud as a child."[72] She then established a connection between "THEO" and "YHWH." "Could our final meeting have also been the scene of a transmission?"[73]

For Kristeva, Benveniste, like Stoyan, was a father, a mediator, a transmitter who directed her "desire to know" towards an unknowable, an unspoken element that she describes as "unconscious": an unconscious that she strives to analyze and interpret in several works, mainly in *Teresa, My Love*. And Theo will return to save her double, Nivi, in danger of drowning, in her novel *The Enchanted Clock*.[74]

I cannot close this section, however, without mentioning another figure who played a great role in Kristeva's "desire to know": that of her son David. Since her child was in a situation of disability, she had to fight for him with all the affection of a mother, and he made her "apprehend worlds that previously, before he came along, were opaque or closed to me."[75] These worlds are particular to handicapped people, to analysands, and beyond them to all the living who in one way or another suffer from an existential deficiency.

"David's thisness, his singularity," she writes, "is my one positive, my ultimate value. My loving empathy led me to guess that despite his neurological troubles he had a sufficiently fine ear to make music."[76] By saying so, she recalls Duns Scotus, her favorite philosopher, who put *ecceitas* at the forefront of his concerns.[77] "For the medieval theologian, truth did not reside in general ideas nor in the opacity of matter, but in *this* man here, *this* woman, *this* object. . . . In Scotist ethics, *thisness* is the only positive, the only 'value.'"[78] In any case, it was for Kristeva the only true answer to the "desire to know." Thanks to David, to his contagious vitality, to his dream world, and his smile, Kristeva found herself in keeping with "this urgency-emergency of life."[79] After which, she included her son in most of her novels under various names: Alex, Jerry, Paul, Stan.

III. The Need to Believe and the Desire to Know

The details of her journey, which Kristeva gives us in *Je me voyage*, reveal to us how, in the same way as the "need to believe" and in connection with it, she experienced a "desire to know" that gave rise to the impressive literary production that we know today. She has always sought to stand between this need to trust and the desire to understand, without sacrificing one phrase to the other. Let's try to see how they mix in her work. Reading the book she wrote in 1998 in collaboration with Catherine Clément, *The Feminine and the Sacred*, may help us in this. It reveals that, at the time Kristeva bathed in a psychoanalytic universe that, in the wake of Freud, had few believers, but that at the same time she wanted to "open the dossier on the Christian female mystics."[80] She began to explore the life and work of Teresa of Avila, which she did more extensively a few years later in *Teresa, My Love*. In Angela of Foligno's work, she discovered "the latencies of a mystic atheism."[81] She also united with Marina Warner—who, in 1976, wrote a eulogistic book on Jesus' mother, *Alone of All Her Sex: The Myth and Cult of the Virgin Mary*—and said she was ready to fight for *her* Virgin in whom she saw an unthinkable side of femininity and an exclusive model of a devoted mother.[82] Catherine of Siena too, in spite of her anorexia, appeared to her to be a "remarkable woman who preached the passionate love of God."[83]

This exchange with Clément confirms the existence that we have found in Kristeva of a singular atheism. Her friend, who defines herself as a "Jewish atheist," describes Kristeva as a "Christian atheist": a rather concise definition but nevertheless an interesting one in that it situates her at the crossroads of psychoanalytic suspicion and Christian faith. Kristeva, as we have seen, is convinced that life can be built only on a primary confidence, but that such trust encourages people to understand, even if such understanding calls into question trust itself.

Caught in the crossfire of her original trust (in the love of her parents and relatives, in the goodness and beauty of life) and her desire to understand (the curiosity and distrust of an exiled migrant, the openness and disillusionment of a Freudian analyst), Kristeva achieved a compromise that led her to call herself an "energetic pessimist": she is pessimistic because she is dispassionate, lucid, bruised, but she is also energetic because she is confident, loved, loving, and potentially active. In doing so, she relates to the great minds of those who have ventured on the frontier between nothingness and being. Like Hegel and Heidegger,[84] she is convinced of the importance of the "negative" in all walks of life, yet she does not go as far as Freud in his pessimism when he states that "the pleasure principle [Eros] seems actually to serve the death drive [Thanatos]."[85] She remains on the ridge between the two abysses of a despairing nihilism and a triumphant dogmatism: a path that the Buddha described as "the middle way," and that Jesus traveled, as evidenced by the two cries of distress and trust uttered on the cross: "My God, my God, why hast thou forsaken me ?"[86] And "Father, into thy hands I commend my spirit."[87] Nisargadatta, the incandescent Hindu sage, said more recently: "When I see that I am nothing, it is wisdom. When I see that I am everything, it is love. Between the two, my life flows."[88] Through these quotations we see that despite the cultural gap that separates them, the mystics of East and West come together.

According to Kristeva, the analytic cure runs along a ridge too: a path of truth whose function is to dissolve the illusions in which the analysand painfully crystallized the desires of his or her ego, but also to cure him or her completely of the injuries produced in him or her by the death drive. When asking herself the question "is psychoanalysis a form of nihilism?" she distinguishes the psychoanalytic theory—the theory of knowledge of psychic objects, which "is part of the nihilist effort to objectify man's being"—from the "analytic language (that spoken by the analysand as well as that spoken by the analyst insofar as the analyst himself remains an analysand)," which "cannot be reduced to objective terms."[89] To her own question, she replies: "In my opinion, therefore, psychoanalysis is the modest if tenacious antidote to nihilism in its most courageously and insolently scientific and vitalist forms. It is the superman's shield and protection."[90]

This is why the death of God the Father, claimed "ad nauseam" by generations of post-Nietzschean thinkers, does not trouble her. She explains: "The death of the Father is also pregnant with the great libertarian potential . . .

only if we can invent fresh versions of the 'loving intelligence' that was once called God . . . the love known as transference is presently making its own modest and markedly unsettling contribution—invented by the still youthful discipline of psychoanalysis."[91] For "it is love that is transferred in the listening we do to the speech, drives, and affects of our patients," she wrote.[92] "There is no way to treat the lovesick except by listening lovingly, a response known as countertransference. The therapist in love with her patient embarks on it because only thus can she pick up the other's truth."[93]

Her autobiography adds: "Via the link of transference/countertransference, analysis heals narcissistic wounds and restores the capacity to love. Through the patient's free association and thanks to the analyst's interpretation, this comes about. Analysis as a state of grace! It's rare, but it exists."[94] For Kristeva, the analyst's interpretation is intended to listen to and translate the repressed traumas, rising to the surface in the free association of the analysand. Such interpretation helps him or her to reach beyond them and makes him or her able to create new links: with humans of course, but also, as did the great Colette, with plants, animals, his or her own animality, and the whole universe.

I would like to note in passing that while the analyst's listening capacity is regarded by Kristeva as "a love of listening," it also includes the interpretive word conceived as "a word of love." "A word of love is often more effective, profound, and durable treatment than electroshock therapy or psychotropic drugs, sometimes it is the only treatment for a condition that is no doubt a consequence not only of our biological nature but also, and *at the same time*, of an inopportune or ill-intentioned word."[95] At the end of *The Enchanted Clock*, Nivi's liberated consciousness gets immersed in a symbiotic universe. The original Eden, enveloping, fusional, the expanding world unfolding in infinite multiverses, the secret, sympathetic limiting family are themes that mix, mingle, and part only to meet anew in the smiling, serene, pure light of a first dawn.

In these discreetly autobiographical texts in which she speaks of detached love and the state of grace, of auroral light and original Eden, Kristeva is a little less atheistic and a little more Christian, a kind of Christian psychoanalyst as Maryse Choisy and Françoise Dolto could be called, a "Christian atheist" says Catherine Clément. Insofar as she defines the analytic countertransference that she practices as a love of listening, Kristeva places it in the context of the Gospel's "agape." This love is not related to its object, it is not the love of the analysand, but in a way a "love of love" on his or her part, the love of God, Saint John would call it.[96]

In *The Old Man and the Wolves*, Kristeva writes: "It's said women don't go in for atheism because they're always in search of an illusion, namely that of a lover who will be both father and mother. But atheism may be a solution for women living in the wilderness bequeathed to them by a dead father."[97] In this desert, which gaped open before her after the murder of her father, Julia-Stephie, a migrant traveler in the novel, claims she has two options: "to hanker after childhood" or "to roam the world."[98] She refuses to choose, or rather, chooses both by trusting "an illusion, namely that of a lover who will be both father and mother" of belief and by traveling in the "dark night" of atheism.[99]

From then on, this Christian atheism with which Clément credits Kristeva makes sense. It is this detached faith that renounces God as one who satisfies all your desires, as an all-powerful idol, in order to join him as an omnicontaining space, the Being of whom Heidegger said he is "the clearing" (*das Offene*), and Spinoza that he loves himself with infinite love, and everything in him. That is why, referring to the God of Teresa of Avila, Kristeva writes that "ideal Fatherhood is no longer punitive for you, but instantly pleasurable and nourishing: it satisfies the person, affirms the advantages of being alive, brings joy."[100]

For Kristeva, "the need to believe and the desire to know, never one without the other, are the universal conditions for humans to be able to speak to each other and to make friends."[101] They are not antinomic—"the 'need to believe': the foundation and condition of the 'desire to know.'"[102] The latter takes root in an original confidence without which it could not arise, and this confidence, tested by this desire, is confirmed. From then on, the potentially mystical "need to believe" and the potentially atheistic "desire to know" can go hand in hand, side by side, like day and night, and lead to a peace that extends far beyond duality and even understanding. In a poem, Saint John of the Cross writes:

> I entered where I did not know
> and I stayed without knowing,
> all science transcending.[103]

But he also writes:

> I went out without being seen,
> my house now being soothed.[104]

Which brings me to a question I would like to ask Julia Kristeva. In the cloud of mystical unknowing in which "the need to believe" and "the desire to know" end up being totally reconciled, is there still room for a "desire to be known"? Do we need then to be looked at by other people in order to exist and to love?

Alain Delaye

L'Université Catholique de L'Ouest
March 2018

NOTES

1. Jacques Derrida, "Faith and Knowledge," in *Acts of Religion* (New York: Routledge, 2001); *Foi et savoir* (Paris: Seuil, 2001).

2. Sigmund Freud, *The Ego and the Id*, in *The Standard Edition of the Complete Psychological Works of Sigmund Freud*, vol. XIX, trans. James Strachey (London: Hogarth, 1961). Julia Kristeva, *This Incredible Need to Believe,* trans. Beverly Bie Brahic (New York: Columbia University Press, 2009), 10–11; *Cet incroyable besoin de croire* (Paris: Bayard, 2007), 37.

3. Sigmund Freud, "On Narcissism: An Introduction," in *The Standard Edition of the Complete Psychological Works of Sigmund Freud*, vol. XIV, trans James Strachey (London: Hogarth, 1961); *Civilization and Its Discontents*, in *Standard Edition*, vol. XXI, trans. James Strachey (London: Hogarth, 1964). Jacques Lacan, *On Feminine Sexuality, The Limits of Love and Knowledge: Encore, The Seminar of Jacques Lacan Book XX*, trans. Bruce Fink (New York: Norton, 1998).

4. This Freud-Rolland correspondence is in Michel Hulin, *La Mystique sauvage* (Paris: PUF, 1993), 29.

5. Kristeva, *This Incredible Need to Believe,* 9; *Cet incroyable besoin de croire,* 35. Freud's atheism is oedipal, it depends on the father. Julia's, she says, *is through the mother*: Freud for a long time protected himself from the "feminine maternal," which he accepted only in his later years and after the death of his mother.

6. Julia Kristeva, *Marriage as a Fine Art*, trans. Lorna Scott Fox (New York: Columbia University Press, 2016), 83–84. She writes in *The Feminine and the Sacred*: God's transfer through Mary's body is "an extraordinary apologia for oblative motherhood, on the brink of primary narcissism: the origin of the love every human being needs to proceed. And the deficiency of same is the sinister source of all depression, if not psychosis." Catherine Clément and Julia Kristeva, *The Feminine and the Sacred,* trans. Jane Marie Todd (New York: Columbia University Press, 2001), 76; *Le Féminin et le sacré* (Paris: Stock, 1998), 125. Some situations illustrate Kristeva's text: the terrible fate of Romanian babies utterly deprived of maternal affection at the time of Ceauşescu, and the experiments on chimpanzees also subjected to a total maternal deprivation by the American army in 1965. See the report made by Peter Singer, *Animal Liberation* (New York: Harper Collins, 2009), ch. 2.

7. See Julia Kristeva, "Intellectual Autobiography," in this volume, 6; *Je me voyage: Mémoires* (Paris: Fayard, 2016), 15–16.

8. Kristeva will plead later for the psychic bisexuality of everybody but also for a sexual singularity: "There are not only two sexes, everyone invents his/her sex in his/her intimacy, that is his/her creativity . . . with a partner, without a partner, with Love etc." Françoise Coblence and Marcela Montes de Oca, "Une Vie psychique est une vie dans le temps: Entretien avec Julia Kristeva," in *La Revue française de psychanalyse* (2017): 357–58 (my translation).

9. As proof: the gratitude expressed in the dedication of *Thérèse mon amour*—"*For my Father*"—and the gratitude felt when, elected honorary doctor at the University of Western Ontario, she declared: "Tears in my eyes thinking of my parents. . . . They would have been so proud! A sacré debt, the debt to one's parents, of which one is never finished paying the sacré dividends." Clément and Kristeva, *The Feminine and the Sacred*, 43; *Le Féminin et le sacré*, 70–71.

10. Julia Kristeva, *Teresa, My Love: An Imagined Life of the Saint of Avila*, trans. Lorna Scott Fox (New York: Columbia University Press. 2014); *Thérèse mon amour: Thérèse d'Avila* (Paris: Fayard, 2008). Teresa of Avila is the author to whom Julia Kristeva has devoted the most space and time and with whom she probably identified herself the most. Perhaps because she found in "La Madre" this maternal fiber that vibrates in her relationships with her son, her students, and her analysands. However, the important transference that she made onto Teresa is not fusional (*psychanalyse oblige*) and she is careful to distance herself from her: by approving the diagnoses of her pathologies, by pointing to her sociohistorical conditioning, by noting the ironic reactions of her psychoanalyst friends, by telling her own erotic emotions, and by calling herself an atheist . . .

11. Ibid., 26, 385; *Thérèse mon amour*, 40, 449.

12. Ibid., 582; *Thérèse mon amour*, 687.

13. Julia Kristeva, "The Contemporary Contribution of Psychoanalysis," in *Passions of Our Time*, trans. Constance Borde and Sheila Malovany-Chevallier (New York: Columbia University Press, 2018), 81; "L'Apport contemporain de la psychanalyse," in *Pulsions du temps* (Paris: Fayard, 2013), 171.

14. Kristeva, *This Incredible Need to Believe*, 26. *Cet incroyable besoin de croire*, 63.

15. Ibid., 53; *Cet incroyable besoin de croire*, 105–6.

16. Kristeva, "The Passion According to Teresa of Avila," in *Passions of Our Time*, 174–76; *Pulsions du temps*, 301–2, 303.

17. Kristeva, *Teresa, My Love*, 12; *Thérèse mon amour*, 23.

18. Coblence and Montes de Oca, "Une Vie psychique est une vie dans le temps: Entretien avec Julia Kristeva," 364 (my translation).

19. Clément and Kristeva, *The Feminine and the Sacred*, 60. *Le Féminin et le sacré*, 99.

20. See St. John of the Cross, *Poems*, trans. Roy Campbell (Baltimore: Penguin, 1951), 46–47.

21. Kristeva, "La Séduction mystique," in *Pulsions du temps*, 466 (my translation).

22. Kristeva, *Teresa, My Love*, 388; *Thérèse mon amour*, 453–54. Sigmund Freud, "A Child is Being Beaten," in *The Standard Edition of the Complete Psychological Works of Sigmund Freud*, vol. XVII, trans. James Strachey (London: Hogarth, 1955).

23. "He, of divine condition, did not jealously hold the rank that equaled him to God. But he annihilated himself (*eauton ekenosen*)." Philippians 2:6–7.

24. John 10:30 and 14:9–10.

25. Kristeva, *Teresa, My Love*, 387; *Thérèse mon amour*, 453.

26. Ibid., 389; *Thérèse mon amour*, 455.

27. Kristeva's approach is similar to that of René Girard on the scenario that is played out in the sacrificial rituals of most religions. A scapegoat is found guilty of the sins of the community and put to death as a result of this imputation. The death of Christ on the cross invalidates this process: He is certainly a victim but an innocent one, and so he abolishes the sacrificial order that presides over the fate of religions and policies of all kinds. With the death of Christ, an innocent victim, the violence that unfolds in the sacred, the prosecution and execution of allegedly guilty victims, loses its legitimacy. To dominate, to kill, to sacrifice no longer makes sense and appeases neither gods nor God since it is He who suffers. It is obvious that He is not an offended and vengeful Creator, but, rather, a loving, suffering, and forgiving Father: the one whom Jesus conjures up in the parable of the prodigal son and whom Saint John describes when he declares: "God is love" (John 4:8). Many Christian theologians went astray in interpreting Christic kenosis as an expiatory process in the face of an offended and righteous God, and many modern thinkers, Nietzschean thinkers among others, followed in their footsteps when they saw Christ's passion as the deadly exaltation of a sacrificial process, whereas it invalidates all kinds of sacrificial theory.

28. Kristeva, *Teresa, My Love*, 397; *Thérèse mon amour*, 465.

29. Ibid, 81; *Thérèse mon amour*, 102.

30. "I regard myself as one of the few remaining atheists on earth," she writes in Coblence and Montes de Oca, "Une Vie psychique est une vie dans le temps: Entretien avec Julia Kristeva," 358 (my translation).

31. Clément and Kristeva, *The Feminine and the Sacred*, letter of January 22, 1997, 33–39.

32. Sigmund Freud, *The Future of an Illusion*, in *Standard Edition of the Complete Works of Sigmund Freud*, vol. XXI, trans. James Strachey (London: Hogarth, 1964), 54.

33. However, one should not be mistaken about this distance. Setting aside Freud's detractors and the smirks of historians about his mythicohistorical reconstructions, Kristeva emphasizes Freud's intention to include psychoanalysis in universal culture. For him, it is not only a therapy offered to disturbed individuals but also a tool to understand and allow the whole human psyche to progress. That is why, despite her reservations, she pleads for Freud's work to be inscribed in the cultural memory of humanity.

34. Julia Kristeva participated in the 2011 interreligious meeting in Assisi to which Pope Benedict XVI invited believers and unbelievers.

35. "Analysis, like illusion, seems interminable. The analyst today is in a position different from that of Freud. . . . What today's analyst must do, I think, is restore to illusion its full therapeutic and epistemological value." Julia Kristeva, *In the Beginning Was Love: Psychoanalysis and Faith*, trans. Arthur Goldhammer (New York: Columbia University Press, 1987), 20–21; *Au commencement était l'amour: Psychanalyse et foi* (New York: Hachette, 1985), 34.

36. Clément and Kristeva, *The Feminine and the Sacred*, 38; *Le Féminin et le sacré*, 65.

37. "*Durch alle Wesen reicht der eine Raum: Weltinnenraum*." R. M. Rilke, *Gedichte 1906–1926*, in *Sämtliche Werke*, vol. 1 (Leipzig: Insel), 683–84 (my translation).

38. See Kristeva, "Intellectual Autobiography," this volume, 73; Kristeva, *Je me voyage*, 152.

39. Kristeva, *Marriage as a Fine Art*, 95.

40. "Identification with this third party separates the child from its jubilant and destructive physical relationship with its mother and subjects it to another dimension, that of symbolization, where, beyond frustration and absence, language unfolds." Kristeva, *In the Beginning Was Love*, 40; *Au commencement était l'amour*, 55.

41. See Kristeva, "Intellectual Autobiography," this volume, 140; Kristeva, *Je me voyage*, 284. "The child must abandon its mother and be abandoned by her in order to be accepted by the father and begin talking." Kristeva, *In the Beginning Was Love*, 41; *Au commencement était l'amour*, 56. See also Julia Kristeva, *Melanie Klein*, trans. Ross Guberman (New York: Columbia University Press, 2001), volume 2 of the "female genius" trilogy.

42. Kristeva, *This Incredible Need to Believe*, 46; *Cet incroyable besoin de croire*, 94.

43. Kristeva, "Intellectual Autobiography," this volume, 90; *Je me voyage*, 188.

44. Ibid, 91; *Je me voyage*, 188.

45. Ibid., 138; *Je me voyage*, 280. However, Kristeva is well aware that the matricide may turn out to be a symbolic infanticide: "Every pregnant woman fantasizes about the death of her baby, but some women, in order to protect their own narcissistic identities, may symbolically murder their offspring. Perhaps we need to invent a new term for them: the Lady Macbeth complex." Kristeva, *In the Beginning Was Love*, 17; *Au commencement était l'amour*, 29.

46. See Kristeva, "Intellectual Autobiography," this volume, 7; *Je me voyage*, 18.

47. Ibid.; *Je me voyage*, 18–19.

48. Which is clearly shown by her important literary production.

49. See Kristeva, "Intellectual Autobiography," this volume, 11–12; *Je me voyage*, 26–27.

50. Ibid., 144; *Je me voyage*, 292.

51. Julia Kristeva, *Murder in Byzantium*, trans. C. Jon Deloguas (New York: Columbia University Press, 2006), 185; *Meurtre à Byzance* (Paris: Fayard, 2004), 283, 284.

52. See Kristeva, "Intellectual Autobiography," this volume, 138; *Je me voyage*, 280. Kristeva's trip seems to be full of the dynamics of several maternities (real and symbolic). Upstream, those of her mother Christine, of Teresa of Avila (la Madre), and of the Virgin Mary (the *Theotokos*). Downstream, those she has experienced and still experiences today with her son David, her students, and analysands.

53. Ibid., 8; *Je me voyage*, 19.

54. Ibid., 8–9; *Je me voyage*, 21.

55. Ibid., 67; *Je me voyage*, 137.

56. Ibid., 56, 58; *Je me voyage*, 117, 119.

57. Kristeva, *This Incredible Need to Believe*, 70. *Cet incroyable besoin de croire*, 132.

58. "I felt myself touch bottom in those days. I thought about exiling myself once again." See Kristeva, "Intellectual Autobiography," this volume, 137; *Je me voyage*, 277.

59. In 1991. See ibid., 52; *Je me voyage*, 108.

60. Julia Kristeva, *The Old Man and the Wolves*, trans. Barbara Bray (New York: Columbia University Press, 1994), 7; *Le Vieil homme et les loups* (Paris: Fayard, 1991), 17.

61. See Kristeva, "Intellectual Autobiography," this volume, 139; *Je me voyage*, 282.

62. Ibid. 32; *Je me voyage*, 68.

63. Ibid.; *Je me voyage*, 67.

64. At the same time, Kristeva confronted the feminism of Simone de Beauvoir and the group of women who gathered around her in Montparnasse. See Julia Kristeva, *Beauvoir présente* (Paris: Fayard, 2016).

65. See Kristeva, "Intellectual Autobiography," this volume, 67–68; *Je me voyage*, 139.

66. Kristeva, *Marriage as a Fine Art*, 94; *Du mariage considéré comme un des beaux-arts* (Paris: Fayard, 2015), 157.

67. See Lacan, *On Feminine Sexuality*.

68. Kristeva, "Intellectual Autobiography," this volume, 37; *Je me voyage*, 78.

69. Ibid., 52; *Je me voyage*, 107.

70. See ibid., 41; *Je me voyage*, 85.

71. Ibid., 47; *Je me voyage*, 98. This led her to postulate the existence of a double level in language: symbolic (its verbal structures) and semiotic (its sensory, instinctual roots). The whole of it produces an "embodied meaning" (the flesh of words). "A stratified concept of significance enables us to understand how logical language, bolstered by infralinguistic (semiotic) representation, can find physical expression. We thus develop a powerful model of the human in which language is not divorced from the body." Kristeva, *In the Beginning Was Love*, 6; *Au commencement était l'amour*, 15.

72. Kristeva, "Intellectual Autobiography," this volume, 50; *Je me voyage*, 102.

73. Ibid.; *Je me voyage*, 103.

74. Julia Kristeva, *The Enchanted Clock*, trans. Armine Kotin Mortimer (New York: Columbia University Press, 2018); *L'Horloge enchantée* (Paris: Fayard, 2015).

75. Kristeva, "Intellectual Autobiography," this volume, 74; *Je me voyage*, 154.

76. Ibid., 81; *Je me voyage*, 167.

77. *Ecceitas*, thisness, singularity, comes from the Latin adverb *ecce:* here is, there is.

78. Kristeva, "Intellectual Autobiography," this volume, 80–81; *Je me voyage*, 154.

79. Ibid., 82; *Je me voyage*, 169.

80. Clément and Kristeva, *The Feminine and the Sacred*, 27; *Le Féminin et le sacré*, 48.

81. Ibid., 37; *Le Féminin et le sacré*, 63.

82. Marina Warner, *Alone of All Her Sex: The Myth and Cult of the Virgin Mary* (New York: Knopf, 1976).

83. Clément and Kristeva, *The Feminine and the Sacred*, 117; *Le Féminin et le sacré*, 118.

84. "Moreover, even the philosopher most attentive to the 'serenity of the being'—Heidegger—does not think of it as devoid of 'negative' but inevitably 'embedded' in 'nothingness.'" Julia Kristeva, "The Contemporary Contribution of Psychoanalysis," in *Passions of our Time*, 78; *Pulsions du temps*, 165–66.

85. Sigmund Freud, *Beyond the Pleasure Principle*, in *The Standard Edition of the Complete Psychological Works of Sigmund Freud*, vol. XVIII, trans. James Strachey (London: Hogarth, 1955), 63; Freud, *Essais de psychanalyse* (Paris: Payot, 1963), 80.

86. Mark 15:34.

87. Luke 23:46.

88. Suyin Lamour, *La Joie d'être* (Paris: Accarias-L'Originel, 2015). See also Nisargadatta Maharaj, *L'Ultime Guérison* (Paris: Almora, 2015).

89. Kristeva, *In the Beginning Was Love*, 59, 60.

90. Ibid., 63.

91. Kristeva, *Teresa, My Love*, 406; *Thérèse mon amour*, 475. "The analytic interpretation is consubstantial with the love of transference/countertransference on which it

rests and which it has to renounce" (Kristeva, *Marriage as a Fine Art*, 94; *Du mariage considéré comme un des beaux-arts*, 157).

92. Kristeva, "Affect, that 'Intense Depth of Words,'" in *Passions of Our Time*, 141; *Pulsions du temps*, 256.

93. Kristeva, *Teresa, My Love*, 66; *Thérèse mon amour*, 84. "Lacan put us on guard: psychoanalysis must not become an 'understanding moralism.' Instead an accompanying—a companionship in love, if I may put it like that. On condition of taking that concept to the edge of the unconscious and of biology, where war, hatred, laughter, and silence play out. A unique companionship, tailored to each individual, to help one become once more capable of forging the ties of love . . ." Kristeva, *Marriage as a Fine Art*, 91–92; *Du mariage considéré comme un des beaux-arts*, 154.

94. Kristeva, "Intellectual Autobiography," this volume, 70; *Je me voyage*, 143. See also the statement that the analyst places "exorbitant confidence in the power of transference and interpretive language" (Kristeva, *In the Beginning Was Love*, 9; *Au commencement était l'amour*, 20).

95. Kristeva, *In the Beginning Was Love*, 49; *Au commencement était l'amour*, 66.

96. "*Ο θεός αγάπη ἐστίν*" (1 John 4:8).

97. Kristeva, *The Old Man and the Wolves* 175; *Le Vieil Homme et les loups*, 257–58.

98. Ibid.; *Le Vieil Homme et les loups*, 258.

99. Ibid.

100. Kristeva, *Teresa, My Love*, 446–47; *Thérèse mon amour*, 522.

101. Coblence and Montes de Oca, "Une Vie psychique est une vie dans le temps: Entretien avec Julia Kristeva," 358 (my translation).

102. Kristeva, *Marriage as a Fine Art*, 84; *Du mariage considéré comme un des beaux-arts*, 141.

103. John of the Cross, *Poems*, 46–47.

104. Ibid., 26–27.

REPLY
TO ROBERT HARVEY AND ALAIN DELAYE

I. A UNIVERSAL ANTHROPOLOGICAL COMPONENT

Robert Harvey interprets my concept of the "need to believe" in light of philosophy and its contemporary debates. Alain Delaye illuminates it with reference to my novels, my personal history, and Catholic spirituality. Their studies bring me back to the genealogy of my work on believing, which I have not sufficiently spoken about and developed up to now, and I welcome their perfect epistemological resonance with my current research.

Each in its specific way, the works of Delaye and Harvey converge in the sense that they offer a veritable panorama of the various aspects of classical and contemporary thought at the crossroads of desire, knowledge, and the need to believe, a panorama that allows me better to situate my hypotheses and understand their scope. Therefore I can only *rebound* in response to their problematics in the attempt to articulate, more clearly than I have done until now, my present preoccupations with their terminology, anchored on the one hand in my psychoanalytic practice and on the other in my attention to certain languages and experiences of modernity.

The *need to believe*, which I understand as a universal anthropological component, is neither an uncertainty nor a hypothesis, and it cannot be reduced merely to the credulous-incredulous duel. It is a truth that "falls upon me" and that I cannot resist, a truth that completely submerges me; vital, absolute, indisputable: *credo quia absurdum*. Like a love, a landscape, a piece of music, a narrative I believe in, lost and fulfilled: an experience, in sum. An experience to situate in my childhood and adolescence, in my marriage with Philippe (considered as one of the fine arts), and in maternity, which continually reveals to me that "no one has yet come to know the structure of the body so accurately that he could explain all its functions" (Spinoza).[1] Delaye rightly emphasizes this, attesting to my writing as a novelist as well as my encounter with the great linguist Émile Benveniste.

The "subjectively sufficient" but "objectively insufficient belief" according to Kant (as Harvey points out) and Heidegger's *clearing* (*das Offene*) (as Delaye reminds us) point toward this horizon of the need to believe, but only Freudian psychoanalysis makes it both an *object of* knowledge and a practice.

Translated from French by Armine Kotin Mortimer.

It is "understood"—or rather, is lived and "transvalued" (Nietzsche)—only in this other, paradoxical experience, psychoanalysis, in which, through the transference/countertransference, the analyst *hears*, in the speaking of the infantile unconscious, the sexuality-language copresence and the *investment* of alterity (of the self and the other). *Investment: Bezetzung* (in German), *cathexis* (in English), *kred* (in Sanskrit), *amuna* (in Hebrew), *credo* (in Latin).[2] "I give to you in expectation of recompense": the nuclear mutuality constitutive of the speaking being.

Freud identifies this neuronal and psychosexual capacity and follows its displacements in the *capacity for representation* and its *cathexis/investment*, which links somatic and memory traces, both free and tied to verbal signs, and produces an endopsychical impression so powerful that it is reflected in the religious myth: the "psychical "revolution" of matter unleashing the "process of thought" that would obtain its recompense in the "beyond."[3] The ultimate result is the repression of the pleasure principle by religion, but also the cathexis of thought—a *jouissance*.

The founder of psychoanalysis points to the investment in "direct and immediate" *Einfühlung* ("becoming one," "identification"—I'll come back to it) with the "father of individual prehistory," an "imaginary" father, who has "the qualities of both parents": dawn of the ego ideal.[4] I insist on the "psychical bisexuality" that Freud attributes to this first occurrence of paternity, and that the clinic confirms: it allows us to envisage a paternal function considerably more subtle than this "obsolete mental formation" denounced by Robert Harvey, which is still parasitical on certain Freudian and Lacanian theories, as well as the unconscious of submissive humanity. He recognizes it in the *believing* and/or anxious *expectation* that "sets the process of the cure in motion."[5] Romain Rolland connects it to the *oceanic feeling* felt for the "maternal container" in early mother-child relations.[6]

When satisfied, the need to believe offers the child the optimal conditions for developing language and thereafter appears as the foundation on which another specific capacity of the speaking being develops (along with so-called "oedipal" desire and revolt): the *desire to know*.

The theoretical fable just elaborated is embodied in the dynamic of the transference/countertransference, which reevaluates the dichotomies of consciousness and metaphysics (body/soul, subject/object, love/hatred, man/woman, life/death), when it doesn't sweep them away, and favors the transformations of psychosexuality that permit the new beginning of psychic life.

Language is not alone in requiring the reciprocal investment of the two protagonists of speaking, as the linguistics of *enunciation* maintains. In this respect, it is important to note that the father of the theory of enunciation, Émile Benveniste, is also the author of *Indo-European Language and Society*,[7] which argues that the "seme" *investment* of the Latin "credo" has its root in the Sanskrit *kred/strada*. The constitutive alterity of the *speaking being* is sketched initially in the mother-child drive investment, in their *reliance*. The mobility of the investment-disinvestment and their interruptions punctuates the psychism understood as *life-and-creativity*, just as its ordeals and catastrophes are translated into symptoms—neurosis or psychosis.

I thank Alain Delaye and Robert Harvey for having insisted on the specific framework of my understanding of the "need to believe" *tributary to psychoanalysis*. The history of religions uses and develops this anthropological dimension of the hominid link but is not reduced to it, and I make no claim for such a reduction. In the history of religions and of the sacred, the different versions of the *divine* are expressed in innumerable sublimities and catastrophes, interpreted by other approaches and disciplines, which could however benefit from this psychosexual dimension of the *need to believe* that I am sketching and that I propose for their purposes as well.

II. Identity: Cult or Interrogation

An idea and a practice of personal *identity* have taken shape in Europe as nowhere else. From the "I am the one who is" by Moses listening to the voice of an unnameable Other (Exodus 3:14), taken up by Jesus (John 8:34), then by Saint Augustine who, relaying the Greek miracle, affirmed: "I have become a question to myself," and continuing to the ferment of the Renaissance and the Enlightenment. Both *cult* and *interrogation*, this idea and this practice have led to an event, also without equivalent: when the Greek-Jewish-Christian culture "cut the thread of religious tradition" (see Tocqueville and Arendt) and inscribed its "values" in the paradigm of the "rights of man." Consequently, the new foundation of humanism demands, imperatively in my opinion, the reevaluation of this heritage—including the "need to believe." And its route necessarily passes through Jerusalem (which called out to Harvey, quite rightly), whatever the sociopolitical conflicts shaking up that part of the world today.

***

I know Islam only through secondhand sources, but it seems to me possible to link the death-dealing symptoms of its radicalization to certain interpretations according to which Allah is closer to the God that Aristotle defines as "First unmovable mover" at the periphery of the universe than to the "paternal function" of the biblical and evangelical Creator.[8] The political events of Islam throughout History have modulated, even altered, the meaning of the Koranic message, and when the mysticism of Ibn Arabi (1165–1240) introduced the "*nafs*" or psyche, the relation of man to God could thenceforth be written in terms of "love" and "nothingness." This other vision of the "need to believe" of a mystical Arabic poet, translated into French, so touched an adolescent girl ready to leave for the jihad—who was being treated at the Maison des Adolescents at the Cochin Hospital in Paris, where I had moved my University of Paris 7 seminar on the "need to believe"—that she quit the burqa, returned to the language courses she had been cutting, and began her studies to become a caregiver. This Sufi mystic and his new reader reminded me of Barthes writing that "only the fullness of language" can respond when "the emptiness of the divine threatens."[9] And I add: the overfullness too. Delaye's insistence on "female jouissance" in Christian mysticism, notably in Teresa of Avila, but also in mobilizing the feminine side of men, fully resonates with my implication with adolescents of both sexes tempted by the "holy war."[10]

***

Freud's Copernican revolution joins in this multiple tradition—Greek, Jewish, and Christian, with its Muslim graft, which it transvalues ceaselessly—even to the scandalous *Moses and Monotheism* (1939). The analysand cathects the analyst, and the need to believe instigates the transference/countertransference, so that the psychoanalytic process will elucidate the sadomasochistic components of the needs and desires. And all without sparing the religious and secularized illusions that subtend the so-called neurotic *Unity*, the *One* of the *parlêtre* (the speaking being) constructed on the refusal of "his human drives of aggression and self-aggression."[11]

Proletarian fraternity seems to have liquidated religion, but the "need to believe" has in fact been displaced onto totalitarian ideology and the death drives onto the prison phenomenon. Today in France, the "yellow vests" believe neither in parties nor in republican institutions and values, they "want to live," converse, and be heard, some of them even search, in vain, for a father among fraternal spectacles. Their war has not (yet?) found a clear and intelligently constructed language. Will it ever, in the era of tweets and selfies? Some believe only in "purchasing power," others in the erotization of destructiveness. And the political, in suspension, withdraws more than ever from inner experience. Another interval in History where the "need to believe" is awaiting the "desire to know."

***

My "Christian" or "singular" atheism (as Delaye senses) is situated in this Greek-Jewish-Christian sphere of which we are not proud enough, perhaps because we have not yet analyzed its summits and its abjections. As concerns my "mysticism"? My reply to Delaye is simple and naïve: the desire to know, for me, is inscribed in the psychoanalytic practice, backed up by the "need to believe" (to *invest*). It is also present in the writing of my novels, where the imaginary is crossed with thought. This state of "*a-thought*" suits me.[12]

I concede that such is not the mystical way of John of the Cross. But "my" Teresa of Avila, who defined herself as a businesswoman, affectionately revolted against the annihilation of "her little Seneca" (the nickname she gave to John) in a probably sadomasochistic asceticism: "The extreme charm of your fraternity frightens me"—"*Espantada estoy de este encontamento de Fray Juan de la Cruz*" (letter 247), she writes.[13] Did this Carmelite realize that her own *ravishments* were inseparable from the *accounts* she gave about them in order to be heard? "To fabricate *this fiction*" ("*hacer esta fiction*" in *The Way of Perfection*). To believe, then, in order to make known.

As for me, make myself heard, what for? "To be looked at"? No. Nor to be *known*, even less to be "seen" (I avoid the media, I don't trust them). But certainly to *invest myself*, curious to *understand*—to analyze ceaselessly—the multiverse of freedom.

III. Metamorphoses of Parentage

Harvey's fine irony echoes my eternal adolescence rebellious to *patriarchy*, still present and always abusive; and I am with him when his irony leads him to "seriously [consider] that matriarchy might make for a worthwhile experiment in the irreligious reeducation of our species."

The Freudian analyst, man or woman, works today with a new version of the *paternal*, an area that Harvey explores elsewhere.[14] Neither a totem animal, nor Laius-Oedipus, nor Abraham-Isaac, nor Jesus and his Father, in the love-hate of the transference the father is not only loved and hated, put to death and resuscitated, but literally atomized on our couches, and nevertheless incorporated . . . by the analysand. As in the primal scene? Why not, if one thinks of the explosion of identities and norms in which the coupling of the man and the woman breaks the community (Freud) and rejoins the zenith of rebirth and procreation.[15]

It is this permanent dissolution-recomposition, this affinity of life with death that the analyst sees herself as guarantee of, that makes possible the treatment of drug addictions, somatizations, criminalities, and other borderlines. The subject of the "need to believe" presents with these "new maladies of the soul":[16] henceforth she puts on a paradoxical identity, which may also bring to mind the Brownian movement of Pollock's "drippings," titled *One*.[17]

Where has the One gone if the beginning/self-beginning has become a dissemination? Am I still One when I analyze or when I am an analysand? Certainly, yes; my identity exists ("There is something of the One") but remains undecidable, deprived of an immobile center, and prey to death-dealing repetitions.[18] A bit like a piece of serial music, or like a dance improvised though sustained by an underlying order. Neither "dead father" nor "Führer," authority doesn't disappear in the analytic cure. No more does it disappear in a society in mutation. It is disseminated in the permanent adjustment of the two parents, charged with reinventing the manner of raising-educating-transmitting (and transmitting themselves) to their progeny, in these new theaters of fecundity.

A veritable Harlequin's coat is taking shape, the improvisations of some borrowing from the models of others and vice versa, interfering, innovating, disastrous, and festive, in which singular, specific parentages appear. It is important to accompany each family, adoption, filiation project with a personalized attention, on a case-by-case basis. As usual? More than ever.[19] Without losing contact with the ungraspable, unperishable need to believe. Last rampart against the rampant transhumanism in the automatization of the species.

J.K.

NOTES

1. Benedict de Spinoza, *A Spinoza Reader: The Ethics and Other Works*, ed. and trans. Edwin Curley (Princeton: Princeton University Press, 1994), 156.

2. [*Cathexis* is the English translation of Freud's *Besetzung* in *The Standard Edition of the Complete Works of Sigmund Freud* translated by James Strachey. This volume in The Library of Living Philosophers uses the less abstractly technical term *investment* where possible.—Ed.]

3. Sigmund Freud, "Formulations on the Two Principles of Mental Functioning," in *The Standard Edition of the Complete Psychological Works of Sigmund Freud*, vol. XII, trans. James Strachey (London: Hogarth, 1958), 223 (translation modified); "Formulations sur les deux principes de l'advenir psychique," in *Oeuvres complètes de Freud: Psychanalyse*, t. XI, trans. Pierre Cotet and René Lainé (Paris: PUF, 2009), 17–18.

4. See Sigmund Freud, *The Ego and the Id*, in *The Standard Edition of the Complete Psychological Works of Sigmund Freud*, vol. XIX, trans. James Strachey (London: Hogarth, 1961), 31 (translation modified); *Le Moi et le ça*, in *Oeuvres complètes de Freud: Psychanalyse*, t. XVI, trans. Catherine Baliteau, Albert Bloch, and Joseph-Marie Rondeau (Paris: PUF, 2010), 275. Julia Kristeva, *Tales of Love*, trans. Leon S. Roudiez (New York: Columbia University Press, 1987), 202.

5. Sigmund Freud, "On Narcissism: An Introduction," in *The Standard Edition of the Complete Psychological Works of Sigmund Freud*, vol. XIV, trans. James Strachey (London: Hogarth, 1957), 86 (translation modified from "starts the process of recovery"); "Pour introduire le narcissisme," *La Vie sexuelle* (Paris: PUF, 1997) 92.

6. See Sigmund Freud, *Civilization and Its Discontents*, in *The Standard Edition of the Complete Psychological Works of Sigmund Freud*, vol. XXI, trans. James Strachey (London: Hogarth, 1961), 64.

7. Émile Benveniste, *Indo-European Language and Society*, trans. Elizabeth Palmaer (London: Faber, 1973).

8. Aristotle, *Physics*, trans. R. P. Hardie and R. K. Gaye, in Richard McKeon, ed., *The Basic Works of Aristotle* (New York: Random House, 1941), Bk. VIII, 10.

9. Roland Barthes, "Loyola," in *Sade, Fourier, Loyola* (Paris: Points Essais, 1971), 78.

10. See Alain Delaye, *La Foi selon Jean de la Croix* (Paris: Carmel, 1975) and *Etty Hillesum: Mystique sans frontières* (Paris: Amalthée, 2014).

11. See Freud, *Civilization and Its Discontents*, 145 (translation modified); *Le Malaise dans la culture*, in *Oeuvres complètes de Freud: Psychanalyse*, t. XVIII, trans. Pierre Cotet, René Lainé, and Johanna Stute-Cadiot (Paris: PUF, 2015), 333.

12. "A-thought" is my way of being in "external inclusion" or "internal exclusion" to genres, communities, disciplines. I have defined mysticism in these terms. See also the chapter on "Blanche ou l'oubli" in Julia Kristeva, *Intimate Revolt*, trans. Jeanine Herman (New York: Columbia University Press, 2002), 217–19; *La Révolte intime* (Paris: Fayard, 1997), 401–5.

13. *The Collected Letters of St. Teresa of Avilia*, trans. Kieran Kavanaught, 2 vols. (Washington: ICS, 2001–2007).

14. See Robert Harvey, *Search for a Father: Sartre, Paternity, and the Question of Ethics* (Ann Arbor: University of Michigan Press, 1991) and *Queer: Repenser les identités*, ed. Robert Harvey and Pascal Le Brun-Cordier (Paris: PUF, 2003).

15. See Sigmund Freud, *Group Psychology and the Analysis of the Ego*, in *The Standard Edition of the Complete Psychological Works of Sigmund Freud*, vol. XVIII, trans. James Strachey (London: Hogarth, 1955), 141 (translation modified); *Psychologie des masses et analyse du moi*, in *Oeuvres complètes de Freud: Psychanalyse*, t. XVI (Paris: PUF, 2010), 80–81.

16. Kristeva, *New Maladies of the Soul*, trans. Ross Guberman (New York: Columbia University Press, 1995); *Les Nouvelles Maladies de l'âme* (Paris: Fayard, 1993).

17. See Julia Kristeva, "La Voie lactée de Jackson Pollock," in *Pulsions du temps* (Paris: Fayard, 2013), 55.

18. [Lacan coined the aphorism "Il y a de l'Un," usually translated as "There is something of the One," in his 1971–1972 seminar. See Jacques Lacan, . . . *or Worse: The Seminar of Jacques Lacan, Book XIX*, ed. Jacques-Alain Miller (Cambridge: Polity, 2018), 110–11.—Tr.]

19. See Julia Kristeva, "Métamorphoses de la parentalité," *Revue française de psychanalyse* 77, no. 5 (December): 1650–57; "Transformations of *Parentality*," in Vaia Tsolas and Christine Anzieu-Premmereur, eds. *A Psychoanalytic Exploration of the Body in Today's World* (New York: Routledge, 2018).

23

Emilia Angelova

ABJECTION AND THE MATERNAL SEMIOTIC IN KRISTEVA'S INTIMATE REVOLT

I. Introduction

Kristeva's concept of "intimate revolt" is first introduced in 1997.[1] It concerns a form of revolt that precisely springs from what is *intimate*: revolt as a form of "questioning" that erupts from within psychic life and overturns it, in contrast to a revolution against an outside regime.[2] Intimate revolt must, then, be understood through its psychoanalytic framing. In psychoanalytic terms, intimate revolt arises because psychic life is driven to persevere, to "relentlessly repeat retrospective return so as to lead it to the limits of the representable/the thinkable/the bearable."[3] Psychic drives thereby rupture the sorts of limits on representation that, in Western philosophy, entail a delimited, unified ego or a linear time that supports its thinking. Intimate revolt instead reveals psychic life as driven by the imaginary and the unconscious: it does not begin in a cause initiated by the ego. One finds oneself in a repetition that ruptures limits, driven by something other than oneself.

Intimate revolt hinges on a distinction and tension central to Kristeva's work and her concept of psychic life. This is the distinction between the *semiotic principle* generative of meaning (negativity) and the symbolic function, which deploys already generated symbols (negations).[4] For Kristeva, semiotic generativity is necessarily copresent with the symbolic function, but, crucially, the semiotic is a transrational and prelinguistic reality that cannot be captured within the limits of rationality or the symbolic order.[5] Intimate revolt erupts when the very semiotic drives that ordinarily generate the symbolic order instead disrupt psychic life and its symbolic order from within. This dissolves symbols and processes of meaning-making, breaching the limits of any discursive structure whatsoever.

This essay traces the psychoanalytic framework and concepts at issue in intimate revolt. I first lay out the basic *logic* of intimate revolt by showing how the tension between the semiotic and symbolic in Kristeva is a matter of a specifically *maternal semiotic* that exceeds symbolization, where, however, the symbolic order can neither negate nor separate itself from the maternal semiotic. This tension drives psychic life to want to return to its maternal semiotic origins, breaching symbolic limits and this separation. I then study the *form* in which this logic is manifest, through Kristeva's discussion of metaphoricity that seeks to figure the semiotic within the terms of the symbolic. This leads to the *abject* as a semiotic material and residue that cannot be symbolized and which disrupts metaphoricity and thereby the symbolic. Finally, I turn to the *process* that drives psychic life to return to a semiotic that cannot be symbolized, namely, melancholy and *traumatism* as the incomplete mourning of maternal loss. This allows me to connect Kristeva to what Levinas calls the "originary traumatism" of the Other.[6] For Levinas, this "originary traumatism" is our opening to the death and alterity of the Other. The connection to Levinas emphasizes that what drives intimate revolt is a relation to alterity that cannot be contained in the symbolic. Kristeva thus sharply diverges from Lacan: intimate revolt is not an egological revolution against symbolic or discursive orders; rather, an identification with the Other erupts within and disturbs symbolic and discursive formations. Kristeva thus stands with Levinas against modernism's tendency to root psychic life in discursive formations, or poststructuralist efforts to reconstruct this modernist myth in new discursive forms (a topic that would have to be taken up in subsequent work).

There are two further introductory points on context and terminology. First, Kristeva's work and the scholarship on it speak of her "turn" from revolution as seeking to overturn symbolic orders to revolt as disrupting symbolization altogether.[7] Revolt always erupts within psychic life; it is always "intimate." I will generally speak of "revolt," with intimacy implied. Second, this contribution to the broader discussion will reveal how the sort of negativity at work in revolt is very different than in revolution. However, instead of discussing negativity against its Hegelian background, I will trace the psychoanalytic sources of negativity through the maternal semiotic, abjection, and traumatism. These psychoanalytic themes become most prominent in Kristeva's 1980s trilogy, *Powers of Horror*, *Tales of Love*, and *Black Sun*.[8] My central focus is *Powers of Horror*, but all three books are involved in her turn to revolt from *Revolution in Poetic Language* (1974). The 1980s trilogy leads to her 1990s trilogy, *The Sense and Non-sense of Revolt*, *Intimate Revolt*, and *Revolt, She Said*, which deepens her concept of revolt.[9] Here, however, discussion is limited to the 1980s work.

II. The Maternal Semiotic, Breaching the Symbolic from Within

While Kristeva's interest in the semiotic and the symbolic is central to *Revolution in Poetic Language*, her 1980s work considerably deepens the role of the Freudian "return" of the maternal repressed in the semiotic. My concern in this section is the basic logic of a *return* from the symbolic to the semiotic, driven by the incompleteness of separation from the mother. This relative and incomplete separation is the specific contribution of *Powers of Horror* to Kristeva's deepening of the Freudian *return* of the maternal repressed in the semiotic (notwithstanding the continuity across the books of the 1980s trilogy, given the role of the dynamic of the mother-child link in her notion of the semiotic). The return of the maternal repressed is refigured in the form of the abject (section III, below), and is central to the process of mourning and melancholy (discussed in section IV). Before drawing out the contribution of *Powers of Horror*, I must first trace the continuity between this book and her earlier view of the semiotic in *Revolution in Poetic Language*.

Revolution in Poetic Language captures the semiotic-symbolic tension by borrowing an important term from Plato's *Timaeus*: the *chora*.[10] We can think of the *chora* as an undivided space-time of becoming that is anterior to social space and time; it is the "bastard child" of reason and is a body in flux. Conceptually, the *chora* serves as the figure of semiotic generativity and negativity. However, it also figures as something material in that the human being at birth is projected out of the *chora*. This is crucial because it lets Kristeva speak of the semiotic negativity inherent in the *chora* as maternal and as an inscription of materiality (for example, a presymbolic that is signified in rhythm, color, intonation, and energy acquired in the womb).[11] It is this semiotic birth in the *chora* as prelinguistic negativity that ties the child to a "wanting to return to origin," classically identified as the maternal body. This semiotic negativity and foundation is the expression of a force and a semiotic field, and inscribes the drives with a significance that is all-pervasive because it is always already underway, mediating the child's relations with others in advance of symbols and negations in language (e.g., saying no *and* meaning no). The semiotic is chronologically and logically anterior to the principle of denotational meaning in language. In contrast, the mind, in the dualist mind/body conception, is a power that must first detach itself from semiotic negativity. It must subdue and master the field of forces in delimited, symbolic negations; it cannot dissolve into a generative, heterogeneous, negativity. That is to say, the symbolic function of language only exists through mastery of the referential meaning of words (negations). The mind, then, works only through abstraction from the givenness of fields such as we find in the *chora*: the mind must step outside of itself to project a transcendent operation of an ideal form (Husserl's *noema*) and a content contained under it, a synthesis or description (*noesis*).[12] However, behind this abstraction, grasping meaning requires grasping the signifying function of the symbol. Because of this, a wanting to "return" to this materiality- or semiotic-based meaning-making, what Kristeva calls the *maternal semiotic*, becomes necessary.

This leads to a central conflict: on the one hand, the symbol and the negation function in language prohibit return to the maternal semiotic since this would overturn meaning. The maternal semiotic is repressed in order to inaugurate social relations that take precedence over it and that are prerequisites for adult life. On the other hand, in the very figuring of meaning in the *chora*, there is a necessity of "wanting to return." It is this conflict that drives a semiotic breaching of the symbolic and, as we will see, drives abjection.[13] This conflict and breaching erupts in a distinctly temporal logic. Insofar as adult life refers back to a moment whose significance is now past, with the dependency upon it supposedly superseded, this foundational operation of the maternal semiotic, with its drives and libidinally invested motility, has no place/time/space to call its own within the social. All the social acknowledges is the mastery of negation as recognized in the syntax and grammar of the proposition and symbols. If the sensuous semiotic foundation were to effect its "return," it would overturn the social, go beyond the limit of what is possible for us in discursive communication. Kristeva accords the semiotic a more basic function of meaning-making than communication in language. For her, its operation is akin to a temporal rhythm, a recursive repetition/return, in part illusory and surreal, which operates "as if" in retroaction (Freud's *Nachträglichkeit*) from the place of the real.[14]

Kristeva's later essay "The Passion According to Motherhood" (2005) illuminates this temporal logic of retroaction by tying it to semiotic motility.[15] Here she argues that the early dyadic relationship between mother and child is the foundation both of the symbolic and for the future subject's capacity to form relationships with others. This semiotic foundation allows for a reflexivity or motility where binary logic has not yet taken place. Early individuation processes are marked by the free passing of opposites into each other (classic examples being the psychical processes of love passing into hate or ego drives into death drives). Semiotic motility assures that future relations are not compromised: the self's relationship to the otherness of the other is already a "reflexive construction" in the very moment it is experienced—it is "as passion, not as emotion."[16] Semiotic negativity is likened to a foundation based on unconscious passions, a "deeper or more archaic, repressed or censored" desire for the primary maternal.[17] Maternal passion and idealization processes, triggered in psychic life to facilitate the separation from the mother, are active in continually (re)investing the operation of the imaginary, a "being on the frontier" of psychic life.[18] That is to say, as the child separates in birth, the mother watches the "object" of her intense desire become another being and, gradually, "a link to the other is constructed" and maternal passion can be (re)directed to the child.[19] The psychic life of the individual achieves independence, but only in relative attachment: "it is from this defusing of passion that maternal love ultimately becomes a force of psychical and vital support."[20] The movement of birth, independence, and separation is retroactive upon this defusing passion, within which there is no separation. This serves to illustrate how, in general, the symbolic order of cleanly separated bodies, and negations, operates in retroaction upon a maternal semiotic that must be repressed—and from which we cannot, in fact, separate.

For Kristeva, this retroaction permanently marks the semiotic as impossible to master through negation in language. It would be wrong, however, to think that this issue of mastery should be understood in terms of any straightforward notion of "action" in the social time of the world. It is not the case that any action *could* master the semiotic—if only it could be more effective, etc. On the contrary, the semiotic is unmasterable and unruly in a much more fundamental sense, one key to the dynamics of intimate revolt since it is the unruliness of the semiotic that ruptures the symbolic from within. Kristeva writes of intimate revolt: "It is not so much in the world of action . . . but in that of psychic life";[21] and that the reality of revolt as psychic, is "not exclusively (*pas exclusivement*) in the world of action."[22] As Beardsworth adds: "The distinction and relation of the 'worlds' of action and revolt cannot be grasped discursively."[23]

Kristeva's *New Maladies of the Soul* (1993) clarifies and deepens this logic of intimate revolt in relation to the maternal semiotic.[24] What Kristeva writes on Freud's case of the Rat Man is illuminating: "my rereadings of Freud enabled me to pinpoint this anonymity, this reversible orality, this nonverbal, impossible-to-represent necrophilia that is *acted out* and that, like an *inaccessible trauma*, characterized the bond between the Rat Man and his mother."[25] She aligns the anonymity of (secondary) repetition with "nonverbal" inaccessible trauma and reversible "orality." Trauma is redefined as the "manifested clash" between "two demands," namely, "the rigorous requirements of the symbolic and the rigorous requirements of excitability."[26] The hysteric is unable to synthesize these demands and "resorts to such compromise" solutions as "anxiety, somatic symptoms, or irreconcilable fantasies."[27] Kristeva here challenges Lacan's formulation that the unconscious is the effect of the signifier (the symbolic): "the Freudian *unconscious* is not a language but a storehouse of drives, the hysterical psyche and its unconscious become a privileged space for recording the transit between the psychic and the extra-psychic."[28] She finds the Freudian unconscious better suited than the Lacanian signifier to founding the mourning processes of the maternal repressed. It would be a "daunting risk" if negation and rejection that underlie symbolic castration were to be taken as rooting the Freudian unconscious "in *mourning* alone."[29] The suffering of the person in the depressive position owes "its benevolent and brutal impact less to its status as a negation than as a *question*," and this allows for opening the Freudian unconscious to the therapeutic benefits of the Kleinians, who place this "at the heart of the capacity to speak."[30]

Kristeva's rereading of Freud allows her to locate a negativity anterior to "symptomatology," that is, anterior to the somatization of the body and to negation (Freud's *Verneinung* as well as Lacan's *Verwerfung* or rejection).[31] Here it verges on where the semiotic bears largely on psychoanalytic practice. For example: "If (and only if) this language can find an analyst who is strong enough, it can turn anal sadomasochism into the ultimate defense against the inaccessible repression represented by the fusion-devouring of the obsessional neurotic and his buried mother."[32] Kristeva is emphasizing a logic of subversion through a negativity, as opposed to negation, that leads to a conversion between the veritable buried mother and the inaccessible trauma and regime of mourning; a logic that nonetheless entails the intervention of a third, such as the analyst, who is, in this configuration, a substitute for the loving, imaginary father (introduced in *Tales of Love* and discussed in many ways since).

As Oliver explains, introducing this splitting of the original mother-child dyad through a relation to the third is "necessary for the transition from the dependence upon the maternal body through the negativity of drive force and then the entrance into signification or language."[33] What is important, for us, is less the consequence of this semiotic-symbolic logic for psychoanalytic practice than the elucidation of this logic and its maternal semiotic source as what drives intimate revolt and the semiotic breaching of the symbolic.

III. Metaphoricity and the Abject as Semiotic Breaching of the Symbolic

We can now deepen this point to see how, for Kristeva, this logic takes form through the semiotic figure of the *abject*. In anthropological and religious contexts, the abject designates what is disgusting, impure, unclean, and must be cast out and rejected. Kristeva appropriates this term and invests it with a psychoanalytic meaning to designate what the subject finds itself drawn to yet cannot grasp: the sort of surreal object that drives the retroaction discussed above as well as what drives retroaction's fantasy that it can master what drives it.

It is Kristeva's theory of the metaphoricity of the maternal in *Powers of Horror* that will now allow me to connect the abject to the maternal semiotic and the semiotic-symbolic tension. There Kristeva diagnoses an "abortive metaphor" at work in Little Hans's phobic relation to the word:[34] his speech is full of unnameables, yet he cannot stop speaking. Language works as an "hallucinatory metaphor."[35] Language concerning the feminine serves as metaphor, naming an unnameable—the sacred, the maternal—that cannot be expressed in language. In doing so it works by paroxysm: it is hallucinatory, language without a signified. The feminine that is thus named is always ambiguous, affective. An affective ambiguity of the feminine serves as metaphor for a sacred that cannot be named in language. This relation of metaphoricity between the sacred and the feminine corresponds to the relation of retroaction between the semiotic and the symbolic. That is to say, the feminine as metaphor is retroactive upon a sacred/semiotic that cannot be contained in symbolic negations.

What is important for our purposes is that Kristeva's discussion of metaphoricity prioritizes "scription" as a theory of "writing" abjection, over and above the structural, anthropological (symbolic) construal of "acts."[36] ("Scription" is her word for inscription when it operates at limits, at borders, and with partial "objects.") Metaphoricity, then, is not a completed, symbolic act. It is an always incomplete scription retroactive upon a semiotic that it never fully grasps. It thus captures the logic of incomplete separation—letting us glimpse this logic in relation to the abject. That is to say, in the metaphoricity of the mother, the abject is what draws this retroaction even as it ensures it can never be complete. The abject thus gives us a new model of the Kristevan negativity and semiotic foundation as transrational poetic reality and precondition of language.

To trace this model in *Powers of Horror*, let me consider its first chapters, which reinstate much of the theory of semiotic significance from *Revolution in Poetic Language*. Kristeva is still bound to the theory that "thetic signification is a stage attained under certain precise conditions during the signifying process."[37] As in Freud and Lacan, these conditions include castration as an initiation into thetic signification, i.e., what allows symbolic enunciation. Following her argument in *Revolution in Poetic Language*, these conditions constitute the subject but cannot be "reduced to this [signifying] process precisely because it [the signifying process] is the threshold of language."[38] What founds the signifying process, semiotic negativity, remains anterior to signification or language. Presumed to be a precondition of language, the semiotic foundation invests the signifying process with a negativity irreducible to any of its acts. Language speaks in denotation and the symbolic operation conditions the subject's ability to "separate himself from the ecosystem into which he was fused, so that, as a result of this separation, he may designate it."[39] Abjection runs against this separation, it pulls the subject back before this separation, and marks the signifying process as not being designatable.

I suggest that in *Powers of Horror* abjection intensifies the overbearing powers of idealization—idealizations that would be dependent on "the subject's ability to separate from the semiotic *chora*," yet the more they are emphasized the more they pull the subject back into abjection, against separation.[40] The ability to separate from the *chora* thus remains irreducible to the ability "to designate an object as real," which "lies in the thetic function of symbolism," as she writes in *Revolution in Poetic Language*.[41] Kristeva will foreground her view on these preconditions of the *chora*—as irreducible and other than the thetic function of symbolism, signifying the real but not as "object," not in a sign structured like a language. It is important to note, however, that in this work Kristeva is engaging with Lacan in this view. Her discussion of the abject involves the Lacanian requirement to designate an object as real. For Kristeva, this becomes a requirement to designate the maternal Thing *and* object of the abjected mother at the borders of the body. This leads to her innovation that what is driving the ego is the abject as the *archaic* maternal that breaches the symbolic—in contrast to the Lacanian view that it is driven by a subject-object correlation that remains within the terms of the symbolic. Briefly, Kristeva arrives at this point through a contrast between *Totem and Taboo* and *Three Essays on the Theory of Sexuality*, aiming to make a correction to Freud and Lacan. She concludes with an expanded notion of primary narcissism.[42] Her focus is on the ability of the speaking being to separate from or enunciate a dynamic object. As she puts it, already in the earliest object relation, we find, as locus of meaning, the early relation to the archaic mother. "By stressing the inherence of language in the human state, by overestimating the subject's having been the slave of language since before his birth, one avoids noting the two moods, active and passive, according to which the subject is constituted in the signifier; by the same token one neglects the economy of narcissism in the elaboration and practice of the symbolic function."[43]

Kristeva charges the Lacanian view with overestimating the subject's having been the slave of language, which is to say, overestimating the primacy of the symbol as negation in language. In contrast to this, she stresses an unacknowledged economy of the sign, without symbol. In the Freudian vocabulary, this "sign without symbol," a pure negativity, is narcissism, an illusion of omnipotence that produces phantasmatic meaning. Kristeva posits, first, a Narcissus who "will always be marked by the uncertainty of his borders, and of his affective valency as well; these are all the more determining as the paternal function was weak or even nonexisting, opening the door to perversion or psychosis."[44] Second, from this uncertainty at borders and affective valency (of love/hate, death/life) in the economy of narcissism, and to compensate for the weak paternal function, she arrives at the deep ambiguity of the "incest prohibition." The social prohibition throws a deep "veil" over primary narcissism as "edenic image," and throws still another "veil" over all the "ambivalent threats with which it menaces subjective identity."[45] For her, the social contract rests on mastery of the logical operation of the symbol and negation in language. Conversely, the mastery of the social order rests on the mastery of negation. This double bind is satisfied, Kristeva adds, "owing to a subjective benefit derived from it [the prohibition] on the level of libidinal economy."[46] The very uncertainty of primary narcissism and the defensive negation against it in neurosis "exploits the affective valency of the subject," who sets himself up "under the aegis of the father."[47]

All of this reveals abjection's unstable logic of dual foundations: the "horror of that dual war, its terror," which Kristeva takes up through what she calls *the borderline case* (on the analyst's couch).[48] The borderline case reveals the residue of a struggle in psychic life, ripe with the negativity of a revolt: that the ability of the subject to sublimate violence through idealization (by transference of love to the maternal other) is correlative to the ability to transform subjective suffering. Narcissism points to abjection as produced in a momentous conversion of the prohibition. Confronting ambivalent threats, and a menace to subjective identity, Narcissus transforms the experience of loss, making it into something else. (Kristeva's interpretation of Narcissus parallels her analysis of ambivalence and loss in the case of Little Hans's "abortive metaphor.") The suffering of the borderline case does not remove the subject from the experience of an ensuing "fear of being rotten, drained, or blocked"—precisely.

To return to our central themes: for Lacan, the symbolic must be anchored in an object that is designated as real, a process rooted in a desire for the desire of the other—in a social other who initiates a symbolic order in linear time. For Kristeva, in contrast, these results concerning loss and the unnameable in her analyses of Little Hans and Narcissus preclude any such anchorage of the symbolic, from either within or outside consciousness. The abject inherently destabilizes the whole process, displacing it toward the archaic maternal, which is archaic precisely in the sense of a mythical principle before the social order and its time, one that must be the principle of that very order and that is disruptive of it.

We can now appreciate the contribution of metaphoricity in *Powers of Horror*: it enables us to see how Kristeva maintains the semiotic *chora* as disclosing "one of the most spectacular shatterings of discourse,"[49] for metaphoricity opens the symbolic to the abject and thereby opens it to the archaic maternal. In this way, the theory of abjection is about "exploding the subject and his ideological limits."[50] This decisively amplifies Kristeva's point in *Revolution in Poetic Language*, that poetic language is not a linguistic code but, rather, is nearer to what we may call a disclosive act in which the semiotic and symbolic are in a constant "dialectical" interplay that "stands for the infinite possibilities of language."[51]

Let us trace how this works by returning to metaphoricity. The key to metaphoricity, we can now see, is that it involves the "return" of the maternal archaic. This return is the "impossibility of losing" maternal loss, the need to hang on to an abject, archaic maternal that cannot (contra Lacan) be grasped in any symbolic order, or even against such an order. In psychoanalytic terms, this points to the interlocking of a dual secret, a space in between two always already interdependent orders. The logic of abjection begins with internal questioning about fears of perviousness (penetration), and points in two directions simultaneously: to two defilements relating to corporeal orifices—the excremental and the menstrual. The Lacanian symbol settles on a narrow mapping of the shaping of the maternal body (becoming the archaic maternal in Kristeva): "neither tears nor sperm, for instance, although they belong to borders of the body, have any polluting value."[52] So Kristeva asks whether the explanation might be delivered by another psychoanalytic approach. Her proposal is that "those *two* defilements stem from the *maternal* and/or the feminine, of which the maternal is the real support."[53] For menstrual blood, this "goes without saying."[54] As for the other explanation—"the anal penis is also the phallus with which infantile imagination provides the feminine sex," and, "on the other hand, maternal authority is experienced first and above all, after the first essentially oral frustrations, as sphincteral training."[55] As she comments a page earlier: "That other sex, the feminine, becomes synonymous with a radical evil that is to be suppressed."[56] That is to say, the sexualization of the feminine is a correlative of sadism. Furthermore, the resulting need to stabilize the inherently ambiguous anality/orality of erotism, solely by means of the logic of binaries, forges the identity of the maternal other on a hallucinatory metaphor that in fact makes it impossible to grasp the maternal other discursively, through any such logic.

To be clear, the metaphoricity of the feminine/mother/maternal other is the result of the excess, over a binary logic, of exclusionary opposites that neither paternal nor symbolic law can manage. At the root of this impossibility is the internal fear of perviousness at bodily and psychic borders. Kristeva seizes on this metaphoricity as she posits a third (aesthetic), law-like purposivity. "It is as if, while having been forever immersed in the symbolics of language, the human being experienced, in addition, an *authority* that was a—chronologically and logically immediate—repetition of the *laws* of language."[57] This authority is a provocation that cannot be located within chronology, but ruptures it, causing the sort of paroxysm noted above in the case of Little Hans. That is to say, the "return" of the maternal archaic introduces a new sort of rupturing conditionality for language "as if" it is conditioned by a "repetition of the *laws* of language" of the preexisting human community—which cannot be repeated. This crucial passage introduces the notion of scription as opposed to acts. I will dwell on this for a moment.

According to Kristeva, the structural anthropologist takes linguistic structure to be defined by rituals as "acts" rather than "symbols."[58] "Through language and within highly hierarchical religious institutions, man hallucinates partial 'objects'—witnesses to an archaic differentiation of the body on its way toward ego identity, which is also sexual identity."[59] This indicates the function of two kinds of law, maternal and paternal, which were crucial in the above discussion of metaphoricity and the semiotic: the paternal law demands representation in language, in symbols, while the maternal law precludes this, remaining in hallucinatory metaphors, hallucinating partial objects. In this context, Kristeva argues further that defilement (from which ritual protects) is the "translinguistic spoor of the most archaic boundaries of the self's clean and proper body. In that sense, if it is a jettisoned object, it is so from the mother."[60] By means of the symbolic institution of ritual and the mother as speaking being, that is, by means of a system of ritual exclusions, the partial object "becomes *scription*—an inscription of limits, an emphasis placed not on the (paternal) Law but on (maternal) Authority through the very signifying order."[61] That is, by means of *scription* and not *acts*, the partial object becomes incarnated in individual and collective life. The mother as a speaking being becomes the abject anterior to scription, in a system of ritual exclusions. Above all, transgressing boundaries here is especially a matter of processing the residual negativity of the semiotic and thus what only appears retrospectively as anterior to "limits" and "borders." Neither limits nor borders are managed by binary logic. Kristeva is frequently misunderstood on this point.[62]

The very force of conditionality of "binary logic" is anterior to the symbolic and yet in no sense preexists it—this force is "not that of *linguistic* signs nor of the *symbolic* order that these signs found."[63] It is the conditionality of the force of the semiotic or the primal mapping of the body as itself older than paternal law, which is secondary to it. "While being the precondition of language, [the maternal semiotic] is dependent upon meaning," and yet it is a dependency upon the maternal body as trustee—which is "distinguished from paternal laws."[64] Loss and the impossibility to lose/mourn the maternal archaic is explained by appeal to conditions of socially imposed abjection.[65] Kristeva speaks of abjection as what takes shape "owing to a subjective benefit derived from it on the level of libidinal economy."[66] Additionally, within these laws, however, this becomes the "royal way" to progress in history—that is "with the phallic phase and acquisition of language, the destiny of man will take shape."[67] On these very premises, the loss of the repressed archaic maternal is impossible.[68]

> Through frustrations and prohibitions, this [semiotic] authority shapes the body into a *territory*, having areas, orifices, points and lines, surfaces and hollows, where the archaic power of mastery and neglect, of the differentiation of proper-clean and improper-dirty, possible and impossible, is impressed and exerted. . . . Maternal [semiotic] authority is the trustee of that mapping of the self's clean and proper body; it is distinguished from paternal laws.[69]

The main point here is that *semiotic authority* presides over a mapping of the maternal body and that of the future subject. Without this authority, the symbolic "exclusionary prohibition" constitutive of collective existence would not have sufficient strength over the "binary logic" of either/or negations. The exclusionary value of the symbol would not have sufficient strength "to dam up the abject or demoniacal potential of the feminine."[70] But setting up a separation, as language—like culture—does, implies that suppressing this insufficiency of strength is dependent upon an archaic repressed and, above all, the authorization of a fiction, illusion, of the return of the maternal archaic repressed. "Such an archaic relationship to the *object* interprets, as it were, the relationship to the *mother*" as an unnamable maternal.[71] And in some societies, Kristeva notes, the "abject" points to attributes of women, to matrilineal or related filiation, or endogamy.

This discussion of act versus scription gives us a different approach to the semiotic-symbolic tension that has been our theme: we have seen that the semiotic authority that enables the symbolic cannot be brought into language in symbolic acts; it can only be alluded to in scription—and this hinges on the maternal. We can now link this back to our beginning point, in the study of the *chora* in *Revolution in Poetic Language*. This allowed us to see how Kristeva's early work already identifies a constitutive tension that forever links symbolic negations back to a semiotic negativity—the semiotic authority just discussed—that generates these negations, where the symbolic cannot designate the semiotic, even as it is retroactive upon it in trying to separate from it. Our study of *Powers of Horror* has shown how in her psychoanalytic work this semiotic-symbolic tension takes the form of the abject as the archaic maternal. The main argument here is that abjection, operating in retroaction upon the archaic maternal (as indicated in her discussion of act and inscription in the anthropological context), and playing out in bodies and on the couch (as in her analysis of Little Hans and Narcissus), is, for Kristeva, what sustains and drives psychic life, yet always threatens to explode the symbolic from within, shattering it, breaching efforts to separate from and master the semiotic. This shattering is central to Kristeva's concept of intimate revolt.

IV. Traumatism, Melancholy, and Maternal Loss: Alterity as Breaching the Symbolic

We are now prepared to see how in her late work this logic of abjection grounds Kristeva's themes of melancholy, maternal loss, and traumatism, and how these processes, in turn, drive the breaching of the symbolic. Crucially, this will enable us to see, once again, how Kristeva diverges from Lacan, in particular how her psychoanalytic framework is rooted in alterity, not in the symbolic.

Critchley's work is important at this juncture. First, his essay "*Das Ding*: Lacan and Levinas" allows me to connect what Levinas calls an "original traumatism" (Levinas's words for exposure to alterity)[72] to Kristeva's essay "L'Impossibilité de perdre" (1988), where she discusses traumatism as an ethical disposition: "Traumatism illuminates the relation of the subject to the thing."[73] Showing the affinity between Levinas and Kristeva will then allow me to connect Kristeva's work to alterity. Second, I am inspired by Critchley's insightful remarks that with *Black Sun* Kristeva is close to Freud and Levinas but not so much Lacan.[74] As we have seen, insofar as Kristeva develops a problematic of negativity that does not reduce to a negation in language, she diverges from the linguistic symbol and its role in Lacan. Her challenge to Lacan is about sublimation: what is involved in "the symbolic repair of the lesions in the imaginary caused by the real of the mother's body."[75]

Melancholy provides a quick way into these issues in *Black Sun*. Melancholy is an effort at separation, at releasing the hold on the maternal thing, *das Ding* (the archaic maternal). For Kristeva, the question is under what conditions the maternal thing becomes a word, insofar as it becomes word (*ein Wort*).[76] We have just seen that this condition cannot be the linguistic symbol: the maternal thing cannot be symbolized yet must be spoken. This conundrum drives melancholy. It also indicates an amplification of issues traced in the above discussion of abjection and the archaic maternal: in melancholy, what cannot be symbolized or separated from, is an undead mother, buried alive, a matricide, or a phantasm of the buried mother within language. This is where the issue of "traumatism" arises in Kristeva: melancholy concerns a separation from a dreamlike disruption, a dream (*Traum*) and trauma that is crucial to every symbolic meaning-making, yet threatens to breach that very order of meaning-making, and even linear time, since this traumatism cannot be located in any sort of designatable meaning or symbolic law.

Traumatism thus marks the speaking subject as open to and shut down by the authority of the mother as speaking being—and to subsequent prohibitions that result in the "impossibility" of finding the phallic mother who would restore the possibility of speech. This traumatism threatens to breach the symbolic, in intimate revolt, and is a double bind that (like abjection) drives the subject to a third, to transference. At this point we can turn to details of Kristeva's *Intimate Revolt* itself, where she writes that transference does not simply draw support from preverbal significances: these allow complex and intraverbal experiences "to be brought to the other"; "they help in forgiving, in transferring," giving pardon.[77] Transference, like forgiveness, is not given by another: "Remission and rebirth are . . . acquired through the putting into words of the unconscious; they are acquired by giving conscious and unconscious meaning to what did not have any, for it is precisely this absence of meaning that was experienced as ill-being. Forgiveness is not given by another."[78] Thus, paradoxically, "one forgives oneself with the help of another (the analyst), by relying on his or her interpretation and on his or her silence (and on his or her love), in order to make sense of the troubling senselessness."[79] Intimate revolt abides by a logic of wanting to "return" that is tied to an impossibility of doing so, to a threat of annihilation.

Going back to Kristeva's question regarding the conditions under which the maternal thing, *das Ding*, can become a word invested with meaning, we find, as Critchley puts it (summarizing Kristeva's view in *Black Sun*), that "we are transfixed by our Thing, standing mute before its affect."[80] This affect, he amplifies, "cannot simply be understood linguistically, but subtends the activity of language. The relation to *das Ding* is not the word, but the subjective affect of [archaic maternal] trauma."[81] The study of melancholia takes to its logical completion the elaboration of the relation to the archaic maternal.

> For Kristeva, *das Ding* [the object and the thing] is "the real in rebellion against signification," the pole of attraction and repulsion, the dwelling place of sexuality from which the object of desire will detach itself. *Das Ding* is the *soleil noir*, the black sun of melancholia, what Kristeva calls "*une instance sans présence*," a light without representation, the unknown object that throws its shadow across the ego. When faced with this seemingly archaic or pre-historic attachment to *das Ding*, the depressive person has the impression of being disinherited from an unnameable supreme good.[82]

As Kristeva herself puts it in "L'Impossibilité de perdre," which articulates her view of traumatism in relation to the archaic maternal: "in commenting on the notion of *das Ding* [the thing] in Freud's *Entwurf*, Lacan claims that however withdrawn the Freudian Thing may be from judging consciousness, it is always already given in the presence of language."[83] In other words, these points from Critchley and Kristeva tell us that affect is anterior to language, it is generative of significance yet it cannot be signified in language. Affect, in this sense, is the port through which traumatism enters, breaching the symbolic.

This analysis of traumatism and the archaic maternal can be amplified through Kristeva's interpretation of the melancholy imagination. For my purposes, this indicates the way that traumatism involves a breach of the symbolic order that arrives by way of alterity, supporting my suggestion (through Critchley) that traumatism in Kristeva has a role similar to originary traumatism in Levinas, which concerns the death of the Other.

The best way to approach this is through Kristeva's introduction of the beautiful and the sublime in a short chapter of *Black Sun* on aesthetic theory, where she specifically attends to allegory and the birth of the mourning-play and of melancholia in eighteenth-century baroque culture in the West.[84] The mourning-play and aesthetics are brought together through a question of aesthetics: "Can the beautiful be sad?"[85] This provokes insights about melancholia and the artistic imagination, which return her to Freud's classic studies "On Transience" and "Mourning and Melancholia."[86] Kristeva suggests that, for Freud, the mourning of the lost love object might extend into melancholia, that is, incomplete mourning, which, for Kristeva, concerns the archaic maternal. Freud connects the enigma of mourning with the enigma of the beautiful, which, insofar as it is ruptured by the sublime, is identified with the ideal and involves sublimation.[87] These links between melancholia, mourning, the archaic maternal, and sublimation lead Kristeva to insights about artistic imagination as driving intimate revolt.[88]

In the aesthetic context, melancholia's incompleteness is manifest in playfulness: "beauty succeed[s] in making its way through the drama that is being played out between the *loss* and the *mastery* over the self's loss/devaluation/execution."[89] Melancholia summons a dynamic of primary processes of idealization, so that it might be able to weave a "*hypersign* around and with the depressive void."[90] This is *allegory*, as "lavishness of that which *no longer is*, but which regains for myself a higher meaning because I am able to remake nothingness, better than it was and within an unchanging harmony, here and now and forever."[91] Kristeva here understands that artistic imagination is capable of a transformation, wherein the individual is confronted with an objectively fragile symbolic order, with fading values, loss of symbolic supports—where "the ambiguity of the 'good' and 'bad' object is displayed."[92] Like Freud, whose theory resulted from the traumas of World War I, Kristeva is concerned with historical reality and destruction. She asks whether the "beautiful object" "is the one that tirelessly returns following destructions and wars in order to bear witness that there is survival after death, that immortality is possible?"—and her answer is affirmative.[93]

In this context, she likens the artistic imagination to the capacity of the beautiful to rupture and be ruptured by the sublime. This rupturing, which is distinctive of allegory, cannot be inscribed in a symbol and rather stands as a hypersign for the restorative capacity associated with the imaginary. "Like feminine finery concealing stubborn depressions, beauty emerges as the admirable face of loss, transforming it in order to make it live."[94] Kristeva here suggests that it is "I [who] bring forth . . . an artifice, an ideal, a 'beyond' that my psyche produces in order to take up a position outside itself—*ek-stasis*"; I do this "in the place of death and so as not to die of the other's death."[95]

Kristeva stresses this capacity of the imaginary to revolt, yet to create, and sublimate, to replace the ephemeral in melancholia, as underlying the capacity for idealization of the artistic and—we must add—the archaic imagination. This capacity for a grandiose aesthetic is a capacity of the melancholic subject, and its model is that of the archaic maternal of "parting sadness": "When we have been able to go through our melancholia to the point of becoming interested in the life of signs, beauty may also grab hold of us to bear witness for someone who grandly discovered the royal way through which humanity transcends the grief of being apart: the way of speech given to suffering, including screams, music, silences, and laughter."[96] Imagination enables sublimation, substitution, transference, and rehabilitates the singularity and infinity of the loving imaginary third, within language: it does with speech what cannot be done with violence, transforming loss into intrasymbolic gain.

> Imagination is that strange place where the subject ventures its identity, loses itself down to the threshold of evil, crime, or asymbolia in order to work through them and to bear witness . . . from elsewhere. A divided space, it is maintained only if solidly fastened to the ideal, which authorizes destructive violence to be *spoken* instead of being *done*. That is sublimation, and it needs *for-giving* [*par-don*].[97]

Imagination thus resolves the sort of conundrum that the archaic maternal provokes, which cannot be discursively resolved. That is to say, imagination provides an archetype of what ensues in intimate revolt, that is, when the semiotic breaches the symbolic order. Psychic life operates according to an established, specific economy of "imaginary discourses," referencing the Western tradition.

> They are consistently close to depression and at the same time show a necessary shift from depression to possible meaning. Like a tense link between Thing and Meaning, the unnameable and the proliferation of signs, the silent affect and an ideality that designates and goes beyond it, the *imaginary* is neither objective description . . . nor theological idealism. . . . The experience of *nameable melancholia* opens up the space of a necessarily heterogeneous subjectivity, torn between the two co-necessary and co-present centers of opacity and ideal.[98]

In a way, Kristeva is saying that in accounts of times of historical crisis, ontogenetic and phylogenetic accounts intertwine. Maternal loss and the impossibility to mourn, to lose loss, which constitutes the subject of traumatism and abjection in *Powers of Horror* is succeeded by and amplified in Kristeva's logic of melancholia. This is the structural insight linking her theory of abjection to melancholia, as we have shown, and anticipating the logic of intimacy of revolt.

In conclusion, we have seen how the works of the 1980s anticipate the logic of intimate revolt, through their focus on semiotic negativity and the maternal semiotic as prior to and generative of the symbolic order. We have also seen how this logic is amplified in her work of the 1990s, which shows how this semiotic-symbolic tension operates in the form of the abject and the archaic maternal, driving the psyche to return to them as prepsychical memory, yet also to separate from these traces. Finally, we have seen that the process behind all this involves imagination and alterity. Contra Lacan, this is not a process rooted in the symbolic, but, rather one that opens psychic life to an imaginary beyond the psyche.

EMILIA ANGELOVA

CONCORDIA UNIVERSITY
AUGUST 2019

NOTES

I thank David Morris for comments on earlier drafts of this essay.

1. Julia Kristeva, *Intimate Revolt: The Powers and Limits of Psychoanalysis Volume 2*, trans. Jeanine Herman (New York: Columbia University Press, 2002).
2. Ibid., 7.
3. Ibid.
4. Julia Kristeva, *Revolution in Poetic Language*, trans. Margaret Waller (Columbia University Press, 1984), 109.
5. Leon Roudiez attributes the term *transrational*, as an influence on the notion of poetic language, to Otto Brik. See his introduction to Kristeva, *Revolution in Poetic Language*, 2.
6. See Simon Critchley, *Ethics–Politics–Subjectivity: Essays on Derrida, Levinas and Contemporary French Thought* (London: Verso, 2009), 195.
7. Kristeva's first explicit thematization of revolt is in *The Sense and Non-sense of Revolt*, trans. Jeanine Herman (Columbia University Press, 2000), ch. 1. There are several views of the shift between revolution and revolt in the scholarship. Beardsworth's notion of the "tendential" severance between the semiotic and symbolic emphasizes the strong

influence of psychoanalysis on this shift. Sara Beardsworth, *Julia Kristeva: Psychoanalysis and Modernity* (Albany: SUNY Press, 2004), 12–25. For another interpretation stressing the contribution of primary narcissism, see Kelly Oliver, "Revolt and Forgiveness," in Tina Chanter and Ewa Ziarek, eds., *Revolt, Affect, Collectivity: The Unstable Boundaries of Kristeva's Polis* (Albany: SUNY Press, 2005).

8. Julia Kristeva, *Powers of Horror: An Essay on Abjection*, trans. Leon S. Roudiez (New York: Columbia University Press, 1982); *Tales of Love*, trans. Leon S. Roudiez (New York: Columbia University Press, 1987); *Black Sun: Depression and Melancholia*, trans. Leon S. Roudiez (New York: Columbia University Press, 1989).

9. Julia Kristeva, *Revolt, She Said* (Los Angeles: Semiotext(e), 2002).

10. Ibid., 25. *Plato's Cosmology: The Timaeus of Plato*, trans. Francis Macdonald Cornford (Indianapolis: Hackett, 1997), 191–97, 52a–52b. Kristeva, *Revolution in Poetic Language*, 239n12.

11. Ibid., 102. For a more complete analysis, see Beardsworth's excellent essay on the semiotic as the logical phase of language. Sara Beardsworth, "From Revolution to Revolt Culture," in Chanter and Ziarek, *Revolt, Affect, Collectivity*, esp. 40–41.

12. Kristeva, *Revolution in Poetic Language*, specifically 245n.60, citing Edmund Husserl, *Ideas: General Introduction to Pure Phenomenology*, trans. W. R. Boyce Gibson (London: Allen & Unwin, 1969), 335, 375.

13. The word for "breaching" in French is *effraction*, a juridical term for "breaking and entering." Kristeva begins using it in *Revolution in Poetic Language* to designate a characteristic function of the semiotic *chora*, namely "pulverizing [the thetic] through the negativity of transgression" (Kristeva, *Revolution in Poetic Language*, 69).

14. For the affinity with Freud, see Vanessa Rumble, "Progress in Spirit: Freud and Kristeva on the Uncanny," in Richard Kearney and Kascha Semonovitch, eds., *Phenomenologies of the Stranger: Between Hostility and Hospitality* (New York: Fordham University Press, 2011), esp. 179–81.

15. Julia Kristeva, "The Passion According to Motherhood," in *Hatred and Forgiveness*, trans. Jeanine Herman (New York: Columbia University Press, 2010).

16. Ibid., 82.

17. Ibid.

18. Ibid., 81.

19. Ibid., 88.

20. Ibid., 89.

21. "*Ce n'est pas dans le monde de l'action . . . mais dans celui de la vie psychique.*" Julia Kristeva, *L'Avenir d'une révolte* (Paris: Flammarion, 2012), 28 (my translation).

22. Kristeva, *Intimate Revolt*, 11.

23. Sara Beardsworth, "The Chiasmus of Action and Revolt: Julia Kristeva, Hannah Arendt, and Gillian Rose," in Sarah K. Hansen and Rebecca Tuvel, eds., *New Forms of Revolt: Essays on Kristeva's Intimate Politics* (Albany: SUNY Press, 2017).

24. Julia Kristeva, *New Maladies of the Soul*, trans. Ross Guberman (New York: Columbia University Press, 1995).

25. Ibid., 54–55.

26. Ibid., 71.

27. Ibid.

28. Ibid., 76.

29. Ibid., 88.

30. Ibid.

31. Ibid., 87–88.

32. Ibid., 54.

33. Oliver, "Revolt and Forgiveness," 86.

34. Kristeva, *Powers of Horror*, 35.

35. Ibid., 44.

36. Ibid., 73.
37. Kristeva, *Revolution in Poetic Language*, 44–45.
38. Ibid., 45.
39. Ibid., 52.
40. Ibid., 52.
41. Ibid., 53–4.
42. Sigmund Freud, *Totem and Taboo*, in *The Standard Edition of the Complete Psychological Works of Sigmund Freud*, vol. XIII, trans. James Strachey (London: Hogarth, 1958); *Three Essays on the Theory of Sexuality*, in *Standard Edition*, vol. VII (London: Hogarth, 1953). For a discussion that defines primary narcissism, see Kristeva, *Tales of Love*, 29–48. Compare *Powers of Horror*, 62.
43. Kristeva, *Powers of Horror*, 62–63.
44. Ibid., 63.
45. Ibid.
46. Ibid.
47. Ibid.
48. Ibid.
49. Kristeva, *Revolution in Poetic Language*, 15.
50. Ibid.
51. Ibid., 15, and Introduction by Leon S. Roudiez to ibid., 2.
52. Kristeva, *Powers of Horror*, 71.
53. Ibid.
54. Ibid.
55. Ibid.
56. Ibid., 70.
57. Ibid., 71–72.
58. Ibid., 73.
59. Ibid.
60. Ibid.
61. Ibid.
62. For an excellent analysis of the problem of transgressing from within, in abjection, see Beardsworth, *Julia Kristeva*, ch. 3.
63. Kristeva, *Powers of Horror*, 72.
64. Ibid.
65. See Kristeva on "the objective frailty of symbolic order," *Powers of Horror*, 70.
66. Ibid., 63.
67. Ibid., 72.
68. Julia Kristeva, "The Speaking Subject is not Innocent," trans. Chris Miller, in Barbara Johnson, ed., *Freedom and Interpretation: The Amnesty Oxford Lectures* (New York: Basic, 1993), 158–59.
69. Kristeva, *Powers of Horror*, 72.
70. Ibid., 65.
71. Ibid., 64.
72. Critchley, *Ethics–Politics–Subjectivity*, 198–216. For the connection to Kristeva, see 199, 214–16.
73. "*Le traumatisme met à jour le rapport du sujet à la chose*" (translated by Critchley in *Ethics–Politics–Subjectivity*, 199), in Julia Kristeva, "L'Impossibilité de perdre," *Les Cahiers de l'Institut de Psycho-Pathologie Clinique*, no. 8 (November 1988): 40. For a different interpretation of the relation to Levinas, see Ewa P. Ziarek, "Kristeva and Fanon: Revolutionary Violence and Ironic Articulation," in Chanter and Ziarek, *Revolt, Affect, Collectivity*.
74. Critchley, *Ethics–Politics–Subjectivity*, 215–16n19.
75. See ibid., 214n8. See also Kristeva, *Black Sun*.

76. See Critchley, *Ethics–Politics–Subjectivity*, 216.
77. Kristeva, *Intimate Revolt*, 19.
78. Ibid., 18–19.
79. Ibid., 19.
80. Critchley, *Ethics–Politics–Subjectivity*, 216n19.
81. Ibid.
82. Ibid. See also Kristeva, *Black Sun*, esp. 13, 5 and 262–63, and compare 43–44.
83. Kristeva, "L'Impossibilité de perdre," 32 (translation by Critchley in *Ethics–Politics–Subjectivity*, 216). Compare Kristeva, *Black Sun*, esp. 15–21.
84. Kristeva, *Black Sun*, ch. 4.
85. Ibid., 97.
86. Sigmund Freud, "On Transience" and "Mourning and Melancholia," in *The Standard Edition of the Complete Psychological Works of Sigmund Freud*, vol. XIV, trans. James Strachey (London: Hogarth, 1957).
87. Kristeva, *Black Sun*, 98.
88. For the relation to revolt, see Beardsworth, "From Revolution to Revolt Culture," 47–48.
89. Kristeva, *Black Sun*, 99.
90. Ibid.
91. Ibid.
92. Ibid.
93. Ibid., 98.
94. Ibid., 99.
95. Ibid.
96. Ibid., 99–100.
97. Ibid., 200.
98. Ibid., 100.

24

Sarah K. Hansen

INTIMATE REVOLT AT THE MARGINS OF COMMUNITY AND THE HOPE OF POSTCOLONIALITY

I. Revolt and the "Hyperbolic We"

Kristeva's notion of intimate revolt emerges in the first two volumes of her series on the powers and limits of psychoanalysis: *The Sense and Non-sense of Revolt* (1996) and *Intimate Revolt* (1997).[1] Here Kristeva describes how dramatic transformations in the nature of power and the subject unsettle some of the conceptual ground of her earlier writing. In *Revolution in Poetic Language* (1974) she famously elaborates the notion of the semiotic *chora*, a space of bodily rhythms, drives, laughter, and music associated with the maternal body and the mother-child relationship.[2] According to Kristeva, the *chora* is necessary for the child's transition into the symbolic, where semiotic drives live on and have the potential to revolutionize symbolic law understood as the form-giving function of social structures and institutions, including language. However, in these two books on *revolt* Kristeva begins to express concerns about the locatability and legitimacy of symbolic law, and thereby the fate of semiotic revolutions. She observes that, today, the dissemination of contemporary disciplinary power obscures and erodes symbolic law so that it no longer supports semiotic drives. As the law suffers the disconnection of drives and affects, bodies suffer from the disconnection of form-giving law. In this context, Kristeva wonders whether revolt is possible. When contemporary subjects are reduced to "patrimonial individuals" (or owners of organs), "who can revolt, and against what? Can a patrimony of organs revolt against a normalizing order? How? Through remote controlled images?"[3]

Inspired by the etymology of the Latin verb *volvere*, to turn or return, and the French meaning of revolt as reversal, detour, cycle, upheaval, and recovery,

Kristeva describes revolt as a psychical event that confronts, displaces, and assimilates an authority in the psychical economy of the individual.[4] During a child's development, the rebellious incorporation of social authority is a condition for entering the symbolic order. In adulthood revolt is a regenerative return to the past that questions and renews symbolic ties. In general, revolt reflects Kristeva's commitment to the idea that the "transformation of man's relationship to meaning . . . intrinsically concerns public life and consequently has profoundly political implications. In fact, it poses the question of another politics, that of permanent conflictuality."[5] It is only through revolt that drives and affects find support in signifying systems, that individuals can find and make meaning in community with one another. These communities of permanently conflictual interlocking alterities are in danger today. Emphasizing the contemporary emergence of vast and nonlocatable normalizing powers as well as the fraying resources of patrimonial individuals, Kristeva warns that the conditions of revolt are deeply uncertain, and contemporary individuals may not know who can revolt and against what. Without greater attention to intimate revolt, the inability to reckon with and reconcile ourselves to our own strangeness leads to the inability to accept and affirm the strangeness of others, especially the strangeness of those at the margins of community.

While Kristeva insists on the political implications of imperiled revolt, anglophone readers in the United States have struggled to appreciate the psyche as political terrain.[6] To some extent, this reception reflects confusions surrounding Kristeva's work that extend well before and beyond the *revolt* books. Since the 1970s she has lamented the rise of identity politics in feminism and other social movements, in particular the way in which group classifications—"woman," "homosexual," "heterosexual"—cover over irreducible differences between individuals.[7] For Kristeva, the personal is political, not in a "dogmatic" or sloganeering sense of identity categories, but in an intimate, psychic, enigmatic, yet analyzable way. Many anglophone readers in the United States take the ambiguity and enigmas of Kristevan revolt to betray a retreat from politics. This is not the case. In a poetic and playful style, Kristeva's writing challenges the fetishization of the political and, in Edmonds's words, "vacuous forms of political correctness."[8] In the logic of fetishized politics, "we think that everything is political. When we say political we say something which cannot be analyzed, it's the final act. This is political . . . stop. [But] it's tremendously important this final enigma, which is politics."[9] Kristeva rejects the assumption that theorists know "the political" in some final sense. Her intimate revolt is a politics of conflictual questioning, especially around the borders and margins of identity and community. She is fond of quoting and revising Camus. "'I revolt, therefore we are.' Or rather: I revolt, therefore we are to *come*."[10]

This essay explores the meaning of the "we" (the community) promised by intimate revolt and threatened by normalizing powers. Our question is, what kind of solidarity is born of an intimate politics that unsettles identity politics? What kind of ethos or way of life might be "to come"? In an autobiographical essay on her experiences with the *Tel Quel* movement, "My Memory's Hyperbole" (1984), Kristeva reflects on "we" as a kind of un/making. "The hyperbolic 'we' is, in effect, only a part of 'me.' It is merely a temporary stability in which projections and identifications are settled among some and allow the history of a perpetually changing whole to be written. A 'we' is alive only if it is never the same."[11] Kristeva's paradoxical shape-shifting "we" is not easy to grasp, especially when considered in normalizing contexts where symbolic law is empty and eroding. With Beardsworth, it's just not clear how to make lives in these contexts.[12] While Kristeva suggests that revolt might forge lives "to be told and written," "biographies with and for others," it is unclear how the "I" and "we" of revolt are more than fragments of suffering and semblance. In her texts, fetishized identities like maternity and femininity may unravel to reveal enigmas and ambiguities but, in the end, who are "we"? Temporarily stable yet permanently conflictual, who says "we," who experiences the liveliness of its change and mutation? These questions are especially important because Kristeva sometimes leaves community feelings and assumptions uninterrogated, especially regarding French, European, and Western identities. Take the closing passage of "My Memory's Hyperbole":

> While the Latin American or Arab Marxist revolution is brewing on the doorstep of the United States, I feel closer to truth and liberty when I work within the space of this challenged giant, which may, in fact, be on the point of becoming a David before the growing Goliath of the Third World. I dream that our children will prefer to join this David, with his errors and impasses, armed with our erring and circling about the Idea, the Logos, the Form: in short, the old Judeo-Christian Europe. If it is only an illusion, I like to think it may have a future.[13]

Here the United States is figured as a giant so challenged and threatened by the Third World that Kristeva dreams of it as a small David standing down a growing Goliath. Kristeva feels "closer to truth and liberty" within a Judeo-Christian frame and expresses her hope that "our" children will feel the same. While Oliver considers this one of Kristeva's "strangest . . . invocation[s] of Biblical metaphor[s]," appearing to contradict her writing on the figure of the stranger/foreigner in *Strangers to Ourselves*, I maintain that it points to a deeper problem of Eurocentrism in Kristeva's writing, even in *Strangers to Ourselves*.[14] Noting that Kristeva writes of her David and Goliath dream during the "full deployment of Operation Desert Storm," Spivak has wondered about the extent of Kristeva's Eurocentrism.[15] She asks: "are we still condemned to circle around 'Idea, Logos, and Form' or can the (ex)orbitant at least be invoked?"[16] This essay considers Spivak's question by putting Kristeva's texts in conversation with the decolonizing intimate politics of Frantz Fanon. The encounter spurs important concerns about the "we" of intimate revolt. If revolt reflects the "transformation of man's relation to meaning," can it participate—intimately, enigmatically—in the transformation of histories of colonialism and Eurocentrism?[17] The ethical bonds born of intimate revolt involve a revaluation of maternity and femininity, but can they also unravel these related stubborn, entangled histories of psychic violence?

II. Strangers to Revolt

Kristeva's writings on revolt during the 1990s are preceded by several texts on the figure of the stranger and the concept of the nation, especially *Strangers to Ourselves* and *Nations Without Nationalism*.[18] Working between the psyche and the social, these texts discuss alterity and community, speaking directly to the phenomena of xenophobia and racism at a time when Jean-Marie Le Pen's National Front political party was growing in popularity and *l'affaire du foulard* (the scarf affair) was unfolding in French public schools.[19] In *Strangers to Ourselves*, Kristeva seeks to identify the psychical conditions of xenophobia. In her view, the disavowal of an uncanny stranger within the self (that is, the unconscious) contributes to the social rejection of strange or foreign others. A different relationship to intimacy might allow for a more tolerant and diverse future. Continuing these arguments, *Nations Without Nationalism* argues for an understanding of the nation as a community of strangers, a definition linked to a universal cosmopolitanism that supports rather than excludes the uncanny. From the fetishized perspective of "the political," the arguments in these books are seen as reductive and psychologizing, offering naïve psychoanalytic solutions to complex political problems. This is Fraser's critique in her widely read essay, "The Uses and Abuses of French Discourse Theories for Feminist Politics," published just as Kristeva's books on strangers and nations appeared in English. To Fraser, Kristeva offers a psychologized subject, "split into two halves, neither of which is a potential political agent."[20] On my reading, these criticisms misapprehend Kristeva's intimate politics as an apolitical "paralyzing oscillation between identity and non-identity," and fail to ask difficult questions about movements of centering and decentering.[21] Kristeva's notion of a community of strangers is Eurocentric.

The ethical concerns of *Strangers to Ourselves* appear to be motivated by a fundamental insight about contemporary individualism. "It is perhaps on the basis of that contemporary individualism's subversion, beginning with the moment when the citizen-individual ceases to consider himself as unitary and glorious but discovers his incoherences and abysses, in short his 'strangeness'—that the question arises again: no longer that of welcoming the foreigner with a system that obliterates him but of promoting the togetherness of those foreigners that we all recognize ourselves to be."[22] This ethical question aims to move beyond identity politics and the objectification of otherness. Kristeva suggests that relations among others may be more like "toccatas and fugues"—lightly brushing by the otherness of the foreigner "without giving it a permanent structure," but also coming back to it in harmonious repetition; "an otherness barely touched upon that already moves away."[23] She reminds readers that "just because one is a foreigner does not mean one is without one's own foreigner" and, thereby, without more toccatas and fugues.[24] The tendency to self-segregate, to form enclaves "of the other within the other"[25] is, in her view, a kind of "fundamentalist" objectification of otherness, an exclusion that parallels the ostracisms of the xenophobe. In order to "be able to live with others, to live *as others*, without ostracism but also without leveling,"[26]

Kristeva calls for individuals to recognize the strangeness in themselves and to return to and mourn the losses and sacrifice that shape subjectivity.

Oliver wonders if Kristeva's own experience of being a foreigner/stranger in France shapes her analysis: many moments in *Strangers to Ourselves* present experiences similar to Kristeva's own, for instance, speaking French as a second language or participating in "mixed marriages that give foreigners some rights of citizenship."[27] Kristeva sometimes distances herself from a French identity, such as when she highlights that she is not a French intellectual because she is not French. Likewise, Kristeva sometimes distances herself from her Bulgarian past, using impersonal language to explore how "the stranger has lost her mother."[28] Oliver asks: "has Kristeva taken on her new skin and shed the old?"[29] Perhaps Kristeva is the figure of the foreigner/stranger who has not mourned the losses that shape her subjectivity or the figure who has not recognized the "incoherences and abysses" of the stranger in herself. After all, years later she will utter angry, pained words about her country of birth that may reveal her valuations of West and East and her identification with the former: "You, Bulgarians, invisible, undesirable, a white patch on brightness, dark Balkans . . . You hurt me, my fellows, my brothers."[30]

If psychobiography illuminates *Strangers to Ourselves*, the text also helps make sense of Kristeva's pain and anger, her ambivalence and dis/identification. In calling for engagement with one's maternal semiotic motherland, Kristeva does not suggest that the reckoning is easy or complete, for herself or any other stranger/foreigner. The end of *Strangers to Ourselves* turns to Freud's discussion of the uncanny to underline how fraught this intimate politics can be. "Freud does not speak of foreigners: he teaches us how to detect foreignness within ourselves," a "strange land of borders and othernesses ceaselessly constructed and deconstructed."[31] With Freud, Kristeva insists that xenophobia includes the unconscious "agony and frightened joyfulness that is called *unheimlich*."[32] While Fraser is concerned that this is a naïve, psychologizing reduction of xenophobia to unconscious dimensions of the political subjectivation, Kristeva is in the process of reshaping the political subject.[33] No longer unitary and glorious, but, rather, divided by a strange and irreducible otherness, this subject-in-process reflects and contributes to social life. "A paradoxical community is emerging, made up of foreigners who are reconciled with themselves to the extent that they recognize themselves as foreigners."[34]

Nations Without Nationalism argues that a revaluation of the idea of a nation is not only compatible with this understanding of the stranger but might also support the revitalization of this ethics of alterity more generally. Nationalism is violent because, in rejecting the stranger within, the nationalist encourages the rejection of strangers without, expelling others. Ahmed comments: "Given that the stranger is already here *and has been here from the beginning*, the nation does not require violence towards strangers, as strangers are part of the nation and are part of the story of its coming into being as a transitional object."[35] To Kristeva, the notion of the nation is composed of—not opposed to—the figure of the stranger/foreigner. In a context of surging racist nationalism in 1990s France, there is a need to rethink the meaning of nationhood, to theorize a nation without violent nationalism. However, while *Nations Without Nationalism* draws on the main arguments of *Strangers to Ourselves*, it also betrays the Western biases of both texts, as the fugues and toccatas of otherness seem to play among *hosts* and strangers. With Ahmed, neither book sufficiently addresses the ways that "strangerness is already *unevenly distributed*. This uneven distribution reminds us that 'who' gets constructed as the host who welcomes the stranger is an effect of relations of power that cannot simply be willed away."[36] In a context of uneven distribution of strangeness, the call to recognize that we are all strangers threatens to cover over the ways that "others have already been recognized as stranger than other others, as border objects that have been incorporated and then expelled from the ideal of the community."[37] Ahmed's criticism is compelling because she does not fetishize community as the political, as though this were "something which cannot be analyzed" or "the final act." Instead, she generates questions that might revitalize intimate politics. In particular, she challenges Kristeva to theorize in the context of histories of bodily movement. In her view, the nation is not an abstract ideal but an expression of bodies themselves; it is "already an effect of the privilege for some bodies to inhabit spaces as hosts (bodies-at-home), and hence to decide who gets let into the body of the nation."[38]

Interestingly, the centering of hosts and decentering of strangers takes place in Freud's "The Uncanny," the essay inspiring Kristeva's discussions.[39] Although Kristeva claims that Freud does not mention foreigners in this essay,[40] Ziarek observes that he raises the issue of foreigners in his terminological discussion. After citing the Greek word *xenos*, he dismisses the term, insisting that "foreign dictionaries tell us nothing new" and other "languages are without a word for this particular variety of what is fearful."[41] His dismissal of *xenos* from consideration reflects how a bias toward what is home-y, familiar, and comfortable can affect even the theorization of what is unfamiliar, disturbing, uncanny. As Ziarek comments, what "good fortune" Freud has to speak German, the only language that could stage an encounter with the aesthetic, psychic, and political shape of the uncanny.[42]

Although Kristeva does not discuss this moment in Freud's text, Ziarek argues that she is much more attuned to the ways that the problematic of otherness is "paradoxically situated at the limits of translatability."[43] Freud's essay is a critique of Jentsch's understanding of the uncanny as an event of "intellectual uncertainty," combining personal narrative, clinical observations, and literary analysis to show the affective and psychical dimensions of the uncanny.[44] In addition to a personal tale of "unintended repetition," stumbling upon an Italian red-light district and then uncannily returning there again, he also explores repetitions in Hoffman's story of "The Sandman."[45] For Freud, the notion of "intellectual uncertainty" not only falls short of capturing the variety of manifestations of the uncanny but locates its effects exclusively within the realm of consciousness and rationality. In contrast, Freud's account of the uncanny's movement of familiarity and unfamiliarity appeals to the unconscious and the early stages of psychic development. In the red-light district and the pages of "The Sandman," he finds the uncanny to be derived from a once familiar early psychic phase that, as repressed, returns again in unfamiliar, uncanny form. To Ziarek, Kristeva deepens Freud's exploration of affect by better posing "the complex relation of the uncanny and the foreign."[46] Her critique of nationalism and her reimagining of the notion of nation consider the psychic, aesthetic, and political affective dimensions of uncanny strangers.

Ziarek's discussion of Kristeva's uncanny strangers is an effective defense against those who criticize *Strangers to Ourselves* and *Nations Without Nationalism* as reductive psychologization of the political. Politics is aestheticized, aesthetics is politicized, and these entanglements are not at all simple or reductive, but shot through with psychic phases that, once familiar, return in uncanny forms. While appreciating Kristeva's deepening of Freud's uncanny affect, there remain concerns about a bias towards her own sense of what is familiar. Who stands in for the abstract figure of the host and who stands in for the abstract figure of the foreigner in her texts? Ahmed puts this critique in terms of the affective dimension that interests both Kristeva and Freud. She agrees with Kristeva's account of the nation as "an effect of the movement of bodies and the direction of that movement—as a transitional object . . . an effect of such 'towardness.'"[47] She disagrees that the promise of the nation is one that can "simply be filled and transformed by others" by saying with good will that "we are all strangers." "Opening the community to others means turning back or turning around, and moving towards those others we have passed and passed by, who have already been recognized as stranger than other others. It means starting again. This promise of new beginnings is the hope of postcoloniality, the hope that coloniality could be posted as we find another way of living with others."[48] Here, we might wonder if Ahmed's description of a more postcolonial understanding of alterity could resonate with Kristeva's understanding of intimate revolt. Perhaps intimate revolt, with all of its *volvere*—reversal, detour, cycle, upheaval, and recovery—can spur a critique of identity that decenters the familiar figures of France, Europe, the West in Kristeva's texts? Perhaps intimate revolt can encounter stranger strangers, in ourselves and others?

III. Revolt at the Margins: Solidarity and Alterity

As a process of regenerative return, Kristeva writes, "revolt twists and turns—indeed, veers off—depending on history."[49] In childhood it is the rebellious incorporation of social authority that conditions entry into the symbolic order. In adult life it is a return to the past that questions and displaces old law and renews symbolic ties. Our question is whether the returns of revolt are not repetitive traumas that deepen the power of the most privileged. To resonate with the hope of postcoloniality and the goal of new beginnings, revolt must genuinely shift and change and veer.[50] Moreover, today it must do so in the hostile conditions of the "power vacuum" in which power is disseminated and nonlocatable. To Kristeva, when authority cannot be located, subjects struggle to revolt. Disempowered, excluded, and lacking social bonds, a depressed culture experiences the symptoms that a depressed individual feels in isolation—despair, symbolic collapse, a severance of social ties. There is also the eruption of abjection and social exclusion. When identification with power no longer works, "'I' feel excluded" in a depressive mode or, in an effort to abolish the feeling of exclusion altogether, "in the renewal of exclusion at the lower echelons of the social edifice . . . 'I' include myself at the top [and] 'I' exclude those at the bottom."[51] In the absence of resources to give meaning to the archaic processes of loss and abjection, "life becomes a life of death, a life of physical and moral violence, barbarity," especially for those at the "lower echelons of the social edifice" whose exclusions are renewed and repeated.[52]

In those moments where Kristeva is more optimistic about the possibility of revolt, it is won in association with loving social support and indefinite questioning. In childhood, the figure of support is the imaginary father or, with Oliver, the "loving third," a conduit that supports the transfer of drives and affects into signification.[53] In effect, to Oliver, the loving third is a figure of the semiotic element within language, "not just the semiotic rhythms of the maternal body, but those rhythms as they show up in the speech of the other."[54] The loving third "supports drives and their affects—which is to say the semiotic element—as they make their way into language" and "the imaginary father is the semiotic as it takes form within the Symbolic."[55] The loving third is an important assistant to the maternal separation necessary for revolt and symbolic authorization. Providing an accepting space for drives in language, the loving third promises resources for the symbolization of loss and abjection, thereby protecting against depressive collapse or abjecting eruptions. Many adults do not have access to abundant loving support. Kristeva describes how artworks and creative experiences in adulthood can revitalize the same sites and processes of symbolic authorization. Throughout her writings, she offers examples of the art of revolt—from "the sacred" and detective novels to uncanny art and paintings of decapitation. These creations and viewers' encounters with them are "fertile moment[s] of depression," ways of forging a more accepting, loved/loving psychic space for the transference of drives to "the place of the Other, of others, of meaning and ultimately to the place of signs themselves."[56] In surprising and sometimes untimely ways, love helps subjects to experience loss, and loss helps subjects to experience love.

In addition to the figure of the loving third, Kristeva emphasizes that contemporary revolt is only possible when it involves indefinite questioning, a reminder that the losses involved in subject formation are neither final nor total. *New Maladies of the Soul* and *Intimate Revolt* reinterpret symbolic castration beyond the paradigm of lack (characteristic of the Lacanian symbolic) and argue that castration is essentially a *question*.[57] That is to say, in a manner consistent with her claim that the child enters language only with loving support, Kristeva suggests that the symbolic order cannot be founded on lack and negation alone. The transition from the presymbolic to the symbolic is spurred and supported by questioning. The "no," reflecting the negativity of maternal separation, opens unto all symbols and introduces negativity into language itself.[58] Questioning calls up an experience of relationality before the "no," which supports the drives in language and, eventually, the reconnection of signs and things in the form of a "negation of negation."[59] In effect, the relational pleasure of questioning counterbalances the impending trauma of separation. Kristeva summarizes this transition: "its value lies not in being a brutal cut. It lies in benevolently generating the capacity of thinking itself, precisely since, beyond negation, what psychoanalysis calls symbolic castration is a question"; "the question opens the *infans* to discourse and allows speech to be taken toward an endless horizon."[60]

We find that Kristeva's writing on revolt associates the transformative role of questioning with French culture.[61] "Open[ing] to the symbolic not as to a fixed truth but as to an indefinite questioning," revolt is a return to the conditions of authorization that questions and displaces old laws for the sake of a future that celebrates questioning.[62] This process is different from the repetition of the "nihilist," who withdraws into old values or unquestioning new ones. The interrogations of revolt "relentlessly repeat retrospective return so as to lead it to the limits of the representable/thinkable/tenable."[63] At the borderline of life and meaning, the experience of the value of questioning introduces a change in the repetition of return, marking the possibility of another economy, one that interrogates the "soft totalitarian" threat of the power vacuum, "the threat of destroying life after having devalued the question of its meaning."[64] At the same time, Kristeva maintains that, as a lifeline to revolt, questioning is a hallmark of French culture and the French intellectual tradition since the Enlightenment. Her remarks upon receiving the Holberg prize in 2004 celebrates the "French tradition of critical questioning [that] continually revives public debate, and maintains it at a very high level."[65] French questioning and self-questioning "is a real antidote to national depression, and to its manic manifestation in nationalism."[66] In the same remarks, she praises French (and US) hospitality as a model of the view of nationhood proposed in *Nations Without Nationalism*, and of the stranger in *Strangers to Ourselves*, where she wrote "one may feel more of a foreigner in France than in any other country, but at the same time one is better as a foreigner in France than any other country."[67]

In our view, Kristeva's commitment to a French perspective and model of questioning as a host to strangers limits the extent to which revolt's transformations of meaning can serve the hope of postcoloniality. In an essay that plays on the title of Kristeva's Holberg remarks, Gratton's "What Are Psychoanalysts for in a Destitute Time?" interrogates the promise and the perils of her French model of revolt with respect to postcoloniality.[68] On the one hand, the "we" of revolt is an "unworking or unworkable community" because it proposes a politics of the "interlocking of alterities" and "permanent conflictuality."[69] While readers like Fraser find that Kristeva's account of conflictuality is a "paralyzing oscillation between identity and non-identity" incapable of practical political action, Gratton finds that revolt's insistent conflictual questioning can be a healing condition for future revolt, an unraveling that builds connection. In his view, the "we" of revolt is an insistent question and "who could resist it?"[70] On the one hand, if the "we" is a perpetual question rather than a tangle of biases, "who are we?" can be a question that connects and inspires. On the other hand, this is the same "we" who worries whether "our" children will prefer something other than the old Judeo-Christian Europe, as

Kristeva put it. If it is only a Western "we," if its unraveling and unworking is a reaction to formerly colonized people challenging contemporary Western hegemony, it seems that a Eurocentric bias circulates in Kristeva's work on revolt. Gratton does not believe this to be the case, however, and suggests that her problematic "we" can be held in suspension to appreciate the possibilities of her "unworkable community."[71]

For Gratton, Fanon's *Black Skin, White Masks* and *The Wretched of the Earth* provide a "decolonial" or postcolonial account of intimate politics that can help us read Kristevan revolt differently. Fanon describes the ways that colonization annihilates the self of colonized persons, trapping them in a "crushing objecthood," while the colonizing subject is "in thrall to its narcissistic dialogue . . . vigilant [and] ready to defend the Greco-Roman pedestal."[72] Reminding us of Kristeva's dire descriptions of a "life of death" deprived of the question of its meaning, Fanon argues that the annihilated colonized self is not fully alive. The closing lines of *Black Skin, White Masks* evoke a new humanism beyond white masks that can be "the open door of every consciousness."[73] Given its brief closing appearance in the text, the status of Fanon's humanist consciousness is less clear than his emphasis on the deep traumas of racist colonization in the black psyche. He shares Kristeva's sense that politics shapes the intimate space of the psyche in radical ways that imperil language, identity, and community. However, his intimate politics requires a reworking of the whiteness of old Judeo-Christian Europe. Black subjects that attempt to heal the traumas of colonization with white masks simply repeat those traumas. Like the revolt of the "nihilist" whose repetitions withdraw into old values, white masks encourage a kind of schizophrenic reaction as the black subject faces the "racist epidermalization of his being in the eyes of the white colonials."[74] Gratton does not pretend to find a similar attention to racism and antiracism in Kristeva's work. Nevertheless, he concludes that intimate revolt could help heal the psychic traumas of colonization. Who needs psychoanalysis in destitute times? Everyone, Kristeva would answer, and Gratton concurs.[75] Although I find their intimate politics resonant with one another, we should be cautious about assimilating Fanon's thinking into Kristeva's as if one is host to the other. Fanon's intimate politics are about understanding himself on his own antiracist and decolonial terms.

The importance of this caution becomes clear in Ziarek's essay on Kristeva and Fanon.[76] She, too, finds that Fanon's work illuminates the question of intimate revolt and racist colonization. Her essay explores how, for Fanon, the conflict between colonizer and colonized is a productive, imaginative reworking of particularity and universality. It is not enough to say, with good will, "we are all humans." To do so minimizes the importance of black identity and risks reaffirming a white colonial understanding of the universal. Fanon and Sartre famously clashed on this issue.[77] In *Black Orpheus*, originally published as an introduction to a collection of Leopold Senghor's poetry, Sartre discounts the importance of black particularity by suggesting that the Negritude movement was a minor stage or episode in a more important human project. "Negritude is for destroying itself, it is a passage and not an outcome, a means and not an ultimate end."[78] "The Lived Experience of the Black," an essay from 1951 that reappears as the fifth chapter of *Black Skin, White Masks*, takes aim at this instrumentalization of black identity and the ways that it obscures the intimate politics of colonization and minimizes how racism is lived in and through the black psyche. "Help had been sought from a friend of the colored peoples, and that friend had found no better response than to point out the relativity of what they were doing"; "Jean-Paul Sartre, in this work, has destroyed black zeal. . . . I needed not to know. . . . At the very moment when I was trying to grasp my own being, Sartre, who remained The Other, gave me my name and thus shattered my last illusion."[79] As Cusick puts it clearly: "Sartre's declaring an end to racialism undermines the power of experiencing blackness positively; rendering it as a temporary move on the way to universal humanism makes it almost powerless. To succeed, *négritude* has to be able to be experienced as absolute."[80] When Fanon imagines a new humanism in the final pages of *Black Skin, White Masks*, it is not a simple affirmation of humanism. It is a tentative possibility to come and an indefinite process of reckoning with particularity and universality. It is a commitment to radical self-questioning and self-transformation in hostile conditions.

On Ziarek's reading, Fanon's project is similar to Kristeva's and, importantly, their revolts might sharpen one another. While Fanon emphasizes but does not theorize the feminization of the excluded other, Kristevan revolt involves the reimagining of femininity in light of its exclusion from the masculine universal subject.[81] While Kristeva emphasizes a French model of revolt, Fanon offers an important critique of the exclusion of colonized peoples from the white French universal subject. Ziarek argues that there is a missed opportunity between Kristeva and Fanon, an opportunity to reckon with the messy traumas of intimate politics and the precarious possibilities of intimate revolt. Considered alongside Fanon, the Eurocentric thematics of Kristeva's account of intimate revolt come to the fore. The French model of self-questioning and permanent restlessness is not on display in Sartre's *destruction of* black zeal.[82] Fanon would like to lose himself in the poetry of Senghor and "the unforeseeable" without the common dismissal, "you'll change, my boy; I was like that too when I was young . . . you'll see, it will all pass."[83] Ziarek argues that Fanon's struggle to experience blackness positively can involve what Kristeva calls a fertile moment of depression.[84] However, it is important to appreciate the ways that Fanon tarries with the unforeseeable. Would an experience of the twists, turns, and detours of black zeal ultimately arrive at a conclusion described as Kristevan or labeled as intimate revolt? For Fanon, pretending to know in advance limits the restless depths at which these questions of identity register.

Ziarek's article begins with a telling epigraph taken from a 2002 interview with Kristeva by Rainer Ganahl, who comments: "There is someone who you don't mention in your book and who I find extremely important: Frantz Fanon, a revolutionary and a psychoanalyst that has written the article 'On Violence.'"[85] Kristeva replies: "I have often heard people speak of him, but I have never read anything by him. He isn't part of the mainstream of Psychoanalytic Studies."[86] Gratton, too, notes Kristeva's disinterest in Fanon and adds that, despite her many engagements with Sartre, she seems to avoid Sartre's texts on Fanon and his other texts on resistance to colonialism. For instance, instead of Sartre's introduction to *Wretched of the Earth,* in which he writes that the great lesson of Fanon "is that we are estranged from ourselves," *The Sense and Non-sense of Revolt* turns to his letter rejecting the Nobel Prize in 1964.[87] Gratton asks: "Is this tied to her resistance to thinking the colonial apparatus, notably absent in works that again and again consider nations and nationality, particularly in the French nation-state? Is this why she can describe the end of French colonialism, without irony, as the 'French returning home'?"[88]

Gratton and Ziarek are right that Kristeva's project of intimate revolt resonates but does not engage with Fanon's thinking. Kristeva's response to Ganahl can be held up to Sartre's reasoning on his refusal of the Nobel Prize—the need to stay true to the affinities and trajectories of one's own writing. "The writer must therefore refuse to let himself be transformed into an institution."[89] In my view, Kristeva falls short of the affinities and trajectories of her notion of intimate revolt, as she actively ignores the work of Fanon in accordance with the psychoanalytic "mainstream." My concern is posed from the perspective of an intimate politics, not that of the identity politics of citation. It is not that black zeal must be represented in discussions of intimate revolt. Rather, a lack of curiosity and a failure of self-questioning seems to decide in advance what it looks like to traverse the limits of the representable/thinkable/tenable vis-à-vis identity.

In "My Memory's Hyperbole," Kristeva describes the "we" as "only a part of 'me.' It is a temporary stability in which projections and identifications are settled among some and allow the history of a perpetually changing whole to be written. A 'we' is alive only if it is never the same."[90] For Fanon, the "we" of black subjectivity is indeed only alive if it is never the same, if it reckons with the unforeseeable, if it finds a way to navigate and veer beyond the sameness of white masks through which blackness has been understood and barely lived as a life of death, traumatizing and retraumatizing through the logics of colonialism. This involves the messy confrontation and displacement of the projections and identifications that settle in the lived bodies and psyches of colonized and colonizing peoples. Here, the difficult work of questioning and self-questioning might change the meaning of blackness, whiteness, and humanity. Fanon aims to transform particularity and universality. The concluding passages of *Black Skin, White Masks* are a declaration of black zeal and black power. The statement "I, the man of color, want only this" precedes Fanon's call for readers to "turn their backs on the inhuman voices," and his final prayer, "O my body, make of me always a man who questions!"[91] In these elliptical moments, it is Fanon's estrangement as a man of color that hosts the tentative possibility of a more enlivened humanism. He is not, with good will, saying "we are all humans" or "we are all strangers." He is disrupting assumptions about who is perpetually changing and who is frozen in time, who is a host and who is a stranger, who is a stranger and who is stranger than other strangers, who is French and who is a foreigner.

IV. Conclusion: Decolonizing Revolt in the Spectacle

Writing in the 1950s and 1960s, Fanon could not have anticipated the spectacular psychosocial changes brought about by technology, media, and globalization.

Indeed, Kristeva's writings on revolt are framed by a concern with not only the power vacuum but also the society of the spectacle. Normalizing mechanisms are diffused throughout mass culture. Power cannot be located in part because it circulates through a vast and overwhelming network of images. The spectacle collapses intimacy and exhausts the imagination. Saturated by media, "the psychic life of modern individuals wavers between somatic symptoms (getting sick and going to the hospital) and the visual depiction of their desires (daydreaming in front of the TV)."[92] In this context, the spectacle is also normalizing theater. "People are increasingly excited when they think they have unearthed a guilty party, a scapegoat" because we live in "a so-called liberal society in which there is no surveillance and no punishment except in these theatrically mediatized cases that become a sort of catharsis of the citizen's nonexistent guilt."[93] In such an environment, forging opportunities for loving support and indefinite questioning is an urgent and incredibly difficult project.

This essay's attention to racism and colonization connects with these Kristevan concerns because, today, colonial logics circulate in the spectacle, threatening to accelerate the repetition of exclusions for the entertainment and consumption of distant viewers. Moreover, the fetishized logic of "the political" also operates at warp speed as incidents of racism and colonial violence "go viral." The hourly and daily cycles of media shock and scapegoating offer little intimate space for remembering, reworking, and reviving psychic space. In this context, it is important to challenge Fraser's influential misreading of Kristeva's subject-in-process as a retreat from politics in the form of an apolitical "paralyzing oscillation" between identity and non-identity. For Kristeva, intimate revolt is an affirmation of the remnants of psychic space that might be reworked and revived toward a transformation of meaning. Intimate, psychic space is important and imperiled political terrain. Reading Kristeva's passionate politicization of intimacy, one senses an opportunity to build connections to histories swallowed by the society of the spectacle. For instance, if we attend to the ways that racism and colonialism shape old laws and if we engage with cultural forms that inspire critical questioning of these histories, suffering psyches might find new, healing meanings in the world. Kristeva's writings do not follow these antiracist, postcolonial trajectories. I have argued here that intimate revolt is limited not by its intimate shape but by its Eurocentric biases. As we have seen, Fanon demands an experience of the unforeseeable or (ex)orbitant, for an absolute but in a deep, restless, curious shape—a question mark.

Fanon and Kristeva, two strangers. What kind of solidarity and community can be found or made between them? What kinds of intimacies might emerge? If we decenter the white European subject, if we traverse the limits of what is representable/tenable, if we twist and turn and veer with no determined itinerary in advance, if "we take a good look at ourselves," then who are we?

Sarah K. Hansen

California State University, Northridge
March 2019

NOTES

1. Julia Kristeva, *The Sense and Non-sense of Revolt: The Powers and Limits of Psychoanalysis Volume 1*, trans. Jeanine Herman (New York: Columbia University Press, 2000); *Intimate Revolt: The Powers and Limits of Psychoanalysis Volume 2*, trans. Jeanine Herman (New York: Columbia University Press, 2002).

2. Julia Kristeva, *Revolution in Poetic Language*, trans. Margret Waller (New York: Columbia University Press, 1984).

3. Kristeva, *The Sense and Non-sense of Revolt*, 8.

4. Ibid, 1.

5. Kristeva, *Intimate Revolt*, 11.

6. See, for example, Cecilia Sjöholm, *Kristeva and the Political* (New York: Routledge, 2005); Kelly Oliver and S. K. Keltner, eds., *Psychoanalysis, Aesthetics, and Politics in the Work of Julia Kristeva* (New York: SUNY Press, 2009); Tina Chanter and Ewa Plonowska Ziarek, eds., *Revolt, Affect, Collectivity: The Unstable Boundaries of Kristeva's Polis* (Albany: SUNY Press, 2005).

7. See Kelly Oliver, "Julia Kristeva's Feminist Revolutions," *Hypatia* 8, no. 3 (Summer 1993): 94–114.

8. Jeff Edmonds, "Kristeva's Uncanny Revolutions: Imagining the Meaning of Politics," in Oliver and Keltner, *Psychoanalysis, Aesthetics, and Politics*, 214.

9. Julia Kristeva, "In Conversation with Rosalind Coward," in Kelly Oliver, ed., *The Portable Kristeva* (New York: Columbia University Press, 2002), 341.

10. Kristeva, *Intimate Revolt*, 224.

11. Julia Kristeva, "My Memory's Hyperbole," in *The Portable Kristeva*, 4.

12. Sara Beardsworth, *Julia Kristeva: Psychoanalysis and Modernity* (Albany: SUNY Press, 2004), 274.

13. Kristeva, "My Memory's Hyperbole," 20–21.

14. See Kelly Oliver, *Reading Kristeva: Unraveling the Double-Bind* (Bloomington: Indiana University Press, 1993), 131.

15. See Gayatri Spivak, *A Critique of Postcolonial Reason* (Cambridge: Harvard University Press, 1999), 66n83.

16. Ibid., 67.

17. Kristeva, *Intimate Revolt*, 11.

18. Julia Kristeva, *Strangers to Ourselves*, trans. Leon S. Roudiez (New York: Columbia University Press, 1991); *Nations Without Nationalism*, trans. Leon S. Roudiez (New York: Columbia University Press, 1993).

19. In 1989 three young women from North African families were expelled from French public school for wearing headscarves. See Norma Clare Moruzzi, "National Abjects: Julia Kristeva on the Process of Political Self-Identification," in Kelly Oliver, ed., *Ethics, Politics and Difference in Julia Kristeva's Writing* (New York: Routledge, 1993), 136–42.

20. Nancy Fraser, "The Uses and Abuses of French Discourse Theories for Feminist Politics," *Theory, Culture, & Society* 9, no. 1 (1992): 51–71.

21. See ibid., 66.

22. Kristeva, *Strangers to Ourselves*, 2–3.

23. Ibid., 3.

24. Ibid., 24

25. Ibid.

26. Ibid., 2.

27. Oliver, *Reading Kristeva*, 134.

28. Ibid., 136.

29. Ibid., 136.

30. Julia Kristeva, *Crisis of the ~~European~~ Subject*, trans. Susan Fairfield (New York: Other Press, 2000), 170.

31. Kristeva, *Strangers to Ourselves*, 191.

32. Ibid.

33. See Fraser, "The Uses and Abuses of French Discourse Theories for Feminist Politics." See also Ewa Ziarek, "The Uncanny Style of Kristeva's Critique of Nationalism," *Postmodern Culture* 5, no. 2 (January 1995): 5.

34. Kristeva, *Strangers to Ourselves*, 195.

35. Sara Ahmed, "The Skin of the Community: Affect and Boundary Formation," in Chanter and Ziarek, *Revolt, Affect, Collectivity*, 96.

36. Ibid., 96.

37. Ibid., 109.

38. Ibid., 108–9.

39. Sigmund Freud, "The 'Uncanny,'" in *The Standard Edition of the Complete Psychological Works of Sigmund Freud*, vol. XVII, trans. James Strachey (London: Hogarth, 1964).

40. Kristeva, *Strangers to Ourselves*, 191.

41. Ewa Ziarek, "The Uncanny Style of Kristeva's Critique of Nationalism," 17n10.

42. Ibid.

43. Ibid.

44. E. Jentsch, "Zur Psychologie des Unheimlichen," *Psychiatrisch-Neurologische Wochenschrift* 8, 22 (August 25, 1906): 195–98, and 8, 23 (September 1, 1906): 203–5. Sigmund Freud, "The 'Uncanny.'"

45. E. T. A. Hoffmann, *The Sandman*, trans. Peter Wortsman (London: Penguin, 2016).

46. Ziarek, "The Uncanny Style of Kristeva's Critique of Nationalism," 17n10.

47. Ahmed, "The Skin of the Community," 108.

48. Ibid., 109.

49. Kristeva, *Sense and Non-sense of Revolt*, 4.

50. For further reading on postcoloniality, see Benedict Anderson, *Imagined Communities: Reflections on the Origin and Spread of Nationalism* (London: Verso, 2000); Homi Bhahba, *The Location of Culture, Nation and Narration* (London: Routledge, 1994); Gayatri Spivak, *A Critique of Postcolonial Reason*; "Can the Subaltern Speak?" in Patrick Williams and Laura Chrisman, eds., *Colonial Discourse and Postcolonial Theory* (New York: Columbia University Press, 1994); Edward Said, *Orientalism* (New York: Pantheon, 1978); Frantz Fanon, *Black Skin, White Masks* (London: Pluto Press, 2008) and *The Wretched of the Earth* (New York: Grove, 1968); Chandra Mohanty, "Under Western Eyes: Feminist Scholarship and Colonial Discourses," in Williams and Chrisman, eds., *Colonial Discourse and Postcolonial Theory*.

51. Kristeva, *Sense and Non-sense of Revolt*, 23.

52. Ibid., 7.

53. Kelly Oliver, "Revolt and Forgiveness," in Chanter and Ziarek, *Revolt, Affect, Collectivity*, 85.

54. Ibid., 83.

55. Ibid.

56. Catherine Clément and Julia Kristeva, *The Feminine and The Sacred*, trans. Jane Marie Todd (New York: Columbia University Press, 2001), 142. Oliver, "Revolt and Forgiveness," 82.

57. Kristeva, *Intimate Revolt*, 146; *New Maladies of the Soul*, trans. Ross Guberman (New York: Columbia University Press, 1995), 88.

58. Kelly Oliver, *The Colonization of Psychic Space: A Psychoanalytic Theory of Oppression* (Minneapolis: University of Minnesota Press, 2004), 146.

59. Kristeva, *New Maladies of the Soul*, 89; *Intimate Revolt*, 213.

60. Kristeva, *Intimate Revolt*, 146–47.

61. Revolt is "free questioning and permanent restlessness," and celebrates "the French tradition of critical questioning, the importance attached to political debate, and the role of intellectuals—exemplified by the Enlightenment philosophers who are so emblematic of French culture—are factors which continually revivify public debate, and maintain it at a very high level." Julia Kristeva, "Thinking about Liberty in Dark Times," in *Hatred and Forgiveness*, trans. Jeanine Herman (New York: Columbia University Press, 2010), 4, 19.

62. Kristeva, *Intimate Revolt*, 146–47.
63. Ibid., 7.
64. Clément and Kristeva, *The Feminine and the Sacred*, 13.
65. Kristeva, "Thinking about Liberty in Dark Times," 4.
66. Ibid.
67. Quoted in ibid, 4.
68. Peter Gratton, "What are Psychoanalysts for in a Destitute Time? Kristeva and the Community in Revolt," *Journal for Cultural Research* 11, no. 1 (January 2007): 1–13.
69. Ibid., 2–3.
70. Gratton, "What are Psychoanalysts for in a Destitute Time?" 12.
71. Ibid., 2. Gratton's view suggests that her Eurocentricism is a momentary lapse in some places within her broader oeuvre.
72. Fanon, *Black Skin, White Masks*, 82; *The Wretched of the Earth*, 40.
73. Fanon, *Black Skin, White Masks*, 181.
74. Gratton, "What are Psychoanalysts for in a Destitute Time?" 8.
75. Ibid., 10, 12.
76. Ewa Ziarek, "Kristeva and Fanon: The Future of the Revolt of the Future of an Illusion*?" Southern Journal of Philosophy* 42, no. 1 (2004): 25–41.
77. See Kathryn Sophia Belle (formerly Kathryn Gines), "Fanon and Sartre 50 Years Later: To Retain or Reject the Concept of Race, *Sartre Studies International* 9, no. 2 (2003): 55–67.
78. Jean-Paul Sartre, "Black Orpheus," in Robert Bernasconi, ed., *Race* (Massachusetts: Blackwell, 2001), 137; "Orphée Noir," in Leopold Senghor, *Anthologie de la nouvelle poésie nègre et malgache de langue française* (Paris: PUF, 1948).
79. Fanon, *Black Skin, White Masks*, 102, 103–5.
80. Carolyn Cusick, "Fanon's Black Skin, White Masks on Race Consciousness," *Americaquests* 3, no. 3 (2006): 1–11, 1.
81. Ziarek, "Kristeva and Fanon," 39.
82. Fanon, *Black Skin, White Masks*, 103.
83. Ibid.
84. Ewa Ziarek, "Kristeva and Fanon." Clément and Kristeva, *The Feminine and The Sacred*, 142.
85. Julia Kristeva, *Revolt, She Said*, trans. Brian O'Keeffe (Los Angeles: Semiotext(e), 2002), 110.
86. Ibid.
87. Gratton, "What are Psychoanalysts for in a Destitute Time?" 9.
88. Ibid., 9.
89. Jean-Paul Sartre, "Sartre on the Nobel Prize," trans. Richard Howard, *New York Review of Books*, December 17, 1964.
90. Kristeva, "My Memory's Hyperbole," 4.
91. Fanon, *Black Skin, White Masks*, 180–81.
92. Kristeva, *New Maladies of the Soul*, 8.
93. Kristeva, *The Sense and Non-sense of Revolt*, 5.

25

Daniel Cohn-Bendit

HANNAH ARENDT PRIZE SPEECH 2006

Julia will understand how difficult it is for a person from Frankfurt to come to Bremen a week after losing the soccer game, but I am happy to do so for her, for you, Julia. There is a wonderful expression of hers, "*je me voyage*," which is practically a definition of what she is. It is originally a character in one of her novels but it is also her. "I travel myself." Let me, then, take you and her on a journey. Because Julia was born in Bulgaria in 1941 and the question is, when you want to introduce yourself, Julia Kristeva, what do you say? Bulgarian? French? I could say: welcome, she's European, because Bulgaria just joined the Union, and it makes it easier for me to say she's European. But it's not that easy.

To figure it out, I'd like to use one of Amin Maalouf's thoughts, he's a . . . But here we go again, it is again a difficult beginning: Amin Maalouf, what is he? A writer born in Lebanon—that's still easy. Is he French? Lebanese? That, he says, is exactly the question that people ask him all the time: yes, what are you actually? Are you Lebanese or are you French? And he answers: as much the one as the other. Yes, understood, you are both, but deep down in your heart, what are you? When you're having a difficult time or when you must identify yourself, what are you? And he answers: I am neither nor. Yes, so you are one-half French and one-half Lebanese. No, there is no such thing as a half identity, with one partial identity here and one partial identity there, I am a whole, and as a whole, I am—and he says, I quote: "I am constantly put under pressure to choose, but this pressure does not come from fanatics or xenophobes, it comes from people like you and me who always ask the same

Translated from German by Daniel Argelès. This is the speech given by Daniel Cohn-Bendit at the ceremony of the Hannah Arendt Prize for Political Thought, when it was awarded to Julia Kristeva in Bremen in 2006. Daniel Cohn-Bendit is laureate of the 2001 Hannah Arendt Prize.

question. Because there is indeed this habit, these bigoted efforts to try to reduce identity to a core. As if there was a core of identity—one must protest against that, and I say it with anger: I don't have one unique unequivocal core, my identity is plural and equivocal."

You will say, this is a platitude, everyone could say that, every intellectual, every well-meaning person, and I found one at the round table of intellectuals, an absolutely brilliant one who actually invented the lightning rod—not bad—and was amongst the first signers of the American Declaration of Independence, and also deeply impressed Tocqueville. His name is Benjamin Franklin and in 1751 he wrote a pamphlet about the Palatine peasants. It was about identity, about being. And I swear, even though I'm completely secular, I swear on anything you'll choose that what I'm about to read to you is not a joke, it is real and was written that way. The context was an argument about Palatine peasants, i.e. German immigrants to America. These German immigrants, most of the time, were Catholics. They were coming from the Palatinate and they were different from the other immigrants, the Anglicans. Different in a simple sense. The Anglicans work seven days a week or six days a week and then on the seventh day they go to church in the morning and then they essentially stay home. You know that: for a long time, it was impossible to organize a soccer game or a tennis match in Wimbledon on a Sunday. The Catholics, the Palatine peasants, had a different tradition. They worked six days a week and on the seventh day they also went to church, but then they went to the beer tent or the wine tent and they let loose. And that upset the Anglicans terribly, they set those tents on fire, it was a real *Kulturkampf*, a real culture war. And that's when this Benjamin Franklin wrote about America's ethnic purity. I'm not making this up: "the Number of purely white People in the World is proportionately very small. All *Africa* is black or tawny . . . *America* (exclusive of the new Comers) wholly so. And in *Europe*, the *Spaniards*, *Italians*, *French*, *Russians* and *Swedes*, are generally of what we call a swarthy Complexion; as are the *Germans* also, the *Saxons* only excepted, who, with the *English*, make the principal Body of White People on the Face of the Earth. I could wish their Numbers were increased." [*Laughter in the audience.*] Well, sometimes it is not funny.

To this, Julia Kristeva responds in *Strangers to Ourselves*:

> In the absence of a new community bond—a saving religion that would integrate the bulk of wanderers and different people within a new consensus, other than "more money and goods for everyone"—we are, for the first time in history, confronted with the following situation: we must live with different people while relying on our personal moral codes, without the assistance of a set that would include our particularities while transcending them. A paradoxical community is emerging, made up of foreigners who are reconciled with themselves to the extent that they recognize themselves as foreigners. The multinational society would thus be the consequence of an extreme individualism, but conscious of its discontents and limits, knowing only indomitable people ready-to-help-themselves in their weakness, a weakness whose other name is our radical strangeness.[1]

This is the challenge that Julia Kristeva set for herself.

Now there is a litmus test to determine whether this is true or not and where the difficulties lie. It is a hellish sort of moment, in which one doesn't know where or how anymore. You will never guess what this litmus test is. Maybe Julia will if I mention a date: November 17, 1993. I also went through a similar hell, on July 8, 1982. You still don't know what this litmus test is. Well, on July 8, 1982 France was playing against Germany, it was the World Cup semifinal in Spain, in Seville, and France was unfairly sent home after the penalty kicks. It was awful. On that day—and it must be faced—why was I French? Maybe because I experienced soccer as a child and a thing from childhood shapes identity more. And now comes my question for Julia: November 17, 1993. As a child, in Bulgaria, she roamed the soccer fields with her father. And on November 17, 1993, during the World Cup qualifiers, Bulgaria sent France packing. I don't know if she was watching. But if she was, because she very often watches soccer, I would like to know whether she was happy or sad on that day. It was her childhood and it was her reality, because, as we know, she has been living in France since 1965.

Let us review Julia Kristeva's journey. She is an intellectual, she embraced political theories, she tried freedom at all levels, she went to China, then wrote a book about it, *About Chinese Women*, she belonged to a group in France, *Tel Quel*, where she tried something, where they tried something crazy, along the lines of: is there something in Maoism, in what is emerging in China, some way of transcending freedom that we could wish for ourselves? After her trip to China she was a bit disappointed, one must say. The Cultural Revolution didn't seem to be the thing after all. But she had this desire to keep thinking further, to keep developing, she explored the most diverse political theories, and she was not afraid when President Jacques Chirac asked her if she would write a report about disabilities, because for her disabled people were not fully represented in our society, and so she accepted. She was not afraid, over the years, to stand up to anybody, she had a feminist point of view but she was not afraid—afraid in the sense of intellectual confrontation—to argue with feminists. She took a stand on the migration process, on political theory, found a way to psychoanalysis, in other words a path to herself, a way to grapple with oneself. Psychoanalysis led her not only to become a psychoanalyst but also to use it in the interpretation of social phenomena. And in her interpretation of literature and of people, in her interpretation of a specific literary moment, she always tried, whether to describe Simone de Beauvoir or Paul Celan, to detect sexuality, emotion, poetry.

And finally, she wrote a trilogy, "Female Genius—Life, Madness, Words," about three women, Hannah Arendt, Melanie Klein, and Colette.[2] I believe Hannah Arendt stands for political philosophy, Melanie Klein for psychoanalysis, and Colette for desire, for fun, for sexuality in the widest sense. And in the course of this confrontation we come to a point where we should ask ourselves: Yes, but where is she? And isn't it at the same time presumptuous and magnificent, this female genius that she describes in three works and three women? That she would say that and that we would accept it and wonder how somebody had the force, the chutzpah, and the courage to say: that's me, I am also these three women or I want to be them, I want to go that road. And I find this to be one of the greatest intellectual challenges that we see ourselves confronted with—and that, to me, is Julia Kristeva.

And when one asks her what defines her thought or when she has to describe it herself—I quote:

> *Je ne me sens pas d'humeur* conclusive, *pas encore: les* épreuves *m'ont appris à vivre dans l'ouvert.*—I don't have the need *to come to an end, to conclude*, not yet: the *challenges* of life have taught me to remain in an open state.[3]

She continues:

> *Celui qui n'a pas d'épreuves ou, plutôt, qui les dénie se contente en realité d'une identité jalousement gardée. Il conserve ainsi ses limites, ses principes, ses protections qui lui servent d'antidépresseurs. Au contraire, l'épreuve* peut *nous offrir l'occasion de 'faire nos preuves,' elle met à mal les frontières et nos défenses et ne nous laisse pas beaucoup de choix; soit on se déprime, soit on met en question valeurs et certitudes. J'essaie, dans ma vie et dans ma pensée, de me tenir dans ce questionnement* —He who doesn't experience trials or, rather, who denies them, accepts a closed identity. He preserves what he keeps inside, his antidepressants, but he can't open up to the world. A trial *can* give us the opportunity to 'prove ourselves,' to give proof of what we are capable of and what we want. Such a trial tests the limits of our boundaries and defenses, and doesn't leave us much choice. Either we can't master this challenge or we are able to question our certainties, our values. I try in my life and my thought, to hold myself in this questioning.[4]

And then she sums up her thought:

> *Un projet sans programme, un* état *de surprise permanente face aux phénomènes, aux discours, au sens et au non-sens, qui me libèrent de ce qui a eu lieu ainsi que de mes jugements antérieurs, et qui m'incitent à une sorte de dépassement. Je vis avec ce désir de sortir de moi.*[5]

Thus: I have a project without a program that is going to close me in, to bring me to a close. What I want is *un état de surprise* (and remember she just quoted Hannah Arendt here), to be able to seize the surprise of being, and this surprise, the acceptance of the surprise is a moment of liberation, a liberation of thought. And she ends by saying: "I live with this desire, this need to come out of myself, to go out of myself."[6]

This is, I think, what Hannah Arendt—you see, I knew this would happen at some point—this is what Julia Kristeva tells us. And then, politically, she stands by it—and it is quite rare for people of our generation to stand by it—Yes, she says, one has the right to revolt. Yes, she says, revolts are part of it, and here I will quote her again because I see there are also a lot of parents here, and what I will quote is difficult for all of us if we agree to it and most of the time we do because we are from the right generation, yes, but in the end:

> *Oui, on a raison de se révolter.*—Yes, one has the right, one is right to revolt.[7] *Et ce n'est pas simplement un bon mot censé flatter.*—This is not just said to please. *La révolte constitue notre intégrité psychique.*—Revolt structures our psychic integrity. *La vie psychique, le psychisme comme vie.*—It is inside our psyche.[8]

And here it comes, parents, pay attention:

> *Si l'enfant ne se révolte pas contre le père ou la mère, si l'adolescent ne crée pas une réalité rebelle contre ses parents, contre l'école et contre l'État, il est tout simplement mort.*—If a child doesn't revolt against his father or mother, if a teenager doesn't create a rebellious reality against her parents, against school, and against the state, she is quite simply dead.[9]

Right? How many adolescent children do we have? And do we suffer from their revolt or not? And are we able to hold out against it? This is, in my opinion, an important question.

> *Il [l'enfant] se prive de la possibilité d'innovation et de création, il devient un robot.*—A child deprived of the possibility of innovation and creation becomes a robot.[10]

Is that what we want?

> *Cette grande question générale est d'une actualité quotidienne, brûlante.*—This is a big question and a burning issue.

For us parents in any case. What I want to show with this, when she then speaks about Sartre in her lectures, or about Simone de Beauvoir, is that she is not blind, she describes how Sartre rejected his Nobel Prize, with this whole antibourgeois attitude, while at the same time accepting communism, totalitarianism—how this antibourgeois stance was coupled with a bourgeois blindness, and so forth. She disenchants the whole enchantment of life, and yet one is enchanted over and over again by this quest for a non-, not only a non-correct thought, but the quest for a thought that is also able to rebel, to say no to what happens in the world.

To conclude, I would like to quote her again, to quote from the book that she wrote about Hannah Arendt. Because it is fascinating how she tries to remove this whole antimotherhood from feminism. A woman, she says, the thing that creates, defines a woman, is precisely to create life. And she analyzes—and it is very interesting—how Hannah Arendt, although she was not a mother, described it very early on as a human gift. And this is how her book about Hannah Arendt ends:

> A full experience of natality would inevitably include birth, life, an affirmation of the uniqueness of each birth, and continual rebirth in the life of the mind—a mind that *is* because it begins again in the plurality of other people, and only then does it act like a living thought that surpasses all other activities. But the

> "miracle" [not the Bern Miracle] also occurs, if only in a single fragment of this "full experience," which justifies the miracle through the promise it provides and the forgiveness it articulates. Arendt shared in that miracle, for she was without a doubt one of the few people of our time to attain the state of bliss in which living is thinking. Did she not write once that, although the rapture of thought is ineffable, "the only possible metaphor one may conceive of for the life of the mind is the sensation of being alive"?
>
> As for a political action that would be tantamount to a birth and that would shelter us from estrangement, Hannah Arendt—without indulging in too many illusions—invites us to think about it and to experience it in the present, while always remaining inside the realm between promise and forgiveness.[11]

This is also Julia Kristeva.

Daniel Cohn-Bendit

Copresident of The Greens/European Free
Alliance in the European Parliament, 2002–2014
December 2006

NOTES

1. Julia Kristeva, *Strangers to Ourselves*, trans. Leon S. Roudiez (New York: Columbia University Press, 1991), 195.
2. Julia Kristeva, *Hannah Arendt*, trans. Ross Guberman (New York: Columbia University Press, 2001); *Melanie Klein*, trans. Ross Guberman (New York: Columbia University Press, 2001); *Colette*, trans. Jane Marie Todd (New York: Columbia University Press, 2004).
3. Julia Kristeva, "La Chine telle quelle," Preface to *Des Chinoises* (Paris: Pauvert, 2005), 9.
4. Julia Kristeva, "Je vis avec ce désir de sortir de moi," *Le Monde*, November 17, 2005.
5. Ibid.
6. Ibid.
7. See, for example, Julia Kristeva, *Revolt, She Said* (Los Angeles: Semiotext(e), 2002), 83.
8. [For these ideas in her writings, see Julia Kristeva, *The Sense and Non-sense of Revolt: The Powers and Limits of Psychoanalysis Volume 1*, trans. Jeanine Herman (New York: Columbia University Press, 2000), 6–17, and *Intimate Revolt: The Powers and Limits of Psychoanalysis Volume 2*, trans. Jeanine Herman (New York: Columbia University Press, 2002), ch. 1.—Ed.]
9. [For this notion in her writings, see Julia Kristeva, *New Maladies of the Soul*, trans. Ross Guberman (New York: Columbia University Press, 1995), ch. 9, and "L'Adolescence, un syndrome d'idéalité," in *La Haine et le pardon* (Paris: Fayard, 2005).—Ed.]
10. Julia Kristeva, *Au risque de la pensée* (Paris: l'Aube, 2001), 40.
11. Kristeva, *Hannah Arendt*, 239–40.

REPLY

TO EMILIA ANGELOVA, SARAH K. HANSEN, AND DANIEL COHN-BENDIT

I. EMILIA ANGELOVA

With remarkable precision and uniquely in this volume, Emilia Angelova addresses the violence of the *traumatism*. Taking up the analysis of the "Rat Man" done by Freud, and in light of the reading I propose in *New Maladies of the Soul* (1993), she returns to the "*inaccessible trauma*" that characterizes the bond between the Rat Man and his mother, "the rigorous requirements of the symbolic and the rigorous requirements of excitability."[1] Comparing my interpretations of the *trauma* (notably in "the impossibility of losing"—"this reversible orality, this nonverbal, impossible-to-represent necrophilia that is *acted out*")[2] with those of Lacan (*das Ding*) and those of Levinas ("original traumatism"), and mentioning analyses by Beardsworth and Oliver, Angelova synthesizes my traversal of the Freudian unconscious and the Kleinian breakthrough. With Angelova, it is a matter of "emphasizing a logic of subversion through a *negativity*, as opposed to *negation*, that leads to a conversion between the veritable buried mother and the inaccessible trauma and regime of mourning, a logic that nonetheless entails the intervention of a *third*, such as the analyst, who is, in this configuration, a substitute for the loving, imaginary father" (my emphasis). The "mourning processes of the maternal repressed" can then continue, owing less to their "status as a negation than as a *question*." This conception of *revolt* as a *questioning* is taken up and closely argued by Sarah Hansen: "Questioning calls up an experience of relationality before [or rather *beyond*?] the 'no,' which supports the drives in language and, eventually, the reconnection of signs and things in the form of a 'negation of negation.' In effect, the relational pleasure of questioning counterbalances the impending trauma of separation."

This trajectory, as clinical as it is philosophical, leads Angelova to mark the stages of the *perpetual detachment of trauma*, that "intimate revolt," according to my terminology, which she detects in the incursion-investment of the drives through the memory traces of emotions and sensations in language: "the semiotic breaching of the symbolic," "the heart of the capacity to speak." Intimate revolt, then, language extending toward the unnameable trauma can become

Translated from French by Armine Kotin Mortimer.

fixed in the phobia of Little Hans, another famous patient of Dr. Freud's, and function like a "hallucinatory metaphor . . . language without a signified."

Having evoked the anthropological and religious contexts of these psychosexual lived experiences, Angelova connects the maternal unnameable to that of the sacred, which one can envision as a "metaphoricity," "always incomplete scription retroactive upon a semiotic that it never fully grasps."

This reflection, which we must indeed call a *semanalysis*, concludes with the *figurability* inherent in language—in its rhetorical figures (according to Aristotle's poetics), in displacements and condensations (according to Freud's primary processes)—which forged and remains implicit in the *morphemes* and *lexemes* of our ordinary codes. Discussing the traumas of the Rat Man and Little Hans, the mourning-abjection of the maternal, and the investment/cathexis of the ideal-loving thirdness, Angelova succeeds in rehabilitating the *metaphoricity* inherent in language as a system of communication and, potentially, as a laboratory of creativity. Infinite adjustment of the drive-*semiotic* with the regulating *symbolic*, the imaginary effectively becomes the laboratory of creativity and is not reduced to *lure* or *illusion*, as those who tend to hypostasize the *symbolic* claim.

Angelova is right to point out that my conceptions of *signifiance* and the *imaginary*, at the crossroads of *fantasy* and the *metaphoricity* of language, can be read as challenges to the Lacanian notions of the "signifier" and the "symbolic." However, when one considers Lacan's allusions to "*lalangue*" (as a single word),[3] which embraces in *his* signifier the *echolalia* anterior to the *system* of language, I would say that my conception of the imaginary—which is not prelinguistic but translinguistic—inscribes itself less against than "right up against" Lacan's Real-Symbolic-Imaginary topology.[4]

The defense and illustration of the imaginary that follow, in Angelova's text, develop both "this metaphoricity as . . . a third (aesthetic), law-like purposivity," and the approach to *traumatism* that "cannot be located in any sort of designatable meaning or symbolic law," as well as to *affect* as "the port through which traumatism enters, breaching the symbolic." Definitively, the imaginary operates in the *sublimation* in which the "artistic imagination as driving intimate revolt" excels. The imaginary, revolt of the drive *chora* against the fixed codes of communities, carves out the bed of intimate freedom; it is freedom's fleeting and shareable form.

I thank Angelova for concluding on the place of the imaginary in Western culture, determining and even central because it is "transformative": this "specific economy of 'imaginary discourses,' referencing the Western tradition." I feel this study resonates with the experience of writing as practiced by two women whose lives and works have marked the women's liberation movement: Beauvoir the novelist and Colette, whose "blossoming" continues to be written.

"Writing has remained the great concern of my life," stated the author of *The Second Sex*.[5] For her, the novel is an act of existential affirmation by which *the unlivable of the intimate is transmuted into political stakes*. This hybrid genre in which Beauvoir risked her intimacy reconnects with the origins of the novel as a dialogical and polyphonic text. Her risks and her blunders are salutary in comparison to numerous feminist novels in which the autofiction goes astray in an indulgent narcissism. Because it is really through the gateway of fiction, its half-spokenness, its displacements, that Beauvoir manifests another facet of her generous vitality: her capacity to embody a political philosophy of liberty within the microcosm of the intimate. Doesn't the ultimate ruse of political fiction consist in foiling the *universalism* of philosophy itself by exploring, well beyond sexual difference and an ethics of ambiguity, some incommensurable *singularities*—hers, ours?

Beauvoir the novelist calls for a *singular universal*. Far from being an admission of a so-called weakness of the theoretician, this tension and this complementarity between philosophy and the novel constituting Beauvoir's oeuvre bear witness to a supreme self-analytical engagement. The novelist circumvents the figure of the militant feminist that her followers have cultivated; "the woman destroyed" comes to light in the figures that her imaginary transmits to us.[6] The latter destroys her status as a feminist, but carries *The Second Sex* into what is irreducible in each woman, each man. Between philosophy and novel—both together, neither one nor the other—Beauvoir becomes more than a myth: a call to singularize the political and to politicize the singular. A self-analysis without end, which invites us to deepen ours and carry it out into the world.

As for Colette, she claimed to have conquered melancholy, the black twin struck down by writing. "Death does not interest me—not even my own."[7] A flagrant denial—wouldn't Dr. Freud, for whom "the pleasure principle seems actually to serve the death drives," have been tempted to analyze it?[8] Another woman, the psychoanalyst Sabina Spielrein (1885–1942), had theorized this in 1912, before Freud. She had even maintained the opposite: "death in the service of the sexual instinct, which includes a destructive component, is a salutary blessing since it leads to a coming into being."[9] More feminine yet, the monstrous Colette lets herself become fascinated by a dismemberer of women, the murderer Landru. And she molds the Inexorable (which she invokes with a capital letter): between "humility" and the pride that this submissiveness induces, she also writes: "For me there is no other destiny."[10] And writing will never cease blossoming in this woman, as long as her hand can guide the pen on the blue paper: "a far less constant turnscrew than pain, an insurrection of the spirit which in the course of my long life I have often rejected, later outwitted, only to accept it in the end, for writing leads only to writing."[11] Finished, a written text? "I used to think that it was the same with the completed book as with other finished ploys, you down tools and raise the joyful cry 'Finished!' then you clap your hands only to find pouring from them grains of sand you believed to be precious. That is the moment when, in the figures inscribed by those grains of sand, you may read the words 'To be continued . . .'"[12] It is the very rhythm of the infinite blossoming that Colette, the least religious human being ever, transmits to us still today.

II. Sarah K. Hansen

After the philosophy of the Enlightenment, especially with the French Revolution, *Politics* became the new religion—the supreme path to the salvation of humanity, taking the place of absolute transcendence. Since the horror of the Holocaust and the Gulag, the society of overconsumption and finance has widened social inequalities and, in the face of an anthropological acceleration without precedent produced by the surge in technologies and hyperconnectivity, the *political device* has not only entered an endemic crisis. It is proving itself to be more and more incapable of *taking a stand*. Could "participatory and interconnected democracy" take its place? When? How? The time of uncertainties is back again . . .

Although my research can have political repercussions because of its ethical connotations, I am not a "political scientist." And I am pleased to read that my work allows readers "to appreciate the psyche as political terrain." Indeed, "the personal is political" in the sense that the *intimate* is *extimate*: simultaneously dependent on the sociopolitical pact *and* susceptible of questioning it, of modulating it. Hence my contribution to the political, today more than ever "in question," can actually only be to "challenge . . . the fetishization of the political" (Hansen). The anxieties that my journey between "I" and "us" generates, it seems, can only be appeased by admitting what I specify in autobiographical terms in *Je Me Voyage* (in Part I of this volume). Namely, that "I" do not *belong* to fetish communities—which are indeed forms of "us"—but that "I travel *myself*" through ensembles that, in my *traversal* and because of it, become "blurry ensembles" ("fuzzy sets)"[13] (if one prefers this metaphor stemming from abstract algebra instead of lending an ear to the evolution of my research and to the *openness* of my writing relayed by the writing of my novels).

I do understand that existence thus understood may seem uncomfortable—it is not, it is true, all restful. But I cannot conceive any other way to lead this "*bios xenikos*," this life in thinking, this life of thought, such as it was from Plato to Arendt.

Hansen discusses in detail the debates and the criticisms or rejections prompted by the political interpretations to which my work lends itself. Many of these questions have stimulated me and encouraged me to develop or change my positions, as I hope the replies in this volume also attest. On the other hand, my detractors are mistaken in their target when they suspect me of devoting some dubious cults to France, to Europe, to the West, even to colonialism, or when they attribute Islamophobic remarks to me.[14] I ask myself: misunderstanding, malevolence, partisan dogmatism?

Let us return to my native Bulgaria. Did I identify with the West (Hansen) in censuring my *roots*, when I wrote: "You, Bulgarians . . . . You hurt me, my fellows, my brothers"?[15] In the text titled "Bulgaria, my Suffering," I took into account the religious heritage (Christian Orthodoxy) and especially the economic and moral troubles that were going to lead to mafia and sovereignty excesses in the formerly communist countries after the fall of the Berlin wall, particularly in Bulgaria. The contextualization that I provide today is not an explanation—such insinuations do not deserve explanations. It just gives me the opportunity to return to the disastrous "Bulgaria affair" of which I was recently the object.

To reprise my responses to this, including in "The Individual Person at the Center" (2019), French and American newspapers reported certain items of information stemming from an official commission of the security archives of the Bulgarian state, according to which I was supposedly recruited as an agent by the Bulgarian secret services during the 1970s. This "affair" reveals that media acceleration prefers to embalm the memory of totalitarian Europe—which reemerges without fail in the form of a nationalist revenge—rather than work on a veritable reevaluation of this historical disaster. I was very shocked that media outlets like *L'Obs*[16] and the *New York Times* jumped on these so-called revelations without first examining the maneuvers of the Bulgarian secret police. The editors of *Le Monde*, having relayed the information, nevertheless paired it with a column by the historian Sonia Combe, which warned readers not to draw hasty conclusions from these rigged and falsified dossiers.[17] Many people today have hooked their anger to obsolete ideologies, but it is inadmissible, in the so-called "advanced" democracies, to ignore, and therefore to validate, the functioning of the Stalinist police forces and to be content to relay the purported purge-"purification" undertaken by the post-communist regimes. Solzhenitsyn warned against the totalitarian system in which the lie is more pernicious than the suppression of freedoms: it impregnates the entire social link, beginning by sucking in, defaming, and abolishing the very existence of the person.

Two "dossiers" were later disclosed. One in particular, which no one speaks of, hurt me deeply; it transformed this bizarre matter into an intimate wound. It contained thirty-two letters, most sent to my parents (to which were added two letters from Philippe Sollers's family), confiscated by the police without my knowing if the letters were extorted during their lifetime or if they were intercepted before they were received. A psychical rape, difficult to understand for those who have not lived through such an intrusion into one's childhood and family intimacy. The other dossier was put together by agents of state security; no fewer than sixteen collaborators claimed to have interrogated me, but my signature is altogether absent and none of my remarks (about Aragon, the Prague Spring, the Palestinians . . .) is authenticated; moreover, no intelligence mission was assigned to me.

As I said in interviews published soon after in the *Journal du Dimanche*, *Vanity Fair*, and *Marianne*,[18] this affair occurred in 1971, the year when Sollers and the *Tel Quel* group founded the Movement of June 1971, fervently Maoist in inspiration. The dossier ends with the following observation: mediocre spy, but my husband should be kept under surveillance, because he has relations with the embassies of China and Albania. We were, in fact, part of the first delegation of intellectuals invited to China in 1974, after its entry into the United Nations. A superior officer concluded: "Empty file."

Although the dossier brought to light is quite obviously a dossier of surveillance, neither *L'Obs* nor the *New York Times* questioned its validity. This is quite obviously a Kafkaesque machination, like so many others, alas, in which functionaries of the Stalinist police created reports in order to justify their travel to the West. No intelligence task or investigative mission, which supposedly would have been assigned to me, appears in these Stalinist archives. They merely ascribe opinions to me in sentences written in the third person, about Aragon, for example, whose participation in the surrealist movement I supposedly revealed (!), or the "Prague Spring" which "is not in keeping with the Bulgarian Communist Party" (!).

***

This murky business occurred in three stages: (1) The secret services fabricate a dossier and hatch bureaucratic reports to shore it up. (2) The "purification" (purge) commissions, in charge of the archives of the secret police, drop these dossiers on the street without interpreting them or alerting the people involved, presented as collaborators or traitors. (3) A certain left-leaning Western press relays all this without doing its job, in the name of a retrospective guilt or from an inability to analyze History.

To understand the ordeal that was inflicted on me, we have to take into account the present context of post-totalitarian Europe, where nostalgia for the communist past intersects with chauvinistic claims and threatens the viability of the European Union. I propose to continue this reflection elsewhere, limiting myself today to pointing out the symptomatic convergence between, on the one hand, the totalitarian systems that scorn the rights of man and woman and, on the other, the media fever for the "scoop" and false reporting that destroy reputations and lives with total impunity and trample upon intimacy. The needed reflection concerns the components of this symptom, while the nationalist movements of Eastern Europe and elsewhere are reborn from the debris of communism and the "fourth estate" of the media loses its independence, tumbling into the dangerous pitfall of overconnected democracy.

As in other countries, notably in Eastern Europe, the ideas of the Enlightenment were imposed by the elites; they have not sufficiently imbued social behaviors and institutional structures. Questioning-thinking develops in the universities; it is absent from the political arena. On this root communism grafted ideals, but the totalitarian drift, quashing social and societal aspirations, turned citizens away from citizenship. Post-communism is today tempted by a return to spirituality. Reactive or communist religious faith progresses in tandem with the spectacle, globalization, and hyperconnected marketing, without putting them into question. More drastically than in the other European countries, the post-totalitarian democracies are confronted with the difficulty of keeping the culture we call humanist alive, the permanent refounding of which demands that we interrogate identity, the nation, faith, and the need to believe.[19]

Europe bears a heavy responsibility in this fracture that is deepening again, threatening Europe's project. If achieving human rights does indeed reside in the respect for the person and their singular creativity, the flow of capital does not guarantee them. An effort of education, training, and culture is needed from everyone, from schools to businesses, to promote the emergence of a reevaluation of the past, so that resentment yields to a democratic political renewal.

Only a constant vigilance, placing the person at the heart of the media-sphere of which we are consummate actors, can still save us.

***

No, I do not belong to that Bulgaria, which apparently isn't forgetting me. I will always be a foreigner in France, and this trial is a chance for me, whereas it is suffering and tragedy for many others whom I try to accompany.

No, I do not feel like a nationalist and I do not deny the fate of foreigners in France; that is obvious for the serious reader of *Strangers to Ourselves*. But yes, I consider just as firmly that the *national* even *nationalist* sentiment is a powerful *antidepressant* that *I must*—that *we* must (here is a "we," a *fuzzy ensemble* or *set*, that I assert!)—accompany with seriousness. So that it doesn't explode into expulsions, even maniacal and death-dealing exterminations against "those who aren't one of us." Do I need to give the references for all my interventions on these themes?

No, I have no secret sympathy for colonialism, notably French colonialism, which supposedly feeds heaven knows what silence on my part about Algeria or the writings of Frantz Fanon. My husband Philippe Sollers had himself declared unfit for service while in military hospitals at the time, so as not to be sent to Algeria, and all our friends from then militated for the "cause of the National Liberation Front of Algeria." I shared with them the memory and the aftereffects of that passion. But I only arrived in France in December 1965, at the time when colonial suffering was succeeded by what was going to become May '68. Fanon's book *Black Skin, White Masks* (1952) was a cult book for me, without being an object of interpretive work. Sartre's preface to Fanon's *The Wretched of the Earth* (1961), denouncing the "striptease of our humanism" under the trappings of colonialism and postcolonialism, seemed to signal the end of an epoch.[20] The founder of third-world thought was later situated at the heart of a theoretical polemic, which I didn't participate in, sparked by a book as symptomatic as it was debatable by the psychoanalyst Octave Mannoni.[21] My "foreignness" found itself exceeded by qualifications and knowledge that I did not possess. One cannot say that I "actively ignore[d] the work of Fanon in accordance with the psychoanalytic 'mainstream.'" The expression "psychoanalytic mainstream" belongs neither to my vocabulary nor to my field of interest. Would I have said (in 2002!) that I had not *worked on* the texts of the psychoanalyst, essayist, and militant that Frantz Fanon was (I certainly had not *ignored* him), and that these texts had mobilized an *important current* of French psychoanalysis in which I did not participate? Hansen's assertion is mistaken about what my positioning was at the time.[22]

I do see myself, on the other hand, when Hansen recalls the "final prayer" by Fanon: "O my body, make of me always a man who questions!" And I hear, in this wish, an ultimate profession of antiracist faith that could never "be transformed into an institution" (as Sartre feared).[23]

On the other hand, the brilliant Angela Davis's cause had won me over, and I did happen to participate in demonstrations, sign petitions in support of the Black Panthers and Black Feminism. Which doesn't make me a militant. But have I ever claimed to be one? What exactly is this ideological-political investigation looking for?

A question for a question, I wonder: why should I ask myself about the admirable Fanon whose trajectory, like many others, did not cross mine? Rather than asking myself about Rafah Nached, for example, the Muslim woman who became a psychoanalyst, whom we helped get out of the Syrian dictator's prisons in 2011? Or about one of the male or female radicalized adolescents who are still being followed at the Maison des Adolescents, not because they are Muslims but because their "malady of ideality" is nurtured or broadly comes from the gaps—even the bankruptcy—of secularized humanism itself?[24]

Yes, I am proud to be European, and I maintain that in the face of the sovereignty excesses, racism, xenophobia, and antisemitism that surface and "go viral" (Hansen) in the disoriented democracies, Europe in difficulty is not knocked out but remains the space where it is still possible to interrogate these excesses. To question *radical evil*, as well as "our *values*." Yes, I am a European who tries to participate in the *epochal* imperative to "transvalue" (Nietzsche) the memory and the potentialities of the Greek-Jewish-Christian *cultures*. Transvalue as well the "break with tradition" (according to Tocqueville and Arendt), which occurred only here, in European culture, with the Enlightenment. For all its irreversibility, this break has allowed men and women of this continent to face the crimes and the times by thinking about them. Beginning with ours. Without forgetting those that emerge in globalization.

III. Daniel Cohn-Bendit

Daniel Cohn-Bendit had received a message of empathy from a friend of his parents, Hannah Arendt, who was averse to modern left tendencies but surely not insensitive to the preoccupations and the ludic sense of the student in revolt. As for me, I had merely read, studiously and passionately, the works of the philosopher, who defined herself as a "political journalist" and who had realized that it was only possible to sur-vive totalitarianisms and the automatization of the species through a "life of the mind" that gives "the sensation of being alive." Two other women of the twentieth century, the psychoanalyst Klein and the writer Colette, bore this "sensation of being alive," and give it to us today, through the life of their works themselves. Thus was born my trilogy on "female genius."

I was listening to the inaugural speech of the European parliamentarian, a committed ecologist, who was introducing me for the award of the Hannah Arendt Prize in Bremen, Germany, and I thought again about the Sorbonne crammed full of students in revolt. I wondered if it was really he—Dany—who had shouted "Sartre, be brief!" to the great philosopher. I could hear the Nanterre student quote Benjamin Franklin, but also the Franco-Lebanese writer Amin Maalouf. About me, he knew the essentials: my foreignness, my *Strangers to Ourselves*, my book on Arendt, my disappointment concerning the cultural revolution, my wager about Chinese women, disability, the psychoanalyst who is launched into "the interpretation of social phenomena," the feminist who promptly "argue[s] with feminists" and who "tries to remove . . . antimotherhood from feminism." But Cohn-Bendit had especially noticed "the chutzpah"—the strength to pose and to claim "female genius."

Yes indeed! I do not claim this genius "in itself" or "for itself," and even less "for me." But so that all the women and men who read me "go that road." To travel oneself toward that "who," that *singularity* in oneself, for men and women to find-recreate, which is not the reified "what" of marketing, consumption, and overproduction. Just a "plural and equivocal" identity.

Yes, dear Dany, with my "nerve," brazen assurance, or *chutzpah*, I confirm: I am European!—"she's European." A *Homo europaeus* exists with a developing culture: European culture. In my childhood, I would hear, at the family table: "To get the children (me and my sister) out of *the guts of hell*[25] (meaning totalitarianism), there is only one solution: that they learn foreign languages." My parents did not give us roots, they gave us wings. I don't see myself as a plant; I am one of those migrating birds that accompany me at the Island of Ré.[26] A swarm of migrators, of migrants.

Beyond our differences, divergences, and singularities, it is in Europe that *we travel ourselves*. "Plural and equivocal" Europe, the most unexpected image of which (in this period of disintegration), but perhaps the most truthful (because playful and worldwide), which came to you spontaneously, is . . . the *soccer game*. Which you had "experienced . . . as a child," as you specify, "and a thing from childhood shapes identity more." I too—did you know?—was a regular fan of soccer matches, beside my father on the seating of the stadiums in Sofia.

From Arendt to *soccer*: to love this Europe, there is nothing more we need, without which the planet risks the chaos of destruction. However, many people are not convinced of it, and I would like briefly to recall, for them, my profession of faith in *Homo europaeus*, before returning to soccer.

In opposition to a certain *identity cult*, in the name of which modern "good conscience" continues to wage freedom-killing and death-dealing wars still today, European culture constantly reveals this paradox: an identity exists—mine, ours—but it is *infinitely constructible and deconstructible*. To the question "Who am I?" the best answer, European, is obviously not certainty but the love of the question mark. After having succumbed to identitarian dogmas to the point of criminality, a European "We" is in the process of emerging. Perhaps it is because Europe succumbed to barbarism (this is to be recalled and analyzed endlessly), and because Europe provided a better analysis of it than many others, that she brings into the world a conception and a practice of identity in the form of a questioning anxiety. It is possible to assume the European patrimony by rethinking it as an antidote to identitarian tensions: ours and those of all persuasions.

I can hear this questioning attitude in the word of the Jewish God: *Ehyeh asher ehyeh*,[27] taken up by Jesus[28]—an identity without definition that returns the "I" to an unrepresentable, eternal return to its very being. I hear it, in another way, in the silent dialogue of the thinking self with itself according to Plato, always "two in one," whose thought does not provide an answer but breaks up. In the *philia politike* according to Aristotle, too, which announces the social space and a political project by appealing to singular memory and the biography of each one. In the voyage, in Saint Augustine's sense, for whom there is only one country, the one of the voyage, precisely: *In via in patria*. In Montaigne's *Essays*, which consecrate the identitarian polyphony of the self: "We are all patchwork, and so shapeless and diverse in composition that each bit, each moment plays its own game."[29] In Descartes's *cogito*, in which one can hear "I am only because I think." But what is thinking? I hear it too in Faust's revolt according to Goethe: "*Ich bin der Geist, der stets verneint*" ("I am the Spirit of Eternal Negation").[30] In the "interminable analysis . . ." of Freud: "Where id was, there ego shall be."[31]

"Diversity, that's my motto," Jean de La Fontaine had said in his "Eel Pâté."[32] Europe is henceforth a political entity that speaks as many languages as it is composed of countries, if not more. This multilingualism is the basis of cultural diversity. We have entered into a new era. European linguistic diversity is in the process of creating kaleidoscopic individuals capable of defying the bilingualism of *Globish English*. Is it possible? Everything seems to prove the contrary today. However, a species is emerging little by little: a polyphonic subject, a polyglot citizen of a plurinational Europe. Will the future European be a singular subject with a psychism that is intrinsically plural, trilingual, quadrilingual, multilingual? Or will she or he be reduced to *Globish*?

Whatever its sustainability, the national character can, like individuals, go through a veritable *depression*. In the face of the depressed patient, the psychoanalyst begins by reestablishing self-confidence, starting from which it is possible to fashion a relation between the two protagonists of the cure. In the same way, the depressed nation requires an optimal image of itself before it will be capable of the effort to undertake, for example, a European integration or an industrial and commercial expansion or a better reception of immigrants. "Nations, like men, die by imperceptible disorders," wrote Giraudoux.[33] A poorly understood universalism and colonial guilt have led numerous political and ideological actors to commit, under cover of cosmopolitanism, such "imperceptible disorders"—even acts of arrogant contempt—with respect to the Nation. They contribute to aggravating the national depression, before pushing the nation toward maniacal, nationalist, and xenophobic exaltation.

Moreover, the fall of the Berlin wall in 1989 sharpened the differences between two models: European culture and North American culture. Different but complementary, these two versions are equally present in international principles and institutions in Europe as well as across the Atlantic.

First, recall that Kant, in identifying "freedom" with "self-beginning," opens the way for an apology of enterprising subjectivity—although subordinate to the freedom of Reason (pure or practical) and a Cause (divine or moral). To be free would mean to be free to obtain the best effects from the enchainment of causes and effects, to adapt to the market of production and for profit. But another model of freedom appears in the Greek world, developing with the Presocratics and through the intermediary of Socratic dialogue. This freedom deploys in the Being of the word that gives of itself, that presents itself to itself and to the other, and in that sense frees itself. As an infinite questioning. Poetry, desire, revolt are its privileged experiences, revealing the incommensurable and yet avowable singularity of each man, of each woman.

We recognize the risks of this second model founded on the questioning attitude: ignoring economic reality; shutting oneself up in corporatist demands; limiting oneself to tolerance and being afraid to question the identitarian claims and cults of the new political and social actors; abandoning worldwide competition and retiring into laziness and archaisms. But one can also see the advantages of this model borne today by European cultures, which does not culminate in a schema but in a *taste for* human *life* and its shareable singularity.

Among the multiple causes that lead to the present discontent, there is one that politicians often pass over in silence: the denial weighing on the universal prereligious and prepolitical "need to believe" inherent in the speaking beings that we are, which is expressed as a "malady of ideality" specific to the adolescent but that also accompanies the adolescent *structure*, across all ages.[34]

Europe is facing a historical challenge. Is it capable of confronting this crisis of belief that the cover of religion no longer keeps in? What seems threatened is the conception of the human forged at the Greek-Jewish-Christian crossroads along with its Muslim graft, this concern for singular and translatable universality. The anxiety that has arrested Europe in these decisive times expresses uncertainty in the face of these stakes. Are we capable of mobilizing all the means, of law and security as well as economic ones, not forgetting those that are given to us by the knowledge of souls, to accompany, with the necessary delicacy and listening, with a suitable education, and with the generosity that is required, this poignant malady of ideality that is unfurling upon us and that the adolescents of the zones where there are no rights express, in Europe itself, in dramatic ways—and not only they?

From the Enlightenment to the suffragists, by way of Marie Curie, Rosa Luxembourg, Simone de Beauvoir, and Simone Weil, the emancipation of women through creativity and the struggle for the political, economic, and social rights, which continues today, offers a federating terrain to the national, religious, and political diversities of female European citizens. This distinctive trait of European culture is also an inspiration and a support for women in the entire world in their aspiration to culture and emancipation. In this spirit, the Simone de Beauvoir Prize for the freedom of women was granted to the young Pakistani girl Malala Yousafzai, seriously wounded by the Taliban because in her blog she demanded the right to education for young girls. Recently the prize was granted to the Salvadoran Sara Garcia Gross, an educator, an academic, and a militant for the rights of women and the right to abortion.

Against the ambient theory of decline, in the face of the two monsters that are finance's lockdown of the political and ecological self-destruction, European cultural space could be an audacious response. Perhaps the only response capable of grasping the complexity of the human condition as a whole, the lessons of its memory, and the risks of its freedoms.

***

And *soccer*, in this fine program? A School of Semiology under the auspices of the New Bulgarian University (!) has imagined that this discipline born in Greece and resuscitated by Saussure and Peirce at the end of the nineteenth century would survive only as an international soccer team!

Composed like this with academics and athletes: "1. Thales of Miletus; 2. Ferdinand de Saussure; 3. Charles Peirce; 4. Kristian Bankov; 5. Umberto Eco; 6. Thomas Sebeok; 7. Cristiano Ronaldo; 8. Francesco Mangiapane; 9. Claudio Guerri; 10. Gianfranco Marrone; 11. Julia Kristeva."

In spite of the thunderous success of women's soccer in the world championship this summer, I must observe that I am the one and only woman in this prestigious selection! In brilliant company, nevertheless, and furthermore with the highly prized number 11, left winger! Like Neymar, Drogba, Ryan Giggs, Pavel Nedvěd, or Miroslav Klose.

Europe was never—and is never—as alive as when it knows how to laugh at itself. N'est-ce pas Dany?

J.K.

NOTES

1. See Julia Kristeva, *New Maladies of the Soul*, trans. Ross Guberman (New York: Columbia University Press, 1995), 54–55, 71.

2. Ibid., 54.

3. See Jacques Lacan, *Encore, The Seminar of Jacques Lacan Book XX: On Feminine Sexuality, The Limits of Love and Knowledge*, trans. Bruce Fink (New York: Norton, 1998), 101; *Séminaire XX (1972–1973): Encore* (Paris: Seuil, 1975), 126–27. Lacan also utilized this concept with regard to James Joyce in *The Sinthome: The Seminar of Jacques Lacan Book XXIII*, trans. A. R. Price (Cambridge: Polity, 2016), 146; *Séminaire XXIII (1975-1976): Le Sinthome* (Paris: Seuil, 2005), 117.

4. "Right up against" translates "tout contre," a French expression that is difficult to translate into English. The plasticity of *signifiance* utilizes the word *contre*, "against," inverting it while assuming it, to say *tout près*: "right up close." Lacan theorizes the "Borromean knot" between the Real, the Imaginary, and the Symbolic in his unpublished Séminaire XXII, RSI, from December 16, 1974. See also Lacan, *Seminar XX*, 127–28; *Séminaire XX*, 115.

5. Simone de Beauvoir, *All Said and Done*, trans. Patrick O'Brian (New York: Paragon, 1993), 114; *Tout compte fait*, in *Mémoires*, t. 2 (Paris: Pléiade, 2018), 606.

6. See Simone de Beauvoir, *The Woman Destroyed*, trans. Patrick O'Brian (New York: Pantheon Books, 1987); *La Femme rompue* (Paris: Gallimard, 1967).

7. See Colette, *Break of Day*, trans. Enid McLeod, in *Break of Day and the Blue Lantern* (New York: Farrar, Straus, and Giroux, 1966), 51; *La Naissance du jour*, in *Oeuvres*, t. III (Paris: Pléiade, 1991), 307.

8. Sigmund Freud, *Beyond the Pleasure Principle*, in *The Standard Edition of the Complete Psychological Works of Sigmund Freud*, vol. XVIII, trans. James Strachey (London: Hogarth, 1955), 63 (translation modified); *Au-delà du principe de plaisir*, in *Oeuvres complètes*, t. XV (Paris: PUF, 2002), 337.

9. See Sabina Spielrein, "Destruction as the Cause of Coming Into Being," *Journal of Analytical Psychology*, vol. 39, no. 2 (1994), 155–86; or "Destruction as Cause of Becoming," *Psychoanalysis and Contemporary Thought* 18 (1995), 85–118; "Die Destruktion als Ursache des Werdens," in *Jahrbuch für Psychoanalitische und Psychopathologische Forschung* IV (1912), 465–503; referred to by Freud, *Beyond the Pleasure Principle*, 55n1; *Au-delà du principe de plaisir*, 338.

10. Colette, *The Blue Lantern*, trans. Roger Stenhouse, in *Break of Day and The Blue Lantern* (New York: Farrar, Straus & Giroux, 1966), 159; *Le Fanal bleu*, in *Oeuvres*, t. IV (Paris: Pléiade, 2001), 1060.

11. Ibid.

12. Ibid.

13. The mathematician Lotfi Zadeh theorized "fuzzy sets" in 1965; they serve as the basis for "fuzzy logic." See, for example, Lotfi A. Zadeh and Rafik A. Aliev, *Fuzzy Logic Theory and Applications: Part I and Part II* (New Jersey: World Scientific, 2018).

14. On this last theme, see my reply to Cecilia Sjöholm and Noëlle McAfee in the section in this volume on Ethics and Politics.

15. Quoted by Hansen from Julia Kristeva, "Bulgaria, My Suffering," in *Crisis of the European Subject*, trans. Susan Fairfield (New York: Other Press, 2000), 170; "Bulgarie, ma souffrance," *L'Infini*, no. 57 (1995).

16. [*L'Obs*, previously known as *Le Nouvel Observateur* (1964–2014).—Tr.]

17. Sonia Combe, "L'Aura de l'archive policière est telle qu'on en oublie qu'elle peut aussi être source de désinformation," *Le Monde*, 4 April 2018. See also the analyses published on thephilosophicalsalon.com (a Los Angeles Review of Books Channel): Sara Beardsworth, "Reflections on the Kristeva Affair," The Philosophical Salon, September 25, 2018, https://thephilosophicalsalon.com/reflections-on-the-kristeva-affair/, and Julia Kristeva, "Bulgaria, Post-Totalitarian Europe and Me," November 26, 2018, https://thephilosophicalsalon.com/bulgaria-post-totalitarian-europe-and-me/. On the blog of the Los Angeles Review of Books: Julia Kristeva, "It's Just Not My Life—Julia Kristeva Responds," November 1, 2018, http://blog.lareviewofbooks.org/essays/just-life-julia-kristeva-responds/. Also: Julia Kristeva, "La Personne au centre: Entretien avec Julia Kristeva," an interview by Georges Nivat and Olivier Mongin. *Esprit*, no. 456 (July–August 2019): 160–75; "The Individual Person at the Center: An Interview with Kristeva," the official Julia Kristeva website, http://www.kristeva.fr/the-individual-person-at-the-center.html; and Julia Kristeva, "La Bulgarie, LEurope Post-Totalitaire et Moi," http://www.kristeva.fr/bulgaria-post-totalitarian-europe-and-me.html (among others).

18. Julia Kristeva, "Julia Kristeva et le fantôme de 'Sabina,'" *Le Journal du Dimanche*, April 22, 2018; "Une Autre Vie que la mienne," *Vanity Fair France* (July 20): 66–73; "'It's Just Not My Life': Julia Kristeva Responds," trans. Patsy Baudoin. *Los Angeles Review of Books* (January 11, 2018). "La Bulgarie, L'Europe Post-Totalitaire et Moi." *Marianne* 1121 (September 7–13): 46–47; "Bulgaria, Post-totalitarian Europe and Me," *Los Angeles Review of Books*, November 26, 2018. All also available on the Julia Kristeva official website, www.kristeva.fr.

19. As Kelly Oliver details in her article in this volume, "Democracy of Proximity and Kristeva's New Humanism."

20. Jean-Paul Sartre, Preface to Frantz Fanon, *The Wretched of the Earth*, trans. Constance Farrington (New York: Grove, 1963), 21.

21. Cf. Octave Mannoni, *Prospero and Caliban: The Psychology of Colonization*, trans. Pamela Powesland (London: Methuen, 1956), which was to have several editions, a lot of criticism as well as prefaces and justifications by the author himself. See also, on this controversy, François Vatin, "Octave Mannoni (1899–1989) et sa *Psychologie de la colonisation*: Contextualisation et décontextualisation," *Revue du MAUSS* 1, no. 37 (2011): 137–78.

22. [The apparent confusion here probably lies in the fact that in the published English translation of the interview referred to by Sarah Hansen, part of Kristeva's response to the interviewer is excised. Before this volume went to press, Donnie McMann, an editorial assistant for The Library of Living Philosophers, found a fuller translation online. At the end of the interview, Rainer Ganahl comments: "There is someone who you don't mention in your book [*The Sense and Non-sense of Revolt*] and who I find extremely important: Frantz Fanon, a revolutionary and a psychoanalyst that has written the article, 'On violence.'" Kristeva replies: "*I do not know him very well.* I have often heard people speak of him, but I have never read anything by him. *Sartre enthusiasts have surely read him.* He isn't part of mainstream Psychoanalytic Studies. *This is neither psychoanalysis, nor sociology, but several things at the same time.*" The italicized sentences are those excised from the published version of the interview in Julia Kristeva, *Revolt, She Said* (Los Angeles: Semiotext(e), 2002). For the fuller version, see http://www.ganahl.info/kristeva_interview.html.—Ed.]

23. Sartre's speech refusing the Nobel Prize in 1964, translated by Richard Howard: "Sartre on the Nobel Prize," *New York Review of Books*, December 17, 1964.

24. See Julia Kristeva, "Can One Be a Muslim Woman and a Shrink?" in *Passions of Our Time*, trans. Constance Borde and Sheila Malovany-Chevallier (New York: Columbia University Press, 2018), 345–51; *Pulsions du temps*, 697–706. See also my reply in the section on Ethics and Politics in this volume.

25. I have found this expression, supposedly from the Bible or the Gospel, only in Dante, in the last canto of the *Inferno*, in the ninth circle. The *intestine*, *burella* in Italian, spilled on the ground, is the image of the "broken heart." I think Judas is present in those places.

26. See Julia Kristeva, *The Samurai*, 308.

27. Exodus 3:14.

28. John 8:23.

29. Michel de Montaigne, "Of the Inconsistency of Our Actions," *Essays*, trans. Donald M. Frame (Stanford: Stanford University Press, 1958), 244.

30. Wolfgang von Goethe, *Faust I and II,* trans. Stuart Atkins, in *Goethe's Collected Works*, vol. 2 (Princeton: Princeton University Press, 1984), 36.

31. Sigmund Freud, *New Introductory Lectures on Psycho-Analysis*, in *The Standard Edition of the Complete Psychological Works of Sigmund Freud*, trans. James Strachey (London: Hogarth, 1964), 80.

32. See Jean de La Fontaine, "Eel Pâté," in *La Fontaine's Complete Tales in Verse*, trans. Randolph Paul Runyon (Jefferson: McFarland, 2009), 181; "Pâté d'anguille," in *Oeuvres complètes*, vol. 1 (Paris: Pléiade, 1954), 594.

33. Jean Giraudoux, *Tiger at the Gates*, trans. Christopher Fry (New York: Oxford University Press, 1955), 70; *La Guerre de Troie n'aura pas lieu*, in *Théâtre complet* (Paris: Gallimard, 1982), act II, scene 13.

34. See also my replies to the sections in this volume on Melancholy, Love, and the Sacred, Desire, Knowledge and Belief, and Ethics and Politics.

26

Rosemary Balsam

THE CONTROVERSIAL NATURE OF KRISTEVA'S "MATERNAL RELIANCE"

In the face of this multiverse of maternal eroticism as reliance—facing its risks, its endurance, and its creativity—psychoanalysis seems to hesitate.

—Julia Kristeva, "Reliance, or Maternal Eroticism"

In 2011 Kristeva presented a fresh focus on mother-child interaction in her paper "Reliance, ou l'érotisme maternel" at the seventy-first Congrès de Psychoanalystes de Langue Française.[1] It first became available to the anglophone world in 2014 as "Reliance, or Maternal Eroticism."[2] This vital concept—employing Kristeva's exquisite attention to the primordial and erotic maternal intensity that is necessary for an infant's unfolding into the world of meaning and meaningful communication—she calls *reliance.* Such interaction remains little elaborated in the psychoanalytic field as a whole, especially concerning its eroticism. Kristeva privileges maternal subjectivity in this scene of the mother with her infant. This lens is still precious and rare in a field that is traditionally mostly interested in the development of the infant towards adulthood. Characteristic of all her writing, Kristeva on maternal eroticism is at once ebullient, emotionally and intellectually appetitive, unbounded, and yet grounded in the world. The appreciation of her concept in this article will be psychoanalytic, although her academic scholarship has a far wider scope. Fortunately for psychoanalysis, her involvement with women does not—because it simply cannot—confine itself to the constraints of the abidingly apologetic tones infiltrating most past and contemporary psychoanalytic theories about women living in their bodies, ironically abundant and procreative though they are. That is why Kristeva comes across as joyfully controversial and upsetting received "truths" of psychoanalysis. Yet again, in this aspect of her work, to quote Barthes, "she changes the order of things" by always linking new theories or approaches to tradition.[3] This paper of 2011 is extremely important in the arc of her work. It forms a later fulcrum to her thinking on the depths of the extravagant experience of a mother in the fullness of her procreative purview and in her embodied contribution to her generation. I will provide a close reading of Kristeva's "Reliance, or Maternal Eroticism," proceeding section by section, followed by a discussion of its significance for psychoanalysis.

I. "In Search of Reliance"

In the first section of her paper, "In Search of Reliance," Kristeva begins: "To live and to think the maternal as *erotic*, wouldn't that be as provocative as to speak of *infantile sexuality*?"[4] She notes that the provenance of sexuality has been the lover and that a major locus of pain in modern times has been seen as the object relationship with the mother. These elements are too limited, however, for understanding a maternality that includes the body, the dimension left out. There is a problem in properly locating "the maternal." She evokes as equal to this primordial arena only the depths of the unconscious, even prior to defining Eros or Thanatos—what Freud has called "the psychic revolution" of materiality.[5] Along this path she associates to Lou Andreas-Salomé's phrase recalling analysts of the era (and us) to "contact with our original, fleshly being,"[6] reconnecting us to our own "materiality" rather than "distinguishing" us from it.[7] Thus Kristeva masterfully evokes the blending of the maternal body and mind. She then takes off in her thesis, elaborating in her singular, scholarly, multifarious, and tumultuous fashion the many splendored dimensions of the archaically strong nuclear psychical force of maternal passion that is both communicable to and preformative for an infant in and close to the mother's body and soul, and in her arms. She detects an interactive and interlacing gap between self and objective reality. She quotes Merleau-Ponty as calling the same space "flesh" in "this transition from the mute world to the speaking world."[8] Unlike most contemporary psychoanalytic writers, from the start she does not shy away from biophysical connections. Her attraction to drive theory allows her to avoid libido as "mere genetics" and her openness to corporeality allows her to avoid "spiritualism."[9] She also references this style in her later forays into "parentality" in 2017, where she comments cogently on the state of the vicissitudes of shifting stabilities in sexual difference in creating modern family life, and plays with a fundamental fragility of heterosexuality and the primal scene due to (speculative) homoerotic bonding preferences within the primal horde.[10] That authorial style is reminiscent of Freud's expansiveness in *Totem and Taboo* or his "lost" 1915 metapsychological paper, "A Phylogenetic Phantasy: Overview of the Transference Neuroses," discovered in the 1980s, which playfully deals with the origins of anxiety as originating in humans aware of extinction in an oncoming ice age.[11]

Kristeva takes the power of the biological body very seriously—more about this being said below in consideration of how controversial this is nowadays in psychoanalysis—while illuminating the "permeability" between biology and the psyche.[12] Her examples about internal reactions in diabetic complications of pregnancy are a little clumsy, but her argument is sustained. A reader can pursue the suggestive direction of a full acknowledgment of psychosomatics as described by Aisenstein and De Aisenberg, for example.[13] Kristeva is trying to note that the primitive psyche deeply affects the body functioning in pregnancy, although these days, especially in medicine, the latter is studied with minimal interest in the psyche. This omission represents a resurgence of an oscillating, widespread unconscious tendency to keep splitting "body" topics and "psychic" topics. She defines her use of "reliance" in this passage:

> Reliance is a specific economy of the drives such that, countercathected by psychical representation and thus *fixed* by psychic inscriptions, the energy of the originary split at once sustains and moves through primary and secondary repression. Without thereby displacing those drives into a psychotic regression, maternal eroticism renders the fixation of the life and death drives both problematic and available, and places them together in the service of the living as an "open structure," related [*reliée*] to others and to the environment.[14]

Her English translators for the 2014 version of her paper—Rachel Boué-Widawsky and Perry Zurn—explain the neologism in this way: "*Reliance* is a French neologism based on Latin and Old French etymology meaning binding or linking. Kristeva is playing on this etymology to speak of sensorial, physical, or mental links."[15]

II. "Life's State of Emergency"

The most compelling, exciting, and poetic section of "Reliance, or Maternal Eroticism" is the second one, "Life's 'State of Emergency,' The Libido, Primary Repression, and the Subliminal Cycle." Kristeva explicates her notion of reliance further:

> By reliance I mean experience in the double sense it has in German. Experience (in the sense of *Erlebnis*) is the eruption of a new pre-object: an emergence, a flash, or an immediate perception. Progressively, in its second phase, experience becomes familiarity [*connaissance*], a patient knowledge [*savoir*] that understands (*Erfahrung*). Whether or not the expectant mother is prepared by a desire to conceive, she is immediately gripped by biopsychic events (like pregnancy, labor, and breast-feeding) in such a way that maternal reliance must be understood not only as irreducible to a "symbolic function" (it is definitively social, like the "paternal function"), but also as a *passion*.[16]

Passion, she declares, "suffers and endures." It is impossible to convey the sensorially rich sentences, elaborations, and flourishes with which this author conveys the communicated passion that emanates from the mother and is in the cradle of the infant's vitality, ultimately translated into its life force. Her metaphors reach to astrophysics to convey the gravitational and primal force of this energy. We deal with a "multiverse."[17] Creative and destructive energies fill this space and demonstrate that "passion is by no means 'passive.'"[18] The Kristevan mother is developmentally a "speaking being" within the *chora*, described in earlier writings, and within the semiotics of the primitive and reverberating interactive communication of human life.[19] The *chora* "is a space before space, a nurturer-and-devourer at once, prior to the One, the Father, the word, and even the syllable. It is a modality of *sense* prior to *signification*, what I call 'the semiotic.'"[20] The semiotic is something to be seized and grasped, such as within Colette's knowledgably charged metaphors. Kristeva's own plunging abilities to swim and dive in the surf of her descriptives sweep her into her own text: "Rather, the self-exile sketched here is a lasting ex-stasis. It regulates the time of death into a temporality of new beginnings: jubilatory affirmations and anxious annihilations that literally put me beside myself, outside myself, and, without annihilating me, multiply me."[21]

Kristeva challenges the masculine origins of psychoanalysis and asks if we dare to "propose new objects of analysis."[22] Her maternal eroticism is deepest in the core of speaking beings—she quotes Heidegger, Lacan, Brusset, and Bion. Plunging again into personal pronouns, it becomes "neither 'I' nor 'you' but 'behind us' and 'beyond the object,'" mobile and interflexible.[23] She is forceful in placing this center deep in the maternal psyche, to be placed deeply into her offspring. Her poetry here is reminiscent of St. Patrick's Breastplate hymn.[24]

Kristeva now leads us into paroxysms of grief experienced mutually in the infant being's separation from this passionate core. "Melancholic jouissance" she calls the state "on the edge of repression."[25] Repression necessary for the formation of language is at stake. The mechanisms involved in her use of primary and secondary repressions are hard to follow here. But there is a build-up coming, to consider the woman/subject/mother in her abject status, her "I" eclipsed.

In these tectonic plates of primary and secondary repression, within the space of splits pointed to by Freud and Laplanche,[26] Kristeva locates maternal eroticism in the unconscious fantastical, often a world without words, communicable by the mother to her infant, or—to their psychological peril—not. This captures her sense of a "state of emergency in life" that inhabits the mother as a resource throughout life. She places the desire to conceive (or not) earlier than self-aware competition with the mother, or any desire to capture the father's penis. It is far more archaic in females. She leaps to Sophocles and, again, Freud's "psychic revolution" of materiality. She draws exquisite contrasts with the sexual libido of the lover and a seduced child's response, and concludes that *tenderness* is "the basic affect of reliance." She says it "'sprouts' [*fait tendre*] its libidinal force."[27]

The next part of her argument contemplates the import of discharge—strongly evoking the act of giving birth. Here "the Thing is delivered from its state of Thing-ness and releases another living subject to the world."[28] Moreover, Kristeva situates the earliest discharge in the psychic sphere as emanating from the depths of maternal reliance and its forces wherein the mother risks her very life in the violence of the birth act, as does the child. In the destined act of becoming a mother, a female human is, as it were, on the barricades of soma and psyche and of life and death drive forces.

Kristeva is in her element on the topic of violence and abjection—an older, formidable idea of hers, which is now integrated into this masterful tapestry.[29] For her, it is "the destiny of the death-drive"—"where there is not yet either a subject or object, or even *objeux*."[30] She continues: "the maternal transforms the abjects (which the death drive has re-jected into the not-yet space of mother-child) into objects of care, into survival, and into life."[31] Invoking Green's "normal maternal madness," she writes of tumultuous processes of interactive separation and rejoining.[32] She encompasses tenderness and hate, closeness, fusion and flinging out. Ever aware of the father, too, Kristeva shows that these maternal echoes go forth through more mature, functional, paternal oedipal levels towards an inclusion of that (oedipal) third, ultimately to be metabolized together with a loving father. Maternal eroticism calls to the father. In that sense it is a "vocation."[33]

Kristeva then returns to the "oedipal dyad" with the mother, and to her ideas about generational language transmission. By speaking the echolalia and the language of her child (and thus rediscovering the drive foundations of phonation, as Sabina Spielrein has demonstrated), each mother in her own way undertakes the Proustian search for "lost time."[34] And, step by step, she resolves the "incongruence" separating affect from cognition—a rift about which the hysteric endlessly complains.[35] The child "loses me, kills me" in order to separate. And I leave him, abject and extrude him.[36]

The transformation of energy—never an either/or set of energies—is key to these understandings that simultaneously fling the mother and child apart and bind them close in an ever differentiating spiral of potential growth. Investment in the father will be by way of the reactivated maternal eroticism within the originary fusion with the mother. Kristeva invokes Green in noting that reliance is also the work of the negative, but rapidly, fluidly can transform this energy into a potentially life-giving infusion between mother and infant. (Or, of course, these same nuclear forces can take a fatal turn that is even more negative and destructive.) She uses Freud's energic concepts of binding, cathexis, and recathexis to capture the volcanic mix. In favorable circumstances, growth and the development of language are hand-in-glove, as the mother intuits, and the mother instinctively "withdraws" and "disinvests in her own message but remains attentive to a single response from the child; the 'incentives' to experimentation, to 'word plays,' to 'the right to error.'"[37] Ultimately, the mother gains in return, through this circulation (which is doubtless perverse in a certain way), a still greater *jouissance* stemming from the response of the child whom she idealizes and encourages.[38] In the absence of a maternal attuned withdrawal from the infant, Kristeva sees out-of-control destruction that malignantly turns towards "possession." The right to create dead matter takes over and flows in these dark possibilities of such a mother's unbounded narcissism. She envisions a future of such a son freeing himself from this quality of incestuous bond only by way of the death of the mother or himself. Summing up:

> It therefore seems justified to me to rehabilitate this word: *reliance*, in the back-and-forth between Old French, French, and English. *Reliance: to link, to gather, to join, to put together*; but also *to adhere, to belong, to depend on*; and therefore *to trust, to feel safe, to share your thoughts and feelings, to assemble together*, and *to be yourself.* After showcasing, with Winnicott, the dynamics of separation and the transitional object, it strikes me today as crucial not only to emphasize this specific aspect of motherhood that *maintains* and re-creates both the cathexis and the countercathexis of the libido, together with *thanatos* itself in more and more extensive psychosomatic links, but also to rethink it. This specific eroticism, which *maintains the urgency of life* up to the limits of life, I call *reliance*.[39]

III. "An Unrepresentable Jouissance, Where Visibility Surfaces"

In the third section of her essay on maternal reliance, Kristeva begins to approach worldly and social implications of reliance in its ferocity and archaic power. There are two common fallouts regarding maternality that are encountered in society, and which are designed to avoid the erotic biopsychical forces she has described: "heroization or sanctification" and what she calls *mère-version* (a kind of turning towards mother, and a pun on Lacan's *père-version*).[40] In *mère-version* the escape is for the mother to kill herself. On sanctification, Kristeva asks the profound question for the ages: "Is man capable of desanctifying maternal eroticism?" Her first comment given this stunning recognition is: "Women themselves bask in it."[41] Freud approaches it through coming to terms with incest.[42] Kristeva takes it back to the Lacanian mirror stage.[43]

She also ranges through other authors' paths of escape from this sarcophagus. Often Céline is on her mind, as he is at the forefront of exploring an abject path to the apocalypse.[44] These passages indulge in more allusory statements that are open to associative interpretation—for example, invocations of biblical Sara's "laugh" at fertility, Isaac's survival, Antigone, the Pietà, Da Vinci's "Virgin and Child" or "Virgin and St. Anne"; a view of the Chinese mother's apparently nonverbal calligraphic "ease"; the circle of smiles in the Virgin and St. Anne; and the many examples of maternal *jouissance* throughout the Christian world with the iconography of Mary the mother of God, child in arms.

What, she suddenly interjects, has happened to these sanctifications in modern life? She riffs as only Kristeva can on happenings in and around the psychoanalytic world in the mid-1930s, just prior to World War II. So where were Freud, Klein, Winnicott, the Tavistock just then, and what were they doing? And she plays with a witty commentary on Beckett's two-year analysis with Bion, from which he broke in dissatisfaction, preferring to dedicate himself further to his mother and literature, and "thus waited for Godot well into the dustbins of old age."[45] We can certainly hear the activity of the negative elements of maternal reliance in that mother-son duo. She concludes that "psychoanalysis today invites us to revitalize our ambitions for freedom in more mobile, more archaic regions, which are nevertheless rich with potential: regions where the One (identity) does not achieve being, or is not content with being simply One."[46]

People have thought that women wanted to be free by opting out of motherhood. We now see that women want to be free to decide to be or not to be mothers.[47] Thus she taps the positions of psychological autonomy and brings us up to date in musing on tolerant attitudes during technologically assisted pregnancies. Searchingly, she asks: "Is this because the presubjective form of feminine eroticism familiarizes them [expectant mothers] with the *self-dispossession* science requires at the most intimate level?"[48] She then leaps to the connections between reliance and the need for religiousness—both of which are universal, but granting reliance a sense of "priorness" and assuming its inherently creative rebelliousness in relation to later chronological dimensions of the law in psychic life.

In this section, I have found that Kristeva has demonstrated a vast range of examples of unconscious *jouissance* in manifestations from the old and contemporary worlds—from the Bible to the Pietà and Beckett's mother fixation, to the psyches of modern women yearning to be pregnant and looking to impersonal science for help.

IV. "Herethic"

In the final section of her essay, "Herethic," Kristeva offers the moral consequence of taking on and developing her metapsychology of the maternal to augment that of the paternal. Maternal reliance, eroticism, or passion is of course strongly repressed in civilization, its only trace, she believes, being left in religions. Secular society lacks a discourse about the maternal.[49] Were its vitality and necessity acknowledged, a different ethical dimension would open up to society (and psychoanalysis) as well as a reinterpretation involving the responsibility for each other within relationships: a concept of responsibility that could be not only dictated by "the law" but also informed by the mutuality of caretaking emanating from the deep connections to maternal passion.

Kristeva wrote in *Tales of Love*: "If ethics amounts to not avoiding the embarrassing and inevitable problematics of the law but giving it flesh, language, and jouissance—in that case its reformulation demands the contributions of women."[50] After introducing *reliance* within her own academic circle in 2011, she explained *herethics* again, and more straightforwardly, to a conference of dancers in Stockholm in 2013: "I recently proposed the existence of a maternal eroticism that I call *reliance*. This word, in French, carries echoes of the word '*lien*,' to link or to connect, and *confiance*, trust or confidence, as well as an alternative to religion (*religion-reliance*). Between biology and sense, attachment and expulsion, love and hate, violent influence and generous transmission, maternal *reliance* is a surprising and necessary version of ethics we might call a *herethic*."[51] Thus in her concept of "her/ethics," Kristeva continues to expound the developmental and fundamental contribution to humanity of the maternal speaking body in connection with the infant. She posits a richness of tender reliance, a place of maternal passion and responsibility within "herethics" that underlies, suffuses, and adumbrates the paternal law encoded in ethics.

VI. Historical Kindred Spirits and Resistance to Maternal Subjectivity

The psychoanalytic world should rejoice in this stunning and helpful contribution Kristeva has given us in her ability to work *maternal reliance* into a theory of mind that remains close to and extends Freud. But not all will delight, for reasons that are old in the field and more entrenched than resistance to Kristeva's work. She writes: "It falls to us to create new metapsychological concepts in order to develop—by paying attention to the sexuality of the lover—the elucidation and support of maternal eroticism, in all its specificity."[52] But she notes how repressed and suppressed is this compelling and emotionally logical experiential aspect of "the maternal" in psychic life. The sad fact is that a motivated blindness overtook the discipline of psychoanalysis, starting with Freud, and is still in effect in different ways in contemporary versions of theories of mind. The unconscious reverberation of maternal eroticism becomes available and detectable only in religion, she feels. Kristeva notes an ignorance within social life, and has said: "Secularization is the only civilization to lack a discourse on motherhood."[53]

There are surprisingly few psychoanalysts who are taken with the vitality and sexuality of the procreative woman. Most cannot appreciate the centrality of this vision and are resistant to the notion. Among the interested were—as well as Lou Andreas-Salomé, whom Kristeva mentions, and Sabina Spielrein—Margarete Hilferding, a medical doctor, the first woman admitted into the Vienna Psychoanalytic Society in 1911, who delivered an initiating talk on birthing women; and the three main dissidents about Freud's phallocentricism in his inner circle of the 1930s, Jung, Jones, and Horney. Fenichel would also have been intrigued by maternal eroticism. Rank, with his birth trauma theories, might have been interested, but he did not focus on the mother's subjectivity. Klein would have liked the passionate drive theory, but the Kristevan mother is more comprehensive then Klein's, both richer in the archaic dimension of the *chora* and more sophisticated in her subjective experience of birthing. There are only a small number of contemporary analysts who appreciate the depths of the procreative body that is simultaneously highly sexual. Most are female—presumably showing that the field is unconsciously responding to or obeying Freud's opinion that women would be the ones to elucidate "the dark continent" for psychoanalysis.

Assessing Hilferding's 1911 work as acutely prescient for Kristeva's, I will also indicate some flash points in the general resistance among analysts to appreciating maternal eroticism.[54] Hilferding was the first woman to graduate from the medical school of the University of Vienna in 1910 and the first female member accepted into the Vienna Psychoanalytic Society,[55] as recorded in their minutes.[56] Her introductory talk in January 1911 (her only talk, it turned out, because of Adler's ouster and her resignation nine months later) was called "On the Basis of Mother Love." She stated boldly that there is no innate mother love. She was prepared to note the subjectivity of mother hatred (as opposed to mother love)—a point traditionally resisted by psychoanalysis. The latter statement was audacious for a medical practitioner in 1911, where some in the Vienna circle still talked of a mental "degenerate" were a woman to reject her child.

Hilferding was prescient about work on female corporeality qua *female*, as featured later by Kristeva, Pines, Raphael-Leff, or writings from the Committee on Women and Psychoanalysis—for example Moeslein-Teising and Thomson Salo.[57] Hilferding said that a woman's *subjective* experience of her body in pregnancy can be experienced differently in birthing, and then again differently in the post-partum period. Like Kristeva, Hilferding focused on the female in her bodily procreative power and emphasized the woman herself. Deutsch kept a focus on the female procreative body in her clinical studies, although her biological essentialism was incorrect in her notions of "female" narcissism and masochism.[58] Langer, too, headlined "sexuality" alongside "motherhood" in her thinking.[59] Others, like Benedek or Stern, merely think of motherhood as a late developmental phase but fail to see its centrality in ego development.[60] Hilferding presented to that very early group a portrait of a mother who can be sexual in her own right, as does Kristeva.

Raw female aggression is of interest to Kristeva. It is one of the newer themes in the analyses of women, in contrast to the limited early descriptions of female aggression, focused as they were on women's attempt to masquerade as men. Their own aggression was obscured by the concept of penis envy. Hilferding never once mentions maternal sexuality or rage as being due to a missing penis or unresolved yearnings to be a man! She said that hatred can exist, especially, if the mother is disappointed in the delivery and feels a radical loss of the pleasures of a pregnant state.

Finally, Hilferding argues that "it is by way of the physical involvement between mother and child that love is called forth," and "certain changes in the mother's sexual life are brought on through the child."[61] Elise responds to Kristeva's similar modern ideas: "Kristeva indicates that a mother relies on her eroticism in mothering her child, but also that the child relies on the mother's eroticism in developing a vibrant sense of self."[62] Hilferding derives her thoughts from the medical clinic, close to the body, and thinks more literally than later analysts about the impact of a mother's sexuality. For example, painful uterine contractions can be brought on by suckling the baby, and frigidity can occur during the nursing period. After delivery, she suggests that the child represents "a natural sexual object for the mother. There must indeed exist between mother and child certain sexual relationships which must also be capable of further development."[63] Hilferding suggests that fetal movements awaken the mother's love and pleasure, and these may be sexual. The loss of bodily pleasure because of the baby's birth may cause aversion to set in. (This is still an unspoken and thus underdeveloped possibility in post-partum depression.) Milk shooting into the breast gives another pleasurable sensation. This close observational method, confirmed by listening to the mother talk about her bodily experience, presages a path for contemporary analysts to learn more about the experience of being female. Hilferding speculates cleverly: "if we assume an Oedipus complex in the child, it finds its origin in sexual excitation by way of the mother, the prerequisite for which is an equally erotic feeling on the mother's part."[64] This theoretical statement is vatic in relation to Kristeva. It is also found in Loewald's 1960 vision of the impact of the mother's necessarily formative force, or in 1992 in Laplanche, who espoused the normative seduction of infants by their parents' sexuality; or in Stein, who appreciated the enigmatic excess and interactive element in sexuality.[65]

Freud must have heard all these suggestions and observations as subversive, even though he did say that it was praiseworthy that "the speaker undertook a psychoanalytic investigation into a topic that, as the result of the convention that we maintain, had been held back from investigation."[66] Her jarring ideas presaged an interactive, two-person psychology. Hilferding's ideas—unknown and undiscovered by subsequent authors—were prescient of Winnicott, Bowlby, Laplanche, the Relational School, and Kristeva.[67] Freud was condescendingly critical and is quoted as saying, strangely: "the only way to find out something about mother love can be only through statistical examination" (this from the man who had derided statistics in letters to colleagues!).[68] Freud steered clear of Hilferding's commentary on the sexuality of the mother, the maternal body, and its impact on the mother-child bond. He even offered that conflictual behavior in motherhood can also occur in "mothers who have experienced the harmful effect of modern literature and who used the yearning for a child as a subterfuge for their sexual cravings"![69]

In the 1940s Deutsch was also vividly interested in female procreation and its pleasures as well as its pains. Today we can strongly dismiss her biologically essentialist and misleading theoretical views, but her clinical cases are worth exploring. She is almost unique in writing about childbirth, for example.[70] Kristeva's form of "female" inflected drive theory would have been positive for her.

VII. Contemporary Kindred Spirits and an Example of Contemporary Resistance

Kristeva's closest contemporary companion in her endeavor to focus on the subjectivity of the mother is Raphael-Leff, the London Middle Group analyst, whose work is not only theoretical but hands-on, as it were, in clinics with actual pregnant and birthing women.[71] North American fellow travelers working on female pleasures (as well as pain) and the sexuality of mothering are Elise (discussed below), Kulish, and myself.[72] From the French schools there is of course the richest representation of mentalized theory (theory about ongoing mental activity) that is at ease with the sexuality of the body—for example, Green in 1986.[73] Laplanche, especially, has (in 1972) conveyed the sexuality of mother-infant life, the mother's "enigmatic messages," and their impact as a central feature in his theories of mind.[74] Contemporary writing from the North American Relational School at times vividly engages with the eroticism of women as a whole, such as in the writings of Dimen or Dimen and Goldner—but their theory does not allow for weaving in the procreativity of women's bodies in as fundamental a manner as Kristeva does.[75] In fact their devotion to a postmodern repudiation of biology has hampered their sense of developmental continuities in body development because it is at odds with their break from allowing *any* manner of bodily sex differentiation that Kristeva, others, and I see as valuable to hold to, alongside a recognized and individualized kaleidoscope of gender expressions.

One contemporary North American relational analyst, who also values elements of ego psychology, and uses Kristeva's insights in a creative fashion, is Elise. Her 2017 paper on the analytic situation suggests that: "the 'multiverse' of mother/child erotic sensibilities—the dance of the semiotic *chora*. . . . *requires* a choreographic engagement by the clinician in interplay with the patient. . . . The embodied art of dance parallels the clinician's creative vitality in contributing to the shaping of the movement of a session."[76] Like Kristeva, Elise describes the deep sensual and sexual reverberations in the mother and child, which, she suggests, echo in the analytic duo, asserting that dance as the most highly embodied aesthetic is an apt metaphor for the communication movements of the analytic pair. Like Kristeva, she freely acknowledges a paternal contribution in addition, although she notes that paternal eroticism is as yet untheorized. The most archaic psychic layer is her interest, and she locates it with the mother and the infant in the mother's body. She is lyrical about the infant waltzing within the mother's body to the sound of her voice and her motion; the first kick experienced as a duet; the musical beat of the mother's heart. The case of Sue, an accountant, is unfolded where the patient progresses from thinking of therapy as "talking heads" to a session deep into the work with Elise, where Sue develops a conviction that the analyst is depressed because she simply *must* have experienced the death of a baby. Sue has read subliminally that the analyst in fact does *feel* like a mother who cannot keep her baby alive, enrapt as she is in this patient's coldness and lifelessness inside the consulting room.

Theory such as Kristeva's semiotic *chora* has the power clinically to open an analyst to the full experience of the patient within her, and within the womb of her room. Thus she opens this embodiment to a fuller and more mutually embodied transference-countertransference, for contemplation. Surprisingly, though, Kristeva's insights still arouse hostility even in this age that has welcomed a vast increase of pre-oedipal insights. How subtle today's resistance is can be exemplified with an article from a contemporary New York psychoanalyst, Adele Tutter, who criticizes Kristeva, Elise, and Loewald (another North American analytic thinker profoundly sensitive to the mutuality of mother and child), among others.[77] Essentially Tutter complains—as some did in Hilferding's Viennese audience of 1911—that too much is being said about the mother's intensity towards the child. She misunderstands the import of these communications. Her aim seems to substitute for the power of bodily issues the more intellectual assertion that "knowing" in the analytic situation or the desire "to know" is itself highly erotic. The intimacy of an analyst "knowing" a patient, then, and vice versa, is a form of eroticism. She also believes that "knowing" has been split-off from eroticism by mechanisms of avoidance of rawer forms of sexuality in psychoanalytic interaction. Perhaps. But she also thinks that erotics with all its adult lust is "quarantined" away by emphasizing accounts of maternal transference. This is her misunderstanding. Occasionally this could be the case. But she fervently describes (and alas misreads) Kristeva, Elise, Loewald, and many others who are involved in articulating the cradle of life force, as if maternal love was too clean and pure—in the way that Tutter sees love of the Virgin for her child as "de-aggressivizing" the elements of lust between adults in the room. "If Klein de-erotizes the breast, Kristeva . . . and Elise de-aggressivize it. The apple of this mother's eye is hardly forbidden: implicitly, the analysand's sexuality is infantilized, as immature as a baby's."[78]

Tutter often, like Kristeva, who writes fulsomely in a cross-disciplinary fashion, using paintings from her knowledge of art history, philosophy, and fiction to illuminate her psychoanalytic points, seems suddenly to misunderstand the depth of reverberance of Kristeva's semiotic *chora*. She overlooks Kristeva's work on "the abject" as it relates to mother and infant as an immersion in aggression and the death drive. I believe that in this criticism, Tutter, who is otherwise very sensitive to nuance, emerges as perhaps threatened by "maternal reliance" in attacking the messengers, as it were! Kristeva is unfortunately accurate in the epigraph to this paper about the hesitancy of psychoanalysts to become involved with the mother in the fullest erotic sense.

VIII. Kristeva's Build-up of Constructs towards Maternal Reliance

It is fitting for the task of forcefully articulating maternal eroticism that Kristeva is grounded and proficient in many European languages and has expertise in linguistics, literary scholarship, theory and criticism, religion, and politico-cultural analysis, as well as philosophy, art, and history. This puts her in tune with the Renaissance scholarship of the early psychoanalysts who, even if they did not grasp female psychology, at least were deeply interested in the functional body as represented in the psyche. However, if one's theory has bleached away the original force of Freud's drive theory—given the centrality of the body in psychic operations—such theoreticians may have thrown away the tools to be able to enter into this crucible of human living.

With Kristeva, the maternally embodied female flies, she expands till bursting, she penetrates, shivers with excitement; she desires an infant or repudiates such desire; she disgorges her vast burdens, she binds herself to an infant as it binds itself to her, she lets go the infant; she enfolds the father; she ignores the world in a singular focus on the helplessness of her tiny charge; yet she encompasses the world for herself and the baby in and out of her arms, her breasts, her entire body. She nurtures, the baby depends, they flourish within her reliance.

Some of the earlier well-known work that is woven into Kristeva's cumulative insights on maternal erotics can be found in, say, *Black Sun*, in her appreciation of the sounds, the stasis, and feelings of melancholia, the darkness of sorrow of the separation that must be effected between mother and child if any growth is to happen;[79] or her work on the abject in *Powers of Horror*, where she may be the only psychoanalytic writer I have encountered who is prepared even to engage the placenta—its waste and its once life-giving force destined for decay and ultimate destruction and disintegration into the earth (if not consumed by the mother as in animal life).

In this essay I have committed the nonsystematic indulgence of picking out just a few works that I think exemplify both the pleasure in these maternal insights of Kristeva's and the resistances. I will close with a loved piece of her writing. Her prose poem "Stabat Mater" thoroughly embodies the woman in the throes of her matricity, in her glorious closeness to all that is central in the earth's existence as she gives birth to the next generation of humans.[80] The passages below are excerpts from "Stabat Mater," which brings the erotic, maternal, semiotic archaic music into the "speaking mother's" birthing experience—ultimate *jouissance*. "Stabat Mater" is a thirteenth-century Latin hymn to the Virgin, "Stabat Mater Dolorosa": the Mother of Sorrows stands in mourning by her dying son.[81] Kristeva asserts that the mother "stands." A woman is stalwart and unwavering in her task of birthing, in her triumphant, joyful, painful, and joyfully painful entry into motherhood. She writes knowingly of the Virgin Mother: "This . . . [consecrated] motherhood is the *fantasy* that is nurtured by the adult, man or woman, of a lost territory" and "involves . . . an idealization of primary narcissism"[82]

Nothing is said directly in the following excerpts about eroticism or reliance or the semiotic per se, but these passages, printed boldface in the original, are integral to this basis of maternality:

> Scent of milk, dewed greenery, acid and clear, recall of wind, air, seaweed . . . it slides under the skin . . . detaches skin from bones, inflates me like an ozone balloon, and I hover with feet planted firmly on the ground . . . to carry him, sure, stable, ineradicable, while he dances in my neck, flutters with my hair . . . slips on the breast, swingles, silver blossom of my belly and finally flies away on my navel in his dream carried by my hands. My son.[83]

> smiles in the blackness of dreams, at night, opaque joy that roots me in her bed, my mother's, and projects him, a son, a butterfly soaking up dew from her hand, there, nearby in the night. Alone: she, I, and he.[84]

> Forgetfulness. . . . Like the fog that devours the park, wolfs down the branches, erases the green . . . and mists up my eyes.[85]

> Who calls such a suffering jouissance? It is the pleasure of the damned. . . . motherhood destines us to demented jouissance, that is answered, by chance, by the nursling's laughter in the sunny waters of the ocean. . . . It is a music from which so-called oriental civility tears away suddenly through violence.[86]

> Let a body venture at last out of its shelter, take a chance with meaning under a veil of words. WORD FLESH.[87]

One can hear the same ferocity in the yearning tonalities of Kristeva's later, explicitly theorized eroticism. One responds to the fierce longing and possession of the erotics of the child, and the erotics with the mother's own mother, in this poem that accompanies her text on the cult of the Virgin Mother. The eroticism of Kristeva's 2011 *maternal reliance* had yet to break forth in its fullness, emerging to be expressed, for her, within the ethics of responsibility, "*une héréthique de l'amour.*"[88]

ROSEMARY BALSAM

YALE UNIVERSITY
FEBRUARY 2019

NOTES

1. Julia Kristeva, "La Reliance, ou l'érotisme maternel," *Revue française de psychanalyse* 75, no. 5 (2011): 1559–70.
2. Julia Kristeva, "Reliance, or Maternal Eroticism," *Journal of the American Psychoanalytic Association* 62, no. 1 (2014): 69–85. See Bonnie Litowitz, "Introduction to Julia Kristeva," ibid., 57–59.
3. See Toril Moi, ed., *The Kristeva Reader* (New York: Columbia University Press, 1986), 1.
4. Kristeva, "Reliance, or Maternal Eroticism," 69.
5. Sigmund Freud, "Formulations on the Two Principles of Mental Functioning," in *The Standard Edition of the Complete Psychological Works of Sigmund Freud*, vol. XII, trans. James Strachey (London: Hogarth, 1964).
6. Lou Andreas-Salomé, *Lettre ouverte à Freud* (Paris: Seuil, 1931) (my translation).
7. Kristeva, "Reliance, or Maternal Eroticism," 70.
8. Maurice Merleau-Ponty, *The Visible and the Invisible*, trans. Alphonso Lingis (Evanston: Northwestern University Press, 1968), 154.
9. Kristeva, "Reliance, or Maternal Eroticism," 70.
10. Julia Kristeva, "Transformations of *Parentality*," in Vaia Tsolas and Christine Anzieu-Premmereur, eds., *A Psychoanalytic Exploration of the Body in Today's World: On the Body*, trans. Edward Kenny (New York: Routledge, 2017), 68–74.
11. Sigmund Freud, *Totem and Taboo*, in *The Standard Edition of the Complete Psychological Works of Sigmund Freud*, vol. XIII, trans. James Strachey (London: Hogarth, 1957); *A Phylogenetic Fantasy: Overview of the Transference Neuroses*, eds. Ilse Grubrich-Simitis, trans. Axel Hoffer (London: Belknap, 1987).
12. Kristeva, "Reliance, or Maternal Eroticism," 71.
13. Marilia Aisenstein and Elsa Rappoport de Aisenberg, *Psychosomatics Today: A Psychoanalytic Perspective* (London: Karnac, 2010).
14. Kristeva, "Reliance, or Maternal Eroticism," 70.
15. Ibid., n. 5. Rachel Boué-Widawsky is a Chicago psychoanalyst and a contributor to this volume. Perry Zurn is an American academic philosopher.
16. Kristeva, "Reliance, or Maternal Eroticism," 71.
17. Ibid.
18. Ibid.
19. Ibid., 72. See also Julia Kristeva, *Revolution in Poetic Language,* trans. Margaret Waller (New York: Columbia University Press 1974), 19–106.
20. Kristeva, "Reliance, or Maternal Eroticism," 72–73.
21. Ibid., 72.
22. Ibid.

23. Ibid.

24. "St. Patrick's Breastplate" or "St. Patrick's Lorica" is translated from Old Irish. These hymns are found in two manuscripts kept in Dublin and published in Whitley Stokes and John Strachan, eds., *Thesaurus Paleohibernicus*, vol. II (Cambridge: Cambridge University Press, 1903), 354–58. The saint was supposed to sing this in the face of an ambush, just as he turned into a wild deer to flee his enemies. An excerpt from the translation (slightly modified):

> I bind to myself to-day. . . .
> Through the strength of heaven,
> light of the sun,
> brilliance of the moon,
> splendour of fire. . . .
> Through God's strength to pilot me. . . .
> Christ with me, Christ before me, Christ behind me,
> Christ in me, Christ beneath me, Christ above me,
> Christ on my right, Christ on my left . . .
> Christ in the heart of every man who thinks of me,
> Christ in the mouth of everyone who speaks of me,
> Christ in every eye that sees me,
> Christ in every ear that hears me.
> I bind to myself to-day . . .
> of the Creator of the creation.

25. Kristeva, "Reliance, or Maternal Eroticism," 74.

26. Sigmund Freud, "Repression," in *The Standard Edition of the Complete Psychological Works of Sigmund Freud*, vol. XIV, trans. James Strachey (London: Hogarth, 1964). Jean Laplanche "The Unfinished Copernican Revolution," trans. L. Thurston, in *Essays on Otherness* (New York: Routledge, 1999), 52–83.

27. Kristeva, "Reliance, or Maternal Eroticism," 75.

28. Ibid., 75–76.

29. For her earlier work on abjection, see Julia Kristeva, *Powers of Horror: An Essay on Abjection*, trans. Leon S. Roudiez (New York: Columbia University Press, 1980).

30. Kristeva, "Reliance, or Maternal Eroticism," 75.

31. Ibid.

32. André Green, *On Private Madness* (London: Karnac, 1997), 245.

33. Kristeva, "Reliance, or Maternal Eroticism," 77. See "Transformations of *Parentality*" for Kristeva on the father.

34. For Sabina Spielrein, see Alexander Etkind, *Eros of the Impossible: The History of Psychoanalysis in Russia* (Boulder: Westview, 1977).

35. Kristeva, "Reliance, or Maternal Eroticism," 78.

36. Ibid., 76.

37. Ibid.

38. Ibid., 78.

39. Ibid., 79.

40. Ibid., 80.

41. Ibid., 80.

42. Sigmund Freud, "On the Universal Tendency to Debasement in the Sphere of Love," in *The Standard Edition of the Complete Psychological Works of Sigmund Freud*, vol. XI, trans. James Strachey (London: Hogarth, 1957).

43. Kristeva, "Reliance, or Maternal Eroticism," 80.

44. See Kristeva, *Powers of Horror*.

45. Kristeva, "Reliance, or Maternal Eroticism," 81.

46. Ibid.

47. Ibid., 82.

48. Ibid.

49. Ibid.

50. Julia Kristeva, "Stabat Mater," in *Tales of Love,* trans. Leon S. Roudiez (New York: Columbia University Press, 1987), 262.

51. Julia Kristeva, "Going Beyond the Human through Dance," *Journal of French and Francophone Philosophy—Revue de la philosophie française et de langue française* 21, no. 1 (2013): 1–12.

52. Kristeva, "Reliance, or Maternal Eroticism," 82.

53. Kristeva, "Going Beyond the Human through Dance," 8.

54. Margarete Hilferding, "On the Basis of Mother Love," in Herman Nunberg and Ernst Federn, eds., *Minutes of the Vienna Psychoanalytic Society*, vol. 3 (1910–11), trans. M. Nunberg and H. Collins (New York: International Universities Press, 1974), 112–25.

55. See Rosemary Balsam, "Women of the Wednesday Society: The Presentations of Drs. Hilferding, Spielrein, and Hug-Hellmuth," *American Imago* 60, no. 3 (2003): 303–42.

56. Hilferding, "On the Basis of Mother Love."

57. See Rosemary Balsam, "The Pregnant Mother and the Body Image of the Daughter," *Journal of the American Psychoanalytic Association* 44, Female Dev. Supplement (1996): 401–27; *Women's Bodies in Psychoanalysis* (New York: Routledge, 2012).

58. Helene Deutsch, *The Psychology of Women: A Psychoanalytic Interpretation*, vols. I and II (New York: Grune and Stratton, 1944/1945).

59. Marie Langer, *Motherhood and Sexuality*, trans. Nancy Hollander (London and New York: Guilford, 1992).

60. Therese Benedek, "The Psychology of Pregnancy," in E. J. Anthony and T. Benedek, eds., *Parenthood, Its Psychology and Psychopathology* (Boston: Little Brown, 1970). Daniel Stern, *The Motherhood Constellation: A Unified View of Parent-Infant Psychotherapy* (London and New York: Routledge, 1995).

61. Hilferding, "On the Basis of Mother Love," 114.

62. Dianne Elise, "Moving from within the Maternal: The Choreography of Analytic Eroticism," *Journal of the American Psychoanalytic Association* 65, no. 1 (2017): 33–60.

63. Hilferding, "On the Basis of Mother Love," 115.

64. Ibid.

65. Hans Loewald, "On the Therapeutic Action of Psychoanalysis," *International Journal of Psychoanalysis* 41 (1960): 16–33. Jean Laplanche, *Seduction, Translation, and the Drives: A Dossier*, trans. M. Stanton (London: Institute of Contemporary Arts, 1992). Ruth Stein, "Moments in Laplanche's Theory of Sexuality," *Studies in Gender and Sexuality* 8, no. 2 (2007): 177–200.

66. As reported by Otto Rank in Nunberg and Federn, eds., *Minutes of the Vienna Psychoanalytic Society*, 118.

67. The 1970s is when one sees papers that challenge received teaching beginning to appear in mainstream journals. It signals the beginnings of all the challenges within the field leading to postmodernist influences and the breakup of monolithic "psychoanalysis"—the beginnings of contemporary pluralism. The Relational School began in the early 1980s.

68. Reported by Otto Rank in Nunberg and Federn, eds., *Minutes of the Vienna Psychoanalytic Society*, 119.

69. Ibid.

70. For a fuller account, see Balsam, *Women's Bodies in Psychoanalysis*.

71. Joan Raphael-Leff, *Pregnancy: The Inside Story* (London: Routledge 2002); *The Dark Side of the Womb: Pregnancy, Parenting, and Persecutory Anxieties* (London: Anna Freud Centre, 2015). Ingrid Moeslein-Teising and Frances Thomson Salo, eds., *The Female Body: Inside and Outside* (London: Karnac, 2013).

72. Nancy Kulish, "Female Sexuality: The Pleasure of Secrets and the Secret of Pleasure," *The Psychoanalytic Study of the Child* 57 (2002): 151–76. Balsam, *Women's Bodies in Psychoanalysis.*

73. Green, *On Private Madness.*

74. Laplanche, *Seduction, Translation, and the Drives.*

75. Muriel Dimen, *Sexuality, Intimacy, Power* (Hillsdale: Analytic, 2003). Muriel Dimen and Virginia Goldner, *Gender in Psychoanalytic Space: Between Clinic and Culture* (New York: Other Press, 2002).

76. Elise, "Moving from within the Maternal," 33.

77. Adele Tutter, "The Erotics of Knowing: A Neglected Contribution to Analytic Erotism," *Journal of the American Psychoanalytic Association* 66, no. 3 (2018): 407–41.

78. Ibid., 441.

79. Julia Kristeva, *Black Sun: Depression and Melancholia*, trans. Leon S. Roudiez (New York: Columbia University Press, 1987).

80. Julia Kristeva "Stabat Mater," 234–64.

81. Kristeva says that her early experience of masses in the Greek Orthodox Church in Bulgaria was formative in her theorizing of "the semiotic." For the close relationship between her religious background and her connection to the procreative female, maternal reliance, love, etc., see Catherine Clément and Julia Kristeva, *The Feminine and the Sacred*, trans. Jane Marie Todd (Columbia University Press, 2001).

82. Kristeva, "Stabat Mater," 234.

83. Ibid., 246.

84. Ibid., 247.

85. Ibid., 249.

86. Ibid., 250, 255, 259.

87. Ibid., 235.

88. Kristeva, "Stabat Mater."

27

Rachel Boué-Widawsky

MATERNAL EROTICISM AND THE JOURNEY OF A CONCEPT IN KRISTEVA'S WORK

As a reader of Kristeva's work for more than twenty-five years, first as a scholar in literature and later as a psychoanalyst, I would like to start by saying that Kristeva's thinking is a passion, understood as an emotional and intellectual activity. What is at the core of this passion, as a motivation and a goal, is an exploration of the otherness within oneself through multiple versions of it, conscious/unconscious, feminine/masculine, rational/emotional, biological/psychical . . . In her entire body of work Kristeva communicates this passion by continuously expanding the limits of the boundaries among disciplines, thus questioning the established forms of knowledge.

The thread of Kristeva's journey among disciplines is led by an insatiable search for an empathic understanding of the human psyche, with its multiple modes of expression. Her limitless exploration of the human psyche is guided by a relentless ethical concern to preserve a place for the singularity of the subject in contemporary human sciences whose epistemology is beleaguered today by the diktat of scientific objectivity. Consequently, Kristeva is a philosopher, a linguist, a psychoanalyst, a literary scholar, and a writer. To do justice to the expansive span of her thinking requires that one humbly keep in mind this intellectual cosmology—she wanted to be an astronaut[1]—within which her thinking activity interconnects with different disciplines. This epistemological position defines Kristeva's ethical approach to the human mind, the exploration of which, in its darkest psychic zones, guarantees the refoundation, according to her, of new forms of humanism. This new humanism that Kristeva advocates in *Passions of Our Time* is necessary to counteract the segregated and positivist modes of thinking, which compartmentalize knowledge into categories.[2]

In this overarching frame of Kristeva's work, the theme of the maternal could be considered at first glance a subtheme, or a controversial political stance in the field of feminist studies, which would argue against a so-called essentialism in her position. For Kristeva, the maternal is a biopsychical thinking modality beyond gender identifications. Thus her exploration of the maternal is not defined by the erasure nor by the promotion of sexual differences on behalf of equality, although Kristeva has been a committed defender of women's rights.[3]

This essay aims at presenting the concept of the maternal as an omnipresent underlying source, desire, and perhaps intentionality of Kristeva's thinking, from her early linguistic research to her later explicit exploration of *maternal reliance*. By tracking the traces of the maternal in her entire work, I hope to show that, for Kristeva, the capacity to think has a maternal origin that has been overshadowed by the logophallocentrism of psychoanalysis and Judeo-Christian philosophy.

In her remarkable book, *Revolution in Poetic Language*, Kristeva introduces into the structural linguistic model (signifier/signified) the subject's nonreferential instincts or bodily drives such as affects, emotions, and sensations.[4] Interested in what contributes to the production of a meaning beyond or behind linguistic forms, Kristeva uses her psychoanalytic knowledge and experience to elaborate a theory for a critique of signification ("*critique du sens*") that includes prelinguistic forms of symbolization. She calls the latter the semiotic as opposed to the symbolic. Being unrepresented in a preset form, the semiotic acts as a disruptive force erupting against the preexistent linguistic or social structures. In *Revolution in Poetic Language*, Kristeva interprets Mallarmé's and Lautréamont's poetic works as illustrations of the capacity of language to construe nonsymbolic phenomena that transgress linguistic structures. For example, she sees in Mallarmé's syntactical deconstruction, or in his use of discordant phonic rhythms, the marks of a nonverbal signifier, a presignifier, which she interprets as a reference to the prohibited maternal. Similarly, her study of Lautréamont's poetry underscores the linguistic dissolution of the speaking subject, which Kristeva interprets as the ultimate alterity, viewed as a sexual confusion that relates to a nonthinkable maternal reference. This maternal unsettling background is seen as "*la doublure du code social*" ("the lining of the social code").[5] For Kristeva, the maternal, as an unsettling state of things, is the fleeting horizon of the major modern texts of the late nineteenth or twentieth centuries: Dostoyevsky, Proust, Céline, Artaud, or Joyce.

Kristeva explores the concept of the semiotic in linguistics and literature further in *Desire in Language*, redefining the typology of genres by emphasizing the concept of the productivity of multiple meanings beyond linguistic denotation and the genre category.[6] She also applies the semiotic to painting viewed as a privileged medium for nonsymbolized expressions. In studying Bellini's Madonnas in "Motherhood According to Bellini," Kristeva finds the opportunity to link the semiotic to the maternal.[7] "'The semiotic' with its maternal ties seems to be the farthest we can reach when we try to imagine and understand the frontiers between nature or 'physis' and meaning."[8] In this article, Kristeva lays out clearly her theoretical approach on motherhood, which she defines as a "pre- and transsymbolic memory" of the speaking subject animal, which explains "this unsettling of the symbolic stratum, this nature/culture threshold, this instilling the subjectless biological program into the very body of a symbolizing subject, this event called motherhood."[9] Comparing Leonardo Da Vinci's male bodies, as a foil to the phallic maternal *jouissance*, with Bellini's Madonnas, Kristeva argues that for both artists the maternal is the bedrock of their art. For her, this underlying theme, manifest as figures of the untouchable body/mother (Bellini) but figurable libido (Leonardo's male bodies), is the drive of the emancipating art of Renaissance painting: "the themes of motherhood, the woman's body, or the mother" is what "determine[d] Western man's vision for four centuries to come."[10]

Kristeva explains biographically that Bellini's Madonnas are characterized by the *absent* mother:[11] "As if there were a maternal *function* that, unlike the mother's solicitude in Leonardo's paintings toward the baby-object of all desire, was merely ineffable jouissance, beyond discourse, beyond narrative, beyond psychology, beyond lived experience and biography—in short beyond figuration."[12] Studying Bellini's pictorial style meticulously, Kristeva differentiates two types of maternal representation: the "possessive" (*Madonna and Child*, Rijksmuseum, Amsterdam) and the "hostile" one (*Madonna and Child*, Bergamo). These two aspects of motherhood testify to the threat that one may feel from the possessive maternal body as from the separation from it—it thus represents the impossible reference, the unrepresentable, which essentially designates what the Freudian theory calls primal repression. Primal repression is considered as a repressed representation of a drive against an excess of stimulation. According to Freud, this operation is the premise of the unconscious formation.

The semiotic is a pervasive function, neither sign nor meaning, which spreads through modalities of expression and that Kristeva attributes to the maternal origin of things. To support her argument, she borrows Plato's concept of *chora* from the *Timaeus*, as a receptacle, a space for things to come into being.[13] The *chora* is "an invisible and characterless sort of thing, one that receives all things and shares in a most perplexing way in what is intelligible, a thing extremely difficult to comprehend."[14] As this intermediate state between the physical and the intelligible, the *chora* is also viewed by Kristeva—who applies a psychoanalytic reading to the concept—as a space for primary processes "ordering the drives."[15] The *chora* is thus considered as a maternal space where the nascent subject (self, ego) is forming through the activity of the instinctual drives and bodily movements. The *chora* organizes this chaotic activity into the premise of a signifying process, prior to the compliance to the symbolic order. The maternal is a primary organizer for the presymbolic function to take place in child development. Partially based on prelinguistic observations in infant language development, Kristeva's argument debunks the prevalent Lacanian phallic symbolic order by claiming that the maternal junction of the physical and the psychical provides the space for the development of prelinguistic forms of symbolization.[16] In many of her books—*Black Sun*, *Tales of Love*, *Hatred and Forgiveness*—she makes us hear these archaic forms of expression through the tonality, rhythms, contradictions, meaninglessness, disruption, silence, and tears of her patients.[17] What leaks in the cracks of the words, from poetic texts or patients' narratives, is not so much the repressed unconscious, but, rather, semicorporeal and psychical affects that underpin and challenge the operations of the psychical apparatus. Seen as a maternal preorganized matrix for the activity of thinking, the maternal semiotic is foundational and heterogeneous, in between sensations and signs, hence its pervasive virtue. It indicates the limits and the origins of our capacity to think by pointing to the crossroads of nature and culture, without the support of an identifiable sign: namely, to the maternal space.

The maternal as both drive and psychic experience, in Kristeva's understanding, has been considered a taboo by civilizations. She explores this taboo aspect of the maternal through the concept of *abjection* in *Powers of Horror*.[18] Abjection is first studied from a psychoanalytic perspective before it is linked to biblical symbolizations and to its literary representations in Céline's work. She explores the concept of abjection beyond the maternal, proper, yet sets the latter as the theoretical horizon of her study. I will underscore the psychoanalytic approach to the concept. *Powers of Horror* has been considered a turning point in Kristeva's style, more lyrical than her previous theoretical texts. The evolution of her style, the power of which is recognized as both vivid and conceptual, corresponds to the nature of her topic, abjection considered as the maternal entrails of culture. Kristeva begins by describing the notion of abjection as a subjective experience before it is a representation, whether theoretical, religious, or artistic: "the abject is not an ob-ject facing me, which I name or imagine. . . . What is *abject* . . . the jettisoned object, is radically excluded and draws me toward the place where meaning collapses."[19] The *abject* is where the delineation between the object and the subject fades, eliciting the power of horror. "On the edge of non-existence and hallucination, of a reality that, if I acknowledge it, annihilates me. There, abject and abjection are my safeguards. The primers of my culture."[20] Because it is the in-between modality of our human condition, the *abject* is the sign of both our cultural and our biological humanity: these "refuse and corpses *show me* what I permanently thrust aside in order to live. These body fluids, this defilement, this shit are what life withstands, hardly and with difficulty, on the part of death. There, I am at the border of my condition as a living being."[21] Here the abject refers to a corporeal experience of the subject, "I," which nevertheless is not limited to its physicality.

As a psychoanalyst who articulates phylogenetic and ontogenetic symbolic representations in the human psyche, Kristeva applies the abject to the self as a marker of an ontological lack within it. "The abjection of self would be the culminating form of that experience of the subject to which it is revealed that all its objects are based merely on the inaugural *loss* that laid the foundations of its own being."[22] This pre-objectal and prerelational loss indicates the maternal abject fabrication of ourselves since it requires the extirpation from it to become a subject. This original experience, forever foreclosed, can nevertheless inspire desire and repulsion.[23] It is also the foundation for religious taboos and prohibitions, which Kristeva studies as a "semiotics of abomination."[24] Thinking of incest, Kristeva here adds to the social function of Lévi-Strauss's view on the psychical experience of this primary prohibition. "What will concern me here is . . . the alterations, within subjectivity and within the very symbolic competence, implied by the *confrontation with the feminine* and the way in which societies code themselves in order to accompany as far as possible the speaking subject on that journey."[25]

The maternal/feminine—as a taboo but also as a source of phobia, "something to be scared of," as Kristeva names one of her chapters—is the root of *abjection*.[26] The maternal body is the mother and the lover of the father. The mother is originally an erotic body and therefore a hiatus between pleasure and repulsion. For artistic examples of the maternal body as a possible source of abjection, Kristeva refers to Max Beckman's sinister representations of mothers (delivering life and death)[27] and to Jackson Pollock's erotic fantasies of a maternal matrix leading to the emergence of abstraction in his art. Analyzing the evolution of Pollock's paintings from *Birth* to *Gothic* and *Cathedral*, Kristeva sees the traces of an effort to approach the maternal/feminine as a gesture in painting "from the symbolism of birth and from the animality of the female desire that erupts in Pollock's painting gesture."[28]

Kristeva's widespread exploration of maternal eroticism, recognized as a fusion of abjection and love, adds to Freud's version of the oedipal complex. For her, the infant's life does not start, as in Freud's theory, in a self-sufficient erotic monad, but, rather, with a necessary separation and loss of the mother in order to be. "For man and for woman the loss of the mother is a biological and psychic necessity, the first step on the way to becoming autonomous. Matricide is our vital necessity, the sine-qua-non condition of our individuation."[29] Following Klein more than Winnicott's idealized mother-child unit, in *Tales of Love* and *New Maladies of the Soul* Kristeva explores, theoretically and clinically, the hidden fantasies of violence and destruction associated with the pre-objectal loved mother.[30] The mother is the first pre-object. On the one hand, an intruder in the infant's first states of being and, on the other hand, the soothing/feeding, repairing presence, she represents the first psychical conflict the child has to resolve. Kristeva's exploration of the pre-oedipal period is inspired by Klein's views on child development and by French psychoanalysis on the prepsychical.[31]

The outset of the universal developmental steps of the infant's life (hate/love, abject/object, me/her) varies depending on the maternal style. "The lesser or greater violence of matricidal drive, depending on individuals and the milieu's tolerance, entails, when it is hindered, its inversion on the self; the maternal object having been introjected, the depressive or melancholic putting to death of the self is what follows, instead of matricide. In order to protect mother I kill myself. . . . Thus my hatred is safe and my matricidal guilt erased."[32] Inspired by Klein here, before writing her extended work on the British psychoanalyst, Kristeva sees the maternal figure, as the necessary figure of abjection, as "an individuating dam against confusional love."[33]

The concept of abjection allows Kristeva to go beyond the drive activity that sustains the first steps of psychical development in Freud's and Klein's theories. For Kristeva, abjection, a nonidentified object that triggers attractive and repulsive affects, negatively defines the preliminaries of a thinking capacity that revolves around the object impossible to represent: the lost and present mother, the hated and needed one. The child attacks her, kisses her, harasses her, kicks her, loves her, misses her . . . In other words, she or he obsessively represents her. These primary forms of representation of the mother relate to the effective expulsion of the child out of her body and to the loss of her in order to become a human being.[34] It is precisely from this loss that the capacity to re-present the mother develops in the child's psyche. This operation is considered by early psychoanalysts and contemporary developmental psychologists as a universal developmental step, occurring between five and eight months.[35] While it is usually understood as a period where the child learns how to differentiate self and other, Kristeva focuses on the semiotic implications of such a development, arguing that the early capacity to fantasize and think requires the psychical *matricide*.[36]

However, at the core of this separation, *maternal reliance* operates as a compensation for the horror of the objectless abject. The maternal caring style determines the outset of such a critical developmental phase. "The loving mother, different from the caring and clinging mother, is someone who has an object of desire; beyond that, she has an Other with relation to whom the child will serve as go-between. She will love her child with respect to that Other. . . . Without the maternal 'diversion' toward a Third Party, the bodily exchange is abjection or devouring."[37] When the maternal/feminine abjection cannot be turned into reliance because of the eviction of the third—namely, the father, as part of the oedipal triangle and as the object of the mother's desire—the child is likely to succumb to the hate of the possessive mother and develop phobic, borderline symptoms to express her/his inability to love.

As we have seen, Kristeva's psychoanalytic concerns are focused on the in-between status of phenomena, oscillating between body and psyche. Like the semiotic, the *chora*, and abjection, maternal reliance indicates a process of transformation of bodily sensations into psychic phenomena. In her essay "Stabat Mater" in *Tales of Love*, she confronts the cult of the immaculate Virgin Mary and her own experience of motherhood opposed to it as a joyfully painful process of ripping apart. She writes in a semiotic, poetic style about the excruciating effort of transforming contradictory drives and emotions (attachment and expulsion) into an idealizing loving process.

> Then, slowly, a shadowy shape gathered, became detached, darkened, stood out: seen from what must be the true place of my head, it was the right side of my pelvis. . . . A piece of my body jutting out unnaturally, asymmetrically, but slit. . . . Frozen placenta, live limb of a skeleton, monstrous graft of life on myself, a living dead. Life . . . death . . . undecidable. . . . The calm of another life, the life of that other who wends his way while I remain henceforth like a framework. Still life. There is him, however, his own flesh, which was mine yesterday. Death, then, how could I yield to it?[38]

It is on this full-bodied experience of motherhood that Kristeva builds her theory with its relevant semiotic style. If she leaves open the old unresolved question of the passage from body to mind, she does not skip it but takes both into consideration in her exploration of maternal reliance.

For her, "maternal embodiment," erotic and abject, is the bedrock of the primary love relationship.[39] As Kristeva's essay on maternal reliance aims to show, maternal reliance derives from her early intuitive inquiries about the role of the maternal experience in the history of the development of human thinking.[40] As she notices in her essay, the first rare human self-representations on prehistoric caves are a gigantic vulva. She interprets this early visual testimony of the capacity to re-present oneself or the other as being linked to the maternal/feminine that plays the role of the intercessor between animality (more often represented in prehistoric caves) and humanity, sexuality and maternality, biology and psyche, drives and thoughts.

Maternality is a separating and a *relating* experience: "*Reliance: to link, to gather, to join, to put together*; but also *to adhere, to belong, to depend on*; and therefore *to trust, to feel safe, to share your thoughts and feelings, to assemble together*, and *to be yourself*."[41] Similar to Winnicott, Kristeva defines *reliance* as a developing binding experience between mother and child but also, primarily and continuously, as an interface between libidinal and aggressive drives. The erotic of maternal reliance is an extension and an enrichment of Winnicott's "maternal preoccupation," defined by him as a "normal illness," or a "dissociated state" where the mother enters a selfless state in order to be in tune with the infant's first moment of life.[42] In addition to being a function for the development of the infant, as a container of his or her not yet fully organized sensations and affects,[43] maternal reliance takes into account the disruptive and chaotic state in which libidinal and aggressive drives lean on each other—thus creating a tension, close to the "state of emergency."[44] The maternal experience is thus at the core of a vital process that depends on necessary destructive drives: separation, violence, and loss are part of the delivery process. While the child has to separate from the mother's body in order to live, the mother has to lose a part of her body to give birth to another life. In this mutual operation of expulsion and separation, life and destructive drives are part of the same act.

For Kristeva, this characteristic of maternal reliance, nourished of oppositional drives and ambivalent feelings, sets the ground for the feminine abjection that, again, many myths, traditions, and religions, as well as literature, have elaborated as a cultural taboo.[45] Registering all these representations of the maternal, Kristeva adds to it the concept of reliance as a corollary of abjection.

> I abject the Thing into which we were fused, the biopsychical *continuum* I had become. In order for psychization to be finalized, and for biopsychical negativity to ensure the creation of links, maternal eroticism lets the death drive loose in the vital process, all while binding [*reliant*] the two together: the maternal transforms the abjects (which the death drive has re-jected into the not-yet space of mother-child) into objects of care, into survival, and into life.[46]

For Kristeva, maternal reliance is the siege where life and death drives are intertwined in the process of giving life and fostering it in order to let the child go on being, as Winnicott puts it.[47]

Owing to the transformation, for the child and the mother, of a sexual intercourse into a psychical relation, this ambivalent combination of abjection and reliance constitutes the erotic substrate of motherhood, inasmuch as the mother relates to her child (with more or less desire and restraint) through her own libidinal drives, her lover's, and through the traces of her own history (as the child of her mother's and father's libidinal drives). This radically regressive experience provides overexcitement, which carries the mother beyond herself into a different place, *unheimlich*, as a stranger to herself, separate from others, father or children. If this "crazy enough mother," to play on Winnicott's expression, tolerates this momentary position in that strange place, she will not passively endure the situation.[48] She might reach the desire to enjoy the ultimate power of defying castration through perhaps endorsing the fantasy of a phallic power, as the genitor. For Kristeva, motherhood might be experienced as a phallic substitute, the desire of which is supposed to be pre-oedipal and stimulated by and within the mother. The phallic desire appears at first "because of the maternal desire for the father (her own and the child's)," she explains in *The Sense and Non-sense of Revolt*.[49]

This erotic reliance (which Freud had registered without further elaboration in *Three Essays on the Theory of Sexuality*) relating in Kristeva to the mother's unconscious sexual fantasy (her desire for the father), is a fundamental substrate to the child's sexual and psychic development. For it introduces into the turbulences of the mother-child dyad the mediation of an imaginary father, differentiated from the real oedipal father.[50] This representation of the imaginary father is viewed by Kristeva as a pre-objectal and presymbolic figure, mediated by maternal eroticism.[51] The function of this imaginary father is to prepare, within the mother-child relationship, for the development of new forms of identification and new object relations before facing the reality of the forbidding oedipal father. By introducing the role of the father as an imaginary function, at first transmitted by the mother's psyche, Kristeva modifies the narcissistic mother-child dyad. She inserts in the mother-child relation the seeds of an alterity.

> At this archaic stage of the psychical evolution, the subject already moves away from the mother/child dyad and toward a third pole, not yet a symbolic agency but already the beginning of the thirdness prefigured by the mother's desire for someone other than the child (her father? the child's father? an extrafamilial or symbolic agency?). In the uncertainty of this disengagement, however, an imaginary space is sketched out where this loving third party is found, the "father of the individual's prehistory," the keystone of our loves and imagination.[52]

The function of this imaginary father, viewed literally as an idealized figure, is seen by her, after Freud, as the possible foundation of monotheist religions.[53]

Kristeva also considers this primary imaginary father as the antidote to the incestuous, tumultuous maternal love and, as such, as instrumental in turning maternal reliance into the first ethical link to our humanity. In "Stabat Mater" she names this immanent ethics of the mother-child relationship an *heretical* ethics or an *herethic* love.[54] Later, in her chapter "On the Extraneousness of the Phallus; or, the Feminine between Illusion and Disillusion" in *The Sense and Non-sense of Revolt*, Kristeva provides the metapsychological foundation of this approach.[55] She presents a new oedipal configuration, called Oedipus 1, where the mother transforms her libidinal and destructive drives into love of the child with the intercession of the erotic psychical link to the lover/father.[56] Her approach is not an erasure of the phallocentric psychoanalytic theory, criticized by feminist ideology; it is an addition of what is prior to it inasmuch as Kristeva's approach makes the infant's first phallic fantasy be the result of the mother's intercession.

With the theoretical, ethical, cultural, and clinical expansion Kristeva gives to maternal reliance, the traces of which I have tried to underscore in this essay, she offers new foundations for revisiting our traditional and contemporary assumptions in art history, in modern literature, in the human sciences (linguistics, anthropology), and in psychoanalysis. In questioning established forms of knowledge through a journey among disciplines, she redesigns culture from a feminine foundation. The final conceptualization of this trajectory in the notion of maternal reliance is an attempt to correct a regrettable omission or eviction of the feminine and the maternal in psychoanalytic theory. In addition to being this counterpoint to a phallocentric psychoanalytic discourse, maternal reliance presents an ethical and metapsychological addition to political and juridical feminist discourse. For Kristeva, maternal reliance brings to the fore the irrevocable existing feminine foundation of civilization. As she writes in *Passions of Our Times*, maternal reliance, in the core of its torments, provides the roots of a new secular humanism.[57]

RACHEL BOUÉ-WIDAWSKY

INSTITUTE FOR PSYCHOANALYTIC TRAINING AND RESEARCH (IPTAR), NEW YORK
JANUARY 2019

NOTES

1. See Julia Kristeva, "Intellectual Autobiography," in this volume, 7.

2. Julia Kristeva, *Passions of Our Time*, trans. Constance Borde and Sheila Malovany-Chevallier (New York: Columbia University Press, 2018).

3. For example, see Kristeva's speech presented in 2011 at the Conference on Rafah Nached, https://www.pep-web.org/document.php?id=dr.004.0004a. A Syrian psychoanalyst, Rafah Nached was a victim of Assad's regime. See also Kristeva's Letter to Malala Yousafzai, written for the latter's reception of the Simone de Beauvoir Prize in 2013. Kristeva established this international prize in 2008 for those, like Malala Yousafzai, who work for women's freedom when such freedom is threatened: http://prixsimonedebeauvoir.blogspot.com/.

4. Julia Kristeva, *Revolution in Poetic Language*, trans. Margaret Waller (New York: Columbia University Press, 1984).

5. See "Le Mystère—doublure du code social," in Julia Kristeva, *La Révolution du langage poétique: L'Avant-garde a la fin du XIXe siècle, Lautréamont et Mallarmé* (Paris: Seuil, 1974).

6. Julia Kristeva, *Desire in Language: A Semiotic Approach to Literature and Art*, ed. Leon S. Roudiez, trans. Thomas Gora, Alice Jardine, and Leon S. Roudiez (New York: Columbia University Press, 1980), 237. This English edition is a combination of early and formative texts published in Julia Kristeva, *Sémiotikè: Recherches pour une sémanalyse* (Paris: Seuil, 1969) and in *Polylogue* (Paris: Seuil, 1977).

7. Kristeva, "Motherhood According to Giovanni Bellini," in *Desire in Language*, 237.

8. Julia Kristeva, "Thinking about Liberty in Dark Times," in *Hatred and Forgiveness*, trans. Jeanine Herman (New York: Columbia University Press, 2010), 12.

9. Kristeva, "Motherhood According to Giovanni Bellini," 241, 242.

10. Ibid., 246.

11. According to biographers, Bellini's maternal origin is uncertain.

12. Kristeva, "Motherhood According to Giovanni Bellini," 247.

13. Plato, *Timaeus*, in John M. Cooper, ed., *Plato: Complete Works* (Indianapolis: Hackett, 1997).

14. Ibid., 51a–b.

15. See the chapter on "The Semiotic *Chora* Ordering the Drives" in Kristeva, *Revolution in Poetic Language*, 25.

16. Ibid., 208.

17. Julia Kristeva, *Black Sun*, trans. Leon S. Roudiez (New York: Columbia University Press, 1989); *Tales of Love*, trans. Leon S. Roudiez (New York: Columbia University Press, 1987).

18. Julia Kristeva, *Powers of Horror*, trans. Leon S. Roudiez (New York: Columbia University Press, 1982).

19. Ibid., 1, 2.

20. Ibid., 2.

21. Ibid., 3.

22. Ibid., 5.

23. It is the material on which artists or writers try to create their medium because it is the first material to be symbolized.

24. The title of chapter 4 of Kristeva, *Powers of Horror*.

25. Ibid., 58.

26. Ibid., ch. 2.

27. See the illustrations of Max Beckman's *Birth* and *Death* in Kristeva, *Passions of Our Time*. She comments on them in two essays: "Reliance: What is Loving for a Mother?" (15) and "Maternal Eroticism" (111).

28. Jackson Pollock's *Birth* (c. 1941, Tate Modern, London), *Gothic* (1944, The Museum of Modern Art, New York), *Cathedral* (1947, Dallas Museum of Art). See Julia Kristeva, "La Voie lactée de Jackson Pollock," *Pulsions du temps* (Paris: Fayard, 2013), 66 (my translation).

29. Kristeva, *Black Sun*, 27–28.

30. Julia Kristeva, *New Maladies of the Soul*, trans. Ross Guberman (New York: Columbia University Press, 1995).

31. For Klein, the child's pre-oedipal development is organized into two phases. The first is the paranoid-schizoid position described in "Notes on some Schizoid Mechanisms" (1946), in Melanie Klein, *Envy and Gratitude and Other Works 1946–1963* (New York: Free Press, 1975). The second is the depressive position, described in "A Contribution to the Psychogenesis of Manic-Depressive States," in Melanie Klein, *Contributions to*

Psychoanalysis, 1921–1945 (Cardiff: Hogarth, 1968). For French psychoanalysis on the prepsychical, see Piera Aulagnier, André Green, Jean Laplanche, and others.

32. Kristeva, *Black Sun*, 28.

33. Ibid. For her later, extended work on Klein, see Julia Kristeva, *Melanie Klein*, trans. Ross Guberman (New York: Columbia University Press, 2001) (volume 2 of the "female genius" trilogy).

34. These early stages of representation of the mother through the immemorial experience of birth, assumed to occur in the child's mind, don't preclude the reciprocal tearing experience of the mother expulsing a part of her body in order to let this part become a human being.

35. For psychoanalysts, see Melanie Klein, D. W. Winnicott, Margaret Mahler, and Edith Jacobson. For developmental psychologists, see John Bolwby, Daniel Stern, Peter Fonagy, and György Gergely and John Watson.

36. See Kristeva, *Melanie Klein*, ch. 6.

37. Kristeva, *Tales of Love*, 34.

38. Ibid., 242–43.

39. On this topic, see Rosemary Balsam, *Women's Bodies in Psychoanalysis* (London: Routledge, 2012).

40. This essay was first published in English as "Reliance, or Maternal Eroticism," *Journal of American Psychoanalytic Association* 62, 1 (2014): 69–85. It is republished as, "Reliance: What is Loving for a Mother?" in *Passions of Our Time*. In this essay I refer to the original publication from 2014.

41. Kristeva, "Reliance, or Maternal Eroticism," 79.

42. D. W. Winnicott, "Primary Maternal Preoccupation," in *Through Pediatrics to Psycho-Analysis* (New York: Brunner/Mazel, 1992), 302.

43. Since Winnicott, psychoanalytic literature has focused on the mother-child unit and the consecutive child development.

44. Kristeva, "Reliance, or Maternal Eroticism," 72. In using this expression, "state of emergency," Kristeva refers to Freud's "*die Not des Lebens*," which Lacan explored for a confrontation with the Freudian concept of the reality principle. See Jacques Lacan, *The Ethics of Psychoanalysis: The Seminar of Jacques Lacan Book VII*, ed. Jacques Alain-Miller, trans. Dennis Porter (New York: Norton, 1997), ch. 4. In my view, Kristeva seems to use the expression in a different way than Lacan in her essay, by referring to it as the least mediated push of life towards reality.

45. See Mary Douglas, *Purity and Danger: An Analysis of the Concepts of Pollution and Taboo* (New York: Routledge, 2002). As an example of religion, read about the feminine taboo in the book of Leviticus in the Old Testament. For literature, see Beckett, Kafka, Bataille, and Artaud, for example.

46. Kristeva, "Reliance, or Maternal Eroticism," 76.

47. Winnicott, "Primary Maternal Preoccupation," 303.

48. Winnicott is known for the famous expression the "good enough mother." See "Primary Maternal Preoccupation," 300–305.

49. See the chapter titled "On the Extraneousness of the Phallus" in Julia Kristeva, *The Sense and Non-Sense of Revolt*, trans. J. Herman (New York: Columbia University Press, 2000), 96.

50. Sigmund Freud, *Three Essays on The Theory of Sexuality*, in *The Standard Edition of the Complete Psychological Works of Sigmund Freud*, vol. VII, trans. James Strachey (London: Hogarth, 1968), 223. Kristeva develops her concept of the imaginary father following Freud's notion of the "father of individual prehistory." See Sigmund Freud, *The Ego and the Id*, in *The Standard Edition of the Complete Psychological Works of Sigmund Freud*, vol. XIX, trans. James Strachey (London: Hogarth, 1961).

51. In exploring the presymbolic modalities of the origin of eroticism in the formation of the psyche, Kristeva differs from Laplanche's theory of seduction, in which he emphasizes

the discontinuity between the child's world and the adult's world, manifest in the impossibility of translating the "enigmatic messages" of sexual signs. See Jean Laplanche, *New Foundations for Psychoanalysis*, trans. Jonathan House (New York: The Unconscious in Translation, 2016).

52. Kristeva, *The Sense and Non-sense of Revolt*, 53.

53. This follows Freud's continuous interest in the psychical roots of religions developed in a number of texts. See Sigmund Freud, *Totem and Taboo*, in *The Standard Edition of the Complete Psychological Works of Sigmund Freud*, vol. XIII, trans. James Strachey (London: Hogarth, 1957); *The Future of an Illusion*, in *Standard Edition*, vol. XXI (London: Hogarth, 1968); *Moses and Monotheism* in *Standard Edition*, vol. XXIII (London: Hogarth, 1964). Kristeva links the early identification to an imaginary ideal third, transmitted by the mother, to the foundation of religious beliefs. See Julia Kristeva, *In the Beginning was Love: Psychoanalysis and Faith*, trans. A. Goldhammer (New York: Columbia University Press, 1987); *New Maladies of the Soul*, 121–23; *This Incredible Need to Believe*, trans. Beverley Bie Brahic (New York: Columbia University Press, 2009); "À Jérusalem: Le Besoin de croire dans les monothéismes et la sécularisation," in *Pulsions du temps*.

54. Kristeva, "Stabat Mater," in *Tales of Love*, 263.

55. Kristeva, *The Sense and Non-sense of Revolt*, ch. 5.

56. Ibid., 99–102.

57. Kristeva, "Dare Humanism," in *Passions of Our Time*, 274–75.

28

Fanny Söderbäck

MATERNAL ENIGMAS: KRISTEVA AND THE PARADOXES OF MOTHERHOOD

Every day the life sciences and obstetrics are gaining growing mastery over the enigma *of gestation which, due to its very status as an* enigma, *formerly conferred power upon the mother while at the same time anxiously taking it away.*

—Julia Kristeva, "Motherhood Today"

Kristeva's engagement with questions of birth, motherhood, and maternal subjectivity spans her entire work. Her views on motherhood cannot be easily summarized, as they have been developed over the course of almost half a century and broached from a variety of perspectives—personal, political, psychoanalytic, aesthetic, theological, anthropological, phenomenological, and so on. In this essay I try to offer something like a systematic analysis of motherhood in Kristeva's corpus. I argue that one important aspect of this analysis—what to me stands out as perhaps the most important contribution of her work on maternal matters—is her insistence that it be treated in all of its complexity, which is to say, that it be examined as an experience defined by ambivalence, ambiguity, and persistent tension. Motherhood, for Kristeva, is full of paradoxes—an *enigma* of sorts. It is these paradoxical-enigmatic features marking the maternal continent that I seek to uncover and examine.

In "Motherhood Today" (the passage cited in the epigraph, above), Kristeva makes two important points, each of which I explore in detail.[1] First, she emphasizes the enigmatic status of pregnancy and childbirth as such. If birth is a riddle, it is not one that Kristeva ever sets out to *solve*, as the life sciences and obstetrics have tried to do. Rather, throughout her work she insists on its riddle-like nature and maintains the need to attend to the enigmatic-ambiguous status of maternal matters rather than attempting to resolve or overcome them. Second, she points to a paradox at the heart of our male-dominated culture, namely that the enigma of gestation has conferred power upon mothers while at the same time being the root cause of their disempowerment. This claim requires historical contextualization, which, in turn, will help us better understand the contested status of motherhood in Western feminist literature in general and in Kristeva's work in particular. In the first section, I examine the second claim, the paradoxical fact that motherhood both empowers and disempowers, with reference both to Kristeva's work and to other feminist literature. In the second section, I discuss the enigmatic nature of gestation, birth, and motherhood as they appear in key moments of Kristeva's corpus.

I hope to show that our only chance of undoing the false dichotomy between reducing women to mothers and robbing them of their maternal powers is, precisely, to emphasize the enigmatic nature of birth and insist that the riddle of motherhood not be resolved. Only if we move beyond the forces of idealization and stigmatization alike can we get to something like the lived experience of motherhood, in all of its messy complexity. These are the stakes of Kristeva's persistent return to questions of birth and motherhood throughout her corpus.

I. Paradoxes of Birth: The Idealization and Erasure of Motherhood

Tuana has argued convincingly that, paradoxically, women have been *reduced* to the role of mothers while simultaneously being *robbed* of their role in procreation, and that upholding them to such a double standard has served to maintain women's perceived inferiority.[2] From ancient Babylonian and Greek creation myths, via the biblical Genesis, to modern science, the female power to give birth has been both *overemphasized* (as a way of establishing women's inferiority to men by tethering them to the embodied realm of biological labor and the survival of the species) and *underemphasized* (as a way of denying such female power and appropriating it to an all-powerful masculine divinity or medical scientific establishment). This seems to be the logic Kristeva has in mind when she claims that the enigma of gestation has conferred power upon women while at the same time anxiously taking it away.

Beauvoir provided a formative work on the reductive identification of women with mothers, her analysis of women's lived experience in *The Second Sex* clearly being guided by an awareness that women have played and continue to play an all too important role in reproduction and childrearing.[3] For Beauvoir, one of the foremost reasons for the oppression and othering of women is their role in procreation, which has locked them in a state of immanence and prevented them from embracing their human capacity for transcendence and freedom. While Beauvoir's rejection of motherhood has been overstated, and interesting analysis has emerged that paints a more complex and ambivalent picture of her views on motherhood,[4] it is clear that, for Beauvoir, reproductive labor as we know it represents an obstacle on the path towards women's liberation. To be sure, the social expectation that women become mothers is far-reaching and powerful. As Battersby puts it, "whether or not a woman is lesbian, infertile, post-menopausal or childless, in modern western cultures she will be assigned a subject-position linked to a body that has perceived potentialities for birth."[5] Such compulsory obligation is, of course, intimately tied to social and economic inequalities between women and men, such that women's liberation ultimately rests on their capacity to reproduce without being swallowed up by the demands of maternal labor, their right to embody motherhood in ways that challenge traditional norms and expectations, or their ability to reject motherhood altogether.

At the same time, however, religious and scientific accounts of reproduction have tended to rob women of their active role in procreation, amounting to the matricidal logic that characterizes patriarchal cultures, alluded to in Kristeva's remarks about the enigma of gestation. The ancients established the long-lasting view that woman is a mere passive receiver while man is the agent in procreation. Feminist assessments of reproductive biology and science therefore tend to bring attention to and challenge the tendency to erase mothers altogether as well as the all too common view that mothers are passive, inferior, and helpless, which arguably has served to justify women's lack of citizenship and rights. It was only in 1883 that the details of the union between sperm and egg (thus the understanding that they play an equally active role in fertilization) were worked out by the Belgian zoologist Van Beneden, but the association of woman with passivity by no means disappeared just because science changed, and remains strongly embedded in Western culture to this day.[6]

Thus women have been reduced to the function of motherhood and the reproductive realm while at the same time being deprived of their active role in procreation, having been allotted instead a docile role as mere receptacles or erased altogether as birthing agents. This paradox is the result of a double repression of sorts: the forgetting of woman *as* mother and, at the same time, the forgetting of woman as anything *other* than mother. This paradoxical double repression has given rise to debate in the feminist literature, where scholars of birth and motherhood are navigating the challenging task of reclaiming women's power to give birth while at the same time liberating women from the social demand that they be mothers.[7] Feminists, then, have been wrestling with the question of whether birth and motherhood pose a threat to or promote women's liberation. With this tension in mind, Rich has argued for the need to distinguish between two meanings of motherhood, namely, "the *potential relationship* of any woman to her powers of reproduction and to children" and "the *institution*, which aims at ensuring that that potential—and all women—shall remain under male control."[8] For her, the former can be liberating while the latter decisively is not. Navigating the minefield between the two typically entails tackling fraught issues such as essentialism, embodiment, and sexuality. It also requires critical attention to the implicit whiteness, heteronormativity, and cis-normativity of motherhood as it appears in contemporary feminist debates.

Kristeva is well aware of this tension between the view that motherhood is liberating and the one that renders it as an emancipatory impasse. Her own work has straddled the line between the two, attending both to the liberatory potential of motherhood and to its dangers. Critics have both accused her of putting too much emphasis on motherhood—to the point of confining women to the maternal function—and suggested that her own work perpetuates a matricide of sorts in that it sacrifices the maternal on the altar of an all too oedipal psychoanalytic framework. It appears that the paradoxes plaguing normative conceptions of motherhood are mirrored in feminist critiques of Kristeva's work. With this in mind, I turn to Kristeva's discourse on motherhood in order both to consider how the paradox we have articulated is treated there and to assess some of the most famous critiques of her alleged tendency to overemphasize *and* underemphasize the role of the mother at once.

Throughout her work, Kristeva appeals to the language of matricide to describe both the vital necessity of individuation and the patriarchal propensity for maternal erasure. A proponent of the former, she is deeply critical of the latter. Noting that "phallic idealization is built upon the pedestal of a putting-to-death of the feminine body," she suggests that this "evacuation of the maternal" results from the fact that, in order to establish the symbolic pact, we have been compelled "to get rid of the domestic, corporal, maternal."[9] This cultural and individual amnesia surrounding the maternal is a core issue. Nikolchina suggests that Kristeva's work be seen as "a theoretic rehabilitation of the maternal figure."[10] Beardsworth argues that Kristeva "returns constantly to the moments at which the maternal . . . itself can be heard, or simply to where the need to hear and elaborate it resounds as loudly as possible."[11] First and foremost, Kristeva addresses our forgetfulness by showing how the work of anamnesis can occur through the practice of psychoanalysis and art or poetic language—revolutionary practices that allow for a movement of return that makes possible renewal and rebirth.

Revolution in Poetic Language provides the first articulation of Kristeva's influential notion of the semiotic *chora*, associated with the maternal body and early heterogeneous drives.[12] Elsewhere, she describes symbolic language as constituting itself "at the cost of repressing instinctual drive and continuous relation to the mother," while, in contrast, "the unsettled and questionable subject of poetic language (for whom the word is never quite uniquely sign) maintains itself at the cost of reactivating this repressed instinctual, maternal element."[13] Insofar as Kristeva traces a matricide of sorts in language, we might say that culture as a whole, understood as a set of discursive practices, is founded on this sacrificial pact. *Powers of Horror* deepens these thoughts, bringing attention to a mother-child relation that is marked by *abjection*, where the distinction between subject and object is not yet developed.[14] Kristeva articulates this ambiguity in terms of an "abject." This text cements her reputation as a psychoanalytic thinker committed to exploring in great detail (and in far from idealizing terms!) a maternal continent that had remained largely silenced in the works of Freud and Lacan. As far as the question of the maternal is concerned, these texts primarily examine what we might call maternal residual traces in language. As Ziarek puts it, Kristeva takes on "the task of rethinking the maternal body as inseparable from the rethinking of language."[15]

Poetic language in particular is described as being shot through with semiotic registers and therefore as exhibiting maternal residual elements that might resurface and push back against an all too paternal-patriarchal discursive apparatus that dominates Western culture and ultimately renders it repetitive and death oriented. Such pushback is the condition of possibility for aliveness. It vitalizes—indeed revolutionizes—an otherwise monotonous social fabric. Motherhood, for Kristeva, is thus never merely about birth—it is always also a matter of rebirth or renewal, and it provides hope for creativity and change.

Nonetheless, she has been under fire for her emphasis on motherhood, particularly in regard to her alleged relegation of the maternal semiotic *chora* to a prediscursive affective realm of bodily proximity. Critics have suggested that this aspect of her work leads to the reduction of women to the biological function of motherhood. Chanter explains: "to the extent that Kristeva seeks to focus upon the maternal experience as a dimension whose significance patriarchal society has tended to overlook, and to the extent that the semiotic is associated with maternity, it is inferred that in embracing the semiotic, Kristeva endorses essentialism."[16] Rose describes "that essentialism and primacy of the semiotic" as "one of the most problematic aspects" of Kristeva's work.[17] Butler argues that Kristeva "delimits maternity as an essentially precultural reality," complaining that her "naturalistic descriptions of the maternal body effectively reify motherhood and preclude an analysis of its cultural construction and variability."[18] Kristeva has noted that "it seems . . . difficult to speak today of maternity without being accused of normativism, read: of regression."[19] She is clearly aware that discourse on motherhood is mined by political divides and ideological schisms. Her more recent work on motherhood, especially, will often bracket her claims with preambles such as "at the risk of shocking some of you," or "at the risk of causing an outrage," as if aware that any and all reference to maternal matters will reawaken the old debates on essentialism or the outcries on how women are trapped in the mores of motherhood.[20]

There is no doubt that the outright rejection of motherhood in the name of feminism troubles Kristeva. In an interview in 1977 she raises the concern that some feminists "are relying too much on an existentialist concept of woman, a concept that attaches a guilt complex to the maternal function. Either one has children, but that means one is not good for anything else, or one does not, and then it becomes possible to devote oneself to serious undertakings."[21] She seeks to formulate a discourse on motherhood that avoids binary presuppositions that assume that women can either choose motherhood and forever be trapped or reject it and achieve liberation. She views such binary options as false, and asserts that what we need "in the West today is a reevaluation of the 'maternal function,' seeing it not as explosive and repressed but as a source of practices considered to be marginal (such as 'aesthetic' practices) and a source of innovation."[22] Motherhood, in other words, entails much more than reproduction and care. It includes creative and artistic practices, modes of sublimation and representation. It is never reducible to a mere biological function, but always situated precariously "at the crossroads of biology and meaning."[23] Moreover, Kristeva never prescribes motherhood as a necessary condition of womanhood, as some critics have suggested she does. She insists that it "is not an 'instinct' and cannot be reduced to a 'desire to have a child,'"—wondering herself: "What about the desire *not* to have a child?"[24] Indeed, Kristeva has consistently insisted on not reducing women to the function of motherhood. Instead, she tends to return to the maternal precisely to free women from this reduction.[25]

What the critics cited above have in common is a suspicion that Kristeva's attention to the semiotic *chora*—and association of it with the maternal body—amounts to a relegation of motherhood to an unspeakable outside that is *prior* and *opposed* to culture and the symbolic order. Rose is concerned that Kristeva assigns to the semiotic "the status of origin" and places it "beyond language," despite Kristeva's clarification that "the position which takes the semiotic as heterogeneous does not arise from a concern to integrate some alleged concreteness, brute corporeality, or energy-in-itself into a language suspected of being too abstract. . . . *This semiotic is without primacy and has no place as origin*."[26] Her whole project is arguably a sustained attempt to avoid such oppositional and exclusive structures, consistently describing the semiotic and the symbolic as *interdependent, coexisting, intertwined*. The alleged exclusivity between the two realms is "relative, precisely because of the necessary dialectic between the two modalities of the signifying process, which is constitutive of the subject. Because the subject is always *both* semiotic *and* symbolic, no signifying system he produces can be either 'exclusively' semiotic or 'exclusively' symbolic, and is instead necessarily marked by an indebtedness to both."[27] No meaning can be produced unless *both* modes are implicated, to a larger or lesser degree.

Kristeva has been accused of what may seem like two contradictory—indeed paradoxical—flaws. On the one hand, she is said to put too much emphasis on the maternal body, leaving little or no space for women to develop subjectivities other than that of motherhood, and relegating maternity to a precultural sphere marked by biological necessity—a critique I have addressed. On the other hand, she is accused of having knowingly sacrificed the maternal, first, by emphasizing the necessity of separating from the mother in her psychoanalytic-developmental account and, second, by idealizing the imaginary father. Chanter explains: "If Kristeva's elaboration of the semiotic is regarded as collapsing onto essentialism, she fares no better in her attempts to acknowledge that, with the subject's entry into language, there is always already present the influence of culture. She is accused of committing the equally grave sin of phallocentrism by accepting the rule of the symbolic."[28] Thus critiques of Kristeva's discourse on motherhood seem to mirror the very paradox we are foregrounding: women simultaneously having been reduced to mothers and robbed of their role as mothers. We now examine this second allegation, namely, that Kristeva is guilty of "matricide."

For important and valuable reasons, feminists have been compelled to correct deeply entrenched views about birth and motherhood embedded in the psychoanalytic tradition, and to challenge an oedipal logic premised by a "silent mother and threatening father."[29] According to the traditional oedipal model formulated by Freud and developed by Lacan, if the child is to enter into the sociolinguistic sphere, separation from the mother is required. With Oliver:

"Because she is associated with nature, the mother must be left behind, killed off, in order for the child to be social."[30] Psychoanalytic theory thus follows the matricidal logic we have spoken of, maternal traces being erased to make room for paternal agency and phallic power. There is no doubt that Kristeva, faithful as she is to the Freudian model of individuation, inscribes what we might call matricide as a necessary condition for subject formation. The little child must separate from the mother in order to gain access to discourse, and this separation is (fantasmatically) experienced as murder. Kristeva does, indeed, describe matricide as "our vital necessity, the sine-qua-non condition of our individuation," asserting that "the loss of the mother is a biological and psychic necessity, the first step on the way to becoming autonomous."[31] This has given rise to a body of critical work of a kind contrasted with the one already examined, for it involves the accusation that Kristeva *underemphasizes* rather than overemphasizes the role of the mother. For example, Stone suggests that "Kristeva defends the necessity of matricide because she retains a version of the traditional psychoanalytic view that the paternal figure is necessary as the 'third term' to break up the mother-child dyad and introduce the child into language and social life."[32] Tyler speaks of a "foundational matricide" in Kristeva's work, and proposes that "her account of the development of subjectivity is in many ways as 'mother free' as Lacan's."[33]

While I think these criticisms are important, it is worth noting that the mother is never actually "left behind" or excluded from the sociosymbolic pact on Kristeva's account. As we have seen, she veers away from fully separating the maternal-semiotic from the paternal-symbolic—the interdependence between the two fundamentally structures her thought. The semiotic traces in language emerge, time and again, in poetic language and other creative discourses. While separation from the mother is necessary for individuation, she insists on the importance of remembering and integrating our relationship to her, even as we distinguish ourselves as individuals. If matricide is necessary for subject formation, it is always in some sense partial, and a continual "return" to the mother is necessary for the possibility of different modes of renewal—rebirth, creativity, revolt.

On the one hand, then, Kristeva inherits the traditional psychoanalytic view that the paternal figure must break up the mother-child dyad in order to introduce symbolic language. As such, she upholds the inevitability of (symbolic) matricide. On the other hand, as Stone has pointed out, Kristeva "qualifies and transforms the idea of the paternal third term, and reappraises early maternal relations, in ways that point in anti-matricidal directions."[34] While those of us who have a mother try to separate from her in order to become differentiated individuals and speaking beings, we also remain entangled with her as we experienced her in the earliest stages of our life—as the organizing force of our most archaic affective and bodily environment. Throughout the course of life, we maintain a complex bond to this archaic relationship, which can erupt in works of art, poetry, and other sublimated forms of expression. Moreover, the process of separation begins early in life and is far from clearcut or absolute, marked instead by an ambivalent process of a continual redrawing of boundaries. Since the infant feels like it is "one" with its mother, the process of separating from her inevitably involves a sort of self-separation or splitting. This process can be violent, painful, and messy. "During that course in which 'I' become, I give birth to myself amid the violence of sobs, of vomit."[35]

Kristeva's work could thus be described as an obituary of sorts. The lost maternal object is inscribed as negation or lack, silent yet threatening. She does speak of matricide, but her own attempt to trace a maternal genealogy bears witness to a loss that (appropriately mourned) could perhaps be overcome. Through the act of recovery, the maternal takes on new meanings, thus becoming incompatible with traditional views on motherhood—views that have served to define and erase the mother in one and the same act. We now explore in more concrete terms what Kristeva means when she speaks of motherhood at different moments in her corpus, and examine more specifically why it is described as *enigmatic*.

II. Enigmatic Motherhood: Negativity, Abjection, Ambiguity

"Stabat Mater," which first appeared in 1976, is arguably her most important essay on maternity. Kristeva explicitly addresses the paradoxical views that we have unpacked here. She clarifies what her own attempt to revisit the maternal amounts to:

> We are caught in a paradox. First, we live in a civilization where the *consecrated* (religious or secular) representation of femininity is absorbed by motherhood. If, however, one looks at it more closely, this motherhood is the *fantasy* that is nurtured by the adult, man or woman, of a lost territory. . . . Now, when feminism demands a new representation of femininity, it seems to identify motherhood with that idealized misconception and, because it rejects the image and its misuse, feminism circumvents the real experience that fantasy overshadows. The result?—a negation or rejection of motherhood by some avant-garde feminist groups. Or else an acceptance—conscious or not—of its traditional representations by the great mass of people, women and men.[36]

In short, the challenge we face today is to refuse the false dichotomy between an all-out rejection of motherhood and the perpetuation of idealized conceptions of it that are ultimately hollow and fail to account for lived experience. As Kristeva has noted, underlining a central point in our discussion, woman as mother tends to be either altogether *absent* or overly *idealized*, depicted either as a *hole* (at the root of the Hebrew word for woman, *nekeva*) or as a divine or royal *whole* (the Virgin Mother).[37] Her work is therefore an attempt to overcome this false and damaging dichotomy, to develop an account of maternity that is more complex, more ambiguous, messier, and more rooted in lived reality in all of its perplexing—indeed enigmatic—heterogeneity. Marked by desire and disgust at once, the maternal cannot be done away with or silenced, nor pinned down in an idealized or frozen image. We must reckon with the mother, wrestle with the experience of motherhood and our relationship to our mothers or else we are missing something about who we are, who we can be, and how we might be otherwise.

The very structure of "Stabat Mater" is meant to illustrate and illuminate two radically different aspects of the maternal: on the one hand, the most idealized and phantasmatic of them all, the figure of the Virgin Mary; on the other, what Kristeva calls "the real experience that fantasy overshadows," in a poetic account of pregnancy and childbirth grounded in her own personal, singular experience. The latter attends to the "impossible" and "unnamable" character of gestation and the "immeasurable" and "unconfinable" nature of the maternal body: the fact that motherhood is an identity crisis of sorts insofar as it splits the self, such that "my body is no longer mine" as the pain of the other (the newborn child) is experienced as arising in my own body, while at the same time a sensuous, indeed erotic luminosity washes through the self and its not-yet-other.[38]

The paradoxes of motherhood appear throughout "Stabat Mater." Childbirth is "deprivation and benefit" at once, the newborn "neither present nor absent," motherhood a "pleasure of the damned" or fearful fascination.[39] The text is sprinkled with contradictions, ambiguities, tensions, and an overall state of liminality. The mother and her infant are "crossroads beings" living on the border, and the mother a "continuous separation" and "division" of both flesh and language, so much so that it becomes "unsettling to say 'I'" as the self is experienced as a "see-saw."[40] Kristeva suggests that Christianity—we might add Western culture as a whole—has attempted "to freeze that see-saw," "to stop it, tear women away from its rhythm, settle them permanently in the spirit."[41] This tendency gives rise to the paradoxical situation wherein woman is either hole or whole rather than somewhere between the two: liminal, paradox, crossroads being. Similarly, woman in such a culture must be either virgin or whore, never a subject of her own erotic pleasures and pains. Thus, when Kristeva takes it upon herself to offer an alternative discourse on maternal subjectivity, it is one that also paints the mother in erotic terms as one capable of "sexual-intellectual-physical passion."[42] Kristeva had already in 1975 explored the enigmas of gestation or what she calls "motherhood's impossible syllogism" in her essay "Motherhood According to Giovanni Bellini."[43] Here, too, she characterizes the pregnant body as fundamentally split—undermining traditional distinctions between subject and object, self and other, inside and outside: "Cells fuse, split, and proliferate; volumes grow, tissues stretch, and body fluids change rhythm, speeding up or slowing down," within the "simultaneously dual and alien space" of gestation.[44]

The characterization of pregnant embodiment, birth, and motherhood in these early essays has been hugely influential for subsequent Western feminist work on such issues. In her wake, feminist phenomenologists tend to challenge and complicate both the reduction of women to passive vessels of gestation and the idealized image of motherhood. They insist on narratives that acknowledge and give voice to the complex, ambiguous, messy nature of motherhood and maternal subjectivity. In her now classic "Pregnant Embodiment: Subjectivity and Alienation," Young draws from Kristeva in considering "some of the experiences of pregnancy from the pregnant subject's viewpoint," describing pregnant bodily existence as "decentered, split, or doubled in several ways."[45] Oliver has pointed out that pregnancy "opens the body to otherness in ways that make the experience porous physically and mentally. This porosity . . . can be a model for more open relationships with others and a more porous notion of subjectivity than philosophers typically provide."[46] What many feminist accounts of pregnancy, childbirth, and mothering have in common—again drawing from Kristeva—is their insistence that these experiences force us to revise basic Western assumptions about personhood, such as the perceived unity of the subject, the boundedness of our bodies, the autonomy and integrity of the self, or the "mineness" that we tend to attribute to the ego. It is evident that pregnancy, childbirth, and mothering put to the test Western dualistic distinctions such as self/other, own/alien, same/different, active/passive, inside/outside, subject/object, reason/affect, and mind/body. If Western philosophy has managed mostly to ignore the phenomenon of pregnancy, feminist philosophies of pregnancy, childbirth, and mothering have put Kristeva's work to use in order to transform, scrutinize, and decenter the very nature of philosophy as we know it, and its most fundamental conceptual presuppositions.

If Kristeva's attention to the enigmas of gestation have proved essential for recent feminist work on pregnant embodiment, her discussion of the early relationship between mother and child has been just as important. Again, she paints a picture that refuses idealization and dichotomization. *Powers of Horror* depicts the subject-to-be as "an inescapable boomerang, a vortex of summons and repulsions" and as one "literally beside himself."[47] And if food loathing is the most archaic form of this vortex of summons and repulsions—what Kristeva calls *abjection*—this is in large part because the first signs of subjectivity entail separation from (indeed rejection of) the maternal, which has been the source of both nourishment and that oceanic feeling of being "one" with her.[48] This marks the very process of subject formation—understood as the untangling of the mother-infant dyad—as paradoxical from the start. Since the mother (and her milk) is not yet an "other" for "me," this means that "I expel *myself*, I spit *myself* out, I abject *myself* within the same motion through which 'I' claim to establish *myself*."[49] Subject formation, in other words, is fraught with an original splitting of sorts, one that entails self-*rejection* as the condition of possibility for self-*formation*.

This all means that abjection is first and foremost aimed at the mother. "When the subject wrests himself away from the maternal . . . he does so in the pulse of ab-jection: the mother is the target of it, so that from her placental and precociously narcissistic envelope the possibility emerges of an object in the face of a subject that 'I' would be."[50] Abjection is the "in-between, the ambiguous, the composite."[51] It is Janus-faced and serves as a reminder that our very being is constituted by impossibility insofar as the foundation of our own being is inaugural *loss*.[52] Here we see one of many clear examples of the manner in which Kristeva is a proponent of matricide in the context of subject formation. If inaugural loss conditions us as individuals, it is easy to see the mother as a mere prop in the drama of subjectivation—one that can be left behind once the subject joins with the father in a symbolic pact. However, we have seen that this is too simplistic a reading. Kristeva is clear that "abjection *preserves* what existed in the archaism of the pre-objectal relationship, in the immemorial violence with which a body becomes separated from another body in order to be."[53] What is at stake here is not simply the birth of a subject but the very possibility of *imagination*, whose foundations are being laid.[54] Our inaugural loss (the matricidal logic) makes possible continual return to the maternal, which gives rise to literature, poetry, art, and other forms of renewal. Thus our separation from the mother simultaneously marks the beginning of a new bond, a creative bond of return that makes possible representation and sublimation.

This also means that representation is rooted in constitutive loss, a loss that cannot be overcome, and is therefore bound up with melancholia. Our "original loss of the *mother*" is "the source of *melancholy*."[55] Kristeva explores both abjection and melancholia in the context of art in *The Severed Head*, written after curating an exhibit at the Louvre on artistic representations of decapitation. The theme of melancholia had been taken up in *Black Sun: Depression and Melancholia*, appearing in French in 1987, where Kristeva already associated melancholia with "*impossible mourning for the maternal object*."[56] In *The Severed Head* she revisits these themes and ties them explicitly to the prevalence of female severed heads in the history of art, suggesting that we view maternity as "an equivalent for decapitation" insofar as "it is the mother's head at which we aim, she is the capital vision."[57] It is perhaps no coincidence that *The Severed Head* is one of very few (just two?) books by Kristeva that has a dedication, and that it is dedicated to her mother, Kristina Kristeva, whom she describes elsewhere as someone "who combined a sharp scientific mind and a strong sense of duty with a gentle nature," and "passed on to me that kind of rigor which is such a necessary part of one's development, especially for a woman, and even more so for a woman in exile."[58] Our discussion thus far portrays how we are all ultimately exiled, all "strangers to ourselves." This is especially true for women insofar as our individuation depends on our separating from (indeed rejecting) a parent with whom we have both erotic ties and ties of identification. By revisiting the maternal continent, time and again, Kristeva explores not only the conditions under which we become exiled in subject formation but also our capacity to sublimate this very experience, which is to say, how we become "capable of bearing the absence of [our] mother."[59]

We have seen that Kristeva's attempt to remove maternity from the false and harmful binary of idealization and erasure tends to lead to an account of maternity and motherhood that is steeped in ambivalence, tension, and complex affective registers such as grief, melancholia, abjection, and disgust. Her attempt at painting a more complex picture of the maternal continent does not end with inscribing negativity in the maternal body in the form of rejection, decapitation, or matricide, however. Abjection always entails repulsion *and* attraction, rejection *and* fascination. While Kristeva has indeed been interested in the structure of loss that organizes the mother-child relation, her autobiographical account of motherhood in "Stabat Mater" is also steeped in an eroticism of sorts, and she has always been interested in maternal desire. One of the things marking the originality of Kristeva's work on motherhood is the way in which the triangulation between mother, father, and child is organized primarily by *maternal* desire—which is why the mother in her work could never be reduced to a passive vessel. Maternal erotic powers are by no means obliterated in her work. The mother is a force to be reckoned with, and she carefully straddles the fine line between pleasure and pain in a maternal *jouissance* that is at the heart of Kristeva's discourse on these matters.

Kristeva's recent work has tended to focus on what she calls *maternal passion*, distinguished from instinct or emotion. In "Motherhood Today" the overevaluation of pregnancy in our culture is symptomatic of a repression of maternal passion.[60] In "The Passion According to Motherhood," she speaks of maternal love as the core passion and as capable of modulating the future subject, adding that in the context of motherhood "passion takes on its most human aspect, that is to say, the furthest from its biological foundation."[61] Maternal passion is thus the prototype of all human passion and sets us apart from nonhuman animals. Moreover, because it necessitates both expulsion and detachment, it is from the outset "inhabited by the *negative*."[62] We are reminded again of the *active* role of the mother in making space for the process of subject formation and in making possible representation. "The 'good enough mother' would be she who knows how to leave to make room for *pleasure*, for the child, for *thought*. To leave room, in other words to disappear. Thus a kind of *symbolic matricide* operates through the child's acquisition of language and thought."[63] This by no means entails reducing oneself to brute facticity or to a merely affective register. Kristeva is careful to distinguish passion from emotion, the former bound up with reflexive consciousness in taking into account "the otherness of the other and the self."[64] This is why passion—and maternal passion as its prototype—sets us apart from nonhuman animals. It is "an emotion put into signs" and is thus fundamentally tied up with sublimation, creativity, and rebirth.[65] As Oliver explains, "it is not primarily passion that is uniquely human but rather dispassion or the sublimation of passion, which is essential to maternal passion as successful mothering."[66]

Kristeva is ultimately concerned that "by turning all our attention on the biological and social aspects of motherhood as well as on sexual freedom and equality, we have become the first civilization which *lacks a discourse on the complexity of motherhood*."[67] Her dream is that the arguments she develops around motherhood and maternal passion "will help to remedy this lack," "will stimulate mothers and those who accompany them (gynecologists, obstetricians, mid-wives, psychologists, analysts) to sharpen our understanding of this passion, pregnant with madness and sublimity."[68] Why? Because mothers today are in dire need of such a discourse.[69]

III. Conclusion

I hope to have shown that Kristeva attends very carefully to the lived experience of motherhood and aims to move beyond hollow expressions of maternity that reproduce the false, harmful dichotomy between idealization and erasure. I have characterized her project as one that seeks to unearth that "real experience that fantasy overshadows"—one that has been covered over and silenced in patriarchal and feminist discourse alike. I have argued, with Kristeva, that doing so requires attending to the enigmatic-paradoxical nature of maternal experience. When she speaks of "experience," it is something deeply rooted in an analysis that ties the maternal to seemingly abstract notions such as language, subject formation, abjection, revolt, and sublimation. She is ultimately not interested in reproducing or contributing to a discourse that approaches motherhood in terms of "its role in and through the banal, domestic heaviness, reduced to basic cares and needs, where we too often tend to relegate the mother's function."[70] Not wanting to "be content with a realist and intersubjective comprehension of mothering," she seeks, rather, to focus on "the negative and its variants in the different phases of development."[71] I take it that the negative, here, entails the concepts I have focused on: abjection, sublimation, passion, revolt . . . Her concern with the experience of motherhood strongly suggests that it is irreducible to the "function" of motherhood—its material and intersubjective conditions—and that we must focus on the role of the negative and its variants (abjection, sublimation, maternal passion, etc.).

In concluding these reflections on motherhood in Kristeva, I wonder nonetheless what it means to offer an account of motherhood that circumvents the false and harmful dichotomy between idealization and erasure *without* also paying attention to that banal, domestic heaviness? Are the negative and its variants (abjection, sublimation, passion . . .) not always already shaped by that heaviness, by that realist and intersubjective comprehension of motherhood that reveals its material conditions of possibility, as well as, importantly, its material conditions of *impossibility*? I think, for example, of racial and economic discrepancies, of heightened maternal mortality in neglected communities, or the intense medicalization of some maternal bodies in stark contrast with the medical oblivion of others.[72] Despite her careful attention to lived experience, it seems to me that Kristeva circumvents an analysis that would acknowledge and account for the power differentials that inevitably shape each and every such experience. While I disagree with those who see Kristeva as placing motherhood "outside" or "before" culture, I worry that "culture" in her analysis is presented in terms that render it "universal" when it is necessarily marked—historically, geographically, and socially.

I am curious to see Kristeva respond to these concerns in light of the need, addressed here, to attend to motherhood in all of its complexity. Does she believe that her own accounts of abjection or maternal passion hold true universally? Or does each maternal context require its own conceptual vocabulary? She has shed important light on the particular challenges that arise from mothering a child with disabilities in an ableist context—speaking from her own experience in powerful ways.[73] Would these reflections on birthing and raising a child with special needs belong only to that banal, domestic heaviness of cares and needs, or do they inform her discussion of "the negative and its variants" in meaningful ways? In other words, when we speak about the "experience" of motherhood—particularly aiming to challenge the false dichotomy of idealization and erasure—are the "basic cares and needs" not necessarily formative of "the negative and its variants," such that abjection, sublimation, passion, as well as revolt are bound to be *situated* and therefore always already bound up with structural racism, ableism, heterosexism, colonialism, and so on? Are these merely "banal" conditions that should be ignored as we elaborate on the experience of motherhood through "the negative and its variants"? Or does our rendering them as "banal" ultimately serve to reproduce, yet again, the harmful logic of idealization and erasure?

FANNY SÖDERBÄCK

DEPAUL UNIVERSITY
MARCH 2019

NOTES

1. Julia Kristeva, "Motherhood Today," paper presented at Gypsy V Colloquium (October 2005), http://kristeva.fr/motherhood.html. Accessed on January 12, 2019.

2. Nancy Tuana, *The Less Noble Sex: Scientific, Religious, and Philosophical Conceptions of Woman's Nature* (Bloomington: Indiana University Press, 1993), 111.

3. Simone de Beauvoir, *The Second Sex*, trans. Constance Borde and Sheila Malovany-Chevallier (New York: Knopf, 2010).

4. See, for example, Sarah LaChance Adams, *Mad Mothers, Bad Mothers, and What a "Good" Mother Would Do: The Ethics of Ambivalence* (New York: Columbia University Press, 2014); Alison Stone, "Beauvoir and the Ambiguities of Motherhood," in Laura Hengehold and Nancy Bauer, eds., *A Companion to Simone de Beauvoir* (Hoboken: Wiley-Blackwell, 2017), 123. In a 1982 interview, Beauvoir herself clarifies that "motherhood in itself is not something negative or something inhuman"; it is, rather, motherhood as a patriarchal reality, "enslaved motherhood," that is a problem. Simone de Beauvoir, Margaret A. Simons, and Jane Marie Todd, "Two Interviews with Simone de Beauvoir," *Hypatia: A Journal of Feminist Philosophy* 3, no. 3 (1989): 18.

5. Christine Battersby, *The Phenomenal Woman: Feminist Metaphysics and the Patterns of Identity* (New York: Routledge, 1998), 16.

6. See Beauvoir, *The Second Sex*, 25.

7. See, for example, the special issue on motherhood and sexuality edited by Anne Ferguson, *Hypatia: A Journal of Feminist Philosophy* 1, no. 2 (1986); the special issue on French Feminism edited by Nancy Fraser and Sandra Bartky, *Hypatia: A Journal of Feminist Philosophy* 3, no. 3 (1989); more recently, the special issue on birth edited by Fanny Söderbäck, *philoSOPHIA: A Journal of Continental Feminism* 4, no. 1 (2014).

8. Adrienne Rich, *Of Woman Born: Motherhood as Experience and Institution* (New York: Norton, 1976), 13.

9. Julia Kristeva, *Tales of Love*, trans. Leon S. Roudiez (New York: Columbia University Press, 1987), 357; *The Sense and Non-sense of Revolt: The Powers and Limits of Psychoanalysis Volume 1*, trans. Jeanine Herman (New York: Columbia University Press, 2000), 21, 45.

10. Miglena Nikolchina, *Matricide in Language: Writing Theory in Kristeva and Woolf* (New York: Other, 2002), 5.

11. Sara Beardsworth, *Julia Kristeva: Psychoanalysis and Modernity* (Albany: SUNY Press, 2004), 261.

12. Julia Kristeva, *Revolution in Poetic Language*, trans. Margaret Waller (New York: Columbia University Press, 1984).

13. Julia Kristeva, "From One Identity to Another," in *Desire in Language: A Semiotic Approach to Literature and Art*, trans. Thomas Gora, Alice Jardine, and Leon S. Roudiez (New York: Columbia University Press, 1980), 136.

14. Julia Kristeva, *Powers of Horror: An Essay on Abjection*, trans. Leon S. Roudiez (New York: Columbia University Press, 1982).

15. Ewa Ziarek, "At the Limits of Discourse: Heterogeneity, Alterity, and the Maternal Body in Kristeva's Thought," *Hypatia: A Journal of Feminist Philosophy* 7, no. 2 (1992): 92–93.

16. Tina Chanter, "Kristeva's Politics of Change: Tracking Essentialism with the Help of a Sex/Gender Map," in Kelly Oliver, ed., *Ethics, Politics, and Difference in Julia Kristeva's Writing* (New York: Routledge, 1993), 183.

17. Jacqueline Rose, "Julia Kristeva—Take Two," in Oliver, *Ethics, Politics, and Difference in Julia Kristeva's Writing*, 53.

18. Judith Butler, *Gender Trouble: Feminism and the Subversion of Identity* (New York: Routledge, 1999), 103.

19. Julia Kristeva, "The Meaning of Parity," in John Lechte and Mary Zournazi, eds., *The Kristeva Critical Reader*, trans. John Lechte (Edinburgh: Edinburgh University Press, 2003), 207.

20. Kristeva, "Motherhood Today."

21. "Julia Kristeva: À quoi servent les intellectuels?" Interview by Jean-Paul Enthoven, *Le Nouvel Observateur* (1977), 106.

22. Julia Kristeva, "'*unes femmes': The Woman Effect*," interview by Elaine Boucquey, in Ross Mitchell Guberman, ed., *Julia Kristeva: Interviews* (New York: Columbia University Press, 1996), 108.

23. Kristeva, "Motherhood Today."

24. Ibid. (my emphasis). Furthermore: "I am emphasizing the structural experience of motherhood: I am not fundamentally 'pro-birth.'" Julia Kristeva, "The Passion According to Motherhood," in *Hatred and Forgiveness*, trans. Jeanine Herman (New York: Columbia University Press, 2010), 87.

25. See Fanny Söderbäck, "Motherhood According to Kristeva: On Time and Matter in Plato and Kristeva," *philoSOPHIA: A Journal of Continental Feminism* 1, no. 1 (2011): 65–87.

26. Rose, "Julia Kristeva—Take Two," 49. Julia Kristeva, "Il n'y a pas de maitre à langage," *Nouvelle revue de psychanalyse: Regards sur la psychanalyse en France* 20 (1979): 130–31 (my emphasis).

27. Kristeva, *Revolution in Poetic Language*, 24.

28. Chanter, "Kristeva's Politics of Change," 184.

29. Kelly Oliver, *Family Values: Subjects Between Nature and Culture* (New York: Routledge, 1997), 56.

30. Ibid., 54.

31. Julia Kristeva, *Black Sun: Depression and Melancholia*, trans. Leon S. Roudiez (New York: Columbia University Press, 1989), 27–28.

32. Alison Stone, "Against Matricide: Rethinking Subjectivity and the Maternal Body," *Hypatia: A Journal of Feminist Philosophy* 27, no. 1 (2012): 118.

33. Imogen Tyler, "Against Abjection," *Feminist Theory* 10, no. 1 (2009): 77–98.

34. Stone, "Against Matricide," 62.

35. Kristeva, *Powers of Horror*, 3.

36. Julia Kristeva, "Stabat Mater," in *Tales of Love*, 234.

37. Julia Kristeva, *This Incredible Need to Believe*, trans. Beverley Bie Brahic (New York: Columbia University Press, 2009), 46–47.

38. Kristeva, "Stabat Mater," 235, 253, 240–41.

39. Ibid., 243, 247, 250.

40. Ibid., 254, 258–59.

41. Ibid., 259.

42. Ibid., 263.

43. Julia Kristeva, "Motherhood According to Giovanni Bellini," in *Desire in Language*, 237.

44. Ibid., 237.

45. Iris Marion Young, "Pregnant Embodiment: Subjectivity and Alienation," in *On Female Body Experience: "Throwing Like a Girl" and Other Essays* (Oxford: Oxford University Press, 2005), 46.

46. Kelly Oliver, "Motherhood, Sexuality, and Pregnant Embodiment: Twenty-Five Years of Gestation," *Hypatia: A Journal of Feminist Philosophy* 25, no. 4 (2010): 772–73.

47. Kristeva, *Powers of Horror*, 1.

48. Ibid., 2.

49. Ibid., 3.

50. Julia Kristeva, *Intimate Revolt: The Powers and Limits of Psychoanalysis Volume 2*, trans. Jeanine Herman (New York: Columbia University Press, 2002), 176.

51. Kristeva, *Powers of Horror*, 4.

52. Ibid., 5.

53. Ibid., 10 (my emphasis).

54. Ibid., 5.

55. Julia Kristeva, *The Severed Head: Capital Visions*, trans. Jody Gladding (New York: Columbia University Press, 2012), 17.

56. Kristeva, *Black Sun*, 9.

57. Kristeva, *The Severed Head*, 73, 82.

58. Julia Kristeva, "Thinking About Liberty in Dark Times," in *Hatred and Forgiveness*, 4. The dedication in *The Severed Head* simply reads: "To my mother." Kristeva speaks of her mother again in her autobiography, where she describes her as combining a propensity for math with artistic talent. See Julia Kristeva, "Intellectual Autobiography," in this volume, 11–12.

59. Kristeva, *The Severed Head*, 5.

60. Kristeva, "Motherhood Today."

61. Kristeva, "The Passion According to Motherhood," 83, 84, 86.

62. Kristeva, "Motherhood Today."

63. Ibid.

64. Kristeva, "The Passion According to Motherhood," 82.

65. Ibid., 94.

66. Kelly Oliver, "Julia Kristeva's Maternal Passions," *Journal of French and Francophone Philosophy* 18, no. 1 (2008–2010): 4.

67. Kristeva, "Motherhood Today."

68. Ibid.

69. Kristeva, *This Incredible Need to Believe*, 47.

70. Kristeva, *Intimate Revolt*, 176.

71. Ibid.

72. For example, black women in the US are three to four times more likely to die from pregnancy or childbirth-related causes than white women are. The imbalance has persisted for decades and the gap is widening in some places, like New York City.

73. See, for example, the interchange between Kristeva and Vanier in *Leur regard perce nos ombres* (Paris: Fayard, 2011), where Kristeva time and again returns to her experience of mothering her son David, who was born with disabilities.

REPLY

TO ROSEMARY BALSAM, RACHEL BOUÉ-WIDAWSKY, AND FANNY SÖDERBÄCK

Rosemary Balsam, Rachel Boué-Widawsky, and Fanny Söderbäck propose interpretations of my work on the maternal that are both sensitive and perspicacious. They return to my *semiological* work (the "semiotic" in the child's learning of language and its resurgence in "poetic language") and consider my *psychoanalytical clinic* on *maternal reliance* ("life's state of emergency," biology and meaning, abjection and subjectivation, the maternal tongue and the new beginning of time). Situating the maternal (motherhood) in the movement of my thought, these authors insist on three aspects that I would like to point out because they eliminate any possibility of essentialism, which certain feminist critics suspect me of.

First, at the crossroads of biology and meaning, the maternal as I understand it participates in the indispensable *reworking of the metaphysical dichotomies* of body/soul and flesh/mind. Its Archimedes lever is the birth of the *infans*, an event in the transgenerational intersubjectivity of speaking beings. Although one cannot dissimulate the physical dimensions of pregnancy, childbirth, and breast-feeding, the *mother* differs from the *genitrix*, for the *maternal* integrates the alterity of the new arrival from the start by relinking the *semiotic* and the *symbolic*. There is no *semiotic* without *symbolic*; the *semiotic* is not pre- but translinguistic. Moreover, the phallic encounter of the girl with the "father of individual prehistory" solicits an "imaginary father" who possesses the characteristics of both parents: thus the feminine constructs itself as a bisexuality (more accentuated in the woman than in the man, according to Freud). My clinical theorization confirms it, amplifying it, in all the facets of maternity.

Second, maternal reliance eludes all idealization. It is a process marked by *negativity* (I use the Freudian terminology, echoing Hegel): *abjection, sublimatory cycle*, and *subjectivation* in which the speaking subject is constituted by violence, expulsion, separation, conflict, an explosive mixture of the "life drive" with the "death drive."

Third, the notion of "reliance" has significance as *experience* in the sense of *Erlebnis* (upsurge, intensity, before becoming knowledge adaptive to the other and to the real—*Erfahrung*) only if the effort to conceptualize is accompanied

Translated from French by Armine Kotin Mortimer.

by a word where fantasy and the imaginary succeed in sublimating the trials of this process by transposing it into the uneven, re-volted, disruptive language of poetry or fiction. That is the vocation of literature and, in a different way, of *interpretation* in the psychoanalytic context, which aims for maximum proximity with the singularity of each analysand's unconscious, and hence is related to *poiesis*.

How do the three authors in this reply achieve this interpretation?

I. Rosemary Balsam

As Rosemary Balsam emphasizes, *reliance* is a "vital concept" that introduces and fosters "an infant's unfolding into the world of meaning and meaningful communication." Balsam insists on the "provocative" connotation of this notion, which convokes the *chora*, a nurturing space anterior to the One and the father (in Plato); "the flesh" (according to Merleau-Ponty); and the permeability between *soma* and *psyche* (Lou Andreas-Salomé), to carefully distinguish the "tectonic plates of primary and secondary repression" through which, and by "exquisite contrasts," "the sexual libido of the lover and a seduced child's response" achieve the *tenderness* that "'sprouts' [*fait tendre*] its libidinal force."

Reliance is also violent for the "female human" who, in the impulse, "risks her very life" "on the barricades of soma and psyche and of life and death drive forces." The *death drive* is not foreign to the experience of motherhood, as Sabina Spielrein's premonitory oeuvre demonstrates. Likewise, Balsam emphasizes the importance of the psychoanalytic concept of *investment* (cathexis), which I elaborate through the different figures and logics of the mother-child relationship: of abjection in the dyad, or at the dawn of pre-oedipal thirdness, or in the new forms of technologically assisted—or refused—motherhood.

This author then addresses the problematic of the *representation* of the maternal in androcentric culture. Balsam takes up my question: Is man capable of desanctifying maternal eroticism? To answer, she does not fail to remind us of the maternal "image" in the Jewish, Christian, and Chinese traditions, as well as in Greek mythology and Renaissance art, and even in the apocalypse (Céline's) and in depressed irony (Beckett's) in the face of modernity. While I affirm that secularized society lacks a coherent discourse on motherhood—and Balsam agrees with this observation—I am nonetheless attentive and indebted to modern female researchers, painters, and novelists who bring out the polyphonic *herethics* of the maternal that "underlies, suffuses, and adumbrates the paternal law encoded in ethics" (Balsam). It is also important to recall the various works of British sociologists inspired by Klein, who propose a "eudemonistic ethics" based on "care" (the Kleinian ego needs to make reparation in order to be happy), the better to dress the wounds of the globalization we are currently experiencing.[1] Not to forget the effervescence of women writers who placed motherhood at the center of their fictions: Colette, an atypical mother, with her *Lettres à sa fille (1916–1953)* (Letters to her daughter), "The Secret Woman" (1924), and *La Chambre éclairée* (The illuminated room) (1922); Anaïs Nin and her *Diary*; Marie Darrieussecq, *Undercurrents* (1999) and *The Baby* (2002); Nancy Huston, *The Mark of the Angel* (1998); as well as Marguerite Duras, *The Sea Wall* (1950), *No More* (1995), and *The Malady of Death* (1982); the famous Christine Angot, *Léonore toujours* (Always Léonore) (1994). And my own works: *The Samurai* (1990), *Possessions* (1996), and *Murder in Byzantium* (2004).

I am particularly grateful to Rosemary Balsam for having given us to discover Margarete Hilferding, who fought to have the bodily experience of maternity recognized by the skeptical Vienna Psychoanalytic Society in 1911. Her oeuvre, though less centered on the immanence of language in this maternal "urgency of life," is "acutely prescient" for mine, she claims. I also thank Balsam for having recalled and hailed the "contemporary resistance" to the repression of *maternal eroticism* among American analysts including Marie Langer, Dianne Elise, Hans Loewald, and others.

II. Rachel Boué-Widawsky

Rachel Boué-Widawsky rightly points out that maternity is not a "subtheme" in my view, but, rather, participates in an "ethical concern" that brings out "a biopsychical thinking modality" and aims to preserve "a place for the singularity of the subject." From the moment of the desire for a child, and all during pregnancy and breast-feeding, the *semiotic meaning* of maternal passion supports *signification* and engages the mother as a speaking subject. It is therefore transversal to the communal code: "semi-corporeal and psychical affects that underpin and challenge the operations of the psychical apparatus." I would specify that the irreconcilable logics of reliance are elaborated "*through* the symbolic," not "*beyond* the symbolic"—the symbolic that they shore up, support, reinforce, back up, or undermine, reject, destroy, displace, and in the best of cases, transform.

The examples that Boué-Widawsky borrows from painting make this *transversality* appear clearly: in the Giovanni Bellini masterpiece where the Madonna of the Byzantine icons is literally transfigured "by the play of the colors" that transmit to the spectator the "ineffable *jouissance*" (of the mother and/or the painter); or in Jackson Pollock's pictorial gesture (from *Birth* to *Gothic* and *Cathedral*), attesting to the "semiotic implications" and the "psychical matricide" in which the male artist engages, appropriating and/or transcending the feminine-maternal. To this I will add the works of women painters: Artemisia Gentileschi, Georgia O'Keeffe, and Louise Bourgeois, who resolve this polemic differently.

The "vignettes" by which Boué-Widawsky revisits with me the history of painting not only contribute to deepening the analysis of Western art confronted with *representation*, namely Renaissance, *impressionist*, or *cubist figuration*, or modern and postmodern dissemination.[2] Indeed, in psychoanalytic terms, my interpretations proceed from a recasting of Freudian theory—which distinguishes the primary processes (displacement and condensation, metonymy and metaphor) from the secondary processes (grammar and logic)—and propose a different approach to what Boué-Widawsky calls "the unresolved question of the passage from body to mind."

In this more broadly epistemological perspective, Boué-Widawsky rightly brings up the nodal role of the notion of *abject-abjection* such as I have conceived it. Following Freud's "Negation" (1925), I identify and develop its facilitation (*Bahnung*) in the early links of maternal passion—entanglement of the "libidinal and aggressive drives," "mutual operation of expulsion," "in-between modality of our human condition," all the while posing as "a marker of an ontological lack within it."

On the two pillars of the instinctual and ontological, Boué-Widawsky develops the enduring dynamic of *abjection*, which "revolves around the object impossible to represent." Abjection persists in the feeling of *separation* and of the *absence* of the object, onto which are grafted fantasies of *decapitation* and *matricide* underlying the psychosexual development of the *infans*' autonomy from the maternal container, then from the maternal object. This analysis complements my interpretation of *decapitation* in Western art[3] as well as the castration complex with which Freudian theory illuminates these cruel or ritual actions and their pictorial sublimations.

The reading Boué-Widawsky proposes of my interpretation of the "father of individual prehistory" is remarkable.[4] She specifies that this imaginary and loving father, preceding the oedipal father of prohibition and law, "modifies the narcissistic mother-child dyad"—but not only that. Endowed with the qualities of both parents, the primary identification with the "father-mother" also implies . . . the maternal itself in the phallic assumption: "the infant's first phallic fantasy . . . [is] the result of the mother's intercession." More than ambivalences, these "*paradoxes*" and "persistent tensions" (taking up Fanny Söderbäck's terms) in maternal reliance reveal here what is specific in my approach to sexual difference: "not an erasure of the phallocentric psychoanalytic theory, criticized by feminist ideology; it is an addition" (Boué-Widawksy). As a result of these particularities, maternal reliance thus preserves sexual difference, deploys psychic bisexuality (more accentuated in the woman than in the man) in what I call the "transformative feminine,"[5] and "redesigns culture from a feminine foundation" (Boué-Widawsky).

III. Fanny Söderbäck

Fanny Söderbäck's study introduces a new critical tonality into my conception and practice of reliance. Inspired by contemporary psychoanalytic theory, but much more so by philosophy, feminism, theory of literature, and her own engagement as a woman and mother, Söderbäck's essay succeeds in extracting from my approach to motherhood an impact I'll call political that "vitalizes—indeed revolutionizes—an otherwise monotonous social fabric." Söderbäck details this impact by demonstrating that my theorization is "never merely about birth—it is always also a matter of rebirth or renewal, and it provides hope for creativity and change." She succeeds in convincing *me*—and I hope that the critics of my supposed "essentialism" will let themselves be convinced as well—that since *Revolution in Poetic Language* (1974) and "Stabat Mater" (1977), I have always refused "the false dichotomy between an all-out rejection of motherhood and the perpetuation of idealized conceptions of it." But Söderbäck the philosopher remains vigilant: this mother with her child, "crossroads beings," "liminal, paradox," which I present as an alternative to the Christian tradition, even to "Western Culture as a whole," is she not too beholden to this same tradition "wherein woman is either hole or whole"?

Söderbäck attentively examines the various "stations" of my maternal experience in order to justify the "aliveness" that stems from it, in her view. The *chora*: "affective realm of bodily proximity," "without primacy" or "place as origin," justifying Ziarek's conclusion according to which "the task of rethinking the maternal body [is] inseparable [in Kristeva] from the rethinking of language."[6] The *semiotic* and the *symbolic* are in no way oppositional, exclusive structures but are always "*interdependent, coexisting, intertwined*." Maternal *desire* is a desire to have, but also *not to* have: "desire *not* to have a child."

"The birth of a subject" like "the very possibility of *imagination*" (Söderbäck) strikes me as one of the most pertinent interpretations of this author, who minutely traces the biopsychical movement of pre-objectal *abjection*. After the latter comes *melancholy* consecutive to the loss of the object, then the psychicization of the *violence* of the drive and of *lack* by *représentance*. The high point being the "impossible mourning for the maternal object" in the *imaginary*, a lining inseparable from thought. Also evoking my "attempt at painting a more complex picture of the maternal continent" by the *triangulation* mother-father-child, which is organized "primarily by *maternal* desire," Söderbäck underscores "the fine line between pleasure and pain in a maternal *jouissance*." And she prolongs this denaturing of maternal passion by pointing to its "reflexivity," which poses "the otherness of the other and the self" and leads to the "dispassion" emphasized by Kelly Oliver: "it is not primarily passion that is uniquely human but rather dispassion or the sublimation of passion, which is essential to maternal passion as successful mothering" (Oliver quoted by Söderbäck).[7]

These pages make it clear that the notions with which I approach "maternal passion" and "reliance" do not ignore but, quite the contrary, support the "domestic heaviness" and the "material conditions" of speaking beings in their daily lives.

For Söderbäck, my "own accounts" are based on clinical experience and its theoretical elaboration, both Freudian and post-Freudian, whose pertinence, although it is debated—and because it is debated—continually innovates and refines its models, attentive to the discontents of our globalized civilization. Theorizations proceed through generalizations, for the most part; as for me, I try to singularize them, persuaded, like Duns Scotus (1266–1308), that the truth of human experience is conjugated in the singular: it resides in the *haecceitas* ("thisness") of each man, each woman. I therefore include clinical vignettes in my research. Necessarily subjective (and starting from the psychoanalytic postulate of the transference-countertransference as the foundation of the analytic process), I felt compelled to write novels for both ethical and subjective reasons: to open and to share the inner space of the analyst that I am and that mobilizes in order to hear, differently, each analysand—each woman, each mother. The "amphibious" text titled "Stabat Mater" is another example: the prose poetry intercuts the theoretical essay devoted to the history of the myth and to the present state of the maternal.

I can hear, in Söderbäck's epistemological anxiety, the concern to take into account the cultural diversity in which subjectivation and the relation it induces are elaborated. We are doing this at the Maison des Adolescents (see my reply to Marie Rose Moro). The multiple steps and facets of the "conceptualization" of motherhood are not "applied" there to be "confirmed" or "refuted." They inhabit and address the men and women who read me, where they can be modulated, innovated, refused, or replaced. The clinic is a living organism, a structure "open" to alterity and the environment: transition and weave of Eros and Thanatos. In other words, I am suggesting that the clinic is one of the possible recreations of the sublimations . . . of maternal reliance!

I refer you to my vignette on Claire, "Mother Courage" of a young girl in a situation of disability.[8] Did I support her with "my own account"? Yes, of course—not only, but not without it. Having analyzed the violence of attachment and expulsion, in my own experience of motherhood, I learned that human life, inseparable from psychic life, is a permanent tension for which adjustments are assumed. The biological variabilities and the familial, social, historical, and political situations are recomposed differently, with the same psychosexual valences but endowed with variable intensities and fragilities. *We are differently universal.*

Returning to *abjection*: the destructiveness of the maternal *hold* is common, in a paroxystic manner in cases of *serious depression* and *maternal madness* (from criminal freezing of fetuses to infanticide) or in a more insidious manner, when it is subsumed under "good intentions" that push *tenderness* itself, necessarily vulnerable and wounded, to explosive acts. This ill-being has multiple causes, social and political, even transgenerational. The psychoanalytic accompaniment of the analysand cannot, of course, ignore them, but through contextualized and individualized interpretation it succeeds in awakening the creative potentialities of the analysand. Moreover, it offers the best, if not the only, resistance to current transhumanism.

Söderbäck's question concerning the social context gives me an opportunity to mention the new ordeals of medically assisted maternity, with the joys, frustrations, failures, and compensations inherent in this experience. Moreover, these ordeals engage the maternal of the man, whether analysand or analyst. Here, briefly, is the example of a female patient facing sterility whose male analyst ran into trouble. An analyst I am supervising confides in me that he has difficulties with Jeanne's cure. After several failures to become a mother by medically assisted procreation (MAP) and surrogate motherhood, his patient has managed to make it through these trials thanks to the psychoanalytic process. But in the end, Jeanne overcathects the analysis—only to make it fail.

She frequently misses the sessions but pays for them meticulously, proclaims that "no child, it's not the end of the world" and that her life from now on depends on two projects: "succeed in her analysis," and "charge ahead in her profession." Jeanne, a freelancer, has just "miraculously landed" a "super job" writing portraits of stars.

For more than two years, my colleague is submerged in the inexhaustible and uninterruptable output of his patient, who is consumed with her frantic compulsion to *do* so as not to *be*, to wipe herself out by *doing*, he says. Throughout her sessions, Jeanne recites the events of her encounters with the stars, the interviews, the steps in the montage of texts and images. "Impossible to bring her back to herself," the young analyst concludes, and in terms of the countertransference he feels alone and "stupid" and adds that he is incapable of "*entering* into the flow" to "carve out the *factual* account from the *imaginary* fabrications" of Jeanne's speech. I hear his desire to "penetrate" feminine desire, hypostatized according to the outdated binary scheme; I also hear the fear of his own feminine (which Jeanne reflects back to him: bereaved and sterile). This aggressive projection prevents him from hearing and supporting the *entanglement* of the "factual" and the "imaginary"—but that is precisely one of those scar-like microsigns that betray the *amplitude* of the feminine, its *oscillation* from the semiotic to the symbolic, under the "performative" armor of the impenetrable patient.

Hallucinated by the void, unrelenting in its bid to survive in the "win-win" (the supreme value that commands the hyperconnected spectacle), the feminine, *broken* in the same way the *life of the soul*[9] is—more than ever—in the empire of images, inhabits our families and our screens. It is watching us. It is down to the analyst, man or woman, to find it and recreate it in their listening. The feminine withdraws, testing and seizing the living with its greater intensity, with or without procreation, with or without sterility.

J.K.

NOTES

1. See Julia Kristeva, *Melanie Klein*, trans. Ross Guberman (New York: Columbia University Press, 2001) (volume 2 of the "female genius" trilogy), 231f; *Le Génie féminin*, t. 2, *Melanie Klein* (Paris: Fayard, 2000), 372f.

2. See my reply to Jean-François Rabain regarding the feminine-maternal of the man's imaginary in the works of Aragon.

3. Julia Kristeva, *The Severed Head: Capital Visions*, trans. Jody Gladding (New York: Columbia University Press, 2011); *Visions capitales* (Paris: Réunion des Musées Nationaux, 1998).

4. See Julia Kristeva, *Tales of Love*, trans. Leon S. Roudiez (New York: Columbia University Press, 1987), 26–56; *Histoires d'amour* (Paris: Denoël, 1983), 32–58. Sigmund Freud, *The Ego and the Id,* in *The Standard Edition of the Complete Psychological Works of Sigmund Freud*, vol. XIX, trans. James Strachey (London: Hogarth, 1961).

5. Julia Kristeva, "Prélude à une éthique du féminin," 51st Congress of the International Psychoanalytical Association, Queen Elizabeth II Center, London, July 24, 2019.

6. Ewa Ziarek, "At the Limits of Discourse: Heterogeneity, Alterity, and the Maternal Body in Kristeva's Thought," *Hypatia: A Journal of Feminist Philosophy* 7, no. 2 (1992): 92–93.

7. Kelly Oliver, "Julia Kristeva's Maternal Passions," *Journal of French and Francophone Philosophy* 18, no. 1 (2008–2010): 4.

8. Julia Kristeva, "Liberty, Equality, Fraternity and . . . Vulnerability," in *Hatred and Forgiveness*, trans. Jeanine Herman (New York: Columbia University Press, 2010), 32; *La Haine et le pardon* (Paris: Fayard, 2005), 99.

9. See Françoise Coblence, "La Vie d'âme: Psyché est corporelle, n'en sait rien," *Revue française de psychanalyse* 74, no. 5 (2010): 1285–356.

29

Charles Gardou

THE "INTIMATE FACE" OF A COMMON THOUGHT AND ACTION

At the borders of life and death, I sometimes have the feeling I'm witnessing the non-sense of Being, revealing the absurdity of connections and beings.

—Julia Kristeva, *Black Sun: Depression and Melancholia*

Three of her works, *Black Sun*, *Strangers to Ourselves*, and *New Maladies of the Soul*, initially brought me to Julia Kristeva.[1] In the course of other readings, I felt closer and closer to a reflection she likes to situate at the crossing of borders: "*I travel myself*," she says.[2] With admiration for the mobility of her oeuvre as a linguist, a semiologist, a philosopher, a psychoanalyst, and a writer, I was naturally delighted to meet this woman who rubbed shoulders with Michel Foucault, Roland Barthes, Jacques Derrida, and Umberto Eco—some of the authors who determined my intellectual course.

Over and above our philosophical and ideological proximities, our first contact revealed human affinities. While Kristeva at that time had not yet written on the subject of disability, our experience as parents made us both sensitive to this form of human frailty. That is why together we decided to create a National Council on Disability to call for and support a "revolution of the gaze" at persons experiencing a disability on a day-to-day basis. This vast project led us to organize a summit in 2005 at the Maison de l'UNESCO in Paris, which brought together almost two thousand participants coming from all regions of France.

With this political and ethical action, we have turned disability and the vulnerability attached to it into a social challenge to be addressed collectively.

Translated from French by Armine Kotin Mortimer.

Vulnerability: this is the concept that unites us, because it is at the heart of our respective work. Because with the force of evidence it specifies the human condition and characterizes our species.

Neither the appearance of power nor our vague ambitions of grandeur succeed in wiping out this constitutive precariousness. Humanity, which would like to be strong and eternal, makes the sound of porcelain breaking. By nature sickly, ephemeral, wounded, weak, deserving of our tears, Man (*l'Homme*) appears as an edifice always threatened with damage, degradation, and ruin. As fragile as his works, said Voltaire. Nothing is definitively assured. Everything turns out to be provisional, contingent, impermanent. Chaotic, imperfect, partial. Never any plenitude. Never to take anything for granted is the wisdom of Siddhartha Gautama, the Buddha: "'Here shall I live during the rains, here in winter and summer'—thus thinks the fool. He does not realize the danger (that death might intervene)."[3] Everything is probable except death; he cannot avoid the face-to-face with death, even when spared from infirmity beforehand. He may die not because he's vulnerable—he's vulnerable because he must die. Such is the most intimate reality, and the strangest. Such is the universal destiny from which none escape.

Yet suspicions continue to weigh on those for whom the mischance of birth or accident amplifies vulnerability, those who are called "disabled." According to a highly regulated social mechanism, which leaves hardly any room for atypical elements, we imagine them stricken with inferiority. As if they are of another nature. As if they constitute a different genus. As if they come from a separate universe, a different humanity. Now they're held in a sort of no man's land, deprived of their rights, cut off from the community like leaves detached from the nourishing plant. Disintegrated. They have to learn to bear their too particular burden in silence, to be content with abandoned expectations, with relations consented to out of compassion but immediately defunct, to be satisfied with an obstructed future. They are made to believe that the "healthy" enjoy not only a privilege, but also, what's more, a merit, a superiority they legitimately glory in.

As if their burden were not enough, we exile them together, by making tacit alliances. Blinded, deafened by the din of their devices, we see only their infirmity, we maintain their disgrace, we aggravate their misfortune. We make them feel that disability also diminishes those who approach them. An irrepressible need to injure in order to bear our own injuries. To inform the other she is unworthy of being, underestimate her to overestimate ourselves. Yet are there other reasons to live besides being recognized, regarded, loved? Are there other motives besides counting for someone else, deserving their interest? An absence of relations is equivalent to an absence of being.

Who are the persons in a situation of disability? What have they done to merit these deprivations, if not that they are marked by fragility more than others? Do we need another Valladolid controversy before we will admit that they embody one of the multiple visages of a single humanity and share its vulnerability, which animates every life to its very depths? To recognize that their disability is only reflecting our universal condition by amplifying it, like a loupe? To concede that it is less an enigma to be deciphered than a challenge to be met? To agree, finally, that our fear of disabilities, proportional to our pathological fear of ourselves, leads us to keep the world of the one apart from that of the others?

Fragility, although unequally distributed, is a common destiny to be confronted in solidarity. An existence is the expression of it, always variable. There are as many vulnerable human beings as there are human beings in the world. No one is immortal or omnipotent. In diverse forms and degrees, each person presents delays, disequilibriums, anomalies, and physical, intellectual, psychological, affective, relational, and economic defects. Once we admit that, a disability ceases to be an inferiority to become a general possibility of existence. It is the metaphor of deficiencies against which we struggle with unequal weapons. Propelling our human condition at times to extremes, it opens onto the universal. What characterizes the problematics of the disability, which we speak of specifically, is its signification of universality. Because it bears within it the entire form of the human condition, it leaves nothing behind—impossible to approach and to comprehend the existential reality that the disability constitutes without inscribing it in the universal cultural chain, without placing it back into the ordinary. It constitutes one of the faces of Man, molded of clay and of marble like the Biblical colossus that inhabits the dream of King Nebuchadnezzar: "This image's head was made of fine gold, his breast and his arms of silver, his belly and his thighs of brass, his legs of iron, his feet part of iron and part of clay." The dream ends like this: "Thou sawest till that a stone was cut out without hands, which smote the image upon his feet that were of iron and clay, and brake them to pieces. Then was the iron, the clay, the brass, the silver and the gold, broken to pieces."[4]

We resemble this statue, at the mercy of the slightest projectile that blind chance may hurl at us. We are embarked on a humanity where at any instant fragility may recur and strike some of us. It lies in wait in the shadows, behind the door of each life.

Butting up against this irreducible part, Man wears himself out fleeing or denying it. In this combat against his own substance, he uses the bulk of his strength. What he is mocks what he may dream of being. A pathetic and at the same time burlesque disconnection. A mere straw at the mercy of a gust of wind, he labors to show his strength—his physical strength, his intellectual strength, his constraining strength, his striking strength. His assurance and his inflexibility. He feeds on relations of strength, trials of strength, acts of strength, shows of strength. He dreams of sovereignty, readily showing himself to be strong with the weak and weak with the strong.

Because he does not succeed in embracing his destiny, he takes refuge in an unreal image of himself. He attempts to protect himself from the vertigo that grabs hold of him when he sees himself as he is. Imperfect, he dreams of perfection. Mortal, he lives in the desperate illusion of immortality. Finite, he aspires to infinity. He hopes for survival beyond the death he tries to evade—or at least wishes to be sudden, unconscious, without decline. Death, the supreme failure, the absolute evil, indelible sign of weakness, haunts him surreptitiously.

He is nevertheless condemned to die, sometimes even in a senseless manner.[5] What a lot of masks, what anesthetics as we attempt to escape from this shadow! What a lot of disguises to avoid the fistfight with this reality! Evasion. Flight. At a distance, to escape from himself. A Danaidean effort. Ensconced in his personage, prisoner of his illusions, he pictures himself dominating his destiny, thinking he can keep himself from dying as long as he doesn't let certain people be born and lets others die.

The absence of any serious tribulations gives him a strange confidence in his resources and his strength. As long as he is protected from important deficiencies of body or mind, he generally settles into a sort of self-assurance. When the distantly threatening danger touches him directly and enters inside his skin, he comprehends, he "grasps for himself" the situation merely glimpsed until then. Because knowing is not the equivalent of feeling, of experiencing in one's very fibers, of bearing within the most intimate self. One can know what disability is while not knowing about the life of those it affects. One can know what they "have" while not knowing what they "are." This ignorance generates individual and collective phantasms, source of all rejections.

Painful reminders of the tragedy of life and of the threats that hover over us, mirrors that reflect our own precariousness are not easy to look at. The one who would like to think of himself as safe and protected is uneasy letting his eyes rest on the other's wounds and, through them, on his own weakness. A piercing fear seizes him when he faces the reality of the words *mental deficiency*, *autism*, *cerebral motor infirmity*, *quadriplegia*, and the myriad of physical or moral tortures that accompany them. Mixing into his fear, which now has a name and a face, is a confused feeling of culpability and responsibility.

The motor that drives human existence resides right there, in this struggle against vulnerability. The hope to succeed in rising above it multiplies our strength tenfold. Some of our strength appears almost without our knowing it, while other forces are discovered and developed only in adversity. Vital forces then take advantage of the slightest gaps to pierce the shell that imprisons them. "What doesn't kill me makes me stronger," Nietzsche liked to say, as he himself lived between illness and health until slipping into another world where he spent eleven years of his life in a twilight state.[6] The human being, thanks to his capital of unsuspected resources and energies, is capable of confronting unexpected situations, perilous circumstances. Out of instinct and free will, he improvises, he reconstructs; he supplements, he adapts. The feeling of a disturbance in the organs can constitute a powerful stimulus: "In developing the psychic phenomena of presentiment and prediction, as well as their functional components like memory, intuition, sensitivity, interest—in short, all the psychic components, an overcompensation leads to the constitution of a super-resistance in the sick organism, to the transformation of inferiority into superiority, to the transformation of the defect into general competence, into talent."[7] On occasion a hindrance may open access to a superior level of functioning, and becomes the motor for psychic development. We notice that when one sense is lacking, another develops; that when one faculty is hindered, another emerges. Disability embodies this blossoming of supplemental faculties and the confrontation with its own reserves. Generally envisioned only as disintegration, paralysis, dependence, sterilization of the possibilities of activity and realization, it can compensate with fruitful aspects. An apparent drying-up can engender a flowering, often enhanced because it was prevented. From the restive and enfeebled body and mind, as they cease to be servants to become stumbling blocks, energies may be born that reach the extreme limits of the human. In contrast, intact faculties and a capable body and mind guarantee neither a thirst for living and self-realization, nor the capacity and the desire for enterprising activity.

While we reject naïve sublimation and idealism, we should recognize that certain lives, reconstructed with effort, out of rubble, represent models of determination and success. Willpower triumphant over manifestations of weakness had to overcome everything. An apparently broken life paradoxically offers reasons to struggle, to resist, to want to reverse the course of things. Perhaps when confronted with the adversity of disabilities or illness, with the inevitability of death, we learn quite simply how to live.

The long history of humankind, which has always illustrated that alloy of clay and marble, also took shape with the capacity for overcoming, with the mobilization of the processes of resilience, with the talents of people presenting deficiencies that are sometimes extreme. Examples abound from all times and cultures: scientists, politicians, inventors, philosophers, painters, sculptors, musicians, writers, poets. Without making a hierarchy of our choice, we have traveled in the footsteps of Robert Schumann, Frida Kahlo, Jean-Jacques Rousseau, Blaise Pascal, Fyodor Dostoyevsky, Joë Bousquet, Helen Keller, and Demosthenes.[8] With the certain knowledge that lived experience gives, each of them knew the place of vulnerability and where the needed resources to overcome it were. Their creative flame was born in adversity, and their work, conquering the weaknesses, grew to rise to the ranks of the finest. Without going into the phantasmatics of supermen, or providing facile interpretations of the relationship between their disability and the extent of what they accomplished, it would be difficult to ignore the cathartic process with them. Their life and their work formed a single adventure.

We see the same ambition in them all: marshal the effort to conquer their limitations, which make them prey to the constant risk of reversal. Intransigent with themselves, they bring together the "materials" they need to reconstruct themselves, which they struggle to tear from the ravages of the disability. If to be resigned means to renounce an ideal, they are never resigned. Even at the lowest point of dispossession they rally to continue creating. They "work at" their feelings of devastation. They rebel. They refuse to submit to the burdens and hindrances of life. But since they are only human, their uneven and fleeting strength can experience frequent pullback movements. At times one finds them as weak as if the blood has deserted their veins, at times so strong that no obstacle would seem capable of stopping their vital and creative force. At times the letting-go and giving up to weakness, at times resistance and the triumph of strength, and at times the one and the other, intertwined.

Robert Schumann, worn out by the burden of his psychical troubles, draws from his anxiety illness the most beautiful musical compositions. Frida Kahlo, victim of poliomyelitis, then crushed in an accident, transforms the degeneration of her body, which devours her femininity, into splendid paintings of blood and colors. Blaise Pascal, stalked in his emotional solitude by illness and prowling death, becomes an inventor, a scholar, and a prodigy of thinking. Jean-Jacques Rousseau, wandering, struggling against his manifold illnesses, leaves behind an immense body of work in the field of ideas and the expression of feelings. Fyodor Dostoyevsky, cowed by destiny, always guilty, constantly suffering from attacks of epilepsy and his pulmonary emphysema, becomes one of the greatest dramatic geniuses. Joë Bousquet, bedridden in his room of exile, walks through his poetry and gives birth to magical words. Helen Keller, deaf, blind, and dumb, walled in by silence, refuses to capitulate in the face of cruel nature, becomes an accomplished lecturer. Demosthenes, struggling mightily against his stammer, opposes the force of his destiny with his own strength to climb to the summit of the art of oratory.

Like so many others, these women and men subject their disabilities to a reversal, an overturning, to open our eyes to the clarity in the midst of the fog that clouds them. They compose, paint, write, invent, to express themselves to be sure, but above all to seize hold of their life and recover its grandeur. They create to restore unity to their dissociated being and accede to another order of existence. Given the façade of their notoriety, they may, it is true, appear like exceptions, people privileged in their capacity for action and creation. Nevertheless, their situation lends a singular breadth to their individual experience and raises it to the level of symbol.

Their unique itineraries illuminate a paradoxical reality: a disability imposes multiple limitations and a loss of power, unspeakable distress, feelings of inferiority. It constrains one to abandon aspirations, it turns to dust desires and projects, it limits certain abilities. However, it does not systematically compromise all the possibilities of a being. Certain possibilities may even increase. Perhaps the disability keeps hidden a fruitful obscurity; as Nietzsche has Zarathustra say: “night is also a sun.”[9] The deviation from equilibrium, from the norm, from the average kills and creates at the same time. It provokes one to exist, to transcend one’s weakness. Even in cases—and we must not forget them—where a deficiency leaves someone entirely bloodless and deprives them of all liberty, the most infinitesimal forces, the most unnoticed, want to live. No human being, as long as he is alive, renounces everything. The wound is not a total negation.

In the end, their life-work uncovers the nature of Man. It shines a harsh light on the gap between his nudity and the heights to which he aspires—the fracture between the consciousness of a constitutive sickliness and the illusory obsession of power and mastery. The vulnerability of Robert, Frida, Blaise, Jean-Jacques, Fyodor, Joë, Helen, and Demosthenes spreads to all, as if to instill the force to overcome it.

A blunt reality can be grasped: every life stripped of its gloss inexorably refers to fragility. Not an accidental fragility, not on the surface, but a fragility of identity, which defines us and anchors humanity in our flesh. That is where the secret of the human being lies and where the source of a real solidarity between humans finds its place, more or less protected from the troubles of life.

As I reach my conclusion, I think about Julia Kristeva's final words in her *Lettre au président de la République sur les citoyens en situation de handicap* (Letter to the President of the Republic about citizens in a situation of disability): "Let everyone slip into their own dreams, the most bizarre or the most repetitive. . . . Let them then return to the surface and listen to those around them who speak, walk, hear, look, act differently, bizarrely, madly, inspiring fear. . . . New worlds will then open to their listening, sorrowful or enchanted, neither normal nor disabled, flowerings of surprises, worlds becoming polyphonies, different resonances, and yet compatible, worlds at last restored to their plurality. Do not tell me I am dreaming or that this is poetry."[10]

Such is the "intimate face" of a common thought and action that it is my good fortune to share with Julia Kristeva.

CHARLES GARDOU

L'UNIVERSITÉ LUMIÈRE LYON 2
APRIL 2018

NOTES

1. Julia Kristeva, *Black Sun: Depression and Melancholia*, trans. Leon S. Roudiez (New York: Columbia University Press, 1989); *Strangers to Ourselves*, trans. Leon S. Roudiez (New York: Columbia University Press, 1991); *New Maladies of the Soul*, trans. Ross Guberman (New York: Columbia University Press, 1995).

2. See Julia Kristeva's Intellectual Autobiography in this volume; *Je me voyage: Mémoires* (Paris: Fayard, 2016).

3. [https://www.accesstoinsight.org/tipitaka/kn/dhp/dhp.20.budd.html. Accessed January 23, 2019—Trans.]

4. Daniel 2:31–35.

5. Socrates's serenity in the face of death brought us the *Phaedo*, Plato's dialogue relating his last moments, during which his master speaks of the immortality of the soul and presents philosophy as a teaching about death: "those who practice philosophy in the right way are in training for dying." Plato, *Phaedo*, in John Cooper, ed., *Complete Works* (Indianapolis: Hackett, 1997), 59 (67e).

6. Friedrich Nietzsche, "Arrows and Epigrams," *Twilight of the Idols*, in Aaron Ridley and Judith Norman, eds., *The Antichrist, Ecce Homo, Twilight of the Idols, and Other Writings*, trans. Judith Norman, Cambridge Texts in the History of Philosophy (Cambridge: Cambridge University Press, 2005), §8, 157.

7. See Koviljka Barisnikov and Geneviève Petitpierre, *Défectologie et déficience mentale: Vygotsky* (*Defectology and mental deficiency: Vygotsky*) (Neuchâtel: Delachaux et Niestlé, 1994), 88. Lev Vygotsky here refers to the German pedagogue Otto Rüle.

8. See Charles Gardou, *Pascal, Frida Kahlo et les autres . . . Ou quand la vulnérabilité devient force* (Toulouse: Érès, 2014).

9. Friedrich Nietzsche, "The Sleepwalker's Song," in *Thus Spoke Zarathustra*, ed. Adrian del Caro and Robert Pippin, trans. Adrian del Caro, Cambridge Texts in the History of Philosophy (Cambridge: Cambridge University Press, 2006), 263.

10. Julia Kristeva, *Lettre au président de la République sur les citoyens en situation de handicap, à l'usage de ceux qui le sont et de ceux qui ne le sont pas* (Paris: Fayard, 2003), 74–75 (translated by Armine Kotin Mortimer).

30

Eivind Engebretsen

EVIDENCE-BASED MEDICINE AND THE IRREDUCIBLE SINGULARITY OF BEING—KRISTEVA'S CONTRIBUTION TO THE MEDICAL HUMANITIES

This essay explores the implications of Kristeva's thinking for the medical humanities and, more precisely, for the discussion about evidence in medical decision making. Medicine and health care play an increasingly significant role in Kristeva's work, and her critique of biomedical reductionism is central to her thought on vulnerability. However, until recently this "medical turn" in her writing has attracted relatively little attention. In this essay, I first give an outline of Kristeva's main criticism of medical discourse and how this criticism is anchored in her work on vulnerability and subjectivity. Second, drawing on examples from my own research on the concept of "evidence" in health care, I demonstrate how Kristeva's theories warrant a radical questioning of fundamental epistemological presuppositions inherent in medical discourse. Finally, I argue how Kristeva's theory about the irreducible singularity of being can provide an alternative approach to evidence-based medical decision making.

The focus of Kristeva's discussion of medical practices is mainly disability and the psychoanalytic treatment of mental disorders, although she also discusses the complexity of treating somatic conditions such as cancer. Her writing on these topics is the main source of this essay.[1] I argue that her thought on disability is in principle translatable for diagnoses and treatment in relation to any defining processes in medical care. On a general level, I demonstrate that her thinking represents a radical break with three important *topoi* or lines of argument within the current debate about evidence-based medicine.

First, Kristeva's theory implies a fundamental critique of what I call *neo-positivist* arguments in favor of the evidence-based medicine movement: the view that clinical experience is subjective and cannot be trusted, and treatment and diagnoses should be built on research results from population-based effect studies (preferably randomized controlled trials) that are summarized and made available through systematic reviews and clinical guideline recommendations. Second, Kristeva's theories challenge another line of argument increasingly emphasized in the debate about medical decision-making—referred to here as a *neoliberal* approach: the view that medical decisions should, as far as possible, be based on the patient's (user's) individual choice of treatment, and that health professionals should not merely provide cure or care but contribute to the patient's empowerment, health literacy, and self-management so that the patient can make informed and rational decisions about his or her own health and treatment. Third, Kristeva's position differs from what I call a *holistic* line of argument used by many of the skeptics of the neopositivist approach to evidence-based medicine: the view that biomedical knowledge is reductionist, focusing on organs rather than persons, and clinical decisions should be based on the patient's total illness experience rather than knowledge about specific pathologies or diseases.

I. Vulnerability

The essential vulnerability of living runs as a conducting line through Kristeva's manifold authorship. For her, vulnerability is integral to "the identity of the human race and, singularly, of the speaking subject."[2] This attention to vulnerability is already implicit in her theories about abjection and the speaking subject emerging through a vulnerable relation to its supposedly exterior others.[3] However, it reaches a new level of explicitness in *Hatred and Forgiveness*, where she declares vulnerability as the fourth term of the French Enlightenment slogan: "liberty, equality, fraternity and . . . vulnerability."[4] In recent years, Kristeva's work has increasingly emphasized the implications of the concept of vulnerability for caregiving practices, including medical care. This turn is clearly visible in her work on disability.[5] As an alternative to a practice of care, "locking the disabled subject into the position of a 'care object,'" Kristeva wants to rethink care as an encounter between singular beings or what she audaciously refers to as love: "Via my love for the singular other, I [the caregiver] bring it to its specific, singular development—and to mine, also specific and singular."[6] By rethinking care in terms of love, Kristeva emphasizes vulnerability as an emotional and epistemological resource in practical caregiving.

The implications of Kristeva's theories of vulnerability for caregiving have been discussed recently by several scholars. In a collection of various case studies, Rudge and Holmes have explored the boundary work of caregivers at the intersection between "filthy" and "clean," and how they manage to cope with this inbetweenness.[7] Stacey has investigated experiences of abjection in cancer treatment as the "horror of not knowing the boundaries of distinguishing 'me' from 'not me.'"[8] The same line of reasoning is reflected in Shildrick's analyses of "monstrous bodies," "those bodies that in their gross failure to approximate to corporeal norms are radically excluded."[9] Based on Kristeva's theories, Shildrick has introduced an "ethics of openness" that acknowledges both vulnerability of the person receiving and the vulnerability of the one giving care. Kristeva's significance for the field of medical humanities more generally has been discussed by Hall and, most recently, in a position paper by Kristeva, Moro, Ødemark, and Engebretsen that introduces a "prolegomenon to a more radical program for the medical humanities, which calls the conventional distinctions between the humanities and the natural sciences into question, acknowledges the pathological and healing powers of culture, and sees the body as a complex biocultural fact."[10] A key element in this project is the rethinking of the concept of *evidence* in health care. The article questions whether the current concept of evidence in medicine is able to capture the vulnerability of the singular subject. I develop this criticism further in this essay.

II. Medical Discourse and the Logic of Privation

Kristeva frames the question of healing as a question of restoring the identity of the subject. She considers illness not only as "the deterioration of an organ but also as the *symptom of the organism* as a whole and, beyond that, a *symptom of the subject*."[11] Thus, healing cannot be obtained by considering patients as "objects under treatment," but only by treating them as "*emerging subjects*."[12] However, this claim should not be confused with a holistic approach to the individual's illness experiences, nor with a neoliberal emphasis on the individual patient's rational choice. In order to understand the profundity of Kristeva's claim and how it relates to medical discourse, it is necessary to explore Kristeva's conception of the subject.

Kristeva rejects any concept of identity "linked to the substantialist, causal and atomist thought of Aristotelian Greece."[13] For her, the subject is defined neither through its possession of a quality—its *whatness* or essence as a human being (Aristotle)—nor through its consciousness or rationality as a transcendental ego (Husserl). The subject is constantly developing through the use of language; it is a "speaking subject" (*un parlêtre*). Drawing particularly on Freudian and Lacanian psychoanalysis, she has developed the concept of the subject in process (*le sujet en procès*), which is constantly under pressure from two linguistic processes that contribute to its formation: the symbolic and the semiotic.[14] The semiotic is the bodily, affectual, and prerepresentational aspect of language associated with rhythms and intonations but also contradictions or ruptures with conventional meanings. The symbolic, on the other hand, is the conventional and communicative function of language expressed through established categories and structures. Thus, the subject in process is split between bodily drives and expressions on the one hand, and, on the other, the symbolic order that arranges these into a coherent and unified structure or voice. This means that the subject to be restored through the healing process is not a unity—in terms of a bodily organism or a coherent illness experience or a rational choice—but an ongoing process or struggle. Human identity cannot be reduced to a category, a symbolic order. Every unity or category is only temporary and is constantly challenged *and* constituted by a continuous process not just of creativity but also of "destructivity, vulnerability, and imbalance."[15] Kristeva therefore rejects the concept of health as a "*definitive state*" and prefers the concept of healing designating a process "*with twists and turns in time*."[16]

In this context, she evokes the ancient myth of the goddess Cura, who mediates between life/light/spirit and death/darkness/matter; Cura is associated with creativity and care, but also with anxiety.[17] According to the myth, Cura created man out of a piece of clay and turned to Jupiter—the God of light—to give life to her creation. As Jupiter grants life to Cura's creature he wants it to bear his name. This results in a quarrel that Tellus (the God of earth) also enters, having provided the material for the creation. Saturn settles the quarrel by offering Jupiter man's soul and Tellus his body, while Cura will possess him as long as he is alive. With Jupiter's "circumscribed act" and Saturn's introduction of the name (*the symbolic*), man is separated from the process of continuous creation and healing that Cura represents. With Jupiter's intrusion, man is cut off from healing as "*a process with twists and turns in time*." Human health is translated into "a *definitive state*"; a condition of full being and illness is consequently conceived as a privation of this state.[18] Hence, Kristeva uses the myth as an allegory of an ontological split inherent in medical discourse: between health as a condition or definitive state outside time, brought about through the introduction of the symbolic (the divine act of naming) and healing as a durative, temporal process with twists and turns in time, in which creativity and destruction are intermingled.[19] The problem with traditional understandings of health and healing is that they are solely based on a symbolic order. Health and illness are understood in dichotomous terms as having/not having. The identity to be restored is considered a full being, a condition of completeness.

Kristeva also traces this understanding of health, disability, and illness back to the Aristotelian concept of *steresis*, a lack of completeness or a privation of having.[20] Blindness is conceived of, for instance, as an incompleteness, a lack of being in one who by nature sees. This ontology of privation found an echo in Christian humanism and inspired the Christian idea of charity as an act of completing or giving to those who have not: "various 'steriles,' defective or poor, share powerlessness in suffering and passion, and in our com-passion with the 'lack of being,' we establish 'good living,' the ethics that will be Christian humanism."[21] However, as Kristeva argues, the idea of illness or disability as a lack of being is visible not only in charity work but also "on the level of knowledge," "through the study of the 'empty' (pathologies)" through which "the sciences appropriate the complexities of the 'full' (normal functioning)."[22] She develops this argument as follows: "Being is perhaps no longer the Divine, but we have replaced it with Biology, when we understand the disabled person as 'lacking' certain biological aptitudes."[23] However, this idea of recreating full being is not only present in the dominant biomedical paradigm. Alternative and more holistic approaches to medicine that emphasize personal illness experiences and the "ethics of care" tend to build on a similar logic by reproducing the idea of charity as an act of completing or giving to those who have not.[24] Moreover, Kristeva emphasizes how neoliberal individualism has contributed to the development of a society that values only rationality, perfection, and productivity at the expense of alterity and vulnerability. Hence, the pathology and charity models of illness and disability combine with neoliberalism, bringing Western culture to an "impasse," which reduces people with illness or disabilities "to either invalids or workers."[25]

Kristeva's theory of the subject and identity fundamentally challenges these different but related notions of fullness and completeness of being as a norm. Medicine tries to restore something that has never existed, she maintains, because human beings are not conditions but constantly emerging subjects. Construed around the master dichotomy of having/not having, medical discourse has developed into a machinery of dividing practices through which those who are different are reduced to what she refers to as "categories of difference."[26] Their lack, their state of nonbeing, makes them different in the same way. Medical discourse "*blends* all disabled people *together* without taking into consideration the *specificity* of their sufferings and exclusions."[27] In this way, medical discourse represents an exclusion of the deepest kind, an exclusion of the "incommensurable singularity of each person."[28] In the following three sections we shall see how this logic is expressed in the three dominant arguments about evidence-based medicine that I briefly outlined above: neopositivism, neoliberal individualism, and the holistic approach.

III. Neopositivist Arguments for Evidence-based Medicine

The current construal of evidence-based medicine is grounded in epidemiological and statistical reasoning. The ultimate method for creating evidence is the so-called randomized controlled trial in which patients are randomly assigned to a treatment group that is exposed to an intervention and a control group that is given a comparable intervention or a placebo. The aim is to determine whether the intervention is more effective on a group of patients than other interventions or lack of intervention. How the intervention works, when, why, and on which patient is considered less relevant. The logic is that the larger the group the less such questions matter. Ideally, results from randomized controlled trials should be aggregated through the use of statistical meta-analysis and subsequently form the basis for clinical guideline recommendations to clinicians with probability estimates for each outcome.

Central to the evidence-based medicine framework is also the evidence hierarchy (often illustrated as a pyramid), with the highest-quality evidence at the top and the lowest-quality evidence at the bottom.[29] On the highest level are randomized controlled trials and the meta-analyses of them, and on the bottom, case studies and anecdotal reports. This hierarchy corresponds to a movement from individual to group, from singularity to generality, from a variety of differences to categorized difference. The evidence comes into being and grows in strength through a process of purification by which singular differences are gradually ruled out and the only ontologies that remain when the top of the pyramid is attained are unified categories of difference (treatment or not treatment, diagnoses or no diagnoses, etc.). In this sense, evidence-based medicine is the name of a process in which individuals are gradually replaced by conditions, and singular difference by generalized "lacks of being."

Hence, medical evidence is by definition concerned with groups or what Kristeva refers to as "categories of difference." For a claim to obtain status as evidence, it must be proven true for a large group of individuals (a population). Moreover, it is assumed that only characteristics that are common to the whole population are relevant in the diagnosis and treatment of the individual patient. The individual is defined through its possession of general qualities. What is true for a group is automatically considered to be true for the individual patient. Evidence is therefore supposed to be moved *from* group *to* individual (from bench to bedside) through so-called *knowledge translation* that designates the "exchange, synthesis and ethically-sound application" of evidence.[30] The process of knowledge-translation hinges upon the mobilization of a chain of textual genres—starting with randomized controlled trials, followed by meta-analyses or systematic reviews (summarizing the scientific state of the art), and culminating in clinical guidelines, which prescribe manners of intervention in concrete cases. It is assumed that all these textual genres transmit the evidence in increasingly condensed and vernacular forms without threatening its universal and general character.[31]

It is also fundamental to the medical concept of evidence that it is "external" to the specific clinical decision.[32] Sackett, one of the pioneers of evidence-based medicine, described it as an "approach that integrates the best *external* evidence with individual clinical expertise and patients' choice."[33] Evidence is external to the individual case, external to the concrete act of relating and to the singular being. This evidence that is external and general is contrasted with clinical expertise and patients' choices, which are *internal* to the individual case. These two latter terms, although included in the evidence-based medicine framework, are excluded from the concept of evidence as such. Evidence-based decisions are based on three sources: external evidence, clinical expertise, and patients' choices. Clinical expertise and patients' choices should be integrated with evidence but do not count *as* evidence. Evidence is by definition blind to the singular case.

IV. Neoliberal Individualism

Of course, this does not mean that modern medicine is not concerned with the individual. On the contrary, there are many neoliberal knowledge practices within modern medicine that aim to put the individual at the center of care. However, these initiatives understand the individual in a way that tends to repeat the same mechanisms of exclusion.

"Patient involvement" is a key word within modern medical discourse. Take, for instance, what the World Health Organization states in the policy brief, *Where are the Patients in Decision-making about their Own Care?* "Patients can play an important role in understanding the causes of illness, protecting their health and taking appropriate action, choosing appropriate treatments for acute episodes of ill health, and managing chronic illness. These roles must be recognized and supported."[34] This overall policy is subsequently specified in three strategies: health literacy, shared decision making, and self-management/empowerment. On the first, "health literacy involves the ability to read, understand, evaluate and use health information to make appropriate decisions about health and health care."[35] On the one hand, the patient is here placed at the center of decisions about health and health care. On the other hand, the concept of health literacy presupposes that in order for the patient's voice to be valuable and form the basis for "appropriate decisions," it must be framed by the right knowledge. The individual voice is not valuable as such but only as a carrier of general knowledge or evidence. Only the literate voice, a voice that is docile and shaped by the medical discourse itself, is included in decision making. The concept of literacy privileges a voice that is framed by rationality, logic, syntax, signification, and representation, or what Kristeva calls the symbolic aspect of discourse. At the same time, following her distinction between the symbolic and the semiotic, the call for literacy excludes aspects of meaning that are more than mere significations: they exclude the semiotic, which she has called the "rhythmical and melodic inflections" of the suffering and singular speaking body, as well as the irrationality and resistance that mark out the illiterate.[36] The call for literacy excludes his or her voice in this sense as "inappropriate" for decisions.

The second strategy—shared decision making—is described and defended in the following way:

> One of the most common sources of patient dissatisfaction is not feeling properly informed about (and involved in) their treatment. Shared decision making, where patients are involved as active partners with the clinician in treatment decisions, can be recommended as an effective way to tackle this problem. . . . Evidence-based patient decision aids facilitate the process of making informed decisions about disease management and treatment.[37]

The aim of so-called "shared decision making" is to involve the patients as active partners. At the same time, "shared decisions" are framed by "evidence-based patient decision aids." Typically, the patient is presented a choice between treatment X and Y based on probabilistic estimates of outcome deduced from current research evidence. Hence, the interaction between the patient and the caregiver is reduced to the weighing of evidence. The encounter is purely contractual, governed by a "logic of choice" and a symbolic language through which the doctor provides "objective" information about the patient's condition. What is excluded from the encounter is the contact aspect, the individual act of relating, the singularity of the patient's suffering, and the semiotic elements of his or her speech.

The third strategy mentioned in the policy is to look for "ways to empower people to manage their own health and health care, by providing them with effective self-management support."[38] The concept of empowerment implies that good health starts with the singular choice of each individual. The individual is encouraged to be singular in a specific way. Singularity is translated into autonomy. It should not be lived or expressed but "managed." The individual that is included in medical decisions is an individual that is shaped by the medical discourse itself: a rational actor that manages his or her own health. Other forms of singularity are categorized as lacks that should be rectified through empowerment and "self-management support."

We see from the WHO policy brief that patient involvement is framed by general norms of standardized knowledge, rational choice, and autonomous conduct. The individual that is included is an individual that fits with a neoliberal notion of a human being: the literate and rational self-managing individual. The singular is created in the image of the general.

V. The Holistic Approach to Patient Experiences

Knowledge practices that explicitly aim to put the patient's experiences at the center of attention are haunted by a similar mechanism of exclusion. Increased focus has lately been put on health and symptoms assessment tools in order to capture and address not only mechanical aspects of the disease but also the patient's own symptom distress and illness experience. This practice encompasses a whole range of measurement instruments—such as quality of life scales, pain and symptom assessment scales, and so on—bound together by a common aim of capturing the subjective experiences of the patients as accurately as possible to prepare for individualized clinical decisions.

Together with colleagues, I have criticized some of the hidden assumptions inherent in symptom assessment instruments that use the Edmonton Symptom Assessment Scale (ESAS) developed for the symptom assessment of cancer patients.[39] The instrument consists of a survey assessing experiences of pain, tiredness, nausea, depression, anxiety, drowsiness, appetite, well-being, and shortness of breath on a scale from 0 to 10.[40] The scale intends to "bring out the patient's subjective experience of their situation."[41] At the same time, it represents a more standardized and supposedly more objective way of measuring the patients' subjective experiences; it aims "to assess the current symptom profile as accurately as possible."[42] Hence, the design of the form is based on the idea that patients speak more accurately through a standardized voice and predefined categories. As a consequence, only the experiences that fit within the form are considered relevant, and the form only allows for subjective differences that can be graded on a standardized scale. It is only capable of capturing differences in degrees of pain. Other differences (such as the type or quality of pain) are not captured.

Ideally, the assessment should be performed by the patient herself or himself. If the patient cannot participate in his or her own symptom assessment, the caregiver should assess the symptoms "as objectively as possible." A list of "objective indicators" is provided in order to ensure objective assessment.[43]

Pain—grimacing, guarding against painful maneuvers
Tiredness—increased amount of time spent resting
Drowsiness—decreased level of alertness
Nausea—retching or vomiting
Appetite—quantity of food intake
Shortness of breath—increased respiratory rate or effort that appears to be causing distress to the patient
Depression—tearfulness, flat affect, withdrawal from social interactions, irritability, decreased concentration and/or memory, disturbed sleep pattern
Anxiety—agitation, flushing, restlessness, sweating, increased heart rate (intermittent), shortness of breath
Wellbeing—how the patient appears overall

The whole concept of "objective indicators" presupposes that symptom experiences have an objective existence independent of the patient's own singular interpretations and descriptions of his or her pain. The form assumes that there is a pure pain experience that exists prior to language and that can be adequately measured given the right assessment tool. Nausea, tiredness, anxiety, and depression are considered to be distinct and clearly distinguishable conditions that exist independently of the categories we use to describe them.

We see that while the patient's subjective experience is said to be the gold standard for treatment, this subjective realm is assumed to have an objective and generalized existence beyond the individual's description of his or her singular sufferings. The truth about the individual's sufferings (the objective indicators) is considered to be outside of the individual. His or her singular mode of expression (the semiotic) is ruled out as noise and falls outside the definition of knowledge. Knowledge is strictly linked to a symbolic order, to clear and universal categories. Moreover, the assessment instrument is based on the idea of a unified individual that is present to itself and has direct access to his or her own pure experiences. It is assumed that, given an accurate assessment instrument, the individual can account for his or her own experiences without any interference of interpretation and language. The experiencing subject is considered a full being, a condition of completeness. The assessment instrument is unable to account for the singular struggles and the "twists and turns in time" that characterize the emerging subject.

Paradoxically, a similar notion of a unified subject can also be found in qualitative research within the medical area. The explicit aim of this type of research is to capture the singularity of the experience of each individual as well as relational aspects of health-care delivery. Patton has stated that qualitative research "is an effort to understand situations in their uniqueness as part of a particular context and the interactions there."[44] Juritzen and colleagues have explored the principles of knowledge underpinning a selection of qualitative studies of rehabilitation interventions, and assessed whether the articles adhere to their own stated principles.[45] The point of departure for the study was a literature review of research about young adults with disabilities, based on a systematic search in medical databases. Of the 104 publications included in the study based on a preliminary screening, only twelve were found to apply qualitative methods. While the quantitative papers were subject to a traditional medical research synthesis, with the aim of describing the state-of-the-art within the field, the team decided to approach the qualitative studies in a different way. The review might be characterized as metaepistemological because it analyzed the knowledge production of the research articles rather than the knowledge content as in a metasynthesis (a summary of the state-of-the-art). This implies an emphasis on how the articles create knowledge rather than what they create knowledge about, and on the principles of knowledge creation in the articles.

The study found that the selected articles demonstrated a tension between the qualitative principles stated in the articles and the way the results were presented. In their objectives and theoretical framing, they emphasized the individual patients' unique experiences, for instance, through the use of a phenomenological approach. However, in the presentation of the results, the intention of exploring singular experiences was partly undermined by an emphasis on categories of experiences and their frequency. This occurs in a number of different ways—for example, through classification into overarching themes, through models/forms, and different methods of quantifying experiences and statements. In the process of describing the singular experiences of the participants, what is unique and different is translated into "categories of difference" that pretend to have universal legitimacy. The studies only highlight the general characteristics of the experiences, not their unique expressions. Hence, the articles undermine the essence of being different: the inability to fit into established categories. Moreover, the young adults' experiences are reduced to general lacks, categories of nonbeing. The singularity of the individual sick or disabled person is almost never considered as a resource in the selected studies; his or her experiences are classified as signs of a lack, a problem to be solved or cared for.

VI. An Epistemology of the Singular Being

To summarize our discussion thus far, medical discourse is governed by a logic of *steresis* that classifies singular difference into categories of difference characterized by a general lack. The only differences that are visible to the medical eye are groups of differences, categories of nonbeing (disabilities, pathologies) that can be clearly distinguished from corresponding categories of full being (i.e. normality). This divide—this categorization—is what Kristeva refers to as the deepest form of exclusion. As I have tried to show, medical discourse is structured around these dividing practices, a machinery of categorization. This is the epistemological face of the exclusion she is referring to. Medical knowledge is by definition knowledge about categories, about groups of difference. The individual we encounter through medical discourse is a generalized individual, an *example* of a general condition, a universal rationality, or a collective experience. Only individuals that fit within established categories and the symbolic order are visible to the medical gaze. Medical discourse seems to be missing an epistemology and a vocabulary for capturing and making sense of singular difference.

This is where Kristeva provides an alternative epistemology, an epistemology of the irreducible singularity of being. In reference to Duns Scotus, she claims that "truth is not in the universal idea, nor in opaque matter, but in a 'this one,' this man here, this woman there.'"[46] With the term *haecceity* (thisness), Scotus refers to characteristics that make a thing into a particular thing, as opposed to *quiddity* (whatness), which refers to the universal qualities of a thing or the aspects by which it falls under a category.[47] *Haecceity* is the idea "that among the properties of an object, there is the property of being that very object."[48] Drawing on Scotus, Kristeva insists on the "positive singularity" of every speaking being. The speaking being is positively given—as a "this one here." At the same time, the subject is never determinate or unified in terms of a "whatness," but, rather, governed by a "*productive dissolution*" or openness.[49] According to Kristeva, the subject *is* this openness: "that which in a man or woman remains open to a search for meaning and sharing."[50]

Moreover, as singular subjects in this sense, we are all essentially vulnerable, according to Kristeva. We are all confronted with "the limits of life, with the fear of deficiency and physical or psychic death."[51] She therefore rejects the idea of an essential divide between those who are lacking and those who are not. She insists that the experience of an essential lack, of a nonbeing, is not something that distinguishes those of us in good health from those who are disabled or sick. Rather, it is something that binds us together: "Not necessarily because 'it could happen to anyone,' but because *it* is already in me/us: in our dreams, our anxieties, our romantic and existential crises, in this *lack of being* that invades us when our resistances crumble and our 'interior castle' cracks."[52] In ignoring alterity and singular difference, we limit not only possible ways of living and imagining good life but also our understanding of what kind of social institutions are needed and how to engage in relationships and care for each other.[53] However, by acknowledging the "difference within us" as a trace—a presence of an absent presence—we can create the foundations for "an ethics of respect for the irreconcilable."[54] As Shildrick explains: "in owning ourselves as dis-integrated, we can give up both the urge to reduce others to the selfsame, or to persecute them as absolutely different."[55] Rather than considering patients as "objects under treatment," care and cure must therefore be based on "interaction." A medicine based on interaction would, in Kristeva's terminology, imply a dynamic and ongoing transformation, as opposed to intervening in a static field of unified identities based on general conditions, universal rationality, or collective experiences.[56]

Such an approach implies acknowledging that "evidence itself is fundamentally singular; it is always evidence *for* a particular decision."[57] Nonetheless, universal categories are not of course irrelevant to medical decision making. Knowledge about universal conditions and pathologies are necessary in order to identify the singular case *as* singular (i.e. as distinct from the general category). It is only by knowing how a population generally reacts to an intervention or treatment that it is possible to identify how *this* patient reacts differently or specifically, given his or her particular illness/healing history. General knowledge frames evidence-based decisions made locally, with reference to a particular patient, but should not be mistaken as evidence per se. This application of general evidence is very different, however, from the neopositivist idea of "translating" knowledge *from* the population *to* the individual case. In Kristeva's point of view, evidence is not based on any unity or similarity with general knowledge. Rather, it relates to the general condition in a way similar to the Derridean trace:[58] the "truth" about the singular patient ("thisness") is marked by an absent presence (i.e., a general condition or a "whatness"). The thisness of the patient is defined by the qualities he or she does *not* possess. Hence, evidence is the property of being *different* from general knowledge.

VII. Treatment as a Work of Art

A treatment is ultimately "an idiolect, a work of art," Kristeva claims, and each analytic situation "a specific microcosm."[59] General categories do not provide evidence for specific analyses or decisions. They can only offer an "initial and rudimentary outline."[60] The specific analysis will always push back on the general category, concretize it, and ultimately challenge it.

In *New Maladies of the Soul*, Kristeva uses the case of Florence, a young woman suffering from depression, to discuss the complex effects of pharmacology and, on a different level, the relation between generalized norms and singular effects in the course of psychoanalytic treatment. Kristeva acknowledges that the antidepressant had the intended effect of reducing Florence's crises of anxiety and enabled her to talk about difficult situations in her life and childhood. "It seemed to me, however," she notes, "that a certain distancing resulted from these chemical interventions—which seemed necessary though provisional."[61] Moreover, the effects of the drug reached beyond the simple and generalized "norm" described in clinical trials, guidelines, and textbooks. The drug entered into a *specific* relation with the patient and the therapist:

> The introduction of a third party (medication, psychiatry) tempered Florence's manic elation—for she was not omnipotent and neither was I; a third party and an alternative reality was involved. This also enabled us to tackle her narcissism, on the one hand, and its projection onto the exaggerated idealization with which she adorned me, on the other. Hence, a modified anxiety threshold made it possible to confront the manic-depressive devices that Florence had put into place in order to deal with loss and separation.[62]

At the same time, the drug had an anesthetic effect on the patient's discourse:

> My feeling arose primarily from the fact that while taking imipramine, Florence was able to have dreams pertaining to anxiety states that she had previously been unable to represent—the anxiety of being swallowed up and devoured by her mother, and inversely, the anxiety of swallowing up and devouring her mother. Yet even though Florence was able to have and report these dreams (which already was a substantial psychic development as compared to the depressive silence and "blank death" of the depressed signifier that had once characterized her), she approached her dreams with a sense of distance and a defensive lack of understanding.[63]

Once Florence decided to stop the pharmacological treatment, the therapy could enter a new phase in which these dreams were analyzed and addressed.

For a thorough discussion of the various psychoanalytic aspects of this case, Kristeva's own essay should be consulted.[64] Here, I only want to make an overall epistemological point: even effects of pharmacological interventions (often considered the most "suitable" object for randomized controlled trials and evidence-based medicine) cannot be generalized in the way that effects on population level are mechanically applied to individual cases. Kristeva's account shows that effects (even those considered the most mechanical) are fundamentally singular. Hence the evidence of these effects cannot be determined by research, "external" to the clinical situation, as Sackett claimed. Such research only provides an "initial and rudimentary outline." Evidence can only be determined within the "specific microcosmos" of the treatment. Kristeva shows that even the most "biomedical" instrument is subject to improvisation.

VIII. Towards a Conclusion: Recapitulating the Double Origin of Evidence-based Medicine

How can medicine incorporate an epistemology of positive singularity and a conception of evidence and truth that is not anchored in a "universal idea," a general category of difference, but starts with "'this one,' this man here, this woman there?" Is such a medicine even possible? I believe that it is. Furthermore, I believe that it has roots in evidence-based medicine itself and its excluded other.

One of the founding figures in evidence-based medicine is Archie Cochrane, the British epidemiologist who gave his name to the Cochrane Collaboration. His book *Effectiveness and Efficiency* from 1972 is often considered a prolegomenon to the celebration of randomized controlled trials as the gold standard of medical evidence.[65] However, as I have argued with others, this is at least partly a misreading of Cochrane's text.[66] He draws a distinction in his text between two aspects of medicine: cure and care. Health care, he insists, is supplying "on the one hand therapy, and on the other board lodging and tender, loving, care."[67] He then states that he will mainly focus on the cure aspect, for practical reasons: "I have devoted most of the space to an analysis of effectiveness and efficiency in the 'cure' section, because so much more is known about it."[68] At that stage, more was known about cure. Later proponents of evidence-based medicine have interpreted Cochrane's *practical* delineation as a *scientific* demarcation: cure is emphasized because more *can* (and should) be known about it.[69] Knowledge about cure can be based on groups, categories of difference. Care is considered to be individual oriented and thus falls outside the scope of medical evidence. This was not Cochrane's intention. He did not consider studies about the effectiveness of a cure as the only legitimate form of medical knowledge. On the contrary, he considered cure and care as equally important dimensions of medical knowledge, though knowledge of different kinds. While the first is group oriented, the second is individual and value oriented, based on personal experience and a relationship to the singular patient and his or her sufferings.

The humanist side of Cochrane's medical philosophy is even more explicit in his memoir, *One Man's Medicine*, published posthumously in 1989. He tells the story of how as a young medical officer in a German war camp, he treated a dying Soviet prisoner.

> The Germans dumped a young Soviet prisoner in my ward late one night. The ward was full, so I put him in my room as he was moribund and screaming and I did not want to wake the ward. I examined him. He had obvious gross bilateral cavitation and a severe pleural rub. I thought the latter was the cause of the pain and the screaming. I had no morphia, just aspirin, which had no effect. I felt desperate. I knew very little Russian then and there was no one in the ward who did. I finally instinctively sat down on the bed and took him in my arms, and the screaming stopped almost at once. He died peacefully in my arms a few hours later. It was not the pleurisy that caused the screaming but loneliness. It was a wonderful education about the care of the dying. I was ashamed of my misdiagnosis and kept the story secret.[70]

As Hurwitz has noted, the story illustrates how medical decisions transcend assessment of research evidence and the calculation of decision options and treatment.[71] In the end, it comes down to a meeting between two singular beings. The decisive moment in the medical encounter was when Cochrane took the solider in his arms. As Hurwitz notes, this was the moment when the "evidence that led Cochrane to this switch in explanatory account became apparent"; he realized that "it was not the pleurisy that caused the screaming but loneliness."[72] The evidence was revealed in this moment of proximity between two singular persons who—although lacking a common code for exchanging information—shared their respective vulnerabilities. The evidence revealed to the caregiver is not based on abstract calculation, but, rather, on what Kristeva refers to as love: "it is mortality in progress that touches me in this; I am it, it falls upon me, I accompany it, I love it as it is."[73]

This is the concept of evidence that seems to be lost within modern evidence-based medicine: an evidence of proximity, of sharing—an evidence that *listens*. Such listening is not only about including the patient's choice in decisions or acknowledging his or her illness experiences as important to the choice of treatment (in addition to mechanical signs of disease). Listening simultaneously involves attending to the patient's singular vulnerability *and* to one's own vulnerability as a caregiver in an interactive social encounter with the patient. Hence, it is not only about changing the patient as an "object of repair" but changing the patient *and* the caregiver through the process of the encounter. Viewed in this way, evidence-based decisions are far from objective or generalized, but, rather, imply a deep personal insight.

EIVIND ENGEBRETSEN

UNIVERSITY OF OSLO
OCTOBER 2018

NOTES

1. Julia Kristeva, *Hatred and Forgiveness*, trans. Jeanine Herman (New York: Columbia University Press, 2010); "A Tragedy and a Dream: Disability Revisited," *Irish Theological Quarterly* 78, no. 3 (2013): 219–30; "At the Limits of Living: To Joseph Grigely," *Journal of Visual Culture* 5, no. 2 (2006): 219–25; *Lettre au président de la république sur les citoyens en situation de handicap: à l'usage de ceux qui le sont et de ceux qui ne le sont pas* (Paris: Fayard, 2003).

2. Julia Kristeva, "Liberty, Equality, Fraternity and . . . Vulnerability," in *Hatred and Forgiveness*, 42.

3. Julia Kristeva, *Powers of Horror: An Essay on Abjection*, trans. Leon S. Roudiez (New York: Columbia University Press, 1982); *Revolution in Poetic Language*, trans. Margaret Waller (New York: Columbia University Press, 1984).

4. Kristeva, "Liberty, Equality, Fraternity and . . . Vulnerability," 29.

5. Ibid., 29–47; "A Tragedy and a Dream"; "At the Limits of Living: To Joseph Grigely"; *Lettre au président de la république sur les citoyens en situation de handicap.*

6. Julia Kristeva, "Reconstructing Identity in Times of Existential Crisis," keynote lecture, Ben Gurion University, Beer Sheva, June 12, 2017.

7. Trudy Rudge and Dave Holmes, *Abjectly Boundless: Boundaries, Bodies and Health Work* (London and New York: Routledge, 2016).

8. Jackie Stacey, *Teratologies: A Cultural Study of Cancer* (New York: Routledge, 2013), 78.

9. Margrit Shildrick, *Embodying the Monster: Encounters with the Vulnerable Self* (London: Sage, 2002), 7.

10. Melinda Hall, "Patient Interpretation: Kristeva's Model for the Caregiver," in Sarah Hansen and Rebecca Tuvel, eds., *New Forms of Revolt: Essays on Kristeva's Intimate Politics* (New York: SUNY Press, 2017). Julia Kristeva, Marie Rose Moro, John Ødemark, and Eivind Engebretsen, "The Cultural Crossings of Care: An Appeal to the Medical Humanities," *BMJ Medical Humanities* 44 (2018): 55, doi:10.1136/medhum-2017-011263.

11. Julia Kristeva, "Healing, a Psychical Rebirth," in *Hatred and Forgiveness*, 153.

12. Ibid., 37.

13. Julia Kristeva, "Word, Dialogue and the Novel," in Toril Moi, ed., *The Kristeva Reader*, trans. Alice Fardine, Thomas Gora, and Leon S. Roudiez (New York: Columbia University Press, 1986), 61.

14. Kristeva, *Revolution in Poetic Language.*

15. Kristeva, "Liberty, Equality, Fraternity and . . . Vulnerability," 42.

16. Kristeva, "Healing, a Psychical Rebirth," 154.

17. Ibid.

18. Ibid., 154.
19. Kristeva, Moro, Ødemark, and Engebretsen, "The Cultural Crossings of Care."
20. See Kristeva, "A Tragedy and a Dream." Aristotle, *Physics* Books I–IV, trans. P. H. Wicksteed and F. M. Cornford (Cambridge: Harvard University Press, 1958), I.5, 188a33–b2; I.7, 191a6–14.
21. Kristeva, "A Tragedy and a Dream," 226.
22. Ibid., 227.
23. Ibid.
24. Carol Gilligan, *In a Different Voice* (Cambridge: Harvard University Press, 1982). Virginia Held, *The Ethics of Care* (New York: Oxford University Press, 2006).
25. Kristeva, "At the Limits of Living: To Joseph Grigely," 221.
26. Kristeva, "A Tragedy and a Dream," 224.
27. Kristeva, "Liberty, Equality, Fraternity and . . . Vulnerability," 36.
28. Ibid., 219.
29. A much quoted article on the pyramid is Gordon H. Guyatt, et al., "Users' Guides to the Medical Literature: IX, A Method for Grading Health Care Recommendations," *JAMA* 274, no. 22 (1995): 1800–1804.
30. Ian D. Graham et al., "Lost in Knowledge Translation: Time for a Map?" *Journal of Continuing Education in the Health Professions* 26, no. 1 (2006): 13–24.
31. Eivind Engebretsen, Tony Joakim Sandset, and John Ødemark, "Expanding the Knowledge Translation Metaphor," *Health Research Policy and Systems* 15, no. 1 (2017): 19.
32. Halvor Hanisch, "Kvalitativ metode i møte med økte krav om evidens og effekt i spesialpedagogisk forskning," University of Oslo, January 18, 2016.
33. David Sackett et al., "Evidence Based Medicine: What it is and What it isn't," *BMJ* 312 (1996): 71–72 (my emphasis).
34. Angela Coulter et al., *Where are the Patients in Decision-making about their Own Care?* (Copenhagen: World Health Organization Regional Office for Europe, 2008).
35. Ibid.
36. Julia Kristeva, "Thinking about Liberty in Dark Times," 11.
37. Coulter et al., *Where are the Patients in Decision-making about Their Own Care?*
38. Ibid.
39. Eivind Engebretsen and Kristin Heggen, "Measuring the Pure Patient Experience—Exploring the Theoretical Underpinnings of Edmonton Symptom Assessment Scale (ESAS)," in Leah McClimans, ed., *Measurement in Medicine: Philosophical Essays on Assessment and Evaluation* (London: Rowman & Littlefield, 2017).
40. See Eduardo Bruera et al., "The Edmonton Symptom Assessment System (ESAS): A Simple Method for the Assessment of Palliative Care Patients," *Journal of Palliative Care* 7, no. 2 (1991): 6–9.
41. *Nasjonalt handlingsprogram med retningslinjer for palliasjon i kreftomsorg* (National program for palliation in cancer care), IS 1529, *Nasjonale faglige retningslinjer* (National guidelines) (Oslo: Helsedirektoratet, 2007), 20.
42. Alberta Health Services, *Guidelines for Using the Revised Edmonton Symptom Assessment System (ESAS-r)* (Canada, 2010), 3.
43. See ibid., 2.
44. Michael Q. Patton, "Quality in Qualitative Research: Methodological Principles and Recent Developments," invited address to the Division J of the American Educational Research Association, Chicago, April 1985.
45. Truls I. Juritzen et al., "The One or the Many: Quantified Subjectivity and Aggregated Uniqueness in Qualitative Rehabilitation Research," *Qualitative Health Research* 27, no. 1 (2017): 51–59.
46. Kristeva, "A Tragedy and a Dream," 224.
47. John Duns Scotus, *Treatise on the Common Nature and Individuation* (*Ordinatio* II, Distinction 3, Part 1, Questions 1–6).

48. Alvin Plantinga, "Haecceity," in Kim Jaegwon, Ernest Sosa, and Gary S. Rosenkrantz, eds., *A Companion to Metaphysics* (Hoboken: John Wiley & Sons, 2009), 74.
49. Julia Kristeva, "The Subject in Process," in Patrick ffrench and Roland-François Lack, eds., *The Tel Quel Reader* (New York: Routledge, 1998), 138.
50. Kristeva, "Liberty, Equality, Fraternity and . . . Vulnerability," 32.
51. Ibid., 36.
52. Ibid., 44.
53. Mary Bunch, "Julia Kristeva, Disability, and the Singularity of Vulnerability," *Journal of Literary and Cultural Disability Studies* 11, no. 2 (2017): 138.
54. Julia Kristeva, *Strangers to Ourselves*, trans. Leon S. Roudiez (New York: Columbia University Press, 1991), 182.
55. Shildrick, *Embodying the Monster*, 83.
56. See Bunch, "Julia Kristeva, Disability, and the Singularity of Vulnerability," 137.
57. Kristeva, Moro, Ødemark and Engebretsen, "The Cultural Crossings of Care."
58. See Jacques Derrida, *Of Grammatology*, trans. G. C. Spivak (Baltimore: Johns Hopkins University Press, 1976).
59. Julia Kristeva, "New Maladies of the Soul," in Kelly Oliver, ed., *The Portable Kristeva* (New York: Columbia University Press, 1997), 216.
60. Ibid.
61. Ibid., 218.
62. Ibid.
63. Ibid.
64. Ibid.
65. Archie Cochrane, *Effectiveness and Efficiency: Random Reflections on Health Services* (London: The Nuffield Provincial Hospital Trust, 1972).
66. See Clemet Askheim, Tony Sandset, and Eivind Engebretsen, "Who Cares? The Lost Legacy of Archie Cochrane," *BMJ Medical Humanities* 43 (2017).
67. Cochrane, *Effectiveness and Efficiency*, 2–3.
68. Ibid.
69. See Askheim, Sandset, and Engebretsen, "Who Cares? The Lost Legacy of Archie Cochrane."
70. Archie Cochrane, *One Man's Medicine* (London: British Medical Journal, Memoir Club, 1989), 82.
71. Brian Hurwitz, "What Archie Cochrane Learnt from a Single Case," *The Lancet* 389, 1086 (2017): 594–95.
72. Ibid., 594. Cochrane, *One Man's Medicine*, 82.
73. Kristeva, "Reconstructing Identity in Times of Existential Crisis."

31

Marie Rose Moro

THE POLYGLOT IMAGINARY, A POETICS, AND A CLINIC

This leads us to consider diverse cultures no longer from the point of view of what their particular identity *may be, always more or less fictive, but of what I will call their fecundity: these diverse cultures are so many* resources *deploying adventurous possibles that any human intelligence can understand and exploit, as long as it concentrates on their coherence, with patience.*

—François Jullien, *Le Pont des singes*

I. Introduction

I have experienced the importance of Kristeva's thought in considering a new clinical epistemology that renews the links among language, culture, clinic, and society. I have had the opportunity to do so in several places, the most recent of which is the seminar we are giving in Paris on the "Need to Believe." This seminar allows professionals—psychoanalysts, clinicians, pediatric psychiatrists, and social workers, but also researchers in the linguistic, clinical, and anthropological domains—to experience this thought, which radiates both in the field of ideas (it being known how much, for Kristeva, "to say is to do") and in the humanities or the medical world. In the latter, we have attempted to show it along with a Norwegian team in a recent article published in the *British Medical Journal*, which argues for the importance of Kristeva's ideas in the medical world, particularly subjectivity and the cultural encoding of care.[1]

We will begin with an affinity that Kristeva feels deeply about, the affinity among three figures—the translator, the foreigner, the writer; an affinity among three experiences—translation, foreignness, writing.[2] And we will show the creativity of such a posture.

Translated from French by Armine Kotin Mortimer.

Finally, I will show the importance of Kristeva's work for a better understanding not only of the "new maladies of the soul" but more precisely of the ideals and sufferings of adolescents.[3] The adolescent is inhabited by the "fanatical belief in absolute satisfaction" characterizing "the open structure" of adolescents of which Kristeva speaks in the "The Adolescent Novel" in her book, *New Maladies of the Soul*;[4] those "believing and nihilistic" adolescents who deploy "their syndrome of ideality."[5]

II. How to Be a Whole Child in a World That Does Not Recognize You

Let us begin with Hado, the child who had lost his appetite for words. Hado is an ordinary boy. In fact, he often goes unnoticed in class or in the courtyard at recess. Hado is doing pretty well in school, and his father, "a man of integrity" from Burkina Faso, is very proud of him. That is how the father designates the men of his country of origin, with pride, at our first meeting. Hado speaks French very well and Mossi sufficiently well for his father and mother to be proud of him. Pride is an important value shared by everyone in the family. "He can go to our country and manage all by himself," the mother tells me. "He can replace me in our country when his turn comes," the father tells me. They perceive the child as comfortable with his parentage, with a feeling of permanence and continuity. The transmission of life is "self-evident." Immigration is not an insurmountable rupture for the parents. Hado is the first child born in France. He therefore has to guide his two little brothers in the ways of France, as his father says with calm and elegance. Monsieur tells his son the story of his paternal grandfather who fought as a "Senegalese infantryman" alongside the French. He was a courageous and loyal man, the father recounts. Everything goes well like this through Hado's fourth year of primary school, when he is among the very first in his class.

Then, brutally, in the fifth year of primary school, in the course of the first trimester, Hado begins to complain a lot about his teacher, who doesn't explain things to him, doesn't let him speak, he says, and sometimes argues with him for no reason. He feels unliked, and after complaining many times for a few days, he grows silent and fades into a sad solitude. Hado was dependent on the teacher to invest in learning at school; the subjects are not familiar enough to him, do not interest him sufficiently for him to invest in them as such.[6] He was among the best students because he liked his teachers and his teachers liked him, but with this new instructor who considers him with mistrust, he experiences discrimination and silently withdraws, like a boy who is "invisible" but in difficulty at school. When I meet him and propose a transcultural consultation[7] with him and his parents in the presence of a translator, he says to me: "Yes, I agree, maybe the translator will help me no longer be afraid of words!" For some time, he was feeling threatened particularly by French words, in speaking but even more in writing. It is as if these words had become less desirable because no longer mediated by a teacher who understands him and appreciates him; those words then became violent. Encountering them, unmediated, frightened him. Such mechanisms can exist, minimally, in all the children of immigrants who seek to conquer on their own these territories unknown to them because written in words that one can encounter only directly, brutally. Hado had lost his appetite for French words. It was by emphasizing the translator's Mossi words valorized by us and by his instructor, to whom we explained what Hado was experiencing, that the fear of words attenuated and he recovered his appetite for the words, for all the words, of the languages and tongues that inhabit him.

III. I Inhabit My Languages

As we know, I am my language, it possesses me at least as much as I possess it. But more than this, I am my languages, all those that traverse me. But what languages? And what happens if I have several languages, if my mother's language, my father's, and the one in which I am immersed are not the same? What happens when I pass from one language to the other? Is my narrative identity actualized in the same way in one language and in the other—and what's more, in their unconscious implicitness? What happens when the language transmitted by my parents and the one that is taught me by schooling and by the world in which I live are not the same? And what will happen if I undergo psychoanalysis in the language that is not the one of my earliest affective attachments? Does this external language have the same consistency for me? Are my associations the same in the inside language, the one of my family, and the outside one, the one of the world that welcomes me and supports me?

A thousand and one questions are raised with the transcultural clinic of children of immigrants and their parents, a clinic that sets as an epistemological framework the obligatory but not simultaneous utilization of psychoanalysis, anthropology, and also (on this point) linguistics. However, we are obliged to recognize that these questions, though deeply contemporary, are too rarely asked in the field of psychoanalysis, too often remaining confined to those who are passionate about this diversity and make it their daily business.

Language is a relationship to the world, a categorization of this world, a genealogy as well, since it positions us in the world designated by this language. It is therefore a lot more than a semiotics and a syntax; it is a framework that allows us to situate ourselves and to construct links within this space. We know how important the feeling of the familiar is in these linguistic questions, that it is reassuring to hear one's maternal tongue spoken when one is far away or in exile. Thus language conjugates a system of signs with sensoriality and affects that latch onto words and images specific to this language code. Language is thus embodied in the very being. Starting from this first language, one can either translate into another language while retaining the concepts and the logics of the first or, if one possesses this second language in a full and complete manner, if one "libidinalizes" this second language, if one makes it desirable, then one can develop the possibility of truly speaking in two or more languages, without translating, putting one's entire being into that language and actualizing competencies in that second language that one perhaps did not have in the first. Then one increases one's freedom to be and to speak in a language that can even allow a new creativity to the extent that, for example, it distances us from unresolved transgenerational traumas or conflicts regarding those who have transmitted this mother tongue to us. This second language then becomes the language of accepted separation.

What does Adelia have to say about it?

IV. Adelia and the Naked Voice of Childhood

Adelia is a young woman of Spanish origin living in France to whom I explained my theories about the importance of the mother tongue as an initial structuring imprint that leaves profound traces for our entire life, traces that I consider creative and the bearer of new freedoms and new cultural blendings (*métissages*) through the necessary recognition of this alterity within us—recalling Kristeva's concept of strangers to ourselves.[8] Adelia told me, almost shamefully, that she adored listening to Spanish radio and that the voices on the radio had a calming effect on her, like a lullaby, like a rope that allowed her to raise herself to a summit in relative security. Radio more than television or film—that is, the naked voice, the voice that lets one dream, lets one be carried off by the materiality of the language and the force of the images that emanate from internal landscapes, infantile fragments. This naked voice that she clothed with her own elements had a calming effect on her. This voice reattached her to the world of childhood installed inside her with nostalgia and security, the world that permits creating even if it is in another language. Indeed, Adelia had started to write plays in French, the language she had learned at school. This passage through writing in the second language had made possible her separation from parental aspirations and had allowed her to authorize herself to write, a process that did not belong to the family tradition nor to the expectations of her mother or her father, who dreamed she would become a doctor. The French language allowed her a veritable psychical separation, permitting writing, authorizing her to cohere with "her little internal voice," as she called the positions of her being, unknown until then. This necessity of writing she discovered in her analysis, which she did in French. But at the conclusion of her psychoanalytic trajectory, she also discovered her need to write in Spanish, returning to its infantile sensations, its images untranslatable into French, those scenes she materialized in theatrical writings à la Don Quixote that could only be realized in Spanish, the language of her parents—and this after their death.

V. A Language Is Also a Tree of Life

For the children of immigrants caught between several worlds, the French language is sometimes the only fixed point. A language is a genealogy, as we know. Being obliged to have several languages, choosing to have several in some cases (but that is a quite different situation), necessarily obliges one to accede to a metalanguage to transcend them. It also obliges one to cross a genealogy transmitted from the inside with the affiliations one acquires from the outside. That increases our freedom, but on the condition of having the means to do it and to cultivate the desire to create a complex, multiple genealogy for oneself, to grow the desire to create interactions among these languages, among these genealogies. Diversity—and this is its charm and its difficulty—leads to complexity.

1. To Resist Is to Be

And beyond words, there is the diversity of concepts. Let us take an example drawn from the ontological vocabulary of Castilian, my mother tongue. The verb *aguantar* can mean "to bear," "to resist," and "to be." The noun *aguante* means "mastery," but it suggests much more, as Michel del Castillo writes:

> [It is] not an event or a misfortune borne with full mastery of self, but an action accomplished by the subject; to resist, in a sense, but with a mixture of defiance and impassible disdain. In bullfighting, it designates the internal force of the *maestro* who withstands the bull's charge not only without flinching, in total immobility, but with a scornful pride. It is with this same tranquil dignity that Don Quixote suffers setbacks and failures, it is this same pride that I find in the Muslim countries. Wherever one looks, one finds the impress of Islam.[9]

This word cannot therefore be understood without the relevant concept. However, in situations where one changes languages, one can keep the word and erase the specificity of the context or, alternatively, keep the concept in its radical difference and modify the word: spoken in French, the word *supporter* ("to bear") does not have the same nuances and does not evoke the same cultural references or images as *aguantar*. It is this dissociation between words and concepts that children of immigrants must manage and, as they do the same with French words and concepts, they find themselves in situations of mixing or blending (*métissage*). So many separations, so many processes that produce newness, movement, even, in certain cases, poetry and new possibilities, links, interactions, encounters.

2. When Words Are Lacking in the Second Language, They Are Reinvented

It is the same with the verb "to be" in Spanish, a language for which the French verb *être* recognizes two different forms: *ser*, which designates an ontological state, and *estar*, which designates an ephemeral state, an attribute of the being that does not contain the being itself but characterizes it at a given moment. When I say *être* in French, I abrade this difference, I flatten the concept and the sense of time: *je suis*, "I am," without any other possible qualification. I redefine what I am differently, without being able to give it the thickness of my mother tongue. I then borrow other linguistic and associative series without knowing where they will lead me but especially without knowing if they will be able to translate my conscious and unconscious internal states. No doubt in certain cases my emotions will be abraded and other emotions magnified. But there will be a separation, a dialogue in Jullien's sense, a separation between words, between logics, whether rational or emotional, conscious or unconscious.[10]

There are also words that don't exist in French because the concept is unclear. The word *Dunanso* in Mossi is lacking in France to the point that it is difficult to transcribe. *Dunanso,* I am told by a Mossi patient, is the house of the foreigner. The house for people passing through, those who come to the village for a few days or a few months without knowing when they are going to leave. It happens that immigrants who are experiencing racism and exclusion in our country, in a very hurtful way, end up asking me where they can stay temporarily, so the indigenous will not feel they are a threat. "There are no *Dunansos* in France?" This space is as symbolic as it is real. They are asking, not to be parked or ghettoized, but quite simply to be in the right place, the place of the foreigner who wishes to live with us. We have neither the notion, nor the location, nor the word that would signify that we owe something to the foreigner. We do not ask ourselves what the ingredients of hospitality are. The word designates not only a space but a manner of thinking. And if it's lacking, it is because this hospitality is not imperative for us.

I heard recently that Freud had learned Spanish to read *Don Quixote* in the original, to gain access to the Don Quixote ontology, which evokes that of the Castilians. To be sure, a good translation can render concepts and images, but not only must one put *Don Quixote* in its historical context, as it is both a very specific and a profoundly universal book, and no doubt universal because it is very specific, one must first of all put it into the linguistic and anthropological context.

A language is thus a system of signs, images, concepts, possible figurations, crypts, a universe one inhabits and transports with oneself. Then the question becomes: what to do when history confronts you with several possible languages, an extremely frequent situation in the world but which, in the eyes of the French language, is always difficult to think. For us it is a matter of passing from the singular to the plural and developing what Chamoiseau might call a polyglot imaginary: "A language that dominates another, we oppose this not by toppling the one that dominates and putting the one that was dominated in its place, but by transmitting to our children, and to ourselves, if it is possible, a multilingual imaginary that will make us fall in love, both phantasmatically and concretely, with all the languages of the world. That changes everything."[11] However, it is not because one is a polyglot that one has an imaginary of diversity. One can be a polyglot and treat languages as objects side by side. The polyglot imaginary is that poetics, that art of living, that look, that clinic that allow us, in this immense shimmering of languages and culture, to be available, to seize what suits us, to go with energy toward what we can recuperate to construct ourselves.

VI. What Becomes of These Implicit Matters in Psychotherapy and Psychoanalysis?

1. Consuelo, the Inconsolable

Consuelo had a very pretty first name, one often heard in Castile, where she was born in the region of Burgos, the heart of Spain, as she liked to say to those who asked about her birth country. Etymologically, *Consuelo* comes from the Castilian root that means "console," to console someone, console oneself, be a consolation—one could hook a lot of meanings onto it. Actually, we understood later during the course of her therapy that this name was a nickname given her after the death of her first two babies, when she had become inconsolable. She laid claim to this nickname and kept it, like a trace of the story, a second nature, as she liked to say. She decided to emigrate to keep her children alive, as if her birth country, like an ogress, swallowed up her children. Against all opposition, she spoke her language to her children, who continued to arrive in the land of exile, a land that did seem to protect her children and allow them to grow up and "be someone," as they say in Spanish. One day, after the departure of all her children for brilliant, international studies, she fell ill. She was losing her taste for life and was no longer able to have desires for anything at all—she who so loved to watch the children and the plants grow up, as she liked to say in her beautiful Castilian language. In French, which she spoke rather well, her words were inconsistent, she said during the first conversation that took place in the French language. She succeeded in convincing the psychiatrists who saw her that she needed psychotherapeutic work in the language of her ancestors with words that also belonged to those who haunted her. That is how Consuelo was able to recover the consistency of her being by going back and forth between the language of her parents and that of her children.

For Consuelo as for all immigrants who have traversed several languages, the mother tongue is an associative support unequal to any other that allows the actualization of certain specific processes and the distancing of others. With respect to unconscious conflicts, the second language permits distance, sometimes favoring their elaboration, at other times freezing this elaboration, which has to return through the fabric of the mother tongue to be actualized in the transference and in a framework that can allow for it. In these situations of emigration or *métissage*, the choice of the psychoanalyst or psychotherapist is important for doing this archeological work. The choice already contains this search for alterity. For example, Consuelo tells me she is looking for a therapist who knows what lack of light is because, she explains to me, no light is equal to the light in Castile. The transference is embodied in the real or imaginary traces of alterity inscribed in the body of the therapist, in his or her name or intonations, but also in the capacity to dream with the patient, to dream on the basis of what the patient says. And in the same way, the countertransference attaches to the marks of alterity in the language of the patient or the body of the patient. As concerns psychotherapeutic or psychoanalytic communication, in Widlöcher's sense, it too is supported by these multiple languages included in the same language and a fortiori by the mother tongue or its traces when patients have multiple language trajectories.[12] It is astonishing that this question of the traces of the first language in the second language is so little considered in current psychoanalytic literature. Language history and intimate history in its conscious and unconscious movements are inscribed in a narrative that is actualized in the countertransferential relation, here and now, which belongs to a psychoanalyst and an analysand, to a psychotherapist and her patient, who have one language or several languages and—singular—bodies.

It is easy to understand how the language that is my own and that was the language of my first exchanges with my mother and my family will be libidinally invested in a very particular way, no doubt prior to language, in sensorial and corporeal feelings, and how much this language, if it is used symbolically or placed in the framework, can potentialize systems of remembering, narrative systems, mechanisms of identification or plural elaboration. What is important for us is therefore its use in a polyglot psychotherapy or its introduction into the framework of the psychotherapy as a particular malleable object (in Roussillon's sense),[13] if this language is no longer used by the patient himself or through a translator when French is not sufficiently invested and mastered by the patient, as in the case of Consuelo. Consuelo's associations in French typically went toward her children and toward the future, those in Spanish usually went to the past and its phantoms, the dead children, the women of the maternal line, and her childhood, the only period of her life when she had the experience of lightness. The passage from one language to the other in Consuelo's psychoanalysis was a powerful factor in the reanimation of associations, in psychical reanimation and reconciliation with the monsters of the past that haunted her and, after eating her children, ate up her life force.

And on the part of children, how are these language trajectories actualized in the investment in the language and the relation to knowledge, to connections, and to the world?

VII. Parvati, an Impeded Odyssey

Parvati has the same first name as her mother, who had the same first name as her own mother, who also had it from her mother . . . "I have this name to honor the goddess Parvati, who protects the first-born daughters of the family," she tells me just before leaving me at the end of her psychotherapy. Parvati was born in France in a corner of the Paris suburbs that everyone calls Little Sri Lanka, so numerous are the Tamil families from that island who live there together. It is a welcoming place where the community organizes celebrations, when possible, to honor the gods and goddesses of the Hindu pantheon. But it is a place where echoes of the war arrived when it raged in the country, though minimally, as if softened by the distance and especially by the daily preoccupations of the families, which are often multiple. Here there's a little war, over there a big one, certainly more murderous and infinitely more cruel, but the war has entered Parvati's home here, says her mother.

Parvati's mother is gravely ill, in fact, and the daily life of the children, already difficult before, has become unbearable. The mother is often in the hospital for treatment of her cancer, the prognosis of which is serious, according to the doctors. This they said in French, a language the family controls poorly. They would have preferred to speak to the doctor in English, a language they control much better, but the doctor speaks to them in French and says only a few words in English. And the words are definitive: *death*, *soon*. Even Parvati, who is ten, has understood what is at stake: her mother is going to die. Parvati is very attached to her mother, for whom she has served as interpreter. In the morning, when she goes by the temple to the goddess, which her mother has installed in the entry of their little house, she speaks to the goddess and tells her that if her mother dies, she will never speak again, neither to her nor to anybody. Parvati's mother also knows she is going to die, and she looks for ways to protect her children. She has three children: a daughter, Parvati, and her two younger brothers, aged five and seven. Her husband cannot stand to see his wife suffer and to think she could die soon. He is completely frightened. He asks himself how he is going to live in a country that is not his with his three children if his wife dies. He is afraid, and Parvati, his wife, sees it in his eyes. She tells him she is not afraid to die because she knows it is her fate and that he should not be afraid either. But nothing calms him. He is constantly with her in the hospital and risks losing his job because of his repeated absences. She tells him to go work. He replies he does not want to leave her alone in this hostile world and that he needs her. He recounts his memories of Sri Lanka and they both escape in thought from this cold hospital bed with memories of celebrations, games, delicious food . . .

When the children are present, the mother translates for them because they cannot understand everything their father tells about this place unknown to them. Parvati, who speaks Tamil well, says she will become a flight attendant so she can travel between Sri Lanka and France, and have her father and mother travel. Her mother smiles; she knows she will not have the time to wait and to see her daughter be a flight attendant. She dreams up a plan. She has an older sister in their native country who has been married for a long time but has no children. She will have her come to look after the children. Her sister and her brother-in-law will live in the house the family rents and look after the children. Parvati's husband does not understand why his wife stubbornly prepares for what is going to happen when she is no longer there. He cannot imagine her death, but he accepts what his wife requests. He cannot contradict her wishes, all the more so since it is very important for him. She also speaks to Parvati and tells her that sometimes adults pass too soon and have to be replaced by other adults. She tells her her sister is going to come look after them. Little Parvati sobs and asks her to stay. The mother talks to her about her sadness in being separated from her own mother, who remained in their native country. The mother asks her to always honor the memory of the goddess, for then she will have a good life. The sister arrives in France, and a few days later Parvati dies and little Parvati stops speaking French, as much in anger as in despair. At school, she in unable to open her mouth; she listens quietly but can no longer speak. She shuts herself in and curls inward in this world that frightens her and could not cure her mother, did not know how to keep her. She has no more tears, and no more words in French either. At home things become complicated. Her father and her aunt do not get along and they argue about the children. She prays to the goddess, she speaks to her mother as if to a goddess and asks her to return. This French world she perceives as hostile without her. She is afraid, she shuts her mouth. For her to speak in French again, we have to be able to help her pass from one world to the other, from one language to the other. First, she will have to be reconciled with her mother, whom she is very angry with for having abandoned her, as if exposed in a world where she risked dying. We will also have to reconcile her with her position as oldest daughter who maintains a privileged connection with the goddess and with the country of her parents, and make the adults around them stop their warring as well so that everyone can return to their place and Parvati can do her work as a girl who has to go from one world to another, from one language to another. She will do this with a certain success by writing beautiful stories she would have loved to tell her mother, stories that take place in an imaginary world. She also dreams of going to the United States to join a part of her family who emigrated there, and become a flight attendant—or a doctor, depending. That is why she is learning English with determination.

For Parvati, the work of separation from her mother and of individuation occurs through investment in a third language. Parvati's language trajectory is also the support for mourning and its elaboration. Her polyglot imaginary will allow her to construct herself and find the forms for her subjectivity to thrive.

What subjective routes will Uma choose?

VIII. Uma, the Sweet Girl with the Closed Mouth

Uma is a very pretty little girl of eight, dressed by her mother like a somewhat old-fashioned doll. Her family is Tamil, from India. She has a pretty Hindu first name. As we know, choosing a first name for a child is one of the most important rites of Hinduism. The choice is determined in agreement with holy writings and, traditionally, with the birth chart that is done at the moment of birth. The latter in particular allows one to determine what the first letter of the name should be. The first name is chosen in such a way that it can serve as a landmark and a compass for the one who bears it. Most first names given to newborns are directly inspired by the divinities of Hinduism, their incarnations, the naming of their qualities or attributes, mythological characters, saints, and sages. The very fact of using this name, repeating it each time one speaks to the child, is a way of paying homage to the divinity and placing the child under its protection. In the first session, we talk a lot about her name and the parents are happy to recount the modalities of naming, the differences between the two families, and, moreover, the conflicts they can engender, but they are in agreement about the fact that the naming is very important for the well-being of the children and for their future. Uma is a Shivaist female name.

The parents tell fragments of the story of Shiva, and the consultation is very animated. Uma comes to consult us with her parents because she does not speak French at school, which makes her parents despair, whereas at home she speaks the two languages relatively well. Her mother is very angry with this daughter who isn't able to acquire what she would have dreamed of having: Western language and knowledge. As for her father, he says he understands his daughter's difficulty confronted with an outside world that no one can introduce her to. He says he is himself frightened by this outside world so different from the one where he was born. Uma is indeed afraid, she shows it in her drawings in which dark colors and shapes that are decked out in large teeth predominate. By her silence, Uma expresses the pain of passage and of renunciation that sometimes constitutes emigration. Uma will start to speak in the outside world when she feels sufficiently reassured about her parents' strength and when she is accompanied in the passage from one language to the other by the liveliness of a French language that has become desirable and a Tamil language that will be the intimate connection with her parents. A connection strong enough that it can be broken without threatening her being as she throws herself whole-heartedly into the language of separation, French.

Investing in the passage between the languages then becomes the very condition of the possibility of speaking them, of using them, of appropriating them, as in the story of Uma.

IX. Conclusion

Thus, this singularity of the languages we traverse and that inhabit us, and the traces they produce, far from being impure, are for us, on the contrary, the grandeur and the complexity of the unique psychoanalytic relation, which cannot be replicated as such—doubtless not possible to model but, on the other hand, contextualized by bodies inscribed in languages and cultures.

This alterity, for Kristeva, refers both to culture in the anthropological sense of the term and to the unconscious. "The foreigner is within us. And when we flee from or struggle against the foreigner, we are fighting our unconscious—that 'improper' facet of our impossible 'own and proper.'"[14]

In sum, art, literature, painting, music: the imaginary. Such is the privileged enunciation that, for Kristeva, restores to language as a system of communication the dynamic of sublimation that constitutes it, from which it arose, and which is permanently at work within it.[15] Kristeva called this work that, unbeknownst to its users, subtends the code of communication, a "potential infinity."[16]

The very same potential infinity opens for us on the basis of Kristeva's oeuvre.

Marie Rose Moro

Medical School, University of Paris and La Maison des Adolescents, Hôpital Cochin
March 2019

NOTES

1. Julia Kristeva, Marie Rose Moro, John Ødemark, and Eivind Engebretsen, "The Cultural Crossings of Care: An Appeal to the Medical Humanities," *BMJ Medical Humanities* 44 (2018), doi:10.1136/medhum-2017- 011263.

2. Julia Kristeva, "L'Impudence d'énoncer: La langue maternelle," *Revue française de psychanalyse* 69, no. 5 (2005): 1655–67; "The Impudence of Uttering: The Mother Tongue," *Psychoanalytic Review* 97, no. 4 (2010): 679–94.

3. Julia Kristeva, *New Maladies of the Soul*, trans. Ross Guberman (New York: Columbia University Press, 1995); *Les Nouvelles Maladies de l'âme* (Paris: Fayard, 1993).

4. Ibid., ch. 9, 135–53; *Les Nouvelles Maladies de l'âme*, 203–28.

5. Julia Kristeva, "L'Adolescence: Un Syndrome d'idéalité," *Conférence Société Psychanalytique de Paris*, February 8, 2010, www.kristeva.fr.

6. For an in-depth understanding of this mechanism of failure among children of immigrants, see Marie Rose Moro, *Aimer ses enfants ici et ailleurs* (Paris: Odile Jacob, 2007). This failure is the consequence of the splitting between their two references: the world of school and the world of what is transmitted at home.

7. A consultation that allies psychoanalysis and anthropology with the help of translators, better to understand and care for immigrants and their children. See Marie Rose Moro, *Nos enfants demain: Pour une société multicuturelle* (Paris: Odile Jacob, 2010).

8. Julia Kristeva, *Strangers to Ourselves*, trans. Leon S. Roudiez (New York: Columbia University Press, 1991); *Étrangers à nous-mêmes* (Paris: Fayard, 1988).

9. Michel del Castillo, *Dictionnaire amoureux de l'Espagne* (Paris: Plon, 2005), 44.

10. François Jullien, *Le Pont des singes: De la diversité à venir, Fécondité culturelle face à l'identité nationale* (Paris: Galilée, 2010), 34.

11. Patrick Chamoiseau, "Pour un imaginaire de la diversité," interview in Abdellatif Chaouite and Marie Virolle, eds., *Allers-Retours* (Paris: Téraèdre Publishing/Revues plurielles, 2008), 16.

12. Daniel Widlöcher, *Métapsychologie du sens* (Paris: PUF, 1986).

13. René Roussillon, "Sur l'opposition entre psychothérapie/psychanalyse," *Carnet Psy* 5, no. 109 (2006): 43–45.

14. Kristeva, *Strangers to Ourselves*, 191; *Étrangers à nous-mêmes*, 283.

15. Kristeva, "The Impudence of Uttering."

16. Julia Kristeva, "Pour une sémiologie des paragrammes," in *Sémiotikè: Essais pour une sémanalyse* (Paris: Seuil, 1969).

32

Jean Vanier

"THEIR LOOK PIERCES OUR SHADOWS"

It is already eight years since we published our correspondence, *Leur regard perce nos ombres* (Their look pierces our shadows)![1] Under the sign of that mournful romantic play by Ibsen that deals with the story of a Rat-Wife (the rat-wife is an abject woman famous in Nordic Romanticism) who falls in love with a disabled child, little Eyolf (Eye/*oeil*), whom she compares to her first lover, who drowned.[2] And the boy, as if to rejoin the psychic depths where abjection, fear, shame, and desires cohabit, decides to drown himself also in the same lake. Eyolf's eyes never leave those of the Rat-Wife: "They stare fixedly into the shadow's depths, and their look pierces our shadows."[3] We have actually made progress since, even if there remains a lot to do, and how quickly time passes!

You evoked one of the two faces of the encounter: separation, mortality "that modifies pleasures and displeasures in the encounters."[4] I replied: "Tagore says that death is not like a lamp that goes out but like the coming of dawn. Yes, life is traversed by death. I remember my first encounter with death—*my* death—but it didn't come."[5] I was a sailor on a warship and I fell into stormy waters, very cold. I lost consciousness, luckily I had an enormous life preserver around me. I continued in my letter to you: "They got me out of the water, gave me a little brandy and brought me back on board. I could have disappeared, carried off by the wind beyond the horizon and there, alone and unconscious, passed through the veil that separates the earth and the sky. This 'gentle' experience of death has perhaps helped me to tame it."[6]

The extreme combat for sur-vival (with a hyphen, the way you write it) that your son David engages in, with the mortal risks he has incurred, has not only bound you and Philippe around him, the proximity of death has also made you live differently, a more intense life, more precious, more sensitive,

Translated from French by Armine Kotin Mortimer.

in a vertical time, as you say, which is a continuous present, a "now" in which sur-vival makes the rest of existence appear like a secondary unreality. A disability teaches us this urgency of life, it confronts us with *mortality*—an underlying mortality, continuous through all of existence—that remains unthinkable and unthought, and makes us afraid. The nonconformity to "the norm" characteristic of persons in a situation of disability is at the intersection of *biology* (biological deficiency) and the response of *society* to this biological deficiency: nature and culture. And that difference, perceived as a *deficit*—although reparable in certain cases and within certain limits—*makes me die if I am alone*, you say, without a prosthesis, without human aid. It is tragically true. The loss of autonomy proves definitively mortal. Their pain is mortal. That's what made me found L'Arche, to offer a place for life, human life in the sense you mean, following Arendt: a *bios*, a life that is thought through, and a thought that can be lived, and not just an organic *zōē*. And I'm with you when you assert that a disability can also be a *chance*, since the situation of disability reveals and can open up the *irreducible singularity* of the speaking being we are, and can reconstruct the social link. Personalized care and the recognition of singularity, and its development, which we put forward at the assembly on "Disability: Time for Engagement" at UNESCO in 2005, which you organized with Charles Gardou from the University of Lyon 2 (a contributor in this volume), have contributed to changing how people look upon disabilities. There you mentioned the creativity David has shown in music, since he has absolute pitch, and in literature since he writes poetry, and the activities of his friends at the *Papotin* newspaper. The film *The Untouchables* (*Intouchables*) found a wide audience; difference can be a source of humor and help us live, one and all.[7]

At L'Arche, we are confronted with the work of death within us, which causes a specific exclusion in our society as concerns persons in a situation of disability. That underlying death provokes fear in a society that advocates performance and excellence. We are often plunged into mourning by the death of our "pals." I have told you about the deaths of our Jacqueline d'Halluin, so devoted, and our Éric, so fragile. As we know, the other face of a true encounter is the inclusion of death and separation; we never possess the other. And there are all sorts of deaths . . . All those we have welcomed, who come from sorrowful institutions, psychiatric hospitals, or difficult situations have often experienced the extinction of the love of their families—they feel guilty that they exist, that they don't have a place here below. However, we, as assistants, cannot replace the family. Imperfect as friends and therapists, we are wounded human beings seeking to live in joy with other wounded human beings, having faith in each human being, and in the unity of the human family. In this life "along with," there exist possibilities of deviance, which is why these relations must be supported in a community through various sorts of supervision. For this, we have a team of professionals whose presence is necessary. Indeed, as you ask, where does the boundary lie between "suggestion, abuse, respect, pleasure"?[8] And I would even add "interpretation," thinking of situations of very great deficiencies, like Éric's, in which we search for the little signs that indicate the desire for an encounter, a reassurance, a greater vitality. As I wrote to you in *Leur regard perce nos ombres*:

> Let's return to death, to the breath that departs like a bird toward the sky. Where is the sky? Where does the monks' chant go? To whom does the song of the birds speak? Is the torn veil only a gentle sleep or the threshold of a place of justice and light? Why are we so afraid of death, when it's for finding another form of happiness? Does this fear come from culpability, failed life, the feeling of inferiority experienced by people, or even from the desire for rejection, scorn, and hatred that can inhabit us? Does it come from the darkness, from the fears buried inside us? Does it also come from our desire to be "like God," death being like the encounter with the Great Rival? Is fear of death the expression of the radical loss of power: absolute impotence? What meaning should we give to impotence? Does the fear of the death of others add to the fear of one's own death—feeling abandoned, or guilty for not having done enough or loved enough?[9]

In our life on earth, the desire for power, the desire to appear like the best, to be recognized, appreciated, cohabits with our astonishment, our wonderment in the face of beauty. Beauty makes us sing, then plunges us into silence and contemplation. Beauty leads to gratuity, to the desire for the encounter. Aristotle says that wonderment is at the very origin of philosophy. When the veil between the earth and the sky is torn, when the breath flies away, when power collapses and total impotence afflicts us, then an even more wonderful wonderment springs forth: the beauty of the presence. Are we not made for the wonder of the presence? You too have spoken of a certain beauty apropos of the life you have been led to experience as a combat with the presence of death and, when all is said and done, a commitment at every instant—the only worthwhile kind. To recall what I wrote to you in *Leur regard perce nos ombres*:

> Of course we know there are limits to wonderment here below. We are not blind to broken relations, anguish, isolation, earthquakes, painful cancers, traffic accidents, Auschwitz and Hiroshima. These all appear as so many lacks, as terrible abysses. Crisis is a rending asunder; it is also the announcement of something new. From chaos springs forth a new life. Crisis and chaos do not bring an end to everything; wonderment is there, ready to emerge through the other who holds out his hand.[10]

Our common desire to make a more human society where "the different other" (that's how David and his friends prefer to identify themselves: different, you wrote me) would be welcomed fully and joyfully should not make us mix up—oh yes, you are right—all the differences, the wall of racism, the exclusion of persons in a situation of disability. There are, however, elements in common: the fear of the other, lived like a danger, like an encumbrance that harms my freedom, impedes my full development. In the face-to-face, heart-to-heart encounter, fear weakens. Still we must live in humility, and I agree with you when you write: "It's not a matter of *accepting* mortality . . . but of *integrating* its ineluctable presence. . . . Only at such a price do I succeed in *taming* depression . . . catastrophes. . . . Through a sort of *serenity*, without pathos or enthusiasm . . . [which is] perhaps the modest face of what you call a 'pleasure.'"[11] Yes, the two faces of the encounter are indeed pleasure and the integration of mortality. To live without allowing oneself to be dominated by the tyranny of normality and mortality, and to integrate mortality, one has to have dared the encounter with this weaker other, who will make possible the welcoming of one's own weaknesses and vulnerabilities.

The encounter of the assistants with persons in the situation of disability is a source of life when there is a true exchange, hand offered, gestures of affection, smiles, tender looks, beginnings of a real relationship. As you say, they help us live better, live our common humanity. But at that moment, fundamental questions may well occur to the assistants: they are living a profoundly human, highly spiritual experience, in which the misery of the flesh is a source of life, whereas they used to live under the tyranny of normality (or mortality) that pushed them toward performance, toward excellence. I wrote to you:

> What education should be given to these disability professionals, as bureaucrats call them? To become competent, to acquire knowledge about the various types of disabilities, to allow persons in the situation of disability to develop are of course the indispensable objectives for all education. But we must, it seems to me, help these professionals be attentive, to experience a relationship of mutual confidence, to discover and listen to the appeal of the person behind the weakened body, so as to create an encounter from one person to another and not just become "normal."[12]

All the more so since, as you believe, there is not *a* disability, nor even *disabilities*, but different, unique people, each time with a specific deficiency. And a vital force, a creativity, also singular.

> All assistants at L'Arche must be able to share with others about their fears, their violence, their disgust, their fatigue, but also about those magic moments when their hearts were opened. They then begin to call into question the tyranny of normality, the functioning of a society that honors the powerful and pushes the weak aside. They discover another world, very diverse, where mortality and pleasure intersect, a place of serenity and peace.[13]

And I continued:

> You spoke about the shock [of exile], the [psychic] "death" the little Bulgarian girl was subjected to, a traumatism, even an ordeal of "dissociation." I was touched by your story, perhaps it's the story of many, many refugees and immigrants. . . . In 1942, at the height of the war . . . I asked my father (during an "official" encounter in his office!) if I could join the Royal Navy. A crazy request on the part of a kid of thirteen! My father said, after having listened to me, "I have confidence in you. If you want to do it, you must." Later, this "I have confidence in you" continued to resonate throughout my life. . . . My father liberated me. . . . I could be myself,

leave my family, follow a path in life that did not conform to normality. I could risk living.[14]

I spent eight years in the Navy, which I left in 1950—my heart had been touched by the reading of the Gospel and the life of Jesus, Prince of Peace, who wills the unity of all human beings. I wanted to become a priest. I joined L'Eau Vive, a community created by Father Thomas Philippe—another encounter.

Is this not what you experience with those men and women who come to you for a liberation—to give them a rebirth, which is to transcend anguish into life? Is this not that "state of grace," like so many other moments of creativity, which transcends time and shatters the walls of finitude and isolation? If my life has gravitated largely around marginal people, is it not in part to seek out these states of grace that are like rebirths?

I am working with you for a new humanism, "together in the train," so that the walls separating the so-called able from men and women who are different because of their weakness and their personal vulnerability continue to fall.[15]

What you say about Voltaire and Mme du Deffand is fascinating.[16] Life is an encounter. Marie awaits a sign, a life-giving letter from Voltaire. The more she goes blind, the more clearly she sees. She lives only because she is the object of his attention, of his love. Society holds no interest for her anymore.

You feel very strongly about the question of the affective and sexual life of persons in the situation of disability. Society, formerly centered on a familial ethic, has become a society of sexual liberation. Not always positive. How can we help each and every one live a dignified and responsible sexuality? The state is still not sufficiently committed to the creation of places where couples or groups of adults in small numbers may live, places adapted to each person's degree of autonomy, in spite of the advances made by the 2005 law in France on the equality of opportunity.[17] Our community life (all our centers are coed) succeeds, with time, in humanizing sexual drives and aggressive drives and puts everyone on the road to better affective health and maturity, often after many humiliations, even abuses. This life in common invites exchanges and sharing through the spoken word by offering personal support and developing a deep sense of solidarity. One and all discover themselves as persons of value with their own freedom and a desire for responsibility. In my book *Man and Woman: God Made Them*, I attempted to address these questions based on my forty years of experience.[18] At L'Arche, we have witnessed beautiful marriages, but sometimes also failures.

Thanks to the profession nourished and elaborated by your intelligence and your listening and loving heart, you rise up against everything that oppresses, encloses, crushes. I perceive in you this desire to give birth to life, life that is liberty, a word spoken and received with respect.

What to do—in developing this "train" project, but also in having recourse to all the means you employ so the weak and the vulnerable will be respected. What ethical markers can we hope to bring together? I admit I'm troubled, like you, when I see people who, with a spirituality of the left hand, act with their right hand as cynical managers of financial markets. It's nothing new: Clair d'Assise, born Chiara Offreduccio di Favarone, ran away at eighteen from her family, who wished for her a marriage of status. Her uncles and cousins, very religious, brought her back to her parents by force and made her submit to the custom among aristocrats at the time.

I am for life, of course, I believe in the integrity of each human being, even the weakest, but I also believe in the importance of being coherent, of finding unity among word, thought, and life. I am touched when you admit to being sometimes annoyed by my smile and my "generous thanks to Destiny." Your annoyance is perhaps a sign that your psychoanalyst's lynx eye suspects there is something unavowed behind the smile and the gratitude. You are not wrong. In me (and maybe in each of us) there are evasions, fears, prejudices, hidden things one isn't able or doesn't want to see. Personally, I don't feel the need to go further in this work of self-examination. At eighty-nine, now, it's the descent into weakness, the welcoming of this weakness, that will finish this work. The accidents and the great weakness that lead to death are a harsh school of truth. There is nothing left to hide there!

We are all full of contradictions, pulled in different directions. There exists in me an attraction for vulnerable people, to reveal to them their value and raise them up, but also a more or less conscious, more or less avowed, desire to be recognized for that. Yes, what a contradiction: to seek glory unconsciously by embracing the "non-glorious." How crazy!

As you know, for a long time now I have not had any responsibilities in my community, neither in L'Arche International nor in Faith and Light. I was recently prescribed complete rest after a heart attack, and I have even had to give up my lecturing within France. I had no difficulty quitting these roles and responsibilities, and no longer traveling. I found a new style of life in my center and my community with the men and women I welcomed, in some cases, more than forty years ago. This community life brings me much joy. Celebrating life together—men and women from all walks of life, whatever their religion or their lack of religion, their visible or invisible difficulties—is the sign that rivalry is not an inevitability and that peace is possible.

I would like my life at L'Arche to be a sign of an alternative way: beyond "normality," beyond the need for excellence, for performances. The human being is quite simply made for living humanly. It is important, to be sure, for everyone to develop their potential and be recognized as unique. To live differently is to live the fidelity to relational life, often by helping others enjoy life in the smallest things. One of the assistants at L'Arche, keen on interreligious dialogue, went to live for a year in Morocco with a Muslim family. Daily life created an interreligious dialogue that became a source of life. This is how one discovers a true complicity and a true presence with the other. That's what life is at Trosly-Breuil.

Now that I no longer have responsibilities in the organization of L'Arche and Faith and Light, I feel more free. With new moments of solitude, I have the time to listen to the birds, to rest, to pray, to read—not so much Voltaire, but, rather, Shakespeare, and especially John, author of the fourth Gospel. This I love! He takes us down the path through humility, the thirst for truth, and the suffering, to achieve a new inspiration. One cannot read John without becoming rooted in what formed his heart and his intelligence: the great prophets of the Old Testament—Isaiah, Ezekiel, Jeremiah, up to Zachariah—and especially Jesus, whose beloved disciple he was. This is a new youthfulness in which I am finding the child in me. Life at L'Arche keeps me on this earth—sufferings and joys—but it also opens me to a blossoming of my heart and my intelligence. It opens me also to the hereafter of death. Where is the sky? Where does the monks' chant go? Where does my prayer go? In me lies a growing desire. A hope, a calling. I await in tranquility and joy.

I think I probably never told you about the Faith and Light movement. And yet, it sprung from my life at L'Arche and really helped me understand persons in a situation of disability. Marie-Hélène Mathieu and I founded it in 1971 when we realized that numerous people suffering from mental difficulties could not join the diocesan pilgrimages to Lourdes. So we organized a great, vast international pilgrimage to the grotto at Lourdes. At Easter in 1971, 12,000 of us met: 4,000 people in a situation of disability, 4,000 parents, and 4,000 friends. We spent five wonderful days full of songs, sharing, liturgies, prayers, and celebrations on the square in front of the Basilica. Never seen before! At the end of these five days, the people at Lourdes, who at the start were petrified with fear by this venture with "crazies," opened their arms wide with joy in their hearts. A malediction was transformed into a benediction.

From the "madness" of this pilgrimage multiple communities were born. Today they number about 1,650, each composed of people in a situation of disability, their parents, and their friends. They meet several times a month. Friendships are forged, people emerge from their isolation and their sadness. For many years, I remained with Marie-Hélène Mathieu at the helm of this vast organization, which has taken root in eighty countries on five continents. I don't dare speak of "destiny" in describing this growth of Faith and Light, but I confess I marvel at this movement spreading soundlessly across the globe. I no longer travel to support and guide these communities. Life is like a river: to retain power is to refuse the movement of life.

I think the men and women who carry the responsibility for our communities today (about 150 communities of L'Arche in the world) are wonderful. L'Arche is necessarily linked to the regional or national authorities from whom we receive subsidies. It isn't always easy to be subordinate to the state, with its norms, and still to preserve the specificity of L'Arche, whose purpose is to connect community and spiritual life with the desire to be competent, capable, and professional. When I created L'Arche in 1964, taking in two men from an institution under lock and key, I wanted to develop a simple, familial space where those two men, and those who would follow, could live as freely, happily, and humanly as possible while developing their potential. With the passing of time, L'Arche was obliged to become an institution recognized by public authorities.

I am happy that a chapter in my life has closed. I am happy to live this new phase, which is going to lead me to the greatest weakness but also to the most hidden and most secret center of myself. I am hoping that, rather than "undergoing" this final phase, I will welcome it with the joy that is mine today.

Thank you, dear Julia, for our correspondence. I hope it will continue in a different form. Yes, you have fostered a new breath of life in me.

JEAN VANIER

FOUNDER OF L'ARCHE AND COFOUNDER OF FAITH AND LIGHT
APRIL 2018

NOTES

The present volume was in proofs when the allegations against Jean Vanier were disclosed.— Ed.

All translations of quotations in this essay are by Armine Kotin Mortimer.

1. Julia Kristeva and Jean Vanier, *Leur regard perce nos ombres* (Paris: Fayard, 2011).
2. Henrik Ibsen, "Little Eyolf (1894)," in *The Complete Major Prose Plays*, trans. Rolf Fjelde (New York: Plume, 1978), 861–936.
3. [In one of her letters in *Leur regard perces nos ombres*, Kristeva cites Ibsen—"*Ils regardent fixement le fond de l'ombre . . . et leur regard pénètre aussi notre ombre* (They stare fixedly into the shadow's depth . . . and their look penetrates our shadow, too)"—and then writes: "Leur regard perce nos ombres *pourrait être le titre de ces lettres qui, nous l'esperons, pourraient contribuer à 'changer le regard'* (*Their look pierces our shadows* could be the title of these letters that, we hope, could contribute to changing the look)." Ibid, 67.—Ed.]
4. Kristeva in *Leur regard perces nos ombres*, 37.
5. Vanier, in ibid., 48.
6. Ibid., 48–49.
7. *Intouchables*, directed by Éric Toledano and Olivier Nakache, Gaumont, 2011.
8. Kristeva, in *Leur regard perce nos ombres*, 35.
9. Vanier, in ibid., 51.
10. Ibid., 52.
11. Kristeva, in ibid., 37–38.
12. Vanier, in ibid., 55.
13. Ibid.
14. Ibid., 55–56.
15. [In a letter published in *Leur regard perce nos ombres*, Kristeva wrote: "I read your letter and I imagine that we are boarding the Disability Challenge train together. For now, it's only a dream, the powers that be aren't budging. . . . Be that as it may, we will take this train, it can't not leave one day or another!" (209). Vanier replied with the desire to work "together in the train" (225)—Trans.]
16. See ibid., 212–15.
17. [On February 11, 2005, France adopted Law 2005-102 for the equal rights and opportunities, participation, and citizenship of people with disabilities.—Ed.]
18. Jean Vanier, *Man and Woman: God Made Them* (New York: Paulist, 2008).

REPLY
TO CHARLES GARDOU, EIVIND ENGEBRETSEN, MARIE ROSE MORO, AND JEAN VANIER

The disabled body has always troubled civilizations. A sacred monster, it inspires all sorts of superstitions; certain civilizations protect it (the Laws of Manu in India), others suppress it (Sparta) or else "export" it and offer it to the divine in the public arena (before the Byzantine martyr Zotikos welcomes the "crippled" as gifts from God). With Saint Augustine, the disabled person becomes lovable, able to be helped. However, the almshouses of the Middle Ages still excluded the leprous, the paralyzed, and the incurable. Medievalists today are asking: where were the disabled? The Franciscans in following Saint Francis did much better than help the disabled and the poor: they glorified them. Epidemics of the fourteenth and fifteenth centuries, mystical burgeoning of the sixteenth—society began at last to be concerned with marginal people, but it was still difficult to distinguish the disabled from the needy. Thus Matthew 25 brings together the poor, the sick, the leprous, the wandering, and the infirm; all who are *excluded* because of a *lack*, the evangelist calls to welcome them, for they are in the image of the Man of Sorrows.

Inaugurated by the Enlightenment, the modern approach to disability carries this compassionate conception forward in demanding political rights for persons with deficiencies. Diderot's *Letter on the Blind for the Use of Those Who Can See* (1749) finally opened the way for education and the development of instructional techniques suited to disabilities. The state's engagement followed, prompting moves of national solidarity, which, in advanced democracies today, lead to "integration in school and work" and to "personalized compensation."

However, in light of the third millennium, persons in a situation of disability reveal the difficulty, if not the impossibility, for modern democracies to apprehend this form of exclusion. When the famous social pact disintegrates, a hostage to finance and hyperconnectivity, the egos are not equal: they are drunk on their "will to power," but realize that their incommensurable singularity survives only by *listening to* other singularities, just as incommensurable. The collective, integrative, and egalitarian solutions are not defunct. They are just insufficient.

Translated from French by Armine Kotin Mortimer.

Because the one who is in a situation of disability is as alone and incurable as an internaut or a Yellow Vest. Because she is super-resistant and endowed with unpredictable faculties, as is the migrant in the flows of globalization. Because he wants and doesn't want to be "integrated" with "people" who are afraid of him, for he dies if he is not bolstered by personalized support. She also proves that the fragility of the human condition is a sur-vival, and has no other way to confront time than by betting on the proximity of an alterity, just as *other* as she is. Whence this poignant paradox: vulnerability aggravated by disability continues to inspire a "piercing fear" (Charles Gardou); but all of us need a specific listening and help for the ordeals of our more or less encumbered and encumbering bodies and souls, and for those prolonged times of dependence and the end of life. In this respect, disability "stricken with inferiority" is revealed to be a "loupe" amplifying our universal condition (Gardou). Immigrants strangled in the bottleneck of globalization join them in a quest for a "polyglot imaginary, a poetics, and a clinic" (Marie Rose Moro). Added to them are the patients for whom "evidence-based medicine" endeavors to *cure* their organs and who deserve that we *listen* and *care* for their biopsychical resources (Eivind Engebretsen). For his part, Jean Vanier[1] creates one hundred forty-seven communities of L'Arche throughout the world and reminds the public powers struggling to create places for the most vulnerable to live that it is time to add to the Republican motto a fourth ethical value: *Liberty, Equality, Fraternity and . . . Vulnerability*.[2] A subtle humanity tries to make itself heard. Are we ready?

I. Charles Gardou

I thought I had reached the depths of the intimate within the labyrinths of writing or through the psychomotor ordeals and critical states of my son David, when Charles Gardou invited me to join the scientific council of his research program on disability at the University of Lyon 2. That was to lead us to the creation of the assembly on disability at UNESCO in 2005. I had written novels to illustrate this nameless intimacy: *The Samurai* (1990), *Possessions* (1996), and *Murder in Byzantium* (2004). For his part, Charles Gardou convinced me, then confirmed me in the idea that it is possible, even necessary, to provide a philosophical and political discourse that would allow "changing the look" at people in a situation of disability. I will never be able to thank him enough, and I am pleased to read him again, here, synthesizing the essential components of his work, which borrows from personal experience, educational sciences, sociology, ethnology, the history of art, and the history of philosophy to develop what he calls disability's "signification of universality." We share the same experience and the same thinking about disability as revelatory of our mortality ("he may die not because he's vulnerable—he's vulnerable because he must die") and as "willpower triumphant over manifestations of weakness," "blossoming of faculties," and astonishing *talent*.

Yes, disability differs from other forms of "vulnerability" because it confronts us more than anything with our mortality. The universalism of human rights succeeds, though not without difficulty, in making people accept differences in race, class, religion, sexual mores. Disability is nonconforming to the norm for a completely different reason: at the intersection of biology (biological deficit and its psychomotor consequences) and the social field, disability defies the norm because while it is reparable within certain limits, it condemns to death the one who is alone, without prosthesis or human help.

The anxiety about death, about finitude, even about repulsion (in the face of certain serious, multiple disabilities) are the hidden face of this panic—the insuperable mixture of indifference, shame, and sometimes arrogance that those not in a situation of disability display in the face of the disabled, and to which the people involved and their families are exposed. To be sure, human beings know they are mortal, and biology has discovered that cellular death (apoptosis) sculpts the living. But the person in a situation of disability has to deal with this mortality that she carries within, the companion to her solitude, like sorrow for Baudelaire: "Give me your hand, my Sorrow; come with me."[3]

In contrast to religions and various spiritualities, which instill the idea of mortality in the minds of more or less receptive adepts, secularization has not constructed a discourse on *mortality*. I am not speaking of *death*. We are experts in celebrations; moreover, the longevity of seniors has seen the rapid expansion of a market dedicated to them, with "institutions" for assisted living; palliative care is being refined as well. I am speaking here of a lifelong mortality from birth, or one connected to "unpredictable genetic biological variabilities" that generate disabilities. This mortality that one calls "disabling" remains unthinkable. A radical change of mentality is needed to assume and accompany the human being in her limits and her finitude. In this sense, disability is a trial but also a chance: the disabled person and his support remind us of the transience constitutive of our human condition. "To philosophize is to learn how to die" (Plato), but that also means, in our postmodern, performative, and pressing era, to domesticate the limit states of life.

When accompanied by complicity, comprehension, and recognition, the cohabitation with mortality elicits contagious "overcompensations" and "superresistances," writes Gardou. Yes, the "hindered" do "'work at' their feelings of devastation." And so intensely that, if they do not achieve great works, like Frida Kahlo, Blaise Pascal, or Fyodor Dostoyevsky, who transcended themselves by "struggling *against* their vulnerability," they nevertheless prove that "the motor that drives human existence resides right there, in this struggle" *with* vulnerability at every moment. A permanent creativity stems from it, necessary for *being*, quite simply. And the "constitutive precariousness" rubs shoulders with this stupefying happiness, which escapes the current derealization and rejects the programmed automatization of our species.

II. Eivind Engebretsen

Eivind Engebretsen has built his critique of biomedical reductionism and its neopositivist, neoliberal, and holistic ideology (based on notions of *evidence* and *choice*) by drawing on my conception of the *singularity* of the "subject in process" and on the necessary reevaluation of notions inherited from ontotheology such as the *norm* and the *lack* (*steresis* in Aristotle).

I trace my understanding of singularity to Duns Scotus (1266–1308), who maintained, against Aquinas, that truth does not reside in the universal idea or in matter but in "such a one": that man, that woman. From this his disciples deduced the notion of "*haecceitas*" or "*ecceitas*," from *hoc, haec*, or *ecce*, "this," in which the demonstrative designates an unnamable singularity. Duns Scotus's discovery is attributed to his reading of the words that God addressed to Moses: "I am that I am" ("*Je suis* Celui *qui est*"). This unpronounceable name is the precise indication of absolute singularity. An ethic of Scotist inspiration was then sketched, which some have designated as "mystical" (certain people, like Gilles Deleuze, called it "atheistic"), whereas others saw in Saint Thomas a "social" ethic. Whatever the case may be, *singularity* appears in Duns Scotus's thought as the unique *positivity*—what today we would call "value." It was in starting from the positivity of the *being* that Duns Scotus applied it to the *Being*-itself, and to God, as the *causa singularitatis*, a singular God, namely Christ. For it is in the passion of death (the *kenosis*) that the Man-God experiences his singularity. Sur-viving, wounded-crucified, he is thus glorified, but this glory is in no case a revelation or a satisfaction, it is the very *evidence* of his singularity. Nancy Eiesland affirms this in *The Disabled God: Toward a Liberatory Theology of Disability*: Jesus appears to his apostles in his glory, but a singular glory, because he is a "disabled god."[4]

An evidence that understandably is not that of "evidence-based medicine," "based on a systematic search of medical databases." But evidence of the *incommensurable singularity* of each person, disability included, who is not reducible to any "norm" or "lack," and which invites the speaking subject to welcome his singular potentialities and sharable initiatives, to the extent of his possibilities.

The reading the young Heidegger did in his *Die Kategorien- und Bedetungslehre des Duns Scotus* (Duns Scotus's doctrine of categories and meanings) (1916), and the reading by Arendt, who stakes her claim on the singularity of the "*who*" proper to "each newborn" against the "*what*" of objectifying, thing-making, objectifying massification, seem to me to denounce both totalitarian regimes and the galloping automatization of transhumanist modernity.[5]

Bringing this *singularity* to the experience of disability allows us to challenge one of the prejudices with which it inexorably collides, that of the *norm*—without romantic refusal or servile submission. The idea of a norm, of a conforming rule, is indispensable in biology as in the social link. In a period witnessing the development of democracies, rich with the promises and advances of the life sciences, *biopolitics* offers a new vision: the norm is no longer a fixed a priori concept; it becomes a dynamic concept. Singularities upset norms and make them evolve.

I understand the militants who reject the term *handicap*, a tributary of the Aristotelian conception (in the *Physics* and the treatise *On the Soul*) that presupposes an archetype built on the idea of a *privation* of possession (*steresis*). I am deaf because I am *deprived* of the sensation or the capacity of hearing.

Without being limited to an ontology of negation, this *ontology of lacking* induces a dichotomy possessing/deprived, powerful/sterile; it limits subjective singularity solely to the paradigm of *lack*—with its necessary counterpart, compassion and/or tenderness. Magnificent charitable works are inspired by it, which found Christian humanism and the church, and which will "com-plete," "give" to those who "don't have."

On the level of knowledge, the study of the "empty" (the pathologies) leads science to appropriate and reconstruct the "full" (normal functioning). Nor is it a matter of abolishing the model of solidarity, which claims to answer the question of poverty/deprivation/"lack of being" and to accede to Being through the accumulation of possessions, but, rather, of adjoining another model to it.

The contingency of the disabled singular person is not a deprivation; it is *positive* when it reveals to me my own singularity as a "possessor," in other words as "valid," which I neither glorify nor deny but which I tame all the better in respect to the singularity of the one designated as "lacking." It is mortality acting in the constitutive precariousness of *this* person that touches me. I accompany him/her, I carry him/her through their specific, singular development—and I pursue mine, equally specific and singular.

I am with Engebretsen when he critiques "some of the hidden assumptions inherent in . . . the Edmonton Symptom Assessment Scale (ESAS) developed for the symptom assessment of cancer patients"; or the supposed "objective indicators . . . independent of the patient's own singular interpretations and descriptions of his or her pain"; or even the efforts to "understand situations in their uniqueness"—particularly among "young adults with disabilities, based on a systematic search in medical databases," which amounts to establishing grids of "'categories of difference' that pretend to have universal legitimacy," but in which "the singularity of the individual . . . [is] classified as sign of a lack."

We are far from the listening and personalized closeness that the "polyglot" clinic of Marie Rose Moro induces in the transference/countertransference between patient and carer. Of which Cochrane himself, "one of the founding figures in evidence-based medicine," seems to recognize the impact when the young Soviet prisoner, "dumped" by the Germans in his ward and dying of pleurisy, stops screaming as soon as Cochrane—then a doctor without "medicine" or morphine—takes him in his arms.

"Cure" and/or "care"? From the general to the "individual case"? Or vice versa (Engebretsen)? "Evidence-based medicine" is itself now questioning the *exceptions* in order to complexify its own statistical procedures. In another way, the *mixed* analysis I conducted with Florence (see Engebretsen), with antidepressants adapted to the "specific microcosm" of the talking cure, attempts to conjugate *evidences*, in the plural.

III. Marie Rose Moro

Could the "polyglot imaginary" whose advent Marie Rose Moro promotes in her psychoanalytic psychotherapies be precisely what the political management of migratory flows is lacking? I am convinced of it, and so I joyfully accepted her invitation to move my seminar on the "need to believe" from the University of Paris 7 to the Maison des Adolescents, which she directs at the Hôpital Cochin, and where she shares her clinical experience with an intercultural and interdisciplinary team, notably among adolescents tempted by jihad.

In the study presented here, her attention is focused on the mother tongue of adolescent or adult immigrants and on the various inhibitions, indeed depressions, they suffer during their exile. Moro develops a conception of the mother tongue in which I recognize my work on the *semiotic* (prelanguage receptacle made of sensorial motions, drives and affects, vocalizations articulated in frequencies and intensities, echolalias anterior to syllables, words and syntax grammatically constructed that will definitively articulate the *symbolic* dimension of the mother tongue—its concepts and its values); and on *maternal reliance* (the weave of attachments and rejections, loves and hatreds, abjections and tendernesses, necessary condition of the *investment* of the community language through the "sublimatory cycle" that is prolonged in the father-mother-child triangulation).

At this dawn of language, strategies of identification, introjection, and projection are elaborated that mobilize the image of the body, that of the emerging self, and that of the *other*. Between biology and language, the imaginary is founded on the "mirror stage." Through the play of representations proposed to the child, the imaginary appeals to the entire gamut of identifications: narcissistic identification, by taking hold of the maternal image or its reduplication; primary identification with the benevolent father in "individual prehistory"; secondary identification in the oedipal phase and particularly its variant, the hysterical identification with the phallic pole; etc. The imaginary is a kaleidoscope of images of the self that then activates prelanguage (the *semiotic*) and language (the *symbolic*), in which the subject of enunciation progressively arrives. I frequently have recourse to this problematic in my clinical practice, in particular in the psychoanalytic psychotherapies with young children or adolescents.

The construction of the speaking subject mobilizes *all the strata of language*, as the phantasms and anxieties of separation and destruction develop. *The imaginary lies nestled in language*, as is shown by the treatment of Paul who, at more than three years of age, "did not know how to speak."[6] He would not come unglued from "his" adored tablet, spending the bulk of his time listening to his favorite songs, tales, and fables, which his parents had installed on it. However, he would not, could not speak. Without being autistic, Paul seemed to be in the throes of a phobic inhibition that hindered his access to speech. His fears were multiple. Fear of separating from the "lullaby," his "native idiom," and from this *tablet*, artificial but ever available mother, coddling new generations. Fear of confronting the "codes," the ones "the rest of us" had set, parents and adults having become inaccessible in our forward flight. Fear of being incapable of using his own "codes," of being "a bad speaker." Paul protected himself by rocking himself with music and indicated to his family, and anyone who would listen, that he lived in a foreign world. An impregnable retreat? It took us some time to unlock the imaginary of this foreignness. I began by recognizing what Paul was capable of and what made him happy in the semiotic resonance with "his" tablet.

The therapist's task consists precisely in identifying the patient's *capacities*, in giving him confidence in his own abilities, in awakening the desire to develop them, first of all with the therapist. I therefore decided to communicate with Paul and his mother by using the means that were at his disposal: *song*, his intimate, secret "code," his inadmissible "foreignness" as a means of communication with the family. The *operas* we improvised, which would have looked ridiculous to a potential audience, bore the *meanings* we wished to exchange, to be sure, but mainly they carried the unsayable *sense* of the affects and drives encrypted in the frequencies, the rhythms, and the vocal intensities that were perceived better (if not exclusively) by Paul. "*Come see me*" (do-re-mi), "*How are you*" (do-si-la), etc. I will not speak of the psychoanalytic work we accomplished over the course of years. I insist on the fact that it is inseparable from the advent of language—favored by my osmotic listening, acted on then distanced, to the semiotic and imaginary links that soldered Paul and his maternal container.

The vignettes that Marie Rose Moro presents do not concern neuropsychical deficits nor any particular psychosexual pathology. They present vulnerabilities caused, revealed, or accentuated by political foreignness: the sensation of exclusion, the trauma of discrimination. In those cases, the between-language is a test that, in a context different from Paul's, mobilizes the need of narcissistic recognition, investment by an other, an existential project. The therapist who begins by "containing" anxiety and "mediating" the investment in the new language (Moro), even "libidinalizing" it so that Hado may find it to his liking—he who had "lost his appetite for [French] words"—is actually not a *translator*. Of course, the "transcultural clinic" practiced by Moro does have recourse to translators to facilitate the exchanges, but through the countertransference the therapist is the one who *transposes* her identification with the early mother-child lived experience into the new language of exile. To accompany the "psychical separation" from the *origin* and let "the little internal voice" (from the semiotic receptacle) express itself, which Adelia recovers in launching into writing (see Moro)—first in French, the language of the therapist, then in recovering her native Spanish and reconstructing the archaic container itself. The analyst-therapist unites with the lost plenitude (real or imaginary) borne by the mother tongue, of which the language of exile has little understanding (Spanish distinguishes between *ser* and *estar*, whereas French abrades them in the single *être*, to be). Thus, the inconsolable Consuelo finds no equivalent to the Castilian light, nor to the Castilian language. But the analyst proceeds above all to a "reanimation of associations," which is equivalent to a "psychical reanimation," by creating an interpretive speaking capable of *transposing* the sensation that is lacking into the specific genius of the second language.

However, this genius that mobilizes the *imaginary* (in the sense mentioned above) is not limited to words and concepts but draws on all the potentialities of the *discourses* (arts and letters) of national cultural textures, which arrive at a *mutual* comprehension (too easily called "universal"). It achieves this through specific translinguistic, historically solidified means, irreducible but not impermeable, then. Thus, certain languages that do not possess a verb to distinguish between *essence* and *existence* have nonetheless elaborated philosophical and aesthetic works devoted to them. The Castilian light is inimitable, but French was able to offer others to the inconsolable Consuelo, thanks to Corneille ("This darkling light that from the star descends"), Rimbaud ("O Sounds and Visions! / Departure amid new noise and affection!"), Mallarmé ("His eye, on the horizon of light, is fed / With golden galleys, beautiful as swans").[7] It's up to "me," Consuelo's analyst, to imagine and to formulate in French the light she is missing, a light she can hear, here and now, *transposed* into this language of exile that my interpretation brings into her reach. If we do not have a *Dunanso* (house for transient people) as in Burkina Faso (see Moro), this does not mean that republican hospitality is condemned to housing them in "disadvantaged suburbs," nor to "opening up" to their conventions by closing swimming pools to women. Hospitality must invent places and construct mentalities that "would signify that we owe something to the foreigner."

I therefore share with Marie Rose Moro the conviction that the *psychoanalytic relation* occupies a "unique" place (as she writes) because it is "third"—neither dominated nor dominating; and that because of this it is capable of *investing* the passage from a language of origin to a "language of separation," even to the "language of adoption" (Parvati's English). Beyond and beneath languages, the polyglot imaginary mobilizes "systems of remembering, narrative systems, mechanisms of identification or plural elaboration." It is urgent to *train go-between-analysts* ready for this embodied *transposition* of diversities, because diversities, in this third millennium, are tending to radicalize rather than get along.

But this blending (*métissage*) is not always peaceful, and aggressiveness also invades the lost container of the maternal semiotic. The transference-countertransference has to become the lightning rod against it. On the condition of not forgetting the *third*: the father of Uma (see Moro), the beautiful survivor of the Hindu Shivaist cult of the female divinity. That poor man is "frightened by this outside [Western] world," with the result that he angers Uma's mother, who in contrast would have dreamed of "acquiring" its knowledge.

I return to my young patient Paul, who, having sung and then spoken, tended to confuse the personal pronouns "I" and "you" while recounting necessarily conflictual stories. Until we found them in the tale of Pinocchio, the famous puppet with whom Paul identified. And notably in the episode where the little boy saved his father Geppetto from the jaws of the whale Monstro. "Help, Pinocchio," the father implored. "I'm coming, Papa, wait for me, don't be afraid, *I* am with *you!*" Paul replied. And he was jubilant, tirelessly repeating to me the imaginary scene and its concluding formula "I am with you, I am with you" . . . which made me laugh—made us laugh. Escape from the famous tablet, as well as from the fearful little boy engulfed in the imposing maternal, who hesitated between the "I" and the "you." From then on the "you" designated the paternal alterity, certainly in danger, but sovereign and lovable: another hero (Geppetto), and the other of the hero (Paul), whose story Paul himself told and to whom my patient spoke by saying "I" in an exchange with "you" as equals, or better as differences. The *third*, then, cornerstone of the (potentially) polyglot imaginary.

IV. Jean Vanier

Jean Vanier reminds me about the correspondence that brought us together. We pursued it aloud or in silence, we pursue it and will pursue it right to the end. I, the confirmed atheist, who claims to question the roots of Christian charity in order to transpose its cardinal *virtues* into *universal values*. He, the man of faith, whom I like to define as a "free electron," who made himself the builder of an absolute fraternity with the limits of life. I tease him, citing Voltaire and Freud; I mistrust the compassion-based "taking charge" that infantilizes; I fear the deviations that brew beneath the immaculate manners of the beautiful souls. I advocate accompanying "hearts" with the advances of science and technology. I recommend the initiation of the staff into psychoanalysis, I criticize "integration" by work alone, and I advocate a true "integration" at school, in business, and in the entire social sphere.

He replies with the Gospel, Shakespeare, and John Paul II, defends his *tenderness* for the most vulnerable by reminding me of Aristotle on this subject, and teaches me about his life in a community with those who seem struck with inferiority. By crisscrossing our differences, which are sure of themselves and proud of it, we try to adjust them to the ambitious "republican worksite" of President Chirac, who wants nothing less than to "change the look" upon the disabled. An unexpected complicity is established between us. The very respectable founder of L'Arche, frequently nominated for the Nobel Peace Prize, becomes, in the course of our epistolary exchanges, "My Jean," and an indispensable landmark in the urgencies of life.

With this new missive prolonging our book, *Leur regard perce nos ombres*, which appeared in 2011,[8] Jean Vanier weaves together once more the links between his life and his work that gave birth to L'Arche: a social practice and a total engagement in what is called "living differently," Faith and Light, at Lourdes, in Morocco . . .

As in his numerous publications (among which my favorites are *Tears of Silence: A Meditation* and, with François-Xavier Maigre, *A Cry Is Heard: My Path to Peace*),[9] Vanier detailed with simplicity his experiences with the intimate-extimate, while exposing the great themes that vulnerability has now imposed on the philosophy of "public health": deficit and difference, the life of relationships, alternative paths . . . However, in the minute, patient, and attentive energy of this letter-reportage, I understand that these innovating "thematics" are being transported by something that surpasses them. Transcended by faith? Certainly, but how?

I had to go to Trosly-Breuil to conceive and name this ontological impact. I'll call it *Jean's joy*. He himself makes no secret of it. "I await in tranquility and joy," my Jean writes. A special joy, full of systematic oscillations with the elementary particles of human dignity, which it recognizes, shares, and celebrates—at the limits of life, with persons diversely polydisabled, bodies without movements, mute anguishes or senseless cries. Everyone, *friends of L'Arche*, as much as Jean and the caregiving personnel, enjoy their meals together, they are at home, a family, a house. This copresence doesn't resorb the deficit, it transforms powerlessness and suffering into dignity. Jean, or the joy of elementary dignity.

Medical-psychological care, like legal and social arrangements, could not *act* without this collusion, a prerequisite sanctuary. I think about the "interveners" living with their *friends* at Trosly-Breuil: difficult to recruit, a majority of them young foreigners, Canadian, German, and Belgian, in "civic service," or who are there by "choice" and "conviction," intimate and unscathed.

We will need a lot of conviction, delicacy, and perseverance for this joy constitutive of dignity to spread. And for the professions of assistance to be renewed and validated, against the present currents of transhumanism.

My Jean will not read this last letter that I send him today. I would like his joy to be my compass, until the end.

J.K.

NOTES

1. Jean Vanier departed from us as I was writing this reply (September 10, 1928 to May 7, 2019).

2. Julia Kristeva, "Liberty, Equality, Fraternity and . . . Vulnerability," in *Hatred and Forgiveness*, trans. Jeanine Herman (New York: Columbia University Press, 2010), 29–45; *La Haine et le pardon* (Paris: Fayard, 2005), 95–118.

3. Charles Baudelaire, "Meditation," *Selected Poems of Charles Baudelaire*, trans. Geoffrey Wagner (New York: Grove, 1974). https://fleursdumal.org/poem/321.

4. Nancy L. Eiesland, *The Disabled God: Toward a Liberatory Theology of Disability* (Nashville: Abingdon, 1994).

5. Martin Heidegger, *Die Kategorien- und Bedetungslehre des Duns Scotus* (Ann Arbor: University of Michigan Library, 1916). Hannah Arendt, *The Human Condition* (Chicago: University of Chicago Press, 1998) and, for a development of these ideas, *The Life of the Mind*, vol. II, "Willing" (New York: Harcourt, Brace, Jovanovich, 1978).

6. See Julia Kristeva, "The Inexpressible Child," *New Maladies of the Soul*, trans. Ross Guberman (New York: Columbia University Press, 1995), 103–12; "L'Enfant au sens indicible," *Les Nouvelles Maladies de l'âme* (Paris: Fayard, 1993), 157–70.

7. Pierre Corneille, *The Cid*, trans. John Cairncross (Harmondsworth: Penguin, 1975), act IV, sc. 3, 88; Arthur Rimbaud, "Departure," in *Illuminations*, trans. John Ashbery (New York: Norton, 2011), 51; Stéphane Mallarmé, "Windows," in *Collected Poems: A Bilingual Edition*, trans. Henry Weinfield (Los Angeles: University of California Press, 1994), 11.

8. Julia Kristeva and Jean Vanier, *Leur regard perce nos ombres* (Paris: Fayard, 2011).

9. Jean Vanier, *Tears of Silence: A Meditation* (Toronto: Griffin House, 1970); Jean Vanier and François-Xavier Maigre, *A Cry is Heard: My Path to Peace* (London: Darton, Longman and Todd, 2018).

33

Cecilia Sjöholm

FROM DENIAL TO FORGIVENESS: KRISTEVA, ARENDT, AND RADICALIZATION

I. Kristeva, Arendt, and the Radical Subject

Few thinkers of our times have been able to pinpoint with the accuracy of Kristeva the change of psychic landscapes. She has identified abjection, melancholy, and narcissism as inherent in the twentieth-century panoply of symptoms. In our view, she has with the same accuracy pointed to *radicalization* as one of the most troubling psychic dispositions of our times. The theme is topical. Radicalization, today, is spreading in multiple forms. It appears not only in forms of fascism, Islamic terror, and other kinds of political or religious extremism but also in a variety of fanatical movements, be they separatist, essentialist, or nationalist. Kristeva has always recognized the phenomenon, not only in her later work but also in her earlier writings on abjection, antisemitism, and misogyny. In what way has Kristeva produced a theory of a radicalized subjectivity? How do figures of radicalization turn up in her present and past writings? How may she help us reread another great thinker of radicalization, Arendt, adding further elements to a theory of radicalized subjectivity? These are the questions in focus in this essay.

Reading Arendt and Kristeva together on radicalization brings out another theme: what takes us beyond radicalization? What might produce an afterness or dissolution of the aggressiveness in the forces involved? The most engaging perspective that Kristeva found in Arendt is that of *life*: an all-dominating force, countering the psychic death observed in Eichmann. The contrast between Arendt's philosophy of life and the presence of death in her times is startling. We may learn from it, for we cannot understand the full extent of the brokenness of our own times unless we go to the ends that produce radicalized subjectivity, on the one hand, and surpass it, on the other. As one enters into definitions and explanations of radicalization, many pitfalls turn up. It is easy to simplify or reduce the mechanisms. The concept of radicalization is used in discourses pitting religious and political beliefs against one another, for instance, anti-Muslim attitudes. We must negotiate not only the terrorist wings of rightwing extremism and Islamism but also the radicalized violent reactions on social media, now all but normalized. Kristeva has not written much on the phenomenon of radicalization as such. My argument finds its origin in a single essay, "Interpreting Radical Evil," which nonetheless fits into her oeuvre.[1] It poses questions about adolescence, brutality, and symptoms of malaise in contemporary society, about belief systems, secularism, and religion, but also about fragile subjectivities in more general terms, and the possibility of finding a means for the "cure" of radicalized subjects in psychoanalysis, literature, and thought.

I focus here on the relation between radicalization and abjection in Kristeva, asking: did she identify a radicalized form of subjectivity in her readings of Céline, and how? What can be traced from those readings that is useful for understanding radicalization today? I place her work alongside another study of radicalization *avant la letter*: Arendt on Eichmann.[2] Arendt is one of the three "female geniuses" chosen by Kristeva for a series of intellectual portraits.[3] The choice may appear curious, unlike that of Klein, whose theory of the object fits many of Kristeva's theorizations on abjection, melancholy, and transference. Arendt does not appear to be an easy friendship. She was not only weary of psychoanalysis but absolutely averse to it. However, aspects of her philosophy lie closer to psychoanalysis than she herself recognized. Her analysis of Eichmann helps elucidate the fact that the Holocaust was made possible by people like him, who represented a radicalized subjectivity. Both Kristeva and Arendt identify the phenomenon of radicalization as adherence to an exclusive belief system and the willingness to use violence to reach ideological goals and to destroy those who oppose the belief system. Kristeva has a psychoanalytic viewpoint, Arendt's is philosophical. Certainly the subjects in their work come from different ends of history as well as the social and political scale. The radicalized subject does not come in only one form and shape. Recently, Kristeva has considered vulnerable and marginalized teenagers, while Arendt analyzed a mass murderer in power. There is, in Kristeva's examples, a possibility of working through as long as there is psychic life. In the case of Eichmann, however, psychic life is shut down and rejected. The comparison becomes interesting because of their differences.

Kristeva's method of understanding subjectivity helps us elucidate the psychoanalytic implications of Arendt's thoughts, pointing to important connections between psychoanalysis and politics. Kristeva's work on radicalization and radical evil and Arendt's work on ideology and terror in the twentieth century identify core challenges at the heart of a contemporary, authoritarian political scene. While Arendt analyzed totalitarianism through its propaganda machine and its shutting down of open spaces, rather than in psychical terms, there is an affinity when it comes to observation, diagnosis, and concern. Psychoanalysis is not a hermeneutics of course. It does not attempt to understand, nor to offer any credible explanation of cause and effect. Instead, it offers an analysis of what cannot be explained in sociological, psychological, political, or cultural terms. Kristeva's way of analyzing radicalization points to what psychoanalysis can do. Arendt indicates what psychoanalysis cannot do, what its limits are—when there is no cure at the level of the subject. Both bring us important suggestions for understanding radicalized subjectivity today.

II. What Is Radicalization? Kristeva's Work

From a sociological and political standpoint, radicalization can be understood as "a dynamic, multi-staged and multifaceted phenomenon that occurs at the interaction of individual vulnerabilities . . . with an encouraging environment and is therefore always context-specific."[4] A subject becomes radicalized because at some level—economically, socially, or psychically—it is vulnerable. Moreover, a radicalized subject is not isolated but inserted in a context that encourages a given belief. As we know, political or religious organizations may provide such an environment. Although we are prone to consider a radicalized subject a terrorist, this is not necessarily the case. Scholars of political extremism and radicalization in sociology and political theory, for instance, debate the relation between radicalization and terrorism, radical beliefs and acts of violence, individual convictions and political contexts, and so on.[5] The concept of radicalization designates a wide diagnosis of multiple groups and subjects.

Kristeva thematizes radicalization in "Interpreting Radical Evil," and it has been discussed in her interviews.[6] The essay emanates from a well-known debate in Europe—how are we to deal with radicalized young adolescents? What are the terms of a practice through which we can stop malignant cycles of marginalization and discontent? Kristeva's essay stems from clinical work engaging with adolescents and thematized in her seminar on "The Need to Believe."[7] The clinical example is a girl with serious anorexia, prone to radical Islamism. Kristeva describes the difficulties in dealing with the girl's lack of investment in the psychoanalyst. She seems incapable of forming bonds. The therapist encounters a person whose sense of the other and of the self appear to be drained. It is at this point, however, that the work can begin: a "restructuring," as Kristeva puts it, which occurs through an "analytic multicultural psychotherapeutic" consultation; that is, with a nonjudgmental group of people from different backgrounds and through a reconnection to literature and language. Slowly, the girl begins to emerge from a violent self-destructiveness towards an ability to form bonds. She engages in literature, theater, and conversation with others.

Radicalization in this case is analyzed in terms of an "ideality disorder" that in itself is characteristic of and endemic to adolescence, a phase that typically comes to an end. Under certain conditions, however, it prevails in a subject as an inability to achieve satisfactions or solutions, taking a turn towards destructiveness. The subject seeking absolute satisfaction, though incapable of achieving it, resolves the tensions "by destroying everything that is not this satisfaction, abolishing the border between self and other, inside and outside, good and evil."[8] Desubjectivation and deobjectivation follow the impossibility of attaching to an object: "only the death drive triumphs, the malignancy of evil."[9] The question is how to move from the impulses of aggression to the acceptance of and fulfillment in a community that may be faulty and incapable of providing complete satisfaction but still provides a context for attachments.

To Kristeva, the secularization of modern society may aggrandize the latent problems of adolescent malaise, cutting short the need to believe that seeks a sense of meaning and context. Religious society responds more readily to the need of idealization, and religious symbols may offer an unexpected appeal to the young. Secular societies even seem to aggrandize the lure of religious extremism, which involves a possible sense of omnipotence: religious extremism may erase the respect for taboos, rules, and norms. It speaks to subjects that have not yet fully internalized the laws and limits of the social world. Extremist forms of religion may speak powerfully to adolescents prone to an ideality disorder. The drive gets open access, allowing for powerful motions of destructivity to have free play. Here Kristeva posits a kind of constitutive split in the subject regarding the relation to an authoritative symbolic order of norms and laws, giving rise to an ambivalent relation to the symbolic. On the one hand, there is a need for a strong symbolic order of laws and limits through a religious belief; on the other, the symbolic order that offers itself in the social context of everyday life in secular society is defiled and ruined.

However, it is impossible to "illuminate" the logic of radicalization though a cultural, religious, or social and political analysis alone. Something in a radicalized subject withdraws from such an explanation. The radicalized subject is characterized by its split between the imaginary ego ideal and the social self, so that radicalization cannot be countered by those analyses. The subject lives in the very split between reverence for a strong symbolic order and the enjoyment that comes with defilement of the symbolic. This means that radicalization is not only about religion or ideology. It lives off a split that only psychoanalysis can demonstrate. A malady of contemporary society, it is not an altogether new phenomenon. Islamist extremism is in focus in "Interpreting Radical Evil," but Kristeva makes clear that radicalization is found in a variety of contemporary ideologies and religions. Her *oeuvre* points to the analysis of other modes of radicalization, like antisemitism, fascism, and nationalism. Current modes of the aggressive domination of the death drive—rationalized into fanatical and exclusionary systems of belief—have elements in common with earlier forms of radicalization. It is not the laws of religion as such that are the problem, but, rather, *the status of the symbolic in the life of the subject*. This topic is much explored in Kristeva's writings since the 1980s, in a terminology preceding the contemporary theorization of radicalization. From her earlier writing on abjection through the identification of the "stranger in ourselves" to the recent writings on adolescence, she moves towards the analysis of a split and vulnerable subject.

Kristeva's work on radicalization resonates, then, with her analysis of abjection: a phenomenon of Western culture returning on many levels. She analyzed its recurrence in Céline, an antisemitic French writer active before and after World War II. Céline desires an unbroken symbolic that would substitute for a faulty and frail society.[10] Lacking a secure self and identity, the voice of abjection is heard in him through "horror, death, madness, orgy, outlaws, war, the feminine threat, the horrendous delights of love, disgust, and fright."[11] He reveals a void of values that has been discussed with regard to nihilism as loss of faith, social texture, and a sense of meaning.[12] One can also note that it is the very instability of the law itself—whether deriving from God, social norms, the state, or family matters—that provokes uncontainable aggression. Abjection in Céline is conjoined with the hatred of a law that is both restraining and weak—a failing paternal law. One could translate this into frustration with a society unable to uphold norms and secure values. He wants to replace the impotent laws with another law, a promise of completion and fullness, a "mystic positivity,"[13] "an idea, a harsh doctrine, a diamond-like doctrine, one even more awesome than the others."[14] Such a law would remedy the frailty of the failing and fragmented subject. Céline's aggression is directed towards his own country, his fellow beings—and himself. He incarnates a form of "ideality disorder." Whether coming from a radicalized Islamic or rightwing individual, someone who is secularly racist or passionately religious, the hatred of Jews, women, homosexuals, or nonbelievers is a symptom of a frail subject. It expresses a radicalized form of hatred for which there is no real satisfaction. To the radicalized subject, an exaggerated hatred is easily reversed into an exaggerated love—of the nation, the people, the flag, God. Exaltation is the mirror image of abjection. Céline longs for a love that is hard and diamond-like, yet that harshness needs to be conquered, achieved, acquired through violence. Here the dream of a "mystic positivity" is a symptom of abjection. It is saturated with the Kleinian death drive and rationalized as ideology.

Fascism and Nazism are discourses of systematic abjection for Kristeva. Abjection in this sense is a sign of radicalization. The same could be said of religious extremism. The systematic and ritual exclusion of real or symbolic dirt—women, foreigners, nonbelievers—is conjoined to ideologies and religions that express hatred, rejection, and disgust. Abjection and its conjoint symptom of radicalization may appeal to a subject that experiences dissolution and fragmentation.

III. Arendt's Unwitting "Psycho" Analysis

The wave of radicalization globally under sway may appear new, yet similar modes have appeared earlier in modern history. Arendt's analysis of Eichmann and *The Origins of Totalitarianism* contain suggestions of what characterizes a radicalized subject. To Kristeva, Arendt sees the need for further analysis of the psychology of the masses, for instance, yet does not perform this work herself.[15] Arendt recognizes a sadomasochistic element in the authoritarian subject, but her unwillingness to see the particularity in Freud's notion of psychic life makes her unable to use psychoanalytic modes of analysis, even where they appear needed.[16] The most pressing issue of radical evil is to be found in the machinery of totalitarian regimes rather than individual subjects. However, with the help of Kristeva and psychoanalysis, one may argue that Arendt's analysis of Eichmann indicates how radicalization works at the level of subjectivity.

Arendt herself is convinced that philosophy is abler than psychoanalysis to communicate across borders of time and space, precisely through its ability to recognize their limits. This differentiates philosophy from the pseudosciences of "Marxian materialism, or psychoanalysis, or logistics, or semantics, or whatnot" that believe they uncover truths outside of historical movements.[17] She is disdainful of psychoanalysis because of its ambition to uncover "a more original reality" beyond that of the common world of publicness.[18] In psychoanalysis the representations of consciousness have no other validity than that of witnessing "repression" or "sublimation." Psychoanalysis relies on universal and ahistorical notions of consciousness. "In its working back toward the unconscious, psychoanalysis penetrates to that very realm over which human beings do not have, and never have had, control, i.e., to the realm of the ahistorical."[19] This makes the "reality" of psychoanalysis alien to thought, a condition from which it can never recover, unlike, for instance, sociology, whose work with the collective subject and its historicity can reach some notion of the relation between thought and the real. Psychoanalysis denies the multiplicity of expressions and appearances that would otherwise influence the human mind. Arendt therefore refers to psychoanalysis as an "iceberg" theory.[20] It undermines any notion of ethical responsibility in attempting to find explanations and causes beyond the actual act.[21] Psychoanalysis is a "pseudoscience" that mistakes distortions, ugliness, and meanness for an inner kind of truth.[22] The "iceberg theory" makes man into a kind of void with no real power over his capacity to think, judge, or act.

Arendt's rebuttal of psychoanalysis seems total. However, Kristeva sees in it a hidden relation to psychoanalysis. Arendt understands psychoanalysis as looking only at appearances, whereas it is looking at a dialectic between the appearing and the unappearing, just as Arendt does. To Kristeva, Arendt looks not only at what appears in the world but also, in her book on totalitarianism for instance, at what is made not to appear. In this sense, there is a paradoxical affinity between Arendt and Freud: "both inscribing, although in different ways, the hidden in the apparent, the repressed in the forbidden."[23] This secret and unacknowledged relation presents itself in Arendt's work on Eichmann. A reading that focuses on the figure of denial in Eichmann will indicate how Kristeva may help us understand Arendt's theory of a radicalized subjectivity.

IV. Arendt and the Split of the Radicalized Subject

Denial is a key concept in psychoanalysis, recognized early on by Freud. Today the concept and phenomenon are so prevalent it has developed its own –ism, "denialism."[24] In psychoanalytic theory it refers also to *disavowal* and goes back to Freud's theory of negation, which identifies a fundamental split in the subject's sense of reality.[25] If I say "it was not my mother in the dream," the signifier "mother" makes something stick—this is the core of its "real." Thus Freud asserts a kind of realist aspect of the unconscious that also comes out in dreams: dreams cannot say "no," everything is simply there. He demonstrates, too, how denial works in language: if I speak about my mother, she sticks to my language. She asserts her insistence in my psychic life through the signifier, which can be negated but cannot disappear. Denial in the sense of disavowal may result in a series of symptoms. The body, through its affects, flickering moves, unwilling gestures and convulsions, gives witness to the kind of detours that the "real" can take. The symptom points to the "detours" of the unconscious. Something approaching the truth of the unconscious demonstrates its place through the symptom of denial.

Arendt's dismissal of psychoanalysis and unwillingness to conduct any open form of self-analysis may itself appear to be a kind of denial—as Kristeva notes when Arendt uses Rahel Varnhagen to mediate her own painful experiences with so-called assimilation.[26] Certainly, Arendt is uninterested in interpreting her life or mode of thinking through a psychoanalytic grid. However, denials tend to be symptoms that come in distinct modes of conversion, for instance projections, or thoughtlessness. Denial or disavowal in this sense is not a feature of Arendt's relation to psychoanalysis. She dismisses it on intellectual not personal grounds. One could imagine psychoanalysis having provided a ground for her analysis of "radical evil"—the topic of Kristeva's notion of radicalization as well as her own. As Bernstein has argued, to Arendt, the ability to encounter evil can never be completed or finished; it is a never-ending work and a process.[27]

Kristeva's reading of Arendt evokes a dimension that may appear provoking. In approaching *The Origins of Totalitarianism*, she gives special attention to its third part, "Totalitarianism," where Arendt considers the ease with which the inhabitant of a totalitarian state is informed by propaganda, ideology, and racism. To Kristeva, Arendt touches on problems that remain acute today but does not develop them further. Questions arise: if we do not return to the traditional laws of religion and their capacity to both interdict and forgive, how are we to steer individual and collective desire past the challenges of melancholic destruction, manic fanaticism, and a tyrannical paranoia?[28] Kristeva sees with stupefaction that Arendt, while clearly introducing these problems, simply leaves them behind. The issues have come further into focus twenty years after the publication of Kristeva's book on Arendt. Whereas societies of totalitarianism erected pseudoscience into natural laws (in the form of racism, for instance), radicalization thrives at the outskirts of political and social reality, collapsing anything from racism to religious commands into natural laws. Recalling that the law and how it structures subjectivities are at the core of radicalization, we need not only the law as foundation of the state, but a law that both guides desire and prevents violence—one not merely judicial but belonging to the structuring of psychic life.[29] It can come from psychoanalysis, but also from religion, social structures, or collective norms.

Arendt's *Eichmann in Jerusalem: A Report on the Banality of Evil* finds the process of radicalization in Eichmann less in aggression and abjection than in a denial of psychic life as such. The symptoms are the renunciation of thought, blankness, the inability to feel, judge, and act. These appear in her idea of how totalitarianism functions. Thought and action are separate processes, freedom and democratic values having to do with the way thinking works. Totalitarian movements wish to cut short and undermine the processes of thought in individual subjects. Eichmann is a subject incarnating a denial of thought—a psyche that is dead and inactive, with a language with no relation to memories, emotions, or events. The chilling observations of the banal in Eichmann belong to Arendt's most famous, debated, and misunderstood propositions. Her stance on Eichmann, although not absolving him from responsibility, has been interpreted as if she thinks that he thinks he was merely following orders.[30] However, to Arendt, banality in this context is not a benign concept. Eichmann's language is not one of extremist conviction, but one devoid of meaning. In this one can trace a feature of "radical evil" that is no less fearful than the conviction of extremism. His bureaucratic language helped produce a foreclosure of thought. "The longer one listened to him, the more obvious it became that his inability to speak was closely connected with an inability to *think*."[31] He was unable to perceive "the words and the presence of others."[32] In other words, Eichmann's mind was mute.

Arendt's analysis resorts unwittingly to the psychoanalytic logic of denial in the sense of disavowal.[33] To Freud, in disavowal reality is both denied and recognized through a fundamental splitting of the ego.[34] We deny not only our participation in an event but its occurrence. Although we know something is happening, we deny it has ever taken place.[35] Arendt *identifies* denial without conceptualizing it—Eichmann is unable to grapple with the reality of his own participation in the Holocaust. He not only denies the event but shuts down his psychic involvement in any reality whatsoever. Arendt recognizes another feature in his behavior: he is a person all too willing to submit, an individual who enthusiastically embraces imaginary laws.[36] Eichmann did not deny the call of conscience—in fact he was obsessed with it.[37] This obsession gives him great satisfaction. At the same time, he fails to recognize the necessary rootedness of any sense of conscience in a *fundamental prohibition*—that of killing the other. Thus Arendt, too, sees the diagnosis of radicalization in relation to the law—law that appears too weak. Moreover, there is, for Eichmann, a gain in shutting down thought. Thoughtlessness as the radical denial of thought was a way for him to maximize pleasure, a feature of radicalization if anything. Brunner observes it conjoined with the collective narcissism that allowed the pathology-ideology of Nazism to prevail: "obliterating human plurality by the denigration, devaluation and dehumanization of others," and producing "their control, domination or extermination."[38] Arendt's analysis of the mechanisms of radicalization in Eichmann suggests a similar perspective.

At this point, we discern a decisive difference in the analysis of radicalization in Arendt and Kristeva, one conditioned by history and ideology no doubt but also by the kind of subjectivities they approach. To Kristeva, a radicalized subject is typically marked by an ideality disorder. The norms and laws upholding society are negated and attacked, and an order of a completely different kind upheld in its place. The split between the ideal and the real contributes to the release of aggressive impulses, often attacking the self. Arendt sees Eichmann's denial of psychic life as total. She, too, conceives of a split: between the negation of psychic life altogether and the enjoyment of following orders. For both, the radicalized subject lives between the idealization of a punishing symbolic order and the denial of reality. The difference is that Kristeva finds vulnerability in the subject, while with Eichmann there is no vulnerability—only the other, disavowed, is vulnerable. In denying the prohibition to kill, Eichmann undoes the most fundamental law of psychic life altogether.

Arendt and Kristeva point, respectively, to the limits of a psychoanalytic and a philosophical perspective. To Arendt, psychoanalysis cannot explain the void in Eichmann's mind. As we have seen, however, Freud's account of denial demonstrates how a psychic depletion is possible. To Kristeva, "thought" does not carry a quality of its own—the subject devoid of loving psychic investments cannot be cured by thought. However, to Arendt, thought is the psychic life of the mind all in all and, as such, cannot be reduced to desires and affective investments. Between them, however, Arendt and Kristeva demonstrate the need and the limits of our understanding of a radicalized subject. Without openings in terms of vulnerabilities and without a language that gives meaning, there is no cure.

V. Faith or Unfaith

According to Kristeva, psychoanalysis and religion represent forms of law that are necessary for society to prevent radicalization. In psychoanalysis the law institutes the name of the father or the function of a founding prohibition that prohibits the free rein of the drive. The founding laws do not only institute fundamental prohibitions, however. They propagate the need for some kind of faith that may serve to give meaning. Kristeva has done a lot of work here, particularly on the function of transference as a cultural mode of creation.[39] In her account, the experience of meaning in relations, literature, philosophy, and religion can be looked at through its origination in primary relations. The experience of meaning originates in love as a transference relation, a loving relation to an object or, perhaps, the figure of an object beginning to take shape. Such a relation is irreducible to the sexualized modes of desire that are related to the Oedipus complex proper.

As for Arendt, a major reason behind her disdain for psychoanalysis lies in her idea that it analyzes emotions. This, however, is not the case. To Lacan, psychoanalysis must resist the urge to fall into a discourse that deals with affects and emotions or that makes normative claims about the "content" of the unconscious.[40] Emotions and experiences of "good" and "bad" belong to the imaginary and thus to a sphere that psychoanalysis must traverse. This is not altogether different from Arendt's viewpoint on the duty of philosophy.

Arendt regards banalization as a destructive aspect of modern life. Rousseau had already reacted in his *Confessions* against society's "perversion of the human heart" and the "leveling demands" that have come to dominate the social sphere.[41] A similar critique is offered by sociologist Illouz.[42] In this light, one might see Kristeva's work as a reaction against a narrow view of emotions. Revaluing the place of affects and emotions in psychoanalysis, she has reclaimed their role. Love, emotions, and affects belong to the domain psychoanalysis must study and interpret. They are not easily banalized: they belong to the sphere of meaning, be it in the form of transference or love, abjection or hatred.

Here, Kristeva and Arendt represent opposed positions. Their view of faith has something to do with it. To Arendt, faith contributes to fanaticism. To Kristeva, faith may contribute to the dissolution of fanaticism. This position—defined here in a much simplified manner—demands to be nuanced and explained. It is important to recognize that a certain form of banalization of emotions may have paved the way for radicalization. When affects and emotions lose their value for the evolving of psychic life and become aspects of ideology, radical separations between good and bad, good and evil, make their way into a social organization. As Kristeva has shown, psychoanalysis, together with literature and philosophy, may present us with a certain protection against a society of aggression by pointing to the complex aspects of emotions and affects. Psychoanalysis opens up the possibility of access to the meaning of emotions, which must be negotiated in societies where emotions are denied or have become commodities. Radicalization may integrate emotions and affects into the service of "radical evil." Their development needs to be integrated into the renegotiation of the life of the subject; they are necessary for new forms of meaning to develop.

In Kristeva's perception, love, conceived as a precocious experience paving the way for a sense of meaning in adult life, is a relation of transference, although it must not solely be conceived in psychoanalytic terms. It is, rather, a subject presenting itself for an object, *parousia*. It is narcissism replaced by *Einfühlung* with a primary object—a term used by Freud to designate precocious bonds in the life of the child. Kristeva develops its meaning: *Einfühlung* is identification with a so-called metaphorical object, not a partial object like a breast. Rather, love is directed towards a metaphorical object that is not a person proper either, but a sense of direction or meaning. *Einfühlung* therefore has less to do with object-relation theory than with the soul and spiritual love. It is "a form, a structure, or an agency (rather than a person)" that "helps to bring about primary stabilization of the subject through its enduring character . . . it both encourages and hinders the disintegrative and aggressive agitation of the instincts."[43] The metaphoric instance of *Einfühlung* is not the mother, but, rather, the third party that the mother respects as coming between her and the child. It serves as a protection against the mother as phallic and devouring. The child identifies itself with the mother's desire for another, with desire as such. That is to say, love is conceived not in terms of desire for an object but in the movement of transposition, the movement towards another body, another love, another capacity to feel.[44] This is a fragile state. Religion may play the role of instituting a metaphorical possibility of *Einfühlung*.

There is no guarantee that the experience of love will institute any belief in the law or in justice, right, or social context. *Einfühlung* is the experience of transferential love as a metaphorical mode of speech.[45] But it must also present a law—which is both promising and prohibiting. This means the void that the law of prohibition institutes must be supplemented by the possibilities of metaphorical identification. Fascism and misogyny like Céline's are a result of the lack not just of law but also of love. In psychoanalytic theory, the law is not merely castrating, it institutes a paternal function that allows for the relation to an object—another human being—to arise at all. It is this precocious relation that is experienced as an identificatory form of love and that can produce a sense of meaning.

We have seen that Arendt does not believe in psychoanalysis. Although some have seen psychoanalytic dimensions in her notion of love of the world, which can be read as a form of affective investment,[46] she dismisses love at a political level. Her suspicion of it is an intellectual, political standpoint. Emotions can be abused in the political domain. Love is never to be used for political purposes.[47] Scholem complains emphatically of the "coldness" in Arendt's report on the Eichmann trial. She is unable to show love for "her own people" and writes in a cold tone. She acts not like a Jew but like a leftist European intellectual, unable to appreciate what it means to belong to a collective emotionally.[48] His accusation is famous, pointing to the massive critique she encountered in Israel after the report's publication. Her response is equally famous: I cannot love an aspect of myself that is merely a given feature; to be Jewish is a given fact; it is meaningless to love a feature of oneself, or for that matter, to simply love oneself. More importantly, the love of a people is meaningless at best. At worst, in a political context, it becomes destructive.[49] Without appealing to the force of the drive (a concept she never uses) her analysis is nonetheless similar. The love of a leader or a people can be turned into aggression against an outsider or intruder. This occurred in Germany in the 1930s and 1940s through the logic of antisemitism.

Kristeva also notes Arendt's refusal to comply with the religious proponents of her time. Arendt sees both the refusal of and the need for religion behind the fanaticism of totalitarianism—a historic event that is unique for its kind.[50] Many fanatical nationalist movements are fueled by a religious perversion.[51] What is interesting to Kristeva is that Arendt's notion of politics is inscribed in a space that is both utopic and necessary: "post-Christian—or perhaps trans-Christian."[52] Arendt elaborates the problems that Kristeva keeps negotiating herself: rejecting the need for a harsh law while avoiding a naïve vision of a society with no need of defining limits. Arendt dismisses psychoanalysis, faith, and emotions, yet deals with the same kind of problems as Kristeva: the danger of radicalization emanates from a society that is both weak in the bonds it installs and authoritarian in the laws it imposes.

VI. The Need for Literature

The key to the creative aspect of Arendt's philosophy, for Kristeva, lies in its closeness to life, which does not imply a cult of birth and maternity. The female genius is dedicated not simply to life as the process of becoming but to *the life* as narrative—*bios*—in Arendt. She displaces politics from representation and governance towards an affirmation of an embodied being whose life, actions, and stories are measurable only against the negative totality of future lives and generations. In this, she conceives of a community that is bound to the future, the past, and the present. Kristeva's celebration of the "female genius" is curious in many ways, celebrating the work of women apparently indifferent to the politics of feminism. To Arendt, feminism is not wrong—simply not a major political movement. There is an element in her work that earns her the title of "female" genius, for she affirms the maternal sphere, if we take the maternal as a metaphor not for nursing but for a philosophical kind of care—care of the singular dimension of life.

Kristeva's appellation "female genius" makes the maternal dimension of the genius into something that goes beyond experience. It offers a point of metaphorical transference, of precocious identification beyond universalism, representation, and affectation. One may thus talk of an experience of meaning rather than identification proper—it is not a question of sexual identity. Kristeva's work on the female genius foregrounds an experience of meaning as an alternative to a political feminism of representation. Psychoanalysis, reading, philosophy, and the creation of art in various forms carry a potential for creating meaning in a cultural environment where, otherwise, meaning appears absent. In this sense, they carry a potential for countering modes of radicalization. Psychoanalysis, literature, and philosophy may identify and pursue a practice that is important not only to the individual but to society at large.

As Kristeva notes, towards the end of her life Arendt inquired into the functions of taste and aesthetic judgment as the basis for a new form of communality based on the futural temporality of forgiveness rather than the endpoint of a tribunal.[53] To Kristeva, Arendtian judgment requires a subject capable of judging. One may be unable to judge because of a politically threatening situation. The subject may then be altogether compromised, even unable to represent, or to figure the vulnerability on which social bonds must be built.[54] Both thinkers see the unhealthy worship of death, whether in the form of totalitarianism or radicalization, as the most direct threat against any principle of life.[55] There is certainly the question of post-radicalization, a need for healing forgiveness, socially, politically, and individually, and both have searched for discourses of a healing forgiveness outside of religious faith. Kristeva argues in "Interpreting Radical Evil" that literature may carry a potential for reconciliation. Despite her own atheism, a discourse of healing and forgiveness prevailed in Arendt, one born, above all, through the concept of natality—a metaphor that associates to a certain notion of maternity. To Kristeva, Arendt's natality is politically poignant because it can be linked to forgiveness and promise. It institutes a new relation to time that makes possible new beginnings, revolts, and revolutions.[56] Beginnings are in focus for Kristeva in *Revolution in Poetic Language*, *In the Beginning Was Love*, and *Intimate Revolt*, to name a few. For her, the maternal position connected with natality is one of productivity, a kind of philosophy of life. To her, Arendt's notion of natality both affirms time and implies the affirmation of a primary alterity that makes metaphor possible. The capacity to "move from standpoint to standpoint"—the Arendtian formula for judgment—points less to empathy than to making thought possible as such.[57] In this sense, natality corresponds not so much to maternity as to a secular notion of faith. Clearly, to Arendt—as shown in her letters with Jaspers—radical evil has become too radical, superseding any possible understanding of the human mind.[58] But natality remains. It signifies an inexhaustible capacity to act and create anew, surpassing the notion of the individual, or community for that matter, and coming close to a semireligious notion of faith. To Kristeva, Arendt—despite her lack of religion—is a woman of God after all, although this God comes in the guise of *Menschenverstand*, human reason.[59]

Kristeva's writings on religion and her work on psychoanalytic transference demonstrate the need for a secular notion of faith. For her, one may trace a similar need in the relation to narrative in Arendt, whose thought implies an inexhaustible link, still to be explored, between natality, new beginnings, and narratives. Narrative links "the destinies of *life* . . . and *politics*: narrative conditions the duration and the immortality of the work of art; but it also accompanies, as historical narrative, the life of the *polis*."[60] Narrative is not reducible to literature, yet literature is a language that actualizes *Einfühlung*, encompassing a metaphoric transposition that makes possible meaning and forgiveness. Arendt and Kristeva share the belief in the capacity of literature to enliven the mind, allowing thought to engage in a social and political reality that does not worship death and destruction.

Between Past and Future makes clear that literature is "thought."[61] Moreover, in the *Denktagebücher* poetic language is speaking *with*. Thought proper strives after a certain congruence with itself, and to accommodate the other in such a way that discord is replaced with differentiation. In *The Life of the Mind*, the thinking ego becomes a two-in-one.[62] Literature may evoke a voice that takes "the standpoint of somebody else," an internalized presence of alterity that "assures us of the reality of the world and of ourselves," and so guides our sense of the real.[63] Such standpoints and alterities are rarely full representations, more often hints of encroachments that appear through poetic sounding. This sense of the real has been cast off in Eichmann's testimony, which offers a dead language of bureaucracy.

To conclude, many have pointed to the moments where Arendt falls short in showing the consequences of her arguments on the forms of radical evil and the denial of thought, not least in her report on Eichmann.[64] Nevertheless, the mechanisms of denial she observed are no less important now, as radicalization spreads in multiple forms. Today the radicalized subject finds a more elaborate analysis in Kristeva. For her, what matters most is not what Arendt fails to do in the domain of psychoanalysis, it is her work on the possibilities of forgiveness and reconciliation, not with evil as such, or figures like Eichmann, but for a secularized society at large. This returns us to the metaphorical dimension of literature, for both Arendt and Kristeva return to the language of natality and of *Einfühlung*. Whether choosing the route to faith, transference, and emotions, like Kristeva, or the path to judgment, like Arendt, literature retains its power. To Kristeva, literature incorporates a transferential relation to a metaphorical object, embodying a sense of meaning through language and imagination as well as emotions and affects. To Arendt, literature promotes a capacity to "move from standpoint to standpoint," to engage in the reflections of imagination, and inhabit new perspectives and points of view.

In sum, as a thinker of what is needed in time, in our own time, by engaging with radicalization Kristeva has approached a topic that is both new and old. There is perhaps no ready cure that psychoanalysis can provide. However, we can learn to approach radicalization through a careful engagement in the *subject*, and an understanding of the splits that leave certain subjects open and vulnerable. Reading Arendt, we get an even more chilling image of radicalization as well as a clear indication of the limits of what psychoanalysis can do: Eichmann presents a denial of psychic life altogether.

It is not surprising that the notion of life guides Kristeva's reading of Arendt, providing a line towards a possible counterpractice to radicalization. Both look at life in language and literature. Philosophy as well as political action must be interpreted through a sense of life. In Kristeva the notions of natality, narrative, and poetic language acquire a new meaning in relation to the dark ends of radicalized subjectivities. Literature, language, and thought might be called on to find new ways of life. Living in times of radicalization, we need also to be able to look beyond and travel into new beginnings.

Cecilia Sjöholm

Södertörn University
March 2019

NOTES

1. Julia Kristeva, "Interpreting Radical Evil," Kristeva Circle, Stockholm, October 13, 2016. For David Maruzalla's English translation, see http://www.kristeva.fr/interpreting-radical-evil.html.

2. Hannah Arendt, *Eichmann in Jerusalem: A Report on the Banality of Evil* (London: Penguin, 1964).

3. Julia Kristeva, *Hannah Arendt*, trans. Ross Guberman (New York: Columbia University Press, 2001); *Melanie Klein*, trans. Ross Guberman (New York: Columbia University Press, 2001); *Colette*, trans. Jane Marie Todd (New York: Columbia University Press, 2004).

4. Rositsa Dzhekova, Nadya Stoynova, Anton Kojouharov, Mila Mancheva, Dia Anagnostou, and Emil Tsenkov, "Understanding Radicalization: Review of Literature" (Sofia: Center for the Study of Democracy, 2016), 7.

5. See, for instance, the wide survey of literature on radicalization in Eastern Europe in ibid.

6. Kristeva explains the disorder thus in "Interpreting Radical Evil": "either ideality is lacking or the ideality at the adolescent's disposal is not adapted to the pubescent drive and to its need to share in an absolutely satisfying object. . . . Since paradise exists (for the unconscious), but 'he' or 'she' disappoints me (in reality) I can only be angry at 'them' and avenge myself: delinquency follows. Or else: since it exists (in the unconscious), but 'he' or 'she' disappoints me or is missing from me, I can only be upset with myself and

take it out on myself which identifies with them: mutilation and self-destructive attitudes follow." See also Gaby Levin, "Julia Kristeva: Humanities Can Help Thwart the Destructive Depression That Feeds Fanaticism," *Haaretz*, June 15, 2017, https://www.haaretz.com/world-news/europe/.premium.MAGAZINE-julia-kristeva-humanities-can-help-thwart-fanaticism-1.5483937.

7. This seminar took place "first at the University of Paris-VII and for three years with Professor Marie Rose Moro at the Maison de Solenn." Julia Kristeva, "The Psychic Life: A Life in Time," *Journal of French and Francophone Philosophy* 26, no. 2 (2018): 86.

8. Kristeva, "Interpreting Radical Evil."

9. Ibid.

10. Julia Kristeva, *Powers of Horror: An Essay on Abjection*, trans. Leon S. Roudiez (New York: Columbia University Press, 1982), 180.

11. Ibid., 137.

12. See, for instance, Sara Beardsworth, *Julia Kristeva: Psychoanalysis and Modernity* (Albany: SUNY Press, 2004), 115–42.

13. Kristeva, *Powers of Horror*, 178.

14. Louis-Ferdinand Céline, interview by Ivan M. Sicard, *L'Emancipation Nationale*, November 21, 1941, quoted in Kristeva, *Powers of Horror*, 178.

15. Kristeva, *Hannah Arendt*, 129.

16. Ibid, 179–81.

17. Hannah Arendt, "Concern with Politics in Recent European Philosophical Thought," in Jerome Kohn, ed., *Essays in Understanding: 1930–1954* (New York: Harcourt Brace, 1994), 444.

18. Hannah Arendt, "Philosophy and Sociology," in *Essays in Understanding*, 33.

19. Ibid.

20. Hannah Arendt, *The Life of the Mind* (San Diego: Harcourt, 1978), 113.

21. Hannah Arendt, *Denktagebuch*, ed. Ursula Ludz and Ingeborg Nordmann (Munich: Piper, 2002), vol. 2, 769. See also Cecilia Sjöholm, *Doing Aesthetics with Arendt: How to See Things* (New York: Columbia University Press, 2015), 45, 169nn71–72.

22. This can be seen in Arendt's rendition of Matisse's sculptures, attempting to unravel the "true" ugly content of a human being. See Sjöholm, *Doing Aesthetics with Arendt*, 45.

23. Julia Kristeva, "Hannah Arendt or Refoundation as Survival" was originally a speech delivered by Kristeva at the reception of the Hannah Arendt Prize for Political Thought in Bremen in 2006. http://www.kristeva.fr/Arendt_en.html.

24. See, for instance, Michael Specter, *Denialism: How Irrational Thinking Hinders Scientific Progress, Harms the Planet, and Threatens our Lives* (London: Penguin, 2009).

25. Sigmund Freud, "Negation," in *The Standard Edition of the Complete Psychological Works of Sigmund Freud*, vol. XIX, trans. James Strachey (London: Hogarth, 1961).

26. Kristeva, *Hannah Arendt*, 51–55.

27. Richard J. Bernstein, "Reflections on Radical Evil: Arendt and Kant," *Soundings: An Interdisciplinary Journal* 85, nos. 1–2 (Spring/Summer 2002): 17–30.

28. Kristeva, *Hannah Arendt*, 122–29.

29. See Kristeva, "Interpreting Radical Evil."

30. As Brunner has argued, Arendt's unwillingness to psychoanalyze Eichmann enlarges his responsibility, making thoughtlessness into a feature of evil. José Brunner, "Eichmann, Arendt and Freud in Jerusalem: On the Evils of Narcissism and the Pleasures of Thoughtlessness," in Gulie Ne'eman Arad, ed., *Hannah Arendt and "Eichmann in Jerusalem,"* special issue, *History and Memory* 8, no. 2 (Fall–Winter 1996): 83.

31. Arendt, *Eichmann in Jerusalem*, 49.

32. Ibid.

33. See Coline Covington, "Hannah Arendt, Evil and the Eradication of Thought," *International Journal of Psychoanalysis* 93 (2012): 1215–36.

34. Sigmund Freud, *An Outline of Psychoanalysis*, in *The Standard Edition of the Complete Psychological Works of Sigmund Freud*, vol. XXIII, trans. James Strachey (London: Hogarth, 1964), 201.

35. See, for instance, Catherine Hall and Daniel Pick, "Thinking about Denial," *History Workshop Journal* 84, no. 1 (October 2017): 1–23.

36. See, for instance, Berkowitz's argument in this contested area apropos Margarethe von Trotta's 2012 film, *Hannah Arendt*. Eichmann subordinates himself to "the fictional truth of the movement." Roger Berkowitz, "Misreading 'Eichmann in Jerusalem,'" *Opinionator* (blog), *New York Times*, July 7, 2013, https://opinionator.blogs.nytimes.com/2013/07/07/misreading-hannah-arendts-eichmann-in-jerusalem/?mcubz=1.

37. Arendt, *Eichmann in Jerusalem*, 280–89.

38. Brunner, "Eichmann, Arendt and Freud in Jerusalem," 68.

39. Julia Kristeva, *Tales of Love*, trans. Leon S. Roudiez (New York: Columbia University Press, 1987); *In the Beginning Was Love: Psychoanalysis and Faith*, trans. Arthur Goldhammer (New York: Columbia University Press, 1987).

40. Jacques Lacan, *The Ego in Freud's Theory and in the Technique of Psychoanalysis: The Seminar of Jacques Lacan Book II*, ed. Jacques-Alain Miller, trans. Sylvana Yomaselli (New York: Norton, 1991).

41. Hannah Arendt, *The Human Condition*, 2nd ed. (Chicago: University of Chicago Press, 1998), 39. See my discussion in Sjöholm, *Doing Aesthetics with Arendt*, 26.

42. Eva Illouz, *Cold Intimacies: The Making of Emotional Capitalism* (Cambridge: Polity, 2007), ch. 1.

43. Kristeva, *In the Beginning Was Love*, 25.

44. Ibid. 26.

45. Kristeva, *Tales of Love*, 29–30.

46. See, for instance, Idit Alphandary, "Love and Worldliness in Psychoanalysis and in the Work of Hannah Arendt," *Philosophy Today* 59, no. 2 (Spring 2015): 227–55.

47. Arendt, *The Human Condition*, 52.

48. See Marie Luise Knott, ed., *Hannah Arendt and Gershom Scholem: Der Briefwechsel*, trans. Anthony David (Chicago: University of Chicago Press, 207), 202.

49. Ibid., 206.

50. Julia Kristeva, *Hatred and Forgiveness*, trans. Jeanine Herman (New York: Columbia University Press, 2010), 25.

51. Kristeva, *Hannah Arendt*, 132.

52. Ibid., 204.

53. Ibid., 223–29.

54. Kristeva, *Hatred and Forgiveness*, 44.

55. Kristeva, *Hannah Arendt*, 32–41.

56. Kristeva, *Hannah Arendt*, 164–65.

57. Hannah Arendt, *Lectures on Kant's Political Philosophy* (Chicago: University of Chicago Press, 1989), 43.

58. Hannah Arendt and Karl Jaspers, *Correspondence: 1926–1969*, ed. Lotte Kohler and Hans Saner, trans. Robert and Rita Kimber (San Diego: Harcourt Brace and Company, 1992). See Kristeva, *Hannah Arendt*, 169.

59. Ibid.

60. Julia Kristeva, *Hannah Arendt: Life Is a Narrative*, trans. Frank Collins (Toronto: University of Toronto Press, 2001), 8.

61. Hannah Arendt, *Between Past and Future* (New York: Viking, 1961), 10–11.

62. Arendt, *The Life of the Mind*, 179–93.

63. Arendt, *The Human Condition*, 50.

64. See, for instance, Bettina Stangneth, *Eichmann Before Jerusalem: The Unexamined Life of a Mass Murderer*, trans. Ruth Martin (New York: Knopf, 2014).

34

Ewa Plonowska Ziarek

A MATERIALIST ETHICS OF PSYCHOANALYSIS? REFLECTIONS ON MATTER, FORGIVENESS, AND VULNERABILITY

From the beginning of her career, ethics has been an ongoing concern of Kristeva's thought. Indeed, as Graybeal points out, "it is impossible to read" Kristeva's work "without becoming aware of the ethical motivation and orientation of her writings."[1] Articulated through psychoanalytic, sociopolitical, and artistic practices, Kristeva's ethics as well as the work of her interpreters have addressed different concerns: "outlaw ethics," ethics of otherness, "herethics," tolerance, solidarity, freedom, hospitality, benevolent listening to the other, forgiveness, revolt, and vulnerable singularity.[2] This diversity of ethical considerations testifies to the difficulty and urgency of her ethical project, which underscores a profound ambiguity of the split, embodied, and relational subject situated at the crossroads of language and biology, politics and the unconscious, intimacy and materiality, that is to say, in what we will call heterogeneous (that is, incompatibly diverse yet inseparable) relations. Kristeva's ethics attends not only to the inassimilable, unconscious, and often intolerable otherness within and without, but also to the unstable inside/outside boundaries and the conflicting character of the drives, simultaneously a source of the creation and of the destruction of meaning.

Despite the ongoing attention to ethics in numerous interpretations of Kristeva's work, what has not been sufficiently addressed is the materialist dimension of her ethics. All too frequently, the materialism of Kristeva's thought has been either confused with charges of essentialism, which dominated feminist debates in the 1980s and 1990s, or limited to the Marxist and post-Marxist engagements in her early thinking.[3] Perhaps only now, in the aftermath of the debates between old (i.e., Marxist) and new materialisms (focused on the "agential" conceptions of body, biology, and matter), can we appreciate the originality of her project, which reconsiders ethics not only in the context of the dialectical materialism of Marx and the Frankfurt school but also from the perspective of the materiality of the body and the dynamic conception of matter itself. Despite her sometimes cursory analysis, the socio-political materialism of Kristeva's ethics is a more familiar part of her theory, ranging from the more optimistic articulation of revolutionary practices in the aftermath of 1968 to her various critiques of new power relations, which hamper these transformations, such as the society of the spectacle (after Guy Debord), nihilism, ableism, and what I propose to call biopolitical neoliberalism. The last can briefly be defined as the unlimited expansion of deregulated economic market forces, investing even the value of bodily organs.[4]

In our view, Kristeva's ethics, in particular its relation to materiality and biology, also has a certain proximity to feminist new materialisms, even though her work is usually ignored in these discussions. Associated with the writings of Alaimo, Barad, Colebrook, Grosz, and Wilson, among others, new materialisms contest the hegemony of the linguistic turn/social construction in feminist theory and the corresponding conception of passive matter, without history or signification, treated at best as a resource for human production. As an alternative, new materialists emphasize the dynamic, agential notion of matter. The idea underscores active coparticipation of matter in the formation of bodies, subjects, and the world, stressing in particular "the ongoing, mutual, co-constitution of mind and matter."[5] By drawing on diverse intellectual sources, ranging from Darwin and Bergson to neuroscience and cognitive sciences, they redefine action and agency in terms of interaction between multiple human and nonhuman, discursive and material forces: "the human, nonhuman, technological, and natural . . . agents . . . jointly construct the parameters of our common world."[6] Insofar as Kristeva has also contested the hegemony of linguistic structuralism in psychoanalysis and in human sciences at least since the 1970s, and has underscored the key role of embodiment, the unconscious, and drives in political, artistic, and economic practices, the encounter between the new materialisms and her work is long overdue and is, in our view, fruitful ground for entering into the variants of her ethics.

Beginning with *Revolution in Poetic Language*, Kristeva has proposed a materialist and embodied approach to the ethics of psychoanalysis by elaborating first of all the dynamic, libidinal forces of the drives, traversing the border between the psyche and the soma, language and matter. Her famous notion of the semiotic precisely aims to theorize the destructive and constructive dynamism of the drives, which are not only agential but also capable of generating protosignifying functions, manifesting themselves as trace, fragmentation, affect, or rhythm. As such, the semiotic precedes and exceeds the symbolic, which is usually understood as the linguistic dimension of social practices. Within this framework, ethics can no longer be limited to anthropocentrism and linguistic construction, but, rather, must be reconsidered in the context of the multiple and unpredictable interactions between political, material, discursive, and biological registers. Nonetheless, as Kristeva also argues, the possibility of ethical transformations is not an effect of mere external causation but requires an engagement of singular, vulnerable, and largely unconscious subjects, even though they might not know what they are doing.

With Kristeva's work, we can articulate the challenge of a materialist ethics of psychoanalysis that takes seriously both materiality and the unconscious in terms of three difficulties: the unpredictability and the opacity of the destructive and generative effects of agential matter and drives; a critique of the implicit cognitivism of materialist interpretations; and the reformulation of the singularity and vulnerability of embodied, desiring subjects.

First, for Kristeva the acknowledgment of the materialist-and-linguistic interaction in the constitution of subjects and the world is an important but insufficient first step in the formulation of ethics. That is why the urgent question she poses is: under which conditions are dynamic entanglements of matter and power, language and drives transformative and under which conditions do they lead to the shattering of the psyche, the destruction of the environment, and the breakdown of social relations. Kristeva's early work, in the aftermath of May '68, is more optimistic, stressing the productive dissolution of social relations and subjective identities, indeed the productive process of negativity itself, which, through action, can lead to the transformation of social relations as well as individual or collective subjectivities. By contrast, her later work takes into account the destructive aspects of the negativity of the death drive, which manifest themselves not only in the oppressive forms of power and the devastation of the world but also in the "new maladies" of the psyche, ranging from anorexia to drug addictions and somatizations.

Second, a materialist ethics of psychoanalysis challenges the implicit or explicit cognitivism of new materialisms, which results from disregarding the opacity of the libidinal forces and the unconscious. That is why, for Kristeva, the main difficulty of an ethics of psychoanalysis consists in a reformulation of an ethical response of subjects who can never be fully aware of psychical and material/social forces conditioning their existence. How can subjects affected by and responding to these multiple agents, surpassing consciousness, be responsible for their effects as well as for the subjective responses? The third question is whether the materialist framework of ethics, which takes into account impersonal, material, and unconscious dimensions of existence, can nonetheless safeguard an ethics of singularity. Is singularity at all possible in the context of the new and old materialisms?

To respond to these challenges, in the first section I address the materialist, destructive, and generative dimensions of Kristeva's theory of drives, exceeding signification and subjectivity. Section II focuses on how Kristeva redefines forgiveness in order to propose an ethical "response-ability"—to use Oliver's apt formulation—to the unknowable, antagonistic entanglements between the unconscious, material, linguistic, and libidinal forces.[7] Here, the task of the psychoanalytic ethics of forgiveness is to attenuate the destructive negativity of the death drive manifesting itself in diverse acts of self-destruction as well as in the destruction of the world. Its difficulty consists in working through the partially unconscious psychic defenses—for instance, paranoid hatred—mobilized not only against the opacity of these unpredictable interactions but also against the threat of dissolution of relationality. The third section discusses the implications of Kristeva's materialism for her conception of the nonpsychic temporality (developing the Freudian "timeless") and its role in psychoanalytic interpretation, which aims to open the consciousness of both the analyst and the analysand toward the unconscious, somatic, physical registers of existence. Ultimately, I suggest that the crucial consequence of Kristeva's materialist ethics of psychoanalysis is her emphasis on sharing the unsharable vulnerability of embodied beings.

I. Ethics and Materialism

In our view, then, to understand the complexity of Kristeva's ethics we must begin with its materialist framework, which is presupposed in her later writings (devoted to more familiar psychoanalytic concerns such as mourning, the uncanny, the maternal, the abject, and so forth). As Beardsworth writes, "the symbolic-and-organic" heterogeneity together with the prominence of the death drive remain, for Kristeva, the most general "form of strangeness."[8] Although ethical considerations are not as strongly foregrounded in *Revolution in Poetic Language*, this work nonetheless gives us the most explicit articulation of the materialist basis of ethics in her writings. The material, affective, and bodily aspects of psychoanalysis are widely recognized by Freud and his followers—for example, the materiality of the symptom, the libidinal character of skin, the materiality of object relations, or the embodied character of the ego itself. (The linguistic reinterpretation of the Freudian legacy by Lacan in symbolic and imaginary terms has somewhat deemphasized this materialist legacy.)[9] Here the radicality of Kristeva's work goes beyond the more familiar negotiation between Freudian thought and the dialectical materialisms devoted to the convergence and divergence of psychoanalysis with the social, cultural, and political forces and relations of power. By proposing the energetic and materialist reformulation of drives, Kristeva confronts us with the emergence and the precarious existence of the subject at the crossroads of heterogeneous antagonistic forces and relations, all of which exceed subjectivity, whether understood in the singular or the collective sense. These dynamic relations traverse the usual oppositions between body and psyche, biology and culture, matter and language, force and signification, energy and trace, political and psychic antagonisms, semiotic and symbolic, the intimate and the impersonal.

The multiplicity of these conflictual relations and the heterogeneity that defines them—from which the dynamic subject on trial emerges and in which she is entangled—cannot be easily converted either into the notion of dialectical contradiction or even into the psychoanalytic notion of the split subject insofar as they also involve the dispersal of matter. Indeed, Kristeva's thought brings us to the limit of familiar discourses, including those of psychoanalysis and material feminisms. She rethinks an embodied subject as part of an "unlimited and unbounded generating process," "a structuring and destructuring *practice*, a passage to the outer *boundaries* of subject and society."[10] Moreover, she attempts to articulate the semiotic and the drives in terms of materialist and affective forces capable of generating and pulverizing significance, as if she were anticipating feminist thinking about materialism or affect theory, and offering an alternative. The Freudian conception of the drives and, in particular, of the process of rejection enables her to formulate the nonreductive materialist interactions between matter, psyche, and language. By moving between Hegel, Marx, and Freud, and especially by linking Hegelian negativity to her own materialist interpretation of the Freudian conception of drives, she proposes to rethink negativity "as the *very movement of heterogeneous matter* inseparable from its differentiation's symbolic function."[11] If we take *matter* seriously in these formulations, the materialist framework of Kristeva's ethics goes beyond the organic body toward the dynamic conception of matter, on the one hand, and socioeconomic relations, on the other. "Drives are material but they are not solely biological since they both connect and differentiate the biological and symbolic within the dialectic of the signifying body invested in a practice. . . . [Drives are] the repeated scission of matter that generates signifiance, the place where an always absent subject is produced."[12] In particular, the materialist process of *rejection* "indicates a basic biological operation of scission, separation, and division; at the same time, it joins the always already splitting body to family structure and to the continuum of nature in a relation of rejection."[13]

Kristeva's Freudian materialist reading of Hegel through the prism of drive theory allows her to posit semiotic "negativity" as "the trans-subjective, trans-ideal, and trans-symbolic movement found in the *separation of matter*, one of the preconditions of symbolicity," which generates and exceeds signification.[14] References to Hegel and Marx become less frequent in her later work, but her materialist interpretation of the Freudian theory of the drives remains one of the crucial coordinates of her thought. Through the concept of the drives, their force and signification, this materialism links soma, psyche, and matter. It situates subjectivity in its conscious and unconscious dimensions in relation to language, biology, and political economy. To be sure, Kristeva's speculations on matter beyond signification and anthropocentrism remain rather general, but the important point is that these impersonal material processes exceed "*the signifying subject, binding him to the laws of objective struggles in nature and society*."[15]

Kristeva's interpreters, including myself, have usually read these passages with the emphasis on the "social" and "signifying" mediations of matter and biology in order to avoid the charges of essentialism. This time, however, it is time to do justice to Kristeva's daring situating of the materialist ethics at "the crossroads between the biological and social order on the one hand, and the thetic and signifying phase of the social order on the other."[16] If, as Oliver suggests, Kristeva's work combines ethics and negativity in order to avoid the twin dangers of the conformity to the law and its opposite, the psychotic rejection of the symbolic, we must emphasize that the dynamism of such negativity operates within historically specific intersubjective and material relations.

Furthermore, this material negativity has concrete affective manifestations such as anguish, lament, disgust, love, hatred, or anxiety.

It is therefore our contention that Kristeva's materialism has often been misunderstood as essentialism in the feminist reception of her work. In our view, her materialism encompasses four notions of materiality: (1) the dynamic, structuring and destructuring, processes of bodies and matter; (2) Marxist economic materialism of forces and antagonistic relations of production; (3) the psychoanalytic notion of the drive; and (4) the materiality of language, sound, and medium.[17] Reading her work retrospectively we have here a blueprint of the nonanthropocentric, materialist conceptions of precarious subjectivity and ethics, which, for Kristeva, is presupposed by psychoanalytic, political, and aesthetic practices. She is nonetheless reluctant to move too quickly to posthumanism because she worries that such a turn might renounce ethical and political responsibility, including the impossible responsibility for crimes against humanity and the destruction of the environment. For instance, how can posthumanism oppose normalizing neoliberal biopolitics, which reduces the human to the value of its organs or what Kristeva calls the "patrimonial" individual? How can it counter the "banality of evil" diagnosed by Arendt? How can it respond to intensified reification, damaging not only interhuman relations but also destroying the world? Or to the erasure of singularity in the predictive technologies driven by big data? In response to all these questions, Kristeva calls for "the laboratory of new forms of humanism" predicated on the materialist, relational conception of speaking beings.[18] Only "this ethical and philosophical horizon" of the materialist conception of the speaking, desiring, and thinking beings "gives us a chance to face up to the new barbarities of automation," "infantilizing conservatism," religiosity, and "mortifying rationalism."[19]

The new materialist feminisms have also stressed the ethical implications of their work. They equally tend "to shift the focus from *ethical principles* to *ethical practices*."[20] The unknowable and sometimes destructive multiple "agencies" of bodies (illness, for example) and nature (toxins, or natural disasters) are acknowledged, and the mastery of the subject in relation to the environment is questioned. However, the unpredictable opacity of material forces is rarely investigated in relation to the unknown within the subject, that is, in relation to the unconscious drives and desires.[21] As a result materialist ethics is all too frequently limited to cognitive interpretations that tend to emphasize the observable "consequences" of known and unknown practices. Alaimo and Hekman write: "a material ethics entails . . . that we can compare the very real material consequences of ethical positions and draw conclusions from those comparisons. We can . . . argue that the material consequences of one ethics is more conducive to human and nonhuman flourishing than that of another."[22] This raises important questions. Does such an ethics of evaluating "material consequences" of practices presuppose the conscious subject who can evaluate "human and nonhuman flourishing" apart from unconscious desires, drives, and affects, including hatred and aggression? To what extent can we really know "material consequences of ethical positions" if these positions, according to the proponents of new materialism themselves, include relations and objects beyond the subject?

II. On the Ethics of Forgiveness and Psychic/Material Heterogeneity

One answer to these questions may emerge from Kristeva's ethics of forgiveness, which precisely aims to formulate an ethical response to the unconscious, material, and unknowable dimensions of human existence. This ethics calls for the suspension of the judgment of the superego in order to enable an analytic listening to the affective intensities of the unconscious drives, resistances, and fantasies. "Interpretation is a pardon whose ambition, through the refinement of its models and formulations, is to make psychical rebirth possible. The gravity of this pardon is perceptible in analytical listening that neither judges nor calculates, but is content to untangle and reconstruct."[23] By drawing on the genealogy of pardon ("*par*, through, *don*, a gift"),[24] Kristeva's ethics of forgiveness has a double meaning. First and foremost, it refers to the process of giving sense to senseless suffering. Cocreated in the process of transference and countertransference, this gift of sense is not limited to psychoanalysis alone since it can emerge from other cultural practices such as art, action, or religion.[25] What is specific to psychoanalytic interpretation is the acknowledgment that the cocreation of meaning emerges from the unnameable aspects of the drive, which not only bridges psyche and soma but is also interconnected with the dynamic movement of matter. Consequently, Kristeva's reformulation of forgiveness offers us insights about the ethical stakes of psychoanalytic interpretation, which is irreducible to cognitivism.

Second, Kristeva's psychoanalytic redefinition of forgiveness, which refers to the irremediable opacity of acts, is partly indebted to Hannah Arendt's political reformulation of forgiveness in *The Human Condition*. As Kristeva and Arendt admit, forgiveness is neither a psychoanalytic nor a political concept because it is inherited from religions, Christianity in particular. Nonetheless, both argue that the secular version of forgiveness is crucial to politics and ethics precisely because human agents do not know the consequences of their political actions (in Arendt) or the interactions with heterogeneous libidinal, natural or sociopolitical conflicts (in Kristeva). Kristeva argues that, for Arendt, forgiveness is an alternative to Nietzsche's active forgetting of the past. For Nietzsche, being trapped in the past and living with its growing burden increases suffering and causes paralyzing resentment.[26] Although Arendt shares Nietzsche's concern about the entrapment in the past, she turns toward forgiveness rather than forgetting in order to seek the possibility of "the freedom from vengeance, which incloses both doer and sufferer in the relentless automatism of the action process."[27] In contrast to vengeance, forgiveness creates a new relation to the past: "forgiving, in other words, is the only reaction which does not merely re-act but acts anew and unexpectedly."[28] Therefore forgiveness, according to Arendt, is an act in its own right, which, by releasing actors from the unintended consequences of the past, enables a new beginning. As the capacity to respond to the unknown and unforeseeable consequences of acts, forgiveness is itself unpredictable.

While both forgetfulness and forgiveness can release us from the past, the crucial difference between them is that forgiveness is a form of action corresponding to the condition of human plurality, for Arendt. Just as we cannot act in isolation from others, so too, Arendt argues, no one could have an experience of forgiveness in isolation. Furthermore, like every other action, forgiveness is closely intertwined with the capacity to create meaning because it is inseparable from "action and speech, which produce meaningful stories."[29] Because of its connection to the renewal and creation of meaning, forgiveness is an alternative not only to determinism but also to violence, which aims to undo the past by destroying the inherited historical world and the very "conditions under which life was given" on earth.[30] Moreover, like every other action, forgiveness discloses the singularity of actors; it is for the sake of "who" they are and not for the sake of what they have done that they are forgiven. Despite the increasing "depersonalization of public and social life," forgiveness discloses human uniqueness in the midst of human plurality.[31]

This cluster of ideas associated with forgiveness in Arendt—not least, the emphasis on the unknown and the unpredictable consequences of acts, the return to the past for the sake of renewal, the disclosure of singularity, and the attenuation of violence thanks to the creation of meaning—is crucial for Kristeva's concept of forgiveness. As a gift of meaning, the psychoanalytic ethics of forgiveness also emerges from the encounter with another, so that its cocreation presupposes human plurality. However, in the context of psychoanalysis, if forgiveness is to enable a new beginning it has to release subjects not only from the unpredictable consequences of acting with others but also from the unknowable and often intolerable interactions between the libidinal and the material forces in "nature and society" from which the psyche emerges and in which it remains entangled. In particular, by confronting hatred and the destructive negativity of the death drive, which does not end with the destruction of interhuman relations but extends to the devastation of the planet, a psychoanalytic ethics of forgiveness works through the unconscious processes of repetition compulsion, psychic defenses and resistances. As an affective manifestation of the death drive, hatred cannot be relegated to a pathology, but, rather, must be regarded as negativity "coextensive" with the human.[32]

What kind of interpretation is capable of dismantling unconscious resistances and releasing us from hatred? As Kristeva has argued from the beginning, what is at stake in the psychoanalytic interpretation is neither linguistic construction nor dialogue between two conscious subjects, but, rather, a cocreation of meaning that arises in unexpected ways from the unconscious negativity and materiality of the drives, bodies, and the extrapsychical processes of separation of matter itself. Unlike the hermeneutic process of understanding or its opposite, the cognitivism of the neurosciences, psychoanalytic interpretation is a heterogeneous "energetic/hermeneutic" practice opening the consciousness of both the analyst and the analysand toward the "unconscious/prepsychical/somatic/physical continuity" of existence and its peculiar prepsychic temporality.[33] If this practice involves intimacy, it is a paradoxical intimacy of the interhuman with the inhuman and nonpsychic, which nonetheless are inscribed as unconscious traces in the psyche. In order to explain these unconscious, somatic, and physical registers of interpretation that are crucial to her ethics of forgiveness, Kristeva gives us a double genealogy: first, the more familiar genealogy of symbols emerging from the material processes of *rejection* in her theory of the signifying process; second, a genealogy of particular symptoms and psychic defenses when the process of affective/symbolic formation breaks down, for instance in cases of paranoid hatred, anorexia, or depression. The pivotal question in these genealogies is: "under what conditions does the rejecting drive become symbolizing negativity" and under what conditions does it shatter subjectivity and the world?[34]

Expanding upon her work on Klein, Kristeva argues that paranoid hatred is a defense against abjection, the earliest psychic elaboration of the impossible, permeable, and abominable limits of being—waste, reject, vomit, corpse—where neither subjects nor objects, neither inside nor outside exist. Abjection is an unnameable, somatic, and affective return to the violent bodily separation of the newborn from the maternal container. The reoccurrence of sensations of disgust "takes the ego back to its source on the abominable limits from which, in order to be, the ego has broken away—it assigns it a source in the non-ego, drive, and death."[35] *Hatred* is an unconscious defense that compensates for the failure of psychic separation and the failure of meaning to emerge from the drive basis of rejection that, according to Kristeva, repeats the division of matter. Such defensive hatred can take different forms, depending on particular psychic structures and personal histories: it can manifest itself as anorexia, phobia, or "paranoid hatred."[36] In contrast to Freud, then, Kristeva suggests that paranoid hatred is not always a defense against homosexual eroticism because it might point to an older and more pervasive unconscious defense against abjection, against the dissolution of differentiations between subjects/objects, inside/outside, psyche/matter, life and death. Vis-à-vis such threatening nondifferentiation, only disgust or the somatic spasm of revulsion can protect subjectivity against shattering. To compensate for miscarried differentiations and identifications, paranoid hatred constructs a rigid "armor of the hateful warrior," which provides "the temporary hiding place for a nonsubject" who "asks only to be born."[37]

Kristeva's most expansive analysis of hatred and the ethics of forgiveness emerges from her case study of Pierre, a failed political scientist at war with himself and the world, a case that inspired *Powers of Horror*. Pierre's paranoid hatred "has transformed the uncertainty of abjection into a reversible dyad" of the two objects, dangerous for each other.[38] In this unconscious defensive structure, "my" sense of tenuous existence is predicated on "my" being a danger to the phantasmatic other, who is likewise dangerous to me but who does not destroy me as long as I remain dangerous for him. The ethics of forgiveness is not limited to naming and sharing with the analysand the analyst's interpretation of his symptoms, however. Rather, through the cocreation of meaning it hopes to soften and change this defensive structure and eventually reconcile the psyche with the unconscious and the nonpsychical, somatic modes of being. What enables both the interpretation and the possibility of working through the resistances it might provoke is the process of transference, thanks to which the unconscious fantasies and defenses underlying the analysand's state of war with the world can emerge.

For Kristeva, a psychoanalytic ethics of forgiveness is intertwined with a heterogeneous hermeneutic/energetic interpretive practice. Its first dimension therefore consists of interpreting transference and countertransference occurring in analysis. For example, during the analysis of Pierre the analyst was solicited to occupy the position of the dangerous object against whom the analysand's hatred is directed. Although such hatred provokes a negative countertransference, the analyst intervenes only through patient listening and subsequent interpretations, which might trigger other resistances, memories, and affects. In this process, the analyst occupies two positions: the object of the analysand's hatred and the listening, speaking, and desiring subject. The hateful dyad in Pierre's unconscious structure is broken insofar as the speaking/listening other is inserted in it. Eventually, analysis creates new transferential links in which the analyst plays the incompatible roles of the abject mother and the idealized and envied intellectual, as well as a symbolic other who might help the analysand in the process of affective and symbolic separation from the abject.

Although the intersubjective interpretation of transference and countertransference is a more conspicuous level of analysis, its energetic, material elements are hardly ignored. As Kristeva claims, in order to unravel the defensive structure of paranoia, forgiveness has to accompany the subject to the unstable borders of existence antithetical to meaning, namely, to the unnameable, abominable limits of being and language where the very distinctions between subjects and objects, psyche and soma, falter. Only by approaching these abject limits of experience can the analysis transform the destructive negativity of the drive "into a start of life, of new significance."[39] To underscore a partial reconciliation of the psyche with the unconscious, somatic, and material relations of existence, Kristeva describes the psychoanalytic ethics of forgiveness as inverted Platonism, a descent into a sensorial cave in order to expand sense to its limits, where meaning encounters the unnameable sensorial experience and perhaps the materiality of the cave itself.

One of the crucial questions Kristeva asks concerns what happens to hatred in the process of interpretation.[40] Although hatred does not disappear, it becomes attenuated and coexists with other affective and erotic relations. Mediated through Eros and meaning, hatred becomes partially sublimated into linguistic expressions of negativity, but only partially since its destructiveness continues to exceed signification and language. The hope of psychoanalysis is that this nonsublimated negativity of hatred "incites me to turn my aggression on all unity, identity, norms, values: in short, to make myself a subject . . . of incessant questioning."[41] Kristeva's ethics of forgiveness is therefore a more modest reformulation of Freudian analysis. For Freud, the analyst "succeeds where the paranoiac fails" insofar as she can relate to the other through language instead of projections.[42] For Kristeva, since the analyst is implicated in paranoid hatred, too, analysis succeeds only insofar as the analyst is able to work through her own negativity and *jouissance* in order to be able to listen to the analysand as other. Because such an ethical transformation depends on moving beyond the consciousness of both the analyst and the analysand "toward unconscious/prepsychical/somatic/physical" registers of existence, psychoanalytic interpretation is irreducible to the lingering cognitivism of new materialism.

III. From Nonpsychic Time to Sharing Vulnerable Singularities

I will now address the implications of Kristeva's materialist ethics both for her conception of nonpsychic temporality and for her notion of the singularity of vulnerable beings. Let us begin with the temporal dimension of Kristeva's ethics of forgiveness, which involves not only a retrospective return to the past but also the possibility of a new beginning, an opening of a future. As she puts it, forgiveness involves "the questioning and displacement of the past. The future, if it exists, depends on it."[43] For Arendt, the new beginning, a release from the consequences of the past, is a political act. For Kristeva, it enables an intimate revolt insofar as the transformation of the unconscious structures, fantasies, and defenses leads to new modes of desire as well as to the questioning of meaning and identities. However, for such a transformation to occur, the process of interpretation has to confront not only the limits of meaning but also the dead time implied by temporal impasse and paralysis: the time that does not temporalize. This is, for Kristeva, the consequence of the Freudian discovery of timelessness (the *Zeitlos*), which does not mean transcendence, but, rather, inertia and stagnation. The real scandal of the *Zeitlos* is that it exceeds psychic time altogether, even the time of the unconscious and drives. In Kristeva's interpretation, the *Zeitlos* suggests nonpsychic temporalities of the traces of matter and energy (including the materiality of memory traces of past excitations), both of which are extraneous to the psyche. Consequently, in exploring the most intimate singularity of speaking beings, Kristeva returns again to a materialism exceeding subjectivity, and rethinks this material excess in the context of unbound time.

Kristeva argues that the Freudian discovery of dead time that does not temporalize—that is, a nonpsychic time that resists recollections of the past and projections of the future—might correspond to the philosophical ambitions of Bergson or Heidegger to expand time beyond subjectivity. In contrast to Bergson's vitalism of matter, Kristeva interprets the *Zeitlos* in terms of "the permanence of . . . timeless biothanatology,"[44] which is nonvitalist and nonteleological. In contrast to Heidegger's temporalization of Being, her "materialist" unbinding of time, expanding it beyond subjectivity, language, cosmology, and organicism, confronts timeless inertia. Nonetheless, such inertia assumes concrete manifestations in psychoanalytic treatment and theory: for instance, in the persistence of the unconscious memory traces of drive excitation; in the inertia of resistances in the process of working through past traumas and symptoms; or in the confrontation with death at the end of analysis. Because these configurations of nonpsychic time cannot be integrated into subjective time, they interrupt not only recollection, perception, and anticipation but also the biological time of the organism. And since working through different configurations of dead time occurs at each step of the analysis, the aim of psychoanalytic ethics does not consist in the conversion of the immemorial past into memory, but, rather, in facilitating an encounter of the psyche with nonpsychic time, which cannot be remembered because it has never been experienced.

Ultimately, what is at stake in the ethics of psychoanalysis is the inscription of the nonpsychic time in the process of psychic temporalization, that is, in the lived experience rather than in somatization or the abolition of the psyche in psychosis or drug addictions. This of course entails a reconfiguration of the very meaning of lived experience, which in the process of analysis becomes reconciled with the endurance of biological and psychic death corresponding to the death drive. By endlessly negotiating between sense and non-sense, forgiveness gives time, which includes the timelessness of death. As Kristeva puts it, an ethics of forgiveness ultimately consists in giving death "its time in time."[45] Consequently, the paradoxical gift of a new beginning and psychic rebirth, so characteristic of the Kristevan "intimate revolt," is inseparable from the gift of death, which is encountered in recollection as so many enduring traces of irrecoverable losses, impasses and traumas, exceeding memory, as we shall see. Thanks to the gift of forgiveness, the unbearable intimacy of lived experience includes intimacy with death and the inorganic. Unbound, lived experience turns into an exorbitant intimacy with what remains beyond experience: the unconscious, but also death, "the biological" and "being itself."[46]

The gift of forgiveness ultimately unbinds intimacy and experience beyond the psyche and toward "biothanatology."[47] By reconciling anamnesis with the traces of dead time, the process of analysis partially inscribes these traces within temporalization. Thanks to this displacement of inertia into temporalization, these traces of dead time appear not only, or no longer, as somatization, drug addictions or the psychotic breakdown of subjectivity. Reconnected in the process of analysis with their unconscious representations, the immemorial traces of drive energies reappear as hallucinations, dreams, gaps of memory, and eventually as the breaches of speech, where they manifest themselves as *jouissance*. To be sure, the displacement of timelessness into temporalization interrupts memory, language, and thinking, yet such interruptions also provoke retroactive questioning of the past and, in this sense, recollection and critical thinking, which can lead to the creation and renewal of psychic life.

Freud's scandal of the *Zeitlos* is certainly a political scandal of ambivalent significance. On the one hand, time that does not budge resists the race of neoliberalism for increased profits and the efficiency of production; it eludes new predictive technologies aiming to capture the future and replace potentialities of being with algorithmic predictions. On the other hand, Kristeva is far from uncritically embracing destructive inertia as a celebration of either posthumanism or new materialism for two reasons. First, what interrupts the linear time of efficiency is not only inertia but, more importantly, the unpredictable occurrence of a new beginning, which is the gift of time that a psychoanalytic ethics of forgiveness hopes to offer. Second, Kristeva's ethics is faithful to the Freudian dualism of psyche and soma, which she reinterprets as the irreducible heterogeneity between materiality and unbearable intimacy of embodied beings.[48] Ultimately what is at stake in Kristeva's account of heterogeneity is not merely a theoretical or an ontological approach, but, rather, political and ethical commitments of psychoanalysis to safeguard both the possibility of renewal and the singularity of embodied human beings. This is an ethics attuned to "the singularity of this experience that emerges . . . where time rejoins the timeless."[49]

Kristeva's investigations of exorbitant intimacy balance inorganic, "extra-psychical" material forces and drives with the singularity of human beings. As she writes, "psychoanalysis is based on the notion that to have a psychical life or an intimacy means to have a singular psychical life, which is precisely what is restored or made possible in treatment."[50] Elaborated in terms of her writings on intimacy, which call for an "art" or "style" of psychoanalytic treatment rather than a scientific method, the ethical concern with the singularity of speaking beings torn between biology and language reveals to us another concern regarding Kristeva's ethics, namely, the relation between singularity and being with others. On the one hand, the unrepeatable, nongeneralizable uniqueness—unlike anything else—cannot be shared with others. On the other hand, singularity cannot exist in isolation because we appear as irreplaceable only if we are regarded as such by others. Just as Arendt's notion of forgiveness discloses the singularity of agents amidst human plurality, so Kristeva's ethos of singularity depends on the "renewed link" with others.

Like other thinkers of singularity—Arendt, Cavarero, or Nancy, for example—Kristeva initially formulates the relation between the singular and the social as the sharing of the unshareable.[51] "To share: to take part in a distinctiveness beyond the separation imposed upon us by our fates; to participate, without erasing the fact that each is 'apart' and recognizing the part that cannot be shared, that is irremediable."[52] The primary psychoanalytic "scene" of such paradoxical sharing of singularities occurs in the process of transference and countertransference. That is why Kristeva argues that transference-countertransference is a psychoanalytic version of the Kantian enlarged mentality. For Kant, the enlarged mentality entails the communicability to others of aesthetic judgments based on pleasure/displeasure. For Kristeva, the psychoanalytic significance of enlarged mentality means that the possibility of the transformation of the unconscious drives and desires presupposes relations to others. Perhaps limited initially to the analyst and other analysands, human plurality, listening, and communicability are a precondition not only of desire but also of a new beginning, which entails the capacity both of making new connections with others and of questioning these connections.[53]

Emerging as it does from the experience of transference and countertransference, Kristeva's formulation of sharing unshareable singularities is attentive to the multiple vulnerabilities of embodied speaking beings in the world. In contrast to philosophy, psychoanalysis is concerned with "the singularity of the vulnerable beings."[54] This intertwining of singularity and vulnerability is already implied in the unbearable intimacy with hatred, pain, and death. Vulnerability is another consequence of the intersection of biology and language, and of timelessness with time. As the ontological condition of finitude of unique human beings, vulnerability is both shared and lived in singular ways: it belongs to "integral parts of the identity of the human race and, singularly, of the speaking subject."[55] As with the destructive negativity of drives and the scattering of matter, Kristeva analyzes equivocal manifestations of vulnerability in psychic and political lives: as hatred, narcissistic crisis, and paranoid projections when such vulnerability is denied; as renewal and the creation of new connections with others and the world when such fragility is acknowledged and worked through. Because of its ambiguity and the potential for destructiveness it harbors, vulnerability constitutes both a condition of possibility and the greatest obstacle to the sharing of the unshareable singularity of embodied beings.

Since vulnerability is a condition we share, it can be a basis for the politics of solidarity. However, when it is denied, solidarity gives way to paranoid projections of hatred mobilized by xenophobic, racist, or ableist politics of imaginary omnipotence, which can underlie the institutions of both national sovereignty and parenthood. Projected onto imaginary others—refugees, Muslims, or people in the situation of disability—these politically and economically mediated denials of vulnerability lead to discrimination, violence, and the construction of new political barriers. If we think that the acknowledgment of vulnerability is too tenuous a basis for the politics of solidarity, we should nonetheless consider Kristeva's argument that the repudiation of vulnerability is at the core of ableist politics, its cultural imaginaries, and political institutions, not to mention neoliberal economics.[56] Given the entwinement of Western political institutions, such as national sovereignty, human rights, or liberty, with ableist values, Kristeva argues that the genuine politics of solidarity among vulnerable singular human beings will not be possible without the inscription of vulnerability in the very structure of democratic citizenship and the corresponding institutional/legal transformations. What if citizenship and the democratic institutions were to include vulnerability with "liberty, equality, fraternity"?

***

From the impersonal movement of heterogeneous matter to the impossible intimacy with the nonhuman, from the explorations of nonpsychic time to the sharing of the vulnerable singularities of embodied beings—such are the crossroads where Kristeva's ethics arises and the parameters of her nonanthropocentric new humanism. As we have seen, what underlies the intersection of these heterogeneous relations is Kristeva's materialist concept of the drive working at the border of psyche and soma. If we reduce these heterogeneous relations to either materialism *or* psyche, biology *or* language, we not only miss the complex situatedness of human beings but, more importantly, we give up on the possibility of renewal emerging from the confrontation with the destruction threatening not only beings but the planet itself. This ethical confrontation is all the more urgent since the death drive and its affective manifestation—hatred—cannot be relegated to a pathology, but, rather, must be regarded as negativity "coextensive" with the human.

EWA PLONOWSKA ZIAREK

UNIVERSITY AT BUFFALO
APRIL 2019

NOTES

1. Jean Graybeal, "Kristeva's Delphic Proposal: Practice Encompasses the Ethical," in Kelly Oliver, ed., *Ethics, Politics and Difference in Julia Kristeva's Writing* (New York: Routledge, 1993), 32.

2. The term "outlaw ethics" comes from Kelly Oliver, "Introduction: Julia Kristeva's Outlaw Ethics," in ibid. For Kristeva's ethics of otherness, in which (in contrast to Levinas), freedom and obligation are inseparable from each other, see, for example, Ewa Ziarek, "Kristeva and Levinas: Mourning Ethics and the Feminine," in ibid., and John Lechte, "Violence, Ethics and Transcendence: Kristeva and Levinas," in John Lechte and Maria Margaroni, *Julia Kristeva: Live Theory* (London: Continuum, 2004). For "herethics," see Julia Kristeva, "Stabat Mater," in *Tales of Love*, trans. Leon S. Roudiez (New York: Columbia University Press, 1987). The other ethical notions appear and are returned to across many of Kristeva's works, for example, those on revolt and those on Arendt.

3. For a response to essentialism in the reception of Kristeva's work, see Tina Chanter, "Kristeva's Politics of Change: Tracking Essentialism with the Help of a Sex/Gender Map," in Oliver, *Ethics, Politics, and Difference*.

4. For the most extensive analysis of nihilism in the context of Kristeva's work, see Sara Beardsworth, *Julia Kristeva: Psychoanalysis and Modernity* (Albany: SUNY Press, 2004). For Kristeva's analysis of "patrimonial" individuals reduced to the value of their organs, see Julia Kristeva, *The Sense and Non-sense of Revolt: The Powers and Limits of Psychoanalysis Volume 1*, trans. Jeanine Herman (New York: Columbia University Press, 2000), 6.

5. Stacy Alaimo and Susan Hekman, "Introduction: Emerging Models of Materiality in Feminist Theory," in Stacy Alaimo and Susan Hekman, eds., *Material Feminisms* (Bloomington: Indiana University Press, 2008), 5. This collection provides a comprehensive overview of different approaches brought under the rubrics of new materialism and material feminisms.

6. Ibid.

7. For the discussion of the response-ability and address-ability in ethics, see Kelly Oliver, *Witnessing: Beyond Recognition* (Minneapolis: University of Minnesota Press, 2001), 6–20 and passim.

8. Beardsworth, *Julia Kristeva*, 195. As she argues, Kristeva's ethics is based not on the abstract universal principle but on the confrontation with the unease with internal otherness, 182–90.

9. One can argue that materialism is limited to the register of the real, which precedes and exceeds the symbolic, in Lacan.

10. Julia Kristeva, *Revolution in Poetic Language*, trans. Leon S. Roudiez (New York: Columbia University Press, 1984), 17.

11. Ibid., 113. For an excellent interpretation of Kristeva's approach to Hegel and Freud, see Elaine P. Miller, *Head Cases: Julia Kristeva on Philosophy and Art in Depressed Times* (New York: Columbia University Press, 2014), 59–63. For an illuminating interpretation

of Kristeva's engagement with the Freudian theory of the drives, see Beardsworth, *Julia Kristeva*, 43–50.

12. Kristeva, *Revolution in Poetic Language*, 167.

13. Ibid., 123.

14. Ibid., 117.

15. Ibid., 119.

16. Ibid., 124.

17. As Miller argues, Kristeva's notion of materiality includes not only external material relations of power but also body and language (*Head Cases*, 61).

18. Julia Kristeva, "A Meditation, a Political Act, an Art of Living," trans. S. K. Keltner, in Kelly Oliver and S. K. Keltner, eds., *Psychoanalysis, Aesthetics, and Politics in the Work of Julia Kristeva* (Albany: SUNY Press, 2009), 22.

19. Ibid., 22.

20. See Alaimo and Hekman, "Introduction," in *Material Feminisms*, 7 (my emphasis).

21. For a rare example of the discussion of psychoanalysis in the context of new materialism, see Elizabeth A. Wilson, "Organic Empathy: Feminism, Psychopharmaceuticals, and the Embodiment of Depression," in Alaimo and Hekman, eds., *Material Feminisms*. However, the question of desire and the drives does not figure significantly in this essay.

22. Alaimo and Hekman, "Introduction," in ibid., 7.

23. Julia Kristeva, "Hatred and Forgiveness; or, From Abjection to Paranoia," in *Hatred and Forgiveness*, trans. Jeanine Herman (New York: Columbia University Press, 2010), 193–94.

24. Ibid., 193.

25. For example, Kristeva argues that the religious myth of the Virgin Mary both acknowledges and elaborates a psychic solution to female paranoia. See Kristeva, "Stabat Mater."

26. For Kristeva's analysis of Arendt's forgiveness in relation to Nietzsche, see Julia Kristeva, *Hannah Arendt*, trans. Ross Guberman (New York: Columbia University Press, 2001), 230–33 (volume 1 of the "female genius" trilogy).

27. Hannah Arendt, *The Human Condition* (Chicago: University of Chicago Press, 1998), 241.

28. Ibid., 241.

29. Ibid., 236.

30. Ibid., 238.

31. Ibid., 243.

32. Kristeva, "Hatred and Forgiveness," 183.

33. Julia Kristeva, "The Scandal of the Timeless," in *Intimate Revolt: The Powers and Limits of Psychoanalysis*, trans. Jeanine Herman (New York: Columbia University Press, 2002), 27, 32.

34. Julia Kristeva, "What Revolt Today?" in *Intimate Revolt*, 9.

35. Julia Kristeva, *Powers of Horror: An Essay on Abjection*, trans. Leon S. Roudiez (New York: Columbia University Press, 1982), 15.

36. Kristeva, "Hatred and Forgiveness," 186.

37. Ibid., 191.

38. Ibid.

39. Kristeva, *Powers of Horror*, 15.

40. Kristeva, "Hatred and Forgiveness," 184.

41. Julia Kristeva, "Psychoanalysis and Freedom," in *Intimate Revolt*, 233.

42. See Kristeva, "Hatred and Forgiveness,"191.

43. Kristeva, "What Revolt Today?" 5.

44. Kristeva, "The Scandal of the Timeless," 33.

45. Ibid., 40.

46. Julia Kristeva, "The Intimate: From Sense to the Sensible," in *Intimate Revolt*, 50.

47. Kristeva, "The Scandal of the Timeless," 41.

48. For excellent discussions of intimacy see S. K. Keltner, "What Is Intimacy?" and Cecilia Sjöholm, "Fear of Intimacy? Psychoanalysis and the Resistance to Commodification," in Oliver and Keltner, *Psychoanalysis, Aesthetics, and Politics.*

49. Kristeva, "The Scandal of the Timeless," 25.

50. Kristeva, "The Intimate: From Sense to the Sensible," 52.

51. Jean-Luc Nancy, *Being Singular Plural*, trans. Robert D. Richardson and Anne E. O'Byrne (Stanford: Stanford University Press, 2000). Adriana Cavarero, *Relating Narratives: Storytelling and Selfhood*, trans. Paul A. Kottoman (London: Routledge, 2000).

52. Julia Kristeva, "Liberty, Equality, Fraternity and . . . Vulnerability," in *Hatred and Forgiveness*, 43.

53. Kristeva, "Psychoanalysis and Freedom," in *Intimate Revolt*, 232–33.

54. Julia Kristeva, "A Meditation, a Political Act, an Art of Living," 22–23.

55. Kristeva, "Liberty, Equality, Fraternity and . . . Vulnerability," 42.

56. In order to transform such ableist culture and to contest discriminations of persons in the situation of disability, the politics of equal rights and access to public, economic, and cultural institutions are necessary but insufficient. Such a politics has to be supplemented by the ethics of solidarity based on the intersubjective interaction and "sharable [*partageable*] singularity." Kristeva, "A Meditation, a Political Act, an Art of Living," 22–23.

35

Noëlle McAfee

KRISTEVA'S LATENT POLITICAL THEORY

The subject of this essay is something that does not seem to exist: Kristeva's political theory. While Kristeva has interrogated a range of subjects, from aesthetics to language, subjectivity to intertextuality, and psychoanalysis to maternity, her writings and addresses on politics tend to begin with assumptions about the superiority of enlightenment universal values embodied in the French Republic and culminate with applying them to issues such as disability, immigration, and the veil.[1]

Kristeva's philosophical genius lies elsewhere: namely in understanding the speaking being, how she is split and on trial, how she is a stranger to herself, why she needs to cultivate a psychic life, and how best she can revolt. Her twin theoretical "super powers" are semiotics and psychoanalysis—semiotics to understand how meaning is made and psychoanalysis to understand how subjectivity develops and what trials it undergoes. Beginning with her early work in semiotics and signification, Kristeva showed how poetic language can shake up the moors of symbolic order and expose sensations and drives; that is, poetic language is itself revolutionary. As she put it later, "the practice of writing can attain non-sense too. By unfolding the meaning of sensations and drives, it can find its pulse in an order that is no longer 'symbolic' but 'semiotic.'"[2] Turning to psychoanalysis in the 1970s, she began to channel and synthesize some of the most important insights of mid-twentieth-century psychoanalytic theory, including those of Lacan, Klein, and Winnicott, the result of which is brilliantly *Freudian*. Where much of contemporary psychoanalytic theory has abandoned two of Freud's central tenets—primary narcissism and the death drive—Kristeva sees them as central to the riddle of human subjectivity. As both Freud and Kristeva understand, the development from a preindividuated state to one of social identifications is rocky and treacherous. It can go badly awry. The death drive can send this development veering into abysses and over precipices, from melancholia to false-self syndromes. Theories that deny primary narcissism (saying we are all social from the start) or the death drive (pure negativity) thus avoid having to tarry with these difficulties. Kristeva's work stares them squarely in the face.

In this essay, it is in this work on subjectivity, not in her writings on French enlightenment values, that one can discern her most important contributions to political theory. These two strands intersect in her recent work on syndromes of ideality. I turn my attention to this intersection in due course. In my own intellectual journey writing on democratic and political theory, I have found Kristeva's work on subjectivity to be a vital traveling companion. My purpose here is to trace the way her work can be an ally in thinking through democratic practices for helping to work through problems that give rise to polarized, intransigent, and Manichaean politics. I find especially useful the link that her work provides between the psyche and the social and the implications of this work for understanding political breakdown. Any theorist who wants to take up this kind of analysis is wise to turn to Kristeva for a latent political theory that is crucial for our times. I begin with an inquiry into Kristeva's own history between politics and psychoanalysis. I then discuss some of her manifest political views—and their limits. In the final section I explore what I see as the lynchpins in her work between the psyche and the political at the heart of this highly productive latent political theory.

I. Cold War Commitments

One might wonder whether the young Kristeva had any political commitments at all. When she arrived in Paris she was no stranger to politics, having grown up in Cold War, communist Bulgaria in an Orthodox Christian family, attending French-speaking Catholic schools and having been a member of a communist youth group (along with nearly every other Bulgarian child). Her family's membership in the Orthodox Church excluded them from many of the perks of the Communist Party. So from the start there was a schism between the Western-oriented Francophile and the good Bulgarian youth who aimed to please with her good grades and intelligence. In 1965 Kristeva won a one-year fellowship to study in France and by Christmas of that year was attending Christmas midnight mass at Notre Dame. She never moved back, instead becoming one of the leading intellectuals of the West in the ensuing decades. Despite more than fifty years of her fealty to the French nation, in early 2018 the *Guardian*, the *New York Times*, and other publications reported that Kristeva had been accused of being a spy for the Bulgarian government during the immediate years following her emigration to France.[3] The allegations came from a Bulgarian commission charged with outing old spies, which had unearthed a file with the name of Sabina, a pseudonym the Bulgarians had supposedly created for her. Kristeva has adamantly denied these allegations.[4] To anyone who knows Kristeva or her writings of the period—and since—the claim that she was a Bulgarian spy is exceedingly hard to believe. In addition to the case she makes in print that in fact the Bulgarians were spying on her and her husband, not she for them, there is her own intellectual history, which makes her being a spy for the Bulgarian secret police unthinkable.

After arriving in Paris in 1965, Kristeva quickly became part of the major left bank circle of prominent intellectuals interested in cultural politics, many seeing an ally for this work in the French Communist Party (PCF). But from the start, Kristeva was wary. As she wrote in a 1984 memoir, when her soon-to-be husband Philippe Sollers proclaimed in 1965 that "only the socialist Revolution could provide a social setting propitious to avant-garde writing," it seemed to her "completely unrealistic from the standpoint of the socialism I had experienced."[5] Maybe it would be different in France, they and others thought; but Kristeva was already being drawn to psychoanalysis, through which she could analyze this quasi-religious, dogmatic obsession with politics.[6] Within a few years, after May '68, she and others in her circle came to see the PCF as a repressive machine, "the killer mechanism of individual difference" and "the essence of the political tie: . . . radical rationalization, the banal hideout, the orthodox lining of perversion."[7] Hence, she writes, her group "kept aloof, from then on, from any other political perversion, even a left-wing one."[8]

After breaking with the PCF altogether, Kristeva and others in her group (Sollers, Barthes, Playnet, Wahl, and Lacan) decided in 1974 to visit Mao's China, not so much to see another version of socialism but, for some in the group, in hopes of glimpsing "a utopia in pure form, which had nothing to do with the sects of the left."[9] For those, such as herself, "who were not interested in political discourse," this trip to China "was a means of finding another set of social and historical roots for 'internal experience.'"[10] (In the end, Lacan could not join them.) But during that trip, she writes, "politically, I saw nothing that might possibly prevent the Cultural Revolution from becoming a national and socialist variation, whose basic reference point remains the province of the Soviets."[11] This, she writes, marked her "farewell to politics."[12]

During those years, then, there was no intellectual on the Left Bank less enthralled by politics or any romantic notions about communism. The trip to China solidified both her antipathy to politics and her growing interest in psychoanalysis. Referring to the trip to China: "This arduous journey, one that from the outset was more cultural than political, definitively inaugurated a return to the only continent we had never left: internal experience."[13] With this her gaze turned decidedly inward, using psychoanalysis—as a theorist and a practicing analyst—to explore the internal landscape of the speaking being. Ironically, although she turned away from politics to focus on the psyche, the central ideas she developed in her psychoanalytic thought are tremendously useful for theorizing politically, especially in our dark times. I will return to this in short order.

II. Kristeva's Manifest Political Views

As her stature as a public intellectual grew, so did her opportunities to address public issues. In these it is possible to discern what I will call her manifest political views, though not quite a political theory. These have several elements: (1) an advocacy for universal and French human values, (2) concern over the experience of foreigners, (3) a focus on disability rights, which I do not have space to address here, and (4) a wariness about feminist politics along with an interest in advocating for what some see as traditional maternal roles.

1. French Values

Kristeva first encountered French values in her home life and schooling in Bulgaria. Referring to her father, Stoyan Kristev, she writes: "This educated member of the Orthodox Church wanted me to learn French from an early age and duly registered me at a primary school run by French nuns, so that I could absorb some of the critical spirit and taste for freedom for which France is rightly famous."[14] This francophone education in Bulgaria prepared her well for taking up intellectual life in the heady 1960s in Paris. Arriving in Paris well versed in all the giants of French literature, she later wrote that she was "in no way" out of her "element in the intellectual climate of Paris."[15] She imagined that her new friends might even have seen her as "a perfect product of the French system."[16] But she also found something new there: "freedom of thought . . . unequalled elsewhere."[17]

While often quite critical of contemporary French politics, Kristeva remains one of the foremost defenders of French enlightenment values of universalism and cosmopolitanism, sometimes to the point of disparaging different cultures' local commitments. Indeed, though continuing to feel as a foreigner within France, she has spent her adult life as one of its greatest ambassadors. On receiving the Holberg Prize, she said: "I have a strong sense of indebtedness to France, and feel proud, in the globalized world in which we live today, to bear the colors of the French Republic in the various countries and continents which I have occasion to visit."[18] The freedom of thought that she found in France became the kernel of one of her most enduring theoretical and practical interests: revolt, which she defines as "return/turning back/displacement/change."[19] In her 2014 essay, "New Forms of Revolt," she writes that revolt "constitutes the internal logic of a certain culture that I would like to revive here and whose acuity seems quite threatened these days."[20] That certain culture is clearly France and by the end of the essay the origin of the threat becomes clear: bearers of extreme evil, supposedly gangster Islamic fundamentalists.

2. Concern over the Foreigner

Herself an *étrangère*, Kristeva has never shied away from the experience of foreignness, both how it is encountered by the native and how the foreigner experiences his or her new land. For quite some time she has been concerned about the children of immigrants, or at least those who have left the developing world for developed societies; these children are young people growing up in foreign worlds, split between tradition, something lost and gone, and modernity. Her views are largely in accord with the French theorist Olivier Roy, who writes of second generation Muslim immigrants: "Contemporary Muslim minorities have to undergo a process of deculturation that has no precedent in history and is not imposed but is the consequence of voluntary displacement and shifts from pristine cultures to a common, uprooted Muslim identity."[21] Roy argues that fundamentalism afflicts uprooted Muslims more than established Muslim societies. To be displaced, to be a stranger in a strange land—the sort of displacement so commonplace in modernity—is to be vulnerable to the lure of fundamentalism.

Speaking of the situation of foreigners in France, Kristeva, herself a foreigner in France, describes the difficulty facing *les étrangers*, the difficulty of finding a safe home in a land where befriendment tends to come from bleeding hearts, paternalist, perverse people, or paranoiacs. One might suggest, in a strange homage to the International Workers of the World, "foreigners of the world, unite," but "things are not so simple," Kristeva writes at the beginning of her book *Strangers to Ourselves*, "one must take into consideration the domination/exclusion fantasy characteristic of everyone."[22] Even the foreigner finds her own foreigner. In France, she notes, "Italians call the Spaniards foreigners, the Spaniards take it out on the Portuguese, the Portuguese on the Arabs or the Jews, the Arabs on the blacks, and so forth and vice versa."[23] Certainly the same has been so in the US, where one people after another scapegoats another people after another. Even where links might be forged between one set of foreigners and another, these links "unfailingly snap when fanatical bonds fuse together again communities cemented by pure, hard fantasies."[24] The phantasies Kristeva refers to, those that some estranged foreigners nurture, are the same ones Roy does post 9/11: a "common, uprooted Muslim identity."[25] But reification of identity is not just something that supposedly plagues immigrants. Roy's and Kristeva's views tend to overlook the reification that happens on the part of the host countries, for example, a hypostatization of "French" identity. In fact, in the years since Kristeva started writing about immigration, the problems globally have escalated, especially with the rise of nationalism in countries that were once paragons of liberalism and openness.

Kristeva writes that "here, on foreign soil, the religion of the abandoned forebears is set up in its essential purity and one imagines that one preserves it better than do the parents who have stayed 'back home.'"[26] But the same could be said of the fantasies of host nations that their own "essential purity" is being attacked. Just consider Trump's call to "make America great again," surely a call to restore the purity of the nation against imagined enemies and persecutors.

Kristeva's concern with immigration took a new turn as she began developing her work on revolt and, with it, a theory of the adolescent syndrome of ideality, the observation that adolescents tend to split the world into perfection, on the one hand, and nihilism, on the other. The parents who once seemed to do no wrong begin to fail and there is either pure redemption or utter loss, for the adolescent. In searching for perfection and certainty, the adolescent is overtaken by the "need to believe" and the temptations of religion. In "New

Forms of Revolt" Kristeva finds that "'disadvantaged teens'" have succumbed to something worse than ideality, "a more radical phase of nihilism."[27] Her prime example of this syndrome is the child of immigrants: "the nihilist believer—who is necessarily nihilist because pathetically idealistic—the disconnected, desocialized teenager in the ruthlessness of global migration."[28]

This is a short step from the syndrome of ideality to immigrant youth uprisings and violence, especially the postcolonial influx of Muslims into France, above all in Marseille, and urban unrest and violence. In my view, diagnosing immigrant youth as suffering from a radical ideality is troubling, especially in not taking into account other factors. Certainly, anyone who becomes rigid and ideological is at great risk of becoming fundamentalist, but is this the root of adolescent uprisings, or might poverty and marginalization be better answers? Kristeva is convinced that the root is a failure to engage in an inner life of revolt. "The pseudo-rebellious nihilist is, in fact, someone who is reconciled by the stability of new values. And this stability, which is illusory, turns out to be deadly and totalitarian. I cannot stress enough the fact that totalitarianism is the result of a certain fixation of revolt precisely in terms of its betrayal, namely, the suspension of retrospective return, which amounts to a suspension of thought."[29] Miller shares my concerns about Kristeva's equation between Muslim unrest and a syndrome of ideality.[30] She sees a contradiction in Kristeva's account of supposed gangster fundamentalism. First, Kristeva's work on the foreigner and on revolt champions crossing boundaries but here she is both worried about global migration and aligning herself with France. Miller is also dismayed that Kristeva did not "consider the legacy of French colonialism in Africa."[31]

> Although this omission allowed her to develop her argument about the relationship between adolescence and the appeal of a seemingly unwavering ideal, her conclusion did not fit the facts in France or accord with her usual careful scholarship. Investing in a chimera, Kristeva turned away from the abject history of her own adopted nation. She seemed to disregard the fact that in the development of the adolescent, it is the parents who must take responsibility in large part for successful socialization.[32]

Miller passes quickly over "the abject history" of Kristeva's own adopted nation, France. But this seems worth pausing over for it is part of a history of colonization, which is itself part of the formation of the modern, liberal, secular nation state. To what extent are "enlightenment values" part and parcel of a history of colonization? Those restless and troublesome youth are the grandchildren of the colonized nations of the Maghreb who, with the end of colonization, were no longer French subjects but, supposedly, French citizens. The tides of history bring undercurrents and riptides of power inversions and anxieties. Subjects turned citizens, no longer there but here, can lead a nation to wonder what is any longer proper to itself. Not coincidentally, there seems to be a French secular obsession with Muslim girls' and women's clothing, not just the veil and the burqa but also a strange valorization of Western clothing; Kristeva seems to share this. In an address to the Kristeva Circle in 2016, Kristeva told the story of a teenage girl named Souad, whom she first encountered wearing a burqa over her jeans and oversized sweater. Apparently Souad had "walled herself up in silence and didn't get off the internet where, with her unknown accomplices, she exchanged furious emails against her family of 'apostates, worse than unbelievers', and prepared her voyage 'over there,' in order to become the mistress of polygamous combatants, the mother of prolific martyrs or a kamikaze herself."[33] But after embarking on a group psychoanalysis, Souad makes progress, which Kristeva gleans from the phenomenon, "she has just put her jeans back on."[34] Apparently, getting rid of the veil and returning to clothes that celebrate rather than hide the body is a step toward mental health. Here Western and non-Western feminisms clash, with many Western feminists seeing freedom as freedom to be seen and some non-Western feminisms as freedom to express one's own desires, including cultural and religious ones. Ultimately this is a clash over when one's desire is really one's own, about who should police and protect it, and the state's role in "protecting" women from their own culture.

Ibrahim sees in Kristeva's writings on religion an orientalism against Islam, an overt preference for Christianity over Islam, and a "colonialist and racist notion that is complicit with a French desire to sustain a sociocultural and political hegemony."[35] Indeed, by pointing to immigrant Muslims as her primary example of the syndrome of ideality, Kristeva does suggest that Islam is susceptible to extremism. In France, even among the left, she is hardly alone, just as populist elements in France are not alone in Europe, nor in the West more broadly. The rise of populism in countries that had previously been bastions of liberalism and multiculturalism could be profitably seen through the lens of a syndrome of ideality. My point is that Kristeva, who has beautifully articulated the theory of ideality, might also be susceptible to the syndrome, just as we all are whenever anxiety over the foreigner emerges.

3. Feminist Politics

Earlier I noted that upon her return from China, Kristeva bid her "farewell to politics." I left out the end of that line: "including feminism."[36] Given that Kristeva has often been referred to in the United States as one of the "French feminists," this is, to say the least, rather surprising. Asked about her relationship to the feminist movement in a 1988 interview, she suggested that her discomfort with it arose from its militancy, leftist ideology, and dogmatism.[37] "At the same time," she added, "I was very interested in the basic questions they were asking: the specificity of the feminine, the mother's influence on her child's development into an independent being, language acquisition, the child's dependency on the mother, the mother's role in language and symbolic processing, the nature of women's writing and women's art, and so forth."[38]

For Kristeva, the maternal function is doubly important: first for delivering the newborn into the social and symbolic world and second for emancipating women themselves.[39] This line of inquiry is anathema to the mainstream of Anglo-American feminist theory, which, beginning in the 1970s, developed a distinction between sex and gender, between biology and cultural meanings, so as to argue that sexism was a problem of bad stereotypes and could not get any validation from biological differences. In other words, biology does not destine human females to the oppressive norms of gender (femininity). Unhappy with Kristeva's invocation of feminine roles such as motherhood, many prominent Anglo-American feminists argued against Kristeva's views. In debates of the 1980s and 1990s charges were hurled at Kristeva that, because of her focus on sexual difference and her theories of the semiotic and the maternal *chora*, she was essentialist.[40] Kristeva's recent writings show that the disputes were not matters of misunderstanding but, instead, of fundamentally different ideas about women's freedom, bodies, and all.[41]

On a surface level, it may seem that Kristeva is a critic of feminism and an upholder of traditional values. Moreover, as I've briefly discussed, her loyalty to French enlightenment values has led her to lament immigrants' local attachments. On the surface, then, it seems that for those interested in radical critique, Kristeva's views on politics are not very helpful and may even be retrograde, Eurocentric, and traditional. However, it is my purpose now to show that there is a political theory, albeit latent, in Kristeva's work on psychoanalysis and meaning.

III. Kristeva's Political Theory

Kristeva's latent political theory is not so much about political issues per se but about the ways in which we all, as members of polities, develop into the kind of people who either can or cannot tolerate difficulty and ambiguity, the latter being seeds of dogmatism and intransigence.

When in the 1970s Kristeva turned away from the politics of Left Bank intellectuals to "the only continent we had never left: internal experience," she did not in fact leave politics behind.[42] Rather, she began an inquiry into the way subjectivity is formed, including our subjectivity as political agents in the world. Her work on revolt suggests that the internal experience of every speaking being profoundly shapes the political. Revolt against both external constraints and internalized and unreflected norms allows for the flourishing of an inner domain of freedom. "We are alive because we have a psychical life," which is "this interior space, this place within, that allows one to take attacks from inside and outside . . . as well as social and political aggression."[43] I read her work on revolt to mean that subjects who are too fearful to speak out and question prevailing norms pave the way for totalitarian regimes and, conversely, totalitarian regimes aim to produce subjects who follow rules unquestioningly. As another example, people born into communities haunted by past shames or glories will anticipate and help reproduce the ghosts of the past. Intimate revolt makes possible a subjectivity that is willing to take a stand in the world and disrupt the status quo, to imagine new possibilities both individually and collectively.

As a whole, Kristeva's work contests one of the most problematic aspects of most liberal political philosophy: the notion, central to social contract theory from Hobbes through Rawls, that individuals can be understood prepolitically; that fully formed individuals can stand outside the political and decide both whether or not to enter into social relations and what form those relations should take. In the nineteenth century, Hegel called that view into question, famously arguing that human beings' self-understanding is shaped through their social relations. This Hegelian insight has continued through social theories that offer a stark contrast to the Anglo-American notion of prepolitical, that is, presocial individuality. Almost anyone steeped in this tradition will take it as given that human beings are shaped through their histories and cultures. Kristeva's work is in this tradition, but in her Freudian commitments it takes a bit of a detour.

In the Freudian story of individual development, infants develop in relationship to their "objects," that is, people in their midst. But at the very dawn of their lives they are born into what he calls primary narcissism. He was never very clear about what he meant by this, and it shifted over the course of his theorizing. But in brief it meant an early psychical period when the infant did not yet have an awareness that its objects were separate entities. While Freud's account of primary narcissism varied over the years, what is constant is a story of the *development* of an ego and its relations to objects, which are not there from the start. Some early ego psychologists, such as René Spitz and Margaret Mahler, developed Freud's notion of primary narcissism by likening it to an early era of infant symbiosis with the mother that would be followed, hopefully, with individuation and independence.[44] The British analyst Winnicott referred to an era of early infantile omnipotence, prior to any individuation, when the mother's preoccupation with the child fostered that child's illusion that all needs were met, therefore having no reason yet to suspect that there was a world separate from itself. However, a later school of psychoanalysis, known as contemporary relational theory, drew on scientific infant observations and argued that there was no early stage of primary narcissism. To the contrary, they argued, infants are relational from the start. Many have been so convinced by these studies that today most schools of psychoanalysis reject Freud's account of primary narcissism, favoring instead a view of the self as object-related, that is, socially oriented from the start.

Kristeva is one of a small group of psychoanalytic thinkers who still believe in something like a stage of primary narcissism. Her readers will recognize it in her concept of the *chora*, a term she takes up from Plato to designate an early holding environment, a space in which individuation can appear, a receptacle for coming into being. This term is often linked with another one: the semiotic, the archaic form of signification that harkens back to the echolalias and nonverbal exchanges between mother and infant. As in primary narcissism, the infant of the semiotic *chora* experiences plenitude: all needs are met, there is not yet a "not me" out in the world, separate from itself. The infant has not yet separated "himself from the ecosystem into which he was fused."[45] The infant of the semiotic *chora* is not yet social. In other words, Kristeva's semiotic *chora* suggests an early stage of connection between infant and mother prior to any entry into the social. This is what Freud described as primary narcissism and Winnicott likened to a holding environment.

The mother or, we may wish to say, whoever is the primary caregiver, helps foster the infant's illusion of fullness, omnipotence, and plenty. Kristeva refers to the maternal position as one of gratifying needs, "holding" (Winnicott).[46] Although the illusion of plenitude is fostered by the mother's care, the infant does not yet know that. That awareness will come with a jolt, with the experience of the mother as "not me" because she has eyes for someone else (whether father, world, job, or other engagements). The impingement on that early holding environment can be terrifying. A gulf opens up, and the infant's salvation will only come from leaping into identifying with mother's other loves, for example, the father. This is the moment of primary repression of the early *chora*, traded away for identifications with and in the sociosymbolic world. Kristeva is one of the few theorists who understand profoundly how fragile the passage is from this early stage of in-differentiation to developing a foothold in the social-symbolic and political world.[47]

From a Kristevan point of view, every person's developmental sojourn is both riven with sociality and shapes the social and political world. But even sociality itself is something socially constructed: we are not born "naturally" social creatures; sociality is an achievement. Contra the school of contemporary relational theory, Kristeva shows that we are not born hardwired to be social and relational. We are made, not born, to connect with others. Social identifications necessitated by the end of the early holding environment make us the kinds of humans Hegel theorized, but not without an early fraught and painful stage.

Elsewhere I have drawn on Kristeva to make the point that in the prehistory of every individual there is an archaic past prior to entry into the social realm.[48] With Freud and Kristeva, I see this archaic past living on timelessly in the unconscious, much as Freud described a timeless Rome in *Civilization and Its Discontents*.[49] Both Freud and Kristeva see that archaic past as the preoedipal relation with the mother. For Freud, this timeless memory may be the source of religious illusion. It is a source of longing. But Kristeva also notes the ways in which the archaic past, namely the semiotic *chora*, continues to threaten to undo or destabilize meaning and the symbolic realm. It is a source for revolt. She turns her theoretical attention to the moments in which this maternal holding environment falters, to the abyss of meaninglessness that opens up, and to the crisis that leads the infant to make its first *social identifications*.

However, this early state, before the "not I," is also a screen over *emptiness*, Kristeva writes, which she believes is at the root of the human psyche.[50] This part of Kristeva's *Tales of Love* strikes me as the most dramatic and even tragic: to become an "I," the illusion of fullness has to be destroyed, which will happen in due course one way or the other, lest one become truly psychotic. The emptiness is revealed, then, when the illusion falters: "the *emptiness* that is intrinsic to the beginnings of the symbolic function appears as the first separation between what is not yet an *Ego* and what is not yet an *object*."[51] Narcissism is the lining of that emptiness, but eventually it too will have to give way, coming to an end with something that triggers loss of plenum. It is this breakup of plenum that gives rise to an I. This may be what must have been felt, if not experienced or thought, as the mother's abandonment—for another lover?

As Castoriadis puts it, "The social individual does not grow like a plant, but is created-fabricated by society . . . this occurs *always* by means of a violent break-up of what is the first state of the psyche and its requirements."[52] The responsibility for this violent end of plenum always falls on the social institution, which is both the source of the need to impinge on the plenum and the recourse the child takes to survive impingement. Using Winnicottian language, Castoriadis adds: "The new-born will *always* have to be torn out of his world . . . under pain of psychosis—to renounce his imaginary omnipotence, to recognize the desire of others as equally legitimate with his own."[53] The only way for the child to bear this loss is to identify with whatever holds the mother's attention. In swift succession, then, there are three moments: primary narcissism, the loss of illusion traded away for identification with the father of one's individual prehistory (returned to below), and hence identification with an avatar of the social. This moment of primal repression inaugurates the unconscious. Thanks to the mother's erotic yet ambivalent eros toward a third, the father, the mother ferries the child over the abyss from plenitude to reality, from echolalias to language.

However, because this transition never goes perfectly, the experience itself can become split off and unlived. Interpreting Winnicott, Ogden argues that this originary loss is akin to one of the primitive agonies that Winnicott lists, primarily the agonizing worry of a return to an unintegrated state. "Feeling states that are tolerable in the context of the mother-infant bond are primitive agonies when the infant must experience them on his own."[54] Because they are intolerable the infant splits them off; the split occurs but it is not experienced, much less remembered. As a result, there is "everywhere the same *impossible mourning for the maternal object*," Kristeva writes, because the moment of loss is one and the same as the moment of primary repression—the schism that creates the ego and the unconscious in one fell swoop.[55] How well, or poorly, this goes has profound political effects. For those who do not make this passage well, psychoanalysis may be called for. Kristeva describes the central task of this work as a loving transference and countertransference that allows the subject to put into the present and metabolize those unlived losses.[56]

Winnicott argued that breakdown "is a fact that is carried round hidden away in the unconscious."[57] Some past breakdown in fact may have inaugurated the unconscious. The conscious ego arises in the wake of the mother's "not me." The cost of becoming an I is repression of what had been before and the ability to split off, thereafter, whatever does not accord with the new (fictively constructed) sense of a boundaried self. After all, "what is primal repression," Kristeva asks, but the "ability of the speaking being, always already haunted by the Other, to divide, reject, repeat?"[58] Infant splits off mother; she becomes abject. Infant is left with emptiness, and narcissism arises in defense against emptiness on the way toward social identifications.

Winnicott, too, notes that emptiness can be looked at through the same lens as a fear of breakdown. "In some patients emptiness needs to be experienced, and this emptiness belongs to the past, to the time before the degree of maturity had made it possible for emptiness to be experienced."[59] It is easier to recall trauma than it is to recall emptiness, for how is one to know that nothing is happening when one does not know yet to expect anything to happen. "Emptiness is a prerequisite for eagerness to gather in. Primary emptiness simply means: before starting to fill up. . . . In practice, the difficulty is that the patient fears the awfulness of emptiness."[60] For Kristeva, the bridge over the abyss of emptiness is identification with a Third Party. For Freud, she writes, "identification with the father in [one's] own personal prehistory" is a "direct and immediate identification and takes place earlier than any object-cathexis."[61] For Kristeva, primary identification allows one to enter into the realm of representations, signs, symbols, language.[62] Emptiness goes underground. Symbolic capacities and sociality arise. Those who fail to make such an identification with a third risk becoming false selves, living in borderline states and psychosomatic conditions. Moreover, "whatever their differences," Kristeva writes, "all these symptomatologies share a common denominator—the inability to represent" rather than the normal development of meaning making heralded by symbolic modes of signification.[63]

Individuation emerges through the infant trying to stand in the place of or identify with what emerges as the mother's desire for another, a third, or what Freud refers to as the father of individual prehistory. To Elliott, Kristeva "describes primary identification as the 'zero degree' that shapes psychic space itself, and links this arising of the subject to Freud's notion of a 'father in individual prehistory.' In this 'prehistory,' the child forges an initial identification, prior to sexual division, with a maternal-paternal container."[64] The loss of plenitude (of the fantasy of omnipotence owed to the mother's early devotion) is compensated with an imaginary identification that makes possible an "I," an identification with a preobject. "The whole symbolic matrix sheltering emptiness is thus set in place in an elaboration that precedes the Oedipus complex," writes Kristeva.[65] What is experienced as human is only possible through this very structure of identification.

In sum, as we transition out of plenum and omnipotence and later, if lucky, to interdependence, we make identifications. This is first, identification with the father of individual prehistory—that is, with whatever it is that is distracting mother from her attention to us, whether work, love, or the law (of the father, of the incest taboo, of the symbolic). Second, as Volkan argues, we come to identify with our groups, our ethnic and religious identifications.[66] These groups provide solace, shelter, safety, meaning, which allow us to split off what we imagine are not the clean and proper parts of our selves. In my view, collective identities are extensions of individual ones—in fact there is hardly such a thing as an individual identity, for "identification," whether external or internal, is always a social relation, a relation with another. Moreover, failures to make identifications during crucial early stages of development lead, following Kristeva's phrase, to maladies of the soul, including depression, false-self syndromes, failures to flourish in the symbolic, all breathtakingly described throughout her work, most dramatically in brief case studies in *Black Sun* and *New Maladies of the Soul*. To these we can add syndromes of ideality, not just (if at all) at the level of individual troubled youth but at the level of politics. Drawing on Kristeva, often a politics of Manichaean divides is fueled by holding on to ideals of perfection as well as visions of demons. Both are manifestations in politics of Kristeva's notion of an adolescent syndrome of ideality, the familiar stage of looking for nirvana or falling into the abyss of nihilism.

In *Fear of Breakdown* I argued that these show up in the rise of nationalism and right-wing populist movements throughout the world. However, unlike Kristeva's application of this concept of an ideality syndrome to individual youth, which I've indicated can be mistaken and problematic, I see it as a phenomenon linked back to those early and difficult passages toward sociality. When "a people" is founded on phantastical ideals, it can become malignant, leading to a collective phenomenon of what Winnicott called a fear of breakdown.[67] Ghosts as well as unmourned wounds and traumas activate fears of breakdown and their concomitant defenses, including idealization and demonization, both resulting from failures to work through imperfection and loss. I am seeking to emphasize that the rise of nationalism, populisms, and other polarizing phenomena taps into a global political problem: the lack of a public and shared means for working through ambiguity and loss, for coming to understand the strangers in our midst; that is, for working through syndromes of ideality. Kristeva calls for a process of such work in her writings on revolt and the adolescent syndrome of ideality. In my view, working through these syndromes calls for a public political process of choice and mourning, a multiplication of the iconic scene, the analytic space: patient on the couch, analyst behind, and the analytic third to their dyad where Manichaean divides can transform into shades of grey; where projected demons can be taken back and metabolized; where the adolescent selves we all are at one time or another might grow up and realize the world is not made of saints and sinners but of complex and imperfect people; and most importantly that there are no perfect solutions that will solve all our troubles.[68] The task is how to take this micropolitics to a macrolevel, how to move to a politics of mourning and working through.

Kristeva argues that to deal with the adolescent syndrome of ideality, first, the analyst must recognize and not dismiss the need to believe, for this idealization is in fact a source of extreme pleasure. This allows for a positive transference that the analyst can use to model another way of thinking that is also pleasurable. As Kristeva writes, "only the analyst's capacity to see through the idealizing course of adolescent drives will allow him to provide a credible and effective transference—and thus be capable of metabolizing the *need to believe* not through acting out but through the pleasure that comes with thinking, questioning and analysing."[69] In other words, to overcome the syndrome of ideality, we need to transform the need to believe into an urge to question and think, that is, to move from seeing the world in black and white terms to seeing its variegated and complex hues. In a dyad of analyst and analysand, this can occur through the transference.

When the adolescent syndrome sweeps up broad swaths of people, the analogue for psychoanalysis is public discourse in an affectively deliberative frame. What I mean by this is something that, however imperfectly, is close to a "talking cure" in the sense that it involves mourning the loss of ideality through the kind of deliberation that elucidates what is gained and what is lost in any course of action we might take. In all our deliberations, private and public, we have to weigh, as on a scale, what will be gained and what will be lost. In making a choice to go in one direction rather than another, we also need to metabolize the loss in advance, thereby giving ourselves the will to move this way rather than that. Otherwise we will be glued in place, unable to take either fork in the road. Such, in my view, are the lessons of Kristeva's deeply political theory, a theory that shows how fraught and treacherous the road to sociality can be, and which argues for the need to metabolize and work through loss.

Noëlle McAfee

Emory University
March 2019

NOTES

1. See Hanan M. Ibrahim, "Foreigners to Kristeva: Refashioning Orientalism and the Limits of Love," *Journal of Commonwealth Literature* (June 2018): 1–12. For Kristeva on disability, see "Liberty, Equality, Fraternity and . . . Vulnerability," in *Hatred and Forgiveness*, trans. Jeanine Herman (New York: Columbia University Press, 2010). On the veil, "What of Tomorrow's Nation?" in *Nations Without Nationalism* (New York: Columbia University Press, 1993): "Can one be sure that even foreigners, who are asking for 'integration,' are aware of and appreciate that French *esprit général* in which they seemingly wish to take their place? . . . It is possible that the 'abstract' advantages of French universalism may prove to be superior to the 'concrete' benefits of a Muslim scarf, for instance" (47). On Kristeva's view on immigration, Honig writes: "The limits of Kristeva's cosmopolitanism emerge again when . . . Kristeva suggests that the '"abstract" advantages of a French universalism may prove to be superior to the "concrete" benefits of a muslim scarf,' implying that the scarf, unlike the nation, is essentially a fetish and is therefore unable, as such, to serve as a healthy transitional object." Bonnie Honig, *Democracy and the Foreigner* (Princeton: Princeton University Press, 2001), 64.

2. Julia Kristeva. "New Forms of Revolt," *Journal of French and Francophone Philosophy* 22, no. 2 (2014): 1–19.

3. "Julia Kristeva Was Communist Secret Agent, Bulgaria Claims," *Guardian*, March 28, 2018, https://www.theguardian.com/world/2018/mar/28/julia-kristeva-communist-secret-agent-bulgaria-claims. Jennifer Schuessler and Boryana Dzhambazova, "Bulgaria Says French Thinker Was a Bulgarian Agent, She Calls It a 'Barefaced Lie,'" *New York Times*, April 1, 2018, https://www.nytimes.com/2018/04/01/arts/julia-kristeva-bulgaria-communist-spy.html. Dimiter Kenarov, "Was the Philosopher Julia Kristeva a Cold War Collaborator?" *New Yorker*, September 5, 2018, https://www.newyorker.com/news/dispatch/was-the-philosopher-julia-kristeva-a-cold-war-collaborator.

4. Julia Kristeva, "Bulgaria, Post-totalitarian Europe and Me," *The Philosophical Salon*, *Los Angeles Review of Books*, November 26, 2018, https://thephilosophicalsalon.com/bulgaria-post-totalitarian-europe-and-me/. See also Julia Kristeva, "It's Not Just My

Life—Julia Kristeva Responds" in the Blog of the *Los Angeles Review of Books*, November 1, 2018, https://blog.lareviewofbooks.org/essays/just-life-julia-kristeva-responds/.

5. Julia Kristeva, "My Memory's Hyperbole," in Kelly Oliver, ed., *The Portable Kristeva* (New York: Columbia University Press, 2002), 13.

6. Ibid., 10–12.

7. Ibid., 17.

8. Ibid.

9. Ibid.

10. Ibid., 18.

11. Ibid., 19.

12. Ibid.

13. Ibid.

14. Julia Kristeva, "Thinking about Liberty in Dark Times," in *Hatred and Forgiveness*, 4.

15. Kristeva, "My Memory's Hyperbole," 6.

16. Ibid.

17. Ibid., 7.

18. Kristeva, "Thinking about Liberty in Dark Times," 4.

19. Kristeva, "New Forms of Revolt," 4.

20. Ibid., 4–5.

21. Olivier Roy, *Globalized Islam: The Search for a New Ummah* (New York: Columbia University Press, 2004), 109.

22. Julia Kristeva, *Strangers to Ourselves*, trans. Leon S. Roudiez (New York: Columbia University Press, 1991), 24.

23. Ibid.

24. Ibid.

25. I use "phantasy" for the largely unconscious frameworks and imaginaries that structure expectations as opposed to "fantasy," which largely refers to daydreams and reverie.

26. Kristeva, *Strangers to Ourselves*, 24.

27. Kristeva, "New Forms of Revolt," 17.

28. Ibid.

29. Ibid., 5.

30. Elaine Miller, "Investing in a Third: Colonization, Religious Fundamentalism, and Adolescence," *Journal of French and Francophone Philosophy* 22, no. 2: 36–45.

31. Ibid., 43.

32. Ibid.

33. Julia Kristeva, "Interpreting Radical Evil," The Kristeva Circle, Stockholm, October 13–15, 2016, http://www.kristeva.fr/interpreting-radical-evil.html.

34. Ibid.

35. Ibrahim, "Foreigners to Kristeva," 4.

36. Kristeva, "My Memory's Hyperbole," 19.

37. Julia Kristeva, "Julia Kristeva in Person," in Ross Guberman, ed., *Julia Kristeva Interviews* (New York: Columbia University Press, 1996), 7.

38. Ibid.

39. See Julia Kristeva, "Reliance, or Maternal Eroticism," *Journal of the American Psychoanalytic Association* 62, no. 1 (2014): 70–71.

40. For an overview of these debates and a defense of Kristeva, see Kelly Oliver, "Julia Kristeva's Feminist Revolutions," *Hypatia*, 8, no. 3 (1993): 94–114.

41. Kristeva, "Reliance, or Maternal Eroticism."

42. Kristeva, "My Memory's Hyperbole," 19.

43. Julia Kristeva, *Intimate Revolt* (New York: Columbia University Press, 2002), 267.

44. R. A. Spitz, "Bridges On Anticipation, Duration, and Meaning," *Journal of the American Psychoanalytic Association* 20, no. 4 (1972): 721–35. M. Mahler, "On Human

Symbiosis and the Vicissitudes of Individuation," *Journal of the American Psychoanalytic Association* 15, no. 4 (1967): 740–63.

45. Julia Kristeva, *Revolution in Poetic Language*, trans. Margaret Waller (New York: Columbia University Press, 1984), 52.

46. Julia Kristeva, *Tales of Love*, trans. Leon S. Roudiez (New York: Columbia University Press, 1987), 29.

47. Members of this small group, in which I include myself, are Winnicott, Castoriadis, Ogden, and Whitebook. It does not include Klein or contemporary Kleinians. Lacan's position is more complicated, though probably closer to Kristeva's. See Amy Allen and Mari Ruti, *Critical Theory Between Klein and Lacan: A Dialogue* (New York: Bloomsbury, 2019).

48. Noëlle McAfee, *Fear of Breakdown: Politics and Psychoanalysis* (New York: Columbia University Press, 2019).

49. Sigmund Freud, *Civilization and Its Discontents*, in *The Standard Edition of the Complete Psychological Works of Sigmund Freud*, vol. XXI, trans. James Strachey (London: Hogarth, 1964), 69–70.

50. Kristeva, *Tales of Love*, 23.

51. Ibid., 24.

52. Cornelius Castoriadis, *The Imaginary Institution of Society* (Cambridge: MIT Press, 1987), 311.

53. Ibid.

54. Thomas Ogden, "Fear of Breakdown and the Unlived Life," *International Journal of Psychoanalysis* 95, no. 2 (2014): 210.

55. Julia Kristeva, *Black Sun*, trans. Leon S. Roudiez (New York: Columbia University Press, 1989), 9.

56. See ibid., ch. 3.

57. D. W. Winnicott, "Fear of Breakdown," *International Review of Psychoanalysis* 1 (1974): 104.

58. Julia Kristeva, *Powers of Horror: An Essay on Abjection*, trans. Leon S. Roudiez (New York: Columbia University Press, 1982), 12.

59. Winnicott, "Fear of Breakdown," 106.

60. Ibid.

61. Freud, "The Ego and the Id," in *The Standard Edition of the Complete Psychological Works of Sigmund Freud*, vol. XIX, trans. James Strachey (London: Hogarth, 1961), 31.

62. Kristeva, *Tales of Love*, 42.

63. Julia Kristeva, *New Maladies of the Soul*, trans. Ross Guberman (New York: Columbia University Press, 1995), 9.

64. Anthony Elliott, "The Affirmation of Primary Repression Rethought: Reflections on the State of the Self in its Unconscious Relational World," *American Imago* 52, no. 1: 55–79.

65. Kristeva, *Tales of Love*, 27.

66. Vamik Volkan, *Bloodlines: From Ethnic Pride to Ethnic Terrorism* (New York: Basic Books, 1998).

67. McAfee, *Fear of Breakdown*, chs. 3 and 12.

68. Ibid., chs. 4–11.

69. Julia Kristeva, "Adolescence, a Syndrome of Ideality," *Psychoanalytic Review* 94, no. 5 (2007): 724–25.

36

Kelly Oliver

THE DEMOCRACY OF PROXIMITY AND KRISTEVA'S NEW HUMANISM

Kristeva argues that we need to rethink the social contract such that it is no longer based on implicit or explicit acceptance of universal laws or presuppositions about rational or autonomous personhood. As an alternative, she proposes that we add vulnerability to the foundations of the social contract (which in France is based on equality, liberty, and fraternity) and thereby transform contractual democracy into democracy based on "proximity." By adding a fourth term, vulnerability, to Enlightenment humanism, Kristeva says, "analytic listening inflects these three toward a concern for sharing."[1] This essay poses and responds to a number of questions raised in and by Kristeva's thought: What is analytic listening? How does it inflect democratic values with sharing? How does sharing vulnerability transform the universal values at the foundation of liberal democracy?

In order to answer these questions, we need to understand Kristeva's notions of vulnerability, proximity, and humanism as hospitality, and how she formulates these concepts in relation to what she calls a "democracy of proximity."[2] Focusing on passages in her recent writings where she invokes a democracy of proximity and a new humanism, I explore what Kristeva might mean by "vulnerability," "proximity," and "new humanism." I interpret vulnerability as the split between being and meaning that makes us human. Following Merleau-Ponty and Levinas, I interpret proximity as affective proximity, which Kristeva associates with psychoanalytic transference. I interpret her new humanism as it revolves around the transfer of affect and hospitality. While I have reservations about endorsing any of these traits as distinctly human, and therefore am skeptical about any sort of humanism or human exceptionalism, nonetheless, I find the role of affects in Kristeva's discussions of a new humanism and of a democracy of proximity promising in rethinking liberal political values. After taking up the task of unpacking Kristeva's notions of vulnerability, proximity, and humanism as hospitality, I will extend her analysis further towards an ethical politics of sharing a home.

Kristeva's thinking about a democracy of proximity is inspired by her own experience living with the "neurological difficulties" of her son and, more recently, by visits to L'Arche community, which motivated her epistolary exchange with its founder, Jean Vanier. The title of the published version of their exchange, *Leur regard perce nos ombres*, is an allusion to Henrik Ibsen's play *Little Eyolf* (1894), in which a disabled son drowns.[3] The boy's mother is haunted by the look in his eyes, which penetrates to the depths of her humanity.

Drawing from this mother's interaction with her son, Kristeva suggests that the encounter with a person in the situation of disability has the potential to challenge traditional notions of humanism—both Christian and Enlightenment—and to inspire a new humanism.[4] Kristeva says that the play changes "the gaze of the non-disabled on persons with disability. Ibsen helps us to do this by reversing the perspective: it is Eyolf who looks at us, it is the look of the little boy with a disability that counts, for it is him who will pierce our shadows."[5] Kristeva is struck by the moment in Ibsen's play when the mother is recalled to her humanity by the look of her disabled son. In her essays on disability, Kristeva explores how interaction with persons in the situation of disability challenges our notion of the human and thereby motivates a new humanism.

Kristeva asks, "how does disability change our experience, and with this, our idea of human being?"[6] She answers that the encounter with disability challenges us to formulate a new humanism, based neither on Christian charity nor on Enlightenment reason, but, rather, on our shared vulnerability, which turns out to be a sharing of what cannot be shared, namely singularity. This new humanism starts from an interaction with people in the situation of disability, which shows us something essential about what it means to be human, namely, what it means to be vulnerable.

In "Liberty, Equality, Fraternity and . . . Vulnerability," Kristeva concludes: "Finding our limits gives us the ability to share those of the disabled subject, failings and flashes of brilliance alike, in the full sense of the word *share*, which is not fusion, osmosis, or identification. To share . . . to participate, without erasing the fact that each is 'apart' and recognizing the part that cannot be shared, that is irremediable."[7] In this passage, Kristeva plays with the word *part*, both in the French *partager*, to share, and as to be a part of or to belong to; but the addition of an "a" in both French (*à part*) and English (apart) transforms the meaning from belonging to, to being separated from.

How can we be both part and apart, together and separate, belonging and isolated? How can we share what is unshareable? In political terms, the question is: how can the social pact take into consideration the singularity of each person? In more philosophical terms, the question is: how can politics become ethical? If politics requires universals or laws, and ethics requires respect for each human being's unique situation, how can we ever reconcile the ethical and political? Recognizing singularity would require acknowledging what sets each one apart without making that uniqueness a reason for exclusion. We would need to recognize what sets each apart and simultaneously recognize that in spite of that—or because of it—each is also a part. Each singular being belongs to the whole of humanity and yet is unique and apart. Kristeva asks us to consider how we can make singularity rather than universality the basis of the social contract. She suggests that we start by acknowledging that what we share through our humanity is what cannot be shared, the singularity of each one. But how is this possible? How can we reconcile the universal and the singular?

Kristeva asks, "Would it be possible that the democracy of proximity and solidarity . . . would realize that the *respect of rights* requires firstly and before anything else *the recognition and the respect for the singular person*?"[8] Kristeva proposes adding vulnerability to the values of liberal democracy insofar as affect is what has been excluded from the social contract, which is based on the ideal citizen or political norm as rational, productive, and able-bodied, etc. As a counterpoint, she insists on an affective engagement with a singular other based on shared vulnerability.

I. Vulnerability

What does she mean by vulnerability, however? Vulnerability is not primarily the consequence of our embodiment or the fact that we can be physically wounded or become ill. Furthermore, her notion of vulnerability cannot be reduced to our dependence or interdependence or that we require or give care—although giving and receiving care are essential for human life and flourishing. Rather, for Kristeva vulnerability is the result of the fact that we are "speaking beings."[9] As speaking beings, we straddle biology and culture, *zōē* and *bios*, such that this split forms a primary wound (to use Kristeva's description from "Stabat Mater").[10] We are vulnerable because we are beings who mean. As beings who mean, our very biology is intrinsically social. She claims that the discovery of the unconscious as the place where biology meets culture is a discovery of "*the essential vulnerability of the speaking body*."[11] Human vulnerability, then, is the unique consequence of our place between nature and culture as speaking bodies or, more generally, as beings who mean. The vulnerability of the speaking being—or the being who means—is its radical dependence upon belonging and being accepted. This vulnerability is the psychical vulnerability that comes with occupying a place between being and meaning, such that we can never fully articulate or communicate our bodily experience.[12]

When discussing people in the situation of disability, however, it is important to acknowledge that not every human being is literally a speaking being. Many people with cognitive disabilities have difficulty speaking, and some disabilities render people speechless. Nonetheless, even people who cannot speak are beings who mean, beings for whom meaning is an issue, beings whose existence straddles biology and culture. Indeed, Kristeva uses the phrase "people in the situation of disability" to signal the place between biology and the social that defines disability or disabilities.

Given her emphasis on human beings as speaking beings, we can see why she values psychoanalysis as the "talking cure." The simplicity of this formulation is deceptive insofar as meaning making involves much more than speaking or signification, for it also takes us into the realms of imagination or fantasy, and affect or emotion. For Kristeva, it is psychoanalysis as the "talking cure" that allows the passions to speak without judgment, and thereby defuses them and thus ushers in a new humanism beyond mere transference.[13] In several places, she suggests that psychoanalysis is not just a practice but also a worldview that goes beyond the analytic session. In her writings on disability, for example, she imagines a cultural psychoanalysis that goes well beyond the couch or the psychoanalytic session. However, thinking through the relationship between speaking beings—or beings who mean—and psychoanalysis is important for rethinking democracy as proximity. Why? The answer is multifaceted and involves expanding our notion of psychoanalysis from the couch to "another way of being in the world."[14]

First, there is transference or, I would prefer to say, the transfer of affect. Until recently, affects were evacuated from political theory. However, as recent highly charged political campaigns in liberal democracies worldwide have made apparent, affects are central to politics. They are also the currency of the unconscious and thus of transference. Transference is unique to speaking beings or, more generally, to beings who mean. We could say that only beings who mean have an unconscious. Moreover, it is the unconscious that makes us vulnerable, or we are vulnerable to the unconscious. Unconscious desires and fears formed in our primary relationships can be transferred onto subsequent relationships. In fact, psychoanalysis relies on this transference to uncover those desires and fears as they manifest themselves in relation to the analyst. However, transference or the transfer of affect is not limited to the psychoanalytic session. Rather, it is inherent in every human relationship.

The psychoanalytic pact proposes that only by attending to our unconscious fears and desires as they affect all of our relationships, whether with others or with ourselves, can we understand why we do what we do and why we want what we want. The postulation of the unconscious is key to thinking through vulnerability in relationship to a democracy of proximity and a new humanism. The liberal individual born out of Enlightenment humanism (and still populating much contemporary political theory) cannot account for its own unconscious fears and desires. Together with the affects associated with them, they have been evacuated from both Enlightenment humanism and the social contract, based as these are on reason and autonomy.

Psychoanalytic listening or benevolent listening, as Kristeva calls it, is attentive to the transfer of affect. In order to support the move of vulnerability into the social pact, Kristeva insists on the necessity of psychoanalytic listening. Thus, benevolent listening on the part of the analyst (and perhaps the analysand listening to himself or herself) is the second aspect of the psychoanalytic setting that we must export to other democratic values, including liberty, equality, and fraternity. These values must be "inflected" with psychoanalytic listening. Analytic listening is not only an attentiveness to the circulation of affect as manifestations of unconscious fears and desires, but is, moreover, nonjudgmental listening, which is why Kristeva also associates analytic listening with forgiveness or pardon as the giving of psychic space and time necessary to make traumatic experiences meaningful.[15] The goal of psychoanalytic listening is to suspend judgment and allow the subject space and time to connect her affect to words. In addition, analytic listening is attentiveness to one's own desires and fears as they are evoked by encounters with others. By both suspending judgment and analyzing one's own fears and desires, psychoanalytic listening opens the political onto the ethical. In fact, analytic listening's suspension of judgment opens up the possibility of analyzing our own investments in violence, abjection, and exclusion.

Kristeva argues that traditional humanism has excluded people with disabilities because it is "incapable of traversing the fears and anxieties that control the unconscious—and often conscious—rejection of the disabled by those who are not. It is precisely here that *psychoanalytic listening to vulnerability* could take on political meaning, addressing not only those affected by a disability but the society of others, who, instead of integrating them, might have real interaction with them."[16] Democratic values must be transformed by considering vulnerability as the dimension of affective transference upon which we are all dependent for meaning making. We are social beings for whom meaning—both referential meaning and existential meaning—is dependent upon the affective realm of experience as it is lived in relation to others. Through interaction with others, we find and create the meaning of our lives with and for each other. Interaction requires being with and living with others. The democracy of sharing is not only sharing resources and physical space but also sharing the emotional support of being with people as they are with both their limitations and their gifts.

Vulnerability brings with it both political rights and responsibilities. In addition to liberty and equality, we have the right to belong and to be accepted by a community. We have the right to have our being supported by meaning-making institutions. We have the right to find ourselves and our bodies "represented" within the social, not as abject and excluded, but, rather, as positive and accepted. Language and meaning preexist us, but we can make meaning our own by making the clichés of culture our own through what Kristeva calls intimate revolt: "'I' will express my specificity by distorting the nevertheless necessary clichés of the codes of communication and by constantly deconstructing ideas/concepts/ideologies/philosophies that 'I' have inherited."[17] However, as her analysis of disability suggests, not everyone has equal opportunity to engage in this intimate revolt, and revolt is more difficult for some than for others.[18]

Furthermore, the support necessary to meaning making for a meaningful life is not facilitated by integration into a capitalist economy that reduces a person's value to how much and how fast they can produce or how much and how fast they can earn. Our culture's "maniacal surge of hyper-productivity" is an attempt to deny our fundamental vulnerability, a disavowal manifest in traditional philosophies based on rational autonomy of the will.[19] Indeed, there is a tension in trying to integrate people with disabilities into an economy that values independence and denigrates dependence. Considering people with disabilities challenges traditional values of rationality, autonomy, and independence as the hallmarks of humanity and criteria for membership in the moral community. While programs of integration are important, it is also crucial to examine their implicit values and priorities. Simply "hiring the handicapped" is not enough.[20]

The risk of integration into this economy of production and consumption is that people with disabilities will be reduced to either "invalids or workers."[21] This form of humanism as *Homo faber* includes people with disabilities and others only insofar as they fit into the economy of performance: "One main current of so-called modern humanism—normative, normalizing, infatuated with performance and entrepreneurial competitiveness in the 'work more to earn more' race—shares this philosophy."[22] Within this economy, only those who are productive or can perform some task have value. Kristeva proposes that the alternative to this integration into capitalist values is interaction. But what is meaningful interaction, and how is it the basis for a democracy of proximity?

II. Proximity

Here we explore what Kristeva might mean by proximity. As we have seen, in *Hatred and Forgiveness*, she associates the democracy of proximity with "a democracy of sharing."[23] We have emphasized that sharing is not only sharing a common space or resources but also sharing a world in the sense of making meaning together. Meaning making is a shared activity that must include persons in the situation of disability. As we have seen, it always involves transference or the transfer of affects, which makes us vulnerable. Moreover, we are vulnerable to meaning itself, or to the big-O Other of language and systems of signification into which we are born but which we do not ourselves create. To paraphrase Wittgenstein, there is no private language. We are social creatures and proximity requires interaction and not just integration; conversely, interaction requires proximity. Integration alone risks automation and standardization that reduce the individual to a cog in the economic machine. Proximity as interaction refers to the sharing of meaning and not just the sharing of space. Proximity is not just physical closeness but, moreover, emotional and intellectual closeness. To be close is not necessarily to be psychically close, but, rather, to be emotionally close. For example, when we ask, "Are you and your sister close?" we don't mean do you live in the same city or state, but, rather, do you live in the same world, are you emotionally close? Your sister might be in the next room and the answer to that question could be "no," while she might be on another continent and the answer could be "yes."[24]

I cannot help but think that Kristeva's notion of proximity is influenced by the notion of proximity prominent in twentieth-century French philosophy, particularly in the work of Merleau-Ponty and Levinas. If we look back at the notion of proximity as it operates in these thinkers, we see a clear association between proximity and affective connection. For example, prefiguring Kristeva's description of abjection, Merleau-Ponty cites Kurt Koffka describing an affective connection prior to perception: "an object looks attractive or repulsive before it looks black or blue, circular or square."[25] This perceptual experience grounds the lived experience of proximity or distance. Lived closeness or lived distance is not defined in terms of physical space, but, rather, in terms of affective space. As Shiloh Whitney notes, also resonant with Kristeva's notion of proximity is Merleau-Ponty's talking of "overwhelming proximity" where emotions overwhelm to the point of being threatening as opposed to a "lived distance" as the ability to step back from that proximity.[26] "What protects the sane man against delirium or hallucination, is not his critical powers, but the structure of his [affective] space."[27] For Merleau-Ponty, we are part of, yet apart from, the flesh of the world, which, in Whitney's words, requires "attending to the intimacy and proximity of flesh as an affective phenomenon."[28]

Like Merleau-Ponty, Kristeva emphasizes the necessity of both connection and distance in relation to affective proximity. For example, her notion of *maternal passion* and *maternal reliance* both revolve around the mother's depassioning or dispassioning as the operation of weaning the child so that it can become separate and more-or-less autonomous.[29] She claims that maternal passion is the prototype for all human passion insofar as it includes both passion and depassion, binding and rebinding, separating human passion from mere animal emotion.[30] Maternal love is the result of a process of transforming animal emotion into passion through the distance from drives and objects initiated through signification. This distance is associated with self-reflectivity that allows us to put emotions into signs.[31]

Following in the steps of biologist Jean-Didier Vincent, she says that emotions belong to all vertebrates, but human beings are the only animals who can turn those emotions into passions through imagination and then signification.[32] Sublimation is uniquely human. Our ability to distance ourselves from our affects through sublimation makes us human. Thus, both proximity and distance are necessary for meaning making. Each individual must be both part of an affective community and yet apart or separated from that affective bind.

For Kristeva, psychoanalysis provides the ultimate distance that allows for an elaboration of drives and affects, bodily sensations and emotions, and thereby gives us distance from our animality. Religion, art, music, writing, and mysticism are other practices that she claims can be sublimatory. Through these various activities, we can redirect drives and affects into creative relations with the other-within (our unconscious) and thereby with others outside of ourselves. She proposes the mother's love as the model of human love that accepts and welcomes the other insofar as the mother's love both binds her to the child and yet necessitates her letting go of the child. In the *ideal* situation of motherhood, the mother welcomes the child's otherness, accepts their difference, and loves them as they are rather than how she might wish them to be. In this regard, the disabled child calls the mother to her own humanity by calling on her to love them not in spite of their difference but because of it. The structure of maternal eros, insofar as it goes beyond self-sovereignty, teaches us that although we do not choose the others or otherness that call to us, we can elect to embrace them. At its limit, the maternal ideal of love is an affirmation of the being of the child as it is above all else.[33]

Kristeva's maternal passion as love and acceptance of difference is reminiscent of what Levinas calls *paternal election.*[34] For Levinas, the father-son relationship requires a choice after the fact in the sense that the father—or parent—does not know who his child is, or will be, yet is called upon to choose it, to love it, to accept it, nonetheless. This relationship is not based on rules or recognition but rather on the embrace of the singularity of the other. The father chooses the son after he has had no choice. His love *elects* this particular child in his uniqueness as the loved one, the one meant to be. In this regard, Levinas suggests that all love for another person must approach paternal love insofar as that love elects the loved one from among all others.[35] This love makes the loved one unique, and makes this love necessary rather than contingent.

Both Kristeva and Levinas describe how the relation with the child requires relinquishing any illusions of control or identification in order to love this other who is "my child" but never mine. This process of undergoing or suffering the passion and dispassion that constitute the eros of paternity and maternity can awaken otherness within the parent that disturbs the parent's sense of self-control, self-identification, and self-ownership—what Kristeva identifies with the instability of identity in maternity, which reaches its peak in pregnancy.[36] For her, this awakening of otherness within is a process of rebirth that comes through various forms of sublimation not limited to maternity or paternity.

When they approach the ideals described by Levinas and Kristeva, the structure of maternity and paternity, the ideals of eros and love beyond sovereignty and self, teach us that although we do not choose the others or otherness that call to us, we can elect to embrace them. For Levinas, it is our face-to-face with the other that initiates the proximity he identifies with ethical responsibility. In *Otherwise than Being*, Levinas describes the face-to-face encounter that initiates the ethical obligation as proximity.[37] As in Merleau-Ponty, Levinasian proximity is beyond critical reasoning or Husserlian intentionality wherein subjects intuit objects. "In starting with *touching*, interpreted not as palpation but as caress, and *language*, interpreted not as the traffic of information but as contact, we have tried to describe *proximity* as irreducible to consciousness and thematization."[38] For Levinas, proximity engenders sensibility, tenderness, caresses, none of which are reducible to knowing or intending subjects or objects. Our relationships with others begin not with intentional consciousness, but, rather, in the proximity of two living bodies. "Only a subject that eats can be for-the-other, or can signify."[39] For Levinas, however, while proximity is an affective phenomenon, it is primarily an ethical phenomenon.

The take away from this quick look back at Merleau-Ponty and Levinas on proximity is that proximity refers not just to physical space but also, and more importantly, to affective space. Moreover, affective connections bring with them ethical obligations. Perhaps this is why at the end of her recent essay on disability, Kristeva turns to love as the basis for an ethics-inflected politics. "Through my love for the other singular, I carry him or her to their specific, singular, development—and to mine, equally specific and singular."[40]

Furthermore, the psychoanalytic listening that suspends judgment and supports the transfer of affects into speech is a loving ear. "Is it not love saturated with affects that Freud put on the couch? Moreover, it is love that is transferred in the listening we do to the speech, drives, and affects of our patients."[41] The love that Kristeva identifies is not love with a capital-L, nor is it romantic or romanticized love.[42] Rather, it is analytic love, which is infused with transferential affect and critical analysis. The love she proposes is a critical love that demands vigilant investigation into our own investments in violence and our own ambivalent desires. This critical love brings with it obligations, not just for what we do or say, not just for what we feel or believe, but also for our unconscious fears and desires and the effects they have on others.

In her discussion of love at the end of "A Tragedy and a Dream," Kristeva associates this love of the singular with what she calls "vigilant transfer" in the maternal relationship or, in other terms, the transfer of affect.[43] This vigilant transfer points to the centrality of transference in human relationships.[44] Transference, specifically the transfer of affects, is what is missing in integration and present in interaction. This is why Kristeva insists on interaction and not merely integration when it comes to people in the situation of disability. The "transferential encounter" revitalizes and jubilates.[45] Operating on the affective level, it imbues signification—and human life itself—with meaning.

Kristeva goes so far as to suggest that caregivers be trained in transference to better understand the needs of the ones they care for and their own relationship to them: "I am thinking of the *training of caregivers* in place of psychoanalysis in this complex and controversial area when broaching the question of love, understood as a continual and elucidated transference, in caring for the disabled person."[46] Moving transference from the psychoanalytic setting into everyday relationships would mean critical reflection on the ways in which we project our own fears and desires onto others. Furthermore, it would require taking responsibility for the ways in which our responses to others engender their responses to us, particularly emotional responses. Taking responsibility for the other's response is a hallmark of Levinasian ethics as first philosophy. It is also the basis for what I have called *witnessing* as attention to a pathos beyond recognition that binds us and obligates us to respond.[47] An ethics of psychoanalysis is even more radical than Levinasian ethics that makes us responsible for the other's response, in that it makes us responsible for our unconscious desires and fears and the process of transference and countertransference, which encompasses our response to others and otherness in ourselves.

Kristeva suggests moving this ethical attention to the singularity of each supported by psychoanalytic listening and attention to the transfer of affects into the political realm in "a politics that has become ethics, in expanding the political pact as far as the boundaries of life," which places "utter singularity at the heart of the social pact."[48] What happens, then, when love of the singular moves into—and moves—the political pact? Can we learn to love others, even those most different from ourselves, even those whom we fear? Can we work through our own projections and abjections and come to terms with others in our midst? Kristeva proposes love over solidarity to transform social bonds and the political pact and make them more inclusive. We need to "reinvent love as *union with singularity* of all others. In other terms: the *love of singulars* must be substituted for *integrating solidarity* with the weak. What love? Love as desire and will so that the singular can elucidate, be recognized, and develop in sharing his own singularity. Far more than solidarity, which itself still has trouble existing, only this love can drive the constitutive singularity."[49] Solidarity with others or the disabled is not enough. Integration is not enough. We must do more than tolerate others. We must embrace them through interaction and ultimately critical analytic love. In other words, we must desire and will their existence and not just tolerate it. We must want them to be . . . to be as they are and not how we might wish. This love of being goes beyond mere acceptance and integration of "deficient" others.

Again, Kristeva turns to a mother's love of her child, and more personally, her own love for her son, when she says "I want that you be," "I love that you be."[50] This is not mere acceptance of or solidarity with those seen as lacking. This love goes beyond accommodating privations and defects, which Kristeva associates with both Aristotelian and Christian approaches to disability.[51] Rather, this love embraces the positive in the person in the situation of disability and wants them to be as they are and not otherwise. It is through interaction with the singularity of each as an act of love that embraces them as they are and thereby transforms the norms of culture. In this dynamic relationship, new political subjects emerge "who push back the limits of former norms and engender new ones," proving that "the norm is no longer an *a priori* fixed concept but a dynamic one."[52]

Another way to describe Kristeva's transformative project is bringing humanism—her new humanism—into politics and culture. In a personal essay on her relationship to her motherland, Bulgaria, she describes a split between the humanism embraced at universities and in the political sphere. When politics does not embrace humanist values, particularly the new humanism founded on the singularity of each person, then it risks totalitarianism and fundamentalism (which could be taken as the extremes of integration). When thinking about integration, we must be careful to ask, integration into what? What are the norms of this integration?

Both totalitarianism and fundamentalism close down questioning and reject singularity in favor of a "solidarity" that doesn't allow for individual differences. In the face of differences of all kinds, and changing norms, today we see reactionary push-back from groups that cling to nationalisms and religious fundamentalisms in the name of an exclusionary politics. With refugees at their highest levels ever and continuing to increase without any signs of abatement, some people are afraid that their way of life is being threatened. Their deep-seated fears manifest as hatred of, and attacks on, those they see as others, those they see as threatening their homes. Discussing post-totalitarian democracies in particular, Kristeva proposes that the antidote is to bring "to life a humanist culture whose refoundation, ever in progress, requires the continual questioning of identity, nation, faith, and the need to believe itself."[53] Continual and vigilant questioning of our own motivations and desires, and of the ways in which transference affects our relationships, wards off dangerous fundamentalisms. Questioning is crucial for a new humanism based on hospitality to the singularity of each.

In light of contemporary fears and hostilities towards immigrants and otherness, living with others might be a prerequisite for integration. In other words, there can be no true integration without interaction. Without interaction, integration is nothing more than a fragile tolerance that, as has been made painfully clear in recent outbursts of racist and sexist hatred on the part of those in power and their followers, easily explodes into its opposite. Living with others and interacting with them, on the other hand, is transformative. This is the principle that motivates Jean Vanier's L'Arche project. Vanier believes that the violence and anger at the lockdown institutions for the disabled is the result of their living situation and not part of the characters of "inmates." Vanier has devoted himself to creating meaningful lives for persons in the situation of disability by creating homes where they are loved. Vanier recounts how his experience living with disabled people is transformative for all involved. For himself, he says he had to learn communion rather than competition; he had to learn simply to be with others, especially those who cannot speak.[54] For the disabled people who moved from institutions into homes, he describes the transformation from anguish and depression to relaxation and trust. "This shows through the expression on the face and through all their flesh. As they discover a sense of belonging, that they are part of a 'family,' then the will to live begins to emerge."[55] His experience has taught him that living with others and a sense of home are essential to well-being.

III. Hospitality

Everyone needs a safe place to call home, a safe place to sleep, and to feel loved. Kristeva points out that "the word 'ethos' originally meant a 'regular sleeping place or animal shelter.'"[56] In this context, she postulates that "the zero degree of humanity" is hospitality.[57] Hospitality is the *quality* of being human, which is a hallmark of the new humanism. Living with others, welcoming them into your home, accepting them as they are, and interacting with them through love—this is what makes us human. It is not our linguistic abilities, our reason, our tool-making, or our productivity, but, rather, our affective connection and the ways in which that connection makes human life meaningful that are distinctive to humanity.

While elsewhere I have challenged the way Kristeva limits the democracy of proximity and affective connection to human beings by excluding other animal beings, here suffice it to say that the new humanism based on affective proximity forces us to consider otherness in all its forms, including our relations with other animals.[58] Furthermore, interaction as living with also forces us to rethink psychoanalysis with its commitment to the "talking cure." Throughout this essay, I have attempted to expand the notion of signification and speech to include all meaning-making activities. What we learn from Vanier's account of living with people in the situation of disability is that it is being with and not speaking to—or even, strictly speaking, listening to—others that gives his life and the lives of those with whom he lives meaning. Our affective connection with others runs deeper than language or thought or reason. It is primal and primary and necessary for survival and thriving. Indeed, in her exchange with Vanier, Kristeva identifies affective connection as fundamental to what it means to be human: "I maintain that the *difference* of disabled people, contrary to all other differences, takes us back not to a struggle for power, but to the meaning we give to the human species. Even when a person doesn't have access to the signification of language and thought, s/he is inhabited by affective meaning: infinitesimal, incommensurable joy and suffering. This meaning inhabits the pre-political and pre-religious foundation where, in effect, the ties of tenderness hide the secret of survival."[59] To live with others is to learn tenderness as a lesson in loving the uniqueness of each person. Again, for Kristeva this lesson in love comes through transference and the dynamic of unconscious affect. For her, "the Freudian discovery of the unconscious . . . makes it possible to rethink the work of the signifying process through love in the singularity of the human adventure."[60] This human adventure is learning to embrace the singularity of each one.

Kristeva's new humanism, in the sense of hospitality that opens onto an interaction with others as being with and embracing (even loving) the singularity of each person as they are, requires an expanded notion not only of humanity and psychoanalysis but also of home. Living with others creates a sense of being at home as belonging. Fundamental to this sense of home and belonging is having a safe place to sleep, both physically and emotionally, a place to let your guard down and be accepted as you are.

In her correspondence with Vanier, she writes that "the caritative approach to disability," as *living with* at L'Arche, "moves beyond a respectful relationship with the disabled by taking 'friendship' to the level of 'love' and 'pleasure' (as you say); this approach accomplishes a true revolution in mentalities, and we will never recognize this enough. This is the very foundation of humanism."[61] This humanism whose foundation is living with as loving friendship resonates with the new humanism based on the human capacity for hospitality as sharing one's home.

Contrary to the sentimental notion of home in popular culture or nationalist movements, *ethos* as habitat or home is based on love as the social bonding agent that brings creatures together and gives them a sense of belonging. Ethos interpreted as a safe place to sleep in a home where one belongs transforms the basis of ethics and politics in responsibilities and rights into a basis in love and caring. Love and caring, however, are not devoid of responsibilities and rights. Rather, "the right to have rights" goes beyond any legal authority, national or transnational, and takes us into the realm of ethical norms grounded in our shared cohabitation on the earth and the unchosen nature of that cohabitation that compels us to choose it, even to love it. This would be Levinasian paternal election and Kristevan maternal eros taken to the level of the social and political.

Democracy based on proximity rather than on contracts challenges us to live with otherness, both our own and that of those around us. Beyond tolerating differences, Kristeva's new humanism challenges us to embrace singularity to the point of loving it, of wanting it to be. The affirmation of the positive uniqueness of each serves as an antidote to Aristotelian norms and their defective or deficient counterparts. Each is both part and apart, belonging yet singular, in this meaning-making adventure we call humanity.

In sum, the democracy of proximity is a political pact based on affective connections stemming from the fact of our vulnerability as meaning makers. This vulnerability points to the centrality of emotions in meaning making, which is possible only by virtue of our relationships with others and otherness. Without considering the ways in which emotions affect our relationships, we risk acting out unconscious desires and fears and projecting them onto others. When we merely project our fears and desires onto others, we are not truly interacting with others. Love and tenderness are not simply given, but, rather, must be cultivated. We have an ethical obligation to love and tenderness. Through cultivating love and tenderness, we can welcome others and extend hospitality, which creates a sense of belonging necessary for human flourishing. Denying the importance of affects in politics, on the other hand, leaves unacknowledged and unexamined the ways in which love and hate determine our political actions and policies.

If, as Kristeva suggests, hospitality is what makes us human, and requires that we open ourselves to otherness (both otherness within ourselves and others), then her new humanism based on hospitality brings with it both ethical and political obligations. In order to welcome others, we must not only accept each person but also affirm the singularity of each. We must love them as they are. Extending this affirmation into the political realm obligates us to provide a loving home for every person and to acknowledge the rights of each to a home, a safe place to sleep. The democracy of proximity and a humanism as hospitality obligate us to share not only material resources but, moreover, our homes and hearts.[62]

Kristeva warns: "The age of suspicion is no longer enough. Faced with increasingly grave crises and threats, the time has come to wager. Let us dare to bet on the continuous renewal of men's and women's ability to believe and know together. So that in the multiverse surrounded by a void, humanity might long continue its creative destiny."[63] She wagers that love will triumph over hate for the survival of our meaning-making species, of which we are all a part through the very singularity that sets each one apart. The question is, who is willing to take this bet? And how can we inspire others to join in the "vigilant transfer" that insists on plumbing the depths of the psyche in search of the meaning of life and love rather than settling for the shallow accumulation of wealth with its valuation of efficient productivity? How can we learn to share, not only our resources, but also our hearts?

Kelly Oliver

Vanderbilt University
March 2019

NOTES

1. Julia Kristeva, "Liberty, Equality, Fraternity and . . . Vulnerability," in *Hatred and Forgiveness*, trans. Jeanine Herman (New York: Columbia University Press, 2010), 42.

2. Julia Kristeva, "A Tragedy and a Dream: Disability Revisited," *Irish Theological Quarterly* 78, no. 3 (2013): 223.

3. Henrik Ibsen, "Little Eyolf (1894)," in *The Complete Major Prose Plays*, trans. Rolf Fjelde (New York: Plume, 1978).

4. In *Leur regard perce nos ombres*, both Kristeva and Vanier use the phrase "the person in the situation of disability" to signal that the meaning of, and response to, disability is a social response to a biological factor that generates the person in the situation of disability. Disability cannot be separated from the social situation that governs its meaning, potentialities, and realities. Julia Kristeva and Jean Vanier, *Leur regard perce nos ombres* (Paris: Fayard, 2011).

5. Ibid., 67 (my translation).

6. Kristeva, "A Tragedy and a Dream," 220.

7. Kristeva, "Liberty, Equality, Fraternity and . . . Vulnerability," 43.

8. Kristeva, "A Tragedy and a Dream," 223.

9. Kristeva, "Liberty, Equality, Fraternity and . . . Vulnerability," 41.

10. Julia Kristeva, "Stabat Mater," in *Tales of Love*, trans. Leon S. Roudiez (New York: Columbia University Press, 1987).

11. Kristeva, "Liberty, Equality, Fraternity and . . . Vulnerability," 41.

12. In the case of people with disability, Kristeva makes the controversial claim that there is a need to learn to live with the mortality encountered through interactions with them. For criticisms of Kristeva's association between disability and mortality, see Jan Grue, "Rhetorics of Difference: Julia Kristeva and Disability," *Scandinavian Journal of Disability Research* 15, no. 1 (2013): 45–57; and Mary Bunch, "Julia Kristeva, Disability, and the Singularity of Vulnerability," *Journal of Literary & Cultural Disability Studies* 11, no. 2 (2017): 133–50.

13. Kristeva goes so far as to say that "the cure defuses passion" in order to sever the transferential link "so as to make others possible." Julia Kristeva, "The Passion According to Motherhood," in *Hatred and Forgiveness*, 94.

14. Kristeva, "Liberty, Equality, Fraternity and . . . Vulnerability," 44.

15. Julia Kristeva, "Hatred and Forgiveness," in *Hatred and Forgiveness*, 191–94. For a discussion of Kristeva's notion of forgiveness in relation to the history of philosophy, see Kelly Oliver, "Forgiveness and Subjectivity," *Philosophy Today* 47, no. 3 (Fall 2003): 280–92.

16. Kristeva, "Liberty, Equality, Fraternity and . . . Vulnerability," 44.

17. Julia Kristeva, *The Sense and Non-sense of Revolt: The Powers and Limits of Psychoanalysis Volume 1*, trans. Jeanine Herman (New York: Columbia University Press, 2000), 19.

18. For example, Frantz Fanon describes coming "too late" to meaning and finding the meaning of his body already set out for him as abject and excluded. Frantz Fanon, *Black Skin, White Masks*, trans. Richard Philcox (New York: Grove, 1967). Elsewhere, I have extended Fanon's analysis and combined it with Kristeva's notion of the imaginary father to argue that meaning requires a loving social support.

19. Julia Kristeva, "At the Limits of Living: To Joseph Grigely," *Journal of Visual Culture* 5, no. 2 (2006): 222.

20. Goodwill Industries is famous for its "hire the handicapped" campaign, which has been transformed into their "help people with disabilities reach their full potential" campaign. See http://www.goodwill.org/blog/advocate/goodwill-helps-people-with-disabilities-reach-their-full-potential/ (accessed March 1, 2019). In 1953 the US Postal Service used

a "Hire the Handicapped" cancel stamp. See https://www.stampcommunity.org/topic.asp?TOPIC_ID=14341 (accessed March 1, 2019).

21. See Julia Kristeva, "Disability Revisited: The Tragic and Chance," in *Passions of Our Time*, trans. Constance Borde and Sheila Malovany-Chevalier (New York: Columbia University Press, 2018).

22. Julia Kristeva, "Dare Humanism," in *Passions of Our Time*, 269.

23. Julia Kristeva, "Secularism: 'Values' at the Limits of Life," in *Hatred and Forgiveness*, 28.

24. See Shiloh Whitney, "Affective Orientation, Difference, and 'Overwhelming Proximity' in Merleau-Ponty's Account of Pure Depth: A New Conception of Intentionality?" *Chiasmi International* 14 (2012): 415–38.

25. Maurice Merleau-Ponty, *Phenomenology of Perception*, trans. Colin Smith (London: Routledge, 1962), 24. Kurt Koffka, *The Growth of the Mind*, trans. Robert Morris Ogden (London: Kegan Paul, Trench, Trubner and Co., 1946), 319.

26. See Whitney, "Affective Orientation, Difference, and 'Overwhelming Proximity.'"

27. Ibid. Merleau-Ponty, *Phenomenology of Perception*, 291.

28. Whitney, "Affective Orientation, Difference, and 'Overwhelming Proximity,'" 431.

29. See Julia Kristeva, "Reliance: What is Loving for a Mother?" in *Passions of Our Time*, 11–20; "Maternal Eroticism," in *Passions of Our Time*, 101–12.

30. Julia Kristeva, "The Passion According to Motherhood," 83, 91.

31. Ibid., 93.

32. Ibid., 80.

33. While Kristeva is clear that she is using maternal eros as a structural model of loving compassion and depassion, there are problems with using the maternal model, including the power dynamics in the mother-child relationship, the fact that most people aren't mothers, and most importantly that many if not most mothers cannot live up to this ideal. Nonetheless, the emphasis on the affective bind between mother and child is very powerful and evocative as a model of love and affirmation.

34. Emmanuel Levinas, *Totality and Infinity: An Essay on Exteriority*, trans. Alphonso Lingis (Pittsburgh: Duquesne University Press, 1969), 267–73.

35. Ibid.

36. Kristeva, "The Passion According to Motherhood," 86.

37. Emmanuel Levinas, *Otherwise than Being or Beyond Essence*, trans. Alphonso Lingis (Pittsburgh: Duquesne University Press, 1998). Levinas also identifies the poor, the widow, and the orphan as emblems of the need that calls on me to respond. With Kristeva, we may wonder if these figures recall the Christian notion of deprivation in the face of which our response would be charity, which she criticizes.

38. Emmanuel Levinas, "Substitution," in Adriaan T. Peperzak, Simon Critchley, and Robert Bernasconi, eds., *Emmanuel Levinas: Basic Philosophical Writings* (Bloomington: Indiana University Press, 1996), 80.

39. Levinas, *Otherwise than Being or Beyond Essence*, 74.

40. Kristeva, "A Tragedy and a Dream," 227.

41. Julia Kristeva, "Affect, That 'Intense Depth of Words,'" in *Passions of Our Time*, 140–41.

42. Kristeva, "A Tragedy and a Dream," 224.

43. Ibid., 229.

44. Ibid.

45. Ibid.

46. Kristeva, "Disability Revisited," 223.

47. See Kelly Oliver, *Witnessing: Beyond Recognition* (Minneapolis: University of Minnesota Press, 2001) and *Response Ethics* (Lanham: Rowman and Littlefield, 2019).

48. Kristeva, "A Tragedy and a Dream," 224.

49. Kristeva, "Disability Revisited," 222–23.
50. Kristeva, "A Tragedy and a Dream," 229.
51. Ibid., 226.
52. Ibid.
53. Julia Kristeva, "La Bulgarie, l'Europe post-totalitaire et moi," *Marianne*, September 7, 2018, 47 (my translation).
54. Jean Vanier, *From Brokenness to Community* (New York: Paulist Press, 1992).
55. Ibid., 15.
56. Julia Kristeva, "Thinking About Liberty in Dark Times," in *Hatred and Forgiveness*, 9.
57. Ibid.
58. See Kelly Oliver, *Animal Lessons: How They Teach Us to Be Human* (New York: Columbia University Press, 2009), and "Service Dogs: Between Animal Studies and Disability Studies," *philoSOPHIA: A Journal of Continental Feminism* 6, no. 2 (Summer 2016): 241–58. See also Cynthia Willett, *Interspecies Ethics* (New York: Columbia University Press, 2014), which is a testament to the need for interspecies ethics by considering our shared "communitarian cohabitation," or proximity.
59. Kristeva and Vanier, *Leur regard perce nos ombres*, 140 (my translation).
60. Julia Kristeva, "The Contemporary Contribution of Psychoanalysis," in *Passions of Our Time*, 80.
61. Kristeva and Vanier, *Leur regard perce nos ombres*, 33 (my translation).
62. Ibid., 200.
63. Kristeva, "Ten Principles for Twenty-First-Century Humanism," in *Passions of Our Time*, 283.

REPLY
TO CECILIA SJÖHOLM, EWA PLONOWSKA ZIAREK, NOËLLE MCAFEE, AND KELLY OLIVER

I. CECILIA SJÖHOLM

Cecilia Sjöholm is the first to think the *radicalization* that I try to accompany by envisaging the "radicalized subjectivity" of "acting out," whether it is a question of the crimes of the Nazi Eichmann or the unleashing of the death drive among the jihadists of political Islam. Shocking, unbearable, this juxtaposition? In no way is it a matter of confusing the historical contexts and the ideological motivations of these criminal radicalizations. Sjöholm takes up my research with regard to Arendt's oeuvre and, without ignoring the geopolitical, philosophical, and theological causes of these phenomena, emphasizes that my reflections concentrate on the *psychosexual microcosm*, whose convergences she identifies.

I try to elucidate how the totalitarian identity tensions of the twentieth century and today, and the technical advances promoted by the hyperconnected ultraliberalism of the postmodern era, defy the *hominid link* (the *conatus* in Hobbes and Spinoza), which explodes into "radical evil." This expression from Kant designates the disaster caused by certain humans who consider other humans *superfluous* and exterminate them. Arendt had denounced this absolute evil in the Holocaust.

In evoking "the banality of evil," this philosopher targets the "good conscience" of "frighteningly normal" individuals. Incapable of "think[ing] from the standpoint of somebody else" or even of judging, they yield to the cult of a supposedly moral authority. Wasn't that Nazism a sacrificial cult devoted to German omnipotence? Eichmann's "guilt came from his obedience, and obedience is praised as a virtue"; "who was he to judge?" Prey to an absolute need to believe, "banal" observance of the Nazi clichés, dispossessed of the capacity to think-judge: "the desubjectivation and the deobjectivation" (Sjöholm) of this *banalized* humanity seizes the supreme power "to determine who should and who should not inhabit the world."[1] And in a context that favors the return to sovereign excesses and religious fundamentalisms, this *perversion of the moral imperative* and the renunciation of the *desire to know* lead to a destructive

Translated from French by Armine Kotin Mortimer.

violence that is neither bestial nor irrational[2]—but spreads in all innocence through human networks.

Arendt remains faithful to the Platonic, then Christian theory of an *unthinkable evil*. However, in her last writings,[3] she includes Being *within* Nothingness and echoes Heidegger's death as "shelter" of Being, or the turn (*Kehre*), while arguing that thought is frustrated in evil since it finds nothing there except its banality and since "only the good is always deep and radical."[4] Arendt constructs an *apologia of narration*, attesting that destructiveness seizes hold of *story* and *history* to purify itself, calm down, and insert itself into History. "The need for literature," as Sjöholm diagnoses it, leads Arendt to Aristotle, Proust, Brecht, Varnhagen, and Isak Dinesen (pseudonym of the novelist Karen Blixen) . . . Thus it is only in the imaginary and in "aesthetic judgment" (Sjöholm) that the *truth* of thought as *life* is unveiled for Arendt: not life-*zōē* but life-*bios*. Only *narrative* life, *bio-graphy*, delivers the *revels* and the *intoxications* of the thinking self.[5]

In emphasizing, quite rightly, "Arendt's rebuttal of psychoanalysis" and her incomprehension of political feminism, Sjöholm develops the "malady of ideality" of radicalized adolescents, the *denial*, the forgiveness, and "faith or unfaith," and reveals that, on the *problematics of the need to believe*, "Kristeva and Arendt represent opposed positions." "Arendt does not believe in psychoanalysis," writes Sjöholm. Neither do I.

***

I will not address here the harsh judgments Arendt addresses to psychoanalysis ("monotonous sameness and pervasive ugliness," "only disorder or abnormality can individualize them"), nor her underestimation of sadomasochism in political violence.[6] No doubt the ordeals this woman philosopher endured made her unreceptive to the Freudian discovery.

Psychoanalysis, while claiming a philosophical dualism (life drive/death drive, among others),[7] and beyond the hypertrophy of the psychical that it is taxed with, resolutely implicates the dualism that is initially given. With and after Freud, the *psyche* lives a new life: the polyphonic *soul*, enriched with multiple interpretations, attentive to the advances in the sciences, participates in the "transubstantiation" of the living body.[8] Subjectivation, which we thought banished from "true" science, comes charging back in biological and neuroscientific theories.[9] Image before object, subject, teleonomy, representation . . . Are you there, soul? What types of representation, what diverse logics constitute the soul? Psychoanalysis does not necessarily have the answers, but it continues this unprecedented recasting of metaphysics. For my part, I try to decompose/recompose this *need to believe*[10] by coupling it with the *desire to know* (without which it risks becoming radicalized), to address the *diversity of radicalizations* that these two universal anthropological components, the prereligious and the prepolitical, undergo. *Defensive radicalizations*, often inhibiting or fractioning the self and the other. But also death-dealing, suicidal, and criminal radicalizations.

As it is not my intention to engage in a frontal, religious, ideological, or political battle, I would like to recall my conception of the *need to believe* as an *investment* by retracing the evolution of this notion in psychoanalytic thought.[11] Before evoking a clinical "vignette" that demonstrates that the *defensive investment*, in the intimacy of subjectivation, can bear on the *image* even more radically than on *ideas*, thus obstructing the *desire to know* that sets into motion thought and life as *bios*.

***

In Freud's prepsychoanalytic texts, the term *investment* evokes a neurological event: the displacement of neuronal energy in view of the "principle of constancy."[12] With the development of psychoanalytic theory, this energetic mobility operates at first between the somatic and the psychical, then in the structuration of psychic spaces, "free cathexes" becoming "bound cathexes" in sensations, memory traces, and the signs of language. Between the two topographies, as soon as the opposition between *sexuality* and *self-preservation* is inverted into *object investment* and *ego investment*, the permanence of *mobile investment* then bears on the link "with verbal residues":[13] psychicization is linked from the start with the verbal. Klein and Segal have unfolded the process of psychical investment by distinguishing the "psychical equations" from their mutations into "veritable symbols" in the course of the "depressive position."[14] In Freud's *The Ego and the Id* (1923), investment traverses the heterogeneous registers of the biological and of narcissism and, underlying the relation to the object, opens the door to "thirdness" by way of the "identification/empathy (*Einfühlung*) with the father of individual prehistory"—the latter not yet an "object" since it is the forerunner of the *ego ideal*.

The transitional space of the construction of the ego is outlined like this and becomes accessible only thanks to Winnicott's genius.[15] If we read too quickly, we forget the economy of the Freudian thought—this *heterogeneity of investment* on which Green insisted when he spoke of the heterogeneity of the drive: energy *and* meaning.[16]

I mention these foundational advances concerning the construction-deconstruction of subjectivity and the research on early mother-child relations to emphasize the experience I call a *maternal eroticism* (central to the vignette that follows). Elucidating its biopsychical complexity is decisive for the well-being of the child and the adolescent, as well as for clarifying the transference, the countertransference, and our interpretive capacity, as Sjöholm suggests.

***

Didier is an "industrial draftsman," well-dressed, in his forties.[17] An amateur painter, I'll discover later. Says he appreciates my books about art. Difficulties "of a relational order" have persuaded him to undergo psychoanalysis. Married, no children, "no sentiment, I just want to know, that's all." A few clichés borrowed from the phraseology of the "great replacement"[18] give me to understand that he constructs for himself a paranoid, persecuted-persecuting false self in conflict with colleagues issuing from "diversity" at the office. Didier's closed speech reveals an obsessional neurosis: dominance of the "procedural" over the "declarative," of ritualized "doing" over technical, defensive "saying." Then, in *disinvested* reports, his masturbatory compulsion appears, "exhausting" and "unavoidable," making me think of those welds between sex drive and sexual object that Freud diagnosed in certain cases of perversion.[19] Without an object, without fantasies, was the industrial draftsman one of those individuals that modernity fosters, saturated with images but lacking in imaginary?

Neither repression nor splitting, the obsessional *isolation* that separates the *psychical representation of affects* from their *verbal representation* had organized around a narcissistic personality, a "perverse combinatory" destined to preserve him from the contained, exciting, and ravaging intimacy with his mother. Didier did not say "my" mother but The Mother. Didier's father, before marrying "The Mother," had been married to "a foreign woman." This romantic aura gave existence to this absent father, protected him from the invasive Mother. Didier spoke to me about her only after a year of learned and polite soliloquies about his industrial drafting and his conflicts at the office, where he described himself as alone, incapable of liking his colleagues and his wife, indifferent even to the death of The Mother. At her death, which had taken place two years before his analysis, he had locked—and never reopened—The Mother's apartment, where the paintings Didier had done since his childhood were stacked up, paintings whose single audience had been The Mother—as I learned much later.

Self-controlled, defended, as if he wanted to persuade himself and persuade me that he had no soul—nothing but an automaton, sometimes sick. This rigidity persisted even after he had confided to me this dream revealing the "icy hole" of his narcissism, under the operative composition. *Didier is leaning out the window of the family home, someone pushes him, he tumbles into the void. Instead of smashing his face in, instead of being anguished or screaming, he suddenly notices that there is no void. He finds himself in front of a mirror, which reflects not his face but . . . the face of his sister. Now Didier does scream, and he wakes up.*

I manage to slip in that Didier is horrified not to see himself as a man but as a woman, was his sister taking his place? Is she the one who pushes him into the void, or is he propelling her so she will fall? Or does his sister's face in the mirror cover the void, does it cover it with the pain left by the death, by The Dead Woman who remains invisible, shut up in her apartment? "I don't see it," he says, still impassive.

In what I would call not "empathy" but an *investment* of the analyst *in the speech* of this analysand, I acquired the countertransferential conviction that Didier was talking *sincerely* to *me* only when he was mentioning the paintings left under lock and key in the apartment of *The* Dead Woman. I said to him: "Your *voice* becomes animated when you speak to me about your *paintings*"—I could hear in the "voice" the unconscious affects, called forth and repressed at the same time by the word "paintings," of the one who claimed "not to see."

Was that all Didier was waiting for? At the next session he brought photos of his works, which he commented on. Collages of shots representing celebrities from the movies, art, and literature that he had cut apart, disfigured, torn, stitched back together, and covered over with paint from a brush or smattered with "dripping." This carnage contrasted sharply with the courteousness of his usual discourse. My interpretation had opened the way to a different modality of representation: the affects that *slept* in Didier's disinvested speech appeared in these collages, on which he commented with learned litanies borrowed from the theories and marketing of art.

While he was "gluing" his collages onto me, I could see and hear the sadistic drive that these projections liberated. And in a new countertransferential movement, I interpreted: "You are making me participate in your massacres. Maybe you need to smash in a woman's face to take your pleasure with her, but glued to me so you won't fall into the void." Didier explodes, he's no longer the same man . . . He missed the next three sessions.

He returned and the analysis took a different path. He returns to "glue-collage" and "smash in the face." Didier starts to tell me some childhood memories: the rituals with The Mother around the potty, the destructive anality strongly eroticized; he also reports to me the fights with his wife, born and having lived in a foreign country: he has never been able to keep himself from "smashing in her face." I restate this: "smashing in the face of a foreigner." Silence. He wipes away a few tears as he gets up from the couch . . .

In the aftermath, Didier opened his mother's apartment and began painting again. We reconsidered his "office wars" under the angle of homoeroticism; a benign but well-placed somatization—a testicular cyst—allowed us to link narcissistic failure and the fear of the feminine with phallic impotence and guilt, while introducing a third party between us: the surgeon, who "unglues." The "globally positive" transference was displaced onto the paternal side. And the "diversity" colleagues were invited to his exhibit of painting, "in a totally new style, you cannot imagine . . ."

At the end of the cure, Didier gave me my portrait. No collage, just the reproduction in painting of a photograph in which I am holding a cigarette in my hand. But in this portrait the cigarette has disappeared, my fingers close on empty space.

The introduction of the image in Didier's psychoanalytic process may be considered as an acting out that breaks the psychoanalytic frame. In hindsight, it appears to me as an *interpretation having recourse to the complexity of signifiance*: as a necessary taking into account of the *image* (or more broadly, as an investment in iconicity), a more "archaic" and fragile degree of the psychic life of the patient, where psychicization risks collapsing into fragmentation-unbinding, prey to the maternal grip in the schizoparanoid position where destructiveness and the death drive threaten. In that sensitive place, when the psychoanalytic process is adjacent to the traumatism, the accompaniment can recreate *maternal reliance* and open the transferential/countertransferential link with the image and in intrapsychical and intersubjective interpretation, to accede to the *drive-flesh* of words. To find languages (*in the plural*) to *name-*

interpret, designate-signify the process of investment that, on this condition only, constitutes psychic life—a life, precisely. To recognize and welcome all the *indices* of subjectivation underlying the rhetoric of defensive language in order to link them to the transferential/countertransferential process. And better to follow the modalities of psychicization specific to these "maladies of the soul" that contemporary history feeds, utilizes, and aggravates.

II. Ewa Plonowska Ziarek

Ewa Plonowska Ziarek takes up several major themes of my research, already discussed in this volume, and innovates them energetically. I will consider only the ones on *ethics* and *forgiveness*, recalling the other replies (see those to the essays on "Desire, Knowledge, and Belief," "Theory of Revolt," "Maternity," "Philosophy of Public Health," and many other places), equally applicable to Ziarek's positions, which nevertheless call for a few clarifications.

I would like to bring out the analyses that Ziarek proposes concerning "the materialism of Kristeva's thought [that] has been . . . confused with charges of essentialism"; "Kristeva's materialist ethics"; its "proximity" to materialisms that "emphasize the dynamic, agential notion of matter"; "the energetic and materialist reformulation of drives" considered as "a critique of the implicit cognitivism of materialist interpretations; and the reformulation of the singularity and vulnerability of embodied, desiring subjects." And, last but not least, the attention I pay, in the transference/countertransference, to the "encounter of the psyche with nonpsychic time" (the *Zeitlos*), "timeless biothanatology," "traces" of death drive in the "hallucinations, dreams, gaps of memory," "drug addictions" or "psychotic breakdown[s]," which "manifest themselves as *jouissance*."

Ziarek's commentary agrees with my convictions according to which the psychoanalytic experience, neither *materialist* nor *essentialist*, proceeds since Freud to a refoundation of materialism and essentialism, but is expressed in no *system*—which it maintains tentatively in the polemics inherent in the social pact and in hyperconnectivity today. Because this *refoundation* operates in an *ethics in action*, which is none other than the *psychoanalytic clinic* itself.

Allow me to underscore the place of *sexuation* and the effects of this problematic on the relations *between the sexes* and on the *metamorphoses of parentality*, onto which are grafted the ethical uncertainties of modern times.

The analyst practices a solitary profession—aggravated by hyperconnected globalization—in which "the only companion he has is his patient and his patient is by definition unreliable," according to Bion.[20] I fully subscribe to this view, and immediately the question arises: *Why?* Why this solitude of the analyst? Because the "unreliable" harnessing of the transference/countertransference does not rest on a particular *organ*, nor on the analyst's *desire*, but on a sort of *ethic in suspension*.[21]

Philosophical reflection on the aspiration for *happiness* (and that is truly what the analysand is looking for!) began almost two thousand years ago. Contemporary thought distinguishes in it the *imperative aim* of morality, founded on the obligation of the *norm*, the *optative aim* of *ethics*, based on *choice* and the *will*, in which *desire*—dear to Freudians—appears, with the concern for the self, for others, and for institutions. The *norm* does not disappear from the ethical quest, but biopolitics today proposes a new conception of it as a *dynamic concept.*

To avoid the active/passive binomial, the rare modern philosophers who take this on classify women in the pre-ethical: guardians of the *dwelling*, experts in *hospitality*, in welcome, and more subtly "in assignment of ambiguity," in the *equivocal* and *fragility* (see Ricoeur, Levinas, Derrida), if not in *care* (see the British theoreticians influenced by "reparation" according to Klein).

However, *sexuation* haunts researchers who sound the depths of the origins of hominization. A strange reverie by Lévi-Strauss affirms that psychosexuality, that is, *denatured* sexuality, is originally . . . feminine! Because "of all mammals, the human animal is the only one . . . that can make love in all seasons. Human females do not have one or several rutting seasons," thus women "could signal their moods with words" (!).[22] No longer any need for sexual organs or "ardors," they are excited with every fiber of their words! It is language—with its singularizing particularities—that operates this psychical revolution of matter (Freud), which displaces the animalistic sexual *instinct* onto the *drive*, henceforth and *definitively psychosexual.* At that point, the geography of the feminine body disintegrates and disseminates the "primacy of the genital" (which certain therapists still privilege). "My whole skin has a soul . . ." wrote Colette the novelist.[23] The tensed strings of the female libido have vibrated so well to receive the penis of the male that the genital organ of these females has migrated . . . into the *vocalizations* of language! With time, the feminine of the man will let itself go there too, even though people still maintain that there is only one libido, the phallic.

The prehistoric imaginary sends us videos of the *human denaturation of sexuality.* A giant vulva topped by the head of a bison (the gate of hell, theologians will say) seems to drag along racing beasts, a zoomorphic representation of human drives. Neither body nor face, this doubled feminine figures and assumes the perpetual excitation into which the male projects himself (the Chauvet cave, 31,000 BP). In this "*origyne*" of the world, doesn't the parietal artist, that excited bison, also exhibit his own castration, panicked and fleeting, which retains only scattered schematic graffiti from his annihilation, as well as a multiplicity of "positive" and "negative" prints of his creating hands? These humans, men and women, prey to their psychicized sexuality, knew *at the same time* that they were mortal (the oldest sepultures date from 115,000 BP).[24]

At the mythic origin of hominization there is the disjunction of the *instinctual* and the sexual (the *denaturation* of human sexuality) and the *splitting* of feminine sexuality: atrophy of the visible organs,[25] haunted by the infinite *iconic quest* for Meaning—unsustainable, impossible authenticity of desire. A structuring splitting appears here, which will not generate psychosis but will be worked through in the transformative structuration of the feminine.

The violence of this splitting is not resorbed in the fantasy of castration or in the murder of the father. Nor in the repugnance and fascination that the boy and the girl feel in noticing that they don't have the same organs. It is not reduced to a psychotic mechanism either. To differentiate it from the latter, let us call it a *refente*—fading and/or splitting—of human psychosexuality. In the unfolding and transmission of human life, it is *heterosexuality* that acts and exhibits this *fading/splitting of being*, whatever the achievements of artificial reproduction and the acceptance of homosexuality may offer. It remains for us to refine how the double feminine Oedipus,[26] modulated by the disturbances of the feminine condition, succeeds in *transforming* this initial *fading/splitting*. And how it manifests as symptoms or manages to take pleasure in heterosexual "comedy."[27]

It would be a mistake to lock up into the category of "materialism/materialist" the psychoanalytic reading of these theoretical and aesthetic fables of hominization that clinical experience confirms.

Today, the "trauma" of the difference of the sexes, which Freud thought about in *Moses and Monotheism* (1939) and *An Outline of Psycho-Analysis* (1939–1940), is eluded, when it doesn't "disappear" in the multiplication of *genders*. However, the liberating import of *gender* destabilizes the "denatured psychic sex" itself, and reveals the traumatic zones of subjectivity where the primordial link of sexuation cracks. Without succumbing to it but brushing up against the splitting, the anguish of castration, of the void, and the phallic show can install symptoms that, far from eroticizing the feminine (Judith Butler), "disassemble" it and push it to withdraw, when they do not condemn it to the *vertigo of being*. The analyst (man or woman) is then inspired to recreate, through listening, the feminine and the masculine, to accompany toward creativity the symptoms of these "*beings otherwise*."

The third millennium will be the one for individual, *singular* chances. Or it will not be[28]—if it lets itself be engulfed by transhumanist automatization that induces the binary domination of "those who have it" over "those who don't have it."

Reprising what I wrote in "Transformations of *Parentality*,"[29] as of now, heterosexuality is no longer perceived as the sure and only way to transmit life and to guarantee the memory of generations. However, whatever variants, acceptances, or rejections of the "heterosexual norm" may exist in the psychosexuality of each one, the mirage of the "primal scene" (Freud) as an original fantasy that structures the unconscious unfailingly connects the diversity of eroticisms "at the zenith of procreation," as Bataille specifies.[30] In vain we seek to know where "values" have gone. What if the *heterosexual couple and its family* were the focal point, precisely, instead and in place of "value" (supposed to mitigate solitude, to prolong, to transmit)? The biotechnology of reproduction and marriage for all change nothing; our fantasies converge unconsciously toward this archaic heritage of parentality. The heterosexual couple continues to fascinate. Not only marriage as an institution but also movies and television series impose it on us as a model to be studied *ad nauseam*. The Couple: enigmatic, scandalous, detestable and, for those very reasons, desirable. *Heterosexuality is and will be the problem.* As a result, starting with the singular transformative feminine, the metamorphoses of parentality are and will be infinite.

In this psychosexual, social, and ethical context, the recognition of *sexual difference* remains the touchstone of our experience. But what becomes of the *paternal*? It is no longer the dominant "principle" but is inscribed with the *maternal* in the *initial* of the primal scene "at the zenith of procreation." This is to say that a structuring *thirdness* supports the unity of the speaking subject with its capacity for language and thought; the One (the Norm, the Law) is disseminated and continually made anew in the modern multiverse (artificial insemination is/remains one of these disseminations of the One).

"Moderns" and "traditionals," "gays" and the "reconstructed," medically assisted procreation and surrogate motherhood on one side and nostalgia for the norm on the other? Rather, what takes shape is a veritable Harlequin's coat, with the improvisations of some borrowing from the models of others: singularly specific parentalities appear. Without yielding to the temptation of a politics of psychoanalysis (incompatible with its deontology), psychoanalysis is perhaps alone able to respond to this urgency—not the disappearance, but the *dissemination of the One* (the Norm, the Law) into incommensurable singularities of which psychoanalysts are—more than the witnesses—the vectors of its emergence.[31]

Thus understood as a "dynamic concept," is this ethic put into action in the clinical experience an "ethics of forgiveness" (Ziarek, following Oliver) that "combines ethics and negativity in order to avoid the twin dangers of the conformity to the law and its opposite"?

As of my study on Dostoyevsky,[32] I have not tried to endorse the economy of forgiveness that certain religions impose, but to analyze its *metamorphoses* in *writing* and more broadly in the diverse variants of *sublimation*. But, above all, to reground it by and in psychoanalytic *interpretation*. Rather than the immemorial ethic of *forgiveness* ("ethics of forgiveness" in Ziarek), I would support an *ethics of interpretation*, as Ziarek specifies: "Kristeva's reformulation of forgiveness offers us insights about the ethical stakes of psychoanalytic interpretation, which is irreducible to cognitivism."

III. Noëlle McAfee

This ethics of *interpretation*, which I conceive of as a transvaluation of the *forgiveness* transmitted by religion, underlies and marks my experience as an analyst, but also my approach to letters and the arts, with an echo in political debate. Never having had the ambition to construct a "political theory" (McAfee notes that it is "latent"), I am honored to read that my "work can be an ally in thinking through democratic practices for helping to work through problems that give rise to polarized, intransigent, and Manichaean politics." In this perspective, it is necessary for the women and men who use my writings to adapt them to their own research. McAfee reignites the polemics opposing me to the *post-totalitarian Bulgarian police manipulation* (see my replies to Sarah Hansen in the section on Theory of Revolt and Marian Hobson in the one on Theory of Literature);[33] to certain feminists who put my universalism into question[34] in the postcolonial French Republic (see my reply to Hansen); or to those who worry "Western and non-Western feminisms clash," and suspect, to use McAfee's words, that my "feminist politics" underestimate "cultural and religious desires."[35]

Elsewhere in her essay, McAfee wonders if I am not "one of a small group of psychoanalytic thinkers who still believe in something like a stage of primary narcissism." Alas, no; as early as *Revolution in Poetic Language* (1974), I undertook a *transvaluation* of narcissism, echoing Klein (before devoting to her the second volume on "female genius" in 2000), and in reinterpreting Plato's *chora*! I detect in it the Presocratism underlying the Platonic oratory dialectic, which designates, with the *chora*, a *rhythm*, a *prespace* before space, a "bastard" concept, because neither the One, nor a name, nor even a syllable works for it! (See my reply to Edward Casey in the section on Melancholy, Love, and the Sacred.)

As for my analysis of the *syndrome of ideality* in adolescents, which doesn't suit McAfee, I take up the problem of ideality or the ego ideal in my replies to the sections on Art and Aesthetics, Theory of Literature, Psychoanalysis, and Desire, Knowledge, and Belief. See also my reply to Melancholy, Love, and the Sacred.

Finally, the problematic of "loss," which McAfee is passionate about, has not escaped my attention; it is inscribed in my developments on *abjection*, in the primary and secondary oedipal phase (*Oedipe prime* and *Oedipe bis*) of the woman, and in *maternal reliance*. In privileging the *economic* dimension of psychic life and its facilitations-inscriptions in languages (whence *significance*, but also *iconicity*, in my clinical and theoretical work), I differentiate myself from the psychosocial approaches McAfee takes. It is precisely this economic approach that modifies my comprehension of the *object* relation in psychoanalysis; *abjection*, maternal *reliance*, and also the syndrome of *ideality* testify to this.

McAfee's remarks on the malady of ideality among radicalized youth and veiled women raise central questions. I would like to provide clarifications, then I will return to the philosophy that underlies the *ethics of interpretation*, which cannot be understood solely in the interface "between politics and psychoanalysis."

Neither ideologue nor prescriptive, neither judging nor neutral, and innocent even less, the psychoanalyst that I am enters *into the factory of jihadism*. I frequently mention the aftereffects of postcolonialism, xenophobia, and racism, which go hand in hand with sovereignty excesses, the mafia seizure of drug traffic, the traffic of arms, and the trafficking of human beings, and I'm not forgetting the bankruptcy of humanism[36] in education, etc. The context of radicalization is inexhaustible. The modest—but decisive—role of psychical and psychoanalytic accompaniment consists in *identifying the psychical collapse underlying* social, legal, and political suffering. With the *fragility*, even the *malignity* of the unconscious and the psychic apparatus. For without the reconstruction of subjectivity (I never speak of "mental health," as McAfee does), no *measure* or *management* could possibly lead to a refoundation of the social pact and the hominid link that is breaking today.

I also note that a quietist Islam can collaborate on the sly ("*taqiyya*," infiltration) with radical Islam and incubate death-dealing jihad.[37] Without professing a static universalism, I am proud to be part of the breakthrough in (religious or ideological) obscurantism that the century of the Enlightenment accomplished by fostering an emancipation of the oppressed: women, children, the colonized, then *genders* and sexual singularities. The renewed putting into question of traditional values should not be perceived as a threat for religious freedom of conscience.

The *need to believe* that I am trying to rehabilitate has no hope of avoiding fundamentalism without the *desire to know*. It is not a matter of letting "the state . . . protect women from their own culture" (McAfee). And I don't understand how one can work for emancipation and the rights of women by reducing them to their *belonging*. With Proust and Arendt, I revolt against those who impose being *one of* (*belonging* to a family, a clan, a group, a sex, a nation, an ideology, a religion), rather than recognizing that this communitarian and constituent *given* is also a necessary *antidepressor*. But on the condition of promoting the risks of freedom by and in the transvaluation, which, for lack of being elucidated, inverts into a maniacal cult, an inexhaustible revenge against the enemy otherness. What if colonial culpability were transformed into complacency with the fundamentalism of formerly colonized religions and cultures? Should one protect the latter from transvaluation on the pretext that they were colonized, and submit to interpretation only the cultures and religions of the colonizers? Or else enter into them with as much delicacy as exigency, as I try to do.

It is not true that I point to "immigrant Muslims as [my] primary example of the syndrome of ideality," and "suggest that Islam is susceptible to extremism" (McAfee). As Sjöholm's analysis shows, the first "radicalized" person who provoked my revolt was . . . Otto Karl Adolf Eichmann![38] His absolute need to believe in the word of the Führer, subjected to a Kantian "moral duty" to which he refers *without thinking* from the point of view of the other or himself, perverts the moral imperative and offers a *structural* example of radicalization. It is possible for all religions and ideologies to open the way for a fanatical overinvestment that annihilates the desire to know. One can avoid it by submitting them to the hermeneutic sieve and by situating them in their history. In probing the *factory of globalization*, I try to address myself to the identitarian catastrophe—neither to protect it nor to save it but to make it hear the possibility of a *becoming*.

I deplore that the story of Souad, who was cared for at the Maison des Adolescents, could be reduced to the caricature McAfee provides of it. I mentioned Souad's trajectory, from her jihadist temptation to the profession of caregiver, in the section on Revolt (see Hansen). Deontological secrecy forces me to conciseness; I was able to provide other scattered elements of her trajectory in various writings and lectures. The clothing detail—"she has just put her jeans back on"—is not anodyne; it offers the proof that the adolescent is in the process of *taking a step* (in the proper and the figurative sense). Souad is preparing to join the interreligious and intercultural questioning of the team, then the writing studio it proposes to her, where she who was tempted by the "holy war" will learn that various currents of Islam exist, and she will discover a Sufi poet translated into French who evokes faith in terms of love. A sort of revelation that leads the *adolescent* to return to school, to become a caregiver. Neither combatted nor denigrated, the religious way is tamed as Souad's creativity becomes emancipated.

The Syrian psychoanalyst Rafah Nached, who studied in "my" university, observes with a group of colleagues that the translations of psychoanalytic texts (Freud, Lacan) into Arabic do not carry the meaning they have in German or in French because "in Arabic language, the metaphors [concerning the unconscious and sexuality] are situated in the area of death."[39] Elsewhere, the sacrificial position and the feminization of the Islamic soul in its subordination to the masculine divinity reveals to her that "psychoanalysis [in the Arabic countries] finds itself perhaps between the rejection of sexuality in the general sense of the term and the esoteric language of divinity."[40] Nached realizes that they must "make something emerge that comes from our language and our culture."[41] Relying on the work of Henry Corbin (Iranologist and philosopher) and Louis Massignon (academic and specialist on Islam), the psychoanalyst discovers the language of Arabic mysticism. She concludes that "it is by passing by the mystical and its 'relationship with *jouissance*' that [the] language of [psychoanalysis] can be understood and accepted by us."[42] Extending her research, she attempts to interpret the religious experience of Islam in light of psychoanalysis.

What interests me, then, is the opening up of feminine emancipation through the creativity of thought and not "the French secular obsession with Muslim girls' and women's clothing" (McAfee). I again quote Nached: "We have discovered that psychoanalysis is a work of civilization, that is, of life"; "which turns on the relation with the Arabic language"; "this society has not yet entered postmodernism"; "We do not want to make psychoanalysis an empire of which Paris is the capital."[43]

Why do feminists not salute the courage of this woman, this Syrian psychoanalyst whom we helped get out of the dictator's prison, preferring as they do to veil the face to the point of letting themselves go with their fantasies imputing to me "a strange valorization of Western clothing"? "Western" or "Global"? None of those is my subject.

***

I dare to take an additional step in the *factory of radicalization*, both before and beyond Islam. Certain people, notably on the left, are fascinated by political Islam, the only one capable, according to them, of leading men and women to sacrifice. At this extreme peak, we are no longer in the "social realm" with its "scale" to weigh "what will be gained and what will be lost" (McAfee). The death drive carries the collapse of subjectivity in an elation and *jouissance* that annul identity, alterity, and the world. The psychoanalytic architecture that limits itself to the *theory of the object* must go further into the *theory of drives*. Secularization prefers to bet on progress and ignore the death drive. Fortunately, we still have art and psychoanalytic interpretation—on the condition that they are capable of recreating the "proximity" that Kelly Oliver reminds us of here.

***

The *representation of murder* and of decapitation is an immemorial treatment of the death drive. The exhibition Capital Visions (Louvre, 1998) gave me the opportunity to emphasize this turning away from the "radical evil" consumed by sublimation—another form of for-giveness. Forms and traversals that, in the twenty-first century, are on their way to being dominated by the image.[44]

Are we slaves to the image? It's not certain, philosophers answer. For the image is potentially a space of freedom: it annihilates the constraint of the object-model and substitutes for it the flight of thought, the vagabondage of the imagination. The image is perhaps the only link that we still have with the sacred—with the *terror* of death and sacrifice, with the *serenity* that stems from the pact of identification between the sacrificed and the sacrificers, with the *joy of representation* inseparable from sacrifice. Images and looks can still offer to humans absorbed by technology an experience of the sacred. What experience?

The sacred is linked with sacrifice. Decapitation rites reveal the fascination that religious mystery exerts. *Homo sapiens*, who is a *Homo religiosus*, has always cut off heads—from Mesopotamia to the Aztecs by way of the Caucasus, but also among the Scythians, the Greeks, and the Celts, and right up to the "infamous insolence" of the "*tricoteuses*" during the Terror, who, during the Revolution, forced "an entire populace to get their eyes dirty." Today also, beheadings, still practiced, recall us to the reality of the world in which we live. Who has never seen terrorist fundamentalists exhibiting the severed heads of their victims before our mesmerized cameras? While the satellite channels turn us into powerless witnesses, this sacralized violence is reestablishing itself on the public stage, which had thought it could do without it.

These cold exhibitions of *radical evil* are always accompanied by a strange *imaginary experience*, which does not erase its abjection but reflects it in gestures, traces, or colors, transcends it, and delivers us from it. These *capital visions* elucidate massacres and sacrificial rites, transposing violence into an object of contemplation and thought. Far from the denial that blinds and the judgment that condemns, art stays close to sacrifice, desacralizes it, and frees us to look at it—hideous or sublime, sometimes grotesque. To abolish it.

The civilization that springs from these capital visions is a prisoner of the sacred, but it doesn't want to capitulate to sacrifice and even less to accept its fundamentalist perversions. It awakens in us an intimate, profound, and lucid resistance, which we are lacking today in the face of modern versions of evil. Unfortunately, neither hyperconnection nor political management seem capable of breathing life into it.

The histories I visited in my Capital Visions are cruel. Through them, a humanity possessed by the death drive and terrorized by murder admits to having arrived at an overwhelming discovery: the only possible resurrection would be . . . representation. The proof lies in the exhibited beheadings. With or without decapitation, any vision is nothing other than a capital transubstantiation. In the process of interpretation, of for-giveness.

***

In this immersion at the limits of psychicization, I can subscribe to McAfee's preoccupations concerning the "public political process" when she warns against "how fraught and treacherous the road to sociality can be" and "argues for the need to metabolize and work through loss."

IV. Kelly Oliver

Kelly Oliver makes an unexpected detour to interpret the humanist import of my work: *proximity*, dear to Merleau-Ponty and Levinas, "beyond critical reasoning or Husserlian intentionality wherein subjects intuit objects." She clarifies this notion by insisting on my approach to *vulnerability* (see also the section in this volume on Philosophy of Public Health) and on the place of *affect* in my accompaniment of subjectivity. Attentive to Green's work,[45] I had indeed introduced this *economic* dimension of subjectivity starting with my first semanalytical writings on the *chora*, then *abjection*, and *maternal eroticism* and *reliance*.

Both a drive motion *and* a qualitative expression, *affect* condenses and concretizes what I consider the major import of Freudian psychoanalysis: the *recasting* of metaphysical categories (body/soul, matter/spirit, inside/outside, interior/exterior).[46] The expression "flesh of words" came to me in what Oliver calls "transferential affect and critical analysis." I try to inhabit it in my clinical listening ("the 'transferential encounter' revitalizes and jubilates," Oliver) and to connect with it in the interpretation of cultural and political facts.[47] Oliver elucidates it by referring to the studies brought together in *Hatred and Forgiveness* (2005) with respect to *vulnerability, adolescence, painting, literature, religions*, and *atheism*.[48] The sociopolitical field broadened in this way makes it clear that "meaning making is a shared activity," an "emotional and intellectual closeness" (Oliver). And it is this "meaning making" in its affective depths that, according to Oliver, is susceptible of "revitalizing" "democratic values" and "transforming contractual democracy into democracy based on 'proximity.'" "Democratic values must be transformed by considering vulnerability as the dimension of *affective* transference upon which we are all dependent for meaning making" (my emphasis).

Does this humanism "based on affective connections" and capable of "affirming the singularity of each" exclude "other animal beings," she asks? The necessary refoundation of humanism connects with the urgency of saving the planet. Ecology is not explicitly present in my writings. However, Oliver attests that "the new humanism [which is sketched in my work] based on *affective proximity* forces us to consider otherness in all its forms, including our relations with other animals." I mistrust those who mock my concern to situate "the person at the center," and the transhumanisms that lead to the automatization of the human species. The *flesh of words* is this dawn of a humanity that offers refuge and hospitality to other living species. My cohabitation with the "female genius" of Colette, in animal and vegetable osmosis with plants and animals, showed that I side with the one who wrote: "One does not love beasts and men at the same time. Day by day, I become suspect to my fellows. But, if they *were* my fellows, I would not be suspect to them."[49]

But let us return to the ethical and political preoccupations of this topic: "How does [my analytic listening] inflect democratic values with sharing?" Oliver asks. I am not going to retell what brought me to the Interreligious Meeting for Peace at Assisi (2011), where I formulated my "Ten Principles for Twenty-First Century Humanism,"[50] but I would like to sketch an ultimate "transvaluation" of for-giveness as *interpretation*,[51] in which my ethicopolitical position resides, addressing it to all the interveners on this topic.

***

My experience as a writer, psychoanalyst, and woman has led me to return to the term forgiveness, which the history of religions has bequeathed to us, convinced that only a reevaluation of tradition (with which we have "cut the thread") can allow us to confront the "discontents of civilization." Can Jankélévitch's cry—"Pardoning died in the death camps"—reawaken "*ontological* wickedness"?[52] Constitutional democracies need a *normative presupposition* (God) to found rational law, but the secularized state no longer has available a *unifying link* (Böckenförde) necessary for a "conservative conscience," whether nurtured by faith (Habermas) or correlating reason and faith (Ratzinger).[53]

In counterpoint, globalized humanity is confronted with prepolitical and transpolitical experiences that render moot any appeal to "normative conscience" and to fideism because they are headed toward a refoundation of humanism arising from the *Aufklärung* without recourse to the irrational. It is at this location of modernity that literary experience and the Freudian discovery of the unconscious are situated—laboratories of new forms of humanism,[54] inseparable from an urgent reappropriation and reevaluation of tradition.

In Leviticus, we read: "Also on the tenth day of this seventh month there shall be a day of atonement: it shall be an holy convocation unto you . . . to make an atonement for you before the LORD YOUR GOD"—DAY OF ATONEMENT OR DAY OF THE GREAT FORGIVENESS.[55]

The Jewish experience of forgiveness recognizes the place of man in and through language: it is not a matter of a personal experience but of a reversal of being (*teshuvah*) at the core of the Israeli community and in the course of life. Only the Roman principle of sparing victims (*parcere subiectis*) prefigures it, from afar (Arendt). This biblical forgiveness implies precise and difficult conditions, inexhaustibly commented on in the Mishnah and perfected by the

Gemara. Asking forgiveness for the harm done and granting one's forgiveness for the harm suffered are two conditions for the future to cease repeating the past and for hope to be reborn. Forgiveness and promise are linked because they modify time: one opens the past, the other stabilizes the future. Arendt pointed out that a "small and closely knit community of [Christ's] followers, bent on challenging the public authorities in Israel," brought an eminently political innovation to this religious practice.[56] God is not the only one to forgive—better, it is because men are capable of forgiving themselves *to begin with* that God will *definitively* forgive them.[57] This philosopher is seeking to define a new political link that should be sketched after the tragedy of the Holocaust, like a "plural communicability" in the "plurality of humans." Its foundation would be *taste*: the most singular, ancient, and sharable of all the senses. It would initiate the *aesthetic judgment* on which this new political philosophy should be founded.

Contrary to what the layperson imagines, the forgiveness defined by theologians does not erase hatred or "radical evil." It's a matter of *temporarily suspending the time* of the Ego, which is the time of hatred, by giving a sinful meaning to the hateful acting out and by referring to God's mercy. However, even when deprived of transcendental protection, the speaking being in secularized societies benefits from the forgiveness and the promise that religious traditions bequeath to him or her. *Guilt*, which results from an infringement of the Law, an interdiction, or morality, shapes the experience of *temporality* coextensive with the vital processes of nonbelievers. To undo this mechanism, an interruption is required: it is not *forgetting*, as Nietzsche believes, but *forgiveness*. It is impossible to undo what has been done, and solipsistic forgetting cannot be envisioned in a plural pact. It is acceptable for men and women, among themselves and at the core of their actions, to *unbind* themselves from their past actions—by forgiving each other, precisely. While forgiveness liberates the past, the promise alleviates the future: in the face of the unpredictability of human actions and the uncertainty of the future, only the promise offers assistance.

This economy of forgiveness, which modifies judgment in the plurality of "human affairs," also operates in the aesthetic ineffable, but by unsuspected means.[58] Dostoyevsky's writings provide a striking example of it.[59] One cannot grasp in what way art is forgiveness if one refers only to the *technique* by which forgiveness operates and is depleted. Beyond the polyphony of the work and the clash of judgments, forgiveness operates through the aesthetic performance in the *jouissance* of abject passion received as beauty. A beauty *beyond* or *across* or even *in spite of* judgment. Potentially immoralist, this last time of *forgiveness-reabsorbed-into-performance* returns to the start of this circular vocation: the suffering and tenderness for the other, for the stranger/foreigner, even for the criminal . . . are henceforth domesticated in me, beauty has just implanted them in me. *I* the artist, *I* the receiver. I am thinking of Willem de Kooning's diabolical women, Francis Bacon's butcheries, Céline's *Fable for Another Time*.

The imaginary is the place where the subject risks her identity and loses herself, as far as the threshold of evil, of crime, or of asymbolism—to traverse them and bear witness to them . . . from an elsewhere. A doubled space, it is attached to the ideal, which authorizes violence to speak itself, rather than the doing of it. It is *sublimation*, which needs *for-giveness*. Let's write it with a hyphen. To reveal that this appropriation-transmutation of theology into aesthetics conceals an undecidable meaning: the endless interpretation of the ineffable put into signs, put into words. The beauty of the sentence and of the narrative consecrates the traversal of passion. And the question remains: nevertheless, *what* happens when the writer lets himself be seduced by criminality and intoxicates us with that? When his ideology justifies but does not interpret?[60]

If psychoanalysis "succeed[s] where the paranoiac fails,"[61] it is not because it teaches us to "love the ego," nor even to "love the other" (as people say familiarly)—which is already difficult to do!—under a heaven without God. The Freudian revolution consists in replacing this *forgiveness*—invented to stop time as judgment in the name of the dogma of love (of God or of the beyond)—with the *interpretation* of the diverse variants of hatred and the death drive, to the point of *radical evil*.

But the analytic ambition to succeed where the paranoiac fails (in uncoupling the "mad truth" from hatred) is inseparable from another ambition: to succeed where theological forgiveness promises a *re-birth of the subject* in a *new temporality*. Religion accomplishes this promise only by subordinating the faithful and/or by sending them to the eternal beyond. But it is indeed through forgiveness that the maximum seduction of this faith operates.

Contrary to what Freud established, religion doesn't fascinate solely because it maintains illusions. *Religion that forgives*, through its pardons and promises of the afterlife, is received as a renewal of psychic life here below. That is how it ensures its hold on individuals in the secularized era, individuals whose psychic space is threatened with destruction by the upsurge of technology and sexual liberation (as testified to by the "new maladies of the soul," among which is the "malady of ideality"—the "need to believe" that secularization has not recognized and that is derailed in jihadism).

Psychoanalytic interpretation is a for-giveness: a re-birth of the psychic apparatus, with and beyond the hatred that carries desire, which religion recognizes-misrecognizes or utilizes in interreligious confrontations. Analytic interpretation has the ambition to make possible the psychic rebirth of the analysand. It recognizes the need to believe and leads it to the desire to know, to create new links, and re-births . . .

***

I return to the anxiety some have expressed: *is radicalization a failure of the French model of secularization, of secularism?*

In question is a more serious phenomenon. "Radicalization" particularly concerns adolescents and those who share in the same psychosocial fragility. It reveals a more radical phase of nihilism, a phase that is present below the "clash of religions." This symptom is more serious because it seizes more deeply the sources of civilization, making evident the destruction and the aberration of the prereligious "need to believe" itself, constitutive of psychic life with and for the other. The need to believe collapses in the *empire of desubjectivation and deobjectalization*, accompanied by a senseless pleasure, or in apathy.

Whence the audacity of psychoanalytic accompaniment, which considers itself much more than an "*all-embracing moralism*."[62] It places the analyst where the deobjectalization-objectalization operates and threatens, but it can inaugurate a *restructuration*. Such is our wager, after the discovery of the *death drive* and the *potential malignity of the psychic apparatus* revealed by maladies of ideality. The latter abolish the *need to believe* and the *desire to know*, with the result that the human, incapable of *investing* and establishing links, dispossessed of the "self" and lacking the sense of the other, wanders in a nonworld without "good" or "evil" or any "value" whatever.

Is it possible to push psychoanalytic listening to these frontiers of *Homo sapiens* and to practice psychoanalysis in these conditions? Are we capable of mobilizing all means, of law and of economics as well as those that the knowledge of souls give us, to accompany this poignant malady of ideality with the necessary listening, an adapted education, and the generosity that is required?

No resignation in the face of destructiveness and extreme evil. Rather, the continuation of the search for that fragile *point* that Pascal defines as "perpetual motion": "He who should find the secret of rejoicing in the good, without troubling himself with its contrary evil, would have hit the mark [*le point*]. It is perpetual motion."[63] What if the ethic that we are lacking today were precisely this "perpetual motion"? An inner experience, to remain vigilant in the chaos of hyperconnection.[64]

J.K.

NOTES

1. See Hannah Arendt, *Eichmann in Jerusalem* (Harmondsworth: Penguin, 1985), 252, 49, 247, 114, 279; *Eichmann à Jérusalem* (Paris: Gallimard, 1991), 408, 400, 188, 448; quoted in Julia Kristeva, *Hannah Arendt*, trans. Ross Guberman (New York: Columbia University Press, 2001), 149–50; *Le Génie féminin*, t. 1, *Hannah Arendt* (Paris: Fayard, 1999), 242–43.

2. Didn't Hegel say that "Terror [in the French Revolution] is Kant put into practice"!? See Maurice Merleau-Ponty, *Humanism and Terror: The Communist Problem*, trans. John O'Neill (Boston: Beacon, 1969), 149; *Humanisme et terreur: Essai sur le problème communiste* (Paris: Gallimard, 1947), 191; and Julia Kristeva, *Time and Sense: Proust and the Experience of Literature* (New York: Columbia University Press, 1997), 274; *Le Temps sensible* (Paris: Fayard, 1994), 336.

3. See in particular Hannah Arendt, "On Violence," in *Crises of the Republic* (New York: Harvest, 1972).

4. See Marie Luise Knott, ed., *The Correspondence of Hannah Arendt and Gershom Scholem*, trans. Anthony David (Chicago: University of Chicago Press, 2017), 209; Gershom Scholem, "Le Procès Eichmann: Un Débat avec Hannah Arendt," in *Fidélité et utopie: Essais sur le judaïsme contemporain*, trans. Marguerite Delmotte and Bernard Dupuy (Paris: Calman-Lévy: 1978), 228; quoted in Kristeva, *Hannah Arendt*, 152; *Hannah Arendt*, 247;

Marie Luise Knott, ed., *The Correspondence of Hannah Arendt and Gershom Scholem*, trans. Anthony David (Chicago: University of Chicago Press,), 209.

5. See Kristeva, *Hannah Arendt*, 200–201; *Hannah Arendt*, 315.

6. See ibid., 179, 194–95, and 224; *Hannah Arendt*, 286–87, 306–7, and 348.

7. See Sigmund Freud, *Beyond the Pleasure Principle*, in *The Standard Edition of the Complete Works of Sigmund Freud*, vol. XVIII, trans. James Strachey (London: Hogarth, 1955), 40; *Au delà du principe de plaisir* (Paris: Payot, 1963), 67.

8. See the section on Psychoanalysis in this volume.

9. See Julia Kristeva, *New Maladies of the Soul*, trans. Ross Guberman (New York: Columbia University Press, 1995), 6; *Les Nouvelles Maladies de l'âme* (Paris: Fayard, 1993), 14–15.

10. See "expectation coloured by faith" (*die glaübige Erwartung*) in Sigmund Freud, "On Psychotherapy," in *Standard Edition of the Complete Psychological Works of Sigmund Freud*, vol. XII, trans. James Strachey (London: Hogarth, 1953), 258; "De la psychothérapie," in *Oeuvres complètes*, t. VI (Paris: PUF, 2006), 45–58; along with "*Das höhere Wesen des Menschen*" ("the higher nature of man") in *The Ego and the Id*, in *Standard Edition*, vol. XIX (London: Hogarth, 1961), 37; *Le Moi et le ça*, in *Oeuvres completes*, t. XVI (Paris: PUF, 1991), 280. These are only some of the stations on the pathways into Freud's work that remain for us to elucidate in depth.

11. *Investment* (cathexis), from the Indo-European root **kredh/*sradh—I give you my vital force in exchange for a recompense*—underlying the Latin *credo*.

12. See Sigmund Freud, "The Neuro-psychoses of Defense," in *The Standard Edition of the Complete Works of Sigmund Freud*, vol. III, trans. James Strachey (London: Hogarth, 1963), 65.

13. See Sigmund Freud, "Formulations on the Two Principles of Mental Functioning," in *The Standard Edition of the Complete Psychological Works of Sigmund Freud*, vol. XII, trans. James Strachey (London: Hogarth, 1958), 221; "Formulations sur les deux principes du cours des événements psychiques," in *Résultats, idées, problèmes*, t. I (Paris: PUF, 1984), 138.

14. See Hanna Segal, "Notes on Symbol Formation," *International Journal of Psycho-Analysis* 38, no. 6 (1957): 391–97; *Revue française de psychanalyse* 34, no. 4, 685–96. See also the section in this volume on Melancholy, Love, and the Sacred.

15. See D. W. Winnicott, "Primitive Emotional Development," *International Journal of Psychoanalysis* 26 (1945): 137–43, and Dominique Cupa, "La Pulsion de cruauté," *Revue Française de Psychanalyse* 66 (2002/2004): 1073–89.

16. See André Green, *Diachrony in Psychoanalysis*, trans. Andrew Weller (London: Free Association Books, 2003); *La Diachronie en psychanalyse* (Paris: Minuit, 2000); *Time in Psychoanalysis: Some Contradictory Aspects*, trans. Andrew Weller (London: Free Association Books, 2002); *Le Temps éclaté* (Paris: Minuit, 2000).

17. See Kristeva, "The Soul and the Image," in *New Maladies of the Soul*, 15–26; *Les Nouvelles Maladies de l'âme*, 20–43.

18. A conspiracy theory according to which the migratory flow onto the French territory could replace the French population with a non-European one.

19. See Sigmund Freud, *Three Essays on the Theory of Sexuality*, in *Standard Edition of the Complete Works of Sigmund Freud*, vol. VII, trans. James Strachey (London: Hogarth, 1953); *Trois Essais sur la théorie de la sexualité* (Paris: Gallimard, 1987).

20. Wilfred R. Bion, *Second Thoughts: Selected Papers on Psycho-analysis* (New York: Jason Aronson, 1984), 138.

21. See my reply to Keren Mock in the section on Melancholy, Love, and the Sacred.

22. See Claude Lévi-Strauss, *We Are All Cannibals and Other Essays*, trans. Jane Marie Todd (New York: Columbia University Press, 2016), 106–7, 111; *Nous sommes tous des cannibales* (Paris: Seuil, 2013), 213–15. The female's cry is no longer a hormonal impulse of the ovarian cycle, but the "sign" of a psychical investment concerning the masculine partner.

23. Colette, *Retreat from Love*, trans. Margaret Crosland (Indianapolis: Bobbs-Merrill, 1974), 121 (translation amended).

24. The grotto at Es Skhul uncovered a Mousterian industry dating from approximately 115,000 years before the present, associated with human remains corresponding to ten individuals (seven adults and three children). These are the oldest known sepultures in the world.

25. "Oh inch of nature!" which Freud attributes to Shakespeare in Sigmund Freud, *Civilization and Its Discontents*, in *The Standard Edition of the Complete Works of Sigmund Freud*, vol. XXI, trans. James Strachey (London: Hogarth, 1964), 91.

26. See Rachel Boué-Widawsky, Rosemary Balsam, and Fanny Söderbäck in the section on Maternity in this volume, and Keren Mock in the section on Melancholy, Love, and the Sacred.

27. See Jacques Lacan, "The Signification of the Phallus," in *Ecrits*, trans. Bruce Fink et al. (New York: Norton, 2006), 582; "La Signification du phallus" (1958), in *Écrits* (Paris: Seuil, 1966), 694.

28. "The two sexes will die separately," wrote Alfred de Vigny in the poem "Samson's Anger," in *Les Destinées*, quoted by Marcel Proust.

29. Julia Kristeva, "Transformations of *Parentality*," in Vaia Tsolas and Christine Anzieu-Premmereur, eds., *A Psychoanalytic Exploration of the Body in Today's World: On the Body* (New York: Routledge, 2018); "Métamorphoses de la parentalité," 73rd Congrès des Psychanalystes de Langue Française on "The Paternal," May 9–12, 2013, http://www.kristeva.fr/metamorphoses.html.

30. See Georges Bataille, *Eroticism* (London: Penguin, 2012); *L'Érotisme* (Paris: Minuit, 2011).

31. See Kristeva, "Transformations of *Parentality*," 68–74.

32. See Julia Kristeva, "Dostoyevsky, the Writing of Suffering and Forgiveness" in *Black Sun: Depression and Melancholia*, trans. Leon S. Roudiez (New York: Columbia University Press, 1989), 190–217; "Dostoïevski, l'écriture de la souffrance et le pardon" in *Soleil noir: Dépression et Mélancolie* (Paris: Fayard, 1987), 201–26.

33. See also, on the relation of philosophy and politics in the countries of Eastern Europe, the chapter by Miglena Nikolchina as well as that of Marian Hobson, both in the section on Theory of Literature.

34. Fanny Söderbäck addresses my universalist conception of culture in the section on Maternity.

35. Elaine Miller addresses my feminism through the perspective of decapitation in the section on Art and Aesthetics, and Ewa Plonowska Ziarek through that of new materialism in this section.

36. See Julia Kristeva, "L'Échec de l'humanisme," Passages 199 (2019), https://signal.sciencespo-lyon.fr/article/713813/L-echec_de_l-humanisme; "De quoi le nationalisme est-il le symptôme?", http://www.kristeva.fr/nationalisme.html.

37. *Taqiyya*, called تقيّة in Arabic, is a practice within Islam that consists in dissimulating or denying one's faith under constraint in order to avoid persecution.

38. See Kristeva, "The Banality of Evil," in *Hannah Arendt*, 143–54; *Hannah Arendt*, 233–49.

39. Rafah Nached, cited in Julia Kristeva, "Can One Be a Muslim Woman and a Shrink?" in *Passions of Our Time*, trans. Constance Borde and Sheila Malovany-Chevallier (New York: Columbia University Press, 2018), 349; *Pulsions du temps* (Paris: Fayard, 2013), 703–4; Rafah Nached, "Histoire de la psychanalyse en Syrie," *Topique* 110 (2010): 117–27; "Dire l'indicible," *Psychanalyse* 21 (May 2011): 33–36.

40. Rafah Nached, cited in Kristeva, "Can One Be a Muslim Woman and a Shrink?" 349; *Pulsions du temps*, 704.

41. See ibid., 350; *Pulsions du temps*, 705.

42. See ibid.

43. See ibid.

44. For the discussion of the image and decapitation in the next paragraphs, see also Julia Kristeva, *The Severed Head: Capital Visions*, trans. Jody Gladding (New York: Columbia University Press, 2012); *Visions capitales* (Paris: Réunion des musées nationaux, 1998).

45. See André Green, *The Fabric of Affect in the Psychoanalytic Discourse*, trans. Alan Sheridan (London: Routledge, 1999); *Le Discours vivant* (Paris: PUF, 1973).

46. See Julia Kristeva, "Affect, That 'Intense Depth of Words,'" in *Passions of Our Time*.

47. See Julia Kristeva, "Speech, That Experience," in ibid.

48. Julia Kristeva, *Hatred and Forgiveness*, trans. Jeanine Herman (New York: Columbia University Press, 2010); *La Haine et le pardon: Pouvoirs et limites de la psychanalyse III* (Paris: Fayard, 2005).

49. See Julia Kristeva, "The Animal, or An Unused Love," in *Colette*, trans. Jane Marie Todd (New York: Columbia University Press, 2004), 215 (emphasis added); "L'Animal, ou un amour sans emploi," in *Le Génie féminin*, t. 3, *Colette* (Paris: Fayard, 2002), 289.

50. See Julia Kristeva, "Dare Humanism" and "Ten Principles For Twenty-First Century Humanism" in *Passions of Our Time*, 263–78, 279–83; *Pulsions du temps*, 539–60, 561–68.

51. See also the section "On Interpretation as *Pardon*" in Julia Kristeva, "Hatred and Forgiveness; Or, From Abjection to Paranoia," in *Hatred and Forgiveness*, 191–94; and the section on "Interpretation and Perversion" in "*Three Essays*; Or, the Victory of Polymorphous Perversion," in ibid., 205–6; *La Haine et le pardon*, 368–73, 390–92; as well as "Interpretation Between Word-Signs and Word-Fetishes: A Source of Beauty," in Kristeva, *Time and Sense*, 245–49; "L'Interprétation entre les mots-signes et les mots-fétiches: une beauté," in *Le Temps sensible*, 301–6.

52. See Vladimir Jankélévitch, "Should We Pardon Them?" trans. Ann Hobart, *Critical Inquiry* 22 (Spring 1996): 567, 556. This is a translation of the section "Pardonner" in Jankélévitch, *L'Imprescriptible: Pardonner? Dans l'honneur et la dignité* (Paris: Seuil, 1986), 49–50.

53. See Joseph Ratzinger and Jürgen Habermas, *Dialectics of Secularization: On Reason and Religion*, ed. Florian Schuller, trans. Brian McNeil (San Francisco: Ignatius 2006); "Les Fondements pré-politiques de l'État démocratique," *Esprit* (July 2004): 5–28.

54. See Julia Kristeva, "Thinking about Liberty in Dark Times," in *Hatred and Forgiveness*, 3–23; *La Haine et le pardon*, 15–22.

55. Leviticus 23: 27–28.

56. Hannah Arendt, *The Human Condition* (Chicago: University of Chicago Press, 1958), 239.

57. See ibid.

58. See Vladimir Jankélévitch, *Music and the Ineffable*, trans. Carolyn Abbate (Princeton: Princeton University Press, 2003), 71f; *La Musique et l'ineffable* (Paris: Seuil, 1983), 92f.

59. See Julia Kristeva, "Dostoyevsky, the Writing of Suffering and Forgiveness," in *Black Sun*, 190–217; *Soleil noir*, 183–226.

60. See the section in this volume on Theory of Literature and my reply to Michal Ben-Naftali in Melancholy, Love, and the Sacred.

61. See Sigmund Freud, letter to Sándor Ferenczi, October 6, 1910, in Eva Brabant, Ernst Falzeder, and Patrizia Giampieri-Deutsch, *The Correspondence of Sigmund Freud and Sándor Ferenczi: Volume I, 1908–1914* (Cambridge: Belknap, 1993), 221; "Lettre à Sandor Ferenczi, 6 octobre 1910," in *Sigmund Freud / Sandor Ferenczi, Correspondance 1908–1914* (Paris: Calmann-Lévy, 1992), 231. Quoted in Julia Kristeva, *The Sense and Non-sense of Revolt*, trans. Jeanine Herman (New York: Columbia University Press, 2000), 58.

62. See Jacques Lacan, *Seminar VII: The Ethics of Psychoanalysis 1959–1960*, trans. Dennis Porter (New York: Norton, 1992), 4; *Le Séminaire VII 1959–1960, L'Éthique de la psychanalyse* (Paris: Seuil, 1986), 13.

63. See Blaise Pascal, *The Thoughts of Blaise Pascal* (Westport: Greenwood, 1978), 66; *Pensées*, in *Oeuvres complètes* (Paris: Pléiade, 1954), 1130.

64. See Julia Kristeva, "Nuit de la justice à l'aube du pardon," 2015, www.kristeva.fr/textes/html.

PART THREE

BIBLIOGRAPHY OF THE WRITINGS OF JULIA KRISTEVA

COMPILED AND EDITED BY

HÉLÈNE VOLAT

BIBLIOGRAPHY OF THE WRITINGS OF JULIA KRISTEVA

The Bibliography is in five parts: Authored Books; Edited Books and Anthologies; Selected Articles; Selected Interviews; Selected Online Publications and Essays.

AUTHORED BOOKS

1964 *Характерни тенденции в западната литература от XX век*. Sofia: DKMS.

1969a *Le Langage, cet inconnu* (Julia Joyaux). Paris: S.G.P.P. Republished as *Le Langage, cet inconnu: Une Initiation à la linguistique*. Paris: Seuil, 1981. *Language, The Unknown: An Initiation into Linguistics.* Translated by Anne M. Menke. New York: Columbia University Press, 1989. London: Harvester, 1989.

História da linguagem. Lisboa: Edições 70, 1969.
La linguistica. Firenze: Sansoni, 1973.
ことば, この未知なるもの: 記号論への招待. Tokyo: Kokubunsha, 1983.
El lenguaje, ese desconocido: introducción a la lingüística. Madrid: Editorial Fundamentos, 1987.
Il Linguaggio, questo sconosciuto: iniziazione alla linguistica, con un'intervista di A. Ponzio a J. Kristeva. Bari: Adriatica Editrice, 1992.
언어 그 미지의 것. Seoul: Minumsa, 1997.
语言,这个未知的世界. Shanghai: Fudan daxue chubanshe, 2015.

1969b *Sémiotikè: Recherches pour une sémanalyse*. Paris: Seuil. Selection in Edited Books 1980 and 1986.

Introdução a semanalise. São Paulo: Editora Perspectivas, 1974.
"Julia Kristeva: Sémeiótiké—Paris, 1969." *Problemi Ljubljana*: *Društvo za teoretsko psihoanalizo* 14, nos. 163–68 (1976): 264–73.
Semiotica do romance. Lisboa: Arcadia, 1977.
Semeiotike: ricerche per una semianalisi. Milano: Feltrinelli, 1978.
Semeiotike = Semiótica. 2 vols. Madrid: Fundamentos, 1978.
記号の解体 学: セメイオチケ. Tokyo: Serika Shobo, 1983.
Σημειωτικη Труды по знаковым системам. Tartu: Universitet, 1992.
علم النص. Casablanca: Les Éditions Toubkal, 1997.
세미오티케 - 기호분석론. Seoul: Dongun Moon, 2005.
符号学: 符义分析探索集. Shanghai: Fudan daxue chubanshe, 2015.
Семиотика: Исследования по семанализу. Moscow: Akademicheskij proekt, 2015.
Séméiotikè: Studia z zakresu semanalizy. Gdansk: Slowo Obraz Terytoria, 2017.

1970 *Le Texte du roman: Approche sémiologique d'une structure discursive transformationnelle*. Paris: Mouton. Chapter 1 translated by Seán Hand as "From Symbol to Sign" in Edited Books 1986, 62–72.

El texto de la novela. Barcelona: Editorial Lumen, 1974.
O text do romance—estudo semiológico de uma estrutura discursiva transformacional. Lisbon: Horizonte, 1984.
テクストとしての小説. Tokyo: Kokubunsha, 1985.

1974a *Des Chinoises*. Paris: Éditions des Femmes. Rev. ed. Paris: J. J. Pauvert, 2001. *About Chinese Women*. Translated by Anita Barrows. New York: Marion Boyars, 1977. Partial translation (first chapter) by Ellen Conroy Kennedy. "On the Women of China." *Signs* 1, no. 1 (Fall 1975): 57–81. Translated (excerpts) by Seán Hand as "About Chinese Women" in Edited Books 1986, 138–59; and in Shelley Saguaro, ed. *Psychoanalysis and Woman: A Reader*. New York: New York University Press, 2000, 24–63.

Donne cinesi. Milan: Feltrinelli, 1975.
Die Chinesin: Die Rolle der Frau in China. Munich: Nymphenburger, 1976; Frankfurt: Ullstein, 1982.
中国の女たち. Tokyo: Serika Shobo, 1981.
中国妇女. Shanghai: Tongji daxue chubanshe, 2010.
Mujeres Chinas: Entre Mao y Tel Quel. Buenos Aires: Capital intelectual, 2016.

1974b *La Révolution du langage poétique: L'Avant-garde à la fin du XIXe siècle, Lautréamont et Mallarmé*. Paris: Seuil. *Revolution in Poetic Language*. First part translated by Margaret Waller. New York: Columbia University Press, 1984. Selections from translation of first part in Edited Books 1986 and 1997. Excerpt from first part translated by Caren Greenberg, Selected Articles 1974g.

Die Revolution der Poetischen Sprache. Frankfurt: Suhrkamp, 1978.
La Rivoluzione del linguaggio poetico: L'avanguardia alla fine del XIX secolo, Lautréamont e Mallarmé. Venice: Marsilio, 1979.
詩的言語の革命. Tokyo: Keisōshobō, 1991 (first part), 2000 (third part).
시적 언어의 혁명. Seoul: Dongun Moon, 2000.
Revolucija pesniškega jezika. Piran: Obalne galerije, 2002.
诗性语言的革命. Chengdu: Sichuan daxue chubanshe, 2016.

1977 *Polylogue*. Paris: Seuil. Selection translated in Edited Books 1980.

Selection translated in *Eretica dell'amore.* Turin: La Rosa, 1979.
Selection translated in *Materia e senso: Pratiche significanti e teoria del linguaggio.* Turin: Einaudi, 1980.
ポリローグ. Tokyo: Hakusuisha, 1999.
Polilog. Kiev: IUnivers, 2004.

1980 *Pouvoirs de l'horreur: Essai sur l'abjection*. Paris: Seuil. *Powers of Horror: An Essay on Abjection.* Translated by Leon S. Roudiez. New York: Columbia University Press, 1982. Selections in Edited Books 1997.

Poteri dell'orrore: Saggio sull'abiezione. Rome: Spirali, 1981.
恐怖の権力—<アブジェクシオン>試論. Tokyo: Hosei University Press, 1984.
Poderes de la perversion: ensayo sobre Louis-Ferdinand Céline. Buenos Aires: Catálogos, 1988; Mexico City: Siglo Veintiuno Editores, 1989.
Moći užasa: ogled o zazornosti. Zagreb: Naprijed, 1989.
Mächte des Grauens: Ein Versuch über den Abscheu. Frankfurt: Suhrkamp, 1990.
Fasans makt: en essä om abjektionen. Göteborg: Daidalos, 1992.
공포의 권력. Seoul: Dongun Moon, 2001.
Силы ужаса: эссе об отвращении. St. Petersburg: Aleteya, 2003.
恐怖的力量. Taipei: Guiguan tushu gongsi, 2003.
Korkunun güçleri: Igrençlik üzerine deneme. Istanbul: Ayrinti Yayinlari, 2004.

כוחות האימה: מסה על הבזות. Tel Aviv: Resling, 2005.
Jälestuse jõud: Essee abjektsioonist. Tallinn: Tänapäev, 2006.
Potega obrzydzenia: esej o wstrecie. Kraków: Wydawnictwo Uniwersytetu Jagiellonskiego, 2007.

1983 *Histoires d'amour*. Paris: Denoël. *Tales of Love*. Translated by Leon S. Roudiez. New York: Columbia University Press, 1987. Selections in Edited Books 1986 and 1997.

Storie d'amore. Rome: Editori Riuniti, 1985.
Historias de amor. Mexico City: Siglo XXI, 1987.
Histórias de amor. Rio de Janeiro: Paz e Terra, 1988.
Geschichten von der Liebe. Frankfurt: Suhrkamp, 1989.
Liefdesgeschiedenissen essay over verleiding en erotiek. Amsterdam: Atlas-Contact, 1991.
爱情传奇. Beijing: Huaxia chubanshe, 1992.
사랑의 역사. Seoul: Minumsa, 1995.
סיפורי אהבה. Tel Aviv: Hakibbutz Hameuhad, 2005.
Ljubavne povesti. Novi Sad: Izdavačka knjižarnica Zorana Stojanovića, 2011.
Ιστορίες αγάπης - μια ψυχαναλυτική ματιά στον έρωτα. Athens: Kedros Publishers, 2012.
Aşk Hikayeleri. Istanbul: Bağlam Yayıncılık, 2016.

1985 *Au commencement était l'amour: Psychanalyse et foi*. Paris: Hachette. Rev. ed. *Au commencement était l'amour: Psychanalyse et foi. Suivi de À propos de l'athéisme de Sartre*. Paris: Librairie Générale Française, 1997. *In the Beginning was Love: Psychoanalysis and Faith*. Translated by Arthur Goldhammer. New York: Columbia University Press, 1988.

Al Comienzo era el amor: psicoanalitica y fe. Buenos Aires: Gedisa, 1986.
In principio era l'amore: Psicanalisi e fede. Bologna: Il Mulino, 1987.
初めに愛が あった:精神分析と信仰. Tokyo: Hosei Daigaku Shuppankyoku, 1987.
No principio era o amor: psicanálise e fé. Sao Paulo: Brasiliense, 1987; Rio de Janeiro: Verus Editora, 2010.
Στην αρχή ήταν η αγάπη: Ψυχανάλυση και πίστ. Athens: Ekdoseis Arga, 1988.
В началото бе любовта: Психоанализа и вяра. Sofia: Kritika i khumanizŭm, 1992.
In den beginne was de liefde: psychoanalyse en geloof. Zoetermeer: Meinema, 1993.
사랑의 정신분석. Seoul: Minumsa, 1999.
בראשית הייתה אהבה. Tel Aviv: Resling, 2004.
Kezdetben volt a szerelem. Pszichanalizis ès hit. Budapest: Napkút, 2012.
در آغاز عشق بود روانکاوی و ایمان. Tehran: Shavand, 2017.

1987 *Soleil noir: Dépression et mélancolie.* Paris: Gallimard. *Black Sun: Depression and Melancholia.* Translated by Leon S. Roudiez. New York: Columbia University Press, 1989. Selections in Edited Books 1986 and 1997.

Sole nero: Depressione e melanconia. Milan: Feltrinelli, 1988; Rome: Donzelli, 2013.
Sol Negro: Depressão e Melancolia. Rio de Janeiro: Rocco, 1989.
Schwarze Sonne: Depression und Melancholie. Frankfurt: Suhrkamp, 1989; Frankfurt: Brandes & Apsel, 2007.
Sort sol: depression og melankoli. Frederiksberg: Det lille Forlag, 1994.
Crno sunce: depresija i melanholija. Novi Sad: Svetovi, 1994.
黒い太陽—抑鬱とメランコリー. Tokyo: Serika Shobo, 1994.
Sol Negro: Depresion y Melancolia. Caracas: Monte Avila Editores, 1997.
Musta Aurinko: Masennus Ja Melankolia. Helsinki: Nemo, 1998.
Черно слънце: Депресия и меланхолия. Sofia: Oksiart, 1999.

Μαύρος ήλιος: Κατάθλιψη και μελαγχολία. Athens: Kastaniotis, 2000.
검은 태양 - 우울증과 멜랑콜리. Seoul: Dongun Moon, 2004.
שמש שחורה: דיכאון ומלנכוליה. Tel Aviv: Resling, 2006.
Remigiusz Ryzinski as Czarne slonce: depresja i melancholia. Kraków: Towarzystwo Autorów i Wydawców Prac Naukowych Universitas, 2007.
黑太陽: 抑鬱症與憂鬱. Taipei: Yuanliu chuban gongsi, 2008.
Kara günes: depresyon ve melankoli. Istanbul: Baglam Yayıncılık, 2009.
خورشید سیاه مالیخولیا. Tehran: Rokhdade No, 2009.
Чёрное солнце: Депрессия и меланхолия. Moscow: Centre Kogito, 2010.

1988 *Étrangers à nous-mêmes*. Paris: Fayard. *Strangers to Ourselves.* Translated by Leon S. Roudiez. New York: Columbia University Press, 1991. Selections in Edited Books 1997.

Fremde sind wir uns selbst. Frankfurt: Suhrkamp, 1990.
Stranieri a se stessi. Milano: Feltrinelli, 1990.
外国人：我らの内なるもの. Tokyo: Hosei Daigaku Shuppankyoku, 1990.
Extranjeros para nostros mismos. Esplugues de Llobregat: Plaza & Janes, 1991.
De vreemdeling in onszelf. Amsterdam: Contact, 1991.
Främlingar för oss själva. Stockholm: Natur & Kultur, 1991.
Muukalaisia itsellemme. Helsinki: Gaudeamus, 1992.
Estrangeiros para Nós Mesmos. Rio de Janeiro: Rocco, 1994.
זרים לעצמנו. Tel Aviv: Resling, 2009.
Önmaga tükrében idegenként. Budapest: Napkút, 2010.
Ξένοι μέσα στον εαυτό μας. Athens: Scripta, 2011.
Stranieri a noi stessi: *L'Europa, l'altro, l'identità.* Milan: Feltrinelli, 1990. Rome: Donzelli, 2014 (new translation with introduction).
Võõrad iseendale. Tallinn: Tallinna Ülikooli Kirjastus, 2017.
Estrangeiros a nós-mesmos. Santo Tirso: De Facto Editores e Centro de Literatura Portuguesa, 2017.

1989 *Georgia O'Keeffe*. In collaboration with Jack Cowart, Juan Hamilton, and Sarah Greenough. Paris: Adam Biro. First published as *Georgia O'Keeffe: Art and Letters*. Washington: National Gallery of Art, 1987. Reprinted as "La Forme inévitable" in Books 2005a, 481–500; and as "Georgia O'Keeffe: La Forme inévitable." In Guy Tosatto and Sophie Bernard, eds. *Georgia O'Keeffe et ses amis photographes.* Paris: Somogy, and Grenoble: Musée de Grenoble, 2015, 23–33.

1990a *Lettre ouverte à Harlem Désir*. Paris: Rivages. Partial translation in Books 1993c.

彼方をめざして：ネーションとは何か. Tokyo: Serika Shobo, 1994.
Έθνη χωρίς εθνικισμό. Athens: Enallaktikes Ekdoseis, 1997.
ملت هایی بدون ملی گرایی. Tehran: Shavand, 2016.

1990b *Les Samouraïs*. Paris: Fayard. *The Samurai: A Novel.* Translated by Barbara Bray. New York: Columbia University Press, 1992.

Os samurais. Sao Paulo: Difusao Cultural, 1991.
Samurajerna. Stockholm: Natur & Kultur, 1991.
Σαμουράι. Athens: Govostis, 1992.
サムライたち. Tokyo: Chikuma Shobō, 1992.
I Samurai. Turin: Einaudi, 1997.
Samuraii. Bucharest: Roa, 1997.
Samuraylar. Istanbul: Sel, 2010.

1991 *Le Vieil Homme et les loups*. Paris: Fayard. *The Old Man and the Wolves*. Translated by Barbara Bray. New York: Columbia University Press, 1994.

Старецът и вълците. Sofia: Hemus, 1993.
Ο γέρος και οι λύκοι. Thessaloniki: Magia, 1993.
Den gamle och vargarna. Stockholm: Natur och Kultur, 1994.
Invazia lupilor. Bucharest: Albatros, 1996.
O Velho e os lobos. Rio de Janeiro: Rocco, 1999.
Bătrânul şi lupii. Bucharest: Univers, 2008.

1993a *Les Nouvelles Maladies de l'âme*. Paris: Fayard. *New Maladies of the Soul*. Translated by Ross Guberman. New York: Columbia University Press, 1995. Selection in Edited Books 1997.

Die neuen Leiden der Seele. Hamburg: Junius, 1994.
Las nuevas enfermedades del alma. Madrid: Cátedra, 1995.
Οι νέες αρρώστιες της ψυχής. Athens: Ekdoseis Kastaniote, 1998.
Le nuove malattie dell'anima. Rome: Borla, 1998.
Νέες αρρώστιες της ψυχής. Athens: Kastaniotis, 2000.
As Novas Doenças da Alma. Rio de Janeiro: Rocco, 2002.
Noile maladii ale sufletului. Bucharest: Editura Trei, 2005.
Ruhun yeni hastaliklari. Istanbul: Ayrinti Yayinlari, 2007.

1993b *Proust and the Sense of Time*. Translated by Stephen Bann. New York: Columbia University Press.

1993c *Nations Without Nationalism*. Translated by Leon S. Roudiez. New York: Columbia University Press.

1994 *Le Temps sensible: Proust et l'expérience littéraire*. Paris: Gallimard. *Time and Sense: Proust and the Experience of Literature*. Translated by Ross Guberman. New York: Columbia University Press, 1996. Selections in Edited Books 1997.

プルースト—感じ られ る時. Tokyo: Chikuma Shobo, 1998.
El tiempo sensible: Proust y la experiencia literaria. Buenos Aires: Eudeba, 2005.
Czas odczuwalny: Proust i doswiadczenie literackie. Kraków: Wydawictwo Eperons-Ostrogi, 2015.

1996a *Possessions*. Paris: Fayard. *Possessions*. Translated by Barbara Bray. New York: Columbia University Press, 1998.

Una donna decapitata. Palermo: Sellerio, 1997.
Εμμονές μυθιστορημα. Athens: Ekdoseis Pataki, 1997.
Obladavane: roman. Sofia: Khemus, 1998.
Apsėdimai. Vilnius: Charibdė, 1998.
포세시옹, 소유라는 악마. Seoul: Minumsa, 1999.
Possessões. Rio de Janeiro: Rocco, 2003.

1996b *Sens et non-sens de la révolte: Pouvoirs et limites de la psychanalyse I*. Paris: Fayard. *The Sense and Non-sense of Revolt: The Powers and Limits of Psychoanalysis Volume 1*. Translated by Jeanine Herman. New York: Columbia University Press, 2000.

반항의 의미와 무의미- 정신분석의 힘과 한계. Paju: Prunsoop Co., 1998.
Sentido y sinsentido de la rebeldía: literatura y psicoanálisis. Santiago: Editorial Cuarto Propio, 1999.
Sentido e contra-senso da Revolta, discorso direto: Poderes e limites de psicanálisa. Rio de Janeiro: Rocco, 2000.
Maišto prasmė ir beprasmybė: psichoanalizės galios ir ribos. Vilnius: Charibdė, 2003.
反抗的意义和非意义. Changchun: Jilin chu ban ji tuan you xian ze ren gong si, 2009.

1997 *La Révolte intime (discours direct): Pouvoirs et limites de la psychanalyse II*. Paris: Fayard. *Intimate Revolt: The Powers and Limits of Psychoanalysis, Volume 2*. Translated by Jeanine Herman. New York: Columbia University Press, 2002. English translation contains texts from Books 1998a.

La revuelta intima: literatura e psicoanálisis. Buenos Aires: Eudeba, 2001.

1998a *L'Avenir d'une révolte*. Paris: Calmann-Lévy. Rev. ed. with preface. Paris: Flammarion, 2012. Translated by Jeanine Herman in Books 1997, part II.

De toekomst van een revolte. Amsterdam: Boom, 1999.
El porvenir de la revuleta. Mexico City: Fondo de Cultura Económica. 1999.
反 抗的未来. Guilin: Guangxi shi fan da xue chu ban she, 2007.
Νόημα και μη νόημα της εξέγερσης. Athens: Scripta, 2010.
El porvenir d'una revuelta. Barcelona: Seix Barral, 2000.
L'avvenire di una rivolta. Genoa: Il Nuovo Melangolo, 2011.
Die Zukunft einer Revolte. Frankfurt: Brandes & Apsel, 2016.
O Futuro de uma Revolta. Santo Tirso: De Facto Editores e Centro de Literatura Portuguesa, 2018.

1998b *Le Féminin et le sacré*. With Catherine Clément. Paris: Stock. Rev. ed. with preface. Paris: Albin Michel, 2015. *The Feminine and the Sacred*. Translated by Jane Marie Todd. New York: Columbia University Press, 2001.

Das Versprechen: vom Erwachen der Frauen. Munich: Matthes und Seitz, 2000.
Lo femenino y lo sagrado. Madrid: Cátedra, Universitat de València, Instituto de la Mujer, 2000.
Το θήλυ και το ιερό. Metamorfosi: Psychogios, 2001.
Femeia şi sacrul. Bucharest: Albatros, 2001.
"母"の根源を求めて—女性と聖なるもの. Tokyo: Kobosha, 2001.
O Feminino e o sagrado. Rio de Janeiro: Rocco, 2001.
여성과 성스러움. Seoul: Munhak Tongne, 2002.

1998c *Proust: Questions d'identité*. Oxford: Legenda.

1998d *Visions capitales*. (Exposition, Musée du Louvre, Département des arts graphiques, Paris, April 27 to July 27, 1998.) Paris: Éditions de la Réunion des Musées nationaux. Rev. ed. with preface. *Visions capitales: Arts et rituels de la décapitation*. Paris: Fayard, 2013. *The Severed Head: Capital Visions*. Translated by Jody Gladding. New York: Columbia University Press, 2012.

La testa senza il corpo. Rome: Donzelli, 2009.

1999 *Le Génie féminin: La Vie, la folie, les mots*, tome 1. *La Vie: Hannah Arendt, ou l'action comme naissance et comme étrangeté*. Paris: Fayard. *Hannah Arendt*. Translated by Ross Guberman. New York: Columbia University Press, 2001.

El genio feminino: la vida, la locura, las palabras. Hannah Arendt. Buenos Aires: Paidós, 2000.
O gênio feminimo: a vida, a loucura, as palavras. Hannah Arendt. Rio de Janeiro: Rocco, 2000.
Das weibliche Genie: das Leben, der Wahn, die Wörter. Hannah Ahrendt. Berlin: Philo, 2001.
Geniul feminine: viața, nebunia, cuvintele. Hannah Arendt, Melanie Klein, Colette. Bucharest: Paralela 1945, 2004–2005.
ハンナ・アーレント—"生"は一つのナラティヴである. Tokyo: Sakuhinsha, 2006.

汉娜·阿伦特. Nanjing: Jiangsu Education Press, 2006.
Geniusz kobiecy Hannah Arendt: biografia. Warsaw: Wydawnictwo KR, 2007.
Das weibliche Genie: Hannah Arendt. Hamburg: Europäische Verlagsanstalt, 2008.
Χάννα Άρεντ. Athens: Kedros, 2008
Hannah Arendt: Il genio femminile. Rome: Donzelli, 2010.
هانا آرنت: زندگی روایت است. Tehran: Rokhdad-e No, 2015.

2000 *Le Génie féminin: La Vie, la folie, les mots*, tome 2. *La Folie: Melanie Klein, ou le matricide comme douleur et comme créativité*. Paris: Fayard. *Melanie Klein.* Translated by Ross Guberman. New York: Columbia University Press, 2001.

El genio femenino: la vida, la locura, las palabras. Melanie Klein. Buenos Aires: Paidós, 2000.
O Gênio Feminino—Tomo II—Melanie Klein. Rio de Janeiro: Rocco, 2002.
Melanie Klein: la madre, la follia. Rome: Donzelli, 2006.
정신병,모친살해,그리고 창조성:멜라니 클라인. Seoul: Ananke, 2006.
Das weibliche Genie Melanie Klein: Das Leben, der Wahn, die Wörter. Gießen: Psychosozial-Verlag, 2008.
メラニー・クライン——苦痛と創造性の母親殺し. Tokyo: Sakuhinsha, 2012.
Melanie Klein: Delilik yahut Acı ve Yaratıcılık Olarak Ana Katli. Istanbul: Pinhan Yayıncılık, 2015.

2001a *Hannah Arendt: Life is a Narrative.* (The Alexander Lectures.) Translated by Frank Collins. Toronto: University of Toronto Press.

2001b *Micropolitique: "Première édition," mercredi 8h25 (2000–2001)*. La Tour-d'Aigues: Éditions de l'Aube.

2002 *Le Génie féminin: La Vie, la folie, les mots*, tome 3. *Colette, ou la chair du monde*. Paris: Fayard. *Colette*. Translated by Jane Marie Todd. New York: Columbia University Press, 2004.

El genio femenino: la vida, la locura, las palabras. Colette. Buenos Aires: Paidós, 2003.
Colette vita di una donna. Rome: Donzelli, 2004.

2003a *Chroniques du temps sensible: Première édition*. La Tour d'Aigues: Éditions de l'Aube.

2003b *Lettre au président de la République sur les citoyens en situation de handicap: À l'usage de ceux qui le sont et de ceux qui ne le sont pas*. Paris: Fayard.

Brev til presidenten: om mennesker med funksjonshemning. Oslo: Cappelen akademisk forlag, 2008.

2004a *Colette: Un génie féminin*. La Tour d'Aigues: Éditions de l'Aube.

Colette: Un genio femminile. Milan: O Barra O Edizioni, 2010.

2004b *Meurtre à Byzance*. Paris: Fayard. *Murder in Byzantium.* Translated by C. Jon Delogu. New York: Columbia University Press, 2006.

Φονικό στο Βυζάντιο. Athens: Ekdoseis Patake, 2004.
Bizans'ta cinayet. Istanbul: YKY, 2004.
Убийство във Византия. Sofia: Ciela, 2005.
Смерть в Византии. Moscow: AST Kranitel', 2007.
비잔틴 살인사건. Seoul: Sodam, 2007.
Gyilkosság Bizáncban. Budapest: Napkút Kiadó, 2014.

2005a *La Haine et le pardon: Pouvoirs et limites de la psychanalyse III*. Paris: Fayard. Selections in *Hatred and Forgiveness*. Translated by Jeanine Herman. New York: Columbia University Press, 2010.

2005b *L'Amour de soi et ses avatars: Démesure et limites de la sublimation*. Nantes: Plein Feux.

2005c *Thinking about Liberty in Dark Times/Penser la liberté en temps de détresse*. Bergen: Bergen University Press.

2006 *Il bisogno di credere: un punto di vista laico*. Translated by M. Guerra. Rome: Donzelli, *Cet incroyable besoin de croire*. Paris: Bayard, 2007. *This Incredible Need to Believe*. Translated by Beverly Bie Brahic. New York: Columbia University Press, 2009. Expanded French ed. Paris: Bayard, 2018.

Esa incredible necesidad de creer: un punto de vista laico. Buenos Aires: Paidós, 2009.

Ta niewiarygodna potrzeba wiary. Kraków: Towarzystwo Autorów I Wydawców Prac Naukowych Universitas, 2010.

Αυτή η απίστευτη ανάγκη για πίστη. Athens: Metaichmio, 2011.

Dieses unglaublieche Bedürfnis zu Glauben. Gießen: Lahn Psychosozial, 2014.

2008 *Thérèse mon amour: Sainte Thérèse d'Avila*. Paris: Fayard. *Teresa, My Love: An Imagined Life of the Saint of Avila*. Translated by Lorna Scott Fox. New York: Columbia University Press, 2014.

Teresa, mon amour: l'estasi come un romanzo. Rome: Donzelli, 2009.

Teresa, Amor Mío: Santa Teresa de Ávila. Barcelona: Paso de Barca, 2015.

2011 *Leur regard perce nos ombres: Échange*. With Jean Vanier. Paris: Fayard.

Il loro sguardo buca le nostre ombre: dialogo tra una non credente e un credente sull'handicap e la paura del diverso. Rome: Donzelli, 2011.

(Bez)sens slabosci: dialog wiary z niewira o wykluczeniu. Poznan: Wydawnictwo Polskiej Prowincji Dominikanów W drodze, 2012.

2014 *A Geruselemme: Il bisogno di credere tra monoteismi e secolarizzazione*. Milano: Mimesis. Translation by Alessandra Luciano of "À Jérusalem. Le Besoin de croire dans les monothéismes et la sécularisation" in Edited Books 2013, 387–419. Translation by Constance Borde and Sheila Malovany-Chevallier as "In Jerusalem: Monotheisms and Secularization and the Need to Believe" in English ed. of Edited Books 2013, 239–62.

2015a *L'Horloge enchantée*. Paris: Fayard. *The Enchanted Clock: A Novel*. Translated by Armine Kotin Mortimer. New York: Columbia University Press, 2018.

2015b *Du mariage considéré comme un des beaux-arts*. Paris: Fayard. *Marriage as a Fine Art*. Translated by Lorna Scott Fox. New York: Columbia University Press, 2016.

Del matrimonio considerato come un'arte. Rome: Donzelli, 2015.

Del matrimonio como una de las bellas artes. Buenos Aires: Interzona, 2017.

Güzel sanatlarin bir dali olarak evlilik: konusmalar. Istanbul: Yapi Kredi Yayıncılık, 2018.

2016a *Je me voyage: Mémoires*. Entretiens avec Samuel Dock. Paris: Fayard, 2016. "*Je me voyage*: A Journey Across Borders and Through Identities. Conversations with Samuel Dock." Translated by Lorna Scott Fox. In *The Philosophy of Julia Kristeva*. Edited by

Sara G. Beardsworth. The Library of Living Philosophers, volume 36. Chicago: Open Court, 2020.

La vita, altrove: autobiografia come un viaggio. Conversazione con Samuel Dock. Rome: Donzelli, 2017.
Пътувам себе си. Спомени. Разговори със Самюел Док. Sofia: Kolibri, 2018.

2016b *Beauvoir présente*. Paris: Fayard.

Simone de Beauvoir: la rivoluzione del feminile. Rome: Donzelli, 2018.
ボーヴォワール. Tokyo: Hōseidaigakushuppankyoku, 2018.
Simone de Beauvoir Aramizda. Istanbul: Sel, 2018.
Beauvoir présente. Rio de Janeiro: Sesc SP, 2019.

EDITED BOOKS AND ANTHOLOGIES

1971a *Épistémologie de la linguistique: Hommage à Émile Benveniste*. Edited by Julia Kristeva. Paris: Didier.

1971b *Essays in Semiotics/Essais de sémiotique*. Edited by Josette Rey-Debove, Julia Kristeva, and Donna J. Umiker. The Hague: Mouton.

Ensaiós de semiologia. Rio de Janeiro: Eldorado, 1971.

1975a *Langue, discours, société: Pour Émile Benveniste*. Edited by Julia Kristeva, Jean-Claude Milner, and Nicolas Ruwet. Paris: Seuil.

Língua, discurso, sociedade. Sao Paulo: Global Editora, 1983.

1975b *La Traversée des signes*. Edited by Julia Kristeva et al. Paris: Seuil.

Prelazenje znakova. Sarajevo: Svjetlost, 1979.
Traversía de los signos. Buenos Aires: La Aurora, 1985.
記号の横断. Tokyo: Serika Shobo, 1987.

1979 *Folle vérité: Vérité et vraisemblance du texte psychotique*. Edited by Julia Kristeva and Jean-Marc Ribettes. Paris: Seuil. Excerpts translated in Edited Books 1986.

Loca verdad: verdad y verosimilitud del texto psicótico/seminario. Madrid: Editorial Fundamentos, 1985.
미친 진실: 정신병적인 텍스트 속의 진실과 진실임직함. Seoul: Dong Sung Cho, 2002.

1980 *Desire in Language*. Edited by Leon S. Roudiez. Translated by Alice Jardine, Thomas Gora, and Leon S. Roudiez. New York: Columbia University Press. Collection of essays from Books 1969b and 1977.

1986 *The Kristeva Reader*. Edited by Toril Moi. Translated by Seán Hand and Leon S. Roudiez. New York: Columbia University Press. Collection of essays from Books 1969b, 1970, 1974a, 1974b, and 1983, and Edited Books 1979.

Puhuva subjekti: tekstejä 1967–1993. Helsinki: Gaudeamus, 1993.

1997 *The Portable Kristeva*. Edited by Kelly Oliver. New York: Columbia University Press. Collection of essays from Books 1974b, 1980, 1983, 1987, 1988, 1993, and 1994, Edited Books 1980, and Selected Articles 1983b. Updated ed. 2002 also includes essays from Books 1996b, 1997, and 1999.

2000a *Crisis of the ~~European~~ Subject*. Translated by Susan Fairfield. Edited by Samir Dayal. New York: Other Press.

2000b *Textuel* 37, special issue, *Où en est la théorie littéraire?* Actes du Colloque organisé à l'Université Paris 7-Denis-Diderot, 27–28 May, 1999. Edited by Julia Kristeva and Evelyne Grossman.

2003a *Le Plaisir des formes*. Edited by Julia Kristeva, Christian de Portzamparc, Umberto Eco, et al. Paris: Seuil.

2003b *The Kristeva Critical Reader*. Edited by John Lechte and Mary Zournazi. Edinburgh: Edinburgh University Press, 2003.

2004 *Notre Colette*. Colloquium, Université Paris 7, April 25–26, 2003. Edited under the direction of Julia Kristeva. Rennes: Presses Universitaires de France.

2006 *Handicap: Le Temps des engagements*. Edited by Brigitte Chapelain, Charles Gardou, and Julia Kristeva. Paris: Presses Universitaires de France.

2007a *Diversité et culture*. Edited by Ulrich Beck, Julia Kristeva, and Krzysztof Pomian. Paris: Éditions Cultures France.

2007b *Seule une femme*. With Marie-Christine Navarro. Paris: Éditions de l'Aube. Contains interviews.

2008a *Europe des cultures et culture européenne: Communité et diversité.* Edited by Julia Kristeva and Frédéric Ogée. Paris: Hachette.

2008b *(Re)Découvrir l'oeuvre de Simone de Beauvoir: Du Deuxième sexe à la cérémonie des adieux*. Edited by Pascale Fautrier, Pierre-Louis Fort, Julia Kristeva, and Anne Strasser. Latresne: Bord de l'eau.

2009 *Guerre et paix des sexes*. Edited by Julia Kristeva. Rennes: Presses Universitaires de Rennes.

2013 *Pulsions du temps*. Paris: Fayard. Edited by David Uhrig and Christina Kkona. Large selection translated by Constance Borde and Sheila Malovany-Chevallier. *Passions of Our Time.* New York: Columbia University Press, 2018.

2016 *Autour d'Émile Benveniste: Sur l'écriture*. Edited by Jean-Claude Coquet, Irène Fenoglio, Julia Kristeva, et al. Paris: Seuil.

SELECTED ARTICLES

1966

1966a "Les Recherches sémantiques de Tzvetan Todorov." *La Pensée* 130 (December): 36–43.

1967

1967a "L'Expansion de la sémiotique." *Information sur les Sciences Sociales* 6, no. 5 (October): 169–81. Reprinted in Books 1969b, 43–59; and in Edited Books 1971b, 31–46.

1967b "Bakhtine, le mot, le dialogue et le roman." *Critique* 23, no. 239 (April): 438–65. Reprinted as "Le Mot, le dialogue et le roman" in Books 1969b, 144–71. Translated by Leon S. Roudiez as "Word, Dialogue, and Novel" in Edited Books 1980, 64–91; and in Edited Books 1986, 34–61.

1967c "Pour une sémiologie des paragrammes." *Tel Quel* 29 (Spring): 53–75. New version in Books 1969b, 174–207. Translated by Roland-François Lack as "Towards a Semiology of Paragrams." In Patrick ffrench and Roland-François Lack, eds., *The Tel Quel Reader.* New York: Routledge, 1998, 25–49.

1967d "Le Sens et la mode." *Critique* 23, no. 247 (December): 1005–31. Reprinted in Books 1969b, 60–89.

1968

1968a "Distance et représentation." *Tel Quel* 32 (Winter): 132–49.

1968b "Du symbole au signe." *Tel Quel* 34 (Summer): 34–40. Reprinted in Books 1970. Translated by Seán Hand as "From Symbol to Sign" in Edited Books 1986, 62–72.

1968c "Le Geste, pratique ou communication?" *Langages*, no. 10 (June): 48–64. Reprinted in Books 1969b, 90–112. "Gesture: Practice or Communication." Translated by Ted Polhemus. In Ted Polhemus, ed., *Social Aspects of the Human Body: A Reader of Key Texts*. Harmondsworth: Penguin Books, 1978, 264–84.

1968d "Linguistique et sémiologie aujourd'hui en U.R.S.S." *Tel Quel* 35 (Fall): 3–8.

1968e "Poésie et négativité." *L'Homme* VIII, no. 2 (April–June): 36–63. Reprinted in Books 1969b, 246–77.

1968f "Pratique et langages gestuels: Bibliographie." With M. Lacoste. *Langages*, no. 10 (June): 132–49.

1968g "Problèmes de la structuration du texte." *La Nouvelle Critique*, special issue, *Linguistique et littérature*: 55–64. Reprinted in Michel Foucault, et al., *Théorie d'ensemble.* Paris: Seuil, 1968, 298–301.

1968h "La Productivité dite texte." *Communications* 11: 59–63. Reprinted in Books 1969b, 208–45.

1968i "La Sémiologie: Science critique ou critique de la science." *La Nouvelle Critique* 16 (September): 15–20. Reprinted in Books 1969b, 27–42; and in Michel Foucault et al., eds., *Théorie d'ensemble*. Paris: Seuil, 1968, 80–93. Translated by Seán Hand as "Semiotics: A Critical Science and/or a Critique of Science" in Edited Books 1986, 74–88.

1968j "Le Texte clos." *Langages*, no. 12 (December): 103–25. Reprinted in Books 1969b, 113–42. Translated by Leon S. Roudiez as "The Bounded Text" in Edited Books 1980, 36–63. Reprinted in Robert Con Davis, ed., *Contemporary Literary Criticism: Modernism through Poststructuralism.* White Plains: Longman, 1986, 448–66.

1969

1969a "À propos de l'idéologie scientifique." *Promesse* 27 (Spring): 53–77.

1969b "L'Engendrement de la formule (Part 1)." *Tel Quel* 37 (Spring): 34–74. Reprinted in Books 1969b.

1969c "L'Engendrement de la formule (Part 2)." *Tel Quel* 38 (Summer): 55–82. Reprinted in Books 1969b, 278–375.

1969d "Narration et transformation." *Semiotica* I: 422–48.

1969e "La Sémiologie comme science des idéologies." *Semiotica* I: 196–204.

1970

1970a "Idéologie du discours sur la littérature." *La Nouvelle Critique* 39: 122–27.

1970b "La Mutation sémiotique." *Annales: Histoire, Sciences Sociales*, no. 6 (November–December): 1497–1522.

1971

1971a "Comment parler à la littérature." *Tel Quel* 47 (Spring): 27–49. Reprinted in Books 1977, 13–21; and as "Comment parler à la littérature avec Roland Barthes" in Edited Books 2013, 39–54. Translated by Leon S. Roudiez as "How Does One Speak to Literature" in Edited Books 1980, 92–123. Translated by Constance Borde and Sheila Malovany-Chevallier as "How to Speak to Literature with Roland Barthes" in English ed. of Edited Books 2013, 21–32.

1971b "Du Sujet en linguistique." *Langages*, no. 24 (December): 107–26. Translated by Anna Strelis as "On the Subject in Linguistics." *Graduate Faculty Philosophy Journal* 31, no. 1 (2010): 61–89. Reprinted in Edited Books 1971a, and in Books 1977, 287–322.

1971c "Les Épistémologies de la linguistique." *Langages*, no. 24 (December): 3–13. Reprinted in Edited Books 1971a.

1971d "Introduction: Le Lieu sémiotique." In Edited Books 1971b, 1–7.

1971e "Matière, sens, dialectique." *Tel Quel* 44 (Winter): 17–35. Reprinted as "Matière, sens, dialectique: Préliminaires" in Books 1977, 263–86.

1971f "Objet, complément, dialectique." *Critique* 27, no. 285 (February): 99–131. Reprinted in Herman Parret, ed., *History of Linguistic Thought and Contemporary Linguistics*. Berlin: de Gruyter, 1976, 431–59. Reprinted as "Objet ou complément" in Books 1977, 225–62.

1971g "The Semiotic Activity: A General Introduction." Translated by Stephen Heath and Christopher Prendergast. In Stephen Heath, Colin McCabe, and Christopher Prendergast, eds., *Signs of the Times: Introductory Readings in Textual Semiotics*. Cambridge: Granta, 1–10.

1972

1972a "La Contradiction et ses aspects chez un auteur des Tang." *Tel Quel* 48–49 (Spring): 59–65.

1972b "L'Espace giotto." *Peinture: Cahiers théoriques* 2–3 (January): 35–51. Reprinted as "La Joie de Giotto" in Books 1977, 383–408. Translated by Leon S. Roudiez as "Giotto's Joy" in Edited Books 1980, 210–36.

1972c "Comptes rendus." *Tel Quel* 48–49 (Spring): 66–71.

1972d "Sémanalyse et production de sens: Quelques problèmes de sémiotique littéraire à propos d'un texte de Mallarmé, *Un Coup de dés*." In Algirdas Julien Greimas, ed., *Essais de sémiotique poétique*. Paris: Larousse, 208–34.

1972e "Le Sujet en procès" (Part 1). *Tel Quel* 52 (Spring): 12–30.

1973

1973a "Bataille, l'expérience et la pratique." In *Bataille*: *Actes du Colloque de Cerisy-la-Salle*. Paris: Union Générale d'Éditions, 267–301. Reprinted as "L'Expérience et la pratique" in Books 1977, 107–36. "Bataille, Experience and Practice." Translated by Leslie-Ann Boldt-Iron. In Leslie-Ann Boldt-Irons, ed., *On Bataille: Critical Essays*. Albany: State University of New York Press, 1995, 237–64.

1973b "La Révolution du langage poétique." *Tel Quel* 56 (Winter): 36–59. Excerpted from Books 1974b. Translated by Margaret Waller as "Revolution in Poetic Language" in Edited Books 1986, 89–136; and in Anthony Elliott, ed., *The Blackwell Reader in Contemporary Social Theory*. Malden: Blackwell, 1999: 67–80; and in Lucy Burke, Tony Crowley, and Alan Girvin, eds., *The Routledge Language and Cultural Theory Reader*. New York: Routledge, 2000: 345–61; and in Kelly Oliver, ed., *French Feminism Reader*. Lamham: Rowman & Littlefield Publishers, 2000, 176–89.

1973c "The Ruin of a Poetics." In Stephen Bann and John E. Bowlt, eds., *Russian Formalism: A Collection of Articles and Texts in Translation.* Translated by Vivienne Mylne. New York: Barnes & Nobles, 102–21.

1973d "The Semiotic Activity." *Screen* 14, nos. 1–2 (Spring–Summer): 25–39.

1973e "Le Sujet en procès" (Part 2). *Tel Quel* 53, no. 3 (Spring): 2–38. Reprinted in *Artaud: Actes du Colloque de Cerisy-la-Salle.* Paris: Union Générale d'Éditions, 43–108; and in Books 1977, 55–106. Reprinted as "Le Sujet en procès: le langage poétique." In *L'Identité: Séminaire interdisciplinaire par Claude Lévi-Strauss, professeur au Collège de France, 1974–1975.* Paris: Grasset, 1977, 223–56. "The Subject in Process." Translated by Patrick ffrench. In Patrick ffrench and Roland-François Lack, eds., *The Tel Quel Reader.* New York: Routledge, 1998, 133–78.

1973f "The System and the Speaking Subject." *Times Literary Supplement* 3736 (October): 1249–52. Reprinted in Thomas A. Sebeok, ed., *The Tell-Tale Sign: A Survey of Semiotics.* Lisse: The Peter de Ridder Press, 1975, 47–55; and in Edited Books 1986, 24–33; and in K. M. Newton, ed., *Twentieth Century Literary Theory: A Reader.* New York: St. Martin's Press, 1997, 24–29.

1974

1974a "D'Ithaca à New York." *Promesse: Pratiques, textes, lectures* 36–37 (Spring): 123–40. Reprinted in Books 1977, 495–515.

1974b "L'Éthique de la linguistique." *Critique* 30, no. 322 (March): 206–16. Reprinted in Books 1977, 357–69. Translated by Leon S. Roudiez as "The Ethics of Linguistics" in Edited Books 1980, 23–35.

1974c "Femmes chinoises." *La Quinzaine littéraire* 192 (August 1–31): 18–20. Reprinted as "Les Chinoises à *contre-courant*," *Tel Quel* 59 (Fall 1974): 26–9; and in Books 1977, 525–29.

1974d "Four Types of Signifying Practices." *Semiotext(e)* 1, no. 1 (February): 65–74.

1974e "Instances du discours et altération du sujet." *Romanic Review* 65, no. 2 (March): 77–95.

1974f "Luttes de femmes." *Tel Quel* 58 (Summer): 99–100.

1974g "Phonetics, Phonology and Impulsional Bases." Translated by Caren Greenberg. *Diacritics* 4, no. 3 (Autumn): 33–37. Excerpt from Books 1974b.

1974h "Polylogue." *Tel Quel* 57 (Spring): 19–55. Reprinted in Books 1977, 173–224. "Polylogue." Translated by Carl R. Lovitt and Ann Reilly. In *Contemporary Literature* 19, no. 3 (Summer 1978): 336–50. "The Novel as Polylogue" (portion of the essay translated by Lovitt and Reilly) in Edited Books 1980, 159–209.

1974i "Pratique signifiante et mode de production." *Tel Quel* 60 (Winter): 21–33. Reprinted in Edited Books 1975b. "Signifying Practice and Mode of Production." *Edinburgh Review* 1 (1976): 64–76.

1974j "Le Sujet dans le langage et pratique politique." *Tel Quel* 58 (Summer): 22–27. Reprinted as "Politique de la littérature" in Books 1977, 13–21.

1975

1975a "À propos du discours biblique." In Edited Books 1975b, 233–37.

1975b "D'une identité l'autre." *Tel Quel* 62 (Summer): 10–27. Reprinted in Books 1977, 149–72. Translated by Leon S. Roudiez as "From One Identity to an Other" in Edited Books 1980, 124–47; in Edited Books 1997: 93–114; in *Wide Angle* 3, no. 3 (1984): 42–47; in Todd May, ed., *Twentieth-Century Continental Philosophy.* Upper Saddle River: Prentice Hall, 1997, 259–77; and in Kelly Oliver, ed., *French Feminism Reader.* Lanham: Rowman & Littlefield Publishers, 2000, 158–65.

1975c "Discours et famille en Chine: Quelques propositions." In Armando Verdiglione, ed. *Psychanalyse et sémiotique*. Paris: Union Générale d'Éditions, 1975, 129–36.

1975d "Ellipse sur la frayeur et la séduction spéculaire." *Communications* 23: 73–78. Reprinted in Books 1977: 373–82.

1975e "La Fonction prédicative et le sujet parlant." In Edited Books 1975a, 229–59. Reprinted in Books 1977, 323–56.

1975f "Maternité selon Giovanni Belli." *Peinture: Cahiers théoriques* 10–11 (December): 11–37. Reprinted in Books 1977, 409–36. "The Maternal Body." Translated by Claire Pajaczkowska. *m/f* 1979: 158–63. Translated by Leon S. Roudiez as "Motherhood according to Giovanni Bellini" in Edited Books 1980, 237–69; in Kelly Oliver, ed., *French Feminism Reader*. Lanham: Rowman & Littlefield Publishers, 2000, 176–89; and (abridged) as "The Maternal Body" in Edited Books 1997, 301–4.

1975g "Remarques sur le mode de production asiatique." In Edited Books 1975b.

1975h "The Subject in Signifying Practice." *Semiotext(e)* 1, no. 3: 19–26. Discussion: 27–30.

1976

1976a "Céline le moderne." *Trente Quatre/Quarante Quatre: Cahiers de recherche des sciences des textes et documents* 1 (Fall): 16–22.

1976b "Contraintes rythmiques et langage poétique." In Pierre Léon and Henri Mitterand, eds., *Analyse du discours: Colloque de Toronto*. Montréal: Centre Éducatif et Culturel, 1976, 215–238. Reprinted in Books 1977, 437–66.

1976c "Lettre à Dominique Aury." *La Nouvelle Revue Française* 286 (October): 244–52.

1976d "Noms de lieu." *Tel Quel* 68 (Winter): 40–57. Revised in Books 1977, 467–91. "Place Names" (revised version). Translated by Alice Jardine and Thomas Gora. *October* 6 (Autumn 1978): 93–111. Reprinted in Edited Books 1980, 271–94.

1976e "Le Père, l'amour, l'exil." *Cahiers de l'Herne ("Beckett")*: 256–68. Reprinted in Books 1977, 137–48. Translated by Leon S. Roudiez as "The Father, Love and Banishment" in Edited Books 1980, 148–58; in Edith Kurtzweil and William Phillips, eds. *Literature and Psychoanalysis*. New York: Columbia University Press, 1983: 183–95; and in Jennifer Birkett, ed., *Samuel Beckett*. London: Longman, 2000, 247–58.

1977

1977a "À la recherche d'une nouvelle dramaturgie des plaisirs." *Libération* (June): 12.

1977b "À partir de Polylogue." *Revue des Sciences humaines* 168: 495–501. "Talking about Polylogue." Translated by Seán Hand. In Toril Moi, ed., *French Feminist Thought: A Reader*. New York: Blackwell Publishers, 115–16.

1977c "Actualité de Céline." *Tel Quel* 71–73 (Fall): 45–52. "The Contemporary Importance of Celine." *Yale Italian Studies* 1, no. 3 (1977): 289–301.

1977d "Des Chinoises à Manhattan." *Tel Quel* 69 (Spring): 11–17. Reprinted as Postface to English ed. of Books 1974a.

1977e "Féminité et écriture: Réponse à deux questions sur *Polylogue*." *Revue des sciences humaines* 4, no. 168 (October–December): 495–501.

1977f "Hérétique de l'amour." *Tel Quel* 74 (Winter): 30–49. Reprinted as "Stabat Mater" in Books 1983, 225–47. "Stabat Mater" (slightly revised version). Translated by Arthur Goldhammer. *Poetics Today* 6, nos. 1–2 (1985): 133–52. Reprinted in Susan Rubin, ed., *The Female Body in Western Culture: Contemporary Perspectives*. Cambridge: Cambridge University Press, 1986, 99–118. Translated by Leon S. Roudiez in Edited Books 1986, 160–86; in Joy Morny, Kathleen O'Grady, and Judith L. Poxon, eds,. *French Feminists on Religion: A Reader.* New York: Routledge, 2000, 120–37; and in Andrea O'Reilly, ed., *Maternal Theory: Essential Readings*. Toronto: Demeter Press, 2007, 163–85.

1977g "La Musique parlée ou remarques sur la subjectivité dans la fiction à propos du *Neveu de Rameau*." In Michèle Duchet and Michèle Jallet, eds., *Langue et langages de Leibniz à l'Encyclopédie: Séminaire de l'Ecole Supérieure de Fontenay*. Paris: Union Générale d'Éditions, 153–206.

1977h "Un Nouveau type d'intellectuel: Le Dissident." *Tel Quel* 74 (Winter): 3–8. Translated by Seán Hand as "A New Type of Intellectual: The Dissident" in Edited Books 1986, 292–300.

1977i "Le Théâtre moderne n'a pas lieu." *Trente Quatre/Quarante Quatre: Cahiers de recherche des sciences des textes et documents* 3 (Winter): 13–16. "Modern Theatre Does Not Take (a) Place." Translated by Alice Jardine and Thomas Gora. *SubStance* 6–7, nos. 18–19 (Winter 1977–Spring 1978): 131–34.

1978

1978a "La Littérature dissidente comme réfutation du discours de gauche." *Tel Quel* 76 (Summer): 40–44.

1978b "Table ronde." *L'Arc* 72: 78, 79, 80, 87, 89. (Contributions by Georges Duby, Jacques Bonnet, Jean-Claude Brinquier, Hubert Damisch, Julia Kristeva, and Michel de Certeau.)

1979

1979a "À vrai dire . . ." In Edited Books 1979: 9–10.

1979b "Le Démon littéraire." In Edited Books 1979: 203–6.

1979c "Il n'y a pas de maître à langage." *Nouvelle Revue de psychanalyse* 20 (Fall): 119–40.

1979d "Le Temps des femmes." *Trente Quatre/Quarante Quatre: Cahiers de recherche des sciences des textes et documents* 5 (Winter): 5–19. Reprinted in a slightly updated version in Books 1993, 297–331; and in Michel de Manassein, ed., *De l'égalité des sexes*. Paris: Centre national de documentation pédagogique, 1995, 23–38. "Women's Time." Translated by Alice Jardine and Harry Blake. *Signs* 7, no. 1 (Autumn 1981): 13–35. Reprinted in Nannerl O. Keohane, Michelle Zimbalist Rosado, and Barbaro Charlesworth Gelpi, eds., *Feminist Theory: A Critique of Ideology*. Chicago: University of Chicago Press, 1982: 31–53; in Edited Books 1986: 187–213; in Claudia Zanardi, ed., *Essential Papers in the Psychology of Women*. New York: New York University Press, 1990: 374–400; in Ann Garry and Marilyn Pearsall, eds., *Women, Knowledge and Reality: Explorations in Feminist Philosophy*. New York: Routledge, 1996, 61–83; and in Matthew Calarco and Peter Atterton, eds., *The Continental Ethics Reader*. New York: Routledge, 2003: 287–296. Excerpted in Catherine Belsey and Jane Moor, eds., *The Feminist Reader: Essays in Gender and the Politics of Literary Criticism*. New York: Blackwell, 1989, 201–16. Translated by Ross Guberman (from Books 1993) in Edited Books 1997, 349–67; in Robin R. Warhol and Diane Herndl, eds., *Feminisms: An Anthology of Literary Theory and Criticism*. New Brunswick: Rutgers University Press, 1997, 860–77; and in Kelly Oliver, ed., *French Feminism Reader*. Lanham: Rowman & Littlefield Publishers, 2000, 181–207.

1979e "Le Vréel." In Edited Books 1979, 11–35. Translated by Seán Hand as "The True-Real" in Edited Books 1986, 214–37.

1980

1980a "Postmodernism?" *Bucknell Review* 25, no. 2: 136–41. Reprinted in Gary Raphael Garvin, ed., *Romanticism, Modernism, Postmodernism*. Lewisburg: Bucknell University Press, 1980, 136–41; and in Peter Brooker, ed., *Modernism/Postmodernism*. New York: Longman, 1992, 197–201.

1981

1981a "L'Abjet d'amour." *Confrontations* 6: 123–25. Reprinted in *Tel Quel* 91 (Spring 1982): 17–33. Reprinted as "Freud et l'amour: le malaise dans la cure" in Books 1983, 27–58. Translated (abridged) from Books 1983 as "Freud and Love: Treatment and Its Discontents" in Edited Books 1986, 238–71; and abridged in Edited Books 1997, 137–61.

1981b "La Littérature souveraine." In *Paris-Paris, 1937–1957: Créations en France*. Paris: Centre Georges Pompidou, 12–18.

1981c "Nom de mort ou de vie." In Jacques Sedat, ed., *Retour à Lacan*. Paris: Fayard, 163–82. "Name of Death or of Life." Translated by John Lechte. In John Lechte, ed., *Writing and Psychoanalysis: A Reader.* New York: St. Martin's Press, 1996, 103–16.

1982

1982a "Approaching Abjection." Translated by John Lechte. *Oxford Literary Review* 5, nos. 1–2: 125–49. Translated by Leon S. Roudiez (from Books 1980) in Sue Vice, ed., *Psychoanalytic Criticism: A Reader*. Cambridge: Blackwell, 1996, 155–58; in Amelia Jones, ed., *The Feminism and Visual Culture Reader*. New York: Routledge, 2003, 389–392; in Catherine Harper, ed., *Textiles: Critical and Primary Sources.* Volume 4. London: Berg, 2012, 309–30; in Asa Simon Mittman and Marcus Hensel, eds., *Classic Readings on Monster Theory: Demonstrare.* Volume I. Leeds: Humanities Press, 2018, 67–74; abridged in Edited Books 1997, 229–31; and (abridged) as "Approaching abjection *and* Semiotics of Biblical Abomination." In Joy Morny, Kathleen O'Grady, and Judith L. Poxon, eds., *French Feminists on Religion: A Reader*. New York: Routledge, 2002, 93–104.

1982b "Condenser et construire: À propos de l'interprétation dans une cure de borderline." *Psychologie médicale* 14, no. 9 (September): 1369–71.

1982c "Lire la Bible." *Esprit* 69, no. 9 (September): 143–52. Reprinted in Books 1993, 173–89. Translated by Ross Guberman as "Reading the Bible" in English ed. of Books 1993. Reprinted in Joy Morny, Kathleen O'Grady, and Judith L. Poxon, eds., *French Feminists on Religion: A Reader.* New York: Routledge, 2000, 161–71; and in Donald Capps, ed., *Freud and Freudians on Religion: A Reader*. New Haven: Yale University Press, 2001, 335–44.

1982d "Maux d'amour." *Furor* 4: 3–22.

1982e "Ne dis rien." *Tel Quel* 91 (Spring): 33–44.

1982f "Psychoanalysis and the Polis." Translated by Margaret Waller. *Critical Inquiry* 9, no. 1 (September): 77–92. Reprinted in an expanded edition in W. J. T. Mitchell, ed., *The Politics of Interpretation*. Chicago: Chicago University Press, 1983, 83–98; in Vassilis Lambropoulos and David Neal Miller, eds., *Twentieth Century Literary Theory: An Introductory Anthology*. Albany: State University of New York Press, 1987, 363–80; and in Edited Books 1986, 301–20.

1982g "La Voie lactée de Jackson Pollock, 1912–1959." *Art Press International* 55 (January): 6. Revised in *L'Infini* 118 (Spring 2012): 43–56. Reprinted as "La Voie lactée de Jackson Pollock" in Edited Books 2013, 55–69. "Jackson Pollock's Milky Way, 1912–1956." Translated by David Macey. *Journal of Philosophy and the Visual Arts* (1989): 35–39.

1982h "La Voix de Barthes." *Communications* 36: 119–23.

1983

1983a "Des E.T. en manque d'amour." *Le Débat* 24 (March): 30–37. Reprinted as "Des extra-terrestres en mal d'amour" in Books 1983, 347–56. Translation by Leon S. Roudiez as "Extraterrestrials Suffering for Want of Love" in English ed. of Books 1983, 372–83; and in Edited Books 1997, 170–79.

1983b "Mémoire." *L'Infini* 1 (Winter): 39–54. "My Memory's Hyperbole." Translated by Athena Viscusi. *New York Literary Forum*, nos. 12–13, 1984: 261–76. Reprinted in Domna Stanton and Jeanine Parisier Plottel, eds., *The Female Autograph*. New York: New York Literary Forum, 1984, 219–36; and in Edited Books 1997, 3–25.

1983c "Responses to 'The Politics of Interpretation.'" With Paul Alpers and Donald Davie. *Critical Inquiry* 9, no. 3 (March): 631–33.

1983d "Within the Microcosm of the 'Talking Cure.'" Translated by Thomas Gora and Margaret Waller. In Joseph H. Smith and William Kerrigan, eds., *Interpreting Lacan*. New Haven: Yale University Press, 33–48.

1984

1984a "De l'identification: Freud, Baudelaire, Stendhal." In Geneviève Haag et al., eds., *Travail de la métaphore: Identification/interprétation*. Paris: Denoël, 53–58.

1984b "Un Docteur subtil." *La Quinzaine littéraire* 419 (June): 14–15.

1984c "Événement et révélation." *L'Infini* 5 (Winter): 3–14.

1984d "Histoires d'amour—Love Stories." In Lisa Appignanesi, *Desire* (ICA Documents 1). London: Institute of Contemporary Arts, 18–21.

1984e "Joyce the Gracehoper ou le retour d'Orphée." *L'Infini* 8 (Fall): 3–13. Reprinted in Books 1993, 255–78. "Joyce the Gracehoper or the Return of Orpheus." Translated by Louise Burchill. In Bernard Benstock, ed., *James Joyce, The Augmented Ninth: Proceedings of the Ninth International James Joyce Symposium, Frankfurt 1984*. Syracuse: Syracuse University Press, 1988, 167–80.

1984f "Le Nouveau monde solitaire." *Le Genre humain* 11 (Fall–Winter): 207–14.

1984g "La Roue des sourires." *Le Nouvel Observateur* 1013 (April): 92–93. Reprinted in Books 1993a, 229–34. Translated by Ross Guberman as "The Wheels of Smiles" in English ed. of Books 1993a. Reprinted in Donald Capps, ed. *Freud and Freudians on Religion: A Reader*. New Haven: Yale University Press, 2001, 345–47.

1984h "Le Sens et l'hétérogène: À propos du statut du sujet de l'énonciation." *Documentation et recherche en Linguistique allemande-Vincennes* 30: 1–25.

1985

1985a "De l'imaginaire mélancolique." *Le Genre humain* 2, no. 13: 65–81. "On the Melancholic Imaginary." Translated by Louise Burchill. In James Donald, ed., *New Formations,* no. 3 (Winter 1987): 5–14; and in Shlomit Rimmon-Kenan, ed., *Discourse and Psychoanalysis in Literature*. New York: Methuen, 1987, 104–23.

1985b "The Speaking Subject." In Marshall Blonsky, ed., *On Signs*. Baltimore: Johns Hopkins University Press, 210–20.

1986

1986a "Le Roman adolescent." *Adolescence* 4, no. 1: 13–28. Reprinted in Books 1993, 203–28. "The Adolescent Novel." In John Fletcher and Andrew Benjamin, eds., *Abjection, Melancholia and Love*. New York: Routledge, 8–23.

1986b "Les Secrets d'une analyste." Preface to Hélène Deutsch, *Autobiographie*. Paris: Mercure de France. Reprinted in Books 1993, 279–95.

1987

1987a "La Femme tristesse." *L'Infini* 17 (Winter): 5–9.

1987b "Holbein, le Christ de Bâle." *Psychologie médicale* 19, no. 7: 1089–97. Reprinted as "*Le Christ mort* de Holbein" in Books 1987. Translated by Leon S. Roudiez as "Holbein's

Dead Christ" in English ed. of Books 1987. Reprinted in Michel Feher, Ramona Nadaff, and Nadia Tazi, eds., *Fragments for a History of the Human Body*. Part 1. Cambridge: MIT Press, 1989, 238–69; and in Donald Capps, ed., *Freud and Freudians on Religion: A Reader*. New Haven: Yale University Press, 2001, 316–26. Abridged in Joy Morny, Kathleen O'Grady, and Judith L. Poxon, eds., *French Feminists on Religion: A Reader*. New York: Routledge, 2002, 139–49.

1987c "The Pain of Sorrow in the Modern World: The Works of Marguerite Duras." Translated by Katherine A. Jensen. *Modern Language Association* 102, no. 2 (March): 138–52; and by Leon S. Roudiez as "The Malady of Grief: Duras" in English ed. of Books 1983.

1987d "Le Réel de l'identification," In Monique David-Ménard et al., eds., *Les Identifications: Confrontations de la Clinique et de la théorie de Freud à Lacan*. Paris: Denoël, 44–63. "Identification and the Real." Translated by Shawn Whiteside. In Peter Collier and Helga Geyer-Ryan, eds., *Literary Theory Today*. Ithaca: Cornell University Press, 167–76.

1987e "La Vierge de Freud." *L'Infini* 18 (Spring): 23–33.

1988

1988a "L'Enfant au sens indicible." *Rééducation orthophonique* 27, no. 154 (June): 203–10. Reprinted in Books 1993, 157–70.

1988b "Étrangers." *L'Infini* 23 (Fall): 11–20. Excerpted from Books 1988. Translated by Leon S. Roudiez in English ed. of Books 1988. Reprinted as "The Strangers." *Partisan Review* 58, no.1 (1991): 88–100.

1988c "Gloire, deuil, écriture: Lettre à un romantique sur Mme de Staël." *Romantisme* 18, no. 62: 7–14. Reprinted in Books 1993, 235–53.

1988d "L'Impossibilité de perdre." *Cahiers de l'IPPC*, Université de Paris 7, no. 8 (November): 29–40.

1988e "L'Obsessionnel et sa mère." *Revue française de psychanalyse* 52, no. 6: 1357–71. Reprinted in Books 1993, 75–99.

1988f "Pourquoi la France?" *Lignes* 3, no. 4: 122–124. Reprinted in Books 1988.

1989

1989a "Des signes au sujet." In Dominique Bourg, Claude Coulot, Antoine Lion, and Joseph Beaude, eds. *Variations johanniques*. Paris: Le Cerf, 147–55. Reprinted in Books 1993, 147–55.

1989b "Les Psychanalystes en temps de détresse." *Lettre international*, no. 21 (Summer): 65–69. Revised as "À quoi bon des psychanalystes en temps de détresse qui s'ignore." In Claude Le Guen, ed,. *La Psychanalyse: Question pour demain*. Colloquium of the Paris Psychoanalytical Society, Paris, January 21–33. Paris: Presses Universitaires de France, 21–33. Reprinted in Books 1993a, 49–74. Translated by Ross Guberman as "In Times Like These, Who Needs Psychoanalysts?" in English ed. of Books 1993a, 27–44; and in Edited Books 1997, 209–28. "Psychoanalysts in Times of Distress." Translated by Michael Münchow. In Sonu Shamdasani and Michael Münchow, eds., *Speculations after Freud: Psychoanalysis, Philosophy and Culture*. New York: Routledge, 2002, 13–26.

1990

1990a "L'Infigurable Mélancolie." *Le Magazine littéraire* 280 (September): 43–45.

1990b "Julia Kristeva." In Marcel and Catherine Jajolet, eds., *40 écrivains parlent de la mort*. Paris: Horay, 157–64.

1990c "Lettre ouverte à Harlem Désir." *L'Infini* 30 (Summer): 67–73. Reprinted in Books 1990a.

1990d "Ours to Jew or Die: Céline and the Categories of Anti-Semitism." In David Theo Goldberg, ed., *Anatomy of Racism*. Minneapolis: University of Minnesota Press, 1990, 171–82. Translated by Leon S. Roudiez (from Books 1980) as "Ours to Jew or Die" in English ed. of Books 1980, 174–87.

1990e "Sartre ou le risque indispensable." *L'Infini* 31 (Fall): 14–16. Also in *Corriere della Sera* 7, no. 14 (April 1990).

1991

1991a "La Castration symbolique: Une question." In Annick Le Guen, Agnès Oppenheimer, and Roger Perron, eds., *Angoisse et complexe de castration*. Paris: Presses Universitaires de France, 101–13. Reprinted in Books 1993, 135–56.

1991b "Clubs et publications insolites en Bulgarie." *L'Infini* 33 (Spring): 119–20.

1991c "Du nouveau à l'Est: Du nouveau?" *L'Infini* 33 (Spring): 73–74.

1991d "Freud revisité." *L'Infini* 36 (Winter): 43–45.

1991e "The Imaginary Sense of Forms With Alain Kirili." Translated by Philip Barnard. *Arts Magazine* 66, no. 1 (September): 28–30.

1991f "La Nation pour inclure ou exclure: Une idée fragile et libre." *Le Monde* (29 March): 21.

1991g "Romeo and Juliet: Love-Hatred in the Couple." Translated by Leon S. Roudiez in English ed. of Books 1983. Reprinted in John Drakakis, ed., *Shakespearean Tragedy*. Harlow: Longman, 1991, 296–315. Roudiez translation reprinted as "Romeo and Juliet: Love-Hatred in the Couple (Le couple amour-haine selon *Roméo et Juliette*)." In R. S. White, ed., *Romeo and Juliet*. Palgrave: Houndmills, 2001, 68–84.

1992

1992a "Apologia for Metaphor." Translated by Stephen Bann. *Women: A Cultural Review* 3, no. 3: 233–37. Reprinted in Books 1993b.

1992b "Le Contre-transfert: Une hystérie réveillée." *Revue internationale de psychopathologie* 5: 43–64. Reprinted in Books 1993, 101–33.

1992c "En deuil d'une langue?" In Nicole Czechowski and Claudie Danziger, eds., *Deuils: Vivre c'est perdre*. Paris: Éditions Autrement, 27–32.

1992d "Hystérie, les signes et le roman." *Les Lettres françaises* (March 18): 22.

1992e "Lettre adressée au Comité de rédaction." *Nouvelle Revue de psychopathologie* 6: 259–60.

1992f "Les Modèles linguistiques et pragmatiques de la communication." With Elizabeth Bélorgey. *Revue internationale de psychopathologie* 7: 381–408. Reprinted in Daniel Widlöcher, ed., *Traité de psychopathologie.* Paris: Presses Universitaires de France, 1994, 865–82.

1992g "Psychoanalysis and the Imaginary." In George Levine, ed., *Constructions of the Self.* New Brunswick: Rutgers University Press, 285–97. Reprinted as "Psychoanalysis and the Imaginary." *Cultural Semiosis: Tracing the Signifier.* New York and London: Routledge, 1998, 181–95.

1992h "Quelques particularités du discours dépressif." *Information psychiatrique* 68, no. 3: 239–50.

1992i "La Sensation est-elle un langage?" *Nouvelle Revue de psychopathologie* 3: 9–30. Reprinted in Books 1994. Translated by Ross Guberman as "Is Sensation a Form of Language?" in English ed. of Books 1994. Translated by John Lechte as "Is Sensation a Language?" In John Lechte, ed., *Writing and Psychoanalysis: A Reader*. New York: St. Martin's Press, 1996, 183–201. Reprinted (abridged) in Edited Books 1997, 116–27.

1992j "What of Tomorrow's Nation?" *Alphabet City* 2 (April): 32–34. Reprinted in Books 1993c.

1993

1993a "Albertine et Charlus." *L'Infini* 44 (Winter): 18–48. Excerpts from Books 1994.
1993b "Psychanalyse et linguistique." In Pierre Kaufman, ed., *L'Apport Freudien: Éléments pour une encyclopédie de la psychanalyse*. Paris: Bordas, 527–35.

1994

1994a "Aimer la vérité cruelle et disgracieuse." *Les Cahiers naturalistes* 68: 7–9.
1994b "Le Bonheur des Béguines." In Paul Vanderbroeck, ed. *Le Jardin clos de l'âme: L'Imaginaire des religieuses dans les Pays-Bas du Sud depuis le 13ème siècle*. Bruxelles: Société des Expositions du Palais des Beaux-Arts, 6–12.
1994c "Entre 'tout' et 'impossible': Le Multiple." *Revue française de psychanalyse* 58, no. 4 (October–December): 1027–32.
1994d "Gérard de Nerval, the Disinherited Poet." (Translated by Leon S. Roudiez in English ed. of Books 1983). In Maud Ellmann, ed., *Psychoanalytic Literary Criticism*. New York: Routledge, 196–220.
1994e "The Importance of Frye." Translated by Joseph Adamson. In Lee Alvin, ed., *The Legacy of Northrop Frye*. Toronto: University of Toronto Press, 335–37.
1994f "Monstrueuse intimité: De la littérature comme expérience." *L'Infini* 48 (Winter): 55–61. Monstrous Intimacy: Of Literature as Experience. Discussion of Joseph Brodsky's Paper 'A Cat's Meow.'" Translated by Marie Michelle Strah. In Sture Allén, ed., *Of Thoughts and Words: The Relation Between Language and Mind. Proceedings of the Nobel Symposium 92, Stockholm, Sweden, 8–12 August 1994*. London: Imperial College, 1995, 55–61.
1994g "Les Nouvelles Maladies de l'âme." *L'Infini* 45 (Spring): 73–75. "The New Maladies of the Soul." Translated by John Corbett. In Jérôme Bindé, ed., *The Future of Values: Twenty-First Century Talks*. New York: Berghahn Books, 303–8.
1994h "On Yuri Lotman." Translated by Martha Noel Evans. *Publications of the Modern Language Association of America* 3, no. 109 (May): 375–84
1994i "Robert Wilson." *artpress* 191 (May): 64–65.
1994j "The Semiotic and the Symbolic." (Translated by Margaret Waller in English ed. of Books 1974b.) In Camille Roman, Suzanne Juhasz, and Christanne Miller, eds., *The Women and Language Debate: A Sourcebook*. New Brunswick: Rutgers University Press, 45–55. Reprinted in Edited Books 1997, 32–69.

1995

1995a "Brouillon d'inconscient ou l'inconscient brouillé." *Genesis*, no. 8: 23–26.
1995b "Bulgarie, ma souffrance." *L'Infini* 51 (Fall): 42–52. "Bulgaria, My Suffering." Translated by Barbara Bray. *Artes* 3 (Stockholm 1996): 121–31. Translated by Susan Fairfield in Edited Books 2000a, 163–83. Translated into Bulgarian in *Europa 2000* (Sofia).
1995c "L'Inquiétante étrangeté avant et après Freud." In Julia Kristeva, Karl-Heinz Kohl, and Ernst Tugendhat, eds., *Festschrift aus Anlass der Verleihung der Dr. Margrit Egnér-Preise 1995 zum Thema "Das Fremde": 9 November 1995*. Zürich: Dr.-Margrit-Egnér-Stiftung, 1995.
1995d "Penser interpreter: L'Expérience analytique au chiasme hallucination/jugement." *Revue française de psychanalyse* 5, no. 59: 1805–10.
1995e "Qui a peur d'une athée?" *Lignes* 1, no. 24: 196–99.
1995f "Les Samouraïs tels quels." *L'Infini* 49–50 (Spring): 57–61. Reprinted in *Lettres actuelles*, no. 6 (May–June): 50–55; and in Philippe Forest, ed., *De 'Tel Quel' à 'L'Infini': L'Avant-garde et après. Colloques de Londres et de Paris, mars 1995*. Nantes: Plein Feux, 2000, 21–33. Translated as "The Samurais 'tels quels.'" *Parallax* 4, no. 1 (January–March 1998): 7–11.

1995g "Le Scandale du hors-temps." *Revue française de psychanalyse* 59, no. 4 (October–December): 1029–44.
1995h "Sémiologie." In *Encyclopaedia universalis* 20. Paris: Encyclopaedia universalis France S.A., 883–86.

1996

1996a "La Fille au sanglot: Du temps hystérique." *L'Infini* 54 (Spring): 27–47. Reprinted (slightly altered) in Edited Books 2005, 247–75.
1996b "L'Intraitable amoureux: Barthes/fragments d'un discours amoureux." *Magazine littéraire*, special issue: 51–59. Reprinted in Books 1997.

1997

1997a "Aragon, *Blanche ou l'oubli*, ou la 'quête bouffonne et farouche d'une conscience.'" In *Le Siècle d'Aragon: Centenaire en Seine-Saint-Denis 1997*. Bobigny: Conseil Général de la Seine-Saint-Denis (n.p.). Reprinted as "Irène, Blanche ou l'oubli." In Carine Trevisan, ed., *Aragon le souci de soi*. Paris: UFR de Sciences de textes et documents, 1999. Reprinted in Books 1997, 336–405. Translated by Jeanine Herman as "Aragon: *Blanche ou l'oubli*; or, 'The Farcical and Ferocious Quest for a Consciousness'" in English ed. of Books 1997, 181–219.
1997b "L'Autre langue, ou traduire le sensible." *L'Infini* 57 (Spring): 15–28. Reprinted in *French Studies* 52, no. 4 (October 1998): 385–96; and in Books 1998a, 61–87. "The Other Language: Or, Translating Sensitivity." Translated by B. Bray, G. Fields, and M. Westlake. *Common Knowledge* 6, no. 3 (Winter 1977): 19–31. Translated by Jeanine Herman as "The Love of Another Language" in English ed. of Books 1997.
1997c "De l'association libre à la culture-révolte." In Catherine Couvreur, Agnès Oppenheimer, Roger Perron, and Jacqueline Schaeffer, eds., *Psychanalyse, neurosciences, cognitivismes*. Paris: Presses Universitaires de France, 99–111.
1997d "Freudian Models of Language: A Conversation." Translated by Claudia Vaughn in *Journal of European Psychoanalysis*, nos. 3–4 (Spring–Winter): 7–19.
1997e "Hannah Arendt's Concept of 'Life.'" Translated by Louise Burchill. *Common Knowledge* 6, no. 2 (Fall): 159–69.
1997f "Intellectuelles, elles." *Lignes* 32 (October): 74–76.
1997g "Les Métamorphoses du Ritz." *Magazine littéraire* 350 (January): 37–43. Reprinted in *Le Trait,* nos. 3–4 (Winter) 1999: 103–9. Enlarged in Edited Books 2005, 541–60.
1997h "La Parole, cette inconnue." *L'Infini* 60 (Winter): 37–42.
1997i "Quelle révolte aujourd'hui?" *Frankfurter Rundschau*, January 21. Reprinted in Books 1998a, 15–31.
1997j "Réponse de Julia Kristeva." *L'Infini* 60 (Winter): 94–100.

1998

1998a "Auto-érotisme et paranoïa dans l'acte narratif." In Michèle Beertrand, ed., *Psychanalyse et réci: Stratégies narratives et processus thérapeutiques*. Besançon: Presses Universitaires Franc-comtoises, 37–49.
1998b "De l'expérience du Phallus ou le Féminin Entre Illusion et Désillusion/Experiencing the Phallus as Extraneous; or, Women's Twofold Oedipus Complex." Translated by Jeanine Herman in English ed. of Books 1996b from chapter 5 of Books 1996b. Translated by Louise Burchill. *Parallax* 4, no. 8 (July–September 1998): 18–42. Louise Burchill translation reprinted in Peter Hartocollis, ed., *Mankind's Oedipal Destiny: Libidinal and Aggressive Aspects of Sexuality.* Madison: International Universities Press, 2001, 37–53.
1998c "Disparition-constellation: Hommage à R. G. Cohn." *Po&sie* 85: 3–5.

1998d "Du sens au sensible: Logiques, jouissance, style." In B. Chouvier, A. Green, Julia Kristeva, et al. *Symbolisation et processus de creation: Sens de l'intime et travail de l'universel dans l'art et la psychanalyse.* Paris: Dunod, 77–98.

1998e "Une étrangère." *La Nouvelle Revue Française* 542 (March): 5–9. Reprinted in Books 2005a, 501–8. Translated by Jeanine Herman as "A Stranger" in English ed. of Books 2005a, 245–50.

1998f "L'Europe divisée: politique, éthique, religion." In Georges Michel Nivat, ed., *Eux et nous: L'Europe face à ses nouvelles déchirures. Textes des conférences et des discussions*: XXXVIe *rencontres de Genève 1997*. Lausanne: L'Age d'homme, 121–58. Reprinted in *L'Infini* 63 (Fall): 38–62; and in Edited Books 2005, 47–82.

1998g "Europhilia-Europhobia." *Constellations* 5, no. 3: 321–32. (Translated by Jeanine Herman in English ed. of Books 1997.) "Europhilie-Europhobie" in Books 1998a.

1998h "La 'Sémanalyse.'" With Dana Rudelic-Fernandez. In Pierre Kaufmann, ed., *L'Apport freudien: Éléments pour une encyclopédie de la psychanalyse*. Paris: Larousse, 747–52.

1998i "The Revolt of Mallarmé." Translated by Louise Burchill. In Robert Greer and Gerald Gillespie, eds. *Mallarmé in the Twentieth Century.* Cranbury: Associated University Press, 31–52.

1999

1999a "Athéisme." *Le Trait*, no. 5 (Fall): 31–34. Reprinted in Books 2005a, 413–18.

1999b "Chanter l'incarnation." Preface to Frank Lalou and Patrick Calame, eds., *Le Grand Livre du Cantique des Cantiques*: *Le Texte hébreu, les traductions historiques et ses commentaires selon les traditions juive et chrétienne*. Paris: Albin Michel.

1999c "Le Contre-transfert et les psychanalystes femmes." In Sophie de Mijolla-Mellor, ed., *Les Femmes dans l'histoire de la psychanalyse*. Bordeaux-le-Bouscat: L'Esprit du temps, 97–100.

1999d "Hannah Arendt, ou la vie est un récit." *L'Infini* 65 (Spring): 42–65. Reprinted in Edited Books 2000a.

1999e "La Passion hystérique." In Jacques André. *De la passion.* Paris: Presses Universitaires de France, 27–62.

1999f "Le Poids mystérieux de l'orthodoxie." *Le Monde* (April 19): 1, 13.

1999g "Psychoanalysis and Freedom." Translated by Charles Levin from "Psychanalyse et liberté" in Books 1998a. *Canadian Journal of Psychoanalysis* 7, no. 1 (Spring): 1–21. French original reprinted in Caroline Jacot Grapa et al., eds., *Le Travail des Lumières*. Paris: Champion, 2002, 823–39.

1999h "Le Sens de la parité." *Le Monde* (March 23, 1999): 1, 16. Abridged version reprinted in *L'Infini* 67 (Fall 1999): 47–54. Reprinted as "Encore de la parité: Des femmes et du sacré" in Books 2005a, 131–41. Translated by John Lechte as "The Meaning of Parity" in Edited Books 2003b. Translated by Jeanine Herman as "On Parity, Again; or, Women and the Sacred" in English ed. of Books 2005a, 49–56.

2000

2000a "Des madones aux nus: Une représentation de la beauté féminine." *L'Infini* 70 (Summer): 22–48. Reprinted in Books 2005a, 143–70; and in Cyrille Michon, ed., *Le Christianisme, héritages et destins*. Paris: Librairie Générale Française, 2002, 185–224. Translated by Jeanine Herman as "From Madonnas to Nudes: A Representation of Female Beauty" in English ed. of Books 2005a, 57–78.

2000b "Dora gynécophile." *Magazine littéraire*, special out of series issue, no. 2: 42–43.

2000c "E comme écrire en français." In Bernard Cerquiglini, Jean-Claude Corbeil, Jean-Marie Klinkenberg, et al., eds., *Le Français dans tous ses états*. Paris: Flammarion, 63–73.

2000d "From Filth to Defilement." (Translated by Leon S. Roudiez in English ed. of Books 1980.) In Kelly Oliver, ed., *French Feminism Reader*. Lanham: Rowman & Littlefield Publishers, 166–75.

2000e "From Symbols to Flesh: The Polymorphous Destiny of Narration." Translated by Paula Barkay. *The International Journal of Psychoanalysis* 81, no. 4 (August): 771–87. Reprinted in Paul Williams and Glenn O. Gabbard, eds., *Key Papers in Literature and Psychoanalysis*. New York: Karnac, 2007, 77–104. Revised as "La Narration en psychanalyse: Des symboles à la chair." In Myriam Revault d'Allonnes and François Azouvi, eds., *L'Herne: Ricœur* (Les Cahiers de l'Herne, 2004), 140–55. Reprinted as "La Narration en psychanalyse: Une Transubstantiation" in Books 2005a, 283–94.

2000f "L'Homme aux collages ou le sens d'une somatisation." *Revue française de psychosomatique* 1, no. 17: 53–65.

2000g "Par-delà la structure: Une renaissance de l'espace psychique." *L'Évolution psychiatrique* 65, no. 3 (July): 469–75.

2000h "Penser la pensée littéraire." In Edited Books 2000b: 26–40. "Thinking about Literary Thought." Translated by Marc Trottier. *American Journal of Semiotics* 18, nos. 1–4 (2002): 1–14; and in *Σημειωτκή—Sign Systems Studies* 30, no. 2 (2002): 405–17.

2000i "Qu'est-ce que raconter sa vie?" *L'Autre: Cliniques, cultures et sociétés* 1, no. 2: 225–37.

2000j "Romeo et Juliette ou l'amour hors-la-loi." *Actes des Congrès de la Société française Shakespeare* 18: 119–30.

2001

2001a "Artaud entre psychose et révolte." *Revue des lettres modernes*, nos. 1517–22: 13–18.

2001b "Charlus et le narrateur." *Textuel*, no. 23: 139–47.

2001c "Credo in Unum Deum." (Translated by Arthur Goldhammer in English ed. of Books 1985.) In Donald Capps, ed., *Freud and Freudians on Religion: A Reader*. New Haven: Yale University Press, 311–15. Reprinted (abridged) as "Credence credit *and* Credo." In Joy Morny, Kathleen O'Grady, and Judith L. Poxon, eds., *French Feminists on Religion: A Reader*. New York: Routledge, 2002: 105–20.

2001d "De la passion selon la maternité." *Revue française de psychanalyse* (July): 105–20. Reprinted in Jean Cournut, Marie-Claire Durieux, and Michèle Emmanuelli, eds. *La Vie amoureuse*. Paris: Presses Universitaires de France, 2001; and in Books 2005a, 175–98. Translated by Jeanine Herman as "The Passion According to Motherhood" in English ed. of Books 2005a, 79–94.

2001e "France-Culture, mercredi 8h25." *L'Infini* 74 (Spring): 28–57.

2001f "La Guerre des sexes depuis l'Antiquité." Preface to François Charpin, ed., *Le Féminin exclu: Essai sur le désir des hommes et des femmes dans la littérature grecque et latine.* Paris: Librairie Calepinus/Michel de Maule, 7–13. Reprinted in Books 2005a, 199–204. Translated as "The War of the Sexes Since Antiquity" in English ed. of Books 2005a, 95–98.

2001g "Les Langues pour seule patrie." Preface to Sylvie Courtine-Denamy, *La Maison de Jacob*. Paris: Éditions Phébus, 9–17. Reprinted in Books 2005b, 37–46.

2001h "Might Not Universality Be . . . Our Own Foreignness?" (Translated by Leon S. Roudiez in English ed. of Books 1988.) In Donald Capps, ed., *Freud and Freudians on Religion: A Reader*. New Haven: Yale University Press, 327–34; in Christina Howells, ed., *French Women Philosophers: A Contemporary Reader. Subjectivity, Identity, Alterity*. New York: Routledge, 2004, 218–35; and abridged in Edited Books 1997, 282–92.

2001i "Paul Celan: Celanie, la douleur du corps nomade." *Magazine littéraire* (July–August): 52–56. Reprinted as "Celanie" in Books 2005a, 577–88.

2001j "La Traversée de la mélancolie." *Figures de la psychanalyse* 1, no. 4: 19–24.

2002

2002a "Le Cantique des Cantiques." *Pardès: Études et culture juives* 1, nos. 32–33: 65–78.

2002b "The Chosen People and the Choice of Foreignness." (Translated by Leon S. Roudiez in English ed. of Books 1988.) In Joy Morny, Kathleen O'Grady, and Judith L. Poxon, eds., *French Feminists on Religion: A Reader.* New York and London: Routledge, 150–59.

2002c "De l'écriture comme étrangeté et comme jouissance." In Marianne Alphant and Nathalie Léger, eds., *R/B, Roland Barthes*. Paris: Seuil, 81–85. Reprinted in Books 2005a, 509–17. Translated by Jeanine Herman as "Writing as Strangeness and Jouissance" in English ed. of Books 2005a, 251–56.

2002d "Faire ce qui n'existe pas." *Le Monde* (December 24): 14. Enlarged as "Peut-on faire la paix?" in Books 2005a, 419–33.

2002e "Guérir, une renaissance psychique." In Samy Abtroun, ed., *Guérir*. Paris: Le Bord de l'eau, 117–29. Reprinted in Books 2005a, 315–22. Translated by Jeanine Herman as "Healing, A Psychical Rebirth" in English ed. of Books 2005a, 153–58.

2002f "Nous deux or a (Hi)story of Intertextuality." *Romanic Review* 93, nos. 1–2 (January–March): 7–13.

2002g "Psychoanalysis: A Counter Depressant." (Translated by Leon S. Roudiez in English ed. of Books 1987.) Abridged in Joy Morny, Kathleen O'Grady, and Judith L. Poxon, eds., *French Feminists on Religion: A Reader.* New York: Routledge. Reprinted in Edited Books 1997, 180–202.

2003

2003a "Après Roland Barthes: Comment parler à la littérature." In Edited Books 2003a, 9–11. Reprinted as "Comment parler à la literature avec Roland Barthes" in Edited Books 2013, 39–54. Translated by Constance Borde and Sheila Malovany-Chevallier as "How to Speak to Literature with Roland Barthes" in English ed. of Books 2013, 21–32.

2003b "Colette et la chair du monde." In Edited Books 2003a, 13–65.

2003c "Habiter les carrefours / Living on Crossroads." *Divinatio*, no. 17: 107–14.

2003d "La Langue, la nation, les femmes." *Divinatio,* no. 17: 99–106.

2003e "Meurtre à Byzance." *L'Infini* 85 (Winter): 3–10.

2003f "Peut-on parler encore d'esthétique? Ou du destin de la sublimation selon Colette." *Revue française de psychanalyse* 67, no. 2 (April–June): 647–61.

2003g "Portrait d'un tueur." *Elle*, June 30, 2003.

2003h "Le Triple arrachement d'Israël (exode, exil, retour)." In Jean-Claude Eslin and Catherine Cornu, eds. *La Bible 2000 ans de lectures*. Paris: Desclée de Brouwer, 413–21. Reprinted as "Le Triple Arrachement d'Israël: Exode, exil et retour (Discours sur les Prophécies)." *L'Infini* 87 (Summer 2004): 60–66. Reprinted in Books 2005a, 435–46. Translated by Jeanine Herman as "The Triple Uprooting of Israel: Exodus, Exile, Return" in English ed. of Books 2005a, 213–21.

2004

2004a "Avec le handicap: Aux frontières du vivant." *Magazine littéraire* 428 (February): 33–36. Revised as "Handicap ou le droit à l'irrémédiable." *Etudes* 402, no. 5 (May 2005): 619–29. Revised as "Liberté, égalité, fraternité et . . . vulnérabilité" in Books 2005a, 95–118. Reprinted as "Liberté, égalité, fraternité et . . . vulnérabilité." In *Recherches en psychanalyse* 2, no. 6, 2006: 11–27. Translated by Claire Potter as "At the Limits of Living: To Joseph Grigley." *Atenea* 25, no.1 (June 2005): 9–15; and in *Journal of Visual Culture* 5, no. 2 (August 2006): 219–25. Translated by Jeanine Herman as "Liberty, Equality, Fraternity, and . . . Vulnerability." *Women's Studies Quarterly* 38, no. 1 (Spring–Summer 2010): 251–68; and in English ed. of Books 2005a, 29–45.

2004b "Beauvoir présente." *Simone de Beauvoir Studies* 20: 11–22. Reprinted in Books 2005a, 205–22; and in Books 2016b. Translated by Jeanine Herman as "Beauvoir, Presently" in English ed. of Books 2005a, 99–113.

2004c "Beyond the Dialectic of Law and Transgression: Forgiveness and Promise." Translated by Ross Guberman. In Cheng, Sinkwan, ed., *Law, Justice, and Power: Between Reason and Will*. Stanford: Stanford University Press, 261–69. (Adapted from chapter 3, "Thinking, Willing, and Judging" in English ed. of Books 1999.)

2004d "De Claudine à Sido: Colette ou la chair du monde." In Edited Books 2004, 39–50.

2004e "Le Désir de loi." In Christian Poncelet, ed., *Vive la loi*: *Actes du Colloque organisé par M. Christian Poncelet*. Paris: Éditions du Sénat and Université de Paris II, 69–72. Reprinted in Books 2005a, 339–56. Translated by Jeanine Herman as "Desire for Law" in English ed. of Books 2005a.

2004f "La Fatigue au féminin." In *Vivre fatigue*: *Actes du Colloque*. Paris: Presses Universitaires de France: 41–53. Reprinted in Books 2005a, 227–43. Translated by Jeanine Herman as "Fatigue in the Feminine" in English ed. of Books 2005a, 114–25.

2004g "Female Genius, Freedom and Culture." *Irish Pages: A Journal of Contemporary Writing* 2, no. 2 (Autumn–Winter): 214–28.

2004h "French Theory." *Irish Pages: A Journal of Contemporary Writing* 2, no. 2 (Autumn–Winter): 201–14. Reprinted in Mary Gallagher, ed., *World Writing: Poetics, Ethics, Globalization*. Toronto: University of Toronto Press, 122–37.

2004i "Introduction: Ni mort ni éternité: '*L'Éclosion*' selon Colette." In Edited Books 2004, 9–12.

2004j "Is There a Feminine Genius?" (Excerpted from English ed. of Books 2002. Translated by Jane Marie Todd.) *Critical Inquiry* 30, no. 3 (Spring): 493–504; and *Proceedings of the British Academy* 122: 117–28.

2004k "Le Langage, la sublimation, les femmes." In François Richard and Fernando Urribarri, eds., *Autour de l'oeuvre d'André Green: Enjeux pour une psychanalyse contemporaine*. Paris: Presses Universitaires de France, 385–97. Reprinted in Books 2005a, 349–56. Translated by Jeanine Herman as "Language, Sublimation, Women" in English ed. of Books 2005a, 177–94.

2004l "Monstrueuse Colette." In Sophie de Mijolla-Mellor, ed., *La Cruauté au féminin*. Paris: Presses Universitaires de France, 9–22.

2004m "Odette, ou comment les idées surprennent l'analyste." In Raymonde Coudert and Guillaume Perrier, eds., special issue on *Marcel Proust, Surprises de la recherche*, *Textuel*, no. 45, Paris: Université de Paris 7-Denis-Diderot, 241–48. Reprinted in Books 2005a, 565–76. Translated by Anne Marie Smith as "Odette, or How Ideas Surprise the Analyst." *Contemporary French and Francophone Studies* 9, no. 2 (April 2005): 131–38.

2004n "Some Observations on Female Sexuality." Translated by Sophie Leighton. *The Annual of Psychoanalysis* 32: 59–68.

2004o "Table ronde: Pourquoi Colette? Sa vie, son oeuvre." With Claude Pichois and Alain Brunet. In Edited Books 2004: 13–23.

2004p "Thinking about Liberty in Dark Times: The Holberg Prize Seminar." Bergen: University of Bergen, 21–36. "Penser la liberté en temps de détresse." In Isabelle Rieusset-Lemarié, ed., *Julia Kristeva: Prix Holberg*. Paris: Fayard, 2005: 145–58; and in Books 2005a, 15–27. Reprinted as "Thinking in Dark Times." *Profession* (2006): 13–21. "A Meditation, a Political Act, an Art of Living." Translated by S. K. Keltner. In Kelly Oliver and S. K. Keltner, eds., *Psychoanalysis, Aesthetics, and Politics in the Work of Kristeva*. Albany: State University of New York Press, 2009, 19–28.

2004q "Towards a Feminization of Values." Translated by John Corbett. In Jérôme Bindé, ed., *The Future of Values: 21st-Century Talks*. New York: Berghahn Books, 80–85.

2004r "Que reste t-il de nos amours?" Preface for Hebrew ed. of Books 1985. Translated into Hebrew by Amos Squverer. Reprinted in French in Books 2005a, 471–78. Translated by Jeanine Herman as "What is Left of Our Loves" in English ed. of Books 2005a, 222–27.

2005

2005a "À la recherche d'une pratique authentique." In Michel Contat, ed., *Sartre*. Paris: Bayard, 266–76.

2005b "Au *Casino*, ou comment une femme joue la comédie humaine." In Annette Messager, Suzanne Pagé, and Béatrice Parent, eds., *Casino*. Paris: Éditions Xavier Barral, Paris Musées, 57–65. Reprinted in Books 2005a, 527–37.

2005c "Au-delà de l'absence." *Recherches en psychanalyse* 1, no. 3: 121–25. Reprinted in Books 2005a, 519–26.

2005d "La Chine telle quelle." *L'Infini* 90 (Spring) 2005: 134–39. First published as Preface to 2001 ed. of Books 1974a. Reprinted in French ed. of Books 2005a, 29–36.

2005e "De l'abjection à la paranoïa." In Alain Fine, Félicie Nayrou, and Georges Pragier, eds., *La Haine: Haine de soi, haine de l'autre, haine dans la culture*. Paris: Presses Universitaires de France, 139–53. Reprinted as "La Haine et le pardon: De l'abjection à la paranoïa" in Books 2005a, 357–73. Translated by Jeanine Herman as "Hatred and Forgiveness; Or, From Abjection to Paranoia" in English ed. of Books 2005a, 183–94.

2005f "Le Génie du catholicisme." *La Croix* (April 8). Reprinted in Books 2005a, 461–64; and in Books 2006, 177–82.

2005g "L'Impudence d'énoncer: La Langue maternelle." *Revue française de psychanalyse* 69, no. 5 (December): 1655–67. Reprinted in Books 2005a, 392–410. "The Impudence of Uttering: The Mother Tongue." Translated by Patricia Viera and Michael Marder. *Psychoanalytic Review* 97, no. 4 (2010): 679–94.

2005h "Ou pourquoi, en roman." *L'Infini* 91 (Summer): 85–99.

2005i "Pourquoi Wu Xian, alias l'infini? Post-scriptum à *Meurtre à Byzance*." *L'Infini* 90 (Spring): 141–47.

2006

2006a "Comptes-rendus des huit forums et rappel des engagements." With Charles Gardou. In Edited Books 2006, 297–324.

2006b "Le Handicap, une idée neuve en France." In Edited Books 2006, 7–11.

2006c "Intimate Revolt: The Future of the Culture of Revolt, the Life of the Mind, and the Species." *International Journal of Baudrillard Studies* 3, no. 1 (January): 1–19. Electronic publication. Longer version from Books 1998a translated by Jeanine Herman as "The Future of Revolt" in English ed. of Books 1997, 221–68.

2006d "Louis-Ferdinand Céline (1894–1961)." Translated by M. B. DeBevoise. In Lawrence Kritzman, ed., *The Columbia History of Twentieth-Century Thought.* New York: Columbia University Press, 2007, 472–74.

2006e "Marcel Proust (1871–1922)." Translated by M. B. DeBevoise. In Lawrence Kritzman, ed., *The Columbia History of Twentieth-Century Thought.* New York: Columbia University Press, 2007, 640–42.

2006f "N'ayez pas peur de la culture européenne." *La Croix* (April 6). Reprinted in French ed. of Books 2006.

2006g "La Passion selon Thérèse d'Avila." *Topique: Revue Freudienne*, no. 96: 39–50. Reprinted in Edited Books 2013, 289–304; and as Preface to *Les Chemins de la perfection: Anthologie établie et traduite de l'espagnol par Aline Schulman.* Paris: Fayard, 2015: 7–16. Revised in *Transversalités* 1, no. 140 (2017): 125–33. "Saint Teresa of Avila." Translated by Anne Marsella. In *Saints: Faith Without Borders.* Chicago: Chicago University Press, 2011, 321–33; reprinted (modified) in Richard Kearney and Brian Treanor, eds., *Carnal Hermeneutics*. New York: Fordham University Press, 2015, 251–262. "The Passion According to St. Teresa of Avila." Translated by Roderick Campbell-Guion. In Peter Tyler and Edward Howells, eds., *Teresa of Avila: Mystical Theology and Spirituality in the Carmelite Tradition.* New York: Routledge, 2017, 99–106. Translated by

Constance Borde and Sheila Malovany-Chevallier as "The Passion According to Teresa of Avila" in English ed. of Edited Books 2013, 165–76.

2006h "Personnes en situation de handicap: L'Heure du rendez-vous." With Charles Gardou. *Empan* 61: 84–86.

2006i "Roland Barthes (1915–1980)." Translated by M. B. DeBevoise. In Lawrence Kritzman, ed., *The Columbia History of Twentieth-Century Thought.* New York: Columbia University Press, 2007, 407–12.

2006j "La Réinvention du couple." *Diogène* 216, no. 4: 36–43. "The Reinvention of the Couple." Translated by Jean Burrell. *Diogenes* 54, no. 4 (2007): 29–34.

2006k "Sacré mère, sacré enfant." *Spirale* 4, no. 40: 37–41.

2006l "Vie affective, familiale et sexuelle." With Hélène Harder. In Edited Books 2006: 89–133.

2007

2007a "À propos des *Bienveillantes* (de l'abjection à la banalité du mal)." *L'Infini* 99 (Summer): 22–35.

2007b "Adolescence: A Syndrome of Ideality." *The Psychoanalytic Review* 94, no. 5 (October): 715–25. (From Books 2005a.) Reprinted (abridged) in Sarah K. Hansen and Rebecca Tuvel, eds., *New Forms of Revolt: Essays on Kristeva's Intimate Politics.* Albany: State University of New York, 2017, 19–20.

2007c "Can We Make Peace? For Teresa Brennan." Translated by Shannon Hoff. In Alice Jardine, Shannon Lundeen, and Kelly Oliver, eds., *Living Attention: On Teresa Brennan.* Albany: State University of New York Press, 117–26.

2007d "Diversité c'est ma devise/My Motto is Diversity." In Edited Books 2007a, 5–23. Reprinted as "Diversité, c'est ma devise" in Edited Books 2013, 601–16. Translated by Constance Borde and Sheila Malovany-Chevallier as "Diversity is My Motto" in English ed. of Books 2013, 311–22.

2007e "Hannah Arendt ou la refondation comme survie." *L'Infini* 98 (Spring): 58–70. "Refoundation as Survival: An Interrogation of Hannah Arendt." *Common Knowledge* 14, no. 3 (Fall 2008): 353–64.

2007f "Louise Bourgeois, Runaway Girl." In Marie-Laure Bernadac and Jonas Storsve, eds., *Louise Bourgeois.* Paris: Centre Pompidou, 261–266. Reprinted as "Une runaway girl" in Books 2008, 477–92; and in Edited Books 2013, 71–83. Translated as "Runaway Girl, Louise Bourgeois: From 'Little Pea' to Runaway Girl." In Frances Morris, Paulo Herkenhoff, and Marie-Laure Bernadac, eds., *Louise Bourgeois.* New York: Rizzoli, 2008, 246–52. Translated by Lorna Scott Fox as "A Runaway Girl" in English ed. of Books 2008.

2007g "Parler en psychanalyse: Des symboles à la chair et retour." *Revue française de psychanalyse* 71, no. 5 (December): 1509–20. Reprinted in Edited Books 2013, 215–34. "Speech in Psychoanalysis: From Symbols to the Flesh and Back." Translated by Andrew Weller. In Dana Birksted-Breen, Sara Flanders, and Alain Gibeault, eds., *Reading French Psychoanalysis.* New York: Routledge, 2010, 423–33. Translated by Constance Borde and Sheila Malovany-Chevallier as "Speaking in Psychoanalysis: From Symbols to Flesh and Back Again" in English ed. of Edited Books 2013, 113–24.

2007h "Le Pas, les larmes, la dette." *Le Monde de la Bible*, no. 180 (November–December). Reprinted in Edited Books 2013, 379–86.

2007i "Postface: Le Débat comme une boussole." In Emmanuel Belluteau, ed. *Quand la Bible parle du handicap: Un autre regard.* Paris: Salvator, 183–85.

2007j "Response by Julia Kristeva. For Shoshana Felman: Truth and Art." (Translated from "La Vérité et l'art" in Books 2005a.) In Emily Sun, Eyal Peretz, and Ulrich Baer, eds., *The Claims of Literature: A Shoshana Felman Reader.* New York: Fordham University Press, 315–25.

2007k "Rethinking 'Normative Conscience': The Task of the Intellectual Today." *Common Knowledge* 13, no. 2 (Spring–Fall): 219–26. Reprinted in *Common Knowledge* 25, nos. 1–3 (April 2019): 192–99.

2008

2008a "Aux risques de la liberté." *Magazine littéraire* 471: 57–60.

2008b "Beauvoir aux risques de la liberté." In Edited Books 2008b, 11–6. Translated by Catherine Porter as "Beauvoir and the Risks of Freedom" and published with "Beauvoir aux risques de la liberté." *Modern Language Association of America* 124, no. 1 (January 2009): 226–30 and 230–33.

2008c "De la 'modernité critique' à la 'modernité analytique.'" *Benjamin-Studien* 1: 251–64. Reprinted in Patricia Farazzi and Michel Valensi, eds., *Retour. Mélanges à la mémoire de Stéphane Mosès*. Paris: Ed. de l'Éclat, 2009: 23–35; and in Edited Books 2013, 519–37. Translated by Constance Borde and Sheila Malovany-Chevallier as "From 'Critical Modernity' to 'Analytical Modernity'" in English ed. of Edited Books 2013, 225–38.

2008d "Existe-t-il une culture européenne?" in Edited Books 2008a: 11–31. Revised as "*Homo europaeus*: Existe-t-il une culture européenne?" *Revue Projet* 339, no. 2 (April 2014): 60–67; also in *La Nouvelle Revue Française* 607 (February 2014): 120–31; and in Edited Books 2013, 635–58. "*Homo Europaeus:* Does European Culture Exist?" In Michael Marder and Patrícia Vieira, eds., *The Philosophical Salon: Speculations, Reflections, Interventions*. London: Open Humanities Press, 2017, 45–49.

2008e "Je vous salue Thérèse." *Magazine littéraire* 481: 68–70.

2008f "Le Maternel séculier." In Paul Denis, Bernard Chervet, and Sylvie Dreyfus-Asséo, eds., *Avancées de la psychanalyse*. Paris: Presses Universitaires de France, 275–86.

2008g "Palin, l'impénétrable pouvoir de la matrone phallique." *Libération* (September 25). Reprinted as "Des femmes, pour quelle civilisation?" in Edited Books 2013, 363–70.

2008h "La Parole, cette expérience." In *Benoît XV, Chercher Dieu: Discours au monde de la culture*. Paris: Parole et Silence/Lethielleux. Reprinted in Edited Books 2013, 495–501.

2008i "La Passion maternelle." *Le Magazine Littéraire,* special issue, no. 14 (August–September): 66–67.

2008j "Le Père de la préhistoire individuelle, ou encore de la sublimation." In Dominique Cupa, ed. *Image du père dans la culture contemporaine: Hommages à André Green*. Paris: Presses Universitaires de France, 189–206.

2009

2009a "A Father is Beaten to Death." (Translated by Lorna Scott Fox in English ed. of Books 2008.) In Lila J. Kalinich and Stuart W. Taylor, eds. *The Dead Father: A Psychoanalytic Inquiry*. New York: Routledge, 175–86. "Un père battu à mort" in Books 2008. Reprinted in Edited Books 2013, 175–96. Translated as "A Father is Being Beaten to Death" by Constance Borde and Sheila Malovany-Chevallier in English ed. of Edited Books 2013, 150–77.

2009b "Décidément la Chine: Une Européenne en Chine." *L'Infini* 107 (Spring): 91–108. Reprinted as "Une Européenne en Chine" in Edited Books 2013, 659–67. "A European in China." Translated by Vernon Cisney and Nicolae Morar. *Critical Inquiry* 37, no. 3 (Spring 2011): 419–33.

2009c "Decollations." (Translated by Caroline Arruda in English ed. of Books 1998d.) In Kelly Oliver and Stacy Keltner, eds., *Psychoanalysis, Aesthetics, and Politics in the Works of Julia Kristeva*. Albany: State University of New York Press, 29–45.

2009d "Foi et raison: Pour quelle inculturation?" *Transversalités* 2, no. 110: 75–90. Reprinted as "Foi et raison avec Jean-Paul II: Pour quelle inculturation?" in Edited Books 2013, 435–54.

2009e As Julia Kristeva-Joyaux. "Le Message culturel de la France et la vocation interculturelle de la francophonie." *Notes d'Iéna*, no. 342 (June 12). Reprinted as "Le Message culturel français" in Edited Books 2013, 617–33.

2009f "Le 11 septembre du World Trade Sex." In Edited Books 2007b, 183–218; and in Edited Books 2009, 16–30.

2009g "Thérèse mon amour." In Frédéric Boyer, ed. *La Littérature contemporaine et le sacré*. Paris: Bibliothèque publique d'information—Centre Pompidou, 35–42. (Excerpts from Books 2008.)

2010

2010a "L'Affect, cette 'intense profondeur des mots.'" Translated from Italian by Lucia Somenzi in P. A. Sequeri, ed., *Esteriorità di Dio: La fede nell'epoca della "perdita del mondo."* Milano: Glossa, 3–26. Reprinted in Edited Books 2013, 235–57. Translated by Constance Borde and Sheila Malovany-Chevallier as "Affect, That 'Intense Depth of Words'" in English ed. of Edited Books 2013, 125–41.

2010b "Antigone, Limit and Horizon" Translated by Ella Brians. In Fanny Söderbäck, ed., *Feminist Readings of Antigone*. New York: State University of New York Press, 215–30. French version, "Antigone, la limite et l'horizon," first published in *L'Infini* 115 (Summer 2011): 64–76; reprinted in Edited Books 2013, 269–87. Translated by Constance Borde and Sheila Malovany-Chevallier as "Antigone, Limit and Horizon" in English ed. of Edited Books 2013, 151–64.

2010c "Enfance et jeunesse d'un écrivain français." *L'Infini* 112 (Fall): 25–29. Reprinted as "Enfance et jeunesse d'un écrivain français: Philippe Sollers" in Edited Books 2013, 31–37.

2010d "L'Érotisme, entre chair et sens." *Sexe et religion, Le Point-Références*, no. 4 (November–December): 6. Reprinted as "Sexe et religion" in Edited Books 2013, 373–78.

2010e "Étrangère au semblant." *Cahiers Bernard Lazare*, no. 320 (November): 13–15.

2010f "Une expérience imaginaire, simple comme un roman, un feuilleton télé, une jalousie." *Le Monde Dossiers et Documents*, no. 398 (June 1): 7.

2010g "Fleur de Chine." *L'Infini* 110 (Spring): 59–61.

2010h "La Séduction mystique." *Le Monde "M"* (supplement), no. 17 (December). Reprinted in Edited Books 2013, 459–68.

2011

2011a "Beauvoir et la psychanalyse: Un défi réciproque." *L'Homme et la société* 1–2, nos. 179–80: 81–98.

2011b "Être mère aujourd'hui." *Revue Française de Psychosomatique* 2, no. 40: 43–51.

2011c "La grammatica del credere: a proposito di Newman." *Vita e Pensiero*, no. 3 (May–June): 74–83. Reprinted as "Moi-même et mon Créateur, selon J. H. Newman" in Edited Books 2013, 421–34.

2011d "L'Humanisme au regard du handicap." With Henri-Pierre Bass. *Le Journal des psychologues* 8, no. 291: 22–28.

2011e "Lacan redonne à la psychanalyse sa portée historique et politique." In Geneviève Fraisse, et al., eds., *Nos derniers maîtres: Les Textes fondamentaux*. Paris: Le Point, 58–65. Reprinted as "L'Événement Lacan" in Edited Books 2013, 259–66. Translated by Constance Borde and Sheila Malovany-Chevallier as "The Lacan Event" in English ed. of Edited Books 2013, 142–47.

2011f "Ni dépression, ni perversion: Éclosion." In Gérard Bonal and Frédéric Maget, eds., *Cahier Colette*. Paris: L'Herne, 19–28. Reprinted as "Ni dépression ni perversion: l'éclosion Colette" in Edited Books 2013, 305–27.

2011g "Oser l'humanisme." *Revue des Deux Mondes* (September): 79–102. Reprinted in Jean-Luc Marion, Julia Kristeva, Alex Kahn, and Jean Clair, eds., *Lumières, religions et raison commune*. Montrouge: Bayard, 2012, 69–97; and in Edited Books 2013, 539–60.

2011h "Reading *The Second Sex* Sixty Years Later." Translated by Timothy Hackett. *philoSOPHIA* 1, no. 2: 137–49.

2011i "La Reliance, ou de l'érotisme maternel." *Revue française de Psychanalyse* 75, no. 5 (December): 1559–70. Reprinted in *Revue du Mauss* 1, no. 39 (2012): 181–95. Reprinted as "L'Érotisme maternel" in Edited Books 2013, 197–214. "Reliance, or Maternal Eroticism." Translated by Rachel Widawsky and Perry Zurn. *Journal of the American Psychoanalytic Association* 62, no. 1 (March 2014): 69–85. Translated by Constance Borde and Sheila Malovany-Chevallier as "Maternal Eroticism" in English ed. of Edited Books, 101–112.

2011j "Sur les pas du passeur." Preface to Stéphane Mosès, *Rêves de Freud: Six Lectures*. Paris: Gallimard, 9–34.

2012

2012a "Азбука/Azbouka, mon alphabet ou comment je suis une lettre." *La Nouvelle Revue Française*, no. 601 (June): 202–14. Reprinted as "Mon alphabet, ou comment je suis une lettre" in Edited Books 2013, 15–23. Translated by Constance Borde and Sheila Malovany-Chevallier as "My Alphabet; Or, How I am a Letter" in English ed. of Edited Books 2013, 3–10.

2012b "La Chair des mots." In Bernard Chervet, Josiane Chambrier, and Sabina Lambertucci-Mann, eds., *L'Interprétation*. Paris: Presses Universitaires de France, 133–50.

2012c "Daniel Widlöcher: L'Imaginaire, les Religions, la Sublimation." *Annales Médico-Psychologiques* 170, no. 6 (August): 440–43.

2012d "Dix principes pour l'humanisme du XXIème siècle." *Études* 416, no. 1: 91–95. Reprinted in *L'Infini* 122 (Spring) 2013: 49–53; and in Edited Books 2013, 561–67. Translated by Constance Borde and Sheila Malovany-Chevallier as "Ten Principles for Twenty-First Century Humanism" in English ed. of Edited Books 2013, 279–83.

2012e "Émile Benveniste un linguiste qui ne dit ni ne cache, mais signifie." Preface to Émile Benveniste, *Dernières Leçons: Collège de France 1968–1969*. Edited by Jean-Claude Coquet and Irène Fenoglio. Paris: Gallimard. Reprinted in Edited Books 2013, 97–132. Translated by Constance Borde and Sheila Malovany-Chevallier as "Emile Benveniste, A Linguist Who Neither Says nor Hides, but Signifies" in English ed. of Edited Books 2013, 33–57.

2012f "In viaggio con Jacqueline Risset." In *I pensieri dell'istante: Scriti per Jacqueline Risset.* Rome: Editori Internazionli Riuniti. Reprinted in Edited Books 2013, 85–90.

2012g "Jean-Jacques Rousseau: Le Subversif." *Le Monde, une vie, une oeuvre*, special issue (May–July): 12. Reprinted as "Une Félicité nommée Rousseau" in Edited Books 2013, 471–94. Translated by Constance Borde and Sheila Malovany-Chevallier as "A Felicity Named Rousseau" in English ed. of Edited Books 2013, 189–207.

2012h "Marcelin Pleynet, une certaine alliance avec le temps." *Faire Part*, nos. 30–31 (Spring): 57–62. Reprinted in *L'Infini* 120 (September 2012): 65–69. Reprinted in Edited Books 2013, 91–96.

2012i "Seuls et reliés." *Ombres et Lumière*, special issue, *Handicap et solitude*, no. 185 (January–February). Reprinted as "Quand leur regard perce nos ombres" in Edited Books 2013, 687–92.

2013

2013a "De l'inviolabilité de la vie humaine" in Edited Books 2013, 569–79. Translated by Constance Borde and Sheila Malovany-Chevallier as "On the Sanctity of Human Life" in English ed. of Edited Books 2013, 284–92. "On the Inviolability of Human Life." Translated by Lisa Walsh. In Geoffrey Adelsberg, Lisa Guenther, and Scott Zeman, eds., *Death and Other Penalties: Philosophy in a Time of Mass Incarceration*. New York: Fordham University Press, 2015, 130–37. "Transformations of *Parentality*." Translated by Edward

Kenny. In Vaia Tsolas and Christine Anzieu-Premmereur, eds., *A Psychoanalytic Exploration of the Body in Today's World: On the Body*. New York: Routledge, 2018, 68–74.
2013b "Métamorphoses de la parentalité." *Revue française de psychanalyse* 77, no. 5 (December): 1650–57. "Transformations of *Parentality*." Translated by Edward Kenny. In Vaia Tsolas and Christine Anzieu-Premmereur, eds., *A Psychoanalytic Exploration of the Body in Today's World: On the Body*. New York: Routledge, 2018, 68–74.
2013c "Rafah Nached." *L'Infini* 123 (Summer): 89–95.
2013d "Stockholm: Going Beyond the Human through Dance." *Journal of French and Francophone Philosophy— Revue de la philosophie française et de langue française* 21, no. 1: 1–12.
2013e "Traduire la douleur, ou le langage comme contre-dépresseur." *Figures de la psychanalyse: Logos-Anankè* 2, no. 26: 13–25.
2013f "A Tragedy and a Dream: Disability Revisited." (Translated from "Le Tragique et la chance: Encore des handicaps" in Edited Books 2013.) *Irish Theological Quarterly* 78, no. 3: 219–30. Reprinted in Richard Kearney and Brian Treanor, eds., *Carnal Hermeneutics*. New York: Fordham University Press, 2015, 115–26. Translated by Constance Borde and Sheila Malovany-Chevallier as "Disability Revisited: The Tragic and Chance" in English ed. of Edited Books 2013.
2013g "Transsubstantiation selon Marcel Proust." (From Books 2005a.) *La Nouvelle Revue Française*, no. 603 (March): 164–83.

2014

2014a "Julia Kristeva Comments on the 'Maternal Reliance.'" Translated by David Maruzzella. *Journal of the American Psychoanalytic Association* 62, no. 3 (June): 60–64.
2014b "Letter to the Editor: Julia Kristeva comments on the 'Maternal Reliance' section of JAPA 62/1." *Journal of the American Psychoanalytic Association* (June 27): 60–64.
2014c "New Forms of Revolt." *Journal of French and Francophone Philosophy—Revue de la philosophie française et de langue française* 22, no. 2: 1–19. Reprinted in Sarah K. Hansen and Rebecca Tuvel, eds., *New Forms of Revolt: Essays on Kristeva's Intimate Politics*. Albany: State University of New York, 2017, 17–22.

2015

2015a "Qui est Méduse?" (From Books 1998d.) *Ars & Humanitas* 9, no. 1: 23–31.
2015b "Une Accélération de l'histoire." *L'Infini* 131 (Spring): 38–47.

2016

2016a "Roland Barthes à contre-courant." In Nathalie Piégay et Laurent Zimmermann, eds., *Roland Barthes aujourd'hui*. Paris: Hermann, 9–20.
2016b "Le Corps d'Adel." In Hans Belting, Emmanuelle Coccia, and Elizabeth de Fontenay et al., eds., *Adel Abdessemed*. Paris: Manuella Editions, 92–143.
2016c "Interpréter le mal radical, *L'Infini* 135 (Spring): 38–47.
2016d "1963, 2016: Deux regards sur Blaga Dimitrova." Translated from Bulgarian by Marie Vrinat and Julia Kristeva. *La Revue de Belles-Lettres*, no. 2: 241–47.
2016e "La Linguistique, l'universel et le 'pauvre linguiste.'" In Edited Books 2016, 97–152.

2017

2017a "Cette Europe où je me voyage: Europe à contre-courant." *La Nouvelle Revue Française*, no. 623 (March): 100–12. Reprinted from French ed. of Books 2006.
2017b "Histoires d'amour et de métamorphoses." Preface to *L'Intime*. Vallet: M-Éditer.
2017c "Motherhood Today." In Sarah K. Hansen and Rebecca Tuvel, eds., *New Forms of Revolt: Essays on Kristeva's Intimate Politics*. Albany: State University of New York.

2018

2018a "Julia Kristeva et le fantôme de 'Sabina.'" *Le Journal du dimanche.* April 22.

2018b "L'Avenir d'une révolte." *L'Infini* 148 (Fall): 3–11.

2018c "The Cultural Crossings of Care: An Appeal to the Medical Humanities." With Marie Rose Moro, John Ødemark, and Eivind Engebretsen. *BMJ Medical Humanities* 44, no. 1: 55–58.

2018d "The Psychic Life: A Life in Time." Translated by Carol Mastrangelo Bové and Anne Marsella. *Journal of French and Francophone Philosophy/Revue de la philosophie française et de langue française* 26, no. 2: 81–90.

2018e "La Bulgarie, L'Europe Post-Totalitaire et Moi." *Marianne* 1121 (September 7–13): 46–47. "Bulgaria, Post-totalitarian Europe and Me." *Los Angeles Review of Books*. November 26, 2018. See also Selected Online Publications 2018b.

2019

2019a "La Culture européenne est la voie pour une Europe plus solide." *Le Monde* (May 24): 30.

2019b "L'Échec de l'humanisme." *Passages*, no. 199 (March): 14–18.

SELECTED INTERVIEWS

1968

1968 "Sémiologie et grammatologie: Entretien avec Julia Kristeva." Interview of Jacques Derrida by Julia Kristeva. *Information sur les sciences sociales* 7, no. 3 (June): 135–48. Reprinted in Jacques Derrida. *Positions: Entretiens avec Julia Kristeva, Henri Ronse, Jean-Louis Houdebine, Guy Scarpetta*. Paris: Minuit, 18–30.

1970

1970 "Littérature, sémiotique, marxisme." Interview by Christine Glucksman and Jean Peytard. *La Nouvelle Critique* 219 (November): 28–35.

1972

1972 "Sémanalyse: Conditions d'une sémiotique scientifique." Interview by Jean-Claude Coquet. *Semiotica* V, no. 4: 324–49.

1974

1974a "Économie et politique du langage poétique." Interview by Jean Houdebine. *Promesse: Pratiques, textes, lectures* 36–37 (Spring): 75–96.

1974b "La Femme, ce n'est jamais ça." Interview by the women of *Psychanalyse et politique*. *Tel Quel* 59 (Fall): 19–26. Reprinted in Books 1977, 517–25. "Woman Can Never Be Defined." Translated by Marilyn August. In *New French Feminisms*. New York: Schocken Books, 1981, 137–41.

1974c "Oscillation du 'pouvoir' au 'refus.'" Interview by Xavière Gauthier. *Tel Quel* 58 (Summer): 99–100. "Oscillation Between Power and Denial." Translated by Marilyn August. In *New French Feminisms*. New York: Schocken Books, 1981, 165–68.

1975

1975 "Unes femme." Interview by Eliane Boucquey. *Les Cahiers du GRIF* 7: 22–27.

1976

1976a "China, Women and the Symbolic: An Interview with Julia Kristeva." Interview by Josette Féral. *SubStance* 5, no. 13 (Fall): 9–18. Translated by Penny Kristzman.

1976b "Deux témoignages sur la société en mouvement. Les intellectuels divisés." Interview by Catherice Francblin. *Art Press International* 1 (Summer): 2–3.

1976c "La Musique et la 'gaffe.'" *Art Press International* 2 (November): 10–11.

1977

1977a "De la généralité à la sémiotique." Interview by Christian Bauer and Pierre Oullet. *Études littéraires* 10, no. 3 (December): 337–46.

1977b "Julia Kristeva: À quoi servent les intellectuels?" Interview by Jean-Paul Enthoven. *Le Nouvel Observateur* (June 20): 98–134.

1977c "Julia Kristeva. Féminité et écriture: En réponse à deux questions sur *Polylogue*." Interview by Françoise van Rossum. *Revue des sciences humaines* 44, no. 168 (October–December): 495–501. "Talking about *Polylogue*." Translated by Seán Hand. In *French Feminist Thought: A Reader*. Oxford: Blackwell, 1987, 110–17.

1977d "Julia Kristeva femme/mère/pensée répond à des questions de Catherine Franblinc." *Art Press International* 5 (March): 6–8.

1977e "Pourquoi les États-Unis?" *Tel Quel* 71–73 (Fall) 3–20. Interview by Marcelin Pleynet and Philippe Sollers. "The U.S. Now: A Conversation." Translated by Phoebe Cohen. *October* 6 (Fall 1978): 3–17. Translated by Seán Hand as "Why the United States" in Edited Books 1986, 272–91.

1984

1984 "*Histoires d'amour*—Love Stories and Julia Kristeva in Conversation with Rosalind Coward." In Lisa Appignanesi. *Desire* (ICA Documents 1). London: Institute of Contemporary Arts, 18–27.

1985

1985 "Entretien avec Julia Kristeva." Interview by Françoise Collin. *Les Cahiers du GRIF* 32: 7–23.

1986

1986a "Interview with Julia Kristeva." Interview by Ina Lipkowitz and Andrea Loselle. *Critical Texts* 3, no. 3 (Spring–Summer): 3–13.

1986b "A Question of Subjectivity: An Interview." Interview by Susan Sellers. *Women's Review* 12: 19–21.

1988

1988 "Exploding the Issue: French Women Writers and the Canon." Interview by Alice A. Jardine and M. Menke. *Yale French Studies* 75: 248–49.

1989

1989 "An Interview with Julia Kristeva." In Patrick O'Donnell and Robert Con Davis, eds., *Intertextuality and Contemporary American Fiction*. Baltimore: Johns Hopkins University Press, 280–93.

1990

1990a "À propos des *Samouraïs*." *L'Infini* 30 (Summer): 56–66. Interview with Elisabeth Bélorgey. Reprinted in Books 1990a, 59–85. Translated by Leon S. Roudiez as "Concerning *The Samurai*" in Books 1993c.

1990b "An Interview with Julia Kristeva: Cultural Strangeness and the Subject in Crisis." Interview by Suzanne Clark and Kathleen Hulley. *Discourse* 13, no. 1 (Fall–Winter): 149–80.

1991

1991a "Entretien avec Julia Kristeva." *Psychanalystes*, no. 39 (July): 51–9.

1991b "Le Rituel galant: Entretien avec Julia Kristeva." In Régine Dhoquois and Annie Prassaloff, eds., *La Politesse, vertu des apparences*. Paris: Éditions Autrement, 76–90.

1992

1992a "Roman noir et temps présent." Interview by Bernard Sichère. *L'Infini* 37 (Spring): 75–86.

1992b "Sofia." *Le Nouvel Observateur*, special issue, *Les 30 Capitales culturelles de l'Europe par les grands écrivains* 13: 36–37.

1993

1993a "Foreign Body." Interview by Scott L. Malcomson. *Transition*, no. 59: 172–83.

1993b "Julia Kristeva." In Alice Jardine and Anne Menke, eds. *Shifting Scenes: Interview on Women, Writing, and Politics in Post-68 France*. New York: Columbia University Press, 113–24.

1993c "*Les Nouvelles Maladies de l'âme*." *Art Press International* 178 (March): 58–60. Reprinted in *L'Infini* 42 (Summer 1993): 67–73.

1995

1995 "Of Word and Flesh: An Interview with Julia Kristeva by Charles Penwarden." In Stuart Morgan and Frances Morris, eds., *Rites of Passage: Art for the End of the Century*. London: Tate Gallery Publications, 21–27.

1996

1996a *Julia Kristeva: Interviews*. Edited by Ross Mitchell Guberman. New York: Columbia University Press, 1996.

1996b "L'Expérience littéraire est-elle encore possible?" Interview by Danielle Sallenave. *L'Infini* 53 (Spring): 20–46.

1998

1998a "Dialogue with Julia Kristeva." Interview by Griselda Pollock. *Parallax* 4, no. 3 (December): 5–16.

1998b *Contre la dépression nationale: Entretien avec Philippe Petit*. Paris: Textuel. Translated by Brian O'Keefe as *Revolt, She Said*. Los Angeles: Semiotext(e), 2002.

علیه افسردگی ملی, Alayh-e Afsordegi-e Melli. Tehran: Shavand, 2016.

1999

1999a "Savoir différer pour mieux désirer: Dialogue avec Marie de Solemne." In Marie de Solemne, ed., *Entre désir et renoncement: Dialogue avec Julia Kristeva et al.* Paris: Éditions Dervy, 75–94.

1999b "La Transsubstantiation de Proust: Une Suspension du refoulement." *Revue française de psychanalyse* 2, no. 63: 429–52.

2001

2001a *Au risque de la pensée*. Interviews by Marie-Christine Navarro. La Tour d'Aigues: Éditions de l'Aube.

思考之危境: 克莉斯蒂娃訪談錄. Taibei Shi: Maitian chuban, 2005.

Il rischio del pensare. Genova: Il melangolo, 2006.

Adalék a Gondolkodás tétjéhez. Budapest: Napkút, 2008

2001b "La Beauté, éclosion de l'insolite: Entretien entre Alain Kirili et Julia Kristeva." In Alain Kirili, Julia Kristeva, and Robert Storr, eds., *Jardin des Tuileries sculptures modernes et contemporaines: Installation conçue par Alain Kirili, 1997–2000*. Paris: Éditions du Patrimoine: 13–27.

2002

2002 "Forgiveness: An Interview." Translated by Alison Rice. *Modern Language Association* 117, no. 2 (March): 278–95.

2003

2003 "The Future of a Defeat: Julia Kristeva Interviewed by Arnaud Spire." *Parallax* 9, no. 2 (December): 21–26.

2005

2005 "*Meurtre à Byzance* ou pourquoi 'Je me voyage' en roman." Interview by Pierre-Louis Fort. *L'Infini* 91 and 92 (Summer and Fall): 85–98 and 609–54. Reprinted in Books 2005a, 610–55. Translated by Jeanine Herman as "Why I 'Ship Myself on a Voyage' in a Novel" in English ed. of Books 2005a, 273–305.

2006

2006a "L'Apport contemporain de la psychanalyse." Interview by Alain Braconnier. *Le Carnet psy* 6, no. 110 (June): 40–47. Reprinted in Edited Books 2013, 153–73.

2006b "Crossing the Borders: An Interview with Julia Kristeva." Interview by Birgitte HuitFeldt Midttun. *Hypatia* 21, no. 4: 164–77.

2006c "De Jésus à Mozart: La Différence du Christianisme. Entretien avec Claire Folscheid." In *Paris Notre-Dame, journal du Diocèse de Paris*, March 16. Reprinted in French ed. of Books 2006.

2008

2008 "Sainte Thérèse sur le divan." Interview by Jacques Nerson. *Le Nouvel Observateur* (May 22): 112–13.

2009

2009 "Comme un polar métaphysique." *Regards*, no. 66 (November): 4–7. Reprinted as "Le Polar métaphysique" in Edited Books 2013, 693–96.

2010

2010a "Freud: Le Débat Onfray-Kristeva." Discussion with Gilles Anquetil and François Armanet. *Le Nouvel Observateur* (April 22): 22–26. Reprinted as "Freud: Le Fond du débat" in Edited Books 2013, 141–52. Translated by Constance Borde and Sheila Malovany-Chevallier as "Freud: The Heart of the Matter" in English ed. of Edited Books 2013, 61–68.

2010b "L'Universel au singulier." *Cahiers Bernard Lazare*, no. 312 (March): 13–15. Reprinted in Edited Books 2013, 679–86. Translated by Constance Borde and Sheila Malovany-Chevallier as "The Universal in the Singular" in English ed. of Edited Books 2013, 339–44.

2011

2011a "Julia Kristeva: 'L'Humanisme ne sait pas accompagner la mortalité.'" Interview by Josyanne Savigneau. *Le Monde* (30 April): 22.

2011b "Simone de Beauvoir, une femme libre." Interview by Josyanne Savigneau. *Le Monde*, special issue, no. 6 (March): 57–62. Reprinted as "On naît femme, mais je le deviens" in Edited Books 2013, 707–22; and in Books 2016b, 83–104. Translated by Constance Borde and Sheila Malovany-Chevallier as "One is Born Woman, But I Become One" in English ed. of Edited Books 2013, 352–62.

2012

2012 "Émile Benveniste: 'Il me lisait le *Rigveda* directement en Sanskrit dans le texte.'" Interview by Julie Clarini. *Le Monde des livres* (April 20): 3.

2013

2013a "Entretien avec Julia Kristeva: Penser en nomade et dans l'autre langue le monde, la vie psychique et la littérature." Interview by Irene Ivantcheva-Merjanska and Michèle E. Vialet. *Kristeva in Process: The Fertility of Thought/La Pensée féconde/Die Fruchtbarkeit des Denkens. Cincinnati Romance Review* 35 (Spring): 158–89.

2013b "L'Europe est le seul endroit au monde où l'identité n'est pas un culte mais une question." Interview by Catherine Calvet and Cécile Daumas. *Libération* (June 28): 18–19.

2013c "Manifeste culturel: Interview." Interview by Catherine Calvet and Cécile Daumas. *L'Infini* 125 (Winter): 32–39.

2013d "Pour une refondation de l'humanisme." Interview by Aurélie Julia. *Revue des Deux Mondes* (September) 2013: 35–48.

2013e "La Révolution est d'abord intérieure." Interview by Patrick Williams. *L'Infini* 122 (Spring): 43–48.

2014

2014 "Pour une académie européenne de la culture." Interview by Olivier Guez and Laure Kaltenbach. *Le Monde*, May 21.

2015

2015a "Certains de mes livres." *L'Infini* 132 (Summer): 32–40.

2015b "Du mariage considéré comme un des Beaux-arts." With Philippe Sollers. Interview by François Armanet and Sylvie Véran. *L'Infini* 131 (Spring): 20–31.

2015c *Julia Kristeva: Les Grands Entretiens d'Artpress*. Edited by Philippe Forest, Jacques Henric, Catherine Francblin, and Laurence Louppe. Paris: Artpress.

2016

2016a "Entretien avec Julia Kristeva." Interview by Anastasia Vécrin. *Le Cahier des Rencontres Philosophiques de Monaco*, no. 1: 90–96.

2016b "*L'Horloge enchantée.*" Interview by Abeline Majorel. *L'Infini* 134 (Summer): 53–57.

2016c "Julia Kristeva: Pour un intellectuel dire c'est faire." Interview by Robert Maggiori and Anastasia Vecrin. *Libération* (February 25): 22–23. Reprinted as "Quand dire c'est faire." *L'Infini* 136 (Summer 2016): 77–81.

2016d "New Humanism and the Need to Believe: Dialogue with Julia Kristeva." Translated by Jennifer McWeeney. In Richard Kearney and Jens Zimmerman, eds., *Reimagining the Sacred: Richard Kearney Debates God*. New York: Columbia University Press, 93–127.

2017

2017a "Humanities Can Help Thwart the Destructive Depression that Feeds Fanaticism." Interview with Gaby Levin. *Haaretz* (June 12).

2017b "La Parole libre est encore à venir." Interview by Jean-Marie Durand. *Les Inrockuptibles* (December 29). Excerpts reprinted in *Cahiers Bernard Lazare* 403 (March 2018): 10–12.

2017c "Une vie psychique est une vie dans le temps." Interview by Françoise Coblence and Marcela Montes de Oca. *Revue française de psychanalyse* 81, no. 2: 351–67. "The Psychic Life: A Life in Time, Psychoanalysis and Culture." Translated by Carol Mastrangelo Bové and Anne Marsella. *Journal of French and Francophone Philosophy—Revue de la philosophie française et de langue française* 26, no. 2 (2018): 81–90.

2018

2018a "Il faut favoriser l'expérience intérieure." Interview by Frederick Casadesus. *Réforme* (May 24).

2018b "Une Autre Vie que la mienne." Interview by Olivier Bouchara. *Vanity Fair France* (July 20): 66–73. "'It's Just Not My Life': Julia Kristeva Responds." Translated by Patsy Baudoin. *Los Angeles Review of Books* (January 11, 2018).

2018c "Mysticism and Anatheism: The Case of Teresa." In Chris Doude van Troostwijk and Matthew Clemente, eds., *Richard Kearney's Anatheistic Wager: Philosophy, Theology, Poetics*. Bloomington: Indiana University Press.

2019

2019a "La Personne au centre: Entretien avec Julia Kristeva." Interview by Georges Nivat and Olivier Mongin. *Esprit*, no. 456 (July–August): 160–75. "The Individual Person at the Center: An Interview with Julia Kristeva." Translated by Patsy Baudoin. Julia Kristeva official website, http://www.kristeva.fr/the-individual-person-at-the-center.html.

2019b "Je suis et resterai une étrangère." Interview by Martin Legros. *Philosophie magazine* 135 (December 2019/January 2020): 69–73.

SELECTED ONLINE PUBLICATIONS AND ESSAYS

2005 "Motherhood Today." Gypsy V Colloquium. October 2005. Julia Kristeva official website, http://kristeva.fr/motherhood.html. See also Selected Articles 2017c.

2006 "Hannah Arendt or Refoundation as Survival." Speech at the reception of the Hannah Arendt Prize for Political Thought. Bremen. December 15–16. Julia Kristeva official website, http://www.kristeva.fr/Arendt_en.html. See also Selected Articles 2007e.

2007 "Pratiques de génie." Interview by Gilles Behnam. *Mag philo*. http://www2.cndp.fr/magphilo/philo17/interview.htm#top.

2010 "De l'affect ou 'L'intense profondeur des mots.'" Lecture at the Facultà Teologica dell'Italia Settentrionale, Milan. February 23–24. Julia Kristeva official website, http://www.kristeva.fr/de-l-affect.html. See also Selected Articles 2010a.

2011 Summary of speech delivered to the Women's Forum. Conference on Rafah Nached. October 9. https://www.pep-web.org/document.php?id=dr.004.0004a.

2012 "Le Langage comme antidépresseur." Lecture at École internationale de Genève. January 14. Julia Kristeva official website, http://www.kristeva.fr/le-langage-comme-antidepresseur.html. See also Selected Articles 2013e.

2014 Letter to Malala Yousafzai. Written for Yousafzai's reception of Simone de Beauvoir Prize 2013. October 14. http://prixsimonedebeauvoir.blogspot.com/.

2015 "Nuit de la justice à l'aube du pardon," www.kristeva.fr/textes/html.

2018a "Alexandre Soljénitsyne: Un Écrivain en lutte avec son siècle." Prison, Écriture, Combat ou La Langue disruptive et la Beauté en Question. Conference on the centenary of Solzhenitsyn's birth. November 21, 2018. Institut de France, Sorbonne. Julia Kristeva official website, http://www.kristeva.fr/soljenitsyne.html.

2018b "La Bulgarie, L'Europe Post-Totalitaire et Moi." Julia Kristeva official website, http://www.kristeva.fr/bulgaria-post-totalitarian-europe-and-me.html. "Bulgaria, Post-Totalitarian Europe and Me." https://thephilosophicalsalon.com/bulgaria-post-totalitarian-europe-and-me/; sur blog.lareviewofbooks.org/. See also Selected Articles 2018e.

2018c "It's Just Not My Life—Julia Kristeva Responds" http://blog.lareviewofbooks.org/essays/just-life-julia-kristeva-responds/. See also Selected Interviews 2018b.

2019a "The Individual Person at the Center." Interview by George Nivat and Olivier Mongin. July 8. Julia Kristeva official website, http://www.kristeva.fr/the-individual-person-at-the-center.html. See also Selected Interviews 2019.

2019b "Prelude to an Ethics of the Feminine." 51st International Psychoanalytical Association Congress. Queen Elizabeth II Centre, London. July 24–27. Julia Kristeva official website, http://www.kristeva.fr/prelude-to-an-ethics-of-the-feminine.html.

INDEX